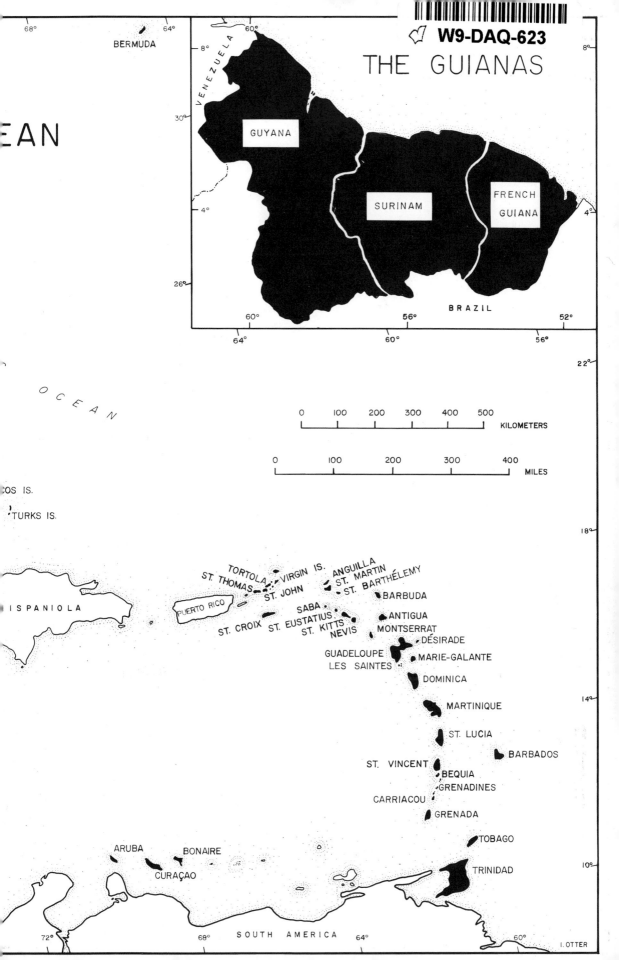

THE COMPLETE
CARIBBEANA
1900–1975

THE COMPLETE CARIBBEANA
1900–1975

A Bibliographic Guide to the Scholarly Literature

LAMBROS COMITAS

*Under the Auspices of The
Research Institute for the Study of Man*

2

INSTITUTIONS • CHAPTERS 19–40

kto press

A U.S. DIVISION OF
KRAUS-THOMSON ORGANIZATION LTD.
MILLWOOD, NEW YORK

Computer production by
Vance Weaver Composition, Inc., New York, New York

Library of Congress Cataloging in Publication Data

Comitas, Lambros.
  The complete Caribbeana, 1900-1975.

    CONTENTS: v. 1. People.—v. 2. Institutions.
—v. 3. Resources.—v. 4. Indexes.
    1. Caribbean area—Bibliography. I. Research
Institute for the Study of Man. II. Title.
Z1595.C63 [F2161]   016.9729'05   76-56709
ISBN 0-527-18820-4 (set)

TABLE OF VOLUMES

TABLE OF CONTENTS

VØLUME THREE • RESOURCES

VOLUME FOUR • INDEXES

CODE TO LIBRARIES

ACM   NEW YORK ACADEMY OF MEDICINE
2 East 103rd Street
New York, New York

AGS   AMERICAN GEOGRAPHICAL SOCIETY
Broadway & 156th Street
New York, New York

AJN   AMERICAN JOURNAL OF NURSING
10 Columbus Circle
New York, New York

AMN   AMERICAN MUSEUM OF NATURAL HISTORY
Central Park West & 79th Street
New York, New York

CEIP   CARNEGIE ENDOWMENT FOR INTERNATIONAL PEACE
345 East 46th Street
New York, New York

COL   COLUMBIA UNIVERSITY
Broadway & 116th Street
New York, New York

IPPF   INTERNATIONAL PLANNED PARENTHOOD FEDERATION
4th Avenue & 11th Street
New York, New York

NYP   NEW YORK PUBLIC LIBRARY
Fifth Avenue & 42nd Street
New York, New York

PhD   *Dissertation Abstracts International*
Comprehensive Dissertation Index
Both published by Xerox University
Microfilms, Ann Arbor, Michigan.

PS   COLUMBIA UNIVERSITY, COLLEGE OF PHYSICIANS & SURGEONS
Broadway & 168th Street
New York, New York

RILA   ROYAL INSTITUTE OF LINGUISTICS AND ANTHROPOLOGY
Stationsplein
Leiden, The Netherlands

RIS   RESEARCH INSTITUTE FOR THE STUDY OF MAN
162 East 78th Street
New York, New York

SCH   SCHOMBURG COLLECTION of the NEW YORK PUBLIC LIBRARY
103 West 135th Street
New York, New York

TCL   TEACHERS COLLEGE (of COLUMBIA UNIVERSITY)
525 West 120th Street
New York, New York
[Includes Educational Resources Information Center (ERIC)]

UCLA   UNIVERSITY OF CALIFORNIA
Los Angeles, California

UNL   UNITED NATIONS LIBRARY
United Nations Plaza
New York, New York

UTS   UNION THEOLOGICAL SEMINARY
Broadway & 120th Street
New York, New York

CODE TO GEOGRAPHICAL UNITS

AG	Anguilla		**LS**	Les Saintes
AR	Aruba		**LW**	Leeward Islands
AT	Antigua			
			MG	Marie Galante
BA	Bahamas		**MS**	Montserrat
BB	Barbados		**MT**	Martinique
BC	British Caribbean			
BE	Bermuda		**NA**	Netherlands Antilles
BN	Bonaire		**NC**	Netherlands Caribbean
BR	Barbuda		**NE**	Netherlands
BQ	Bequia		**NL**	Netherlands Leeward Islands
BV	British Virgin Islands		**NV**	Nevis
BZ	Belize (British Honduras)		**NW**	Netherlands Windward Islands
CA	Canada		**PA**	Panama
CC	Caicos Islands			
CM	Cayman Islands		**SA**	Saba
CO	Costa Rica		**SB**	Saint Barthelemy
CR	Carriacou		**SC**	Saint Croix
CU	Curacao		**SE**	Saint Eustatius
			SJ	Saint John
DM	Dominica		**SK**	Saint Kitts
DR	Dominican Republic		**SL**	Saint Lucia
DS	Desirade		**SM**	Saint Martin/St. Maarten
			SR	Surinam (Dutch Guiana)
FA	French Antilles		**ST**	Saint Thomas
FC	French Caribbean		**SV**	Saint Vincent
FG	French Guiana			
FR	France		**TB**	Tobago
			TC	Turks and Caicos Islands
GC	General Caribbean		**TR**	Trinidad and Tobago
GD	Guadeloupe		**TT**	Tortola
GG	Guianas—General			
GN	Grenadines		**UK**	United Kingdom
GR	Grenada		**US**	United States of America
GU	Guyana (British Guiana)		**UV**	United States Virgin Islands
JM	Jamaica		**VI**	Virgin Islands—General
KNA	St. Kitts—Nevis—Anguilla		**WW**	Windward Islands

THE COMPLETE
CARIBBEANA
1900–1975

ELEMENTS
OF
CULTURE

Chapter 19

CULTURAL CONTINUITIES

Works on African and other Old World cultural persistences or adaptations, particularly in the areas of art, music and language.
See also: **[8]** The nature of society; **[11]** Population segments: Afro-Caribbean; **[14]** Population segments: Maroon; **[22]** Creative arts and recreation; **[23]** Religion; **[24]** Folklore; **[25]** Language and linguistics; **[26]** Culture change; **[29]** Folk medicine.

Abrahams, Roger D.
24.0002   **BC**   1967   The shaping of folklore traditions in the British West Indies.

Adhin, J. H.
19.0001   **SR**   1954-55 De culturele invloed van de Aziatische bevolkingsgroep op Suriname [The cultural influence of the Asiatic population group upon Suriname]. *Vox Guy* 1(4-5), Nov.-Jan.: 29-34.   **[12,15]**

Alexis, Gerson
23.0002   **MT**   1975   Avatars du voudou en Martinique.

Alleyne, Mervin C.
25.0007   **JM**   1970   The linguistic continuity of Africa in the Caribbean.

Amersfoort, J. M. M. van
12.0004   **SR**   1970   Hindostaanse Surinamers in Amsterdam [Hindustani Surinamese in Amsterdam].
17.0006   **SR,NE**   1974   IMMIGRATIE EN MINDERHEIDSVORMING: EEN ANALYSE VAN DE NEDERLANDSE SITUATIE 1945-1973 [IMMIGRATION AND MINORITY FORMATION: AN ANALYSIS OF THE DUTCH SITUATION 1945-1973].

Archambault, Jean
52.0011   **GD**   1972   De la voile au moteur: Technologie et changement social aux Saintes [From sail to motor: Technology and social change in the Saintes].

Bagley, Christopher
18.0012   **BC,UK**   1975   Sequels of alienation: a social psychological view of the adaptation of West Indian migrants in Britain.

Barrett, Leonard
29.0007   **JM**   1973   The portrait of a Jamaican healer: African medical lore in the Caribbean.

Bastide, Roger
11.0003   GC   1971[?]   AFRICAN CIVILISATIONS IN THE NEW WORLD.

Bastien, Rémy
19.0002 GC   1964   Procesos de aculturación en las Antillas [Processes of acculturation in the Antilles. *Revta Indias* 95-96, Jan.-June: 177-196.   [*RIS*]
11.0004   GC   1969   Estructura de la adaptación del negro en América Latina y del afroamericano en Africa [Structure of the adaptation of the negro in Latin America and of the Afro-American in Africa].

Baxter, Ivy
19.0003 JM   1970   THE ARTS OF AN ISLAND: THE DEVELOPMENT OF THE CULTURE AND OF THE FOLK AND CREATIVE ARTS IN JAMAICA, 1494-1962 (INDEPENDENCE). Metuchen, New Jersey, Scarecrow Press: 407p.   [22]   [*RIS*]

Beckwith, Martha Warren
23.0010   JM   1924   THE HUSSAY FESTIVAL IN JAMAICA.

Beckwith, Martha Warren & Roberts, Helen H.
22.0019   JM   1923   CHRISTMAS MUMMINGS IN JAMAICA.

Berghe, Pierre L. van den
16.0007   GC   1963   Racialism and assimilation in Africa and the Americas.

Bertrand, Anca
22.0026   GC   1968   Notes pour une définition du folklore antillais [Notes for a definition of West Indian folk music].

Biharie, S.
12.0012   SR   1971   Hindostaanse muziekinstrumenten en zang in Suriname [Hindustani musical instruments and song in Surinam].

Bourguignon, Erika
23.0014   GC   1967   RELIGIOUS SYNCRETISM AMONG NEW WORLD NEGROES.

Bowen, Calvin
22.0035   JM   1954   Jamaica's John Canoe.

Braithwaite, Lloyd E.
8.0018   TR   1954   Cultural integration in Trinidad.
8.0021   TR   1975   SOCIAL STRATIFICATION IN TRINIDAD: A PRELIMINARY ANALYSIS.

Brathwaite, Edward
6.0022   JM   1970   FOLK CULTURE OF THE SLAVES IN JAMAICA.
22.0039   BC   1970   Timehri.
26.0001   GC   1974   CONTRADICTORY OMENS: CULTURAL DIVERSITY AND INTEGRATION IN THE CARIBBEAN.
19.0004 BC   1974   Timehri. *In* Coombs, Orde, ed. IS MASSA DAY DEAD? BLACK MOODS IN THE CARIBBEAN. Garden City, New York, Anchor Press/Doubleday: 29-45.   [21,26]   [*CEIP*]

Brathwaite, Edward K.
19.0005 GC   1974   The African presence in Caribbean literature. *Daedulus* 103(2), Spring: 73-109.   [11,22]   [*RIS*]

Bryce-Laporte, R. S.
23.0022   **GC,PA**   1970   Crisis, contraculture, and religion among West Indians in the Panama Canal Zone.

Buhler, Richard O.
23.0024   **BZ**   1976   *Primicias* in Belize.

Bunel, Francois
19.0006   **GD**   1962[?]   RECUEIL DE SCÈNES VÉCUES À LA GUADELOUPE [TRUE EPISODES OF GUADELOUPE—A MISCELLANY]. Pointe-à-Pitre, Guad., Impr. Parisienne Anibal Lautric. **[25]**   [*RIS*]

Butt, Audrey J.
13.0023   **GU**   1957   The Mazaruni scorpion (a study of the symbolic significance of tattoo patterns among the Akawaio).

Butt Colson, Audrey J.
13.0030   **GG**   1971   Comparative studies of the social structure of Guiana Indians and the problem of acculturation.

Cameron, Norman E.
11.0014   **GC**   1929-34   THE EVOLUTION OF THE NEGRO.
11.0015   **GC**   1950   The background of the Afro-American.

Carr, Andrew T.
19.0007   **TR**   1953   A Rada community in Trinidad. *Car Q* 3(1): 36-54. **[11,23]**   [*RIS*]
22.0058   **TR**   1956   Pierrot Grenade.

Cassidy, Frederic G.
25.0054   **JM**   1957   Iteration as a word-forming device in Jamaican folk speech.
25.0057   **JM**   1961   Some footnotes on the "junjo" question.

Cecil, C. H.
22.0061   **BC**   1937   I—you, and the Devil take the loser!

Cheetham, Juliet
18.0057   **BC,UK**   1972   Immigrants, social work, and the community.

Clark, Astley
22.0065   **JM**   1975   Extract from *The Music and Musical Instruments of Jamaica*.

Clarke, Colin G.
12.0018   **TR**   1967   Caste among Hindus in a town in Trinidad: San Fernando.

Clarke, John Henrik
6.0034   **GC**   1973   THE INFLUENCE OF AFRICAN CULTURAL CONTINUITY ON THE SLAVE REVOLTS IN SOUTH AMERICA AND IN THE CARIBBEAN ISLANDS.

Cloak, F. T., Jr.
19.0008   **TR**   1966   A NATURAL ORDER OF CULTURAL ADOPTION AND LOSS IN TRINIDAD. Chapel Hill, University of North Carolina, Institute for Research in Social Sciences: 177p. (Working papers in methodology, 1) **[9,26]**
[*RIS*]

Collier, H. C.
22.0070	TR	1939	Trinidad fantasia.
22.0074	TR	1943	Carnival capers in calypso land.
22.0075	BC	1967	"Warri," an African game transplanted to the West Indies.

Comitas, Lambros
52.0037	JM	1962	FISHERMEN AND COOPERATION IN RURAL JAMAICA.

Comvalius, Th. A. C.
22.0079	SR	1946	Oud-Surinaamsche rhythmische dansen in dienst van de licha-melikje opvoeding [Old Surinamese rhythmic dances in the service of physical education].

Connell, Neville
19.0009	BC	1957	Punch drinking and its accessories. *J Barb Mus Hist Soc* 25(1), Nov.: 1-17. **[30]** [*AMN*]

Coombs, Orde
18.0066	BC,US	1976	Illegal immigrants in New York: the invisible subculture.

Coulthard, G. R.
20.0015	FA	1961	The French West Indian background of negritude.
21.0016	GC	1968	Parallelisms and divergencies between *négritude* and *indigenismo*.

Cregan, K. H.
13.0039	GU	1931	Blowpipes, spears, bows and arrows, and clubs: weapons of the aboriginals of Guiana.

Crowley, Daniel J.
49.0022	JM,TR	1953	American credit institutions of Yoruba type.
12.0020	TR	1954	East Indian festivals in Trinidad life.
22.0085	TR	1954	THE MEANINGS OF CARNIVAL.
23.0058	SL	1955	Festivals of the calendar in St. Lucia.
22.0087	TR	1956	The midnight robbers.
19.0010	SL	1956	Naming customs in St. Lucia. *Social Econ Stud* 5(1), Mar.: 87-92. **[9]** [*RIS*]
22.0088	TR	1956	The traditional masques of Carnival.
8.0050	TR	1957	Plural and differential acculturation in Trinidad.
22.0089	SL	1957	Song and dance in St. Lucia.
19.0011	BA	1958-59	L'héritage africaine dans les Bahamas [African heritage in the Bahamas]. *Presence Afr* 23, Dec.-Jan.: 41-58. [*COL*]
24.0055	SL	1958	La Rose and La Marguerite Societies in St. Lucia.
8.0051	GC	1960	Cultural assimilation in a multiracial society.
24.0056	GC	1962	Negro Folklore: an Africanist's view.

Cruickshank, J. Graham
25.0075	BB	1911	Negro English, with reference particularly to Barbados.
25.0076	GU,BB	1916	"BLACK TALK": BEING NOTES ON NEGRO DIALECT IN BRITISH GUIANA, WITH (INEVITABLY) A CHAPTER ON THE VERNACULAR OF BARBADOS.
19.0012	GU	1917	Among the "Aku" (Yoruba) in Canal No. 1, West Bank, Demerara River. *Timehri* 3d ser., 4(21), June: 70-82. **[11]** [*AMN*]
22.0094	GU	1924	An African dance in the colony.

| 19.0013 | GU | 1929 | Negro games. *Man* 29(141), Oct.: 179-180. **[14,22]** | [*COL*] |
| 8.0053 | GU | 1933 | "Good time" in slavery days. | |

Cundall, Frank
19.0014	BB	1924	An historic dripstone. *W I Comm Circ* 39(683), Dec. 4: 481-482.
				[*NYP*]
53.0155	JM	1939	PLACE-NAMES OF JAMAICA.

Dalby, David
| 14.0004 | JM | 1971 | Ashanti survivals in the language and traditions of the Windward Maroons of Jamaica. |

Dam, Theodore van
| 22.0099 | GC | 1954 | The influence of the West African songs of derision in the New World. |

Dark, Philip J. C.
| 22.0101 | SR | 1954 | BUSH NEGRO ART: AN AFRICAN ART IN THE AMERICAS. |

Dathorne, Oscar Ronald
| 22.0102 | BC | 1965 | Africa in the literature of the West Indies. |
| 22.0103 | GC | 1965 | The theme of Africa in West Indian literature. |

Davenport, William Hunt
| 52.0044 | JM | 1971 | A COMPARATIVE STUDY OF TWO JAMAICAN FISHING COMMUNITIES. |

Davids, Leo
| 9.0039 | GU,TR | 1964 | The East Indian family overseas. |

DeCamp, David
| 19.0015 | JM | 1960 | Cart names in Jamaica. *Names* 8(1), Mar.: 15-23. | [*AGS*] |

Delafosse, Maurice
| 14.0005 | SR | 1925 | Survivances africaines chez les Nègres "Bosch" de la Guyane [African survivals among the Bush Negroes of Guiana]. |

Despres, Leo A.
| 37.0196 | GU | 1964 | The implications of nationalist politics in British Guiana for the development of cultural theory. |
| 26.0003 | GU | 1969 | Differential adaptations and micro-cultural evolution in Guyana. |

Dillard, J. L.
| 25.0093 | BC | 1966 | English in the West Indies, or the West Indies in English? |

Dolphin, Celeste
| 48.0048 | GU | 1959 | Good afternoon, schools. |

Donicie, A. C.
| 19.0016 | SR | 1953 | Iets over de taal en de sprookjes van Suriname [On the language and the fairy-tales of Surinam]. *W I G* 33: 153-173. **[14,24,25]** |
| | | | | [*COL*] |

Doran, Edwin Beal, Jr.
| 35.0027 | GC | 1962 | The West Indian hip-roofed cottage. |

Drimmelen, C. van

11.0027   SR   1925-26 De Neger en zijn cultuur geschiedenis [The Negro and his cultural history].

Duckworth, John

19.0017   BA   1973   An inquiry into the African origins of San Salvador culture. *In* Thomas, Garry, L., ed. ANTHROPOLOGICAL FIELD REPORTS FROM SAN SALVADOR ISLAND. San Salvador, Bahamas, Island Environment Studies, Reports 1973: 6-8.   [*RIS*]

Egan, Cecilia M.

23.0078   MT   1943   Martinique—the isle of those who return.

Ehrlich, Allen S.

12.0026 GU,JM,TR 1971   History, ecology, and demography in the British Caribbean: an analysis of East Indian ethnicity.

Ekwueme, Laz. E. N.

19.0018   GC   1972   African sources in New World black music. *Black Images* 1(3-4), Autumn & Winter: 3-12.   **[11,22]**   [*RIS*]

Elder, J. D.

22.0123   TR   1971   Color, music, and conflict: a study of aggression in Trinidad with reference to the role of traditional music.

Emanuel, Lezmore Evan

25.0111   VI   1972   SURVIVING AFRICANISMS IN VIRGIN ISLANDS ENGLISH CREOLE.

Espinet, Charles S.

22.0128   TR   1953   Masquerade—origin and development of Trinidad's Carnival.

Espinet, Charles S. & Pitts, Harry

22.0129   TR   1944   LAND OF THE CALYPSO: THE ORIGIN AND DEVELOPMENT OF TRINIDAD'S FOLK-SONG.

Feaster, J. Gerald

19.0019   BZ   1968   Measurement and determinants of innovativeness among primitive agriculturists. *Rural Sociol* 33(3), Sept.: 339-348.   **[13,20]**   [*TCL*]

Fock, Niels

13.0061   GU   1958   Cultural aspects and social functions of the "oho" institution among the Waiwai.

9.0047   GG   1960   South American birth customs in theory and practice.

Fortuné, Roger

30.0090   GC   1961   Les bons plats de chez nous [Our tasty dishes].

Frampton, H. M.

22.0135   DM   1957   Carnival time in Dominica.

Freilich, Morris

44.0024   TR   1960   Cultural models and land holdings.

10.0014   TR   1970   Mohawk heroes and Trinidadian peasants.

Fried, Morton H.
15.0035   **GU**   1956   Some observations on the Chinese in British Guiana.

Frucht, Richard, ed.
6.0085   **GC**   1971   Black society in the New World.

Gardner, M. M.
22.0137   **TR**   1954   The greatest show of its kind on earth—Trinidad's Carnival.

Garrett, Clara Maude
19.0020   **JM**   1935   Caribbean Christmas. *Can-W I Mag* 25(1), Dec.: 22-23.   **[23]**
                                                                        [*NYP*]

Goodman, Eileen
19.0021   **BC**   1953   What's in a name?—millions! *Can-W I Mag* 43(5), May: 9, 11.
                                                                        [*NYP*]

Gregory, James R.
19.0022   **BZ**   1972   Pioneers on a cultural frontier: the Mopan Maya of British
                        Honduras. Ph.D. dissertation, University of Pittsburgh:
                        327p.   **[13,20,26]**   [*PhD*]

Groot, Silvia W. de
14.0013   **SR**   1969   Djuka society and social change: history of an attempt to
                        develop a Bush Negro community in Surinam, 1917-1926.
2.0178   **SR**   1974   Surinaamse Granmans in Afrika: vier Groot-Opperhoofden
                        bezoeken het land van hun voorouders [Surinamese
                        Granmans in Africa: four Headmen visit the country of their
                        ancestors].

Gúerin, Daniel
19.0023   **GC**   1956   Un futur pour les Antilles? [A future for the Antilles?] *Présence Afr*
                        6, Feb.-Mar.: 20-27.   **[23,25]**   [*COL*]

Hall, Jerry Alan
43.0182   **BZ**   1973   Mennonite agriculture in a tropical environment: an anal-
                        ysis of the development and productivity of a mid-latitude
                        agricultural system in British Honduras.

Harris, Wilson
24.0084   **GC**   1970   History, fable and myth in the Caribbean and Guianas.

Haweis, Stephen
19.0024   **DM**   1947   The death of a basket. *Can-W I Mag* 37(3), May: 21,23.   **[13]**
                                                                        [*NYP*]

Hearne, John
19.0025   **JM**   1963   European heritage and Asian influence in Jamaica. *In* Our
                        Heritage. Kingston, Dept. of Extra-mural Studies, University of
                        the West Indies, p.7-37. (Public affairs in Jamaica, no. 1.)   **[5]**
                                                                        [*RIS*]

Henriques, Fernando
9.0067   **JM**   1951   Kinship and death in Jamaica.

Henry, Bessie M.
45.0077   **BV**   1957   English ceramics in the British Virgin Islands.

Henry, Frances
19.0026   **GC**   1972   Cultural variation. *In* Resource development in the Caribbean.
                                       Montreal, McGill University, Centre for Developing-Area Studies:
                                       100-105. **[21,26]**   [*RIS*]

Herskovits, Melville Jean
19.0027   **SR**   1928-29   Preliminary report of an ethnological expedition to Suriname, 1928.
                                       W I G 10: 385-390. **[14]**   [*COL*]
19.0028   **SR**   1929   Adjiboto, an African game of the Bush-Negroes of Dutch Guiana.
                                       Man 29(7), July: 122-127. **[14,22]**   [*COL*]
11.0040   **GC**   1931   The New World Negro as an anthropological problem.
22.0172   **GC**   1932   Wari in the New World.
11.0041   **GC**   1938   African ethnology and the New World Negro.
19.0029   **GC**   1938   Les noirs du Nouveau Monde: sujet de recherches africanistes [The
                                       New World Negroes: a subject for Africanist research]. *J Soc Afr*
                                       8(1): 65-82. **[11]**   [*AMN*]
22.0173   **GC**   1941   El estudio de la música negra en el hemisferio occidental [The study
                                       of Negro music in the Western Hemisphere].
22.0174   **GC**   1941   Patterns of Negro music.
11.0042   **GC**   1946   Problem, method and theory in Afroamerican studies.
11.0043   **GC**   1948   The contribution of Afroamerican studies to Africanist research.
11.0044   **GC**   1951   The present status and needs of Afroamerican research.
11.0045   **GC**   1960   The ahistorical approach to Afroamerican studies: a critique.

Herskovits, Melville Jean & Herskovits, Frances S.
22.0176   **SR**   1930   Bush-Negro art.
14.0019   **SR**   1934   Rebel destiny: among the Bush Negroes of Dutch Guiana.
11.0047   **TR**   1947   Trinidad village.

Hill, Errol
22.0183   **TR**   1967   On the origin of the term calypso.

Hill, Luke M.
36.0046   **GU**   1911   Nomenclature of Georgetown: its streets and districts.

Hogg, Donald William
23.0126   **JM**   1956   A West Indian shepherd.
23.0127   **JM**   1960   The Convince Cult in Jamaica.
23.0130   **JM**   1969   Jamaican religions: a study in variations.

Holmer, Nils M.
19.0030   **GC**   1960   Indian place names in South America and the Antilles. *Names* 8(3),
                                       Sept.: 133-149. **[13,25,53]**   [*RIS*]
19.0031   **GC**   1960   Indian place names in South America and the Antilles. *Names* 8(4),
                                       Dec.: 197-219. **[13,25,53]**   [*RIS*]

19.0032   GC   1961   Indian place names in South America and the Antilles. *Names* 9(1), Mar.: 37-52. **[13,25,53]**   [*RIS*]

Horowitz, Michael M.
23.0133   MT   1963   The worship of South Indian deities in Martinique.

Horowitz, Michael M. & Klass, Morton
23.0134   MT   1961   The Martiniquan East Indian cult of Maldevidan.

Howard, Joseph H.
22.0190   GC   1967   DRUMS IN THE AMERICAS.

Hurault, Jean
19.0033   FG   1960   Histoire des noirs réfugiés Boni de la Guyane Francaise [History of the black Boni refugees of French Guiana]. *Rev Fr Hist O-M* 47(166): 76-137. **[5,14]**   [*RIS*]
14.0021   FG   1961   Canots africaines en Guyane [African canoes in Guiana].

Hurston, Zora Neale
19.0034   JM   1938   TELL MY HORSE. Philadelphia, J. B. Lippincott, 301p.   [*AGS*]

James, Eric George
37.0432   JM   1956   ADMINISTRATIVE INSTITUTIONS AND SOCIAL CHANGE IN JAMAICA, BRITISH WEST INDIES—A STUDY IN CULTURAL ADAPTATION.

Jayawardena, Chandra
23.0146   GU   1966   Religious belief and social change: aspects of the development of Hinduism in British Guiana.
17.0052   GC   1967   Migration and social change: a review of Indian communities overseas.

Jha, J. C.
12.0036   TR   1973   Indian heritage in Trinidad, West Indies.
12.0037   TR   1974   The Indian heritage in Trinidad.
12.0038   TR   1976   The Hindu festival of Divali in the Caribbean.
12.0039   TR   1976   The Hindu sacraments (*rites de passage*) in Trinidad and Tobago.

Jones, Catherine Joy
18.0156   BC,UK   1971   IMMIGRATION AND SOCIAL ADJUSTMENT: A CASE STUDY OF WEST INDIAN FOOD HABITS IN LONDON.

Junker, L.
14.0027   SR   1924-25   Godsdienst, zeden en gebruiken der Boschnegers [Religion, manners and customs of the Bush Negroes].

Justus, Joyce Bennett
18.0163   GC,US   1975   Strategies for survival: West Indians in Los Angeles.

Kahn, Morton Charles
14.0031   SR   1928   The Bush Negroes of Dutch Guiana.
22.0211   SR   1931   Art of the Dutch Guiana Bush Negro.
14.0033   SR   1931   DJUKA, THE BUSH NEGROES OF DUTCH GUIANA.
19.0035   SR   1939   Africa's lost tribes in South America. *Nat Hist* 43(4), Apr. 209-215, 232. **[14]**   [*AGS*]

| 19.0036 | SR | 1954 | Little Africa in America: the Bush Negroes. *Américas* 6(10), Oct.: 6-8, 41-43. **[14]** [*AGS*] |
| 19.0037 | SR | 1959 | The Djukas of Surinam. *Explor J* 37(1), Feb.: 12-18. **[14]** [*AGS*] |

Kerns, Virginia & Dirks, Robert

| *24.0101* | BZ | 1975 | John Canoe. |

Klass, Morton

| *8.0117* | TR | 1960 | East and West Indian: cultural complexity in Trinidad. |
| *12.0045* | TR | 1961 | EAST INDIANS IN TRINIDAD: A STUDY OF CULTURAL PERSISTENCE. |

Klerk, Cornelis Johannes Maria de

| *23.0164* | SR | 1951 | CULTUS EN RITUEEL VAN HET ORTHODOXE HINDOEÏSME IN SURINAME [CULTS AND RITUAL OF ORTHODOX HINDUISM IN SURINAM]. |
| *46.0133* | SR | 1953 | DE IMMIGRATIE DER HINDOESTANEN IN SURINAME [THE IMMIGRATION OF HINDUS TO SURINAM]. |

Köbben, A. J. F.

| *14.0038* | SR | 1968 | Continuity in change: Cottica Djuka society as a changing system. |

Kruijer, G. J.

| *23.0175* | NA | 1953 | Kerk en religie op de Bovenwindse Eilanden der Nederlandse Antillen [Church and religion of the Windward Islands of the Netherlands Antilles]. |

Kunike, Hugo

| 19.0038 | GG | 1912 | Der Fisch als Fruchtbarkeitssymbol bei den Waldindianern Sudamerikas [The fish as a fertility symbol among the South American forest Indians]. *Anthropos* 7(1-2), Jan.-Apr.: 206-229. **[13,23,34]** [*AMN*] |

La Guerre, John Gaffar, ed.

| *12.0051* | TR | 1974 | CALCUTTA TO CARONI: THE EAST INDIANS OF TRINIDAD. |

Latour, M. D.

24.0103	CU	1937	Cuenta di Nanzi [Tales of Anansi].
24.0104	CU	1938	Cuenta di Nanzi [Tales of Anansi].
24.0105	CU	1940	Cuenta di Nanzi [Tales of Anansi].

Leach, MacEdward

| *24.0107* | JM | 1961 | Jamaican duppy lore. |

Leiris, Michel

| 19.0039 | FA | 1950 | Martinique, Guadeloupe, Haiti. *Temps Mod* 5(52), Feb.: 1345-1368. **[11]** [*COL*] |

Lekis, Lisa

| *22.0223* | GC | 1955 | The dance as an expression of Caribbean folklore. |
| 19.0040 | GC | 1956 | THE ORIGIN AND DEVELOPMENT OF ETHNIC CARIBBEAN DANCE AND MUSIC. Ph.D. dissertation, University of Florida: 294p. **[21,22]** [*PhD*] |

Lelyveld, Th. van

19.0041   SR   1919   De kleeding der Surinaamsche bevolkingsgroepen [The way of dressing of the Surinam population groups]. *W I G* 1(1): 247-268, 458-470.   [*COL*]

19.0042   SR   1919-20   De kleeding der Surinaamsche bevolkingsgroepen [The way of dressing of the Surinam population groups]. *W I G* 1(2): 20-34, 125-143.   [*COL*]

Leschaloupe, Constance Marie

22.0224   TR   1953   Carnival in Trinidad—masquerades and steelbands.

Lewin, Olive

22.0225   JM   1968   Jamaican folk music.

Lewis, Gordon K.

37.0484   GC   1961   The Caribbean: colonization and culture.

Lichtveld, Lou

25.0236   SR   1928-29   Afrikaansche resten in de Creolentaal van Suriname [African survivals in the Creole language of Surinam].

25.0237   SR   1929-30   Afrikaansche resten in de Creolentaal van Suriname [African survivals in the Creole language of Surinam].

29.0031   SR   1930-31   Een Afrikaansch bijgeloof: snetji-koti [An African superstition: "snakebite cure"].

24.0108   SR   1930-31   Op zoek naar de spin [Looking for the spider].

35.0052   SR   1960   Native arts in modern architecture.

Lier, Willem F. van

14.0046   SR   1921-22   Bij de Aucaners [Among the Aucanians].

14.0047   SR   1922-23   Bij de Aucaners [Among the Aucanians].

Lindblom, K. G.

19.0043   GC   1924   Uber eine alte ethnographische Sammlung aus dem nördlichsten Südamerika im Ethnographischen Reichsmuseum in Stockholm [On an old ethnographic collection from northernmost South America in the National Ethnographic Museum in Stockholm]. *Ymer* 44(2): 153-180. **[1]**   [*COL*]

22.0227   SR   1926   Einige Details in der Ornamentik der Buschneger Surinams [Some details of the ornaments of the Bush Negroes of Surinam].

Louden, Delroy M.

18.0197   BC,UK   1975   Adjustment of West Indian migrants to Britain: an account of some British studies.

McBurnie, Beryl

24.0110   TR   1973   West Indian dance.

McCallan, E. A.

3.0371   BE   1948   Life on old St. David's, Bermuda.

McEleney, J. J.

19.0044   JM   1953   From Jamaica to Canada. *Can-W I Mag* 43(5), May: 5-7.   [*NYP*]

Malefijt, Annemarie de Waal

15.0061   SR   1963   THE JAVANESE OF SURINAM: SEGMENT OF A PLURAL SOCIETY.
23.0190   SR   1971   Animism and Islam among the Javanese in Surinam.

Mathurin, Lucille

8.0155   JM   1971   Creole authenticity: a review of Edward Brathwaite's *The Development of Creole Society in Jamaica 1770-1820.*
6.0196   BC   1975   THE REBEL WOMAN IN THE BRITISH WEST INDIES DURING SLAVERY.

Matthews, Basil

9.0100   TR   1953   CRISIS OF THE WEST INDIAN FAMILY.

May, Arthur J.

35.0054   BC   1933   The architecture of the West Indies.

Mazzarelli, Marcella

8.0156   BZ   1967   Intercommunity relations in British Honduras.

Meiden, J. A. van der

23.0195   SR   1960   Kerken, tempels en heiligdommen in Suriname [Churches, temples and sacred places in Surinam].

Merriam, A. P.; Whinery, Sara & Fred, B. G.

22.0254   TR   1956   Songs of a Rada community in Trinidad.

Merrill, Gordon Clark

19.0045   BC   1961   The survival of the past in the West Indies. *In* Lowenthal, David, ed. THE WEST INDIES FEDERATION. New York, Columbia University Press, p.17-34.   **[5,38,41]**   [*RIS*]

Messenger, John C.

15.0066   MS   1967   The influence of the Irish in Montserrat.
15.0067   MS   1975   Montserrat: the most distinctively Irish settlement in the New World.

Mintz, Sidney W.

17.0068   SC   1955   Puerto Rican emigration: a threefold comparison.
11.0068   GC   1964   Melville J. Herskovits and Caribbean studies: a retrospective tribute.
11.0069   GC   1971[?] Afroamerikaner auf den Antillen [Afro-Americans in the Antilles].
10.0034   GC   1974   Les rôles économiques et la tradition culturelle [Economic roles and cultural tradition].

Mischel, Frances

23.0199   TR   1957   African "powers" in Trinidad: the Shango cult.

Moodie, Silvia María

22.0259   TR   1970   Canciones tradicionales en la isla de Trinidad [Traditional songs on the island of Trinidad].

Moore, Joseph Graessle

23.0202   JM   1953   RELIGION OF JAMAICAN NEGROES: A STUDY OF AFRO-JAMAICAN ACCULTURATION.

Moore, Joseph Graessle & Simpson, George E.

23.0204   JM   1957   A comparative study of acculturation in Morant Bay and West Kingston, Jamaica.

23.0205   JM   1958   A comparative study of acculturation in Morant Bay and West Kingston, Jamaica.

Morpurgo, A. J.

19.0046   SR   1958   Legkaart der beschaving [Mosaic of civilization]. *In* Walle, J. van de & Wit, H. de, eds. SURINAME IN STROOMLIJNEN. Amsterdam, Wereld Bibliotheek, p.76-85.

Myers, Iris

13.0147   GU   1944   The Makushi of British Guiana—a study in culture contact.

13.0148   GU   1946   The Makushi of British Guiana—a study in culture contact.

Naidoo, M. B.

12.0061   TR   1960   The East Indian in Trinidad—a study of an immigrant community.

Nettleford, Rex

19.0047   JM   1963   The African connexion—the significance for Jamaica. *In* OUR HERITAGE. Kingston, Dept. of Extra-mural Studies, University of the West Indies, p.39-55. (Public affairs in Jamaica, no. 1.)   **[5,11]**
                                              [*RIS*]

Newson, Linda A.

26.0007   TR   1972   ABORIGINAL AND SPANISH COLONIAL TRINIDAD: A STUDY IN CULTURAL EVOLUTION.

Niehoff, Arthur

12.0067   TR   1959   The survival of Hindu institutions in an alien environment.

12.0068   TR   1967   The function of caste among the Indians of the Oropuche Lagoon, Trinidad.

Niehoff, Arthur & Niehoff, J.

12.0069   TR   1960   EAST INDIANS IN THE WEST INDIES.

Oudschans Dentz, Fred

19.0048   SR   1955-56 De naam van het land Suriname als geslachtsnaam [The name of the country Surinam as family name]. *W I G* 36: 65-71.   [*COL*]

Panhuys, L. C. van

14.0054   SR   1904   About the ornamentation in use by savage tribes in Dutch Guiana.

14.0055   SR   1906   NÄHERES ÜBER DIE ORNAMENTE DER NATURVÖLKER SURINAMS [DETAILS ON THE ORNAMENTS OF THE PRIMITIVE PEOPLES OF SURINAM].

14.0056   SR   1910   MITTEILUNGEN ÜBER SURINAMSCHE ETHNOGRAPHIE UND KOLONISATIONSGESCHICHTE. . .[NOTES ON THE ETHNOGRAPHY AND COLONIAL HISTORY OF SURINAM].

14.0057   SR   1934   Die Beduetung einiger Ornamente der Buschneger von Niederländisch Guyana [The significance of some Bush Negroes' ornaments from Dutch Guiana].

19.0049   SR   1935-36 De grondslag van de wiskunde in Suriname [The foundations of mathematics in Surinam]. *W I G* 17: 149-158.   **[25]**   [*COL*]

Patient, Serge

19.0050   FC   1971   Assimilation ou négritude?: la culture antilloguyanaise en question
[Assimilation or negritude?: the Antillean-Guyanese culture in
question]. *Afr Lit Art* 17, June: 11-16.   **[21]**   [*COL*]

Patterson, H. Orlando

6.0225   JM   1966   Slavery, acculturation and social change: the Jamaican case.
6.0226   JM   1967   THE SOCIOLOGY OF SLAVERY: AN ANALYSIS OF THE ORIGINS, DEVEL-
OPMENT AND STRUCTURE OF NEGRO SLAVE SOCIETY IN JAMAICA.

Patterson, Sheila

18.0222   BC,UK   1963   DARK STRANGERS: A SOCIOLOGICAL STUDY OF THE ABSORPTION OF A
RECENT WEST INDIAN MIGRANT GROUP IN BRIXTON, SOUTH LONDON.

Pearse, Andrew C.

2.0355   GC   1955   Caribbean folk culture.
32.0453   BC   1956   Ethnography and the lay scholar in the Caribbean.
22.0293   TR   1971   Carnival in nineteenth century Trinidad.

Penard, A. P. & Penard, T. E.

24.0137   SR   1926-27   Negro riddles from Surinam.

Penard, F. P. & Penard, A. P.

23.0223   SR   1913   Surinaamsch bijgeloof: iets over *winti* en andere natuurbegrippen
[Surinam superstition: about *winti* and other supernatural notions].

Pendergast, David M.

19.0051   BZ   1972   The practice of *primicias* in San José Succotz, British Honduras
(Belize). *Ethnos* 37(1-4): 88-96.   **[13,23,29]**   [*COL*]

Petzoldt, T. R.

19.0052   SR   1970   Cultureel patroon [Cultural pattern]. *Schakels* S73: 1-4.   [*NYP*]

Phillips, Leslie H. C.

23.0226   GU   1960   Kali-mai puja.

Pollak-Eltz, Angelina

19.0053   GC   1967   Las culturas negras en las Américas [Black cultures in the Amer-
icas]. *Eco* 15(4), August: 430-452.   [*NYP*]
23.0231   GC   1970   AFRO-AMERIKAANSE GODSDIENSTEN EN CULTEN [AFRO-AMERICAN
RELIGIONS AND CULTS].
23.0232   TR,GR   1970   Shango-Kult und Shouter-Kirche auf Trinidad und Grenada.
[Shango-cult and Shouter-church on Trinidad and Grenada].
23.0233   GR,TR   1971   The Yoruba religion and its decline in the Americas.
23.0234   GC   1972   CULTOS AFROAMERICANOS [AFRO-AMERICAN CULTS].
23.0235   GC   1974   EL CONCEPTO DE MÚLTIPLES ALMAS Y ALGUNOS RITOS FÚNEBRES
ENTRE LOS NEGROS AMERICANOS [THE CONCEPT OF MULTIPLE SOULS
AND SOME FUNERAL RITES OF NEGROES IN THE AMERICAS].

Pope, Pauline Holman

6.0234   SC   1972   CRUZAN SLAVERY: AN ETHNOHISTORICAL STUDY OF DIFFERENTIAL
RESPONSES TO SLAVERY IN THE DANISH WEST INDIES.

Post, Ken

19.0054   **GC**   1967   The second triangular trade: some notes on the links between the Caribbean and Africa. *B Afr Stud Assoc WI* 1, Dec.: 8-14. **[11]**
            [*RIS*]

Powrie, Barbara E.

20.0067   **TR**   1956   The changing attitude of the coloured middle class towards Carnival.

Price, Richard & Price, Sally

14.0062   **SR**   1972   Kammbá: the ethnohistory of an Afro-American art.

Prins, J.

9.0119   **SR**   1965   Twintig jaar praktijk van de Aziatische huwelijkswetgeving in Suriname [Assessing 20 years of the Surinam "Asiatic marriage law"].

Procope, Bruce

22.0297   **TR**   1956   The Dragon Band or Devil Band.
22.0298   **TR**   1959   Ken Morris—metalworker.

Ramchand, Kenneth

22.0304   **GC**   1970   THE WEST INDIAN NOVEL AND ITS BACKGROUND.

Randel, William

53.0462   **JM**   1960   Survival of pre-English place names in Jamaica.

Rauf, Mohammad Abdur

12.0076   **GU**   1972   CRABWOOD CREEK: A STUDY OF CULTURAL CONTINUITY AND ETHNIC IDENTITY ON DIFFERENT GENERATIONAL LEVELS AMONG EAST INDIANS IN GUYANA.

Ray, Michael

19.0055   **GU**   1934   Black Scots. *Can-W I Mag* 23(11), Oct.: 341-342.   [*NYP*]

Reisman, Karl

25.0289   **AT**   1965   'THE ISLE IS FULL OF NOISES': A STUDY OF CREOLE IN THE SPEECH PATTERNS OF ANTIGUA, WEST INDIES.

Revert, Eugene

24.0141   **MT**   1951   DE QUELQUES ASPECTS DU FOLK-LORE MARTINIQUAIS: LE MAGIE ANTILLAISE [ON SOME ASPECTS OF MARTINIQUE FOLKLORE: ANTILLEAN MAGIC].

Rivière, P. G.

13.0169   **SR**   1966   A policy for the Trio Indians of Surinam.

Roberts, Helen H.

22.0308   **JM**   1924   Some drums and drum rhythms of Jamaica.
22.0311   **JM**   1926   Possible survivals of African song in Jamaica.

Rodway, James

53.0484   **GU**   1906   The river-names of British Guiana.
42.0133   **GU**   1911   Names of our plantations.

53.0485	**GU**	1911	Our river names.
13.0175	**GU**	1917	Indian Charms.

Römer, R. A.

8.0190	**CU**	1971	KORSOW: EEN SOCIOLOGISCHE VERKENNING VAN EEN CARIBISCHE MAATSCHAPPIJ [CURAÇAO: A SOCIOLOGICAL RECONNOITERING OF A CARIBBEAN SOCIETY].

Rosenberger, Daniel Ginter

6.0251	**BZ**	1958	AN EXAMINATION OF THE PERPETUATION OF SOUTHERN UNITED STATES INSTITUTIONS IN BRITISH HONDURAS BY A COLONY OF EX-CONFEDERATES.

Roth, Walter Edmund

13.0180	**GU**	1921	Some examples of Indian mimicry, fraud and imposture.
13.0181	**GU**	1924	An introductory study of the arts, crafts, and customs of the Guiana Indians.
13.0182	**GU**	1929	ADDITIONAL STUDIES OF THE ARTS, CRAFTS, AND CUSTOMS OF THE GUIANA INDIANS, WITH SPECIAL REFERENCE TO THOSE OF SOUTHERN BRITISH GUIANA.

Rubin, Vera

8.0194	**GC**	1960	Cultural perspectives in Caribbean research.

Ruiz, R. E.

11.0079	**GC**	1965[?]	A historical perspective on Caribbean Negro life.

Saint-Pierre, Madeleine

25.0302	**MT**	1972	Créole ou français? Les cheminements d'un choix linguistique [Creole or French? Approaching a linguistic choice].

Sanford, Margaret

19.0056	**BZ**	1974	Revitalization movements as indicators of completed acculturation. *Comp Stud Soc Hist* 16(4), Sept.: 504-518. **[26]** [*COL*]

Schipper, Ary

22.0324	**SR**	1944-45	Enkele opmerkingen over Surinaamsche muziek [Some observations about Surinam's music].

Schwartz, Barton M.

8.0196	**TR**	1963	THE DISSOLUTION OF CASTE IN TRINIDAD.
23.0264	**TR**	1964	Ritual aspects of caste in Trinidad.
37.0764	**TR**	1965	Extra-legal activities of the village pandit in Trinidad.
12.0081	**TR**	1967	Differential socio-religious adaptation.

Seaga, Edward

29.0045	**JM**	1955	Jamaica's primitive medicine.

Sedoc-Dahlberg, Betty

18.0256	**SR,NE**	1971	SURINAAMSE STUDENTEN IN NEDERLAND: EEN ONDERZOEK ROND DE PROBLEMATIEK VAN DE TOEKOMSTIGE INTELLEKTUELE KADER-VORMING IN SURINAME [SURINAMESE STUDENTS IN THE NETHER-LANDS: RESEARCH ON THE PROBLEMS OF THE SHAPING OF THE INTELLECTUAL FRAMEWORK OF SURINAM IN THE FUTURE].

Senior, Clarence
17.0095 SC 1947 THE PUERTO RICAN MIGRANT IN ST. CROIX.

Simmons, Harold F. C.
22.0331 SL 1960 Térré bois bois.

Simpson, George Eaton
23.0271 JM 1950 The acculturative process in Jamaican revivalism.
23.0272 JM 1955 Culture change and reintegration found in the cults of West Kingston, Jamaica.
23.0275 JM 1956 Jamaican revivalist cults.
23.0276 JM 1957 The nine night ceremony in Jamaica.
29.0046 TR 1962 Folk medicine in Trinidad.
8.0201 GC 1962 The peoples and cultures of the Caribbean area.
23.0278 TR 1962 The shango cult in Nigeria and in Trinidad.
23.0279 TR 1964 The acculturative process in Trinidadian Shango.
23.0280 TR 1965 THE SHANGO CULT IN TRINIDAD.
8.0203 GC 1970 CARIBBEAN PAPERS.
23.0282 TR,JM 1970 RELIGIOUS CULTS OF THE CARIBBEAN: TRINIDAD, JAMAICA AND HAITI.

Singaravélou
12.0086 GD 1975 LES INDIENS DE LA GUADELOUPE [THE INDIANS OF GUADELOUPE].

Singer, Philip & Araneta, Enrique
12.0089 GU 1967 Hinduization and creolization in Guyana: the plural society and basic personality.

Singh, Kelvin
12.0091 TR 1974 East Indians and the larger society.

Singh, Paul G.
37.0788 BC 1970 Problems of institutional transplantation: the case of the Commonwealth Caribbean local government system.

Skinner, Elliott P.
8.0205 GU 1955 ETHNIC INTERACTION IN A BRITISH GUIANA RURAL COMMUNITY: A STUDY OF SECONDARY ACCULTURATION AND GROUP DYNAMICS.

Smith, M. G.
8.0209 GC 1955[?] A FRAMEWORK FOR CARIBBEAN STUDIES.
19.0057 GC 1960 The African heritage in the Caribbean. *In* Rubin, Vera, ed. CARIBBEAN STUDIES: A SYMPOSIUM. 2D ED. Seattle, University of Washington Press, p.34-53. **[11]**   [*RIS*]

Smith, Raymond Thomas
19.0058 BC 1967 Social stratification, cultural pluralism, and integration in West Indian societies. *In* Lewis, Sybil & Mathews, Thomas G., eds. CARIBBEAN INTEGRATION: PAPER ON SOCIAL, POLITICAL, AND ECONOMIC INTEGRATION. Third Caribbean Scholars' Conference, Georgetown, Guyana, April 4-9, 1966. Rio Piedras, University of Puerto Rico, Institute of Caribbean Studies: 226-258. **[8,16,38]**
                                                                    [*RIS*]
9.0159 GC 1971 Culture and social structure in the Caribbean: some recent work on family and kinship studies.

Smith, Robert Jack

12.0094   TR   1963   MUSLIM EAST INDIANS IN TRINIDAD: RETENTION OF ETHNIC IDENTITY UNDER ACCULTURATIVE CONDITIONS.

Snelleman, J. F.

19.0059   SR   1928-29 De West-Indische zaal in het Museum van het Koloniaal Instituut [The West Indian room in the museum of the Colonial Institute]. *W I G* 10: 149-157. **[1]**   [*COL*]

Solien, Nancie L.

13.0198   JM,BZ,TR   1971   West Indian characteristics of the Black Carib.

Speckmann, Johan Dirk

12.0096   SR   1963   The Indian group in the segmented society of Surinam.

Stone, Linda S.

12.0100   SV   1973   East Indian adaptations on St. Vincent: Richland Park.

Taylor, Douglas

13.0208   DM,BZ   1950   The meaning of dietary and occupational restrictions among the Island Carib.

53.0570   DM   1954   Names on Dominica.

Tholenaar-van Raalte, J.

18.0272   GC,UK,NE   1968   De integratie van Westindische immigranten in Groot-Brittannië en in Nederland [The integration of West Indian immigrants in Great Britain and the Netherlands).

Thomas-Hope, Elizabeth

18.0273   BC,UK,US   1975   The adaptation of migrants from the English-speaking Caribbean in select urban centres of Britain and North America.

Thompson, Robert Wallace

24.0156   GC   1955-56 The mushroom and the parasol: a West Indian riddle.

19.0060   GC   1956   Duckanoo—a word and a thing. *Caribbean* 9(10), May: 218-219, 229.   [*COL*]

25.0368   GC   1958   Mushrooms, umbrellas and black magic: a West Indian linguistic problem.

Tracey, Kenneth A.

8.0239   GC   1975   Race problems in anthropological perspective.

Triseliotis, J. P.

18.0276   BC,UK   1972   The implications of cultural factors in social work with immigrants.

Tucker, Terry

19.0061   BE   1951   Early Bermuda Christmases. *Bermuda Hist Q* 8(4), Oct.-Dec.: 140-142.   [*COL*]

22.0358   BE   1955   Guy Fawkes Day.

19.0062   BE   1968   Old Bermuda traditions (sports, wedding and domestic). *Bermuda Hist Q* 25(3), Autumn: 86-89.   [*COL*]

Tull, Marc

19.0063   BA   1973   San Salvadorian reactions to the American: a brief look at American influence on San Salvador. *In* Thomas, Garry L., ed. ANTHROPOLOGICAL FIELD REPORTS FROM SAN SALVADOR ISLAND. San Salvador, Bahamas, Island Environment Studies Reports 1973: 1-5. **[26]**   [*RIS*]

Vries, Jan de

14.0075   SR   1970   Het medisch werk in Suriname's bosland: Een sociopedagogische beschouwing [The medical work in the inland of Surinam: A socio-educational analysis].

Walker, Della

13.0218   GU   1972   Guyana: problems in Amerindian acculturation.

Warner, Maureen

19.0064   TR   1970   Some Yoruba descendants in Trinidad. *B Afr Stud Assoc WI* 3, Dec.: 9-16. **[11,25]**   [*RIS*]

19.0065   TR   1971   African feasts in Trinidad. *B Afr Stud Assoc WI* 4, Dec.: 85-94. **[23,25]**   [*RIS*]

25.0401   TR   1971   Trinidad Yoruba—notes on survivals.

Waterman, Richard Alan

22.0371   TR   1943   AFRICAN PATTERNS IN TRINIDAD NEGRO MUSIC.

Watson, Karl S.

15.0089   BB   1970   THE REDLEGS OF BARBADOS.

Wengen, G. D. van

15.0092   SR   [n.d.]   DE JAVANEN IN DE SURINAAMSE SAMENLEVING [THE JAVANESE IN THE SURINAMESE SOCIETY].

Wesche, Marjorie Bingham

5.0969   BC   1972   Place names as a reflection of cultural chance: an example from the Lesser Antilles.

Whipple, Emory

22.0375   BZ   1976   Pia Manadi.

White, Landeg E.

22.0376   TR   1969   Steelbands: a personal record.

Whitten, Norman E., Jr. & Szwed, John F., eds.

11.0089   GC   1970   AFRO-AMERICAN ANTHROPOLOGY: CONTEMPORARY PERSPECTIVES.

Wickham, John

19.0066   BC   1958   Growing up in the West Indies. *Shell Trin* 5(2), Mar.: 26-28.

Wilbert, Johannes

13.0219   GU   1967   Secular and sacred functions of the fire among the Warao.

Williams, James

19.0067   GU   1922   The name "Guiana." *W I Comm Circ* 37(612), Mar. 16: 127. **[13]**
                                                                                          [*NYP*]

19.0068	**GU**	1922	The name "Guiana." *W I Comm Cir* 36(613), Mar. 30: 151. **[13]** *[NYP]*
19.0069	**GU**	1922	The name "Guiana." *W I Comm Circ* 37(614), Apr. 13: 173-174. **[13]** *[NYP]*
53.0651	**GG**	1923	The name "Guiana."

Williams, Joseph J.

23.0328	**JM**	1934	PSYCHIC PHENOMENA OF JAMAICA.
23.0329	**JM**	1970	VOODOOS AND OBEAHS; PHASES OF WEST INDIAN WITCHCRAFT.

Wood, B. R.

13.0225	**GU**	1944	Curare.

Wood, Richard E.

25.0419	**CU**	1972	Dutch syntactic loans in Papiamentu.

Wynter, Sylvia

22.0385	**JM**	1970	Jonkonnu in Jamaica: towards the interpretation of folk dance as a cultural process.

Yde, Jens

13.0226	**GU**	1959	Resist-dyed bark costumes of the Waiwai Indians.

Chapter 20

VALUES AND NORMS

Attitudes in general; status and values; racial and political attitudes; cultural responses; social psychology.

See also: [11] Population segments: Afro-Caribbean; [12] Population segments: East Indian; [15] Population segments: Other; [21] Ethnic and national identity; [23] Religion; [31] Psychiatry and mental health.

Abbenhuis, Fulgentius

20.0001   SR   1970   Surinaamse mentaliteit [Surinamese mentality]. *In* Janssen, Cornelius, ed. SURINAME: HET WERK VAN DE FRATERS VAN TILBURG ONDER DE VIJFSTERRENVLAG. Tilburg, The Netherlands, Fraters van O.L. Vrouw, Moeder van Barmhartigheid: 17-22. (Intercom-Fraters No. 7)   [23]   [*RILA*]

Abrahams, Peter

20.0002   JM   1961[?]   The influence of ideas. *In* Cumper, George, ed. REPORT OF THE CONFERENCE ON SOCIAL DEVELOPMENT IN JAMAICA. Kingston, Standing Committee on Social Services, p.98-100.   [21]   [*RIS*]

Abrahams, Roger D.

8.0001   SV   1970   A performance-centered approach to gossip.

Abrahams, Roger D. & Bauman, Richard

25.0001   SV   1971   Sense and nonsense in St. Vincent: speech behavior and decorum in a Caribbean community.

Abraham-van der Mark, Eva E.

9.0002   CU   1970   Differences in the upbringing of boys and girls in Curaçao, correlated with differences in the degree of neurotic instability.

Adhin, J. H.

9.0009   SR   1969   Huwelijksontbinding door verstoting [Dissolution of marriage by repudiation].

Alderman, Michael H. & Ferguson, Robert

34.0001   JM   1976   The impact of a family planning clinic in rural Jamaica.

Alexander, Henry Jacob

9.0016   JM   1973   THE CULTURE OF MIDDLE-CLASS FAMILY LIFE IN KINGSTON, JAMAICA.

Alleyne, Mervin C.
25.0005   **SL**   1961   Language and society in St. Lucia.

Allison, Audrey M.
20.0003   **JM**   1968   The smiling Englishman. *Engl Immigr* 2, Spring: 22-24.   [*TCL*]

Anderson, L. E.
32.0022   **JM**   1973   Authoritarianism and achievement in a Jamaica Teachers'
                              College.

Anderson, William A. & Dynes, Russell R.
46.0006   **CU**   1973   Organizational and political transformation of a social movement: a
                              study of the 30th of May Movement in Curaçao.

Angrosino, Michael V.
12.0007   **TR**   1975   The case of the healthy Hindu.

Archambault, Jean
52.0010   **GD**   1967   Un village de pêcheurs (Deshaies) en Guadeloupe [A village
                              of fishermen (Deshaies) on Guadeloupe].

Ashton, Guy T.
17.0008   **BZ**   1967   Consecuencias de la emigración de zapateros adolescentes a Belice
                              [Consequences of the migration of adolescent shoemakers to
                              Belize].

Austin, Diane Joyce
10.0001   **JM**   1974   Symbols and ideologies of class in urban Jamaica: a cultural
                              analysis of class.

Back, Kurt W. & Stycos, J. Mayone
34.0005   **JM**   1959   The survey under unusual conditions: the Jamaica Human
                              Fertility Investigation.

Bacus, M. Kazim
32.0038   **GU**   1974   The primary school curriculum in a colonial society.

Bagley, Christopher & Coard, Bernard
21.0002   **BC,UK**   1975   Cultural knowledge and rejection of ethnic identity in West Indian
                                  children in London.

Bagley, Christopher & Verma, Gajendra K.
16.0002   **BC,UK**   1975   Inter-ethnic attitudes and behaviour in British multi-racial schools.

Baksh, Ishmael
32.0041   **TR**   1974   Some factors related to educational expectation among East
                              Indian and negro students attending public secondary
                              school in Trinidad.
32.0043   **TR**   1975   Selected variables and educational expectation among high school
                              students in Trinidad.

Barrow, Christine
20.0004   **BB**   1976   Reputation and ranking in a Barbadian locality. *Social Econ Stud*
                              25(2), June: 106-121.   **[8]**   [*RIS*]

Bartels, Dennis

20.0005   GU   1974   The influence of folk models upon historical analysis: a case study from Guyana. *W Can J Anthrop* 4(1), Jan.: 73-81. **[37]**   [*COL*]

Baugh, Edward

20.0006   BC   1968   Review article: Towards a West Indian criticism. *Car Q* 14(1-2), March-June: 140-144.   [*RIS*]

Bayley, George D.

20.0007   GU   1911   Census comicalities. *Timehri* 3d ser., 1(18B), July: 86-88. **[7]**   [*AMN*]

Beal, John F. & Dickson, S.

28.0104   BC,UK   1975   Differences in dental attitudes and behaviour between West Midland mothers of various ethnic origins.

Bell, Wendell

38.0020   JM   1960   Attitudes of Jamaican elites toward the West Indies Federation.

37.0042   JM   1960   Images of the United States and the Soviet Union held by Jamaican elite groups.

37.0043   JM   1962   Equality and attitudes of elites in Jamaica.

37.0044   JM   1964   JAMAICAN LEADERS: POLITICAL ATTITUDES IN A NEW NATION.

37.0045   GC   1967   Ethnicity, decisions of nationhood, and images of the future.

40.0004   BC   1973   New states in the Caribbean: a grounded theoretical account.

Bell, Wendell, ed.

37.0046   BC   1967   THE DEMOCRATIC REVOLUTION IN THE WEST INDIES: STUDIES IN NATIONALISM, LEADERSHIP, AND THE BELIEF IN PROGRESS.

Bell, Wendell & Moskos, C. C., Jr.

40.0005   BC   1965   Some implications of equality for political, economic and social development.

Bell, Wendell & Oxaal, Ivar

37.0047   BC   1964   DECISIONS OF NATIONHOOD: POLITICAL AND SOCIAL DEVELOPMENT IN THE BRITISH CARIBBEAN.

Bengtsson, Bo

54.0095   TR   1966   A SURVEY OF CULTURAL PRACTICES AND UTILIZATION OF EDIBLE AROIDS IN TRINIDAD.

Benoist, Jean

56.0019   GC   1972   Dynamique bio-culturelle de la région Caraïbe: essai d'anthropobiologie écologique [Bio-cultural dynamics of the Caribbean: ecological anthropobiological trial].

Bertrand, Anca

20.0008   FA   1969   Notes sur le costume créole. [Notes of Creole dress]. *Parallèles* 30: 4-17.   [*RIS*]

Bickerton, Y. J.

47.0023   GU   1971   Ethnic images in Guyanese advertising.

Birbalsingh, F. M.

16.0008   **BC**   1968   Review article: To John Bull, with hate.

Biswamitre, C. R.

12.0013   **SR**   1937   Miskenning [Misjudgment].

Blake, Judith; Stycos, J. Mayone & Davis, Kingsley

34.0010   **JM**   1961   FAMILY STRUCTURE IN JAMAICA: THE SOCIAL CONTEXT OF REPRO-
                              DUCTION.

Blom, F. E. A.

31.0027   **GC**   1963   Conflicting values and cultural identifications facing the Caribbean
                              adolescent today.

Bonaparte, Tony H.

20.0009   **TR**   1969   The influence of culture on business in a pluralistic society: a study
                              of Trinidad. *Am J Econ Sociol* 28(3), July: 285-300.   **[8,45]**   [*COL*]

Booy, Theodoor de

24.0029   **JM**   1915   Certain West-Indian superstitions pertaining to celts.

Braithwaite, Lloyd E.

32.0077   **BC**   1958   The development of higher education in the British West Indies.
31.0030   **GC**   1963   The changing social scene.

Brana-Shute, Gary

9.0027   **BC**   1976   Domesticity, drinking, and systemic equilibrium: some ideas on
                              lower class Caribbean male behavior.

Brathwaite, Edward

22.0037   **BC**   1963   Roots.

Bremmer, Theodore A.

32.0082   **BC**   1975   Science education in the Caribbean: curricular and other concerns.

Brody, Eugene B.

34.0015   **JM**   1974   Mental health and population control.
34.0016   **JM**   1974   Psychocultural aspects of contraceptive behavior in Jamaica.

Brody, Eugene B.; Ottey, Frank & Lagranade, Janet

34.0017   **JM**   1974   Couple communication in the contraceptive decision making of
                              Jamaican women.

Brody, Grace F.

20.0010   **JM**   1972   THE DEVELOPMENT OF AESTHETIC PREFERENCES: A COMPARISON OF
                              AMERICAN AND JAMAICAN CHILDREN. Paper presented at the (80th)
                              Annual Convention of the American Psychological Association,
                              Honolulu, Hawaii, September 1972: 8p.   [*TCL*]

Brown, Marvin & Amoroso, Donald M.

20.0011   **TR**   1975   Attitudes toward homosexuality among West Indian male and
                              female college students. *J Social Psychol* 97 (Second Half), Dec.:
                              163-168.   **[31]**   [*COL*]

Camacho, Andrew
46.0031   BC   1970   Work and society.

Cameron, Norman E.
20.0012   GU   1965   AN INTRODUCTION TO OUR SOCIAL PHILOSOPHY. Georgetown, Labour Advocate Printing Dept.: 33p. **[21]**   [*NYP*]

Carew, Jan
16.0016   GC   1975   The origins of racism in the Americas.

Carter, Bernard W.
61.0027   GU   1971   Factors related to the adoption of recommended rice farming practices on a land settlement scheme in Guyana.

Chambertrand, Gilbert de
22.0062   FA   1963   MI 10!

Chartrand, Francine
15.0019   GD   1965   Le choix du conjoint chez les Blancs-Matignons de la Guadeloupe: critères éconimiques et critères raciaux [The choice of spouse among the Blancs-Matignons of Guadeloupe: economic and racial criteria].

Cheetham, Juliet
18.0057   BC,UK   1972   Immigrants, social work, and the community.

Ciski, Robert
15.0021   SV   1975   THE VINCENTIAN PORTUGUESE: A STUDY IN ETHNIC GROUP ADAPTATION.

Ciski, Robert & Mulcahy, F. David
20.0013   SV   1972   Adaptándose al Soufriere [Adapting to Soufriere]. *Ethnica* 4: 27-45. (reprint) **[53]**   [*RIS*]
20.0014   SV   1972[?]   Reactions in Villo Point. *In* Fraser, Thomas M.; Ciski, Robert; Hourihan, John J.; Morth, Grace E. & Mulcahy, F. David. LA SOUFRIERE: CULTURAL REACTIONS TO THE THREAT OF VOLCANIC ERUPTION ON THE ISLAND OF SAINT VINCENT, 1971-1972. Amherst, University of Massachusetts: 19-31. **[53]**   [*RIS*]

Clarke, Anthony Stephen
32.0119   TR   1973   AN ANALYSIS OF STUDENTS' SELF-ESTEEM AND STUDENTS' ATTITUDES TOWARD CULTURE IN SECONDARY SCHOOLS IN TRINIDAD.

Clarke, Colin G.
8.0035   TR   1973   PLURALISM AND STRATIFICATION IN SAN FERNANDO, TRINIDAD.

Cohen, Yehudi A.
8.0038   JM   1971   Four categories of interpersonal relationships in the family and community in a Jamaican village.

Coleridge, P. E.
8.0039   **SR**   1958   Vrouwenleven in Paramaribo [Women's life in Paramaribo].

Cook, A. P.
33.0048   **BC**   1975   Some influences on the behaviour of the West Indian adolescent
—and some problems.

Corbin, Carlyle G., Jr.
32.0130   **UV**   1975   INSTITUTIONAL CONSEQUENCES OF IMPORTED EDUCATION TO THE U.S.
VIRGIN ISLANDS.

Coulthard, G. R.
20.0015 **FA**   1961   The French West Indian background of negritude. *Car Q* 7(3),
Dec.: 128-136.   **[11,19,21]**   [*RIS*]

Crane, Julia G.
8.0046   **SA**   ·1971   EDUCATED TO EMIGRATE: THE SOCIAL ORGANIZATION OF SABA.

Cross, Malcolm
8.0048   **GC**   1968   Cultural pluralism and sociological theory: a critique and re-
evaluation.

Cumper, George E.
20.0016 **JM**   1970   Work attitude in Jamaica: a critical sidelight on the 'human
resources' approach. *In* Harewood, Jack, ed. HUMAN RESOURCES IN
THE COMMONWEALTH CARIBBEAN. St. Augustine, Trinidad, U.W.I.,
Institute of Social and Economic Research: 14p.   **[7]**   [*RIS*]

Dalton, Robert H.
32.0152   **ST**   1968   EDUCATION AND THE SOCIAL CLIMATE: A FOLLOW-UP STUDY OF
CHILDREN FIVE YEARS LATER.

Danns, Kens
20.0017 **BC**   1975   Charisma and West Indian leadership. *Guy J Sociol* 1(1), Oct.:
42-50.   [*RIS*]

Darlington, Charleen Arnett
20.0018 **BA**   1973   A brief examination of political attitudes on San Salvador on the
eve of political independence. *In* Thomas, Garry L., ed. ANTHRO-
POLOGICAL FIELD REPORTS FROM SAN SALVADOR ISLAND. San
Salvador, Bahamas, Island Environment Studies, Reports 1973:
106-109.   **[37]**   [*RIS*]

Davidson, J. R. T.
31.0049   **JM**   1972   Post-partum mood change in Jamaican women: a description and
discussion on its significance.

Davidson, Lewis
33.0059   **JM**   1961[?] Acceptance of social change.

Dew, Edward
20.0019 **SR**   1974   Testing elite perceptions of deprivation and satisfaction in a
culturally plural society. *Comp Polit* 6(2), Jan.: 271-285.   **[8]** [*COL*]

Dirks, Robert

8.0063   TT   1972   Networks, groups, and adaptation in an Afro-Caribbean community.

Dodd, David J.

33.0061   GU   1975   Some reflections on the evolution of delinquent careers in greater Georgetown.

Domingos, Robert

25.0100   CU   1974   ATTITUDE AND LANGUAGE CHOICE IN A MULTILINGUAL SOCIETY: URBAN CURAÇAO.

Dubreuil, Guy

9.0042   MT   1965   La famille martiniquaise: analyse et dynamique [The Martiniquan family: analysis and dynamics].

Duke, James T.

20.0020   JM   1963   EQUALITARIANISM AMONG EMERGENT ELITES IN A NEW NATION. Ph.D. dissertation, University of California, Los Angeles, 265p.   **[8,32]**

37.0207   JM   1967   Egalitarianism and future leaders in Jamaica.

Duncan, Neville C.

37.0209   JM   1970   The political process, and attitudes and opinions in a Jamaican Parish Council.

Dunwoodie, Peter

22.0115   GC   1975   Commitment and confinement: two West Indian visions.

Eckstein, Michael Eusey

33.0065   SC   1967   VIOLATIONS OF VALUES: A STUDY OF THE DIVERSE SOCIAL CONSEQUENCES OF CRIME IN ST. CROIX.

Ehrlich, Allen S.

12.0029   JM   1976   Race and ethnic identity in rural Jamaica: the East Indian case.

Elder, J. D.

22.0121   TR   1968   The male/female conflict in calypso.

Epstein, Erwin H.

21.0026   SL   1972   SENSE OF NATIONALITY AMONG SCHOOLCHILDREN: 'CENTER'-'PERIPHERY' DIFFERENCES WITH SPECIAL REFERENCE TO ST. LUCIA, WEST INDIES.

Espinet, Adrian

20.0021   BC   1965   Honours and Paquotille. *New Wld Q* 2(1), Dead Season: 19-22.

[*RIS*]

Evans, Peter

18.0094   BC,UK   [n.d.]   ATTITUDES OF YOUNG IMMIGRANTS.

Feaster, J. Gerald

19.0019   BZ   1968   Measurement and determinants of innovativeness among primitive agriculturists.

Finkel, Herman J.

20.0022 SK,NV 1964 Attitudes toward work as a factor in agricultural planning in the West Indies. *Car Stud* 4(1), Apr.: 49-53. **[43,46]** [*RIS*]

Fischer, Michael M. J.

20.0023 JM 1974 Value assertion and stratification: religion and marriage in rural Jamaica. *Car Stud* 14(1), April: 7-37. **[9,23]** [*RIS*]

Fisher, Lawrence E.

31.0061 BB 1973 THE IMAGERY OF MADNESS IN VILLAGE BARBADOS.

Fonaroff, Arlene

30.0088 JM 1975 Cultural perceptions and nutritional disorders: a Jamaican case study.

Fonaroff, L. Schuyler

28.0445 TR 1968 Man and malaria in Trinidad: ecological perspectives on a changing health hazard.

Foner, Nancy

8.0074 JM 1971 SOCIAL CHANGE AND SOCIAL MOBILITY IN A JAMAICAN RURAL COMMUNITY.

32.0210 JM 1972 Competition, conflict, and education in rural Jamaica.

32.0211 JM 1973 STATUS AND POWER IN RURAL JAMAICA: A STUDY OF EDUCATIONAL AND POLITICAL CHANGE.

32.0212 JM,UK 1975 The meaning of education to Jamaicans at home and in London.

Forsythe, Dennis

20.0024 GC 1974 Repression, radicalism and change in the West Indies. *Race* 15(4), April: 401-429. **[38,40]** [*COL*]

21.0028 GC 1975 Alienation and ideology among four West Indian activists.

8.0075 BC 1975 Race, colour and class in the British West Indies.

Forsythe, Dennis, ed.

21.0029 GC 1975 BLACK ALIENATION, BLACK REBELLION.

Fraser, Thomas M.

33.0076 SV 1972[?] Conclusion: the volcano takes its toll.

53.0215 SV 1972[?] Introduction: "Soufriere comes alive".

Fraser, Thomas M.; Ciski, Robert; Hourihan, John J.; Morth, Grace E. & Mulcahy, F. David

20.0025 SV 1972[?] LA SOUFRIERE: CULTURAL REACTIONS TO THE THREAT OF VOLCANIC ERUPTION ON THE ISLAND OF SAINT VINCENT, 1971-1972. Amherst, University of Massachusetts: 113p. **[53]** [*RIS*]

Frechette, Errol James

18.0109 BC,CA 1970 ATTITUDES OF FRENCH AND ENGLISH SPEAKING CANADIANS TOWARD WEST INDIAN IMMIGRANTS: A GUTTMAN FACET ANALYSIS.

Fredericks, Marcel A.; Mundy, Paul & Lennon, John J.

28.0458 GU 1969 Los médicos en una nación en desarrollo: trasfondo social y actitudes [Doctors in a developing nation: social background and attitudes].

		Freilich, Morris
9.0048	**TR**	1968 Sex, secrets and systems.

Freilich, Morris & Coser, Lewis A.
9.0049   **TR**   1972   Structured imbalances of gratification: the case of the Caribbean mating system.

Gemmink, Joh.
7.0056   **SR**   1970   COPULATIE—PATRONEN BIJ RACIALE—EN CULTUREELE ASSIMILATIE [MATING PATTERNS ASSOCIATED WITH RACIAL AND CULTURAL ASSIMILATION].

Gerber, Stanford N. & Stanton, Howard R.
8.0078   **ST**   1973   Ethnic structure and social change in the U.S. Virgin Islands.

Girvan, Norman
20.0026   **GC**   1975   ASPECTS OF THE POLITICAL ECONOMY OF RACE IN THE CARIBBEAN AND IN THE AMERICAS. Mona, Jamaica, University of the West Indies, Institute of Social and Economic Research: 33p. **[16,40]**
[*RIS*]

Glantz, Oscar
20.0027   **GC,US**   1976   Personal efficacy, system-blame, and violence orientation: a test of the ·blocked-opportunity theory. *Social Econ Stud* 25(2), June: 122-133. **[37]**   [*RIS*]

Glass, Ruth
21.0032   **JM**   1962   Ashes of discontent.

Goeje, C. H. de
20.0028   **GC**   1943   Philosophy, initiation and myths of the Indians of Guiana and adjacent countries. *Int Archiv Ethnogr* 44: 1-136. **[13,23,24,29]**
[*AMN*]

Gomes, Ralph C.
20.0029   **GU**   1975   A social psychology of leadership: elite attitudes in Guyana. *In* Singham, A. W., ed. THE COMMONWEALTH CARIBBEAN INTO THE SEVENTIES. Montreal, McGill University, Centre for Developing Area Studies: 119-142. **[37,40]**   [*RIS*]

Gorsuch, Richard L. & Barnes, M. Louise
20.0030   **BZ**   1973   Stages of ethical reasoning and moral forms of· Carib youths. *J Cross-Cult Psychol* 4(3), Sept.: 283-301. **[13]**   [*TCL*]

Graham, Sara
8.0085   **GU**   1973   OCCUPATIONAL MOBILITY IN GUYANA.

Graham, Sara & Beckles, David
46.0086   **GU**   1968   The prestige ranking of occupations: problems of method and interpretation suggested by a study in Guyana.

Green, Helen Bagenstose
31.0067   **TR**   1964   Socialization values in the Negro and East Indian subcultures of Trinidad.

20.0031   TR   1965   Values of Negro and East Indian school children in Trinidad. *Social Econ Stud* 14(2), June: 204-216. **[11,12,32]**   [*RIS*]

Greene, J. E.
18.0118   BC,CA   1970   Political perspectives on the assimilation of immigrants: a case study of West Indians in Vancouver.

Gregory, James R.
19.0022   BZ   1972   PIONEERS ON A CULTURAL FRONTIER: THE MOPAN MAYA OF BRITISH HONDURAS.
20.0032   BZ   1975   Image of limited good, or expectation of reciprocity? *Curr Anthrop* 16(1), March: 73-83. **[10,13]**   [*COL*]

Gresle, François
8.0090   MT   1971   Ambiguïtés des modèles et spécificité de la société martiniquaise [Ambiguous models and specifications in Martiniquan society].

Hanson, David
20.0033   BZ   1974   Politics, partisanship, and social position in Belize. *J Inter-Amer Stud* 16(4), Nov.: 409-435. **[8,37]**   [*COL*]

Haynes, Lilith M.
25.0160   BB,GU   1973   LANGUAGE IN BARBADOS AND GUYANA: ATTITUDES, BEHAVIOURS AND COMPARISONS.

Heckscher, Bridget Tancock
9.0064   BB   1967   Household structure and achievement orientation in lower-class Barbadian families.

Henderson, T. H.
43.0194   BC   1970   Selecting extension workers for the development of small scale farming in the West Indies.

Henriques, Fernando
8.0097   BC   1969   Colour and contemporary society in the Caribbean.

Herskovits, Melville Jean & Herskovits, Frances S.
14.0019   SR   1934   REBEL DESTINY: AMONG THE BUSH NEGROES OF DUTCH GUIANA.

Hill, Carole E., ed.
20.0034   BB,TR   1975   SYMBOLS AND SOCIETY: ESSAYS ON BELIEF SYSTEMS IN ACTION. Athens, University of Georgia Press: 140p. (Southern Anthropological Society, Proceedings, No. 9)   [*COL*]

Hill, David
20.0035   BC,UK   1970   The attitudes of West Indian and English adolescents in Britain. *Race* 11(3), Jan.: 313-321. **[18]**   [*COL*]

Hill, Donald R.
9.0071   CR   1974   More on truth, fact, and tradition in Carriacou.

Hill, Errol
22.0185   BC   1972   Cultural values and the theatre arts in the English-speaking Caribbean.

Hilton, Jennifer

20.0036　BC,UK　1972　The ambitions of school children. *Race Today* 4(3), March: 79-81. **[32]** *[RIS]*

Hinds, Donald

18.0140　BC,UK　1966　Journey to an illusion: the West Indian in Britain.

Hodge, Merle

9.0073　GC　1974　Male attitudes in Caribbean family life.

9.0074　GC　1974　The shadow of the whip: a comment on male-female relations in the Caribbean.

Hoetink, Harry

20.0037　GC　1961　"Colonial psychology" and race. *J Econ Hist* Dec.: 629-640. **[21]** *[RIS]*

21.0044　GC　1974　National identity and somatic norm image.

Horowitz, Michael M.

9.0077　MT　1971　A decision model of conjugal patterns in Martinique.

Hoyt, Elizabeth E.

41.0247　JM　1959　Changing standards of living in Jamaica.

Isaacs, Ian

32.0309　JM　1976　Environmental and other factors affecting the performance in mathematics of third-year students in Jamaican post-primary schools.

Jacobs, Sharon

20.0038　BA　1973　San Salvador Island: from culture contact to alienation. *In* Thomas, Garry L., ed. Anthropological field reports from San Salvador Island. San Salvador, Bahamas, Island Environment Studies, Reports 1973: 110-119. **[26]** *[RIS]*

James, C. L. R.

20.0039　BC　1963　Beyond a boundary. London, Hutchinson, 365p. **[22]**

Jayawardena, Chandra

8.0114　GU　1963　Conflict and solidarity in a Guianese plantation.

John, Gus

18.0155　BC,UK　1972　The social worker and the young blacks.

Jordan, Winthrop D.

16.0052　BC　1962　American chiaroscuro: the status and definition of mulattoes in the British Colonies.

5.0493　GC　1968　White over black: American attitudes toward the Negro, 1550-1812.

Justus, Joyce Bennett

20.0040　DM　1973　The utmost for the highest: a study of adolescent aspirations in Dominica, West Indies. Ann Arbor, Michigan, University Microfilms: 179p. (PhD dissertation, University of Calif., Los Angeles, 1971.) **[32]** *[RIS]*

Kreiselman, Mariam J.

9.0087   MT   1958   THE CARIBBEAN FAMILY: A CASE STUDY IN MARTINIQUE.

Krimpen, A. van

20.0041   SR   1974   VERSLAG VAN EEN ENQUÊTE ONDER LEERLINGEN VAN SURINAAMSE SCHOLEN [ACCOUNT OF A QUESTIONNAIRE AMONG STUDENTS OF SURINAMESE SCHOOLS]. Amsterdam, Universiteit van Amsterdam, Sociografisch Instituut FSW: 117p. [Onderzoekprojekt Sociale Ontwikkelingsstrategie Suriname 1969, Deelrapport nr. 16]. **[9,32]**
                                              [RIS]

Kruijer, G. J.

34.0046   JM   1958   Family size and family planning: a pilot survey among Jamaican mothers.

9.0088   JM   1968   JAMAICA'S SOCIAL PROBLEMS: A REPORT INDICATING A WAY OUT; PART I [PART II: CLARIFICATIONS AND ADDITIONAL DETAILS; PART III: SCIENTIFIC EVIDENCE].

Kruijf, Hans de & Arends, Harold

54.0603   CU   1975   The attitude of the people in Curaçao towards "naturalesa": a qualitative psychological study.

Kumar, Sushil

34.0047   AT   1973   A SURVEY OF USERS AND NONUSERS OF CONTRACEPTIVES IN ANTIGUA.

LaFlamme, A. G.

16.0055   BA   1972   GREEN TURTLE CAY: A BI-RACIAL COMMUNITY IN THE OUT-ISLAND BAHAMAS.

Laishley, Jennie

20.0042   BC,UK   1975   Cognitive processes in adolescent ethnic attitudes. *In* Verma, Gajendra K. & Bagley, Christopher, eds. RACE AND EDUCATION ACROSS CULTURES. London, Heinemann Educational Books Ltd.: 263-282. **[16,18]**   *[RIS]*

Landis, Joseph B.

20.0043   GU   1973   Racial attitudes of Africans and Indians in Guyana. *Social Econ Stud* 22(4), Dec.: 427-439. **[11,12]**   *[RIS]*

Langton, Kenneth P.

37.0470   JM   1966   Political partisanship and political socialization in Jamaica.

Lawton, David

22.0220   JM   1976   White man, black man, coolie man—pejorative terms in a Creole society.

Lefley, Harriet P.

31.0087   BA   1972   Modal personality in the Bahamas.

Lengermann, Patricia Madoo

20.0044   TR   1971   Working-class values in Trinidad and Tobago. *Social Econ Stud* 20(2), June: 151-163. **[10]**   *[RIS]*

20.0045   TR   1972   The debate on the structure and content of West Indian values: some relevant data from Trinidad and Tobago. *Br J Sociol* 23(3), Sept.: 298-311. **[8]**   *[COL]*

Lieber, Michael
10.0025   **TR**   1973   STYLES AND ADAPTATIONS: ASPECTS OF LOWER-CLASS SOCIAL LIFE IN PORT-OF-SPAIN, TRINIDAD.

Lieberman, Dena
20.0046   **SL**   1975   Language attitudes in St. Lucia. *J Cross-Cult Psychol* 6(4), Dec.: 471-481.   **[25]**   [*TCL*]

Lightbourne, Robert
9.0092   **JM**   1972   La relación entre cinco tipos de hijos y el deseo de tener más hijos, en Jamaica [The relationship between 5 types of children and the wish to have more children in Jamaica].

Lowe, Gilbert Antonio
20.0047   **JM**   1966   Education, occupation of fathers and parental contributions to educational expenses as factors in career aspiration among male Jamaican students. *J Negro Educ* 35(3), Summer: 230-236.   **[9,32]**   [*TCL*]

Lowenthal, David
20.0048   **BC**   1961   Caribbean views of Caribbean land. *Can Geogr* 5(2): 1-9.   **[21,44,57]**   [*RIS*]
37.0500   **BC**   1962   Levels of West Indian Government.

Lynch, Louis
32.0368   **BB**   1963   Parent-pupil-teacher relationships.

McCartney, Timothy O.
31.0096   **BA**   1971   NEUROSES IN THE SUN.

MacDonald, Judy Smith
25.0242   **GR**   1973   Cursing and context in a Grenadian fishing community.

McKenzie, Earl
20.0049   **JM**   1973   Time in European and African philosophy: a comparison. *Car Q* 19(3), Sept.: 77-85.   [*RIS*]

Macridis, Roy C.
37.0532   **UV**   1970   Political attitudes in the Virgin Islands.

Madoo, Patricia
20.0050   **TR**   1970   MODERNIZATION AND VALUE CHANGES IN TRINIDAD AND TOBAGO. Ann Arbor, Michigan, University Microfilms: 308p. (Ph.D. Dissertation, Cornell University, 1969)   **[26]**   [*RIS*]

Malik, Yogendra K.
12.0058   **TR**   1970   Socio-political perceptions and attitudes of East Indian elites in Trinidad.

Manning, Frank E.
23.0191   **BB**   1975   The prophecy and the law: symbolism and social action in Seventh-Day Adventism.

Maslin, Simeon J.
21.0060   **GC**   1965-66 Caribbean Jewry: scandal and challenge.

Mason, Philip
8.0153   **GC**   1970   PATTERNS OF DOMINANCE.

Matthews, Harry G.
39.0108   **JM**   1969   JAMAICA IN THE UNITED NATIONS, 1962-1966.

Mau, James A.
20.0051   **JM**   1965   The threatening masses: myth or reality? *In* Andic, F. M. &
                                Mathews, T. G., eds. THE CARIBBEAN IN TRANSITION: PAPERS ON
                                SOCIAL, POLITICAL AND ECONOMIC DEVELOPMENT. Second Caribbean
                                Scholars' Conference, Mona, Jamaica, April 14-19, 1964. Rio
                                Piedras, University of Puerto Rico, Institute of Caribbean Studies:
                                258-270. **[8,37]**   [*RIS*]
37.0561   **JM**   1967   Images of Jamaica's future.
37.0562   **JM**   1968   SOCIAL CHANGE AND IMAGES OF THE FUTURE: A STUDY OF THE
                                PURSUIT OF PROGRESS IN JAMAICA.

Mau, James A.; Hill, Richard J. & Bell, Wendell
20.0052   **JM**   1961   Scale analyses of status perception and status attitude in Jamaica
                                and the United States. *Pacif Sociol Rev* 4(1), Spring: 33-40. **[8]**
                                                                                              [*RIS*]

Maynard, Edward Samuel
9.0101   **BB,US**   1974   ENDOGAMY AMONG BARBADIAN IMMIGRANTS TO NEW YORK CITY:
                                AN EXPLORATORY STUDY OF MARRIAGE PATTERNS AND THEIR RELA-
                                TIONSHIP TO ADJUSTMENT TO AN ALIEN CULTURE.

Menkman, W. R.
11.0066   **SR**   1927-28 Lanti sa pai [The country will pay for it].

Metraux, Rhoda
26.0006   **MS**   1957   Montserrat, B.W.I.: some implications of suspended culture change.

Metraux, Rhoda & Abel, Theodora M.
31.0102   **MS**   1957   Normal and deviant behavior in a peasant community: Montserrat,
                                B.W.I.

Miller, Errol L.
32.0397   **JM**   1967   Ambitions of Jamaican adolescents and the school system.
20.0053   **JM**   1969   Body image, physical beauty and colour among Jamaican adoles-
                                cents. *Social Econ Stud* 18(1), March: 72-89.   [*RIS*]
20.0054   **JM**   1970   A STUDY OF SELF CONCEPT AND ITS RELATIONSHIP TO CERTAIN
                                PHYSICAL, SOCIAL, COGNITIVE AND ADJUSTMENT VARIABLES IN A
                                SELECTED GROUP OF JAMAICAN SCHOOLGIRLS. Ph.D. dissertation,
                                University of the West Indies. **[32]**
20.0055   **JM**   1971   Experimenter effect and the reports of Jamaican adolescents on
                                beauty and body image. *Social Econ Stud* 21(4), Dec.: 353-390.
                                                                                              [*RIS*]
20.0056   **JM**   1971   Self and identity problems in Jamaica—the perspective of shame.
                                Car Q 17(3-4), Sept.-Dec.: 15-35. **[8]**   [*RIS*]
21.0065   **JM**   1973   Self and identity problems in Jamaica.

20.0057   **JM**   1973   Self evaluation among Jamaican high school girls. *Social Econ Stud* 22(4), Dec.: 407-426.   **[10]**   [*RIS*]

Millette, James
20.0058   **TR**   1974   The black revolution in the Caribbean. *In* Coombs, Orde, ed. Is MASSA DAY DEAD? BLACK MOODS IN THE CARIBBEAN. Garden City, New York, Anchor Press/Doubleday: 47-67.   **[5,21]**   [*CEIP*]

Mills, G. E. & Robertson, Paul D.
37.0582   **JM**   1974   The attitudes and behaviour of the senior civil service in Jamaica.

Minchin-Comm, Dorothy
6.0203   **BC**   1972   THE CHANGING CONCEPTS OF THE WEST INDIAN PLANTOCRACY IN ENGLISH POETRY AND DRAMA, 1740-1850.

Morris, Miriam
30.0179   **BC**   1971   Cultural differences and the feeding of young children in the Caribbean.

Morth, Grace E.
20.0059   **SV**   1972[?]   Reactions in Georgetown. *In* Fraser, Thomas M.; Ciski, Robert; Hourihan, John J.; Morth, Grace E. & Mulcahy, F. David, eds. LA SOUFRIERE: CULTURAL REACTIONS TO THE THREAT OF VOLCANIC ERUPTION ON THE ISLAND OF SAINT VINCENT, 1971-1972. Amherst, University of Massachusetts: 32-62.   **[53]**   [*RIS*]

Moses, Yolanda T.
10.0037   **MS**   1975   What price education: the working women of Montserrat.

Moskos, Charles C., Jr.
37.0595   **BC**   1963   THE SOCIOLOGY OF POLITICAL INDEPENDENCE: A STUDY OF INFLU- ENCE, SOCIAL STRUCTURE AND IDEOLOGY IN THE BRITISH WEST INDIES.
37.0596   **BC**   1967   Attitudes toward political independence.

Moskos, Charles C., Jr. & Bell, Wendell
37.0597   **BC**   1964   Attitudes towards democracy among leaders in four emergent nations.
37.0598   **BC**   1965   Attitudes toward democracy among leaders in four emergent nations.
8.0167   **BC**   1965   Some implications of equality for political, economic, and social development.
37.0599   **BC**   1967   Attitudes toward democracy.
37.0600   **BC**   1967   Attitudes toward equality.
37.0601   **BC**   1967   Attitudes toward global alignments.
20.0060   **BC**   1967   Political attitudes in new nations: examples from the British Caribbean. *In* Sherif, Carolyn W. & Sherif, Muzafer, eds. ATTITUDE, EGO-INVOLVEMENT AND CHANGE. New York, John Wiley and Sons, Inc.: 271-296.   **[10,37,40]**   [*COL*]
20.0061   **BC**   1968   Ideological foundations of development in the West Indies. *In* Greer, Scott; McElrath, Dennis L.; Minar, David W. & Orleans, Peter, eds. THE NEW URBANIZATION. New York, St. Martin's Press: 89-110.   **[8,37]**   [*AGS*]

Moyston, B.

31.0108   **JM**   1963   Problems of the Jamaican adolescent.

Nettleford, Rex

5.0651   **JM**   1974   Aggression, violence and force: containment and eruption in Jamaican history of protest.

Nisbet, Richard

6.0221   **BC**   1970   THE CAPACITY OF NEGROES FOR RELIGIOUS AND MORAL IMPROVEMENT CONSIDERED.

Nunes, F. E.

20.0062   **BC**   1973   Social structure, values and business policy in the Caribbean. *Car Q* 19(3), Sept.: 62-76.   **[8,45]**   [*RIS*]

37.0628   **JM**   1974   The declining status of the Jamaican Civil Service.

O'Connell, Victor E.

11.0072   **GU**   1972   SOME DEVELOPMENTS IN THE IDEOLOGY OF AFRICAN ETHNIC GROUPS IN GUYANA.

O'Mard, C. M.

31.0115   **AT**   1963   Special problems of the senior school child in Antigua.

Omoruyi, Omo

9.0104   **GU**   1975   A common experiential setting as a source of discontinuity in the socialization process in a plural society: Guyana as a case study.

20.0063   **GU**   1975   Use of multiple symbols of association as a measure of cohesion in a plural society. *Sociologus* 25(1): 62-76.   **[8,21,37]**   [*RIS*]

Otterbein, Charlotte Swanson & Otterbein, Keith F.

20.0064   **BA**   1973   Believers and beaters: a case study of supernatural beliefs and child rearing in the Bahama Islands. *Am Anthrop* 75(5), October: 1670-1681.   **[9]**   [*COL*]

Pastner, Stephen L.

20.0065   **TR**   1967   PROCESS AND VALUE IN A TRINIDAD MOUNTAIN COMMUNITY. M.A. Thesis, Brandeis University: 37p.   **[10,43]**   [*RIS*]

Patterson, H. Orlando

8.0179   **JM**   1965   Outside history: Jamaica today.

22.0290   **BC**   1969   The ritual of cricket.

Paula, A. F.

11.0074   **CU**   1972   FROM OBJECTIVE TO SUBJECTIVE SOCIAL BARRIERS: A HISTORICO-PHILOSOPHICAL ANALYSIS OF CERTAIN NEGATIVE ATTITUDES AMONG THE NEGROID POPULATION OF CURAÇAO.

Perinbam, B. Marie

10.0043   **GC**   1973   Parrot or phoenix? Frantz Fanon's view of the West Indian and Algerian woman.

Phillips, A. S.

10.0044   **JM**   1974   ADOLESCENCE IN JAMAICA.

Phillips, Andrew P.
46.0180   **AT**   1964   THE DEVELOPMENT OF A MODERN LABOR FORCE IN ANTIGUA.

Philpott, Stuart B.
18.0232   **MS,UK**   1968   Remittance obligations, social networks and choice among Montserratian migrants in Britain.

Powell, Dorian L.
20.0066   **JM**   1972   Occupational choice and role conceptions of nursing students. *Social Econ Stud* 21(3), Sept.: 284-312.   **[28,32]**   [*RIS*]

Powrie, Barbara E.
20.0067   **TR**   1956   The changing attitude of the coloured middle class towards Carnival. *Car Q* 4(3-4). Mar.-June: 224-232.   **[8,10,11,19]**   [*RIS*]

Ramcharan-Crowley, Pearl
32.0471   **SL,DM**   1973   Creole culture: outcast in West Indian schools.

Richards, Leopold A.
32.0483   **JM**   1974   THE CAREER ASPIRATIONS OF SECONDARY SCHOOL STUDENTS IN JAMAICA IN RELATION TO EDUCATIONAL PROGRAMMES AND MANPOWER NEEDS.

Riske, Roger & Rust, Val D.
32.0485   **TR**   1975   Nonformal education and the labor force in Port of Spain, Trinidad.

Rivière, R. E. & Yankey, J. Bernard
10.0048   **DM**   1970   A comparative study of two rural farming communities—the social dimension.

Roberts, George W.
34.0077   **BC**   1955   Cultural factors in fertility in the British Caribbean.

Robertson, Paul D.
20.0068   **JM**   1975   Ruling class attitudes in Jamaica: the bureaucratic component. *In* Singham, A. W., ed. THE COMMONWEALTH CARIBBEAN INTO THE SEVENTIES. Montreal, McGill University, Centre for Developing Area Studies: 94-118.   **[37,41]**   [*RIS*]

Robillard, Micheline
9.0127   **GD**   1967   ENFANCE ET SOCIALISATION DANS UNE COMMUNAUTÉ GUADELOUPÉENNE: ANALYSE DE CAS [CHILDHOOD AND SOCIALIZATION IN A COMMUNITY IN GUADELOUPE: CASE ANALYSIS].

Rodgers, William B.
20.0069   **BA**   1967   Changing gratification orientations: some findings from the Out Island Bahamas. *Hum Org* 26(4), Winter: 200-205.   **[11,26]**   [*COL*]
20.0070   **BA**   1969   Developmental exposure and changing vocational preferences in the Out Island Bahamas. *Hum Org* 28(4): 270-278.   **[11,41]**   [*COL*]
41.0436   **DM**   1971   Incipient development and vocational evolution in Dominica.

Rodgers, William B. & Gardner, Richard E.

20.0071   BA   1969   Linked changes in values and behavior in the Out Island Bahamas. *Am Anthrop* 71(1), Feb.: 21-35.   [*COL*]

Rodgers, William B. & Morris, Miriam

41.0437   DM   1971   Environmental modification and system response: developmental change in Dominica.

Rodman, Hyman

9.0132   TR   1971   LOWER-CLASS FAMILIES: THE CULTURE OF POVERTY IN NEGRO TRINIDAD.

Rodney-Edwards, Thelma

20.0072   GC   1972[?]   The attitude of Caribbean society to the illegitimate child. *In* Haynes, Lilith M., ed. FAMBLI: THE CHURCH'S RESPONSIBILITY TO THE FAMILY IN THE CARIBBEAN. Trinidad, CARIPLAN: 120-123.   **[9]**   [*RIS*]

Rottenberg, Simon

20.0073   AT   1952   Income and leisure in an underdeveloped economy. *J Polit Econ* 60(2), Apr.: 95-101.   [*COL*]

Rubin, Vera

20.0074   TR   1961   Family aspirations and attitudes of Trinidad youth. *In* CHILDREN OF THE CARIBBEAN—THEIR MENTAL HEALTH NEEDS: PROCEEDINGS OF THE SECOND CARIBBEAN CONFERENCE FOR MENTAL HEALTH, Apr. 10-16, 1959. Saint Thomas, Virgin Islands. San Juan, P.R., Dept. of the Treasury, Purchase and Supply Service—Printing Division, p.59-68.   **[9,10,32]**   [*RIS*]

20.0075   BC   1962   Culture, politics and race relations. *In* Singham, A. & Braithwaite, L. E., eds. Special number [of *Social Econ Stud*] on the Conference of Political Sociology of the British Caribbean, Dec. 1961. *Social Econ Stud* 11(4), Dec.: 433-455.   **[8,16,37]**   [*RIS*]

31.0127   TR   1963   The adolescent: his expectations and his society.

9.0134   GC   1965[?]   The West Indian family retrospect and prospect.

20.0076   JM   1975   The "*ganja* vision" in Jamaica. *In* Rubin, Vera, ed. CANNABIS AND CULTURE. The Hague, Mouton: 257-266.   **[29]**   [*RIS*]

Rubin, Vera & Zavalloni, Marisa

20.0077   TR   1969   WE WISH TO BE LOOKED UPON: A STUDY OF THE ASPIRATIONS OF YOUTH IN A DEVELOPING SOCIETY. New York, Teacher's College Press: 257p.   **[32]**   [*RIS*]

Schwartzbaum, Alan M. & Cross, Malcolm

32.0511   TR   1970   Secondary school environment and development; the case of Trinidad and Tobago.

Scroggs, William

20.0078   JM   1961   Imprudent jurisprudence: an outline of an illegal fiction. *W I Econ* 4(1-2), July-Aug.: 6-7.   **[46]**   [*RIS*]

Sedoc-Dahlberg, Betty

18.0256   SR,NE   1971   SURINAAMSE STUDENTEN IN NEDERLAND: EEN ONDERZOEK ROND DE PROBLEMATIEK VAN DE TOEKOMSTIGE INTELLEKTUELE KADER-VORMING IN SURINAME [SURINAMESE STUDENTS IN THE NETHER-LANDS: RESEARCH ON THE PROBLEMS OF THE SHAPING OF THE INTELLECTUAL FRAMEWORK OF SURINAM IN THE FUTURE].

Sherlock, Philip M.

37.0775	JM,TR	1963	Prospects in the Caribbean.
20.0079	BC	1972	The socio-cultural environment of the 1970's. *In* TRAINING OF PUBLIC SERVICE TRAINERS: REPORT ON A PILOT COURSE, ST. AUGUSTINE, TRINIDAD, AUG. 10-SEPT. 18, 1970. New York, United Nations: 44-48. **[37]** [*UNL*]

Silverman, Marilyn

8.0200	GU	1967	DEVIANCE AND CONFORMITY IN A CARIBBEAN MINING TOWN.
9.0146	GU	1969	Adolescent groups and delinquency in MacKenzie, Guyana.

Simpson, George Eaton

36.0080	JM	1954	Begging in Kingston and Montego Bay.
8.0201	GC	1962	The peoples and cultures of the Caribbean area.

Smith, Karl A. & Johnson, Raymond L.

34.0107	JM	[n.d.]	MEDICAL OPINION ON ABORTION IN JAMAICA: A NATIONAL DELPHI SURVEY OF PHYSICIANS, NURSES, AND MIDWIVES.

Smith, M. G.

20.0080	JM	1960	Education and occupational choice in rural Jamaica. *Social Econ Stud* 9(3), Sept.: 332-354. **[8,32,41]** [*RIS*]

Smith, Raymond Thomas

8.0221	GU	1964	Ethnic difference and peasant economy in British Guiana.
9.0159	GC	1971	Culture and social structure in the Caribbean: some recent work on family and kinship studies.

Spackman, Ann

37.0819	TR	1967	The Senate of Trinidad and Tobago.

Sparer, Joyce L.

22.0337	GU	1968	Attitudes toward 'race' in Guyanese literature.

St. George, John

34.0110	TR	1969	Factors influencing the high incidence of grand multiparity in Trinidad and Tobago.

Stoffle, Richard William

8.0229	BB	1969	BARBADIAN SOCIAL NETWORKS: AN ANALYSIS OF MALE CLIQUE AND FAMILY PARTICIPATION.
9.0174	BB	1972	INDUSTRIAL EMPLOYMENT AND INTER-SPOUSE CONFLICT: BARBADOS, WEST INDIES.

Stone, Carl

37.0829	JM	1974	ELECTORAL BEHAVIOUR AND PUBLIC OPINION IN JAMAICA.
21.0089	JM	1974	Race and nationalism in urban Jamaica.
36.0085	JM	1975	Urbanization as a source of political disaffection—the Jamaican experience.

Strumpel, Burkhard

41.0481	BZ	1965	Consumption aspirations: incentives for economic change.
20.0081	BZ	1965	Preparedness for change in a peasant society. *Econ Dev Cult Chg* 13(2), Jan.: 203-216. **[10,41]** [*COL*]

Stycos, J. Mayone
34.0113   **JM**   1968   HUMAN FERTILITY IN LATIN AMERICA: SOCIOLOGICAL PERSPECTIVES.

Stycos, J. Mayone & Back, Kurt
34.0114   **JM**   1958   Contraception and Catholicism in Jamaica.

Sutton, Constance R.; Makiesky, Susan; Dwyer, Daisy & Klein, Laura
10.0053   **BB**   1975   Women, knowledge and power.

Thakur, Parsram Sri
32.0565   **US,BC**   1975   A COMPARISON OF WEST INDIAN AND AMERICAN UNDERGRADUATES ON SELECTED COGNITIVE FACTORS.

Theuns, H. L.
16.0092   **SR**   1975   Ras, politiek en ideologie in Suriname [Race, politics and ideology in Surinam].

Thom, James Theophilus
32.0566   **GU**   1969   THE PARENTAL, SOCIO-ECONOMIC, ENVIRONMENTAL AND OTHER FACTORS DETERMINING THE NATURE AND EXTENT OF THE DISPARITY IN THE PERFORMANCE OF PRIMARY SCHOOL CHILDREN IN SELECTION TESTS FOR SECONDARY SCHOOL ENTRANCE IN GUYANA.

Thomas, Clive Y.
37.0843   **GU**   1973   Meaningful participation: the fraud of it.

Thorne, Alfred P.
43.0435   **JM**   1960   An economic phenomenon.

Tidrick, Kathryn
31.0138   **JM**   1973   Skin shade and need for achievement in a multiracial society: Jamaica, West Indies.

Tobias, Peter Michael
17.0108   **GR**   1975   "HOW YOU GONNA KEEP EM DOWN IN THE TROPICS ONCE THEY'VE DREAMED NEW YORK?": SOME ASPECTS OF GRENADIAN MIGRATION.

Triseliotis, J. P.
18.0276   **BC,UK**   1972   The implications of cultural factors in social work with immigrants.

Tucker, Gerald Etienne
20.0082   **JM**   1973   AFRO-EUROPEAN POLITICAL CULTURE AND DEVELOPMENT IN JAMAICA. Ph.D. dissertation, McGill University.   **[37]**   [*PhD*]

Vérin, Pierre
25.0380   **BC,MT**   1958   The rivalry of Creole and English in the West Indies.

Verma, Gajendra
16.0095   **BC,UK**   1975   Inter-group prejudice and race relations.

Verma, Gajendra & Bagley, Christopher, eds.
16.0096   **BC,UK**   1975   RACE AND EDUCATION ACROSS CULTURES.

Vuorinen, Saara Sofia

18.0281   BC,CA   1974   ETHNIC IDENTIFICATION OF CARIBBEAN IMMIGRANTS IN THE KITCHENER-WATERLOO AREA.

Walcott, Derek

21.0093   GC   1974   The Caribbean: culture or mimicry?

20.0083   GC   1974   The muse of history: an essay. *In* Coombs, Orde, ed. IS MASSA DAY DEAD? BLACK MOODS IN THE CARIBBEAN. Garden City, New York, Anchor Press/Doubleday: 1-28. **[22]**   [*CEIP*]

Walters, Enid

20.0084   JM   1971   The political attitudes of Jamaican sixth formers. *In* Munroe, Trevor & Lewis, Rupert, eds. READINGS IN GOVERNMENT AND POLITICS OF THE WEST INDIES. Mona, Jamaica, University of the West Indies: 12-15. **[37]**   [*RIS*]

Walvin, James

18.0282   BC,UK   1973   BLACK AND WHITE: THE NEGRO AND ENGLISH SOCIETY 1555-1945.

Watson, G. Llewellyn

15.0088   UK   1975   The sociological relevance of the concept of *Half-Caste* in British society.

Watts, Francis

20.0085   BC   1926   History as affecting outlook in the West Indies. *Can-W I Mag* 15(3), Jan.: 59-60. **[5,47]**   [*NYP*]

Weisbord, Robert G.

16.0098   BC   1960   British West Indian reaction to the Italian-Ethiopian War: an episode in pan-Africanism.

Wells, Henry

37.0884   UV   1955   Outline of the nature of United States Virgin Islands politics.

Whetton, Jim

20.0086   JM   1968   A perspective on violence. *Jam J* 2(1), March: 46-50.   [*RIS*]

Williams, Eric Eustace

40.0086   GC   1961   MASSA DAY DONE.

Willis, Margaret

20.0087   JM   1971   Housing aspirations and changing life-styles in Jamaica. *Jam Archi* 8: 59-61. **[26,35]**   [*NYP*]

Wilson, Peter J.

20.0088   GC   1969   Reputation and respectability: a suggestion for Caribbean ethnology. *Man* 4(1), March: 70-84. **[8]**   [*NYP*]

8.0245   BC   1973   CRAB ANTICS: THE SOCIAL ANTHROPOLOGY OF ENGLISH-SPEAKING NEGRO SOCIETIES OF THE CARIBBEAN.

Windt, H. L. de

20.0089   NA   1974   Enkele charmante hebbelijke onhebbelijkheden van de Antilliaan [Some charming habits of the Antillean, by others considered to be ill-mannered]. *Kristòf* 1(1), Feb.: 7-10.   [*RIS*]

Wong, Walter

20.0090   JM   1963   The adolescent in the family. *In* Carter, Samuel E., ed. THE ADOLESCENT IN THE CHANGING CARIBBEAN: PROCEEDINGS OF THE THIRD CARIBBEAN CONFERENCE FOR MENTAL HEALTH, Apr. 4-11, 1961, UCWI, Jamaica. Kingston, The Herald, p.68-71. **[9]**   [*RIS*]

Yawney, Carole D.

20.0091   JM   1976   Remnants of all nations: Rastafarian attitudes to race and nationality. *In* Henry, Frances, ed. ETHNICITY IN THE AMERICAS. The Hague, Mouton: 231-262. **[11,21,23]**   [*RIS*]

Zavalloni, Marisa

20.0092   TR   1960   Youth and the future: values and aspirations of high school students in a multicultural society in transition—Trinidad, W.I. Ph.D. dissertation, Columbia University, 141p. **[10,32]**   [*RIS*]

20.0093   TR   1968   ADOLESCENTS' VALUES IN A CHANGING SOCIETY: A STUDY OF TRINIDAD YOUTH. Paris, Mouton and Co.: 67p. **[8,10]**   [*RIS*]

Zoller, Peter T.

5.1019   JM   1970   REVOLT IN JAMAICA: A STUDY OF CARLYLE, RUSKIN, MILL AND HUXLEY.

Chapter 21

ETHNIC AND NATIONAL IDENTITY

Nationalism; cultural identity; problems of identity.
See also: **[19]** Cultural continuities; **[20]** Values and norms; **[26]** Cultural change.

		Abrahams, Peter
20.0002	**JM**	1961[?] The influence of ideas.
		Alexander, Henry Jacob
9.0016	**JM**	1973 THE CULTURE OF MIDDLE-CLASS FAMILY LIFE IN KINGSTON, JAMAICA.
		Anderson, Dale
21.0001	**BC**	1963-64 The reality of a West Indian culture. *Social Sci* 2: 18-20. [*RIS*]
		Andrews, Valerie; Brodie, Ben & Forde, Kenneth
40.0001	**BC**	1975 On the tasks facing Caribbean students and intellectuals.
		Angrosino, Michael V.
22.0011	**BC**	1975 V. S. Naipaul and the colonial image.
		Auguste, Armet
37.0025	**MT**	1971 Césaire et le Parti Progressiste Martiniquais: le nationalisme progressiste [Cesaire and the PPM: the progressive nationalism].
		Bagley, Christopher & Coard, Bernard
21.0002	**BC,UK**	1975 Cultural knowledge and rejection of ethnic identity in West Indian children in London. *In* Verma, Gajendra K. & Bagley, Christopher, eds. RACE AND EDUCATION ACROSS CULTURES. London, Heinemann Educational Books Ltd.: 322-331. **[11,18,20,26]** [*RIS*]
		Bastien, Elliot
18.0020	**BC,UK**	1965 The weary road to whiteness and the hasty retreat into nationalism.
		Baugh, Edward
22.0016	**BC**	[n.d.] WEST INDIAN POETRY: A STUDY IN CULTURAL DECOLONISATION.
		Beaubrun, Michael H.
16.0005	**TR**	1965 Interpersonal relationships within the nation.
		Bell, Wendell
37.0044	**JM**	1964 JAMAICAN LEADERS: POLITICAL ATTITUDES IN A NEW NATION.
37.0045	**GC**	1967 Ethnicity, decisions of nationhood, and images of the future.

Bell, Wendell, ed.
37.0046   **BC**   1967   THE DEMOCRATIC REVOLUTION IN THE WEST INDIES: STUDIES IN NATIONALISM, LEADERSHIP, AND THE BELIEF IN PROGRESS.

Bell, Wendell & Freeman, Walter E., eds.
21.0003   **GC**   1974   ETHNICITY AND NATION-BUILDING: COMPARATIVE, INTERNATIONAL, AND HISTORICAL PERSPECTIVES. Beverly Hills, California, Sage Publications: 400p.   **[16,37]**   [*COL*]

Beloux, François
37.0049   **MT**   1969   Un poète politique: Aimé Césaire [Political poet: Aimé Césaire].

Berrian, Albert H. & Long, Richard A., eds.
21.0004   **GC**   1967   NÉGRITUDE: ESSAYS AND STUDIES. Hampton, Va., Hampton Institute Press: 115p.   **[11]**   [*RIS*]

Birbalsingh, F. M.
22.0029   **BC**   1970   The novels of Ralph DeBoissière.

Blackett, Richard
21.0005   **GC**   1971   Some of the problems confronting West Indians in the black American struggle. *Black Lines* 1(4), Summer: 47-52.   [*NYP*]

Blanc, O.
21.0006   **GD,MT**   1965   La France des Antilles [The France of the Antilles]. *Transmondia* 126, March: 50-55.   **[38]**   [*AGS*]

Bolden, Bertram
18.0029   **BC,CA**   1971   Black immigrants in a foreign land.

Bonaparte, Tony H.
16.0009   **TR**   1972   AN ANALYSIS OF THE RACIAL AND CULTURAL INFLUENCES ON THE BUSINESS SYSTEM OF TRINIDAD, WEST INDIES.

Boodhoo, Isaiah James
32.0073   **TR**   1974   A CURRICULUM MODEL IN ART EDUCATION FOR THE PRIMARY SCHOOLS OF TRINIDAD AND TOBAGO.

Boxill, Courtney
12.0015   **TR**   1975   From East Indian to Indo-Trinidadian.

Brathwaite, Edward
19.0004   **BC**   1974   Timehri.

Brathwaite, Edward K.
2.0043   **GC**   1975   Caribbean man in space and time.

Brathwaite, J. Ashton
21.0007   **BC**   1970   SOULS IN THE WILDERNESS. Toronto, 21st Century Book: 80p.   **[11,18]**   [*NYP*]

Brathwaite, L. Edward
22.0043   **BC**   1969   Caribbean critics.

Brereton, Ashton S.
37.0088   BC   1963-64 West Indian perspective.
21.0008   BC   1963-64 West Indians—a people with no self respect. *Social Scient* 1: 5-6.

Brereton, Bridget
22.0045   TR   1975   The Trinidad Carnival 1870-1900.

Brown, John
32.0088   LW   1961   THE MEANING OF 'EXTRA-MURAL' IN THE LEEWARD ISLANDS.

Brown, Lloyd W.
22.0046   BC,US   1970   The West Indian novel in North America: a study of Austin Clarke.

Bryce-Laporte, R. S.
18.0042   GC,US   1972   Black immigrants: the experience of invisibility and inequality.

Burrough, Josephine Boenisch
10.0009   GU   1973   Ethnicity as a determinant of peasant farming characteristics: the Canals Polder, Guyana.

Butcher, LeRoi
11.0013   BC,CA   1971   The Congress of Black Writers.

Byles, G. Louis
16.0012   BC   1946   Way to real unity in the West Indies.

Cameron, Norman E.
20.0012   GU   1965   AN INTRODUCTION TO OUR SOCIAL PHILOSOPHY.

Carew, Jan
21.0009   BC   1953   British West Indian poets and their culture. *Phylon* 14(1) 1st quarter: 71-73.   **[22]**   [*COL*]
16.0016   GC   1975   The origins of racism in the Americas.
32.0108   BC   1976   Identity, cultural alienation and education in the Caribbean.

Carr, Bill
22.0059   BC   1968   A complex fate: the novels of Andrew Salkey.

Cartey, Wilfred
11.0017   GC   1970   BLACK IMAGES.

Césaire, Aimé
21.0010   MT   1967   AIMÉ CÉSAIRE, ÉCRIVAIN MARTINIQUAIS [AIMÉ CÉSAIRE, MARTINIQUAN WRITER]. Paris, Fernand Nathan, Classiques du Monde: 64p.   **[22]**   [*NYP*]

Chapman, Esther
21.0011   BC   1957   Matters of some importance: the West Indian. *W I Rev* new ser., 2(10), Oct.: 13, 15.   [*NYP*]

Chartol, Edouard
21.0012   GD   1966   Traditions et culture... [Traditions and culture...] *Rev Fr* 194, Supplement, December.   [*RIS*]

Chevannes, Alston Barrington
23.0046   JM   1976   The repairer of the breach: Reverend Claudius Henry and
Jamaican society.

Ciski, Robert
15.0021   SV   1975   THE VINCENTIAN PORTUGUESE: A STUDY IN ETHNIC GROUP ADAP-
TATION.

Clarke, Colin G.
21.0013   GC   1976   Insularity and identity in the Caribbean. *Geography* 61(1), Jan.:
8-16.   [40]   [*NYP*]

Coombs, Orde
18.0065   GC,US   1970   West Indians in New York: moving beyond the limbo pole.

Coombs, Orde, ed.
21.0014   GC   1974   IS MASSA DAY DEAD? BLACK MOODS IN THE CARIBBEAN. Garden
City, New York, Anchor Press/Doubleday: 260p.   [5,26,40]
[*CEIP*]

Cooper, Wayne & Reinders, Robert C.
18.0067   JM,UK   1967   A Black Briton comes 'home': Claude McKay in England, 1920.

Corbin, Carlyle G., Jr.
32.0130   UV   1975   INSTITUTIONAL CONSEQUENCES OF IMPORTED EDUCATION TO THE U.S.
VIRGIN ISLANDS.

Corzani, Jacques
21.0015   GD,MT   1970   Guadeloupe et Martinique: la difficile voie de la négritude et de
l'Antillanité [Guadeloupe and Martinique: the difficult way of
negritude and antillianity]. *Presence Afr* 76(4): 16-42.   [11]   [*TCL*]

Coulthard, G. R.
20.0015   FA   1961   The French West Indian background of negritude.
22.0083   GC   1962   RACE AND COLOUR IN CARIBBEAN LITERATURE.
21.0016   GC   1968   Parallelisms and divergencies between *négritude* and *indigenismo*.
Car Stud 8(1), April: 31-55.   [5,19]   [*RIS*]

Creary, John
22.0084   BC   1968   A prophet armed: the novels of Roger Mais.

Cross, Malcolm
12.0019   GU,TR   1972   THE EAST INDIANS OF GUYANA AND TRINIDAD.

Crowley, Daniel J.
22.0085   TR   1954   THE MEANINGS OF CARNIVAL.
8.0050   TR   1957   Plural and differential acculturation in Trinidad.
24.0058   BC   1967   The view from Tobago: national character in folklore.

Cruse, Harold
11.0024   GC   1967   Ideology in black: African, Afro-American and Afro-West Indian
and the nationalist mood.

Dabreo, Sinclair
40.0017   **BC**   1974[?] LESSONS FROM THE CARIBBEAN REVOLUTION.

Daniel, George T.
46.0052   **BC**   1957   Labor and Nationalism in the British Caribbean.

Dash, J. Michael
21.0017   **GC**   1974   Marvellous realism—the way out of négritude. *Car Stud* 13(4), Jan.: 57-70. **[22]**   [*RIS*]

Dathorne, Oscar Ronald
22.0102   **BC**   1965   Africa in the literature of the West Indies.

Davies, Barrie
22.0105   **BC**   1968   The seekers: the novels of John Hearne.

Dawes, Neville
21.0018   **JM**   1975   The Jamaican cultural identity. *Jam J* 9(1), March: 34-37.   [*RIS*]

Demas, William G.
38.0057   **BC**   1974   WEST INDIAN NATIONHOOD AND CARIBBEAN INTEGRATION.
40.0020   **BC**   1975   CHANGE AND RENEWAL IN THE CARIBBEAN.

Dennert, H. & Habibe, H.
21.0019   **NA**   1970   De eigen identiteit van de Nederlandse Antillen [The identity of the Netherlands Antilles]. *Schakels* NA56: 1-24.   [*NYP*]

Despres, Leo A.
37.0196   **GU**   1964   The implications of nationalist politics in British Guiana for the development of cultural theory.
8.0061   **GU**   1975   Ethnicity and ethnic group relations in Guyana.

Dirks, Robert
21.0020   **VI**   1975   Ethnicity and ethnic group relations in the British Virgin Islands. *In* Bennett, John W., ed. THE NEW ETHNICITY: PERSPECTIVES FROM ETHNOLOGY. PROCEEDINGS OF THE AMERICAN ETHNOLOGICAL SOCIETY, 1973. New York, West Publishing Co.: 95-109. **[8,17]** [*RIS*]

Doelwijt, Thea
18.0079   **SR,NE**   1968   Een eigen gezicht [An identity].

Doran, Edwin Beal, Jr.
21.0021   **GC**   1958   Cultural connections in the Leeward Islands. *Caribbean* 11(12), July: 274-277.   [*COL*]

Dostal, W., ed.
13.0047   **GG**   1972   THE SITUATION OF THE INDIAN IN SOUTH AMERICA: CONTRIBUTIONS TO THE STUDY OF INTER-ETHNIC CONFLICT IN THE NON-ANDEAN REGIONS OF SOUTH AMERICA.

Drayton, Arthur D.
21.0022   **BC**   1963   West Indian fiction and West Indian society. *Kenyon Rev* 25(1), Winter: 129-141. **[22]**   [*COL*]
22.0114   **BC**   1970   West Indian consciousness in West Indian verse: a historical perspective.

Dunwoodie, Peter

22.0115   **GC**   1975   Commitment and confinement: two West Indian visions.

Edmondson, Locksley

21.0023   **GC**   1974   Caribbean nation-building and the internationalization of race: issues and perspectives. *In* Bell, Wendell & Freeman, Walter E., eds. ETHNICITY AND NATION-BUILDING: COMPARATIVE, INTERNATIONAL, AND HISTORICAL PERSPECTIVES. Beverly Hills, California, Sage Publications: 73-86.   **[11,39]**   [*COL*]

21.0024   **GC**   1974   The internationalization of black power: historical and contemporary perspectives. *In* Coombs, Orde, ed. Is MASSA DAY DEAD? BLACK MOODS IN THE CARIBBEAN. Garden City, New York, Anchor Press/Doubleday: 205-244.   **[39]**   [*CEIP*]

32.0184   **GC**   1976   Educational challenges of the Caribbean connection with Africa.

Ehrlich, Allen S.

12.0025   **JM**   1971   ETHNIC IDENTITY AND THE EAST INDIAN IN RURAL JAMAICA.

12.0027   **JM**   1974   Ecological perception and economic adaptation in Jamaica.

12.0029   **JM**   1976   Race and ethnic identity in rural Jamaica: the East Indian case.

Elder, J. D.

21.0025   **TR**   1972   The people and their culture. *In* Boyke, Roy, ed. PATTERNS OF PROGRESS. Port-of-Spain, Trinidad, Key Caribbean Publications: 80-84.   [*RIS*]

Epstein, Erwin H.

21.0026   **SL**   1972   SENSE OF NATIONALITY AMONG SCHOOLCHILDREN: 'CENTER'-'PERIPHERY' DIFFERENCES WITH SPECIAL REFERENCE TO ST. LUCIA, WEST INDIES. Paper prepared for the Third World Congress for Rural Sociology, Baton Rouge, Louisiana, Aug. 22-27: 29p.   **[9,20]**
                                                                          [*TCL*]

Esedebe, Peter Olisanwuche

21.0027   **UK,GC** 1968   A HISTORY OF THE PAN-AFRICAN MOVEMENT IN BRITAIN, 1900-1948. Ph.D. dissertation, University of London: 288p.   **[11,16,18]**

Farley, Rawle

45.0048   **BC**   1958   NATIONALISM AND INDUSTRIAL DEVELOPMENT IN THE BRITISH CARIBBEAN.

Farrugia, Laurent

13.0055   **GD,MT** 1975   LES INDIENS DE GUADELOUPE ET DE MARTINIQUE [THE INDIANS OF GUADELOUPE AND MARTINIQUE].

Figueroa, John Joseph

22.0132   **GC**   1975   Introduction to George Lamming.

Forsythe, Dennis

11.0033   **BC,CA** 1971   The Black Writers Conference: days to remember.

17.0036   **BC**   1972   Migration and radical politics.

21.0028   **GC**   1975   Alienation and ideology among four West Indian activists. *In* Forsythe, Dennis, ed. BLACK ALIENATION, BLACK REBELLION. Washington, D.C., College and University Press: 127-156.   **[16,20]**   [*RIS*]

18.0106   **GC,US** 1976   West Indian radicalism in America: an assessment of ideologies.

Forsythe, Dennis, ed.
21.0029 GC 1975 BLACK ALIENATION, BLACK REBELLION. Washington, D.C., College and University Press: 177p. **[11,16,20]** [*RIS*]

Frucht, Richard, ed.
6.0085 GC 1971 BLACK SOCIETY IN THE NEW WORLD.

Frutkin, Susan
11.0034 MT 1973 AIMÉ CÉSAIRE: BLACK BETWEEN WORLDS.

Furley, Peter
21.0030 BZ 1971 A capital waits for its country. *Geogr Mag* 43(10), July: 713-716. **[36]** [*COL*]

Garebian, Keith
22.0138 BC 1975 V. S. Naipaul's negative sense of place.

Garvey, Amy Jacques, comp.
11.0036 JM 1967 PHILOSOPHY AND OPINIONS OF MARCUS GARVEY OR AFRICA FOR THE AFRICANS.

Gerig, Zenas E.
32.0224 JM 1967 AN ANALYSIS OF SELECTED ASPECTS OF JAMAICAN CULTURE WITH IMPLICATIONS FOR ADULT EDUCATIONAL PROGRAMS IN THE CHURCH.

Gilkes, Michael
22.0141 BC 1975 RACIAL IDENTITY AND INDIVIDUAL CONSCIOUSNESS IN THE CARIBBEAN NOVEL.
22.0142 BC 1975 The spirit in the bottle—a reading of Mittelholzer's. *A Morning at the Office.*
22.0143 GC 1975 WILSON HARRIS AND THE CARIBBEAN NOVEL.

Gillin, John P.
21.0031 GC 1951 Is there a modern Caribbean culture? *In* Wilgus, A. Curtis, ed. THE CARIBBEAN AT MID-CENTURY [PAPERS DELIVERED AT THE FIRST ANNUAL CONFERENCE ON THE CARIBBEAN HELD AT THE UNIVERSITY OF FLORIDA, DEC. 7-9, 1950]. Gainesville, University of Florida Press, p.129-135. (Publications of the School of Inter-American Studies, ser. 1, v. 1.) **[8]** [*RIS*]

Glass, Ruth
21.0032 JM 1962 Ashes of discontent. *Listener BBC Telev Rev* 67(1714), Feb. 1: 207-209. **[5,8,20,37]** [*NYP*]

Glissant, Edouard
21.0033 FC 1962 Culture et colonisation: l'équilibre antillais [Culture and colonization: the Antillean balance]. *Esprit* 30(305), Apr.: 588-595. [*COL*]

Gomes, Albert
18.0114 TR,UK 1973 I am an immigrant.

Gomes, Ralph C.
21.0034 GU 1972 Colonialism, nationalism, fractionalism, and self-identity among Guyanese leaders. *In* McDonald, Vincent R., ed. THE CARIBBEAN ECONOMIES: PERSPECTIVES ON SOCIAL, POLITICAL AND ECONOMIC CONDITIONS. New York, MSS Information Corporation: 128-147. **[37]** [*COL*]

Goonewardene, James

21.0035   GC   1975   Nationalism and the writer in Sri Lanka and the West Indies. *Savacou* 11-12, Sept.: 12-17.   **[22]**   [*RIS*]

Gordon, Derek Stuart

8.0082   GU   1973   ETHNICITY AND OCCUPATIONAL ATTAINMENT IN GEORGETOWN, GUYANA.

Green, Vera M.

17.0045   NA   1975   Racial versus ethnic factors in Afro-American and Afro-Caribbean migration.

Groot, Silvia W. de

14.0015   SR   1973   The Bush Negro Chiefs visit Africa: diary of an historic trip.

Guérin, Daniel

21.0036   FC   1971   The dawning of social consciousness. *In* Frucht, Richard, ed. BLACK SOCIETY IN THE NEW WORLD. New York, Random House: 345-364.   [*COL*]

Gurr, A. J.

22.0159   BC   1972   Third-World novels: Naipaul and after.

Habibe, H.

22.0160   CU   1975   Algun aspekto sosial den poesia na papiamento [Some social aspects of Papiamento poetry].

Hale, Thomas A.

21.0037   MT   1974   Aimé Césaire: a bio-bibliography. *Afr J* 5(1), Spring: 3-29.   **[5,22]**
                                                                                   [*COL*]

Hall, Kenneth

32.0265   JM   1975   African studies in the Jamaican curriculum.

Hartog, J.

21.0038   CU   [n.d.]   Cultural life in Curacao. *Car Q* 1(3): 36-38.   **[22]**

Hearne, John

21.0039   BB   1966-67   What the *Barbadian* means to me. *New Wld Q* 3(1-2), Dead Season and Croptime, Barbados Independence Issue: 6-9.   [*RIS*]

22.0171   BC   1968   The fugitive in the forest.

Hélène, Appolon

21.0040   GC   1970   "L'ANTILLAITISME": PRÉFIGURATION DU MONDE DE DEMAIN ["L'ANTILLAITISME": VISION OF TOMORROW'S WORLD]. Paris, Editions Louis Soulanges: 217p.   **[40]**   [*NYP*]

Henriques, Fernando

8.0098   GC   1973   Contemporary social problems.

Henry, Frances

19.0026   GC   1972   Cultural variation.

Henry, Frances, ed.
21.0041   GC   1976   ETHNICITY IN THE AMERICAS. The Hague, Mouton: 456p.   [37]
                                                                                    [*RIS*]

Herrenberg, Henk F.
18.0134   **SR,NE**   1968   Studenten en arbeiders [Students and workers].

Hill, Donald R.
9.0071   **CR**   1974   More on truth, fact, and tradition in Carriacou.

Hill, Errol
22.0180   **BC**   1955   Drama round the Caribbean.
22.0186   **BC**   1972   The emergence of a national drama in the West Indies.

Hockey, Sidney W.
21.0042   BC   1958   An emerging culture in the British West Indies. *In* Wilgus, A.
                         Curtis, ed. THE CARIBBEAN: BRITISH, DUTCH, FRENCH, UNITED
                         STATES [papers delivered at the Eighth Conference on the Carib-
                         bean held at the University of Florida, Dec. 5-7, 1957]. Gainesville,
                         University of Florida Press, p.39-50. (Publications of the School of
                         Inter-American Studies, ser. 1, v. 8.)   **[8,22]**   [*RIS*]

Hoetink, Harry
20.0037   GC   1961   "Colonial psychology" and race.
21.0043   GC   1972   National identity, culture, and race in the Caribbean. *In* Campbell,
                         Ernest Q., ed. RACIAL TENSIONS AND NATIONAL IDENTITY: PRO-
                         CEEDINGS OF THE SECOND ANNUAL VANDERBILT SOCIOLOGY CON-
                         FERENCE, NOVEMBER 4-6, 1970. Nashville, Tennessee, Vanderbilt
                         University Press: 17-44.   **[16,40]**   [*RIS*]
21.0044   GC   1974   National identity and somatic norm image. *In* Bell, Wendell and
                         Freeman, Walter E., eds. ETHNICITY AND NATION-BUILDING. Beverly
                         Hills, California, Sage Publication: 29-45.   **[8,20]**   [*COL*]

Holzberg, C. S.
15.0042   **JM,CU**   1976   Societal segmentation and Jewish ethnicity: ethnographic illustra-
                                  tions from Latin America and the Caribbean.

Hosein, Everold Naffath
48.0079   **BC**   1973   AN EXPLORATORY STUDY OF THE SIGNIFICANCE AND FEASIBILITY OF A
                               REGIONAL TELEVISION PROGRAMMING SYSTEM FOR THE COMMON-
                               WEALTH CARIBBEAN.

Howard, Michael C.
13.0085   **BZ**   1975   ETHNICITY IN SOUTHERN BELIZE: THE KEKCHI AND THE MOPAN.

Hunte, George Hutchinson
16.0050   **BC**   1946   West Indian unity: measures and machinery.

Ingram, Robert P.
21.0045   TR   1972   THE QUALITY OF LIFE. *In* Boyke, Roy, ed. PATTERNS OF PROGRESS.
                         Port-of-Spain, Trinidad, Key Caribbean Publications: 77-79.   [*RIS*]

James, C. L. R.

21.0046   GC   1970   *The Black Scholar* interviews: C. L. R. James. *Black Scholar* 2(1), Sept.: 35-43.   [*NYP*]

21.0047   GC   1971   From Toussaint l'Ouverture to Fidel Castro. *In* Frucht, Richard, ed. Black society in the New World. New York, Random House: 324-344.   **[6]**   [*COL*]

37.0431   BC   1975   The revolutionary.

James, C. L. R. & Anthony, Michael

22.0196   TR   1969   Discovering literature in Trinidad: two experiences.

James, Louis

22.0197   JM   1968   Of redcoats and leopards: two novels by V. S. Read.

James, Louis, ed.

22.0198   BC   1968   The islands in between: essays on West Indian literature.

Jones, Edward H.

22.0204   MT   1970   Afro-French writers of the 1930's and creation of the négritude school.

Jones, Rhett S.

6.0155   JM   1975   The transformation of Maroon identity in Jamaica, 1738-1795.

Karner, Frances P.

15.0049   CU   1969   The Sephardics of Curaçao: a study of socio-cultural patterns in flux.

King, Cameron & James, Louis

22.0216   BC   1968   In solitude for company: the poetry of Derek Walcott.

Knight, Vere

21.0048   FC   1975   French-Caribbean literature: a literature of commitment. *Revta Interam Rev* 5(1), Spring: 67-92.   **[22]**   [*RIS*]

Koenig, Edna Louise

25.0204   BZ   1975   Ethnicity and language in Corozal District, Belize: an analysis of code switching.

Kroll, Morton

37.0460   TR   1967   Political leadership and administrative communications in new nation states: the case study of Trinidad and Tobago.

Lacour, Pierre

2.0259   GD,MT,BC   1972   La Guadeloupe et ses problèmes [Guadeloupe and its problems].

LaFlamme, A. G.

16.0056   BA   1975   Black and white on Green Turtle Cay.

La Guerre, John Gaffar

12.0050   TR   1974   The East Indian middle class today.

Lamine, Mahmadou

12.0052   GC   1975   The place of the Indian community in JHAC's philosophy of Black Power.

Lamming, George

11.0055   GC   1966   Caribbean literature: the black rock of Africa.
22.0219   GC   1975   On West Indian writing.

Lashley, Cliff

1.0169   JM   1972   West Indian national libraries and the challenge of change.

Lassale, Jean-Pierre

32.0341   FC   1975   Problèmes de coopération culturelle [Problems of cultural cooperation].

Leborgne, Yvon

21.0049   FA   1962   Le climat social [The social environment]. *Esprit* 30(305), Apr.: 537-550.   **[37]**   [*NYP*]

Lekis, Lisa

19.0040   GC   1956   THE ORIGIN AND DEVELOPMENT OF ETHNIC CARIBBEAN DANCE AND MUSIC.

Lenoir, J. D.

14.0044   SR   1975   Surinam national development and maroon cultural autonomy.

Lewis, Gordon K.

2.0281   BB   1966   The struggle for freedom (a story of contemporary Barbados).
8.0131   GC   1974   On the dangers of composing a West Indian anthology.

Lewis, Vaughan A.

21.0050   JM   1965   Nettleford's Mirror. *Savacou* 11-12, Sept.: 72-77.   [*RIS*]

Lewis, W. Arthur

21.0051   GC   1973   On being different. *In* Lowenthal, David & Comitas, Lambros, eds. THE AFTERMATH OF SOVEREIGNTY: WEST INDIAN PERSPECTIVES. Garden City, N.Y., Anchor Press/Doubleday: 293-302.   [*RIS*]

Lichtveld, Lou

21.0052   GC   1959   Cultural relations within the Caribbean. *Caribbean* 13(4), Apr.: 73-77.   [*COL*]

Lirus, Julie

18.0190   MT,FR   1975   Identité culturelle chez le Martiniquais [Cultural identity of the Martiniquan people].

Lotan, Yael

21.0053   JM   1964   Jamaica today. *Freedomways* 4(3), 3d quarter, Summer: 370-374.   **[37]**   [*RIS*]
40.0052   JM   1972   Jamaica today.

Lowenthal, David

20.0048   BC   1961   Caribbean views of Caribbean land.
38.0138   BC   1961   The social background of West Indian Federation.

37.0500	BC	1962	Levels of West Indian Government.
11.0061	GC	1972	Black power in the Caribbean context.
21.0054	GC	1972	Some problems of identity in relation to resource perception. *In* RESOURCE DEVELOPMENT IN THE CARIBBEAN. Montreal, McGill University, Centre for Developing-Area Studies: 51-61. **[56]**

[*RIS*]

Lumumba, Carl

11.0062 BC,CA 1971   The West Indies and the Sir George Williams affair: an assessment.

McCartney, Timothy O.

21.0055 BA 1974   What is the relevance of black power to the Bahamas? *In* Coombs, Orde, ed. IS MASSA DAY DEAD? BLACK MOODS IN THE CARIBBEAN. Garden City, New York, Anchor Press/Doubleday: 165-187. **[11]**

·[*CEIP*]

MacDonald, Bruce F.

22.0236 TR 1975   Symbolic action in three of V. S. Naipaul's novels.

McDonald, Frank

37.0520 TR 1970   TRINIDAD: BLACK POWER AND NATIONAL RECONSTRUCTION.

Mahabir, Dennis J.

21.0056 BC 1957   Cultural mosaic. *Caribbean* 10(12), July: 295-296.   [*COL*]

Mainberger, Gonsalv

21.0057 MT 1963   Mythe et realité de l'homme noir; à la memoire de Frantz Fanon [Myth and reality of the Negro; in memory of Frantz Fanon]. *Presénce Afr* 18(46), 2d quarter: 211-224. **[11]**   [*COL*]

Malik, Yogendra K.

12.0057 TR 1969   Agencies of political socialization and East Indian ethnic identification in Trinidad.

Manning, Frank E.

21.0058 BE 1974   Entertainment and black identity in Bermuda. *In* Fitzgerald, Thomas, ed. SOCIAL AND CULTURAL IDENTITY. Athens, University of Georgia Press: 39-50. (Southern Anthropological Society, Proceedings No. 8) **[11,22]**   [*COL*]

Manyoni, Joseph R.

21.0059 GC 1973   Emergence of Black Power. *In* Moss, Robert, ed. THE STABILITY OF THE CARIBBEAN· REPORT OF A SEMINAR HELD AT DITCHLEY PARK, OXFORDSHIRE, U. K. MAY 18-20, 1973. Washington D.C., Georgetown University, Center for Strategic and International Studies: 101-115. **[40]**   [*RIS*]

Marshall, Woodville K.

22.0250 BC 1965   Gary Sobers and the Brisbane Revolution.

Martin, Leann Thomas

14.0048 JM 1973   MAROON IDENTITY: PROCESSES OF PERSISTENCE IN MOORE TOWN.

Maslin, Simeon J.

21.0060   GC   1965-66 Caribbean Jewry: scandal and challenge. *Reconstructionist* 31(17-18), Dec. 24: 7-12. Jan. 7: 24-29. **[15,20,23]**   [*COL*]

Matthews, Basil

21.0061   BC   1942   Calypso and Pan America. *Commonweal* 37(4), Nov. 13: 91-93. **[22]**   [*COL*]

Memmi, Albert

21.0062   MT   1973   The impossible life of Frantz Fanon. *Mass Rev* 14(1), Winter: 9-39. **[11]**   [*COL*]

Messenger, John C.

15.0067   MS   1975   Montserrat: the most distinctively Irish settlement in the New World.

Meyer, A.

21.0063   CU   1969   Enige socio-psychologische opmerkingen over Curaçao [Some sociopsychological remarks about Curaçao]. *N W I G* 47(1), Sept.: 60-66. **[31]**   [*RIS*]

21.0064   NA   1973   De Antilliaanse persoonlijkheid [The Antillean personality]. *In* Statius van Eps, L. W. & Luckman-Maduro, E., eds. VAN SCHEEPSCHIRURGIJN TOT SPECIALIST. Assen, the Netherlands, Van Gorcum & Comp. B.V.: 149-153. (Anjerpublikatie 15) **[31]**
                                                                              [*RILA*]

Midgett, Douglas

18.0210   BC,UK   1975   West Indian ethnicity in Great Britain.

Miller, Errol L.

21.0065   JM   1973   Self and identity problems in Jamaica. *Car Q* 19(2), June: 108-142. **[11,20]**   [*RIS*]

Millette, James

20.0058   TR   1974   The black revolution in the Caribbean.

Mintz, Sidney W.

37.0583   GC   1967   Caribbean nationhood in anthropological perspective.

Morris, Kerwyn L.

21.0066   GC   1973   On Afro-West Indian thinking. *In* Lowenthal, David & Comitas, Lambros, eds. THE AFTERMATH OF SOVEREIGNTY: WEST INDIAN PERSPECTIVES. Garden City, N.Y., Anchor Press/Doubleday: 277-281. **[11]**   [*RIS*]

Morris, Mervyn

11.0071   JM   1968   Black power and us.
22.0262   BC   1968   The poet as novelist: the novels of George Lamming.

Moskos, Charles C., Jr.

37.0595   BC   1963   THE SOCIOLOGY OF POLITICAL INDEPENDENCE: A STUDY OF INFLUENCE, SOCIAL STRUCTURE AND IDEOLOGY IN THE BRITISH WEST INDIES.
37.0596   BC   1967   Attitudes toward political independence.

21.0067   JM   1967   THE SOCIOLOGY OF POLITICAL INDEPENDENCE: A STUDY OF NATIONALIST ATTITUDES AMONG WEST INDIAN LEADERS. Cambridge, Massachusetts, Schenkman Publishing Co., Ltd.: 120p.   [37]   [RIS]

Moskos, Charles C., Jr. & Bell, Wendell
21.0068   BC   1964   West Indian nationalism. *New Soc* 69, Jan. 23: 16-18.   [8,37]
8.0166   GU,TR   1965   Cultural unity and diversity in new states.

Munroe, Trevor
40.0059   BC   1971   DEVELOPED IDEALISM AND EARLY MATERIALISM: 'LEFT' CARIBBEAN THOUGHT IN TRANSITION.

Murch, Arvin
40.0060   FA   1972   POLITICAL INTEGRATION AS AN ALTERNATIVE TO INDEPENDENCE IN THE FRENCH ANTILLES.

Naipaul, V. S.
21.0069   BC,UK   1972   THE OVERCROWDED BARRACOON AND OTHER ARTICLES. London, André Deutsch: 286p.   [12,18,22]   [RIS]

Nantet, Jacques
22.0266   FC   1972   Le monde noir des Antilles et de l'Amérique du Sud [The Black world of the Antilles and South America].

Narasimhaiah, C. D.
22.0267   BC   1971   A.C.L.A.L.S. Conference on Commonwealth Literature, Kingston, Jamaica, 3-9 January 1971.

Nettleford, Rex
21.0070   JM   1965   National identity and attitudes to race in Jamaica. *Race* 7(1): 59-72.   [16]   [RIS]
16.0073   JM   1970   MIRROR, MIRROR: IDENTITY, RACE AND PROTEST IN JAMAICA.
21.0071   BC   1971   Caribbean perspectives: the creative potential and the quality of life. *Car Q* 17(3-4), Sept.-Dec.: 114-127.   [22]   [RIS]

Ngugi, Wa Thiong'o
22.0271   GC   1972   HOMECOMING: ESSAYS ON AFRICAN AND CARIBBEAN LITERATURE, CULTURE AND POLITICS.

Norris, Katrin
21.0072   JM   1962   JAMAICA: THE SEARCH FOR AN IDENTITY. London, Oxford University Press, 103p.   [8,16,37]   [RIS]

Oakley, Leo
21.0073   JM   1970   Ideas of patriotism and national dignity in some Jamaican writings. *Jam J* 4(3), Sept.: 16-21.   [RIS]

Omoruyi, Omo
20.0063   GU   1975   Use of multiple symbols of association as a measure of cohesion in a plural society.

Ormerod, Beverley
21.0074   FC   1975   Beyond *négritude*: some aspects of the work of Edouard Glissant. *Savacou* 11-12, Sept.: 39-45.   [22]   [RIS]

Owen, Nancy H.
13.0154   **DM**   1975   Land, politics, and ethnicity in a Carib Indian community.

Owens, J. V.
23.0217   **JM**   1975   Literature on the Rastafari: 1955-1974.

Oxaal, Ivar
5.0693   **TR**   1968   BLACK INTELLECTUALS COME TO POWER: THE RISE OF CREOLE NATIONALISM IN TRINIDAD AND TOBAGO.
16.0078   **TR**   1971   RACE AND REVOLUTIONARY CONSCIOUSNESS: A DOCUMENTARY INTERPRETATION OF THE 1970 BLACK POWER REVOLT IN TRINIDAD.

Parmasad, K. V.
21.0075   **GC**   1973   By the light of a deya. *In* Lowenthal, David & Comitas, Lambros, eds. THE AFTERMATH OF SOVEREIGNTY: WEST INDIAN PERSPECTIVES. Garden City, N.Y., Anchor Press/Doubleday: 283-291.   **[12]**
[*RIS*]

Parris, D. Elliott
22.0288   **BC**   1973   THE IDEOLOGY OF CREATIVE WRITERS OF THE ENGLISH-SPEAKING CARIBBEAN, 1950-1972: A SOCIOLOGICAL ANALYSIS.
22.0289   **BC**   1975   Perspectives of the creative writers.

Patient, Serge
19.0050   **FC**   1971   Assimilation ou négritude?: la culture antilloguyanaise en question [Assimilation or negritude?: the Antillean-Guyanese culture in question].

Patterson, H. Orlando
8.0180   **JM,GU**   1975   Context and choice in ethnic allegiance: a theoretical framework and Caribbean case study.

Phillips, Andrew P.
21.0076   **AT**   1967   Management and workers face an independent Antigua. *In* Bell, Wendell, ed. THE DEMOCRATIC REVOLUTION IN THE WEST INDIES. Cambridge, Mass., Schenkman Pub. Co., Inc.: 165-196.   **[37,40,46]**
[*RIS*]

Price, Thomas J.
14.0064   **FG,SR**   1968   How three Negro cultures view their African heritage.
14.0065   **FG,SR**   1970   Ethnohistory and self-image in three new world negro societies.

Proudfoot, Mary
21.0077   **BC**   1956   The British Caribbean—general conspectus. *Statist* Sept. 5-6.

Ramphal, S. S.
21.0078   **BC**   1972   The search for Caribbean identity. *In* CALLED TO BE. REPORT OF THE CARIBBEAN ECUMENICAL CONSULTATION FOR DEVELOPMENT, CHAGUARAMAS, TRINIDAD, NOVEMBER 1971. Bridgetown, Barbados, CADEC: 23-26.   [*RIS*]

Ramraj, Victor
21.0079   **BC**   1963-64   Satire and tradition in West Indies society. *Social Scient* 2: 10-12.
[*RIS*]

Ramsaran, J. A.
22.0305   **BC**   1975   West Indian gallery: the works of Derek Walcott.

Rauf, Mohammad Abdur
12.0076   **GU**   1972   CRABWOOD CREEK: A STUDY OF CULTURAL CONTINUITY AND ETHNIC
                                  IDENTITY ON DIFFERENT GENERATIONAL LEVELS AMONG EAST INDIANS
                                  IN GUYANA.

Roback, Judith
23.0248   **GU**   1973   THE WHITE-ROBED ARMY: CULTURAL NATIONALISM AND A RELIG-
                                  IOUS MOVEMENT IN GUYANA.

Robinson, Arthur N. R.
32.0488   **TR**   1967   THE ROLE OF THE TEACHER IN THE DEVELOPMENT OF A NATIONALIST
                                  SPIRIT: LECTURE DELIVERED TO THE TEACHERS AT THE TEACHERS'
                                  TRAINING COLLEGE, WRIGHTSON ROAD, ON THURSDAY, 22ND JUNE,
                                  1967.

Rodney, Walter
11.0078   **JM,GC**   1969   THE GROUNDINGS WITH MY BROTHERS.

Rogers, Claudia
23.0249   **JM**   1975   What's a Rasta?

Rohlehr, Gordon
22.0314   **BC**   1968   The ironic approach.

Romalis, Coleman
21.0080   **GC**   1976   Some comments on race and ethnicity in the Caribbean. *In* Henry,
                                    Frances, ed. ETHNICITY IN THE AMERICAS. The Hague, Mouton:
                                    417-427.   [*RIS*]

Römer, R. A.
21.0081   **CU**   1974   Het "wij" en de Curaçaoenaar [The "we" of the inhabitants of
                                    Curaçao]. *Kristòf* 1(2), April: 49-60.   [*RIS*]

Roo, B. Jos de
22.0316   **NA**   1975   Een belangrijk werk voor de Antillen: Kenneth Ramchand's *The
                                  West Indian novel and its background* [An important work for the
                                  Antilles: Kenneth Ramchand's *The West Indian novel and its
                                  background*].
21.0082   **CU**   1976   Dubbelspel—dubble politiek [Double game—double politics].
                                    Kristòf 3(1), Feb.: 32-45.   **[22]**   [*RIS*]

Rubin, Vera
21.0083   **TR**   1959   Approaches to the study of national characteristics in a
                                    multicultural society. *Int J Social Psych* 5(1), Summer: 20-26.   **[31]**
                                                                                            [*RIS*]

Ryan, Selwyn
21.0084   **GC**   1971   Politics in the Caribbean: black power or black powerlessness.
                                    Black Lines 1(4), Summer: 19-34.   **[40]**   [*NYP*]
37.0747   **BE**   1976   Politics in an artificial society: the case of Bermuda.

Scroggs, William
37.0766   **JM**   1962   Jamaicans are English.

Searle, Chris
21.0085   **TB**   1972   THE FORSAKEN LOVER: WHITE WORDS AND BLACK PEOPLE. London, Routledge & Kegan Paul Ltd.: 108p. **[32]**   [*RIS*]

Sertima, Ivan van
22.0328   **BC**   1968   CARIBBEAN WRITERS: CRITICAL ESSAYS.

Shapiro, Norman R.
11.0081   **GD,MT**   1967   Negro poets of the French Caribbean: a sampler.

Sherlock, Philip M.
32.0518   **BC**   1955   The dynamic of nationalism in adult education.
21.0086   **BC**   1956[?]   Federation: let's meet the family. *Extra-Mural Reptr* 3(2), Apr. **[38]**   [*RIS*]
2.0425   **GC**   1963   CARIBBEAN CITIZEN.
37.0775   **JM,TR**   1963   Prospects in the Caribbean.

Shoman, A.
37.0779   **BZ**   1973   The birth of the nationalistic movement in Belize, 1950-1954.

Silverman, Marilyn
12.0085   **GU**   1976   The role of factionalism in political encapsulation: East Indian villagers in Guyana.

Singaravélou
12.0086   **GD**   1975   LES INDIENS DE LA GUADELOUPE [THE INDIANS OF GUADELOUPE].

Singer, Philip
12.0088   **GU**   1967   Caste and identity in Guyana.

Singer, Philip & Araneta, Enrique
12.0089   **GU**   1967   Hinduization and creolization in Guyana: the plural society and basic personality.

Singham, A. W., ed.
2.0432   **BC**   1975   THE COMMONWEALTH CARIBBEAN INTO THE SEVENTIES: PROCEEDINGS OF A CONFERENCE HELD ON 28-30 SEPTEMBER, 1973, AT HOWARD UNIVERSITY, WASHINGTON, D. C.

Skinner, Elliott P.
8.0207   **GU**   1971   Social stratification and ethnic identification.

Smith, M. G.
8.0214   **GC**   1961   West Indian culture.

Smith, Raymond Thomas
21.0087   **GU**   1958   British Guiana. *In* SUNDAY GUARDIAN OF TRINIDAD, THE WEST INDIAN FEDERATION SUPPLEMENT, April 20. Port of Spain, Sunday Guardian, p.25, 33, 63. **[8,38]**   [*RIS*]

Smith, Rowland, ed.

22.0334   GC   1976   EXILE AND TRADITION: STUDIES IN AFRICAN AND CARIBBEAN LITERATURE.

Snyder, Emile

22.0335   FC   1976   Aimé Césaire: the reclaiming of the land.

Sparer, Joyce L.

22.0337   GU   1968   Attitudes toward 'race' in Guyanese literature.

Springer, Hugh W.

21.0088   BC   1953   On being a West Indian. *Car Q* 3(3), Dec.: 181-183.   [*RIS*]

Steger, Hanns-Albert

23.0292   GC   1970   Revolutionäre Hintergründe des kreolischen Synkretismus [Revolutionary background of Creole Syncretism].

Stone, Carl

21.0089   JM   1974   Race and nationalism in urban Jamaica. *Car Stud* 13(4), Jan.: 5-32. **[8,16,20]**   [*RIS*]

33.0187   JM   1975   Urban social movements in post-War Jamaica.

St. Pierre, Maurice

22.0342   BC   1973   West Indian cricket—a socio-historical appraisal. Part I.

22.0343   BC   1973   West Indian cricket. Part II—An aspect of creolization.

Sutton, Constance R. & Makiesky, Susan R.

17.0100   BC   1975   Migration and West Indian racial and ethnic consciousness.

Sypher, W.

21.0090   BC   1939   The West Indian as a character in the 18th century. *Stud Philol* 34(3), July: 503-520. **[5]**   [*COL*]

Taylor, Edward

17.0102   JM   1976   The social adjustment of returned migrants to Jamaica.

Thieme, John

22.0348   BC   1975   V. S. Naipaul's Third World: a not so free state.

Thomas, J. J.

21.0091   BC   1969   FROUDACITY: WEST INDIAN FABLES EXPLAINED. London, New Beacon Books: 195p. (Originally published in 1889)   [*RIS*]

Thorpe, Michael

22.0351   BC   1976   V. S. NAIPAUL.

Tinker, Hugh

12.0107   BC   1975   British policy towards a separate Indian identity in the Caribbean, 1920-1950.

Verlooghen, Corly

21.0092   SR   1970   DE GLINSTERENDE REVOLUTIE: IDENTITEITS-POËZIE [THE GLITTERING REVOLUTION: IDENTITY POEMS]. Amsterdam, The Netherlands: 283p. **[22]**   [*COL*]

Voorhoeve, Jan & Renselaar, H. C. van
23.0312   SR   1962   Messianism and nationalism in Surinam.

Vuorinen, Saara Sofia
18.0281   BC,CA   1974   ETHNIC IDENTIFICATION OF CARIBBEAN IMMIGRANTS IN THE KITCHENER-WATERLOO AREA.

Walcott, Derek
21.0093   GC   1974   The Caribbean: culture or mimicry? *J Inter-Amer Stud* 16(1), Feb.: 3-13.   **[20]**   [*COL*]

Watson, G. Llewellyn
18.0284   BC,UK   1972   THE SOCIOLOGY OF BLACK NATIONALISM: IDENTITY, PROTEST AND THE CONCEPT OF "BLACK POWER" AMONG WEST INDIAN IMMIGRANTS IN BRITAIN.

Williamson, Karina
22.0380   BC   1965   Roger Mais: West Indian novelist.

Wynter, Sylvia
22.0383   BC   1968   Reflections on West Indian writing and criticism. Part 1.
22.0384   BC   1969   Reflections on West Indian writing and criticism. Part 2.
22.0385   JM   1970   Jonkonnu in Jamaica: towards the interpretation of folk dance as a cultural process.
21.0094   BC   1972   Creole criticism—a critique. *New Wld Q* 5(4), Cropover: 12-36.
                                                                             [*RIS*]

Yawney, Carole D.
20.0091   JM   1976   Remnants of all nations: Rastafarian attitudes to race and nationality.

Chapter 22

CREATIVE ARTS AND RECREATION

Literary commentary, criticism, biography; music, dance and theater;
festivals; sports and games.
See also: [24] Folklore.

Abrahams, Roger D.

22.0001	BC	1968	Charles Walters—West Indian Autolycus. *West Folk* 27(2), April: 77-95. [*NYP*]
24.0005	NV,TB	1968	Public drama and common values in two Caribbean islands.
24.0007	TB	1968	Speech Mas' on Tobago.
22.0002	BC	1969	West Indian music on records. *J Am Folk* 82(325), July-Sept.: 295-298. [*COL*]
22.0003	TB,NV	1970	Patterns of performance in the British West Indies. *In* Whitten, Norman, E., Jr. & Szwed, John F., eds. AFRO-AMERICAN ANTHRO-POLOGY: CONTEMPORARY PERSPECTIVES. New York, The Free Press: 163-179. **[8]** [*RIS*]
22.0004	BC	1974	DEEP THE WATER, SHALLOW THE SHORE: THREE ESSAYS ON SHANTYING IN THE WEST INDIES. Austin, Texas, University of Texas Press: 125p. **[24]** [*RIS*]

Adams, Alton A.

22.0005	TR	1955	Whence came the calypso? *Caribbean* 8(10), May, 218-220, 230, 235. [*COL*]

Akong, Roy

22.0006	TR	1972	Pan. *In* Boyke, Roy, ed. PATTERNS OF PROGRESS. Port-of-Spain, Trinidad, Key Caribbean Publications: 89-91. [*RIS*]

Alladin, M. P.

32.0014	GC	1968	Research in arts and crafts.
22.0007	TR	1969	FOLK CHANTS AND REFRAINS OF TRINIDAD AND TOBAGO. Trinidad, CSO: 39p. **[24]** [*RIS*]
22.0008	TR	1974	Festivals of Trinidad and Tobago. *New Vision* 1(1), Jan.-March: 3-10. **[23,24]** [*NYP*]

Alleyne, Alvona & Ramchand, Kenneth, comps.

1.0005	BC	1973	The West Indies.
1.0006	BC	1974	The West Indies.

Amelunxen, C. P.

22.0009   CU   1934-35 De verdediging van Curacao bezongen [The defense of Curacao is
                          sung (praised)]. *W I G* 16: 250-254.   **[5]**   [*COL*]

Anderson, Peter

22.0010   GU   1965   Portrait of an artist: Ken Corsbie. *New Wld F* 1(8), Feb. 19: 27-31.
                                                                                               [*RIS*]

Angrosino, Michael V.

22.0011   BC   1975   V. S. Naipaul and the colonial image. *Car Q* 21(3), Sept.:
                          1-11. **[16,21]**   [*RIS*]

Arya, U.

12.0008 SR   1968   Ritual songs and folksongs of the Hindus of Surinam.

Asein, S. O.

1.0010   BC   1972   West Indian poetry in English, 1900-1970: a selected bibliography.

**Ashcroft, M. T.; Hendriks, D. W. A.; Herbert, E. J.; Hodgson, D. P.; Lodge,
E.; Perry, J. H. E. & Swindells, R.**

53.0010 JM   1965   Jackson's Bay Great Cave.

Attaway, William

22.0012   BC   1957   Calypso song book. New York, McGraw-Hill, 64p.

Baker, E. C.

2.0016   DM   1970   Stephen Haweis of Dominica.

Barbanson, W. L. de

22.0013   GD   1950   Frans-creoolse versjes van Guadeloupe [French-Creole verses of
                          Guadeloupe]. *W I G* 31(1), Apr.: 3-20. **[24,25]**   [*COL*]

Barker, J. S.

22.0014   BC   1963   Summer spectacular: the West Indies v. England, 1963.
                          London, Collins, 128p.

22.0015   BC   1968   In the main: West Indies v M.C.C. 1968. London, Pelham Books:
                          163p.   [*RIS*]

Baugh, Edward

22.0016   BC   [n.d.]   West Indian poetry: a study in cultural decolonisation.
                          Kingston, Jamaica, Savacou Publications: 20p. (Savacou Pamphlet
                          No. 1) **[21]**   [*RIS*]

Baxter, Ivy

19.0003 JM   1970   The arts of an island: the development of the culture and of
                          the folk and creative arts in Jamaica, 1494-1962 (Independ-
                          ence).

Beckwith, Martha Warren

22.0017   JM   1922   Folk games in Jamaica. Poughkeepsie, N.Y., Vassar College, 79p.
                          (Field-work in folk-lore; publications of the Folklore Foundation,
                          no. 1.) **[24]**   [*COL*]

22.0018   JM   1924   English ballad in Jamaica; a note upon the origin of the ballad
                          form; with music and texts. *Pubs Mod Lang Assoc Am* 39, June:
                          455-483.   [*NYP*]

23.0010   **JM**   1924   THE HUSSAY FESTIVAL IN JAMAICA.
24.0022   **JM**   1924   JAMAICA ANANSI STORIES.

Beckwith, Martha Warren & Roberts, Helen H.
22.0019   **JM**   1923   CHRISTMAS MUMMINGS IN JAMAICA. Poughkeepsie, N.Y., Vassar College, 46p. (Field-work in folk-lore; publications of the Folklore Foundation, no. 2.) **[19,24]**   [*COL*]

Bedell, Eugenia
22.0020   **GC**   1967   Yachting unlimited. *Car Beachcomb* 3(6), Nov.-Dec.: 15-16.   [*NYP*]

Benjamin, Elsie
22.0021   **JM**   1945   Toward a native drama. *Theatre Arts* 29(5), May: 313-314.   [*COL*]

Bennett, Louise
24.0027   **JM**   1961   LAUGH WITH LOUISE: A POT-POURRI OF JAMAICAN FOLKLORE.

Bennett, Wycliffe
22.0022   **JM**   1974   The Jamaican theatre: a preliminary overview. *Jam J* 8(2-3), Summer: 3-9.   [*RIS*]

Bernard, C. M.
22.0023   **GU**   1948   Music in British Guiana. *Timehri* 4th ser., 1(28), Dec.: 28-34.

Bertrand, Anca
22.0024   **GD,MT**   1967   Les bijoux créoles [Creole jewelry]. *Parallèles* 22: 5-21.   [*RIS*]
22.0025   **GD,MT**   1967   Carnaval à la Martinique et à la Guadeloupe [Carnival in Martinique and Guadeloupe]. *Parallèles* 21: 4-15.   [*RIS*]
22.0026   **GC**   1968   Notes pour une définition du folklore antillais [Notes for a definition of West Indian folk music]. *Parallèles* 28: 5-19. **[19,24]**   [*RIS*]
22.0027   **MT**   1968   A propos des ballets folkloriques martiniquais [About the ballets folkloriques martiniquais]. *Parallèles* 26, 1st trimester: 74-77.   [*RIS*]
22.0028   **GC**   1968   Le théatre lyrique aux Antilles [Lyric theatre in the Antilles]. *Parallèles* 28, 3rd trimester: 29-31.   [*RIS*]

Biharie, S.
12.0012   **SR**   1971   Hindostaanse muziekinstrumenten en zang in Suriname [Hindustani musical instruments and song in Surinam].

Birbalsingh, F. M.
22.0029   **BC**   1970   The novels of Ralph DeBoissière. *J Commonw Lit* 9, July: 104-108. **[21]**   [*COL*]

Birkett, T. Sydney
22.0030   **GC**   1927   RESUME OF BIG CRICKET IN THE WEST INDIES AND BRITISH GUIANA SINCE THE WEST INDIES TOUR OF 1923 IN ENGLAND. [Bridgetown?] Barbados, Advocate Co., 61p.

Blofeld, Henry
22.0031   **BC**   1970   CRICKET IN THREE MOODS. London, Hodder and Stoughton: 192p.   [*NYP*]

Bonsignori, Umberto

22.0032   BC   1972   DEREK WALCOTT: CONTEMPORARY WEST INDIAN POET AND PLAY-
WRIGHT. Ph.D. dissertation, University of California (Los Angeles):
249p.   [*PhD*]

Boodhoo, Isaiah James

32.0073   TR   1974   A CURRICULUM MODEL IN ART EDUCATION FOR THE PRIMARY
SCHOOLS OF TRINIDAD AND TOBAGO.

Boomert, A.

13.0018   SR   1975   Indian art in Suriname.

Boskaljon, R.

22.0033   CU   1948   Het muziekleven [The music world]. *In* ORANJE EN DE ZES
CARAÏBISCHE PARELEN. Amsterdam, J. H. de Bussy: 356-366.
                                                                [*UCLA*]

22.0034   CU   1958   HONDERD JAAR MUZIEKLEVEN OP CURACAO [HUNDRED YEARS OF
MUSIC ON CURACAO]. Assen [Netherlands], VanGorcum, 188p.

Bowen, Calvin

22.0035   JM   1954   Jamaica's John Canoe. *Car Commn Mon Inf B* 8(1), Aug.: 11-
12. **[19,23]**   [*COL*]

Boxill, Anthony

22.0036   TR   1975   V. S. Naipaul's starting point. *J Commonw Lit* 10(1), Aug.:
1-9. **[12]**   [*COL*]

Brathwaite, Edward

22.0037   BC   1963   Roots. *Bim* 10(37), July-Dec.: 10-21. **[20]**
22.0038   BC   1968   The Caribbean Artists Movement. *Car Q* 14(1-2), March-June:
57-59.   [*RIS*]
22.0039   BC   1970   Timehri. *Savacou* 2, Sept.: 35-44. **[19]**   [*RIS*]

Brathwaite, Edward K.

19.0005   GC   1974   The African presence in Caribbean literature.

Brathwaite, L. Edward

22.0040   GC   1967   Jazz and the West Indian novel. *Bim* 11(44), Jan.-June: 275-284.
                                                                [*RIS*]
22.0041   GC   1967   Jazz and the West Indian novel—II. *Bim* 12(45), July-Dec.:
39-51. **[11]**   [*RIS*]
22.0042   BC   1968   Jazz and the West Indian novel—III. *Bim* 12(46), Jan.-June:
115-126.   [*RIS*]
22.0043   BC   1969   Caribbean critics. *New Wld Q* 5(1-2), Dead Season and Croptime:
5-12. **[21]**   [*RIS*]

Brathwaite, P. A. & Brathwaite, Serena U., comps. & eds.

22.0044   GU   1967   FOLK SONGS OF GUYANA IN WORDS AND MUSIC. Georgetown,
Brathwaite: 20p. **[24]**   [*RIS*]

Brereton, Bridget

22.0045   TR   1975   The Trinidad Carnival 1870-1900. *Savacou* 11-12, Sept.:
46-57. **[5,21]**   [*RIS*]

Brown, Lloyd W.

22.0046   BC,US   1970   The West Indian novel in North America: a study of Austin Clarke. *J Commonw Lit* 9, July: 89-103.   **[18,21]**   [*COL*]

Brown, Wayne

5.0110   JM   1975   EDNA MANLEY. THE PRIVATE YEARS: 1900-1938.

Brownell, Willard N. & Rainey, William E.

52.0028   VI   1971   RESEARCH AND DEVELOPMENT OF DEEP WATER COMMERCIAL AND SPORT FISHERIES AROUND THE VIRGIN ISLANDS PLATEAU.

Brulin, Tone

22.0047   NA   1971   Toneel in de Nederlandse Antillen [Theatre in the Netherlands Antilles]. *In* STICUSA JAARVERSLAG 1971. Amsterdam, The Netherlands, Nederlandse Stichting voor Culturele Samenwerking met Suriname en de Nederlandse Antillen: 54-58.   [*NYP*]

Brunings, D. A.

22.0048   SR   1970   Zeilen in Suriname [Sailing in Surinam]. *Suralco Mag* 2, Aug.: 24-31.   [*UCLA*]

Bueno, Salvador

22.0049   GC   1966   Raza, color y literatura antillana [Race, color and Caribbean literature]. *Casa Américas* 6(36-37), May-Aug.: 186-189.   **[11]**
                                                                       [*COL*]

Bullard, M. Kenyon

22.0050   BZ   1975   Marbles: an investigation of the relationship between marble games and other aspects of life in Belize. *J Am Folk* 88(350), Oct.-Dec.: 393-400.   **[8]**   [*COL*]

Caboo, Roy

22.0051   TR   1975   The making of a Caribbean artist. *Race Today* 7(2), Feb.: 36-39.
                                                                       [*RIS*]

Cameron, D. J.

22.0052   BC   1972   CARIBBEAN CRUSADE: THE NEW ZEALAND CRICKETERS IN THE WEST INDIES 1972. Auckland, Hodder and Stoughton Ltd.: 166p.   [*NYP*]

Cameron, N. E.

22.0053   TR   1955   Harmony in steel bands. *New Commonw* British Caribbean Supplement 30(11), Nov. 28: xviii-xix.   [*AGS*]

Caple, S. Canynge

22.0054   BC   1957   ENGLAND V. THE WEST INDIES 1895-1957. Worcester, Littlebury, 206p.   **[5]**

Carew, Jan

21.0009   BC   1953   British West Indian poets and their culture.
22.0055   GU   1965   An artist in exile—from the West Indies. *New Wld F* 1(27-28), Nov.12: 23-30.   **[18]**   [*RIS*]

Carnegie, James

22.0056   JM   1970   Notes on the history of jazz and its role in Jamaica. *Jam J* 4(1), March: 20-29.   [*RIS*]

Carr, Andrew T.

22.0057   TR   1954   Trinidad calypso is unique folk culture. *Car Commn Mon Inf B* 7(7), Feb.: 162-164. **[24]**   [*COL*]

22.0058   TR   1956   Pierrot Grenade. *Car Q* 4(3-4), Mar.-June: 281-314. **[19,25]**   [*RIS*]

Carr, Bill

22.0059   BC   1968   A complex fate: the novels of Andrew Salkey. *In* James, Louis, ed. THE ISLANDS IN BETWEEN: ESSAYS ON WEST INDIAN LITERATURE. London, Oxford University Press: 100-108. **[21]**   [*NYP*]

Castagne, Patrick

22.0060   TR   1962   This is calypso! *Chron W I Comm* 77(1377): Oct.: 518-519.   [*NYP*]

Cecil, C. H.

22.0061   BC   1937   I—you, and the Devil take the loser! *Can-W I Mag* 26(12), Dec.: 25-26. **[19]**   [*NYP*]

Césaire, Aimé

21.0010   MT   1967   AIMÉ CÉSAIRE, ÉCRIVAIN MARTINIQUAIS [AIMÉ CÉSAIRE, MARTINIQUAN WRITER].

Chambertrand, Gilbert de

22.0062   FA   1963   MI IO! New ed. by Bettino Lara & Rober Fortuné. [Basse-Terre] Guadeloupe, Impr. officielle, 94p. **[20,25]**   [*RIS*]

Chang, Carlisle

22.0063   TR   1963[?]   Painting in Trinidad. *In* Hill, Errol, ed. THE ARTIST IN WEST INDIAN SOCIETY: A SYMPOSIUM [seminars held in Port of Spain, Trinidad, May-June 1963, and in Jamaica, Oct. 1962-Jan. 1963]. [Mona?] Dept. of Extra-mural Studies, University of the West Indies, p. 25-37.   [*RIS*]

Chevrette, Valerie

1.0057   GC   1971   ANNOTATED BIBLIOGRAPHY OF THE PRECOLUMBIAN ART AND AR-CHAEOLOGY OF THE WEST INDIES.

Chumaceiro, N.

22.0064   CU   1948   De sport [Sports]. *In* ORANJE EN DE ZES CARAÏBISCHE PARELEN. Amsterdam, J. H. de Bussy: 397-399.   [*UCLA*]

Clark, Astley

22.0065   JM   1975   Extract from *The Music and Musical Instruments of Jamaica. Jam J* 9(2-3): 59-67. **[19]**   [*RIS*]

Clarke, John

22.0066   BC   1963   CRICKET WITH A SWING: THE WEST INDIES TOUR, 1963. London, Stanley Paul, 200p.

Clarke, John & Scovell, Brian

22.0067 BC 1966 EVERYTHING THAT'S CRICKET: THE WEST INDIES TOUR 1966. London, Stanley Paul: 192p. [*RIS*]

Coffey, Edmund Patrick

22.0068 TR 1968 REPORT OF THE COMMISSION OF ENQUIRY INTO THE HORSE-RACING INDUSTRY IN TRINIDAD AND TOBAGO. Trinidad, Government Printery: 35p. [*RIS*]

Collier, H. C.

22.0069 JM 1937 Cristallized poetry. *Can-W I Mag* 26(12): Dec.: 28-30. [*NYP*]

22.0070 TR 1939 Trinidad fantasia. *Can-W I Mag* 28(2), Feb.: 7-11. **[19]** [*NYP*]

22.0071 JM 1940 The sculptural art of Edna Manley. *Can-W I Mag* 29(1), Feb.: 24-26. [*NYP*]

22.0072 TR 1940 Tropical trove. *Can-W I Mag* 29(6), June: 21-23. [*NYP*]

22.0073 GU 1941 Arts and crafts in British Guiana. *Can-W I Mag* 30(4), Apr.: 21-23. [*NYP*]

22.0074 TR 1943 Carnival capers in calypso land. *Can-W I Mag* 32(1), Jan.: 19-22. **[19]** [*NYP*]

22.0075 BC 1967 "Warri," an African game transplanted to the West Indies. *Can-W I Mag* 24(6), May: 23-24. **[19]** [*NYP*]

Comvalius, Th. A. C.

22.0076 SR 1935-36 Het Surinaamsche Negerlied: de banja en de doe [The Surinam Negro song: the banja and the doe]. *W I G* 17: 213-230. **[14]** [*COL*]

22.0077 SR 1938 Twee historische liederen in Suriname [Two historical songs in Surinam]. *W I G* 20: 291-295. **[5]** [*COL*]

22.0078 SR 1939 Een der vormen van het Surinaamsche lied na 1863 [One of the types of the Surinam song after 1863]. *W I G* 21: 355-360. [*COL*]

22.0079 SR 1946 Oud-Surinaamsche rhythmische dansen in dienst van de lichamel-ikje opvoeding [Old Surinamese rhythmic dances in the service of physical education]. *W I G* 27: 97-103. **[19,32]** [*COL*]

Connell, Neville

23.0054 BB 1953 St. George's Parish Church, Barbados.

22.0080 BB 1954 Church plate in Barbados. *Connoisseur* 134(539), Aug.: 8-13. **[23]**

22.0081 GC 1957 Caribbean artists paint action and colour. *Studio* 153(770), May: 129-135.

Connor, Edric

22.0082 TR 1958 SONGS FROM TRINIDAD. London, Oxford University Press, 76p.

Cook, Mercer

37.0153 FA 1940 The literary contribution of the French West Indian.

Cororan, T. C.

32.0131 TR 1966 Our school choirs and the Music Festival.

Coulthard, G. R.

22.0083 GC 1962 RACE AND COLOUR IN CARIBBEAN LITERATURE. London, Oxford University Press, 152p. **[11,16,21]** [*RIS*]

Creary, John

22.0084   BC   1968   A prophet armed: the novels of Roger Mais. *In* James, Louis, ed. THE ISLANDS IN BETWEEN: ESSAYS ON WEST INDIAN LITERATURE. London, Oxford University Press: 50-63.   **[21]**   [*NYP*]

Crowley, Daniel J.

12.0020   TR   1954   East Indian festivals in Trinidad life.

22.0085   TR   1954   THE MEANINGS OF CARNIVAL. Port of Spain, 3p.   **[19,21]**   [*RIS*]

22.0086   GU   1956   Bush Negro combs: a structural analysis. *Vox Guy* 2(4), Dec.: 145-161.   **[14]**   [*RIS*]

22.0087   TR   1956   The midnight robbers. *Car Q* 4(3-4), Mar.-June: 263-274.   **[19]** [*RIS*]

22.0088   TR   1956   The traditional masques of Carnival. *Car Q* 4(3-4), Mar.-June: 194-223.   **[5,19]**   [*RIS*]

22.0089   SL   1957   Song and dance in St. Lucia. *Ethnomusicology* 9, Jan.: 4-14.   **[19]** [*RIS*]

22.0090   TR   1958   Calypso: Trinidad Carnival songs and dances. *Dance Notat Rec* 9(2), Summer: 3-7.   [*RIS*]

3.0133   BA   1958   Guy Fawkes Day at Fresh Creek, Andros Island, Bahamas.

22.0091   BB,TR,WW   1958   The shak-shak in the Lesser Antilles. *Ethnomusicology* 2(3), Sept.: 112-115.   [*RIS*]

22.0092   TR   1959   Toward a definition of "calypso." *Ethnomusicology* 3(2), May: 57-66.   [*RIS*]

22.0093   TR   1959   Toward a definition of "calypso." *Ethnomusicology* 3(3), Sept.: 117-124.   [*RIS*]

Cruickshank, J. Graham

22.0094   GU   1924   An African dance in the colony. *W I Comm Circ* 39(662, suppl.), Feb. 14: 8-9.   **[11,19]**   [*NYP*]

19.0013   GU   1929   Negro games.

Cumper, Pat

22.0095   JM   1975   Cecil Baugh, master potter. *Jam J* 9(2-3): 18-27.   [*RIS*]

Cundall, Frank

22.0096   JM   1907   Sculpture in Jamaica. *Art J* 69, Mar.: 65-70.   [*COL*]

22.0097   JM   1924   Pine's painting of Rodney and his officers. *W I Comm Circ* 39(670), June 5: 219.   **[5]**   [*NYP*]

22.0098   JM   1924   Pine's painting of Rodney and his officers. *W I Comm Circ* 39(671), June 19: 242-243.   **[5]**   [*NYP*]

Dam, Theodore van

22.0099   GC   1954   The influence of the West African songs of derision in the New World. *Afr Music* 1(1): 53-56.   **[19]**   [*NYP*]

Daniskas, J.

32.0154   NC   1970   Muziekonderwijs in Suriname en de Nederlandse Antillen [Music education in Surinam and the Netherlands Antilles].

Dark, Philip J. C.

22.0100   SR   1951   Some notes on the carving of calabashes by the Bush Negroes of Surinam. *Man* 51(97), May: 57-60.   **[14]**   [*COL*]

| 22.0101 | SR | 1954 | BUSH NEGRO ART: AN AFRICAN ART IN THE AMERICAS. London, Alec Tiranti, 65p. **[14,19]** [*NYP*] |

Dash, J. Michael

| *21.0017* | GC | 1974 | Marvellous realism—the way out of négritude. |

Dathorne, Oscar Ronald

22.0102	BC	1965	Africa in the literature of the West Indies. *J Commonw Lit* 1, Sept.: 95-116. **[19,21]** [*COL*]
22.0103	GC	1965	The theme of Africa in West Indian literature. *Phylon* 26(3), Fall: 255-276. **[19]** [*COL*]
22.0104	GC	1966	A SURVEY OF WEST AFRICAN AND WEST INDIAN LITERATURE. Ph.D. dissertation, University of Sheffield: 1160p. **[1]**

Davies, Barrie

| 22.0105 | BC | 1968 | The seekers: the novels of John Hearne. *In* James, Louis, ed. THE ISLANDS IN BETWEEN: ESSAYS ON WEST INDIAN LITERATURE. London, Oxford University Press: 109-120. **[21]** [*NYP*] |

Davis, Margo & Davis, Gregson

| 22.0106 | AT | 1973 | ANTIGUA BLACK: PORTRAIT OF AN ISLAND PEOPLE. San Francisco, The Scrimshaw Press: 141p. **[3]** [*RIS*] |

De Challes, Macé

| 22.0107 | GC | 1972 | Cockfighting in the 19th century Caribbean. *Car R* 4(4), Oct.-Nov.-Dec.: 12-14. **[5]** [*RIS*] |

Dennert, H.

22.0108	NA	1968	Hedendaagse muziek [Contemporary music]. *Schakels* NA52: 12-16. [*NYP*]
22.0109	CU	1968	Muzikaal verleden [Musical past]. *Schakels* NA52: 1-11. [*NYP*]
22.0110	NA	1968	Steelbands in opkomst [The development of steel bands]. *Schakels* NA52: 20-23. [*NYP*]

Dirks, Robert

| *6.0058* | JM | 1975 | Slaves' holiday. |

Dolphin, Celeste

| 22.0111 | GU | 1946 | Arawak rhythm. *Can-W I Mag* 36(8), Oct.: 19-22. **[13]** [*NYP*] |

Donawa, Wendy

| 22.0112 | BB | 1969 | Viewpoint. *Bim* 13(49), July-Dec.: 53-57. [*RIS*] |

Drayton, Arthur D.

21.0022	BC	1963	West Indian fiction and West Indian society.
22.0113	BC	1970	The European factor in West Indian literature. *Rev Lang Viv* 36(6): 582-601. [*COL*]
22.0114	BC	1970	West Indian consciousness in West Indian verse: a historical perspective. *J Commonw Lit* 9, July: 66-88. **[21]** [*COL*]

Dunwoodie, Peter

| 22.0115 | GC | 1975 | Commitment and confinement: two West Indian visions. *Car Q* 21(3), Sept.: 15-27. **[20,21]** [*RIS*] |

Duperly, Doris

32.0175   **JM**   1973   An account of the Secondary Schools' Drama Festival committee.

Du Quesnay, F. J.

22.0116   **JM**   1968   Four illustrators of the Jamaican scene. *Jam J* 2(2), June: 55-60. **[5]**   [*RIS*]

Easby, Elizabeth Kennedy

4.0099   **GC**   1972   Seafarers and sculptors of the Caribbean.

Easby, Elizabeth Kennedy & Scott, John F.

4.0100   **GC**   1970   BEFORE CORTÉS: SCULPTURE OF MIDDLE AMERICA: A CENTENNIAL EXHIBITION AT THE METROPOLITAN MUSEUM OF ART FROM SEPTEMBER 30, 1970 THROUGH JANUARY 3, 1971.

Edwards, Charles L.

24.0072   **BA**   1942   BAHAMA SONGS AND STORIES: A CONTRIBUTION TO FOLK-LORE.

Ekwueme, Laz. E. N.

19.0018   **GC**   1972   African sources in New World black music.

Elder, J. D.

22.0117   **TR**   1961   SONG-GAMES OF TRINIDAD AND TOBAGO. Delaware, Ohio, Cooperative Recreation Service, 15p.   [*RIS*]

22.0118   **BC**   1963[?]   The future of music in the West Indies. (i) Folk music. *In* Hill, Errol, ed. THE ARTIST IN WEST INDIAN SOCIETY; A SYMPOSIUM [seminars held in Port of Spain, Trinidad, May-June 1963, and in Jamaica, Oct. 1962-Jan. 1963]. [Mona?] Dept. of Extra-mural Studies, University of the West Indies, p.38-45.   [*RIS*]

22.0119   **TR**   1965   Song-games from Trinidad and Tobago. *Pubs Am Folk Soc,* Bibliographical and special series, 16(119p.)   [*RIS*]

22.0120   **TR**   1966   EVOLUTION OF THE TRADITIONAL CALYPSO OF TRINIDAD AND TOBAGO: A SOCIO-HISTORICAL ANALYSIS OF SONG-CHANGE. Ph.D. dissertation, University of Pennsylvania: 316p.   [*RIS*]

24.0073   **TR**   1966   *Kalinda*—song of the battling troubadours of Trinidad.

22.0121   **TR**   1968   The male/female conflict in calypso. *Car Q* 14(3), Sept.: 23-41. **[20,31]**   [*RIS*]

22.0122   **TR**   1969   FROM CONGO DRUM TO STEEL-BAND: A SOCIO-HISTORICAL ACCOUNT OF THE EMERGENCE AND EVOLUTION OF THE TRINIDAD STEEL ORCHESTRA. St. Augustine, Trinidad, Univ. of the West Indies: 47p.
                                                                            [*RIS*]

22.0123   **TR**   1971   Color, music, and conflict: a study of aggression in Trinidad with reference to the role of traditional music. *In* Frucht, Richard, ed. BLACK SOCEITY IN THE NEW WORLD. New York Random House: 315-323. **[5,6,16,19]**   [*COL*]

22.0124   **TB**   1972   FOLK SONG AND FOLK LIFE IN CHARLOTTEVILLE (ASPECTS OF VILLAGE LIFE AS DYNAMICS OF ACCULTURATION IN A TOBAGO FOLK SONG TRADITION). Port-of-Spain, National Cultural Council of Trinidad and Tobago: 62p. (Paper presented at the Twenty-first Conference of the International Music Council, Kingston, Jamaica, August 27-Sept. 3, 1971) **[24]**   [*RIS*]

24.0075   **TR**   1972   MA ROSE POINT: AN ANTHOLOGY OF RARE AND STRANGE LEGENDS FROM TRINIDAD AND TOBAGO.

Elie, Louis

22.0125   MT   1976   Vers une association départementale de la musique à la Martinique [Towards a Departmental society of music in Martinique]. *B Inf Cenaddom* 31, May-June: 23-27.   [*RIS*]

Ellam, Patrick

3.0169   GC   1957   THE SPORTSMAN'S GUIDE TO THE CARIBBEAN.

Escoffery, Gloria

22.0126   BC   1968   The bicycle lamp: an artist's reflections on art teaching. *Car Q* 14(4), Dec.: 49-55.   **[32]**   [*RIS*]

Espinet, Charles S.

22.0127   TR   1951[?]   Trinidad's tinpany. *Esso Ant* 1(5), [Sept.?].   [*RIS*]
22.0128   TR   1953   Masquerade—origin and development of Trinidad's Carnival. *Can-W I Mag* 43(13), Jan.: 22-23, 25.   **[19]**   [*NYP*]

Espinet, Charles S. & Pitts, Harry

22.0129   TR   1944   LAND OF THE CALYPSO: THE ORIGIN AND DEVELOPMENT OF TRINIDAD'S FOLK-SONG. Port of Spain, Guardian Commercial Printery, 74p.   **[5,19]**   [*COL*]

Evans, Vernon

22.0130   TR   1963[?]   The future of music in the West Indies. (ii) Art music. *In* Hill, Errol, ed. THE ARTIST IN WEST INDIAN SOCIETY: A SYMPOSIUM [seminars held in Port of Spain, Trinidad, May-June 1963, and in Jamaica Oct. 1962-Jan. 1963]. [Mona?] Dept. of Extra-mural Studies, University of the West Indies, p.46-50.   **[32]**   [*RIS*]

Eytle, Ernest

22.0131   BC   1963   FRANK WORRELL. London, Hodder and Stoughton, 192p.

Figueroa, John Joseph

22.0132   GC   1975   Introduction to George Lamming. *Revta Interam Rev* 5(2), Summer: 146-148.   **[21]**   [*RIS*]

Flagler, J. M.

22.0133   BC   1954   A reporter at large: Well caught, Mr. Holder! *New Yorker* 30, Sept. 25: 65-85.

Forbes, Ronald

13.0063   GU   1965   Art and the Akawaio.

Fowler, Henry

22.0134   JM   1968   A history of theatre in Jamaica. *Jam J* 2(1), March: 53-59.   **[5]**
                                                                        [*RIS*]

Frampton, H. M.

22.0135   DM   1957   Carnival time in Dominica. *Can-W I Mag* 47(5), May: 9, 11.   **[19]**
                                                                        [*NYP*]

Gabb, George & Lizama, Frank

22.0136   BZ   1974   Belizean art. *National Stud* 2(1), January: 16-26.   [*RIS*]

Gardner, M. M.

22.0137 TR 1954 The greatest show of its kind on earth—Trinidad's Carnival. *Can-W I Mag* 44(5), May: 26-27, 29-31. **[19]**   [*NYP*]

Garebian, Keith

22.0138 BC 1975 V. S. Naipaul's negative sense of place. *J Commonw Lit* 10(1), Aug.: 23-25. **[12,21]**   [*COL*]

Gelman, Kenneth J.; Marcus, Joel A. & Schwerin, Charles N.

56.0124 ST 1970 Recreational watercraft and pollution: Charlotte Amalie, St. Thomas, Virgin Islands.

Gilchrist, Roy

22.0139 BC 1963 HIT ME FOR SIX. London, Stanley Paul, 126p.

Gilkes, Michael

22.0140 GU 1973 THE CARIBBEAN SYZYGY: A STUDY OF THE NOVELS OF EDGAR MITTELHOLZER AND WILSON HARRIS. Ph.D. dissertation, University of Kent: 468p.

22.0141 BC 1975 RACIAL IDENTITY AND INDIVIDUAL CONSCIOUSNESS IN THE CARIBBEAN NOVEL. Georgetown, Guyana, Ministry of Information and Culture, National History and Arts Council: 51p. (Edgar Mittelholzer Memorial Lectures, 1974) **[21]**   [*RIS*]

22.0142 BC 1975 The spirit in the bottle—a reading of Mittelholzer's. *A Morning at the Office. Car Q* 21(4), Dec.: 1-12. **[21]**   [*RIS*]

22.0143 GC 1975 WILSON HARRIS AND THE CARIBBEAN NOVEL. Longman Caribbean: 159p. **[21]**   [*RIS*]

Giuseppi, Undine

22.0144 TR 1969 SIR FRANK WORRELL. London, Thomas Nelson and Sons: 92p. **[2]**
                                                                                [*RIS*]

Glazema, P.

22.0145 SR 1970 Openluchtmuseum Nieuw Amsterdam [Open Air Museum New Amsterdam]. *Schakels* S74: 15-18.   [*NYP*]

Goeje, C. H. de

22.0146 CU 1948 De wiri-wiri, een muziek-instrument van Curacao [The wiri-wiri, a musical instrument of Curacao]. *W I G* 29: 225-228.   [*COL*]

22.0147 GC 1950 Verwanten van de Curacaose wiri [Relatives of the Curacao wiri]. *W I G* 31: 180. **[13]**   [*COL*]

Goonewardene, James

21.0035 GC 1975 Nationalism and the writer in Sri Lanka and the West Indies.

Gordijn, W.

22.0148 NC 1965 Tien jaar Statuut 1954-1964. Culturele ontwikkelingen in Rijksverband [Ten years of Statute 1954-1964. Cultural developments in context of the Kingdom]. *N W I G* 44(1-2), April: 60-74. **[37]**
                                                                                [*RIS*]

Gordijn, W., ed.

1.0122 NC 1970[?] CULTURELE KRONIEK '48-'68 [CULTURAL CHRONICLE '48-'68].

Gradussov, Alex

22.0149	JM	1969	Carl Abrahams: painter and cartoonist. *Jam J* 3(1), March: 43-46.
			[*RIS*]
23.0103	JM	1969	Kapo; cult leader, sculptor, painter.
22.0150	JM	1969	Osmond Watson talks to Alex Gradussov. *Jam J* 3(3), Sept.: 47-53.
			[*RIS*]
22.0151	JM	1970	Looking forward: Alex Gradussov talks to Harry and Elma Thubron. *Jam J* 4(2), June: 49-56. [*RIS*]
22.0152	JM	1970	Thoughts about the theatre in Jamaica. *Jam J* 4(1), March: 46-52.
			[*RIS*]
22.0153	JM	1971	Gloria Escoffery talks to Alex Gradussov. *Jam J* 5(1), March: 34-40. [*RIS*]
22.0154	JM	1971	A talk with two photographers: Amador Packer and Errol Harvey. *Jam J* 5(4), Dec.: 37-44. [*RIS*]

Graham, S. P.

22.0155	GU	1965	Portrait of an artist—Hugh Sam. *New Wld F* 1(9), March 5: 35-38.
			[*RIS*]

Grimes, John

22.0156	GC	1964	Caribbean music and dance. *Freedomways* 4(3), Summer: 426-434.
			[*RIS*]

Guckian, Patrick

22.0157	GU	1970	The balance of colour: a re-assessment of the work of Edgar Mittleholtzer. *Jam J* 4(1), March: 38-45. **[16]** [*RIS*]

Guggenheim, Hans

22.0158	TR	1968	SOCIAL AND POLITICAL CHANGE IN THE ART WORLD OF TRINIDAD DURING THE PERIOD OF TRANSITION FROM COLONY TO NEW NATION. Ph.D. dissertation, New York University, Department of Sociology: 172p. **[26,37]** [*RIS*]

Guggenheim, Hans & Carr, Andrew T.

23.0105	TR	1965	Tribalism in Trinidad.

Gurr, A. J.

22.0159	BC	1972	Third-World novels: Naipaul and after. *J Commonw Lit* 7(1), June: 6-13. **[21]** [*COL*]

Habibe, H.

22.0160	CU	1975	Algun aspekto sosial den poesia na papiamento [Some social aspects of Papiamento poetry]. *Kristòf* 2(1), Feb.: 31-40. **[21]**
			[*RIS*]
22.0161	NA	1975	Kenshinan literario di Dr. J. de Palm [Literary mime of Dr. J. de Palm]. *Kristòf* 2(6), Dec.: 266-271. [*RIS*]
22.0162	NA	1975	Ta ken ta falsifika istoria, Habibe o Smit??? [Who commits falsification of history, Habibe or Smit???] *Kristòf* 2(3), June: 148-153. [*RIS*]

Hale, Thomas A.

21.0037	MT	1974	Aimé Césaire: a bio-bibliography.

Hamner, Robert D.

22.0163   TR   1975   V. S. Naipaul: a selected bibliography. *J Commonw Lit* 10(1), Aug.: 36-44. **[1,12]**   [*COL*]

Handler, Jerome S. & Frisbie, Charlotte J.

6.0127   BB   1972   Aspects of slave life in Barbados: music and its cultural context.

Hanson, Donald R. & Dash, Robert

22.0164   TR   1955   The saga of the steelband. *Caribbean* 8(8), Mar.: 173, 176-177, 184.
                                                                                            [*COL*]

Harley, Milton; Hyde, Eugene & Segree, Norma

32.0271   JM   1968   The Jamaica School of Arts and Crafts (a discussion).

Harris, Wilson

22.0165   GU   1966   Impressions after seven years. *New Wld F* 1(44), July 25: 17-20.
                                                                                            [*RIS*]
22.0166   GC   1967   TRADITION, THE WRITER AND SOCIETY: CRITICAL ESSAYS. London, New Beacon Publications: 75p.   [*COL*]

Harrison, John

22.0167   BC   1950[?]   Art for West Indian children. *Car Q* 1(3): 19-31.   **[32]**
22.0168   BC   1952   Last thoughts on art in the British West Indies. *J Barb Mus Hist Soc* 19(2), Feb: 53-57.   [*AMN*]

Hartog, J.

21.0038   CU   [n.d.]   Cultural life in Curacao.
5.0384   GU   1971   HONDERD JAAR GEZELLIGHEID IN DE GEZELLIGHEID 1871-1971 [HUNDRED YEARS OF CONVIVIALITY IN "DE GEZELLIGHEID" 1871-1971].

Hatterman, Nola

22.0169   SR   1975   Ontwikkeling van de beeldende kunst in Suriname [Development of the art of design in Surinam]. *Suralco Mag* Sept.: 12-17.   [*UCLA*]

Hearne, John

22.0170   BC   1967   Home from the wars. . .an epitaph. *Jam J* 1(1), Dec.: 82-84.   [*RIS*]
22.0171   BC   1968   The fugitive in the forest. *In* James, Louis, ed. THE ISLANDS IN BETWEEN: ESSAYS ON WEST INDIAN LITERATURE. London, Oxford University Press: 140-153. **[21]**   [*NYP*]

Henriques, Fernando, comp.

1.0133   BC   1965   The West Indies.
1.0134   BC   1966   The West Indies.
1.0135   BC   1967   The West Indies.

Herskovits, Melville Jean

19.0028   SR   1929   Adjiboto, an African game of the Bush-Negroes of Dutch Guiana.
22.0172   GC   1932   Wari in the New World. *J Roy Anthrop Inst Gr Br Ire* 62, Jan.-June: 23-37. **[19]**   [*AGS*]
22.0173   GC   1941   El estudio de la música negra en el hemisferio occidental [The study of Negro music in the Western Hemisphere]. *Boln Latam Mus Amer Music* 5, Oct. 133-142. **[11,19]**   [*COL*]

22.0174 GC 1941 Patterns of Negro music. *Trans Ill St Acad Sci* 34(1), Sept.: 19-23. **[11,19]** [*NYP*]

22.0175 SR 1949 Afro-American art. *In* Wilder, Elizabeth, ed. STUDIES IN LATIN AMERICAN ART. Proceedings of a conference held in the Museum of Modern Art, New York, 28-31 May 1945. Washington, D.C., American Council of Learned Societies. p.58-64. **[14]** [*SCH*]

Herskovits, Melville Jean & Herskovits, Frances S.

22.0176 SR 1930 Bush-Negro art. *Arts* 17(1), Oct.: 25-37, 48-49. **[14,19]** [*COL*]

24.0089 SR 1936 SURINAME FOLK-LORE (with transcriptions and Suriname songs and musicological analysis by Dr. M. Kolinski).

Heuvel, Pim

22.0177 CU 1974 De trilogie van een displaced person [The trilogy of a displaced person]. *Kristòf* 1(6), Dec.: 282-291. [*RIS*]

22.0178 NA 1975 Afschuw van licht [Abhorrence of light]. *Kristòf* 2(3), June: 133-142. [*RIS*]

Heyl, Edith S.

22.0179 BE 1944 Bermuda's early literary associations. *Bermuda Hist Q* 1(2), May-July: 95-99. [*NYP*]

Hill, Errol

22.0180 BC 1955 Drama round the Caribbean. *Car Commn Mon Inf B* 8(6), Jan.: 112-113, 120-121. **[21]** [*COL*]

22.0181 BC 1963[?] West Indian drama. *In* Hill, Errol, ed. THE ARTIST IN WEST INDIAN SOCIETY: A SYMPOSIUM [seminars held in Port of Spain, Trinidad, May-June 1963, and in Jamaica, Oct. 1962-Jan. 1963]. [Mona?] Dept. of Extra-mural Studies, University of the West Indies, p.7-24. [*RIS*]

22.0182 TR 1966 THE TRINIDAD CARNIVAL: A STUDY OF ITS FORM AND CONTENT AS THE BASIS FOR A NATIONAL THEATRE. Ph.D. dissertation, Yale University: 118p.

22.0183 TR 1967 On the origin of the term calypso. *Ethnomusicology* 11(3), September: 359-367. **[19]** [*COL*]

22.0184 TR 1971 Calypso. *Jam J* 5(1), March: 23-27. [*RIS*]

22.0185 BC 1972 Cultural values and the theatre arts in the English-speaking Caribbean. *In* RESOURCE DEVELOPMENT IN THE CARIBBEAN. Montreal, McGill University, Centre for Developing-Area Studies: 113-124. **[20]** [*RIS*]

22.0186 BC 1972 The emergence of a national drama in the West Indies. *Car Q* 18(4), Sept.: 9-40. **[21]** [*RIS*]

22.0187 TR 1972 THE TRINIDAD CARNIVAL: MANDATE FOR A NATIONAL THEATRE. Austin, University of Texas Press: 139p. [*RIS*]

Hill, Errol, ed.

22.0188 BC 1963[?] THE ARTIST IN WEST INDIAN SOCIETY: A SYMPOSIUM [seminars held in Port of Spain, Trinidad, May-June 1963, and in Jamaica, Oct. 1962-Jan. 1963]. [Mona?] Department of Extra-mural Studies, University of the West Indies, 79p. [*RIS*]

Hill, Robert
22.0189   JM,CA   1973   Jamaican art in Canada. *In* Salkey, Andrew, ed. CARIBBEAN ESSAYS: AN ANTHOLOGY. London, Evans Brothers: 74-77.   **[18]**   [*RIS*]

Hockey, Sidney W.
21.0042   BC   1958   An emerging culture in the British West Indies.

Howard, Joseph H.
22.0190   GC   1967   DRUMS IN THE AMERICAS. New York, Oak Publications: 319p.   **[19]**
                                                                                    [*COL*]

Hurston, Zora Neale
24.0092   BZ   1930   Dance songs and tales from the Bahamas.

Hylton, Patrick
22.0191   BC   1975   The politics of Caribbean music. *Black Scholar* 7(1), Sept.: 23-29.   **[8,37]**   [*NYP*]

Im Thurn, Everard F.
22.0192   GU   1901   Games of the red-men of Guiana. *Folk-Lore* 12(2), June: 132-161.   **[13]**   [*COL*]

Irish, J. A. George
22.0193   JM   1975   Notes on a historic visit: Nicolás Guillén in Jamaica. *Car Q* 21(1-2), March-June: 74-84.   [*RIS*]

James, C. L. R.
20.0039   BC   1963   BEYOND A BOUNDARY.
22.0194   BC   1966   Kanhai: a study in confidence. *New Wld Q* 2(3), May, Guyana Independence Issue: 13-15.   [*RIS*]
22.0195   GC   1970   The artist in the Caribbean (1959). *Radical America* 4(4), May: 61-66.   [*RIS*]

James, C. L. R. & Anthony, Michael
22.0196   TR   1969   Discovering literature in Trinidad: two experiences. *J Commonw Lit* 7, July: 73-87.   **[21]**   [*COL*]

James, Louis
22.0197   JM   1968   Of redcoats and leopards: two novels by V. S. Read. *In* James, Louis, ed. THE ISLANDS IN BETWEEN: ESSAYS ON WEST INDIAN LITERATURE. London, Oxford University Press: 64-72.   **[21]**   [*NYP*]

James, Louis, comp.
1.0152   BC   1972   The West Indies.

James, Louis, ed.
22.0198   BC   1968   THE ISLANDS IN BETWEEN: ESSAYS ON WEST INDIAN LITERATURE. London, Oxford University Press: 166p.   **[21]**   [*NYP*]

Jekyll, Walter
24.0096   JM   1907   JAMAICAN SONG AND STORY.

Jekyll, Walter, ed.
24.0097   **JM**   1966   JAMAICAN SONG AND STORY: ANNANCY STORIES, DIGGING SINGS, RING TUNES, AND DANCING TUNES.

Jephcott, Pearl
33.0105   **GU**   1956   REPORT ON THE NEEDS OF THE YOUTH OF THE MORE POPULATED COASTAL AREAS OF BRITISH GUIANA: WITH PARTICULAR REFERENCE TO THE RECREATION AND INFORMAL EDUCATION OF THOSE AGED 13-19.

Jesse, C.
4.0172   **SL**   1973   Pre-Columbian stone artifacts put to strange uses.

Johnson, Linton Kwesi
22.0199   **JM**   1976   Jamaica rebel music. *Race and Class* 17(4), Spring: 397-412.   [*COL*]

Johnson, Robert
22.0200   **JM,TR**   1939   Imperial Bisley, 1939—how Jamaica and Trinidad shot. *W I Comm Circ* 54(1065), July 27: 325-326.   [*NYP*]

Johnston, Robert A.
22.0201   **BZ**   1973   THE THEATER OF BELIZE. North Quincy, Massachusetts, The Christopher Publishing House: 96p.   [*RIS*]

Johnstone, Robert
22.0202   **BC**   1955   Rifle shooting in the West Indies. *W I Comm Circ* 70(1288), Apr.: 109-110.   [*NYP*]

Jones, Bridget
22.0203   **GC**   1975   Some French influences in the fiction of Orlando Patterson. *Savacou* 11-12, Sept.: 27-38.   [*RIS*]

Jones, Edward H.
22.0204   **MT**   1970   Afro-French writers of the 1930's and creation of the négritude school. *CLA J* 14(1), Sept.: 18-34.   **[11,21]**   [*COL*]

Jonson, Bari
22.0205   **JM**   1973   The entertainers 1973. *Jam J* 7(4), Dec: 38-46.   [*RIS*]

Joubert, Sidney M.
25.0193   **NC**   1976   Asentuashon na Papiamentu [Accent in Papiamentu].
22.0206   **NA**   1976   Literatura neerlandoantillana [Netherlands Antillean literature]. *Kristòf* 3(2), April: 75-95.   **[25]**   [*RIS*]

Jourdain, Elodie
22.0207   **TR,FA**   1954   Trinidad calypso *not* unique. *Car Commn Mon` Inf B* 7(10), May: 221-222, 232.   [*COL*]

Joyau, Auguste
22.0208   **MT**   1974   PANORAMA DE LA LITTÉRATURE À LA MARTINIQUE, XVIIe ET XVIIIe SIÈCLES [PANORAMA OF LITERATURE IN MARTINIQUE, 17TH AND 18TH CENTURY]. Morne-Rouge, Martinique, Editions des Horizons Caraïbes: 428p.   [*UCLA*]

Juliana, Elis

22.0209	CU	1975	Bastèl. *Kristòf* 2(2), April: 65-69.	[*RIS*]
22.0210	CU	1975	Tambú. *Kristòf* 2(1), Feb.: 43-45.	[*RIS*]

Kahn, Morton Charles

22.0211　SR　1931　Art of the Dutch Guiana Bush Negro. *Nat Hist* 31(2), Mar.-Apr.: 155-168. **[14,19]**　　　　　　　　　　　　　　　　　　　[*AGS*]

Kalff, S.

22.0212　SR　1922-23　Vroegere kunst in West-Indie [Early art in West India]. *W I G* 4: 353-372.　　　　　　　　　　　　　　　　　　　　　　[*COL*]

Keator, Dolores

22.0213　JM　1965　Skin diving. *In* Cargill, Morris, ed. IAN FLEMING INTRODUCES JAMAICA. New York, Hawthorn Books, Inc.: 181-188.　[*RIS*]

Kemoli, Arthur M.

22.0214　GC　1973　CRITICISM IN AFRO-CARIBBEAN LITERATURE: SATIRE AND THE PROPHETIC. D.Phil. dissertation, University of Sussex: 462p.

Kesteloot, Lilyan

22.0215　FC　1974　BLACK WRITERS IN FRENCH: A LITERARY HISTORY OF NÉGRITUDE. Philadelphia, Temple University Press: 401p. **[11]**　　[*COL*]

Kiban, Robert Janki

13.0110　SR　1966　MUZIEK, ZANG EN DANS VAN DE KARAIBEN IN SURINAME [MUSIC, SONG AND DANCE OF THE CARIBS IN SURINAM].

King, Cameron & James, Louis

22.0216　BC　1968　In solitude for company: the poetry of Derek Walcott. *In* James, Louis, ed. THE ISLANDS IN BETWEEN: ESSAYS ON WEST INDIAN LITERATURE. London, Oxford University Press: 86-99. **[21]** [*NYP*]

Knight, Vere

21.0048　FC　1975　French-Caribbean literature: a literature of commitment.

Kruijer, G. J.

32.0337　JM　1952　De 4-H Clubs van Jamaica.

17.0057　NW　1953　Enquête onder be Bovenwinders op Curacao en Aruba [Juli-Augustus 1951) [Investigation among Windward Islanders on Curacao and Aruba (July-August 1951)].

Lacovia, R. M.

22.0217　BC　1972　English Caribbean literature. *Black Images* 1(1), Jan.: 15-22.　[*RIS*]

LaFay, Howard & Parks, Winfield

22.0218　TR　1971　Carnival in Trinidad. *Natn Geogr Mag* 140(5), Nov.: 693-701.　　　　　　　　　　　　　　　　　　　　　　　　[*COL*]

Lamming, George

11.0055　GC　1966　Caribbean literature: the black rock of Africa.

22.0219　GC　1975　On West Indian writing. *Revta Interam Rev* 5(2), Summer: 149-162. **[21]**　　　　　　　　　　　　　　　　　　　　[*RIS*]

Lawton, David

22.0220 JM 1976 White man, black man, coolie man—pejorative terms in a Creole society. *Univ Mich Papers Linguistics* 2(1): 64-67. **[16,20,25]** [*RIS*]

Layng, Judith

22.0221 GC 1975-76 The American Company of Comedians and the disruption of empire. *Revta Interam Rev* 5(4), Winter: 665-675. **[5]** [*RIS*]

Leaf, Earl

22.0222 GC 1948 Isles of rhythm. New York, A. S. Barnes, 211p. **[23]**

Lekis, Lisa

22.0223 GC 1955 The dance as an expression of Caribbean folklore. *In* Wilgus, A. Curtis, ed. The Caribbean: its culture [papers delivered at the Fifth Conference on the Caribbean held at the University of Florida, Dec. 2-4, 1954]. Gainesville, University of Florida Press, p.43-73. (Publications of the School of Inter-American Studies, ser. 1, v. 5.) **[13,19,24]** [*RIS*]

19.0040 GC 1956 The origin and development of ethnic Caribbean dance and music.

Lemmon, Alfred E.

13.0130 BZ 1973 Maya music and dance.

Leschaloupe, Constance Marie

22.0224 TR 1953 Carnival in Trinidad—masquerades and steelbands. *Can-W I Mag* 43(10), Oct.: 11, 13-14. **[19]** [*NYP*]

Lewin, Olive

22.0225 JM 1968 Jamaican folk music. *Car Q* 14(1-2), March-June: 49-56. **[19]** [*RIS*]

Lewis, Lesley

22.0226 JM 1972 English commemorative sculpture in Jamaica. *Jam Hist Rev* 9: 8-124. **[5]** [*RIS*]

Lichtveld, Lou

35.0052 SR 1960 Native arts in modern architecture.

Lindblom, K. G.

22.0227 SR 1926 Einige Details in der Ornamentik der Buschneger Surinams [Some details of the ornaments of the Bush Negroes of Surinam]. Stockholm, 12p. (Riksmuseets Etnografiska Avdelning, no. 1). **[14,19]** [*COL*]

Locke, Donald

22.0228 GU 1965 Art in Guyana today. *New Wld F* 1(27-28), Nov. 12: 30-36. [*RIS*]
22.0229 GU 1965 Portrait of an artist (no. 5): Philip Moore. *New Wld F* 1(11), April 2: 34-39. [*RIS*]
22.0230 GU 1965 Portrait of an artist (no. 8): E. R. Burrowes—the first artist of Guiana. *New Wld F* 1(22), Sept.: 13-27. [*RIS*]

Luquet, G.-H.

22.0231   SR   1933   Exposition d'ethnographie guyanaise au Trocadéro [Exhibit of Guianese ethnography at the Trocadéro]. *Nature* 61(2896, pt. 1), Jan. 1: 30-32.   **[14]**   [*COL*]

Lutz, Franke

22.0232   GU   1912   String-figures from the upper Potaro. *Timehri* 3d ser., 2(19A), July: 117-127.   **[13]**   [*AMN*]

McBurnie, Beryl

22.0233   TR   1958   The Belaire. *Shell Trin* 5(2), Mar.: 12-15.

22.0234   GU   1963[?] West Indian dance. *In* Hill, Errol, ed. THE ARTIST IN WEST INDIAN SOCIETY: A SYMPOSIUM [seminars held in Port of Spain, Trinidad, May-June 1963, and in Jamaica, Oct. 1962-Jan. 1963]. [Mona?] Dept. of Extra-mural Studies, University of the West Indies, p.51-54.   [*RIS*]

22.0235   TR   1968   The Little Carib and West Indian dance. *Car Q* 14(1-2), March-June: 136-139.   [*RIS*]

24.0110   TR   1973   West Indian dance.

McCormack, Ed

37.0511   JM   1976   Bob Marley with a bullet.

MacDonald, Bruce F.

22.0236   TR   1975   Symbolic action in three of V. S. Naipaul's novels. *J Commonw Lit* 9(3), April: 41-52.   **[21]**   [*COL*]

McFarlane, Basil

22.0237   JM   1970   Edna Manley's retrospective. *Jam J* 4(1), March: 33-37.   [*RIS*]

22.0238   JM   1974   A fanatic for colour and form: A. D. Scott, Jamaica's leading art patron. *Jam J* 8(2-3), Summer: 14-18.   [*RIS*]

22.0239   JM   1974   Interview with a Jamaican master: Albert Huie discusses his life and art. *Jam J* 8(1), March: 42-47.   [*RIS*]

McKay, Claude

22.0240   JM   1912   SONGS OF JAMAICA. Kingston, Aston W. Gardner, 140p.   **[25]**
                                                                          [*NYP*]

5.0574   GC   1970   CLAUDE MCKAY EXHIBIT MATERIALS.

McNamara, Rosalind

22.0241   GC   1960   Music in the Caribbean. *Caribbean* 14(3), Mar.: 45-49.   [*COL*]

22.0242   GC   1960   Music in the Caribbean. *Caribbean* 14(4), Apr.: 69-70, 84-85, 100.
                                                                          [*COL*]

McWhinnie, Harold J.

32.0373   GR   1962   Teaching art in Grenada.

Maes-Jelinek, Hena

22.0243   BC   1971   The myth of El Dorado in the Caribbean novel. *J Commonw Lit* 6(1), June: 113-128.   [*COL*]

Mallett, R. H.

22.0244   BC   1923   The West Indies cricket tour: critical survey and a retrospect. *W I Comm Circ* 38(656), Nov. 22: 501-502.   [*NYP*]

22.0245	BC	1923	The West Indies cricket tour: critical survey and a retrospect. *W I Comm Circ* 38(657), Dec. 6: 520-521. [*NYP*]
22.0246	BC	1924	The West Indies cricket tour: critical survey and a retrospect. *W I Comm Circ* 39(659), Jan. 3: 12-13. [*NYP*]
22.0247	BC	1924	The West Indies cricket tour: critical survey and a retrospect. *W I Comm Circ* 39(660), Jan. 17: 32-33. [*NYP*]

Manley, Edna
22.0248 JM 1968 Henry Daley, the artist. *Jam J* 2(4), Dec.: 33-36. [*RIS*]

Manley, Edna; Parboosingh, Karl & Verity, Robert
22.0249 BC 1968 "The fine arts" (A discussion). *Car Q* 14(1-2), March-June: 63-76.
 [*RIS*]

Manning, Frank E.
21.0058 BE 1974 Entertainment and black identity in Bermuda.

Maronier, J. H.
1.0178 NC 1967 PICTURES OF THE TROPICS: A CATALOGUE OF DRAWINGS, WATER-COLOURS, PAINTINGS, AND SCULPTURES IN THE COLLECTION OF THE ROYAL INSTITUTE OF LINGUISTICS AND ANTHROPOLOGY IN LEIDEN.

Marshall, Woodville K.
22.0250 BC 1965 Gary Sobers and the Brisbane Revolution. *New Wld Q* 2(1), Dead Season: 35-42. **[21]** [*RIS*]

Marti-Ibañez, Feliz M. D.
3.0386 TR 1970 Elegy to Trinidad with calypso accompaniment.

Matthews, Basil
21.0061 BC 1942 Calypso and Pan America.

Maxwell, Marina
22.0251 GC 1970 Towards a revolution in the arts. *Savacou* 2, Sept.: 19-32. [*RIS*]

Meeteren, N. van
22.0252 NA 1948 Literatuur [Literature]. *In* ORANJE EN DE ZES CARAÏBISCHE PARELEN. Amsterdam, J. H. de Bussy: 521-527. [*UCLA*]

Meijer, W.
22.0253 CU 1948 Verenigingsleven [Club memberships]. *In* ORANJE EN DE ZES CARAÏBISCHE PARELEN. Amsterdam, J. H. de Bussy: 374-392. **[46]**
 [*UCLA*]

Merriam, A. P.; Whinery, Sara & Fred, B. G.
22.0254 TR 1956 Songs of a Rada community in Trinidad. *Anthropos* 51(1-2): 157-174. **[19]** [*COL*]

Micaux, Maurice; Pentier, Fernand & Lara, Bettino
22.0255 GD 1965 HOMMAGE À UN ANIMATEUR DE LA JEUNESSE GUADELOUPIÉNNE, JOSEPH BOURGEOIS [HOMAGE TO A LEADER OF GUADELOUPEAN YOUTH, JOSEPH BOURGEOIS]. Imprimerie Officielle: 47p. **[2]** [*RIS*]

Midas, André

22.0256   BC   1958   Festival of arts in retrospect. *Caribbean* 11(12), July: 266-270.

[*COL*]

Mighty Sparrow

22.0257   TR   1963   ONE HUNDRED AND TWENTY CALYPSOES TO REMEMBER. [Port of Spain, Trinidad, National Recording Co.] 92p.   [*RIS*]

Milner, Harry

22.0258   JM   1968   Jamaica and "The New Wave". *Jam J* 2(4), Dec.: 51-56.   [*RIS*]

Minchin-Comm, Dorothy

6.0203   BC   1972   THE CHANGING CONCEPTS OF THE WEST INDIAN PLANTOCRACY IN ENGLISH POETRY AND DRAMA, 1740-1850.

Moerheuvel, L. H.

48.0118   NC   1937   De PHOHI in de West [The PHOHI in the West].

Moodie, Silvia María

22.0259   TR   1970   Canciones tradicionales en la isla de Trinidad [Traditional songs on the island of Trinidad]. *Revta Dialect Trad Pop* 26(3-4): 323-361.   **[19]**   [*COL*]

Moore, Ruth S. & Hough, David M.

22.0260   UV   1967   ARTS IN THE U.S. VIRGIN ISLANDS. St. Thomas, College of the Virgin Islands, Caribbean Research Institute. (For the Virgin Islands Council on the Arts).   [*RIS*]

Morris, Mervyn

22.0261   JM   1967   On reading Louise Bennett seriously. *Jam J* 1(1), Dec.: 69-74.   **[25]**
[*RIS*]

22.0262   BC   1968   The poet as novelist: the novels of George Lamming. *In* James, Louis, ed. THE ISLANDS IN BETWEEN: ESSAYS ON WEST INDIAN LITERATURE. London, Oxford University Press: 73-85.   **[21]**   [*NYP*]

Morris, Robert K.

22.0263   GC   1975   PARADOXES OF ORDER: SOME PERSPECTIVES ON THE FICTION OF V. S. NAIPAUL. Columbia, Mo., University of Missouri Press: 105p.   [*RIS*]

Mungra, M.

22.0264   SR   1970   Vrijetijdsbesteding [Recreation]. *Schakels* S73: 40-46.   [*NYP*]

Muntslag, F. H. J.

14.0051   SR   1966   TEMBE: SURINAAMSE SURINAM WOODCARVING: SYMBOLISM OF THE MOST FREQUENT MOTIFS [TEMBE: SURINAAMSE HOUTSNIJKUNST: SYMBOLIEK VAN DE MEEST VOORKOMENDE MOTIEVEN].

Murray, Rudy G.

1.0199   BC   1972   A bibliography of Caribbean novels in English.

Murray, Tom

22.0265   JM   1951   FOLK SONGS OF JAMAICA. London, Oxford University Press, 59p.

[*RIS*]

Naipaul, V. S.
21.0069 **BC,UK** 1972 THE OVERCROWDED BARRACOON AND OTHER ARTICLES.

Nantet, Jacques
22.0266 **FC** 1972 Le monde noir des Antilles et de l'Amérique du Sud [The Black world of the Antilles and South America]. *In* Nantet, Jacques, ed. PANORAMA DE LA LITTÉRATURE NOIRE D'EXPRESSION FRANÇAISE. Paris, Librairie Arthème Fayard: 205-236. (Chapter 8) **[11,21]**
[*COL*]

Narasimhaiah, C. D.
22.0267 **BC** 1971 A.C.L.A.L.S. Conference on Commonwealth Literature, Kingston, Jamaica, 3-9 January 1971. *J Commonw Lit* 6(2), Dec.: 120-126. **[21]**   [*COL*]

Nettleford, Rex
22.0268 **BC** 1968 The dance as an art form—its place in the West Indies. *Car Q* 14(1-2), March-June: 127-135.   [*RIS*]
22.0269 **JM** 1969 Pocomania in dance-theatre. *Jam J* 3(2), June: 21-24. **[23]** [*RIS*]
22.0270 **JM** 1969 ROOTS AND RHYTHMS: JAMAICA'S NATIONAL DANCE THEATRE. London, André Deutsch: 128p.   [*RIS*]
21.0071 **BC** 1971 Caribbean perspectives: the creative potential and the quality of life.

Ngugi, Wa Thiong'o
22.0271 **GC** 1972 HOMECOMING: ESSAYS ON AFRICAN AND CARIBBEAN LITERATURE, CULTURE AND POLITICS. London, Heinmann Educational Books Ltd.: 155p. **[21]**   [*COL*]

Nicolas, Maurice
22.0272 **MT** 1968-69 Le Festival de Noel An I [The first Christmas Festival]. *B Cham Com Indus Mart* 4th trimester/1st trimester: 7-28.   [*RIS*]

Nicole, Christopher
22.0273 **BC** 1957 WEST INDIAN CRICKET. London, Phoenix Sports Books, 256p. **[5]**

Niven, Alastair Neil Robertson
22.0274 **BC** 1972 A STUDY OF THE RELATIONSHIP BETWEEN THE INDIVIDUAL AND HIS COMMUNITY AS DEPICTED IN SELECTED ENGLISH-LANGUAGE NOVELS FROM ASIA, AFRICA AND THE WEST INDIES. Ph.D. dissertation, University of Leeds: 503p.

Norman, Alma
32.0429 **JM** 1965 History can be fun.
22.0275 **JM** 1967 BALLADS OF JAMAICA. London, Longmans, Green and Co., Ltd.: 35p. **[5]**   [*COL*]

North, Lionel
22.0276 **GC** 1932 Songs of the Afro-Indian. *Can-W I Mag* 21(3), Feb.: 96-98. **[11]**
[*NYP*]

O'Gorman, Pamela
22.0277 **JM** 1972 An approach to the study of Jamaican popular music. *Jam J* 6(4), Dec.: 50-54.   [*RIS*]

22.0278   **JM**   1975   The introduction of Jamaican music into the established churches. *Jam J* 9(1), March: 40-44.   **[23]**   [*RIS*]

Olsen, Fred
4.0245   **GC**   1973   Petroglyphs of the Caribbean Islands and Arawak deities.

Ormerod, Beverley
21.0074   **FC**   1975   Beyond *négritude*: some aspects of the work of Edouard Glissant.

Oudschans Dentz, Fred
25.0264   **SR**   1937   De plaats van de Creool in de literatuur van Suriname [The place of Creole in the literature of Surinam].

22.0279   **SR**   1943   De loopbaan van Krayenhoff van Wickera in Suriname [The career of Krayenhoff van Wickera in Surinam]. *W I G* 25: 117-121.   **[5]**
[*COL*]

22.0280   **SR**   1949   Geschiedkundige aantekeningen over het cultureele leven in Suriname [Historical annotation about the cultural life in Surinam]. *W I G* 30: 42-50.   **[32]**   [*COL*]

Panhuys, L. C. van
22.0281   **SR**   1905   About the ornamentation in use by savage tribes in Dutch Guiana and its meaning. *In* PROCEEDINGS OF THE INTERNATIONAL CONGRESS OF AMERICANISTS, 13th Session, New York, Oct. 1902. Easton Pa., Eschenbach Print Co. p.209-212.   **[14]**   [*AGS*]

22.0282   **SR**   1912   Les chansons et la musique de la Guyane Néerlandaise [The songs and music of Dutch Guiana]. *J Soc Am* new ser., 9: 27-39.   [*AGS*]

22.0283   **SR**   1913   Development of ornament amongst the Bush Negroes in Suriname. *In* PROCEEDINGS OF THE INTERNATIONAL CONGRESS OF AMERICANISTS, XVIII Session, London, 1912. London, Harrison, pt. 2, p.380-381.   **[14]**   [*AGS*]

22.0284   **SR**   1930   Ornaments of the Bush Negroes in Dutch Guiana; a further contribution to research in Bush-Negro art. *In* PROCEEDINGS OF THE 23rd INTERNATIONAL CONGRESS OF AMERICANISTS, New York, 1928. New York, p.728-735.   **[14]**   [*AGS*]

22.0285   **SR**   1931-32   Boschnegerkunst [Bush Negro art]. *W I G* 13: 153-162.   **[14]**
[*COL*]

24.0124   **SR**   1934-35   Het kikvorschmotief in Suriname en elders [The frog motif in Surinam and elsewhere].

22.0286   **SR**   1934   Quelques chansons et quelques danses dans la Guyane Neerlandaise [A few songs and dances of Dutch Guiana]. *In* VERHANDLUNGEN DES XXIV INTERNATIONALEN AMERIKANISTEN-KONGRESSES. Hamburg, 1930. Hamburg, Friederichsen, de Gruyter, p.207-211.   **[25]**   [*AGS*]

24.0126   **SR**   1935-36   Surinaamsche folklore (liederenver zameling Van Vliet) [Folklore of Surinam (Song collection of Van Vliet)].

22.0287   **SR**   1936-37   Aard en karakter van Surinaamsche liederen [Nature and character of Surinam songs]. *W I G* 18: 1-12.   [*COL*]

Parris, D. Elliott
22.0288   **BC**   1973   THE IDEOLOGY OF CREATIVE WRITERS OF THE ENGLISH-SPEAKING CARIBBEAN, 1950-1972: A SOCIOLOGICAL ANALYSIS. Ph.D. dissertation, University of California (Los Angeles): 271p. **[16,21]**   [*PhD*]

22.0289   BC   1975   Perspectives of the creative writers. *In* Singham, A. W., ed. THE COMMONWEALTH CARIBBEAN INTO THE SEVENTIES. Montreal, McGill University, Centre for Developing Area Studies: 145-169. **[21]**
[RIS]

Pass, Mrs. E. A. de
8.0178   TR   1929   The West Indies Boy Scouts.

Patterson, H. Orlando
22.0290   BC   1969   The ritual of cricket. *Jam J* 3(1), March: 22-25. **[20]**   *[RIS]*

Patterson, Massie & Belasco, Lionel
22.0291   GC   1943   CALYPSO SONGS OF THE WEST INDIES. New York, M. Baron, 25p.
[NYP]

Pearse, Andrew C.
22.0292   GR,CR,TR   1955   Aspects of change in Caribbean folk music. *J Int Folk Music Coun* 8: 29-36.   *[RIS]*
32.0453   BC   1956   Ethnography and the lay scholar in the Caribbean.
22.0293   TR   1971   Carnival in nineteenth century Trinidad. *In* Horowitz, Michael M., ed. PEOPLES AND CULTURES OF THE CARIBBEAN: AN ANTHROPOLOGICAL READER. New York, Natural History Press for the American Museum of Natural History: 528-552. **[5,19,24]**   *[RIS]*

Pearson, Ross
51.0086   JM   1957   The geography of recreation on a tropical island: Jamaica.

Peberdy, P. Storer
4.0255   GU   1948   Discovery of Amerindian rock-paintings in British Guiana.

Pelage, Al.
2.0357   GD   [n.d.]   LA GUADELOUPE VUE PAR AL. PELAGE: GRAVURES ET DESSINS HUMORISTIQUES [GUADELOUPE AS SEEN BY AL. PELAGE: HUMOROUS PRINTS AND DRAWINGS].

Penard, Thomas E. & Penard, Arthur P.
22.0294   SR   1925-26 Four Arawak Indian songs. *W I G* 7: 497-500. **[13]**   *[COL]*

Pharand, Sylvie
13.0159   MT   1974   LA VANNERIE CARAÏBE DU MORNE-DES-ESSES, MARTINIQUE [CARIB BASKETRY OF MORNE-DES-ESSES, MARTINIQUE].

Powell, Dulcie
22.0295   JM   1974   The preservation of Fern Gully. *Jam J* 8(2-3), Summer: 66-71. **[56]**
[RIS]

Prasad, Usha
22.0296   JM   1975   National exhibition of paintings, 1975. *Jam J* 9(2-3): 28-35.   *[RIS]*

Price, Richard
14.0059   SR   1970   Saramaka woodcarving: the development of an Afroamerican art.

Price, Richard & Price, Sally

14.0062   SR   1972   Kammbá: the ethnohistory of an Afro-American art.

Procope, Bruce

22.0297   TR   1956   The Dragon Band or Devil Band. *Car Q* 4(3-4), Mar.-June: 275-280.   **[19]**   [*RIS*]

22.0298   TR   1959   Ken Morris—metalworker. *Shell Trin* 5(9), Christmas: 10-12.   **[19]**

38.0176   BC   1960   The temporary federal mace.

Punch, L. D. "Lully"

32.0468   TR   [n.d.]   SCOUTING MEMORIES.

Quirarte, Jacinto

4.0299   BZ   1975   The wall paintings of Santa Rita, Corozal.

Rae, Norman

22.0299   JM   1965   Contemporary Jamaican art. *In* Cargill, Morris, ed. IAN FLEMING INTRODUCES JAMAICA. New York, Hawthorn Books, Inc.: 165-173.
                                                                                [*RIS*]

Ramaya, Narsaloo

22.0300   TR   1974   Indian music and Western music: a comparison. *New Vision* 1(1), Jan.-March: 30-32.   [*NYP*]

Ramchand, Kenneth

22.0301   BC   1968   A BACKGROUND TO THE NOVEL IN THE WEST INDIES. Ph.D. dissertation, University of Edinburgh: 426p.

22.0302   JM   1969   Obeah and the supernatural in West Indian literature. *Jam J* 3(2), June: 52-54.   **[23]**   [*RIS*]

22.0303   BC   1969   Terrified consciousness. *J Commonw Lit* 7, July: 8-19.   **[14]**   [*COL*]

22.0304   GC   1970   THE WEST INDIAN NOVEL AND ITS BACKGROUND. London, Faber & Faber: 295p.   **[19]**   [*RIS*]

Ramchand, Kenneth, comp.

1.0234   BC   1969   The West Indies. *J Commonw Lit* 6.

1.0235   BC   1969   The West Indies. *J Commonw Lit* 8.

1.0236   BC   1970   The West Indies. *J Commonw Lit* 10.

Ramchand, Kenneth & Durrant, Fay, comps.

1.0237   BC   1971   The West Indies. *J Commonw Lit* 6(2).

Ramsaran, J. A.

22.0305   BC   1975   West Indian gallery: the works of Derek Walcott. *Black Wld* 24(8), June: 39-48.   **[21]**   [*NYP*]

Ray, Michael

22.0306   GU   1940   Sugar cane cricket. *Can-W I Mag* 29(12), Dec.: 23-24, 28.   [*NYP*]

Renselaar, H. C. van

14.0067   SR   1966   Tembe, bosnegerkunst in hout [Tembe, Bush Negro art in wood].

5.0761   SR   1968   Théodore Bray, planter and draughtsman in Surinam.

Reuters, H. M. J.

22.0307	SR	1967

Welzijnszorg bij de Troepenmacht in Suriname [Welfare of the military forces in Surinam]. *Schakels* S65/NA49: 26-31. **[37]**

[NYP]

Roberts, Helen H.

22.0308   JM   1924   Some drums and drum rhythms of Jamaica. *Nat Hist* 24(2), Mar.-Apr. 241-251. **[19]**   *[AGS]*

22.0309   JM   1925   A study of folk song variants based on field work in Jamaica. *J Am Folk* 38(148), Apr.-June: 149-216.   *[COL]*

22.0310   JM   1926   Lullabies in Jamaica. *J Am Folk* 41(162), Oct.-Dec.: 588-591. **[24]**   *[COL]*

22.0311   JM   1926   Possible survivals of African song in Jamaica. *Mus Q* 12(3), July: 340-358. **[19]**   *[COL]*

Roberts, L. D.

22.0312   BC   1961   CRICKET'S BRIGHTEST SUMMER. Kingston, United Printers, 158p.

Robinson, Alban

22.0313   GU   1918   Some figures in string from the Makushis on the Ireng and Takuto Rivers. *Timehri* 3d ser., 5(22), Aug.: 140-152. **[13]**   *[AMN]*

Rohlehr, Gordon

22.0314   BC   1968   The ironic approach. *In* James, Louis, ed. THE ISLANDS IN BETWEEN: ESSAYS ON WEST INDIAN LITERATURE. London, Oxford University Press: 121-139. **[12,21]**   *[NYP]*

22.0315   TR   1970   Sparrow and the language of calypso. *Savacou* 2, Sept.: 87-99.

[RIS]

Roo, B. Jos de

22.0316   NA   1975   Een belangrijk werk voor de Antillen: Kenneth Ramchand's *The West Indian novel and its background* [An important work for the Antilles: Kenneth Ramchand's *The West Indian novel and its background*]. *Kristòf* 2(5), October: 244-251. **[21]**   *[RIS]*

21.0082   CU   1976   Dubbelspel—dubble politiek [Double game—double politics].

Rooy, René de

22.0317   CU   1954-55 Letterkundig leven op Curacao [Literary life on Curacao]. *Vox Guy* 1(4-5), Nov.-Jan.: 17-24.

Ross, Alan

22.0318   BC   1960   THROUGH THE CARIBBEAN: THE M.C.C. TOUR OF THE WEST INDIES 1959-60. London, Hamish Hamilton, 296p.

Ross, Charlesworth

22.0319   BC   1968 . The first West Indian novelist. *Car Q* 14(4), Dec.: 56-60. **[5]** *[RIS]*

Ross, Gordon

22.0320   BC   1976   A HISTORY OF WEST INDIES CRICKET. London, Arthur Barker Ltd.: 175p.   *[RIS]*

Roth, Vincent, ed.

22.0321   GU   1949   GRAPHIC ART IN BRITISH GUIANA: A COLLECTION OF WORK BY LOCAL ARTISTS 1944-1948. Georgetown, Daily Chronicle, 54p.

Roth, Walter Edmund

13.0181   **GU**   1924   An introductory study of the arts, crafts, and customs of the Guiana Indians.

13.0182   **GU**   1929   ADDITIONAL STUDIES OF THE ARTS, CRAFTS, AND CUSTOMS OF THE GUIANA INDIANS, WITH SPECIAL REFERENCE TO THOSE OF SOUTHERN BRITISH GUIANA.

Rouse, Irving

4.0340   **GC**   1965   Caribbean ceramics: a study in method and theory.

Roussier, Paul

22.0322   **MT**   1935   Fêtes d'autrefois à la Martinique [Festivals of the past in Martinique]. *In* Denis, Serge, ed. NOS ANTILLES. Orleans, Luzeray, p.217-220.   **[5]**   [*AGS*]

Rowland, John T.

55.0158   **BE**   1923   The proper course to Bermuda: some hints on what the navigators in the Bermuda race may expect.

Samson, Ph. A.

22.0323   **SR**   1954   Aantekeningen over kunst en vermaak in Suriname voor 1900 [Notes on art and entertainment in Surinam prior to 1900]. *W I G* 35: 154-165.   **[5]**   [*RIS*]

37.0756   **SR**   1956-57 Iets over de Surinaamsche Scherpschuttersvereeniging [About the Rifle-Club in Surinam].

Satterthwaite, Linten, Jr.

4.0348   **BZ**   1954   A modified interpretation of the "giant glyph" altars at Caracol, British Honduras.

4.0349   **BZ**   1954   Sculptured monuments from Caracol, British Honduras.

Schipper, Ary

22.0324   **SR**   1944-45 Enkele opmerkingen over Surinaamsche muziek [Some observations about Surinam's music]. *W I G* 26: 209-221.   **[19]**   [*COL*]

Sealy, Clifford

22.0325   **TR**   1963[?] Art and the community. *In* Hill, Errol, ed. THE ARTIST IN WEST INDIAN SOCIETY: A SYMPOSIUM [seminars held in Port of Spain, Trinidad, May-June 1963, and in Jamaica, Oct. 1962-Jan. 1963]. [Mona?] Dept. of Extra-mural Studies, University of the West Indies, 68.   [*RIS*]

Seeger, Peter

22.0326   **TR**   1958   The steel drum: a new folk instrument. *J Am Folk* 71: 52-57.
                                                                            [*COL*]

22.0327   **TR**   1961   THE STEEL DRUMS OF KIM LOY WONG: AN INSTRUCTION BOOK. New York, Oak Publications, 40p.   [*SCH*]

Sertima, Ivan van

22.0328   **BC**   1968   CARIBBEAN WRITERS: CRITICAL ESSAYS. London, New Beacon Books Ltd.: 67p.   **[21]**   [*UCLA*]

Shapiro, Norman R.
11.0081   GD,MT   1967   Negro poets of the French Caribbean: a sampler.

Sharp, Stanley
22.0329   BZ   1952[?]   Art in British Honduras. *Car Q* 2(2): 30-31.   [*RIS*]

Sherlock, Philip M.
22.0330   JM   1943   Art in Jamaica. *Can-W I Mag* 32(7), July: 19-20.   [*NYP*]

Simmons, Harold F. C.
22.0331   SL   1960   Térré bois bois. *Car Q* 6(4): 282-285.   **[19]**   [*RIS*]

Sjiem Fat, P. V.
33.0180   NA   1972   De Landsverordening Hazardspelen 1948, P. B. 1948 no. 138 [The
                          Land regulation games of chance 1948, P. B. 1948 no. 138].

Smit, C. G. M.
22.0332   NA   1975   Habibe pleegt geschiedvervalsing [Habibe commits falsification of
                         history]. *Kristòf* 2(3), June: 144-147.   [*RIS*]

Smith, Mrs. Allan F.
5.0852   BE   1965   Bermuda silversmiths and their silver.

Smith, Lloyd Sidney
22.0333   BC   1922   WEST INDIES CRICKET HISTORY AND CRICKET TOURS TO ENGLAND,
                         1900, 1906, 1923. Port of Spain, Yuille's Printerie, 240p.   **[5]**

Smith, Rowland, ed.
22.0334   GC   1976   EXILE AND TRADITION: STUDIES IN AFRICAN AND CARIBBEAN LIT-
                         ERATURE. London, Longman & Dalhousie University Press:
                         190p.   **[21]**   [*RIS*]

Snyder, Emile
22.0335   FC   1976   Aimé Césaire: the reclaiming of the land. *In* Smith, Rowland, ed.
                         EXILE AND TRADITION: STUDIES IN AFRICAN AND CARIBBEAN LIT-
                         ERATURE. London, Longman & Dalhousie University Press: 30-
                         43.   **[21]**   [*RIS*]

Sobers, Garfield & Barker, J. S., eds.
22.0336   BC   1967   CRICKET IN THE SUN: A HISTORY OF WEST INDIES CRICKET. London,
                         Arthur Barker, Ltd.: 127p.   [*RIS*]

Sparer, Joyce L.
22.0337   GU   1968   Attitudes toward 'race' in Guyanese literature. *Car Stud* 8(2), July:
                         23-63.   **[20,21]**   [*RIS*]

Stanford, Olly N.
32.0548   TR   1945   The 4-H clubs movement.

Steenmeijer, F.
22.0338   AR   1948   Verenigingsleven en clubs [Club life and membership]. *In* ORANJE
                         EN DE ZES CARAÏBISCHE PARELEN. Amsterdam, J. H. de Bussy:
                         470-478.   [*UCLA*]

Stewart, C. Thornley & Murray, R. M., eds.

22.0339   JM   1915   PEPPERPOT: A MAGAZINE DEPICTING MAINLY THE PERSONAL AND LIGHTER SIDE OF JAMAICAN LIFE. Kingston, Jamaica, The Jamaica Times, Limited: 52p.   [*NYP*]

Stillwell, H. Daniel

22.0340   GC   1971   Recreational geography in Latin America. *In* Lentnek, Barry; Carmin, Robert L. & Martinson, Tom L., eds. GEOGRAPHIC RESEARCH ON LATIN AMERICA: BENCHMARK 1970: PROCEEDINGS OF THE CONFERENCE OF LATIN AMERICANIST GEOGRAPHERS, VOLUME ONE. Muncie, Indiana, Ball State University: 309-314.   **[51,56]**
                                                                         [*COL*]

Stimpson, Alison

32.0553   JM   1974   Making the scene in art education.

Stoelting, Winifred L.

22.0341   GC   [n.d.]   A CHECKLIST OF THE WEST INDIAN FICTION (EXCLUDING CUBA, PUERTO RICO, AND HAITI). Atlanta University, Center for African and African-American Studies: 8p. (CAAS Bibliography No. 8)   **[1]**   [*RIS*]

Stone, Herbert L.

3.0580   BE   1923   The Bermuda race.
55.0189   BE   1923   The inside story of the Bermuda race.

Stow, John

23.0293   BE   1954   A catalog of the treasures.

St. Pierre, Maurice

22.0342   BC   1973   West Indian cricket—a socio-historical appraisal. Part I. *Car Q* 19(2), June: 7-27.   **[21]**   [*RIS*]
22.0343   BC   1973   West Indian cricket. Part II—An aspect of creolization. *Car Q* 19(3), Sept: 20-35.   **[21]**   [*RIS*]

Street, Donald M.

22.0344   GC   1966   A CRUISING GUIDE TO THE LESSER ANTILLES. New York, Dodd, Mead and Co.: 242p.   [*RIS*]

Strologo, Sergio dello

22.0345   JM   1968   Designing in Jamaica. *Jam J* 2(4), Dec.: 43-48.   [*RIS*]

Swanton, E. W.

22.0346   BC   1960   WEST INDIES REVISITED: THE M.C.C. TOUR 1959-60. London, Heinemann, 288p.

Theroux, Paul

22.0347   BC   1972   V. S. NAIPAUL: AN INTRODUCTION TO HIS WORK. New York, Africana Publishing Corporations: 144p.   [*COL*]

Thieme, John

22.0348   BC   1975   V. S. Naipaul's Third World: a not so free state. *J Commonw Lit* 10(1), Aug.: 10-22.   **[21]**   [*COL*]

Thompson, Donald

22.0349   VI   1970   Gottschalk in the Virgin Islands. *Yrbk Inter-Am Mus Res* 6: 95-103. **[5]**   [*COL*]

Thompson, Paul Lawrence

22.0350   FG   1974   THREE NOVELS BY DR. BERTÈNE JUMINER AND THE THEMES OF ASSIMILATION, ALIENATION AND REVOLT. Ph.D. dissertation, Pennsylvania State University: 210p. **[16]**   [*RIS*]

Thorpe, Michael

22.0351   BC   1976   V. S. NAIPAUL. Harlow, Essex, Longman Group Ltd. *for* The British Council: 47p. **[12,21]**   [*RIS*]

Timmerman, Henri Th.

22.0352   SR   1966   Volksmuziek in de West (I): de vijf sterren van Suriname [Folk music in the West (I): the five stars of Surinam]. *Euphonia* 48(9), Sept.: 8-11.   [*NYP*]

22.0353   NL   1966   Volksmuziek in de West (II): Aruba, Bonaire en Curaçao [Folk music in the West (II): Aruba, Bonaire and Curaçao]. *Euphonia* 48(10), Oct.: 5-8.   [*NYP*]

22.0354   NW   1966   Volksmuziek in de West (III): Saba, Sint Eustatius en Sint Maarten [Folk music in the West (III): Saba, Saint Eustatius and Saint Maarten]. *Euphonia* 48(11), Nov: 5-6.   [*NYP*]

22.0355   TR   1966   Volksmuziek in de West (IV): Steelbands: de mens achter de muziek [Folk music in the West (IV): steel bands: the folk behind the music]. *Euphonia* 48(12), Dec.: 6-7.   [*NYP*]

Todd, Edwin

22.0356   JM   1968   Dunkley. *Jam J* 2(3), Sept.: 44-47.   [*RIS*]
22.0357   JM   1970   Abstract art, the avant garde and Jamaica. *Jam J* 4(4), Dec.: 27-39.
                                                                [*RIS*]

Tucker, Terry

22.0358   BE   1955   Guy Fawkes Day. *Bermuda Hist Q* 12(4), Winter: 135-138. **[19]**
                                                                [*COL*]
22.0359   BE   1964   Shakespeare, St. George's Day and Bermuda. *Bermuda Hist Q* 21(1), Spring: 9-10.   [*COL*]

Tull, Marc

22.0360   BA   1973   Fun take, puttin-in-jail, ring take and knocks hole: the role played by marbles in child socialization on San Salvador. *In* Thomas, Garry L., ed. ANTHROPOLOGICAL FIELD REPORTS FROM SAN SALVADOR ISLAND. San Salvador, Bahamas, Island Environment Studies Reports 1973: 59-68. **[9]**   [*RIS*]

Vatuk, Ved Prakash

12.0109   GU   1964   Protest songs of East Indians in British Guiana.

Vérin, Pierre

22.0361   SL   1967   Quelques aspects de la culture matérielle de la région de Choiseul, Ile de Sainte-Lucie, Antilles [Some aspects of the material culture of the Choiseul region of the island of Saint Lucia, Antilles]. *J Soc Amer* 56(2): 461-494.   [*AMN*]

Verlooghen, Corly

21.0092   SR   1970   DE GLINSTERENDE REVOLUTIE: IDENTITEITS-POËZIE [THE GLITTERING REVOLUTION: IDENTITY POEMS].

Vervoorn, A. J.

25.0381   SR   [n.d.]   Het Nederlands en de Surinaamse letterkunde [The Dutch language and Surinamese literature].

Vieira, Philip I.

22.0362   TR   1941   Songs of the West. *Can-W I Mag* 30(8), Aug.: 21-23.   [*NYP*]

22.0363   BC   1958   The West Indies Festival of Arts, 1958. *Caribbean* 11(8), Mar.: 177-179.   [*COL*]

Vincent, Mary Louise

22.0364   MT   1970   Two painters of the tropics: Lafcadio Hearn and Paul Gauguin in Martinique. *Car Stud* 10(3), Oct.: 172-181.   **[5]**   [*RIS*]

Vincke, Gaston

3.0625   FG   1935   AVEC LES INDIENS DE LA GUYANE [WITH THE INDIANS OF GUIANA].

Voorhoeve, Jan

6.0291   SR   1966   Fictief verleden: De slaventijd in de Surinaamse bellettrie [Fictitious past: The period of slavery in Surinam literature & drama].

Vries-Hamburger, L. de

22.0365   SR   1959   Voklskunst en huisnijverheid [Folk art and handicrafts]. *Schakels* S-35: 13-16.

Waart, P. de

48.0168   NC   1937   De West en de KRO [The West and the Catholic Broadcasting Corporation].

Wagar, Constance Edwarda

32.0583   TR   1970   A HISTORY OF ART EDUCATION IN TRINIDAD, 1851-1968.

Wagenaar Hummelinck, P.

4.0384   NL   1972   Rotstekeningen van Curaçao, Aruba en Bonaire: deel IV [Linear rock designs of Curaçao, Aruba and Bonaire: part IV].

Walcott, Clyde A.

22.0366   BC   1958   ISLAND CRICKETERS. London, Hodder and Stoughton, 188p.

22.0367   BB   1966-67   The home of the heroes. *New Wld Q* 3(1-2), Dead Season and Croptime, Barbados Independence Issue: 51-53.   [*RIS*]

Walcott, Derek

22.0368   BC   1970   Meanings. *Savacou* 2, Sept: 45-51.   [*RIS*]

20.0083   GC   1974   The muse of history: an essay.

Walke, Olive

22.0369   TR   1959   Christmas music of Trinidad. *Shell Trin* 5(9), Christmas: 5-6.   **[23]**

Walle, J. van de

22.0370   CU   1954   Walsen, danza's en tuma's der Antillen [*Walsen, donzas and tumas* of the Antilles]. *Oost West* 47(5): 11-12.

Walsh, William
5.0944   TR   1973   V. S. NAIPAUL.

Warner, Keith Q.
11.0084   FC   1974   Négritude: a new dimension in the French classroom.

Waterman, Richard Alan
22.0371   TR   1943   AFRICAN PATTERNS IN TRINIDAD NEGRO MUSIC. Ph.D. dissertation, Northwestern University, 261p.   **[11,19]**

Watson, Karl S., comp.
1.0297   BC,FC   1971   LITERATURE OF THE ENGLISH AND FRENCH-SPEAKING WEST INDIES IN THE UNIVERSITY OF FLORIDA LIBRARIES: A BIBLIOGRAPHY.

Weatherhead, Basil
22.0372   BB   1954   Inter-colonial tournament. *Can-W I Mag* 44(10), Oct.: 19-20.
[*NYP*]

Webster, Aimée
22.0373   JM   1973   Ikebana. *Jam J* 7(4), Dec.: 47-49.   [*RIS*]

Wengen, G. D. van
22.0374   CU   1968   Typico-muziek van Curaçao [Typico-music of Curaçao]. *Schakels* NA52: 26-32.   [*NYP*]

Whipple, Emory
22.0375   BZ   1976   Pia Manadi. *Belizean Stud* 4(4), July: 1-18.   **[13,19,24]**   [*RIS*]

White, Landeg E.
22.0376   TR   1969   Steelbands: a personal record. *Car Q* 15(4), Dec.: 32-39.   **[19]**
[*RIS*]

Williams, Aubrey
22.0377   GC   1968   The predicament of the artist in the Caribbean. *Car Q* 14(1-2), March-June: 60-62.   [*RIS*]
22.0378   GC   1970   The artist in the Caribbean. *Savacou* 2, Sept.: 16-18.   [*RIS*]

Williams, Denis
22.0379   GU   1969   IMAGE AND IDEA IN THE ARTS OF GUYANA. Georgetown, Guyana, The National History and Arts Council, Ministry of Information: 39p.   [*SCH*]

Williamson, Karina
22.0380   BC   1965   Roger Mais: West Indian novelist. *J Commonw Lit* 2, Dec.: 138-147.   **[21]**   [*COL*]

Worrel, Frank
22.0381   BC   1959   CRICKET PUNCH. London, Stanley Paul, 144p.

Wright, Richardson
22.0382   JM   1937   REVELS IN JAMAICA, 1682-1838. New York, Dodd, Mead, 378p.   **[5]**
[*COL*]

Wynter, Sylvia

22.0383	BC	1968	Reflections on West Indian writing and criticism. Part 1. *Jam J* 2(4), Dec.: 23-32. **[21]** [*RIS*]
22.0384	BC	1969	Reflections on West Indian writing and criticism. Part 2. *Jam J* 3(10), March: 27-42. **[21]** [*RIS*]
22.0385	JM	1970	Jonkonnu in Jamaica: towards the interpretation of folk dance as a cultural process. *Jam J* 4(2), June: 34-48. **[19,21]** [*RIS*]

Yeaton, Leander

26.0009	BA	1973	Gambling: a brief case study in cultural change.

Zuill, Kitty

22.0386	BE	1944	Christmas in Bermuda. *Bermuda Hist Q* 1(4), Oct.-Dec.: 199-200. [*NYP*]

Chapter 23

RELIGION

Church history; missionary concerns; social role of churches; religious sects and cults; religio-political groups; magic.

See also: [11] Population segments: Afro-Caribbean; [12] Population segments: East Indian; [13] Population segments: Amerindian and Black Carib; [14] Population segments: Maroon; [15] Population segments: Other; [19] Cultural continuities; [24] Folklore.

Abbenhuis, Fulgentius

20.0001   SR   1970   Surinaamse mentaliteit [Surinamese mentality].

Abbenhuis, M. F.

6.0001   CU,SR   1953   De requesten van Pater Stöppel en Perfect Wennekers in 1817 en 1819 [The petitions of Father Stöppel and Perfect Wennekers in 1817 and 1819].

Adams-Gordon, Veneta H.

23.0001   UV   1963   The history of the African Methodist Episcopal Church in the Virgin Islands. *Vc Miss* 64 [i.e. 65] (2), Feb.: 10-11.   [*NYP*]

Adhin, J. H.

33.0003   SR   1969   Juridische organisatie-vormen van godsdienstige groeperingen in Surineme [Legal organizational forms of religious groups in Surinam].

Alexis, Gerson

23.0002   MT   1975   Avatars du voudou en Martinique. *Conjonction* 126, June: 33-48. **[19]**   [*RIS*]

Alladin, M. P.

22.0008   TR   1974   Festivals of Trinidad and Tobago.

Alland, Alexander

15.0001   ST   1940   The Jews of the Virgin Islands; a history of the islands and candid biographies of outstanding Jews born there. *Am Heb* 146(20).

15.0002   ST   1940   The Jews of the Virgin Islands; a history of the islands and candid biographies of outstanding Jews born there. *Am Heb* 146(21).

15.0003   ST   1940   The Jews of the Virgin Islands; a history of the islands and candid biographies of outstanding Jews born there. *Am Heb* 146(24).

15.0004   ST   1940   The Jews of the Virgin Islands; a history of the islands and candid biographies of outstanding Jews born there. *Am Heb* 147(1).

Allen, E. Anthony

23.0003   GC   1972   The future role of the churches. *In* Haynes, Lilith M., ed. FAMBLI: THE CHURCH'S RESPONSIBILITY TO THE FAMILY IN THE CARIBBEAN. Trinidad, CARIPLAN: 227-234.   [9]   [*RIS*]

Andrade, Jacob A. P. M.

15.0006   JM   1941   A RECORD OF THE JEWS IN JAMAICA FROM THE ENGLISH CONQUEST TO THE PRESENT TIME.

Anthon, Michael

23.0004   GU   1957   The Kanaima. *Timehri* 4th ser., 1(36), Oct.: 61-65.   [13]

Appleton, S. E.

5.0019   TR   1938   Old Tobago—some notes based on a perusal of the church registers. *W I Comm Circ* 53(1044).

5.0020   TR   1938   Old Tobago—some notes based on a perusal of the church registers. *W I Comm Circ* 53(1045).

Asbeck, W. D. H. van

23.0005   SR   1919   De Evangelische of Moravische Broeder-Gemeente in Suriname [The Evangelical or Moravian Brethern in Surinam]. *W I G* 1(1): 197-207.   [5,32]   [*COL*]

Bailey, Joyce

23.0006   GC   1972[?]   An exercise in theologizing. *In* Haynes, Lilith M., ed. FAMBLI: THE CHURCH'S RESPONSIBILITY TO THE FAMILY IN THE CARIBBEAN. Trinidad, CARIPLAN: 173-181.   [*RIS*]

Bain, Rodney

23.0007   BA   1967   Missionary activity in the Bahamas, 1700-1830. *In* Holmes, Brian, ed. EDUCATIONAL POLICY AND THE MISSION SCHOOLS. New York, Humanities Press: 47-75.   [5,32]   [*UCLA*]

Barbanson, W. L. de

7.0010   SB   1958   Grafschriften op Saint Barthélémy [Gravestone inscriptions on St. Barthelemy].

Barrett, Leonard

23.0008   JM   1968   THE RASTAFARIANS: A STUDY IN MESSIANIC CULTISM IN JAMAICA. Rio Piedras, P.R., Institute of Caribbean Studies, University of Puerto Rico (Caribbean monograph series No. 6): 238p.   [11,16,37]   [*RIS*]

Barry, Colman

15.0009   BE   1973   UPON THESE ROCKS: CATHOLICS IN THE BAHAMAS.

Bastide, Roger

11.0003   GC   1971[?]   AFRICAN CIVILISATIONS IN THE NEW WORLD.

Beck, Jane C.

24.0021   BC   1975   The West Indian supernatural world: belief integration in a pluralistic society.

Beckwith, Martha Warren
23.0009   JM   1923   Some religious cults in Jamaica. *Am J Psychol* 34(1), Jan.: 32-45.
  [COL]
23.0010   JM   1924   THE HUSSAY FESTIVAL IN JAMAICA. Poughkeepsie, N.Y., Vassar College, 17p. (Field-work in folk-lore; (Publications of the Folk-lore Foundation, no. 4)). **[12,19,22]**

Bell, Hesketh J.
23.0011   GC   1970   OBEAH: WITCHCRAFT IN THE WEST INDIES. Westport, Connecticut, Negro Universities Press: 200p. (Originally published in 1889) **[3,11]**   *[COL]*

Bennett, Harold Repton
23.0012   BC   1971   A RHETORICAL ANALYSIS OF THE PREACHING OF EVANGELIST HIRAM S. WALTERS, PRESIDENT OF THE WEST INDIES UNION CONFERENCE OF SEVENTH-DAY ADVENTISTS. Ph.D. dissertation, Michigan State University: 285p.   *[PhD]*

Bennett, J. Harry, Jr.
23.0013   BB   1951   The S.P.G. and Barbadian politics, 1710-1720. *Hist Mag Prot Epsc Ch* 20(2), June: 190-206. **[5,37]**   *[COL]*

Bethencourt, Cardozo de
15.0013   GC   1925   Notes on the Spanish and Portuguese Jews in the United States, Guiana, and the Dutch and British West Indies during the seventeenth and eighteenth centuries.

Bijlsma, R.
15.0014   SR   1920-21   De stichting van de Portugeesch-Joodsche gemeente en synagoge in Suriname [The founding of the Portuguese-Jewish community and synagogue in Surinam].

Bourguignon, Erika
23.0014   GC   1967   RELIGIOUS SYNCRETISM AMONG NEW WORLD NEGROES. Paper presented at Annual Meeting of the American Anthropological Association: 14p. **[11,19]**   *[RIS]*
23.0015   GC   1968   Trance dance. *Dance Persp* 35, Autumn: 1-61. **[24]**   *[NYP]*
11.0011   GC   1970   Ritual dissociation and possession belief in Caribbean Negro religion.
23.0016   SV   1973   An assessment of some comparisons and implications. *In* Bourguignon, Erika, ed. RELIGION, ALTERED STATES OF CONSCIOUSNESS, AND SOCIAL CHANGE. Columbus, Ohio State University Press: 321-339. **[10,31]**   *[COL]*

Bourguignon, Erika, ed.
23.0017   SV   1973   RELIGION, ALTERED STATES OF CONSCIOUSNESS, AND SOCIAL CHANGE. Columbus, Ohio State University Press: 389p. **[10,31]**   *[COL]*

Bowen, Calvin
22.0035   JM   1954   Jamaica's John Canoe.

Bowen, W. Errol
23.0018   JM   1971   Rastafarism and the new society. *Savacou* 5, June: 41-50. **[11]**
  [RIS]

Braithwaite, Lloyd E.
38.0033   **BC**   1957   'Federal' associations and institutions in the West Indies.

Brana-Shute, Gary
9.0028   **SR**   1976   Social conflict and ritual restoration: a case of lower class Creole mating in disequilibrium.

Brathwaite, Joan, ed.
23.0019   **GC**   1973   HANDBOOK OF CHURCHES IN THE CARIBBEAN. FIRST EDITION. Bridgetown, Barbados, Christian Action for Development in the Caribbean (CADEC): 234p.   [*RIS*]

Brou, Alexandre
23.0020   **BC,FG**   1935   CENT ANS DE MISSIONS 1815-1934: LES JÉSUITES MISSIONAIRES AU XIXᴱ ET AU XXᴱ SIÈCLES [ONE HUNDRED YEARS OF MISSION WORK, 1815-1934: THE JESUIT MISSIONAIRES IN THE 19TH AND 20TH CENTURIES]. Paris, Editions Spes, 312p.   [**5**]   [*NYP*]

Brown, Beverley
5.0102   **JM**   1975   George Liele: Black Baptist and Pan-Africanist 1750-1826.

Brown, Brian A.
12.0016   **TR**   1972   INTERFACE IN TRINIDAD: A STUDY OF THE 100 YEAR RELATIONSHIP BETWEEN HINDU AND PRESBYTERIAN ELEMENTS OF THE EAST INDIAN COMMUNITY OF TRINIDAD.

Brown, Samuel Elisha
23.0021   **JM**   1966   Treatise on the Rastafarian movement. *Car Stud* 6(1), April: 39-40.   [**11**]   [*RIS*]

Bryce-Laporte, R. S.
23.0022   **GC,PA**   1970   Crisis, contraculture, and religion among West Indians in the Panama Canal Zone. *In* Whitten, Norman, E., Jr. & Szwed, John F., eds. AFRO-AMERICAN ANTHROPOLOGY: CONTEMPORARY PERSPECTIVES. New York, The Free Press: 103-118.   [**18,19,26**]   [*RIS*]

Buchner, J. H.
23.0023   **JM**   1971   THE MORAVIANS IN JAMAICA. Freeport, New York, Books for Libraries Press: 175p.   [**5,15**]   [*RIS*]

Buhler, Richard O.
23.0024   **BZ**   1976   *Primicias* in Belize. *Belizean Stud* 4(4), July: 25-32.   [**19,24**]   [*RIS*]

Bullard, M. Kenyon
23.0025   **BZ**   1974   Hide and secrete: Women's sexual magic in Belize. *J Sex Res* 10(4), Nov.: 259-265.   [**10,29**]   [*PS*]

Burkhardt, W.
23.0026   **SR**   1927   Surinam. *Int Rev Missions* 16(63), July: 415-424.   [*NYP*]

Butt, Audrey J.
23.0027   **GU**   1953   "The burning fountain from whence it came;" a study of the beliefs of the Akawaio. *Social Econ Stud* 2(1), Sept.: 102-116.   [**13**]   [*RIS*]

23.0028	GU	1954	The burning fountain from whence it came (a study of the system of beliefs of the Carib-speaking Akawaio of British Guiana). *Timehri* 4th ser., 1(33), Oct.: 48-60. **[13]**
23.0029	GU	1959	The birth of a religion (the origins of 'Hallelujah' the semi-Christian religion of the Carib-speaking peoples of the borderlands of British Guiana, Venezuela and Brazil.) *Timehri* 4th ser., no. 38, Sept.: 37-48; no. 39, Sept.: 37-48. **[5,13]** *[AMN]*
23.0030	GU	1961-62	Symbolism and ritual among the Akawaio of British Guiana. *N W I G* 41: 141-161. **[4,13,25]** *[COL]*
13.0026	GU	1965-66	The Shaman's legal role.
13.0027	GU	1966-67	Akawaio charm stones.

Butt Colson, Audrey J.

13.0031	GU	1971	Hallelujah among the Patamona Indians.

Cabon, A.

23.0031	FG	1950	La clergé de la Guyane sous la Révolution [The Guiana clergy during the Revolution]. *Rev Hist Colon Fr* 37(3-4): 173-202. **[5]** *[NYP]*

Cadbury, Henry J.

23.0032	BB	1940	Quakers, Jews and freedom of teaching in Barbados, 1686. *B Friends Hist Assoc* 29(2), Autumn: 97-106. **[5,15]**
23.0033	BB	1941	Barbados Quakers—1683 to 1761: Preliminary list. *J Barb Mus Hist Soc* 9(1), Nov.: 29-31. **[5]** *[AMN]*
23.0034	BB	1942	186 Barbados Quakeresses in 1677. *J Barb Mus Hist Soc* 9(4), Aug.: 195-197. **[5]** *[AMN]*
3.0077	BB	1943	A Quaker account of Barbados in 1718.
23.0035	BB	1946-47	Witnesses of a Quaker marriage in 1689. *J Barb Mus Hist Soc* 14(1-2), Nov.-Feb.: 8-10. **[5]** *[AMN]*
23.0036	BB	1948	Clergymen licensed to Barbados, 1694-1811. *J Barb Mus Hist Soc* 15(2), Feb.: 62-69. **[5]** *[AMN]*
23.0037	BB	1948-49	Further lists of early clergy. *Barb Mus Hist Soc* 16(1-2), Nov.-Feb.: 21-24. **[5]** *[AMN]*
23.0038	BB	1953	Glimpses of Barbados Quakerism 1676-9. *J Barb Mus Hist Soc* 20(2), Feb.: 67-70. **[5]** *[AMN]*
15.0017	JM	1971	Quakers and the earthquake at Port Royal, 1692.

Caine, W. Ralph Hall

3.0078	JM	1908	THE CRUISE OF THE PORT KINGSTON.

Caires, H. S. de

23.0039	GU	1941	The Jesuits in British Guiana. *Month* 177(923), Sept.-Oct.: 455-462. *[NYP]*

Caldecott, A.

23.0040	BC	1970	THE CHURCH IN THE WEST INDIES. London, Frank Cass & Co. Ltd.: 275p. (Originally published in 1898) **[5]** *[RIS]*

Calley, Malcolm J. C.

18.0051	BC,UK	1962	Pentecostal sects among West Indian migrants.
18.0052	BC,UK	1965	GOD'S PEOPLE: WEST INDIAN PENTECOSTAL SECTS IN ENGLAND.

Cameron, Norman E.

23.0041   GU   1968   A HISTORICAL ACCOUNT OF THE PARISH OF CHRIST CHURCH GUYANA. Georgetown, Guyana, Christ Church Vestry: 43p.   [RIS]

Campbell, Carl

23.0042   JM   1971   Denominationalism and the Mico Charity schools in Jamaica, 1835-1842. *Car Stud* 10(4), Jan.: 152-172.   [5,32]   [RIS]

Carmichael, Gertrude

5.0149   TR   1965   Trinidad's two cathedrals.

Carr, Andrew T.

19.0007   TR   1953   A Rada community in Trinidad.

Case, Henry W.

3.0089   BB,GU   1910   ON SEA AND LAND, ON CREEK AND RIVER.

Catherall, Gordon A.

23.0043   JM   1970   BRITISH BAPTIST INVOLVEMENT IN JAMAICA, 1783-1865. Ph.D. dissertation, University of Keele: 318p.   [5]

Chan, V. O.

16.0017   GU   1970   The riots of 1856 in British Guiana.

Chandool, Earl

23.0044   BC   1968   Resources available to the churches of the Eastern Caribbean. *In* REPORT OF CONSULTATION ON SOCIAL AND ECONOMIC DEVELOPMENT IN THE EASTERN CARIBBEAN HELD IN ST. VINCENT NOV. 26-30, 1968. Port-of-Spain, Trinidad, Superservice Printing Co.: 17-20.   [RIS]

Chevannes, Alston Barrington

23.0045   JM   1971   JAMAICAN LOWER CLASS RELIGION: STRUGGLES AGAINST OPPRESSION. Masters Thesis, University of the West Indies (Mona): 155p.   [10]
                                                                                                                    [RIS]

5.0165   JM   1971   Revival and black struggle.
23.0046   JM   1976   The repairer of the breach: Reverend Claudius Henry and Jamaican society. *In* Henry, Frances, ed. ETHNICITY IN THE AMERICAS. The Hague, Mouton: 263-289.   [11,21]   [RIS]

Cleghorn, Robert

23.0047   BZ   1939   A SHORT HISTORY OF BAPTIST MISSIONARY WORK IN BRITISH HONDURAS 1822-1939. London, Kingsgate Press, 71p.   [5]   [UTS]

Cochran, Hamilton

23.0048   VI   1968   Obeah in the Virgin Islands. *V I View* 3(9), Feb.: 30-41.   [NYP]

Cole, George Watson

23.0049   BE   1928   LEWIS HUGHES; THE MILITANT MINISTER OF THE BERMUDAS AND HIS PRINTED WORKS. Worcester, Massachusetts, American Antiquarian Society: 67p.   [5]   [NYP]

Colley Hutchinson, R. & Krafft, A. J. C.

23.0050   BC,SM,SE   1948   De Methodistische kerk van de Engelse Antillen, van Sint Maarten en van St. Eustatius [The Methodist church of the British Antilles, St. Martin and St. Eustatius]. *In* ORANJE EN DE ZES CARAÏBISCHE PARELEN. Amsterdam, J. H. de Bussy: 512-514.   [UCLA]

Collier, H. C.

23.0051   BC   1939   Duppy-hunting in paradise. *Can-W I Mag* 28(10), Nov.: 22-24.
   [*NYP*]

23.0052   BC   1939   Poltergeist—or "duppy 'pon de 'ouse." *Can-W I Mag* 28(7), Aug.: 11-13.   [*NYP*]

23.0053   BC   1941   Obeah—the witchcraft of the West Indies—plain bugaboo between me and you. *Can-W I Mag* 30(8), Aug.: 24-25.   [*NYP*]

Collins, Rev.

32.0125   JM   1907   The agricultural and industrial experiment.

Connell, Neville

23.0054   BB   1953   St. George's Parish Church, Barbados. *J Barb Mus Hist Soc* 20(3), May: 133-136. **[5,22,35]**   [*AMN*]

22.0080   BB   1954   Church plate in Barbados.

3.0114   BB   1957   Father Labat's visit to Barbados in 1700.

Costa, S. C. da

5.0187   SR   1973   Joden Savanne: een historische plaats in het oerwoud van Suriname [Joden Savanne: a historical place in the Surinam jungle].

Courtenay, Harrison

23.0055   BZ   1974   The Church of St. Mary the Virgin. *National Stud* 2(3), May: 21-25.
   [*RIS*]

Crabb, J. A., ed.

23.0056   JM   1951   CHRIST FOR JAMAICA. Kingston, The Pioneer Press, 102p. **[5]**

Crow, Paul A., Jr.

23.0057   JM   1966   The venture of church union in Jamaica. *Lex Theol Q* 1, July: 89-98.
   [*UTS*]

Crowley, Daniel J.

23.0058   SL   1955   Festivals of the calendar in St. Lucia. *Car Q* 4(2), Dec.: 99-121. **[19]**   [*RIS*]

23.0059   SL   1955   Supernatural beings in St. Lucia. *Caribbean* 8(11-12), June-July: 241-244, 264-265.   [*RIS*]

Cundall, Frank

23.0060   JM   1922   THE LIFE OF ENOS NUTTALL, ARCHBISHOP OF THE WEST INDIES. London, Society for Promoting Christian Knowledge: 256p. **[5]**
   [*NYP*]

23.0061   JM   1930   Three fingered Jack. *W I Comm Circ* 45(816), Jan. 9: 9-10. **[5,11,24]**   [*NYP*]

23.0062   JM   1930   Three fingered Jack. *W I Comm Circ* 45(817), Jan. 23: 36-37. **[5,11,24]**   [*NYP*]

23.0063   JM   1930   Three fingered Jack. *W I Comm Circ* 45(818), Feb. 6: 55-56. **[5,11,24]**   [*NYP*]

23.0064   JM   1931   A BRIEF HISTORY OF THE PARISH CHURCH OF ST. ANDREW, JAMAICA. Kingston, Institute of Jamaica, 75p. **[5]**   [*NYP*]

Cundall, Frank; Davis, N. Darnell & Friedenberg, Albert M.

15.0024   JM,BB   1915   Documents relating to the history of the Jews in Jamaica and Barbados in the time of William III.

Cuthbert, Robert

23.0065   BC   1968   The Christian imperative for social action. *In* REPORT OF CONSUL-
TATION ON SOCIAL AND ECONOMIC DEVELOPMENT IN THE EASTERN
CARIBBEAN HELD IN ST. VINCENT NOV. 26-30, 1968. Port-of-Spain,
Trinidad, Superservice Printing Co.: 8-10.   [*RIS*]

Cuthbert, Robert & Cuthbert, Marlene

23.0066   BC   1968   REPORT OF CONSULTATION ON SOCIAL AND ECONOMIC DEVELOPMENT
IN THE EASTERN CARIBBEAN HELD IN ST. VINCENT NOV. 26-30, 1968.
Port-of-Spain, Trinidad, Superservice Printing Co.: 52p.   **[41]**
                                                                          [*RIS*]

Davidson, Lewis

23.0067   JM   1945   FIRST THINGS FIRST: A STUDY OF THE PRESBYTERIAN CHURCH IN
JAMAICA. Edinburgh, William Blackwood, 46p.   [*UTS*]

Davis, J. Merle

23.0068   JM   1942   THE CHURCH IN THE NEW JAMAICA: A STUDY OF THE ECONOMIC AND
SOCIAL BASIS OF THE EVANGELICAL CHURCH IN JAMAICA. New York,
International Missionary Council, Dept. of Social and Economic
Research & Counsel, 100p.   [*UTS*]

Davis, N. Darnell

15.0025   BB   1909   Notes on the history of the Jews in Barbados.

Davis, Stephen

37.0186   JM   1976   Roots of reggae: the extraordinary Rastafarians.

Debien, Gabriel

5.0239   FA   1965   Les papiers de l'abbé Renard et l'histoire religieuse des Antilles
Françaises [The papers of Father Renard and the religious history
of the French Antilles].

6.0051   FA   1967   La christianisation des esclaves des Antilles françaises aux 17è et
18è siècles [The christianization of the slaves in the French Antilles
during the 17th and 18th centuries].

Delany, Francis X.

23.0069   JM   1930   A HISTORY OF THE CATHOLIC CHURCH IN JAMAICA B.W.I., 1494 TO
1929. New York, Jesuit Mission Press, 292p.   **[5]**   [*UTS*]

Dellinger, N. T.

23.0070   BZ   1976   Belizean Baptists. *Belizean Stud* 4(2), March: 10-20.   [*RIS*]

Desroches, Rosny

23.0071   GC   1972   The future role of the churches. *In* Haynes, Lilith M., ed. FAMBLI:
THE CHURCH'S RESPONSIBILITY TO THE FAMILY IN THE CARIBBEAN.
Trinidad, CARIPLAN: 221-226.   **[9]**   [*RIS*]

Devas, Raymund P.

23.0072   GR   1927   The Catholic Church in Grenada, B.W.I. (1650-1927) by R. C.
Devas. *Ir Eccles Rec* 5th ser., 30, Aug.: 188-199; 30, Sept.:
288-307.   **[5]**   [*NYP*]

23.0073   GR   1928   The Catholic Church in Grenada, B.W.I. (1650-1927) by R. C.
Devas. *Ir Eccles Rec* 5th ser., 31, May: 474-481; 32, July:
51-56.   **[5]**   [*NYP*]

23.0074   GR   1932   CONCEPTION ISLAND; OR, THE TROUBLED STORY OF THE CATHOLIC
                          CHURCH IN GRENADA. London, Sands, 436p.   **[5]**   [*RIS*]

Dix, Jabez
23.0075   SL   1933   Adolphe—one of the most terrible of Obeah-men. *Can-W I Mag*
                          22(2), Jan.: 53-55.   [*NYP*]

Donicie, A. C.
23.0076   SR   1948   Sterfhuis en begrafenis bij de Saramakkanen [House of the de-
                          ceased and funeral among the Saramaccans]. *W I G* 29: 175-
                          182. **[14]**   [*COL*]

Driessen, W. C. H.
33.0064 AR   1970   Alcoholism, guilt and disease.

Durham, Harriet F.
15.0027 GC   1972   CARIBBEAN QUAKERS.

Easton, Wilfred
23.0077   GC   1956   WEST INDIES: WHAT OF THE CHURCH? London, Edinburgh House
                          Press, 24p.   [*UTS*]

Edwards, P. A.
32.0185 BC   1971   EDUCATION FOR DEVELOPMENT IN THE CARIBBEAN.

Egan, Cecilia M.
23.0078   MT   1943   Martinique—the isle of those who return. *Nat Hist* 52(2), Sept.:
                          52-53, 96. **[11,19]**   [*COL*]

Elder, J. D.
23.0079   TR   1970   The Yoruba ancestor cult in Gasparillo (Its structure, organization,
                          and social function in community life). *Car Q* 16(3), Sept.:
                          5-20. **[9,11]**   [*RIS*]

Ellis, J. B.
23.0080   BZ,JM 1913   THE DIOCESE OF JAMAICA: A SHORT ACCOUNT OF ITS HISTORY,
                          GROWTH, AND ORGANISATION. London, Society for Promoting
                          Christian Knowledge, 237p. **[5]**   [*NYP*]

Elsenhout, R.
23.0081   SR   1970   Een visie op het werk van de fraters in Suriname [An opinion on the
                          work of the fathers in Surinam]. *In* Janssen, Cornelius, ed.
                          SURINAME: HET WERK VAN DE FRATERS VAN TILBURG ONDER DE
                          VIJFSTERRENVLAG. Tilburg, The Netherlands, Fraters van O.L.
                          Vrouw, Moeder van Barmhartigheid: 74-86. **[33]**   [*RILA*]

Elst, Dirk H. van der
14.0009 SR   1975   The Coppename Kwinti: notes on an Afro-American tribe in
                          Surinam. II. Organization and ideology.

Emanuels, D. H.
33.0068 SR   1969   Afwijkend recht voor afzonderlijke bevolkingsgroepen in de
                          geschiedenis van Suriname [Special laws for different population
                          groups in the history of Surinam].

Emmanuel, Isaac S.

15.0028   **GC**   1955   New light on early American Jewry.

23.0082   **CU**   1957   PRECIOUS STONES OF THE JEWS OF CURACAO; CURACAON JEWRY
1656-1957. New York, Bloch, 584p.   **[5,15]**   [*NYP*]

Emmanuel, Isaac S. & Emmanuel, Susan A.

15.0029   **NA**   1970   HISTORY OF THE JEWS OF THE NETHERLANDS ANTILLES: VOL.
1—HISTORY; VOL. 2—APPENDICES.

Essed, W. F. R.

28.0370   **SR**   1930-31 Eenige opmerkingen naar aanleiding van de artikelen over treef en
lepra in dit tijdschrift verschenen [Some remarks in connection with
the articles about treyf and leprosy that appeared in this magazine].

Euwens, P. A.

23.0083   **CU**   1934-35 De Joodsche Synagoge op Curacao [The Jewish Synagogue on
Curacao]. *W I G* 16: 222-231.   **[5]**   [*COL*]

Farquar, David U.

23.0084   **LW**   1971   CHRISTIAN MISSIONS IN THE LEEWARD ISLANDS, 1810-1850: A SOCIAL
AND ECCLESIASTICAL ANALYSIS. D.Phil. dissertation, University of
York: 418p.   **[5]**

Farrar, P. A.

23.0085   **BB**   1935   Christ church. *J Barb Mus Hist Soc* 2(3), May: 143-154.   **[5,35]**
[*AMN*]

15.0031   **BB**   1942   The Jews in Barbados.

Findlay, G. G. & Holdsworth, W. W.

23.0086   **BC**   1921   THE HISTORY OF THE WESLEYAN METHODIST MISSIONARY SOCIETY,
v. 2. London, Epworth Press, 534p.   **[5,6]**   [*UTS*]

Findling, John E.

37.0237   **BB**   1973   The Lowther-Gordon controversy: church and state in Barbados,
1711-1720.

Fischer, Michael M. J.

20.0023   **JM**   1974   Value assertion and stratification: religion and marriage in rural
Jamaica.

Fisher, Ruth Anna

15.0033   **JM**   1943   Note on Jamaica.

Fock, Niels

23.0087   **GU**   1963   WAIWAI: RELIGION AND SOCIETY OF AN AMAZONIAN TRIBE.
Copenhagen, National Museum, 584p.   **[13]**   [*COL*]

13.0062   **GU**   1971   Authority, its magico-religious, political and legal agencies among
Caribs in northern South America.

Fort, Rev.

23.0088   **DM,SV**   1903   La Dominique et Sainte Lucie [Dominica and St. Lucia]. *In* Piolet,
J.-B., ed. LA FRANCE AU DEHORS: LES MISSIONS CATHOLIQUES
FRANCAISES AU XIXᴱ SIÈCLE. Vol. 6: MISSIONS D'AMÉRIQUE. Paris,
Librairie Armand Colin, 331-332.   **[5]**   [*NYP*]

Franklin, C. B.

23.0089   TR   1934   A CENTURY AND A QUARTER OF HANOVER METHODIST CHURCH HISTORY 1809-1934. Port of Spain, 32p.   **[5]**

Froidevaux, Henri

3.0201   FG   1901   Les "lettres édifiantes" et la description de la mission de Kourou [The "edifying letters" and a description of the Kourou mission].

Furley, Oliver

5.0304   BC   1965   Moravian missionaries and slaves in the West Indies.

23.0090   BC   1965   Protestant missionaries in the West Indies. *Race* 6(3), Jan.: 232-242.   **[6,16]**   [*COL*]

Gaay Fortman, B. de

23.0091   CU   1941   Lutherschen op Curacao [Lutherans on Curacao]. *W I G* 23: 280-288.   **[7]**   [*COL*]

23.0092   GU,SE   1941   Lutherschen op St. Eustatius en in Essequebo [Lutherans on St. Eustatius and in Essequibo]. *W I G* 23: 346-352.   **[7]**   [*COL*]

23.0093   GU   1942   De geschiedenis der Luthersche gemeente in Berbice [The history of the Lutheran congregation in Berbice]. *W I G* 24: 20-27, 51-62, 65-89.   **[5]**   [*COL*]

Galton, C. T., Bp.

32.0221   GU   1912   Elementary education in British Guiana.

Garrett, Clara Maude

19.0020   JM   1935   Caribbean Christmas.

Goeje, C. H. de

23.0094   SR   1929-30   A. Ph. Penard over inwijding en wereld-beschouwing der Karaïben [A. Ph. Penard on initiation and worldview of the Caribs]. *W I G* 11: 275-286.   **[13]**   [*COL*]

23.0095   SR   1942   De inwijding tot medicijnman bij de Arawakken (Guyana) in tekst en mythe [The initiation of medicinemen among the Arawaks (Guiana) in word and myths]. *Bijd Volk* 101: 211-276.   **[13]**

20.0028   GC   1943   Philosophy, initiation and myths of the Indians of Guiana and adjacent countries.

23.0096   SR   1947   Negers in Amerika [Negroes in the Americas]. *W I G* 28: 217-221.   **[14]**   [*COL*]

23.0097   SR   1948   ZONDVLOED EN ZONDEVAL BIJ DE INDIANEN VAN WEST-INDIE [THE DELUGE AND THE FALL AMONG THE INDIANS OF THE WEST INDIES]. Amsterdam, Indisch Instituut, 64p. (Mededeling no. 79, Afdeling Volkenkunde no. 28.).   **[13]**   [*NYP*]

23.0098   GC   1952   The physical world, the world of magic, and the moral world of Guiana Indians. *In* Tax, Sol, ed. INDIAN TRIBES OF ABORIGINAL AMERICA: Selected papers of the XXIXth International Congress of Americanists. Chicago, University of Chicago Press, 266-270.   **[13,24]**   [*AGS*]

23.0099   NA   1956-57   Enkele beschouwingen over de Indianen der Nederlandse Antillen en hun geestesleven [Some observations about the Indians in the Netherlands Antilles and their spiritual life]. *W I G* 37: 41-50.   **[13]**   [*COL*]

Gomez Canedo, P. Lino

5.0332   GU   1966   Los franciscanos en Guayana [The Franciscans in Guyana].

Goodman, F. D.

23.0100   SV   1969   Glossolalia: speaking in tongues in four cultural settings. *Con Psych* 12(2-4): 113-129.   **[31]**   [*PS*]

Goodridge, Sehon

23.0101   BC   1971   POLITICS AND THE CARIBBEAN CHURCH: A CONFESSION OF GUILT. Bridgetown, Barbados, Caribbean Ecumenical Consultation for Development, Study Paper No. 2: 20p.   [*RIS*]

Goslinga, Cornelius Ch.

23.0102   GC   1956   Kerk, Kroon en Cariben [Church, crown and Caribs]. *W I G* 36: 147-161.   **[5,13,37]**   [*COL*]

Gradussov, Alex

23.0103   JM   1969   Kapo; cult leader, sculptor, painter. *Jam J* 3(2), June: 46-51.   **[22]**
                                                                            [*RIS*]

Guasco, Alexandre

23.0104   FG   1903   La Guyane francaise [French Guiana]. *In* Piolet, J.-B., ed. LA FRANCE AU DEHORS: LES MISSIONS CATHOLIQUES FRANCAISES AU XIXE SIÈCLE, Vol. 6: MISSIONS D'AMÉRIQUE. Paris, Librairie Armand Colin, 395-415.   **[5]**   [*NYP*]

Gúerin, Daniel

19.0023   GC   1956   Un futur pour les Antilles? [A future for the Antilles?]

Guggenheim, Hans & Carr, Andrew T.

23.0105   TR   1965   Tribalism in Trinidad. *MD Med News Mag* 9(2), Feb.: 138-143.   **[22]**   [*RIS*]

Hall, Michelle

23.0106   BA   1973   The role of religion on San Salvador. *In* Thomas, Garry L., ed. ANTHROPOLOGICAL FIELD REPORTS FROM SAN SALVADOR ISLAND. San Salvador, Bahamas, Island Environment Studies, Reports 1973: 69-76.   [*RIS*]

Hamid, Idris

23.0107   GC   1971   IN SEARCH OF NEW PERSPECTIVES. Bridgetown, Barbados, Caribbean Ecumenical Consultation for Development: 20p.   [*RIS*]

23.0108   GC   1972   Decolonializing the Christian faith: a fresh approach to the Christian faith in the context of the Caribbean. *In* Haynes, Lilith M., ed. FAMBLI: THE CHURCH'S RESPONSIBILITY TO THE FAMILY IN THE CARIBBEAN. Trinidad, CARIPLAN: 152-172.   [*RIS*]

Hanrath, Johannes J.

23.0109   SR   1967   Iets over vrijmetselarij in Suriname [Some remarks on freemasonry in Surinam]. *Oost West* 60(9), May: 15-17.   [*NYP*]

Hartog, J.

23.0110   NL   1947   De godsdiensten in Curacao [The religions of Curacao]. *W I G* 28: 1-8.   [*COL*]

23.0111	AR	1952	Aruba's oudste kerk 1750-1816-1952 [Aruba's oldest church 1750-1816-1952]. *W I G* 33: 191-198. **[5]** [*COL*]
23.0112	NA	1970	MOGEN DE EILANDEN ZICH VERHEUGEN: GESCHIEDENIS VAN HET PROTESTANTISME OP DE NEDERLANDSE ANTILLEN [LET THE ISLANDS REJOICE: HISTORY OF PROTESTANTISM IN THE NETHERLANDS ANTILLES]. Curaçao, Kerkeraad van de Verenigde Protestantse Gemeente: 286p. **[5]** [*RILA*]

Hartog, John

23.0113	SE	1967	The Honen Daliem congregation of St. Eustatius. *Am Jew Arch* 19(1), April: 60-77. **[5]** [*COL*]

Haynes, Lilith M.

23.0114	GC	1972[?]	The future role of the churches. *In* Haynes, Lilith M., ed. FAMBLI: THE CHURCH'S RESPONSIBILITY TO THE FAMILY IN THE CARIBBEAN. Trinidad, CARIPLAN: 217-220. [*RIS*]

Haynes, Lilith M., ed.

23.0115	GC	1972[?]	FAMBLI: THE CHURCH'S RESPONSIBILITY TO THE FAMILY IN THE CARIBBEAN. Trinidad, CARIPLAN: 241p. **[9]** [*RIS*]

Hayward, W. B.

23.0116	BE	1954	Additional great days. *Bermuda Hist Q* 11(1), Spring: 49-51. **[5]** [*COL*]
23.0117	BE	1954	St. Peter's churchyard. *Bermuda Hist Q* 11(1), Spring: 41-43. **[5]** [*COL*]

Hendrick, S. Purcell

23.0118	JM	1911	A SKETCH OF THE HISTORY OF THE CATHEDRAL CHURCH OF ST. JAGO DE LA VEGA, SPANISH TOWN IN THE PARISH OF ST. CATHERINE, JAMAICA. Kingston, Jamaica Times, 52p. **[5,35]** [*NYP*]

Henney, Jeannette H.

23.0119	SV	1968	"MOURNING" A RELIGIOUS RITUAL AMONG THE SPIRITUAL BAPTISTS OF ST. VINCENT: AN EXPERIENCE IN SENSORY DEPRIVATION. Columbus, Ohio, Department of Anthropolgy, The Ohio State University (Cross-Cultural Study of Dissociational States, Working Paper 21): 26p. **[31]** [*RIS*]
23.0120	SV	1968	SPIRIT POSSESSION BELIEF AND TRANCE BEHAVIOR IN A RELIGIOUS GROUP IN ST. VINCENT, BRITISH WEST INDIES. Ann Arbor, Michigan, University Microfilms, Inc.: 216p. (Ph.D. dissertation, The Ohio State University)
23.0121	SV	1973	The Shakers of St. Vincent: a stable religion. *In* Bourguignon, Erika, ed. RELIGION, ALTERED STATES OF CONSCIOUSNESS, AND SOCIAL CHANGE. Columbus, Ohio State University Press: 219-263. **[10,31]** [*COL*]
23.0122	SV	1974	Spirit-possession belief and trance behavior in two fundamentalist groups in St. Vincent. *In* Goodman, Felicitas D.; Henney, Jeanette H. & Pressel, Esther. TRANCE, HEALING AND HALLUCINATION: THREE FIELD STUDIES IN RELIGIOUS EXPERIENCE. New York, John Wiley and Sons, Inc.: 1-111. [*COL*]

Henriques, Fernando

9.0070   **GC**   1972   Sociological excursus of research on the family in the Caribbean.

Henry, Frances

8.0099   **TR**   1965   Social stratification in an Afro-American cult.
23.0123   **TR**   1969   Stress and strategy in three field situations. *In* Henry, Frances &
                                  Saberwal, Satish, eds. STRESS AND RESPONSE IN FIELDWORK. New
                                  York, Holt, Reinhart and Winston, Inc.: 35-46.   **[2,11]**   [*RIS*]

Heusden, Edgard van

32.0290   **SR**   1970   De Stichting voor Buitengewoon Onderwijs [The Foundation for
                                  Extraordinary Education].

Hilfman, P. A.

15.0041   **SR**   1909   Notes on the history of the Jews in Surinam.

Hill, Clifford

18.0136   **BC,UK**   1963   WEST INDIAN MIGRANTS AND THE LONDON CHURCHES.
18.0139   **BC,UK**   1971   BLACK CHURCHES: WEST INDIAN AND AFRICAN SECTS IN BRITAIN.
23.0124   **BC,UK**   1971   From church to sect: West Indian religious sect development. *J
                                         Scient Stud Relig* 10(2), Summer: 114-123.   **[18]**   [*COL*]
23.0125   **BC,UK**   1971   Pentecostal growth—result of racialism? *Race Today* 3(6), June:
                                         187-190.   **[16,18]**   [*RIS*]

Hoad, John

9.0072   **GC**   1972[?]   The attitude of Caribbean churches to the illegitimate child.

Hogg, Donald William

23.0126   **JM**   1956   A West Indian shepherd. *In Context* 4(2), Mar.: 12-15.   **[19]**   [*RIS*]
23.0127   **JM**   1960   The Convince Cult in Jamaica. *In* Mintz, Sidney W., comp. PAPERS
                                  IN CARIBBEAN ANTHROPOLOGY. New Haven, Dept. of Anthropology,
                                  Yale University, no. 58 (24p.) (Yale University Publications in
                                  Anthropology, no. 57-64.)   **[19]**   [*RIS*]
23.0128   **JM**   1961   Magic and "science" in Jamaica. *Car Stud* 1(2), July: 1-5.   [*RIS*]
23.0130   **JM**   1969   JAMAICAN RELIGIONS: A STUDY IN VARIATIONS. Ann Arbor, Mich-
                                  igan, University Microfilms, Inc.: 466p. (Ph.D. dissertation, Yale
                                  University, 1964)   **[8,19]**   [*RIS*]
23.0131   **JM**   1970   Elegy for a Christian pagan. *Car R* 2(2), Summer: 1-3.   [*RIS*]

Holzberg, C. S.

15.0042   **JM,CU**   1976   Societal segmentation and Jewish ethnicity: ethnographic illustra-
                                      tions from Latin America and the Caribbean.

Hooker, Bernard

23.0132   **JM**   1969   THE BIBLE, JUDAISM, AND JAMAICA; A SERIES OF RADIO TALKS
                                  WHICH RELATE BIBLE STORIES TO EVERYDAY LIFE. Jamaica, Moore
                                  Business Forms Caribbean: 255p.   [*NYP*]

Hooper, Rachel

18.0144   **BC,UK**   1969   ACT NOW: A REPORT ON RACE RELATIONS IN BRITAIN FOLLOWING A
                                      SURVEY AUGUST-SEPTEMBER 1969 WITH SPECIAL REFERENCE TO THE
                                      RESPONSE OF THE CHURCHES AND OF THE CHURCH MISSIONARY
                                      SOCIETY.

Horowitz, Michael M.

23.0133   **MT**   1963   The worship of South Indian deities in Martinique. *Ethnology* 2(3), July: 339-346. **[12,19]**   [*RIS*]

Horowitz, Michael M. & Klass, Morton

23.0134   **MT**   1961   The Martiniquan East Indian cult of Maldevidan. *Social Econ Stud* 10(1), Mar.: 93-100. **[12,19]**   [*RIS*]

Horst, Raoul van der

32.0292   **SR**   1970   Het studieconvict Boniface te Paramaribo [The Boniface religious boarding school in Paramaribo].

Hoster, William

23.0135   **UV**   1926   Our mission work in Puerto Rico and the Virgin Islands. *Sp Miss* 91(1), Jan.: 19-26.   [*NYP*]

Houtzager, J. C.

23.0136   **CU**   1939   Het Gereformeerd kerkelijk leven in Curacao [The Reformed Church on Curacao]. *W I G* 21: 43-47.   [*COL*]

Howard, Michael C.

23.0137   **BZ**   1975   Kekchi religious beliefs and lore regarding the jungle. *National Stud* 3(2), March: 34-49. **[13,24]**   [*RIS*]

Hughes, H. B. L.

23.0138   **JM**   1945   The Impact on Jamaica of the Evangelical Revival. *Jam Hist Rev* 1(1), June: 7-23. **[5]**   [*AMN*]

Hulse, Gilbert R.

23.0139   **BZ**   1973   The Cathedral of St. John the Baptist. *National Stud* 1(4), July: 24-28.   [*RIS*]

Hunte, Keith D.

23.0140   **BB**   1975   Church and society in Barbados in the eighteenth century. *In* Social groups and institutions in the history of the Caribbean: papers presented. . .at the VI Annual Conference of Caribbean Historians. Puerto Rico, April 4-9, 1974. Rio Piedras, Puerto Rico, Association of Caribbean Historians: 13-25. **[5,6]**   [*RIS*]

Hurwitz, Samuel J. & Hurwitz, Edith

15.0043   **JM**   1965   The New World sets an example for the old: the Jews of Jamaica and political rights 1661-1831.

23.0141   **JM**   1966   A beacon for Judaism; the first fruits of the west. *Am Jew Hist Q* 56(1), Sept.: 3-26. **[15]**   [*COL*]

Hutchinson, Frank L.

33.0100   **JM**   1956   Hunger and help in the Caribbean: Jamaica, Puerto Rico, Haiti.

Hutton, J. E.

23.0142   **GC**   1922   A HISTORY OF MORAVIAN MISSIONS. London, Moravian Publ. Office, 550p. **[5]**   [*UTS*]

Jacobs, H. P.

23.0143   JM   1965   Dialect, magic and religion. *In* Cargill, Morris, ed. IAN FLEMING INTRODUCES JAMAICA. New York, Hawthorn Books, Inc.: 79-101. **[3]**   [*RIS*]

Jakobsson, Stiv

6.0152   BC   1972   AM I NOT A MAN AND A BROTHER? BRITISH MISSIONS AND THE ABOLITION OF THE SLAVE TRADE AND SLAVERY IN WEST AFRICA AND THE WEST INDIES, 1786-1838.

Janssen, Cornelius

45.0081   SR   1970   De bedrijven: TIM-IN, de sigarenfabriek "Leo Victor" en de drukkerij "Leo Victor". [The companies: TIM-IN, the cigar factory "Leo Victor" and the printer "Leo Victor"].

Janssen, Cornelius, ed.

23.0144   SR   1970   SURINAME: HET WERK VAN DE FRATERS VAN TILBURG ONDER DE VIJFSTERRENVLAG [SURINAM: THE WORK OF THE FATHERS FROM TILBURG UNDER THE FIVE STAR FLAG]. Tilburg, The Netherlands, Fraters van O. L. Vrouw, Moeder van Barmhartigheid: 96p. (Intercom-Fraters No. 7)   [*RILA*]

Japal, L.

23.0145   GR   1968   The Grenada Inter-Church Council: a pattern for inter-church action. *In* REPORT OF CONSULTATION ON SOCIAL AND ECONOMIC DEVELOPMENT IN THE EASTERN CARIBBEAN HELD IN ST. VINCENT Nov. 26-30, 1968. Port-of-Spain, Trinidad, Superservice Printing Co.: 25-29.   [*RIS*]

Jayawardena, Chandra

23.0146   GU   1966   Religious belief and social change: aspects of the development of Hinduism in British Guiana. *Comp Stud Soc Hist* 8(2), Jan.: 211-240. **[12,19]**   [*COL*]

Jenkins, Charles Francis

23.0147   TT   1923   Tortola, the chief of the British Virgin Islands. *B Geogr Soc Phila* 21(1), Jan.: 1-20. **[5]**   [*AGS*]

Jesse, C.

23.0148   FA   1960   Religion among the early slaves in the French Antilles. *J Barb Mus Hist Soc* 28(1), Nov.: 4-10. **[5,6]**   [*AMN*]

5.0477   GC   1965   The Papal Bull of 1493 appointing the first Vicar Apostolic in the New World.

Jessurun Cardozo, Is.; Maduro, S. A. L. & Maduro, J. M. L.

23.0149   CU   1948   Ons Joods leven [Our Jewish life]. *In* ORANJE EN DE ZES CARAÏBISCHE PARELEN. Amsterdam, J. H. de Bussy: 106-121. **[15]**
                                                                         [*UCLA*]

Jha, J. C.

12.0038   TR   1976   The Hindu festival of Divali in the Caribbean.

12.0039   TR   1976   The Hindu sacraments (*rites de passage*) in Trinidad and Tobago.

Jordan, W. F.

3.0311 FC 1922 CRUSADING IN THE WEST INDIES.

Josa, F. P. Luigi

23.0150 BC 1910 ENGLISH CHURCH HISTORY OF THE WEST INDIAN PROVINCE. Georgetown, Argosy Co., 143p. **[5]** [*SCH*]

Judah, George Fortunatus

15.0046 JM 1909 The Jews' tribute in Jamaica.

Junker, L.

23.0151 SR 1925-26 De godsdienst der Boschnegers [The religion of the Bush Negroes]. *W I G* 7: 81-95, 127-137, 153-164. **[14]** [*COL*]

Kalff, S.

15.0047 CU 1926-27 Joden op het eiland Curacao [Jews on the island of Curacao].
23.0152 SR,CU 1928-29 Westindische predikanten [West Indian preachers]. *W I G* 10: 413-416, 465-476. [*COL*]

Kane, Arthur

23.0153 JM 1969 Leadership training group dynamics and cursillos. *In* CARIBBEAN DEVELOPMENT AND THE FUTURE OF THE CHURCH: PROCEEDINGS OF A CONFERENCE HELD IN GEORGETOWN, JAN. 6-8. Georgetown, Guyana, Guyana Institute for Social Research and Action. [*SCH*]
23.0154 JM 1969 Social action and the church in Jamaica. *In* CARIBBEAN DEVELOPMENT AND THE FUTURE OF THE CHURCH: PROCEEDINGS OF A CONFERENCE HELD IN GEORGETOWN, JAN. 6-8. Georgetown, Guyana, Guyana Institute for Social Research and Action. **[33]**

[*SCH*]

36.0050 JM 1973 The church and urbanization in the Caribbean.

Karner, Frances P.

15.0049 CU 1969 THE SEPHARDICS OF CURAÇAO: A STUDY OF SOCIO-CULTURAL PATTERNS IN FLUX.

Kennedy, Jean de Chantal

23.0155 BE 1970 Presbyterians and Independents in early Bermuda history. *Bermuda Hist Q* 27(1), Spring: 20-22. **[5]** [*COL*]

Kesler, C. K.

23.0156 SR 1923-24 Nils Otto Tank (1800-1864). *W I G* 5: 65-76. **[5]** [*COL*]
23.0157 NC,ST 1933-34 Graaf von Zinzendorf in Holland [Count von Zinzendorf in Holland]. *W I G* 15: 1-10. **[5]** [*COL*]
23.0158 SR 1939 Een Moravische Zuster uit de 18e eeuw: Anna Maria Kersten geb. Tonn 1723-1807 [A Moravian Sister from the 18th century: Anna Maria Kersten née Tonn, 1723-1807] *W IG* 21: 206-217. **[5]**

[*COL*]

23.0159 GU 1942 Moeilijkheden met betrekking tot eedsaflegging en het dragen van wapenen in Berdice 18de eeuw [Problems about oath-taking and carrying of weapons in Berbice in the 18th century]. *W I G* 24: 129-142. **[5]** [*COL*]

Kiemen, Mathias C.
32.0330   GC   1960   Catholic schools in the Caribbean.

Kiev, Ari
31.0083   JM,UK   1963   Beliefs and delusions of West Indian immigrants to London.
18.0167   BC,UK   1964   Psychotherapeutic aspects of Pentecostal sects among West Indian immigrants to England.
23.0160   JM   1969   Ras Tafari. *In* PAPERS OF THE FIRST CARIBBEAN PSYCHIATRIC ASSOCIATION MEETING, OCHO RIOS, JAMAICA: 11p.   **[11,31]**   [*RIS*]

King, R. O. C.
23.0161   BC   1948   The church in the British West Indies. *Int Rev Miss* 37(145), Jan.: 80-85.   [*NYP*]

Kitzinger, Sheila
23.0162   JM   1969   Protest and mysticism: the Rastafari cult of Jamaica. *J Scient Stud Relig* 8(2), Fall: 240-262.   **[11,16,37]**   [*RIS*]
23.0163   JM   1971   The Rastafarian brethren of Jamaica. *In* Horowitz, Michael M., ed. PEOPLES AND CULTURES OF THE CARIBBEAN: AN ANTHROPOLOGICAL READER. New York, Natural History Press for the American Museum of Natural History: 580-588.   **[11]**   [*RIS*]

Klerk, Cornelis Johannes Maria de
23.0164   SR   1951   CULTUS EN RITUEEL VAN HET ORTHODOXE HINDOEÏSME IN SURINAME [CULTS AND RITUAL OF ORTHODOX HINDUISM IN SURINAM]. Amsterdam, Urbi et Orbi, 292p.   **[12,19]**   [*RIS*]
23.0165   SR   1963   Over de religie der Surinaamse Hindostanen [On the religion of the Hindustanis in Surinam]. *In* Lutchman, W. I., ed. VAN BRITS-INDISCH EMIGRANT TOT BURGER VAN SURINAME. The Hague, Drukkerij Wieringa, p.61-80.   **[12]**

Kleyntjens, J.
23.0166   NA   1931-32 Het apostolische vicariaat van Curacao [The aspostolic vicariate of Curacao]. *W I G* 13: 123-137.   [*COL*]

Klingberg, Frank J.
32.0333   BC   1939   The Lady Mico Charity Schools in the British West Indies, 1835-1842.
6.0166   JM   1942   As to the state of Jamaica in 1707.

Klingberg, Frank J., ed.
42.0084   BB   1949   CODRINGTON CHRONICLE: AN EXPERIMENT IN ANGLICAN ALTRUISM ON A BARBADOS PLANTATION, 1710-1834.

Kloos, Peter
13.0112   SR   1968   Becoming a Piyei: variability and similarity in Carib shamanism.

Knappert, L.
23.0167   CU   1925-26 Koning Willem I en de Protestantsche gemeente op Curacao [King William the First and the Protestant community on Curacao]. *W I G* 7: 193-206.   **[5]**   [*COL*]
23.0168   SR   1926-27 De Labadisten in Suriname [The Labadists in Surinam]. *W I G* 8: 193-218.   [*COL*]

23.0169	SM	1928-29	Een heksenproces op Sint Maarten [A witch trial on St. Maarten]. *W I G* 10: 241-264. **[5,37]** [*COL*]
23.0170	CU	1939	Wigboldt Rasvelt en zijne gemeente op Curacao, 1730-1757 [Wigboldt Rasvelt and his congregation on Curacao]. *W I G* 21: 1-11, 33-42. **[5]** [*COL*]

Köbben, A. J. F.
14.0040   SR   1975   Opportunism in religious behaviour.

Koch, L.
23.0171   UV   1905   Den danske mission i Vestindien [The Danish mission in the West Indies]. *Kirk Saml* 5th ser., 3(1): 144-180. **[5]** [*NYP*]

Korn, Bertram W.
23.0172   JM   1966   The Haham de Cordova of Jamaica. *Am Jew Archs* 18(2), Nov.: 141-154. **[5]** [*COL*]

Krafft, A. J. C.
23.0173   CU   1948   Het Protestantisme [Protestantism]. *In* ORANJE EN DE ZES CARAÏBISCHE PARELEN. Amsterdam, J. H. de Bussy: 93-98. [*UCLA*]
23.0174   AR   1948   Het Protestantisme [Protestantism]. *In* ORANJE EN DE ZES CARAÏBISCHE PARELEN. Amsterdam, J. H. de Bussy: 409-411.
   [*UCLA*]

Kruijer, G. J.
23.0175   NA   1953   Kerk en religie op de Bovenwindse Eilanden der Nederlandse Antillen [Church and religion of the Windward Islands of the Netherlands Antilles]. *W I G* 34(4): 238-251. **[19]** [*RIS*]
56.0199   JM   1956   Met bulldozers en sociologie de bergen in [Trip into the mountains with bulldozers and sociology].

Kunike, Hugo
19.0038   GG   1912   Der Fisch als Fruchtbarkeitssymbol bei den Waldindianern Sudamerikas [The fish as a fertility symbol among the South American forest Indians].

Laing, Edward A.
23.0176   BZ   1974   Methodism in Belize. *National Stud* 2(1), January: 3-7. [*RIS*]

Lanternari, Vittorio
23.0177   JM   1971   Religious movements in Jamaica. *In* Frucht, Richard, ed. BLACK SOCIETY IN THE NEW WORLD. New York, Random House: 308-312. **[8,11]** [*COL*]

Larsen, Jens P. M.
23.0178   UV   1950   VIRGIN ISLAND STORY: A HISTORY OF THE LUTHERAN STATE CHURCH, OTHER CHURCHES, SLAVERY, EDUCATION AND CULTURE IN THE DANISH WEST INDIES, NOW THE VIRGIN ISLANDS. Philadelphia, Muhlenberg Press, 250p.

Latimer, J.
6.0173   BC   1965   The foundation of religious education in the British West Indies.

Latour, M. D.

23.0179 CU 1948 De R. K. Missie [The Roman Catholic Mission]. *In* ORANJE EN DE ZES CARAÏBISCHE PARELEN. Amsterdam, J. H. de Bussy: 99-105.
[*UCLA*]

32.0343 CU 1948 Het R. K. bijzonder onderwijs [Roman Catholic private schools].

Law, Esther K.

23.0180 BE 1969 Presbyterianism in Bermuda: Christ Church, Warwick, 1719-1969. *Bermuda Hist Q* 26(2), Summer: 43-53. **[5]** [*COL*]

Lawrence, George E.

23.0181 MS 1956 THOMAS O'GARRA: A WEST INDIAN LOCAL PREACHER. London, Epworth Press, 59p.

Leach, MacEdward

24.0107 JM 1961 Jamaican duppy lore.

Leaf, Earl

22.0222 GC 1948 ISLES OF RHYTHM.

Levy, Babette M.

23.0182 BC 1960 The West Indies and Bahamas: Puritanism in conflict with tropical island life. *In* Proceedings of the American Antiquarian Society, vol. 70. Worcester, Mass., p.278-348. **[5]** [*COL*]

Lewin, R. J. M.

5.0547 JM 1968 Notes on St. Peter's Church, Alley (1671-).

Lichtveld, Lou (Albert Helman, pseudonym)

5.0554 SR 1968 ZAKEN, ZENDING EN BEZINNING: DE ROMANTISCHE KRONIEK VAN EEN TWEEHONDERDJARIGE SURINAAMSE FIRMA [MERCHANT, MISSION AND MEDITATION: THE ROMANCE OF A TWO HUNDRED YEAR OLD SURINAMESE COMPANY].

Lier, Willem F. van & Goeje, C. H. de

23.0183 SR 1940 Aantekeningen over het geestelijk leven en de samenleving der Djoeka's in Suriname [Notes on the spiritual life and society of the Djukas in Surinam]. *Bijd Volk* 99(2): 129-294. **[14]**

Linde, J. M. van der

6.0182 SR 1953 De emancipatie der Negerslaven in Suriname en de zendingsarbeid der Moravische Broeders [The emancipation of the Negro slaves in Surinam and the missionary work of the Moravian Brethren].

5.0558 SR 1966 SURINAAMSE SUIKERHEREN EN HUN KERK: PLANTAGEKOLONIE EN HANDELSKERK TEN TIJDE VAN JOHANNES BASSELIERS, PREDIKANT EN PLANTER IN SURINAME 1667-1689 [SURINAMESE SUGAR LORDS AND THEIR CHURCH: PLANTATION COLONY AND MERCHANTS CHURCH AT THE TIME OF JOHANNES BASSELIERS, MINISTER AND PLANTER IN SURINAM 1667-1689].

Linyard, Fred

15.0058 JM 1969 The Moravians in Jamaica from the beginning to emancipation, 1754 to 1838.

Livingston, Noel B.

23.0184   JM   1946   Records of the Kingston vestry. *Jam Hist Rev* 1(2), Dec.: 181-186. **[5]** [*COL*]

Lohier, Michel

5.0562   FG   1969   Mana, début de la colonisation—ses échecs. Oeuvre éman-cipatrice de la Mère Javouhey, Supérieure de la Congré-gation des Soeurs de Saint-Joseph de Cluny [Mana. Beginning of colonisation—its failures. Emancipatory work of Mother Javouhey, Superior of the Congregation of Sisters of Saint Joseph of Cluny].

Long, Joseph K.

23.0185   JM   1972   Medical anthropology, dance, trance in Jamaica. *B Int Comm Urg Anthrop Ethnol Res* 14: 17-23. **[29]** [*COL*]

Lynden, J. W. van

23.0186   SR   1939   De Evangelische Broedergemeente in Suriname [The United Breth-ren in Surinam]. *W I G* 221: 161-172. **[5]** [*COL*]

McCallan, E. A.

23.0187   BE   1950   Association of a Bermuda Church with one in Virginia. *Bermuda Hist Q* 7(1), Jan.-March: 24-29. [*COL*]

McCormack, Ed

37.0511   JM   1976   Bob Marley with a bullet.

McCormack, Michael

23.0188   GC   1971   Liberation or development: the role of the church in the new Caribbean. Bridgetown, Barbados, Caribbean Ecumenical Consultation for Development, Study Paper no. 5: 24p.   [*RIS*]

McNeill, George

23.0189   JM   1911   The story of our missions: the West Indies. Edinburgh, Foreign Mission Committees at the Offices of the United Free Church of Scotland, 93p. **[5]** [*UTS*]

McTurk, Michael

5.0577   GU   1912   Some old graves in the Colony.

Makin, William J.

3.0378   JM   1939   Caribbean nights.

Malefijt, Annemarie de Waal

23.0190   SR   1971   Animism and Islam among the Javanese in Surinam. *In* Horowitz, Michael M., ed. Peoples and cultures of the Caribbean: an anthropological reader. New York, Natural History Press for the American Museum of Natural History: 553-559. **[15,19]** [*RIS*]

Manning, Frank E.

23.0191   BB   1975   The prophecy and the law: symbolism and social action in Seventh-Day Adventism. *In* Hill, Carole E., ed. Symbols and society: essays on belief systems in action. Athens, University of Georgia Press: 30-43. (Southern Anthropological Society Proceed-ings No. 9). **[20]** [*COL*]

Marcus, Jacob Rader
15.0063   **GC**   1953   The West India and South America expedition of the American Jewish Archives.

Marks, A. F.
23.0192   **CU**   1971   Enkele oud-curaçaose geloofsels en gebruiken rond ziekte en dood (Some old Curaçao beliefs and customs regarding illness and death). *Oost West* 64, Jan.-Feb.: 3-6.   [*NYP*]

Martin, Kingsley
23.0193   **JM**   1961   The Jamaican volcano. *New Stsm* 61(1566), Mar. 17: 416-418. **[11,16,37]**   [*RIS*]

Maslin, Simeon J.
21.0060   **GC**   1965-66 Caribbean Jewry: scandal and challenge.
15.0064   **GC**   1969   Toward the preservation of Caribbean Jewish monuments.

May, Fred
23.0194   **GU**   1918   The Lutherans of Berbice. *Timehri* 3d ser., 5(22), Aug.: 74-77.   **[5]**
                                                                              [*AMN*]

Meiden, J. A. van der
23.0195   **SR**   1960   Kerken, tempels en heiligdommen in Suriname [Churches, temples and sacred places in Surinam]. *Schakels* S-38: 17-22.   **[19]**

Menkman, W. R.
23.0196   **SM,SB**   1958   St. Maarten en St. Barthélemy, 1911-1951. *W I G* 38: 151-162.   **[5]**
                                                                              [*COL*]

Merrill, Gordon Clark
15.0065   **GC**   1964   The role of Sephardic Jews in the British Caribbean area during the seventeenth century.

Mességué, Maurice & Gayot, André
23.0197   **GC**   1968   Ce soir, le diable viendra te prendre: la sorcellerie aux Antilles [Tonight, the devil will get you: sorcery in the Antilles]. Paris, Robert Laffont: 291p.   [*RIS*]

Metraux, A.
23.0198   **FG**   1928   La Religion des Tupinamba et ses rapports avec celle des autres tribus Tupi-Guarani [The religion of the Tupinamba and its relationship to that of the other Tupi-Guarani tribes]. Paris, Librairie Ernest Leroux, 260p.   **[13]**   [*COL*]

Meyer, A.
31.0103   **MT,CU**   1968   Superstition and magic in the Caribbean—some psychiatric consequences.

Meyer, J.
7.0125   **SR**   1954   Pioneers of Pauroma, contribution to the earliest history of the Jewish colonization of America.

Mintz, Sidney W.

8.0157   **JM**   1958   Historical sociology of the Jamaican church-founded free village system.

Mischel, Frances

23.0199   **TR**   1957   African "powers" in Trinidad: the Shango cult. *Anthrop Q* 30(2), Apr.: 45-59. **[11,19]**   [*RIS*]

Mischel, Walter & Mischel, Frances

31.0107   **TR**   1958   Psychological aspects of spirit possession.

Mitchell, David I.

23.0200   **BC**   1964   PRINCIPLES AND POLICIES FOR A PROGRAM OF LEADERSHIP EDUCA-TION FOR THE SUNDAY CHURCH SCHOOLS OF THE METHODIST CHURCH IN THE ENGLISH-SPEAKING CARIBBEAN. Ph.D. dissertation, Columbia University. **[32]**   [*PhD*]

23.0201   **BC**   1968   The challenge of development in the Eastern Caribbean. *In* REPORT OF CONSULTATION ON SOCIAL AND ECONOMIC DEVELOPMENT IN THE EASTERN CARIBBEAN HELD IN ST. VINCENT NOV. 26-30, 1968. Port-of-Spain, Trinidad, Superservice Printing Co.: 12-16. **[41]**
                                                                                   [*RIS*]

Moore, Joseph Graessle

23.0202   **JM**   1953   RELIGION OF JAMAICAN NEGROES: A STUDY OF AFRO-JAMAICAN ACCULTURATION. Ph.D. dissertation, Northwestern University, 284p. **[11,19]**

23.0203   **JM**   1965   Religious syncretism in Jamaica. *Prac Anthrop* 12(2), March-April: 63-70.   [*AMN*]

Moore, Joseph Graessle & Simpson, George E.

23.0204   **JM**   1957   A comparative study of acculturation in Morant Bay and West Kingston, Jamaica. *Zaire* 9-10: 979-1019. **[19]**   [*RIS*]

23.0205   **JM**   1958   A comparative study of acculturation in Morant Bay and West Kingston, Jamaica. *Zaire* 11: 65-87. **[19]**   [*RIS*]

Moore, Robert J.

6.0211   **GC**   1972   An historical appraisal of the role of the churches in the Caribbean.

Morsink, F.

14.0050   **SR**   1934-35 Nogmaals: de dood van Jankosoe. En: nog niet het einde van een dynastie [Once again: the death of Jankosoe. And: not yet the end of a dynasty].

Mothon, R. P.

23.0206   **TR**   1903   La Trinidad. *In* Piolet, J.-B., ed. LA FRANCE AU DEHORS: LES MISSIONS CATHOLIQUES FRANCAISES AU XIXᴱ SIÈCLE. Vol. 6: MISSIONS D'AMÉRIQUE. Paris, Librairie Armand Colin, p.353-382. **[5]** [*NYP*]

Muller, Karl

23.0207   **GC**   1931   Westindien. Suriname [West Indies. Surinam]. *In his* 200 JAHRE BRÜDERMISSION. Herrnhut [Ger.], Missionsbuchhandlung, p.19-109. **[5]**   [*NYP*]

Murphy, Patricia Shaubah

6.0218   UV   1969   THE MORAVIAN MISSION TO THE AFRICAN SLAVES OF THE DANISH
                              WEST INDIES, 1732-1828.

Neehall, Roy

23.0208   GC   1972   The call is proclaimed; justice, liberation and the Christian Gospel.
                             In CALLED TO BE. REPORT OF THE CARIBBEAN ECUMENICAL CON-
                             SULTATION FOR DEVELOPMENT, CHAGUARAMAS, TRINIDAD, NOVEM-
                             BER 1971. Bridgetown, Barbados, CADEC: 20-22.   [*RIS*]

Nelson, Vernon H.

23.0209   AT   1966   Samuel Isles, first Moravian missionary on Antigua. *Morav Hist Soc
                             Trans* 21(1): 3-27.   **[5]**   [*COL*]

Nettleford, Rex

22.0269   JM   1969   Pocomania in dance-theatre.

Niehoff, Arthur

23.0210   TR   1959   The spirit world of Trinidad. *Shell Trin* 5(7), June: 17-19.

Nimar, Nicole

44.0050   MT,GD   1971   PROPRIÉTÉ ET EXPLOITATION DE LA TERRE EN MARTINIQUE ET EN
                             GUADELOUPE [OWNERSHIP AND EXPLOITATION OF LAND IN
                             MARTINIQUE AND GUADELOUPE].

Noussanne, Henri de

23.0211   FA,TR   1936   LA FRANCE MISSIONNAIRE AUX ANTILLES: GUADELOUPE, MARTIN-
                             IQUE, TRINIDAD [FRENCH MISSIONARIES IN THE WEST INDIES:
                             GUADELOUPE, MARTINIQUE, TRINIDAD]. Paris, P. Lethielleux,
                             173p.   **[5]**   [*NYP*]

Nowicka, Ewa

23.0212   JM   1974   The Ras Tafari movement—its genesis and functions. *Estud
                             Latamer* 2: 61-90.   **[11,16,37]**   [*RIS*]

O'Gorman, Pamela

22.0278   JM   1975   The introduction of Jamaican music into the established churches.

Oliver, Vere Langford

23.0213   BB   1915   THE MONUMENTAL INSCRIPTIONS IN THE CHURCHES AND CHURCH-
                             YARDS OF THE ISLAND OF BARBADOS, BRITISH WEST INDIES. London,
                             Mitchell Hughes and Clarke, 223p.   **[5]**   [*NYP*]

Oppenheim, Samuel

15.0071   GG,TB   1907   An early Jewish colony in Western Guiana 1658-1666: and its
                             relation to the Jews in Surinam, Cayenne and Tobago.

15.0072   GU   1908   An early Jewish colony in Western Guiana: supplemental data.

Otterbein, Keith F.

23.0214   BA   1965   Conflict and communication: the social matrix of obeah. *Kansas J
                             Sociol* 1(3), Summer: 112-118.   [*COL*]

Oudschans Dentz, Fred

28.0955   **SR**   1930-31   Dr. Constantin Hering en Christiaan Johannes Hering.

23.0215   **SR**   1948   Wat er overbleef van het kerkhof en de synagoge van de Joden-Savanne in Suriname [What is left of the cemetery and the synagogue of the Jewish-Savannah in Surinam]? *W I G* 29: 210-224. **[3,7,15]**   *[COL]*

23.0216   **SR**   1949   De Hervormde Kerk in Suriname in Haar begintijd [The Dutch Reformed Church in Surinam in her early years]. *W I G* 30: 353-361. **[5]**   *[COL]*

Owens, J. V.

23.0217   **JM**   1975   Literature on the Rastafari: 1955-1974. *Savacou* 11-12, Sept.: 86-105. **[1,11,21]**   *[RIS]*

Panhuys, L. C. van

23.0218   **SR**   1913   The heathen religion of the Bush Negroes in Dutch Guiana. *In* Actes du IVᴱ Congrès international d'histoire des religions, Leide, Sept. 1912. Leiden, E. J. Brill, p.53-57. **[14]**   *[NYP]*

23.0219   **SR**   1936-37   De opoffering van een R.K. priester in Suriname [The sacrifice of a Roman Catholic priest in Surinam]. *W I G* 18: 200-206. **[28]**   *[COL]*

Payne, Ernest A.

23.0220   **JM**   1946   Freedom in Jamaica; some chapters in the story of the Baptist Missionary Society. 2d ed. London, Carey Press, 112p. **[5,6]**   *[UTS]*

Pelleprat, P. Pierre

23.0221   **GC**   1965   Relato de las misiones de los Padres de la Compañía de Jesus en las islas y en tierra firme de América Meridional [Tale of the missions of the Fathers of the Company of Jesus in the islands and in Middle America]. Caracas, Venezuela, Academia Nacional de la Historia: 110p. (Originally published in 1660) **[5]**   *[NYP]*

Penard, A. P.

23.0222   **SR**   1928   Het pujai-geheim der Surinaamsche Caraiben [The pujai-secret of the Caribs of Surinam]. *Bijd Volk Ned-Indie* 84: 625-671. **[13]**

Penard, F. P. & Penard, A. P.

23.0223   **SR**   1913   Surinaamsch bijgeloof: iets over *winti* en andere natuurbegrippen [Surinam superstition: about *winti* and other supernatural notions]. *Bijd Volk Ned-Indie* 67: 157-183. **[19]**

Pendergast, David M.

19.0051   **BZ**   1972   The practice of *primicias* in San José Succotz, British Honduras (Belize).

Perowne, Stewart

23.0224   **BB**   1952   Monuments in Barbados. *Country Life* 110(2864), Dec. 7: 1939-1942.

Peters, Fred E.

35.0061   **MS**   1931   SAINT ANTHONY'S CHURCH, MONTSERRAT, WEST INDIES.

Petitjean-Roget, Jacques

23.0225   **MT**   1956   Les protestants à la Martinique sous l'ancien régime [The Protestants in Martinique under the old regime]. *Rev Hist Colon* 40(3): 220-265. **[5]**   [*RIS*]

Phillips, Anthony de V.

6.0231   **GC**   1972[?]   Reactions [to Robt. J. Moore: An historical appraisal of the role of the churches in the Caribbean].

Phillips, Leslie H. C.

23.0226   **GU**   1960   Kali-mai puja. *Timehri* 4th ser., no. 39, Sept.: 37-46. **[12,19]**
          [*AMN*]

Pierson, Roscoe M.

23.0227   **JM**   1969   Alexander Bedward and the Jamaica Native Baptist Free Church. *Lex Theol Q* 4, July: 65-76. **[5]**   [*UTS*]

Pierson, Roscoe M., comp.

1.0225   **BC**   1968   WEST INDIAN CHURCH HISTORY: A FINDING LIST OF PRINTED MATERIALS RELATING TO THE HISTORY OF THE CHURCH IN THE ENGLISH-SPEAKING CARIBBEAN AREA.

Pilkington, Frederick

23.0228   **JM**   1950   DAYBREAK IN JAMAICA. London, Epworth Press, 220p. **[3]**   [*SCH*]

Pinnington, John

6.0232   **JM**   1968   The Anglican struggle for survival in Jamaica in the period of abolition and emancipation, 1825-50.

23.0229   **GU**   1968   Factors in the development of the Catholic movement in the Anglican church in British Guiana. *Hist Mag Prot Epsc Ch* 37(4), Dec.: 355-369.   [*COL*]

23.0230   **UV**   1968   A note on Anglicanism in the Danish West Indies and the ecclesiological problems posed by it. *Hist Mag Prot Epsc Ch* 37(1), March: 67-72. **[5]**   [*COL*]

5.0736   **TR**   1970   Anglican problems of adaptation in the Catholic Caribbean—the C. M. S. in Trinidad, 1836-1844.

Pitman, Frank Wesley

6.0233   **BC**   1926   Slavery on the British West India plantation in the eighteenth century.

Pollak-Eltz, Angelina

23.0231   **GC**   1970   AFRO-AMERIKAANSE GODSDIENSTEN EN CULTEN [AFRO-AMERICAN RELIGIONS AND CULTS]. Roermond, The Netherlands, J. J. Romen & Zonen: 221p. **[11,14,19]**   [*RIS*]

23.0232   **TR,GR**   1970   Shango-Kult und Shouter-Kirche auf Trinidad und Grenada. [Shango-cult and Shouter-church on Trinidad and Grenada]. *Anthropos* 65: 814-832. **[19]**   [*COL*]

23.0233   **GR,TR**   1971   The Yoruba religion and its decline in the Americas. *In* VERHANDLUNGEN DES XXXVIII. INTERNATIONALEN AMERIKANISTENKONGRESSES, SPUTTGART-MÜNCHEN, 12. BIS 18. AUGUST 1968. Munich, Kommissionsverlag Klaus Renner, Vol. 3: 423-427. **[19]**   [*COL*]

23.0234   **GC**   1972   CULTOS AFROAMERICANOS [AFRO-AMERICAN CULTS]. Caracas, Universidad Católica "Andrés Bello", Instituto de Investigaciones Históricas: 258p. **[11,14,19]**   [*RIS*]

23.0235   **GC**   1974   EL CONCEPTO DE MÚLTIPLES ALMAS Y ALGUNOS RITOS FÚNEBRES ENTRE LOS NEGROS AMERICANOS [THE CONCEPT OF MULTIPLE SOULS AND SOME FUNERAL RITES OF NEGROES IN THE AMERICAS]. Caracas, Universidad Católica "Andrés Bello", Instituto de Investigaciones Históricas: 52p. **[11,14,19]**   [*RIS*]

Price, Ernest
23.0236   **JM**   1930[?]   BANANALAND: PAGES FROM THE CHRONICLES OF AN ENGLISH MINISTER IN JAMAICA. London, Carey Press: 186p. **[3]**   [*NYP*]

Price, Richard
52.0096   **MT**   1964   Magie et pêche à la Martinique [Magic and fishing in Martinique].
23.0237   **MT**   1966   Fishing rites and recipes in a Martiniquan village. *Car Stud* 6(1), April: 3-24. **[11,52]**   [*RIS*]

Prince, Raymond
23.0238   **JM**   1969   The Ras Tafari of Jamaica: a study of group beliefs and social stress. *In* PAPERS OF THE FIRST CARIBBEAN PSYCHIATRIC ASSOCIATION MEETING, OCHO RIOS, JAMAICA: 10P. **[11,31]**   [*RIS*]

Prins, J.
23.0239   **BB**   1961-62   De Islam in Suriname: een Oriëntatie [Islam in Surinam: an orientation]. *N W I G* 41(1): 14-37. **[12,15]**   [*COL*]
9.0118   **SR**   1963   Een Surinaams rechtsgeding over een Moslimse verstoting [A Surinam lawsuit about a Moslem divorce].

Quandt, Ch.
5.0747   **SR**   1968   NACHRICHT VON SURINAME UND SEINEN EINWOHNERN, SONDERLICH DEN ARAWACKEN, WARAUEN UND KARAIBEN [AN ACCOUNT OF SURINAM AND ITS INHABITANTS, PARTICULARLY THE ARAWAKS, WARAO AND CARIBS].

Raalte, J. van
23.0240   **SR**   1973   SECULARISATIE EN ZENDING IN SURINAME [SECULARIZATION AND MISSION IN SURINAM]. Wageningen, the Netherlands, H. Veenman & Zonen B.V.: 276p. **[2]**   [*RILA*]

Ramchand, Kenneth
22.0302   **JM**   1969   Obeah and the supernatural in West Indian literature.

Ramos, Carlos G.
34.0073   **CU**   1975   The Catholic church and birth control: Curaçao and Puerto Rico.

Ramrekersingh, Augustus
6.0242   **GC**   1968   Christianity and slavery, yesterday and today.

Ras Dizzy
11.0076   **JM**   1967   Notes and commentary. II. The Rastas Speak.
23.0241   **JM**   1970   RUN WIDE RUN DEEP. Jamaica: 34p.   [*RIS*]

Rauschert, Manfred

23.0242   GC   1967   Materialien zur geistigen Kultur der ostkaraibischen Indianerstämme [Materials concerning spiritual culture of Eastern Caribbean Indian tribes]. *Anthropos* 62(1-2): 165-206. **[13]**   [*COL*]

Ray, Michael

9.0121   GU   1935   Bamboo marriage.

Reece, J. E. & Clark-Hunt, C. G., eds.

23.0243   BB   1925   BARBADOS DIOCESAN HISTORY. London, West India Committee, 136p. **[5]**

Reid, G. B.

23.0244   TR   1969   Social action and the church in Trinidad and Tobago. *In* CARIBBEAN DEVELOPMENT AND THE FUTURE OF THE CHURCH: PROCEEDINGS OF A CONFERENCE HELD IN GEORGETOWN, JAN. 6-8. Georgetown, Guyana, Guyana Institute for Social Research and Action. **[33]**
[*SCH*]

Rennard, J.

23.0245   FA   1935   Organisation des paroisses [The parish organization]. *In* Denis, Serge, ed. NOS ANTILLES. Orleans, Luzeray, 131-159. **[5]**   [*AGS*]

23.0246   MT   1951   LA MARTINIQUE HISTORIQUE DES PAROISSES: DES ORIGINES À LA SEPARATION [PARISH HISTORY OF MARTINIQUE: FROM CONTACT TO SEPARATION]. Thonon-les-Bains (Haute-Savoie), Société d'édition savoyarde, 349p. **[5]**   [*RIS*]

Revert, Eugene

24.0141   MT   1951   DE QUELQUES ASPECTS DU FOLK-LORE MARTINIQUAIS: LE MAGIE ANTILLAISE [ON SOME ASPECTS OF MARTINIQUE FOLKLORE: ANTILLEAN MAGIC].

Rijnders, B. J. C.

23.0247   SR   1947   Het werk van de Evangelische Broedergemeente in Suriname [The work of the United Brethren in Surinam]. *W I G* 28: 300-311.
[*COL*]

Rivière, P. G.

13.0171   SR   1970   Factions and exclusions in two South American village systems.

13.0172   SR   1971   The political structure of the Trio Indians as manifested in a system of ceremonial dialogue.

Roback, Judith

23.0248   GU   1973   THE WHITE-ROBED ARMY: CULTURAL NATIONALISM AND A RELIGIOUS MOVEMENT IN GUYANA. Ph.D. dissertation, McGill University. **[21]**   [*PhD*]

Rogers, Claudia

23.0249   JM   1975   What's a Rasta? *Car R* 7(1), Jan.-Feb.-March: 9-12. **[11,21]**   [*RIS*]

Roopchand, T.

23.0250   GU   1976   The Hindu temple service: a functionalist approach. *Guy J Sociol* 1(2), April: 93-122. **[8,12]**   [*RIS*]

Roos, J. S.
15.0079   **SR**   1905   Additional notes on the history of the Jews in Surinam.

Roth, Henry D.
23.0251   **GU**   1950   The kanaima. *Timehri* 4th ser., 1(29), Aug.: 25-26.   **[13]**

Roth, Walter Edmund
23.0252   **GU**   1970   AN INQUIRY INTO THE ANIMISM AND FOLK-LORE OF THE GUIANA INDIANS. New York, Johnson Reprint Corporation: 453p. (Originally published in 1915).   **[13,24]**   [*RIS*]

Russell, H. O.
23.0253   **BC**   1972   THE MISSIONARY OUTREACH OF THE WEST INDIAN CHURCHES TO WEST AFRICA IN THE NINETEENTH CENTURY, WITH PARTICULAR REFERENCE TO THE BAPTISTS. D.Phil. dissertation, University of Oxford: 517p.

Rycroft, W. Stanley
23.0254   **GC**   1955   The contribution of Protestantism in the Caribbean. *In* Wilgus, A. Curtis, ed. THE CARIBBEAN: ITS CULTURE [papers delivered at the Fifth Conference on the Caribbean held at the University of Florida, Dec. 2-4, 1954]. Gainesville, University of Florida Press, 158-168. (Publications of the School of Inter-American Studies, ser. 1, v. 5.)   [*RIS*]

Samaroo, Brinsley
23.0255   **BC**   1975   Missionary methods and local responses: the Canadian Presbyterians and the East Indians in the Caribbean. *In* EAST INDIANS IN THE CARIBBEAN: A SYMPOSIUM ON CONTEMPORARY ECONOMIC AND POLITICAL ISSUES, JUNE 25-28, 1975. St. Augustine, Trinidad, University of the West Indies, Faculty of Social Sciences and Institute of African and Asian Studies: 41p.   **[12]**   [*RIS*]

Samson, Ph. A.
7.0183   **SR**   1939   Uit het verleden van Suriname [From Surinam's past].
23.0256   **SR**   1940   De oplossing van het eedsvraagstuk in Suriname [The solution of the problem of oath-taking in Surinam]. *W I G* 22: 284-286.   **[37]**
      [*COL*]
23.0257   **SR**   1946   Afgoderij als strafbaar feit [Idolatry as a penal offense]. *W I G* 27: 378-381.   **[37]**   [*COL*]
23.0258   **SR**   1946   Bijgeloof in de rechtszaal [Superstition in the courtroom]. *W I G* 27: 141-146.   [*COL*]

Samuel, Wilfred S.
15.0080   **BB**   1936   A REVIEW OF THE JEWISH COLONISTS IN BARBADOS IN THE YEAR 1680.

Sawatzky, Harry Leonard
17.0091   **BZ**   1969   MENNONITE SETTLEMENT IN BRITISH HONDURAS.
17.0092   **BZ**   1971   Mennonite colonization in British Honduras.

Schlesinger, Benjamin
15.0081   **JM**   1967   The Jews of Jamaica: a historical view.

Schoelcher, Victor
6.0258   **GD**   1935   LETTRES INÉDITES À VICTOR SCHOELCHER (1848-1851) [UNPUB-
                                LISHED LETTERS TO VICTOR SCHOELCHER (1848-1851)].

Schulze, Adolf
23.0259   **GC**   1931-32 200 JAHRE BRÜDERMISSION [200 YEARS OF THE BROTHERS' MISSIONS].
                                Herrnhut, [Ger.], Verlag der Missionsbuchhandlung, 2v.   **[5]**
                                                                                        [*COL*]

Schutz, H.
23.0260   **SR**   1934-35 Herrnhutter nederzetting leiding 7B [The Moravian settlement Line
                                7B]. *W I G* 16: 273-281.   **[5]**   [*COL*]
23.0261   **SR**   1935-36 Sporen van tweehonderd jaar Herrnhutterzending [Traces of two
                                hundred years of Moravian missionary work]. *W I G* 17: 221-
                                227.   **[5]**   [*COL*]

Schutz, John A.
23.0262   **BB**   1946   Christopher Codrington's will: launching the S.P.G. into the
                                Barbadian sugar business. *Pacif Hist Rev* 15(2), June: 192-
                                200.   **[5,42]**   [*COL*]

Schutz, John A. & O'Neil, Maud E., eds.
23.0263   **BB**   1946   Arthur Holt, Anglican clergyman, reports on Barbados, 1725-1733.
                                J Negro Hist 31(4), Oct: 444-469.   **[5,11]**   [*COL*]

Schwartz, Barton M.
23.0264   **TR**   1964   Ritual aspects of caste in Trinidad. *Anthrop Q* 37(1), Jan.: 1-
                                15.   **[8,12,19]**   [*RIS*]
12.0081   **TR**   1967   Differential socio-religious adaptation.

Seaga, Edward
23.0265   **JM**   1969   Revival cults in Jamaica: notes towards a sociology of religion. *Jam
                                J* 3(2), June: 3-13.   [*RIS*]

Sereno, Renzo
23.0266   **GC**   1948   Obeah: magic and social structure in the Lesser Antilles. *Psychiatry*
                                11(1), Feb.: 15-31.   **[8,28,31]**   [*COL*]

Shilstone, E. M.
23.0267   **BB**   1936   Parish churches in Barbados. *J Barb Mus Hist Soc* 4(1), Nov.:
                                5-8.   **[5]**   [*AMN*]
23.0268   **BB**   1958   MONUMENTAL INSCRIPTIONS IN THE BURIAL GROUND OF THE JEWISH
                                SYNAGOGUE AT BRIDGETOWN, BARBADOS. London, Jewish Historical
                                Society of England, University College, London.   **[5,15]**   [*COL*]
15.0084   **BB**   1971   Some early records of the Friends in Barbados.

Shorrocks, Francis
23.0269   **BB**   1958   History of the Catholic Church in Barbados during the 19th
                                century. *J Barb Mus Hist Soc* 25(3), May: 102-122.   **[5]**   [*AMN*]

Sibley, Inez K.
23.0270   **JM**   1965   THE BAPTISTS OF JAMAICA. Kingston, Jamaica, The Jamaica Baptist
                                Union: 91p.   **[5]**   [*RIS*]

Simpson, George Eaton

23.0271	JM	1950	The acculturative process in Jamaican revivalism. *In* Wallace, Anthony F. C., ed. MEN AND CULTURES: SELECTED PAPERS OF THE FIFTH INTERNATIONAL CONGRESS OF ANTHROPOLOGICAL AND ETHNOLOGICAL SCIENCES, Philadelphia, Sept. 1-9, 1956. Philadelphia, University of Pennsylvania Press, p.332-341. **[19]** [*RIS*]
23.0272	JM	1955	Culture change and reintegration found in the cults of West Kingston, Jamaica. *Proc Am Phil Soc* 99(2), Apr. 15: 89-92. **[11,16,19,37]** [*RIS*]
23.0273	JM	1955	Political cultism in West Kingston, Jamaica. *Social Econ Stud* 4(2), June: 133-149. **[11,16,37]** [*RIS*]
23.0274	JM	1955	The Ras Tafari movement in Jamaica: a study of race and class conflict. *Social Forces* 34(2), Dec.: 167-170. **[11,16,37]** [*RIS*]
23.0275	JM	1956	Jamaican revivalist cults. *Social Econ Stud* 5(4), Dec.: iv, 442, v-xi p. **[19]** [*RIS*]
23.0276	JM	1957	The nine night ceremony in Jamaica. *J Am Folk* 70(278), Oct.-Dec.: 329-335. **[19]** [*RIS*]
23.0277	JM	1962	The Ras Tafari movement in Jamaica in its millennial aspect. *In* Thrupp, Sylvia L., ed. MILLENNIAL DREAMS IN ACTION: ESSAYS IN COMPARATIVE STUDY. The Hague, Mouton, p.160-165. (Comparative studies in society and history, Supplement 2.) **[11,16,37]** [*RIS*]
23.0278	TR	1962	The shango cult in Nigeria and in Trinidad. *Am Anthrop* 64(6), Dec.: 1204-1219. **[11,19]** [*RIS*]
23.0279	TR	1964	The acculturative process in Trinidadian Shango. *Anthrop Q* 37(1), Jan.: 16-27. **[11,19]** [*RIS*]
23.0280	TR	1965	THE SHANGO CULT IN TRINIDAD. Rio Piedras, University of Puerto Rico, 140p. (Institute of Caribbean Studies, Caribbean monograph series no. 2.) **[11,19]** [*RIS*]
23.0281	TR	1966	Baptismal, "mourning", and "building" ceremonies of the Shouters in Trinidad. *J Am Fold* 79(314), Oct.-Dec.: 537-550. [*RIS*]
8.0203	GC	1970	CARIBBEAN PAPERS.
23.0282	TR,JM	1970	RELIGIOUS CULTS OF THE CARIBBEAN: TRINIDAD, JAMAICA AND HAITI. Rio Piedras, Puerto Rico, Institute of Caribbean Studies, University of Puerto Rico: 308p. **[11,19]** [*RIS*]
23.0283	GC	1972	Afro-American religions and religious behavior. *Car Stud* 12(2), July: 5-30. **[8,11]** [*RIS*]

Sloman, E.

35.0074	GU	1912	St. George's Cathedral.

Smailus, Ortwin

24.0152	BZ	1975	The spirits of the mountain (aluxoob) in Maya mythology.

Smart, Lawrence H.

35.0075	BE	1954	Structural problems.

Smith, G. W.

23.0284	GC	1939[?]	CONQUESTS OF CHRIST IN THE WEST INDIES: A SHORT HISTORY OF EVANGELICAL MISSIONS. Brown's Town, St. Ann, Jamaica, Evangelical Book-Room, 125p. **[5]** [*UTS*]

Smith, M. G.

23.0285   GR   1963   DARK PURITAN. Kingston, Dept. of Extra-mural Studies, University
of the West Indies, 139p. **[11]**   [*RIS*]

Smith, M. G.; Augier, F. R. & Nettleford, Rex

23.0286   JM   1960   THE RAS TAFARI MOVEMENT IN KINGSTON, JAMAICA. Kingston,
University of the West Indies, 54p. **[11,16,33,37]**   [*RIS*]

Smith, Peter J. C.

23.0287   BE   1969   Presbyterianism in Bermuda: early religious history. *Bermuda Hist
Q* 26(2), Summer: 36-42. **[5]**   [*COL*]

Smith, Raymond Thomas

12.0092   GU   1959   Some social characteristics of Indian immigrants to British Guiana.

Smith, Raymond Thomas & Jayawardena, C.

9.0163   GU   1958   Hindu marriage customs in British Guiana.

Smith, Robert Jack

12.0094   TR   1963   MUSLIM EAST INDIANS IN TRINIDAD: RETENTION OF ETHNIC IDENTITY
UNDER ACCULTURATIVE CONDITIONS.

Smith, Robert Worthington

23.0288   BC   1950   Slavery and Christianity in the British West Indies. *Church Hist*
19(3), Sept.: 171-186.   [*COL*]

Smits, Guibert

23.0289   SR   1970   Godsdiensten in Suriname [Religions in Suriname]. *In* Janssen,
Cornelius, ed. SURINAME: HET WERK VAN DE FRATERS VAN TILBURG
ONDER DE VIJFSTERRENVLAG. Tilburg, The Netherlands, Fraters van
O. L. Vrouw, Moeder van Barmhartigheid: 12-16. (Intercom-
Fraters No. 7)   [*RILA*]

Springer, James L.

23.0290   GC   1972[?] The future role of the churches. *In* Haynes, Lilith M., ed. FAMBLI:
THE CHURCH'S RESPONSIBILITY TO THE FAMILY IN THE CARIBBEAN.
Trinidad, CARIPLAN: 211-215. **[9]**   [*RIS*]

9.0172   GC   1972[?] The relevance of existing sociological research and findings to the
life and ministry of the churches in the Caribbean.

Staehelin, F.

23.0291   SR,GU   1912[?] Die Mission der Brüdergemeine in Suriname und Berbice im
achtzehnten Jahrundert [The Moravian Brethren mission in
Surinam and Berbice in the 18th century]. Paramaribo, Verlag von
C. Kersten & Co. in Kommission bei der Missionsbuchlandlung in
Herrnhut und für den Buchhandel bei der Unitätsbuchhandlung in
Gnadau, 7 pts. in 3v. **[5,13,14]**   [*SCH*]

Steele, Beverly

12.0099   GR   1976   East Indian indenture and the work of the Presbyterian Church
among the Indians in Grenada.

Steger, Hanns-Albert
23.0292   GC   1970   Revolutionäre Hintergründe des kreolischen Synkretismus [Revolutionary background of Creole syncretism]. *Int Jb Religsoziol* 6: 99-141. **[11,21]**   [*COL*]

Stewart, John
26.0008   GC   1974   Where goes the indigenous black church?

Stewart, T. D. & Groome, John R.
27.0139   GR   1968   The African custom of tooth mutilation in America.

Stow, John
23.0293   BE   1954   A catalog of the treasures. *Bermuda Hist Q* 11(1), Spring: 19-24. **[22]**   [*COL*]
23.0294   BE   1954   Great days. *Bermuda Hist Q* 11(1), Spring: 44-49. **[5]**   [*COL*]
23.0295   BE   1954   Some former ministers. *Bermuda Hist Q* 11(1), Spring: 51-62. **[5]**   [*COL*]
23.0296   BE   1954   The spirit of the founders; the first few years; the growth of the building. *Bermuda Hist Q* 11(1), Spring: 2-16. **[5,35]**   [*COL*]
23.0297   BE   1954   The wall tablets. *Bermuda Hist Q* 11(1), Spring: 28-40. **[5]**   [*COL*]
23.0298   BE   1969   Bermuda's Bishops. *Bermuda Hist Q* 26(4), Winter: 111-114. **[5]**   [*COL*]

Stycos, J. Mayone & Back, Kurt
34.0114   JM   1958   Contraception and Catholicism in Jamaica.

Sukul, J. P. Kaulesar
23.0299   SR   1974   ENKELE BESCHOUWINGEN OVER HET HOLIFEEST [SOME REMARKS ABOUT THE HOLI HOLIDAY]. Utrecht, The Netherlands, Shri Sanatan Dharm Nederland: 19p. **[12]**   [*RILA*]

Summit, Alphons
15.0086   SR   1940   The Jews of Surinam.

Swellengrebel, N. H. & Kuyp, E. van der
28.1256   SR   1940   HEALTH OF WHITE SETTLERS IN SURINAM.

Talbot, Frederick; Mc Neil, Jesse Jai & Talbot, Sylvia
34.0116   BC   1967   THE WANTED CHILD. REPORT OF 1967 FAMILY PLANNING SURVEY OF FIVE ISLANDS IN THE CARIBBEAN.

Tannenbaum, Frank
6.0280   ⤴ GC   1947   SLAVE AND CITIZEN: THE NEGRO IN THE AMERICAS.

Taylor, Douglas
23.0300   DM   1945   Carib folk beliefs and customs from Dominica, B.W.I. *Sw J Anthrop* 1(4), Winter: 507-530. **[13,24,29]**

Thoden van Velzen, H. U. E.
23.0301   SR   1966   Het geloof in wraakgeesten: bindmiddel en splijtzwam van de Djuka matri-lineage [The belief in vengeance spirits: integrative and disruptive force in the Djuka matrilineage]. *N W I G* 45(1), Oct.: 45-51. **[9,14]**   [*RIS*]
14.0071   SR   1966   POLITIEKE BEHEERSING IN DE DJUKA MAATSCHAPPIJ: EEN STUDIE VAN EEN ONVOLLEDIG MACHTSOVERZICHT [POLITICAL CONTROL IN THE DJUKA SOCIETY: STUDY OF AN INCOMPLETE SPHERE OF INFLUENCE].

Thomas, Michael

37.0846   **JM**   1976   Jamaica at war: the Rastas are coming!

Thompson, E. W.

23.0302   **BC**   1940   The return of the West Indies. *Int Rev Missions* 29(116), Oct.: 452-462. **[33]**   [*NYP*]

23.0303   **GC**   1943   Eyes on the West Indies. *Int Rev Missions* 32(127), July: 293-300. **[33]**   [*NYP*]

Tucker, Arthur Tudor

23.0304   **BE**   1955   Parson Richardson, 1755-1805, Rector of the Parish of St. George, Bermuda: "His Life and Times". *Bermuda Hist Q* 12(2), Summer: 64-74. **[5]**   [*COL*]

Tucker, Leonard, comp.

23.0305   **JM**   1914   "Glorious liberty": the story of a hundred years' work of the Jamaica Baptist Mission. London, Baptist Missionary Society, 168p. **[5]**   [*UTS*]

Tucker, Terry

23.0306   **BE**   1964   Witchcraft in the Somers Isles. *Bermuda Hist Q* 21(3), Autumn: 67-70. **[5]**   [*COL*]

23.0307   **BE**   1974   St. Anne's Church. *Bermuda Hist Q* 31(2), Summer: 44-46. **[35]**
[*COL*]

Tuyl, Ethelbert van

32.0575   **SR**   1970   Taman Putro: hoe ons Javaans Internaat onstond en tot bloei kwam [Taman Putro: how our Javanese Boarding school came into existence and prospered].

Underhill, Edward Bean

5.0923   **GC**   1970   The West Indies: their social and religious condition.

Vandercook, John Womack

23.0308   **SR**   1925   White magic and black, the jungle science of Dutch Guiana. *Harper's Mag* 151, Oct.: 548-554. **[29]**   [*COL*]

29.0048   **SR**   1927   Magic is the jungle science: the black tribes of Guiana do not believe in death.

Vassady, Bela, Jr.

23.0309   **BC**   1972   The role of the black West Indian missionary in West Africa, 1840-1890. Ph.D. dissertation, Temple University: 372p.   [*PhD*]

Vaughan, B. N. Y.

32.0578   **JM**   1966   Ecumenical conference on education.

Vaughan, David

5.0925   **JM,UK**   1950   Negro victory: the life story of Dr. Harold Moody.

Veer, Johan J. van der

23.0310   **SR**   1968   De daad bij het woord: zendingswerk in Suriname [Suiting the act to the word: missionary work in Surinam]. Baarn, The Netherlands, Bosch & Keuning N.V.: 63p. **[14,33]**   [*NYP*]

Veerasawmy, J. A.
37.0859   GU   1919   The Noitgedacht murder.

Vérin, Pierre
23.0311   SL   1965   Les croyances populaires de Sainte-Lucie (Antilles) [Popular beliefs in St. Lucia]. *Ann Fac Lett Sci Hum Mad* 4: 87-112. **[24]**   *[RIS]*

Vismans, R.
33.0201   AR   1970   Pastoral care and alcoholism in Aruba.

Voorhoeve, Jan
25.0385   SR   1957   Missionary linguistics in Surinam.

Voorhoeve, Jan & Renselaar, H. C. van
23.0312   SR   1962   Messianism and nationalism in Surinam. *Bijd Volk* 118: 193-216. **[21]**

Voullaire, R.
23.0313   SR   1907   A journey among the bush men of Surinam. *Miss Rev Wld* new ser., 20(11), Nov.: 815-819. **[14]**   *[NYP]*

Voullaire, W. R.
23.0314   SR   1926   SURINAM: LE PAYS, LES HABITANTS ET LA MISSION MORAVE [SURINAM: THE LAND, THE INHABITANTS, AND THE MORAVIAN MISSION]. Lausanne, Impr. La Concorde, 94p. **[5]**   *[AGS]*

Vuijsje, H.
23.0315   SR   1974   ONTWIKKELINGSFUNKTIES VAN RELIGIEUZE ORGANISATIES IN SURI-NAME [DEVELOPMENT FUNCTIONS OF RELIGIOUS ORGANIZATIONS IN SURINAM]. Amsterdam, Universiteit van Amsterdam, Sociografisch Instituut FSW: 84p. (Onderzoekprojekt Sociale Ontwikkelings-strategie Suriname 1969, Deelrapport nr. 9)   *[RIS]*

Waddell, Hope Masterton
6.0292   JM   1970   TWENTY-NINE YEARS IN THE WEST INDIES AND CENTRAL AFRICA: A REVIEW OF MISSIONARY WORK AND ADVENTURE 1829-1858.

Walke, Olive
22.0369   TR   1959   Christmas music of Trinidad.

Wallbridge, Edwin Angel
6.0293   GU   1969   THE DEMERARA MARTYR: MEMOIRS OF THE REV. JOHN SMITH, MISSIONARY TO DEMERARA.

Warner, Maureen
19.0065   TR   1971   African feasts in Trinidad.

Watlington, Hereward T.
23.0316   BE   1956   Old Devonshire Church. *Bermuda Hist Q* 13(4), Winter: 159-181. **[5,35]**   *[COL]*

Watson, G. Llewellyn
23.0317   JM   1973   Social structure and social movements: the Black Muslims in the USA and the Ras-Tafarians in Jamaica. *Br J Sociol* 24(2), June: 188-204. **[8,11]**   *[COL]*

Wavell, Stewart; Butt, Audrey & Epton, Nina
23.0318   GU   1967   TRANCES. New York, E. P. Dutton and Co.: 253p.   [13]   [COL]

Weiss, H.
23.0319   SR   1919   Het zendingswerk der Herrnhutters in de Oerwouden van de
                            Boven-Suriname [Missionary work of the Moravian Brethren in the
                            jungles of the Upper-Surinam River]. *W I G* 1(1): 102-110.   [5]
                                                                                              [COL]
23.0320   SR   1920-21 De zending der Hernhutters onder de Indianen in Berbice en
                            Surinam, 1738-1816 [The mission of the Moravians among the
                            Indians in Berbice and Surinam, 1738-1816]. *W I G* 2: 36-44,
                            109-121, 187-197, 249-264.   [5]   [COL]

Wel, F. J. van
23.0321   SR   1966   Herkomst en werk der Evangelische Broedergemeenschap in
                            Suriname [Origin and work of the Moravian Brethren in Suriname].
                            Oost West 59(11-12), July-Aug.: 18-20.   [15]   [NYP]
23.0322   SR   1967   De missie [The mission]. *Schakels* S66: 16-22.   [NYP]

Welsh, Philip C.
5.0968   JM   1967   The Roman Catholic Church and the Kingston earthquake of 1907.

Wesley, Charles H.
32.0600   BC   1932   Rise of Negro education in the British Empire.
32.0601   BC   1933   Rise of Negro education in the British Empire.

Wetering, W. van
14.0076   SR   1973   HEKSERIJ BIJ DE DJUKA: EEN SOCIOLOGISCHE BENADERING [DJUKA
                            WITCHCRAFT BELIEF: A SOCIOLOGICAL APPROACH].
14.0077   SR   1973   Witchcraft among the Tapanahoni Djuka.

White, Ralph J.
23.0323   GU   1919   The Berbice Lutheran Church. *Timehri* 3d ser., 6(23), Sept.:
                            196-201.   [5]   [AMN]

White, Walter Grainge
3.0647   GU   [n.d.]   AT HOME WITH THE MACUCHI.

Whitefield, George
23.0324   BE   1927   A LETTER FROM THE REVEREND MR. WHITEFIELD TO A REVEREND
                            DIVINE IN BOSTON; GIVING A SHORT ACCOUNT OF HIS LATE VISIT TO
                            BERMUDA. Boston: 7p. (Originally published in 1748)   [NYP]

Wilkinson, Henry
23.0325   BE   1954   The communion cup and Sir Thomas Smith. *Bermuda Hist Q* 11(1),
                            Spring: 24-28.   [5]   [COL]

Willeford, Mary Jo
23.0326   GC   1969   Negro New World religions and witchcraft. *Bim* 12(48), Jan.-June:
                            216-222.   [11]   [RIS]

Williams, Cicely
29.0049   JM   1973   Witch doctors.

Williams, Joseph J.

23.0328 JM 1934 PSYCHIC PHENOMENA OF JAMAICA. New York, Dial Press, 309p. **[19]** [*AMN*]

23.0329 JM 1970 VOODOOS AND OBEAHS; PHASES OF WEST INDIAN WITCHCRAFT. New York, AMS Press: 257p. (Originally published in 1922) **[5,19]** [*COL*]

Winkel, C. N. & Schrils, J. H. P.

23.0330 CU 1948 De Vrijmetselarij [Freemasonry]. *In* ORANJE EN DE ZES CARAÏBISCHE PARELEN. Amsterdam, J. H. de Bussy: 122-125. [*UCLA*]

Wooding, C. J.

23.0331 SR 1970 Winti. *Gids* 133(9):286-288. [*COL*]

23.0332 SR 1972 WINTI: EEN AFROAMERIKAANSE GODSDIENST IN SURINAME; EEN CULTUREEL-HISTORISCHE ANALYSE VAN DE RELIGIEUZE VERSCHIJN-SELEN IN DE PARA [WINTI: AN AFROAMERICAN RELIGION IN SURINAM; A CULTURAL-HISTORICAL ANALYSIS OF RELIGIOUS PHENOMENA IN THE PARA DISTRICT]. Meppel, The Netherlands, Krips Repro B. V.: 565p. [*RIS*]

Wright, Philip

6.0307 JM 1973 KNIBB 'THE NOTORIOUS': SLAVES' MISSIONARY 1803-1845.

Yarnley, J. R.

23.0333 JM 1939 Behind the cactus hedge. *Can-W I Mag* 28(6), July: 7-10. [*NYP*]

Yawney, Carole D.

20.0091 JM 1976 Remnants of all nations: Rastafarian attitudes to race and nationality.

Young, Everild & Helweg-Larsen, Kjeld

5.1015 GC 1965 THE PIRATES' PRIEST: THE LIFE OF PÈRE LABAT IN THE WEST INDIES, 1693-1705.

Zeefuik, Karel August

6.0311 SR 1973 HERNHUTTER ZENDING EN HAAGSCHE MAATSCHAPPIJ 1828-1867: EEN HOOFDSTUK UIT DE GESCHIEDENIS VAN ZENDING EN EMANCIPATIE IN SURINAME [MORAVIAN MISSION AND "HAAGSCHE MAATSCHAPPIJ" 1828-1867: A CHAPTER IN THE HISTORY OF MISSION AND EMANCIPATION IN SURINAM].

Zerries, Otto

23.0334 GC 1961 Die Religionen der Naturvölker Südamerikas und Westindiens. *In* Krickeberg, Walter, ed. DIE RELIGIONEN DES ALTEN AMERIKA [THE RELIGIONS OF THE PRIMITIVE PEOPLES OF SOUTH AMERICA AND THE WEST INDIES]. Stuttgart, W. Kohlhammer, p.269-376. (Die Religionen des Menschheit, v.7.) **[13]** [*NYP*]

Zylberberg, Jacques

8.0250 GD 1966 Esquisse d'une sociologie de la Guadeloupe [Outline of the sociology of Guadeloupe].

Chapter 24

FOLKLORE

Folk tales; proverbs.

See also: **[11]** Population segments: Afro-Caribbean; **[12]** Population segments: East Indian; **[13]** Population segments: Amerindian and Black Carib; **[14]** Population segments: Maroon; **[15]** Population segments: Other; **[19]** Cultural continuities; **[22]** Creative arts and recreation; **[23]** Religion; **[25]** Language and linguistics.

Abbenhuis, F. R. M.

24.0001   SR   1935-36 Nog eens: folklore in Suriname [Once again: folklore in Surinam]. *W I G* 17: 367-373.   [*COL*]

Abrahams, Roger D.

24.0002   BC   1967   The shaping of folklore traditions in the British West Indies. *J Inter-Amer Stud* 9(3), July: 456-480.   **[19]**   [*COL*]

24.0003   BC   1968   British West Indian proverbs and proberb collections. *Proverbium* 10: 239-243.   [*COL*]

24.0004   BC   1968   Introductory remarks to a rhetorical theory of folklore. *J Am Folk* 81(320), April-June: 143-158.   [*COL*]

24.0005   NV,TB   1968   Public drama and common values in two Caribbean islands. *Trans-action* July-Aug: 62-71.   **[22]**   [*RIS*]

24.0006   BC   1968   "Pull out your purse and pay": a St. George mumming from the British West Indies. *Folklore* 79, Autumn: 176-201.   [*COL*]

24.0007   TB   1968   Speech Mas' on Tobago. *In* Hudson, Wilson M., ed. TIRE SHRINKER TO DRAGSTER. Austin, Texas, Encino Press: 125-144. (Publications of the Texas Folklore Society No. 34.)   **[22]**   [*COL*]

22.0004   BC   1974   DEEP THE WATER, SHALLOW THE SHORE: THREE ESSAYS ON SHANTYING IN THE WEST INDIES.

Alladin, M. P.

24.0008   TR   1968   FOLK STORIES AND LEGENDS OF TRINIDAD. Trinidad, C.S.O. Printing Unit: 27p.   [*RIS*]

22.0007   TR   1969   FOLK CHANTS AND REFRAINS OF TRINIDAD AND TOBAGO.

22.0008   TR   1974   Festivals of Trinidad and Tobago.

Allsopp, Richard

24.0009   GU   1967   Folklore in Guyana: building a Guyanese tradition. *Kaie* 4, July: 37-41.   [*RIS*]

Anderson, Izett & Cundall, Frank, comps.

24.0010   JM   1910   JAMAICA NEGRO PROVERBS AND SAYINGS, COLLECTED AND CLASSI-
                         FIED ACCORDING TO SUBJECTS. Kingston, Institute of Jamaica,
                         48p. **[11,25]**   [*NYP*]

24.0011   JM   1972   JAMAICA PROVERBS AND SAYINGS. Shannon, Ireland, Irish University
                         Press: 128p. (Originally published in 1910)   [*COL*]

Anthony, Michael

24.0012   TR   1976   FOLK TALES AND FANTASIES. Port of Spain, Columbus Publishers:
                         65p.   [*RIS*]

Archer, A. Clifford

24.0013   BB   1937   "Bugaboo in Barbados." *Can-W I Mag* 26(5), May: 24-26; 26(6),
                         June: 27-29.   [*NYP*]

Arya, U.

12.0008   SR   1968   RITUAL SONGS AND FOLKSONGS OF THE HINDUS OF SURINAM.

Ashtine, Eauline

24.0014   TR   1966   CRICK-CRACK!: TRINIDAD AND TOBAGO FOLK TALES. University of
                         the West Indies, Extra-Mural Department: 60p.   [*RIS*]

24.0015   TR   1968   NINE FOLK TALES. Trinidad and Tobago, Ministry of Education and
                         Culture, The Publication Unit: 72p.   [*RIS*]

Aspinall, Algernon E.

5.0025   GC   1969   WEST INDIAN TALES OF OLD.

Augustus, Earl

24.0016   TR   [n.d.]   BAKA. Port-of-Spain, The Vanguard Publishing Co., Ltd: 30p.
                                                                                       [*RIS*]

24.0017   TR   1966   GAMBAGE. Trinidad and Tobago, University of the West Indies,
                         Extra-Mural Department: 30p. (New World Life and Lore Series:
                         vol. one)   [*RIS*]

Ayuso, Miriam

24.0018   BZ   1976   The legend of X-tabay. *Belizean Stud* 4(5), September: 6-12. **[13]**
                                                                                       [*RIS*]

Banks, E. P.

24.0019   GC   1955   Islands Carib folk tales. *Car Q* 4(1), Jan.: 32-39.   **[13]**   [*RIS*]

Barbanson, W. L. de

22.0013   GD   1950   Frans-creoolse versjes van Guadeloupe [French-Creole verses of
                         Guadeloupe].

Barbotin, Maurice (Zagaya, pseudonym)

24.0020   GD   1965   PROVERBES CRÉOLES EN GUADELOUPE [CREOLE PROVERBS IN
                         GUADELOUPE]. Madrid, Ediciones Castilla, S.A.: 275p.   [*RIS*]

Bastide, Roger

11.0003   GC   1971[?]   AFRICAN CIVILISATIONS IN THE NEW WORLD.

Beck, Jane C.

24.0021   BC   1975   The West Indian supernatural world: belief integration in a pluralistic society. *J Am Folk* 88(349), July-Sept.: 235-244. **[23]**
[*COL*]

Beckwith, Martha Warren

22.0017   JM   1922   FOLK GAMES IN JAMAICA.

24.0022   JM   1924   JAMAICA ANANSI STORIES. New York, American Folk-lore Society, 295p. (Memoirs of the American Folk-lore Society, v. 17.) **[22]**

24.0023   JM   1928   JAMAICA FOLK-LORE. New York, American Folk-lore Society, 95, 67, 137, 47p. (Memoirs of the American Folk-lore Society, v. 21.)
[*COL*]

11.0007   JM   1970   BLACK ROADWAYS: A STUDY OF JAMAICAN FOLK LIFE.

Beckwith, Martha Warren, comp.

24.0024   JM   1970   JAMAICA PROVERBS. New York, Negro Universities Press: 137p. (Originally published in 1925). [*RIS*]

Beckwith, Martha Warren & Roberts, Helen H.

22.0019   JM   1923   CHRISTMAS MUMMINGS IN JAMAICA.

Bennetot, Arlette de

24.0025   FG   1968   CONTES ET LÉGENDES DE LA GUYANE FRANÇAISE [STORIES AND LEGENDS OF FRENCH GUIANA]. Paris, Fernand Nathan: 252p.
[*COL*]

Bennett, Louise

24.0026   JM   1957   ANANCY STORIES AND DIALECT VERSE. (New series.) Kingston, Pioneer Press, 94p. **[25]** [*NYP*]

24.0027   JM   1961   LAUGH WITH LOUISE: A POT-POURRI OF JAMAICAN FOLKLORE. Kingston, City Printery, 56p. **[22]** [*RIS*]

Bertrand, Anca

22.0026   GC   1968   Notes pour une définition du folklore antillais [Notes for a definition of West Indian folk music].

Black, Clinton V.

5.0066   JM   1952   TALES OF OLD JAMAICA.

Blackman, Margot

24.0028   BB   1966   Barbadian proverbs. *Bim* 11(43), July-Dec.: 158-163. [*RIS*]

Booy, Theodoor de

24.0029   JM   1915   Certain West-Indian superstitions pertaining to celts. *J Am Folk* 28(107), Jan.-Mar., 78-82. **[4,20]** [*COL*]

Bourguignon, Erika

23.0015   GC   1968   Trance dance.

Brathwaite, P. A. & Brathwaite, Serena U., comps. & eds.

22.0044   GU   1967   FOLK SONGS OF GUYANA IN WORDS AND MUSIC.

24.0030   GU   1967   GUYANESE PROVERBS AND STORIES. Georgetown, Brathwaite: 80p.
[*RIS*]

Breinburg, Petronella
24.0031   SR   1971   LEGENDS OF SURINAME. London, New Beacon Books Ltd.: 47p.
                                                                            [*RIS*]

Brenneker, Paul
24.0032   NL   1969   SAMBUBU NO. 1: VOLKSKUNDE VAN CURAÇAO, ARUBA EN BONAIRE
                         [SAMBUBU NO. 1: FOLKLORE OF CURAÇAO, ARUBA AND BONAIRE].
                         Curaçao, Paul Brenneker: 7-304.   [*RILA*]
24.0033   NL   1970   SAMBUBU NO. 2: VOLKSKUNDE VAN CURAÇAO, ARUBA EN BONAIRE
                         [SAMBUBU NO. 2: FOLKLORE OF CURAÇAO, ARUBA AND BONAIRE].
                         Curaçao, Paul Brenneker: 310-500.   [*RILA*]
24.0034   NL   1972   SAMBUBU NO. 4: VOLKSKUNDE VAN CURAÇAO, ARUBA EN BONAIRE
                         [SAMBUBU NO. 4: FOLKLORE OF CURAÇAO, ARUBA AND BONAIRE].
                         Curaçao, Paul Benneker: 814-1004.   [*RILA*]
24.0035   NL   1972   SAMBUBU NO. 5: VOLKSKUNDE VAN CURAÇAO, ARUBA EN BONAIRE
                         [SAMBUBU NO. 5: FOLKLORE OF CURAÇAO, ARUBA AND BONAIRE].
                         Curaçao, Paul Benneker: 1009-1294.   [*RILA*]
24.0036   NL   1973   SAMBUBU NO. 7: VOLKSKUNDE VAN CURAÇAO, ARUBA EN BONAIRE
                         [SAMBUBU NO. 7: FOLKLORE OF CURAÇAO, ARUBA AND BONAIRE].
                         Curaçao, Paul Brenneker: 1595-1886.   [*RILA*]
24.0037   NL   1974   SAMBUBU NO. 8: VOLKSKUNDE VAN CURAÇAO, ARUBA AND BONAIRE
                         [SAMBUBU NO. 8: FOLKLORE OF CURAÇAO, ARUBA AND BONAIRE].
                         Curaçao, Paul Brenneker: 1892-2082.   [*RILA*]

Brett, William Henry & Lambert, Leonard, eds.
24.0038   GU   1931   GUIANA LEGENDS. London, Society for the Propagation of the
                         Gospel in Foreign Parts, 49p. **[13]**   [*NYP*]

Buhler, Richard O.
29.0016   BZ   1975   Belizean folk remedies.
24.0039   BZ   1975   Ixtabi. *National Stud* 3(6), November: 16-18.   [*RIS*]
23.0024   BZ   1976   *Primicias* in Belize.

Cappelle, H. van
24.0040   SR   1916   Surinaamsche Negervertellingen [Folktales of the Surinam Ne-
                         groes]. *Bijd Volk Ned-Indie* 72: 233-379. **[14]**
24.0041   SR   1926   MYTHEN EN SAGEN UIT WEST-INDIË [MYTHS AND LEGENDS FROM THE
                         WEST INDIES]. Zutphen, W. J. Thieme, 416p.   [*NYP*]

Carr, Andrew T.
22.0057   TR   1954   Trinidad calypso is unique folk culture.

Cassidy, Frederic G.
25.0053   JM   1953[?] Language and folklore.
25.0060   JM   1967   Some new light on old Jamaicanisms.

Chambertrand, Gilbert de
24.0042   FA   1935   Manzè Elodie. *In* Denis, Serge, ed. NOS ANTILLES. Orléans,
                         Luzeray, p.307-317. **[25]**   [*AGS*]
24.0043   FA   1935   Proverbes et dictons antillais [Proverbs and sayings of the [French]
                         Antilles]. *In* Denis, Serge, ed. NOS ANTILLES. Orléans, Luzeray,
                         p.289-304. **[25]**   [*AGS*]

Clavel, M.

24.0044   BA   1904   Items of folk-lore from Bahama Negroes. *J Am Folk* 17(64), Jan.-March: 36-38. **[11]**   [*COL*]

Cleare, W. T.

24.0045   BA   1917   Four folk-tales from Fortune Island, Bahamas. *J Am Folk* 30(116), April-June: 228-229.   [*COL*]

Collier, H. C.

24.0046   GU   1938   The woman who stuck in the sky. *Can-W I Mag* 27(12), Dec.: 4-8. **[13]**   [*NYP*]

Cooksey, C.

24.0047   GU   1921   Warao stories. *Timehri* 3d ser., 7(24), Aug.: 90-97. **[13]**   [*AMN*]

Cromer, Peggo

24.0048   JM   1974   National dances of the Caribbean and Latin America. *Car R* 6(3), July-Aug.-Sept.: 26-32.   [*RIS*]

Crooks, Kenneth B. M.

24.0049   JM   1933   Forty Jamaican proverbs: interpretations and inferences. *J Negro Hist* 18(2), Apr.: 132-143. **[25]**

Crowley, Daniel J.

24.0050   BA   1954   Form and style in a Bahamian folktale. *Car Q* 3(4), Aug.: 218-234.   [*RIS*]

24.0051   SL   1955   "The good child and the bad" in the West Indies. *Extra-Mural Reptr* 2(1), Feb.: 27-29.   [*RIS*]

24.0052   SL   1955   "The good child and the bad" in the West Indies. *Extra-Mural Reptr* 2(2), Apr.: 17-20.   [*RIS*]

24.0053   TR   1955   A Trinidad Hindi riddle tale. *Caribbeana* 9(2), Sept.: 28-29, 41. **[12]**   [*COL*]

24.0054   BA   1956   TRADITION AND INDIVIDUAL CREATIVITY IN BAHAMIAN FOLKTALES. Ph.D. dissertation, Northwestern University : 213p.   [*PhD*]

24.0055   SL   1958   La Rose and La Marguerite Societies in St. Lucia. *J Am Folk* 71(282), Oct.-Dec.: 541-552. **[8,19]**   [*RIS*]

24.0056   GC   1962   Negro Folklore: an Africanist's view. *Tex Q* Autumn: 65-71. **[11,19]**   [*RIS*]

24.0057   BA   1966   I COULD TALK OLD-STORY GOOD: CREATIVITY IN BAHAMIAN FOLK-LORE. Berkeley, Calif., Univ. of California Press: 157p.   [*RIS*]

24.0058   BC   1967   The view from Tobago: national character in folklore. *In* Wilgus, D. K., ed. FOLKLORE INTERNATIONAL: ESSAYS IN TRADITIONAL LITERATURE, BELIEF AND CUSTOM IN HONOR OF WAYLAND DEBS HAND. Hatboro, Pennsylvania, Folklore Associates, Inc.: 29-39. **[21]**   [*COL*]

Cruickshank, J. Graham

24.0059   BC   1918   "B'ru Nansi." *W I Comm Circ* 33(504), Jan. 24: 34-35.   [*NYP*]

24.0060   BC   1918   "B'ru Nansi." *W I Comm Circ* 33(505), Feb. 7: 53-54.   [*NYP*]

Cundall, Frank

23.0061   JM   1930   Three fingered Jack. *W I Comm Circ* 45(816).

23.0062   JM   1930   Three fingered Jack. *W I Comm Circ* 45(817).

23.0063   **JM**   1930   Three fingered Jack. *W I Comm Circ* 45(818).

Damas, L.-G.
24.0061   **FG**   1943   Veilles noires [Black evenings]. Paris, Editions Stock, 220p.
                                                                    [*NYP*]

David, B.
24.0062   **MT**   1967   Proverbes et dictons de la Martinique [Proverbs and sayings of
                                Martinique]. *Notes Afr* 116, Oct.: 110-117.   [*AMN*]

David, B. & Jardel, J.-P.
24.0063   **MT**   1969[?]   Les proverbes créoles de la Martinique: language et société
                                [Creole proverbs of Martinique: language and society].
                                Martinique, C.E.R.A.G.: 355p.   **[25]**   [*RIS*]

Debrot, R.
24.0064   **CU**   1968   Feest van maisoogst [Feast of the corn harvest]. *Schakels* NA53:
                                21-26.   [*NYP*]

DeCamp, David
24.0065   **JM**   1968   "Mock bidding in Jamaica." *In* Hudson, Wilson M., ed. Tire
                                shrinker to dragster. Austin, Texas, Encino Press: 145-153.
                                (Publication of the Texas Folklore Society No. 34.)   [*COL*]

Delmond, Stany
25.0088   **MT**   1935   Language et folklore martiniquais [Language and folklore of
                                Martinique].

Dennert, H.
24.0066   **CU**   1968   De oude Curaçaose klederdracht [The old Curaçao costume].
                                Schakels NA53: 15-17.   [*NYP*]
24.0067   **CU**   1968   Het oude Curaçaose Luango-verhaal [The old Curaçao Luango
                                story]. *Schakels* NA53: 27-29.   [*NYP*]
24.0068   **CU**   1968   Van geboorte tot de dood [From birth to death]. *Schakels* NA53:
                                2-5.   [*NYP*]

Dillard, J. L.
24.0069   **GC**   1962   Some variants in concluding tags in Antillean folk tales. *Car Stud*
                                2(3), Oct.: 16-25.   [*RIS*]
24.0070   **GC**   1963   Beginning formulas for Antillean folk tales, etc. *Car Stud* 3(3), Oct.:
                                51-55.

Donicie, A. C.
19.0016   **SR**   1953   Iets over de taal en de sprookjes van Suriname [On the language
                                and the fairy-tales of Surinam].

Dubelaar, C. N.
24.0071   **SR**   1972   Negersprookjes uit Suriname [Negro fables from Surinam].
                                Neerlands Volksleven 22(3-4) Special issue: 66p. **[11]**   [*NYP*]

Edwards, Charles L.
24.0072   **BA**   1942   Bahama songs and stories: a contribution to folk-lore. New
                                York, G. E. Stechert and Co.: 111p. **[22]**   [*RIS*]

Elder, J. D.

1.0100   GC   1965   The value of Caribbean folk archives and the mechanics of setting up such a collection.

24.0073   TR   1966   *Kalinda*—song of the battling troubadours of Trinidad. *J Folk Inst* 3(2), August: 192-203. **[22]**   [*RIS*]

24.0074   TR   1968   The folklore of Trinidad and Tobago, Part 1. *Tchr J* March: 16-18.   [*RIS*]

22.0124   TB   1972   FOLK SONG AND FOLK LIFE IN CHARLOTTEVILLE (ASPECTS OF VILLAGE LIFE AS DYNAMICS OF ACCULTURATION IN A TOBAGO FOLK SONG TRADITION).

24.0075   TR   1972   MA ROSE POINT: AN ANTHOLOGY OF RARE AND STRANGE LEGENDS FROM TRINIDAD AND TOBAGO. Port-of-Spain, National Cultural Council of Trinidad and Tobago: 79p. **[22]**   [*RIS*]

Engels, C. J. H.

24.0076   CU   1954   De culturele plaats van de Antillen in het Koninkrijk [The cultural position of the Antilles in the Kingdom]. *Vox Guy* 1(4-5), Nov.-Jan.: 25-28. **[3]**

Finlay, H. H.

24.0077   BA   1925   Folklore from Eleuthera, Bahamas. *J Am Folk* 38(148), April-June: 293-299.   [*COL*]

Franck, Harry A.

24.0078   JM   1921   Jamaica proverbs. *Dialect Notes* 5(4): 98-108. **[25]**   [*COL*]

Funk, Henry Elwell

25.0115   MT   1953   THE FRENCH CREOLE DIALECT OF MARTINIQUE: ITS HISTORICAL BACKGROUND, VOCABULARY, SYNTAX, PROVERBS AND LITERATURE WITH A GLOSSARY.

Georgel, Thérèse

24.0079   FC   1955[?]   CONTES ET LÉGENDES DES ANTILLES [STORIES AND LEGENDS OF THE ANTILLES]. Paris, Fernand Nathan: 255p.   [*NYP*]

Goeje, C. H. de

20.0028   GC   1943   Philosophy, initiation and myths of the Indians of Guiana and adjacent countries.

24.0080   SR   1947   Anansi, l'araignée rusée [Anansi, the wily spider]. *Revta Mus Paul* new ser., 1: 125-126. **[11]**   [*AMN*]

23.0098   GC   1952   The physical world, the world of magic, and the moral world of Guiana Indians.

Goldenberg, Marcel

24.0081   MT   1973   Nature et culture dans les contes populaires du Compère Lapin [Nature and culture in the folk stories of Compere Lapin]. *Rec Cent Etud Reg Ant-Guy* 1: 37-45.   [*RIS*]

Gray, Cecil

24.0082   BC   1968   "Folk" themes in West Indian drama: an analysis. *Car Q* 14(1-2), March-June: 102-109.   [*RIS*]

Hadel, Richard E.
24.0083   BZ   1974   Tataduhende and Sissimite. *National Stud* 2(4), July: 14-21.   [*RIS*]

Harris, Wilson
24.0084   GC   1970   History, fable and myth in the Caribbean and Guianas. *Car Q* 16(2), June: 1-32.   **[19]**   [*RIS*]

Heath, Roy
24.0085   GU   1973   The function of myth. *In* Salkey, Andrew, ed. CARIBBEAN ESSAYS: AN ANTHOLOGY. London, Evans Brothers: 86-94.   [*RIS*]

Henriquez, P. Cohen & Hesseling, D. C.
24.0086   CU,SR   1935-36   Papiamentse en Negerengelse spreekworden [Papiamento and Negro-English proverbs]. *W I G* 17: 161-172.   **[25]**   [*COL*]
24.0087   CU   1936-37   Nog enige Papiamentse spreekwoorden [Some more Papiamento proverbs]. *W I G* 18: 82-84.   **[25]**   [*COL*]

Herskovits, Melville Jean
24.0088   TR   1945   Trinidad proverbs ("Old time saying so"). *J Am Folk* 58(299), July-Sept.: 195-207.   [*COL*]

Herskovits, Melville Jean & Herskovits, Frances S.
24.0089   SR   1936   SURINAME FOLK-LORE (with transcriptions and Suriname songs and musicological analysis by Dr. M. Kolinski). New York, Columbia University Press, 766p.   **[11,14,22,25,32]**   [*RIS*]

Hills, Theo L.
56.0151   GU   1961   The interior of British Guiana and the myth of El Dorado.

Holder, Geoffrey & Harshman, Tom
24.0090   TR   1959   BLACK GODS, GREEN ISLANDS. Garden City, N.Y., Doubleday, 235p.

Horowitz, Michael M.
24.0091   MT   1959   Humor and riddles in Martiniquan folk literature. *Midwest Folk* 9(3): 149-154.   **[25]**   [*RIS*]

Howard, Michael C.
23.0137   BZ   1975   Kekchi religious beliefs and lore regarding the jungle.

Hurston, Zora Neale
24.0092   BZ   1930   Dance songs and tales from the Bahamas. *J Am Folk* 43(169), July-Oct.: 294-312.   **[22]**   [*COL*]

Iremonger, Lucille
24.0093   BC   1956   WEST INDIAN FOLK TALES: ANANSI STORIES, TALES FROM WEST INDIAN FOLKLORE RETOLD FOR ENGLISH CHILDREN. London, George G. Harrap, 64p.

Jacobs, H. P.
24.0094   JM   1945   The untapped sources of Jamaican history. *Jam Hist Rev* 1(1), June: 92-98.   [*AMN*]
24.0095   JM   1948   An early dialect verse. *Jam Hist Rev* 1(3), Dec.: 274-288.   [*COL*]

Jekyll, Walter
24.0096 JM 1907 JAMAICAN SONG AND STORY. London, David Nutt, 288p. (Publication of the Folk-Lore Society 55.) **[22]** [*COL*]

Jekyll, Walter, ed.
24.0097 JM 1966 JAMAICAN SONG AND STORY: ANNANCY STORIES, DIGGING SINGS, RING TUNES, AND DANCING TUNES. New York, Dover Publications, Inc.: 288p. **[22]** [*RIS*]

Jha, J. C.
12.0038 TR 1976 The Hindu festival of Divali in the Caribbean.

Johnson, John H.
24.0098 AT 1921 Folklore from Antigua, British West Indies. *J Am Folk* 34(131), Jan.-Mar.: 40-88. [*COL*]

Josselin de Jong, J. P. B. de
24.0099 SR 1938 Folklore van Suriname [Folklore of Surinam]. *W I G* 20: 1-8. [*COL*]

Jourdain, Elodie
24.0100 MT 1954 Story-tellers of Martinique. *Car Comm Mon Inf B* 7(12), July: 265-266, 268. [*COL*]

Kerns, Virginia & Dirks, Robert
24.0101 BZ 1975 John Canoe. *National Stud* 3(6), November: 1-15. **[13,19]** [*RIS*]

Kesler, C. K.
25.0201 NA 1926-27 De naam Antillen [The name "Antilles"].

Laplante, André
24.0102 MG 1972 L'univers marie-galantais: Quelques notes sur la cosmologie des Marie-Galantais de la région des Bas [The Marie-Galantean universe: Some notes on the cosmology of the Marie-Galanteans of the Bas region]. *In* Benoist, Jean, ed. L'ARCHIPEL INACHEVÉ: CULTURE ET SOCIÉTÉ AUX ANTILLES FRANÇAISES. Montreal, Canada, Univ. of Montreal: 205-232. [*RIS*]

Latour, M. D.
24.0103 CU 1937 Cuenta di Nanzi [Tales of Anansi]. *W I G* 19: 33-43. **[19]** [*COL*]
24.0104 CU 1938 Cuenta di Nanzi [Tales of Anansi]. *W I G* 20: 9-18, 103-108, 143-147, 296-305. **[19]** [*COL*]
24.0105 CU 1940 Cuenta di Nanzi [Tales of Anansi]. *W I G* 22: 47-52, 86-91, 134-140. **[19]** [*COL*]
24.0106 CU 1948 Folklore. *In* ORANJE EN DE ZES CARAÏBISCHE PARELEN. Amsterdam, J. H. de Bussy: 83-92. [*UCLA*]

Leach, MacEdward
24.0107 JM 1961 Jamaican duppy lore. *J Am Folk* 74(293), July-Sept.: 207-215. **[11,19,23]** [*RIS*]

Lekis, Lisa
22.0223 GC 1955 The dance as an expression of Caribbean folklore.

Lemmon, Alfred E.
13.0130   **BZ**   1973   Maya music and dance.

Lichtveld, Lou
24.0108   **SR**   1930-31 Op zoek naar de spin [Looking for the spider]. *W I G* 12: 209-230, 305-324. **[19]**   [*COL*]

Lindeijer, Tom
24.0109   **CU**   1968   Viering van de jaarwisseling [Celebration of the new year]. *Schakels* NA53: 18-20.   [*NYP*]

McBurnie, Beryl
24.0110   **TR**   1973   West Indian dance. *In* Salkey, Andrew, ed. Caribbean essays: an anthology. London, Evans Brothers: 95-99. **[19,22]**   [*RIS*]

McLellan, G. H.
24.0111   **GU**   1943   Old time story: some old Guianese yarns re-spun. 2d ed. Georgetown, Daily Chronicle, 266p.   [*RIS*]

McTurk, Michael
24.0112   **GU**   1949   Essays and fables in the vernacular. Georgetown, Daily Chronicle, 97p. **[25]**   [*RIS*]

Meade, Florence O.
24.0113   **UV**   1932   Folk tales from the Virgin Islands. *J Am Folk* 45(177), July-Sept.: 363-371.   [*COL*]

Meikle, H. B.
24.0114   **TR**   1958   Mermaids and fairymaids or water gods and goddesses of Tobago. *Car Q* 5(2), Feb.: 103-108.   [*RIS*]

Menkman, W. R.
24.0115   **GC**   1937   Nog eens het eiland der reuzen [Once again the island of the giants]. *W I G* 19: 85-86. **[5]**   [*COL*]

Morpurgo, A. J.
24.0116   **SR**   1935-36 Folklore in Suriname. *W I G* 17: 116-125. **[14]**   [*COL*]

Nodal, Roberto
1.0212   **GC**   1975   A tentative bibliography of Caribbean folklore.

Ottley, C. R.
24.0117   **TR**   1950   Tobago legends and West Indian lore. Georgetown, Daily Chronical, 137p.   [*RIS*]
24.0118   **TR**   1962   Legends: true stories and old sayings from Trinidad and Tobago. Port of Spain, College Press, 71p.   [*RIS*]

Panhuys, L. C. van
24.0119   **NC**   1932-33 Folklore in Nederlandsch West-Indië [Folklore in the Netherlands West Indies]. *W I G* 14: 124-130. **[11]**   [*COL*]
24.0120   **NC**   1933-34 Aanvulling Folklore in Nederlandsch West Indië [Addition to folklore in the Netherlands West-Indies]. *W I G* 15: 16-17. **[11]**
                                                                                              [*COL*]

| 24.0121 | BN | 1933-34 | Folklore van Bonaire [Folklore of Bonaire]. *W I G* 15: 97-101. |

[RIS]

24.0122	SR	1934-35	Folklore in Suriname. *W I G* 16: 17-32. **[14]** [COL]
24.0123	BN	1934-35	Folklore van Bonaire [Folklore of Bonaire]. *W I G* 16: 65-71, 318-320. [RIS]
24.0124	SR	1934-35	Het kikvorschmotief in Suriname en elders [The frog motif in Surinam and elsewhere]. *W I G* 16: 361-366. **[13,22]** [COL]
24.0125	SR	1934-35	Surinaamsche folklore [Surinam folklore]. *W I G* 16: 315-317.

[COL]

| 24.0126 | SR | 1935-36 | Surinaamsche folklore (liederenver zameling Van Vliet) [Folklore of Surinam (Song collection of Van Vliet)]. *W I G* 17: 282-289. **[14,22]** [COL] |

Parsons, Elsie Clews

24.0127	BA	1918	FOLK-TALES OF ANDROS ISLAND, BAHAMAS. Lancaster, Pennsylvania, American Folklore Society: 170p. [NYP]
24.0128	BA	1919	Riddles and proverbs from the Bahama Islands. *J Am Folk* 32(125), July-Sept.: 439-441. [COL]
24.0129	BB	1925	Barbados folklore. *J Am Folk* 38(148), Apr.: 267-292. [COL]
24.0130	BE	1925	Bermuda folklore. *J Am Folk* 38(148), April-June: 239-266. [COL]
24.0131	BZ	1928	Spirituals and other folk-lore from the Bahamas. *J Am Folk* 41(162), Oct.-Dec.: 453-524. [COL]
24.0132	BB,BA	1930	Proverbs from Barbados and the Bahamas. *J Am Folk* 43(169), July-Oct.: 324-325. [COL]
24.0133	GC	1933-43	FOLK-LORE OF THE ANTILLES, FRENCH AND ENGLISH. New York, American Folk-lore Society, 3v. (Memoirs of the American Folk-lore Society, v. 26.) [COL]

Pearse, Andrew C.

| *32.0453* | BC | 1956 | Ethnography and the lay scholar in the Caribbean. |
| *22.0293* | TR | 1971 | Carnival in nineteenth century Trinidad. |

Penard, A. P. & Penard, T. E.

24.0134	SR	1917	Popular notions pertaining to primitive stone artifacts in Surinam. *J Am Folk* 30(116), Apr.-June: 251-261. [COL]
24.0135	SR	1917	Surinam folk-tales. *J Am Folk* 30(116), Apr.-June: 239-250. [COL]
24.0136	SR	1924	Surinaamsche volksvertellingen [Surinam folktales]. *Bijd Volk Ned-Indie* 80: 325-363.
24.0137	SR	1926-27	Negro riddles from Surinam. *W I G* 7: 411-432. **[14,19]** [COL]
24.0138	SR	1926	Surinaamsche voklsvertellingen [Surinam folktales]. *Bijd Volk Ned-Indie* 82: 48-94.

Penard, Thomas E. & Penard, Arthur P.

| 24.0139 | SR | 1928-29 | Popular beliefs pertaining to certain places in Suriname. *W I G* 10: 17-33. [COL] |

Pugh, Emily

| *29.0041* | BE | 1957 | St. David's Island remedies. |
| 24.0140 | BE | 1960 | Nineteenth century folk-lore of St. David's Island. *Bermuda Hist Q* 17(4), Winter: 136-146. **[3]** [COL] |

Revert, Eugene

24.0141   MT   1951   DE QUELQUES ASPECTS DU FOLK-LORE MARTINIQUAIS: LE MAGIE ANTILLAISE [ON SOME ASPECTS OF MARTINIQUE FOLKLORE: ANTILLEAN MAGIC]. Paris, Editions Bellenand, 201p.   **[19,23,29]**   [*RIS*]

Roberts, Helen H.

24.0142   JM   1925   A study of folk song variants based on field work in Jamaica. *J Am Folk* 38(148), April-June: 149-216.   [*COL*]

22.0310   JM   1926   Lullabies in Jamaica.

Roth, Walter Edmund

23.0252   GU   1970   AN INQUIRY INTO THE ANIMISM AND FOLK-LORE OF THE GUIANA INDIANS.

Rowe, Charles G. & Horth, Auguste

24.0143   FG   1951   'Dolos': Creole proverbs of French Guiana. *J Am Folk* 64(253), July-Sept.: 253-264.   **[25]**   [*COL*]

Salkey, Andrew

24.0144   GC   1973   HOW ANANCY BECAME A SPIDER INDIVIDUAL PERSON. London, Bogle-L'Ouverture Publications: 178p.   [*RIS*]

Schont, Mme.

24.0145   GD   1935   QUELQUES CONTES CRÉOLES [CREOLE TALES]. Basse-Terre, Impr. catholique, 110p.   **[25]**   [*NYP*]

Sherlock, Philip M.

24.0146   JM   1924   Jamaica superstitions. *Liv Age* 423(4169), Dec. 6: 529-534.

24.0147   JM   1956   ANANSI THE SPIDER MAN: JAMAICA FOLK TALES. London, Macmillan, 85p.   [*NYP*]

24.0148   BC   1966   WEST INDIAN FOLK-TALES. London, Oxford University Press: 151p.   [*RIS*]

24.0149   BC   1969   THE IGUANA'S TAIL: CRICK CRACK STORIES FROM THE CARIBBEAN. New York, Thomas Y. Crowell Company: 97p.   [*RIS*]

Sherlock, Philip M. & Sherlock, Hilary

24.0150   GC   1974   EARS AND TAILS AND COMMON SENSE: MORE STORIES FROM THE CARIBBEAN. New York, Thomas Y. Crowell Company: 121p.   [*RIS*]

Sibley, Inez K.

24.0151   JM   1968   QUASHIE'S REFLECTIONS IN JAMAICAN CREOLE. Kingston, Jamaica, Bolivar Press: 61p. (Originally published in 1939).   **[25]**   [*NYP*]

Singham, A. W.

37.0790   GU,GR   1965   Three cases of constitutionalism and cuckoo politics: Ceylon, British Guiana and Grenada.

Smailus, Ortwin

24.0152   BZ   1975   The spirits of the mountain (aluxoob) in Maya mythology. *National Stud* 3(5), September: 11-20.   **[13,23]**   [*RIS*]

Speirs, James

24.0153   GU   1902   THE PROVERBS OF BRITISH GUIANA WITH AN INDEX OF PRINCIPAL WORDS, AN INDEX OF SUBJECTS, AND A GLOSSARY. Demerara, Argosy, Co., 88p.   **[25]**   [*NYP*]

Taylor, Douglas

23.0300	DM	1945	Carib folk beliefs and customs from Dominica, B.W.I.
24.0154	DM	1946	Notes on the star lore of the Caribbees. *Am Anthrop* new ser., 48(2), Apr.-June: 215-222. **[13]** *[COL]*
24.0155	DM	1952	Tales and legends of the Dominica Caribs. *J Am Folk* 65(257), July-Sept.: 267-279. **[13]** *[COL]*

Thompson, Robert Wallace

24.0156	GC	1955-56	The mushroom and the parasol: a West Indian riddle. *W I G* 35-36(2-4): 162-164. **[19]** *[COL]*

Turenne des Prés, F.

24.0157	JM	1952	The tale—a West Indian folk story. *Phylon* 13(4),: 293-297. *[COL]*

Twining, Mary

1.0275	GC	[n.d.]	CARIBBEAN FOLKLORE.
1.0276	GC	1971	Toward a working folklore bibliography of the Caribbean area.

Vatuk, Ved Prakash

12.0109	GU	1964	Protest songs of East Indians in British Guiana.

Vérin, Pierre

24.0158	SL	1960	Une histoire de diablesse (A she-devil]. *Rev Guad* 39, Jan.-Mar.: 42-43. *[RIS]*
24.0159	SL	1961	Littérature orale de l'île de Sainte-Lucie [Oral literature of the island of St. Lucia]. *Rev Guad* 45, 3-4 trimesters: 23-26. **[25]** *[RIS]*
23.0311	SL	1965	Les croyances populaires de Sainte-Lucie (Antilles) [Popular beliefs in St. Lucia].

Voorhoeve, Jan & Lichtveld, Ursy M., eds.

24.0160	SR	1975	CREOLE DRUM: AN ANTHOLOGY OF CREOLE LITERATURE IN SURINAM. New Haven and London, Yale University Press: 308p. **[5,25]** *[RIS]*

Wel, F. J. van

24.0161	SR	1973	Er tin tin. . .negersprookjes in Suriname [Er tin tin. . .Negro fables from Surinam]. *Schakels* S79: 1-20. **[11]** *[NYP]*

Whipple, Emory

22.0375	BZ	1976	Pia Manadi.

Whitehead, Henry S.

25.0407	UV	1932	Negro dialect of the Virgin Islands.

Wilbert, Johannes

13.0219	GU	1967	Secular and sacred functions of the fire among the Warao.
13.0220	GU	1970	FOLK LITERATURE OF THE WARAO INDIANS: NARRATIVE MATERIAL AND MOTIF CONTENT.

Yvandoc, C.

24.0162	FA	1962	On ti coutt langue. *Rev Guad* 13(48), 3d trimester: 35. **[25]** *[RIS]*

Chapter 25

LANGUAGE AND LINGUISTICS

Amerindian and Creole language studies; dialectology; bilingualism; grammars; language learning; speech behavior; naming patterns; dictionaries and lexicography.

See also: **[11]** Population segments: Afro-Caribbean; **[12]** Population segments: East Indian; **[13]** Population segments: Amerindian and Black Carib; **[14]** Population segments: Maroon; **[15]** Population segments: Other; **[19]** Cultural continuities.

Abrahams, Roger D.
8.0001   **SV**   1970   A performance-centered approach to gossip.

Abrahams, Roger D. & Bauman, Richard
25.0001   **SV**   1971   Sense and nonsense in St. Vincent: speech behavior and decorum in a Caribbean community. *Am Anthrop* 73(3), June: 762-772. **[8,20]**
[*COL*]

Adam, Lucien
25.0002   **WW**   1906   Le caraïbe du Honduras et le caraïbe des îles [The Carib [language] of Honduras and the Carib of the islands]. *In* INTERNATIONALER AMERIKANISTEN-KONGRESS, 14TH SESS., STUTTGART, 1904. [PROCEEDINGS.] Berlin, W. Kohlhammer, pt. 2, p.357-371. **[13]**

Adhin, J. H.; Tuinman, J. & Witte, C. J. de
25.0003   **SR**   1972   NEDERLANDS VOOR DE KLEUTER IN SURINAME [DUTCH FOR THE TODDLER IN SURINAM]. Gronigen, The Netherlands, Wolters-Noordhoff N.V.: 187p. **[32]**   [*RILA*]

Alers, M. H.
25.0004   **SR,NE**   1974   TAALPROBLEMEN VAN SURINAAMSE KINDEREN IN NEDERLAND [LANGUAGE PROBLEMS OF SURINAMESE CHILDREN IN THE NETHERLANDS]. Amsterdam Universiteit van Amsterdam, Antropologisch-Sociologisch Centrum, Afdeling Culturele Antropologie: 51p. (Uitgave 4) **[18,32]**   [*RIS*]

Alleyne, Mervin C.
25.0005   **SL**   1961   Language and society in St. Lucia. *Car Stud* 1(1), Apr.: 1-10. **[8,20]**   [*RIS*]
37.0007   **JM**   1963   Communication and politics in Jamaica.

25.0006   GC   1965   Communication between the elite and the masses. *In* Andic, F. M. & Mathews, T. G. eds. THE CARIBBEAN IN TRANSITION: PAPERS ON SOCIAL, POLITICAL AND ECONOMIC DEVELOPMENT. SECOND CARIBBEAN SCHOLARS' CONFERENCE, MONA, JAMAICA, APRIL 14-19, 1964. Rio Piedras, University of Puerto Rico, Institute of Caribbean Studies: 12-19.   [8]   [*RIS*]

25.0007   JM   1970   The linguistic continuity of Africa in the Caribbean. *Black Acad Rev* 1(4), Winter: 3-16.   [11,19]   [*NYP*]

25.0008   GC   1971   Acculturation and the cultural matrix of creolization. *In* Hymes, Dell, ed. PIDGINIZATION AND CREOLIZATION OF LANGUAGES: PROCEEDINGS OF A CONFERENCE HELD AT THE UNIVERSITY OF THE WEST INDIES, MONA, JAMAICA, APRIL 1968. London, Cambridge University Press: 169-186.   [*RIS*]

Allsopp, Richard

25.0009   GU   1958   The English language in British Guiana. *Engl Lang Tch* 12(2), Jan.-Mar.: 59-66.   [*TCL*]

25.0010   JM   1970   A critical commentary on the dictionary of Jamaican English. *Car Stud* 10(2), July: 90-117.   [*RIS*]

25.0011   BC   1971   Some problems in the lexicography of Caribbean English. *Car Q* 17(2), June: 10-24.   [*RIS*]

25.0012   BC   1971   What dictionary should West Indians use? *J Commonw Lit* 6(2), Dec.: 133-143.   [*COL*]

25.0013   BC   1972   WHY A DICTIONARY OF CARIBBEAN ENGLISH USAGE? Cave Hill, Barbados, University of the West Indies: 7p.   [*RIS*]

Allsopp, S. R. R.

25.0014   BZ   1965   British Honduras—the linguistic dilemma. *Car Q* 11(3-4), Sept.-Dec.: 54-61.   [*RIS*]

25.0015   GU   1965   Research in British Guiana Creole (BGC): methods and results. *In* Jones, J. Allen, ed. LANGUAGE TEACHING, LINGUISTICS AND THE TEACHING OF ENGLISH IN A MULTILINGUAL SOCIETY: REPORT OF THE CONFERENCE, APRIL 6-9, 1964. Kingston, Jamaica, University of the West Indies, Faculty of Education: 47-51.   [*RIS*]

Alvarez Nazario, Manuel

25.0016   GC   1969   El arahuaco insular: sustrato lingüístico de las Antillas mayores y menores [Insular Arawak: linguistic substratum of the Greater and Lesser Antilles]. *Revta Inst Cult Puerto* 12(45), Oct.-Dec.: 45-53.   [13]   [*COL*]

Andersen, Roger William

25.0017   CU   1974   NATIVIZATION AND HISPANIZATION IN THE PAPIAMENTU OF CURACAO, NETHERLANDS ANTILLES: A SOCIOLINGUISTIC STUDY OF VARIATION. Ph.D. dissertation, University of Texas (Austin): 299p.   [*PhD*]

Anderson, Betty

32.0019   SL   1962   Literacy teaching.

Anderson, Izett & Cundall, Frank, comps.

24.0010   JM   1910   JAMAICA NEGRO PROVERBS AND SAYINGS, COLLECTED AND CLASSIFIED ACCORDING TO SUBJECTS.

Armstrong, Percy E.

25.0018 BC 1941 English as she is spoke. *Can-W I Mag* 30(5), May: 25-27. [*NYP*]

Ashcraft, Norman & Jones, Grant

25.0019 BZ 1966 Linguistic problems in British Honduras. *Car Q* 12(4), Dec.: 55-58.
[*RIS*]

Ashruf, G. J.; Dors, H. G.; Eersel, Chr. H.; Sietaram, K.; Muntslag, F. G. & Chin A Foeng, J. A.

25.0020 SR 1972 PRATEN EN SCHRIJVEN: KLAS 2, DEEL A. [TALKING AND WRITING: CLASS 2, VOLUME A]. Alphen aan den Rijn, The Netherlands, Samson Leersystemen N. V.: 51p. **[32]** [*RILA*]

Aub-Büscher, Gertrud

25.0021 TR 1968 Notes pour un glossaire du parler créole de la Trinité [Notes on a glossary of the Creole dialect of Trinidad]. *Rev Ling Rom* 32(127-128), July-Dec.: 334-340. [*UCLA*]

25.0022 TR 1970 A propos des influences du français dialectal sur un parler créole des Antilles [The influence of French dialect on Creole speech in the Antilles]. *In* PHONÉTIQUE ET LINGUISTIQUE ROMANES: MÉLANGES OFFERTS À M. GEORGES STRAKA. TOME 1. Lyon-Strasbourg, Société de Linguistique Romane: 360-369. [*UCLA*]

Bailey, Beryl Loftman

25.0023 JM 1962 A LANGUAGE GUIDE TO JAMAICA. New York, Research Institute for the Study of Man, 74p. **[32]** [*RIS*]

25.0024 GC 1962 Language studies in the independent university. *Car Q* 8(1): 38-42. **[32]** [*RIS*]

32.0040 JM 1963 Teaching of English noun-verb concord in primary schools in Jamaica.

25.0025 JM 1966 JAMAICAN CREOLE SYNTAX: A TRANSFORMATIONAL APPROACH. Cambridge, University Press: 164p. [*RIS*]

25.0026 JM 1966[?] Some problems involved in the language teaching situation in Jamaica. *In* Shuy, Roger W., ed. SOCIAL DIALECTS AND LANGUAGE LEARNING. PROCEEDINGS OF THE BLOOMINGTON, INDIANA CONFERENCE, 1964. Champaign, Illinois, National Council of Teachers of English: 105-111. **[32]** [*COL*]

25.0027 JM 1971 Jamaican Creole: can dialect boundaries be defined? *In* Hymes, Dell, ed. PIDGINIZATION AND CREOLIZATION OF LANGUAGES: PROCEEDINGS OF A CONFERENCE HELD AT THE UNIVERSITY OF THE WEST INDIES, MONA, JAMAICA, APRIL 1968. London, Cambridge University Press: 341-348. [*RIS*]

Baird, Keith

25.0028 NC [n.d.] ANTICIPATIONS OF PAPIAMENTO IN THE AFRO-PORTUGUESE OF GIL VICENTE. Atlanta University, Center for African and African-American Studies: 6p. (CAAS Papers in Linguistics No. 6) **[6]**
[*RIS*]

Balen, W. J. van

25.0029 CU 1940 Papiamentoe en Portugeesch [Papiamento and Portuguese]. *W I G* 22: 371-376. [*COL*]

Barbanson, W. L. de

22.0013   **GD**   1950   Frans-creoolse versjes van Guadeloupe [French-Creole verses of Guadeloupe].

Barnett, A. G.

25.0030   **SR**   1932   Colonial survivals in Bush-Negro speech. *Am Speech* 7(6), Aug.: 393-397.   [*COL*]

Baum, Paul

25.0031   **NA**   1974   Dos corrientes de literatura en papiamento [Two literary currents in Papiamentu]. *Revta Interam Rev* 4(3), Fall: 330-339.   [*RIS*]

Beardsley, Theodore S.

25.0032   **GC**   1975   French *R* in Caribbean Spanish. *Revta Interam Rev* 5(1), Spring: 101-109.   [*RIS*]

Benn, Bernard W.

32.0051   **BC**   1971   Metropolitan standards and their effects on Caribbean teaching.

Bennett, Louise

24.0026   **JM**   1957   ANANCY STORIES AND DIALECT VERSE.

Benoist, Jean & Lefebvre, Gilles

25.0033   **SB**   1972   Organisation sociale, évolution biologique et diversité linguistique à Saint-Barthélemy [Social organization, biological evolution and linguistic diversity in Saint-Barthelemy]. *In* Benoist, Jean, ed. L'ARCHIPEL INACHEVÉ: CULTURE ET SOCIÉTÉ AUX ANTILLES FRAN-ÇAISES. Montreal, Canada, Univ. of Montreal: 93-105.   **[8]**   [*RIS*]

Bentolila, Alain

25.0034   **MT**   1969   La spirante vélaire en créole martiniquais [The velar spirant in Martinican Creole]. *Linguistique* 2: 123-126.   [*UCLA*]

Bentz, Dorothy

25.0035   **BB,US**   1938   American English as spoken by the Barbadians. *Am Speech* 13(4), Dec.: 310-312.   **[18]**   [*COL*]

Bickerton, Derek

25.0036   **GU**   1973   The nature of creole continuum. *Language* 49(3), Sept.: 640-669.
                                                                                           [*NYP*]
25.0037   **GU**   1975   DYNAMICS OF A CREOLE SYSTEM. New York, Cambridge University Press: 224p.   [*COL*]
25.0038   **GC**   1976   Pidgin and Creole studies. *In* ANNUAL REVIEW OF ANTHROPOLOGY. VOLUME 5. Palo Alto, California, Annual Reviews Inc.: 169-193.   **[1]**   [*RIS*]

Birmingham, John Calhoun, Jr.

25.0039   **NA**   1970   THE PAPIAMENTU LANGUAGE OF CURAÇAO. Ph.D. dissertation, University of Virginia: 185p.   [*PhD*]

Boheemen, H. van

32.0070   **SR**   1951   Surinaamse onderwijszorgen [Education Problems in Surinam].

Bonne, C.

25.0040   **SR**   1920-21 Het Boschnegerschrift van Afaka [The Bush Negro writing system of Afaka]. *W I G* 2: 391-396. **[14]**   [*COL*]

Borely, Clive

32.0075   **TR**   1966   Teaching Trinidadian(s) English.

Boyce, Rubert W.

28.0147   **BC**   1910   HEALTH PROGRESS AND ADMINISTRATION IN THE WEST INDIES.

Breton, Raymond

25.0041   **FC**   1900   DICTIONAIRE FRANÇAIS-CARAÏBE [FRENCH-CREOLE DICTIONARY]. Leipzig, B. G. Teubner: 415p.   [*COL*]

Brunot, Ferdinand

25.0042   **FA**   1935   Le francais hors d'Europe [French outside of Europe]. *In his* HISTOIRE DE LA LANGUE FRANCAISE DES ORIGINES À 1900. Paris, Librairie A. Colin, v. 8, pt. 3, p.1037-1194. **[5]**   [*TCL*]

Bruton, J. G.

25.0043   **JM**   1945   Influencias españoles sobre el inglés de Jamaica [Spanish influences on Jamaican English]. *Boln Inst Caro Cuerva* 1(2), May-Aug.: 375-376.   [*NYP*]

Bryan, T. Avril

25.0044   **TR**   1974   French, Spanish, and Trinidad English. *Americas* 26(9), Sept.: 25-31. **[3]**   [*RIS*]

Bunel, Francois

19.0006   **GD**   1962[?] RECUEIL DE SCÈNES VÉCUES À LA GUADELOUPE [TRUE EPISODES OF GUADELOUPE—A MISCELLANY].

Butt, Audrey J.

23.0030   **GU**   1961-62 Symbolism and ritual among the Akawaio of British Guiana.

Caluwé, Jan de

25.0045   **NA**   1975   Taaldidaktiek voor de Antillen [Language didactics for the Antilles]. *Kristòf* 2(5), October: 224-231.   [*RIS*]

Carew, Jan

32.0108   **BC**   1976   Identity, cultural alienation and education in the Caribbean.

Carlson, Paul E.

25.0046   **SV**   1973   Cognition and social function in the West Indian dialect: Stubbs. *In* Fraser, Thomas M., ed. WINDWARD ROAD: CONTRIBUTIONS TO THE ANTHROPOLOGY OF SAINT VINCENT. Amherst, University of Massachusetts, Department of Anthropology: 123-147. (Research Reports No. 12)   [*RIS*]

Carr, Andrew T.

22.0058   **TR**   1956   Pierrot Grenade.

Carrington, Lawrence D.

25.0047   SL   1967   ST. LUCIAN CREOLE: A DESCRIPTIVE ANALYSIS OF ITS PHONOLOGY AND MORPHO-SYNTAX. Ph.D. dissertation, University of the West Indies (Mona).

25.0048   SL,DM   1969   Deviations from standard English in the speech of primary school children in St. Lucia and Dominica: a preliminary survey. Part I. *IRAL* 7(3), Aug.: 165-184.   **[32]**   [*TCL*]

Carrington, Lawrence D. & Borely, C. B.

32.0111   TR   1969   AN INVESTIGATION INTO ENGLISH LANGUAGE LEARNING AND TEACHING PROBLEMS IN TRINIDAD AND TOBAGO.

Carrington, Lawrence D.; Borely, C. B. & Knight, H. E.

32.0112   TR   1972   AWAY ROBIN RUN! A CRITICAL DESCRIPTION OF THE TEACHING OF THE LANGUAGE ARTS IN THE PRIMARY SCHOOLS OF TRINIDAD AND TOBAGO.

25.0049   TR   1972   LINGUISTIC EXPOSURE OF TRINIDADIAN CHILDREN. St. Augustine, Trinidad, University of the West Indies, Institute of Education, Project 15: 25p.   **[32]**   [*TCL*]

25.0050   TR   1974   Linguistic exposure of Trinidadian children. *Car J Educ* 1, June: 12-22.   **[32]**   [*RIS*]

Cary-Elwes, C. I.

25.0051   GU   1917   On the correct method of spelling the Indian languages. *Timehri* 3d ser., 4(21), June: 87-97.   [*AMN*]

Casseres, R.

25.0052   NA   1974   De moedertaal: een pedagogisch uitgangspunt [The mother tongue: from an educational point of view]. *Kristòf* 1(2), April: 83-93.   **[32]** [*RIS*]

Cassidy, Frederic G.

25.0053   JM   1953[?]   Language and folklore. *Car Q* 3(1): 4-12.   **[24]**   [*RIS*]

25.0054   JM   1957   Iteration as a word-forming device in Jamaican folk speech. *Am Speech* 32(1), Feb.: 49-53.   **[19]**   [*COL*]

25.0055   GC   1959   English language studies in the Caribbean. *Am Speech* 34(3), Oct.: 163-171.   **[32]**   [*COL*]

25.0056   JM   1961   JAMAICA TALK: THREE HUNDRED YEARS OF THE ENGLISH LANGUAGE IN JAMAICA. London, Macmillan, 468p.   [*RIS*]

25.0057   JM   1961   Some footnotes on the "junjo" question. *Am Speech* 36(2), May: 101-103.   **[19]**   [*COL*]

25.0058   BC   1966   "Hipsaw" and "John Canoe". *Am Speech* 41(1), Feb.: 45-51. [*COL*]

25.0059   JM   1966   Multiple etymologies in Jamaican Creole. *Am Speech* 41(3), Oct.: 211-215.   [*COL*]

25.0060   JM   1967   Some new light on old Jamaicanisms. *Am Speech* 42(3), Oct.: 190-201.   **[24]**   [*COL*]

25.0061   JM   1971   Tracing the pidgin element in Jamaica Creole (with notes on method and the nature of pidgin vocabularies). *In* Hymes, Dell, ed. PIDGINIZATION AND CREOLIZATION OF LANGUAGES: PROCEEDINGS OF A CONFERENCE HELD AT THE UNIVERSITY OF THE WEST INDIES, MONA, JAMAICA, APRIL 1968. London, Cambridge University Press: 203-221.   [*RIS*]

Cassidy, Frederic G. & DeCamp, David

25.0062   JM   1966   Names for an albino among Jamaican Negroes. *Names* 14: 129-133. **[11]**   [*COL*]

Cassidy, Frederic G. & LePage, R. B.

25.0063   JM   1967   DICTIONARY OF JAMAICA ENGLISH. Cambridge, University Press: 489p.   [*RIS*]

Castillo Mathieu, Nicolás del

25.0064   BZ   1975   Léxico caribe en el caribe negro de Honduras Británica [Carib lexicon in Black Carib in British Honduras]. *Thesaurus* 30(3), Sept.-Dec.: 401-470.   [*UCLA*]

Cave, George N.

25.0065   GU   1970   Some sociolinguistic factors in the production of standard language in Guyana and implications for the language teacher. *Language Learning* 20(2), Dec.: 249-263. **[32]**   [*COL*]

32.0114   GU   1971   PRIMARY SCHOOL LANGUAGE IN GUYANA: AN INVESTIGATION OF ORAL LANGUAGE AT THE STANDARD ONE LEVEL.

Chambertrand, Gilbert de

24.0042   FA   1935   Manzè Elodie.

24.0043   FA   1935   Proverbes et dictons antillais [Proverbs and sayings of the [French] Antilles].

22.0062   FA   1963   Mi io!

Christie, Pauline Grace

25.0066   DM   1969   A SOCIO-LINGUISTIC STUDY OF SOME DOMINICAN CREOLE SPEAKERS. D. Phil. dissertation, University of York: 228p.

Collymore, Frank A.

25.0067   BB   1955   NOTES FOR A GLOSSARY OF WORDS AND PHRASES OF BARBADIAN DIALECT. Bridgetown, Advocate Co., 80p.   [*RIS*]

25.0068   BB   1965   NOTES FOR A GLOSSARY OF WORDS AND PHRASES OF BARBADIAN DIALECT. Bridgetown, Barbados, Advocate Co.: 122p.   [*RIS*]

25.0069   BB   1967   Postscript to "Notes". *Bim* 12(45), July-Dec.: 58-60.   [*RIS*]

Coomans, H. E.

54.0218   NA   1970   Volksnamen voor weekdieren op de Nederlandse Antillen [Vernacular names of molluscs in the Netherlands Antilles].

Corne, Chris

25.0070   FG   1971   Le patois créole français de la Guyane (St-Laurent-du-Maroni): esquisse de grammaire [The Creole French patois of Guyana (St-Laurent-du-Maroni): outline of grammar]. *Te Reo* 14: 81-103.   [*UCLA*]

Craig, Dennis R.

32.0133   JM   1965   The written English of some 14-year-old Jamaican and English children.

32.0134   BC   1966   Some developments in language teaching in the West Indies.

32.0135   JM   1966   Teaching English to Jamaican Creole speakers: a model of a multi-dialect situation.

32.0136   JM   1967   Some early indications of learning a second dialect.

32.0138	BC	1971	Education and Creole English in the West Indies: some sociolinguistic factors.
32.0139	GU	1971	English in secondary education in a former British colony: a case study of Guyana.
25.0071	JM	1971	THE USE OF LANGUAGE BY 7 YEAR-OLD JAMAICA CHILDREN LIVING IN CONTRASTING SOCIO-ECONOMIC ENVIRONMENTS. Ph.D. dissertation, University of London: 476p.
32.0140	JM	1973	Reading and the creole speaker.
25.0072	JM	1974	Developmental and social-class differences in language. *Car J Educ* 1(2), Dec.: 5-23. **[8]** [*RIS*]
32.0141	BC	1974	Language education research in the Commonwealth Caribbean.

Craig, Dennis R. & Carter, Sheila

32.0142	JM	1976	The language learning aptitudes of Jamaican children at the beginning of secondary school.

Craig, Dennis R. & Wilson, Donald G.

25.0073	GC	1971	Report on Annual Conference on Caribbean Linguistics held at U.W.I., Mona—17th to 21st May, 1971. *Car Q* 17(2), June: 4-9. **[1]** [*RIS*]

Crawford, John R.

25.0074	BC	1976	When is a bluggo not a bluggo? *Car J Educ* 3(1), Jan.: 66-69. [*RIS*]

Creary, Jean

32.0143	JM	1965	Mathematics for children speaking Jamaican creole.

Crooks, Kenneth B. M.

24.0049	JM	1933	Forty Jamaican proverbs: interpretations and inferences.

Cruickshank, J. Graham

25.0075	BB	1911	Negro English, with reference particularly to Barbados. *Timehri* 3d ser., 1(18B), July: 102-106. **[11,19]** [*AMN*]
25.0076	GU,BB	1916	"BLACK TALK": BEING NOTES ON NEGRO DIALECT IN BRITISH GUIANA, WITH (INEVITABLY) A CHAPTER ON THE VERNACULAR OF BARBADOS. Demerara, Argosy Co., 76p. **[11,19]** [*SCH*]

Dalby, David

14.0004	JM	1971	Ashanti survivals in the language and traditions of the Windward Maroons of Jamaica.

Dam, C. F. A. van & Goilo, E. R.

25.0077	NL	1953	2000 ZINNEN [2000 SENTENCES]. Willemstad, Curaçao, Hollandsche Boekhandel: 221p. [*UCLA*]

David, B. & Jardel, J.-P.

24.0063	MT	1969[?]	LES PROVERBES CRÉOLES DE LA MARTINIQUE: LANGUAGE ET SOCIÉTÉ [CREOLE PROVERBS OF MARTINIQUE: LANGUAGE AND SOCIETY].

Davy, Pierre

25.0078	GD	1971	Créole et français en Guadeloupe: une complicité périlleuse [Creole and French in Guadeloupe: a perilous complicity]. *In* FRANÇAIS ET CRÉOLE DANS LA CARAÏBE: VIᴱ SYMPOSIUM INTER-AMÉRICAIN DE LINGUISTIQUE, PORTO-RICO, JUNE 1971 [FRENCH AND CREOLE IN THE CARIBBEAN: SIXTH INTER-AMERICAN SYMPOSIUM ON LINGUISTICS, PUERTO RICO, JUNE 1971]. Fort-de-France, Martinique, Centre d'Etudes Régionales Antilles-Guyane: 59-66. (Documents du CERAG No. 4) [*RIS*]

D'Costa, Jean
25.0079   JM   1968   Language and dialect in Jamaica. *Jam J* 2(1), March: 71-74.   [*RIS*]

DeCamp, David
25.0080   JM   1961   Social and geographical factors in Jamaican dialects. *In* Le Page, R. B., ed. PROCEEDINGS OF THE CONFERENCE ON CREOLE LANGUAGE STUDIES. London, Macmillan, p.61-84. (Creole language studies, no. 2.) **[5,56]**   [*RIS*]
25.0081   JM   1967   African day-names in Jamaica. *Language* 43(1): 139-149.   [*NYP*]
25.0082   GC   1968   The field of creole language studies. *Latin Amer Res Rev* 3(3), Summer: 25-46.   [*COL*]
25.0083   JM   1969   Diasystem vs. overall pattern: the Jamaican syllabic nuclei. *In* Atwood, E. Bagby & Hill, Archibald A., ed. STUDIES IN LANGUAGE, LITERATURE, AND CULTURE OF THE MIDDLE AGES AND LATER. Austin, University of Texas: 3-12.   [*COL*]
25.0084   GC   1971   Introduction: the study of pidgin and creole languages. *In* Hymes, Dell, ed. PIDGINIZATION AND CREOLIZATION OF LANGUAGES: PROCEEDINGS OF A CONFERENCE HELD AT THE UNIVERISITY OF THE WEST INDIES, MONA, JAMAICA, APRIL 1968. London, Cambridge University Press: 13-39.   [*RIS*]
25.0085   JM   1971   Toward a generative analysis of a post-creole speech continuum. *In* Hymes, Dell, ed. PIDGINIZATION AND CREOLIZATION OF LANGUAGES: PROCEEDINGS OF A CONFERENCE HELD AT THE UNIVERSITY OF THE WEST INDIES, MONA, JAMAICA, APRIL 1968. London, Cambridge University Press: 349-370.   [*RIS*]
25.0086   JM   1974   Neutralizations, iteratives, and ideophones: the locus of language in Jamaica. *In* De Camp, David, & Hancock, Ian F., eds. PIDGINS AND CREOLES: CURRENT TRENDS AND PROSPECTS. Washington, D.C., Georgetown University Press: 46-60.   [*RIS*]

DeCamp, David & Hancock, Ian F., eds.
25.0087   GC   1974   PIDGINS AND CREOLES: CURRENT TRENDS AND PROSPECTS. Washington, D. C., Georgetown University Press: 137p.   [*RIS*]

Delmond, Stany
25.0088   MT   1935   Language et folklore martiniquais [Language and folklore of Martinique]. *Mercure Fr* 264(898), Nov. 15: 83-95. **[24]**   [*NYP*]

Denis, Serge
25.0089   NA   1935   Notre créole [Our Creole language]. *In* Denis, Serge, ed. NOS ANTILLES. Orléans, Luzeray, p.325-376.   [*AGS*]

Derrick, June
18.0076   BC,UK   1966   TEACHING ENGLISH TO IMMIGRANTS.

Deutch, Rachel F.
32.0166   FC   1969   Suggestions for the teaching of Negro literature of French expression.

Dillard, J. L.
25.0090   GC   1962   Purism and prescriptivism as applied to the Caribbean Creoles—a tentative classification. *Car Stud* 1(4), Jan.: 3-10.   [*RIS*]

25.0091   GC   1964   The writings of Herskovits and the study of the language of the Negro in the New World. *Car Stud* 4(2), July: 35-41. **[11]**   [*RIS*]

25.0092   GC   1965   Additional notes on stepping and bending. *Car Stud* 4(4), Jan.: 74-76.   [*RIS*]

25.0093   BC   1966   English in the West Indies, or the West Indies in English? *In* Emig, Janet A.; Fleming, James T. & Popp, Helen M., eds. LANGUAGE AND LEARNING. New York, Harcourt, Brace and World, Inc.: 282-286. **[19]**   [*COL*]

25.0094   BC,CA   1970-71   The history of Black English in Nova-Scotia—a first step. *Afr Lang Rev* 9: 263-279. **[6]**   [*COL*]

25.0095   GC   1970   Names or slogans: some problems from the Cameroun, the Caribbean, Burundi, and the United States. *Car Stud* 9(4), Jan.: 104-110.   [*RIS*]

25.0096   JM   1970   Observations on the dictionary of Jamaican English. *Car Stud* 10(2), July: 118-124.   [*RIS*]

25.0097   BC   1975   CREOLE PORTUGUESE AND CREOLE ENGLISH: THE EARLY RECORDS. Atlanta University, Center for African and African-American Studies: 14p. (CAAS Papers in Linguistics No. 3) **[6]**   [*RIS*]

Dilworth, W. W.
32.0168   JM   1965   Teaching language arts on the basis of pupils' needs, errors and background experiences.

Diniz, Edson Soares
9.0040   GU   1968   A terminologia de parentesco dos índios wapitxâna [Wapishana kinship terminology].

Di Pietro, Robert J.
25.0098   GC   1968   Bilingualism. *In* Sebeok, Thomas A., ed. CURRENT TRENDS IN LINGUISTICS, IV: IBERO-AMERICAN AND CARIBBEAN LINGUISTICS. The Hague, Mouton: 399-414.   [*RIS*]

25.0099   SC   1968   Multilingualism in St. Croix. *Am Speech* 43(2), May: 127-137.
                                                                          [*COL*]

Domingos, Robert
25.0100   CU   1974   ATTITUDE AND LANGUAGE CHOICE IN A MULTILINGUAL SOCIETY: URBAN CURAÇAO. Ph.D. dissertation, Claremont Graduate School: 116p. **[20]**   [*PhD*]

Donicie, A.
25.0101   SR   1967   DE CREOLENTAAL VAN SURINAME: SPRAAKKUNST [THE CREOLE LANGUAGE OF SURINAM: GRAMMAR]. Paramarbio, Surinam, Radhakishun & Co. N. V.: 152p.   [*UCLA*]

Donicie, A. C.
19.0016   SR   1953   Iets over de taal en de sprookjes van Suriname [On the language and the fairy-tales of Surinam].

25.0102   SR   1953   Kanttekeningen bij "De klanken van het Neger-Engels" [Notes about "The sounds of Negro-English"]. *Taal Tong* 5: 4-7.

25.0103   SR   1955   De partikels *sa* en *(de)go* in de Creolentaal van Suriname [The particles *sa* and *(de)go* in the Creole language of Surinam]. *W I G* 36: 183-191.   [*COL*]

Doob, Leonard William
31.0054   JM   1958   The effect of the Jamaican patois on attitude and recall.

Doran, Edwin Beal, Jr.
25.0104   CM   1954   Notes on an archaic island dialect. *Am Speech* 29(1), Feb.: 82-85.
[*COL*]

Dubelaar, C. N.
25.0105   SR   1970   Het Afakaschrift in de Afrikanistiek [The Afaka script in the African studies]. *N W I G* 47(3), Nov.: 294-303.   **[14]**   [*RIS*]
1.0096   SR   1970   Lijst van geschriften van Justus Wilhelm Gonggryp met beknopts biografie [List of writing by Justus Wilhelm Gonggryp with a short biography].

Dubelaar, C. N. & Gonggryp, J. W.
25.0106   SR   1968   Het Afaka-schrift: Een nadere beschouwing [The Afaka script: A further analysis]. *N W I G* 46(3), Dec.: 232-260.   **[14]**   [*RIS*]

Durbin, Mridula Adenwala
25.0107   TR   1973   Formal changes in Trinidad Hindi as a result of language adaptation. *Am Anthrop* 75(5), Oct.: 1290-1304.   **[12]**   [*RIS*]

Dwyer, Audley Lloyd
32.0177   JM   1973   A PROPOSAL FOR IMPROVING THE TEACHING OF ENGLISH IN THE LOWER PRIMARY GRADES IN JAMAICAN SCHOOLS.

Echteld, J. J. M.
25.0108   SR   1962   THE ENGLISH WORDS IN SRANAN (NEGRO-ENGLISH OF SURINAM). Groningen, J. B. Wolters, 219p. (Ph.D. dissertation, University of Amsterdam, September 1961).   [*COL*]

Edwards, W. J.
32.0187   GU   1975   A guided composition programme for Form I children in Guyana.

Edwards, Walter F.
25.0109   GU   1976   Sociolinguistics and its application to the study of some aspects of social behaviour in Guyana. *Guy J Sociol* 1(2), April: 1-18.   [*RIS*]

Eersel, Christian
25.0110   SR   1971   Varieties of creole in Suriname: prestige in choice of language and linguistic form. *In* Hymes, Dell, ed. PIDGINIZATION AND CREOLIZATION OF LANGUAGES: PROCEEDINGS OF A CONFERENCE HELD AT THE UNIVERSITY OF THE WEST INDIES, MONA, JAMAICA, APRIL 1968. London, Cambridge University Press: 317-322.   [*RIS*]

Emanuel, Lezmore Evan
25.0111   VI   1972   SURVIVING AFRICANISMS IN VIRGIN ISLANDS ENGLISH CREOLE. Ann Arbor, Michigan, University Microfilms: 177p. (Ph.D. dissertation, Howard University, 1970)   **[19]**   [*RIS*]

Fanshawe, D. B.

54.0327	GU	1947	Arawak Indian plant names.
54.0329	GU	1953	Akawaio Indian plant names.

Figueroa, John Joseph

32.0204   BC   1966   Notes on the teaching of English in the West Indies.

Fisher, Lawrence E.

25.0112   BB   1976   *Dropping remarks* and the Barbadian audience. *Am Ethnol* 3(2), May: 227-242.   **[10]**   [*COL*]

Fokker, A. A.

25.0113   NL   1914   Het Papiamentoe of basterd-Spaans der West-Indische eilanden [The Papiamento or bastard-Spanish of the West Indian islands]. *Tijdschr Ned Taal Lettk* 33: 54-79.   [*UCLA*]

Franck, Harry A.

24.0078   JM   1921   Jamaica proverbs.

Frank, Francine Wattman

25.0114   NL   1974   Language and education in the Leeward Netherlands Antilles. *Car Stud* 13(4), Jan.: 111-117.   **[32]**   [*RIS*]

Funk, Henry Elwell

25.0115   MT   1953   THE FRENCH CREOLE DIALECT OF MARTINIQUE: ITS HISTORICAL BACKGROUND, VOCABULARY, SYNTAX, PROVERBS AND LITERATURE WITH A GLOSSARY. Ph.D. dissertation, University of Virginia, 294p.   **[24]**

Gáldi, L.

25.0116   FC   1949   De l'importance des parlers français-créoles pour la linguistique générale [About the importance of French Creole dialects for general linguistics]. *In* ACTES DU SIXIÈME CONGRÈS INTERNATIONAL DES LINGUISTES, PARIS, 19-24 JUILLET 1948. Paris, Librarie C. Klincksieck: 307-315.   [*UCLA*]

Gannon, Roger E.

25.0117   DM,UK   1972   DEVIANT FEATURES OF THE ENGLISH SPEECH OF SELECTED SPEAKERS OF DOMINICAN CREOLE RESIDENT IN LONDON. Ph.D. dissertation, University of Essex: 578p.   **[18]**

Germain, Robert

25.0118   FA   1976   GRAMMAIRE CRÉOLE [CREOLE GRAMMAR]. Villejuif, France, Editions du Levain: 319p.   [*RIS*]

Glock, Naomi

25.0119   SR   1972   Clause and sentence in Saramaccan. *J Afr Lang* 11, part 1: 45-61.
                                                                    [*AMN*]

25.0120   SR   1972   Role structure in Saramaccan verbs. *In* Grimes, Joseph E.; ed. LANGUAGES OF THE GUIANAS. Norman, Oklahoma, University of Oklahoma: 28-34 (Summer Institute of Linguistics Publications, 35).   **[14]**   [*COL*]

Göbl, L.

25.0121   FA   1933   Problemi di sostrato mel creolo-francese (Problems of the linguistic substratum in French Creole]. *Rev Ling Rom* 9(35-36), July-Dec.: 336-345.   [*NYP*]

Göbl-Galdi, L.

25.0122   FC   1934   Esquisse de la structure grammaticale des patois francais-creoles [Outline of the grammatical structure of the Creole French dialects]. *Z Franz Spr* 58(5-6): 257-295.   [*COL*]

Goeje, C. H. de

25.0123   GG   1909   ETUDES LINGUISTIQUES CARAÏBES [CARIB LINGUISTIC STUDIES]. [Part 1.] Amsterdam, Noord-Hollandsche Uitg. Mij., 307p. (Verhandelingen der Koninklijke Akademie van Wetenschappen, Afdeeling Letterkunde, new ser., v. 10, no. 3.) **[13]**   [*COL*]

13.0072   GG   1924   Guayana and Carib tribal names.

13.0073   GG   1924-25 Karaïben en Guiana [Caribs and Guyana].

25.0124   GU,SR   1928   THE ARAWAK LANGUAGE OF GUIANA. Amsterdam, Noord-Hollandsche Uitg. Mij., 309p. (Verhandelingen der Koninklijke Akademie van Wetenschappen te Amsterdam, Afdeeling Letterkunde, new ser., v. 28, no. 2.) **[13]**   [*COL*]

25.0125   SR   1929-30 Het merkwaardige Arawaksch [The remarkable Arawak (language)]. *W I G* 11: 11-28. **[13]**   [*COL*]

25.0126   GU,SR   1930   The inner structure of the Warrau language of Guiana. *J Soc Am* new ser., 22: 33-72. **[13]**   [*AGS*]

25.0127   GU,SR   1930-31 Het merkwaardige Warau [The remarkable Warau (language)]. *W I G* 12: 1-16. **[13]**   [*COL*]

25.0128   SR   1932-33 Het merkwaardige Karaïbisch [The remarkable Carib language]. *W I G* 14: 99-123. **[13]**   [*COL*]

25.0129   GG   1934-35 Curiositeiten uit Guyana [Curiosities from Guiana]. *W I G* 16: 72-76.

25.0130   GC   1935   Fünf Sprachfamilien Südamerikas [Five South American linguistic families]. *Meded Kon Akad Wetensch Afd Lettk* ser. A, 77(5): 149-177. **[13]**   [*COL*]

25.0131   GC   1935-36 Het merkwaardige Eiland-Karaïbisch [The remarkable Island-Carib language]. *W I G* 17: 241-249. **[13]**   [*COL*]

25.0132   GG   1937   Laut und Sinn in Karibischen Sprachen [Sound and meaning in Carib languages]. *In* MÉLANGES DE LINGUISTIQUE ET DE PHILOLOGIE OFFERTS À JACQUES VAN GINNEKEN. Paris, Librairie C. Klincksieck, p.335-339. **[13]**   [*AMN*]

25.0133   GC   1939   Nouvel examen des langues des Antilles avec notes sur les langues arawak-maipure et caribes et vocabulaires shebayo et guayana (Guyane) [A new examination of Caribbean languages, with notes on the Arawak-Maypure and Carib languages and on Shebayo [?] and Guiana vocabularies]. *J Soc Am* new ser., 31: 1-120. **[13]**   [*AGS*]

25.0134   GG   1946   ETUDES LINGUISTIQUES CARIBES [CARIB LINGUISTIC STUDIES]. [Part 2.] Amsterdam, Noord-Hollandsche Uitg. Mij., 274p. (Verhandelingen der Koninklijke Nederlandsche Akademie van Wetenschappen, Afdeeling Letterkunde, new ser., v. 49, no. 2.) **[13]**   [*NYP*]

Goilo, E. R.

25.0135   CU   1951   PAPIAMENTS LEERBOEK [PAPIAMENTO GRAMMAR]. Willemstad, Curacao, 168p.   [*NYP*]

25.0136   NL   1974   HABLEMOS PAPIAMENTO [LETS SPEAK PAPIAMENTO]. Aruba, De Wit Stores N.V.: 88p.   **[32]**   [*RILA*]

Gonggrijp, J. W.

25.0137   SR   1960   The evolution of Djuka-script in Surinam, by J. W. Gonggryp. *N W I G* 40: 63-72.   **[14]**   [*RIS*]

Gonggrijp, J. W. & Dubelaar, C. N.

25.0138   SR   1960   Pater Morssink en Afaka [Pater Morssink and Afaka]. *Opbouw* Christmas: 11p.   **[14]**   [*RIS*]

25.0139   SR   1963   De geschriften van Afaka in zijn Djoeka-schrift [The papers of Afaka in Djuka script], [by] J. W. Gonggryp & C. Dubelaar. *N W I G* 42(3), May: 213-254.   **[14]**   [*RIS*]

Goodman, Morris F.

25.0140   TR   1958   On the phonemics of French Creole of Trinidad. *Word* 14(2-3), Aug.-Dec.: 208-212.   [*RIS*]

25.0141   FC   1961   A COMPARATIVE STUDY OF CREOLE FRENCH. Ph.D. dissertation, Columbia University: 295p.   [*PhD*]

25.0142   GC   1964   A COMPARATIVE STUDY OF CREOLE FRENCH DIALECTS. The Hague, Mouton, 281p.   [*RIS*]

25.0143   GC   1964   A COMPARATIVE STUDY OF CREOLE FRENCH DIALECTS. The Hague, Mouton & Co.: 143p.   [*RIS*]

Granda, Germán de

25.0144   NA   1973   Papiamento en Hispanoamérica (siglos XVII-XIX) [Papiamento in Spanish-America (17th-19th century)]. *Thesaurus* 28(1), Jan.-April: 1-13.   **[5]**   [*UCLA*]

25.0145   CU   1974   El repertorio lingüistico de los sefárditas de Curaçao durante lost siglos XVII y XVIII y el problema del origen del papiamento [The linguistic repertoire of the sephards of Curacao in the 17th and 18th centuries and the problem of the origin of Papiamento]. *Romance Philology* 28(1), Aug.: 1-16.   **[15]**   [*COL*]

Grant, D. R. B.

32.0248   JM   1964   Some problems in the teaching of English.

Gray, Cecil

32.0253   BC   1963   Teaching English in the West Indies.

32.0256   JM   1971   Jamaican English—a report of a pilot experiment in remedial English teaching through role-playing and dialogues.

32.0257   BC   1975   Curricula, syllabuses and examinations in English.

Green, John

32.0259   BC   1973   The language situation in English-speaking Caribbean.

Grimes, Joseph E.

25.0146   SR   1972   Writing systems for the interior of Surinam. *In* Grimes, Joseph E., ed. LANGUAGES OF THE GUIANAS. Norman, Oklahoma, University of Oklahoma: 85-91 (Summer Institute of Linguistics Publications, 35).   **[13]**   [*COL*]

Grimes, Joseph E., ed.

25.0147 GG 1972 LANGUAGES OF THE GUIANAS. Norman, Oklahoma, University of Oklahoma: 91p. (Summer Institute of Linguistics Publications, 35)
[COL]

Grimes, Joseph E. & Glock, Naomi

25.0148 SR 1970 A Saramaccan narrative pattern. *Language* 46(2), Part 1, June: 408-425. [13]
[NYP]

Gúerin, Daniel

19.0023 GC 1956 Un futur pour les Antilles? [A future for the Antilles?]

Gullick, Charles John M. R.

25.0149 BZ 1976 Maltese and Creole. *Belizean Stud* 4(3), May: 25-36.
[RIS]

Hadel, Richard E.

25.0150 BZ 1975 Male and female speech in Carib. *National Stud* 3(4), July: 32-36. [13]
[RIS]

Hall, Robert A., Jr.

25.0151 SR 1948 The linguistic structure of Taki-Taki. *Language* 24: 92-116. [COL]
25.0152 GC 1952 Pidgin English and linguistic change. *Lingua* 3, Feb.: 138-146.
[COL]
25.0153 GC 1958 Creolized languages and "genetic relationships." *Word* 14(2-3), Aug.-Dec.: 367-373.
[RIS]
25.0154 GC 1966 PIDGIN AND CREOLE LANGUAGES. Ithaca, New York, Cornell University Press: 188p.
[RIS]
25.0155 GC 1968 Creole linguistics. *In* Sebeok, Thomas A., ed. CURRENT TRENDS IN LINGUISTICS, IV: IBERO-AMERICAN AND CARIBBEAN LINGUISTICS. The Hague, Mouton & Co.: 361-371.
[RIS]

Hancock, Ian F.

25.0156 GC 1969 A provisional comparison of the English-based Atlantic Creoles. *Afr Lang Rev* 8: 7-72. [6]
[COL]
25.0157 JM,SR 1971 A provisional comparison of the English-derived Atlantic creoles. *In* Hymes, Dell, ed. PIDGINIZATION AND CREOLIZATION OF LANGUAGES: PROCEEDINGS OF A CONFERENCE HELD AT THE UNIVERSITY OF THE WEST INDIES, MONA, JAMAICA, APRIL 1968. London, Cambridge University Press: 287-291.
[RIS]

Harris, Charles C.

25.0158 SR 1952 PAPIAMENTU PHONOLOGY. Ph.D. dissertation, Cornell University.
[PhD]

Hartog, J.

25.0159 NA 1965 Enquête over het gebruik van Nederlands of Papiament onder het bibliotheekpubliek op de Nederlandse Antillen [Survey about the use of Dutch or Papiamento among library users in the Netherlands Antilles]. *Bibliotheekleven* 50(1), Jan.: 17-20.
[COL]

Haynes, Lilith M.

25.0160 BB,GU 1973 LANGUAGE IN BARBADOS AND GUYANA: ATTITUDES, BEHAVIOURS AND COMPARISONS. Ph.D. dissertation, Stanford University: 155p. [20]
[PhD]

Hazaël-Massieux, Guy

25.0161   GD,MT   1969   Remarques sur les créoles français des Antilles: problèmes de convergence linguistique [Remarks on the French Creole languages of the Antilles: the problems of linguistic convergence]. *In* ACTES DU XE CONGRÈS INTERNATIONAL DES LINGUISTES, BUCAREST, 28 AOÛT-2 SEPTEMBRE 1967. I. Bucarest, Romania, Éditions de l'Académie de la République Socialiste de Roumanie: 727-731.   [*UCLA*]

25.0162   GD   1972   LA PHONÉTIQUE ET LA PHONOLOGIE DU CRÉOLE DE LA GUADELOUPE [PHONETICS AND PHONOLOGY OF CREOLE IN GUADELOUPE]. Thèse, 3ème cycle, Université de Grenoble: ca. 400p.

Hearn, Lafcadio

25.0163   MT,TR,GU   1960[?]   "GOMBO ZHÈBES." LITTLE DICTIONARY OF CREOLE PROVERBS, SELECTED FROM SIX CREOLE DIALECTS. TRANSLATED INTO FRENCH AND INTO ENGLISH, WITH NOTES, COMPLETE INDEX TO SUBJECTS AND SOME BRIEF REMARKS UPON THE CREOLE IDIOMS OF LOUISIANA. DeBrun: 42p. (Originally published in 1885).   [*UCLA*]

Hellinga, W. Gs.

25.0164   NC   1951   De waarde van de z.g. Mengtalen in de West [The value of the so-called mixed language in the West]. *Taal Tong* 3: 133-137.

32.0282   SR   1955   LANGUAGE PROBLEMS IN SURINAM: DUTCH AS THE LANGUAGE OF THE SCHOOLS.

25.0165   SR   1958   Kansen voor het Nederlands in Suriname [Changes for the Dutch language in Surinam]. *In* ALBUM EDGARD BLANQUAERT. Tongeren, [Belgium], George Miciels.

Hellinger, Marlis; Hadel, Richard E. & Young, Colville

25.0166   BZ   1974   How to write Belizean Creole; and, Comments. *National Stud* 2(4), July: 22-34.   [*RIS*]

Hellinger, Marlis & Young, Colville

25.0167   BZ   1974   The future of Belizean Creole; and Comment. *National Stud* 2(3), May: 11-18.   [*RIS*]

Henriquez, P. Cohen & Hesseling, D. C.

24.0086   CU,SR   1935-36   Papiamentse en Negerengelse spreekworden [Papiamento and Negro-English proverbs].

24.0087   CU   1936-37   Nog enige Papiamentse spreekwoorden [Some more Papiamento proverbs].

Herskovits, Melville Jean

25.0168   SR   1930-31   On the provenience of the Portuguese in Saramacca Tongo. *W I G* 12: 545-557.   [*COL*]

Herskovits, Melville Jean & Herskovits, Frances S.

24.0089   SR   1936   SURINAME FOLK-LORE (with transcriptions and Suriname songs and musicological analysis by Dr. M. Kolinski).

Hesseling, D. C.

25.0169   UV   1905   HET NEGERHOLLANDS DER DEENSE ANTILLEN: BIJDRAGE TOT DE GESCHIEDENIS DER NEDERLANDSE TAAL IN AMERIKA [THE NEGRO-DUTCH OF THE DANISH ANTILLES: CONTRIBUTION TO THE HISTORY OF THE DUTCH LANGUAGE IN AMERICA]. Leiden, A. W. Sijthoff, 290p.   [*COL*]

| 25.0170 | NA | 1933 | Papiaments en Negerhollands [Papiamento and Negro-Dutch]. *Tijdschr Ned Taal Lettk* 52: 265-288. [*UCLA*] |
| 25.0171 | NL | 1933 | Een Spaans boek over het Papiaments [A Spanish book about Papiamento]. *Tijdschr Ned Taal Lettk* 52: 40-69. [*UCLA*] |

Hoff, B. J.

25.0172	SR	1955	The languages of the Indians of Surinam and the comparative study of the Carib and Arawak languages. *Bijd Volk* 111(4): 325-355. **[13]** [*RIS*]
25.0173	SR	1961	Dorsal phonemes, with special reference to Carib. *Lingua* 10(4): 403-419. **[13]** [*RIS*]
25.0174	SR	1962	The nominal word-groups in Carib; a problem of delimitation of syntax and morphology. *Lingua* 11: 157-164. **[13]** [*RIS*]

Hollyman, K. J.

| 1.0144 | FC | 1965 | Bibliographie des créoles et dialectes régionaux française d'outre-mer moderne [Bibliography of creoles and regional French dialects of modern overseas departments]. |

Holmer, Nils M.

19.0030	GC	1960	Indian place names in South America and the Antilles. *Names* 8(3).
19.0031	GC	1960	Indian place names in South America and the Antilles. *Names* 8(4).
19.0032	GC	1961	Indian place names in South America and the Antilles. *Names* 9(1).

Horowitz, Michael M.

| 24.0091 | MT | 1959 | Humor and riddles in Martiniquan folk literature. |

Houte, I. C. van

| 25.0175 | SR | 1963 | Het bilinguisme van de Hindostaanse kinderen in Suriname [Bilingualism of Hindustani children in Surinam]. *In* Lutchman, W. I., ed. VAN BRITS-INDISCH EMIGRANT TOT BURGER VAN SURINAME. The Hague, Drukkerij Wieringa, p.90-98. **[12,32]** |

Hoyer, W. M.

25.0176	NA	1922	WOORDENLIJST EN SAMENSPRAAK, HOLLANDSCH-PAPIAMENTSCH-SPAANSCH [VOCABULARY AND CONVERSATION, DUTCH-PAPIAMENTO-SPANISH]. [Willemstad?] Curacao, Libería Bethencourt, 74p. [*NYP*]
2.0218	AR	1945	A BRIEF HISTORICAL DESCRIPTION OF THE ISLAND OF ARUBA IN ENGLISH AND PAPIAMENTO.
25.0177	NL	1958	A LITTLE GUIDE: ENGLISH-PAPIAMENTO-NETHERLANDS. Curaçao, Boekhandel Bethencourt: 96p. [*UCLA*]

Hughes, Alister

| 25.0178 | GR | 1966 | Non-standard English of Grenada. *Car Q* 12(4), Dec.: 47-54. [*RIS*] |
| 25.0179 | BC | 1971 | Eastcaribbeanese. *Car Cons Assoc Environ Newsl* 2(1), Jan.: 19-23. [*RIS*] |

Hull, Alexander

| 25.0180 | FC | 1968 | The origins of New World French phonology. *Word* 24(1-2-3), April-Aug.-Dec.: 255-269. [*COL*] |

Hummelen, J. A.

| 25.0181 | NA | 1967 | Veeltaligheid en taalproblemen [Polyglottism and language problems]. *Schakels* NA47: 14-26. **[32]** [*NYP*] |

Huttar, George L.

25.0182   SR   1972   A comparative word list for Djuka. *In* Grimes, Joseph E., ed. LANGUAGES OF THE GUIANAS. Norman, Oklahoma, University of Oklahoma: 12-21 (Summer Institute of Linguistics Publications, 35). **[14]**   [*COL*]

Huttar, George L. & Huttar, Mary L.

25.0183   SR   1972   Notes on Djuka phonology. *In* Grimes, Joseph E., ed. LANGUAGES OF THE GUIANAS. Norman, Oklahoma, University of Oklahoma: 1-11 (Summer Institute of Linguistics Publications, 35). **[14]**
[*COL*]

Hymes, Dell, ed.

25.0184   GC   1971   PIDGINIZATION AND CREOLIZATION OF LANGUAGES: PROCEEDINGS OF A CONFERENCE HELD AT THE UNIVERSITY OF THE WEST INDIES, MONA, JAMAICA, APRIL 1968. London, Cambridge University Press: 530p.   [*RIS*]

Isaac, Emile

25.0185   FA   1961   Rapport sur les envois en langue créole [Notes on envois in the Creole language]. *Rev Guad* 43, Jan.-Mar.: 33-37.   [*RIS*]

Jackson, Walter S.

25.0186   SR   1972   A Wayana grammar. *In* Grimes, Joseph E., ed. LANGUAGES OF THE GUIANAS. Norman, Oklahoma, University of Oklahoma: 47-77 (Summer Institute of Linguistics Publications, 35). **[13]**   [*COL*]

Jansen, G. P.

25.0187   CU   1945   DICCIONARIO PAPIAMENTU-HOLANDÉS [PAPIAMENTO-DUTCH DICTIONARY]. 2d ed. [Willemstad? Curacao, St. Vincentiusgesticht?] 166p.   [*AGS*]

Jardel, Jean-Pierre

1.0154   FA,TR   1973   Bibliographie créole succincte [Concise Creole bibliography].

Johnson, Mary Canice

25.0188   GC   1974   Two morpheme structure rules in an English proto-creole. *In* De Camp, David & Hancock, Ian F., eds. PIDGINS AND CREOLES: CURRENT TRENDS AND PROSPECTS. Washington, D.C., Georgetown University Press: 118-129.   [*RIS*]

Jones, J. Allen

32.0317   BC   1965   The need for a Standard.
32.0318   JM   1966   English in the Commonwealth: 9. The West Indies.

Jones, J. Allen, ed.

32.0319   BC   1965   LANGUAGE TEACHING, LINGUISTICS AND THE TEACHING OF ENGLISH IN A MULTILINGUAL SOCIETY: REPORT OF THE CONFERENCE, APRIL 6-9, 1964.

Jones, Morgan W.

25.0189   SR   1972   Trio phonology. *In* Grimes, Joseph E., ed. LANGUAGES OF THE GUIANAS. Norman, Oklahoma, University of Oklahoma: 42-46. (Summer Institute of Linguistics Publications, 35) **[13]**   [*COL*]

Jonis, S. F.

25.0190   CU   1974   Plural na papiamentu [The plural in Papiamento]. *Kristòf* 1(4), Aug.: 167-171.   [*RIS*]

Josselin de Jong, J. P. B. de

25.0191   ST,SJ   1924   HET NEGERHOLLANDSCH VAN ST. THOMAS EN ST. JAN [THE NEGRO-DUTCH OF ST. THOMAS AND ST. JOHN]. Amsterdam, Noord-Hollandsche Uitg. Mij., (Mededeelingen der Koninklijke Akademie van Wetenschappen, Afdeeling Letterkunde, ser. A., v. 57, no. 3.)   [*AMN*]

25.0192   NC   1926   HET HUIDIGE NEGERHOLLANDSCH (TEKSTEN EN WOORDENLIJST) [THE PRESENT-DAY NEGRO DUTCH (TEXTS AND VOCABULARY)]. Amsterdam, 124p. (Verhandelingen der Koninklijke Akademie van Wetenschappen, Afdeeling Letterkunde, new ser., v. 26, no. 1)   [*NYP*]

Joubert, Sidney M.

25.0193   NC   1976   Asentuashon na Papiamentu [Accent in Papiamentu]. *Kristòf* 3(3), Sept.: 127-138. **[22]**   [*RIS*]

22.0206   NA   1976   Literatura neerlandoantillana [Netherlands Antillean literature].

25.0194   NL   1976   El papiamento, lengua criolla de Curazao, Aruba y Bonaire [Papiamentu, creole language of Curaçao, Aruba and Bonaire]. *Kristòf* 3(1), Feb.: 11-24.   [*RIS*]

Jourdain, Elodie

25.0195   GC   1953[?]   Creole—a folk language. *Car Q* 3(1): 24-30.   [*RIS*]

25.0196   FA   1954   Is Creole a key to education? *Car Commn Mon Inf B* 7(11), June: 243-244, 246, 249. **[32]**   [*COL*]

25.0197   FA   1954   Notes on Creole speech. *Car Commn Mon Inf B* 8(2), Sept.: 42-44, 46.   [*COL*]

25.0198   MT   1954   Le verbe en créole martiniquais [The verb in the Creole language of Martinique]. *W I G* 35(1-2), Apr.: 39-58.   [*RIS*]

25.0199   FA   1956   DU FRANCAIS AUX PARLERS CRÉOLES [FROM FRENCH TO THE CREOLE LANGUAGES.] Paris, Librairie C. Klincksieck, 334p.   [*RIS*]

25.0200   FA   1956   LE VOCABULAIRE DU PARLER CRÉOLE DE LA MARTINIQUE [THE VOCABULARY OF THE CREOLE LANGUAGE OF MARTINIQUE]. Paris, Librairie C. Klincksieck, 303p.   [*RIS*]

Karsten, Rudolf

12.0043   SR   1930   DE BRITISCH-INDIERS IN SURINAME, BENEVENS EEN HANDLEIDING VAN DE BEGINSELEN VAN HET HINDOSTAANS [THE BRITISH INDIANS IN SURINAM, AND A MANUAL OF THE PRINCIPLES OF THE HINDOSTANI LANGUAGE].

Kesler, C. K.

25.0201   NA   1926-27   De naam Antillen [The name "Antilles"]. *W I G* 8: 567-569. **[5,24]**   [*COL*]

Knight, H. E.; Carrington, L. D. & Borely, C. B.

32.0335   TR   1972   PRELIMINARY COMMENTS ON LANGUAGE ARTS TEXTBOOKS IN USE IN THE PRIMARY SCHOOLS OF TRINIDAD AND TOBAGO.

32.0334   **TR**   1974   Preliminary comments on Language Arts textbooks in use in the primary schools of Trinidad and Tobago.

Koefoed, G.
25.0202   **SR**   1973   De eenlettergrepige Engelse woorden in het Surinaams [The one syllable English words in the Surinamese language]. *Bijd Volk* 129(2-3): 321-339.   [*COL*]

Koenig, Duane
25.0203   **BZ**   1975   Malta as a model for Belize. *National Stud* 3(5), September: 28-31.
                                                                                                     [*RIS*]

Koenig, Edna Louise
25.0204   **BZ**   1975   ETHNICITY AND LANGUAGE IN COROZAL DISTRICT, BELIZE: AN ANALYSIS OF CODE SWITCHING. Ph.D. dissertation, University of Texas (Austin): 243p.   **[21]**   [*PhD*]

Kroon, E. W.
25.0205   **NA**   1972   PAPYAMENTU VOOR BEGINNERS [PAPIAMENTO FOR BEGINNERS]. Amsterdam, The Netherlands, Antilliaans Contact Centrum; 30p.   **[32]**   [*RILA*]

Lapierre, Robert
25.0206   **FC**   1971   Questions de méthode touchant l'origine et la formation du créole-français des Antilles et de la Guyane [Methodological questions on the origin and formation of French Creole in the Antilles and (French) Guiana]. *In* FRANÇAIS ET CRÉOLE DANS LA CARAÏBE: VIᴱ SYMPOSIUM INTER-AMÉRICAIN DE LINGUISTIQUE, PORTO-RICO, JUNE 1971 [FRENCH AND CREOLE IN THE CARIBBEAN: SIXTH INTER-AMERICAN SYMPOSIUM ON LINGUISTICS, PUERTO RICO, JUNE 1971]. Fort-de-France, Martinique, Centre d'Etudes Régionales Antilles-Guyane: 43-51 [Documents du CERAG No. 4].   [*RIS*]

Lastra, Yolanda
32.0342   **GC**   1968   Literacy.

Latour, M. D.
25.0207   **CU**   1935-36 Oorsprong en betekenis van het woord *macamba* [Origin and meaning of the word *macamba*]. *W I G* 17: 256-260.   [*COL*]
25.0208   **NL**   1935-36 Vreemde invloeden in het Papiamento [Foreign influences on Papiamento]. *W I G* 17: 387-396.   [*COL*]
25.0209   **CU**   1936-37 De taal van Curacao [The language of Curacao]. *W I G* 18: 231-239.
                                                                                                     [*COL*]
25.0210   **CU**   1937   Portuguese taalresten in het Papiamento [Portuguese language survivals in Papiamento]. *W I G* 19: 212-214.   [*COL*]
25.0211   **NL**   1940   Het Papiamento [Papiamento]. *W I G* 22: 220-225.   [*COL*]
25.0212   **NL**   1948   Het Papiamento [Papiamento]. *In* ORANJE EN DE ZES CARAÏBISCHE PARELEN. Amsterdam, J. H. de Bussy: 75-82.   [*UCLA*]

Laurence, K. M.
25.0213   **TR**   1967   Notes of Iere, the Amerindian name for Trinidad. *Car Q* 13(3), Sept.: 45-51.   [*RIS*]

25.0214	TR	1970	SPANISH IN TRINIDAD: THE SURVIVAL OF A MINORITY LANGUAGE IN A MULTI-LINGUAL SOCIETY. Ph.D. dissertation, University of London: 428p.
25.0215	TR	1971	Trinidad English—the origin of "mamaguy" and "picong". *Car Q* 17(2), June: 36-39. [RIS]
25.0216	TR	1975	Continuity and change in Trinidadian toponyms. *N W I G* 50(2-3), Sept.: 123-142. **[56]** [RIS]

Lawton, David

25.0217	JM	1963	SUPRASEGMENTAL PHENOMENA IN JAMAICAN CREOLE. Ph.D. dissertation, Michigan State University: 67p. [PhD]
25.0218	JM	1964	Some problems of teaching a creolized language to Peace Corps members. *Language Learning* 14(1-2): 11-19. **[32]** [COL]
25.0219	JM	1968	The implications of tone for Jamaican Creole. *Anthrop Ling* 10(6), June: 22-26. [COL]
25.0220	GC	1975	Linguistic developments in the Caribbean: 1950-1975. *Revta Interam Rev* 5(1), Spring: 93-100. [RIS]
25.0221	JM	1976[?]	Language attitude, utterance recognition, and the Creole continuum in Jamaica: fact or fiction? *Univ Mich Papers Linguistics* 2(2): 48-57. [RIS]
22.0220	JM	1976	White man, black man, coolie man—pejorative terms in a Creole society.

Lefebvre, Claire

25.0222	MT	1974	Discreteness and the linguistic continuum in Martinique. *Anthrop Ling* 16(2), Feb.: 47-78. [COL]

Lefebvre, Gilles

25.0223	FC	1971	Les diglossies françaises dans la Caraïbe [French diglosses in the Caribbean]. *In* FRANÇAIS ET CRÉOLE DANS LA CARAÏBE: VIᴱ SYMPOSIUM INTER-AMÉRICAIN DE LINGUISTIQUE, PORTO-RICO, JUNE 1971 [FRENCH AND CREOLE IN THE CARIBBEAN: SIXTH INTER-AMERICAN SYMPOSIUM ON LINGUISTICS, PUERTO RICO, JUNE 1971]. Fort-de-France, Martinique, Centre d'Etudes Régionales Antilles-Guyane: 21-33 [Documents du CERAG No. 4]. [RIS]

Lenz, Rudolfo

25.0224	CU	1926	El papiamento, la lengua criolla de Curazao (la gramática más sencilla) [Papiamento, the Creole language of Curacao (the simplest grammar)]. *An Univ Chile* 2d ser., 4(3): 695-768; 4(4): 1021-1090. [NYP]
25.0225	CU	1927	El papiamento, la lengua criolla de Curazao (la gramática más sencilla) [Papiamento, the Creole language of Curacao (the simplest grammar)]. *An Univ Chile* 2d ser., 5(1), 287-327; 5(2): 365-412; 5(4): 889-990. [NYP]

Le Page, R. B.

18.0186	BC,UK	[n.d.]	Linguistic problems.
25.0226	BC	1952	A survey of dialects in the British Caribbean. *Car Q* 2(3): 49-51. [RIS]
25.0227	BC	1955	The language problem of the British Caribbean. *Car Q* 4(1), Jan.: 40-49. [RIS]

| 25.0228 | BC | 1957 | General outlines of Creole English dialects in the British Caribbean. *Orbis Bel* 6(2): 373-391. [*UCLA*] |

25.0228 **BC** 1957 General outlines of Creole English dialects in the British Caribbean. *Orbis Bel* 6(2): 373-391.   [*UCLA*]

25.0229 **BC** 1958 General outlines of Creole English dialects in the British Caribbean. *Orbis Bel* 7(1): 54-64.   [*UCLA*]

32.0351 **BC** 1968 Problems to be faced in the use of English as the medium of education in four West Indian territories.

25.0230 **BC** 1969 Dialect in West Indian literature. *J Commonw Lit* 7, July: 1-7.
[*COL*]

25.0231 **TR,JM,BZ** 1969 Problems of description in multilingual communities. *Trans Philol Soc Lond* 1968: 189-212.   [*UCLA*]

Le Page, R. B., ed.
25.0232 **GC** 1961 PROCEEDINGS OF THE CONFERENCE ON CREOLE LANGUAGE STUDIES HELD AT THE UNIVERSITY COLLEGE OF THE WEST INDIES, MAR. 28-APR. 4, 1959. London, Macmillan, 130p. (Creole language studies, no. 2.)   [*RIS*]

Le Page, R. B. & Cassidy, F. G.
25.0233 **JM** 1961 Lexicographic problems of "The dictionary of Jamaican English." *In* Le Page, R. B., ed. PROCEEDINGS OF THE CONFERENCE ON CREOLE LANGUAGE STUDIES, held at the University College of the West Indies, Mar. 28-Apr. 4, 1959. London, Macmillan, p.17-36. (Creole language studies, no. 2.)   [*RIS*]

Le Page, R. B. & DeCamp, David
25.0234 **JM** 1960 JAMAICAN CREOLE: AN HISTORICAL INTRODUCTION TO JAMAICAN CREOLE BY R. B. LE PAGE, AND FOUR JAMAICAN CREOLE TEXTS, WITH INTRODUCTION, PHONEMIC TRANSCRIPTIONS AND GLOSSES BY DAVID DECAMP. London, Macmillan, 182p. (Creole language studies, no. 1.) **[5]**   [*RIS*]

Letang, Casimir
25.0235 **GD** [n.d.] NOUS BITACO: POÈMES CRÉOLES ["NOUS BITACO." CREOLE POEMS]. Pointe-a-Pitre, Guad., Impr. Paran.   [*RIS*]

Lichtveld, Lou
25.0236 **SR** 1928-29 Afrikaansche resten in de Creolentaal van Suriname [African survivals in the Creole language of Surinam]. *W I G* 10: 391-402, 507-526. **[19]**   [*COL*]

25.0237 **SR** 1929-30 Afrikaansche resten in de Creolentaal van Suriname [African survivals in the Creole language of Surinam]. *W I G* 11: 72-84, 251-262. **[19]**   [*COL*]

32.0356 **SR** 1950 Educational problems in bilingual countries in the Caribbean.

25.0238 **GC** 1954 Enerlei Creools [One kind of Creole]. *W I G* 35(1-2), Apr.: 59-71.
[*RIS*]

Lieberman, Dena
20.0046 **SL** 1975 Language attitudes in St. Lucia.

Littman, Jerome
25.0239 **CU** 1945 The wind-blown language: Papiamento. *Hispania* 20(1), Feb.: 50-59.   [*COL*]

Loftman, Beryl I.
25.0240   GC   1953   CREOLE LANGUAGES OF THE CARIBBEAN AREA. M.A. thesis, Columbia University, 79p.   [*COL*]

Longacre, Robert E.
25.0241   GC   1968   Comparative reconstruction of indigenous languages. *In* Sebeok, Thomas A., ed. CURRENT TRENDS IN LINGUISTICS, IV: IBERO-AMERICAN AND CARIBBEAN LINGUISTICS. The Hague, Mouton & Co.: 320-360.   [*RIS*]

Lowenthal, David & Comitas, Lambros, eds.
2.0295   GC   1973   CONSEQUENCES OF CLASS AND COLOR: WEST INDIAN PERSPECTIVES.

MacDonald, Judy Smith
25.0242   GR   1973   Cursing and context in a Grenadian fishing community. *Anthropologica* 15(1): 89-127.   **[8,20,33]**   [*COL*]
9.0096   GR   1973   Inlaw terms and affinal relations in a Grenadian fishing community.

McKay, Claude
22.0240   JM   1912   SONGS OF JAMAICA.

McTurk, Michael
24.0112   GU   1949   ESSAYS AND FABLES IN THE VERNACULAR.

Maduro, A. J.
25.0243   NA   1971   Enkele opmerkingen over Richard Wood's artikel over "The English loanwords in Papiamentu" [Some remarks about Richard Wood's article on "The English loanwords in Papiamentu"]. *N W I G* 48(2-3), Dec.: 190-192.   [*RIS*]

Marckwardt, Albert H.
25.0244   JM   1962   Applied linguistics. *Car Q* 8(2), June: 111-120.   **[32]**   [*RIS*]

Martinet, André, ed.
25.0245   GC   1968   LE LANGAGE [THE LANGUAGE]. Paris, France, Éditions Gallimard: 1525p. (Encyclopédie de la Pléiade, 25).   [*UCLA*]

Martinus, Frank
1.0183   NA   1972[?]   BIBLIOGRAFIE VAN HET PAPIAMENTU BEVATTENDE TITELS EN BESCHRIJVINGEN VAN DE MEESTE WERKEN DIE IN HET PAPIAMENTU VERSCHENEN ZIJN VANAF HET VROEGSTE BEGIN TOT HEDEN, RELIGIEUS EN PROFAAN, ALSMEDE EEN LIJST VAN TONEELSTUKKEN EN TONEEL-GROEPEN, MET VOORTS EEN GESELELECTEERDE BIBLIOGRAFIE VAN STUDIES EN ARTIKELEN OVER HET PAPIAMENTU [BIBLIOGRAPHY OF PAPIAMENTO CONTAINING TITLES AND DESCRIPTIONS OF MOST WORKS PUBLISHED IN PAPIAMENTO FROM THE EARLIEST START TO THE PRESENT, RELIGIOUS AND PROFANE, AND ALSO A LIST OF PLAYS AND THEATRE GROUPS AND A SELECTED BIBLIOGRAPHY OF STUDIES AND ARTICLES ABOUT PAPIAMENTO].

Meikle, H. B.
25.0246   TR   1955   Tobago villagers in the mirror of dialect. *Car Q* 4(2), Dec.: 154-160.
                                                                          [*RIS*]

Menkman, W. R.

25.0247   SR   1932-33 De Surinaamsche taaltuin [The Surinam language and idiom].
                 W I G 14: 244-252.   [*COL*]
25.0248   CU   1936-37 Curacao, zijn naam en zijn taal [Curacao, its name and its
                 language]. *W I G* 18: 38-50.   **[2,5]**   [*COL*]
25.0249   SR   1937   Surinaamsche talltuin [Surinam language and idiom]. *W I G* 19:
                 243-246.   [*COL*]

Mezzera, Baltasar Luis

25.0250   JM   1965   PUERTO RICO, JAMAICA. Montevideo, Artes Gráficas Covadonga:
                 37p.   [*NYP*]

Midgett, Douglas

25.0251   SL   1970   Bilingualism and linguistic change in St. Lucia. *Anthrop Ling* 12(5),
                 May: 158-170.   [*COL*]

Mintz, Sidney W.

25.0252   GC   1971   The socio-historical background to pidginization and creolization.
                 In Hymes, Dell, ed. PIDGINIZATION AND CREOLIZATION OF LAN-
                 GUAGES: PROCEEDINGS OF A CONFERENCE HELD AT THE UNIVERSITY
                 OF THE WEST INDIES, MONA, JAMAICA, APRIL 1968. London,
                 Cambridge University Press: 481-496.   [*RIS*]

Moodie, Sylvia María

25.0253   TR   1973   I. The Spanish language as spoken in Trinidad. II. The phonemic
                 system of the Spanish dialect of Trinidad. *Car Stud* 13(1), April:
                 88-98.   [*RIS*]

Mordecai, Pamela

32.0409 JM   1975   The use of electronic media; T.V., radio and films in the teaching of
                 English—an overview.

Morgan, Raleigh, Jr.

25.0254   SM   1959   Structural sketch of St. Martin Creole. *Anthrop Ling* 1(8), Nov.:
                 20-24, 24a-24f.   [*COL*]
25.0255   SM   1960   The lexicon of St. Martin Creole. *Anthrop Ling* 2(1), Jan.: 7-29.
                                                                                            [*COL*]

Morpurgo, A. J.

25.0256   SR   1932-33 Eenige opmerkingen over de Surinaamsche Negertaal [A few
                 remarks about the Surinam Negro-language]. *W I G* 14: 397-408.
                                                                                            [*COL*]

Morris, Mervyn

22.0261 JM   1967   On reading Louise Bennett seriously.

Navarro, Tomas

25.0257   CU   1953   Observaciones sobre el papiamento [Notes on Papiamento]. *Nueva
                 Revta Filol Hispan* 7: 183-189.   [*COL*]

Nichols, Donald Arthur

25.0258   SC   1974   AUDITORY DISCRIMINATION BY VIRGIN ISLANDS CHILDREN OF DIF-
                 FERENT DIALECTS OF ENGLISH. Ed.D. dissertation, Boston Univer-
                 sity, School of Education: 59p.   **[32]**   [*PhD*]

Nodal, Roberto

1.0208   GC   1972   A BIBLIOGRAPHY (WITH SOME ANNOTATIONS) ON THE CREOLE LAN-
GUAGES OF THE CARIBBEAN, INCLUDING A SPECIAL SUPPLEMENT ON
GULLAH.

Nordenskiold, Erland

25.0259   GG   1922   DEDUCTIONS SUGGESTED BY THE GEOGRAPHICAL DISTRIBUTION OF
SOME POST-COLUMBIAN WORDS USED BY THE INDIANS OF AMERICA.
Göteberg, Sweden; Elanders boktr. aktiebolag, 176p. (Comparative
ethnographical studies, v. 5.) **[13]**   [COL]

Norris, R. A.

32.0430   BC,UK   1971   Developing a curriculum in English for West Indian children.

Otterbein, Keith F.

9.0109   BA   1964   Principles governing the usage of in-law terminology on Andros
Island, Bahamas.

Ottley, C. R.

25.0260   TR   1965   TRINIBAGIANESE: WORDS AND PHRASES, OLD AND NEW, PECULIAR TO
THE SPEECH OF TRINIDADIANS AND TOBAGONIANS, VOL. 1. Fairview,
Diego Martin, Trinidad, C. R. Ottley, Feb.: 32p. (Little Books on
Trinidad and Tobago No. 1)   [RIS]

25.0261   TR   1966   SAYINGS OF TRINIDAD AND TOBAGO: OLD AND NEW. Fairview, Diego
Martin, Trinidad, C. R. Ottley, July: 11p. (Little Books on Trinidad
and Tobago No. 3)   [RIS]

25.0262   TR   1966   TRINIBAGIANESE: WORDS AND PHRASES, OLD AND NEW, PECULIAR TO
THE SPEECH OF TRINIDADIANS AND TOBAGONIANS, VOL. 2. Fairview,
Diego Martin, Trinidad, C. R. Ottley, June: 26p. (Little Books on
Trinidad and Tobago No. 2)   [RIS]

Ottley, C. R., ed.

25.0263   TR   1965   TRINIDADIANESE: HOW TO OLD TALK IN TRINIDAD. [Port of Spain?]
Trinidad, Granderson, 32p.   [RIS]

Oudschans Dentz, Fred

25.0264   SR   1937   De plaats van de Creool in de literatuur van Suriname [The place of
Creole in the literature of Surinam]. *W I G* 19: 208-211. **[11,22]**
          [COL]

Palm, J. Ph. de

25.0265   CU   1969   HET NEDERLANDS OP DE CURAÇAOSE SCHOOL [THE DUTCH LAN-
GUAGE IN THE CURAÇAO SCHOOL]. Groningen, The Netherlands,
Wolters-Noordhoff N.V.: 105p. **[32]**   [NYP]

Panhuys, L. C. van

25.0266   SR   1904   Indian words in the Dutch language. *Bijd Volk Ned-Indie* 56:
611-614. **[13]**

25.0267   SR   1905   Indian words in the Dutch language and in use at Dutch Guiana. *In*
PROCEEDINGS OF THE INTERNATIONAL CONGRESS OF AMERICANISTS,
13th Session, New York, Oct. 1902. Easton, Pa., Eschenbach Print.
Co., p.205-208. **[13]**   [AGS]

25.0268	SR	1913	A few observations on Carib numerals. *In* PROCEEDINGS OF THE INTERNATIONAL CONGRESS OF AMERICANISTS. XVIII Session, London, 1912. London, Harrison, pt. 1, p.109-110. **[13]** [*AGS*]
22.0286	SR	1934	Quelques chansons et quelques danses dans la Guyane Neerlandaise [A few songs and dances of Dutch Guiana].
19.0049	SR	1935-36	De grondslag van de wiskunde in Suriname [The foundations of mathematics in Surinam].

Pastner, Carroll McClure

| 25.0269 | TR | 1967 | A SOCIOLINGUISTIC STUDY OF A RURAL TRINIDAD COMMUNITY. M.A. Thesis, Brandeis University: 44p.   [*RIS*] |

Pavy, David

| 25.0270 | GC | 1967 | ON A LINGUISTIC ASPECT OF RACIAL PERCEPTION IN THE AMERICAS. Paper presented at the 1967 meeting of the American Anthropological Association: 11p.   [*RIS*] |

Peasgood, Edward T.

| 25.0271 | GG | 1972 | Carib phonology. *In* Grimes, Joseph E., ed. LANGUAGES OF THE GUIANAS. Norman, Oklahoma, University of Oklahoma: 35-41 (Summer Institute of Linguistics Publications, 35). **[14]** [*COL*] |

Pée, Willem et al.

| 25.0272 | SR | 1951 | Opstellen over het Surinaams [Essays about the Surinam language]. *Taal Tong* 3: 130-192. |
| 25.0273 | SR | 1953 | Opstellen over het Surinaams [Essays about the Surinam language]. *Taal Tong* 5: 4-19. |

Pée, Willem; Hellinga, W. Gs. & Donicie, A.

| 25.0274 | SR | 1951 | Het Neger-Engels van Suriname [Negro-English of Surinam]. *Taal Tong* 3: 130-192. |
| 25.0275 | SR | 1953 | Voorstellen tot een nieuwe systematische spelling van het Surinaams (Neger-Engels) op linguistische grondslag [Proposals for a new and systematic spelling of the Surinam language (Negro English) on a linguistic basis]. *Taal Tong* 5(1), Mar.: 8-19.   [*COL*] |

Pelage, Al.

| *2.0357* | GD | [n.d.] | LA GUADELOUPE VUE PAR AL. PELAGE: GRAVURES ET DESSINS HUMORISTIQUES [GUADELOUPE AS SEEN BY AL. PELAGE: HUMOROUS PRINTS AND DRAWINGS]. |

Penard, Thomas E.

| 25.0276 | SR | 1926-27 | Note on words used by South American Indians for banana. *W I G* 8: 375-377. **[13]**   [*COL*] |
| 25.0277 | TR | 1927-28 | Remarks on an old vocabulary from Trinidad. *W I G* 9: 265-270. **[13]**   [*COL*] |

Penard, Thomas E. & Penard, Arthur P.

| 25.0278 | SR | 1926-27 | European influence on the Arawak language of Guiana. *W I G* 7: 165-176. **[13,26]**   [*COL*] |

Perego, Pierre

| 25.0279 | GC | 1968 | Les créoles [The Creole languages]. *In* Martinet, André, ed. LE LANGAGE. Paris, France, Éditions Gallimard: 608-619 (Encyclopédie de la Pléiade, 25).   [*UCLA*] |

Petitjean-Roget, Jacques
4.0281   **DM,GD**   1963   The Caribs as seen through the dictionary of the Reverend Father Breton.

Ponge, Robert
25.0280   **GC**   1975   Foreign language teaching and the two cultures. *Savacou* 11-12, Sept.: 18-26. **[32]**   *[RIS]*

Price, Richard
25.0281   **SR**   1975   KiKóongo and Saramaccan: a reappraisal. *Bijd Volk* 131(4): 461-478. **[14]**   *[COL]*

Price, Richard & Price, Sally
25.0282   **MT**   1966   A note on canoe names in Martinique. *Names* 14: 157-160. **[52]**
                                                                        [COL]
14.0063   **SR**   1972   Saramaka onomastics: an Afro-American naming system.

Prince, John Dyneley
25.0283   **SR**   1934   Surinam Negro-English. *Am Speech* 9(3), Oct.: 181-186.   *[COL]*

Prins-Winkel, A. C.
25.0284   **NL**   1973   KABES DURU? VERSLAG VAN EEN ONDERZOEK NAAR DE ONDER-WIJSSITUATIE OP DE BENEDENWINDSE EILANDEN VAN DE NEDER-LANDSE ANTILLEN, IN VERBAND MET HET PROBLEEM VAN DE VREEMDE VOERTAAL BIJ HET ONDERWIJS [KABES DURU? REPORT OF AN INVESTIGATION OF THE EDUCATIONAL SITUATION IN THE LEEWARD ISLANDS OF THE NETHERLANDS ANTILLES, IN CONNECTION WITH THE FOREIGN LANGUAGE USED IN EDUCATION. Assen, The Netherlands, Van Gorcum & Comp. B.V.: 179p. (Dissertation, Universiteit van Amsterdam) **[32]**   *[RILA]*

Ramchand, Kenneth
25.0285   **JM**   1970   The Negro and the English language in the West Indies. *Savacou* 1(1), June: 33-44. **[11]**   *[RIS]*

Ratelband, K.
25.0286   **SR**   1944-45   Een Boschnegerschrift van West-Afrikaanschen oorsprong [A Bush Negro system of writing of West African origin]. *W I G* 26: 193-208. **[14]**   *[COL]*

Reinecke, John E.
25.0287   **GC**   1938   Trade jargons and Creole dialects as marginal languages. *Social Forces* 17(1), Oct.: 107-118.   *[COL]*

Reinecke, John E.; Tsuzaki, Stanley M.; DeCamp, David; Hancock, Ian F. & Wood, Richard E., comps.
25.0288   **GC**   1975   A BIBLIOGRAPHY OF PIDGIN AND CREOLE LANGUAGES. Honolulu, University Press of Hawaii: 804p. **[1]**   *[RIS]*

Reisman, Karl
25.0289   **AT**   1965   'THE ISLE IS FULL OF NOISES': A STUDY OF CREOLE IN THE SPEECH PATTERNS OF ANTIGUA, WEST INDIES. Ph.D. dissertation, Harvard University: 301p. **[19]**

25.0290   AT   1970   Cultural and linguistic ambiguity in a West Indian village. *In*
                      Whitten, Norman E., Jr. & Szwed, John F., eds. AFRO-AMERICAN
                      ANTHROPOLOGY: CONTEMPORARY PERSPECTIVES. New York, The
                      Free Press: 129-144.   **[11]**   [*RIS*]

Rens, L. L. E.
25.0291   SR   1953   THE HISTORICAL AND SOCIAL BACKGROUND OF SURINAM'S NEGRO-
                      ENGLISH. Amsterdam, North-Holland Pub. Co., 155p.   [*COL*]

Richards, Henry J.
25.0292   TR   1966   Some vestiges of Spanish in the dialect of Trinidad. *Hispania* 49(3),
                      Sept.: 481-483.   [*TCL*]
25.0293   TR   1970   Some Spanish words in the English-based dialect of Trinidad.
                      Hispania 53(2), May: 263-266.   [*TCL*]
25.0294   TR   1970   Trinidadian folk usage and Standard English: a contrastive study.
                      Word 26(1), April: 79-87.   [*COL*]

Rivet, P. & Reinburg, P.
25.0295   FG   1921   Les Indiens Marawan [The Marawan Indians]. *J Soc Am* new ser.,
                      13: 103-118.   **[13]**   [*AGS*]

Roberts-Holmes, Joy
18.0246   JM,UK   1973   Culture shock: remedial teaching and the immigrant child.

Robson, Barbara Lynn Baker
25.0296   JM   1971   A LINGUISTIC STUDY OF VARIATION IN SPOKEN STYLES WITHIN THE
                      INDIVIDUAL. Ph.D. dissertation, University of Texas (Austin): 106p.
                                                                                 [*PhD*]

Rochefort, César de
25.0297   GC   1941   Remarques sur la langue caraïbe [Observations on the Carib
                      language]. *Rev Soc Hist Geogr Haiti* 12(41), Apr.: 13-16.   **[13]**
                                                                                 [*AGS*]

Rodway, James
53.0484   GU   1906   The river-names of British Guiana.
53.0485   GU   1911   Our river names.

Rountree, S. Catherine
25.0298   SR   1972   The phonological structure of stems in Saramaccan. *In* Grimes,
                      Joseph E., ed. LANGUAGES OF THE GUIANAS. Norman, Oklahoma,
                      University of Oklahoma: 22-27 (Summer Institute of Linguistics
                      Publications, 35).   **[14]**   [*COL*]

Rowe, Charles G. & Horth, Auguste
24.0143   FG   1951   'Dolos': Creole proverbs of French Guiana.

Rubin, Joan
1.0249   GC   1963   A bibliography of Carribbean Creole languages.

Saint-Jacques Fauquenoy, Marguérite
25.0299   GU   1972   ANALYSE STRUCTURALE DU CRÉOLE GUYANAIS [STRUCTURAL ANAL-
                      YSIS OF GUYANESE CREOLE]. Paris, Editions Klincksieck: 142p.
                      (Etudes linguistiques, 13)   [*COL*]

25.0300   FC   1972   Le verbe "être" dans les créoles français [The verb "to be" in French Créole]. *In* LANGUES ET TECHNIQUES, NATURE ET SOCIÉÏE: APPROCHE LINGUISTIQUE. Paris, Éditions Klincksieck: 225-231.
                             [COL]

25.0301   FG   1974   Guyanese: a French creole. *In* De Camp, David and Hancock, Ian F., eds. PIDGINS AND CREOLES: CURRENT TRENDS AND PROSPECTS. Washington, D.C., Georgetown University Press: 27-37.   [RIS]

Saint-Pierre, Madeleine

25.0302   MT   1972   Créole ou français? Les cheminements d'un choix linguistique [Creole or French? Approaching a linguistic choice]. *In* Benoist, Jean, ed. L'ARCHIPEL INACHEVÉ: CULTURE ET SOCIÉTÉ AUX ANTILLES FRANÇAISES. Montreal, Canada, Univ. of Montreal: 251-266. **[19]**
                             [RIS]

Schoen, Elin

25.0303   CU   1972   The melted language of Curacao. *Am Way* 5(3), March: 18-20
                             [RIS]

Schont, Mme.

24.0145   GD   1935   QUELQUES CONTES CRÉOLES [CREOLE TALES].

Schuchardt, Hugo

25.0304   SR   1914   DIE SPRACHE DER SARAMAKKANEGER IN SURINAM [THE LANGUAGE OF THE SARAMACCA NEGROES OF SURINAM]. Amsterdam, Noord-Hollandsche Uitg. Mij., 120. (Verhandelingen der Koninklijke Akademie van Wetenschappen te Amsterdam, Afdeeling Letterkunde, new ser., v. 14, no. 6.) **[11]**   [NYP]

25.0305   ST   1914   Zum Negerholländischen von St. Thomas [Concerning the Negro-Dutch of St. Thomas.] *Tijdschr Ned Taal Lettk* new ser., 33(25): 123-135.   [COL]

Seaman, G. A.

25.0306   VI   1968   VIRGIN ISLANDS DICTIONARY. G. A. Seaman: 17p.   [RIS]

Sebeok, Thomas Albert, ed.

25.0307   GC   1968   CURRENT TRENDS IN LINGUISTICS, IV: IBERO-AMERICAN AND CARIBBEAN LINGUISTICS. The Hague, Mouton and Co.: 659p.   [RIS]

Sibley, Inez K.

24.0151   JM   1968   QUASHIE'S REFLECTIONS IN JAMAICAN CREOLE.

Silva-Fuenzalida, Ismael

25.0308   SR   1952   PAPIAMENTU MORPHOLOGY. Ph.D. dissertation, Northwestern University.   [PhD]

Simons, R. D.

25.0309   SR   1954   Het partikel 'sa' in het Surinaams [The particle 'sa' in the Surinam language]. *W I G* 35(3), Oct.: 167-170.   [RIS]

Simons, R. D. & Voorhoeve, J.

25.0310   SR   1955-56   Ontleningen van Nederlandse samenstellingen in het Surinaams [Adoption of Dutch compounds in the Surinam language]. *W I G* 36: 61-64. **[13,26]**   [COL]

Sluisdom, E.

25.0311   SR   1970   De best gesproken taal in Suriname [The most well-spoken language in Surinam]. *Geogr Tijdschr* Nieuwe Reeks, 4(4), Sept.: 349-353.

[*AGS*]

Smith, M. G.

25.0312   GC   1966   The communication of new techniques and ideas: some cultural and psychological factors. *In* Vries, Egbert de, ed. Social research and rural life in Central America, Mexico and the Caribbean Region. Proceedings of a seminar organized by UNESCO in co-operation with the United Nations Economic Commission for Latin America, Mexico City, 17-27 Oct., 1962. Paris, UNESCO: 121-130.   [*RIS*]

Solien, Nancie L.

9.0167   BZ   1960   Changes in Black Carib kinship terminology.

Solomon, Denis

32.0538   BC   1975   Foreign language teaching: a plea for new objectives.

Speckmann, Johan Dirk

25.0313   SR   1966   Het taalgebruik bij de Hindostanen in Suriname [The language use of the Hindustani in Surinam]. *N W I G* 45(1), Oct.: 60-65.   **[12]**

[*RIS*]

Speirs, James

24.0153   GU   1902   The proverbs of British Guiana with an index of principal words, an index of subjects, and a glossary.

Sprauve, Gilbert A.

25.0314   UV   1974   Towards a reconstruction of Virgin Islands English Creole phonology. Ph.D. dissertation, Princeton University: 163p.   [*PhD*]

Staffeleu, P.

54.0948   SR   1975   Surinaamse zoogdiernamen [Surinam vernacular names of mammals].

Standish, P.

25.0315   BC   1973   Foreign language acquisition and some sociolinguistic factors affecting the case of the English speaking Caribbean. *Car Stud* 13(1), April: 99-109.   **[32]**   [*RIS*]

Taylor, Douglas

13.0204   DM   1935   The Island Caribs of Dominica.
13.0205   DM   1936   Additional notes on the Island Carib of Dominica, B.W.I.
25.0316   GC   1945   Certain Carib morphological influences on Creole. *Int J Am Ling* 11(3), July: 140-155.   **[13]**   [*COL*]
25.0317   DM   1946   Loan words in Dominica Island Carib. *Int J Am Ling* 12(4), Oct.: 213-216.   **[13,26]**   [*COL*]
25.0318   DM   1947   Phonemes of Caribbean Creole. *Word* 3(3), Dec.: 173-179.   [*COL*]
25.0319   DM   1951   Structural outlines of Caribbean Creole. *Word* 7(1), April: 43-59.

[*COL*]

25.0320   DM   1952   A note on the phoneme [r] in Dominica Creole. *Word* 8(3), Dec.: 224-226.   [*COL*]

53.0570	**DM**	1954	Names on Dominica.
25.0321	**DM**	1955-56	Names on Dominica. *W I G* 36: 121-124. **[7]** [*COL*]
25.0322	**GC**	1955	On the etymology of some Arawakan words for three. *Int J Am Ling* 21(2), Apr.: 185-187. **[13]** [*COL*]
25.0323	**BZ**	1955	Phonemes of the Hopkins (British Honduras) dialect of Island Carib. *Int J Am Ling* 21(3), July: 233-241. **[13]** [*COL*]
25.0324	**DM**	1955	Phonic interference in Dominican Creole. *Word* 11(1), Apr.: 45-52. [*COL*]
25.0325	**GC**	1956	Island Carib II: Word-classes, affixes, nouns, and verbs. *Int J Am Ling* 22(1), Jan.: 1-44. **[13]** [*COL*]
25.0326	**GC**	1956	Island Carib morphology III: Locators and particles. *Int J Am Ling* 22(2), Apr.: 138-150. **[13]** [*COL*]
25.0327	**GC**	1956	Language contacts in the West Indies. *Word* 12(3), Dec.: 399-414. [*COL*]
25.0328	**GC**	1956	Languages and ghost-languages of the West Indies. *Int J Am Ling* 22(2), Apr.: 180-183. [*COL*]
25.0329	**GC**	1956	Spanish Huracán and its congeners. *Int J Am Ling* 22(4), Oct.: 275-276. [*COL*]
25.0330	**GC**	1957	Ballyhoo. *Int J Am Ling* 23(4), Oct.: 302-303. [*COL*]
25.0331	**GC**	1957	Languages and ghost-languages of the West Indies: a postscript. *Int J Am Ling* 23(2), Apr.: 114-116. [*COL*]
9.0178	**GC**	1957	Marriage, affinity, and descent in two Arawakan tribes: a sociolinguistic note.
25.0332	**GC**	1957	A note on some Arawakan words for *man*, etc. *Int J Am Ling* 23(1), Jan.: 46-48. **[9,13]** [*COL*]
25.0333	**GC**	1957	On the affiliation of "Island Carib." *Int J Am Ling* 23(4), Oct.: 297-302. **[13]** [*COL*]
25.0334	**GC**	1957	Spanish Canoa and its congeners. *Int J Am Ling* 23(3), July: 242-244. [*COL*]
25.0335	**GC**	1957	Spanish Hamaca and its congeners. *Int J Am Ling* 23(2), Apr.: 113-114. [*COL*]
25.0336	**GC**	1958	Carib, Caliban, Cannibal. *Int J Am Ling* 24(2), Apr.: 156-157. [*COL*]
25.0337	**GC**	1958	A case of reconstitution. *Int J Am Ling* 24(4), Oct.: 323-324. [*COL*]
25.0338	**GC**	1958	Compounds and comparison. *Int J Am Ling* 24(1), Jan.: 77-79. [*COL*]
25.0339	**GC**	1958	Corrigenda to Island Carib I-IV. *Int J Am Ling* 24(4), Oct.: 325-326. **[13]** [*COL*]
25.0340	**GC**	1958	Island Carib IV: Syntactic notes, texts. *Int J Am Ling* 24: (1), Jan.: 36-60. **[13]** [*COL*]
25.0341	**GC**	1958	Iwana-Yuana *iguana*. *Int J Am Ling* 24(2), Apr.: 157-158. [*COL*]
25.0342	**GC**	1958	Lines by Black Carib. *Int J Am Ling* 24(4), Oct.: 324-325. **[13]** [*COL*]
25.0343	**SV**	1958	Names on Saint Vincent. *W I G* 38: 97-105. **[7]** [*COL*]
25.0344	**GC**	1958	The place of Island Carib within the Arawakan family. *Int J Am Ling* 24(2), Apr.: 153-156. **[13]** [*COL*]
25.0345	**GC**	1958	Some problems of sound correspondence in Arawakan. *Int J Am Ling* 24(3), July: 234-239. **[13]** [*COL*]
25.0346	**GC**	1958	Use and disuse of languages in the West Indies. *Car Q* 5(2), Feb.: 67-77. [*RIS*]
25.0347	**GC**	1959	Homophony or polysemy. *Int J Am Ling* 25(2), Apr.: 134-135. [*COL*]

| 25.0348 | GC | 1959 | On dialectal divergence in Island Carib. *Int J Am Ling* 25(1), Jan.: 62-67. **[13]** [*COL*] |

25.0348 GC 1959 On dialectal divergence in Island Carib. *Int J Am Ling* 25(1), Jan.: 62-67. **[13]**   [*COL*]

25.0349 GC 1960 Compounds and comparison again. *Int J Am Ling* 26(3), July: 252-256.   [*COL*]

25.0350 GC 1960 Language shift or changing relationships? *Int J Am Ling* 26(2), Apr.: 155-161.

25.0351 GC 1960 On consonantal correspondences in three Arawakan languages. *Int J Am Ling* 26(3), July: 244-252. **[13]**   [*COL*]

25.0352 GC 1960 On the history of Island-Carib consonantism. *Int J Am Ling* 26(2), Apr.: 146-155. **[13]**   [*COL*]

25.0353 GC 1960 Some remarks on the spelling and formation of Taino words. *Int J Am Ling* 26(4), Oct.: 345-348. **[13]**   [*COL*]

25.0354 GC 1961 Arawakan for *path, bone, hand:* a semantic problem of reconstruction. *Int J Am Ling* 27(4), Oct.: 365-367. **[13]**   [*COL*]

25.0355 GC 1961 A problem in relationship. *Int J Am Ling* 27, July: 284-286.   [*COL*]

25.0356 DM 1961 Some Dominican-Creole descendants of the French definite article. *In* Le Page, R. B., ed. PROCEEDINGS OF THE CONFERENCE ON CREOLE LANGUAGE STUDIES held at the University College of the West Indies, Mar.28-Apr. 4, 1959. London, Macmillan, p.85-90. (Creole language studies, no. 2.)   [*RIS*]

9.0179 GC 1961 Some remarks on teknonymy in Arawakan.

25.0357 DM,SV 1962 Lexical borrowings in Island-Carib. *Romance Philology* 16(2), Nov.: 143-152. **[13]**   [*UCLA*]

25.0358 SR 1962 Surinam Arawak as compared with different dialects of Island Carib. *Bijd Volk* 118: 362-372. **[13]**

25.0359 MT,SR 1963 The origin of West Indian Creole languages: evidence from grammatical categories. *Am Anthrop* 65(4), Aug.: 800-814.   [*RIS*]

25.0360 DM 1968 Le créole de la Dominique [Dominican Creole]. *In* Martinet, André. LE LANGAGE. Paris, France, Éditions Gallimard: 1022-1049 (Encyclopédie de la Pléiade, 25).   [*UCLA*]

25.0361 SR 1969 A preliminary view of Arawak phonology. *Int J Am Ling* 35(3), July: 234-238. **[13]**   [*COL*]

13.0210 SR 1970 Arawak grammatical categories and translation.

25.0362 SR 1970 The postpositions of Arawak. *Int J Am Ling* 36(1), Jan: 31-37. **[13]**
                                                                            [*COL*]

25.0363 GC 1971 Grammatical and lexical affinities of creoles. *In* Hymes, Dell, ed. PIDGINIZATION AND CREOLIZATION OF LANGUAGES: PROCEEDINGS OF A CONFERENCE HELD AT THE UNIVERSITY OF THE WEST INDIES, MONA, JAMAICA, APRIL 1968. London, Cambridge University Press: 293-296.   [*RIS*]

25.0364 GC 1971 New languages for old in the West Indies. *In* Horowitz, Michael M., ed. PEOPLES AND CULTURES OF THE CARIBBEAN: AN ANTHROPOLOGICAL READER. New York, Natural History Press for the American Museum of Natural History: 77-91.   [*RIS*]

13.0211 DM 1972 The Island Caribs of Dominica, B.W.I.

Taylor, Douglas & Keller, Hans Erich
25.0365 DM 1963 Remarks on the lexicon of Dominican French Creole. *Romance Philology* 16(4), May: 402-415.   [*UCLA*]

Taylor, Douglas & Rouse, Irving
4.0362   GC   1955   Linguistic and archeological time depth in the West Indies.

Thomas, J. J.
25.0366   TR   1969   THE THEORY AND PRACTICE OF CREOLE GRAMMAR. London, New Beacon Books Ltd: 134p. (Originally published in 1869)   [*RIS*]

Thompson, Robert Wallace
25.0367   TR   1957   A preliminary survey of the Spanish dialect of Trinidad. *Orbis Bel* 6(2): 353-372.   [*UCLA*]
25.0368   GC   1958   Mushrooms, umbrellas and black magic: a West Indian linguistic problem. *Am Speech* 33(3), Oct.: 170-175.   **[19]**   [*COL*]
25.0369   GC   1961   A note on some possible affinities between the Creole dialects of the Old World and those of the New. *In* Le Page, R. B., ed. PROCEEDINGS OF THE CONFERENCE ON CREOLE LANGUAGE STUDIES held at the University College of the West Indies, Mar. 28-Apr. 24, 1959. London, Macmillan, p.107-113. (Creole language studies, no. 2.)   [*RIS*]
25.0370   JM   1962   Sobre la no-hispanidad del inglés acriollado de Jamaica [On the non-Hispanicity of the Creolized English in Jamaica]. *Thesaurus* 17(1), Jan.-April: 139-143.   [*UCLA*]

Thompson, Wally
25.0371   GC   1966   Creoles and pidgins, East and West. *New Wld Q* 2(4), Cropover: 11-16.   [*RIS*]

Todd, Loreto
25.0372   BC,NC   1974   PIDGINS AND CREOLES. London, Routledge & Kegan Paul: 106p.   [*RIS*]

Tracey, Frances V.
25.0373   GU   1972   Wapishana phonology. *In* Grimes, Joseph E., ed. LANGUAGES OF THE GUIANAS. Norman, Oklahoma, University of Oklahoma: 78-84. (Summer Institute of Linguistics Publications, 35)   **[13]**   [*COL*]

Valdman, Albert
25.0374   FA   1971   Sur l'évolution sociolinguistique des dialectes français créoles aux Antilles [On the sociolinguistic evolution of French creole dialects in the Antilles]. *In* FRANÇAIS ET CRÉOLE DANS LA CARAÏBE: VIᴱ SYMPOSIUM INTER-AMÉRICAIN DE LINGUISTIQUE, PORTO-RICO, JUNE 1971 [FRENCH AND CREOLE IN THE CARIBBEAN: SIXTH INTER-AMERICAN SYMPOSIUM ON LINGUISTICS, PUERTO RICO, JUNE 1971]. Fort-de-France, Martinique, Centre d'Etudes Régionales Antilles-Guyane: 5-20 (Documents du CERAG No. 4).   **[8]**   [*RIS*]
25.0375   FC   1973   Certains aspects sociolinguistiques des parlers créoles français aux Antilles [Certain sociolinguistic aspects of spoken French creoles in the Antilles]. *Ethnies* 3: 7-21.   **[8]**   [*COL*]
25.0376   FA   1973   Créole et français aux Antilles [Creole and French in the Antilles]. *Rec Cent Etud Reg Ant-Guy* 1: 1-25.   [*RIS*]
25.0377   FC   1973   Some aspects of decreolization in Creole French. *In* Sebeok, Thomas A., ed. CURRENT TRENDS IN LINGUISTICS. The Hague, Mouton: 507-536.   [*RIS*]

Valkhoff, Marius

| 25.0378 | GC | 1960 | Contributions to the study of Creole. I. Contributions to the study of Creole. *Afr Stud* 19(2): 77-87. **[1]** [*COL*] |
| 25.0379 | GC | 1960 | Contributions to the study of Creole. III. Some notes on Creole French. *Afr Stud* 19(4): 230-244. **[1]** [*COL*] |

Vérin, Pierre

| 25.0380 | BC,MT | 1958 | The rivalry of Creole and English in the West Indies. *W I G* 38(3-4): 163-167. **[20,32]** [*RIS*] |
| *24.0159* | SL | 1961 | Littérature orale de l'île de Sainte-Lucie [Oral literature of the island of St. Lucia]. |

Vervoorn, A. J.

| 25.0381 | SR | [n.d.] | Het Nederlands en de Surinaamse letterkunde [The Dutch language and Surinamese literature]. *In* HET NEDERLANDS IN SURINAME. Den Haag, the Netherlands, Kabinet voor Surinaamse en Nederlands-Antilliaanse Zaken: 27-63. **[22]** [*RILA*] |
| 25.0382 | SR | 1974 | Surinaamse schrijvers en het Nederlands [Surinamese writers and the Dutch language]. *Ons Erfdeel* 17(2), March-April: 165-180. [*NYP*] |

Voorhoeve, Jan

25.0383	SR	1952	De studie van het Surinaams [The study of the Surinam language]. *W I G* 33: 175-182. [*COL*]
25.0384	SR	1953	VOORSTUDIES TOT EEN BESCHRIJVING VAN HET SRANAN TONGO (NEGERENGELS VAN SURINAME) [PRELIMINARY STUDIES OF SRANAN TONGO (SURINAM NEGRO ENGLISH)]. Amsterdam, North Holland Pub. Co., 108p. [*COL*]
25.0385	SR	1957	Missionary linguistics in Surinam. *Bib Transl* 8(4), Oct.: 179-190. **[23]** [*NYP*]
25.0386	SR	1957	Spellingsmoeilijkheden in het Sranan [Spelling difficulties in Sranan]. *Taal Tong* 9: 147-158.
25.0387	SR	1957	Structureel onderzoek van het Sranan [Structural analysis of Sranan]. *W I G* 37: 189-211. [*COL*]
25.0388	SR	1957	The verbal system of Sranan. *Lingua* 6(4), July: 374-396. [*COL*]
25.0389	SR	1959	An orthography for Saramaccan. *Word* 15(3), Dec.: 436-445. [*COL*]
25.0390	SR	1961	A project for the study of Creole language history in Surinam. *In* Le Page, R. B., ed. PROCEEDINGS OF THE CONFERENCE ON CREOLE LANGUAGE STUDIES held at the University College of the West Indies. Mar. 28-Apr. 4, 1959. London, Macmillan, p.99-106. (Creole language studies, no. 2.) **[32]** [*RIS*]
25.0391	SR	1961	Spelling difficulties in Sranan. *Bib Transl* 12, Jan.: 1-11.
25.0392	SR	1961	Le ton et la grammaire dans le Saramaccan [Pitch and grammar in Saramaccan]. *Word* 12(2), Aug.: 146-163. [*COL*]
25.0393	SR	1962	SRANAN SYNTAX. Amsterdam, North-Holland Pub. Co., 91p.
25.0394	SR	1970	The regularity of sound correspondences in a Creole language (Sranan). *J Afr Lang* 9(2): 51-69. [*COL*]
25.0395	SR	1971	Het Surinaams [The Surinam vernacular]. *Intermediair* 7(12), March 26: 23-27. [*RILA*]
25.0396	SR	1971	Varieties of creole in Suriname: church creole and pagan cult languages. *In* Hymes, Dell, ed. PIDGINIZATION AND CREOLIZATION OF LANGUAGES: PROCEEDINGS OF A CONFERENCE HELD AT THE UNIVERSITY OF THE WEST INDIES, MONA, JAMAICA, APRIL 1968. London, Cambridge University Press: 305-315. [*RIS*]

25.0397	SR	1971	Varieties of creole in Suriname: the art of reading creole poetry. *In* Hymes, Dell, ed. PIDGINIZATION AND CREOLIZATION OF LANGUAGES: PROCEEDINGS OF A CONFERENCE HELD AT THE UNIVERSITY OF THE WEST INDIES, MONA, JAMAICA, APRIL 1968. London, Cambridge University Press: 323-326. [*RIS*]
25.0398	SR	1973	Historical and linguistic evidence in favour of the relexification theory in the formation of creoles. *Lang Soc* 2(1), April: 133-145. [*AGS*]

Voorhoeve, Jan & Lichtveld, Ursy M.

25.0399	SR	1970	Het Surinaams (Sranan-tongo) [The Surinam language (Sranan-tongo)]. *Gids* 133(9): 280-285. [*COL*]

Voorhoeve, Jan & Lichtveld, Ursy M., eds.

24.0160	SR	1975	CREOLE DRUM: AN ANTHOLOGY OF CREOLE LITERATURE IN SURINAM.

Voskuil, J. J.

25.0400	SR	1956	HET NEDERLANDS VAN HINDOESTAANSE KINDEREN IN SURINAME: ONDERZOEK NAAR DE INVLOED VAN DE MOEDERTAAL BIJ HET AANLEREN VAN EEN VREEMDE CULTUURTAAL [THE DUTCH OF THE HINDUSTANI CHILDREN IN SURINAM: STUDY OF THE INFLUENCE OF THE MOTHER LANGUAGE ON THE LEARNING OF A FOREIGN LANGUAGE]. Amsterdam, Noord-Hollandsche Uitg. Mij., 138p. [12,32] [*NYP*]

Warner, Maureen

19.0064	TR	1970	Some Yoruba descendants in Trinidad.
19.0065	TR	1971	African feasts in Trinidad.
25.0401	TR	1971	Trinidad Yoruba—notes on survivals. *Car Q* 17(2), June: 40-49. [19] [*RIS*]

Wel, F. J. van

25.0402	SR	[n.d.]	Het Nederlands in Suriname [The Dutch language in Surinam]. *In* HET NEDERLANDS IN SURINAME. The Hague, The Netherlands, Kabinet voor Surinaamse en Nederlands-Antilliaanse Zaken: 5-26. [32] [*RILA*]

Wel, Freek van

25.0403	SR	1974	De toekomst van het Nederlands in Suriname [The future of the Dutch language in Surinam]. *Ons Erfdeel* 17(1), Jan.-Feb.: 23-32. [32] [*NYP*]

Wells, J. C.

25.0404	JM,UK	1973	JAMAICAN PRONUNCIATION IN LONDON. Oxford, Blackwell: 150p. (Publication of the Philological Society 25) [18] [*RIS*]

White, Walter Grainge

25.0405	GU	1917	Fringes of Makuchi. *Timehri* 3d ser., 4(21), June: 98-106. [13] [*AMN*]
25.0406	GU	1918	Articles on Indian languages. *Timehri* 3d ser., 5(22), Aug.: 98-103. [13] [*AMN*]

Whitehead, Henry S.

25.0407	UV	1932	Negro dialect of the Virgin Islands. *Am Speech* 7(3), Feb.: 175-179. [24] [*COL*]

Wight, J.
25.0408   JM   1971   Dialect in school. *Educ Rev* 24(1), Nov.: 47-58.   **[32]**   [*UCLA*]

Wijk, H. L. A. van
25.0409   CU   1958   Orígenes y evolución del papiamentu [Origins and development of Papiamento]. *Neophilologues* 42, July: 169-182.   **[5]**

Willeford, Mary Jo
25.0410   BB   1967   Archaic words in Bajan dialect. *Bim* 12(45), July-Dec.: 21-26.   [*RIS*]
25.0411   BB   1967   Bajan dialect: English or Sudanic? *Bim* 11(44), Jan.-June: 268-272.
                                                                                                [*RIS*]
25.0412   BB   1968   Africanisms in the Bajan dialect. *Bim* 12(46), Jan.-June: 90-97.
                                                                                                [*RIS*]

Williams, James
1.0304   GG   1924   The Arawak Indians and their language.
13.0223   GU   1928   The Warau Indians of Guiana and vocabulary of their language.
13.0224   GU   1929   The Warau Indians of Guiana and vocabulary of their language.
25.0413   GU   1932   GRAMMAR NOTES AND VOCABULARY OF THE LANGUAGE OF THE MAKUCHI INDIANS OF GUIANA. St. Gabriel-Mödling bei Wien, Verlag der Internationalen Zeitschrift "Anthropos", 413p. (Linguistische Anthroposbibliothek, v. 8.)   **[13]**   [*AMN*]

Wilson, D. G.
25.0414   JM   1969   Bi-lingualism. *Car Q* 15(1), March: 45-50.   **[32]**   [*RIS*]

Wilson, Donald
32.0616   BC   1975   Role playing and second dialect teaching in the West Indies.

Winford, Donald
25.0415   TR   1972   A SOCIOLINGUISTIC DESCRIPTION OF TWO COMMUNITIES IN TRINIDAD. D.Phil. dissertation, University of York: 502p.

Wood, Richard E.
25.0416   NA   1969   Linguistic problems in the Netherlands Antilles. *Mond Ling-Prob* 1(2), March: 77-86.   [*COL*]
25.0417   NA   1970   PAPIAMENTU: DUTCH CONTRIBUTIONS. Ph.D. dissertation, Indiana University: 258p.   [*PhD*]
25.0418   NA   1971   The English loanwords in Papiamentu. *N W I G* 48(2-3), Dec.: 173-189.   [*RIS*]
25.0419   CU   1972   Dutch syntactic loans in Papiamentu. *Rev Lang Viv* 38(6): 635-647.   **[19]**   [*COL*]
25.0420   NL   1972   The hispanization of a creole language: Papiamentu. *Hispania* 55(4), Dec.: 857-864.   [*TCL*]
25.0421   NA   1972   New light on the origins of Papiamentu: an eighteenth-century letter. *Neophilologus* 56(1), Jan.: 18-30.   [*NYP*]

Young, Colville Norbert
25.0422   BZ   1973   BELIZE CREOLE: A STUDY OF THE CREOLISED ENGLISH SPOKEN IN THE CITY OF BELIZE, IN ITS CULTURAL AND SOCIAL SETTING. D.Phil. dissertation, University of York: 312p.

Yvandoc, C.

25.0423	**GD**	1962	Aporta a Feri. *Rev Guad* 46, Jan.-Mar.: 26-27.
24.0162	**FA**	1962	On ti coutt langue.

Ziel, Henny F. de

18.0292	**SR,NE**	1968	Sranan-patatania.

Zonneveld, J. I. S.

56.0347	**SR**	1967	Toponymen in Suriname [Toponyms in Surinam].

Chapter 26

CULTURAL CHANGE

Works which focus on aspects of socio-cultural change.
See also: **[19]** Cultural continuities; **[21]** Ethnic and national identity.

Abrams, Ira Rance
13.0001   **BZ**   1973   CASH CROP FARMING AND SOCIAL AND ECONOMIC CHANGE IN A YUCATEC MAYA COMMUNITY IN NORTHERN BRITISH HONDURAS.

Adams, Kathleen Joy
13.0002   **GU**   1972   THE BARAMA RIVER CARIBS OF GUYANA RESTUDIED: FORTY YEARS OF CULTURAL ADAPTATION AND POPULATION CHANGE.

Aiken, James
48.0002   **GU**   1915   "Timehri" and development.

Alleyne, J. M.
8.0003   **GC**   1975   The creolization of Africans and Indians.

Astruc, M.
48.0006   **FC**   1975   La radio et la télévision française dans les départements d'Outre-Mer [French radio and television in the French Overseas departments].

Bagley, Christopher & Coard, Bernard
21.0002   **BC,UK**   1975   Cultural knowledge and rejection of ethnic identity in West Indian children in London.

Bastide, Roger
11.0003   **GC**   1971[?]   AFRICAN CIVILISATIONS IN THE NEW WORLD.

Bastien, Rémy
11.0004   **GC**   1969   Estructura de la adaptación del negro en América Latina y del afroamericano en Africa [Structure of the adaptation of the negro in Latin America and of the Afro-American in Africa].

Beaucage, Pierre
13.0011   **GC**   1966   Les Carïbes noirs: trois siècles de changement social [The Black Caribs: Three centuries of social change].

Boxill, Courtney
12.0015   **TR**   1975   From East Indian to Indo-Trinidadian.

Brathwaite, Edward
26.0001   GC   1974   CONTRADICTORY OMENS: CULTURAL DIVERSITY AND INTEGRATION IN THE CARIBBEAN. Mona, Jamaica, Savacou Publications: 80p. (Monograph No. 1)   **[5,8,19]**   [*RIS*]
19.0004   BC   1974   Timehri.

Brathwaite, Edward K.
8.0024   JM   1971   THE DEVELOPMENT OF CREOLE SOCIETY IN JAMAICA, 1770-1820.

Bryce-Laporte, R. S.
23.0022   GC,PA   1970   Crisis, contraculture, and religion among West Indians in the Panama Canal Zone.

Butt Colson, Audrey J.
13.0030   GG   1971   Comparative studies of the social structure of Guiana indians and the problem of acculturation.

Carew, Jan
32.0108   BC   1976   Identity, cultural alienation and education in the Caribbean.

Ciski, Robert
15.0021   SV   1975   THE VINCENTIAN PORTUGUESE: A STUDY IN ETHNIC GROUP ADAPTATION.

Clarke, Colin G.
12.0018   TR   1967   Caste among Hindus in a town in Trinidad: San Fernando.

Cloak, F. T., Jr.
19.0008   TR   1966   A NATURAL ORDER OF CULTURAL ADOPTION AND LOSS IN TRINIDAD.

Coombs, Orde, ed.
21.0014   GC   1974   IS MASSA DAY DEAD? BLACK MOODS IN THE CARIBBEAN.

Crowley, Daniel J.
26.0002   SL   1959[?]   CONSERVATISM AND CHANGE IN SAINT LUCIA: ACTAS DEL XXXIII CONGRESO INTERNACIONAL DE AMERICANISTAS, SAN JOSÉ, COSTA RICA, JULY 20-27, 1958. [n.p.] Editorial Lehmann, p.704-715.   **[5,11]**   [*RIS*]

Davison, Betty
17.0028   JM   1968   No place back home: a study of Jamaicans returning to Kingston, Jamaica.

Despres, Leo A.
26.0003   GU   1969   Differential adaptations and micro-cultural evolution in Guyana. *Sw J Anthrop* 25(1), Spring: 14-44.   **[8,19,42]**   [*COL*]

Dirks, Robert & Kerns, Virginia
9.0041   TT   1976   Mating patterns and adaptive change in Rum Bay, 1823-1970.

Dostal, W., ed.
13.0047   GG   1972   THE SITUATION OF THE INDIAN IN SOUTH AMERICA: CONTRIBUTIONS TO THE STUDY OF INTER-ETHNIC CONFLICT IN THE NON-ANDEAN REGIONS OF SOUTH AMERICA.

Duchemin, Philippe
13.0049   FG   1972   The Indians of French Guiana and the policy of assimilation. II. The situation of the Indian groups in French Guiana in 1971.

Elst, Dirk H. van der
14.0010   SR   1975   The Coppename Kwinti: notes on an Afro-American tribe in Surinam. III. Culture change and viability.

Eyre, L. Alan
50.0049   JM   1973   The impact of modern mining industries on simple societies.

Gregory, James R.
19.0022   BZ   1972   PIONEERS ON A CULTURAL FRONTIER: THE MOPAN MAYA OF BRITISH HONDURAS.

Grodd, Gabriele
26.0004   SR   1971   KULTURWANDEL DER INDONESISCHEN EINWANDERER IN SURINAM: KULTURELLE UND GESELLSCHAFTLICHE VERÄNDERUNGEN EINER JAVANISCHEN MINDERHEIT IN LATEIN-AMERIKA [CULTURAL ADAPTATION OF THE INDONESIAN IMMIGRANTS IN SURINAM: CULTURAL AND SOCIOLOGICAL CHANGES OF A JAVANESE MINORITY IN LATIN-AMERICA]. Freiburg im Breisgau, Albert-Ludwigs-Universität: 159p (Ph.D. dissertation). **[15]**   [*RIS*]

Groot, Silvia W. de
14.0013   SR   1969   DJUKA SOCIETY AND SOCIAL CHANGE: HISTORY OF AN ATTEMPT TO DEVELOP A BUSH NEGRO COMMUNITY IN SURINAM, 1917-1926.

Guggenheim, Hans
22.0158   TR   1968   SOCIAL AND POLITICAL CHANGE IN THE ART WORLD OF TRINIDAD DURING THE PERIOD OF TRANSITION FROM COLONY TO NEW NATION.

Gullick, Charles John M. R.
13.0077   SV   1974   TRADITION AND CHANGE AMONG THE CARIBS OF ST. VINCENT.

Hartog, J.
5.0377   BN   1957[?]   BONAIRE VAN INDIANEN TOT TOERISTEN [BONAIRE FROM INDIANS TO TOURISTS].

Henry, Frances
19.0026   GC   1972   Cultural variation.

Hurault, Jean
13.0090   FG   1963   Les Indiens de Guyane Francaise: problèmes pratiques d'administration et de contacts de civilisation [The Indians of French Guiana: practical problems of administration and culture contact].
13.0097   FG   1972   The Indians of French Guiana and the policy of assimilation. I. The "Francization" of the Indians.

Jacobs, Sharon
20.0038   BA   1973   San Salvador Island: from culture contact to alienation.

Jha, J. C.
12.0038   TR   1976   The Hindu festival of Divali in the Caribbean.
12.0039   TR   1976   The Hindu sacraments (*rites de passage*) in Trinidad and Tobago.

Johnstone, H. M.
35.0044   TR   1959   Queens Hall, Trinidad—the beginning of a new era of cultural development.

Jones, Grant D.
13.0106   BZ   1974   Revolution and continuity in Santa Cruz Maya society.

Karner, Frances P.
15.0049   CU   1969   THE SEPHARDICS OF CURAÇAO: A STUDY OF SOCIO-CULTURAL PATTERNS IN FLUX.

Köbben, A. J. F.
14.0038   SR   1968   Continuity in change: Cottica Djuka society as a changing system.

Kuper, Adam
2.0257   JM   1976   CHANGING JAMAICA.

La Guerre, John Gaffar
12.0050   TR   1974   The East Indian middle class today.

La Guerre, John Gaffar, ed.
12.0051   TR   1974   CALCUTTA TO CARONI: THE EAST INDIANS OF TRINIDAD.

Lassale, Jean-Pierre
32.0341   FC   1975   Problèmes de coopération culturelle [Problems of cultural cooperation].

Lefley, Harriet P.
31.0087   BA   1972   Modal personality in the Bahamas.

Levy, Joseph Josy
2.0277   MT   1976   UN VILLAGE DU BOUT DU MONDE: MODERNISATION ET STRUCTURES VILLAGEOISES AUX ANTILLES FRANÇAISES [A VILLAGE AT THE END OF THE EARTH: MODERNIZATION AND VILLAGE STRUCTURES IN THE FRENCH ANTILLES].

Livingstone, W. P.
5.0559   JM   1900   BLACK JAMAICA; A STUDY IN EVOLUTION.

McCaffrey, Colin
26.0005   BZ   1967   POTENTIALITIES FOR COMMUNITY DEVELOPMENT IN A KEKCHÍ INDIAN VILLAGE IN BRITISH HONDURAS. Ph.D. dissertation, University of California, Berkeley: 443p.   **[15]**   [*PhD*]

MacDonald, John S. & MacDonald, Leatrice D.
9.0095   BB,GR,TR   1973   Transformation of African and Indian family traditions in the Southern Caribbean.

Madoo, Patricia
20.0050   TR   1970   MODERNIZATION AND VALUE CHANGES IN TRINIDAD AND TOBAGO.

Marcus, George E.
8.0151   **GU**   1970   Incomplete transformation: social change in a Guyanese rural community.

Maynard, Edward Samuel
9.0101   **BB,US**   1974   Endogamy among Barbadian immigrants to New York City: an exploratory study of marriage patterns and their relationship to adjustment to an alien culture.

Metraux, Rhoda
26.0006   **MS**   1957   Montserrat, B.W.I.: some implications of suspended culture change. *Trans N Y Acad Sci* 2d ser., 20(2), Dec.: 205-211.   **[20]**   [*RIS*]

Mintz, Sidney W.
8.0163   **GC**   1974   Caribbean transformations.
10.0034   **GC**   1974   Les roles économiques et la tradition culturelle [Economic roles and cultural tradition].

Newson, Linda A.
26.0007   **TR**   1972   Aboriginal and Spanish colonial Trinidad: a study in cultural evolution. Ph.D. dissertation, University of London: 461p. **[5,19]**

Oakley, Robin, ed.
18.0218   **BC,UK**   1968   New backgrounds: the immigrant child at home and at school.

Otterbein, Keith F.
35.0057   **BA**   1975   Changing house types in Long Bay Cays: the evolution of folk housing in an Out Island Bahamian community.

Parris, Ronald Glenfield
16.0079   **BB**   1974   Race, inequality and underdevelopment in Barbados, 1627-1973.

Patterson, Sheila
18.0222   **BC,UK**   1963   Dark strangers: a sociological study of the absorption of a recent West Indian migrant group in Brixton, South London.

Penard, Thomas E. & Penard, Arthur P.
25.0278   **SR**   1926-27 European influence on the Arawak language of Guiana.

Price, Richard
9.0117   **SR**   1970   Saramaka emigration and marriage: a case study of social change.

Ramesar, Marianne D.
12.0074   **TR**   1976   The impact of the Indian immigrants on colonial Trinidad society.

Read, Margaret
32.0472   **BC**   1955   Education and social change in tropical areas.

Renselaar, H. C. van
15.0078   **SR**   1969   Geschiedenis van de Creolen en Creoolse volkscultuur [History of the Creoles and Creole culture].

Rivière, P. G.

13.0169   **SR**   1966   A policy for the Trio Indians of Surinam.

Rodgers, William B.

8.0187   **BA**   1965   THE WAGES OF CHANGE: AN ANTHROPOLOGICAL STUDY OF THE EFFECTS OF ECONOMIC DEVELOPMENT ON SOME NEGRO COMMUNITIES IN THE OUT ISLAND BAHAMAS.

20.0069   **BA**   1967   Changing gratification orientations: some findings from the Out Island Bahamas.

Samaroo, Brinsley

12.0079   **GC**   1974   Hindu marriage in the Caribbean.

Sanford, Margaret

19.0056   **BZ**   1974   Revitalization movements as indicators of completed acculturation.

Schwartz, Barton M.

12.0081   **TR**   1967   Differential socio-religious adaptation.

12.0082   **TR**   1967   The failure of caste in Trinidad.

Schwartz, Barton M., ed.

12.0083   **GU,TR,SR**   1967   CASTE IN OVERSEAS INDIAN COMMUNITIES.

Scott, Gloria

41.0447   **BC**   1966   Problems of economic and cultural change in the West Indies and the Atlantic Provinces.

Seggar, W. H.

13.0196   **GU**   1965   The changing Amerindian.

Silin, Robert H.

15.0085   **JM,US**   [n.d.]   THE CHINESE IN JAMAICA: A STUDY OF SELECTED PROBLEMS.

Simons, R. D. & Voorhoeve, J.

25.0310   **SR**   1955-56 Ontleningen van Nederlandse samenstellingen in het Surinaams [Adoption of Dutch compounds in the Surinam language].

Singer, Philip

12.0088   **GU**   1967   Caste and identity in Guyana.

Singer, Philip & Araneta, Enrique

12.0089   **GU**   1967   Hinduization and creolization in Guyana: the plural society and basic personality.

Smith, Raymond Thomas

8.0222   **GU**   1966   People and change.

Solien, Nancie L.

13.0198   **JM,BZ,TR**   1971   West Indian characteristics of the Black Carib.

Speckmann, Johan Dirk

12.0097   **SR**   1963   Het proces van sociale verandering bij de Hindostaanse bevolkingsgroep in Suriname [The process of social change among the Hindustanis in Surinam].

Stewart, John
26.0008   GC   1974   Where goes the indigenous black church? *In* Coombs, Orde, ed. Is MASSA DAY DEAD? BLACK MOODS IN THE CARIBBEAN. Garden City, New York, Anchor Press/Doubleday: 189-204.   **[10,23]**   [*CEIP*]

Stewart, John Othneil
10.0052   TR   1973   COOLIE AND CREOLE: DIFFERENTIAL ADAPTATIONS IN A NEO-PLANTATION VILLAGE—TRINIDAD, WEST INDIES.

Stone, Linda S.
12.0100   SV   1973   East Indian adaptations on St. Vincent: Richland Park.

Taylor, Douglas
25.0317   DM   1946   Loan words in Dominica Island Carib.
53.0570   DM   1954   Names on Dominica.

Thompson, Robert Wallace
56.0300   TR   1959   Pre-British place-names in Trinidad.

Tucker, Terry
48.0165   BE   1967   Motoring comes of age in Bermuda.

Tull, Marc
19.0063   BA   1973   San Salvadorian reactions to the American: a brief look at American influence on San Salvador.

Walker, Della
13.0218   GU   1972   Guyana: problems in Amerindian acculturation.

Williams, James
1.0303   GU   1917   Indian languages.
53.0651   GG   1923   The name "Guiana."

Willis, Margaret
20.0087   JM   1971   Housing aspirations and changing life-styles in Jamaica.

Yeaton, Leander
26.0009   BA   1973   Gambling: a brief case study in cultural change. *In* Thomas, Garry L., ed. ANTHROPOLOGICAL FIELD REPORTS FROM SAN SALVADOR ISLAND. San Salvador, Bahamas, Island Environment Studies, Reports 1973: 91-94.   **[22]**   [*RIS*]

HEALTH,
EDUCATION
AND
WELFARE

Chapter 27

HUMAN BIOLOGY

Bone and skeletal studies; body measurement; genetics; hematology; sickle cell studies.

See also: [4] Archaeology and ethnohistory; [28] Health and public health; [30] Food and nutrition.

Abrahams, Dawne E. & Kean, E. A.
27.0001   JM   1969   Hypoglycin A in biological material: its detection and assay. *W I Med J* 18(3), Sept.: 147-151.   [*PS*]

Ahern, E. J.; Herbert, R.; McIver, C.; Ahern, V.; Wardle, J. & Seakins, M.
28.0007   JM   1975   Beta-thalassaemia of clinical significance in adult Jamaican negroes.

Ahern, E. J.; Holder, W.; Ahern, V.; Serjeant, G. R.; Serjeant, B. E.; Forbes, M.; Brimhall, B. & Jones, R. T.
27.0002   JM   1975   Haemoglobin F Victoria Jubilee (α_2 $^A\gamma_2$ 80 Asp $\rightarrow$ Tyr). *Biochim Biophys Acta* 393(1), 30 May: 188-194.   [*ACM*]

Ahern, E. J.; Swan, A. V. & Ahern, V.
27.0003   JM   1973   The prevalence of the rarer inherited haemoglobin defects in adult Jamaicans. *Br J Haematol* 25(4), Oct.: 437-444.   [11,28]   [*PS*]

Aleksev, V. P.
27.0004   GG   1969   Antropologicheskie ocobennosti korennovo naceleniya Gviani [Anthropological characteristics of the primitive peoples of Guyana]. *In* Grigulevich, I. R., ed. GVIANA: GAIANA, FRANTZUZKAYA-GAIANA, SURINAM. Moscow, Izdatelstvo "Natchka": 197-212.   [13]   [*UNL*]

Arends, Tulio
27.0005   GC   1966   Haemoglobinopathies, thalassaemia and glucose-6-phosphate deficiency in Latin America and the West Indies. *N Z Med J* 65(412), Dec. Supplement: 831-844.   [28]   [*PS*]

Arneaud, John D. & Young, Oswald
27.0006   TR   1955   A preliminary survey of the distribution of ABO and Rh blood groups in Trinidad, B.W.I. *Docum Med Geogr Trop* 7(4), Dec.: 375-378.   [*COL*]

Ashcroft, M. T. & Antrobus, A. C. K.

27.0007   SV,GC   1970   Heights and weights of schoolchildren in St. Vincent. *J Biosoc Sci* 2(4): 317-328.   **[32,28]**   [*PS*]

Ashcroft, M. T.; Beadnell, H. M. S. G.; Miller, G. J. & Bell, R.

27.0008   GU   1969   Anthropometric measurements of Guyanese adults of African and East Indian origins. *Trop Geogr Med* 21(2), June: 169-176.   **[11,12,28]**   [*PS*]

Ashcroft, M. T.; Bell, R. & Nicholson, C. C.

27.0009   GU   1968   Anthropometric measurements of Guyanese schoolchildren of African and East Indian racial origins. *Trop Geogr Med* 20(2), June: 159-171.   **[11,12,28]**   [*PS*]

Ashcroft, M. T.; Bell, R.; Nicholson, C. C. & Pemberton, S.

27.0010   GU   1968   Growth of Guyanese infants of African and East Indian racial origins, with some observations on mortality. *Trans Roy Soc Trop Med Hyg* 62(5): 607-618.   **[11,12]**   [*PS*],

Ashcroft, M. T.; Buchanan, I. C. & Lovell, H. G.

27.0011   KNA   1965   Heights and weights of primary schoolchildren in St. Christopher-Nevis-Anguilla, West Indies. *J Trop Med Hyg* 68(11), Nov.: 277-283.   **[28,32]**   [*PS*]

Ashcroft, M. T.; Buchanan, I. C.; Lovell, H. G. & Welsh, B.

27.0012   KNA   1966   Growth of infants and preschool children in St. Christopher-Nevis-Anguilla, West Indies. *Am J Clin Nutr* 19(1), July: 37-45.   **[28]**   [*PS*]

Ashcroft, M. T.; Heneage, P. & Lovell, H. G.

27.0013   JM   1966   Heights and weights of Jamaican schoolchildren of various ethnic groups. *Am J Phys Anphrop* 24(1), Jan.: 35-44.   **[8]**   [*COL*]

Ashcroft, M. T.; Ling, J.; Lovell, H. G. & Miall, W. E.

27.0014   JM   1966   Heights and weights of adults in rural and urban areas of Jamaica. *Br J Prev Social Med* 20(1), Jan.: 22-26.   **[28]**   [*PS*]

Ashcroft, M. T. & Lovell, H. G.

27.0015   JM   1965   Changes in mean size of children in some Jamaican schools between 1951 and 1964. *W I Med J* 14(1), March: 48-52.   **[32]**   [*PS*]

27.0016   JM   1966   Heights and weights of Jamaican primary schoolchildren. *J Trop Pediat* 12(2), Sept.: 37-43.   **[28,32**   [*PS*]

27.0017   JM   1966   The validity of surveys of heights and weights of Jamaican schoolchildren. *W I Med J* 15(1), March: 27-33.   **[32]**   [*PS*]

Ashcroft, M. T.; Lovell, H. G.; George, M. & Williams, A.

27.0018   JM   1965   Heights and weights of infants and children in a rural community of Jamaica. *J Trop Pediat* 11(3), Dec.: 56-68.   **[28,32]**   [*PS*]

Ashcroft, M. T.; Miall, W. E. & Milner, P. F.

27.0019   JM   1969   A comparison between the characteristics of Jamaican adults with normal hemoglobin and those with sickle cell trait. *Am J Epidemiol* 90(3), Sept.: 236-243.   **[28]**   [*PS*]

Ashcroft, M. T. & Serjeant, G. R.

28.0056   JM   1972   Body habitus of Jamaican adults with sickle cell anemia.

Bateson, E. M.

28.0098   JM   1970   Comparative radiology of the proximal gastro-intestinal tract in Jamaica: a review of 3,800 barium examinations.

Bellon, R.; Pericarpin, S. & Fauran, P.

27.0020   FA   1965   Etude familiale d'hémoglobinopathies SC [Family study of SC hemoglobinopathies]. *J Med Bord Sud-Ouest* 142(6), June: 953-955.
[PS]

Bennett, M. A.; Heslop, R. W. & Meynell, M. J.

28.0118   JM   1967   Massive haematuria associated with sickle-cell trait.

Benoist, Jean

27.0021   MT   1957   Stature et corpulence à la Martinique: données anthropométriques globales et incidence des conditions sociales [Height and weight in Martinique: overall anthropometric data and incidence of social factors]. *Biotypologie* 18(4): 237-246.
[RIS]

27.0022   MT   1958[?] DONNÉES COMPARATIVES SUR LA CROISSANCE SOMATIQUE DES ENFANTS DE COULEUR ET DES ENFANTS DE RACE BLANCHE NÉS ET ÉLEVÉS À LA MARTINIQUE [COMPARATIVE DATA ON THE SOMATIC GROWTH OF COLORED CHILDREN AND WHITE CHILDREN BORN AND RAISED IN MARTINIQUE]. Société des Africanistes, p.[7-9]. **[11,15]**
[RIS]

27.0023   MT   1959   Notes pour l'étude de la croissance chez les enfants martiniquais: étude préliminaire chez les enfants du sexe masculin de Fort-de-France [Notes for the study of growth among Martinique children. Preliminary study among the male children of Fort-de-France]. *Archs Inst Past Mart* 12(1-2), Jan.-Apr.: 43-46.   [RIS]

27.0024   MT   1961   L'étude de la structure génétique d'une population métissée [Study of the genetic structure of a hybrid population]. *Anthropologica* new ser., 3(1): 55-64.
[COL]

27.0025   MT   1963   Les Martiniquais: anthropologie d'une population métissée [The people of Martinique: the anthropology of a hybrid population]. *B Mem Soc Anthrop Paris* II. ser., 4(2), Apr.-June: 241-432.   [RIS]

27.0026   FA   1964   Quelques facteurs sociaux de la différenciation raciale aux Antilles Francaises [Some social aspects of racial differentiation in the French Antilles]. *In* ACTAS Y MEMORIAS, XXXV CONGRESO INTERNACIONAL DE AMERICANISTAS, México, 1962. México, p.87-94.
[RIS]

27.0027   SB   1964   Saint-Barthélemy: physical anthropology of an isolate. *Am J Phys Anthrop* new ser., 22(4), Dec.: 473-487.   [RIS]

27.0028   SB   1965   Répartition des groupes sanguins ABO à Saint-Barthélémy [Distribution of the blood type A B O on Saint Barthelemy]. *Archs Inst Past Guad:* 113-118.   [AMN]

9.0022   SB   1966   Du social au biologique: étude de quelques interactions [From social to biological: study of some interactions].

Benoist, Jean & Dansereau, Gilles

27.0029   SB   1972   Données qualitatives et quantitatives sur les dermatoglyphes digitaux et palmaires de Saint-Barthélemy (Antilles Françaises) [Quantitative and qualitative data on finger and palmar dermatoglyphics from Saint-Barthelemy (French West Indies)]. *B Mem Soc Anthrop* 9(12): 165-176.   [COL]

Bideau, J. & Courmes, E.

27.0030   GD   1965   Enquête sur la fréquence des hémoglobines anormales observées chez les Guadeloupéens [Investigation of the frequency of abnormal hemoglobins observed in natives of Guadeloupe]. *J Med Bord Sud-Ouest* 142(6), June: 961-966.   **[28]**   [*PS*]

Bois, Etienne P.

13.0016   FG   1967   LES AMÉRINDIENS DE LA HAUTE-GUYANE FRANÇAISE: ANTHRO-POLOGIE, PATHOLOGIE, BIOLOGIE [THE AMERINDIANS OF UPPER FRENCH GUIANA: ANTHROPOLOGY, PATHOLOGY, BIOLOGY].

Bone, R. A. & Sparrock, J. M.

27.0031   GC   1971   Comparison of macular pigment densities in human eyes. *Vision Res* 11(10), Oct.: 1057-1064.   **[11]**   [*PS*]

Boyd, P. I.

27.0032   GC   1971   HEALTH PROBLEMS IN THE DEVELOPING CARIBBEAN. Bridgetown, Barbados, CADEC (Caribbean Ecumenical Consultation for Development): 11p. (Study Paper No. 7)   [*RIS*]

Braconnier, F.; Cohen-Solal, M.; Schlegel, N.; Blouquit, Y.; Thillet, J.; De Linval, J. C. & Rosa, J.

28.0153   GD,MT   1975   Hemoglobine J. Broussaic α_2 90 Lys →Asn β_2A (FG2) découvert dans une famille martiniquaise. Comparaison des différentes techniques analytiques utilisées [Hemoglobin J. Broussais alpha-2 90 Lys leads to Asn beta-2A (FG2) discovered in a Martinique family. Comparison of several analytical techniques].

Brimhall, B.; Vedvick, T. S.; Jones, R. T.; Ahern, E.; Palomino, E. & Ahern, V.

27.0033   JM   1974   Haemoglobin F Port Royal (alpha 2G gamma 2 125 Glu leads to Ala). *Br J Haematol* 27(2), June: 313-318.   **[28]**   [*PS*]

Brothwell, D. R.

27.0034   GU   1967   The Amerindians of Guyana: a biological review. *Eug Rev* 59(1), March: 22-45.   **[9,13,28,30]**   [*COL*]

Bullbrook, John Albert

4.0044   TR   1953   ON THE EXCAVATION OF A SHELL MOUND AT PALO SECO, TRINIDAD, B.W.I.

Bullen, Adelaide K.

27.0035   GR   1968   Field comments on the skull excavated in 1967 at Caliviny Island, Grenada, W.I. *In* PROCEEDINGS OF THE SECOND INTERNATIONAL CONGRESS FOR THE STUDY OF PRE-COLUMBIAN CULTURES IN THE LESSER ANTILLES; ST. ANN'S GARRISON, BARBADOS, JULY 24-28, 1967. Barbados Museum: 44-46.   [*RIS*]

Butts, Donald C. A.

27.0036   SR   1955   Blood groups of the Bush Negroes of Surinam. *Docum Med Geogr Trop* 7(1), Mar.: 43-49.   **[14]**   [*COL*]

Buxton, L. H. Dudley; Trevor, J. C. & Julien, Alvarez H.
27.0037   ST   1938   Skeletal remains from the Virgin Islands. *Man* 38(47), Apr.: 49-51.
               [COL]

Byas, Vincent W.
27.0038   MT   1943   Ethnologic aspects of the Martinique Creole. *J Negro Hist* 28(3), July: 261-283. **[11]**   [COL]

Cabannes, Raymond J. R.
13.0033   FG   1971   Genetic polymorphisms in Indian populations of French Guiana and Bolivia.

Cabannes, Raymond J. R.; Beurrier, A. & Larrouy, G.
27.0039   FG   1965   La thalassémie chez les Indiens de Guyane Française [Thalassemia in the Indians of French Guiana]. *Nou Rev Fr Hemat* 5(4), July-Aug.: 617-629. **[13,28]**   [PS]

Chen, W. N. & James, O. B. O'L.
27.0040   JM   1972   Histoplasmin sensitivity in the Jamaican population. *W I Med J* 21(4), Dec.: 220-224. **[28]**   [PS]

Clarke, Eric E.
28.0247   GU,JM   1973   A comparative analysis of the age distribution and types of primary glaucoma among populations of African and Caucasian origins.

Clegg, J. B. & Weatherall, D. J.
27.0041   JM   1974   Hemoglobin Constant Spring, an unusual a-chain variant involved in the etiology of hemoglobin H disease. *Ann NY Acad Sci* 232(0), May 24: 168-178. **[28]**   [ACM]

Clegg, J. B.; Weatherall, D. J. & Milner, P. F.
27.0042   JM   1971   Haemoglobin Constant Spring—a chain termination mutant? *Nature* 234(5328), Dec. 10: 337-340. **[15,28]**   [PS]

Clegg, Legrand H., II
11.0019   GC   1969   The beginning of the African diaspora: black men in ancient and medieval America? Part I.

Clermont, Norman
1.0058   GC   1972   BIBLIOGRAPHIE ANNOTÉE DE L'ANTHROPOLOGIE PHYSIQUE DES ANTILLES [ANNOTATED BIBLIOGRAPHY OF THE PHYSICAL ANTHROPOLOGY OF THE ANTILLES].

Cohen, Joel E.
27.0043   GC   1973   Heterologous immunity in human malaria. *Q Rev Bio* 48(3), Sept.: 467-489. **[28,54]**   [ACM]

Collier, W. A.
27.0044   SR   1955   The M-N blood-groups in the Arawaks of Matta, Surinam. *Docum Med Geogr Trop* 7(4), Dec.: 359-360. **[13]**   [COL]

Collier, W. A.; Fros, J. & Schipper, J. F. A.
27.0045   SR   1952   Blood groups of some American Indian settlements. *Docum Med Geogr Trop* 4(3), Sept.: 225-226. **[13]**   [COL]

Collier, W. A. & La Parra, D. A. de

27.0046   SR   1952   Sickle-cell trait in Surinam Creoles. *Docum Med Geogr Trop* 4(3), Sept.: 223-225. **[11]** [*COL*]

Collier, W. A.; Wolff, A. E. & Zaal, A. E. G.

27.0047   SR   1952   Contributions to the geographical pathology of Surinam. I: Blood groups of the Surinam population. *Docum Med Geogr Trop* 4(1), Mar.: 92-95. [*COL*]

Condon, P. I.; Gray, Robert & Serjeant, G. R.

27.0048   JM   1974   Ocular findings in children with sickle cell haemoglobin C in disease in Jamaica. *Br J Opthal* 58(7), July: 644-649. **[28]** [*PS*]

Condon, P. I. & Serjeant, G. R.

27.0049   JM   1972   Ocular findings in homozygous sickle cell anemia in Jamaica. *Am J Ophthal* 73(4), April: 533-543. **[28]** [*PS*]

27.0050   JM   1975   The progression of sickle cell eye disease in Jamaica. *Doc Ophthalmol* 39(1), 21 Nov.: 203-210. **[28]** [*PS*]

Cook, J. A.; Kellermeyer, W. F.; Warren, K. S. & Kellermeyer, R. W.

27.0051   SL   1972   Sickle cell haemoglobinopathy and schistosoma mansoni infection. *Ann Trop Med Paras* 66(2), June: 197-202. **[28]** [*PS*]

Daveau, M.; Rivat, L.; Langaney, A.; Afifi, N.; Bois, E. & Ropartz, C.

27.0052   FG   1975   Gm and Inv allotypes in French Guiana Indians. *Hum Hered* 25(2): 88-92. **[13]** [*ACM*]

Davenport, C. B.

27.0053   JM   1928   Race crossing in Jamaica. *Scient Mon* 27(3), Sept.: 225-238. [*AGS*]

Davenport, C. B. & Steggerda, Morris

27.0054   JM,CM   1929   RACE CROSSING IN JAMAICA. Washington, D.C., Carnegie Institution of Washington, 516p. **[11]** [*RIS*]

Dawber, Rodney P. R.

27.0055   BC,UK   1974   Knotting of scalp hair. *Br J Derm* 91(2), Aug.: 169-173. **[18]** [*PS*]

Debrot, A.

27.0056   CU   1969   Time interval between the eruption of homologous teeth. *J Dent Res* 48(2), March-April: 291-293. **[11]** [*PS*]

Desai, Patricia; Miall, W. E. & Standard, K. L.

30.0065   JM   1969   The social background of malnutrition in Jamaica.

Doornbos, L.; Jonxis, J. H. P. & Visser, H. K. A.

14.0006   SR   1968   Growth of Bushnegro children on the Tapanahony River in Dutch Guyana.

Doran, Edwin Beal, Jr.

27.0057   CM   1952   Inbreeding in an isolated island community. *J Hered* 43(6), Nov.-Dec.: 263-266. **[7,28]** [*RIS*]

Droogleever Fortuyn, A. B.

27.0058   SR   1946   SOME DATA ON THE PHYSICAL ANTHROPOLOGY OF OAJANA INDIANS. Amsterdam, Koninklijke Vereeniging Indisch Instituut, 24p. (Mededeeling no. 69, Afdeeling Volkenkunde no. 22.) **[13]** *[COL]*

27.0059   SR   1952   AGE, STATURE, AND WEIGHT IN SURINAM CONSCRIPTS. Amsterdam, Koninklijk Instituut voor de Tropen, 126p. (Mededeling no. 101, Afdeling Culturele en physische anthropologie no. 44.) *[SCH]*

Ekker, I.

30.0067   CU   1966   Voeding en voedingstoestand van Curaçaose schoolkinderen [Nutrition and nutritional state of Curaçao schoolchildren].

Ennis, J. T.; Serjeant, G. R. & Middlemiss, Howard

27.0060   JM   1973   Homozygous sickle cell disease in Jamaica. *Br J Radiol* 46(551), Nov.: 943-950. **[11,28]** *[PS]*

Erkelens, D. W.

28.0365   CU   1973   Melkintolerantie op Curaçao [Lactose intolerance in Curaçao].

Firschein, I. Lester

27.0061   BZ   1961   Population dynamics of the sickle-cell trait in the Black Caribs of British Honduras, Central America. *Am J Hum Gntcs* 13(2), June: 233-254. **[13]** *[COL]*

Floch, Hervé Alexandre & Lajudie, P. de

27.0062   FG   1947   Répartition des groupes sanguins en Guyane Francaise [Distribution of blood groups in French Guiana]. *Inst Past Guy Ter L'In* 145, Jan.: 3p. *[ACM]*

Florey, Charles du V.; Ashcroft, M. T. & Miller, G. J.

28.0438   GU   1971   Blood pressure levels of Guyanese adults of African and Indian origin.

Fonaroff, L. Schuyler

28.0441   TR   1966   BIOGEOGRAPHIC ASPECTS OF MALARIA IN TRINIDAD.
28.0442   BB   1966   Geographic notes on the Barbados malaria epidemic.
28.0444   TR   1968   The historical geography of malaria risk in Trinidad: three maps of change.
28.0445   TR   1968   Man and malaria in Trinidad: ecological perspectives on a changing health hazard.

French, E. A. & Lehmann, H.

27.0063   JM   1971   Is haemoglobin G_a Philadelphia linked to alpha-thalassaemia? *Acta Haematol* 46(3), 149-156. **[18,28]** *[PS]*

Gabuzda, Thomas G.

28.0474   JM   1975   Sickle cell leg ulcers: current pathophysiologic concepts.

Garrow, J. S.

27.0064   JM   1954   Some haematological and serum protein values in normal Jamaicans. *W I Med J* 3(2), June: 104-107. *[COL]*

Geerdink, R. A.; Bartstra, H. A. & Hopkinson, D. A.

27.0065   SR   1974   Phosphoglucomutase (PGM$_2$) variants in Trio Indians from Surinam. *Hum Hered* 24(1): 40-44.   **[13]**   [*ACM*]

Geerdink, R. A.; Breel, P. M.; Sander, P. C. & Schillhorn-Van Veen, Joke M.

28.0483   SR   1973   Comparison of serum cholesterol values in Amerindians from Surinam with those of Dutch controls.

Geerdink, R. A.; Nijenhuis, Lourens E.; Loghem, Erna van &
Li Fo Sjoe, Eddy

27.0066   SR   1974   Blood groups and immunoglobulin groups in Trio and Wajana Indians from Surinam. *Am J Hum Genet* 26(1), Jan.: 45-53.   **[13]**
                                                                                                                  [*PS*]

Geerdink, R. A.; Okhura, K.; Li Fo Sjoe, E.; Schillhorn van Veen, J. M. &
Bartstra, H. A.

27.0067   SR   1975   Serum factors and red cell enzymes in Carib and Arowak Indians from Surinam. *Trop Geogr Med* 27(3), Sept.: 269-273.   **[13]**   [*PS*]

Gibbs, W. N.

27.0068   JM   1963   ABO and Rh blood group distribution in a rural Jamaican community. *W I Med J* 12(2), June: 103-108.   [*COL*]

27.0069   GC   1969   Hb A$_2$ and the diagnosis of β-thalassaemia trait. *W I Med J* 18(3), Sept.: 177-180.   **[28]**   [*PS*]

Gibbs, W. N.; Ottey, F. & Dyer, H.

27.0070   JM   1972   Distribution of glucose-6-phosphate dehydrogenase phenotypes in Jamaica. *Am J Hum Genet* 24(1), Jan.: 18-23.   **[11,28]**   [*PS*]

Giglioli, George

28.0506   GU   1972   Changes in the pattern of mortality following the eradication of hyperendemic malaria from a highly susceptible community.

28.0507   GU   1974   The impact of malaria eradication on patterns of natality, mortality, and morbidity on the sugar plantations of the coastlands of Guyana, South America.

Glanville, E. V. & Geerdink, R. A.

27.0071   SR   1969   Dermatoglyphics of the Trio Indians of Surinam. *Proc Kon Ned Akad Wetensch* C, 72(4): 445-450.   **[13]**   [*AMN*]

13.0068   SR   1970   Skinfold thickness, body measurements and age changes in Trio and Wajana Indians of Surinam.

27.0072   SR   1972   Blood pressure of Amerindians from Surinam. *Am J Phys Anthrop* 37(2), Sept.: 251-254.   **[13]**   [*COL*]

Goyheneche, E. & Nicolas, Maurice

5.0340   FA   1956   DES ÎLES ET DES HOMMES [THE ISLANDS AND THE PEOPLE].

Grantham-McGregor, Sally M. & Back, E. H.

28.0557   JM   1971   Gross motor development in Jamaican infants.

Grantham-McGregor, Sally M. & Desai, Patricia

27.0073   JM   1973   Head circumferences of Jamaican infants. *Dev Med Child Neurol* 15(4), Aug.: 441-446.   **[28]**   [*PS*]

Grantham-McGregor, Sally M.; Desai, Patricia & Back, E. H.

27.0074   JM   1972   A longitudinal study of infant growth in Kingston, Jamaica. *Hum Biol* 44(3), Sept.: 549-562.   [*PS*]

Grantham-McGregor, Sally M. & Hawke, W. A.

28.0560   JM   1971   Developmental assessment of Jamaican infants.

Gray, R. H.

28.0561   JM   1971   Clinical features of homozygous SS disease in Jamaican children.

Grinder, Robert E.

27.0075   JM   1964   Negro-white differences in intellectual performance: a receding controversy. *Int Ment Heal Res Newsl* 6(4), Winter: 2, 5-6. **[11,16,31]**   [*RIS*]

Gueri, Miguel

28.0568   JM   1970   The leg ulcer problem in Jamaica.

Gueri, Miguel & Serjeant, G. R.

28.0569   JM   1970   Leg ulcers in sickle-cell anaemia.

Guerra, Francisco

28.0571   GC   1966   The influence of disease on race, logistics and colonization in the Antilles.

Gurney, J. M.; Fox, Helen & Neill, J.

30.0110   JM   1972   A rapid survey to assess the nutrition of Jamaican infants and young children in 1970.

Halberg, F. & Simpson, H.

27.0076   SR   1967   Circadian acrophases of human 17-hydroxycorticosteriod excretion referred to midsleep rather than midnight. *Hum Biol* 39(4), Dec.: 405-413. **[13]**   [*COL*]

Hambly, Wilfrid D.

27.0077   BZ   1937   Skeletal material from San José ruin, British Honduras. Chicago, Field Museum of Natural History, 19p. (Publication no. 380, Anthropological series, v. 25, no. 1.)   [*AGS*]

Haneveld, G. T.

27.0078   NA   1965   Verdichtsel en waarheid over de eerste Antillianen [Fiction and truth about the first Antilleans]. *Schakels* NA42: 13-24.   [*NYP*]

Harper, W. F.

27.0079   JM   1959   Cranial vault sutures in the Jamaica Negro. *W I. Med J* 8(4), Dec.: 267-271. **[11]**   [*COL*]

27.0080   JM   1962   Aboriginal Amerindian skulls of Jamaica. *Inf B Scient Res Coun* 2(4), Mar.: 66-69. **[13]**   [*RIS*]

Harrison, G. Ainsworth

27.0081   BA,GC   1971   The application of spectrophotometry to studies of skin color in Latin American populations. *In* Salzano, Francisco M., ed. The ongoing evolution of Latin American populations. Springfield, Illinois, Charles C. Thomas: 455-469. **[7]**   [*NYP*]

Harvey, R. G.; Godber, Marilyn J.; Kopec, A. C.; Mourant, A. E. & Tills, D.

13.0079   DM   1969   Frequency of genetic traits in the Caribs of Dominica.

Hayes, J. A.

27.0082   JM   1969   Distribution of bronchial gland measurements in a Jamaican population. *Thorax* 24(5), Sept.: 619-625.   **[28]**   [*PS*]

28.0618   JM   1970   Racial, occupational and environmental factors in relation to emphysema in Jamaica.

Hayes, J. A. & Lovell, H. G.

28.0619   JM   1966   Heart weight of Jamaicans. Autopsy study of normal cases and cases of hypertension and chronic lung disease.

Helminiak, Thomas Walter

28.0629   SL   1972   THE SUGAR-BANANAS SHIFT OF ST. LUCIA, WEST INDIES: BILHARZIA AND MALARIA DISEASE CAUSAL LINKAGES.

Henry, M. U.

28.0632   TR   1963   The haemoglobinopathies in Trinidad.

Ho Ping Kong, H. & Alleyne, G. A. O.

27.0083   JM   1969   Acid-base status of adults with sickle-cell anaemia. *Br Med J* 3, Aug. 2: 271-273.   **[28]**   [*PS*]

30.0121   JM   1971   Studies on acid excretion in adults with sickle-cell anaemia.

Jelliffe, E. F. Patrice & Jelliffe, D. B.

27.0084   SV   1968   Anthropometry in action. (I) Dental second year malnutrition (practical age-grouping in young children in areas without birth verification). *J Trop Pediat* 14(2), June: 71-74.   **[28,30]**   [*PS*]

27.0085   GC   1969   The arm circumference as a public health index of protein-calorie malnutrition of early childhood. (IX) Experience in the Caribbean. *J Trop Pediat* 15(4), Dec.: 209-212.   **[28,30]**   [*PS*]

Jensen, A. R.

27.0086   JM   1975   A theoretical note on sex linkage and race differences in spatial visualization ability. *Behav Genet* 5(2), Apr.: 151-164.   **[11]**   [*AMN*]

Johnson, Benjamin Charles

27.0087   BA   1959   A SAMPLING SURVEY STUDY OF ARTERIAL BLOOD PRESSURE LEVELS IN NASSAU, NEW PROVIDENCE, BAHAMAS, 1958 FOR DESCRIPTION OF LEVELS OF BLOOD PRESSURE IN A POPULATION IN RELATIONSHIP TO AGE, SEX, RACE AND OTHER FACTORS. Ph.D. dissertation, University of Michigan: 134p.   **[28]**   [*PhD*]

Johnston, Judith Cowan

27.0088   TR   1974   THE SOCIAL ECOLOGY OF EAST INDIAN INFANT STATURE IN SOUTH TRINIDAD. Ph.D. dissertation, Harvard University.

Jones, T. C. & M, Nancy S. F.

54.0557   GU   1975   Cytogenetics of the squirrel monkey (*Saimiri sciureus*).

Kahn, A.; Boivin, P. & Lagneau, J.

27.0089   FC,FR   1973   Phénotypes de la glucose-6-phosphate déshydrogénase érythro-cytaire dans la race noire. Etude de 301 noirs vivants en France et description de 9 variantes différentes. Fréquence élevée d'une enzyme déficitaire de migration "B" [Phenotypes of erythrocyte glucose-6-phosphate dehydrogenase in black people. Examination of 301 black people living in France and description of 9 different variants. High incidence of deficiency of an enzyme of "B" mobility]. *Humangenetik* 18(3), May 25: 261-270.   **[11,18,28]**

[*ACM*]

Knip, Agatha S.

27.0090   SR   1972   Quantitative considerations on functioning eccrine sweat glands in male and female migrant Hindus from Surinam. *Proc Kon Ned Akad Wetensch* C, 75(1): 44-54. **[12]**   [*AMN*]

27.0091   SR   1974   Quantitative considerations on functioning eccrine sweat glands in male Bushnegroes from Surinam. *Proc Kon Ned Akad Wetensch* C, 77(1): 29-38. **[14]**   [*AMN*]

Lang, A.; Lehmann, H. & King-Lewis, P. A.

28.0765   BC,UK   1974   Hb K Woolwich the cause of a thalassaemia.

Leslie, J.; Langler, D.; Serjeant, G. R.; Serjeant, B. E.; Desai, P. & Gordon, Y. B.

28.0795   JM   1975   Coagulation changes during the steady state in homozygous sickle-cell disease in Jamaica.

Liachowitz, Claire et al.

28.0800   SR   1958   Abnormal hemoglobins in the Negroes of Surinam.

Luyken, R.; Luyken-Koning, F. W. M. & Immikhuizen, M. J. T.

28.0814   SR   1971   Lactose intolerance in Surinam.

MacIver, J. E. & Went, L. N.

28.0823   JM   1958   Further observations on abnormal haemoglobins in Jamaica.

Marshall, W. A.; Ashcroft, M. T., & Bryan, Glenda

27.0092   JM   1970   Skeletal maturation of the hand and wrist in Jamaican children. *Hum Biol* 42(3), Sept.: 419-435.   [*PS*]

Massiah, V. I.

28.0845   TR   1968   Haemophilia *A* and *B* in the Port-of-Spain General Hospital in the period—1962 to 1967.

Mathews, Henry M.; Fisher, George U. & Kagan, Irving G.

28.0849   TB   1970   Persistence of malaria antibody in Tobago, West Indies, following eradication, as measured by the indirect hemagglutination test.

Matson, G. Albin; Sutton, H. Eldon; Swanson, Jane & Robinson, A. R.

27.0093   BZ   1965   Distribution of haptoglobin, transferrin, and hemoglobin types among Indians of Middle America: in British Honduras, Costa Rica, and Panama. *Am J Phys Anthrop* 23(2), June: 123-129. **[12]**   [*COL*]

Mazess, Richard B.

27.0094   BA   1967   Skin color in Bahamian Negroes. *Hum Biol* 39(2), May: 145-154. **[11]**   [*COL*]

Meredith, Howard V.

27.0095   GC   1968   Body size of contemporary groups of pre-school children studied in different parts of the world. *Child Dev* 39(2), June: 335-377. **[30]**   [*COL*]

27.0096   GC   1969   Body size of contemporary youth in different parts of the world. *Soc Res Child Dev* 34(7), Oct.: 120p. **[30]**   [*PS*]

27.0097   GC   1970   Body size of contemporary groups of one-year-old infants studied
                         in different parts of the world. *Child Dev* 41(3), Sept.: 551-600.   **[30]**
                                                                                                          [*COL*]

Miller, Colin G.
27.0098   JM   1960   Observations on liver size in Healthy Jamaican Children Hermitage
                         Survey. *W I Med J* 9(2): 124-130.   [*COL*]

Miller, G. J.; Ashcroft, M. T.; Swan, A. V. & Beadnell, H. M. S. G.
27.0099   GU   1970   Ethnic variation in forced expiratory volume and forced vital
                         capacity of African and Indian adults in Guyana. *Am Rev Resp Dis*
                         102(6), Dec.: 979-981.   **[11,12]**   [*PS*]

Miller, G. J.; Cotes, J. E.; Hall, A. M.; Salvosa, C. B. & Ashworth, A.
28.0880 JM,TR 1972   Lung function and exercise performance of healthy Caribbean men
                         and women of African ethnic origin.

Milner, P. F.
27.0100   JM   1965   The human blood groups—their importance in Jamaica. *Inf B*
                         Scient Res Coun 6(2), Sept.: 53-55.   [*RIS*]
28.0883 JM   1967   High incidence of haemoglobin G Accra in a rural district in
                         Jamaica.

Milner, P. F.; Back, E. H. & Carpenter, R.
27.0101   JM   1970   Beta-thalassaemia Hb E disease. *W I Med J* 19(3), Sept.: 147-
                         157.   **[28]**   [*PS*]

Milner, P. F.; Miller, C.; Grey, R.; Seakins, M.; De Jong, W. W. &
Went, L. N.
27.0102   JM   1970   Hemoglobin O Arab in four Negro families and its interaction with
                         hemoglobin S and hemoglobin C. *New Eng J Med* 283(26), Dec. 24:
                         1417-1425.   **[11,28]**   [*PS*]

Montestruc, Etienne & Berdonneau, Robert
27.0103   MT   1957   Premier cas d'hémoglobinose C, S à La Martinique [First instance
                         of hemoglobinosis C, S in Martinique]. *B Soc Path Exot Fil* 50(1),
                         Jan.-Feb.: 94-95.   [*ACM*]
27.0104   MT   1958   Quelques considérations sur les groupes sanguins A, B, O et sur le
                         facteur *Rhesus* chez le Martiniquais [Some comments on blood
                         groups A, B, O, and on the Rh factor among the people of
                         Martinique]. *B Soc Path Exot Fil* 51(6), Nov.-Dec.: 917-920.   [*ACM*]

Montestruc, Etienne; Berdonneau, Robert; Benoist, Jean & Collet, André
27.0105   MT   1959   Hémoglobines anormales et groupes sanguins A, B, O, chez les
                         Martiniquais [Abnormal hemoglobins and blood groups A, B, O,
                         among the people of Martinique]. *B Soc Path Exot Fil* 52(2),
                         Mar.-Apr.: 156-158.   [*ACM*]

Morris, David; Persaud, Trivedi V. N. & Roopnarinesingh, Syam
27.0106   JM   1971   Length of Jamaican babies at birth. *W I Med J* 20(1), March:
                         35-40.   **[28]**   [*PS*]

Nehaul, B. B. G.

27.0107 GU 1947 Physical measurements of East Indian boys in Leguan, British Guiana. *Br Gui Med Annual* 152-161. **[12]** [*RIS*]

Nijenhuis, L. E. & Gemser-Runia, Jeltje

27.0108 SR 1975 Hereditary and acquired blood factors in the negroid population of Surinam: III. Blood group studies. *Trop Geogr Med* 17(1), March: 69-79. **[11]** [*PS*]

Panhuys, L. C. van

27.0109 FG 1905 Are there pygmies in French Guiana? *In* PROCEEDINGS OF THE INTERNATIONAL CONGRESS OF AMERICANISTS, 13th Session, New York, Oct. 1902. Easton, Pa., Eschenbach Print. Co., p.131-133. **[13]** [*AGS*]

Peetoom, F.; Crommelin, S.; Fontijn, A. & Prins, H. K.

27.0110 SR 1965 Hereditary and acquired blood factors in the negroid population of Surinam: VI. Serum group-specific components and transferrin types. *Trop Geogr Med* 17(3), Sept.: 243-245. **[11]** [*PS*]

Pendergast, David M.; Bartley, Murray H. & Armelagos, George J.

4.0274 BZ 1968 A Maya tooth offering from Yakalche, British Honduras.

Perronnette, H.

27.0111 MT 1968 The community weight-profile of children in rural Martinique. *J Trop Pediat* 14(1), March: 43-46. **[28]** [*PS*]

Pik, C.; Loos, J. A.; Jonxis, J. H. P. & Prins, H. K.

27.0112 SR 1965 Hereditary and acquired blood factors in the negroid population of Surinam. II. The incidence of haemoglobin anomalies and the deficiency of glucose-6-phosphate dehydrogenase. *Trop Geogr Med* 17(1), March: 61-68. **[11]** [*PS*]

Pollak, Margaret & Mitchell, Susan

27.0113 BC,UK 1974 Early development of Negro and white babies. *Archs Dis Child* 49(1), Jan.: 40-45. **[9,18]** [*PS*]

Poonai, A.; Morris, D.; Persaud, T. V. N. & Poonai, P. V.

27.0114 JM 1973 Birth weight in Jamaican twins. *W I Med J* 22(2), June: 77-83. **[28]** [*PS*]

Prabhakar, V.; Persaud, Vasil; Indira, C. & Davis, N. E.

28.1035 JM 1976 Incidence of atherosclerosis in the Circle of Willis.

Ribstein, Michel; Yoyo & Levigneron

28.1067 MT 1965 Complications nerveuses et complications mentales de l'hémoglobinose hétérozygote AS [Nervous and mental complications in heterozygote hemoglobinose AS].

Richards, Charles S.

27.0115 SL 1975 Genetic factors in susceptibility of *Biomphalaria glabrata* for different strains of *Schistosoma mansoni*. *Parasitology* 70(2): Apr.: 231-241. **[28,54]** [*AMN*]

Ricketson, Oliver, Jr.

27.0116   BZ   1931   Excavations at Baking Pot, British Honduras. *In* CARNEGIE INSTI-
                      TUTION OF WASHINGTON, PUBLICATION NO. 403; CONTRIBUTIONS TO
                      AMERICAN ARCHAEOLOGY, Washington, D.C., v. 1, no. 1, p.3-
                      27. **[4]**   [*AGS*]

Rife, David C.

27.0117   AR,CU   1972   Genetic variability among peoples of Aruba and Curaçao. *Am J
                         Phys Anthrop* 36(1), Jan.: 21-30.   [*COL*]

Rivat, L.; Rivat, C. & Ropartz, C.

27.0118   FR,FC   1975   An abnormal Cγ4 gene among the Negro population. *Ann Immunol*
                         126(1), Jan.: 41-44.   [*ACM*]

Robson, J. R. K.; Bazin, M. & Soderstrom, R.

27.0119   DM   1971   Ethnic differences in skin-fold thickness. *Am J Clin Nutr* 24(7),
                      July: 864-868. **[11]**   [*PS*]

Roopnarinesingh, S. S.; Morris, D. & Persaud, Trivedi V. N.

27.0120   JM   1971   Birth weight of Jamaican babies. *J Trop Pediat* 17(1), March:
                      11-14. **[28]**   [*PS*]

Ruiz, L.; Miall, W. E. & Swan, A. V.

28.1112   JM   1973   Quantitative aspects of electrocardiograms of adults in a Jamaican
                      rural population.

Salzano, Francisco M., ed.

7.0182   GC   1971   THE ONGOING EVOLUTION OF LATIN AMERICAN POPULATIONS.

**Salzano, Francisco M.; Woodall, J. P.; Black, F. L.; Weitkamp, L. R. &
Franco, M. Helena**

27.0121   SR   1974   Blood groups, serum proteins and hemoglobins of Brazilian Tiriyo
                      Indians. *Hum Biol* 46(1) Feb.: 81-87. **[13]**   [*COL*]

Sar, A. van der

27.0122   CU   1967   Aplastic sickle cell crisis: a report of four cases. *Trop Geogr Med*
                      19(4), Dec.: 273-285. **[11,28]**   [*PS*]

27.0123   CU   1970   The sudden rise in platelets and reticulocytes in sickle cell crises.
                      Trop Geogr Med 22(1), March: 30-40. **[28]**   [*PS*]

Saul, Frank P. & Hammond, Norman

4.0350   BZ   1974   A classic Maya tooth cache from Lubaantún, Belize.

Serjeant, Beryl E.; Forbes, Miriam; Williams, Leslie L. & Serjeant, G. R.

27.0124   JM   1974   Screening cord bloods for detection of sickle cell disease in Jamaica.
                      Clin Chem 20(6), June: 666-669. **[11,28]**   [*ACM*]

Serjeant, G. R.

28.1160   JM   1970   The clinical features in adults with sickle cell anaemia in Jamaica.
28.1161   JM   1973   Duodenal ulceration in sickle cell anaemia.
28.1162   JM   1974   Leg ulceration in sickle cell anemia.

Serjeant, G. R. & Ashcroft, M. T.

27.0125   JM   1973   Delayed skeletal maturation in sickle cell anemia in Jamaica. *John Hopkins Med J* 132(2), Feb.: 95-102. **[11,28]**   [*ACM*]

Serjeant, G. R.; Ashcroft, M. T. & Serjeant, B. E.

28.1163   JM   1973   The clinical features of haemoglobin SC disease in Jamaica.

Serjeant, G. R.; Ashcroft, M. T.; Serjeant, B. E. & Milner, P. F.

28.1164   JM   1973   The clinical features of sickle-cell/β-thalassaemia in Jamaica.

Serjeant, G. R.; Ennis, J. T. & Middlemiss, Howard

27.0126   JM   1973   Haemoglobin SC disease in Jamaica. *Br J Radiol* 46(551), Nov.: 935-942. **[11,28]**   [*PS*]

27.0127   JM   1973   Sickle cell beta thalassemia in Jamaica. *Br J Radiol* 46(551), Nov.: 951-959. **[11,28]**   [*PS*]

Serjeant, G. R.; Richards, R.; Barbor, P. R. H. & Milner, P. F.

27.0128   JM   1968   Relatively benign sickle-cell anaemia in 60 patients aged over 30 in the West Indies. *Br Med J* 3(5610), July 13: 86-91. **[28]**   [*PS*]

Serjeant, G. R. & Serjeant, B. E.

27.0129   JM   1972   A comparison of erythrocyte characteristics in sickle cell syndromes in Jamaica. *Br J Haematol* 23(2), Aug: 205-213. **[28]**   [*PS*]

Serjeant, G. R.; Serjeant, B. E. & Condon, P. I.

28.1165   JM   1972   The conjunctival sign in sickle cell anemia. A relationship with irreversibly sickled cells.

Sharpe, L. J.

27.0130   BC,UK   1965   Brixton. *In* Deakin, Nicholas, ed. Colour and the British electorate, 1964: six case studies. New York, Frederick A. Praeger: 12-30. **[16,18]**   [*COL*]

Smals, A. G. H. & Lustermans, F. A. Th.

27.0131   SR   1969   Een volwassen vrouw met homozygote β-Thalassemie en hetero-zygote G6PD-deficiëntie [An adult woman with homozygotic beta-thalassaemia and heterozygotic G6PD deficiency]. *Ned Tijdschr Geneesk* 113(7), Feb. 15: 290-298. **[28]**   [*PS*]

Sprauve, M. E. & Dodds, M. L.

30.0210   VI   1965   Dietary survey of adolescents in the Virgin Islands.

Stafford, J. L.; Hill, K. R. & Arneaud, J. D.

27.0132   GC   1955   Rhesus factor distribution in the Caribbean: preliminary communication. *W I Med J* 4(2), June: 119-125.   [*COL*]

Standard, K. L.

27.0133   BB   1964   Weights and heights of children in Barbados, West Indies, 1961. *W I Med J* 13(2), June: 77-83. **[30]**   [*COL*]

Standard, K. L.; Desai, Patricia & Miall, W. E.

27.0134   JM   1969   A longitudinal study of child growth in a rural community in Jamaica. *J Biosoc Sci* 1(2), April: 153-176. **[28,30]**   [*PS*]

Standard, K. L.; Lovell, H. G. & Garrow, J. S.

27.0135   BB,JM   1966   The validity of certain physical signs as indices of generalised malnutrition in young children. *J Trop Pediat* 11(4), March: 100-106. **[30]**   [*PS*]

Standard, K. L.; Lovell, H. G. & Harney, L.

27.0136   BB   1966   Heights and weights of Barbadian schoolchildren. *Br J Prev Social Med* 20(3), July: 135-140. **[28,32]**   [*PS*]

Statius van Eps, L. W.

28.1213   CU   1967   Investigations in Curaçao on renal functions in patients suffering from sickle-cell anaemia and other haemoglobin diseases.

Steggerda, Morris

27.0137   JM   1928   Physical development of Negro-white hybrids in Jamaica, British West Indies. *Am J Phys Anthrop* 12(1), July: 121-138.   [*COL*]

Stewart, T. D.

27.0138   GC   1939   Negro skeletal remains from Indian sites in the West Indies. *Man* 39(52), Apr.: 49-51. **[11]**

Stewart, T. D. & Groome, John R.

27.0139   GR   1968   The African custom of tooth mutilation in America. *Amer J Phys Anthrop* 28, Jan.: 31-42. **[11,23]**   [*ACM*]

St. George, John; St. John, E. H. & Josa, D.

28.1227   TR   1970   Factors influencing birth weight in normal pregnacy.

Stuart, J.; Schwartz, F. C. M.; Little, A. J. & Raine, D. N.

27.0140   BC,UK   1973   Screening for abnormal haemoglobins: a pilot study. *Br Med J* 4(5887), Nov. 3: 284-287. **[11,18,28]**   [*PS*]

Sutter, Jean

7.0202   FG   1967   Interprétation démographique de la fréquence des groupes sanguins chez les Wayana et les Emerillon de la Guyane [Demographic interpretation of blood group frequencies among the Wayana and Emerillon of Guiana].

Swellengrebel, N. H.

17.0101   SR   1940   Over de vraag of een proefneming tot vestiging van politieke uitgewekenen in Suriname hygienisch te verantwoorden is [On the question whether an attempt to settle political refugees in Surinam is advisable from a hygienic viewpoint].

Tacoma, J.

27.0141   AR   1959   Indian skeletal remains from Aruba. *W I G* 39: 95-112. **[13]**   [*RIS*]
27.0142   AR   1964   Kunstmatige schedeldeformatie in Aruba [Artificial skull deformation in Aruba]. *N W I G* 43(3), May: 211-222. **[13]**   [*RIS*]
27.0143   AR   1965   Craniology of Aruban Indians. *In* HOMENAJE A JUAN COMAS EN SU 65 ANIVERSARIO: VOL. 2-ANTROPOLOGÍA FÍSÍCA [HOMMAGE TO JUAN COMAS ON HIS 65TH BIRTHDAY: VOL. 2-PHYSICAL ANTHROPOLOGY]. Mexico, Instituto Indigenista Interamericano: 367-376.   [*AMN*]

Tanis, R. J.; Neel, J. V.; Dovey, H. & Morrow, M.

27.0144   GU   1973   The genetic structure of a tribal population, the Yanomama Indians. IX. Gene frequencies for 18 serum protein and erythrocyte enzyme systems in the Yanomama and five neighboring tribes: nine new variants. *Am J Hum Genet* 25(6), Nov.: 655-676.   **[13]**   *[PS]*

Thorburn, Marigold J.

28.1280   JM   1969   The pathology of sickle cell anaemia in Jamaican adults over 30.

Tjong Tjin Joe, J.; Prins, H. K. & Nijenhuis, L. E.

27.0145   SR   1965   Hereditary and acquired blood factors in the negroid population of Surinam. I. Origin, collection, and transport of the blood samples; characteristic blood groups. *Trop Geogr Med* 17(1), March: 56-60.   **[11]**   *[PS]*

Vernon, Philip E.

27.0146   BC   1965   Environmental handicaps and intellectual development: part I. *Br J Educ Psych* 35(1), Feb.: 9-20.   **[32]**   *[COL]*

27.0147   BC   1965   Environmental handicaps and intellectual development: part II. *Br J Educ Psych* 35(2), June: 117-126.   **[32]**   *[COL]*

Verrill, Alpheus Hyatt

4.0379   GU   1918   Prehistoric mounds and relics of the north west district of British Guiana.

Vinke, B. & Sar, A. van der

28.1350   CU   1966   Peptic ulcer and gastric cancer in the negroid population of Curaçao.

Vollum, Dorothy I.

27.0148   BC,UK   1972   Skin markings in negro children from the West Indies. *Br J Derm* 86(3), March: 260-263.   **[11,18]**   *[PS]*

Vu Tien, Jacqueline; Pison, Gilles; Lévy, Dany; Darcos, Jean-Claude; Constans, Jacques & Bernard, Jean

27.0149   GG   1975   Etude quantitative du système génétique "haptoglobine" [Quantitative study of the genetics of haptoglobin levels]. *Comptes Rendus Acad Sci* [D] 280(20), 26 May: 2417-2419.   *[PS]*

Vu Tien, Jacqueline; Pison, Gilles; Lévy, Dany; Darcos, Jean-Claude; Constans, Jacques & Mauran-Sendrail, Anne

27.0150   GG   1975   Le phénotype H_pO dans quelques populations d'Afrique et d'Amérique centrale [The phenotype H_pO in several African and Central American populations]. *Comptes Rendus Acad Sci* [D] 280(19), 21 May: 2281-2284.   *[PS]*

Wagenaar Hummelinck, P.

27.0151   AR,CU   1959   Indiaanse skeletvondsten op Aruba en Curacao [Indian skeletal discoveries in Aruba and Curacao]. *W I G* 39: 72-94.   **[13]**   *[RIS]*

Waterman, James A.

28.1398   TR   1967   Malaria—and its eradication in Trinidad and Tobago.

Weatherall, D. J. & Clegg, J. B.

28.1413   JM   1975   The α-chain-termination mutants and their relation to the α-thalassaemias.

Wells, A. V.

27.0152   BB   1963   Study of birthweights of babies born in Barbados, West Indies. *W I Med J* 12(3), Sept.: 194-199.   [*COL*]

Went, L. N. & MacIver, J. E.

28.1424   JM   1956   Investigation of abnormal haemoglobins in Jamaica: a preliminary survey.

Whimster, William F.

28.1429   JM   1971   Normal lung weights in Jamaicans.

Whimster, William F. & Macfarlane, Alison J.

27.0153   JM   1974   Normal lung weights in a white population. *Am Rev Resp Dis* 110(4), Oct.: 478-483.   **[28]**   [*PS*]

Young, Valentine H.

28.1483   GC   1966   Plasma 11-hydroxycorticoid levels in coloured West Indians.

Zanen, G. E. van

27.0154   CU   1962   EXPRESSION OF THE HAEMGLOBIN S GENE ON THE ISLAND OF CURACAO. Amsterdam, Drukkerij J. Ruysendaal, 113p. (Ph.D. thesis, University of Groningen, 1962.)   [*RIS*]

Zeegelaar, F. J.; Sanchez, H.; Luyken, R.; Luyken-Koning, F. W. M. & Staveren, W. A. van

30.0244   SR   1967   Studies on physiology of nutrition in Surinam. XI. The skeleton of aged people in Surinam.

Zegers, B. J.; Geerdink, R. A. & Sander, P. C.

27.0155   SR   1973   Serum immunoglobulin levels in Trio and Wajana Indians of Surinam. *Vox Sang* 24(5), May: 457-467.   **[13]**   [*ACM*]

Chapter 28

HEALTH AND PUBLIC HEALTH

Clinical studies of disease; epidemiological studies; sanitation and hygiene; water supply and health; insect control.

See also: [27] Human biology; [29] Folk medicine; [30] Food and nutrition; [31] Psychiatry and mental health; [33] Social and legal issues; [34] Fertility and family planning.

Abonnenc, E.

7.0002	FG	1948	Aspects démographiques de la Guyane Francaise [Demographic aspects of French Guiana]. I. Historique [Historical].
7.0003	FG	1948	Aspects démographiques de la Guyane Francaise [Demographic aspects of French Guiana]. II. Demographic actuelle [Present day demography].
7.0004	FG	1949	Aspects démographiques de la Guyane Francaise [Demographic aspects of French Guiana]. III. Avenir de la population [Future of the population].

Abraham, E. A. V.

29.0001	GU	1912	Materia medica Guian. Britt.

Achard, Ch.

28.0001	FG	1939	Mission en Guyane [Guiana expedition]. *B Acad Natn Med* 3d ser., 122(32), Nov.: 401-411. **[17]** [*ACM*]

Adam, Malcolm

28.0002	JM	1973	Mongolism, thyrotoxicosis and diabetes mellitus. *W I Med J* 22(1), March: 37-40 [*PS*]

Adam, Malcolm; Grell, Gerald C.; Burgess, I. B. & Walter, E.

28.0003	JM	1973	The effects of sulphonylurea drugs on thyroid function in diabetics. *W I Wed J* 22(2), June: 67-72. [*PS*]

Adam, Malcolm & McIver, Cecil

28.0004	JM	1973	Impotence in diabetes mellitus. *W I Med J* 22(4), Dec.: 157-160. [*PS*]

Adam, Malcolm & Moule, N.J.

28.0005	JM	1975	Feminization in Cushing's syndrome due to bilateral adrenocortical hyperplasia. *W I Med J* 24(1), March: 30-33. [*PS*]

Adams, Anthony C. I.

28.0006   JM   1965   Teaching international community medicine. *Archs Environ Heal* 10, Jan.: 95-103   **[32]**   *[PS]*

Adamson, A. M.

54.0005   TR   1941   Observations on biting sandflies (*Ceratopogonidae*) in Trinidad, British West Indies.

Ahern, E. J.; Herbert, R.; McIver, C.; Ahern, V.; Wardle, J. & Seakins, M.

28.0007   JM   1975   Beta-thalassaemia of clinical significance in adult Jamaican negroes. *Br J Haematol* 30(2), June: 197-213.   **[27]**   *[PS]*

Ahern, E. J. & Persaud, Vasil

28.0008   JM   1972   Acute leukaemia and alkali resistant haemoglobin: report of a case and a review of the literature. *W I Med J* 21(4), Dec.: 257-261.   *[PS]*

Ahern, E. J.; Swan, A. V. & Ahern, V.

28.0009   JM   1972   The prevalence of iron deficient erythropoiesis and anaemia in a rural Jamaican community. *Br J Haematol* 22(3), March: 273-280.   **[30]**   *[PS]*

27.0003   JM   1973   The prevalence of the rarer inherited haemoglobin defects in adult Jamaicans.

Aitken, T. H. G.

28.0010   TR   1957   Virus transmission studies with Trinidadian mosquitoes. *W I Med J* 6(4), Dec.: 229-232.   *[COL]*

28.0011   GC   1961   The public health importance of *Culex quinquefasciatus say* in the West Indies. *W I Med J* 10(4), Dec.: 264-268.   *[COL]*

28.0012   TR   1965   A survey of Trinidadian arthropods for natural virus infections (August, 1953 to December, 1958. *Car Med J* 27(1-4): 147-156.   *[ACM]*

28.0013   TR   1965   Virus transmission studies with Trinidadian mosquitoes. *Car Med J* 27(1-4): 137-140.   *[ACM]*

28.0014   TR   1966   Notas sobre el *Culex (Melanoconium) portesi* Senevet & Abonnenc, vector del arbovirus. [Report of *Culex (Melanoconion) portesi* Senevet and Abonnenc, vector of the arbovirus.] *Revta Venez Sanid Asist Social* 31(3), Supplement, Sept: 935-938.   *[PS]*

Aitken, T. H. G. & Anderson, C. R.

28.0015   TR   1965   Virus transmission studies with Trinidadian mosquitoes. Part II. Further observations. *Car Med J* 27(1-4): 141-145.   *[ACM]*

Aitken, T. H. G.; Jonkers, A. H.; Tikasingh, E. S. & Worth, C. B.

28.0016   TR   1968   Hughes virus from Trinidadian ticks and terns. *J Med Entomol* 5(4), Oct.: 501-503.   **[54]**   *[PS]*

Aitken, T. H. G. & Spence, L.

28.0017   TR   1963   Virus transmission studies with Trinidadian mosquitoes pt. III: Cache Valley virus. *W I Med J* 12(2), June: 128-132.   *[COL]*

Aitken, T. H. G.; Spence, L.; Jonkers, A. H. & Anderson, C. R.

28.0018   TR   1968   Wyeomyia-virus isolations in Trinidad, West Indies. *Am J Trop Med Hyg* 17(6), Nov: 886-888.   *[PS]*

Aitken, T. H. G.; Spence, L.; Jonkers, A. H. & Downs, W. G.
28.0019   TR   1969   A 10-year survey of Trinidadian arthropods for natural virus infections (1953-1963). *J Med Entomol* 6(2), May: 207-215.   [*PS*]

Aitken, T. H. G.; Worth, C. B.; Jonkers, A. H.; Tikasingh, E. S. & Downs, W. G.
28.0020   TR   1968   Arbovirus studies in Bush Bush Forest, Trinidad, W.I., September 1959-December 1964. II. Field program and techniques. *Am J Trop Med Hyg* 17(2), March: 237-252.   [*PS*]

Aitken, T. H. G.; Worth, C. B. & Tikasingh, E. S.
28.0021   TR   1968   Arbovirus studies in Bush Bush Forest, Trinidad, W.I., September 1959-December 1964. III. Entomologic studies. *Am J Trop Med Hyg* 17(2), March: 253-268.   [*PS*]

Alcala, V. O.
28.0022   GC   1959   Instructional material for healthy living. *Caribbean* 13(2), Feb.: 34-35, 44. **[1]**   [*COL*]

Alderman, Michael H.; Cadien, S.; Haughton, P. B. H.; Johnston, H. M. & Johnson, K. G.
28.0023   JM   1972   A student rural health project in Jamaica. *W I Med J* 21(1), March: 20-24.   [*PS*]

Alderman, Michael H.; Levy, Barry; Husted, James; Searle, Ryan & Minott, Owen D.
30.0002   JM   1973   A young-child nutrition programme in rural Jamaica.

Alexander, Brenda
18.0005   BC,UK   1974   Help for immigrant families.

Ali, M. E. & Sibbald, J. C.
28.0024   GU   1970   The management of orthopaedic problems from the 1962 epidemic of poliomyelitis in Guyana. *W I Med J* 19(2), June: 94-100.   [*PS*]

Alleyne, G. A. O.
28.0025   JM   1966   The excretion of water and solute by malnourished children. *W I Med J* 15(3), Sept.: 150-154. **[30]**   [*PS*]
30.0005   JM   1966   Plasma and blood volumes in severely malnourished Jamaican children.
30.0006   JM   1967   The effect of severe protein calorie malnutrition on the renal function of Jamaican children.
30.0008   JM   1970   Some features of infantile malnutrition in Jamaica.

Alleyne, G. A. O.; Halliday, D. & Waterlow, J. C.
30.0009   JM   1969   Chemical composition of organs of children who died from malnutrition.

Amblard, P.; Ambroise-Thomas, P.; Desire, C.; Gout, M.; Monrose, M. & Schneider, R.
28.0026   MT   1975   Aspects actuels de la lèpre à la Martinique [Present-day aspects of leprosy in Martinique]. *B Soc Path Exot* 68(2), March-April: 164-171.   [*PS*]

Anderson, C. R. & Downs, W. G.

28.0027   TR   1965   The isolation of yellow fever virus from the livers of naturally infected red howler monkeys. *Car Med J* 27(1-4): 75-77.   [*ACM*]

Anderson, C. R.; Downs, W. G.; Wattley, G. H.; Ahn, N. W. & Reese, A. A.

28.0028   TR   1965   Mayaro virus: a new human disease agent. II. Isolation from blood of patients in Trinidad, B.W.I. *Car Med J* 27(1-4): 111-115.   [*ACM*]

Anderson, C. R.; Spence, L. & Downs, W. G.

28.0029   TR   1965   Report of a case of yellow fever in Trinidad, B.W.I. *Car Med J* 27(1-4): 55-64.   [*ACM*]

Anderson, C. R.; Spence, L.; Downs, W. G. & Aitken, T. H. G.

28.0030   TR   1965   Oropouche virus: a new human disease agent from Trinidad, W.I. *Car Med J* 27(1-4): 126-130.   [*ACM*]

Anderson, Charles R.

28.0031   TR   1957   St. Louis virus in Trinidad. *W I Med J* 6(4), Dec.: 249-253.   [*COL*]

Anderson, M. F.

28.0032   JM   1962   Haemoglobinopathies in pregnacy. *W I Med J* 11(4), Dec.: 265-274.
                                                                   [*COL*]
28.0033   JM   1971   The foetal risks in sickle cell anaemia. *W I Med J* 20(4), Dec.: 288-295.   [*PS*]

Anduze, Roy

28.0034   UV   1955   Health in the Virgin Islands. *Caribbean* 9(2), Sept.: 37-39.   [*COL*]

Angrosino, Michael V.

12.0005   TR   1972   OUTSIDE IS DEATH: ALCOHOLISM, IDEOLOGY AND COMMUNITY ORGANIZATION AMONG THE EAST INDIANS OF TRINIDAD.

12.0006   TR   1974   OUTSIDE IS DEATH: COMMUNITY ORGANIZATION, IDEOLOGY AND ALCOHOLISM AMONG THE EAST INDIANS OF TRINIDAD.

Annamunthodo, H.

28.0035   JM   1958   Observations on carcinoma of the breast in Jamaica. *W I Med J* 7(2), June: 93-108.   ·[*COL*]
28.0036   JM   1958   Surgical treatment of chronic peptic ulcer in Jamaica. *W I Med J* 7(1), Mar.: 53-67.   [*COL*]
28.0037   JM   1959   Carcinoma of penis. *W I Med J* 8(3), Sept.: 149-160.   [*COL*]
28.0038   JM   1959   Observations on cancer of the oesophagus in Jamaica. *W I Med J* 8(2), June: 92-100.   [*COL*]
28.0039   JM   1959   Observations on cancer of the stomach in Jamaica. *W I Med J* 8(1), Mar.: 17-32.   [*COL*]
28.0040   JM   1962   Rectal lymphogranuloma venereum in Jamaica. *W I Med J* 11(2), June: 73-85.   [*COL*]

Antonio, D. R.; Branday, J. M. & Chung, E. E.

28.0041   JM   1974   Chronic subdural haematoma—a clinical survey. *W I Med J* 23(1), March 1-7.   [*PS*]

Antrobus, A. C. K.

30.0015   SV   1971   Child growth and related factors in a rural community in St. Vincent.

30.0016   **BC**   1974   Corrective measures for childhood malnutrition.

Archimède
28.0042   **GD**   1965   L'hygiène scolaire dans le département de la Guadeloupe. Bilan
général de l'année scolaire 1962-1963 [School hygiene in the
department of Guadeloupe. General review of the 1962-1963 school
year]. *J Med Bord Sud-Ouest* 142(6), June: 1001-1007. **[32]**   *[PS]*

Arends, Tulio
27.0005   **GC**   1966   Haemoglobinopathies, thalassaemia and glucose-6-phosphate deficiency in Latin America and the West Indies.
28.0043   **GC**   1971   Hemoglobinopathies and enzyme deficiencies in Latin America
populations. *In* Salzano, F. M., ed. THE ONGOING EVOLUTION OF
LATIN AMERICAN POPULATIONS. Springfield, Illinois, Charles C.
Thomas: 509-559. **[7,15,17]**   *[NYP]*

Armenta, George
28.0044   **GU**   1970   "Puma"—a high protein drink for Guyana. *Cajanus* 3(5), Oct.:
289-292. **[30]**   *[RIS]*

Armstrong, J. A.
28.0045   **CM**   1969   The effectiveness of Flit® MLO against *Aedes taeniorhynchus* larvae
on Grand Cayman, British West Indies. *Mosq News* 29(3), Sept.:
489-490.   *[PS]*
28.0046   **CM**   1971   Insecticide studies at the Mosquito Research and Control Unit,
Grand Cayman, B.W.I. *Mosq News* 31(1), March: 1-11. **[54]** *[PS]*

Ashcroft, M. T.
28.0047   **GU**   1962   The morbidity and mortality of enteric fever in British Guiana. *W I
Med J* 11(1), Mar.: 62-71. **[5,7]**   *[COL]*
28.0048   **GC**   1965   A history and general survey of the helminth and protozoal
infections of the West Indies. *Ann Trop Med Paras* 59(4), Dec.:
478-493.   *[PS]*
2.0011   **BC**   1971   Some aspects of growth and development in different ethnic groups
in the Commonwealth West Indies.

Ashcroft, M. T. & Antrobus, A. C. K.
27.0007   **SV,GC** 1970   Heights and weights of schoolchildren in St. Vincent.

Ashcroft, M. T.; Beadnell, H. M. S. G.; Bell, R. & Miller, G. J.
28.0049   **GU**   1970   Characteristics relevant to cardiovascular disease among adults of
African and Indian origin in Guyana. *B WHO* 42(2): 205-
223. **[11,12]**   *[PS]*

Ashcroft, M. T.; Beadnell, H. M. S. G.; Miller, G. J. & Bell, R.
27.0008   **GU**   1969   Anthropometric measurements of Guyanese adults of African and
East Indian origins.

Ashcroft, M. T.; Beadnell, H. M. S. G.; Miller, G. J. & Urquhart, A. E.
28.0050   **GU**   1969   VDRL tests in representative communities of Guyanese adults. *Br J
Ven Dis* 45(2), June: 140-143.   *[PS]*

Ashcroft, M. T.; Bell, R. & Nicholson, C. C.

27.0009   GU   1968   Anthropometric measurements of Guyanese schoolchildren of African and East Indian racial origins.

Ashcroft, M. T.; Buchanan, I. C. & Lovell, H. G.

27.0011   KNA   1965   Heights and weights of primary schoolchildren in St. Christopher-Nevis-Anguilla, West Indies.

Ashcroft, M. T.; Buchanan, I. C.; Lovell, H. G. & Welsh, B.

27.0012   KNA   1966   Growth of infants and preschool children in St. Christopher-Nevis-Anguilla, West Indies.

Ashcroft, M. T.; Cruickshank, E. K.; Hinchcliffe, R.; Jones, W. I.; Miall, W. E. & Wallace, J.

28.0051   JM   1967   A neurological, ophthalmological and audiological survey of a suburban Jamaican community. *W I Med J* 16(4), Dec.: 233-245.
                                                                                                                    [*PS*]

Ashcroft, M. T.; Ling, J.; Lovell, H. G. & Miall, W. E.

27.0014   JM   1966   Heights and weights of adults in rural and urban areas of Jamaica.

Ashcroft, M. T. & Lovell, H. G.

27.0016   JM   1966   Heights and weights of Jamaican primary schoolchildren.

Ashcroft, M. T.; Lovell, H. G.; George, M. & Williams, A.

27.0018   JM   1965   Heights and weights of infants and children in a rural community of Jamaica.

Ashcroft, M. T. & Miall, W. E.

28.0052   JM   1969   Cardiothoracic ratios in two Jamaican communities. *Am J Epidemiol* 89(2), Feb.: 161-167.   [*PS*]

Ashcroft, M. T.; Miall, W. E. & Milner, P. F.

27.0019   JM   1969   A comparison between the characteristics of Jamaican adults with normal hemoglobin and those with sickle cell trait.

Ashcroft, M. T.; Miall, W. E.; Standard, K. L. & Urquhart, A. E.

28.0053   JM   1967   Serological tests for treponemal disease in adults in two Jamaican communities. *Br J Ven Dis* 43(2), June: 96-104.   [*PS*]

Ashcroft, M. T.; Milner, P. F. & Wood, C. W.

28.0054   JM   1969   Haemoglobin concentration, eosinophilia and intestinal helminths in children in rural Jamaica. *Trans Roy Soc Trop Med Hyg* 63(6): 811-820.   [*PS*]

Ashcroft, M. T.; Nicholson, C. C. & Stuart, C. A.

28.0055   GU   1963   Typhoid antibodies in British Guiana school children. *W I Med J* 12(4), Dec.: 247-252.   [*COL*]

Ashcroft, M. T. & Serjeant, G. R.

28.0056   JM   1972   Body habitus of Jamaican adults with sickle cell anemia. *South Med J* 65(5), May: 579-582.   **[27]**   [*PS*]

Ashcroft, M. T.; Serjeant, G. R. & Desai, P.

28.0057   JM   1972   Heights, weights, and skeletal age of Jamaican adolescents with sickle cell anaemia. *Archs Dis Childh* 47(254), Aug.: 519-524.   **[28]**
[*PS*]

Ashcroft, M. T.; Singh, Balwant; Nicholson, C. C.; Ritchie, J. M.; Sobryan, E. & Williams, F.

28.0058   GU   1967   A seven-year field trial of two typhoid vaccines in Guyana. *Lancet* II for 1967 (7525), Nov. 18: 1056-1059.   [*PS*]

Ashcroft, M. T. & Stuart, K. L.

28.0059   JM   1973   Acute myocardial infarction in the University Hospital, Jamaica, 1968-1970. *W I Med J* 22(2), June: 60-66.   [*PS*]

Ashcroft, M. T.; Urquhart, A. E. & Gentle, G. H. K.

28.0060   JM   1965   Treponemal serological tests in Jamaican school children. *Trans Roy Soc Trop Med Hyg* 59(6), Nov.: 649-656.   **[32]**   [*PS*]

Ashworth, Ann

30.0019   JM   1968   Dietary survey methods: a comparison of the caloric and protein contents of some rural Jamaican diets.

30.0020   JM   1968   An investigation of very low calorie intakes reported in Jamaica.

30.0021   JM   1969   Growth rates in children recovering from protein-calorie malnutrition.

Ashworth, Ann & Harrower, A. D. B.

30.0023   JM   1967   Protein requirements in tropical countries: nitrogen losses in sweat and their relation to nitrogen balance.

Ashworth, Ann; Milner, P. F.; Waterlow, J. C. & Walker, R. B.

30.0025   JM   1973   Absorption of iron from maize (*Zea mays* L.) and soya beans (*Glycine hispida* Max.) in Jamaican infants.

Ashworth, Ann & Picou, D.

30.0026   JM   1976   Nutritional status in Jamaica (1968-74).

Ashworth, Ann & Waterlow, J. C.

30.0027   JM   1974[?]   NUTRITION IN JAMAICA, 1969-70.

Asin, H. R. G. & Thiel, P. H. van

28.0061   SR   1963   On intestinal protozoa in the urban and bushland population in Surinam. *Trop Geogr Med* 15(2), June: 108-120.   [*COL*]

Asprey, G. F. & Thornton, Phyllis

29.0003   JM   1953   Medicinal plants of Jamaica. Part 1.

29.0004   JM   1954   Medicinal plants of Jamaica. Part 2.

29.0005   JM   1955   Medicinal plants of Jamaica. Part 3.

29.0006   JM   1955   Medicinal plants of Jamaica. Part 4.

Asregadoo, E. R.

28.0062   GU   1964   Congenital cataracts associated with rubella. *W I Med J* 13(1), Mar.: 22-24.   [*COL*]

Atkinson, D. W.

28.0063   JM   1966   Ureterocoele with reports of three unusual adult cases. *W I Med J* 15(4), Dec.: 221-225.   [*PS*]

28.0064   JM   1967   Cancer of the bladder in Jamaica. *Br J Urol* 39(6), Dec.: 768-771.
                                                                                      [*PS*]

Attaway, David Henry

28.0065   GC   1968   ISOLATION AND PARTIAL CHARACTERIZATION OF CARIBBEAN PALYTOXIN. Ph.D. dissertation, University of Oklahoma: 52p.
                                                                                     [*PhD*]

Ayre, J. E. & Burrowes, J. T.

28.0066   CM   1968   Preliminary report on detection and elimination programme on cervical cancer in the Cayman Islands. *W I Med J* 17(1), March: 21-25.   [*PS*]

Back, E. H.

28.0067   JM   1971   Childhood tetanus in Jamaica. *W I Med J* 20(2), June: 111-122.
                                                                                      [*PS*]

Back, E. H. & Brooks, S. E. H.

28.0068   JM   1962   The pattern of infantile gastro-enteritis in Jamaica. *W I Med J* 11(3), Sept.: 179-187.   [*COL*]

Back, E. H. & DePass, E. E.

28.0069   JM   1957   Acute rheumatic fever in Jamaican children. *W I Med J* 6(2), June: 98-104.   [*COL*]

Back, E. H. & Hill, K. R.

28.0070   JM   1956   A case of glycogen storage disease in a West Indian infant. *W I Med J* 5(1), Mar.: 59-64.   [*COL*]

Back, E. H. & Ward, E. E.

28.0071   JM   1962   Electrolyte and acid-base disturbances occurring in infantile gastroenteritis in Jamaica. *W I Med J* 11(4), Dec.: 228-234.   [*COL*]

Bailey, C. E. Stanley

28.0072   LW   1944   Tuberculosis in the Leeward Islands colony. *Car Med J* 6(3): 178-182.   [*COL*]

28.0073   AT   1960   Tuberculosis in Antigua. *Car Med J* 22(1-4): 93-95.   [*COL*]

Bailey, D. L.

28.0074   JM   1965   Deformity of the nose and face due to nasal polyposis. *W I Med J* 14(2), June: 118-123.   [*PS*]

Bailey, W. R.

28.0075   JM   1973   The geography of fevers in early Jamaica. *Jam Hist Rev* 10: 23-31. **[5]**   [*RIS*]

Baldwin, Robert E. & Weisbrod, Burton A.

28.0076   SL   1974   Disease and labor productivity. *Econ Dev Cult Chg* 22(3), April: 414-435. **[46]**   [*RIS*]

Bangou

28.0077   GD   1965   Bilan des cardiopathies opérées en métropole depuis 7 ans sur des sujets guadeloupéens, et réflexions sur ce bilan [Summary of cardiopathies in Guadeloupean patients operated on in metropolitan France during the past 7 years and thoughts on this summary]. *J Med Bord Sud-Ouest* 142(6), June: 1011-1014.   **[18]**   [*PS*]

28.0078   GD   1965   Contrôle cardio-vasculaire du sportif guadeloupéen [Cardio-vascular examination of Guadeloupean sportsmen]. *J Med Bord Sud-Ouest* 142(6), June: 996-1000.   [*PS*]

Barnes, S.

28.0079   SR   1968   Malaria eradication in Surinam; prospects of success after five years of health education. *Int J Heal Educ* 11(1): 20-31.   **[32]**   [*PS*]

Barnes, Seymour T. & Jenkins, C. David

28.0080   SR   1972   Changing personal and social behavior: experiences of health workers in a tribal society. *Social Sci Med* 6(1), Feb.: 1-15.   **[14]**
                                                                                     [*COL*]

Barratt, Norma

28.0081   TR   1971   The role of parainfluenza viruses in respiratory disease in Trinidad. *W I Med J* 20(4), Dec.: 279-287.   [*PS*]

Barrière, H.

28.0082   FC   1974   Creeping disease, myase cutanée. Une nouvelle pathologie de vacances [Creeping disease, cutaneous myasis. A new holiday disease]. *Sem Hop Paris* 50(12), March 8: 827-829.   [*PS*]

Barron, Bruce A. & Richart, Ralph M.

28.0083   BB   1971   An epidemiologic study of cervical neoplastic disease. Based on a self-selected sample of 7,000 women in Barbados, West Indies. *Cancer* 27(4), April: 978-986.   [*PS*]

Barrow, Nita

28.0084   GC   1968   The role of the nurse in the changing Caribbean. *Jam Nurse* 8(2), Sept.: 6 passim.   [*AJN*]

Bartholomew, C.

28.0085   TR   1970   Acute scorpion pancreatitis in Trinidad. *Br Med J* 1(5697), March 14: 666-668.   [*PS*]

28.0086   TR   1970   Experience with 100 cases of gastroscopy with the GTFA gastrocamera. *W I Med J* 19(3), Sept.: 167-174.   [*PS*]

28.0087   TR,GC   1972   Treatment of diabetes mellitus in the tropics. *Cajanus* 5(3), July-Sept.: 179-186.   [*RIS*]

Bassett, D. C. J.

28.0088   TR   1970   *Hippelates* flies and streptococcal skin infection in Trinidad. *Trans Roy Soc Med Hyg* 64(1): 138-147.   [*PS*]

Bateson, E. M.

28.0089   JM   1966   Non-rachitic bow leg and knock-knee deformities in young Jamaican children. *Br J Radiol* 39(458), Feb.: 92-101.   [*PS*]

28.0090   JM   1966   Radiological case reports: a case of dissecting aneurism of the aorta. *W I Med J* 15(3), Sept.: 121-124.   [*PS*]

28.0091	JM	1967	Radiological case report: a case of intralobar pulmonary sequestration. *W I Med J* 16(1), March: 33-38. [*PS*]

28.0092   SK   1967   Radiological case report: a case of saccular aneurism of the ascending aorta which presented as a pulsating tumour in the neck. *W I Med J* 16(3), Sept.: 145-149. [*PS*]

28.0093   JM   1967   Radiological case report: two emergency femoral arteriograms. *W I Med J* 16(4), Dec.: 246-249. [*PS*]

28.0094   JM   1968   Radiological case report: a case of tracheo-bronchomegaly presenting as cystic bronchiectasis. *W I Med J* 17(2), June: 120-123. [*PS*]

28.0095   JM   1968   Radiological presentation of bronchogenic carcinoma in Jamaica. *W I Med J* 17(3), Sept.: 143-148. [*PS*]

28.0096   JM   1968   The relationship between Blount's disease and bow legs. *Br J Radiol* 41(482), Feb.: 107-114. [*PS*]

28.0097   JM   1969   Concomitant gastric and duodenal ulcers. *Br J Radiol* 42(500), Aug.: 598-604. [*PS*]

28.0098   JM   1970   Comparative radiology of the proximal gastro-intestinal tract in Jamaica: a review of 3,800 barium examinations. *Trop Geogr Med* 22(3), Sept.: 276-280. **[27]** [*PS*]

28.0099   JM   1974   The anatomical localization of carcinoma of the stomach: a comparison of radiological series in Jamaican and Australian patients. *Med J Aus* 1(17), April 27: 647-650. [*ACM*]

Bateson, E. M. & Woo-Ming, Michael
28.0100   JM   1969   "Coin" lesions of the chest. A review of fifteen cases seen in the University Hospital of the West Indies. *W I Med J* 18(2), June: 82-94. [*PS*]

Bauckham, John F.
28.0101   SL   1960   Tuberculosis in St. Lucia. *Car Med J* 22(1-4): 118-119. [*COL*]

Bayer, Frederick M. & Weinheimer, Alfred J., eds.
54.0071   GC   1974   PROSTAGLANDINS FROM *Plexaura homomalla:* ECOLOGY, UTILIZATION AND CONSERVATION OF A MAJOR MEDICAL MARINE RESOURCE. A SYMPOSIUM.

Bayley, H. H.
28.0102   BB   1939   An investigation of the infectious jaundice of Barbados. *Car Med J* 1(2): 135-142. [*COL*]

Beadnell, H. G.
28.0103   GU   1962   Industrial injuries in the sugar industry of British Guiana. *W I Med J* 11(1), Mar.: 15-21. **[42,46]** [*COL*]

Beal, John F. & Dickson, S.
28.0104   BC,UK   1975   Differences in dental attitudes and behaviour between West Midland mothers of various ethnic origins. *Public Health* 89(2), Jan.: 65-70. **[9,18,20]** [*ACM*]

Beaubrun, Michael H.
28.0105   TR   1962   Huntington's chorea in Trinidad. *Car Med J* 24(1-4): 45-50. **[31]** [*COL*]

| 28.0106 | TR,GR | 1963 | Huntington's chorea in Trinidad. *W I Med J* 12(1), Mar. 39-46. [COL] |

33.0026	TR	1967	Alcohol treatment in Trinidad and Tobago.
33.0027	TR	1967	Treatment of alcoholism in Trinidad and Tobago, 1956-65.
33.0028	JM	1968	Alcoholism and drinking practices in a Jamaican suburb. *Alcoholism* 4.
33.0029	JM	1968	Alcoholism and drinking practices in a Jamaican suburb. *Alcoholism* 5.
33.0031	GC	1971	Problems of drug use and abuse.
8.0009	JM	1975	Cannabis or alcohol: the Jamaican experience.

Beaubrun, Michael H. & Firth, Hedy
| 33.0033 | TR | 1969 | A transcultural analysis of Alcoholics Anonymous Trinidad/London. |

Becquet, R. & Lescaux, F.
| 28.0107 | GD | 1966 | Considérations cliniques, diagnostiques et therapeutiques sur la bilharziose intestinale en Guadeloupe. A propos de trente observations [Clinical, diagnostic and therapeutic considerations on intestinal bilharziasis in Guadeloupe. A propos of 30 cases]. *J Sci Med Lille* 84(1), Jan.: 29-36. [PS] |

Been, T. W.; Clark, B. M.; Grant, L. S. & Broom, J. C.
| 28.0108 | JM | 1960 | Leptospira kremastos infection in Jamaica, West Indies. *W I Med J* 9(1), Mar.: 25-30. [COL] |

Beijering, J.
| 28.0109 | CU | 1950 | Het vraagstuk van het behoud van het water op Curacao [The problem of water conservation on Curacao]. *W I G* 31: 65-79. [56] [COL] |

Belle, Edward A.; Grant, Louis S. & Griffiths, Bertie B.
| 28.0110 | JM | 1966 | The isolation of Cache Valley virus from mosquitoes in Jamaica. *W I Med J* 15(4), Dec.: 217-220. [PS] |

Belle, Edward A.; Grant, Louis S.; Thomas, Kendrick J. & Minott, Owen S.
| 28.0111 | JM | 1964 | Laboratory investigation of the 1963 influenza epidemic in Jamaica, West Indies. *W I Med J* 13(1), Mar.: 63-69. [COL] |

Belle, Edward A.; Khan, R. & Grant, L. S.
| 28.0112 | JM | 1967 | A clinical trial to study the effectiveness of CI-158 in the treatment of ascaris and/or oxyuris infections. *W I Med J* 16(4), Dec.: 222-224. [PS] |

Benbow, Colin
| 28.0113 | BE | 1971 | A sidelight on the Spanish 'flu. *Bermuda Hist Q* 28(3), Autumn: 81-86. [5] [COL] |

Benjamins, H. D.
29.0010	SR	1929-30	"Sneki-koti", inenting tegen de beet van vergiftige slangen ["Snakebite cure", inoculation against the biting of poisonous snakes].
29.0011	SR	1929-30	Treef en lepra in Suriname [Treyf and leprosy in Surinam].
29.0012	SR	1931-32	"Sneki-koti", inenting tegen de beet van vergiftige slangen ["Snakebite cure", inoculation against the biting of poisonous snakes].

Bennett, B. A.

28.0114   BC   1966   Journey to the West Indies. *Nurs Mirror* 121(3166), March 11: i-v.
                                                                                                    [*PS*]

28.0115   JM   1966   Journey to the West Indies. *Nurs Mirror* 121(3167), March 18: x-xii.
                                                                                                    [*PS*]

28.0116   TR,BB,AT   1966   Journey to the West Indies. *Nurs Mirror* 121(3168), March 25: i-iv.
                                                                                                    [*PS*]

28.0117   GR,GU   1966   Journey to the West Indies. *Nurs Mirror* 122(3169), April 1: iv-vi.
                                                                                                    [*PS*]

18.0025   BC   1966   Journey to the West Indies.

Bennett, C. V.

31.0023   BB   1965[?]   Nursing and mental health in the family.

Bennett, M. A.; Heslop, R. W. & Meynell, M. J.

28.0118   JM   1967   Massive haematuria associated with sickle-cell trait. *Br Med J* 1,
                      March 18: 677-679.   **[18,27]**   [*PS*]

Beresford, C. H.; Milner, P. F.; Gurney, M. & Fox, H.

28.0119   JM   1972   Haemoglobin, iron, folate and vitamin B12 levels in pregnant and
                      lactating women in Jamaica. *W I Med J* 21(2), June: 70-76.   **[30]**
                                                                                                    [*PS*]

Beresford, C. H.; Neale, R. J. & Brooks, O. G.

30.0032   JM   1971   Iron absorption and pyrexis.

Bergmans, Wilko A. G. M.

28.0120   CU   1965   Ervaringen van een huisarts op Curaçao [Experiences of a general
                      practitioner on Curaçao]. *Schakels* NA42: 1-5.   [*NYP*]

Bertram, D. S.

54.0097   BZ   1971   Mosquitoes of British Honduras, with some comments on malaria,
                       and on arbovirus antibodies in man and equines.

Beuze, Renée

29.0013   FA   1973   LA SANTÉ PAR LES PLANTES DES ANTILLES FRANÇAISES [HEALTH
                       THROUGH PLANTS OF THE FRENCH ANTILLES].

Bevier, George

28.0121   GC   1943   Some international aspects of yellow fever control. *Br Gui Med
                      Annual 1943* 26: 13-31.   [*ACM*]

Bhagwansingh, Andrew

28.0122   TR   1974   Maternal and child health and family planning programme
                      —Trinidad and Tobago. *In* INTERNATIONAL CONFEDERATION OF
                      MIDWIVES. Report of the Caribbean Working Party, Bridgetown,
                      Barbados, 16-24 May, 1974. [Bridgetown, Barbados]: 79-83.   **[34]**
                                                                                                    [*RIS*]

Bhattacharya, B. P.

28.0123   GU   1962   Clinical aspects of the problem of multiparity in British Guiana.
                      Car Med J 24(1-4): 72-75.   [*COL*]

Bideau, J. & Courmes, E.

27.0030 GD 1965   Enquête sur la fréquence des hémoglobines anormales observées chez les Guadeloupéens [Investigation of the frequency of abnormal hemoglobins observed in natives of Guadeloupe].

Bisno, A. L.; Barratt, Norma; Swanston, William H. & Spence, Leslie P.

28.0124 TR 1970   An outbreak of acute respiratory disease in Trinidad associated with para-influenza viruses. *Am J Epidemiol* 91(1), Jan.: 68-77.   [*PS*]

Bisno, A. L. & Grant, L. S.

28.0125 JM 1968   Human salmonellosis in Jamaica 1962-1966. *W I Med J* 17(4), Dec.: 215-228.   [*PS*]

Bisno, A. L.; Spence, Leslie P.; Stewart, John A. & Casey, Helen L.

28.0126 TR 1969   Rubella in Trinidad: sero-epidemiologic studies of an institutional outbreak. *Am J Epidemiol* 89(1), Jan.: 74-81.   [*PS*]

Blaine, George

28.0127 JM 1957   Tropical phagaedenic ulcer in Jamaica: evaluation of new ambulatory methods of treatment. *W I Med J* 6(4), Dec.: 285-296.   [*COL*]

Blanchy, S. & Bourgeois, M.

31.0026 FG 1975   La psychiatrie en Guiane Française. Aspects formales, institutionnels et statistiques [Psychiatry in French Guiana. Formal, institutional and statistical aspects].

Bleiker, M. A. & Erpecum, C. P. van

28.0128 SR 1965   Tuberculin sensitivity in Surinam. An investigation with sensitins prepared from atypical mycobacteria. *Roy Neth Tub Assoc* 9: 45-63.
                                                                                              [*PS*]

Blin, G.

28.0129 FG 1914   L'uncinariose chez les chercheurs d'or et les forcats du Maroni [Uncinariasis among the gold prospectors and convicts of Maroni]. *Ann Hyg Med Colon* 17(1), Jan.-Mar.: 149-176.   [37]   [*ACM*]

Blumberg, B.; McGiff, J. & Guicherit, I.

28.0130 SR 1951   Filariasis in Moengo (Surinam) in 1950. *Docum Ned Indo Morbis Trop* 3(4), Dec.: 368-372.   [*RIS*]

28.0131 SR 1952   Malaria survey among the Bush Negroes of Marowyne District, Surinam, S.A. in 1950. *Docum Med Geogr Trop* 4(1), Mar.: 2-4.   [14]ʼ   [*COL*]

28.0132 SR 1953   A survey of intestinal parasites in the school children of Moengo, Surinam, 1950. *Docum Med Geogr Trop* 5(2), June: 137-140.   [9]
                                                                                              [*RIS*]

Bodkin, G. E.

28.0133 GU 1921   Some recent entomological surveys bearing on malarial incidence in British Guiana. *J Bd Agric Br Gui* 14(4), Oct.: 226-229.   [54]
                                                                                              [*AMN*]

Boltanski, Etienne

28.0134 FA 1970   Rôle de l'hygiène scolaire dans l'éradication de la bilharziose intestinale aux Antilles françaises [The role of school hygiene in the eradication of intestinal bilharzia (schistosomiasis) in the French Antilles]. *B Acad Natn Med* 154(30-31): 786-789.   [*PS*]

Bolten, D. G. J.

28.0135   SR   1925-26 Muggenbestrijding [The fight against gnats]. *W I G* 7: 567-570.   **[33]**   [*COL*]

28.0136   SR   1926-27 Eene waterleiding voor Paramaribo [Waterworks for Paramaribo]. *W I G* 8: 119-124.   **[48]**   [*COL*]

Bond, James O.

28.0137   GC   1969   St. Louis encephalitis and dengue fever in the Caribbean area: evidence of possible cross-protection. *B WHO* 40(1): 160-163.   [*PS*]

Bonne, C.

28.0138   SR   1919   De maatschappelijke beteekenis der Surinaamsche ziekten [The social implications of the Surinam diseases]. *W I G* 1(1): 291-310.   [*COL*]

28.0139   SR   1923-24 Hygienische ervaring te Moengo [Hygienic experience in Moengo]. *W I G* 5: 394-404.   **[3,15]**   [*COL*]

28.0140   SR   1923-24 Organizatie van den geneeskundigen dienst in Suriname [Organization of the medical services in Surinam]. *W I G* 5: 289-294.   **[33]**   [*COL*]

28.0141   SR   1925-26 De opleiding en de positie van den districtsgeneesheer in Suriname [The training and the position of the district medical officer in Surinam]. *W I G* 7: 432-439.   **[33]**   [*COL*]

Bools, Mary M.

28.0142   BB   1960   Sensitivity tests on *Tubercle bacilli* in Barbados. *Car Med J* 22(1-4): 96-99.   [*COL*]

Borghans-Delvaux, J. M.; Borghans, J. G. A. & Vinke, B.

28.0143   NA   1959   Q-Fever in the Netherlands Antilles. *Trop Geogr Med* 11(3), Sept.: 253-258.   [*COL*]

Boucaud, J. E. A.

28.0144   TR   1942   Treatment of war casualties in Trinidad. *Car Med J* 4(2): 49-57.   [*COL*]

28.0145   BC   1962   The practice of medicine in the British West Indies 1814-1953. *Car Med J* 24(1-4): 40-44.   **[5]**   [*COL*]

Bower, B. D.

28.0146   JM   1958   Tay-Sach's disease in a West Indian of African origin. *W I Med J* 7(1), Mar.: 68-70.   **[11]**   [*COL*]

Boyce, Rubert W.

28.0147   BC   1910   HEALTH PROGRESS AND ADMINISTRATION IN THE WEST INDIES. New York, Dutton, 328p.   **[25]**   [*AGS*]

Boyd, Mark F. & Aris, F. W.

28.0148   JM   1929   A malarial survey of the island of Jamaica, B.W.I. *Am J Trop Med* 9(5), Sept.: 309-399.   **[56]**   [*COL*]

Boyd, P. I.

28.0149   BC   1972   Priorities among the health problems in the Commonwealth Caribbean. *W I Med J* 21(3), Sept.: 137-146.   [*PS*]

28.0150   BC   1975   The health programme of the Caricom Secretariat. *Cajanus* 8(6): 370-379.   **[33,38]**   [*RIS*]

Braaksma, H. E.
28.0151 SR 1957 Myiasis caused by dermatobia cyaniventris in Surinam. *Docum Med Geogr Trop* 9(1), Mar.: 97-99.

Bracken, Michael B.
28.0152 GC 1970 Health education—old wine in new medicine bottles? *W I Med J* 19(3), Sept.: 188-191. **[32]**   [*PS*]

Braconnier, F.; Cohen-Solal, M.; Schlegel, N.; Blouquit, Y.; Thillet, J.; De Linval, J. C. & Rosa, J.
28.0153 GD,MT 1975 Hemoglobine J. Broussaic α_2 90 Lys →Asn β_2A (FG2) découvert dans une famille martiniquaise. Comparaison des différentes techniques analytiques utilisées [Hemoglobin J. Broussais alpha-2 90 Lys leads to Asn beta-2A (FG2) discovered in a Martinique family. Comparison of several analytical techniques]. *Nou Rev Fr Hemat* 15(3), May-June: 333-342. **[27]**   [*PS*]

Brahman, A. P.
28.0154 GU 1961 A report of three fatal cases of human paralytic rabies occurring in one family from British Guiana (1960). *W I Med J* 10(3), Sept.: 149-155.   [*COL*]

Brand, C. A.
28.0155 SL 1958 An outbreak of typhoid fever in St. Lucia (summer, 1957). *W I Med J* 7(2), June: 142-148.   [*COL*]

Branday, W. J.
30.0034 JM 1968 Some early efforts to improve nutrition in Jamaica.

Branday, William Joseph
28.0156 JM 1944 Tuberculosis in Jamaica. *Car Med J* 6(3): 153-169.   [*COL*]
28.0157 TR 1951 Tuberculosis in Trinidad. *Car Med J* 13(3-4): 119-127. [*COL*]
28.0158 TR 1960 Tuberculosis in Trinidad. *Car Med J* 22(1-4): 41-48.   [*COL*]
28.0159 TR 1961 Notes on X-ray campaign in Port-of-Spain. *Car Med J* 23(1-4): 71-73.   [*COL*]

Branday, William Joseph; Dasent, L. E.; Pierre, Henry & Richardson, R. K.
28.0160 TR 1958 Results of 200 resections for pulmonary tuberculosis. *W I Med J* 7(2), June: 149-156.   [*COL*]

Bras, G.
28.0161 JM 1974 Some investigations into liver disease in the West Indies. *W I Med J* 23(3), Sept.: 160-164.   [*PS*]

Bras, G. et al.
28.0162 JM 1959 Medical Research Society of the University College of the West Indies: proceedings of the second meeting held at the University College of the West Indies on 6th June, 1959. *W I Med J* 8(3), Sept.: 218-220.   [*COL*]

Bras, G.; Brooks, S. E. H. & DePass, E. E.
28.0163 JM 1955 Data about malignant neoplasms and the incidence of cirrhosis of the liver in Jamaica. *W I Med J* 4(3), Sept.: 173-181.   [*COL*]

Bras, G. & Clearkin, K. P.

28.0164   JM   1954   Histopathology of the pancreas in Jamaican infants and children. *Docum Med Geogr Trop* 6(4), Dec.: 327-330.   [COL]

Bras, G.; Cole, H.; Ashmeade-Dyer, A. & Watler, D. C.

28.0165   JM   1969   Report on 141 childhood malignancies observed in Jamaica. *J Natn Cancer Inst* 43(2), Aug.: 417-421.   [PS]

Bras, G.; Gordon, C. C.; Emmons, C. W.; Prendegast, K. M. & Sugar, M.

28.0166   JM,CM   1965   A case of phycomycosis observed in Jamaica: infection with *Entomophthora coronata. Am J Trop Med Hyg* 14(1), Jan.: 141-145.   [PS]

Bras, G.; Jelliffe, D. B. & Stuart, K. L.

28.0167   JM   1954   Histological observations on hepatic disease in Jamaican infants and children. *Docum Med Geogr Trop* 6(1), Mar.: 43-60.   [COL]

Bras, G.; Murray, S. M. & McDonnough, L. T.

28.0168   JM   1965   Sporadic occurrence in Jamaica of neoplasms resembling Burkitt's tumour. *Lancet,* II for 1965 (7413), Sept. 25: 619-620.   [PS]

Bras, G.; Stewart, D. B. & Antrobus, A. C. K.

28.0169   JM   1956   Observations on carcinoma of the cervix in Jamaica. Pt. I: Incidence and morbid anatomical data. *W I Med J* 5(1), Mar.: 1-9.   [COL]

Bras, G.; Waterlow, J. C. & DePass, E.

30.0035   JM   1957   Further observations on the liver, pancreas and kidney in malnourished infants and children.

Bras, G. & Watler, D. C.

28.0170   JM   1955   Further observations on the morphology of veno-occlusive disease of the liver in Jamaica. *W I Med J* 4(4), Dec.: 201-211.   [COL]

28.0171   JM   1967   The five most frequent cancers in Jamaica. *W I Med J* 16(4), Dec.: 200-209.   [PS]

Bras, G.; Watler, D. C. & Ashmeade-Dyer, A.

28.0172   JM   1965   The incidence of malignant neoplasms in Jamaica. *Br J Cancer* 19(4), Dec.: 681-694.   [PS]

Bras, G.; Watler, D. C. & Brooks, S. E. H.

28.0173   JM   1965   La incidencia del cáncer de cuello uterino en Jamaica con comentarios de la epidemiología y patología [The incidence of cervix uteri cancer in Jamaica with comments on epidemiology and pathology]. *Prensa Med Argent* 52(11), April 9: 610-613.   [PS]

Bras, G.; Whimster, W. F.; Patrick, A. L. & Woo-Ming, M.

28.0174   JM   1972   Aspects of lung cancer in Jamaica. *Cancer* 29(6), June: 1590-1596.   [PS]

Bray, J. P.; Burt, E. G.; Potter, E. V.; Poon-King, T. & Earle, D. P.

28.0175   TR   1972   Epidemic diphtheria and skin infections in Trinidad. *J Infect Dis* 126(1), July: 34-40.   [PS]

Bremner, J. M.; Lawrence, J. S. & Miall, W. E.
28.0176   JM   1968   Degenerative joint disease in a Jamaican rural population. *Ann Rheum Dis* 27(4), July: 326-332.   [*ACM*]

Bremont, E.
28.0177   FG   1918   La syphilis à la Guyane Francaise [Syphilis in French Guiana]. *B Soc Path Exot* 11(9), Nov.: 784-788.   [*ACM*]

Bressler, R.; Corredor, C. & Brendel, K.
28.0178   JM   1969   Hypoglycin and hypoglycin-like compounds. *Pharmacol Rev* 21(2), June: 105-130.   **[30]**   [*PS*]

Brimhall, B.; Vedvick, T. S.; Jones, R. T.; Ahern, E.; Palomino, E. & Ahern, V.
27.0033   JM   1974   Haemoglobin F Port Royal (alpha 2G gamma 2 125 Glu leads to Ala).

Brinkman, G. L.; Sharadambal, B. & Madhave, V.
30.0036   TR   1970   A feeding trial of fish protein concentrate with preschool children.

Brody, Robert W.
28.0179   LW,VI   1972   Food poisoning in the eastern Caribbean. *In* PROCEEDINGS OF THE GULF AND CARIBBEAN FISHERIES INSTITUTE, 24TH ANNUAL SESSION, NOVEMBER, 1971. Coral Gables, Florida, University of Miami, Rosenstiel School of Marine and Atmospheric Sciences: 100-116.   **[30,52]**   [*AMN*]

Brooke, O. G.
30.0037   JM   1972   Hypothermia in malnourished Jamaican children.
28.0180   JM   1972   Thermoregulatory instability in kernicterus. *W I Med J* 21(4), Dec.: 253-256.   [*PS*]

Brooks, G. D.; Schoof, H. F. & Smith, E. A.
28.0181   UV   1965   Effectiveness control of various insecticides against *Aedes aegypti* infestations in water storage drums in the U.S. Virgin Islands. *Mosq News* 25(4), Dec.: 423-427.   [*PS*]

Brooks, S. E. H. & Audretsch, Johanna J.
28.0182   JM   1970   Studies on hypoglycin toxicity in rats. *Am J Path* 59: 161-180.   **[54]**
                                                                              [*PS*]

Brooks, S. E. H.; Miller, C. G.; McKenzie, K.; Audretsch, J. J. & Bras, G.
28.0183   JM   1970   Acute veno-occlusive disease of the liver. Fine structure in Jamaican children. *Archs Path* 89(6), June: 507-520.   [*PS*]

Brooks, S. E. H.; Pegg, P. J. & Ward, E. E.
28.0184   JM   1968   The syndrome of inappropriate secretion of antidiuretic hormone, associated with a cerebral aneurysm. *W I Med J* 17(4), Dec.: 193-203.   [*PS*]

Brooks, S. E. H. & Ramphal, P. J.
28.0185   JM   1965   The Guillain-Barré syndrome in Jamaica. *W I Med J* 14(2), June: 89-95.   [*PS*]

Brooks, V. E. & Butler, A.

28.0186   JM   1966   Acute intestinal obstruction in Jamaica. *Surg Gynec Obstet* 22, Feb.:
                         261-263.   [*PS*]

Brothwell, D. R.

27.0034   GU   1967   The Amerindians of Guyana: a biological review.

Brown, Harold W.

28.0187   GC   1965   Government and medicine in the Caribbean. *In* Wilgus, A. Curtis,
                         ed. THE CARIBBEAN: ITS HEALTH PROBLEMS. Gainesville, University
                         of Florida Press: 191-199. (Caribbean Conference Series 1, Vol.
                         15) **[32]**   [*RIS*]

Brown, I. D. & Shaw, D. G.

28.0188   BC,UK 1973   Multiple osteochondroses of the feet in a West Indian family. *J
                         Bone Joint Surg* 55-B(4), Nov.: 864-870.   **[18]**   [*PS*]

Brown, John

32.0089   SL   1962   Education and development of St. Lucia.

Brown, P.

28.0189   JM   1968   Accidental poisoning in children in Jamaica and Belfast—a com-
                         parative study. *Ulster Med J* 37, Summer: 126-133.   [*PS*]

Browne, J. A.

28.0190   GU   1933   The common causes of blindness in British Guiana. *Br Gui Med
                         Annual 1932* 25: 25-34.   [*ACM*]

28.0191   GU   1939   Three every-day eye diseases in British Guiana. *Car Med J* 1(3):
                         218-222.   [*COL*]

Bruijning, C. F. A.

28.0192   SR   1952   Some observations on the distribution of *A. Darlingi* root in the
                         Savannah region of Surinam. By C. F. A. Bruyning. *Docum Med
                         Geogr Trop* 4(2), June: 171-174.   **[54]**   [*COL*]

28.0193   SR,FG 1957   Man-biting sandflies *(Phlebotomus)* in the endemic Leishmaniasis
                         area   of   Surinam.   *Docum   Med   Geogr   Trop* 9(3), Sept.:
                         229-236. **[14,54]**   [*COL*]

28.0194   SR   1957   Notes on the common species of Culicoides (*Diptera:* Cerato-
                         pogonidae) from Surinam in relation to Ozzardi-Filariasis. *Docum
                         Med Geogr Trop* 9(2), June: 169-172.   [*COL*]

Bruinsma, John H.

28.0195   GC   1970   A study of the movement and location of U.W.I. medical graduates,
                         classes 1954-1965. *W I Med J* 19(2), June: 91-93.   **[32]**   [*PS*]

Brumpt, Lucien-C. & Brunet, F.

28.0196   FG   1968   La risque d'implantation de la bilharziose intestinale à la Guyane
                         Française [The risk of introducing intestinal bilharzia (schisto-
                         somiasis) to French Guiana]. *B Acad Natn Med* 152(9-10): 134-137.
                                                                                        [*PS*]

Buchler, Ira R.

29.0015   CM   1964   Caymanian folk medicine: a problem in applied anthropology.

Bullamore, Henry W.

28.0197   JM   1973   The inequality of access to public services: the case of Port Antonio, Jamaica. *In* Roseman, Curtis C., et al. SOCIAL PROBLEMS IN A SMALL JAMAICAN TOWN. Urbana-Champaign, University of Illinois: 17-40. (Department of Geography Paper No. 6) **[33]** *[AGS]*

Buma, S.

28.0198   NA   1975   Het schaal-probleem in de organisatie van de volksgezondheid [The problem of scale in the organization of public health]. *Kristòf* 2(2), April: 53-62.   *[RIS]*

28.0199   NA   1975   Het schaal-probleem in de organisatie van de volksgezondheid II [The problem of scale in the organization of public health II]. *Kristòf* 2(3), June: 115-121.   **[32]**   *[RIS]*

Burke, L. M.

28.0200   JM   1962   The acute phase of poliomyelitis. *W I Med J* 11(2), June: 123-128.   *[COL]*

Burrowes, J. T.

28.0201   JM   1951   Hysterectomy in Jamaica. *W I Med J* 1(1), Sept.: 26-32.   *[COL]*

28.0202   JM   1966   The intra-uterine contraceptive device in Jamaica (a preliminary review). *W I Med J* 15(1), March: 1-10.   **[34]**   *[PS]*

Burton, C. A.

28.0203   BC   1967   Structural organization and administration services of health in Antigua, St. Lucia, and Trinidad and Tobago. *In* SECOND SEMINAR ON ORGANIZATION AND ADMINISTRATION OF HEALTH SERVICES —CARIBBEAN. Port-of-Spain, Trinidad, 14-19 Nov.: 174-177.   *[RIS]*

Burton, George J.

28.0204   GU   1967   Observations on the habits and control of *Culex pipiens fatigans* in Guyana. *B WHO* 37(2): 317-322.   *[PS]*

Butcher, Leonard V.

28.0205   TR   1958   The present status of paralytic rabies (bat-transmitted in Trinidad). *W I Med J* 7(1), Mar.: 17-20.   *[COL]*

Butler, A. K.

28.0206   JM   1967   Malignant melanoma in Jamaica. *Postgrad Med J* 43(501), July: 449-453.   *[PS]*

Butler, C. S. & Hakansson, E. G.

28.0207   UV   1917   Some first impressions of the Virgin Islands, medical, surgical and epidemiological. *U S Navl Med B* 11(4), Oct.: 465-475.   **[29]**

   [ACM]

Butler, K. A.

28.0208   BZ   1966   Retropubic prostatectomy in patients with long standing suprapubic cystostomy. *W I Med J* 15(1), March: 40-44.   *[PS]*

28.0209   JM   1969   Non-parasitic cyst of liver treated by hemihepatectomy. *W I Med J* 18(4), Dec.: 235-237   *[PS]*

Butt, Audrey J.
29.0018   **GU**   1956   Ritual blowing: taling—a causation and cure of illness among the
Akawaio.

Byam, Neville
28.0210   **TR**   1969   Obesity and diabetes mellitus in Trinidad and Tobago. *Cajanus*
2(6), Dec.: 449-464.   [*RIS*]

Byer, M. A.
28.0211   **TR**   1952   Hookworm disease in county Caroni. *Car Med J* 14(3-4): 87-89.
[*COL*]
28.0212   **BB**   1957   Public health problems encountered during the first two and a half
years at the Health Centre at Speighstown, Barbados. *Car Med J*
19(1-2): 40-52.   [*COL*]

Cabannes, Raymond J. R.
13.0033   **FG**   1971   Genetic polymorphisms in Indian populations of French Guiana
and Bolivia.

Cabannes, Raymond J. R.; Beurrier, A. & Larrouy, G.
27.0039   **FG**   1965   La thalassémie chez les Indiens de Guyane Française [Thalassemia
in the Indians of French Guiana].

Cable, R. M. & Michaelis, Mary B.
28.0213   **JM,CU**   1967   *Plicatobothrium cypseluri* n. gen., n. sp. (Cestoda: Pseudophyllidea)
from the Caribbean Flying Fish, *Cypselurus bahiensis* (Ranzani,
1842). *Proc Helm Soc Wash* 34(1), Jan.: 15-18.   [*PS*]

Caires, P. F. de
28.0214   **GU**   1947   Yellow fever service in British Guiana. *Br Gui Med Annual* 188-200.
[*RIS*]
28.0215   **GC**   1951   The international yellow fever problem in the Caribbean islands.
W I Med J 1(1), Sept.: 3-14.   [*COL*]

Campbell, Betty
30.0042   **TR**   1948   Malnutrition and allied problems in Trinidad and Tobago.

Campbell, C. K.
28.0216   **JM,UK**   1974   Studies on *Hendersonula toruloidea* isolated from human skin and
nail. *Sabouraudia* 12(2), July: 150-156.   **[54]**   [*ACM*]

Campbell, Marie; Summerell, J. M.; Bras, G.; Hayes, J. A. & Stuart, K. L.
28.0217   **JM**   1971   Pathology of idiopathic cardiomegaly in Jamaica. *Br Heart J* 33(1),
Jan.: 193-202.   [*PS*]

Carey, Ellen
28.0218   **GU**   1961   Health for British Guiana's children. *Corona* 13(7), July: 257-260.
[*AGS*]

Carley, Mary Manning
28.0219   **JM**   1943   MEDICAL SERVICES IN JAMAICA. Kingston, Institute of Jamaica with
the assistance of Jamaica Welfare, 19p. (Social survey series, no.
2.)   **[30]**   [*COL*]

Carmen, Mrs.
28.0220   **JM**   1974   Family life education—its relevance for health workers. *In* International Confederation of Midwives. REPORT OF THE CARIBBEAN WORKING PARTY, BRIDGETOWN, BARBADOS, 16-24 MAY, 1974. (Bridgetown, Barbados): 123-129.   **[32]**   [*RIS*]

Carnegie, A. L.
28.0221   **JM**   1963   Poisoning by barracuda fish. *W I Med J* 12(4), Dec.: 217-224.   **[52,54]**   [*COL*]

Carpenter, Reginald & Annamunthodo, Harry
28.0222   **JM**   1962   Ano rectal carcinoma in Jamaica. *W I Med J* 11(3), Sept.: 188-198.   [*COL*]

Carpenter, Reginald & Brooks, Stanley E. H.
28.0223   **JM**   1970   Fibrous tissue tumours of the neck in children. *W I Med J* 19(3), Sept.: 141-146.   [*PS*]

Carrington, Charles, ed.
3.0086   **GU,MT**   1972   DOCUMENTS ON MEDICAL ANTHROPOLOGY (UNTRODDEN FIELDS OF ANTHROPOLOGY) BY A FRENCH ARMY-SURGEON.)

Carroll, F. D.
18.0054   **JM,US**   1971   Jamaican optic neuropathy in immigrants to the United States.

Carteron, B. & Courmes, E.
28.0224   **GD**   1970   Les *Moraxella* dans la pathologie infectueuse Guadeloupéenne [*Moraxella* in infectious pathology in Guadeloupe]. *Med Trop* 30(3): 341-346.   [*PS*]

Casals, Jorai & Whitman, Loring
28.0225   **TR**   1965   Mayaro virus: a new human disease agent. I. Relationship to other arboviruses. *Car Med J* 27(1-4): 103-110.   [*ACM*]

Cazanove, Dr.
28.0226   **FC**   1935   Les épidémices de fièvre jaune aux Antilles et à la Guyane Francaise [Yellow fever epidemics in the Antilles and in French Guiana]. *In* Denis, Serge, ed. NOS ANTILLES. Orléans, Luzeray, 179-213.   **[5]**   [*AGS*]

Cecil, C. H.
28.0227   **TR**   1942   Health and hygiene in Trinidad. *Can-W I Mag* 31(3), Mar.: 9-12.   [*NYP*]

Chalchat, P.; Colas-Belcour, J.; Destombes, P.; Drouhet, E.; Fromentin, H.; Martin, L.; Ravisse, P. & Silverie, J.
28.0228   **FG**   1965   A propos d'un cas guyanais de leishmaniose cutanéo-muqueuse résistant aux antimoniaux et guéri par l'amphotéricine B. [A propos of a Guyanese case of mucocutaneous leishmaniasis resistant to antimonials and cured by Amphotericin-B.]. *B Soc Path Exot* 58(1), Jan.-Feb.: 73-80.   [*PS*]

Chalmers, A. H.; Harris, J. C.; Swanton, R. H. & Thorley, A. P.

28.0229   BZ   1968   A survey of the distribution of dermal leishmaniasis in British Honduras. *Trans Roy Soc Trop Med Hyg* 62(2): 213-220.   [*PS*]

Chambers, H. D.

28.0230   JM   1953   The syndrome called "vomiting sickness." *W I Med J* 2(1), Mar.: 37-42.   [*COL*]

28.0231   JM   1960   A clinical type of hypertension observed in Jamaica—illustrated by the most outstanding of the cases observed. *W I Med J* 9(1), Mar.: 67-72.   [*COL*]

28.0232   JM   1962   Malignant lymphocytic lymphoma. *W I Med J* 11(1), Mar. 27-29.   [*COL*]

Champagnie, L. E.

28.0233   JM   1967   Area study of Montego Bay in the parish of St. James. *Jam Nurse* 7(3), Dec.: 23-28.   **[33]**   [*AJN*]

Charles, E. D. B. & Grant, L. S.

28.0234   JM   1962   Poliomyelitis in Jamaica, W.I. *W I Med J* 11(3), Sept.: 203-212.   [*COL*]

Charles, L. J.

28.0235   LW,WW   1952   Malaria in Leeward and Windward Islands, British West Indies. *Am J Trop Med Hyg* 1(6), Nov.: 941-961.   [*COL*]

28.0236   GU   1953   Re-infestation problems in an *Aedes Aegypit*-free area in British Guiana. *W I Med J* 2(1), Mar.: 1-10.   [*COL*]

Check, T. M. & Day, H. V.

28.0237   JM   1967   Dental ambassadors. *J Am Dent Assoc* 75(1), July: 90-94.   [*PS*]

Chen, Gerald

28.0238   TR   1967   Organization for health planning in Trinidad and Tobago: working document. *In* SECOND SEMINAR ON ORGANIZATION AND ADMINISTRATION OF HEALTH SERVICES—CARIBBEAN. Port-of-Spain, Trinidad, 14-19 Nov.: 178-200.   **[32]**   [*RIS*]

Chen, W. N. & James, O. B. O'L.

27.0040   JM   1972   Histoplasmin sensitivity in the Jamaican population.

Chen, W. N.; Moodie, K.; Nicholson, G. D.; Alisharan, R.; Harmon, R. E. & Alleyne, G. A. O.

28.0239   JM   1976   Two cases of Pasteurella multocida infections in Jamaica. *W I Med J* 25(2), June: 87-91.   **[54]**   [*RIS*]

Chopra, J. G. & Byam, N. T. A.

28.0240   TR   1968   Anemia survey in Trinidad and Tobago. *Am J Publ Heal* 58(10), Oct.: 1922-1936.   **[30]**   [*PS*]

Chopra, J. G.; Noe, E.; Matthew, J.; Dhein, C.; Rose, J.; Cooperman, J. M. & Luhby, A. L.

28.0241   TR   1967   Anemia in pregnancy. *Am J Publ Heal* 57(5), May: 857-868.   **[30]**   [*PS*]

Chopra, J. G.; Tantiwongse, P.; Everette, M. S. & Villegas, N.
30.0048   TR   1965   Anaemia in malnutrition.

Chruściel, T. L.
28.0242   JM   1975   Recent progress in the long-term pharmacological research on cannabis. *Int J Clin Pharmacol Biopharm* 12(1-2), July: 57-62.   **[31]**
[*ACM*]

Chutkan, W. B.
28.0243   JM   1973   Patients requiring lower limb prostheses in Jamaica. *W I Med J* 22(3), Sept.: 116-118.
[*PS*]

Cirera, P.; Larrouy, G. & Le Gonidec, G.
28.0244   FG,DM   [n.d.]   Sur la fréquence de la syphilis dans certaines populations de la région des Caraïbes [On the frequency of syphilis in various populations in the Caribbean area]. *B Soc Path Exot* 61(2), March-April: 169-176.
[*PS*]

Clarac
28.0245   FG   1902   La Guyane Francaise: notes de géographie médicale, d'ethnographie et de pathologie [French Guiana: medical geography, ethnography, and pathology]. *Ann Hyg Med Colon* 5: 5-108.   **[7]**
[*ACM*]

Clare, Lionel A.
28.0246   BZ   1974   Maternal and child health—family planning programme in Belize. *In* International Confederation of Midwives. REPORT OF THE CARIBBEAN WORKING PARTY, BRIDGETOWN, BARBADOS, 16-24 MAY, 1974. [Bridgetown, Barbados]: 95-100.   **[34]**   [*RIS*]

Clarke, Eric E.
28.0247   GU,JM   1973   A comparative analysis of the age distribution and types of primary glaucoma among populations of African and Caucasian origins. *Ann Ophthal* 5(10), Oct.: 1055-1071.   **[27]**   [*ACM*]

Clarke, F. J.
28.0248   SL   1962   Adult education and the health of the community. *In* Brown, John, ed. AN APPROACH TO ADULT EDUCATION. Castries, St. Lucia, Govt. Print. Off., 15-19.   **[32]**   [*RIS*]

Clarke, T. L. E.
28.0249   BV   1918   Some observations on fish poisoning in the British Virgin Islands. *W I B* 17(2): 56-67.   **[52,54]**   [*AMN*]

Clastrier, J.
28.0250   FG   1970   *Culex guyanensis* n. sp. *(Diptera, Culicidae)* nouveau moustique de la Guyane Française [*Culex (Eubonnea) guyanensis* n. sp. *(Diptera, Culicidae)*, new mosquito of French Guiana]. *Ann Paras Hum Comp* 45(1), Jan.-Feb.: 115-118.   **[54]**   [*PS*]
28.0251   FG   1970   *Culex (Melanoconium) dolichophyllus* n. sp. et *Culex (Microculex) stonei* Lane et Whitman, 1943 *(Diptera, Culicidae)* en Guyane Française [*Culex (Melanoconium) dolichophyllus* n. sp. and *Culex (Microculex) stonei* Lane and Whitman, 1943 *(Diptera, Culicidae)* in French Guiana]. *Ann Paras Hum Comp* 45(6), Nov.-Dec.: 857-861.   **[54]**   [*PS*]

28.0252   FG   1970   Quatre nouveaux *Melanoconium (Diptera, Culicidae)* de la Guyane Française [Four new *Melanoconium (Diptera, Culicidae)* of French Guiana]. *Ann Paras Hum Com* 45(4), July-Aug.: 463-476.   **[54]**
[PS]

28.0253   FG   1971   Deux nouveaux *Culicoides (Diptera, Ceratopogonidae)* de la Guyana Française [Two new *Culicoides (Diptera, Ceratopogonidae)* of French Guiana]. *Ann Paras Hum Comp* 46(3), May-June: 285-294.   **[54]**
[PS]

Clayson, David
32.0121   JM   1973   Public health training among the rural poor in Jamaica: some effects on medical students' concept modification and self-evaluation.

32.0122   JM   1973   Public health training in the urban ghetto and among the rural poor: comparative effects on medical students' concept modification and self-evaluation.

Cleare, L. D.
54.0198   GU   1919   Some parasites of man and animals in British Guiana.

Clegg, J. B. & Weatherall, D. J.
27.0041   JM   1974   Hemoglobin Constant Spring, an unusual a-chain variant involved in the etiology of hemoglobin H disease.

Clegg, J. B.; Weatherall, D. J. & Milner, P. F.
27.0042   JM   1971   Haemoglobin Constant Spring—a chain termination mutant?

Clunie-Francis, H. M.
28.0254   JM   1966   May Pen, Clarendon. Area study. *Jam Nurse* 6(2), April: 26-27 passim.   [AJN]

Cobb, J. S.; Adam, M.; Pegg, P. J.; Keane, P. M. & Massey, J. C.
28.0255   JM   1970   Thyroid function in euthyroid Jamaicans. *J Clin Endocrinol* 31(4), Oct.: 450-452.   **[11]**   [PS]

Cochrane, E.
28.0256   GR   1941   Is *A. argyritarsis* a malarial vector in Grenada? *Car Med J* 3(4): 193-195.   [COL]

28.0257   GR   1942   Notes on *A. argyritarsis* and *A. pseudopunctipennis* in Grenada. *Car Med J* 4(3): 97-100.   [COL]

Cochrane, E. & Stuart, K. L.
28.0258   BB   1963   Cardiovascular disorders in Barbados. *W I Med J* 12(4), Dec.: 275-284.   [COL]

Cohen, Joel E.
27.0043   GC   1973   Heterologous immunity in human malaria.

Coia, A. G.
28.0259   GU   1933   Nephritis in British Guiana. *Br Gui Med Annual 1932* 25: 45-50.
[ACM]

28.0260   GU   1933   Some racial statistics of uterine fibroids in British Guiana. *Br Gui Med Annual 1932* 25: 106-109.   [ACM]

Cole, F. M.

| 28.0261 | JM | 1969 | Spontaneous intracerebral haemmorrhage. A review. *W I Med J* 18(3), Sept.: 129-137.   [*PS*] |

Cole, F. M. & Cole, H. L.

| 28.0262 | JM | 1969 | The pattern of fetal cerebrovascular disease in Jamaica. *W I Med J* 18(4), Dec.: 202-209.   [*PS*] |

Collier, H. C.

29.0020	BC	1941	Nature, her own apothecary.
55.0049	GU	1942	Climate and health in British Guiana.
29.0021	GU	1942	Copper skin's secret.
29.0022	GU	1946	Jungle dope.
29.0023	GU	1948	Curare—the story of a reformation.

Collier, W. A.; Collier, E. E. & Tjong A Hung, T.

| 28.0263 | SR | 1956 | Serological research on encephalitis in Surinam. *Docum Med Geogr Trop* 8(1), Mar.: 39-44.   [*COL*] |

Collier, W. A. & Fuente, A. A. de la

| 28.0264 | SR | 1953 | The histoplasmine test in Surinam. *Docum Med Geogr Trop* 5(2), June: 103-108.   [*COL*] |

Collier, W. A. & Tiggelman-Van Krugten, V. A. H.

| 28.0265 | SR | 1955 | De vleermuizenlyssa in Suriname [The lyssa virus carried by bats in Surinam]. *Vox Guy* 1(6): 149-159. |

Collier, W. A. & Tjong A Hung, T.

| 28.0266 | SR | 1953 | Serological brucella tests in Surinam. *Docum Med Geogr Trop* 5(4), Dec.: 321-322.   [*COL*] |

Collier, W. A.; Winckel, W. E. F. & Blom, F. A. E.

| 28.0267 | SR | 1953 | Two cases of St. Louis encephalitis in Surinam. *Docum Med Geogr Trop* 5(3), Sept.: 225-234.   [*COL*] |

Collier, W. A.; Winckel, W. E. F. & Kafiluddi, S.

| 28.0268 | SR | 1954 | Coxsackie infections (pseudopoliomyelitis) in Surinam. *Docum Med Geogr Trop* 6(2), June: 97-105.   [*COL*] |

Colwell, Miles; Guicherit, Iwan & Cralley, Lester V.

| 28.0269 | SR | 1967 | Practical application of an integrated environmental health control program in Suriname. *In* INDUSTRY AND TROPICAL HEALTH, VI. PROCEEDINGS OF THE SIXTH CONFERENCE OF THE INDUSTRIAL COUNCIL FOR TROPICAL HEALTH, OCTOBER 25-27, 1966, BOSTON. Boston, Harvard School of Public Health: 78-87.   [*PS*] |

Comitas, Lambros

| *33.0047* | JM | 1976 | Cannabis and work in Jamaica: a refutation of the amotivational syndrome. |

Commissiong, L. M.

| 28.0270 | GC | 1968 | Health services in the British Caribbean 1935-1969. *Car Med J* 30: 40-42.   [*PS*] |

Condon, P. I.; Gray, Robert & Serjeant, G. R.

27.0048   **JM**   1974   Ocular findings in children with sickle cell haemoglobin C in disease in Jamaica.

Condon, P. I. & Serjeant, G. R.

27.0049   **JM**   1972   Ocular findings in homozygous sickle cell anemia in Jamaica.

27.0050   **JM**   1975   The progression of sickle cell eye disease in Jamaica.

Cook, J. A.

5.0183   **GC**   1968   John Esquemeling, buccanner's surgeon and historian.

Cook, J. A.; Baker, S. T.; Warren, K. S. & Jordan, P.

28.0271   **SL**   1974   A controlled study of morbidity of schistosomiasis mansoni in St. Lucian children, based on quantitative egg excretion. *Am J Trop Med Hyg* 23(4), July: 625-633.   [*PS*]

Cook, J. A. & Jordan, Peter

28.0272   **SL**   1971   Clinical trial of hycanthone in schistosomiasis mansoni in St. Lucia. *Am J Trop Med Hyg* 20(1), Jan.: 84-88.   [*PS*]

Cook, J. A.; Kellermeyer, W. F.; Warren, K. S. & Kellermeyer, R. W.

27.0051   **SL**   1972   Sickle cell haemoglobinopathy and schistosoma mansoni infection.

Cook, Martin J.

28.0273   **TR**   1945   Sulfonamide failures in the treatment of gonorrhea in Trinidad, B.W.I. *Car Med J* 7(2-3): 88-94.   [*COL*]

Cook, Robert

30.0053   **BC**   1968   The financial cost of malnutrition in the "Commonwealth Caribbean."

30.0054   **GC**   1969   Nutrition and mortality under five years in the Caribbean area.

30.0055   **BC**   1970   Nutrition and mortality under five years in the English-speaking Caribbean area.

Cook, Robert & Yang, Yueh-Heng

30.0057   **BC**   1973   National food and nutrition policy in the Commonwealth Caribbean.

Cooke, W. T.; Asquith, P.; Ruck, Nicola; Melikian, V. & Swan, C. H. J.

30.0058   **BC,UK**   1974   Rickets, growth, and alkaline phosphatase in urban adolescents.

Cooke, W. T.; Swan, C. H. J.; Asquith, P.; Melikian, V. & McFreely, W. E.

30.0059   **BC,UK**   1973   Serum alkaline phosphatase and rickets in urban schoolchildren.

Cool, P.

28.0274   **SR**   1923-24 De Geneeskundige Dienst in Suriname [The Medical Service in Surinam]. *W I G* 5: 653-657.   [*COL*]

28.0275   **SR**   1924-25 De nieuwe afdeling van het militaire hospitaal te Paramaribo voor besmettelijke ziekten [The new section for contagious diseases in the military hospital in Paramaribo]. *W I G* 6: 433-440.   [*COL*]

Coomans, H. E.

5.0184   **SM**   1973   H. E. van Rijgersma, gouvernementsarts op St.-Maarten, 1863-1877 [H. E. van Rijgersma, government doctor on St. Maarten, 1863-1877].

Corniou, B.; Ardoin, P.; Bartholomew, C.; Ince, W. & Massiah, V.

28.0276   TR   1972   First isolation of a South American strain of eastern equine virus from a case of encephalitis in Trinidad. *Trop Geogr Med* 24(2), June: 162-167.   [*PS*]

Cory, Richard A. S.

28.0277   JM   1960   Surgical treatment of respiratory tuberculosis over a quarter of a century in Jamaica, West Indies. *Car Med J* 22(1-4): 75-80.   [*COL*]

Cosminsky, Sheila

1.0074   GC   1976   Latin American and the Caribbean.

Cottman, Evans W. & Blassingame, Wyatt

3.0118   BA   1963   OUT ISLAND DOCTOR.

Coura, J. R. & Petana, W. B.

28.0278   BZ   1967   American trypanosomiasis in British Honduras. II.—The prevalance of Chagas' disease in Cayo District. *Ann Trop Med Paras* 61(3), Sept.: 244-250.   [*PS*]

Courmes, E.

28.0279   GD   1965   Rapport technique [Technical report]. *Archs Inst Past Guad:* 5-44. **[7]**   [*ACM*]

28.0280   GD   1966   Rapport technique [Technical report]. *Archs Inst Past Guad;* 5-37. **[7]**   [*ACM*]

Courmes, E.; Fauran, P. & Lespinasse, J.-P.

28.0281   GD   1966   Contribution à l'étude des filarioses humaines dans le département de Guadeloupe [Contribution to the study of human filariasis in Guadeloupe]. *Archivs Inst Past Guad:* 39-66.   [*ACM*]

Courmes, E.; Escudie, A.; Fauran, P. & Monnerville, A.

28.0282   GD   1965   Premier cas autoctone de leishmaniose viscerale humaine en Guadeloupe [First native case of human visceral leishmaniasis in Guadeloupe]. *Archs Inst Past Guad:* 49-63.   [*ACM*]

Cox, Frederick & Gold, Eli

28.0283   BB   1973   Incidence and types of Group A streptococcal pyoderma and pharyngitis in children in Barbados. *W I Med J* 22(2), June: 99-106.
                                                                                       [*PS*]

Coye, Alexandra

8.0045   BZ   1973   Socio-economic classes in Belize and their influence on health.

Craigen, A. J.

28.0284   GU   1912   Practice of midwifery at the Public Hospital, Georgetown. *Br Gui Med Annual 1910* 17: 25-33. **[34]**   [*ACM*]

Crane, Alfred V.

28.0285   GU   1924   The Georgetown sewerage scheme. *W I Comm Circ* 39(671), June 19: 237-238. **[36]**   [*NYP*]

Craton, Michael
5.0196   JM   1974   Dr. John Quier, 1739-1822.

Crisfield, R. J.
28.0286   JM   1974   Scoliosis with progressive external ophthalmoplegia in four siblings.
                                         J Bone Joint Surg 56B(3), Aug.: 484-489.   [*PS*]

Cruickshank, E. K.
28.0287   JM   1952   The University College Hospital of the West Indies. *W I Med J* 1(3),
                                         Oct.: 274-280.   [32]   [*COL*]
28.0288   JM   1956   A neuropathic syndrom of uncertain origin: review of 100 cases.
                                         W I Med J 5(3), Sept.: 147-159.   [*COL*]
28.0289   JM   1970   Clinical syndromes associated with plant toxins in Jamaica. *Trans
                                         Am Clin Climatol Assoc* 81: 67-84.   [*PS*]
28.0290   JM   1975   A neurological retrospect of Jamaica. *W I Med J* 24(1), March:
                                         3-15.   [*PS*]

Cruickshank, E. K. et al.
28.0291   JM   1955   Sickle cell anaemia: symposium at the University College of the
                                         West Indies, May 26th, 1954. *W I Med J* 4(1), Mar.: 25-37.   [11]
                                                                                                                                      [*COL*]

Cruickshank, E. K. & Montgomery, R. D.
28.0292   JM   1961   Multiple sclerosis in Jamaica. *W I Med J* 10(3), Sept.: 211-214.
                                                                                                                                      [*COL*]

Cummins, G. T. M.
28.0293   BC   1971   The feedings of the newborn in hospital—an obstetrician's view.
                                         W I Med J 20(3), Sept.: 170-173.   [*PS*]
34.0019   GC   1974   What constitutes maternal and child care in the Caribbean.

Cummins, G. T. M. & Vaillant, Henry W.
34.0021   BB   1966   The training of the nurse-midwife for a national program in
                                         Barbados combining the IUD and cervical cytology.

Currie, Leonard J.
35.0021   GC   1965   Housing and health in the Caribbean.

Curtin, Philip D.
6.0042   GC   1968   Epidemiology and the slave trade.

Curzen, Peter & Knight, L. Patrick
28.0294   JM   1967   Induction of labour with buccal syntocinon. *W I Med J* 16(2), June:
                                         107-109.   [*PS*]

Da Costa, L. R.
28.0295   JM   1972   Cell turnover in the normal human small intestinal mucosa. *W I
                                         Med J* 21(2), June: 66-69.   [11]   [*PS*]
28.0296   JM   1972   Small intestinal villous pattern and mucosal dynamics in healthy
                                         Jamaicans. *Am J Dig Dis* 17(2), Feb.: 105-110.   [*PS*]

Da Costa, L. R. & Bluestone, R.
28.0297   JM   1966   A double-blind clinical trial of long-acting isoprenaline in bronchial
                                         asthma. *W I Med J* 15(3) Sept.: 170-172.   [*PS*]

Dalhuysen, B.
33.0057   AR   1970   Internal medical aspects of alcoholism and experiences with it in Aruba.

Dalton, Peter
28.0298   SL   1971   Socio-cultural aspects of bilharzial transmission in St. Lucia. Paper presented at the Society of Applied Anthropology meeting, Miami, Florida: 10p.   [*RIS*]

Dan, M.
28.0299   TR   1960   A study of P.A.S. intake of patients in South Trinidad. *Car Med J* 22(1-4): 38-40.   [*COL*]

Daniels, C. W.
28.0300   GU   1902   Notes on malaria and other tropical diseases. *Br Gui Med Annual* [12]: 40-46.   [*ACM*]

Dautheuil
28.0301   FG   1936   Comment on devenait médecin au XVIIᵉ siècle "en l'isle de Cayenne" [How one became a physican in the 17th century on "Cayenne island"]. *Chron Med* 43(9), Sept. 1: 227-230.   [5]   [*COL*]

Davidson, J. R. T.
31.0049   JM   1972   Post-partum mood change in Jamaican women: a description and discussion on its significance.

Davies, J. N. P. & Hollman, A.
28.0302   GC   1965   Becker type cardiomyopathy in a West Indian woman. *Am Heart J* 70(2): 225-232.   [*PS*]

Davies, John B.
28.0303   JM   1967   The distribution of sandflies (Culicoides spp.) breeding in a tidal mangrove swamp in Jamaica and the effect of tides on the emergence of C. furens Poey and C. barbosi (Wirth & Blanton). *W I Med J* 16(1), March: 39-50.   [*PS*]
28.0304   JM   1969   Effect of felling mangroves on emergence of *culicoides* spp. in Jamaica. *Mosq News* 29(4), Dec.: 566-571.   [*PS*]

Davies, John E.; Edmundson, Walter F. & Raffonelli, Americo
28.0305   BA   1975   The role of house dust in human DDT pollution. *Am J Publ Heal* 65(1), Jan.: 53-57.   [58]   [*PS*]

Davis, N. Darnell
28.0306   NV   1911   Nevis as West Indian health resort. *Timehri* 3d ser., 1(18C), Dec.: 285-294.   [5]   [*AMN*]

Davis, W. G. & Persaud, Trivedi V. N.
28.0307   JM   1970   Recent studies on the active principles of Jamaican medicinal plants. *W I Med J* 19(2), June: 101-110.   [29,54]   [*PS*]

Dawson, C. R. & Schachter, J.
28.0308   JM   1967   Trachoma in Jamaica. Epidemiologic and microbiologic observations on mild disease. *Am J Ophthal* 63(5, part 2), May: 1408-1413.
                                                                [*PS*]

Deane, C. G.
30.0062   TR   1938   Deficiency diseases in East Indians of the labouring class.

Debrot, A.
28.0309   CU   1968   Eruption sequences in children of Curaçao, Netherlands Antilles.
                            J Dent Res 47(1), Jan.-Feb.: 83-86.   **[11]**   [*PS*]

Degazon, D. W.
28.0310   JM   1952   Primary glaucoma: pathogenesis and Jamaican aspects. *W I Med J*
                            1(2), Apr.: 178-194.   [*COL*]

DePass, E. E.
28.0311   JM   1962   Some effects in rats of the administration of Crotalaria fulva extract
                            by mouth. *W I Med J* 11, Mar.: 12-14.   [*COL*]

Desai, Patricia
28.0312   JM   1969   A five-year study of infant growth in rural Jamaica. *W I Med J*
                            18(4), Dec.: 210-221.   [*PS*]

Desai, Patricia; Clarke, L. M. & Heron, C. E.
28.0313   JM   1970   Do child welfare clinics influence growth? *J Biosoc Sci* 2(4):
                            305-315.   **[33]**   [*PS*]

Desai, Patricia; Standard, K. L. & Miall, W. E.
28.0314   JM   1970   Socio-economic and cultural influences on child growth in rural
                            Jamaica. *J Biosoc Sci* 2(2), April: 133-143.   **[9,32,35]**   [*COL*]

Destombes, P.
28.0315   FA   1965   Adénites avec surcharge lipidique, de l'enfant ou de l'adulte jeune,
                            observées aux Antilles et au Mali (Quatres observations) [Adenitis
                            with lipid excess, in children or young adults, seen in the Antilles
                            and in Mali—four cases]. *B Soc Path Exot* 58(6), Nov.-Dec.:
                            1169-1175.   [*PS*]

Devine, Fred W.
28.0316   GC   1965   CARE in the Caribbean. *In* Wilgus, A. Curtis, ed. THE CARIBBEAN:
                            ITS HEALTH PROBLEMS. Gainesville, University of Florida Press:
                            233-245. (Caribbean Conference Series 1, Vol. 15)   **[30,39]**   [*RIS*]

Dias, Emmanuel
28.0317   GG   1952   Doenca de chagas nas Américas. IV: Colδumbia, Venezuela e
                            Guianas [Running sores in the Americas. IV: Colombia, Venezuela,
                            and the Guianas]. *Revta Brasil Mala Do Trop* 4(3), July: 255-
                            280.   **[54]**   [*COL*]

Disney, R. H. L.
54.0278   BZ   1966   A trap for phlebotomine sandflies attracted to rats.
28.0318   BZ   1968   Observations on a zoonosis: leishmaniasis in British Honduras.
                            J Appl Ecol 5(1), April: 1-59.   **[54]**   [*COL*]

Dolly, Reynold Cartwright
28.0319   TR   1961   Some aspects of industrial medicine as seen in the oil industry. *Car
                            Med J* 23(1-4), 59-63.   **[45]**   [*COL*]

Donovan, Anthony

28.0320   GU   1939   Health aspects of the proposed large-scale settlement in British Guiana of European refugees. *In* REPORT OF THE BRITISH GUIANA COMMISSION TO THE PRESIDENT'S ADVISORY COMMITTEE ON POLITICAL REFUGEES. Washington, D.C., [no. 2] (39p.)   [*AGS*]

Doran, Edwin Beal, Jr.

27.0057   CM   1952   Inbreeding in an isolated island community.

Dowdle, W. R.; Ferreira, W.; De Salles Gomes, L. F.; King, D.; Kourany, M.; Madalengoitia, J.; Pearson, E.; Swanston, W. H.; Tosi, H. C. & Vilches, A. M.

28.0321   GC   1970   WHO collaborative study on the sero-epidemiology of rubella in Caribbean and Middle and South American populations in 1968. *B WHO* 42(3): 419-422.   [*PS*]

Downs, W. G.

28.0322   TR   1965   Epidemiological notes in connection with the 1954 outbreak of yellow fever in Trinidad, B.W.I. *Car Med J* 27(1-4): 65-72.   [*ACM*]

28.0323   TR   1965   Human infections with arbovirus in Trinidad, W. I. *Car Med J* 27(1-4): 14-19.   [*ACM*]

Downs, W. G.; Aitken, T. H. G.; Worth, C. B.; Spence, L. & Jonkers, A. H.

28.0324   TR   1968   Arbovirus studies in Bush Bush Forest, Trinidad, W.I., September 1959-December 1964. I. Description of the study area. *Am J Trop Med Hyg* 17(2), March: 224-236. (See Aitken et al for Parts II and III.)   [*PS*]

Downs, W. G. & Anderson, C. R.

28.0325   BC   1958   Distribution of immunity to Mayaro virus infection in the West Indies. *W I Med J* 7(3), Sept.: 190-194.   [*COL*]

28.0326   GR   1959   Arthropod-borne encephalitic viruses in the West Indies area. Part I: A serological survey of Grenada, W. I. *W I Med J* 8(2), June: 101-109.   [*COL*]

28.0327   GR   1965   Arthropod-borne encephalitic viruses in the West Indies area. Part I: A serological survey of Grenada, W.I. *Car Med J* 27(1-4): 30-38.   [*ACM*]

28.0328   GC   1965   Distribution of immunity to Mayaro virus infection in the West Indies. *Car Med J* 27(1-4): 116-121.   [*ACM*]

Downs, W. G.; Anderson, C. R.; Aitken, T. H. G. & Delpeche, K. A.

28.0329   TR   1956   Notes on the epidemiology of ilhéus virus infection in Trinidad, B.W.I. *Car Med J* 18(3-4): 74-79.   [*COL*]

28.0330   TR   1965   Notes on the epidemiology of Ilhéus virus infection in Trinidad, B.W.I. *Car Med J* 27(1-4): 85-90.   [*ACM*]

Downs, W. G.; Anderson, C. R.; Delpeche, K. A. & Byer, M. A.

28.0331   BB   1962   Arthropod-borne encephalitis viruses in the West Indies area. Pt. II: A serological survey of Barbados, W.I. *W I Med J* 11(2), June: 117-122.   [*COL*]

Downs, W. G.; Anderson, C. R.; Delpeche, K. A. & Byer, M. A.
28.0332   BB   1965   Arthropod-borne encephalitic viruses in the West Indies area. Part II: A serological survey of Barbados, W.I. *Car Med J* 27(1-4): 20-29.
[*ACM*]

Downs, W. G.; Anderson, C. R. & Theiler, M.
28.0333   TR   1965   Neutralizing antibodies against certain viruses in the sera of residents of Trinidad, B.W.I. *Car Med J* 27(1-4): 39-54.   [*ACM*]

Downs, W. G.; Delpeche, K. A. & Uttley, K. H.
28.0334   AT   1963   Arthropod-borne encephalitis viruses in the West Indies area. Pt. IV: A serological survey of Antigua, W.I. *W I Med J* 12(2), June: 109-116.   [*COL*]

Downs, W. G. & Grant, L. S.
28.0335   JM   1962   Arthropod-borne encephalitis viruses in the West Indies area. Pt. III: A serological survey of Jamaica, W.I. *W I Med J* 11(4), Dec.: 253-264.   [*COL*]

Downs, W. G. & Spence, L.
28.0336   SV   1963   Arthropod-borne encephalitis viruses in the West Indies area. Pt. VI: A serological survey of St. Vincent, W.I. *W I Med J* 12(3), Sept.: 148-155.   [*COL*]
28.0337   SL   1964   Arthropod-borne encephalitis viruses in the West Indies area Pt. VII. A serological survey of St. Lucia, W.I. *W I Med J* 13(1), Mar.: 25-32.   [*COL*]

Downs, W. G.; Spence, L. & Aitken, T. H. G.
62.0036   TR   1965   Studies on the virus of Venezuelan equine encephalomyelitis in Trinidad, W.I.

Downs, W. G.; Spence, L.; Aitken, T. H. G. & Whitman, L.
28.0338   TR   1961   Cache Valley virus, isolated from a Trinidadian mosquito, *Aedes scapularis*. *W I Med J* 10(1), Mar.: 13-15.   [*COL*]

Downs, W. G.; Spence, L. & Borghans, J. G. A.
28.0339   CU   1963   Arthropod-borne encephalitis viruses in the West Indies area. Pt. V: A serological survey of Curacao, N.W.I. *Trop Geogr Med* 15(3), Sept.: 237-242.   [*COL*]

Downs, W. G.; Turner, L. H. & Green, A. E.
28.0340   TR   1962   Leptospirosis in Trinidad: a preliminary report. *W I Med J* 11(1), Mar.: 51-54.   [*COL*]

Drayton, Harold A.
28.0341   GU   1969   Equine encephalitis in coastal and hinterlands areas of Guyana. *W I Med J* 18(3), Sept.: 171-176.   **[62]**   [*PS*]

Drew, F. L.; Raizman, R.; Agnew, D.; Solters, J.; Weitzel, G.; Hawk, R. & Dulabon, D.
28.0342   JM   1974   Prevalence of positive treponemal serological tests in a rural Jamaican community. *W I Med J* 23(4), Dec.: 238-244.   [*PS*]

Duchassin, M.; Lataste-Dorolle, C. & Silverie, C. R.

28.0343   FG   1965   Indice d'infection par *L. icterohaemorrhagiae* du rat de Cayenne. Quelques aspects épidémologiques des leptospiroses en Guyane Française [Incidence of infection caused by *L. icterohaemorrhagiae* in rats in Cayenne. Some epidemiological aspects of leptospirosis in French Guiana]. *B Soc Path Exot* 58(2), March-April: 170-177.
          [*PS*]

Duck, E. F.

28.0344   BA   1967   Bahamas approach to cervical cytology. *W I Med J* 16(3), Sept.: 162-165.
          [*PS*]

Dufougeré, W.

28.0345   FG   1920   Ankylostomiase et béribéri en Guyane Francaise [Ankylostomiasis and beriberi in French Guiana]. *B Soc Path Exot* 13(7), July: 603-617. **[30]**
          [*ACM*]

37.0206   FG   1921   De l'utilisation rationnelle de la main-d'oeuvre pénale en Guyane [On the rational use of forced labor in Guiana].

Duncan, W. J.

7.0037   GU   1916   The public health statistics of the colony.

7.0038   GU   1919   The public health and medical statistics of the colony.

Dunham, Lucia J.; Sheets, Ray H. & Morton, Julia F.

28.0346   CU   1974   Proliferative lesions in cheek pouch and esophagus of hamsters treated with plants from Curaçao, Netherlands Antilles. *J Natn Cancer Inst* 53(5), Nov.: 1259-1269. **[54]**
          [*PS*]

Duperrat, B. & Labouche, F.

28.0347   FC,FR   1975   Le granulome venerien (Donovanose) en France [Venereal granuloma (donovaniasis) in France]. *Ann Derm Syph* 102(3): 241-250.
          [*ACM*]

Earle, D. P.; Potter, E. V.; Poon-King, T.; Finklea, J. F.; Sharrett, A. R. & Ortiz, J.

28.0348   TR   1970   Streptococcal skin infections and epidemic acute nephritis in Trinidad. *Trans Am Clin Climatol Assoc* 81: 184-195.
          [*PS*]

Earle, K. Vigors

28.0349   BC   1939   Esthiomène as seen in the West Indies. *Car Med J* 1(4): 310-320.
          [*COL*]

28.0350   TR   1939   Notes on the dengue epidemic at Point Fortin. *Car Med J* 1(3): 245-249.
          [*COL*]

28.0351   TR   1941   Infectious mononucleosis: some cases observed in Trinidad. *Car Med J* 3(2): 94-101.
          [*COL*]

28.0352   TR   1965   Notes on the dengue epidemic at Point Fortin. *Car Med J* 27(1-4): 157-163.
          [*ACM*]

Eddey, L. G.

28.0353   GU   1947   An example of effective disease control in a tropical mining community. *Br Gui Med Annual,* 162-181.
          [*RIS*]

Edge, P. Granville

7.0046   BC   1944   Infant mortality in British West Indies.

28.0354   BC   1944   Malaria and nephritis in the British West Indies. *Car Med J* 6(1): 32-43.   [*COL*]

Edghill, H. B.

28.0355   GU   1961   Filariasis at Port Mourant and its environs Corentyne coast, British Guiana. *W I Med J* 10(1), Mar.: 44-54.   [*COL*]

Ehrenkranz, N. J.; Ventura, A. K.; Cuadrado, R. R.; Pond, W. L. & Porter, J. E.

28.0356   GC   1971   Pandemic dengue in Caribbean countries and the southern United States. Past, present and potential problems. *New England J of Med* 285(26), Dec.: 1460-1469.   [*PS*]

Ekker, I.

30.0067   CU   1966   Voeding en voedingstoestand van Curaçaose schoolkinderen [Nutrition and nutritional state of Curaçao schoolchildren].

Elder, J. D.

33.0067   TR   1970   Drug addiction and society.

Ellinas, Symeon & Cummins, Gordon T. M.

28.0357   BB   1974   Oral prostaglandins in induction of labour. *W I Med J* 23(1), March: 15-21.   [*PS*]

Ellington, E. V.

28.0358   JM   1961   Estimation of hypoglycin "A" in *Blighia sapida*: (ackee). *W I Med J* 10(3), Sept.: 184-188.   **[60]**   [*COL*]

28.0359   GC   1968   The identification and isolation of hypotensive and hypertensive principles in Phorodendron rubrum var. gracile—a West Indian medicinal plant. *W I Med J* 17(3), Sept.: 155-157.   **[54]**   [*PS*]

Engels, C. J. H.

28.0360   CU   1973   Samenwerken om milieuvervuiling te voorkomen [Cooperation to avoid pollution]. *In* Statius van Eps, L. W. & Luckman-Maduro, E., eds. Van scheepschirurgijn tot specilaist. Assen, The Netherlands, Van Gorcum & Comp. B.V.: 59-63. (Anjerpublikatie 15)
                                                                                                             [*RILA*]

English, E. W. F. et al.

7.0047   GU   1907   Report of the Mortality Commission.

Ennever, Olive N.

32.0190   JM   1968   Training of the assistant nurse—developments in Jamaica.

Ennever, Olive; Marsh, M. & Standard, K. L.

28.0361   JM   1969   A community health aide training programme. *W I Med J* 18(4), Dec.: 193-201.   [*PS*]

28.0362   JM   1969   Programa de adiestramiento de asistentes en salud de la comunidad [Training program for assistants in community health]. *Educ Med Salud* 3, Oct.-Dec.: 324-335.   **[32]**   [*PS*]

Ennever, Olive & Standard, Kenneth L.

28.0363   BC   1975   An analysis of health problems of Commonwealth Caribbean countries and the priorities. *W I Med J* 24(3), Sept.: 115-121.   [*PS*]

Ennis, J. T.; Gueri, M. C. & Serjeant, G. R.

28.0364   JM   1972   Radiological changes associated with leg ulcers in the tropics. *Br J Radiol* 45(529), Jan.: 8-14.   [*PS*]

Ennis, J. T.; Serjeant, G. R. & Middlemiss, Howard

27.0060   JM   1973   Homozygous sickle cell disease in Jamaica.

Erkelens, D. W.

28.0365   CU   1973   Melkintolerantie op Curaçao [Lactose intolerance in Curaçao]. *In* Statius van Eps, L. W. & Luckman-Maduro, E., eds. VAN SCHEEPSCHIRURGIJN TOT SPECIALIST. Assen, The Netherlands, Van Gorcum & Comp. B.V.: 117-119. (Anjerpublikatie 15) **[27]**
                          [*RILA*]

Escudie, A.

28.0366   GD   1966   Fréquence des sensibilisations à quelques allergènes en Guadeloupe [Frequency of sensitivity to several allergens in Guadeloupe]. *Archs Inst Past Guad:* 78-86.   [*ACM*]

Escudie, A. & Courmes, E.

28.0367   GD   1966   Observations sur l'allergie tuberculinique et léprominique des enfants cliniquement sains, vivant sau contact de lépreux en Guadeloupe [Observations on tuberculin and lepromin allergies in clinically healthy children living in contact with lepers in Guadeloupe]. *B Soc Path Exot* 59(3), May-June: 290-296.   [*PS*]

Escudie, A.; Segretain, G.; Destombes, P.; Proye, G.; Chatillon, M. & Courmes, E.

28.0368   GD   1967   Premier cas de mycétome fongique à grains blancs en Guadeloupe, probabilité d'un nouvel agent maduromycose [First case of white grained fungal mycetoma in Guadeloupe. Probability of a new agent of maduramycosis]. *B Soc Path Exot* 60(1), Jan.-Feb.: 13-20.
                          [*PS*]

Esdras, Marcel

28.0369   FA   1960   Les congrès des médecins de langue francaise de l'hémisphere Américain [Congresses of French-speaking physicians in the Western Hemisphere]. *Rev Guad* 39, Jan.-Mar.: 35-39.   [*RIS*]

Essed, W. F. R.

28.0370   SR   1930-31 Eenige opmerkingen naar aanleiding van de artikelen over treef en lepra in dit tijdschrift verschenen [Some remarks in connection with the articles about treyf and leprosy that appeared in this magazine]. *W I G* 12: 257-267.   **[14,23]**   [*COL*]

Etges, Frank J.; Bell, Emily J. & Ivins, Bruce

28.0371   GC   1969   A field survey of molluscicide-degrading micro-organisms in the Caribbean area. *Am J Trop Med Hyg* 18(3), May: 472-476.   [*PS*]

Eustace, P.

18.0091 GC,UK 1972 Myopia and divergent squint in West Indian children.

Evans, Alfred; Cox, Frederick; Nankervis, George; Opton, Edward; Shope, Robert; Wells, A. V. & West, Bernice

28.0372 BB 1974 A health and seroepidemiological survey of a community in Barbados. *Int J Epidemiol* 3(2), June: 167-175. [*ACM*]

Everard, C. O. R. & Baer, George M.

54.0311 GR 1974 Epidemiology of mongoose rabies in Grenada.

Ewan, H. M. Gordon

28.0373 JM 1967 Methods of contraception: an assessment of their usefulness in Jamaica. *W I Med J* 16(1), March: 1-9. [34] [*PS*]

Fairfield, Letitia D.

28.0374 BC 1921 Venereal diseases—the West Indian Commission. *W I Comm Circ* 36(596), Aug. 4: 321-322. [*NYP*]

Farooq, M.

28.0375 GC 1969 Pre-control investigations in Bilharziasis. *J Trop Med Hyg* 72(1), Jan.: 14-18. [2] [*PS*]

Fauran, P.

28.0376 FG 1965 Etude d'une collection de Trombiculidae de Guyane Française [Study of a collection of Trombiculidae of French Guiana]. *Archs Inst Past Guad:* 96-103. [*ACM*]

Fauran, P. & Courmes, E.

28.0377 GD 1965 Notes sur les Culicidae de Guadeloupe [Notes on the Culicidae of Guadeloupe]. *Archs Inst Past Guad:* 104-112. [*ACM*]

28.0378 GD 1966 Notes sur les Culicidae de Guadeloupe [Notes on the Culicidae of Guadeloupe]. *Archs Inst Past Guad:* 70-72. [*ACM*]

Fauran, P.; Courmes, E. & Escudie, A.

28.0379 GD 1965 Vecteurs possibles de la leishmaniose viscérale en Guadeloupe [Possible vectors of visceral leishmaniasis in Guadeloupe]. *Archs Inst Past Guad:* 64-67. [*ACM*]

Fauran, P.; Courmes, E. & Mille, R.

28.0380 JM 1966 Note sur la présence in Martinique de *Phlebotomus atroclavatus (Diptera: Psychodidae)* [Note on the presence of *Phlebotomus atroclavatus (Diptera: Psychodidae)* on Martinique]. *B Soc Path Exot* 59(5), Sept.-Oct.: 904-908. [*PS*]

Fawkes, M. A.

28.0381 TR 1949 Acute gonorrhoea in the male—analysis of 500 cases. *Car Med J* 11(2): 64-69. [*COL*]

28.0382 TR 1957 A short history of yaws in Trinidad. *W I Med J* 6(3), Sept.: 189-204. [5] [*COL*]

Feldman, Roger A.; Bray, Juanita P.; Poon-King, Theo & Potter, Elizabeth V.

28.0383 TR 1973 Epidermic diptheria and skin infections in Trinidad. *J Infect Dis* 127(2), Feb.: 207-209. [*PS*]

Feldman, Roger A.; Mootoo, C. Leslie & Gelfand, Henry M.
28.0384   GU   1965   Control of a Type 1 poliomyelitis epidemic in British Guiana, 1962-63, with trivalent oral poliovirus vaccine. 2. Virological aspects. *B WHO* 33(1): 13-19.   [*PS*]

Feng, P. C.
28.0385   JM   1969   Hypoglycin- from ackee: a review. *W I Med J* 18(4), Dec.: 238-241. **[30]**   [*PS*]

Feorino, Paul M. & Palmer, Erskine L.
28.0386   BB   1973   Incidence of antibody to envelope antigen of herpes simplex virus type 2 among patients with cervical carcinoma and matched controls. *J Infect Dis* 127(6), June: 732-735. **[54]**   [*PS*]

Ferguson, J. E. A.
28.0387   GU   1906   The climate of the Peter's Hall District and its effects on the inhabitants. *Br Gui Med Annual 1905* 14: 84-114. **[52]**   [*ACM*]
28.0388   GU   1916   The treatment of anchylostomiasis in the Peter's Hall Medical District. *Br Gui Med Annual 1915* 21: 43-48.   [*ACM*]

Ferguson, Stephen
32.0199   BC,UK   1974   West Indian medical graduates of Edinburgh to 1800.

Fernandes, H. P.
28.0389   GU   1951   Streptomycin in the treatment of tuberculosis in British Guiana. *Car Med J* 13(1-2): 52-78.   [*COL*]

Field, C. D.
32.0201   JM   1967   Biophysical science in the University of the West Indies.

Field, F. E.
28.0390   GU   1913   Observations on dysentery, with a special reference to its treatment by hypodermic injections of emetine. *Br Gui Med Annual 1912* 19: 1-7.   [*ACM*]
28.0391   GU   1916   Report on the amelioration and control of ankylostomiasis in the Belle Vue (West Bank) District of British Guiana. *Br Gui Med Annual 1915* 21: 49-95.   [*ACM*]

Fields, D. N.; Snelly, G. W. & Guicherit, I. D.
28.0392   SR   1956   The treatment of ascariasis with piperazine. *Docum Med Geogr Trop* 8: 80-84.   [*RIS*]

Fields, J. P. & Hellreich, P. D.
28.0393   JM   1969   Sarcoidosis masquerading as Hansen's disease. *Archs Derm* 100(5), Nov.: 649-651. **[18]**   [*PS*]

Finnie, Evelyn & Grant, L. S.
28.0394   JM   1966   A review of staphylococcal infections in the University Hospital of the West Indies. *W I Med J* 15(3), Sept.: 141-146.   [*PS*]

Fistein, Boris
28.0395   TR   1960   Toxic hypoglycaemia (Jamaican vomiting sickness): first case reported from the territory of Trinidad and Tobago. *W I Med J* 9(1), Mar.: 62-66.   [*COL*]

28.0396   TR   1966   *Trypanosoma cruzi* infection in blood-sucking reduviid bugs in Trinidad. *Trans Roy Soc Trop Med Hyg* 60(4), July: 536-538.   [*PS*]

Fitzmaurice, L. W. et al.
28.0397   JM   1953   The vomiting sickness of Jamaica: symposium at the University College of the West Indies, Mar. 27th, 1953. *W I Med J* 2(2), June: 93-124.   [*COL*]

Fleming, W. L.; Brathwaite, A. R.; Martin, J. E. & Collier, J.
28.0398   JM   1974   Penicillin and tetracycline sensitivity of Jamaican strains of gonococci. *W I Med J* 23(4), Dec.: 226-231.   [*PS*]

Fletcher, K.
30.0069   JM   1966   Observations on the origin of liver fat in infantile malnutrition.

Fletcher, P.; McCall, I. W. & Perks, W. D.
28.0399   JM   1975   Jejuno-gastric intussusception. *W I Med J* 24(1), March: 21-25.
                                                                                                  [*PS*]

Flew, G. P. & Grundy, J. H.
28.0400   GU   1967   Infection with *Dermatobia hominis* occurring in British Guiana. *J Roy Army Med Corps* 113(3): 148-155.   [*PS*]

Floch, Hervé Alexandre
28.0401   GD   1942   Apercu de pathologie médicale rurale en Guadeloupe [Sketch of the rural medical pathology in Guadeloupe]. *Inst Past Guy Ter L'In* 50, July (15p.)
28.0402   FG   1944   L'endémie palustre dans les communes rurales et l'intérieur de la Guyane Francaise [Endemic malaria in the rural communities and the interior of French Guiana]. *Inst Past Guy Ter L'In* 78, June (5p.)
28.0403   FG   1947   L'endémo-épidémie palustre en Guyane Francaise [Endemo-epidemic malaria in French Guiana]. *Inst Past Guy Ter L'In* 163, Oct. (12p.)
28.0404   FG   1948   La pathologie humaine en Guyane Francaise [Human pathology in French Guiana]. *Rev Med Fr* 29(7), July: 99-100, 102.   [*ACM*]
28.0405   FG   1949   Particularités épidémiologiques de la lèpre en Guyane Francaise [Epidemiological characteristics of leprosy in French Guiana]. *Inst Past Guy Ter L'In* 189, Apr. (7p.)
28.0406   FG   1950   Lutte antiamarile et lutte antipaludique en Guyane Francaise [Flight against yellow fever and malaria in French Guiana]. *Inst Past Guy Ter L'In* 213 (105p.)
28.0407   FG   1951   L'assistance sociale aux lépreux et à leurs familles [Social welfare for the lepers and their families]. *Arch Ins Past Guy* 241, Sept. (6p.)   [33]
28.0408   FG   1952   La fièvre jaune en Guyane Francaise [Yellow fever in French Guiana]. I: Rappel historique [Historical view]. *Arch Inst Past Guy* 266, July.   [5]   [*ACM*]
30.0070   FG   1953   Etude du problème de l'alimentation en Guyane Francaise [Study of the nutritional problem in French Guiana].
28.0409   FG   1953   La fièvre jaune en Guyane Francaise [Yellow fever in French Guiana]. II: Résultats de l'enquête épidémiologique de 1951 [Results of the 1951 epidemiological survey]. *Archs Inst Past Guy* 278, Feb. (19p.)   [5]   [*ACM*]

28.0410	FG	1954	La cinquiéme campagne de pulvérisations d'insecticides à effet remanent dans les habitations en Guyane Francaise [The fifth campaign of residual insecticide spraying of dwellings in French Guiana]. *Archs Inst Past Guy* 317, Feb. (68p.)
28.0411	FG	1954	Evolution de la lutte antipaludique en Guyane Francaise de 1950 à 1954 [Development of the fight against malaria in French Guiana from 1950 to 1954]. *Archs Inst Past Guy* 345, Nov. (8p.)
28.0412	FG	1954	Salmonellosis in French Guiana. *W I Med J* 3(4), Dec.: 277-278. [COL]
30.0071	FG	1955	Aspects nutritionnels de problèmes de pathologie guyanaise [Nutritional factors in the problems of Guianese pathology].
28.0413	FG	1955	La lutte antipaludique en Guyane Francaise [The fight against malaria in French Guiana]. I. La septième campagne de "dedetisation" [The seventh campaign of DDT spraying]. *Archs Inst Past Guy* 369, Aug. (75p.)
28.0414	FG	1955	Yellow fever control in French Guiana. *Caribbean* 8(9), Apr.: 196-197, 208. [COL]
28.0415	FG	1956	French Guiana malaria control. *Caribbean* 9(12), July: 270-271, 276. [COL]
28.0416	FG	1956	Influence de la lutte antipaludique sur la natalité, la mortinatalité et la mortalité infantile en Guyane Francaise [Influence of the fight against malaria on birthrate, stillbirth rate, and infantile mortality in French Guiana]. *B Soc Path Exot* 49(4), July-Aug.: 647-651. **[7,34]** [ACM]
28.0417	FG	1956	Influence du paludisme sur la natalité, mortinatalité et mortalité infantile [The influence of malaria on the birthrate, stillbirth rate, and infantile mortality]. *Revta Brasil Mala Do Trop* 8(4), Oct.: 541-544. **[7,34]** [COL]
28.0418	FG	1956	La lutte antipaludique en Guyane Francaise [The fight against malaria in French Guiana]. II. Notre huitième campagne de pulverisations d'insecticides à effet remanent dans les habitations [Our eighth campaign of residual insecticide spraying of dwellings]. *Archs Inst Past Guy* 404, Aug. (80p.)
28.0419	FG	1956	Natalité, mortinatalité, mortalité infantile et paludisme [Birthrate, stillbirth rate, infantile mortality, and malaria]. *Archs Inst Past Guy* 408, Sept. (5p.) **[7,34]**
30.0074	FG	1956	Sur l'avitaminose PP en Guyane Francaise [On avitaminosis PP in French Guiana].
28.0420	FG	1956	Le traitement suppressif du paludisme chez les immigrants en Guyane Francaise [Medical control of malaria among the immigrants in French Guiana]. *Archs Inst Past Guy* 17(397), June (4p.) **[18]** [ACM]
28.0421	FG	1965	Intoxication par la "Lépiote de Morgan" en Guyane Française [Poisoning by"Morgan's lepiote" in French Guiana). *B Soc Path Exot* 58(6), Nov.-Dec.: 1020-1025. [PS]
28.0422	FG	1966	Sur quelques composés chimiques doués de propriétés molluscicides et larvicides susceptibles d'utilisations practiques dans la lutte contre certains moustiques [On some chemical compounds having molluscoid and larvicidal properties which lend themselves to practical application in the fight against certain mosquitos]. *B Soc Path Exot* 59(6): 997-1002. **[54]** [PS]

28.0423   GD   1971   Sur la nécessité d'entreprendre en Guadeloupe une lutte effective contre la bilharziose intestinale à *S. mansoni* [On the necessity of beginning an efficient control against intestinal bilharziasis due to *S. mansoni* in Guadeloupe]. *B Soc Path Exot* 64(1), Jan.-Feb.: 71-79.
   [*PS*]

28.0424   GD   1972   Sur la lèpre en Guadeloupe [Leprosy in Guadeloupe]. *B Soc Path Exot* 65(1), Jan.-Feb.: 35-46.   [*PS*]

Floch, Hervé Alexandre & Abonnenc, E.

28.0425   FG   1946   Sur la lèpre en Guyane Francaise [Concerning leprosy in French Guiana]. III: Influence du traitement par l'huile de chaulmoogra [Results of chaulmoogra oil treatment]. *Inst Past Guy Ter L'In* 135, Sept. (11p.)   [*ACM*]

Floch, Hervé Alexandre & Camain, R.

28.0426   FG   1947   Maladies vénériennes autres que la syphilis en Guyane Francaise [Venereal diseases other than syphilis in French Guiana]. *Inst Past Guy Ter L'In* 165, Dec. (4p.)   [*ACM*]

Floch, Hervé Alexandre & Cornu, G.

35.0031   FG   1956   Problèmes de l'habitat à Cayenne. Le Casier sanitaire des immeubles [Housing problems in Cayenne. A sanitation register of the property].

Floch, Hervé Alexandre & Duchassin, M.

28.0427   FG   1965   La situation de l'endémie lépreuse en Guyane Française en 1965. [The status of leprous endemic disease in French Guiana in 1965]. *B Soc Path Exot* 58(3), May-June: 401-409.   [*PS*]

Floch, Hervé Alexandre; Durieux, C. & Koerber, R.

28.0428   FG   1953   Enquête épidémiologique sur la fièvre jaune en Guyane Francaise [Epidemiological survey of yellow fever in French Guiana]. *Ann Inst Past* 84(3), Mar.: 495-508.   [*ACM*]

Floch, Hervé Alexandre & Fauran, P.

28.0429   FG   1954   Lutte antipaludique et lutte antiamarile en Guyane Francaise. Les moustiques vecteurs du virus de la fièvre jaune en Guyane Francaise [The fight against malaria and yellow fever in French Guiana. Mosquito vectors of the yellow fever virus in French Guiana]. *Archs Inst Past Guy* 322, Apr. (67p.)   **[54]**

Floch, Hervé Alexandre & Kramer, René

28.0430   FG   1966   Présence de *Culex (M.) vomerifer* Komp 1932, *Culex (M.) portesi* Senevet et Abonnenc 1941 et *Culex (M.) cayennensis* Floch et Abonnenc 1945, en Guyane Française [The occurrence of *Culex (M.) vomerifer* Komp 1932, *Culex (M.) portesi* Senevet and Abonnenc 1941 and *Culex (M.) cayennensis* Floch and Abonnenc 1945 in French Guiana]. *B Soc Path Exot* 59(3), May-June: 384-387.
   [*PS*]

Floch, Hervé Alexandre & Lajudie, P. de

28.0431   FG   1942   Sur le paludisme à la Guyane Francaise et spécialement à Cayenne [On malaria in French Guiana, particularly in Cayenne]. *Inst Past Guy Ter L'In* 47, July (8p.)

28.0432   FG   1945   L'endémo-épidémie typhoïdique en Guyane Francaise. Sur le niveau moyen des agglutinines naturelles [Endemo-epidemic typhoid in French Guiana. On the standard method of natural agglutination]. *Inst Past Guy Ter L'In* 105, May (8p.)

28.0433   FG   1945   Sur la filariose à *W. bancrofti* en Guyane Francaise, la lymphangite endémique et l'éléphantiasis des pays chauds [On *W. bancrofti* filariasis in French Guiana, endemic lymphangitis and elephantiasis in tropical countries]. *Inst Past Guy Ter L'In* 109, Aug. (17p.)

28.0434   FG   1946   Sur la lèpre en Guyane Francaise [Regarding leprosy in French Guiana]. I. Généralités. Répartition par âge. Dépistage. Contamination [Generalities. Distribution by age. Case findings. Contamination]. *Inst Past Guy Ter L'In* 131, July (6p.)   [*ACM*]

28.0435   FG   1946   Sur la lèpre en Guyane Francaise [Regarding leprosy in French Guiana]. II. Incubation. Symptôme initial. Formes cliniques. Diagnostic. Evolution et pronostic. Syphilis et lèpre. Cause des décès [Incubation. Initial symptom. Clinical forms. Diagnosis. Evolution and prognosis. Syphilis and leprosy. Cause of decease]. *Inst Past Guy Ter L'In* 133, Aug. (10p.)   [*ACM*]

28.0436   FG   1946   Sur la syphilis en Guyane Francaise [Regarding syphilis in French Guiana]. *Inst Past Guy Ter L'In* 123, Mar. (4p.)   [*ACM*]

Floch, Hervé Alexandre; Riviérez, E. & Sureau, P.
30.0085   FG   1952   Pellagre et vitamine PP en Guyane Francaise [Pellagra and vitamin PP in French Guiana].

Floch, Hervé Alexandre; Riviérez, Maurice & Sureau, Pierre
30.0086   FG   1953   Sur la pellagre en Guyane Francaise [Concerning pellagra in French Guiana].

Flores, H.; Seakins, Anne; Brooke, O. G. & Waterlow, J. C.
28.0437   JM   1974   Serum and liver triglycerides in malnourished Jamaican children and fatty liver. *Am J Clin Nutr* 27(6), June: 610-614.   [*PS*]

Florey, Charles du V.; Ashcroft, M. T. & Miller, G. J.
28.0438   GU   1971   Blood pressure levels of Guyanese adults of African and Indian origin. *Am J Epidemiol* 94(5), Nov.: 419-424. **[11,12,27]**   [*PS*]

Florey, Charles du V.; Gerassimos, Michael M. & Cuadrado, Raul R.
28.0439   BA   1966   Report of a serological survey of the southern half of Eleuthera Island, Bahamas. *W I Med J* 15(2), June: 71-82.   [*PS*]

Florey, Charles du V.; McDonald, H.; Miall, W. E. & Milner, R. D. G.
28.0440   JM   1973   Serum lipids and their relation to blood glucose and cardio-vascular measurements in a rural population of Jamaican adults. *J Chronic Dis* 26(2), Feb.: 85-100.   [*ACM*]

Flu, P. C.
3.0184   SR   1922-23 Sanitaire verhoudingen in Suriname [Sanitary situations in Surinam].

Fonaroff, Arlene
30.0088   JM   1975   Cultural perceptions and nutritional disorders: a Jamaican case study.

Fonaroff, L. Schuyler

28.0441   TR   1966   BIOGEOGRAPHIC ASPECTS OF MALARIA IN TRINIDAD. Berkeley, University of California, Department of Geography: 67p.   **[27,56]**
                                                                                        [*AGS*]

28.0442   BB   1966   Geographic notes on the Barbados malaria epidemic. *Prof Geogr* 18(3), May: 155-163.   **[27,56]**   [*AGS*]

28.0443   JM   1968   ECOLOGICAL PARAMETERS OF THE KWASHIORKOR—MARASMUS SYNDROME IN JAMAICA. Berkeley, University of California, Department of Geography: 92p.   **[7,30]**   [*AGS*]

28.0444   TR   1968   The historical geography of malaria risk in Trinidad: three maps of change. *W I Med J* 17(1), March: 14-20.   **[27,56]**   [*PS*]

28.0445   TR   1968   Man and malaria in Trinidad: ecological perspectives on a changing health hazard. *Ann Assoc Am Geogr* 58(3), Sept.: 526-556.   **[20,27,54,56]**   [*COL*]

28.0446   TR   1972   The decline of malaria in Trinidad. *In* McGlashan, N. D., ed. MEDICAL GEOGRAPHY. London, Methuen and Co. Ltd.: 165-172.   **[7]**   [*PS*]

28.0447   BB   1973   Did Barbados import its malaria epidemic? *J Barb Mus Hist Soc* 34(3), March: 122-130.   **[5]**   [*NYP*]

Forde, H. McD. & Williams, H. M.

28.0448   BB   1960   Tetanus in Barbados. *W I Med J* 9(1), Mar.: 9-13   [*COL*]

Francis, A. G.

28.0449   TR   1938   A brief summary of common diseases in Trinidad. *Car Med J* 1(1): 55-62.   [*COL*]

28.0450   TR   1939   Some cases of interest. *Car Med J* 1(3): 234-244.   [*COL*]

Francis, Ettle

32.0214   JM   1970   Baccalaureate degree for West Indian nurses.

Francis, Oliver M.

28.0451   GU   1943   Social, economic and dietetic features of tuberculosis in British Guiana. *Br Gui Med Annual 1943* 26: 43-71.   **[8,30]**   [*ACM*]

28.0452   GU   1943   Tuberculin tests in British Guiana. *Br Gui Med Annual 1943* 26: 72-82.   [*ACM*]

28.0453   GU   1944   Tuberculosis in British Guiana. *Car Med J* 6(3): 183-190.   **[10]**
                                                                                        [*COL*]

28.0454   GU   1947   Comments on the state of the public health of British Guiana. *Br Gui Med Annual* 1-12.   [*RIS*]

Fraser, H. Aubrey

33.0074   BC   1974   The law and cannabis in the West Indies.

Frazer, A. C. et al.

28.0455   BC   1957   Proceedings of the Second Annual Scientific Meeting of the Caribbean Medical Research Committee, held in Trinidad on Apr. 6th, 7th, 1957. *W I Med J* 6(2), June: 133-140.   [*COL*]

28.0456   BC   1958   Standing Advisory Committee for Medical Research in the British Caribbean: proceedings of the Scientific Meeting Apr. 12th and 13th, 1958. *W I Med J* 7(2), June: 157-165.   [*COL*]

Fredericks, Marcel A. & Mundy, Paul

28.0457   GU   1967   Social backgrounds and some selected attitudes of physicians in a developing nation, their bearing on medical education for the Caribbean. *W I Med J* 16(4), Dec.: 216-221. **[32]**   [*PS*]

Fredericks, Marcel A.; Mundy, Paul & Lennon, John J.

28.0458   GU   1969   Los médicos en una nación en desarrollo: trasfondo social y actitudes [Doctors in a developing nation: social background and attitudes]. *América Indígena* 29(3), July: 699-709. **[20]**   [*NYP*]

Freitas, Q. B. de

28.0459   GU   1904   Notes on and classification of malarial fever cases treated in the Public Hospital, Georgetown. *Br Gui Med Annual* 13: 75-82.
     [*ACM*]

28.0460   GU   1909   Record of the work of the maternity ward of the Public Hospital, Georgetown, from June, 1905, to March, 1906, and January, 1908, to May, 1908. *Br Gui Med Annual 1908* 16: 26-28.   [*ACM*]

28.0461   GU   1933   Former contributors to the British Guiana Annual. *Br Gui Med Annual 1932* 25: 1-5.   [*ACM*]

28.0462   GU   1933   Notes on cardiac dilation. *Br Gui Med Annual 1932* 25: 70-73. **[11,12]**   [*ACM*]

28.0463   GU   1936   A retrospect of medical practice in British Guiana, 1900-1935. *Br Gui Med Annual 1936* 26: 148-152.   [*ACM*]

28.0464   GU   1940   Report of the Sub-committee of the Infant Welfare and Maternity League of British Guiana. *Car Med J* 2(4): 174-185.   [*COL*]

28.0465   GU   1940   Return of post mortem examinations made on coroner's order and classification of death from 1933 to 1935 in British Guiana. *Car Med J* 2(4): 191-192.   [*COL*]

37.0250   GU   1941   Notes on the trial of a nurse-midwife on the charge of murder held in the Criminal Court of Georgetown, Demarara, from 22nd April to 5th May, 1941.

28.0466   GU   1942   Some observations on the proposed scheme for British Guiana for the improvement of public health and sanitary measures. *Car Med J* 4(2): 58-61. **[33]**   [*COL*]

28.0467   GU   1943   Progress of the Medical and Public Health Services in British Guiana. *Br Gui Med Annual 1943* 26: 172-180.   [*ACM*]

28.0468   GU   1944   Review of the salient stages in the medical history of the colony from 1900-1944. *Timehri* 4th ser., 1(26), Nov.: 61-65.   [*AMN*]

3.0200   GU   1948   Early experiences of a government medical officer in British Guiana.

French, E. A. & Lehmann, H.

27.0063   JM   1971   Is haemoglobin G_a Philadelphia linked to alpha-thalassaemia?

Fros, J.

28.0469   SR   1954   Filariasis in Suriname. *Vox Guy* 1(1), May: 39-47.   [*RIS*]

28.0470   SR   1956   Filariasis in South American Indians in Surinam. *Docum Med Geogr Trop* 8(1), Mar.: 63-69. **[13]**   [*COL*]

Fry, L. & Rodin, P.

28.0471   SV   1966   Early yaws. *Br J Ven Dis* 42(1), March: 28-30.   [*PS*]

Fuente, L. A. de la

28.0472   CU   1973   De medische dienst van Shell Curaçao N.V. [The medical service of Shell Curaçao N.V.]. *In* Statius van Eps, L. W. & Luckman-Maduro, E., eds. VAN SCHEEPSCHIRURGIJN TOT SPECIALIST. Assen, The Netherlands, Van Gorcum & Comp. B.V.: 63-66. (Anjerpublikatie 15)   [*RILA*]

Fung-Kee-Fung, C. O.

28.0473   GU   1962   Observations on endometrioses in British Guiana and a suggested origin. *Car Med J* 24(1-4): 56-71.   [*COL*]

Gabuzda, Thomas G.

28.0474   JM   1975   Sickle cell leg ulcers: current pathophysiologic concepts. *Int J Dermatol* 14(5), June: 322-325. **[27]**   [*ACM*]

Gaikhorst, G.

28.0475   AR   1960   The presence of *Trypanosoma cruzi* on the island of Aruba and its importance to man. *Trop Geogr Med* 12(1), Mar.: 59-61.   [*COL*]

Gallagher, Bernadette A. & Miller, C. G.

28.0476   JM   1967   Acute glomerulonephritis in Jamaican children. *W I Med J* 16(1), March: 17-32.   [*PS*]

Gan, K. H.; Gani, K. S.; Hansen, A. L.; Suharto & Sulastri, D.

28.0477   AR   1971   Observations on the A2 (Hong Kong) 68—influenza epidemic of 1969-70 in Indonesia and Aruba (Netherlands Antilles). *J Hyg Epidemiol Microbiol Immunol* 15(3): 267-270.   [*PS*]

Gans, J. C. & Karbaat, J.

28.0478   SR   1967   Histoplasmosis in Dutch servicemen returning from Surinam. *Trop Geogr Med* 19(3), Sept.: 177-186. **[15]**   [*PS*]

Gardiner, J.

28.0479   JM   1966   Induction of labour up to thirty-six weeks. *W I Med J* 15(2), June: 108-111. **[34]**   [*PS*]

Gardner, C. C.

28.0480   JM   1956   The principle of central sterile supply and its application in the University College Hospital of the West Indies. *W I Med J* 5(4), Dec.: 231-239.   [*COL*]

28.0481   JM   1956   The surgical treatment of chronic duodenal ulcer in Jamaica. *W I Med J* 5(2), June: 90-96.   [*COL*]

Garrow, J. S.

30.0096   JM   1965   Total body-postassium in kwashiorkor and marasmus.

28.0482   JM   1966   "Kwashiorkor" and "marasmus" in Jamaican infants. *Archs Latam Nutr* 16(1), Sept.: 145-154. **[30]**   [*PS*]

30.0097   JM   1967   Loss of brain potassium in Kwashiorkor.

Garrow, J. S.; Fletcher, K. & Halliday, D.

30.0098   JM   1965   Body composition in severe infantile malnutrition.

Garrow, J. S.; Picou, D. & Waterlow, J. C.
30.0099   JM   1962   The treatment and prognosis of infantile malnutrition in Jamaican children.

Garrow, J. S. & Pike, M. C.
30.0100   JM   1967   The long-term prognosis of severe infantile malnutrition.
30.0101   JM   1967   The short-term prognosis of severe primary infantile malnutrition.

Geerdink, R. A.; Breel, P. M.; Sander, P. C. & Schillhorn-Van Veen, Joke M.
28.0483   SR   1973   Comparison of serum cholesterol values in Amerindians from Surinam with those of Dutch controls. *Atherosclerosis* 18(2), Sept.-Oct.: 173-178.   [13,27]   [*ACM*]

Gentilini, M.
28.0484   FC,FR   1971   Aspects épidémiologiques des migrants en France [Epidemiological aspects of migrants in France]. *B Inst Natn Sante* 26(2), March-April: 431-522.   [17,18]   [*ACM*]

Gentilini, M.; Danis, M.; Dürr, J. M. & Garabiol, B.
28.0485   FA,FR   1971   Traitement de l'ankylostomiase par l'association thiabendazole-lévamisole [Treatment of ancylostomiasis with a combination of thiabendazole-levamisole (200 cases)]. *B Soc Path Exot* 64(6), Nov.-Dec.: 891-900.   [18]   [*PS*]

Gentilini, M.; Richard-Lenoble, D.; Danis, M.; Ducosson, P. & Volkowa, V.
28.0486   FA,FR   1975   Les hémoglobinopathies chez l'adulte jeune, antillais, migrant en métropole (à propos de 1,000 électrophorèses) [Heminoglobino-pathies of young adults migrating from the Antilles to the metrop-olis (apropos of 1,000 cases of electrophoresis)]. *B Soc Path Exot* 68(2), March-April: 210-214.   [18]   [*PS*]

Gentle, G. H. K.
28.0487   TR   1956   Yellow fever vaccination programme: Trinidad, B.W.I.—1954/55. *Car Med J* 18(1-2): 13-18.   [*COL*]
28.0488   TR   1957   The significance of asymptomatic serum-positivity in Trinidad and Tobago with special reference to yaws. *W I Med J* 6(4), Dec.: 217-224.   [*COL*]
28.0489   JM   1965   Yaws survey—Jamaica, 1963. *Br J Ven Dis* 41(3), Sept.: 155-162.
                                                                      [*PS*]

George, Walter F.
28.0490   JM   1974   An approach to VD control based on a study in Kingston, Jamaica. *Br J Ven Dis* 50(3), June: 222-227.   [32,33]   [*ACM*]

Gervaise, Guy
28.0491   MT   1965   Maladie de Weber-Christian à form viscérale pure. Premier cas observé à la Martinique [The Weber-Christian syndrome in pure visceral form. First case observed in Martinique]. *J Med Bord Sud-Ouest* 142(6): 989-991.   [*PS*]

Gibbs, W. N.
27.0069   GC   1969   Hb A_2 and the diagnosis of β-thalassaemia trait.

Gibbs, W. N.; Cole, F. & McIver, C.

28.0492   JM   1970   Histiocytosis X—acute disseminated variant. *W I Med J* 19(4), Dec.: 212-218.   [*PS*]

Gibbs, W. N.; Ottey, F. & Dyer, H.

27.0070   JM   1972   Distribution of glucose-6-phosphate dehydrogenase phenotypes in Jamaica.

Gibson, Eunice

28.0493   BB   1945   The Barbados Nurses Association. *Am J Nurs* 45(1), Jan.: 16-17.
                                                                                    [*COL*]

Giglioli, George

28.0494   GU   1923   Ankylostome inspection in Mackenzie, Rio Demerara (Report on carbon tetrachloride in the treatment of hook worm). *Br Gui Med Annual 1923* 23: 151-173.   [*ACM*]

28.0495   GU   1926   Report on hookworm survey carried out at Mackenzie and Akyma. *Br Gui Med Annual 1925* 24: 34-36.   [*ACM*]

28.0496   GU   1933   Statistical data on the incidence of various malarial parasites in the river areas of the interior. *Br Gui Med Annual 1932* 25: 98-102. **[54]**   [*ACM*]

28.0497   GU   1939   Notes on health conditions on the southern Rupununi savannahs. *In* REPORT OF THE BRITISH GUIANA COMMISSION TO THE PRESIDENT'S ADVISORY COMMITTEE ON POLITICAL REFUGEES. Washington, D.C., [no. 6.] (10p.)   [*AGS*]

28.0498   GU   1941   Malaria in British Guiana. *Car Med J* 3(1): 49-51.   [*COL*]

28.0499   GU   1946   Malaria and agriculture in British Guiana. *Timehri* 4th ser., 1(27), July: 46-52. **[43]**

28.0500   GU   1948   Immediate and long-term economic effects accruing from the control of mosquito-transmitted diseases in British Guiana. *Timehri* 4th ser., 1(28), Dec.: 5-8. **[41]**

28.0501   GU   1951   The influence of geological formation and soil characteristics on the distribution of malaria and its mosquito carrier in British Guiana. *Timehri* 4th ser., 1(30), Nov.: 48-56. **[53,54,57]**

28.0502   GU   1956   Medical services on the sugar estates of British Guiana. *Timehri* 4th ser., 1(35), Oct.: 7-31. **[42,43]**

28.0503   GU   1958   The mosquito and sand-fly nuisance in Georgetown and its suburbs. *Timehri* 4th ser., no. 37, Sept.: 7-11. **[36,54]**   [*AMN*]

30.0102   GU   1958   An outline of the nutritional situation on the sugar estates of British Guiana in respect to the eradication of malaria: recent developments in the production of green vegetables and fruit by individual units.

28.0504   GU   1958   Post-mortem and histo-pathological notes on twenty fatal cases of *Bact. Paratyphosum C* infection in British Guiana. *W I Med J* 7(1), Mar.: 29-38.   [*COL*]

28.0505   GU   1962   Trends in the incidence of hookworm and ascaris infestation in British Guiana. *W I Med J* 11(1), Mar.: 30-39.   [*COL*]

28.0506   GU   1972   Changes in the pattern of mortality following the eradication of hyperendemic malaria from a highly susceptible community. *B WHO* 46(2): 181-202. **[7,27,56]**   [*PS*]

28.0507   GU   1974   The impact of malaria eradication on patterns of natality, mortality, and morbidity on the sugar plantations of the coastlands of Guyana, South America. *W I Med J* 23(3), Sept.: 174-187. **[7,27,56]**   [*PS*]

Giglioli, George; Ch'en, Wan-i; Howell, P. & Marchant, D.

28.0508   GU   1974   Malaria eradication under continental equatorial conditions in Guyana. *W I Med J* 23(1), March: 25-34.   [*PS*]

Giglioli, George; Dyrting, A. E.; Rutten, Frans J. & Gentle, G. H. K.

28.0509   GU   1967   Photo-allergic dermatitis during a chloroquinized salt anti-malarial campaign in Guyana. *Trans Roy Soc Trop Med Hyg* 61(3): 313-330.
[*PS*]

Giglioli, George; Rutten, Frans J. & Ramjattan, S.

28.0510   GU   1967   Interruption of malaria transmission by chloroquinized salt in Guyana (with observations on a chloroquine-resistant strain of *Plasmodium falciparum*). *B WHO* 36(2): 283-301.   [*PS*]

Gilkes, C. D.; Kellett, F. R. S. & Gillette, H. P. S.

28.0511   TR   1956   Yellow fever in Trinidad and the development of resistance in Aedes Aegypti Linn, to D.D.T. formulations. *W I Med J* 5(2), June: 73-89.   [*COL*]

Gillette, H. P. S.

28.0512   TR   1945   The progress of malaria control measures in Trinidad and Tobago with special references to county St. David. *Car Med J* 4-6: 212-230.
[*COL*]

28.0513   TR   1949   A short review of DDT residual house spraying for malaria control in Trinidad 1945-1948. *Car Med J* 11(1): 6-26.   [*COL*]

28.0514   BC   1960   Comments of Dr. Thomas's report of the chest service for the Federation of the West Indies. *Car Med J* 22(1-4): 16-19. **[38]**
[*COL*]

Gilmour, John

28.0515   JM   1969   Colorectal cancers in Jamaica: a review (1958-1967). *Dis Colon Rectum* 12(5), Sept.-Oct.: 357-363.   [*PS*]

Gilmour, Mavis G.

28.0516   JM   1965   Some aspects of appendicitis. *W I Med J* 14(1), March: 53-56. [*PS*]

Gilmour, W. Santon

28.0517   BB   [n.d.]   TUBERCULOSIS SURVEY AND RECOMMENDATIONS. [Bridgetown?] Barbados. Advocate Co., 19p.   [*RIS*]

28.0518   BC   1944   Tuberculosis survey in the British West Indies. *Car Med J* 6(3): 171-177.   [*COL*]

Giraud, R.

28.0519   MT   1965   Les lesions pseudo-tumorales de caecum [Pseudo-tumorous cecal lesions]. *J Med Bor Sud-Ouest* 142(6), June: 970-975.   [*PS*]

Giroud, P.; Capponi, M.; Escudié, A.; Fauran, P. & Morel, P. C.

28.0520   GD   1966   Isolement d'une souche de R. conori de larves d'amblyomma variegatum de la Guadeloupe [Isolation of a strain of "Rickettsia conori" from ticks in Guadeloupe]. *B Soc Path Exot* 59(3), May-June: 283-286.   [*PS*]

Godfrey, J. E.

28.0521　GU　1904　A few introductory remarks on the regulations passed by the recent Quarantine Conference. *Br Gui Med Annual* 13: 1-23.　**[37,48]**
　　　　　　　　　　　　　　　　　　　　　　　　　　　　　　　　　[*ACM*]

28.0522　GU　1913　Tuberculosis in British Guiana. *Br Gui Med Annual 1912* 19: 65-74.
　　　　　　　　　　　　　　　　　　　　　　　　　　　　　　　　　[*ACM*]

Goerke, Heinz

28.0523　JM　1956　The life and scientific works of Dr. John Quier, practitioner of physic and surgery, Jamaica: 1738-1822. *W I Med J* 5(1), Mar.: 23-27.　**[5]**　　　　　　　　　　　　　　　　　　　　[*COL*]

Goethals, H. W.

28.0524　BC　1968　Caribbean report. *Wld Heal* Dec.: 30-35.　　　　　　[*RIS*]

Goldberg, J. & Sutherland, E. S.

28.0525　JM　1963　Studies on Gonorrhoea. I: Some social and sexual parameters of male patients in Kingston, Jamaica. *W I Med J* 12(4), Dec.: 228-246.　**[37]**　　　　　　　　　　　　　　　[*COL*]

Golding, J. S. R.

28.0526　JM　1974　Changing incidence and pattern of trauma in Jamaica. *Br Med J* 4(5940), Nov. 9: 333-335.　　　　　　　　　　　[*PS*]

28.0527　JM　1974　Twenty-five years of orthopaedic surgery. *W I Med J* 23(3), Sept.: 148-150.　　　　　　　　　　　　　　　　　　　[*PS*]

Golding, J. S. R. & Stafford, J. L.

28.0528　JM　1955　Christmas disease (haemophilia B.). *W I Med J* 4(3), Sept.: 188-192.
　　　　　　　　　　　　　　　　　　　　　　　　　　　　　　　　　[*COL*]

Golding, J. S. R. & Weston, Peter M.

28.0529　JM　1958　Skeletal tuberculosis in Jamaica. *W I Med J* 7(1): 21-28.　[*COL*]

Golding, John

28.0530　JM　1961　The problem of treating the disabled child. *W I Med J* 10(3), Sept.: 172-174.　　　　　　　　　　　　　　　　　　　[*COL*]

Gomes, G. A.

28.0531　GU　1934　Some medical worthies of the past in the Colony: notes and reminiscenses. *Timehri* 4th ser., no. 25, Dec.: 31-37.　**[5]**　　[*RIS*]

Gordon, C. C. & Grant, L. S.

28.0532　JM　1954　A preliminary survey of fungus infections in Jamaica. *W I Med J* 3(2), June: 95-97.　　　　　　　　　　　　　　　[*COL*]

Gore, Don

28.0533　JM　1962　Hidradenitis suppurativa. *W I Med J* 11(4), Dec.: 249-252.　[*COL*]

28.0534　JM　1965　Vagectomy with drainage procedure for duodenal ulceration. *W I Med J* 14(4), Dec.: 247-256.　　　　　　　　　　　[*PS*]

Gosden, Minnie

28.0535　TR　1938　An account of tuberculosis lesions found in post mortem examinations on children in Trinidad. *Car Med J* 1(1): 88-95.　[*COL*]

Gourlay, R. John
28.0536   JM   1961[?]   The importance of health in a developing community. *In* Cumper, George, ed. REPORT OF THE CONFERENCE ON SOCIAL DEVELOPMENT IN JAMAICA. Kingston, Standing Committee on Social Services, p.101-104.   **[31]**   *[RIS]*
30.0104   JM   1963   Haemoglobin levels in relation to dietary iron and protein in a semiurban community in Jamaica.

Gourlay, R. John & Hall, Ruth
28.0537   JM   1966   Ampicillin in the treatment of a chronic faecal excretor of *S. typhosa. J Trop Med Hyg* 69(4), April: 117-119.   *[PS]*

Gourlay, R. John & Marsh, Monica
28.0538   JM   1965   An outbreak of yaws in a suburban community in Jamaica. *Am J Trop Med Hyg* 14(5), Sept.: 777-779.   *[PS]*

Grace, A. W. & Grace, Feiga Berman
28.0539   GU,SK   1931   RESEARCHES IN BRITISH GUIANA, 1926-1928 ON THE BACTERIAL COMPLICATIONS OF FILARIASIS AND THE ENDEMIC NEPHRITIS; WITH A CHAPTER ON EPIDEMIC ABSCESS AND CELLULITIS IN ST. KITTS, BRITISH WEST INDIES. London, London School of Hygiene and Tropical Medicine, 75p. (Memoir series no. 3.)   *[AGS]*

Grant, Louis Strathmore
28.0540   JM   1956   An analysis and interpretation of some public health laboratory reports, Jamaica, B.W.I. (1940-1954). *W I Med J* 5(2), June: 97-112.   *[COL]*
28.0541   JM   1956   Modern trends in preventive medicine in the Caribbean: a review. *W I Med J* 5(1), Mar.: 44-58.   *[COL]*
28.0542   JM   1958   A bacteriological analysis of urinary infections (University College Hospital of the West Indies). *W I Med J* 7(4), Dec.: 285-290.   *[COL]*
28.0543   JM   1961   A serological survey for Q. fever antibodies in man and animals in Jamaica, West Indies. *W I Med J* 10(4), Dec.: 234-239.   *[COL]*
32.0251   BC   1966   Training for medicine in the West Indies.

Grant, Louis Strathmore & Anderson, S. E.
28.0544   BC   1955   Medical care insurance. Pt. I: The approach in developing a programme for the Caribbean. *W I Med J* 4(2), June: 109-118; 4(3), Sept.: 169-172.   **[49]**   *[COL]*
28.0545   BC   1955   The problem of medical care in the Caribbean. *W I Med J* 4(2), June: 105-108.   **[33]**   *[COL]*

Grant, Louis Strathmore; Beck, J. W.; Chen, W. N. & Belle, E. A.
28.0546   JM   1963   A survey of parasitic infection in two communities in Jamaica and a drug trial on positive cases. *W I Med J* 12(3), Sept.: 185-193.   *[COL]*

Grant, Louis Strathmore; Been, T. E.; Bezjak, V. & Belle, E. A.
28.0547   JM   1965   The microbiology of diseases in Jamaican children. *W I Med J* 14(1), March: 63-72.   *[PS]*

Grant, Louis Strathmore & Belle, E. A.
28.0548   JM   1966   Role of insects in the transmission of virus disease in Jamaica. *Inf B Scient Res Coun* 6(4), March: 110-114.   **[54]**   *[RIS]*

Grant, Louis Strathmore; Belle, E. A. & Ramprashad, C.

28.0549   DM,GC   1968   The effectiveness of CI-433 versus enter-vioform in the control of diarrhoeal disease. *W I Med J* 17(1), March: 31-34.   [*PS*]

Grant, Louis Strathmore & Bras, G.

28.0550   JM   1957   Leptospirosis in Jamaica. *W I Med J* 6(2), June: 129-132.   [*COL*]

Grant, Louis Strathmore & Caselitz, F.-H.

28.0551   JM   1954   Preliminary survey of Salmonella types in Jamaica. *W I Med J* 3(3), Sept.: 201-206.   [*COL*]

28.0552   JM   1954   A preliminary survey of the occurrence of typhoid vi-phage types and biochemical types in the British Caribbean territories with special reference to Jamaica. *W I Med J* 3(3), Sept.: 145-152.

                                                                        [*COL*]

Grant, Louis Strathmore & Chen, W.

28.0553   JM   1965   Staphylococcal infection in the University Hospital of the West Indies. *W I Med J* 14(2), June: 96-103.   [*PS*]

Grant, Louis Strathmore; Chen, W. N. & Urquhart, A. E.

28.0554   JM   1964   The epidemiology of leptospirosis in Jamaica (preliminary findings). *W I Med J* 13(2), June: 90-96.   [*COL*]

Grant, Louis Strathmore; Gracey, L. & Clark, Betty M.

28.0555   JM   1957   The prevalence of salmonella, shigella and typhoid phage types in Jamaica. *W I Med J* 6(4), Dec.: 233-236.   [*COL*]

Grant, Louis Strathmore & Peat, A. A.

28.0556   JM   1957   The epidemiology of the first poliomyelitis epidemic (Jamaica) 1954. *W I Med J* 6(4), Dec.: 257-271.   [*COL*]

Grantham-McGregor, Sally M. & Back, E. H.

30.0105   JM   1970   Breast-feeding in Kingston, Jamaica.
30.0106   JM   1970   A note on infant feeding in Kingston.
28.0557   JM   1971   Gross motor development in Jamaican infants. *Dev Med Child Neurol* 13(1), Feb.: 79-87.   [11,27]   [*PS*]

Grantham-McGregor, Sally M. & Desai, Patricia

27.0073   JM   1973   Head circumferences of Jamaican infants.
28.0558   JM   1975   A home-visiting intervention programme with Jamaican mothers and children. *Dev Med Child Neutrol* 17(5), Oct.: 605-613.   [9] [*PS*]

Grantham-McGregor, Sally M.; Desai, Patricia & Milner, P. F.

28.0559   JM   1974   Haematological levels in Jamaican infants. *Arch Dis Childh* 49(7), July: 525-530.   [*PS*]

Grantham-McGregor, Sally M. & Hawke, W. A.

28.0560   JM   1971   Developmental assessment of Jamaican infants. *Dev Med Child Neurol* 13(5), Oct.: 582-589.   [11,27]   [*PS*]

Gray, R. H.

28.0561   JM   1971   Clinical features of homozygous SS disease in Jamaican children. *W I Med J* 20(1), March: 60-68.   [27]   [*PS*]

Greenbaum, D. M.

28.0562   BA   1968   Ascariasis. *Med Ann DC* 37(8), Aug.: 405-410 passim.   [*PS*]

Grewal, N.

28.0563   GU   1959   Surgical treatment of peptic ulcer in British Guiana. *W I Med J* 8(4), Dec.: 262-266.   [*COL*]

Grewal, Nicholas

28.0564   GU   1966   Bilateral congenital dislocation of head of radius with brachy-dactylia in British Guiana case report. *W I Med J* 15(3), Sept.: 147-149.   [*PS*]

Griffin, Philip Norman

28.0565   MS   1960   Tuberculosis in Montserrat. *Car Med J* 22(1-4): 114-115.   [*COL*]

Griffiths, Bertie B.

28.0566   JM   1972   COMPARISON OF TWO HUMAN PATHOGENIC STRAINS WITH A COMMENSAL STRAIN OF *Herpes simplex* VIRUS ISOLATED AT THE UNIVERSITY HOSPITAL OF THE WEST INDIES. Ph.D. dissertation, University of the West Indies.

Griffiths, Bertie B.; Grant, Louis S.; Minott, Owen D. & Belle, Edward A.

28.0567   JM   1968   An epidemic of dengue-like illness in Jamaica—1963. *Am J Trop Med Hyg* 17(4), July: 584-589.   [*PS*]

Gueri, Miguel

28.0568   JM   1970   The leg ulcer problem in Jamaica. *W I Med J* 19(4), Dec.: 221-227. **[27]**   [*PS*]

Gueri, Miguel & Serjeant, G. R.

28.0569   JM   1970   Leg ulcers in sickle-cell anaemia. *Trop Geogr Med* 22(2), June: 155-160. **[27]**   [*PS*]

Gueri, Miguel; Van Devanter, S.; Serjeant, B. E. & Serjeant, G. R.

28.0570   JM   1975   Oral zinc sulphate treatment of chronic non-sickle cell ulcers in Jamaica. *W I Med J* 24(1), March: 26-29.   [*PS*]

Guerra, Francisco

28.0571   GC   1966   The influence of disease on race, logistics and colonization in the Antilles. *J Trop Med Hyg* 69(2), Feb.: 23-35. **[7,27,56]**   [*PS*]

Guilbride, P. D. L.

28.0572   GC   1952   Veterinary public health: the importance of animal disease to public health in the Caribbean with special reference to Jamaica. I. Tuberculosis and brucellosis. *W I Med J* 1(2), Apr.: 105-137. **[62]**
          [*COL*]

28.0573   GC   1952   Veterinary public health: the importance of animal disease to public health in the Caribbean with special reference to Jamaica. II. Anthrax; tetanus leptospirosis (Weil's disease). *W I Med J* 1(3), Sept.: 291-316. **[62]**   [*COL*]

28.0574   GC   1953   Veterinary public health: the importance of animal disease to public health in the Caribbean with special reference to Jamaica. III. Virus infections. Rabies and paralytic rabies. *W I Med J* 2(1), Mar.: 11-36. **[62]**   [*COL*]

28.0575	GC	1953	Veterinary public health: the importance of animal disease to public health in the Caribbean with special reference to Jamaica. IV. Fungus infections. Sylvatic plague and salmonellosis. *W I Med J* 2(2), June: 135-154. **[62]** [*COL*]
28.0576	GC	1953	Veterinary public health: the importance of animal disease to public health in the Caribbean with special reference to Jamaica. V. Parasitic infections. *W I Med J* 2(3), Sept.: 205-223. **[62]** [*COL*]
28.0577	GC	1953	Veterinary public health: the importance of animal disease to public health in the Caribbean with special reference to Jamaica. VI. Milkborne diseases. Other zoonoses. General summary. Additions. *W I Med J* 2(4), Dec. 259-268. **[62]** [*COL*]

Gunness, Robert N.

28.0578	TR	1967	Rehabilitation of the disabled in Trinidad and Tobago. *Car Med J* 29(1-4): 42-71. [*PS*]

Guppy, P. Lechmere

52.0059	TR	1922	A naturalist in Trinidad and Tobago.

Haas, R. A. de

28.0579	SR	1971	Studies on the distribution of polioviruses in Surinam. *Arch Ges Virusforsch* 33(1-2): 72-76. [*PS*]

Haas, R. A. de & Arron-Leeuwin, A. E.

28.0580	SR	1975	Arboviruses isolated from mosquitos and man in Surinam. *Trop Geogr Med* 27(4), Dec.: 409-412. **[54]** [*PS*]

Haas, R. A. de; Jonkers, A. H. & Heinemann, D. W.

28.0581	SR	1966	Kwatta virus, a new agent isolated from *Culex* mosquitoes in Surinam. *Am J Trop Med Hyg* 15(6), Nov.: 954-957. [*PS*]

Haas, R. A. de & Kruyf, H. A. M. de

28.0582	SR	1971	Isolation of Guama-group viruses in Surinam during 1967 and 1968. *Trop Geogr Med* 23(3), Sept.: 268-271. [*PS*]

Haas, R. A. de; Oostburg, B. F. J.; Sitalsing, A. D. & Bellot, S. M.

28.0583	SR	1971	Isolation of yellow fever virus from a human liver obtained by autopsy in Surinam. *Trop Geogr Med* 23(1), March: 59-63. [*PS*]

Habib, George G.

28.0584	TR	1962	Aseptic meningitis and acute encephalitis in Trinidad, West Indies. *W I Med J* 11(1), Mar.: 4-11. [*COL*]
28.0585	TR	1962	Neurosyphilis (clinical experience in the diagnosis and treatment). *W I Med J* 11(2), June: 100-116. [*COL*]
28.0586	TR	1964	Nutritional vitamin B12 deficiency among Hindus. *Trop Geogr Med* 16(3), Sept.: 206-215. **[12,30]** [*COL*]

Hadel, Richard E.

28.0587	BZ	1974	Builders of Belize (3): Nurse Seay. *National Stud* 2(1), January: 8-11. **[5]** [*RIS*]

Hall, J. A. S.

28.0588	JM	1961	The role of infection in myelomatosis. *W I Med J* 10(4), Dec.: 240-246. [*COL*]

28.0589	JM	1963	Diphtheritic pseudo-tables. *W I Med J* 12(1), Mar.: 47-49. [*COL*]
28.0590	JM	1963	Plasma fibrinogen in cerebral catastrophes: a preliminary report. *W I Med J* 12(2), June: 124-127. [*COL*]
28.0591	JM	1967	Myasthenia Gravis in Kingston, Jamaica. *W I Med J* 16(1), March: 51-56. [*PS*]

Hall, J. St. Elmo; Sandison, J. W.; Sivapragasam, S. & Ling, J.

| 28.0592 | JM | 1972 | Elective Caesarean section and haemodynamic studies in a case of "tight" mitral stenosis. *W I Med J* 21(4), Dec.: 231-235.   [*PS*] |

Hall, John S.

| 28.0593 | JM | 1969 | Facial palsy: a multifactorial entity. *W I Med J* 18(4), Dec.: 231-234.   [*PS*] |
| 28.0594 | JM | 1969 | Primary hepatoma. *W I Med J* 18(2), June: 112-115.   [*PS*] |

Halley; Kuhlmann; LeMaistre & Nègre

| 28.0595 | GD | 1965 | Possibilités actuelles du radio-diagnostic par les substances de contraste en Guadeloupe [Present possibilities of X-ray diagnosis with contrast media in Guadeloupe]. *J Med Bord Sud-Ouest* 142(6), June: 1023-1025.   [*PS*] |

Halliday, D.

| *30.0112* | JM | 1967 | Chemical composition of the whole body and individual tissues of two Jamaican children whose death resulted primarily from malnutrition. |

Hamilton, Gertrude

| 28.0596 | JM | 1960 | The University College Hospital Domiciliary Midwifery Service. Pt. I: A follow-up survey of eighty patients. *W I Med J* 9(1), Mar.: 17-21.   [*COL*] |

Haneveld, G. T.

28.0597	CU	1965	Kaleidoscoop van de gezondheid op Curaçao [Kaleidoscope of the health situation on Curaçao]. *Schakels* NA42: 6-8. [*NYP*]
5.0362	NA	1973	De Antilliaanse geneesheer [The Antillean doctor].
54.0439	NA	1973	Giftige dieren [Poisonous animals].

Harewood, Jack & Heath, K.

| 28.0598 | TR | 1967 | Recent trends in infectious and degenerative diseases as causes of death in Trinidad Tobago. *Car Med J* 29: 79-89.   [*PS*] |

Harkness, J. W. P.

| 28.0599 | BC | 1949 | Montego Bay Conference report. E: Report of the Fourth Conference of Heads of British West Indian Medical Departments. *Car Med J* 11(2): 77-94.   [*COL*] |
| 28.0600 | BC | 1950 | Some aspects of public health progress in the British Caribbean territories during the period 1947-50. *Car Med J* 12(5): 178-189.   [*COL*] |

Harland, W. A.; Richards, R. & Goldberg, I. J.

| 28.0601 | JM | 1971 | Reduced thyroid activity in Jamaicans. *J Endocrinol* 49(3), March: 537-544.   [*PS*] |

Harney, Lenore

30.0113   **KNA**   1958   The effect of additional dietary skimmed milk on the nutrition of
children of the colony of St. Kitts Nevis Anguilla using deaths from
malnutrition in the age-group 1-4 years as indicator.

28.0602   **BB**   1965   The problem of gonorrhoea control in Barbados. *W I Med J* 14(3),
Sept.: 154-157.   [*PS*]

Harris, M.

28.0603   **JM**   1972   The clinical and pathological features of dissecting aneurysms of
the aorta in Jamaica. *W I Med J* 21(1), March: 40-44.   [*PS*]

Harrison, John B.

28.0604   **GU**   1926   A report on the working of septic tanks at various properties in
Georgetown as indicated by the chemical examination of their
effluents. *Br Gui Med Annual 1925* 24: 1-28.   [*ACM*]

Harry, G. V.

28.0605   **JM**   1947   Gastro-enterostomy from the economic viewpoint: a plea for its
more extensive use, with a review of 104 cases. *Car Med J* 9(1-2):
21-31.   [*COL*]

Hart, Clinton; Lindo, Vernon & Fletcher, Douglas

28.0606   **JM**   1967   The Hart Report. Report of the committee appointed to inquire into
the terms and conditions of service of nurses in the employment of
the Jamaican government. *Jam Nurse* 7(2), Aug.-Sept.: 24-30.
[*AJN*]

Hartz, Ph. H.

28.0607   **CU**   1948   De geneeskunde [The medical science]. *In* Oranje en de zes
Caraïbische parelen. Amsterdam, J. H. de Bussy: 170-175.
[*UCLA*]

28.0608   **CU**   1948   Het St. Elisabeth's Gasthuis [St. Elisabeth's Hospital]. *In* Oranje en
de zes Caraïbische parelen. Amsterdam, J. H. de Bussy: 176-178.
[*UCLA*]

Hartz, Philip H.

28.0609   **CU**   1950   The incidence of sarcoma, leucaemia and allied diseases in the
native population of Curacao, N.W.I. *Docum Ned Indo Morbis Trop*
2(2), June: 159-165.   [*COL*]

Hartz, Philip H. & Sar, A. van der

28.0610   **CU**   1946   Occurrence of rheumatic carditis in the native population of
Curacao, Netherlands West Indies. *Archs Path* 41(1), Jan.: 32-36.
[*COL*]

Hassall, C. H. & Reyle, K.

28.0611   **JM**   1955   The toxicity of the ackee (*Blighia sapida*) and its relationship to the
vomiting sickness of Jamaica. *W I Med J* 4(2), June: 83-90.   **[60]**
[*COL*]

Hassell, T. A.; Renwick, S. & Stuart, K. L.

28.0612   **BB**   1972   Rheumatic fever and rheumatic heart disease in Barbados: detection and prophylaxis. *Br Med J* 3(5823), Aug. 12: 387-389.   [*PS*]

Hay, David M.

28.0613 JM 1969 The mortality of vulva carcinoma. *W I Med J* 18(3), Sept.: 161-166.
[*PS*]

28.0614 JM 1973 Amniotic fluid analysis for the prediction of foetal maturity. *W I Med J* 22(1), March: 20-23. [*PS*]

Hay, David M. & Boyd, John J.

28.0615 JM 1973 A comparative study of the obstetric performance of the adolescent Jamaican primigravida. *W I Med J* 22(2), June: 84-92. [*PS*]

28.0616 JM 1973 A study of the obstetric performance of the adolescent Jamaican primigravida. *Am J Obstet Gynec* 116(1), May 1: 34-38. [*ACM*]

Hay, David M. & Cole, F. M.

28.0617 JM 1969 Primary invasive carcinoma of the vulva in Jamaica. *J Obstet Gynaec Br Commonw* 76(9), Sept.: 821-830. [*PS*]

Hayes, J. A.

27.0082 JM 1969 Distribution of bronchial gland measurements in a Jamaican population.

28.0618 JM 1970 Racial, occupational and environmental factors in relation to emphysema in Jamaica. *Chest* 57(2), Feb.: 136-140. **[8,27]** [*PS*]

Hayes, J. A. & Lovell, H. G.

28.0619 JM 1966 Heart weight of Jamaicans. Autopsy study of normal cases and cases of hypertension and chronic lung disease. *Circulation* 33(3), March: 450-454. **[11,27]** [*PS*]

Hayes, J. A. & Ragbeer, M. M. S.

28.0620 JM 1966 Deaths from amoebiasis. *W I Med J* 15(3), Sept.: 155-159. [*PS*]

Hayes, J. A. & Summerell, J. M.

28.0621 JM 1963 Emphysema in Jamaica: a preliminary report. *W I Med J* 12(1), Mar.: 34-38. [*COL*]

28.0622 JM 1966 Myocarditis in Jamaica. *Br Heart J* 28(2): 172-179. [*PS*]

28.0623 JM 1969 Emphysema in a non-industrialized tropical island. *Thorax* 24(5), Sept.: 623-625. [*PS*]

Hayes, J. S.; Persaud, M. P. & Omess, P. J.

28.0624 TR 1975 Post-streptococcal glomerulonephritis in North Trinidad. *Trop Geogr Med* 27(3), Sept.: 253-256. [*PS*]

Hayes, John S. A.

28.0625 TR 1967 A case of diabetic neuropathy. *Car Med J* 29(1-4): 75-78. [*PS*]

Hearn, C. E.

28.0626 JM 1968 Bagassosis—an epidemiological, environmental and clinical survey. *Br J Indus Med* 25, Oct.: 267-282. **[42]** [*PS*]

Hearn, C. E. & Keir, W.

28.0627 TR 1971 Nail damage to spray operators exposed to paraquat. *Br J Indus Med* 28(4), Oct.: 399-403. **[42]** [*PS*]

Heinemann, Deryck Waldemar

28.0628   SR   1971   Epidemiologie en bestrijding van schistosomiasis in Suriname [Epidemiology and control of schistosomiasis in Surinam]. Enkhuizen, The Netherlands, Drukkerij Th. Visser N.V.: 107p. (Dissertation, Rijksuniversiteit Leiden)   **[54]**   [*RILA*]

Helminiak, Thomas Walter

28.0629   SL   1972   The sugar-bananas shift of St. Lucia, West Indies: bilharzia and malaria disease causal linkages. Ph.D. dissertation, University of Wisconsin: 319p.   **[27,38]**   [*PhD*]

Hemmes, J.

28.0630   NA   1973   Infectie-ziekten: algemene inleiding [Infectious-diseases: general introduction]. *In* Statius van Eps, L. W. & Luckman-Maduro, E., eds. Van scheepschirurgijn tot specialist. Assen, The Netherlands, Van Gorcum & Comp. B.V.: 120-122 (Anjerpublikatie 15).
                                                                    [*RILA*]

Henry, Joseph L.

28.0631   JM   1975   Prevention and control of dental disease in Jamaica. *J Natn Med Assoc* 67(4), July: 294-297.   [*ACM*]

Henry, M. U.

28.0632   TR   1963   The haemoglobinopathies in Trinidad. *Car Med J* 25(1-4): 26-40.   **[27]**   [*COL*]

30.0116   GC   1973   The role of nutritionists and dietitians in Caribbean health services.

Henry, M. U. & Poon-King, T.

28.0633   TR   1961   Blood groups in diabetes (a preliminary survey in South Trinidad). *W I Med J* 10(3), Sept.: 156-160.   [*COL*]

Hernández-Morales, Federico

28.0634   GC   1965   Intestinal disorders in the Caribbean. *In* Wilgus, A. Curtis, ed. The Caribbean: its health problems. Gainesville, University of Florida Press: 152-160. (Caribbean Conference Series 1, Vol. 15)   [*RIS*]

Hilburg, Carlos J.

28.0635   GC   1965   Water and sewage problems in the Caribbean. *In* Wilgus, A. Curtis, ed. The Caribbean: its health problems. Gainesville, University of Florida Press: 97-109. (Caribbean Conference Series 1, Vol. 15)   **[43]**   [*RIS*]

Hill, A. Edward

28.0636   TR   1956   Dengue and related fevers in Trinidad and Tobago. *Car Med J* 18(3-4): 80-85.   [*COL*]

28.0637   TT   1965   Dengue and related fevers in Trinidad and Tobago. *Car Med J* 27(1-4): 91-96.   [*ACM*]

Hill, Kenneth R.

28.0638   JM   1952   The vomiting sickness of Jamaica: a review. *W I Med J* 1(3), Oct.: 243-264.   [*COL*]

28.0639   JM   1953   Non-specific factors in the epidemiology of yaws. *W I Med J* 2(3), Oct.: 155-183.   [*COL*]

Hill, Kenneth R.; Bras, G. & Clearkin, K. P.

28.0640   JM   1955   Acute toxic hypoglycaemia occurring in the vomiting sickness of Jamaica: morbid anatomical aspects. *W I Med J* 4(2), June: 91-104.
[COL]

Hill, Kenneth R.; Rhodes, Katerina; Stafford, J. L. & Aub, R.

28.0641   JM   1951   Liver disease in Jamaican children (serous hepatosis). *W I Med J* 1(1), Sept.: 49-63.
[COL]

Hill, Kenneth R.; Still, W. J. S. & McKinney, Brian

28.0642   JM   1967   Jamaican cardiomyopathy. *Br Heart J* 29(4): 594-601.   [PS]

Hill, Rolla B.

28.0643   GC   1947   The International Health Division of the Rockefeller Foundation in the Caribbean. *Car Commn Mon Inf B* 1(3), Oct.: 18-19.   [COL]

Hill, Vincent G.

28.0644   JM   1962   Sewage stabilization ponds and their application to Jamaica. *Inf B Scient Res Coun* 2(4), Mar.: 78-80.   [RIS]

Hinchcliffe, R.

28.0645   JM   1971   Quelques aspects de la surdité causée par le bruit [Various aspects of deafness caused by noise]. *Acta Oto-Rhino-Laryng Belg* 25(1-2): 172-180.   [PS]

28.0646   JM   1972   Some geographical aspects of neuro-otology with particular reference to the African. *Afr J Med Sci* 3(2), April: 137-146. **[11]**
[PS]

28.0647   JM   1973   Epidemiology of sensorineutral hearing loss. *Audiology* 12(5-6), Sept.-Dec.: 446-452.   [ACM]

Hinchcliffe, R. & Miall, W. E.

28.0648   JM   1965   Deafness in Jamaica (A pilot survey of a sample rural population). *W I Med J* 14(4), Dec.: 241-246.   [PS]

Hinds, P.

34.0039   BB   1974   The role of the hospital midwife in family planning programmes.

Hofmeister, F. J.

28.0649   GC   1973   Editorial: Welcome to our new sections. Mexico and the West Indies. *Obstet Gynecol* 42(5), Nov. 770-773.   [PS]

28.0650   JM   1974   Pursuit of excellence: 1973 Grabham Oration. *W I Med J* 23(2), June: 98-105.   [PS]

Holding, M. & Morris, D.

28.0651   JM   1974   Hospital deaths from cerebrovascular accidents: some associated factors. *W I Med J* 23(2), June: 80-84.   [PS]

Hommel, M.

28.0652   GD   1971   Contribution à l'étude de parasitoses intestinales en Guadeloupe [Contribution to the study of intestinal parasitoses in Guadeloupe]. *B Soc Path Exot* 64(3), May-June: 331-337.   [PS]

Hood, Catriona
18.0142   GC,UK   1971   Social and cultural factors in health of children of immigrants.

Hood, Catriona; Oppé, T. E.; Pless, I. B. & Apte, Evelyn
18.0143   BC,UK   1970   CHILDREN OF WEST INDIAN IMMIGRANTS: A STUDY OF ONE-YEAR-OLDS IN PADDINGTON.

Hood, Catriona; Oppé, T. E.; Pless, J. B. & Apte, Evelyn
28.0653   BC,UK   1969   West Indian children and the health services in Paddington. *Race Today* 1(7), Nov.: 195-199.   **[18]**   [*RIS*]

Ho Ping Kong, H. & Alleyne, G. A. O.
27.0083   JM   1969   Acid-base status of adults with sickle-cell anaemia.

Horowitz, H. S.; Law, F. E. & Pritzker, T.
28.0654   ST   1965   Effect of school water fluoridation on dental caries, St. Thomas, V.I. *Publ Heal Rpts* 80(5), May: 381-388.   [*PS*]

Horwitz, Abraham & Burke, Mary H.
28.0655   GC   1966   Health, population and development. *In* Stycos, J. Mayone & Arias, Jorge, eds. POPULATION DILEMMA IN LATIN AMERICA. Washington, D. C., Potomac Books, Inc.: 145-195.   **[7]**   [*RIS*]

Hourrigan, J. L.; Strickland, R. K.; Kelsey, O. L.; Knisely, B. E.; Crago, C. C.; Whittaker, S. & Gilhooly, D. J.
62.0057   UV   1969   Eradication efforts against tropical bont tick, amblyomma variegatum, in the Virgin Islands.

Howell, S. B. & Cook, J. A.
28.0656   SL   1971   Treatment of schistosomiasis mansoni with hycanthone in glucose-6-phosphate dehydrogenase deficiency in St. Lucia. *Trans Roy Soc Trop Med Hyg* 65(3), 331-333.   [*PS*]

Hoyos, M. D. & Armstrong, G. A.
34.0040   BB   1975   The profile of family planning defaulters in a Barbadian general practice.

Hoyte, D. A. N. & Persaud, T. V. N.
32.0299   BC   1972   A survey of teaching in human anatomy at University of the West Indies.

Huisman, J.
28.0657   SR,NE   1966   Een explosie van varicellen onder een groep in Nederland verblijvende Westindiërs [An outbreak of varicella among a group of West Indians residing in The Netherlands]. *Ned Tijdschr Geneesk* 110(47), Nov. 19: 2099-2101.   **[18]**   [*PS*]

Humphreys, G. S.
28.0658   TR   1965   Chronic diffuse progressive interstitial pulmonary fibrosis in a child. *W I Med J* 14(1), March: 18-21.   [*PS*]

Humphreys, G. S. & Delvin, D. G.
28.0659   JM   1968   Ineffectiveness of propranolol in hypertensive Jamaicans. *Br Med J* 2, June 8: 601-603.   [*PS*]

Hurst, E. Weston & Pawan, J. L.

28.0660   TR   1959   A further account of the Trinidad outbreak of acute rabic myelitis: histology of the experimental disease. *Car Med J* 21(1-4): 25-45.

[*COL*]

28.0661   TR   1959   An outbreak of rabies in Trinidad without history of bites, and with the symptoms of acute ascending myelitis. *Car Med J* 21(1-4): 11-24.   [*COL*]

Hutchings, R. F.; Gordon, C. C. & Thwaits, R. E. D.

28.0662   JM   1970   The "Uroscreen" test for significant bacteriuria in pregnancy. *W I Med J* 19(2), June: 71-77.   [*PS*]

Hyde, H. A.

28.0663   JM   1973   Atmospheric pollen grains and spores in relation to allergy. II. *Clin Allergy* 3(2), June: 109-126.   **[54]**   [*ACM*]

Hyronimus, R.

28.0664   FC   1958   Maintaining health standards in the French Caribbean Departments. *Caribbean* 11(8), Mar.: 170-173.   [*COL*]

Ibáñez, Boris

28.0665   TR   1967   Report and recommendations on the organization and administration of the Ministry of Health and Housing of Trinidad and Tobago. *In* SECOND SEMINAR ON ORGANIZATION AND ADMINISTRATION OF HEALTH SERVICES—CARIBBEAN. Port-of-Spain, Trinidad, 14-19, Nov.: 81-125.   [*RIS*]

28.0666   AT   1967   Report and recommendations on the organization and administration of the Medical Department of Antigua. *In* SECOND SEMINAR ON ORGANIZATION AND ADMINISTRATION OF HEALTH SERVICES —CARIBBEAN. Port-of-Spain, Trinidad, 14-19 Nov.: 126-150.   [*RIS*]

28.0667   SL   1967   Report and recommendations on the organization and administration of the Medical Department of St. Lucia. *In* SECOND SEMINAR ON ORGANIZATION AND ADMINISTRATION OF HEALTH SERVICES —CARIBBEAN. Port-of-Spain, Trinidad, 14-19 Nov.: 151-173.   [*RIS*]

28.0668   BC   1967   Structural organization and administrative services of health in Antigua, St. Lucia, and Trinidad and Tobago. *In* SECOND SEMINAR ON ORGANIZATION AND ADMINISTRATION OF HEALTH SERVICES —CARIBBEAN. Port-of-Spain, Trinidad, 14-19 Nov.: 63-80.   [*RIS*]

Inalsingh, C. H. Amar

28.0669   TR   1974   An experience in treating five hundred and one patients with keloids. *Johns Hopkins Med J* 134(5), May: 284-290.   [*ACM*]

Irvine, R. A. & Tang, K.

28.0670   JM   1957   Datura poisoning; a case report. *W I Med J* 6(2), June: 126-128.   **[29]**   [*COL*]

Jacobs, Philip

28.0671   BC,UK   1974   Some lesions of the spine in immigrants. *Proc Roy Soc Med* 67(9), Sept.: 862-866.   **[18]**   [*ACM*]

Jacobson, F. W.

28.0672   JM   1951   Ringworm disease in Jamaican schoolchildren. *W I Med J* 1(1),
                         Sept.: 64-74.   [*COL*]

Jacobson, F. W.; Clearkin, K. P. & Annamunthodo, H.

28.0673   JM   1954   Chromomycosis: report of four more cases in Jamaica. *W I Med J*
                         3(3), Sept.: 153-158.   [*COL*]

James, O. B. O'L. & Chessells, Judith

28.0674   JM   1968   Mixed bacterial meningitis due to haemophilus influenzae and
                         salmonella typhimurium. *W I Med J* 17(3), Sept.: 172-174.   [*PS*]

James, O. B. O'L.; Grant, L. S. & Hultqvist, E.

28.0675   JM   1967   A bacterial survey of selected areas of a hospital. *W I Med J* 16(2),
                         Sept.: 129-138.   [*PS*]

James, O. B. O'L.; Segree, W. & Ventura, A. K.

28.0676   JM   1972   Some anti-bacterial properties of Jamaican honey. *W I Med J* 21(1),
                         March: 7-17.   [*PS*]

James, O. B. O'L.; Wells, D. M. & Grant, L. S.

28.0677   JM   1975   Resistance factors in the hospital and non-hospital environment.
                         Trop Geogr Med 27(1), March: 39-46.   [*PS*]

James, W. P. T.

30.0125   JM   1968   Intestinal absorption in protein-calorie malnutrition.
28.0678   JM   1968   Patterns of infant feeding in Jamaica. *Cajanus* 2, April, 50-54.   **[30]**
                                                                                     [*RIS*]

James, W. P. T. & Coore, H. G.

30.0127   JM   1970   Persistent impairment of insulin secretion and glucose tolerance
                         after malnutrition.

James, W. P. T.; Drasar, B. S. & Miller, C.

28.0679   JM   1972   Physiological mechanism and pathogenesis of weanling diarrhea.
                         Am J Clin Nutr 25(6), June: 564-571.   **[30]**   [*PS*]

James, W. P. T.; Ragbeer, M. M. S. & Walshe, M. M.

28.0680   JM   1969   Acrodermatitis enteropathica. *W I Med J* 18(1), March: 17-24.   [*PS*]

Jean, Sally Lucas

28.0681   UV   1933   Virgin Islands: school health program—utilization of existing
                         facilities. *Education* 54(4), Dec.: 205-209.   **[30,32]**   [*TCL*]

Jelliffe, D. B.

31.0077   JM   1954   Mongolism in Jamaican children.
28.0682   BC   1971   The biological basis and public health aims of young child feeding.
                         W I Med J 20(3), Sept.: 132-134.   **[30]**   [*PS*]
30.0130   BC   1971   Guidelines to young child feeding in the contemporary Caribbean.

**Jelliffe, D. B.; Wynter-Wedderburn, L. E.; Young, V. M.; Grant, L. S. &
Caselitz, F. H.**

28.0683   JM   1954   Salmonellosis in Jamaican children. *Docum Med Geogr Trop* 6(4),
                         Dec.: 315-326.   [*COL*]

Jelliffe, E. F. Patrice

28.0684   GC   1970   Dental health and fluoridation. *Cajanus* 3(2), April: 91-100.   [*RIS*]

30.0132   **GC**   1971   A new look at weaning multimixes for the Caribbean—a means of improving child nutrition.

28.0685   JM   1971   Nutrition education on the maternity ward (or what mothers believe they have learnt on the maternity ward). *W I Med J* 20(3), Sept.: 177-183. **[30]**   [*RIS*]

30.0133   **BC**   1971   Nutritional status of infants and pre-school children: a review of surveys since 1960.

Jelliffe, E. F. Patrice & Jelliffe, D. B.

27.0084   **SV**   1968   Anthropometry in action. (I) Dental second year malnutrition (practical age-grouping in young children in areas without birth verification).

27.0085   **GC**   1969   The arm circumference as a public health index of protein-calorie malnutrition of early childhood. (IX) Experience in the Caribbean.

Jenney, E. Ross

28.0686   GC   1965   The Pan American Health Organization in WHO and the Caribbean. *In* Wilgus, A. Curtis, ed. THE CARIBBEAN: ITS HEALTH PROBLEMS. Gainesville, University of Florida Press: 227-232 (Caribbean Conference Series 1, Vol. 15.) **[39]**   [*RIS*]

Jennings, Roy

28.0687   JM   1967   THE ROLE OF RESPIRATORY VIRUSES IN JAMAICA. Ph.D. dissertation, University of the West Indies.

28.0688   JM   1968   Respiratory viruses in Jamaica: a virologic and serologic study. 3. Hemagglutination-inhibiting antibodies to type B and C influenza viruses in the sera of Jamaicans. *Am J Epidemiol* 87(2), March: 440-446.   [*PS*]

28.0689   JM   1972   Adenovirus, parainfluenza virus and respiratory syncytial virus antibodies in the sera of Jamaicans. *J Hygiene* 70(3), Sept.: 523-529.   [*PS*]

Jennings, Roy & Grant, L. S.

28.0690   JM   1967   Respiratory viruses in Jamaica: a virologic and serologic study. 1. Virus isolations and serologic studies on clinical specimens. *Am J Epidemiol* 86(3), Nov.: 691-699.   [*PS*]

28.0691   JM   1967   Respiratory viruses in Jamaica: a virologic and serologic study. 2. Hemagglutination-inhibiting antibodies to influenza A viruses in the sera of Jamaicans. *Am J Epidemiol* 86(2), Nov.: 700-709.   [*PS*]

Jenny Weyerman, J. W.

28.0692   SR   1923-24   Eene waterleiding voor Paramaribo [Water works for Paramaribo]. *W I G* 5: 295-309, 648-652. **[48]**   [*COL*]

28.0693   SR   1927-28   Van waar moet het water komen voor eene waterleiding te Paramaribo? [From where do we get the water for waterworks in Paramaribo?] *W I G* 9: 271-286. **[48]**   [*COL*]

Johnson, Benjamin Charles

27.0087   **BA**   1959   A SAMPLING SURVEY STUDY OF ARTERIAL BLOOD PRESSURE LEVELS IN NASSAU, NEW PROVIDENCE, BAHAMAS, 1958 FOR DESCRIPTION OF LEVELS OF BLOOD PRESSURE IN A POPULATION IN RELATIONSHIP TO AGE, SEX, RACE AND OTHER FACTORS.

Johnson, J. T. C.
28.0694   BB   1926   A REPORT TO THE PUBLIC HEALTH COMMISSIONERS ON THE ORGAN-
                       IZATION OF THE MEDICAL AND SANITARY SERVICES OF THE COLONY OF
                       BARBADOS, WITH RECOMMENDATIONS. [Bridgetown?] Barbados,
                       Cole's Printery.

Johnstone, Robert E. & Gutsche, Brett B.
28.0695   JM   1975   Missionary anesthesia. *Anesth Analg* 54(2), March-April: 184-188.
                                                                                          [*ACM*]

Jones, C. June
28.0696   BB   1974   Preliminary report on the isolation of twelve leptospira serotypes in
                       Barbados. *W I Med J* 23(2), June: 65-68.   [*PS*]

Jones, C. R.
28.0697   GU   1954   The health of the Amerindian. *Timehri* 4th ser., 1(33), Oct.:
                       23-27.   **[13]**
28.0698   GU   1954   Tuberculosis amongst the Amerindians of British Guiana. *W I Med
                       J* 3(2), June: 77-87.   **[13]**   [*COL*]

Jones, K.
18.0159   BC,UK   1967   Immigrants and the social services.

Jones, T. R.
28.0699   GU   1960   Tuberculosis in British Guiana. *Car Med J* 22(1-4): 105-111.   [*COL*]

Jonkers, A. H.; Aitken, T. H.; Spence, L. & Worth, C.
28.0700   TR   1966   Estudios ecológicos del virus de la encefalitis equina venezolana
                       (EEV) en la selva de Bush Bush, Trinidad [Ecological studies of
                       Venezuelan equine encephalitis virus (EEV) in the Bush Bush forest
                       of Trinidad]. *Revta Venez Sanid Asist Social* 31(3), Supplement,
                       Sept.: 929-933.   [*PS*]

Jonkers, A. H.; Alexis, F. & Loregnard, R.
28.0701   GR   1969   Mongoose rabies in Grenada. *W I Med J* 18(3), Sept.: 167-170.
                                                                                          [*PS*]

Jonkers, A. H.; Casals, J.; Aitken, T. H. G. & Spence, L.
54.0559   TR   1973   Soldado virus, a new agent from Trinidadian *Ornithodoros* ticks.

Jonkers, A. H.; Downs, W. G.; Aitken, T. H. G. & Spence, L.
28.0702   SR   1964   Arthropod-borne encephalitis viruses in northeastern South Amer-
                       ica. Part I: A serological survey of northeastern Surinam. *Trop
                       Geogr Med* 16(2): 135-145.   [*COL*]

Jonkers, A. H.; Metselaar, D.; Pães de Andrade, A. H. & Tikasingh, E. S.
28.0703   TR,SR   1967   Restan, a new group C arbovirus from Trinidad and Surinam. *Am J
                         Trop Med Hyg* 16(1), Jan.: 74-78.   [*PS*]

**Jonkers, A. H.; Spence, L.; Downs, W. G.; Aitken, T. H. G. &
Tikasingh, E. S.**
28.0704   TR   1968   Arbovirus studies in Bush Bush Forest, Trinidad, W.I., September
                       1959-December 1964. V. Virus isolations. *Am J Trop Med Hyg*
                       17(2), March: 276-284.   [*PS*]

Jonkers, A. H.; Spence, L.; Downs, W. G.; Aitken, T. H. G. & Worth, C. B.

28.0705   TR   1968   Arbovirus studies in Bush Bush Forest, Trinidad, W.I., September 1959-December 1964. VI. Rodent-associated virus (VEE and agents of groups C and Guamá): Isolations and further studies. *Am J Trop Med Hyg* 17(2), March: 285-298.   [PS]

Jonkers, A. H.; Spence, L. & Karbaat, J.

28.0706   SR   1968   Arbovirus infections in Dutch military personnel stationed in Surinam: further studies. *Trop Geogr Med* 20(3), Sept.: 251-256. **[15]**   [PS]

Jonkers, A. H.; Spence, L. & Olivier, O.

28.0707   TR   1968   Laboratory studies with wild rodents and viruses native to Trinidad. *Am J Trop Med Hyg* 17(2), March: 299-307.   [PS]

Jordan, P.; Woodstock, Lilian; Unrau, G. O. and Cook, J. A.

28.0708   SL   1975   Control of *Schistosoma mansoni* transmission by provision of domestic water supplies. A preliminary report of a study in St. Lucia. *B WHO* 52(1): 9-20. **[48]**   [PS]

Junker, L.

28.0709   SR   1941   Malaria in Suriname [Malaria in Surinam]. *W I G* 23: 23-30.   [COL]

Kahn, A.; Boivin, P. & Lagneau, J.

27.0089   FC,FR   1973   Phénotypes de la glucose-6-phosphate déshydrogénase érythro-cytaire dans la race noire. Etude de 301 noirs vivants en France et description de 9 variantes différentes. Fréquence élevée d'une enzyme déficitaire de migration "B" [Phenotypes of erythrocyte glucose-6-phosphate dehydrogenase in black people. Examination of 301 black people living in France and description of 9 different variants. High incidence of deficiency of an enzyme of "B" mobility].

Kahn, Morton Charles

3.0317   SR   1936   Where black man meets red.

Karbaat, J.

28.0710   SR   1965   Amerikaanse huidleishmaniose [American skin leishmaniasis]. *Med Mil Geneesk Tijdschr* 18(1): 17-23.   [ACM]

28.0711   SR   1965   Histoplasmosis in Suriname. *Med Mil Geneesk Tijdschr* 18(5): 135-147.   [ACM]

Karmody, C. S.

28.0712   TR   1968   Subclinical maternal rubella and congenital deafness. *New Eng J Med* 278(15), April 11: 809-814.   [PS]

28.0713   TR   1969   Asymptomatic maternal rubella and congenital deafness. *Archs Otolaryng* 89(5), May: 720-726.   [PS]

Kass, Edward H.

28.0714   JM   1973   Should bacteriuria be treated? *Med J Aus* 1(2) Supplement, June 30: 38-43. **[10]**   [ACM]

Kaude, Jüri V. & Johnson, Clive

32.0324   JM   1973   The launching of a postgraduate training program in diagnostic radiology in the West Indies.

Keane, P. M.; Pegg, P. J.; Johnson, E. & Adam, M.

28.0715   JM   1971   The binding characteristics of transcortin, thyroxine binding globulin and pre-albumin in Jamaicans. *W I Med J* 20(4), Dec.: 271-275.   [*PS*]

Kellermeyer, R. W.; Warren, K. S.; Waldmann, T. S.; Cook, J. A. & Jordan, P.

28.0716   SL,SV   1973   Concentration of serum immunoglobulins in St. Lucians with schistosomiasis mansoni compared with matched uninfected St. Vincentians. *J Infect Dis* 127(5), May: 557-562.   **[11]**   [*PS*]

Kellett, F. R. S. & Omardeen, T. A.

28.0717   TR   1957   Tree hole breeding of *Aedes Aegypti* (Linn) in Arima, Trinidad, B.W.I. *W I Med J* 6(3), Sept.: 179-188.   [*COL*]

Kelly, F. James

55.0114   GU   1933   Climate and health in British Guiana.

Kelly, P. J. et al.

28.0718   GU   1926   Leprosy in British Guiana (report of a Departmental Medical Conference held in Georgetown, September, 1924—May, 1925). *Br Gui Med Annual 1925* 24: 86-105.   [*ACM*]

Kendall, M. N.

32.0326   BC   1972   Overseas nursing students in Britain.

Kennard, C. P.

28.0719   GU   1902   Fever cases. *Br Gui Med Annual* [12?]: 10-25.   **[55]**   [*ACM*]
28.0720   GU   1906   Acute anaemia. *Br Gui Med Annual 1905* 14: 49-60.   [*ACM*]
28.0721   GU   1906   Typhoid fever. *Br Gui Med Annual 1905* 14: 74-83.   [*ACM*]
28.0722   GU   1909   Continous fever—with special reference to the typhoid group. *Br Gui Med Annual 1908* 16: 54-87.   [*ACM*]
28.0723   GU   1911   Rice fields and malaria. *Timehri* 3d ser., 1(18C), Dec.: 280-284.   **[61]**   [*AMN*]

Kesler, C. K.

28.0724   GU   1929-30   Een Duitsch medicus in Essequebo in de laatste jaren der 18e eeuw [A German medical doctor in Essequibo during the last years of the 18th century]. *W I G* 11: 241-250.   **[5,6]**   [*COL*]
28.0725   SR   1931-32   Een paar opmerkingen [A few remarks]. *W I G* 13: 534-536.   [*COL*]

Kettle, D. S. & Linley, J. R.

28.0726   JM   1969   The biting habits of some Jamaican culicoides. I. C. barbosai wirth. *B Entomol Res* 58, May: 729-753.   **[54]**   [*ACM*]

Kildare-Donaldson, Evan; Daley, Errol A. & Sorhaindo, B. A.

28.0727   DM   1972   Tubal ligations in Dominica. *W I Med J* 21(4), Dec.: 236-239.   **[34]**
                                                                             [*PS*]

King, Robert L.
28.0728   GC   1965   Health facilities construction in the Caribbean. *In* Wilgus, A. Curtis, ed. THE CARIBBEAN: ITS HEALTH PROBLEMS. Gainesville, University of Florida Press: 176-190 [Caribbean Conference Series 1, Vol. 15]. **[35]**   [*RIS*]

King, S. D.
28.0729   JM   1972   Rubella antibody levels in Jamaican females. *W I Med J* 21(2), June: 82-86.   [*PS*]
28.0730   JM   1973   A comparative study on lymphogranuloma venereum (LGV) in Jamaica, 1970-72. *W I Med J* 22(4), Dec.: 161-165.   [*PS*]

King, S. D. & Grant, L. S.
28.0731   JM   1963   A review of salmonella, shigella, pathogenic escherichia coli and typhoid phage types. *W I Med J* 12(2), June: 90-97.   [*COL*]

King, S. D. & Urquhart, A. E.
28.0732   JM   1975   Laboratory investigations on four cases of leptospiral meningitis in Jamaica. *W I Med J* 24(4), Dec.: 196-201.   [*PS*]

Knobloch, Natalie A.
28.0733   BZ   1969   *Peltamigratus thornei* sp. n. (Nematoda: Hoplolaimidae) from soil in Central America. *Proc Helm Soc Wash* 36(2), July: 208-210.   [*PS*]

Kol, H. van
28.0734   NC   1919   De Volksgezonheid in onze West-Indische kolonien [Public health in our West-Indian colonies]. *W I G* 1(1): 269-290.   [*COL*]

Kooy, P.
28.0735   SR   1970   Brucellosis, treponematosis, rickettsiosis, and psittacosis in Surinam: a serological survey. *Trop Geogr Med* 22(2), June: 172-178.   [*PS*]

Kooy, P. & Oedayarajsingh Varma, A.
28.0736   SR   1965   Quelques données sur le sérodiagnostic de la syphilis en Surinam [Some data on the serum diagnosis of syphilis in Surinam]. *B Soc Path Exot* 58(6), Nov.-Dec.: 1026-1031.   [*PS*]
28.0737   SR   1966   Quelques données sur le sérodiagnostic de la syphilis en Surinam, II [Some data on the serum diagnosis of syphilis in Surinam]. *B Soc Path Exot* 59(1), Jan.-Feb.: 65-70.   [*PS*]

Kooy, P. & Wesenhagen, W.
28.0738   SR   1966   Anonymous mycobacteria in Surinam. *Trop Geogr Med* 18(1), March: 71-76.   [*PS*]

Koplik, B. S.
28.0739   JM   1967   An island in the sun—impressions of Jamaican dentistry. *New York J Dent* 37(5), May: 189-190 passim.   [*PS*]

Krogh, A. L.
28.0740   TR   1944   Social medicine in Trinidad. *Car Med J.* 6(2): 75-86.   [*COL*]

Kroon, T. A. J.

28.0741   CU   1973   Tuberculose op Curaçao [Tuberculosis in Curaçao]. *In* Statius van
Eps, L. W. & Luckman-Maduro, E., eds. VAN SCHEEPSCHIRURGIJN
TOT SPECIALIST. Assen, The Netherlands, Van Gorcum & Comp.
B.V.: 125-130. [Anjerpublikatie 15].   [*RILA*]

Kuil, H.

28.0742   SR   1966   The prevalence of antibodies against *Toxoplasma* in stray dogs in
Paramaribo, Surinam, Dutch Guiana. *Ann Trop Med Paras* 60(1),
March: 22-24.   [*PS*]

Kuip, E. van der

28.0743   SR   1969   *Schistosomiasis mansoni* in the Saramacca district of Surinam. *Trop
Geogr Med* 21(1), March: 88-92.   **[8]**   [*PS*]

28.0744   AR,CU   1969   *Trypanosomiasis cruzi* in Aruba and Curacao. *Trop Geogr Med* 21(4),
Dec.: 462-469.   **[35]**   [*PS*]

Kulkarni, Dattatreya Vithalrao

28.0745   TR   1969   COMPARATIVE STUDY OF TREATMENT MODELS IN LEPROSY WITH
SPECIAL REFERENCE TO TRINIDAD (WEST INDIES). Ph.D. dissertation,
Brandeis University: 403p.   [*PhD*]

Kuyp, Edwin van der

28.0746   SR   1950   CONTRIBUTION TO THE STUDY OF THE MALARIAL EPIDEMIOLOGY IN
SURINAM. Amsterdam, Koninklijke Vereeniging Indisch Instituut,
146p. (Mededeling no. 89, Afdeling Tropische hygiëne no. 18.)
                                                                        [*AGS*]

28.0747   SR   1950   Iets over de malaria in Suriname [About malaria in Surinam]. *W I G*
31: 181-192.   [*COL*]

28.0748   SR   1951   Yellow fever in Surinam. *Trop Geogr Med* 10(2), June: 181-194.
                                                                        [*COL*]

28.0749   SR   1954   Malaria in Nickerie (Surinam). *Docum Med Geogr Trop* 7(3), Sept.:
259-262.   [*COL*]

28.0750   SR   1961   Schistosomiasis in the Surinam district of Surinam. *Trop Geogr Med*
13(4), Dec.: 357-373.   [*COL*]

1.0167   SR   1962   Literatuuroverzicht betreffende de voeding en de voedingsgewoonten van de Boslandcreool in Suriname [Bibliography about
nutrition and food habits of the Bush Negroes in Surinam].

28.0751   SR   1964   Report on malaria radiation in Surinam. *Trop Geogr Med* 16(2):
172-173.   [*COL*]

28.0752   SR   1969   FUTUROLOGIE VAN DE GEZONDHEID IN SURINAME DEEL I: REDE
UITGESPROKEN TER GELEGENHEID VAN DE PROKLAMATIE VAN DE
FAKULTEIT DER MEDISCHE WETENSCHAPPEN VAN DE UNIVERSITEIT
VAN SURINAME OP VRIJDAG 26 SEPTEMBER 1969 [THE FUTURE OF
HEALTH IN SURINAM PART I: SPEECH AT THE OPENING OF THE
MEDICAL FACULTY OF THE UNIVERSITY OF SURINAM ON FRIDAY,
SEPTEMBER 26, 1969]. Druk Leo-Victor: 61p.   **[32]**   [*RILA*]

13.0126   SR   1971   HET GEVAAR VAN TOERISME VOOR DE BOVENLANDSE INDIANEN IN
SURINAME: REDE UITGESPROKEN BIJ DE AANVAARDING VAN HET AMBT
VAN GEWOON HOOGLERAAR IN DE GEZONDHEIDSLEER EN SOCIALE
GENEESKUNDE AAN DE UNIVERSITEIT VAN SURINAME OP DINSDAG 4
MEI 1971 [THE RISKS OF TOURISM FOR THE SURINAM HINTERLAND
AMERINDIANS: ACCEPTANCE SPEECH FOR THE POSITION OF PROFESSOR
IN HYGIENE AND SOCIAL MEDICINE AT THE UNIVERSITY OF SURINAM,
TUESDAY, MAY 4, 1971].

54.0607   **NA**   1973   Muskieten of muggen van de Nederlandse Antillen en hun betekenis voor de volksgezondheid [Mosquitoes of the Netherlands Antilles and their impact on public health].

Kuyp, Edwin van der; Erpecum, C. P. van & Bleiker, M. A.
28.0753   **SR**   1967   A medical expedition with special reference to tuberculosis among the Oajana and Trio Amerindians in South-east Surinam. *Roy Neth Tub Assoc* 10: 49-60.   **[13]**   [*PS*]

Laarschot, E. C. J. M. van de
28.0754   **CU**   1948   Het Wit Gele Kruis [The White Yellow Cross]. *In* ORANJE EN DE ZES CARAÏBISCHE PARELEN. Amsterdam, J. H. de Bussy: 184-190.
                                                                                                    [*UCLA*]

La Frenais, A. C. L.
28.0755   **GU**   1907   Some remarks on nervous diseases of British Guiana. *Br Gui Med Annual 1906* [15:] 85-97.   [*ACM*]

Lainson, R.
28.0756   **BZ**   1965   Parasitological studies in British Honduras. I.—A parasite resembling *Trypanosoma (Schizotrypanum) cruzi* in the coati, *Nasua narica* (Carnivora, Procyonidae), and a note of *Trypanosoma legeri* from the ant-eater, *Tamandua tetradactyla* (Edentata). *Ann Trop Med Paras* 59(1), March: 37-42.   **[54]**   [*PS*]
28.0757   **BZ**   1965   Parasitological studies in British Honduras. II.—*Cyclospora niniae* sp. nov. (Eimeriidae, Cyclosporinae) from the snake *Ninia sebae sebae* (Colubridae). *Ann Trop Med Paras* 59(2), June: 159-163.   **[54]**
                                                                                                    [*PS*]
28.0758   **BZ**   1968   Parasitological studies in British Honduras. III.—Some coccidial parasites of mammals. *Ann Trop Med Paras* 62(2), June: 252-259.   **[54]**   [*PS*]
28.0759   **BZ**   1968   Parasitological studies in British Honduras. IV.—Some coccidial parasites of reptiles. *Ann Trop Med Paras* 62(2), June: 260-266.   **[54]**   [*PS*]

Lambert, B.
33.0111   **NA**   1952   Situation sociale et médicale aux Antilles Néerlandaises [The social and medical situation in the Dutch West Indies].

Lampe, P. H. J.
28.0760   **SR**   1926-27 Enkele opmerkingen over den sociaal-hygienischen toestanden en de geneeskundige verzorging van Suriname [Some remarks about the social-hygienic conditions and medical care in Surinam]. *W I G* 8: 249-276.   **[33]**   [*COL*]
28.0761   **SR**   1927   SURINAME, SOCIAAL-HYGIENISCHE BESCHOUWINGEN [SURINAM, SOCIAL-HYGIENIC OBSERVATIONS]. Amsterdam, de Bussy, 590p. (Kolonial Instituut, Afdeling Tropische hygiene, no. 14.)   **[7,33]**
28.0762   **SR**   1927-28 Suriname, sociaal-hygienische beschouwingen [Surinam, social-hygienic observations]. *W I G* 9: 465-487.   **[15,33]**   [*COL*]
29.0030   **SR**   1928-29 "Het Surinaamsche treefgeloof", een volksgeloof betreffende het ontstaan van de melaatschheid ["The treyf belief in Surinam," a superstition about the cause of leprosy].

28.0763   SR   1950   Study on filariasis in Surinam. *Docum Ned Indo Mortis Trop* 2(3),
                         Sept.: 193-208.   [*COL*]
35.0047   GC   1951   Housing and health in the Caribbean.

Landauer, Stella
28.0764   BC   1970   Recent nursing developments in the English-speaking Caribbean.
                         Int Nurs Rev 17(2): 172-184.   [*PS*]

Landman, Jacqueline P. & Shaw-Lyon, Violet
30.0137   JM   1976   Breast feeding in decline in Kingston, Jamaica, 1973.

Lang, A.; Lehmann, H. & King-Lewis, P. A.
28.0765   BC,UK 1974   Hb K Woolwich the cause of a thalassaemia. *Nature* 249(5456),
                         May 31: 467-469.   **[18,27]**   [*PS*]

Lanjouw, J. & Uittien, H.
54.0617   SR   1935-36 Surinaamsche geneeskruiden in den tijd van Linnaeus [Surinam's
                         medicinal herbs during the age of Linnaeus].

Lapierre, J.; Hien, Tran Vinh; Holler, C. & Saison, E.
28.0766   FA,FR 1973   La pathologie antillaise observée en métropole: Considérations
                         épidémiologiques générales [Antillean pathology observed in met-
                         ropolitan France: General epidemiologic considerations]. *B Soc
                         Path Exot* 66(1), Jan.-Feb.: 216-226.   **[18]**   [*PS*]

Larkin, Frances A.
28.0767   DM   1971   Pattern of weaning in Dominica. *W I Med J* 20(3), Sept.:
                         229-236.   **[30]**   [*PS*]

Lassalle, C. F.
28.0768   TR   1915   Malaria. *Proc Agric Soc Trin Tob* 15(3), Mar.: 69-73.   [*AMN*]
54.0618   TR   1921   A mosquito survey of Trinidad.

La Touche, C. J.; Tyagi, S. C. & Gentles, J. C.
28.0769   GC   1967   Quelques données mycologiques et histologiques à propos de deux
                         cas de maduromycose à *Madurella grisea* provenant des îles
                         Caraïbes [Some mycologic and histologic data regarding 2 cases of
                         maduromycosis caused by *Madurella grisea* from the Caribbean
                         islands]. *B Soc Path Exot* 60(1), Jan.-Feb.: 9-12.   [*PS*]

Latour, M. D.
28.0770   CU   1955-56 Het Sint Elisabeths Gasthuis op Curacao 1855-1955 [The St.
                         Elisabeth's Hospital on Curacao, 1855-1955]. *W I G* 36: 46-52.   **[5]**
                                                                                      [*COL*]

Laurence, Stephen M.
28.0771   TR   1938   Quarantine as part of the colony's public health service. *Car Med J*
                         1(1): 106-110.   [*COL*]
28.0772   TR   1941   The evolution of the Trinidad midwife. *Car Med J* 3(4): 204-
                         208.   **[5]**   [*COL*]

Lawrence, A. W. W.
28.0773   JM   1966   Adamantinoma. *W I Med J* 15(4), Dec.: 226-230.   [*PS*]

Lawrence, J. S.; Bremner, J. M.; Ball, J. & Burch, T. A.

28.0774   JM   1966   Rheumatoid arthritis in a subtropical population. *Ann Rheum Dis* 25(1), Jan.: 59-66.   [*ACM*]

Lee, C. U.

28.0775   GU   1923   A preliminary report on the incidence of filarial infection amongst Chinese, East Indians, Portuguese, blacks and mixed races in Georgetown. *Br Gui Med Annual 1923* 23: 32-34.   **[11,12,15]**
                                                                                  [*ACM*]

Leedom, John M.; Graham, Albert C. & Byer, M. A.

28.0776   BB   1965   Epidemia de poliomielitis en Barbada, Indias Occidentales [Epidemic of poliomyelitis in Barbados, W.I.]. *Boln Ofic Sanit Panam* 59(1), July: 22-33.   [*PS*]

28.0777   BB   1965   1963 epidemic of poliomyelitis in Barbados, West Indies. *Publ Heal Rpts* 80(5), May: 423-431.   [*PS*]

Lees, Ronald E. M.

30.0138   SL   1964   Malnutrition: the pattern and prevention in St. Lucia.

28.0778   SL   1965   S. mansoni and other helminthiasis within one watershed in St. Lucia. *W I Med J* 14(2), June: 82-88.   [*PS*]

28.0779   SL   1966   Lucanthone hydrochloride in the treatment of *Schistosoma mansoni* infection. *Trans Roy Soc Trop Med Hyg* 60(2), March: 233-237.
                                                                                  [*PS*]

30.0139   SL   1966   Malnutrition: the infant at risk.

28.0780   SL   1967   Trial of an enteric-coated preparation of lucanthone hydrochloride in *Schistosoma mansoni* infections. *Trans Roy Soc Trop Med Hyg* 67(6): 806-811.   [*PS*]

28.0781   SL   1968   Suppressive treatment of *Schistosomiasis mansoni* with spaced doses of lucanthone hydrochloride. *Trans Roy Soc Trop Med Hyg* 62(6): 782-785.   [*PS*]

28.0782   SL   1968   Symptoms and clinical and laboratory findings in 123 cases of schistosomiasis mansoni in St. Lucia. *J Trop Med Hyg* 71(2), Feb.: 40-43.   [*PS*]

28.0783   SL   1973   A selective approach to yaws control. *Can J Publ Heal* 64 Supplement, Oct.: 52-56.   [*ACM*]

Lees, Ronald E. M. & DeBruin, A. M.

28.0784   SL   1963   Review of yaws in St. Lucia five years after an eradication campaign. *W I Med J* 12(2), June: 98-102.   [*COL*]

28.0785   SL   1963   Skin disease in school children in St. Lucia. *W I Med J* 12(4), Dec.: 265-267.   [*COL*]

Lees, Ronald E. M. & Gentle, G. H. K.

28.0786   SL   1967   Yaws control: a report of a mass juvenile sweep in St. Lucia. *W I Med J* 16(4), Dec.: 228-232.   [*PS*]

Leeuwin, R. S.

18.0185   SR,NE   1962   Microfilaraemia in Surinamese living in Amsterdam.

Leger, Marcel

28.0787   FG   1917   La lèpre à la Guyane Francaise et ses réglementations successives [Leprosy in French Guiana and successive regulations about it]. *B Soc Path Exot* 10(8), Oct.: 733-749.   **[5]**   [*ACM*]

28.0788   **FG**   1917   Le paludisme à la Guyane Francaise: index endémique des diverses localités [Malaria in French Guiana: Endemic indices for the various localities]. *B Soc Path Exot* 10(8), Oct.: 749-756.   [*ACM*]

28.0789   **FG**   1917   Parasitisme intestinal à la Guyane Francaise dans la population locale et dans l'élément pénal [Intestinal parasitism in French Guiana, among the local population and among the penal element]. *B Soc Path Exot* 10(7), July: 557-560.   **[33]**   [*ACM*]

28.0790   **FG**   1918   La lèpre à la Guyane Francaise dans l'élément penal: documents statistiques [Leprosy in French Guiana among the penal element: statistical documentation]. *B Soc Path Exot* 11(9), Nov.: 793-799.   **[33]**   [*ACM*]

28.0791   **FG**   1920   La Guyane Francaise: questions de salubrité et de réglementations sanitaires [French Guiana: matters of sanitation and public health regulations]. *B Soc Path Exot* 13(3), Mar.: 199-204.   **[33]**   [*ACM*]

28.0792   **FG**   1921   Parasitisme intestinal chez les enfants à la Guyane Francaise: Sa relation avec la pureté des eaux de boisson [Intestinal parasitism among the children of French Guiana: its relation to the purity of drinking waters]. *B Soc Path Exot* 14(2), Feb.: 85-89.   [*ACM*]

LeMaistre & Nère

28.0793   **FA**   1965   Les dysplasies fibreuses viscérales en milieu antillais [Visceral fibrous dysplasias in the Antillian setting]. *J Med Bord Sud-Ouest* 142(6), June: 1021-1023.   [*PS*]

Lescene, G. T.

28.0794   **JM**   1955   Brief historical retrospect of the medical profession in Jamaica. *W I Med J* 4(4), Dec.: 217-240.   **[5]**   [*COL*]

Leslie, J.; Langler, D.; Serjeant, G. R.; Serjeant, B. E.; Desai, P. & Gordon, Y. B.

28.0795   **JM**   1975   Coagulation changes during the steady state in homozygous sickle-cell disease in Jamaica. *Br J Haematol* 30(2), June: 159-166.   **[27]**   [*PS*]

L'Etang, E.

28.0796   **GD**   1965   Bilharziose à la Guadeloupe. Traitement accéléré en milieu hospitalier [Bilharziasis in Guadeloupe. Accelerated treatment in a hospital setting]. *J Med Bord Sud-Ouest* 142(6), June: 1049-1060.   [*PS*]

Lewis, L. F. E.

28.0797   **SL**   1943   Chemotherapy of pneumonia in district practice. *Car Med J* 5(2): 55-61.   [*COL*]

31.0089   **TR**   1953   Psychiatry in relation to the general practitioner.

31.0090   **TR**   1956   The use of chlorpromazine and of serpasil in the treatment of psychotic patients.

Lewis, Thomas H.

31.0092   **SR**   1975   A culturally patterned depression in a mother after loss of a child.

Lewis, Thomas H. & Brannon, William L.

28.0798   **SR**   1974   Poliomyelitis in an isolated Amerindian population. *J A M A* 230(9), Dec. 2: 1295-1297.   **[13]**   [*PS*]

Lewthwaite, R.
28.0799   BC   1956   Address to the inaugural meeting of the Caribbean Research
                            Committee. *W I Med J* 5(2), June: 129-134.   [*COL*]

Lherisson, Fritz
30.0141   GC   1972   Child nutrition in the Caribbean: a résumé of the present situation
                          and UNICEF'S current role.

Liachowitz, Claire et al.
28.0800   SR   1958   Abnormal hemoglobins in the Negroes of Surinam. *Am J Med*
                            24(1), Jan.: 19-24.   **[14,27]**   [*RIS*]

Lichtveld, Lou
29.0031   SR   1930-31 Een Afrikaansch bijgeloof: snetji-koti [An African superstition:
                            "snakebite cure"].
29.0032   SR   1932   Een oude getuigenis over de genezing van slagenbeet en aardeten
                          [An old testimony about the cure of snakebite and the eating of
                          earth].

Lindo, Victor & Bras, G.
28.0801   JM   1966   Further investigations into the toxicity of Crotalaria fulva in
                            Jamaica. *W I Med J* 15(1), March: 34-39.   [*PS*]

Llewellyn, C. H.; Spielman, A. & Frothingham, T. E.
54.0641   BA   1970   Survival of arboviruses in *Aedes algonotatus,* a peri-domestic
                          Bahaman mosquito.

Lloyd-Still, R. M.
31.0094   BC   1955   The mental hospital.

Long, Joseph K.
29.0033   JM   1973   JAMAICAN MEDICINE: CHOICES BETWEEN FOLK HEALING AND MODERN
                          MEDICINE.

Lord, Rexford D.
62.0080   GC   1974   History and geographic distribution of Venezuelan equine en-
                          cephalitis.

Loret, H.
28.0802   FA,MT   1965   A propos de deux cas de primo-infestation bilharzienne chez des
                               sujets neufs [Two cases of bilharzian primo-infestation in new
                               subjects]. *Med Bord Sud-Ouest* 142(6), June: 1014-1020.   [*PS*]
28.0803   GD   1965   Réflexions sur la pathologie virale en Guadeloupe: Isolement de
                            quelques souches d'enterovirus [Reflections on viral pathology in
                            Guadeloupe: Isolation of several strains of enterovirus]. *J Med Bord
                            Sud-Ouest* 142(6), June: 1061-1068.   [*PS*]

Losonczi, E.
28.0804   BZ   1956   Report on the BCG campaigns in British Honduras. *W I Med J*
                            5(4), Dec.: 271-283.   [*COL*]

Lovell, Belle
34.0058   BZ   1974   The traditional birth attendant—Belize.

Lovell, H. G.; Miall, W. E. & Stewart, D. B.

28.0805   JM   1966   Arterial blood pressure in Jamaican women with and without uterine fibroids. *W I Med J* 15(1), March: 45-51.   [*PS*]

Low, Deen

30.0144   DM   1969   Daily food for Dominican families.

Low, Doreen Iris Deen

30.0145   SL,SK   1970   EVALUATING NUTRITION EDUCATION PROGRAMS ON TWO CARIBBEAN ISLANDS.

Lowe, A.

28.0806   SV   1960   Tuberculosis in St. Vincent. *Car Med J* 22(1-4): 120-122.   [*COL*]

Lowry, M. F.

28.0807   JM   1974   University Hospital newborn services: present and future. *W I Med J* 23(3), Sept.: 142-144.   [*PS*]

Lowry, M. F.; Hall, J. St. Elmo & Sparke, B.

28.0808   JM   1976   Perinatal mortality in the University Hospital of the West Indies: 1973-75. *W I Med J* 25(2), June: 92-100.   [*RIS*]

Lowry, M. F.; Howell, Valerie & Bird, Sybil

28.0809   JM   1976   Paramedical assessment of gestational age in the newborn. *W I Med J* 25(1), March: 17-22.   [*PS*]

Lowry, M. F. & Miller, Colin G.

28.0810   JM   1975   Measles in Jamaican children. *W I Med J* 24(2), June: 90-93.   [*PS*]

Luck, Donald

28.0811   JM   1966   Poliomyelitis in Jamaica. A short history with comments upon the effects of immunization. *W I Med J* 15(4), Dec.: 189-196.   [*PS*]

Luckman-Maduro, E.

5.0570   NA   1973   Minibiografieën van doktoren die in de Nederlandse Antillen leefden en werkten [Mini-biographies of doctors who lived and worked in the Netherlands Antilles].

Lunn, John A.; Miridjanian, Anoush; Fontares, Presentación; Jacobs, Elliot; Rosen, Samuel & Christakis, George

28.0812   BA   1974   Epidemiologic reconnaissance of hypertension in the Bahamas: with special reference to depot fat composition and its implications in relation to cardiovascular disease prevalence. *Mt Sinai J Med NY* 41(3), May-June: 444-452.   **[30]**   [*ACM*]

Luty, Ella

28.0813   MS   1968   The role of the nurse in the past—flashback: Montserrat. *Jam Nurse* 8(2), Sept.: 10.   **[5]**   [*AJN*]

Luyken, R.

30.0146   NW   1958   Over voedingsproblemen in de tropen in verband met het voedingsonderzoek op de Bovenwindse Eilanden [On problems of nutrition in the tropics in relationship to the nutritional research on the Windward Islands].

30.0147   SR   1962-63 Voedingsfysiologisch onderzoek in Suriname [Research in nutritional physiology in Suriname].

Luyken, R. & Luyken-Koning, F. W. M.
30.0150   SR   1960   Studies on the physiology of nutrition in Surinam. I. General remarks.
30.0151   SR   1960   Studies on the physiology of nutrition in Surinam. II. Serum protein levels.
30.0152   SR   1960   Studies on the physiology of nutrition in Surinam. III. Urea excretions.
30.0153   SR   1960   Studies on the physiology of nutrition in Surinam. IV. Nitrogen balance studies.
30.0154   SR   1960   Studies on the physiology of nutrition in Surinam. V. Amylase, lipase and cholinesterase activity of the serum of diverse population growth.
30.0155   SR   1960   Studies on the physiology of nutrition in Surinam. VI. Cholestrol content of the blood serum.
30.0156   SR   1961   Studies on the physiology of nutrition in Surinam. VII. Serum iron.
30.0157   SR   1961   Studies on the physiology of nutrition in Surinam. VIII. Metabolism of calcium.
30.0158   SR   1961   Studies on the physiology of nutrition in Surinam. IX. Somato-metrical data.

Luyken, R.; Luyken-Koning, F. W. M. & Dam-Bakker, A. W. I. van
30.0161   NW   1959   Nutrition survey on the Windward Islands (Netherlands Antilles).

Luyken, R.; Luyken-Koning, F. W. M. & Immikhuizen, M. J. T.
28.0814   SR   1971   Lactose intolerance in Surinam. *Cajanus* 4(5-6): 336-344.   **[27,30]**
                                                                                              [*RIS*]

Lynch-Brathwaite, B. A.; Duncan, E. J. & Seaforth, C. E.
54.0654   TR   1975   A survey of ferns of Trinidad for antibacterial activity.

Maal, W. P.
28.0815   CU   1948   Het Nederlandse Rode Kruis: afdeling Curaçao [The Dutch Red Cross: section Curaçao]. *In* ORANJE EN DE ZES CARAÏBISCHE PARELEN. Amsterdam, J. H. de Bussy: 193-197.   [*UCLA*]
28.0816   CU   1948   Ziekenhuis van de N. V. Sanatorium "Het Groene Kruis" [The hospital of the Sanitarium "The Green Cross"]. *In* ORANJE EN DE ZES CARAÏBISCHE PARELEN. Amsterdam, J. H. de Bussy: 179-183.
                                                                                              [*UCLA*]

McCarthy, M. C.
30.0163   TR   1966   Dietary and activity patterns of obese women in Trinidad.

McCulloch, W. E.
28.0817   GC   1955   YOUR HEALTH IN THE CARIBBEAN. Kingston, Pioneer Press, 149p. **[30]**
30.0164   BC   1958   Thirty-five years' experience of colonial nutrition.

McDonald, H.
28.0818   JM   1975   Serum protein fractionation and quantitation by cellulose acetate electrophoresis on normal Jamaicans. *W I Med J* 24(1), March: 55-60.   [*PS*]

McDowall, M. F.

28.0819   TR   1964   The care of the child in health and disease. *In* REPORT OF CONFERENCE ON CHILD CARE IN TRINIDAD AND TOBAGO [HELD BY] TRINIDAD AND TOBAGO ASSOCIATION FOR MENTAL HEALTH, SUB-COMMITTEE ON CHILDREN AND YOUTH. COMMUNITY EDUCATION CENTRE, ST. ANNE'S, APR. 18TH, 1964. [Port of Spain?] Government Printery, 11-13.   [*RIS*]

28.0820   TR   1971   Feeding of the newborn in hospital—paediatrician's view. *W I Med J* 20(3), Sept.: 174-176.   **[30]**   [*PS*]

McFarlane, H.

28.0821   JM   1966   Multiple myeloma in Jamaica—a study of 40 cases with special reference to the incidence and laboratory diagnosis. *J Clin Path* 19(3), May: 268-271.   [*PS*]

McFarlane, H.; Talerman, A. & Steinberg, A. G.

28.0822   JM   1970   Immunoglobulins in Jamaicans and Nigerians with immunogenetic typing of myeloma and lymphoma in Jamaicans. *J Clin Path* 23(2), March: 124-126.   **[11]**   [*PS*]

MacIver, J. E. & Went, L. N.

28.0823   JM   1958   Further observations on abnormal haemoglobins in Jamaica. *W I Med J* 7(2), June: 109-122.   **[27]**   [*COL*]

McKay, David A.; Warren, Kenneth S.; Cook, Joseph A. & Jordan, Peter

28.0824   SL   1973   Immunologic diagnosis of schistosomiasis. III. The effects of nutritional status and infection intensity on intradermal test results in St. Lucian children. *Am J Trop Med Hyg* 22(2), March: 205-210.   **[30,54]**   [*PS*]

MacKenzie, A. D. & Phillips, C. I.

28.0825   JM   1968   West Indian amblyopia. *Brain* 91(2), June: 249-260.   **[18]**   [*PS*]

MacKenzie, C. F.

28.0826   JM   1975   A review of 100 cases of cardiac arrest and the relation of potassium, glucose and haemoglobin levels to survival. *W I Med J* 24(1), March: 39-45.   [*PS*]

McKenzie, H. I.

28.0827   JM   1963   A new health programme in Lawrence Tavern. *Car Q* 9(4), Dec.: 3-9.   [*RIS*]

McKenzie, H. I.; Alleyne, S. I. & Standard, K. L.

28.0828   JM   1967   Reported illness and its treatment in a Jamaican community. *Social Econ Stud* 16(3), Sept.: 262-279.   **[29]**   [*RIS*]

McKenzie, H. I.; Lovell, H. G.; Standard, K. L. & Miall, W. E.

28.0829   JM   1967   Child mortality in Jamaica. *Millbank Mem Fund Q* 45(3), July: 303-320.   **[7]**   [*PS*]

McKenzie, Keith

28.0830   JM   1974   Priorities for child care. *In* International Confederation of Midwives. REPORT OF THE CARIBBEAN WORKING PARTY, BRIDGETOWN, BARBADOS, 16-24 MAY, 1974. [Bridgetown, Barbados]: 59-64.   **[7,30]**   [*RIS*]

McKigney, John I.

30.0165   GC   1968   Economic aspects of infant feeding practices in the West Indies.

30.0168   JM   1971   The uniqueness of human milk. Economic aspects.

MacNamara, B. G. P.

28.0831   GC   1968   The treatment of poisoning in children. *W I Med J* 17(3), Sept.: 166-171.   [PS]

McShine, L. A. H.

28.0832   TR   1961   Cardiac surgery in Trinidad with an analysis of my first 25 cases. *Car Med J* 23(1-4): 49-54.   [COL]

Mahadevan, P.

30.0170   GC   1968   Animal protein supplies for the Caribbean.

Mahy, G. E.

28.0833   GR,BC   1975   Fluphenazine enanthate in a community psychiatric programme. *W I Med J* 24(1), March: 61-64.   [PS]

Mailloux, M.

28.0834   FA   1973   État actuel des leptospiroses humaines aux Antilles Françaises [Current status of human leptospirosis in the French Antilles]. *B Soc Path Exot* 66(1), Jan.-Feb.: 46-54. **[54]**   [PS]

28.0835   FG   1973   Sur un cas de leptospirose humaine à Saint-Laurent-du-Maroni (Guyane Française) [A case of human leptospirosis in Saint-Laurent-du-Maroni (French Guiana)]. *B Soc Path Exot* 66(2), March-April: 269-272.   [PS]

Manchester, K. L.

28.0836   JM   1974   Biochemistry of hyoglycin. *FEBS Lett* 40 Supplement, March 23: S133-S139.   [ACM]

Mandle, Jay R.

7.0118   GU   1970   The decline in mortality in British Guiana, 1911-1960.

Mapp, Lionel McHenry

28.0837   TR   1952   Midwives versus middies in a rural community. *Car Med J* 14(3-4): 139-144. **[34]**   [COL]

Marcano, Roderick G.

28.0838   TR   1960   Rehabilitation in Trinidad. *Car Med J* 22(1-4): 53-58.   [COL]

28.0839   TR   1963   Twenty-five years of public health in the city of Port-of-Spain. *Car Med J* 25(1-4): 10-25.   [COL]

Markowski, B.

28.0840   BZ   1959   Ruptured ectopic pregnancy: analysis of 100 operated cases in British Honduras, Central America. *W I Med J* 8(4), Dec.: 229-234.   [COL]

Marriott, J. A. S.

31.0100   JM   1968   Psychiatric symptomatology in Jamaican medical patients.

Martin, C. R. A.

28.0841   BC,UK   1965   Child health among West Indian immigrants. *Med Officer* August 20: 113-116. **[18]**   *[PS]*

Martin, P. A.; Thorburn, M. J.; Hutchinson, S.; Bras, G. & Miller, C. G.

28.0842   JM   1972   Preliminary findings of chromosomal studies on rats and humans with veno-occlusive disease. *Br J Exp Path* 53(4), Aug.: 374-380. **[29]**   *[PS]*

Martinez, G. S.

28.0843   SL   1970   Blindness in St. Lucia. *W I Med J* 19(1), March: 14-18.   *[PS]*

Mason, G. B.

28.0844   BC   1922   The British West Indies medical services. *United Emp* new ser., 13(11), Nov.: 692-698. **[33]**   *[AGS]*

Massiah, V. I.

28.0845   TR   1968   Haemophilia *A* and *B* in the Port-of-Spain General Hospital in the period—1962 to 1967. *Car Med J* 30: 49-62. **[27]**   *[PS]*

Masson, George H.

28.0846   TR   1910   Indentured labour and preventable diseases. *Proc Agric Soc Trin Tob* 10(6), June: 209-219. **[12]**   *[AMN]*

28.0847   TR   1913   Tuberculosis. *Proc Agric Soc Trin Tob* 13(10), Oct.: 501-508.

                                                                      [AMN]

28.0848   TR   1922   The treatment of ankylostomiasis on the high seas by the intensive method of thymol administration. *Proc Agric Soc Trin Tob* 22(7), July: 563-569. **[12,17]**   *[AMN]*

Mathews, Henry M.; Fisher, George U. & Kagan, Irving G.

28.0849   TB   1970   Persistence of malaria antibody in Tobago, West Indies, following eradication, as measured by the indirect hemagglutination test. *Am J Trop Med Hyg* 19(4), July: 581-585. **[27]**   *[PS]*

Mauze, J. & Pilin, E.

28.0850   GD   1948   Les fièvres typho-exanthématiques en Guadeloupe [Typho-exanthematous fevers in Guadeloupe]. *B Soc Path Exot Fil* 41(7-8), July-Aug.: 442-445.   *[ACM]*

Mauze, J.; Ruggiero, D. & Pilin, E.

28.0851   GD   1948   Le typhus tropical en Guadeloupe [Tropical typhus in Guadeloupe]. *B Soc Path Exot Fil* 41(7-8), July-Aug.: 563-564.   *[ACM]*

May, T.

28.0852   SR   1926-27   De lepra, haar voorkomen, verspreiding, en bestrijding, in 'tbijzonder in Suriname [The occurence of leprosy, its spread, and the fight against it, specifically in Surinam]. *W I G* 8: 546-556.

                                                                      [COL]

28.0853   SR   1927-28   De lepra, haar voorkomen, verspreiding, en bestrijding, in 'tbijzonder in Suriname [The occurrence of leprosy, its spread, and the fight against it, specifically in Surinam]. *W I G* 9: 17-37. *[COL]*

Meertens, L.
28.0854   SL   1968   The appearance of Katayama Syndrome in St. Lucia. *W I Med J*
17(2), June: 117-119.   [*PS*]

Meeteren, N. van
28.0855   CU   1950   Grondwaterpeil en watervoorziening op Curacao voorheen en thans
[The level of groundwater and the water supply on Curacao in the
past and at present]. *W I G* 31: 129-169.   **[53]**   [*COL*]

Melnick, Joseph L.
28.0856   BC   1959   Studies on the serological epidemiology of poliomyelitis as an index
of immunity in certain Caribbean islands, British Guiana, and
Ecuador. *W I Med J* 8(4), Dec.: 275-298.   [*COL*]

Menkman, W. R.
7.0122   SR   1949   Een buitengewoon Surinaams verslag [A special report on Surinam].

**Merson, M. H.; Tenney, J. H.; Meyers, J. D.; Wood, B. T.; Wells, J. G.;
Rymzo, W.; Cline, B.; De Witt, W. E.; Skaliy, P. & Mallison, F.**
28.0857   GC   1975   Shigellosis at sea: an outbreak aboard a passenger cruise ship. *Am J
Epidemiol* 101(2), Feb.: 165-175.   [*PS*]

Messmer, William J.
28.0858   BZ   1974   Intestinal parasites in Belizean children. *National Stud* 2(1), January: 12-15.   [*RIS*]

Metivier, Vivian M.
28.0859   TR   1939   Notes on ocular tuberculosis in Trinidad. *Car Med J* 1(2): 184-191.
[*COL*]
28.0860   TR   1940   Intra-ocular foreign bodies in Trinidad and Tobago. *Car Med J*
1(3): 110-115.   [*COL*]
28.0861   TR   1941   Prevention of blindness in Trinidad and Tobago—ophthalmia
neonatorum: babies' sore eyes. *Car Med J* 3(2): 91-93.   [*COL*]

Metselaar, D.
28.0862   SR   1966   Isolation of arboviruses of Group A and Group C in Surinam. *Trop
Geogr Med* 18(2), June: 137-142.   **[15]**   [*PS*]

Metselaar, D.; Wilterdink, J. B. & Verlinde, J. D.
28.0863   SR   1964   Virological and serological observations made during the development and control of an outbreak of poliomyelitis in Surinam.
Trop Geogr Med 16(2): 129-134.   [*COL*]

Miall, W. E.
28.0864   JM,GU   1970   Electrocardiographic abnormalities in Jamaican and Guyanese
population samples. *In* PROCEEDINGS, FIFTH INTERNATIONAL SCI-
ENTIFIC MEETING OF THE INTERNATIONAL EPIDEMIOLOGICAL ASSO-
CIATION. Belgrade, Yugoslavia: 277-291.   [*ACM*]

**Miall, W. E.; Del Campo, E.; Fodor, J.; Nava Rhode, J. R.; Ruiz, L.;
Standard, K. L. & Swan, A. U.**
28.0865   JM   1972   Longitudinal study of heart disease in a Jamaican rural population.
2. Factors influencing mortality. *B WHO* 46(6): 685-694. **[7]** [*PS*]

Miall, W. E.; Del Campo, E.; Fodor, J.; Nava Rhode, J. R.; Ruiz, L. & Standard, K. L.

28.0866   JM   1972   Longitudinal study of heart disease in a Jamaican rural population. 3. Factors influencing changes in serial electrocardiograms. *B WHO* 46(6): 695-708.   [PS]

Miall, W. E.; Desai, Patricia & Standard, K. L.

30.0176   JM   1970   Malnutrition, infection and child growth in Jamaica.

Miall, W. E.; Milner, P. F.; Lovell, H. G. & Standard, K. L.

28.0867   JM   1967   Haematological investigations of population samples in Jamaica. *Br J Prev Social Med* 21(2), April: 45-55.   [PS]

Miall, W. E. & Rerrie, J. I.

28.0868   JM   1962   The prevalence of pulmonary tuberculosis in a rural population in Jamaica. *W I Med J* 11(3), Sept.: 145-156.   [COL]

Miles, R. P. M.

28.0869   JM   1956   Rectal lymphogranuloma venereum in Jamaica. *W I Med J* 5(3), Sept.: 183-188.   [COL]

Millard, D. Ralph & McNeill, Kenneth A.

28.0870   JM   1965   The incidence of cleft lip and palate in Jamaica. *Cleft Palate J* 2, Oct.: 384-388.   **[11]**   [PS]

Miller, B. R.; Moseley, H. S.; DaCosta, L. R.; Sandison, J. W. & Stuart, K. L.

28.0871   JM   1970   The prognosis in idiopathic cardiomyopathy in Jamaica. *Path Microbiol* 35(1-3); 49-54.   [PS]

Miller, Colin G.

28.0872   JM   1974   University of the West Indies, Department of Paediatrics: past —present—and future. *W I Med J* 23(3), Sept.: 137-141.   **[32]**   [PS]

Miller, Colin G.; Grant, L. S. & Irvine, R. A.

28.0873   JM   1961   Typhoid fever. *W I Med J* 10(3): Sept.: 189-197.   [COL]

Miller, Colin G. & Sue, S. Lim

28.0874   JM   1964   The clinical estimation of neonatal jaundice in Jamaica. *W I Med J* 13(1), Mar.: 59-62.   [COL]

Miller, Colin G. & Thorburn, Marigold J.

28.0875   JM   1966   An outbreak of congenital rubella in Jamaica. *W I Med J* 15(4), Dec.: 177-188.   [PS]

Miller, Colin G.; Woo-Ming, Michael O. & Carpenter, Reginald A.

28.0876   JM   1968   Lobar emphysema of infancy: case report of bilateral involvement with congenital heart disease. *W I Med J* 17(1), March: 35-41.   [PS]

Miller, G. J.

28.0877   GU,JM   1974   Cigarette smoking and irreversible airways obstruction in the West Indies. *Thorax* 29(5), Sept.: 495-504.   [PS]

Miller, G. J. & Ashcroft, M. T.
28.0878 GU 1971 A community survey of respiratory disease among East Indian and African adults of Guyana. *Thorax* 26(3): 331-338. **[11,12]** [*PS*]

Miller, G. J.; Ashcroft, M. T.; Beadnell, H. M. S. G.; Wagner, J. C. & Pepys, J.
28.0879 GU 1971 The lipoid pneumonia of blackfat tobacco smokers in Guyana. *Q J Med* 40(160), Oct.: 457-470. [*PS*]

Miller, G. J.; Cotes, J. E.; Hall, A. M.; Salvosa, C. B. & Ashworth, A.
28.0880 JM,TR 1972 Lung function and exercise performance of healthy Caribbean men and women of African ethnic origin. *Q J Exp Physiol* 57(3), July: 325-341. **[11,27]** [*PS*]

Miller, G. J. & Persaud, V.
28.0881 JM 1968 Hereditary hepatolenticular degeneration (Wilson's disease): a report of the first case in Jamaica. *Trop Geogr Med* 20(3), Sept.: 225-232. **[11]** [*PS*]

Milner, P. F.
28.0882 JM 1965 Modern laboratory methods in clinical haematology (The assay of serum vitamin B-12). *W I Med J* 14(4), Dec.: 231-240. [*PS*]
28.0883 JM 1967 High incidence of haemoglobin G Accra in a rural district in Jamaica. *J Med Genet* 4(2), June: 88-90. **[11,27]** [*PS*]

Milner, P. F.; Back, E. H. & Carpenter, R.
27.0101 JM 1970 Beta-thalassaemia Hb E disease.

Milner, P. F.; Miller, C.; Grey, R.; Seakins, M.; De Jong, W. W. & Went, L. N.
27.0102 JM 1970 Hemoglobin O Arab in four Negro families and its interaction with hemoglobin S and hemoglobin C.

Milroy, E.
28.0884 JM 1969 Achalasia of the cardia—the long-term result of Heller's operation. *W I Med J* 18(2), June: 65-81. [*PS*]

Milroy, E. J. G.
28.0885 JM 1968 Treatment of the enlarged benign prostate using local injections: a preliminary report. *W I Med J* 17(4), Dec.: 241-245. [*PS*]

Minett, E. P.
28.0886 GU 1912 Mosquito prophylaxis. *Timehri* 3d ser., 2(19A), July: 172-178. **[41]**
28.0887 GU 1912 Three cases of anthrax infection in man from the Public Hospital, Georgetown. *Br Gui Med Annual 1910* 17: 100-106. [*ACM*]
28.0888 GU 1913 The frequency of bacillus violaceous in the water and milk supplies of British Guiana. *Br Gui Med Annual 1911* 18: 44-46. [*ACM*]
28.0889 GU 1913 The treatment of leprosy by nastin and benzoyl chloride. *Br Gui Med Annual 1911* 18: 24-33. [*ACM*]
28.0890 GU 1914 The progress of village sanitation. *Br Gui Med Annual 1913* 20: 90-98. [*ACM*]
28.0891 GU 1920 Health problems in British Guiana. *J Bd Agric Br Gui* 13(1), Jan.: 20-24. [*AMN*]

| 28.0892 | GU | 1921 | Agriculture versus malaria. *J Bd Agric Br Gui* 14(4), Oct.: 289-291. **[61]** [*AMN*] |
| 7.0127 | GU | 1923 | Brief review of the public health statistics of the colony. |

Minott, O. D. & Gueri, M.

| 28.0893 | JM | 1968 | Carcinoma of the cervix uteri—diagnosis and disposal in a busy casualty department. *W I Med J* 17(1), March: 26-30. [*PS*] |

Mischel, Frances

| 29.0035 | TR,GR | 1959 | Faith healing and medical practice in the southern Caribbean. |

Moffie, D.

| 28.0894 | NA | 1966 | De geografische verbreiding van multipele sclerose [The geographical distribution of multiple sclerosis]. *Ned Tijdschr Geneesk* 110(33), Aug. 13: 1454-1457. [*PS*] |

Möhlmann, M.

| 28.0895 | CU | 1973 | Het St.-Elisabeth Hospitaal [The St. Elisabeth's Hospital]. *In* Statius van Eps, L. W. & Luckman-Maduro, E., eds. VAN SCHEEP-SCHIRURGIJN TOT SPECIALIST. Assen, The Netherlands, Van Gorcum & Comp. B.V.: 91-97. (Anjerpublikatie 15) [*RILA*] |

Molengraaff, G. J. H.

| 28.0896 | CU | 1930-31 | Korte uiteenzetting van de destijds door den mijnbouwkundigen dienst opgestelde plannen tot waterverzorging van de haven van Willemstad en van die stad zelve op het eiland Curacao [Short explanation of the former plans of the mining department for the water supply of the port of Willemstad and of that city itself on the island Curacao]. *W I G* 12: 25-30. **[5]** [*COL*] |

Monekosso, G. L.

| 28.0897 | JM | 1962 | A clinical comparison of obscure myelopathies in Jamaica and western Nigeria. *W I Med J* 11(4), Dec.: 240-248. [*COL*] |

Montaigne, E. L. de

| 28.0898 | JM | 1953 | Leprosy in Jamaica. *W I Med J* 2(2), June: 125-133. [*COL*] |

Montaigne, E. L. de & Hill, Kenneth R.

| 28.0899 | JM | 1958 | A study of the blood in leprosy: cytology and clotting. *W I Med J* 7(3), Sept.: 195-199. [*COL*] |

Montestruc, Etienne

| 28.0900 | MT | 1949 | La géographie médicale de la Martinique [The medical geography of Martinique]. *Cah O-M* 2(5), Jan.-Mar.: 54-62. [*AGS*] |

Montgomery, R. D.

| 28.0901 | JM | 1959 | Some observations on medical outpatient practice at the University College Hospital of the West Indies. *W I Med J* 8(2), June: 119-123. [*COL*] |
| 28.0902 | GC | 1964 | Observations on the cyanide content and toxicity of tropical pulses. *W I Med J* 13(1), Mar.: 1-11. [*COL*] |

Moody, L. M. et al.
28.0903 JM 1954 Salmonellosis in Jamaica: symposium at the University College of the West Indies, February 10th 1954. *W I Med J* 3(2), June: 108-136. [*COL*]

Moore, J. R. & Lowry, M. F.
28.0904 JM 1975 Prognosis for extremely low birth weight babies in Jamaica. *W I Med J* 29(4), Sept.: 138-143. [*PS*]

Moorehead, George A.
28.0905 SC,ST 1973 Utilization of Methadone Hydrochloride for opiate addiction. *In* NATIONAL CONFERENCE ON METHADONE TREATMENT PROCEEDINGS. New York, National Association for the Prevention of Addiction to Narcotics: 645-651. Vol. 1. **[33]** [*PS*]

Mootoo, C. L.
28.0906 GU 1967 Maternal mortality in Guyana: a social, superstitious and a public health problem. *W I Med J* 16(3), Sept.: 139-144. [*PS*]

Mootoo, C. L. & Singh, B.
28.0907 GU 1966 Review of 210 deaths by poisoning in British Guiana (1959-1964). *W I Med J* 15(1), March: 11-17. [*PS*]

Morgan, O. S.; Hall, J. St. Elmo & Gibbs, W. N.
28.0908 JM 1976 Hodgkin's Disease in pregnancy: a report of three cases. *W I Med J* 25(2), June: 121-124. [*RIS*]

Morris, David
28.0909 JM 1972 Observations on gestational age in a series of Jamaican births. *W I Med J* 21(2), June: 77-81. **[11]** [*PS*]

Morris, David; Persaud, Trivedi V. N. & Roopnarinesingh, Syam
27.0106 JM 1971 Length of Jamaican babies at birth.

Morris, David & Standard, K. L.
28.0910 BC 1974 Notifiable diseases in the English-speaking Caribbean for the two-year period 1972 and 1973. *W I Med J* 23(4), Dec.: 212-216. [*PS*]

Morrison, C. J.
30.0180 JM 1970 Improving nutrition in Jamaica—suggestions towards a strategy of action.

Morton, Julia F.
28.0911 CU 1968 Plants associated with esophageal cancer cases in Curaçao. *Cancer Res* 28(11), Nov.: 2268-2271. **[29,54]** [*PS*]
28.0912 CU 1968 A survey of medicinal plants of Curaçao. *Econ Botany* 22(1): 87-102. **[29,54]** [*PS*]

Moser, C. A.
41.0356 JM 1957 THE MEASUREMENT OF LEVELS OF LIVING WITH SPECIAL REFERENCE TO JAMAICA.

Muhler, J. C.; Kelley, G. E.; Stookey, G. K.; Lindo, F. I. & Harris, N. O.

28.0913 UV 1970 The clinical evaluation of a patient-administered SNF2-ZRSIO4 prophylactic paste in children. I. Results after one year in the Virgin Islands. *J Am Dent Assoc* 81(1), July: 142-145.   [*PS*]

Muir, Ernest

28.0914 TR 1941 Leprosy. *Car Med J* 3(1): suppl. (25p.)   [*COL*]
28.0915 TR 1942 Leprosy control in Trinidad. *Car Med J* 4(3): 83-91.   [*COL*]
28.0916 BC 1944 Leprosy in the British West Indies and British Guiana. *Car Med J* 6(1): 17-31.   [*COL*]

Munro, D. C.

28.0917 SV 1969 Medical mission to St. Vincent. *Can Med Assoc J* 101, Nov. 29: 76-78.   [*PS*]

Murray, Wm. C. G.

30.0181 SV 1942 Infant feeding and nutrition in St. Vincent.

Murray, Wm. C. G. & Asregadoo, E. R.

28.0918 GU 1959 Some common eye diseases in British Guiana. *W I Med J* 8(4), Dec.: 225-228.   [*COL*]

Muskiet, A. B.

28.0919 NA 1973 Andere ziekenhuizen in de Nederlandse Antillen [Other hospitals in the Netherlands Antilles]. *In* Statius van Eps, L. W. & Luckman-Maduro, E., eds. VAN SCHEEPSCHIRURGIJN TOT SPECIALIST. Assen, The Netherlands, Van Gorcum & Comp. B.V.: 97-100. (Anjer-publikatie 15)   [*RILA*]

Myers, Donald M. & Jones, C. June

28.0920 BB 1975 *Leptospira fort-bragg* isolated from a rat in Barbados. *B Pan Am Heal Org* 9(3): 208-211.   [*ACM*]

Nahas, Gabriel G. & Greenwood, Albert

33.0142 JM 1974 The first report of the National Commission on marihuana (1972): signal of misunderstanding or exercise in ambiguity.

Nalin, D. R.

31.0112 GU 1973 Epidemic of suicide by malathion poisoning in Guyana. Report of 264 cases.

Nègre, André

5.0646 FA 1965 Les médecins aux Antilles au 17ᵉ siècle [Doctors in the Antilles in the 17th century].

Nehaul, B. B. G.

28.0921 GU 1943 Report on the physical development and health of a sample of school children in the Island of Leguan, British Guiana, 1941. *Br Gui Med Annual 1943* 26: 95-113. **[30,32]**   [*ACM*]
28.0922 GU 1951 Cancer in British Guiana—pathological studies. *Car Med J* 13(3-4): 90-94.   [*COL*]
28.0923 GU 1951 A short history of the British Guiana Branch of the British Medical Association. *Timehri* 4th ser., 1(30), Nov.: 60-63.

28.0924	GU	1954	Village administration and sanitation. *Timehri* 4th ser., 1(33), Oct.: 45-47.
28.0925	GU	1955	Datura poisoning in British Guiana. *W I Med J* 4(1), Mar.: 57-59. **[29]** [*COL*]
28.0926	GU	1955	History of the British Guiana of the British Medical Association. *Car Med J* 17(1-2): 31-38. **[5]** [*COL*]
28.0927	GU	1955	Influence of Indian immigration. *Timehri* 4th ser., 1(34), Sept.: 35-40. **[12,17]**
28.0928	GU	1956	Filariasis in British Guiana: clinical manifestations of filariasis due to *Wuchereria Bancrofti*. *W I Med J* 5(3), Sept.: 201-206. [*COL*]
28.0929	GU	1956	Some public health legislation of British Guiana in the nineteenth century. *Timehri* 4th ser., 1(35), Oct.: 76-81. **[5]**
28.0930	GU	1958	Serum protein levels in a group of East Indians in a hospital. *W I Med J* 7(3), Sept.: 228-231. **[12]** [*COL*]
28.0931	GU	1960	Infantile diarrhoea in British Guiana; bacteriological findings. *W I Med J* 9(1), Mar.: 51-54. [*COL*]

Nehaul, B. B. G. et al.

| 28.0932 | GU | 1962 | Conference of the Council of Caribbean Branches of the British Medical Association. *Car Med J* 24(1-4): 11-39. [*COL*] |

Neilson, Helen R.

| *30.0182* | GC | 1972 | Candi's role and contribution to improved nutrition and dietary services. |

Newbold, C. E. & Gillette, H. P. S.

| 28.0933 | TR | 1949 | Self-clearing sea heads for low drainage through surf and consequent effects on the incidence of malaria. *Car Med J* 11(4): 137-153. **[53]** [*COL*] |

Newman, Peter

| *7.0131* | GU | 1965 | MALARIA ERADICATION AND POPULATION GROWTH. WITH SPECIAL REFERENCE TO CEYLON AND BRITISH GUIANA. |

Nicholson, C. C.

30.0184	GU	1947	Nutritional survey of pupils of elementary schools, Mahaicony District, February-March, 1947.
30.0185	GU	1956	Assessment of the nutritional status of elementary school children of British Guiana by periodic sampling surveys, and evaluation of the beneficial effects of supplementary feeding.
28.0934	GC	1957	Observations on the incidence, aetiology and prevention of typhoid fever and the diarrhoeal diseases in British Guiana. *Car Med J* 19(1-2): 24-39. [*COL*]

Nicholson, G. D.

| 28.0935 | JM | 1972 | Re-use of coil dialyzers in long-term haemodialysis. *W I Med J* 21(4), Dec.: 240-244. [*PS*] |

Nicholson, G. D. & Amin, U. F.

| 28.0936 | JM | 1974 | The management of Acute Intrinsic Renal Failure. *W I Med J* 23(4), Dec.: 196-205. [*PS*] |

Noel, Desmond

28.0937 GR,GN 1974   Maternal and child health/family planning programme in Grenada, Carriacou and Petit Martinique. *In* International Confederation of Midwives. REPORT OF THE CARIBBEAN WORKING PARTY, BRIDGE-TOWN, BARBADOS, 16-24 MAY, 1974. [Bridgetown, Barbados]: 84-88. **[34]**   [*RIS*]

Noel, Gloria E.

28.0938 GU   1970   The need for continuity of nursing care between hospital and home as an established pattern of service in the Republic of Guyana. *Jam Nurse* 10(3), Dec.: 10-11 passim.   [*AJN*]

Norris, J. R. & Cunningham, K.

28.0939 JM   1963   Idiopathic hypoparathyroidism and pseudohypoparathyroidism: case reports and review of the literature. *W I Med J* 12(1), Mar.: 13-22.   [*COL*]

O'Gara, R. W.

28.0940 NA   1968   Biologic screening of selected plant material for carcinogens. *Cancer Res* 28(11), Nov.: 2272-2275. **[29,54]**   [*PS*]

O'Gara, R. W.; Lee, C. & Morton, J. F.

28.0941 CU   1971   Carcinogenicity of extracts of selected plants from Curaçao after oral and subcutaneous administration to rodents. *J Natn Cancer Inst* 46(6), Jun.: 1131-1137. **[54]**   [*PS*]

O'Gara, R. W.; Lee, C.; Morton, J. F.; Kapadia, Govind J. & Dunham, Lucia J.

28.0942 CU   1974   Sarcoma induced in rats by extracts of plants and by fractionated extracts of *Krameria ixina. J Natn Cancer Inst* 52(2), Feb.: 445-448. **[54]**   [*PS*]

Ogilvie, J. A.

28.0943 BC   1930   A peep into West Indian medical history. *Am J Publ Heal* 20(11), Nov.: 1207-1208.   [*COL*]

Omardeen, T. A.; Kellett, F. R. S. & Gillette, H. P. S.

28.0944 TR   1957   Precipitin studies on *Anopheles aquasalis* Curry, the coastal vector of malaria in Trinidad. B.W.I. *W I Med J* 6(3), Sept.: 205-214. [*COL*]

Omphroy-Spencer, G.

28.0945 JM,BC 1974   What are the priorities for maternal care? *In* International Con-federation of Midwives. REPORT OF THE CARIBBEAN WORKING PARTY, BRIDGETOWN, BARBADOS, 16-24 MAY, 1974. [Bridgetown, Barbados]: 51-58. **[7,34]**   [*RIS*]

Oostburg, Baltus F. J.

28.0946 SR   1971   Thiabendazole therapy of *Lagochilascaris minor* infection in Surinam. Report of a case. *Am J Trop Med Hyg* 20(2), March: 580-583.   [*PS*]

28.0947 SR   1973   Case report; a snakebite in Surinam. *Trop Geogr Med* 25(2), June: 187-189. **[54]**   [*PS*]

Oostburg, Baltus F. J. & Varma, Andre A. O.

28.0948 SR 1968 *Lagochilascaris minor* infection in Surinam. Report of a case. *Am J Trop Med Hyg* 17(4), July: 548-550.   [*PS*]

Orihel, Thomas C.

28.0949 GU 1967 Infections with *Dipetalonema perstans* and *Mansonella ozzardi* in the aboriginal indians of Guyana. *Am J Trop Med Hyg* 16(5), Sept.: 628-635. **[13]**   [*PS*]

Orr, David

28.0950 JM 1967 Lumbar epidural analgesia (citanest and amethocaine combined for a single injection). *W I Med J* 16(2), June: 110-112.   [*PS*]

Ortiz, J. S.; Finklea, J. F.; Potter, E. V.; Poon-King, T.; Ali, D. & Earle, D. P.

28.0951 TR 1970 Endemic nephritis and streptococcal infections in South Trinidad. Surveillance studies during the first year following a major epidemic. *Archs Intern Med* 126(4), Oct.: 640-646.   [*PS*]

Ory, H.; Conger, B.; Richart, R. & Barron, B.

28.0952 BB 1974 Relation of type 2 Herpesvirus antibodies to cervical neoplasia Barbados, *West Indies, 1971. Obstet Gynecol* 43(6), June: 901-904.
                                                                         [*PS*]

Ossenfert, W. F.

28.0953 AR,CU 1950 Health conditions in Aruba and Curacao. *Car Commn Mon Inf B* 4(3), Oct.: 529-530.   [*COL*]

Ottley, J.

28.0954 GU 1909 A short account of the diseases which appear to be prevalent in the Puruni district, and particularly at the Peters' Mine. *Br Gui Med Annual 1908* 16: 103-110.   [*ACM*]

Oudschans Dentz, Fred

28.0955 SR 1930-31 Dr. Constantin Hering en Christiaan Johannes Hering. *W I G* 12: 147-160. **[5,23]**   [*COL*]

Ovens, Gerald H. C.

32.0440 JM 1955 A colonial medical school.

Owen, R. A.

28.0956 GC 1966 Defective vision in West Indian immigrants. *Br J Ophthal* 50(10), Oct.: 561-569. **[18]**   [*PS*]

Ozzard, A. T.

28.0957 GU 1902 The mosquito and malaria. *Br Gui Med Annual* [12?]: 26-39. **[54]**
                                                                        [*ACM*]
28.0958 GU 1904 Notes on the tropical diseases of British Guiana. *Br Gui Med Annual* 13: 43-49.   [*ACM*]
28.0959 GU 1911 Some of the preventable diseases of British Guiana and what we can do to prevent them. *Timehri* 3d ser., 1(18B), July: 136-148.
                                                                        [*AMN*]
28.0960 GU 1912 Village sanitation in British Guiana. *Br Gui Med Annual 1910* 17: 34-42.   [*ACM*]

28.0961　GU　1914　Enteric fever in the Public Hospital, Georgetown. *Br Gui Med Annual 1913* 20: 75-86.　　　　　　　　　　　　[*ACM*]

28.0962　GU　1916　Rural sanitation in British Guiana. *Br Gui Med Annual 1915* 21: 17-23.　　　　　　　　　　　　　　　　　[*ACM*]

Paanakker, L. A.

28.0963　AR　1948　Ziekenverzorging en ziekenverpleging [Health care and nursing]. *In* Oranje en de zes Caraïbische parelen. Amsterdam, J. H. de Bussy: 421-429.　　　　　　　　　　　[*UCLA*]

Panhuys, L. C. van

28.0964　SR　1913　Recent discoveries in Dutch Guiana. *In* Proceedings of the international Congress of Americanists, XVIII session, London. 1912. London, Harrison, pt. 2, p. 376-379.　[*AGS*]

29.0039　SR　1935-36　Opvattingen van Zuid-Amerikaansche Indianen nopens ziekten en geneeswijzen [South American Indian ideas about illness and cures].

23.0219　SR　1936-37　De opoffering van een R.K. priester in Suriname [The sacrifice of a Roman Catholic priest in Surinam].

28.0965　SR　1943　Malaria het beletsel voor Suriname's bloei [Malaria, the obstacle to Surinam's advancement]. *W I G* 25: 303-319.　　　[*COL*]

29.0040　SR　1943　"Sneki-koti", inenting tegen den bijt van vergiftige slangen ["Sneki-koti", immunization against the bite of poisonous snakes].

Parker, M. Murray & Godsen, Minnie

28.0966　TR　1941　An account of cases of congenital urethral obstruction in male infants and children. *Car Med J* 3(2): 61-67.　　　[*COL*]

Parker, M. T.

28.0967　TR　1969　Streptococcal skin infection and acute glomerulonephritis. *Br J Derm* 81, Supplement No. 1: 37-46.　　　　　　[*PS*]

Parker, M. T.; Bassett, D. C. J.; Maxted, W. R. & Arneaud, J. D.

28.0968　TR　1968　Acute glomerulonephritis in Trinidad: serological typing of group A streptococci. *J Hygiene* 66(4), Dec.: 657-675.　　　[*PS*]

Pathak, U. N.

28.0969　JM　1966　Intra-amniotic saline induction for termination of early pregnancy. *W I Med J* 15(2), June: 89-93. **[34]**　　　　　[*PS*]

28.0970　JM　1970　Case report: stones in the diverticulum of the female urethra. *W I Med J* 19(3), Sept.: 180-183.　　　　　　　　[*PS*]

Pathak, U. N. & Hayes, J. A.

28.0971　JM　1968　Umbilical endometriosis. *Br J Clin Pract* 22(3), March: 117-120.　　　　　　　　　　　　　　　　　　[*PS*]

Pathak, U. N. & Singh, S. R.

28.0972　JM,GC　1967　The role of hysterectomy in obstetrics. *W I Med J* 16(4), Dec.: 210-215.　　　　　　　　　　　　　　　　[*PS*]

Patterson, A. W.

28.0973　JM　1974　Maternal and child health and family planning. *In* International Confederation of Midwives. Report of the Caribbean Working Party, Bridgetown, Barbados, 16-24 May, 1974. [Bridgetown, Barbados]: 71-74. **[34]**　　　　　　　　　　　[*RIS*]

Paul, George P.
28.0974   BB   1917   REPORT ON ANKLOSTOMIASIS INFECTION SURVEY OF BARBADOS FROM SEPTEMBER 4, TO NOVEMBER 16, 1916. New York, Rockefeller Foundation, International Health Board, 54p.

Paul, M.; Finnie, E. & Grant, L. S.
28.0975   BC   1973   Bacteriophage (phage) typing of typhoid bacilli isolated in the Caribbean between 1962-1970. *W I Med J* 22(1), March: 15-19.
[PS]

Pautrizel, R.; Szersnovicz, F.; Courmes, E.; Couprie, F. & Hippomene, R.
28.0976   FA   1966   Les résultants d'une enquête séro-épidémiologique de la polio-myélite aux Antilles Françaises: les problèmes qui en découlent [Results of a sero-epidemiologic survey of poliomyelitis in the French Antilles—evolving problems]. *B Inst Natn Sante* 21(1), Jan.-Feb.: 33-46. [ACM]

Pawan, J. L.
28.0977   TR   1959   The transmission of paralytic rabies in Trinidad by the vampire bat (*Desmodus rotundus murinus* Wagner, 1840). *Car Med J* 21(1-4): 110-136. [COL]

Payne, George C.
28.0978   TR   1919   Ankylostomiasis and the planter. *Proc Agric Soc Trin Tob* 19(4), Apr.: 81-87. **[46]** [AMN]

Pearson, R. S. Bruce
28.0979   BB   1973   Asthma in Barbados. *Clin Allergy* 3(3), Sept.: 289-297. [ACM]

Pearson, R. S. Bruce & Cunnington, A. M.
28.0980   BB   1973   The importance of mites in house dust sensitivity in Barbadian asthmatics. *Clin Allergy* 3(3), Sept.: 299-306. **[54]** [ACM]

Pecker, J.; Bouckson, G.; Girard; Ferrand, B.; Aninat, J. C. & Lesbonis
28.0981   MT   1969   La forme neuro-chirurgicale des bilharizioses medullaires. A propos d'un cas observé en Martinique [Neurosurgical form of medullary bilharziosis. A propos of a case observed in Martinique]. *Neurochirurgia* 12(6), Nov.: 201-208. [PS]

Peixotto, Daniel L. M.
28.0982   CU   1973   Waarnemingen op het luchtgestel en ziektens van het eiland Curaçao [Observations on the air quality and diseases on the island Curaçao]. *In* Statius van Eps, L. W. & Luckman-Maduro, E., eds. VAN SCHEEPSCHIRURGIJN TOT SPECIALIST. Assen, The Netherlands, Van Gorcum & Comp. B.V.: 21-40. (Anjerpublikatie 15) **[5]**
[RILA]

Pena, Patricia
30.0190   GC   1972   Teaching the diabetic diet in the Caribbean.

Pennec, Dr.
28.0983   GD   1957   The new leprosarium at Pointe Noire, Guadeloupe. *Caribbean* 10(9), Apr.: 222-225. [COL]

Penrose, Clement A.

28.0984   BA   1905   Sanitary conditions in the Bahama Islands. *In* Shattuck, George
Burbank, ed. THE BAHAMA ISLANDS. New York, Macmillan (*for the
Geographical Society of Baltimore*): 387-416.   **[8,33]**   [*NYP*]

Perronette, H.

28.0985   MT   1948   Public health services in Martinique have been reorganised. *Car
Commn Mon Inf B* 1(12), July: 15-16.   [*COL*]

Perronnette, H.

27.0111   MT   1968   The community weight-profile of children in rural Martinique.

Persaud, Clement Ramdat

28.0986   JM   1973   LABORATORY AND FIELD STUDIES ON THE JAMAICAN STRAIN OF
HUMAN *strongyloides*. Ph.D. dissertation, University of the West
Indies.

Persaud, Trivedi V. N.

28.0987   JM   1967   Foetal abnormalities caused by the active principle of the fruit of
Blighia sapida (ackee). *W I Med J* 16(4), Dec.: 193-197.   **[60]**   [*PS*]

28.0988   JM   1968   Hypoglycin-A and foetal development in rabbits. *W I Med J* 17(1),
March: 52-56.   [*PS*]

28.0989   JM   1968   Non-teratogenicity of hypoglycin-A in mice. *W I Med J* 17(3),
Sept.: 163-165.   [*PS*]

32.0456   BC   1970   Medical education in the English-speaking Caribbean.

Persaud, Trivedi V. N. & Ellington, A. C.

28.0990   JM   1968   The effects of Cannabis sativa L. (ganja) on developing rat
embryos—preliminary observations. *W I Med J* 17(4), Dec.:
232-234.   [*PS*]

Persaud, Vasil

28.0991   JM   1970   Etiology of tubal ectoptic pregnancy. Radiologic and pathologic
studies. *Obstet Gynec* 36(2), Aug.: 257-263.   [*PS*]

28.0992   JM   1974   Incidence of cancer of the uterine cervix in Kingston, Jamaica,
1958-1970. *W I Med J* 23(1), March: 8-14.   [*PS*]

28.0993   JM   1974   Intra-epithelial and early invasive carcinoma of the uterine cervix.
W I Med J 23(4), Dec.: 232-237.   [*PS*]

28.0994   JM   1974   Population screening for cervical cancer in Jamaica: results of two
separate surveys. *W I Med J* 23(2), June: 85-91.   [*PS*]

28.0995   JM   1975   Epidemiology of cancer of the uterine cervix in Jamaica. *W I Med J*
24(4), Dec.: 171-178.   [*PS*]

Persaud, Vasil & Bras, G.

28.0996   JM   1966   Juvenile nasopharygeal angiofibroma (Report of a case with
unusual features). *W I Med J* 15(3), Sept.: 125-127.   [*PS*]

Persaud, Vasil & Burkett, Gene

28.0997   JM   1971   A case of primary carcinoma of the Fallopian tube with a review of
the literature. *W I Med J* 20(1), March: 46-50.   [*PS*]

Persaud, Vasil & Knight, L. Patrick

28.0998   JM   1968   Carcinoma of the body of the uterus in Jamaica. *W I Med J* 17(1),
March: 42-51.   [*PS*]

28.0999   JM   1968   Malignant mesenchymal tumours of the corpus uteri. *W I Med J* 17(2), June: 96-102.   [*PS*]

Persaud, Vasil & Patrick, A. L.
28.1000   JM   1967   Lipoma of the corpus callosum. *W I Med J* 16(3), Sept.: 173-176.   [*PS*]

Persaud, Vasil & Patterson, Adeline W.
28.1001   JM   1970   Feminizing mesenchymal tumours of the ovary. A clinico-pathological review. *W I Med J* 19(1), March: 37-47.   [*PS*]

Persaud, Vasil & Woo-Ming, Michael
28.1002   JM   1973   Plasma cell granuloma of the lung. *W I Med J* 22(4), Dec.: 169-177.   [*PS*]

Petana, W. B.
28.1003   BZ   1967   American trypanosomiasis in British Honduras. III. Unusual morphology in a strain of *Trypanosoma (Schizotrypanum) cruzi* from a white mouse infected with the gut contents of a wild-caught *Triatoma dimidiata* (Hemiptera, Reduviidae). *Ann Trop Med Paras* 61(4), Dec.: 409-412. **[54]**   [*PS*]

28.1004   BZ   1967   American trypanosomiasis in British Honduras. IV. Laboratory observations on *Triatoma dimidiata* (Hemiptera, Reduviidae) and its efficiency as a vector of Chagas' disease in British Honduras. *Ann Trop Med Paras* 61(4), Dec.: 413-416.   [*PS*]

28.1005   BZ   1968   A survey for intestinal parasites in two communities in British Honduras, Central America. *Ann Trop Med Paras* 62(4), Dec.: 518-521.   [*PS*]

28.1006   BZ   1969   American trypanosomiasis in British Honduras. V.—Development of *Trypanosoma (Schizotrypanum) cruzi* in animals infected with strains isolated from the El Cayo District, and the occurrence of crithidia forms in the tissues. *Ann Trop Med Paras* 63(1), March: 39-45. **[54]**   [*PS*]

28.1007   BZ   1969   American trypanosomiasis in British Honduras. VI.—A natural infection with *Trypanosoma (Schizotrypanum) cruzi* in the opossum *Didelphis marsupialis* (Marsupialia, Didelphoidea), and experimental investigations of different wild-animal species as possible reservoirs for the parasite. *Ann Trop Med Paras* 63(1), March: 47-56. **[54]**   [*PS*]

28.1008   BZ   1969   American trypanosomiasis in British Honduras. VII.—A natural infection in a wild cotton rat *Sigmodon hispidus* (Rodentia, Cricketidae) with a trypanosome morphologically resembling *Trypanosoma sigmondi* Culbertson, 1941. *Ann Trop Med Paras* 63(1), March: 57-61. **[54]**   [*PS*]

28.1009   BZ   1971   American trypanosomiasis in British Honduras. VIII.—The morphogenesis of *Trypanosoma (Schizotrypanum) cruzi* in the tissues of animals experimentally infected with British Honduras strains of the parasite. *Ann Trop Med Paras* 65(1), March: 21-24.   [*PS*]

28.1010   BZ   1971   American trypanosomiasis in British Honduras. IX. Development of *Trypanosoma (Schizotrypanum) cruzi* in *Triatoma dimidiata* (Hemiptera, Reduviidae), and a note on the occurrence of dividing trypomastigote forms in the gut of some naturally infected bugs. *Ann Trop Med Paras* 65(1), March: 25-30.   [*PS*]

28.1011 BZ 1971 American trypanosomiasis in Brisith Honduras. X. Natural habitats and ecology of *Triatoma dimidiata* (Hemiptera, Reduviidae) in the El Cayo and Toledo Districts, and the prevalence of infection with *Trypanosoma (Schizotrypanum) cruzi* in the wild-caught bugs. *Ann Trop Med Paras* 65(2), June: 169-178. **[54]**   [*PS*]

28.1012 BZ 1971 American trypanosomiasis in British Honduras. XI. Observation on the viability and morphology of *Trypanosoma sigmondi* Culbertson 1941, *in vitro. Ann Trop Med Paras* 65(2), June: 179-183.   [*PS*]

Petana, W. B. & Coura, J. R.

28.1013 BZ 1967 American trypanosomiasis in British Honduras. I. Isolation of a strain of *Trypanosoma (Schizotrypanum) cruzi* from a triatomine bug, *Triatoma dimidiata* (Hemiptera, Reduviidae). *Ann Trop Med Paras* 61(3), Sept.: 235-243. **[54]**   [*PS*]

Peterson, E.

28.1014 ST,SJ 1919 Infectious and contagious diseases on the islands of St. Thomas and St. John, Virgin Islands of the United States, March-September 1918. *U S Navl Med B* 13(4), Oct. 682-706. **[33]**   [*ACM*]

Pickering, George et al.

28.1015 BC 1959 Standing Advisory Committee for Medical Research in the British Caribbean: [report]. *In* PROCEEDINGS OF THE FOURTH SCIENTIFIC MEETING Apr. 5th and 6th, 1959, held at Georgetown, British Guiana. *W I Med J* 8(2), June: 135-143.   [*COL*]

Picou, D.

28.1016 BC 1965 Medical research in the British Caribbean. *J Trop Med Hyg* 68(8), Aug.: 208-210.   [*ACM*]

Pike, Lennox A.

28.1017 BZ 1967 Observations on the feeding of babies with gastroenteritis on an acidified milk formula. *W I Med J* 16(4), Dec.: 225-227. **[30]** [*PS*]

Pineau, A.

28.1018 GD 1960 Médecine et psychiatrie rurale en Guadeloupe [Rural medicine and psychiatry in Guadeloupe]. *Concours Méd* 82(4), Jan. 23: 413-416. **[30,31]**   [*COL*]

28.1019 GD 1960 Médecine et psychiatrie rurale en Guadeloupe [Rural medicine and psychiatry in Guadeloupe]. *Concours Méd* 82(5), Jan. 30: 533-544. **[30,31]**   [*COL*]

Pinkerton, J. H. M. & Miller, Colin G.

28.1020 JM 1956 Observations on carcinoma of the cervix. Pt. II: A report on 73 consecutive cases of carcinoma of the cervix uteri seen at the University College Hospital of the West Indies. *W I Med J* 5(1), Mar.: 10-18.   [*COL*]

Pitt, D. T.

28.1021 BC 1943 Comment on medical section of Sir F. Stockdale's report. *Car Med J* 5(3): 121-127.   [*COL*]

Pitts, O. M.; Ravenel, J. M. & Finklea, J. F.

28.1022   TR   1969   Rubella immunity in Trinidad. *Am J Epidemiol* 89(3), March: 271-275.   [*PS*]

Pless, I. B. & Hood, C.

28.1023   GC   1967   West Indian one-year-olds. A comparative analysis of health and service utilisation. *Lancet,* I for 1967 (7504), June 24: 373-376.   **[18]**   [*PS*]

Pletsch, D. J.

28.1024   GC   1971   A.M.C.A.'s response to the current ecological era: Latin America-Caribbean region. *Mosq News* 31(3), Sept.: 343-44.   [*PS*]

Plotz, Harry; Woodward, Dore E.; Philip, Cornelius B. & Bennett, Byron L.

28.1025   JM   1943   Endemic typhus fever in Jamaica, B.W.I. *Am J Publ Heal* 43(7), July: 812-814.   [*COL*]

Plus, N.; Croizier, G.; Duthoit, J. L.; David, J.; Anxolabehere, D. & Periquet, G.

54.0782   FG   1975   Découverte, chez la Drosophile, de virus appartenant à trois nouveaux groupes [The discovery, in Drosophila, of viruses belonging to three new groups].

Poonai, A.; Morris, D.; Persaud, T. V. N. & Poonai, P. V.

27.0114   JM   1973   Birth weight in Jamaican twins.

Poon-King, T.; Henry, M. V. & Rampersad, F.

28.1026   TR   1968   Prevalence and natural history of diabetes in Trinidad. *Lancet,* I for 1968 (7535), Jan. 27: 155-160.   [*PS*]

Poon-King, T.; Mohammed, I.; Cox, R.; Potter, E. V.; Simon, N. M.; Siegel, A. C. & Earle, D. P.

28.1027   TR   1967   Recurrent epidemic nephritis in South Trinidad. *New Eng J Med* 277(14), Oct.: 728-733.   [*PS*]

Poon-King, T.; Svartman, Mauri; Mohammed, Isahak; Potter, Elizabeth V.; Achong, Joyce; Cox, Reginald & Earle, David P.

28.1028   TR   1973   Epidemic acute nephritis with reappearance of M-type 55 streptococci in Trinidad. *Lancet* 1(7801), March 3: 475-479.   [*PS*]

Portner, Stuart

28.1029   TR   1967   Organization for health planning in Trinidad and Tobago: summary of contents. *In* SECOND SEMINAR ON ORGANIZATION AND ADMINISTRATION OF HEALTH SERVICES—CARIBBEAN. Port-of-Spain, Trinidad, 14-19 Nov.: 201-203.   [*RIS*]

Pot, A. W.; Raalte, S. W. G. van & Sar, A. van der

28.1030   NA   1942   Bijdrage tot de kennis der bacillaire dysenterie op Curacao [Contribution to the knowledge about amoebic dysentery on Curacao]. *Geneesk Tijdschr Ned-Indie* 82(6): 234-250.

Potter, E. V.; Moran, A. F.; Poon-King, T. & Earle, D. P.

28.1031   TR   1968   Characteristics of beta hemolytic streptococci associated with acute glomerulonephritis in Trinidad, West Indies. *J Lab Clin Med* 71(1), Jan.: 126-137.   [*PS*]

Potter, E. V.; Ortiz, J. S.; Sharrett, A. R.; Burt, E. G.; Bray, J. P.; Finklea, J. F.; Poon-King, T. & Earle, D. P.

28.1032   TR   1971   Changing types of nephritogenic streptococci in Trinidad. *J Clin Invest* 50(6), June: 1197-1205.   [*PS*]

Potter, E. V.; Siegal, A. C.; Simon, N. M.; McAninch, J.; Earle, D. P.; Poon-King, T.; Mohammed, I. & Abidh, S.

28.1033   TR   1968   Streptococcal infections and epidemic acute glomerulonephritis in South Trinidad. *J Pediat* 72(6): 871-884.   [*PS*]

Potter, E. V.; Svartman, M.; Burt, E. G.; Finklea, J. F.; Poon-King, T. & Earle, D. P.

28.1034   TR   1972   Relationship of acute rheumatic fever to acute glomerulo-nephritis in Trinidad. *J Infect Dis* 125(6), June: 619-625.   [*PS*]

Powell, Dorian L.

20.0066   JM   1972   Occupational choice and role conceptions of nursing students.

Prabhakar, V.; Persaud, Vasil; Indira, C. & Davis, N. E.

28.1035   JM   1976   Incidence of atherosclerosis in the Circle of Willis. *W I Med J* 25(2), June: 73-77.   [27]   [*RIS*]

Pradinaud, R.; Joly, F.; Basset, M.; Basset, A. & Grosshans, E.

28.1036   FG   1969   Les chromomycoses et la maladie de Jorge Lobo en Guyanes Française [Chromomycosis and Jorge Lobo disease in French Guiana]. *B Soc Path Exot* 62(6), Nov.-Dec.: 1054-1063.   [*PS*]

Pradinaud, R. & Rivierez, E.

28.1037   FG   1968   Miyase furonculeuse de la paupière supérieure en Guyane Française [Furuncular myiasis of the upper eyelid in French Guiana]. *B Soc Derm Syph* 75(6): 808-810.   [*PS*]

Puffer, Ruth R.

28.1038   GC   1965   Morbidity and mortality in the Caribbean. *In* Wilgus, A. Curtis, ed. THE CARIBBEAN: ITS HEALTH PROBLEMS. Gainesville, University of Florida Press: 133-146. (Caribbean Conference Series 1, Vol. 15)   [7]   [*RIS*]

Pyke, D. A. & Wattley, G. H.

28.1039   TR   1962   Diabetes in Trinidad. *W I Med J* 11(1), Mar.: 22-26.   [*COL*]

Quénum, C. & N'Diaye, P.-D.

28.1040   JM   1973   Approche épidémiologique du cancer de l'enfant [Epidemiological approach to cancer in children]. *B Soc Med Afr Noire* 18(2): 129-136.   [*ACM*]

Quigley, Lawrence F.; Shklar, Gerald & Cobb, Carolus M.

28.1041   NA   1966   Reverse cigarette smoking in Caribbeans: clinical, histologic, and cytologic observations. *J Am Dent Assoc* 72(4), April: 867-873.   [13]   [*PS*]

Quinn, Sheila

28.1042   GC   1968   The role of the professional nurses' association in the changing Caribbean. *Jam Nurse* 6(2), Sept.: 14-25 passim.   [*AJN*]

Ragbeer, M. M. S.
32.0469	BC	1972	Post-graduate medical education in the Commonwealth Caribbean.
32.0470	BC	1974	The medical faculty U.W.I.—a brief review of twenty-five years of activity—1949-1974.

Ragbeer, M. M. S. & Brooks, S. E. H.
28.1043	JM	1968	Granular cell "myoblastoma" of the breast. *W I Med J* 17(1), March: 1-13. [*PS*]

Ragbeer, M. M. S. & Singh, S. M.
28.1044	JM	1968	Dygerminoma of the ovary. *W I Med J* 17(3), Sept.: 149-154. [*PS*]

Ragbeer, M. M. S.; Walrond, E. R. & Bateson, E. M.
28.1045	GC	1970	Kaposi's sarcoma in West Indians. *W I Med J* 19(1), March: 54-63. [*PS*]

Ramkeesoon, Gemma
33.0156	TR	1964	Voluntary welfare services for the child.

Ramkissoon, Ramdath
28.1046	TR	1963	Gastroenteritis at the General Hospital, Port-of-Spain. *Car Med J* 25(1-4): 69-74. [*COL*]

Ramkissoon, Ramdath & McDowall, Milton F.
28.1047	TR	1968	Respiratory disease in children caused by parainfluenza viruses. Description of an acute outbreak. *Clin Pediat* 7(9), Sept.: 518-524. [*PS*]

Ramprashad, C.; Grant, L. S. & Belle, E. A.
28.1048	DM	1968	The treatment of (intestinal amoebiasis) with a single dose of humatin. *W I Med J* 17(1), March: 57-60. [*PS*]

Ramsey, F. C.
30.0195	BC	1974	The place of nutrition in the priorities of maternal and child health.

Ramsey, Frank C.
28.1049	BB	1962	Scarlet fever in Barbados. *W I Med J* 11(3), Sept.: 199-202. [*COL*]
28.1050	JM	1962	Trichuris dysentery syndrome. *W I Med J* 11(4), Dec.: 235-239. [*COL*]
28.1051	JM	1963	Organic phosphorus insecticide poisoning in infants. *W I Med J* 12(1), Mar.: 50-52. [*COL*]

Rang, Mercer
28.1052	JM	1967	Current practice in orthopaedics: compound fractures. *W I Med J* 16(2), June: 102-106. [*PS*]

Reddy, S. K.
30.0198	JM,BB	1971	Artificial feeding in Jamaica and Barbados.

Reekie, Robert Andrew & Miller, Colin G.
28.1053	JM	1971	Cor pulmonale secondary to chronic nasopharyngeal obstruction in a child. *W I Med J* 20(1), March: 41-45. [*PS*]

Reijenga, T. W.

28.1054   SR   1971   VERSPREIDINGSOECOLOGIE VAN *Biomphalaria glabrata* (SAY, 1818) IN RELATIE TOT BILHARZIASIS IN SURINAME [DISTRIBUTION AND ENVIRONMENT OF *Biomphalaria glabrata* (SAY, 1818) IN RELATION TO BILHARZIASIS IN SURINAM]. Nijmegen, The Netherlands, Thoben Offset: 128p. (Dissertation, Rijksuniversiteit Leiden). **[56]** [*RILA*]

Reijenga, T. W. & Asselt, W. P. van

28.1055   SR   1968   *Schistosomiasis mansoni* in a Surinam polder. *Trop Geogr Med* 20(1), March: 28-34. **[35]** [*PS*]

Reijenga, T. W.; Vas, I. E. & Wiersema, J. P.

28.1056   SR   1962   On injuries caused by predatory salmon (*Serrasalmo rhombeus L.*) in the rivers of Surinam. *Trop Geogr Med* 14(2), June: 105-110. **[52,54]** [*COL*]

Reisel, J. H.

28.1057   NA   1969   Epidemiological and psychosomatic aspects in essential hypertension. *Psychother Psychosom* 17(3-4): 169-177. **[31]** [*PS*]

Rep, B. H.

28.1058   NA   1975   Intestinal helminths in dogs and cats on the Antillian Islands Aruba, Curaçao and Bonaire. *Trop Geogr Med* 27(3), Sept.: 317-323. **[54]** [*PS*]

28.1059   SR   1978   Hookworms and other helminths in dogs, cats and man in Surinam. *Trop Geogr Med* 20(3), Sept.: 262-270. **[54]** [*PS*]

Rerrie, I. J.

28.1060   JM   1960   Review of adult tuberculosis in Jamaica. *Car Med J* 22(1-4): 64-69. [*COL*]

28.1061   JM   1960   Review of childhood type tuberculosis in Jamaica. *Car Med J* 22(1-4): 70-74. [*COL*]

Restrepo, Carlos & Tracy, Richard E.

28.1062   JM   1975   Variations in human aortic fatty streaks among geographic locations. *Atherosclerosis* 21(2), March-April: 179-193. **[11]** [*ACM*]

Reus, Tjeerd de

28.1063   CU   1970   GESLACHTSZIEKTEN OP CURAÇAO [VENEREAL DISEASES ON THE ISLAND OF CURAÇAO]. Assen, The Netherlands, Van Gorcum & Comp. N.V./Dr. H. J. Prakke & H.M.G. Prakke: 163p. (Dissertation, Rijksuniversiteit Leiden) [*RILA*]

28.1064   NL   1973   Geslachtsziekten en geslachtsziektenbestrijding [Venereal disease and how it is controlled]. *In* Statius van Eps, L. W. & Luckman-Maduro, E., eds. VAN SCHEEPSCHIRURGIJN TOT SPECIALIST. Assen, The Netherlands, Van Gorcum & Comp. B.V.: 131-134. (Anjerpublikatie 15) [*RILA*]

Reynolds, R. M. P.

28.1065   BB   1967   Some notes about eye diseases in Barbados. *Barb Nurs J* 1, Sept.-Oct.: 5-6. [*AJN*]

Rhodes, Katerina
30.0202   **JM**   1957   Two types of liver disease in Jamaican children.

Ribstein, Michel; Certhoux, A. & Lavenaire, A.
31.0120   **MT**   1967   Alcoolisme au rhum: étude de la symptomologie et analyse de la personalité de l'homme martiniquais alcoolique au rhum [Alcoholism caused by rum. Study of the symptomatology and analysis of the personality of the male rum alcoholic of Martinique].

Ribstein, Michel & Foucault, J. M.
28.1066   **MT**   1965   Synostoses et fusions rachidiennes cervicales. Etude critique de sept observations [Synostosis and cervical rachidian fusions. Critical study of seven observations]. *J Med Bord Sud-Ouest* 142(6), June: 948-953.   [*PS*]

Ribstein, Michel; Yoyo & Levigneron
28.1067   **MT**   1965   Complications nerveuses et complications mentales de l'hémoglobinose hétérozygote AS [Nervous and mental complications in heterozygote hemoglobinose AS]. *J Med Bord Sud-Ouest* 142(6), June, 955-961.   **[27]**   [*PS*]

Rice, N. S.; Jones, B. R. & Ashton, N.
28.1068   **GC**   1968   Punctate keratopathy of West Indians. *Br J Ophthal* 52(12), Dec.: 865-875.   **[18]**   [*PS*]

Rice, Paul L.
28.1069   **GC**   1965   Control of insects of public health importance in the Caribbean. *In* Wilgus, Curtis, ed. THE CARIBBEAN: ITS HEALTH PROBLEMS. Gainesville, University of Florida Press: 110-123. (Caribbean Conference Series 1, Vol. 15)   [*RIS*]

Richards, Charles S.
27.0115   **SL**   1975   Genetic factors in susceptibility of *Biomphalaria glabrata* for different strains of *Schistosoma mansoni.*

Richards, R. & Brooks, S. E. H.
28.1070   **JM**   1966   Ferrous sulphate poisoning in pregnancy (with afibrinogenaemia as a complication). *W I Med J* 15(3), Sept.: 134-140.   [*PS*]

Richardson, Evelyn
28.1071   **SC**   1971   ONE MOMENT OF GLORY. Brooklyn, New York, Theo. Gaus' Sons, Inc.: 83p.   **[29]**   [*NYP*]

Richardson, R. K.
28.1072   **TR**   1966   The results of treatment by resection of two hundred cases of pulmonary tuberculosis in Trinidad and Tobago. *Dis Chest* 50(3), Sept.: 281-288.   [*PS*]
28.1073   **TR**   1966   The results of treatment by resection of two hundred cases of tuberculosis in Trinidad and Tobago. *W I Med J* 15(1), March: 18-26.   [*PS*]

Richardson, Stephen A.
30.0203   **JM**   1975   Physical growth of Jamaican school children who were severely malnourished before 2 years of age.

Richardson, Stephen A.; Birch, H. G. & Hertzig, Margaret E.

28.1074   JM   1973   School performance of children who were severely malnourished in infancy. *Am J Ment Def* 77(5), March: 623-632.   **[30,32]**   [*ACM*]

Ríos Vargas, Antonio

28.1075   GC   1965   Status and need of medical care facilities in the Caribbean. *In* Wilgus, A. Curtis, ed. THE CARIBBEAN: ITS HEALTH PROBLEMS. Gainesville, University of Florida Press: 163-175. (Caribbean Conference Series 1, Vol. 15)   **[7]**   [*RIS*]

Roberts, D. F.; Triger, D. R. & Morgan, R. J.

28.1076   JM   1970   Glucose-6-phosphate dehydrogenase deficiency and haemoglobin level in Jamaican children. *W I Med J* 19(4), Dec.: 204-211.   **[30]**
[*PS*]

Robertson, E. L. S.

28.1077   TR   1964   The care of the physically handicapped child. *In* REPORT OF CONFERENCE ON CHILD CARE IN TRINIDAD AND TOBAGO [HELD BY] TRINIDAD AND TOBAGO ASSOCIATION FOR MENTAL HEALTH, SUB-COMMITTEE ON CHILDREN AND YOUTH, COMMUNITY EDUCATION CENTRE, ST. ANN'S, APR. 18TH, 1964. [Port of Spain?] Government Printery, p.19-21.   [*RIS*]

Robertson, W. B.

28.1078   JM   1961   Some factors influencing the development of atherosclerosis: a survey in Jamaica, West Indies. *W I Med J* 10(4), Dec.: 269-275.
[*COL*]

Robinson-Von Avery, J.

28.1079   JM   1974   University Hospital: the future of paediatrics. *W I Med J* 23(3), Sept.: 145-147.   [*PS*]

Robles, R. M.

28.1080   AR   1948   Geneeskunde en hygiëne [Medicine and hygiene]. *In* ORANJE EN DE ZES CARAÏBISCHE PARELEN. Amsterdam, J. H. de Bussy: 417-420.
[*UCLA*]

Rodgers, P. E. B.

28.1081   JM   1965   The clinical features and aetiology of the neuropathic syndrome in Jamaica. *W I Med J* 14(1), March: 36-47.   [*PS*]

Rodgers, P. E. B. & Cruickshank, E. K.

28.1082   JM   1962   Spinal arachnoiditis. *W I Med J* 11(3), Sept.: 164-170.   [*COL*]

Roethof-Ensing, Dokie

28.1083   SR   1970   Medische hulp in het binnenland [Medical aid in the interior]. *Schakels* S75: 35-38.   [*NYP*]

Roever-Bonnet, H. de

28.1084   SR   1967   Toxoplasmosis in Surinam (Netherlands Guyana): a serological survey. *Trop Geogr Med* 19(3), Sept.: 221-228.   **[13,14]**   [*PS*]

Rombouts, H. E.

28.1085   SR   1939   Medische notites over de grens-expedities [Medical notes about the border expedities]. *Tijdschr Ned Aar Genoot* 2d ser., 56(6), Nov.: 876-882.   [*AGS*]

Römer, R.

28.1086   SR   1919-20   Sanitaire beschouwing in verband met immigraties van werkkrachten in Suriname [Essay on sanitation in connection with the immigration of labor forces into Surinam]. *W I G* 1(2): 101-124, 214-240, 380-400, 436-485.   **[17]**   [*COL*]

Romiti, Cesare

28.1087   GU   1933   Rare hernias in aboriginal Indians of British Guiana. *Br Gui Med Annual 1932* 25: 6-24.   **[13]**   [*ACM*]

28.1088   GU   1933   Three cases of pleuricystic adamantinomata of the jaw, observed in Negroes. *Br Gui Med Annual 1932* 25: 51-66.   **[11]**   [*ACM*]

28.1089   GU   1936   Filariasis in British Guiana. *Br Gui Med Annual 1936* 26: 54-65.   [*ACM*]

28.1090   GU   1957   Post-operative malaria. *W I Med J* 6(4), Dec.: 272-284.   [*COL*]

28.1091   GU   1957   Statistical report on the incidence of fibroids and malignant tumors of the uterus in British Guiana. *W I Med J* 6(4), Dec.: 243-248.   **[11,12]**   [*COL*]

Roopnarinesingh, S. S.

28.1092   JM   1969   Hydatidiform mole: a review of the literature and report on twenty-nine cases treated at the University Hospital of the West Indies. *W I Med J* 18(4), Dec.: 222-230.   [*PS*]

28.1093   JM   1970   The young Negro primigravida in Jamaica. *J Obstet Gynaec Br Commonw* 77(5), May: 424-426.   **[11]**   [*PS*]

28.1094   JM   1970   The young primigravida. *W I Med J* 19(2), June: 78-83.   [*PS*]

28.1095   JM   1971   Foetal mortality in breech. *W I Med J* 20(2), June: 87-90.   [*PS*]

34.0091   TR   1975   Teenage pregnancy in Trinidad.

Roopnarinesingh, S. S.; Morris, D. & Chang, E.

28.1096   JM   1971   The underweight Jamaican parturient. *J Obstet Gynaec Br Commonw* 78(4), April: 379-382.   **[30]**   [*PS*]

Roopnarinesingh, S. S.; Morris, D. & Persaud, Trivedi V. N.

27.0120   JM   1971   Birth weight of Jamaican babies.

Roopnarinesingh, S. S. & Pathak, U. N.

28.1097   JM   1970   Obesity in the Jamaican parturient. *J Obstet Gynaec Br Commonw* 77(10), Oct.: 895-899.   **[30]**   [*PS*]

Rose, F. G.

28.1098   GU   1919   An investigation into the causes of still-birth and abortion in the city of Georgetown. *Br Gui Med Annual 1919* 22: 33-47.   **[10]**   [*ACM*]

28.1099   GU   1921   The progress of sanitation in British Guiana. *Timehri* 3d ser., 7(24), Aug.: 61-64.   [*AMN*]

28.1100   GU   1926   Leprosy statistics and legislation in British Guiana. *Br Gui Med Annual 1925* 24: 118-121.   **[33,37]**   [*ACM*]

28.1101   GU   1933   Six years of leprosy work in British Guiana. *Br Gui Med Annual 1932* 25: 35-44.   [*ACM*]

Rose, F. G. & Chow, J. E.
28.1102   GU   1923   A résumé of the scientific work published by medical men in British Guiana from 1769 to the present day. *Br Gui Med Annual 1923* 23: 53-62.   **[1,5]**   [*ACM*]

Ross, Evelyn
28.1103   JM   1966   The Mona Rehabilitation Centre in Kingston, Jamaica. *Nurs Mirror* 123(13), Dec. 30: 288-290.   [*PS*]

Rostant, Maurice & René-Boisneuf, Jean
28.1104   GD   1965   Réflexions à propos de quelques manifestations séreuses dans la maladie de Hansen [Reflections on several serious manifestations of Hansen's disease]. *J Med Bord Sud-Ouest* 142(6), June: 967-970.
                                                                                                          [*PS*]

Rotchell, Yvonne E.
28.1105   BB   1976   An evaluation of paracervical block anaesthesia for use in minor gynaecological surgery. *W I Med J* 25(1), March: 35-38.   **[34]**   [*PS*]

Roth, Walter Edmund
29.0042   GU   1919   A few notes on the medical practises of the Guiana Indians.

Rowe, Monica Elaine Hamilton
28.1106   JM   1967   A STUDY OF MACROGLOBULINS IN JAMAICANS. Ph.D. dissertation, University of the West Indies.

Rowland, E. D.
28.1107   GU   1912   Remarks on sixty-four cases of enteric fever treated in the Public Hospital, Georgetown, from December, 1908, to June, 1910. *Br Gui Med Annual 1910* 17: 1-24.   [*ACM*]
28.1108   GU   1913   Enteric fever in the Public Hospital, Georgetown. *Br Gui Med Annual 1912* 19: 8-53.   [*ACM*]
28.1109   GU   1914   Pneumonia in British Guiana. *Br Gui Med Annual 1913* 20: 38-74.
                                                                                                          [*ACM*]

Royes, K. C.
28.1110   JM   1948   Infantile hepatic cirrhosis in Jamaica. *Car Med J* 10(1-2): 16-48.
                                                                                                          [*COL*]

Royes, Veronica I. Joy
28.1111   JM   1971   SOME COMPONENTS OF THE AIR SPORA IN JAMAICA AND THEIR POSSIBLE MEDICAL APPLICATION. Ph.D. dissertation, University of the West Indies.   **[54]**

Rubin, Vera
31.0128   GC   1963   Report on the census of Caribbean mental hospitals.

Rubin, Vera & Comitas, Lambros
33.0170   JM   1976   GANJA IN JAMAICA: THE EFFECTS OF MARIJUANA USE.

Ruiz, L.; Miall, W. E. & Swan, A. V.

28.1112 JM 1973 Quantitative aspects of electrocardiograms of adults in a Jamaican rural population. *Br Heart J* 35(8), Aug.: 829-839. **[11,27]** [*PS*]

Saleh, A. E. C.

28.1113 CU 1974 Enkele doelstellingen in de Curaçaosche gezondheidszorg [Some objectives of health care in Curaçao]. *Kristòf* 1(4), Aug.: 149-158. [*RIS*]

Salmond, R. W. A.

28.1114 BB 1941 The new X-ray department at the General Hospital, Barbados. *Car Med J* 3(3): 149-150. [*COL*]

Salzano, Francisco M., ed.

7.0182 GC 1971 THE ONGOING EVOLUTION OF LATIN AMERICAN POPULATIONS.

Sampath, Martin

28.1115 TR 1953 The influence of socio-anthropological factors on the incidence of syphilis in a heterogenous group of pregnant women in Trinidad. *Car Med J* 15(1-2): 47-49. **[9,11,12]** [*COL*]

Sampath, S. D.

28.1116 TR 1960 Accidents among children. *Car Med J* 23(1-4): 64-70. [*COL*]

Samuels, G. A. S.

28.1117 JM 1971 Appendicitis in children. *W I Med J* 20(2), June: 101-105. [*PS*]

Sandison, John W.

28.1118 JM 1965 A combined recovery and intensive therapy ward. *W I Med J* 14(4), Dec: 277-286. [*PS*]

Sandison, John W.; James, O. B. O'L.; Grant, L. S. & Hultqvist, E.

28.1119 JM 1967 A bacterial survey of the recovery ward of the University College Hospital of the West Indies. *W I Med J* 16(2), June: 92-101. [*PS*]

Sandt, Donald G.

28.1120 SL 1973 Direct filtration for recovery of *Schistosoma mansoni* cercariae in the field. *Bull WHO* 48(1): 27-34. **[54]** [*PS*]

Sar, A. van der

28.1121 NA 1945 Lepra en las Antillas Neerlandesas [Leprosy in the Netherlands Antilles]. *Revta Policl Cara* 13(76), May-June: 1-17. [*RIS*]

28.1122 CU 1951 Incidence and treatment of kwashiorkor in Curacao. *Docum Ned Indo Morbis Trop* 3(1), Mar.: 25-44. **[30]**

28.1123 CU 1955 The agranulocytoid type of bacillary dysentery. *W I Med J* 4(1), Mar.: 49-54. [*COL*]

28.1124 CU 1962 Sur l'étiologie de l'éosinophilie tropicale à Curacao [On the etiology of tropical eosinophilia in Curacao]. *B Soc Path Exot* 55(4), July-Aug.: 646-655. [*RIS*]

27.0122 CU 1967 Aplastic sickle cell crisis: a report of four cases.

27.0123 CU 1970 The sudden rise in platelets and reticulocytes in sickle cell crises.

28.1125 CU 1973 An outbreak of dengue haemorrhagic fever on Curaçao. *Trop Geogr Med* 25(2), June: 119-129. [*PS*]

Sar, A. van der & Kroon, T. A. J.
30.0207   CU   1956   Avitaminosis A and subclinical vitamin C deficiency in Curacao.
28.1126   CU   1957   The incidence of scarlet fever in Curacao (with a report on a Dick test survey). *J Trop Pediat* 2(4), Mar.: 203-207.   [*COL*]

Sar, A. van der & Vinke, B.
28.1127   CU   1965   Investigation into the occurrence of *Trypanosoma cruzi* in Curaçao. *Trop Geogr Med* 17(3), Sept.: 225-228.   [*PS*]

Sar, A. van der & Winkel, C. A.
28.1128   CU   1959   Non-specific spondylitis in Negroid children in Curacao. *Trop Geogr Med* 11(3), Sept.: 263-275.   **[11]**   [*COL*]

Sar, T. van der
28.1129   SR   1974   Het gebruick van zeis en houwer bij het maaien van gras [The use of scythe and machete for mowing grass]. *Sur Landb* 22(1): 40-43.   **[43]**   [*RILA*]

Sausse, André
28.1130   FG   1951   Pathologie comparée des populations primitives noires et indiennes de la Guyane Francaise [Comparative pathology of the primitive Negro and Indian populations of French Guiana]. *B Soc Path Exot* 44(7-8), July: 455-460.   **[13,14]**   [*ACM*]
13.0190   FG   1951   Populations primitives du Maroni (Guyane Francaise) [Primitive peoples of the Maroni (French Guiana)].

Sautet, Jacques
28.1131   GD,DS   1951   Les traitements modernes doivent-ils faire abandonner la ségrégation des lépreux et amener une refonte totale de la prophylaxie de la lèpre? [Will modern therapy lead to the abandonment of the segregation of lepers and to a complete change in the treatment of leprosy?] *Presse Med* 63(17), Mar. 5: 339-441.   [*ACM*]
28.1132   GC   1953   Health of the worker and industrial medicine. *Car Econ Rev* 5(1-2), Dec.: 145-157.   **[45,46]**   [*RIS*]
28.1133   FC,TR   1955   L'épidémie de fièvre jaune de Trinidad menace-t-elle dans l'immédiat nos Départements américains? [Does the yellow fever epidemic in Trinidad represent an immediate threat to our American territories?] *Presse Med* 63(17), Mar. 5.: 339-441.   [*ACM*]

Saward, E. Joyce
28.1134   JM   1960   Rehabilitation in Jamaica. *Car Med J* 22(1-4): 81-83.   [*COL*]

Scantlebury, Elayne
28.1135   BB   1974   Maternal child health/family planning in Barbados. *In* International Confederation of Midwives. Report of the Caribbean Working Party, Bridgetown, Barbados, 16-24 May, 1974. [Bridgetown, Barbados]: 75-78.   **[34]**   [*RIS*]

Schaad, J. D. G.
28.1136   SR   1960   Epidemiological observations in Bush Negroes and Amerindians in Surinam. *Trop Geogr Med* 12(1), Mar.: 38-46.   **[13,14]**   [*RIS*]

Schallibaum, E. M.

28.1137   JM   1968   Preliminary survey of sensitivity to local strains of Pseudomonas pyocyanea to carbenicillin. *W I Med J* 17(4), Dec.: 229-231.   [*PS*]

Scherer, W. F.; Anderson, K.; Dickerman, R. W. & Ordonez, J. V.

28.1138   BZ   1972   Studies of Patois group arboviruses in Mexico, Guatemala, Honduras and British Honduras. *Am J Trop Med Hyg* 21(2), March: 194-200.   [*PS*]

Scherer, W. F.; Dickerman, R. W. & Ordonez, J. V.

28.1139   BZ   1970   Discovery and geographic distribution of Venezuelan encephalitis virus in Guatemala, Honduras and British Honduras during 1965-68, and its possible movement to Central America and Mexico. *Am J Trop Med Hyg* 19(4), July: 703-711.   [*PS*]

Schmid, Janeiro B.

1.0259   GC   1965   Bibliography and reference sources in the Caribbean.

Schouten, H.; Suriel-Smeets, R. M. & Kibbelaar, M. A.

28.1140   CU   1968   The simultaneous occurrence of ova resembling *Dicrocoelium dendriticum* or *Capillaria hepatica* in the stools of inhabitants of Curaçao. *Trop Geogr Med* 20(3), Sept.: 271-275.   [*PS*]

Schuitemaker, F. S.

28.1141   FG   1929-30 Bezoek aan St. Louis, het leprozen eiland in de Marowijne; Melattschen etablissement van de Fransche strafkolonie St. Laurent, Fransch-Guyana [Visit to St. Louis, the leper island in the Marowijne river; leper asylum of the French penal colony St. Laurent, French Guiana]. *W I G* 11: 177-186.   [*COL*]

Scott, Henry Harold

28.1142   JM   1913   Fulminating cerebro-spinal meningitis in Jamaica. *Ann Trop Med Paras* 7(1), Mar. 31: 165-181.   [*COL*]

28.1143   JM   1915   An investigation into the causes of the prevalence of enteric fever in Kingston, Jamaica; with special reference to the question of unrecognised carriers. *Ann Trop Med Paras* 9(2), June 30: 239-284.   [*COL*]

28.1144   JM   1916   On the "vomiting sickness" of Jamaica. *Ann Trop Med Paras* 10(1), Apr. 29: 1-78.   [*COL*]

28.1145   JM   1917   The vomiting sickness of Jamaica. *Trans Roy Soc Trop Med Hyg* 10(3), Jan.: 47-66.   [*ACM*]

28.1146   JM   1918   An investigation into an acute otubreak of "central neuritis." *Ann Trop Med Paras* 12(2), Oct. 31: 109-196.   [*COL*]

Scott, O. D.; Moodie, K. & Bissessar, R.

28.1147   JM   1968   A preliminary qualitative survey of the bacterial flora of restaurants and bakeries in the city of Kingston, Jamaica. *W I Med J* 17(3), Sept.: 158-162.   [*PS*]

Seaforth, Compton E.

28.1148   GC   1962   Drugs from the West Indies. *Car Q* 7(4), Apr.: 198-202.   **[57]**   [*RIS*]
28.1149   GC   1967   Drugs from the West Indies. *Car Q* 13(3), Sept.: 52-56.   **[29]**   [*RIS*]

Seaga, Edward
29.0045   **JM**   1955   Jamaica's primitive medicine.

Sebastian, S. & Buchanan, I. C.
28.1150   **AG**   1965   Feasibility of concrete septic privies for sewage disposal in Anguilla, B.W.I. *Publ Heal Rpts* 80(12), Dec.: 1113-1118.   **[36]**   [*PS*]

Seheult, R.
28.1151   **TR**   1938   A historical review of ankylostomiasis in Trinidad. *Car Med J* 1(1): 46-54.   [*COL*]
28.1152   **TR**   1940   A brief historical survey of the surgeons-general of Trinidad. *Car Med J* 2(3): 105-109.   **[5]**   [*COL*]
28.1153   **TR**   1940   A short historical survey of three notable medical men of the past century. *Car Med J* 2(4): 157-163.   **[5]**   [*COL*]
28.1154   **GC**   1944   A brief sketch of the history of yellow fever in the West Indies. *Car Med J* 6(3): 132-139.   **[5]**   [*COL*]
28.1155   **TR**   1945   Observations on the incidence of cancer in Trinidad. *Car Med J* 7(2-3): 72-79.   [*COL*]
28.1156   **TR**   1946   A review of the evolution of health services in Trinidad—1814-1934. *Car Med J* 8(2): 41-47.   **[5]**   [*COL*]

Seidelin, Harald
28.1157   **JM**   1913   On "vomiting sickness" in Jamaica. *Ann Trop Med Paras* 7(3B), Nov. 7: 377-478.   [*COL*]

Seivwright, Mary
17.0093   **JM,US**   1965   Project report on factors affecting mass migration of Jamaican nurses to the U.S. *Jam Nurse* 5(2).
17.0094   **JM,US**   1965   Project report on factors affecting mass migration of Jamaican nurses to the U.S. *Jam Nurse* 5(3)

Sengupta, Bijoy; Persaud, Vasil & Burrowes, James
28.1158   **BC**   1976   The use of colposcopy in early cervical cancer detection. *W I Med J* 25(2), June: 78-86.   [*RIS*]

Senior, Clarence
35.0072   **GC**   1954   Housing and sanitation in the Caribbean.

Sereno, Renzo
23.0266   **GC**   1948   Obeah: magic and social structure in the Lesser Antilles.

Série, Ch.; Sabourin, G.; Dujeu, G. & Mercier, J.
28.1159   **FG**   1973   Considérations sur l'endémie hansénienne en Guyane Française [Considerations on endemic Hansen's disease in French Guyana]. *B Soc Path Exot* 66(3), May-June: 371-380.   [*PS*]

Serjeant, Beryl E.; Forbes, Miriam; Williams, Leslie L. & Serjeant, G. R.
27.0124   **JM**   1974   Screening cord bloods for detection of sickle cell disease in Jamaica.

Serjeant, G. R.
28.1160   **JM**   1970   The clinical features in adults with sickle cell anaemia in Jamaica. *W I Med J* 19(1), March: 1-8.   **[27]**   [*PS*]

| 28.1161 | JM | 1973 | Duodenal ulceration in sickle cell anaemia. *Trans Roy Soc Trop Med Hyg* 67(1): 59-63. **[11,27]** [*PS*] |

| 28.1162 | JM | 1974 | Leg ulceration in sickle cell anemia. *Archs Intern Med* 133(4), April: 690-694. **[11,27]** [*PS*] |

Serjeant, G. R. & Ashcroft, M. T.
| 27.0125 | JM | 1973 | Delayed skeletal maturation in sickle cell anemia in Jamaica. |

Serjeant, G. R.; Ashcroft, M. T. & Serjeant, B. E.
| 28.1163 | JM | 1973 | The clinical features of haemoglobin SC disease in Jamaica. *Br J Haematol* 24(4), April: 491-501. **[11,27]** [*PS*] |

Serjeant, G. R.; Ashcroft, M. T.; Serjeant, B. E. & Milner, P. F.
| 28.1164 | JM | 1973 | The clinical features of sickle-cell/β-thalassaemia in Jamaica. *Br J Haematol* 24(1), Jan.: 19-30. **[11,27]** [*PS*] |

Serjeant, G. R.; Ennis, J. T. & Middlemiss, Howard
| 27.0126 | JM | 1973 | Haemoglobin SC disease in Jamaica. |
| 27.0127 | JM | 1973 | Sickle cell beta thalassemia in Jamaica. |

Serjeant, G. R.; Richards, R.; Barbor, P. R. H. & Milner, P. F.
| 27.0128 | JM | 1968 | Relatively benign sickle-cell anaemia in 60 patients aged over 30 in the West Indies. |

Serjeant, G. R. & Serjeant, B. E.
| 27.0129 | JM | 1972 | A comparison of erythrocyte characteristics in sickle cell syndromes in Jamaica. |

Serjeant, G. R.; Serjeant, B. E. & Condon, P. I.
| 28.1165 | JM | 1972 | The conjunctival sign in sickle cell anemia. A relationship with irreversibly sickled cells. *JAMA* 219(11), March 13: 1428-1431. **[27]** [*PS*] |

Sexton, Thomas
| 28.1166 | SR | 1966 | Analysis of a communications breakdown in the Surinam malaria eradication programme. *Int J Heal Educ* 9(3), July-Sept.: 122-129. **[14]** [*PS*] |

Shaffer, Alice
| 28.1167 | GC | 1952 | UNICEF in the Caribbean. *Car Med J* 14(1-2): 51-53. [*COL*] |

Sharrett, A. Richey; Finklea, John F.; Potter, Elizabeth V.; Poon-King, Theo & Earle, David P.
| 28.1168 | TR | 1974 | Control of streptococcal skin infections in South Trinidad. *Am J Epidemiol* 99(6), June: 408-413. [*PS*] |

Sharrett, A. Richey; Poon-King, Theo; Potter, Elizabeth V.; Finklea, John F. & Earle, David P.
| 28.1169 | TR | 1971 | Subclinical nephritis in South Trinidad. *Am J Epidemiol* 94(3), Sept.: 231-245. [*PS*] |

Shaw, G. Ingram
| 28.1170 | KNA | 1960 | Tuberculosis in St. Kitts-Nevis-Anguilla. *Car Med J* 22(1-4): 116-117. [*COL*] |

Sheridan, Richard B.

6.0267   **BC**   1975   Mortality and the medical treatment of slaves in the British West Indies.

Shope, Robert E. & Whitman, Loring

28.1171   **TR**   1966   Nepuyo virus, a new group C agent isolated in Trinidad and Brazil. II. Serological studies. *Am J Trop Med Hyg* 15(5), Sept.: 772-774.

       [*PS*]

Silverie, Charles & Duchassin, Marcel

28.1172   **FG**   1966   Enquête sur l'incidence en Guyane Française de l'histoplasmose en milieu militaire au moyen de tests cutanés à l'histoplasmine [A survey of histoplasmosis frequency in a military environment by means of histoplasmin skin tests, in French Guiana]. *B Soc Path Exot* 59(2), March-Apr.: 199-206.   [*PS*]

Simons, R. D. G. Ph.

28.1173   **SR**   1932-33 De maatschappelijke betekenis der Surinaamsche ziekten (van 1919 tot 1931) [The social significance of the Surinam diseases (from 1919 to 1931)]. *W I G* 14: 429-439.   [*COL*]

Simpson, George Eaton

29.0046   **TR**   1962   Folk medicine in Trinidad.

Simpson, J. M.

28.1174   **JM**   1970   Environmental temperature and response to premedicant drugs. *Anaesthesia* 25(4), Oct.: 508-517. **[18]**   [*PS*]

Sinclair, Hazel

34.0097   **JM**   1974   The role of the district midwife in family planning.

Sivapragasam, S.

28.1175   **JM**   1973   The fat embolism syndrome. *W I Med J* 22(1), March: 41-44. [*PS*]

Slavin, G.; Klenerman, L.; Darby, A. & Bansal, S.

28.1176   **BB,UK**   1973   Tumoral calcinosis in England. *Br Med J* 1(5846), Jan. 20: 147-149. **[11,18]**   [*PS*]

Smals, A. G. H. & Lustermans, F. A. Th.

27.0131   **SR**   1969   Een volwassen vrouw met homozygote β-Thalassemie en heterozygote G6PD-deficiëntie [An adult woman with homozygotic β-thalassaemia and heterozygotic G6PD deficiency].

Smink, D. A. & Prins, H. K.

28.1177   **SR**   1965   Hereditary and acquired blood factors in the negroid population of Surinam: V. Electrophoretic heterogeneity of glucose-6-phosphate dehydrogenase. *Trop Geogr Med* 17(3), Sept.: 236-242. **[11]**   [*PS*]

Smith, John Morrison

28.1178   **BC,UK**   1973   Skin tests and atopic allergy in children. *Clin Allergy* 3(3), Sept.: 269-275. **[18]**   [*ACM*]

Smith, Karl A.

28.1179   GC   1975   Health priorities in the poorer countries. *Soc Sci Med* 9(3), March: 121-132.   [*COL*]

Smith, Karl A. & Johnson, Raymond L.

34.0107   JM   [n.d.]   MEDICAL OPINION ON ABORTION IN JAMAICA: A NATIONAL DELPHI SURVEY OF PHYSICIANS, NURSES, AND MIDWIVES.

Smith, M. W.

28.1180   TR   1975   Some aspects of the ecology and lifecycle of *Amblyomma cajennense* (Fabricius 1787) in Trinidad and their influence on tick control measures. *Ann Trop Med Paras* 69(1), March: 121-129.   **[58,62]**   [*PS*]

Smith, P. T.

28.1181   BV   1972   Medical services in the British Virgin Islands. *Int J Heal Serv* 2(1): 111-118   **[5]**   [*PS*]

Sneath, P. A. T.

7.0195   GU   1941   A study of crude birth/death ratio (vital index) in British Guiana.
28.1182   GU   1943   Contemporary facts on the incidence of tuberculosis in British Guiana. *Br Gui Med Annual* 26: 32-42.   [*ACM*]

Soper, Fred L.

28.1183   GC   1952   Yellow fever in the Caribbean. *In* Wilgus, A. Curtis, ed. THE CARIBBEAN; PEOPLES, PROBLEMS AND PROSPECTS [PAPERS DELIVERED AT THE SECOND ANNUAL CONFERENCE ON THE CARIBBEAN, HELD AT THE UNIVERSITY OF FLORIDA, DEC. 1951]. Gainesville, University of Florida Press, p.13-17. (Publications of the School of Inter-American Studies, ser. 1, v. 2.)   [*RIS*]

Spence, L.

28.1184   TR   1972   Studies on poliomyelitis in Trinidad and Tobago. *W I Med J* 21(4), Dec.: 211-215.   [*PS*]

Spence, L.; Anderson, C. R.; Aitken, T. H. G. & Downs, W. G.

28.1185   TR   1966   Aruac virus, a new agent isolated from Trinidadian mosquitoes. *Am J Trop Med Hyg* 15(2), March: 231-234.   [*PS*]
28.1186   TR   1966   Nepuyo virus, a new group C agent isolated in Trinidad and Brazil. I. Isolation and properties of the Trinidadian strain. *Am J Trop Med Hyg* 15(1), Jan.: 71-74.   [*PS*]
28.1187   TR   1967   Bush bush, Ieri and Lukuni viruses, three unrelated new agents isolated from Trinidadian forest mosquitoes. *Proc Soc Exp Biol Med* 125(1), May: 45-50.   [*PS*]

Spence, L.; Anderson, C. R. & Downs, W. G.

28.1188   TR   1957   The isolation of influenza virus during an epidemic in Trinidad, British West Indies. *Car Med J* 19(3-4): 174-179.   [*COL*]
28.1189   TR   1965   Isolation of Ilhéus virus from human beings in Trinidad, West Indies. *Car Med J* 27(1-4): 97-102.   [*ACM*]

Spence, L. & Barratt, Norma

28.1190   TR   1968   Respiratory syncytial virus associated with acute respiratory infections in Trinidadian patients. *Am J Epidemiol* 88(2), Sept.: 257-266.

Spence, L. & Downs, W. G.

28.1191 GU 1968 Virological investigations in Guyana, 1956-1966. *W I Med J* 17(2), June: 83-89.   [*PS*]

Spence, L.; Downs, W. G. & Aitken, T. H. G.

28.1192 GU 1961 Eastern equine encephalitis virus in the West Indies and British Guiana. *W I Med J* 10(4), Dec.: 227-229.   [*COL*]

62.0125 GC,GU 1965 Eastern equine encephalitis virus in the West Indies and British Guiana.

Spence, L.; Downs, W. G. & Anderson, C. R.

28.1193 TR 1959 The isolation of Coxsackie viruses from human beings in Trinidad. *W I Med J* 8(4), Dec.: 235-237.   [*COL*]

Spence, L.; Downs, W. G. & Boyd, C.

28.1194 TR 1965 Isolation of St. Louis encephalitis virus from the blood of a child in Trinidad. *Car Med J* 27(1-4): 122-125.   [*ACM*]

Spence, L.; Downs, W. G.; Boyd, C. & Aitken, T. H. G.

28.1195 TR 1960 Description of human yellow fever causes seen in Trinidad in 1959. *W I Med J* 9(4), Dec.: 273-277.   [*COL*]

28.1196 TR 1965 Description from human yellow fever cases seen in Trinidad in 1959. *Car Med J* 27(1-4): 78-82.   [*ACM*]

Spence, L.; Downs, W. G. & Green, A. E.

28.1197 TR 1972 Leptospirosis in Trinidad: further studies resulting in recognition of two new serotypes. *W I Med J* 21(4), Dec.: 216-219.   [*PS*]

Spence, L.; Jonkers, A. H. & Casals, J.

28.1198 AT 1969 Dengue type 3 virus isolated from an Antiguan patient during the 1963-64 Caribbean epidemic. *Am J Trop Med Hyg* 18(4), July: 584-587.   [*PS*]

Spence, L.; Jonkers, A. H. & Grant, L. S.

28.1199 GC 1968 Arboviruses in the Caribbean Islands. *Progr Med Virol* 10: 415-486.   [*PS*]

Spence, L.; McDowall, M. F. & Barrat, N.

28.1200 TR 1963 Prevalence of enteroviruses in children at the General Hospital, Port-of-Spain, Trinidad, in 1960. *W I Med J* 12(3), Sept.: 183-187   [*COL*]

Sprent, J. F.

28.1201 TR,SR 1971 Speciation and development in the genus Lagochilascaris. *Parasitology* 62(1), February: 71-112. **[54]**   [*PS*]

Springett, V. H.

28.1202 BC,UK 1973 Tuberculosis in immigrants in Birmingham 1970-1972. *Br J Prev Social Med* 27(4), Nov.: 242-246. **[18]**   [*PS*]

Stafford, J. L.; Hill, K. R. & DeMontaigne, E. L.

28.1203 TC 1955 Microfilariasis in the Turks Islands. *W I Med J* 4(3), Sept.: 183-187.   [*COL*]

Stage, H. H. & Giglioli, George
28.1204   GU   1947   Observations on mosquito and malaria control in the Caribbean area. Part II: British Guiana. *Mosq News* 7(2), June: 73-76.   [*COL*]

Stamm, H.
28.1205   JM   1952   Clinical analysis of a general practice in a West Indian town. *W I Med J* 1(3), Oct.: 281-290.   [*COL*]
28.1206   JM   1955   Calls after hours. *W I Med J* 4(4), Dec.: 212-216.   [*COL*]

Standard, K. L.
7.0197   BB   1961   An analysis of child mortality in Barbados, West Indies.
28.1207   GC   1966   Promoting health in the Caribbean. *Jam Nurse* 6(2), Aug: 28-30.   [*AJN*]
28.1208   BC   1971   Problems of health and disease in the Commonwealth Caribbean. *Trop Doc* 1(3), July: 131-133.   [*PS*]

Standard, K. L.; Cruickshank, R. & Ennever, O.
28.1209   JM   1969   Evaluación por los alumnos de una pasantía de medicina de la comunidad en Jamaica [Evaluation by the students of a community medicine clerkship in Jamaica]. *Educ Med Salud* 3(1), Jan.-March: 8-21.   **[32]**   [*PS*]
28.1210   JM   1970   Analysis of students' evaluation of a five-week clerkship in community medicine in Jamaica, West Indies. *In* PROCEEDINGS, FIFTH INTERNATIONAL SCIENTIFIC MEETING OF THE INTERNATIONAL EPIDEMIOLOGICAL ASSOCIATION, Belgrade, Yugoslavia: 519-528.   **[32]**   [*ACM*]

Standard, K. L.; Desai, Patricia & Miall, W. E.
27.0134   JM   1969   A longitudinal study of child growth in a rural community in Jamaica.

Standard, K. L. & Ennever, O.
28.1211   BC   1971   Community medicine in the Commonwealth Caribbean. *W I Med J* 20(1), March: 1-4.   [*PS*]
32.0547   JM   1974   Training health auxiliaries.
28.1212   JM   1975   Training of health auxiliaries in the West Indies. *Educ Med Salud* 9(3): 285-295.   **[32]**   [*PS*]

Standard, K. L.; Lovell, H. G. & Harney, L.
27.0136   BB   1966   Heights and weights of Barbadian schoolchildren.

Statius van Eps, L. W.
28.1213   CU   1967   Investigations in Curaçao on renal functions in patients suffering from sickle-cell anaemia and other haemoglobin diseases. *Neth Found Adv Trop Res* (WOTRO), Report for the Year 1966: 40-45.   **[27]**   [*RIS*]
28.1214   NA   1973   Lepra. *In* Statius van Eps, L. W. & Luckman-Maduro, E., eds. VAN SCHEEPSCHIRURGIJN TOT SPECIALIST. Assen, The Netherlands, Van Gorcum & Comp. B.V.: 17-21. (Anjerpublikatie 15)   **[5]**   [*RILA*]
28.1215   NA   1973   Vroedvrouwen in de Nederlandse Antillen [Midwives in the Netherlands Antilles]. *In* Statius van Eps, L. W. & Luckman-Maduro, E., eds. VAN SCHEEPSCHIRURGIJN TOT SPECIALIST. Assen, The Netherlands, Van Gorcum & Comp. B.V.: 103-105. (Anjerpublikatie 15)   [*RILA*]

28.1216   NA   1973   Zuigelingensterfte [Infant mortaility]. *In* Statius van Eps, L. W. &
                      Luckman-Maduro, E., eds. VAN SCHEEPSCHIRURGIJN TOT SPECIAL-
                      IST. Assen, The Netherlands, Van Gorcum & Comp. B.V.: 70-73.
                      (Anjerpublikatie 15)   [*RILA*]

                      Statius van Eps, L. W. & Haneveld, G. T.
28.1217   NA   1973   Gezondheidszorg [Health care]. *In* Statius van Eps, L. W. &
                      Luckman-Maduro, E., eds. VAN SCHEEPSCHIRURGIJN TOT SPECIAL-
                      IST. Assen, The Netherlands, Van Gorcum & Comp. B.V.: 41-46.
                      (Anjerpublikatie 15)   **[5]**   [*RILA*]

                      Statius van Eps, L. W. & Luckman-Maduro, E., eds.
28.1218   NA   1973   VAN SCHEEPSCHIRURGIJN TOT SPECIALIST: 333 JAAR NEDERLANDS-
                      ANTILLAANSE GENEESKUNDE [FROM SHIP'S SURGEON TO SPECIALIST:
                      333 YEARS OF NETHERLANDS-ANTILLEAN HEALTH CARE]. Assen, The
                      Netherlands, Van Gorcum & Comp. B.V.: 196p. (Anjerpublikatie
                      15)   **[5]**   [*RILA*]

                      Staudt, F. J.
28.1219   SR   1974   Ergonomisch onderzoek in de Surinaamse bosbouw [Ergonomic
                      research in Surinam forestry]. *Sur Landb* 22(1): 23-33.   **[43]**
                                                                              [*RILA*]

                      Stephenson, Derick
28.1220   JM   1969   Dental caries, environment and diet in Jamaica. *W I Med J* 18(2),
                      June: 116-118.   **[30]**   [*PS*]

                      Steven, George H.
28.1221   GU   1933   Pathological notes on cases resembling wet beriberi occurring in
                      British Guiana. *Br Gui Med Annual 1932* 25: 84-91.   [*ACM*]
28.1222   GU   1936   Post-mortem notes on the spleen in various races of British Guiana:
                      a comparison with 1893. *Br Gui Med Annual 1936* 26: 137-143.
                                                                              [*ACM*]

                      Stewart, D. B.
28.1223   JM   1960   The University College Hospital domiciliary midwifery services.
                      Part II: A comment on domiciliary midwifery services. *W I Med J*
                      9(1), Mar.: 22-24.   [*COL*]
32.0551 JM   1962   A developing medical school in the tropics.
28.1224   JM   1965   The organization of obstetric care in Jamaica. *J Ind Fed Gynec
                      Obstet* 2(3), April: 93-99.   [*PS*]
28.1225   GC   1968   Specialist training in obstetrics and gynaecology. *W I Med J* 17(2),
                      June: 65-73.   [*PS*]

                      St. George, John
28.1226   TR   1970   The problems of grand multiparity. An analysis of 2,582 cases
                      delivered in General Hospital, Port-of-Spain, Trinidad, from 1965-
                      67. *W I Med J* 19(2), June: 84-90.   [*PS*]
30.0214 TR   1971   Dietary deficiency and pre-eclamptic toxaemia—a preliminary
                      communication.

St. George, John; St. John, E. H. & Josa, D.

28.1227   TR   1970   Factors influencing birth weight in normal pregnacy. *J Trop Pediat* 16(3), Sept.: 93-102.   **[27]**   [*PS*]

St. Henley, A.

28.1228   GU   1960   Cancer of the stomach in British Guiana: a review of cases admitted to the Georgetown Hospital 1956-1959. *W I Med J* 9(4), Dec.: 236-243.   [*COL*]

Stirling, G. A.

28.1229   JM   1960   The adrenals in hypertensive Jamaicans. *Trop Geogr Med* 12(2), June: 114-118.   [*COL*]

Stirling, G. A. & Castor, Ursula S.

28.1230   JM   1962   Tubal pregnancy in Jamaicans. *W I Med J* 11(1), Mar.: 45-47.   [*COL*]

Stockdale, Frank A.

28.1231   BC   1943   Development and welfare in the West Indies 1940-1942. *Car Med J* 5(1): 8-30.   **[33]**   [*COL*]

Stockhausen, B. Y.

28.1232   JM   1968   Cancer involving the vulva. *W I Med J* 17(2), June: 103-108.   [*PS*]

Stoehl, G.

28.1233   NC   1937   Over de veelvuldigheid van kanker [On the frequency of cancer]. *Geneesk Tijdschr Ned-Indie* 77: 2292-2304.

Stolnitz, George J.

28.1234   GC   1958   The revolution in death control in nonindustrial countries. *Ann Am Acad Polit Social Sci* 316, Mar.: 94-101.   **[7]**   [*RIS*]

Stolze, E.

28.1235   SR   1958   Histological report on 152 post-mortem liver punctures in Surinam. *Trop Geogr Med* 10(3), Se:t.: 272-276.   [*COL*]

Stoopler, Mark; Frayer, William & Alderman, Michael H.

30.0215   JM   1974   Prevalence and persistence of lactose malabsorption among young Jamaican children.

Stout, Robert J.

28.1236   JM   1963   Some clinical evidence for a quantitative relationship between dose of relaxant and plasma protein. *W I Med J* 12(4), Dec.: 256-264.   [*COL*]

Strangways-Dixon, J. & Lainson, R.

28.1237   BZ   1966   The epidemiology of dermal leishmaniasis in British Honduras. Part III. The transmission of *Leishmania mexicana* to man by *Phlebotomus pessoanus*, with observations of the development of the parasite in different species of *Phlebotomus*. *Trans Roy Soc Trop Med Hyg* 60(2), March: 192-201.   [*PS*]

Stuart, J.; Schwartz, F. C. M.; Little, A. J. & Raine, D. N.
27.0140   **BC,UK**   1973   Screening for abnormal haemoglobins: a pilot study.

Stuart, K. L.
32.0556   **JM**   1974   The Department of Medicine—the University of the West Indies 1948-1973.

Stuart, K. L. & Bras, G.
28.1238   **JM**   1971   Prognosis of idiopathic cardiomegaly in Jamaica with reference to the coronary arteries and other factors. *Br Heart J* 33(Supplement): 187-193.   [*PS*]

Stuart, K. L.; MacIver, C. & Nicholson, J. A.
28.1239   **JM**   1972   Outpatient treatment trial of mild and severe hypertension. *Br Med J* 2(5804), April 1: 21-24.   [*PS*]

Sturrock, R. F.
28.1240   **SL**   1973   Control of *Schistosoma mansoni* transmission: strategy for using molluscicides on St. Lucia. *Int J Paras* 3(6), Nov.: 795-801.   **[54]**
                                                                                                                                                                              [*AMN*]
54.0992   **SL**   1973   Field studies on the population dynamics of *Biomphalaria glabrata*, intermediate host of *Schistosoma mansoni* on the West Indian island of St. Lucia.
54.0993   **SL**   1973   Field studies on the transmission of *Schistosoma mansoni* and on the bionomics of its intermediate host, *Biomphalaria glabrata*, on St. Lucia, West Indies.

Sturrock, R. F.; Barnish, G. & Upatham, E. S.
28.1241   **SL**   1974   Snail findings from an experimental mollusciciding programme to control *Schistosoma mansoni* transmission on St. Lucia. *Int J Paras* 4(3), June: 231-240.   **[54]**   [*AMN*]

Sturrock, R. F. & Sturrock, B. M.
28.1242   **SL**   1970   Observations on the susceptibility to *Schistosoma mansoni* from St. Lucia of several Caribbean strains of snails of the genus *Biomphalaria*. *W I Med J* 19(1), March: 9-13.   [*PS*]
28.1243   **SL**   1972   The influence of temperature on the biology of *Biomphalaria glabrata* (Say), intermediate host of *Schistosoma mansoni* on St. Lucia, West Indies. *Ann Trop Med Parasitol* 66(3), Sept.: 385-390.   **[54]**   [*PS*]

Stycos, J. Mayone & Arias, Jorge, eds.
7.0200   **GC**   1966   POPULATION DILEMMA IN LATIN AMERICA.

Sudia, W. Daniel; Coleman, P. H. & Grant, L. S.
28.1244   **JM**   1966   The recurrence of St. Louis encephalitis virus in *Culex Nigripalpus* mosquitoes in Jamaica, 1963. *Mosq News* 26(1): 39-42.   [*PS*]

Summerell, J. & Gibbs, W. N.
28.1245   **JM**   1972   Splenic histiocytosis associated with thrombocytopenia. *Acta Haematol* 48(1): 34-38.   [*PS*]

Summerell, J.; Hayes, J. A. & Bras, G.

28.1246   JM   1968   Autopsy data on heart disease in Jamaica. *Trop Geogr Med* 20(2), June: 127-132.   [*PS*]

Suriel-Smeets, R. M. & Schouten, H.

28.1247   CU   1972   The simultaneous occurrence of ova resembling dicrocoelium dentriticum and capillaria hepatica in the stools of inhabitants of Curaçao. II. Identification of the D-trematode: didymozoon Sp. *Trop Geogr Med* 24(2), June: 192-193.   [*PS*]

Sutton, R. N. P.

28.1248   TR   1965   Minor illness in Trinidad: a longitudinal study. *Trans Roy Soc Trop Med Hyg* 59(2), March: 212-220.   [*PS*]

Sutton, R. N. P.; Barratt, Norma & Schild, G. C.

28.1249   TR   1967   Enteroviruses in a Trinidad nursery. *Trans Roy Soc Trop Med Hyg* 61(5): 718-724.   [*PS*]

Svartman, Mauri; Potter, Elizabeth; Finklea, J. F.; Poon-King, Theo & Earle, D. P.

28.1250   TR   1972   Epidemic scabies and acute glomerulonephritis in Trinidad. *Lancet*, I for 1972 (7744), Jan 29: 249-251.   [*PS*]

Swaby, Gertrude

28.1251   JM   1968   The role of the nurse in the past—flashback: Jamaica. *Jam Nurs* 8(2), Sept: 11 passim. **[5]**   [*AJN*]

Swanston, W. H. & Drysdale, H.

28.1252   TR   1968   Virological investigations during the 1966 epidemic of influenza in Trinidad. *W I Med J* 17(4), Dec.: 235-240.   [*PS*]

Sweet, R. D.

28.1253   JM   1966   A pattern of eczema in Jamaica. *Br J Derm* 78(2), Feb.: 93-100.   [*PS*]

Swellengrebel, N. H.

28.1254   SR   1940   The efficient parasite. *Science* new ser., 92(2395), Nov. 22: 465-469. **[11]**   [*AGS*]

17.0101   SR   1940   Over de vraag of een proefneming tot vestiging van politieke uitgewekenen in Suriname hygienisch te verantwoorden is [On the question whether an attempt to settle political refugees in Surinam is advisable from a hygienic viewpoint].

28.1255   NC   1952   De Pan Amerikaanse Sanitare Organisatie (P.A.S.O.) in verband met Suriname en de Nederlandse Antillen [The Pan-American Sanitary Organisation (P.A.S.O.) in relation to Surinam and the Dutch Antilles]. *W I G* 33: 1-11.   [*COL*]

Swellengrebel, N. H. & Kuyp, E. van der

28.1256   SR   1940   HEALTH OF WHITE SETTLERS IN SURINAM. Amsterdam, 118p. (Colonial Institute at Amsterdam, Special publication no. 53, Dept. of Tropical Hygiene no. 16.) **[15,23]**   [*AMN*]

CARIBBEANA 1900–1975

Swellengrebel, N. H. & Rijpstra, A. C.
28.1257   SR   1965   Lateral-spined schistosome ova in the intestine of a squirrel monkey from Surinam. *Trop Geogr Med* 17(1), March: 80-84.   **[54]**   [*PS*]

Symonds, Bruce
28.1258   TR   1956   Fatty liver disease in South Trinidad. *Car Med J* 18(1-2): 9-12.   **[30]**   [*COL*]

Symonds, Bruce & Mohammed, I.
30.0218   TR   1956   "Sugar babies" in South Trinidad.

Talerman, A.
28.1259   JM   1969   Clinico-pathological study of multiple myeloma in Jamaica. *Br J Cancer* 23(2), June: 285-293.   [*PS*]
28.1260   JM   1970   Clinico-pathological study of malignant lymphoma in Jamaica. *Br J Cancer* 24(2), March: 37-47.   [*PS*]

Talerman, A.; Finnie, E. & Wontumi, J. A.
28.1261   JM   1968   Multiple liver abscesses caused by klebsiella aerogenes. *J Med Microbiol* 1(1), Aug.: 164-167.   [*PS*]

Talerman, A.; Hayes, J. A. & Lindo, V.
28.1262   JM   1968   Aortic aneurysms in Jamaica. *Trans Roy Soc Trop Med Hyg* 62(4): 522-527.   [*PS*]

Talerman, A.; Serjeant, G. R. & Milner, P. F.
28.1263   JM   1971   Normal pregnancy in a patient with multiple myeloma and sickle cell anaemia. *W I Med J* 20(2), June: 97-100.   [*PS*]

Tanaka, Kay; Isselbacher, Kurt J. & Shih, Vivian
28.1264   JM   1972   Isovaleric and a-methybutyric acidemias induced by hypoglycin A: mechanism of Jamaican vomiting sickness. *Science* 175(4017), Jan. 7: 69-71.   **[60]**   [*RIS*]

Taylor, Andrew, Jr.; Santiago, Alejandro; Gonzales-Cortes, Abel & Gangarosa, Eugene J.
28.1265   TR   1974   Outbreak of typhoid fever in Trinidad in 1971 traced to a commercial ice cream product. *Am J Epidemic* 100(2), Aug.: 150-157.   [*PS*]

Teixeira, J.
28.1266   GU   1904   The recent epidemic of small-pox. *Br Gui Med Annual* 13: 24-31.   [*ACM*]
28.1267   GU   1906   Report on smallpox treated at the Isolation Hospital at the "Best". *Br Gui Med Annual 1905* 14: 39-48.   [*ACM*]

Terpstra, Wiepko Jelle
28.1268   SR   1972   INTESTINAL PARASITES IN AMERINDIANS OF THE INTERIOR OF SURINAM. Dissertation, Rijksuniversiteit Leiden: 120p.   **[13]**   [*RILA*]

Thézé, J.
28.1269   FG   1916   Pathologie de la Guyane Francaise [Pathology of French Guiana]. I. Paludisme. Fièvres continues et eaux de Cayenne. Dysenterie. Helminthiase intestinale [Malaria. Continuous fevers and the waters of Cayenne. Dysentery. Intestinal helminthiasis]. *B Soc Path Exot* 9(6), June: 376-402.   [*ACM*]

28.1270   FG   1916   Pathologie de la Guyane Francaise [Pathology of French Guiana].
                         II. Lèpre, filariose, etc. [Leprosy, filariasis, etc.) *B Soc Path Exot*
                         9(7), July: 449-469.   [*ACM*]

Thiel, P. H. van
28.1271   SR   1971   History of the control of endemic diseases in the Netherlands
                         Overseas Territories. *Ann Soc Belg Med Trop* 51(4-5): 451-457. **[5]**
                                                                                        [*PS*]

Thom, Herbert C. S.
55.0200 GC   1965   Some aspects of Caribbean area climate.

Thomas, Anthony & Krieger, Laurie
28.1272   JM   1976   Jamaican vomiting sickness: a theoretical investigation. *Social Sci*
                         Med 10(3-4), March-April: 177-183. **[29]**   [*COL*]

Thomas, J. H.
28.1273   BC   1960   Respiratory tuberculosis in the Caribbean. *Car Med J* 22(1-4):
                         20-23. **[10]**   [*COL*]

Thomas, Mary Elizabeth
28.1274   JM   1965   Quarantine in old Jamaica. *Car Stud* 4(4), Jan: 77-92. **[5]**   [*RIS*]

Thomas, Richard & Chesher, Gregory
28.1275   JM   1973   The pharmacology of marihuana. *Med J Aus* 2(5), Aug. 4:
                         229-237. **[33]**   [*ACM*]

Thompson, Janet
28.1276   GC   1968   The role of the nurse at present in the changing Caribbean. *Jam*
                         Nurse 8(2), Sept: 12 passim.   [*AJN*]

Thomson, David
28.1277   GU,TR 1913   Sanitation on the Panama Canal Zone, Trinidad and British
                         Guiana. *Ann Trop Med Paras* 7(1), Mar. 31: 125-152.   [*COL*]

Thorburn, Marigold J.
28.1278   JM   1965   Chromosome analyses in the University College Hospital of the
                         West Indies. *W I Med J* 14(1), March: 11-17.   [*PS*]
28.1279   JM   1969   Mental retardation in Jamaica. *Jam Nurse* 9(1), April-May: 18-22.
                                                                                        [*AJN*]
28.1280   JM   1969   The pathology of sickle cell anaemia in Jamaican adults over 30.
                         Trans Roy Soc Trop Med Hyg 63(1): 102-111. **[27]**   [*PS*]
28.1281   JM   1970   The pathology and incidence of the D & E trisomies in Jamaica.
                         W I Med J 19(3), Sept. 130-140.   [*PS*]
28.1282   JM   1974   Jamaican bushes and human chromosomes. *Jam J* 8(4): 18-
                         21. **[29,54]**   [*RIS*]

Thorburn, Marigold J.; Carpenter, Reginald A., & Williams, Samuel I.
28.1283   JM   1969   Clinical and cytogenic observations on four true hermaphrodites.
                         W I Med J 18(1), March: 5-16.   [*PS*]

Thorburn, Marigold J. & Curzen, Peter
28.1284   JM   1966   Perinatal mortality in the University College Hospital of the West
                         Indies, Jamaica. *W I Med J* 15(4), Dec.: 202-210.   [*PS*]

Thorburn, Marigold J.; Gwynn, R. V. & Ragbeer, M. S.

28.1285   JM   1968   Pathological and cytogenetic observations on the naturally occurring canine venereal tumour in Jamaica (Sticker's tumour). *Br J
Cancer* 22(4), Dec.: 720-727.   **[54]**   [*PS*]

Thorburn, Marigold J. & Hayes, J. A.

28.1286   JM   1968   Causes of death in Jamaica, 1953-1964: an analysis of the post-
mortem diagnosis at the University Hospital of the West Indies.
Trop Geogr Med 20(1), March: 35-49.   [*PS*]

Thorburn, Marigold J.; Hutchinson, S. & Alleyne, G. A. O.

30.0220   JM   1972   Chromosome abnormalities in malnourished children.

Thorburn, Marigold J. & Johnson, B. E.

28.1287   JM   1966   Apparent monosomy of a G autosome in a Jamaican infant. *J Med
Genet* 3(4), Dec.: 290-292.   [*PS*]

Thorburn, Marigold J. & Miller, C. G.

28.1288   JM   1967   Pathology of congenital rubella in Jamaica. *Arch Dis Childh*
42(224), Aug.: 389-396.   **[7]**   [*PS*]

Thorburn, Marigold J.; Miller, C. G. & Bras, G.

28.1289   JM   1967   Congenital hepatic fibrosis in Jamaican children. *Archs Dis Childh*
42(224), Aug.: 379-396.   [*PS*]

Thorburn, Marigold J.; Wright, E. S.; Miller, C. G. & Smith-Read, E. H.

28.1290   JM   1970   Exomphalos-macroglossia-gigantism syndrome in Jamaican infants.
Amer J Dis Child 119(4), April: 316-321.   [*PS*]

Thorburn, Marigold J.; Wynter, H. H. & Bell, Ruth

28.1291   JM   1969   Congenital malformations in Jamaica: an analysis of the perinatal
population of the University Hospital of the West Indies. *Trop
Geogr Med* 21(2), June: 147-156.   [*PS*]

Tiggelman-van Krugten, V. A. H. & Collier, W. A.

28.1292   SR   1955   The search for antibodies to the parapoliomyelitis group in human
and animal sera in Surinam. *Docum Med Geogr Trop* 7(3), Sept.:
270-272.   [*COL*]

Tikasingh, E. S.

28.1293   TR   1974   Enzootic rodent leishmaniasis in Trinidad, West Indies. *B Pam Am
Heal Org* 8(3): 232-242.   **[54]**   [*ACM*]

54.1014   SR,FG   1975   Observations on *Lutzomyia flaviscutellata* (Managabeira) (Diptera:
Psychodidae), a vector of enzootic leishmaniasis in Trinidad, West
Indies.

Tikasingh, E. S.; Aitken, T. H. G.; Butcher, L. V. & Gonzalez, F. O.

28.1294   TR   1968   Epidemiologic investigations relating to a case of eastern equine
encephalitis in a Trinidadian horse. *W I Med J* 17(2), June: 90-95.
                                                                               [*PS*]

Tikasingh, E. S.; Aitken, T. H. G.; Worth, C. Brooke; Spence, L. & Mongul, F. E.

28.1295   GU   1965   An outbreak of eastern equine encephalitis on the Courantyne coast of British Guiana. *W I Med J* 14(3), Sept.: 158-166.   **[62]**   [*PS*]

Tikasingh, E. S.; Ardoin, P.; Everard, C. O. R. & Davies, J. B.

62.0130   TR   1973   Eastern equine encephalitis in Trinidad. Epidemiological investigations following two human cases of South American strain in Santa Cruz.

Tikasingh, E. S.; Jonkers, A. H.; Spence, L. & Aitken, T. H. G.

28.1296   TR   1966   Nariva virus, a hitherto undescribed agent isolated from the Trinidadian rat, *Zygodontomys b. brevicauda* (J. A. Allen and Chapman). *Am J Trop Med Hyg* 15(2), March: 235-238.   [*PS*]

Tikasingh, E. S.; Spence, L.; Jonkers, A. H. & Green, A. E.

28.1297   MS   1966   Arthropod-borne encephalitis viruses in the West Indies area. Part VIII: A serological survey of Montserrat. *W I Med J* 15(2), June: 112-117.   [*PS*]

Tikasingh, E. S.; Worth, C. B.; Jonkers, A. H.; Aitken, T. H. G. & Spence, L.

62.0131   TR   1973   A three-year surveillance of eastern equine encephalitis virus activity in Trinidad.

Tillema, D. A.

28.1298   JM   1970   Slipped capital femoral epiphysis. *W I Med J* 19(1), March: 25-31.   [*PS*]

Tillema, D. A. & Golding, J. S.

28.1299   JM   1971   Chondrolysis following slipped capital femoral epiphysis in Jamaica. *J Bone Joint Surg* (American volume) 53-A(8), Dec.: 1528-1540.   [*PS*]

Tirolien, Camille

51.0103   GD   1961   Thermalisme [Mineral springs].

Tisseuil, M. J.

28.1300   GD,GU   1973   A propos du procès-verbal sur le mémoire de M. H. Floch: "Sur la lèpre en Guadeloupe." (Séance du 9 février 1972) [Apropos of the commentary of M. H. Floch's dissertation on leprosy in Guadeloupe (session of February 9, 1972)]. *B Soc Path Exot* 66(1), Jan.-Feb.: 9-11.   [*PS*]

Tjon Sie Fat, Howard Cyril

28.1301   NW   1954   ONDERZOEK NAAR DE SOCIAAL-HYGIENISCHE TOESTAND OP DE BOVENWINDSE EILANDEN DER NEDERLANSE ANTILLEN [INVESTIGATION OF SOCIAL-HYGIENIC CONDITIONS ON THE WINDWARD ISLANDS OF THE NETHERLANDS ANTILLES]. Amsterdam, Uitgeverij Argus, 176p.   **[33]**   [*RIS*]

Toby, D.; Hosien, E. & Foster, K.

32.0571   GC   1974   The student in the Medical Faculty of the University of the West Indies—after 25 years.

Todd, G. B.; Serjeant, G. R. & Larson, M. R.

28.1302   JM   1973   Sensori-neural hearing loss in Jamaicans with SS disease. *Acta Oto-Lar* 76(4), Oct.: 268-272.   **[11]**   [*ACM*]

Tom, F. & Tom, P.

28.1303   JM   1966   The age of the menarche in Jamaica. *W I Med J* 15(2), June: 83-88.
                                                                                                                        [*PS*]

Tongeren, H. A. E. van

28.1304   SR   1965   Arbovirus group A spectrum in the province of Brokopondo, Surinam: a serological survey. *Trop Geogr Med* 17(2), June: 172-185.
                                                                                                                        [*PS*]

28.1305   SR   1965   Arbovirus group B spectrum in the province of Brokopondo, Surinam: a serological survey. *Trop Geogr Med* 17(4), Dec.: 339-352.
                                                                                                                        [*PS*]

28.1306   SR   1967   Occurrence of arboviruses belonging to the C-, Bunyamwera and Guama groups, and of Oropouche, Junin, Tacaiuma and Kwatta viruses in man in the province of Brokopondo, Surinam: a serological survey. *Trop Geogr Med* 19(4), Dec.: 309-325.   [*PS*]

Tribouley, J.; Tribouley-Duret, J.; Bernard, D.; Appriou, M. & Pautrizel, R.

28.1307   GD   1975   La bilharziose intestinale en Guadeloupe [Intestinal bilharziasis in Guadeloupe]. *B Soc Path Exot* 68(2), March-April: 180-193.   [*PS*]

Tulloch, E. E.

28.1308   JM   1971   Historical perspectives of nursing in Jamaica. *Int Nurs Rev* 18(1): 49-58.   **[5]**   [*PS*]

Tulloch, J. A.

28.1309   JM   1958   Heart disease in Jamaica. *W I Med J* 7(3), Sept.: 169-181.   [*COL*]
28.1310   JM   1958   Myocardial infarction in Jamaica: the clinical features. *W I Med J* 7(4), Dec.: 244-250.   [*COL*]
30.0221   JM   1958   Some aspects of myocardial infarction in Jamaica.

Tulloch, J. A. & Douglas, C. P.

28.1311   JM   1963   A study of pregnancy in relation to the prediabetic state. *W I Med J* 12(2), June: 133-136.   [*COL*]

Tulloch, J. A. & Gay, K.

28.1312   JM   1956   An analysis of the admissions to a male and female medical ward of the University College Hospital of the West Indies during 1955. *W I Med J* 5(3), Sept.: 207-211.   [*COL*]

Tulloch, J. A.; Gay, K. & Irvine, R. A.

28.1313   JM   1956   Some aspects of diabetes in Jamaica. *W I Med J* 5(4), Dec.: 256-264.   [*COL*]

Tulloch, J. A. & Johnson, H. M.

28.1314   JM   1958   A pilot survey of the incidence of diabetes in Jamaica. *W I Med J* 7(2), June: 134-136.   [*COL*]

Tulloch, J. A. & Luck, D. E.

28.1315   JM   1959   The problem of diabetic control in the Caribbean. *W I Med J* 8(3), Sept.: 179-188.   [*COL*]

Turiaf, J.; Battesti, J. P. & Menault
28.1316   FA   1970   La sarcoïdose des sujets natifs des Antilles françaises [Sarcoidosis in natives of the French Antilles]. *Presse Med* 78(22), May 2: 1003-1008.   [*PS*]

Turk, D. C. & Wynter, H. H.
28.1317   JM   1961   Meningitis in Jamaica, 1958-1960. *W I Med J* 10(2), June: 118-131.
                                                                                [*COL*]

Unrau, G. O.
28.1318   SL   1975   Individual household water supplies as a control measure against *Schistosoma mansoni*. A study in rural St. Lucia. *B WHO* 52(1): 1-8.   **[48]**   [*PS*]

Upatham, Edward Suchart
54.1026   SL   1973   The effect of water temperature on the penetration and development of St. Lucian *Schistosoma mansoni* miracidia in local *Biomphalaria glabrata*.
54.1027   SL   1973   Location of *Biomphalaria glabrata* (Say) by miracidia of *Schistosoma mansoni* Sambon in natural standing and running waters on the West Indian Island of St. Lucia.
28.1319   SL   1974   Studies on the effects of cercarial concentration and length of exposure on the infection of mice by St. Lucian *Schistosoma mansoni* cercariae in a natural running-water habitat. *Parasitology* 68(2), April: 155-159.   **[54]**   [*PS*]

Urquhart, A. E. & Grant, L. S.
28.1320   JM   1965   The use of the Reiter Protein Complement Fixation Test in the diagnosis of syphilis in Jamaica. *W I Med J* 14(1), March: 22-28.
                                                                                [*PS*]
28.1321   GC   1966   Leptospirosis in the West Indies—a preliminary survey. *W I Med J* 15(2), June: 94-96.   [*PS*]

Usborne, Vivian
30.0223   SV   1963   The home treatment of infant malnutrition in a rural district of St. Vincent.

Uttley, K. H.
28.1322   AT   1958   The mortality from erysipelas over the last hundred years in Antigua, the West Indies. *W I Med J* 7(4), Dec.: 276-280.   **[5]**
                                                                                [*COL*]
28.1323   AT   1959   The epidemiology of tetanus in the Negro race over the last hundred years in Antigua, the West Indies. *W I Med J* 8(1), Mar.: 41-49.   **[5,11]**   [*COL*]
28.1324   AT   1959   The mortality and epidemiology of filariasis over the last hundred years in Antigua, British West Indies. *W I Med J* 8(4), Dec.: 238-248.   **[5]**   [*COL*]
28.1325   AT   1960   The epidemiology and mortality of whooping cough in the Negro over the last hundred years in Antigua, British West Indies. *W I Med J* 9(2), June: 77-95.   **[5,11]**   [*COL*]
28.1326   AT   1960   The mortality and epidemiology of diptheria since 1857 in the Negro population of Antigua, British West Indies. *W I Med J* 9(3), Sept.: 156-163.   **[5,11]**   [*COL*]

28.1327   AT   1960   The mortality and epidemiology of typhoid fever in the coloured inhabitants of Antigua, West Indies, over the last hundred years. *W I Med J* 9(2), June: 114-123.   **[5,11]**   [*COL*]

28.1328   AT   1960   The mortality of yellow fever in Antigua, West Indies, since 1857. *W I Med J* 9(3), Sept.: 184-188.   **[5]**   [*COL*]

28.1329   AT   1960   Smallpox mortality in the Negro population of Antigua, West Indies; a historical note. *W I Med J* 9(3), Sept.: 169-171.   **[5,11]**
[*COL*]

28.1330   AT   1961   Epidemiology and mortality of malaria in Antigua, BWI, 1857-1956. *Am J Publ Heal* 51(4), Apr.: 577-585.   **[5]**   [*COL*]

28.1331   AT   1961   The epidemiology of puerperal fever and maternal mortality in Antigua, West Indies, over the last hundred years, including a comparison with recent trends in neighbouring territories. *W I Med J* 10(1), Mar.: 63-71.   **[5]**   [*COL*]

28.1332   AT   1961   Tuberculosis mortality in the Negro population of Antigua, British West Indies, over the last hundred years. *Tubercle* 42(4), Dec.: 444-456.   **[11]**   [*COL*]

28.1333   AT   1966   The incidence and mortality of disease in Antigua, West Indies, in recent years. *W I Med J* 15(2), June: 97-107.   [*PS*]

Vaillant, Henry W.; Cummins, G. T. & Richart, R. M.
28.1334   BB   1968   An island-wide screening program for cervical neoplasia in Barbados. *Am J Obstet Gynec* 101(7), Aug. 1: 943-946.   [*PS*]

Vallejo, Nilo
28.1335   GC   1965   Health education in the Caribbean. *In* Wilgus, A. Curtis, ed. THE CARIBBEAN: ITS HEALTH PROBLEMS. Gainesville, University of Florida Press: 200-212. (Caribbean Conference Series 1, Vol. 15)   **[32]**
[*RIS*]

Varma, M. G. R.
54.1033   BZ   1973   Ticks (*Ixodidae*) of British Honduras.

Veeder, Nancy Walker
34.0123   JM   1974   PRENATAL CARE UTILIZATION AND PERSISTENCE PATTERNS IN A DEVELOPING NATION: A STUDY OF ONE HUNDRED AND EIGHTY-FIVE PREGNANT WOMEN ATTENDING TWO PRENATAL CLINICS IN KINGSTON, JAMAICA, WEST INDIES.

Ventura, Arnoldo K.
28.1336   JM   1965   St. Louis encephalitis virus in Jamaican birds. *Am J Trop Med Hyg* 14(2), March: 297-302.   **[54]**   [*PS*]

28.1337   JM   1969   A new group of viruses in Jamaica. I. Initial Studies. *W I Med J* 18(2), June: 95-104.   [*PS*]

Ventura, Arnoldo K. & Hewitt, Colin M.
28.1338   JM   1970   Recovery of Dengue-2 and Dengue-3 viruses from man in Jamaica. *Am J Trop Med Hyg* 19(4), July: 712-715.   [*PS*]

Verlinde, J. D.
28.1339   SR   1968   Susceptibility of Cynomolgus monkeys to experimental infection with arboviruses of Group A (Mayaro and Mucambo), group C (Oriboca and Restan) and an unidentified arbovirus (Kwatta) originating from Surinam. *Trop Geogr Med* 20(4), Dec.: 385-390.
[*PS*]

Verlinde, J. D.; Kooij, P. & Versteeg, J.

28.1340   SR   1970   Vampire-bat transmitted rabies virus from Surinam: comparison of properties with European street virus and fixed virus. *Trop Geogr Med* 22(1), March: 119-122.   **[54]**   [*PS*]

Verlinde, J. D.; Li-Fo-Sjoe, E.; Versteeg, J. & Dekker, S. M.

28.1341   SR   1975   A local outbreak of paralytic rabies in Surinam children. *Trop Geogr Med* 27(2), June: 137-142.   **[14,54]**   [*PS*]

Vernon, Cynthia

28.1342   JM   1965   The public health nurse in the community. *Int Nurs Rev* 12(6), Dec.: 35-37.   [*PS*]

28.1343   JM   1971   Special needs of the young child in Jamaica. *Jam Nurse* 11(3), Dec.: 12-16.   **[30]**   [*AJN*]

Verteuil, Eric de

28.1344   TR   1934   Agriculture and health. *Proc Agric Soc Trin Tob* 34(8), Aug.: 307-314.   **[43]**   [*AMN*]

28.1345   TR   1941   Trinidad malaria in prospect and retrospect. *Car Med J* 3(3), 139-147.   **[5]**   [*COL*]

28.1346   TR   1943   The urgent need for a medical health policy for Trinidad. *Car Med J* 5(3): 107-119.   **[33]**   [*COL*]

Verteuil, Eric de & Urich, F. W.

28.1347   TR   1959   The study and control of paralytic rabies transmitted by bats in Trinidad, British West Indies. *Car Med J* 21(1-4): 85-109.   [*COL*]

Vinke, B. & Jansen, W.

28.1348   CU   1960   Comparison of an intradermal test for *Schistosoma Mansoni* with the results of faecal examinations in Curacao. *Trop Geogr Med* 12(2), Sept.: 217-221.   [*COL*]

Vinke, B.; Piers, A. & Irausquin-Cath, H.

28.1349   CU   1969   Folic acid and Vitamin B_{12} deficiences in negroid hospital patients on Curaçao. *Trop Geogr Med* 21(4), Dec.: 401-406.   **[11,30]**   [*PS*]

Vinke, B. & Sar, A. van der

28.1350   CU   1966   Peptic ulcer and gastric cancer in the negroid population of Curaçao. *Trop Geogr Med* 18(3), Sept.: 221-226.   **[11,27]**   [*PS*]

Vinke, B.; Sar, A. van der; Faber, J. G. & Vries, J. A. de

30.0227   CU   1960   Penicillin in nutritional megaloblastic anaemia in Curacao.

30.0228   CU   1960   Serum vitamin B_{12} levels and response to the treatment of megaloblastic anaemia in Curacao.

Visser, W. J.; Bellot, S. M.; Duursma, S. A. & Luyken, R.

30.0229   SR   1974   Osteoporosis in Surinam.

Volz, P. A.

28.1351   BA   1971   A preliminary study of keratinophilic fungi from Abaco Island, the Bahamas. *Mycopathol Mycol Appl* 43(3-4), March 25: 337-339.   **[54]**
[*PS*]

Voogt, H. J. de

28.1352   SR   1967   Osteomyelitis in the tropics. *Trop Geogr Med* 19(4), Dec.: 352-356. **[14]**   [*PS*]

Vries, Jan de

14.0075   SR   1970   Het medisch werk in Suriname's bosland: Een sociopedagogische beschouwing [The medical work in the inland of Surinam: A socio-educational analysis].

Vyse, H. G.

28.1353   JM   1952   Comprehensive medical services in Jamaica. *Car Med J* 14(3-4): 119-121.   [*COL*]

28.1354   JM   1953   The incidence of diptheria in Jamaica. *W I Med J* 2(1), Mar.: 67-79.   [*COL*]

Waal, I. van der; Bruggenkate, C. M. ten & Kwast, W. A. van der

28.1355   NE,SR   1975   Focal epithelial hyperplasia in a child from Surinam. *Int J Oral Surg* 4(4), Sept.: 168-171.   [*ACM*]

Wagenaar Hummelinck, P.

54.1078   SR   1942   Studies over de patatta-luis [Studies of the patatta louse].

28.1356   CU   1947   Medisch werk op Curacao in 1939-1946 [Medical work on Curacao]. *W I G* 28: 329-334.   [*COL*]

Wallace, J. & Lovell, H. G.

28.1357   JM   1969   Glaucoma and intraocular pressure in Jamaica. *Am J Ophthalmol* 67(1), Jan.: 93-100.   [*PS*]

Wallbridge, J. S.

7.0210   GU   1907   Remarks on the Mortality Commission Report.

Walrond, E. R.

28.1358   JM   [n.d.]   Carcinoma of the oesophagus in Jamaica. *W I Med J* 21(2), June: 109-113.   [*PS*]

28.1359   JM   1970   Pyloric stenosis in Jamaica. *W I Med J* 19(3), Sept.: 175-179.   [*PS*]

28.1360   JM   1971   Development of progressive care in the general surgical wards at the University Hospital, Jamaica. *W I Med J* 20(2), June: 106-110.   [*PS*]

28.1361   JM   1972   Abdominal aortic eneurysm involving the renal arteries. *W I Med J* 21(4), Dec.: 245-248.   [*PS*]

28.1362   JM   1973   An unusual case of traumatic haemobilia. *W I Med J* 21(1), March: 34-36.   [*PS*]

28.1363   JM   1974   Progressive care surgical wards at the University Hospital, Jamaica. *W I Med J* 23(4), Dec.: 245-249.   [*PS*]

Walrond, E. R. & Jordon, R.

28.1364   JM   1969   Carcinoma of the colon and rectum at the University Hospital, Jamaica. *W I Med J* 18(3), Sept.: 152-160.   [*PS*]

Walrond, E. R. & Sahoy, R.

28.1365   JM   1973   Gall bladder disease at the University Hospital—Jamaica. *W I Med J* 22(3), Sept.: 119-124.   [*PS*]

Walrond, Mickey

28.1366   BB   1966-67 Health and freedom. *New Wld Q* 3(1-2), Dead Season and Croptime, Barbados Independence Issue: 106-109.   [*RIS*]

Walshe, Margaret M.

28.1367   JM   1967   Infective dermatitis in Jamaican children. *Br J Derm* 79(4), April: 229-236.   [*PS*]

28.1368   JM   1967   Norwegian scabies. *W I Med J* 16(1), March: 57-61.   [*PS*]

28.1369   JM   1968   Dermatology in Jamaica. *Trans St John Hosp Derm Soc* 54(1): 46-53.   [*PS*]

Walshe, Margaret M. & Hayes, J. A.

28.1370   JM   1967   Respiratory symptoms and smoking habits in Jamaica. *Am Rev Resp Dis* 96(4), Oct.: 640-644.   [*PS*]

Walshe, Margaret M. & Milner, P. F.

28.1371   JM   1967   The management of leg ulcers in sickle cell anaemia. *W I Med J* 16(1), March: 10-16.   [*PS*]

Ward, D. M.

28.1372   JM   1967   Bilateral amblyopia occurring in aphakic West Indians. *Br J Ophthal* 51(5), May: 343-347.   [*PS*]

Ward, E. E.

28.1373   JM   1963   Serum gamma globulins and infection in Jamaica. *W I Med J* 12(1), Mar.: 59-62.   [*COL*]

Warner, Henry

28.1374   TR   1919   Water supply and sanitary reform. *Proc Agric Soc Trin Tob* 19(5), May: 110-122.   **[43,44]**   [*AMN*]

Warner, Joyce; Brooks S. E. H.; James, W. P. T. & Louisy, Sheila

28.1375   JM   1972   Juvenile dermatitis herpetiformis in Jamaica: clinical and gastro-intestinal features. *Br J Derm* 86(3), March: 226-237.   **[30]**   [*PS*]

Warren, Kenneth S.; Cook, Joseph A. & Jordan, Peter

28.1376   SL   1972   Passive transfer of immunity in human Schistosomiasis mansoni: effect of hyperimmune anti-schistome gamma globulin on early established infections. *Trans Roy Soc Trop Med Hyg* 66(1): 65-74.
                                                                                  [*PS*]

Warren, Kenneth S.; Cook, Joseph A.; Littell, Arthur S.; Kagan, Irving G. & Jordan, Peter

28.1377   SL,SV   1973   Immunologic diagnosis of schistosomiasis. II. Further studies on the sensitivity and specificity of delayed intradermal reactions. *Am J Trop Med Hyg* 22(2), March: 199-204.   **[54]**   [*PS*]

Warren, Kenneth S.; Kellermeyer, Robert W.; Jordan, Peter; Littell, Arthur S.; Cook, Joseph A. & Kagan, Irving G.

28.1378   SL,SV   1973   Immunologic diagnosis of schistosomiasis. I. A Controlled study of intradermal (immediate and delayed) and serologic tests in St. Lucians infected with *Schistosoma mansoni* and in uninfected St. Vincentians. *Am J Trop Med Hyg* 22(2), March: 189-198.   **[54]**
                                                                                  [*PS*]

Washburn, B. E.

32.0595	JM	1929	JAMAICA HEALTH STORIES AND PLAYS.
28.1379	JM	1930	THE HEALTH GAME. London, J. & A. Churchill: 202p. [*NYP*]
28.1380	JM	1933	An epidemic of malaria at Falmouth, Jamaica, British West Indies. *Am J Hyg* 17(3), May: 656-665. [*COL*]
28.1381	GU,TR	1960	AS I RECALL. New York, Rockefeller Foundation, 183p. **[11,12]** [*COL*]

Waterlow, J. C.

28.1382	JM	1961	The Tropical Metabolism Research Unit. *Inf B Scient Res Coun* 2(1), June: 5-7. [*RIS*]
28.1383	JM	1974	Some aspects of childhood malnutrition as a public health problem. *Br Med J* 4(5936), Oct. 12: 88-90. **[30]** [*PS*]
30.0233	JM	1975	Amount and rate of disappearance of liver fat in malnourished infants in Jamaica.

Waterman, I. D.

28.1384	TR	1958	A century of service. *Car Med J* 20(1-4): 36-41. **[5]** [*COL*]

Waterman, James A.

28.1385	TR	1938	Some notes on maternal mortality in Trinidad with a note on the maternity department and the training of midwives at the Colonial Hospital, Port-of-Spain. *Car Med J* 1(1): 74-81. [*COL*]
28.1386	TR	1940	A statistical analysis of eclampsia cases treated at the Colonial Hospital, Port-of-Spain, from 1924 to 1938. *Car Med J* 2(3): 137-146. [*COL*]
28.1387	TR	1941	Haemophilia in the Afro-West Indian. *Car Med J* 3(3): 167-171. **[11]** [*COL*]
28.1388	BC	1942	A suggested maternity scheme for the West Indies. *Car Med J* 4(4): 140-147. **[34]** [*COL*]
28.1389	TR	1943	Acute rheumatic fever and rheumatic carditis in the tropics with special reference to Trinidad. *Car Med J* 5(4): 204-232. [*COL*]
28.1390	TR	1943	The disorders of cardiac rhythm confirmed by electrocardiography as seen in Trinidad. *Car Med J* 5(4): 233-247. [*COL*]
28.1391	TR	1944	A national health service with special reference to Trinidad. *Car Med J* 6(4): 304-309. **[33]** [*COL*]
28.1392	TR	1944	Notes on tuberculosis in Trinidad. *Car Med J* 6(3): 204-215. [*COL*]
30.0235	TR	1945	Nutrition in Trinidad, with special reference to milk during pregnancy and infancy.
28.1393	TR	1948	Peroneal palsy complicating labour and the puerperium. *Car Med J* 10(3-4): 88-108. **[30]** [*COL*]
28.1394	TR	1957	Some notes on scorpion poisoning in Trinidad. *Car Med J* 19(1-2): 113-128. [*COL*]
28.1395	BC	1958	The impact of federation on medicine in the West Indies. *Car Med J* 20(1-4): 42-48. **[38]** [*COL*]
28.1396	TR	1959	The history of the outbreak of paralytic rabies in Trinidad transmitted by bats to human beings and the lower animals from 1925. *Car Med J* 21(1-4): 1-6. [*COL*]
28.1397	TR	1965	The history of the outbreak of paralytic rabies in Trinidad transmitted by bats to human beings and the lower animals from 1925. *Car Med J* 27(1-4): 164-169. [*ACM*]
28.1398	TR	1967	Malaria—and its eradication in Trinidad and Tobago. *Car Med J* 29(1-4): 19-35. **[27]** [*PS*]

Waterman, James A. et al.

28.1399 TR 1963 Voluntary pre-payment health insurance scheme. *Car Med J* 25(1-4): 41-69. **[33,49]** [*COL*]

Waterman, N.

28.1400 CU 1919-20 De geneeskundige organisatie in de kolonie Curacao [The medical organization in the colony of Curacao]. *W I G* 1(2): 35-47. [*COL*]

28.1401 CU 1973 De geneeskundige organisatie in de kolonie Curaçao [The health care organisation in the colony Curaçao]. *In* Statius van Eps, L. W. & Luckman-Maduro, E., eds. VAN SCHEEPSCHIRURGIJN TOT SPECIALIST. Assen, The Netherlands, Van Gorcum & Comp. B. V.: 47-58. (Anjerpublikatie 15) **[5]** [*RILA*]

Watler, D. C.

28.1402 JM 1958 Leukaemia in Jamaica: a statistical survey of seventy cases. *W I Med J* 7(4), Dec.: 267-275. [*COL*]

28.1403 JM 1960 Congenital heart disease in Jamaica (observation on post mortem incidence, with a report of an unusual case of *cor triloculare biatriatum*). *W I Med J* 9(3), Sept.: 194-200. [*COL*]

Watler, D. C.; Bras, G. & McDonald, H. G.

28.1404 JM 1959 The incidence of malignant neoplasms in Jamaica. *W I Med J* 8(4), Dec.: 249-261. [*COL*]

Watler, D. C.; Burrowes, A. S. & Bras, G.

28.1405 JM 1960 Analysis of 136 consecutive cases of malignant neoplasm of the stomach. *W I Med J* 9(3), Sept.: 164-168. [*COL*]

Watler, D. C.; McNeil-Smith, E. & Wynter, L.

28.1406 JM 1958 Haemophilia in Jamaica. *W I Med J* 7(1), Mar.: 1-16. [*COL*]

Wattley, G. H.

28.1407 TR 1959 Myocardial infarction in south Trinidad. *W I Med J* 8(1), Mar.: 33-40. [*COL*]

28.1408 TR 1959 The pattern of skin disease in south Trinidad. *W I Med J* 8(3), Sept.: 199-202. [*COL*]

28.1409 TR 1960 Heart disease in Trinidad. *W I Med J* 9(3), Sept.: 189-193. [*COL*]

28.1410 TR 1968 The arrhythmias in consulting practice. *Car Med J* 30: 43-48. [*PS*]

Watty, E. I.

28.1411 DM 1960 Tuberculosis in Dominica. *Car Med J* 22(1-4): 112-113. [*COL*]

Ways, P.; Bryant, J. & Guicherit, I. D.

28.1412 SR 1956 Histoplasmin sensitivity among the Bush Negroes of Surinam. *Docum Med Geogr Trop* 8(4), Dec.: 383-391. **[14]** [*COL*]

Weatherall, D. J. & Clegg, J. B.

28.1413 JM 1975 The α-chain-termination mutants and their relation to the α-thalassaemias. *Phil Trans Roy Soc Lord Biol* 271(913), Aug. 7: 411-455. **[27]** [*COL*]

Webster, W. A.

28.1414   JM   1971   Studies on the parasites of Chiroptera. I. Helminths of Jamaican bats of the genera *Tadarida, Chilonycteris,* and *Monophyllus. Proc Helm Soc Wash* 38(2), July: 195-199.   [*PS*]

Weinheimer, Alfred J.

28.1415   GC   1974   The discovery of 15-epi PGA$_2$ in *Plexaura homomalla. In* Bayer, Frederick M. & Weinheimer, Alfred J., eds. PROSTAGLANDINS FROM *Plexaura homomalla:* ECOLOGY, UTILIZATION AND CONSERVATION OF A MAJOR MEDICAL MARINE RESOURCE. A SYMPOSIUM. Coral Gables, University of Miami Press: 17-21. (Studies in Tropical Oceanography, 12).   **[54]**   [*UCLA*]

Weinstein, B.

28.1416   GU   1962   Diabetes: a regional survey in British Guiana (preliminary report). *W I Med J* 11(2), June: 88-93.   **[11,12]**   [*COL*]

Weisbrod, Burton A.; Andreano, Ralph L.; Baldwin, Robert E.; Epstein, Erwin H. & Kelley, Allen C.

28.1417   SL   1973   DISEASE AND ECONOMIC DEVELOPMENT: THE IMPACT OF PARASITIC DISEASES IN ST. LUCIA. Madison, Wisconsin, University of Wisconsin Press: 218p.   **[41]**   [*RIS*]

Weller, Thomas H.

28.1418   GC   1961   Research in the health services in the Caribbean. *W I Med J* 10(2), June: 73-75.   [*COL*]

Wellin, Edward et al.

28.1419   GC   1960   Sociocultural factors in public health. *In* Rubin, Vera, ed. CULTURE, SOCIETY AND HEALTH. New York, New York Academy of Sciences, p.1044-1060. (Annals of the New York Academy of Sciences, v. 84, art. 17.)   [*RIS*]

Wells, A. V.

28.1420   SL   1959   Antibodies to poliomyelitis viruses in St. Lucia. *W I Med J* 8(3), Sept.: 161-170.   [*COL*]

28.1421   SL   1961   Malaria eradication in St. Lucia, West Indies. *W I Med J* 10(2), June: 103-111.   [*COL*]

Wenger, O. C.

28.1422   TR   1944   The role of the private practitioner in a modern venereal disease control programme. *Car Med J* 6(3): 87-94.   [*COL*]

28.1423   TR   1946   CARIBBEAN MEDICAL CENTER. Washington, Caribbean Commission, 74p.   [*COL*]

Went, L. N.; Channer, D. M.; Harding, R. Y. & Clunes, B. E.

30.0236   JM   1960   The effect of iron and protein supplementations on the haemoglobin level of healthy female students.

Went, L. N. & MacIver, J. E.

28.1424   JM   1956   Investigation of abnormal haemoglobins in Jamaica: a preliminary survey. *W I Med J* 5(4), Dec.: 247-255.   **[27]**   [*COL*]

Wertheimer, F. W.; Brewster, R. H. & White, C. L.
30.0237 TR 1967 Periodontal disease and nutrition in Trinidad.

West, M. E.; Garvey, H. Lloyd & Ling, George M.
28.1425 GC 1973 Cardiovascular and antiarrhythmic effects of an active principle from the bark of anacardium occidentale. *W I Med J* 22(2), June: 49-59. **[29]**   [PS]

West, M. E. & Sidrak, G. H.
28.1426 JM 1970 Some biological observations on hypoglycin-A in the presence of leucine. *W I Med J* 19(1), March: 19-24.   [PS]

West, M. E.; Sidrak, G. H. & Street, S. P. W.
28.1427 JM 1971 The anti-growth properties of extracts from *Momordica charantia L.* *W I Med J* 20(1), March: 25-34. **[54]**   [PS]

Weston, Peter M.
28.1428 JM 1961 Carcinoma of the urinary bladder in Jamaica. *W I Med J* 10(2), June: 112-117.   [COL]

Wever, O. R.
33.0213 AR 1970 Some medical and sociopathological aspects of alcoholism in Aruba and its actual treatment.

Whimster, William F.
28.1429 JM 1971 Normal lung weights in Jamaicans. *Am Rev Resp Dis* 103(1), Jan.: 85-90. **[27]**   [ACM]

Whimster, William F. & Macfarlane, Alison J.
27.0153 JM 1974 Normal lung weights in a white population.

Whitbourne, Dahlia
28.1430 JM 1965 History of the school medical services, Kingston, Jamaica (1934-1959). *W I Med J* 14(3), Sept.: 167-179. **[32]**   [PS]

White, Senior
28.1431 TR 1947 Malaria work in Trinidad. *Car Commn Mon Inf B* 1(4), Nov.: 14-16.   [COL]

Whitelocke, H. I. et al.
28.1432 JM 1954 Peptic ulcer in Jamaica: symposium at the University College of the West Indies, March 3rd, 1954. *W I Med J* 3(3), Sept.: 166-184.
[COL]

Wickstrom, Per Henrik
28.1433 JM 1968 THE EPIDEMIOLOGY OF DIABETES IN JAMAICA. Ph.D. dissertation, Yale University: 158p.

Wiersema, J. P. & Barrow, R. S.
28.1434 SR 1961 Cancer, especially of the cervix uteri, in Surinam. *Trop Geogr Med* 13(4), Dec.: 347-350.

Wiersema, J. P. & Niemel, P. L. A.

28.1435   **SR**   1965   Lobo's disease in Surinam patients. *Trop Geogr Med* 17(2), June:
89-111. **[14]**   *[PS]*

Wijers, D. J. B. & Huisenga, J.

54.1109   **SR**   1967   A new species of *Lutzomyia* from Surinam (Diptera, Psychodidae).

Wijers, D. J. B. & Linger, R.

28.1436   **SR**   1966   Man-biting sandflies in Surinam (Dutch Guiana): *Phlebotomus anduzei* as a possible vector of *Leishmania braziliensis. Ann Trop Med Paras* 60(4), Dec.: 501-508.   *[PS]*

Wildervanck, A.; Collier, W. A. & Winckel, W. E. F.

28.1437   **SR**   1953   Two cases of histoplasmosis on farms near Paramaribo (Surinam): investigations into the epidemiology of the disease. *Docum Med Geogr Trop* 5(2), June: 108-115.   *[COL]*

Wilgus, A. Curtis, ed.

28.1438   **GC**   1965   THE CARIBBEAN: ITS HEALTH PROBLEMS. Gainesville, University of Florida Press: 273p. (Caribbean Conference Series 1, Vol. 15)
                                                             [RIS]

Willcox, R. R.

28.1439   **GC,UK**   1974   Effective treatment of gonorrhoea in London with two oral doses of amoxycillin. *Br J Ven Dis* 50(2), April: 120-124. **[18]**   *[PS]*

Williams, Cicely

28.1440   **JM**   1952   Vomiting in children. *W I Med J* 1(3), Oct.: 265-273.   *[COL]*

Williams, Denis

28.1441   **GU**   1972[?]   GIGLIOLI IN GUYANA, 1922-1972. Georgetown, National History and Arts Council: 68p.   *[RIS]*

Williams, F. M. W.; Hamilton, H. F.; Singh, Balwant & Herlinger, R.

28.1442   **GU**   1960   Tropical eosinophilia in British Guiana; a preliminary report. *W I Med J* 9(3), Sept.: 149-155.   *[COL]*

Williams, L. L.

34.0124   **JM**   1966   Post-partum insertion of a standard Lippes loop.

28.1443   **JM**   1973   Some observations on maternal mortality in Jamaica. *W I Med J* 22(1), March: 1-14. **[7]**   *[PS]*

Williams, Paul

28.1444   **BZ**   1965   Observations on the phlebotomine sandflies of British Honduras. *Ann Trop Med Paras* 59(4), Dec.: 393-404.   *[PS]*

28.1445   **BZ**   1966   The biting rhythms of some anthropophilic phlebotomine sandflies in British Honduras. *Ann Trop Med Paras* 60(3), Sept.: 357-364.
                                                             [PS]

28.1446   **BZ**   1966   The distribution on the human body of bites by phlebotomine sandflies in British Honduras. *Ann Trop Med Paras* 60(2), June: 219-222.   *[PS]*

28.1447   **BZ**   1966   Experimental transmission of *Leishmania mexicana* by *Lutzomyia cruciata. Ann Trop Med Paras* 60(3), Sept.: 365-372.   *[PS]*

28.1448   BZ   1970   Phlebotomine sandflies and leishmaniasis in British Honduras (Belize). *Trans Roy Soc Trop Med Hyg* 64(3), June: 317-364. **[54]**
[PS]

Williams, Paul; Lewis, D. J. & Garnham, P. C. C.
28.1449   BZ   1965   On dermal leishmaniasis in British Honduras. *Trans Roy Trop Med Hyg* 59(1), Jan.: 64-71.
[PS]

Williamson, Frances E.
28.1450   SL   1965   Educational campaigns in St. Lucia. *In* Wilgus, A. Curtis, ed. THE CARIBBEAN: ITS HEALTH PROBLEMS. Gainesville, University of Florida Press: 124-129. (Caribbean Conference Series 1, Vol. 15) [RIS]

Wilson, John F.
28.1451   BC   1954   Blindness in the British Caribbean territories. *W I Comm Circ* 69(1281), Sept.: 245-246.
[NYP]

Wilson, M. B. & Stuart, K. L.
28.1452   JM   1970   Immunological studies on leakage of heart antigens in Jamaican cardiomyopathies. *W I Med J* 19(4), Dec.: 236-239.
[PS]

Wilson, Phyllis
28.1453   JM   1969   Some aspects of physiotherapy in Jamaica. *Physiotherapy* 55(2), Feb.: 60-63.
[PS]

Wilterdink, J. B.; Metselaar, D.; Kuyp, E. van der & Verlinde, J. D.
28.1454   SR   1964   Poliomyelitis in Surinam. *Trop Geogr Med* 16(2), June: 120-128. **[10]**
[COL]

Winckel, W. E. F. & Aalstein, M.
28.1455   SR   1953   Contribution to the geographical pathology of Surinam: first case of kala-azar in Surinam. *Docum Med Geogr Trop* 5(4), Dec.: 339-342.
[COL]

Wise, K. S.
28.1456   GU   1907   Acute anaemia. *Br Gui Med Annual 1906* 15: 103-117.   [ACM]
62.0148   GU   1907   Observations on the milk supply of Georgetown.
28.1457   GU   1909   *Filaria bancroftii. Br Gui Med Annual 1908* 16: 35-50.   [ACM]
28.1458   GU   1912   The nastin treatment of leprosy in British Guiana. *Br Gui Med Annual 1910* 17: 45-99.   [ACM]
7.0216   GU   1912   The public health, statistics, and medical institutions of the Colony. *Br Gui Med Annual* 17.
7.0217   GU   1913   The public health, statistics, and medical institutions of the Colony. *Br Gui Med Annual* 18.
7.0218   GU   1913   The public health, statistics, and medical institutions of the Colony. *Br Gui Med Annual* 19.
54.1122   GU   1914   A list of the commoner invertebrate animals of medical interest identified in British Guiana.
28.1459   GU   1914   The pathological effects of *Filaria bancroftii* with reference to septic complications. *Br Gui Med Annual 1913* 20: 1-27.   [ACM]
28.1460   GU   1919   Malaria, the problem of British Guiana. *Br Gui Med Annual 1919* 22: 1-28.   [ACM]

Wise, K. S. & Minett, E. P.

28.1461   GU   1912   Drinking water supplies: a chemical and bacteriological study of the drinking water supplies on estates from a hygienic point of view. *Timehri* 3d ser., 2(19B), Dec.: 247-254. **[42,54]**   [*AMN*]

28.1462   GU   1913   Review of the milk question in British Guiana. *Br Gui Med Annual 1911* 18: 47-59. **[62]**   [*ACM*]

Wishart, W. de W.

7.0219   GU   1902   The influence of rainfall on death-rate in the tropics.

28.1463   GU   1923   Infant welfare work in Georgetown: past, present and future. *Br Gui Med Annual 1923* 28: 35-42.   [*ACM*]

28.1464   GU   1923   Some aspects of the sanitary and public health problems of Georgetown. *Br Gui Med Annual 1923* 23: 43-52.   [*ACM*]

28.1465   GU   1926   Recommendations for mosquito prophylaxis in Georgetown. *Br Gui Med Annual 1925* 24: 29-33.   [*ACM*]

7.0220   GU   1943   The Georgetown vital index as related to rainfall.

Witte, John J.; Page, Malcolm I. & Gelfand, Henry M.

28.1466   GU   1965   Control of a Type 1 poliomyelitis epidemic in British Guiana, 1962-63, with trivalent oral poliovirus vaccine. 1. Epidemiological aspects. *B WHO* 33(1): 1-11.   [*PS*]

Wittkower, Eric D.

31.0145   GC   1970   Transcultural psychiatry in the Caribbean: past, present, and future.

Wolfe, Martin S. & Wershing, Julie M.

28.1467   BA   1974   Mebendazole: treatment of trichuriasis and ascariasis in Bahamian children. *J A M A* 230(10), Dec. 9: 1408-1411.   [*PS*]

Wolff, J. W. & Bohlander, H. J.

28.1468   SR   1969   A survey for leptospiral antibodies in sera from the bushland population of Surinam. *Trop Geogr Med* 21(2), June: 199-202. **[14]**
                                                                                            [*PS*]

Wolff, J. W.; Collier, W. A.; Bool, P. H. & Bohlander, H.

28.1469   SR   1958   Investigations on the occurrence of leptospirosis in Surinam. *Trop Geogr Med* 10(4), Dec.: 341-346.   [*COL*]

Wolff, J. W.; Collier, W. A.; Roever-Bonnet, H. de & Hoekstra, J.

28.1470   SR   1958   Yellow fever immunity in rural population groups of Surinam (with a note on other serological investigations). *Trop Geogr Med* 10(4), Dec.: 325-331.   [*COL*]

Wood, J. K.

28.1471   JM   1968   Paroxysmal cold haemoglobinuria in Jamaica—a case report. *W I Med J* 17(3), Sept.: 175-179.   [*PS*]

Wood, J. K.; Milner, P. F. & Pathak, U. N.

30.0242   JM   1968   The metabolism of iron-dextran given as a total-dose infusion to iron deficient Jamaican subjects.

Wood, R. J.

28.1472   TR   1967   A comparative genetical study on DDT resistance in adults and larvae of the mosquito *Aedes aegypti* L. *Genet Res* 10: 219-228.   [*PS*]

54.1127   TR   1968   Heterogeneity in the Trinidad DDT-resistant strain and QS susceptible strain of *Aedes aegypti* L. The isolation of highly resistant and highly susceptible substrains.

Woodruff, A. W.

28.1473   TT   1973   Lettsom and his family in Tortola. *Proc Roy Soc Med* 66(1), Jan.: 41-46. **[5]**   [*ACM*]

Woo-Ming, M. O.

28.1474   JM   1966   Cardiorespiratory resuscitation in the prone position in small children. *W I Med J* 15(4), Dec.: 197-200.   [*PS*]

Woo-Ming, M. O.; Miller, C. G.; Sivapragasam, S. & Doobay, B.

28.1475   BC   1973   Pulmonary artery banding for ventricular septal defect in infancy. *W I Med J* 22(3), Sept.: 133-136.   [*PS*]

Worth, C. B.; Downs, W. G.; Aitken, T. H. G. & Tikasingh, E. S.

28.1476   TR   1968   Arbovirus studies in Bush Bush Forest, Trinidad, W. I., September 1959-December 1964. IV. Vertebrate populations. *Am J Trop Med Hyg* 17(2), March: 269-275.   [*PS*]

Wortman, Judith

34.0126   TR,JM   1975   Training nonphysicians in family planning services and a directory of training programs.

Wright, H. B. & Taylor, Belle

28.1477   TR   1958   The incidence of diabetes in a sample of the adult population in south Trinidad. *W I Med J* 7(2), June: 123-133.   [*COL*]

Wulff, H.; Chin, T. D. & Wenner, H. A.

28.1478   JM   1969   Serologic responses of children after primary vaccination and revaccination against smallpox. *Am J Epidemiol* 90(4), Oct.: 312-318.   [*PS*]

Wylie, A.

28.1479   GU   1906   On cataract disease in British Guiana. *Br Gui Med Annual 1905* 14: 65-69.   [*ACM*]

Wynter, Hugh H.

28.1480   JM   1969   Prolapsed urethral mucosa. *W I Med J* 18(2), June: 105-111.   [*PS*]
28.1481   JM   1971   Carcinoma-in-situ of the uterine cervix. *W I Med J* 20(2), June: 91-96.   [*PS*]

Wynter, Hugh H. & Hew, L. R.

28.1482   JM   1968   Fetal mortality and morbidity in twin pregnancy. *W I Med J* 17(4), Dec.: 204-214.   [*PS*]

Young, Valentine H.

28.1483   GC   1966   Plasma 11-hydroxycorticoid levels in coloured West Indians. *W I Med J* 15(3), Sept.: 128-133. **[11,27]**   [*PS*]

Zaal, G. Ph.

28.1484   SR   1937   Het drinkwatervraagstuk in Suriname en het stadium zijner oplossing [The problem of drinking water in Surinam and the stage of its solution]. *W I G* 19: 65-79. **[33]**   [*COL*]

Zanen, G. E. van

5.1017   CU   1969   DAVID RICARDO CAPRILES: STUDENT—GENEESHEER—SCHRIJVER, CURAÇAO 1837-1902 [DAVID RICARDO CAPRILES: STUDENT —DOCTOR—WRITER, CURAÇAO 1837-1902].

Zephirin, M.

28.1485   GC   1969   Hospital food service in the Caribbean. *Cajanus* 2(5), Oct.: 381-390. **[30]**   [*RIS*]

28.1486   GC   1972   The food service supervisor. *Cajanus* 5(3), July-Sept.: 200-208. **[30]**   [*RIS*]

Chapter 29

FOLK MEDICINE

Medicinal plants; native and folk pharmacopoeia.

See also: [24] Folklore; [28] Health and public health; [54] Plant and animal life.

Abraham, E. A. V.

29.0001 GU 1912 Materia medica Guian. Britt. *Timehri* 3d ser. 2(19a), July: 179-196. **[13,28,54]** *[AMN]*

Adams, C. D. & Magnus, K. E.

29.0002 JM 1966 Some Jamaican herb remedies are poisonous. *Inf B Scient Res Coun* 6(4), March: 105-109. *[RIS]*

Asprey, G. F. & Thornton, Phyllis

29.0003 JM 1953 Medicinal plants of Jamaica. Part 1. *W I Med J* 2(4), Dec.: 233-252. **[28,54]** *[COL]*

29.0004 JM 1954 Medicinal plants of Jamaica. Part 2. *W I Med J* 3(1), Mar.: 17-41. **[28,54]** *[COL]*

29.0005 JM 1955 Medicinal plants of Jamaica. Part 3. *W I Med J* 4(2), June: 69-82. **[28,54]** *[COL]*

29.0006 JM 1955 Medicinal plants of Jamaica. Part 4. *W I Med J* 4(3), Sept.: 145-168. **[28,54]** *[COL]*

Barrett, Leonard

29.0007 JM 1973 The portrait of a Jamaican healer: African medical lore in the Caribbean. *Car Q* 19(3), Sept.: 6-19. **[19]** *[RIS]*

Bayley, Iris

29.0008 BB 1949 The bush-teas of Barbados. *J Barb Mus Hist Soc* 16(3), May: 103-109. **[54]**

Beaubrun, Michael H.

8.0009 JM 1975 Cannabis or alcohol: the Jamaican experience.

31.0020 GC 1975 The view from Monkey Mountain.

Beckwith, Martha Warren

29.0009 JM 1927 NOTES ON JAMAICAN ETHNOBOTANY. Poughkeepsie, N.Y., Vassar College, 47p. (Field-work in folk-lore; Publications of the Folklore Foundation no. 8.) **[30,54]** *[COL]*

Benjamins, H. D.

29.0010   SR   1929-30 "Sneki-koti", inenting tegen de beet van vergiftige slangen ["Snakebite cure", inoculation against the biting of poisonous snakes]. *W I G* 11: 497-512.   **[28]**   [*COL*]

29.0011   SR   1929-30 Treef en lepra in Suriname [Treyf and leprosy in Surinam]. *W I G* 11: 187-218.   **[5,14,28]**   [*COL*]

29.0012   SR   1931-32 "Sneki-koti", inenting tegen de beet van vergiftige slangen ["Snakebite cure", inoculation against the biting of poisonous snakes]. *W I G* 13: 3-23, 317-324.   **[28]**   [*COL*]

Beuze, Renée

29.0013   FA   1973   LA SANTÉ PAR LES PLANTES DES ANTILLES FRANÇAISES [HEALTH THROUGH PLANTS OF THE FRENCH ANTILLES]. Pointe-à-Pitre, Emile Desormeaux: 80p.   **[28]**

Boghen, Dan & Boghen, Miriam

29.0014   MT   1972   Notes sur la médecine populaire à la Martinique [Notes on popular/folk medicine on Martinique]. *In* Benoist, Jean, ed. L'ARCHIPEL INACHEVÉ: CULTURE ET SOCIÉTÉ AUX ANTILLES FRANÇAISES. Montreal, Canada, University of Montreal: 233-248.   [*RIS*]

Bois, Etienne P.

13.0016   FG   1967   LES AMÉRINDIENS DE LA HAUTE-GUYANE FRANÇAISE: ANTHROPOLOGIE, PATHOLOGIE, BIOLOGIE [THE AMERINDIANS OF UPPER FRENCH GUIANA: ANTHROPOLOGY, PATHOLOGY, BIOLOGY].

Buchler, Ira R.

29.0015   CM   1964   Caymanian folk medicine: a problem in applied anthropology. *Hum Org* 23(1), Spring: 48-49.   **[28]**   [*RIS*]

Buhler, Richard O.

29.0016   BZ   1975   Belizean folk remedies. *National Stud* 3(3), May: 17-21.   **[24]**   [*RIS*]

Bullard, M. Kenyon

23.0025   BZ   1974   Hide and secrete: Women's sexual magic in Belize.

Burland, Barbara

29.0017   BE   1965   SOME INFORMATION ON HERBS, MEDICINAL PLANTS AND OTHER TYPES OF REMEDIES USED IN THE PAST IN BERMUDA FOR VARIOUS AILMENTS. Hamilton, Bermuda Historical Society: 32p. (Occasional Publication No. 6)   **[54]**   [*NYP*]

Butler, C. S. & Hakansson, E. G.

28.0207   UV   1917   Some first impressions of the Virgin Islands, medical, surgical and epidemiological.

Butt, Audrey J.

29.0018   GU   1956   Ritual blowing: taling—a causation and cure of illness among the Akawaio. *Man* 56(48), Apr.: 49-55.   **[13,28]**   [*COL*]

Campbell, Sadie

29.0019   JM   1974   Bush teas: a cure-all. *Jam J* 8(2-3), Summer: 60-65.   [*RIS*]
30.0044   JM   1974   Folk-lore and food habits.

Collier, H. C.

29.0020	BC	1941	Nature, her own apothecary. *Can-W I Mag* 30(1), Jan.: 8-10. **[28,54]** [*NYP*]
29.0021	GU	1942	Copper skin's secret. *Can-W I Mag* 31(4), Apr.: 19-22. **[13,28]** [*NYP*]
29.0022	GU	1946	Jungle dope. *Can-W I Mag* 36(1), Feb.: 21-24. **[13,28]** [*NYP*]
29.0023	GU	1948	Curare—the story of a reformation. *Can-W I Mag* 38(3), Mar.: 7-10. **[28]** [*NYP*]

Comitas, Lambros

8.0044 JM 1975 The social nexus of *ganja* in Jamaica.

Cosminsky, Sheila

1.0074 GC 1976 Latin American and the Caribbean.

Davis, W. G. & Persaud, Trivedi V. N.

28.0307 JM 1970 Recent studies on the active principles of Jamaican medicinal plants.

Eldridge, Joan

29.0024 BA 1975 Bush medicine in the Exumas and Long Island, Bahamas, a field study. *Econ Botany* 29(4), Oct.-Dec.: 307-332. **[54]** [*COL*]

Feng, P. C.

29.0025 GU 1956 A preliminary survey of the medicinal plants of British Guiana. *W I Med J* 5(4), Dec.: 265-270. **[54]** [*COL*]

Fonaroff, Arlene

30.0088 JM 1975 Cultural perceptions and nutritional disorders: a Jamaican case study.

Goeje, C. H. de

20.0028 GC 1943 Philosophy, initiation and myths of the Indians of Guiana and adjacent countries.

Haneveld, G. T.

29.0026 GU 1965 Curaçao in kleuren [Curaçao in colors]. *Schakels* NA42: 9-12. [*NYP*]

29.0027 NA 1966 De aloëcultuur in de Nederlandse Antillen [The aloe culture in the Netherlands Antilles]. *Schakels* S62/NA45: 11-14. [*NYP*]

Hershenson, Benjamin Robert

54.0477 GC 1968 A PHARMACOGNOSTICAL INVESTIGATION OF TEN WEST INDIAN PLANTS WITH SPECIAL EMPHASIS ON *Suriana maritima* L. (SIMARUBACEAE).

Heyde, H.

29.0028 SR [n.d.] SURINAAMSE PLANTEN ALS VOLKSMEDICIJN: NENGRE OSO DRESI [SURINAMESE PLANTS AS FOLK MEDICINE]. R. F. L. Mungra and E. K. Madarie: 32p. **[54]** [*RILA*]

Irvine, R. A. & Tang, K.

28.0670 JM 1957 Datura poisoning; a case report.

Kloos, Peter

13.0112   SR   1968   Becoming a Piyei: variability and similarity in Carib shamanism.

29.0029   SR   1970   Search for health among the Maroni River Caribs, etiology and medical care in a 20th century Amerindian group in Surinam. *Bijd Volk* 126(1): 115-141.   **[13]**   [*COL*]

Lampe, P. H. J.

29.0030   SR   1928-29   "Het Surinaamsche treefgeloof", een volksgeloof betreffende het ontstaan van de melaatschheid ["The treyf belief in Surinam," a superstition about the cause of leprosy]. *W I G* 10: 545-568.   **[14,28]**   [*COL*]

Lewis, Thomas H.

31.0092   SR   1975   A culturally patterned depression in a mother after loss of a child.

Lichtveld, Lou

29.0031   SR   1930-31   Een Afrikaansch bijgeloof: snetji-koti [An African superstition: "snakebite cure"]. *W I G* 12: 49-52.   **[14,19,28]**   [*COL*]

29.0032   SR   1932   Een oude getuigenis over de genezing van slagenbeet en aardeten [An old testimony about the cure of snakebite and the eating of earth]. *W I G* 14: 1-7.   **[14,28]**   [*COL*]

Long, Joseph K.

23.0185   JM   1972   Medical anthropology, dance, trance in Jamaica.

29.0033   JM   1973   JAMAICAN MEDICINE: CHOICES BETWEEN FOLK HEALING AND MODERN MEDICINE. Ph.D. dissertation, Southern Methodist University: 278p.   **[28]**   [*RIS*]

Lovell, Belle

34.0058   BZ   1974   The traditional birth attendant—Belize.

Lowe, H. I. C.

29.0034   JM   1972   Jamaican folk medicine. *Jam J* 6(2), June: 20-24.   **[54]**   [*RIS*]

McKenzie, H. I.; Alleyne, S. I. & Standard, K. L.

28.0828   JM   1967   Reported illness and its treatment in a Jamaican community.

Martin, P. A.; Thorburn, M. J.; Hutchinson, S.; Bras, G. & Miller, C. G.

28.0842   JM   1972   Preliminary findings of chromosomal studies on rats and humans with veno-occlusive disease.

Mischel, Frances

29.0035   TR,GR   1959   Faith healing and medical practice in the southern Caribbean. *Sw J Anthrop* 15(4), Winter: 407-417.   **[11,28]**   [*COL*]

Morton, Julia F.

28.0911   CU   1968   Plants associated with esophageal cancer cases in Curaçao.

28.0912   CU   1968   A survey of medicinal plants of Curaçao.

54.0708   NL   1973   Geneeskrachtige kruiden en giftige planten [Medicinal herbs and poisonous plants].

Mulcahy, F. David

29.0036   SV   1973   A sketch of Vincentian-Portuguese folk botany and medicine. *In* Fraser, Thomas M., ed. WINDWARD ROAD: CONTRIBUTIONS TO THE ANTHROPOLOGY OF SAINT VINCENT. Amherst, University of Massachusetts, Department of Anthropology: 108-122. (Research Reports No. 12)   [*RIS*]

Nehaul, B. B. G.
28.0925   GU   1955   Datura poisoning in British Guiana.

O'Gara, R. W.
28.0940   NA   1968   Biologic screening of selected plant material for carcinogens.

Panhuys, L. C. van
29.0037   SR   1924   About the "trafe" superstition on the colony of Surinam. *Janus* 28: 357-368.   [*NYP*]
29.0038   SR   1924   The trafe-superstition in Surinam. *In* PROCEEDINGS OF THE TWEN-TY-FIRST INTERNATIONAL CONGRESS OF AMERICANISTS, [1ST SESS.,] THE HAGUE, AUG. 12-16, 1924. The Hague, p.182-185.   [14]   [*AGS*]
29.0039   SR   1935-36 Opvattingen van Zuid-Amerikaansche Indianen nopens ziekten en geneeswijzen [South American Indian ideas about illness and cures]. *W I G* 17: 51-57.   [13,28]   [*COL*]
29.0040   SR   1943   "Sneki-koti", inenting tegen den bijt van vergiftige slangen ["Sneki-koti", immunization against the bite of poisonous snakes]. *W I G* 25: 122-128.   [14,28]   [*COL*]

Pendergast, David M.
19.0051   BZ   1972   The practice of *primicias* in San José Succotz, British Honduras (Belize).

Pugh, Emily
29.0041   BE   1957   St. David's Island remedies. *Bermuda Hist Q* 14(4), Winter: 123-128.   [24]   [*COL*]

Revert, Eugene
24.0141   MT   1951   DE QUELQUES ASPECTS DU FOLK-LORE MARTINIQUAIS: LE MAGIE ANTILLAISE [ON SOME ASPECTS OF MARTINIQUE FOLKLORE: ANTIL-LEAN MAGIC].

Richardson, Evelyn
28.1071   SC   1971   ONE MOMENT OF GLORY.

Roth, Walter Edmund
13.0179   GU   1913   The narcotics and stimulants of the Guianese Indian.
29.0042   GU   1919   A few notes on the medical practises of the Guiana Indians. *Br Gui Med Annual 1919* 22: 48-57.   [13,28]   [*ACM*]

Rubin, Vera
20.0076   JM   1975   The "*ganja* vision" in Jamaica.

Rubin, Vera, ed.
29.0043   JM   1975   CANNABIS AND CULTURE. The Hague, Mouton: 598p.   [11]   [*RIS*]

Schaeffer, Joseph
29.0044   JM   1975   The significance of marihuana in a small agricultural community in Jamaica. *In* Rubin, Vera, ed. CANNABIS AND CULTURE. The Hague, Mouton: 355-388.   [9]   [*RIS*]

Seaforth, Compton E.
28.1149   GC   1967   Drugs from the West Indies.

Seaga, Edward
29.0045   JM   1955   Jamaica's primitive medicine. *Tomorrow* 3(3): 70-78.   **[19,28]**   [*RIS*]

Simpson, George Eaton
29.0046   TR   1962   Folk medicine in Trinidad. *J Am Folk* 75(298), Oct.-Dec.: 326-340.   **[8,19,28]**   [*RIS*]

Singer, Philip; Aarons, Louis & Araneta, Enrique
31.0134   GU   1967   Integration of indigenous healing practices of the Kali cult with Western psychiatric modalities in British Guana.

Spencer, D. J.
31.0135   BA   1970   Cannabis induced psychoses.

Steggerda, Morris
29.0047   JM   1929   Plants of Jamaica used by natives for medicinal purposes. *Am Anthrop* new ser., 31(3), July-Sept.: 431-434.   [*COL*]

Sturtevant, William C.
60.0216   GC   1969   History and ethnography of some West Indian starches.

Taylor, Douglas
23.0300   DM   1945   Carib folk beliefs and customs from Dominica, B.W.I.

Thomas, Anthony & Krieger, Laurie
28.1272   JM   1976   Jamaican vomiting sickness: a theoretical investigation.

Thorburn, Marigold J.
28.1282   JM   1974   Jamaican bushes and human chromosomes.

Vandercook, John Womack
23.0308   SR   1925   White magic and black, the jungle science of Dutch Guiana.
29.0048   SR   1927   Magic is the jungle science: the black tribes of Guiana do not believe in death. *Mentor* 14(12, serial no. 287), Jan.: 18 +.   **[14,23]**   [*NYP*]

West, M. E.; Garvey, H. Lloyd & Ling, George M.
28.1425   GC   1973   Cardiovascular and antiarrhythmic effects of an active principle from the bark of anacardium occidentale.

Williams, Cicely
29.0049   JM   1973   Witch doctors. *Nutr Rev* 31(11), Nov.: 369-371.   **[23]**   [*ACM*]

Wong, Wesley
29.0050   TR   1967   The folk medicine of Blanchisseuse, Trinidad. M.A. Thesis, Brandeis University: 81p. & 213p. (appendix)   [*RIS*]
29.0051   TR   1976   Some folk medicinal plants from Trinidad. *Econ Botany* 30(2), April-June: 103-142.   **[54]**   [*COL*]

Chapter 30

FOOD AND NUTRITION

Food supplies; cookbooks; malnutrition and associated medical problems.
See also: **[27]** Human biology; **[28]** Health and public health; **[60]** Fruits, vegetables and root crops; **[61]** Sugar, rice and fibers; **[62]** Dairy, livestock and pasturage.

Ahern, E. J.; Swan, A. V. & Ahern, V.

28.0009 JM 1972 The prevalence of iron deficient erythropoiesis and anaemia in a rural Jamaican community.

Aiken, James

30.0001 GU 1912 Food and labour. *Timehri* 3d ser., 2(19B), Dec.: 287-291. **[41]**
[*AMN*]

Alderman, Michael H.; Levy, Barry; Husted, James; Searle, Ryan & Minott, Owen D.

30.0002 JM 1973 A young-child nutrition programme in rural Jamaica. *Lancet* 1(7813), May 26: 1166-1169. **[28]** [*PS*]

Aletrino-Coronel, H. E.

30.0003 SR 1967 MIJN KEUKENGEHEIMEN [MY KITCHEN SECRETS]. Paramaribo, Suriname, N.V. Varekamp & Co.: 80p. [*RILA*]

Alleyne, G. A. O.

30.0004 JM 1966 Cardiac function in severely malnourished Jamaican children. *Clin Sci* 30(3), June: 553-562. [*PS*]
28.0025 JM 1966 The excretion of water and solute by malnourished children.
30.0005 JM 1966 Plasma and blood volumes in severely malnourished Jamaican children. *Archs Dis Childh* 41(217), June: 313-315. **[28]** [*PS*]
30.0006 JM 1967 The effect of severe protein calorie malnutrition on the renal function of Jamaican children. *Pediatrics* 39(3), March: 400-411. **[28]** [*PS*]
30.0007 JM 1968 Studies on total body potassium in infantile malnutrition: the relation to body fluid spaces and urinary creatinine. *Clin Sci* 34(1), Feb: 199-209. [*PS*]
30.0008 JM 1970 Some features of infantile malnutrition in Jamaica. *W I Med J* 19(1), March: 32-36. **[28]** [*PS*]

Alleyne, G. A. O.; Halliday, D. & Waterlow, J. C.

30.0009   JM   1969   Chemical composition of organs of children who died from malnutrition. *BR J Nutr* 23: 783-790. **[28]**   [*PS*]

Alleyne, G. A. O. & Scullard, G. H.

30.0010   JM   1969   Alterations in carbohydrate metabolism in Jamaican children with severe malnutrition. *Clin Sci* 37(3), Dec.: 631-642.   [*PS*]

30.0011   JM   1969   Blood keto acids in malnutrition. *Am J Clin Nutr* 22(8), Aug.: 1139-1141.   [*PS*]

Alleyne, G. A. O.; Viteri, F. & Alvarado, J.

30.0012   JM   1970   Indices of body composition in infantile malnutrition: Total body potassium and urinary creatinine. *Am J Clin Nutr* 23(7), July: 875-878.   [*PS*]

Alleyne, G. A. O. & Young, V. H.

30.0013   JM   1967   Adrenocortical function in children with severe protein-calorie malnutrition. *Clin Sci* 33, Aug.: 189-200.   [*PS*]

Andrews, R.

30.0014   TR   1976   Food and nutrition activities in Trinidad and Tobago. *Cajanus* 9(3): 158-163.   [*RIS*]

Antrobus, A. C. K.

30.0015   SV   1971   Child growth and related factors in a rural community in St. Vincent. *J Trop Pediat* 17(4), Dec.: 188-210. **[28]**   [*PS*]

30.0016   BC   1974   Corrective measures for childhood malnutrition. *Cajanus* 7(1), Feb.: 12-17. **[28]**   [*RIS*]

30.0017   GC   1974   Food, nutrition and people. *Cajanus* 7(6), Dec.: 245-251.   [*RIS*]

Antrobus, K.

30.0018   SV   1971   Experiences with the use of soyameal and skimmed milk in St. Vincent. *W I Med J* 20(3), Sept.: 237-240.   [*PS*]

Armenta, George

28.0044   GU   1970   "Puma"—a high protein drink for Guyana.

Ashcroft, M. T.

2.0011   BC   1971   Some aspects of growth and development in different ethnic groups in the Commonwealth West Indies.

Ashworth, Ann

30.0019   JM   1968   Dietary survey methods: a comparison of the caloric and protein contents of some rural Jamaican diets. *Arch Latam Nutr* 18(2), June: 165-172. **[28]**   [*PS*]

30.0020   JM   1968   An investigation of very low calorie intakes reported in Jamaica. *Br J Nutr* 22(3), Sept.: 341-355. **[28]**   [*PS*]

30.0021   JM   1969   Growth rates in children recovering from protein-calorie malnutrition. *Br J Nutr* 23: 835-844. **[28]**   [*PS*]

Ashworth, Ann; Bell, Ruth; James, W. P. T. & Waterlow, J. C.

30.0022   JM   1968   Calorie requirements of children recovering from protein-calorie malnutrition. *Lancet* II for 1968 (7568), Sept. 14: 600-603.   [*PS*]

Ashworth, Ann & Harrower, A. D. B.

30.0023   JM   1967   Protein requirements in tropical countries: nitrogen losses in sweat and their relation to nitrogen balance. *Br J Nutr* 21: 833-843. **[28]**

[*PS*]

Ashworth, Ann & March, Yvette

30.0024   JM   1973   Iron fortification of dried skim milk and maize-soya-bean-milk mixture (CSM): availability of iron in Jamaican infant. *Br J Nutr* 30(3), Nov.: 577-584. [*PS*]

Ashworth, Ann; Milner, P. F.; Waterlow, J. C. & Walker, R. B.

30.0025   JM   1973   Absorption of iron from maize (*Zea mays* L.) and soya beans (*Glycine hispida* Max.) in Jamaican infants. *Br J Nutr* 29(2), March: 269-278. **[28]** [*PS*]

Ashworth, Ann & Picou, D.

30.0026   JM   1976   Nutritional status in Jamaica (1968-74). *W I Med J* 25(1), March: 23-34. **[28]** [*PS*]

Ashworth, Ann & Waterlow, J. C.

30.0027   JM   1974[?]   NUTRITION IN JAMAICA, 1969-70. [Mona, Jamaica], University of the West Indies, Extra-Mural Department: 102p. **[28,33]** [*RIS*]

Aykroyd, W. R.

30.0028   GC   1965   Nutrition in the Caribbean. *J Hygiene* 63(1), Mar.: 137-153. [*PS*]

Back, E. H.

30.0029   JM   1956   A nutritional survey of small farmers in Jamaica in 1955. *W I Med J* 5(3), Sept.: 189-195. **[10]** [*COL*]

30.0030   JM   1961   The dietary of small farmers in Jamaica. *W I Med J* 10(1), Mar.: 28-43. **[10]** [*RIS*]

Beckford, George L. & Brown, E. A.

41.0033   JM   1968   Economic aspects of food availability in Jamaica.

Beckwith, Martha Warren

29.0009   JM   1927   NOTES ON JAMAICAN ETHNOBOTANY.

Bengtsson, Bo

54.0095   TR   1966   A SURVEY OF CULTURAL PRACTICES AND UTILIZATION OF EDIBLE AROIDS IN TRINIDAD.

Benoist, Jean

30.0031   GC   1969   Université de Montréal: le Centre de Recherches Caraïbes [The University of Montreal Center for Caribbean Research]. *Parallèles* 32, 3rd trimester: 36-39. [*RIS*]

Beresford, C. H.; Milner, P. F.; Gurney, M. & Fox, H.

28.0119   JM   1972   Haemoglobin, iron, folate and vitamin B12 levels in pregnant and lactating women in Jamaica.

Beresford, C. H.; Neale, R. J. & Brooks, O. G.

30.0032   JM   1971   Iron absorption and pyrexis. *Lancet* 1(7699), March 20: 568-572. **[28]** [*PS*]

Bertrand, Anca

30.0033   FC   1971   Cuisine et boissons créoles [Creole cuisine and beverages]. *Parallèles* 38, 1st trimester: 5-8.   [*RIS*]

Branday, W. J.

30.0034   JM   1968   Some early efforts to improve nutrition in Jamaica. *Cajanus* 6, Dec.: 40-44.   **[28]**   [*RIS*]

Bras, G.; Waterlow, J. C. & DePass, E.

30.0035   JM   1957   Further observations on the liver, pancreas and kidney in malnourished infants and children. *W I Med J* 6(1), Mar.: 33-42.   **[28]**   [*COL*]

Bressler, R.; Corredor, C. & Brendel, K.

28.0178   JM   1969   Hypoglycin and hypoglycin-like compounds.

Brinkman, G. L.; Sharadambal, B. & Madhave, V.

30.0036   TR   1970   A feeding trial of fish protein concentrate with preschool children. *Am J Clin Nutr* 23(4), April: 395-399.   **[28]**   [*PS*]

Brody, Robert W.

28.0179   LW,VI   1972   Food poisoning in the eastern Caribbean.

Brooke, O. G.

30.0037   JM   1972   Hypothermia in malnourished Jamaican children. *Archs Dis Childh* 47(254), Aug.: 525-530.   **[28]**   [*PS*]

30.0038   JM   1973   Thermal insulation in malnourished Jamaican children. *Archs Dis Child* 48(11), Nov.: 901-905.   [*PS*]

Brooke, O. G. & Ashworth, Ann

30.0039   JM   1972   The influence of malnutrition on the postprandial metabolic rate and respiratory quotient. *Br J Nutr* 27(2), March: 407-415.   [*PS*]

Brooke, O. G. & Salvosa, Carmencita B.

30.0040   JM   1974   Response of malnourished babies to heat. *Archs Dis Childh* 49(2), Feb.: 123-127.   [*PS*]

Brothwell, D. R.

27.0034   GU   1967   The Amerindians of Guyana: a biological review.

Cabannes, Raymond J. R.; Schmidt-Beurrier, A. & Monnet, B.

30.0041   FG   1966   Etude des protéines, des haptoglobines, des transferrines et des hémoglobines d'une population noire de Guyane Française (Boni) [Study of the proteins, haptoglobins, transferrins and hemoglobins of a Negro population of French Guiana (Boni)]. *B Soc Path Exot* 59(5), Sept.-Oct.: 908-916.   **[14]**   [*PS*]

Campbell, Betty

30.0042   TR   1948   Malnutrition and allied problems in Trinidad and Tobago. *Car Commn Mon Inf B* 1(10), May: 17-19.   **[28]**   [*COL*]

Campbell, J. A.

30.0043   BC   1974   Recommended dietary allowances for Caribbean countires. *Cajanus* 7(1), Feb.: 18-20.   [*RIS*]

Campbell, Sadie
30.0044   JM   1974   Folk-lore and food habits. *Jam J* 8(2-3), Summer: 56-59.   **[29]**
                                                                                                          [RIS]

Cannon, Poppy
30.0045   JM   1965   The cooking in paradise. *In* Cargill, Morris, ed. IAN FLEMING
                         INTRODUCES JAMAICA. New York, Hawthorn Books, Inc.: 189-196.
                                                                                                          [RIS]

Carley, Mary Manning
28.0219   JM   1943   MEDICAL SERVICES IN JAMAICA.

Chan, H.
30.0046   JM   1968   Adaptation of urinary nitrogen excretion in infants to changes in
                         protein intake. *Br J Nutr* 22(2), May: 315-323.   *[PS]*

Chopra, J. G. & Byam, N. T. A.
28.0240   TR   1968   Anemia survey in Trinidad and Tobago.

Chopra, J. G. & Gist, C. A.
30.0047   TR   1966   Food practices among Trinidadian children. *J Am Diet Assoc* 49(6):
                         497-501.   **[11,12]**   *[PS]*

**Chopra, J. G.; Noe, E.; Matthew, J.; Dhein, C.; Rose, J.; Cooperman, J. M. &
Luhby, A. L.**
28.0241   TR   1967   Anemia in pregnancy.

Chopra, J. G.; Tantiwongse, P.; Everette, M. S. & Villegas, N.
30.0048   TR   1965   Anaemia in malnutrition. *J Trop Pediat* 11(1), June: 18-24.   **[28]**
                                                                                                          [PS]

Christian, H. L.
30.0049   DM   1953   The La Plaine 3-F Campaign. *Community Dev B* 5(1), Dec.: 20-22.
                                                                                                          [NYP]

Cochrane, E.
30.0050   GC   1943   The diet of the mental worker in the tropics. *Car Med J* 5(3):
                         128-135.   *[COL]*

Cohen, Mervyn D.; Morgan, P. & Baker, P.
30.0051   TC   1974   The nutritional status of children in the Turks and Caicos Islands.
                         W I Med J 23(2), June: 92-97.   *[PS]*

Collymore, Yvonne
30.0052   GC   1972   COOKING OUR WAY: A COURSE IN CARIBBEAN COOKERY AND
                         NUTRITION. Barbados, Caribbean Universities Press: 144p.   *[RIS]*

Connell, Neville
19.0009   BC   1957   Punch drinking and its accessories.

Cook, Robert
30.0053   BC   1968   The financial cost of malnutrition in the "Commonwealth Car-
                         ibbean." *J Trop Pediat* 14(2), June: 60-65.   **[28]**   *[PS]*

30.0054   GC   1969   Nutrition and mortality under five years in the Caribbean area. *J Trop Pediat* 15(3), Sept.: 109-117. **[7,28]**   [*PS*]

30.0055   BC   1970   Nutrition and mortality under five years in the English-speaking Caribbean area. *Cajanus* 3(1), Feb.: 2-9. **[7,28]**   [*RIS*]

30.0056   BC   1971   Some information about feeding practices in the Eastern Caribbean. *W I Med J* 20(3), Sept.: 208-212.   [*PS*]

Cook, Robert & Yang, Yueh-Heng

30.0057   BC   1973   National food and nutrition policy in the Commonwealth Caribbean. *Cajanus* 7(2), April-June: 77-94. **[28]**   [*RIS*]

Cooke, W. T.; Asquith, P.; Ruck, Nicola; Melikian, V. & Swan, C. H. J.

30.0058   BC,UK   1974   Rickets, growth, and alkaline phosphatase in urban adolescents. *Br Med J* 2(5914), May 11: 293-297. **[18,28]**   [*ACM*]

Cooke, W. T.; Swan, C. H. J.; Asquith, P.; Melikian, V. & McFreely, W. E.

30.0059   BC,UK   1973   Serum alkaline phosphatase and rickets in urban schoolchildren. *Br Med J* 1(5849), Feb. 10: 324-327. **[18,28]**   [*PS*]

Cross, Lawrence & Wilson, L.

30.0060   TR   1967   Some nutritional experiments with aeroids at Central Experiment Station. *In* Proceedings of the Caribbean Food Crops Society: Fifth Annual Meeting, Paramaribo, Surinam, July 24-31: 162-166.   [*RIS*]

Cruickshank, E. K.

30.0061   JM   1973   Cicely D. Williams, grand lady of medicine. *Nutr Rev* 31(11), Nov.: 378-381. **[5]**   [*ACM*]

Deane, C. G.

30.0062   TR   1938   Deficiency diseases in East Indians of the labouring class. *Car Med J* 1(1): 34-45. **[10,12,28]**   [*COL*]

Debien, Gabriel

30.0063   FC   1964   La nourriture des esclaves sur les plantations des Antilles Francaises aux XVIIᵉ et XVIIIᵉ siècles [The diet of slaves on the plantations of the French Antilles in the 17th and 18th centuries]. *Car Stud* 4(2), July: 3-27. **[5,6,42]**   [*RIS*]

DeCastro, Steve & Lauritz, John

47.0082   TR   1967   Some steps towards an optimal foodstuffs consumption, production and importation programme for Trinidad and Tobago.

Degras, L.

30.0064   GC   1971   Données sur la valeur alimentaire de quelques productions végétales des Antilles [Data on the alimentary value of some Antillean vegetable products]. *Parallèles* 38, 1st trimester: 9-14.
                                                                       [*RIS*]

Desai, Patricia; Miall, W. E. & Standard, K. L.

30.0065   JM   1969   The social background of malnutrition in Jamaica. *Cajanus* 2(4), Aug.: 303-318. **[27]**   [*RIS*]

Devine, Fred W.
28.0316   **GC**   1965   CARE in the Caribbean.

Doornbos, L.; Jonxis, J. H. P. & Visser, H. K. A.
14.0006   **SR**   1968   Growth of Bushnegro children on the Tapanahony River in Dutch Guyana.

Dorff, Ilse Marie
30.0066   **SR**   1972   SURINAAMS KOKEN [SURINAMESE COOKING]. Bussum, The Nether-lands, C.A.J. van Dishoeck: 72p.   [*NYP*]

Dufougeré, W.
28.0345   **FG**   1920   Ankylostomiase et béribéri en Guyane Francaise [Ankylostomiasis and beriberi in French Guiana].
37.0206   **FG**   1921   De l'utilisation rationnelle de la main-d'oeuvre pénale en Guyane [On the rational use of forced labor in Guiana].

Ekker, I.
30.0067   **CU**   1966   Voeding en voedingstoestand van Curaçaose schoolkinderen [Nu-trition and nutritional state of Curaçao schoolchildren]. *Voeding* 27(7), July 15: 255-401.   **[27,28]**   [*NYP*]

English, E. W. F. et al.
7.0047   **GU**   1907   Report of the Mortality Commission.

Eyre, L. Alan
30.0068   **JM**   1970   How long can Jamaica feed itself? *Cajanus* 3(2), April: 77-86.   **[43]**
[*RIS*]

Feng, P. C.
28.0385   **JM**   1969   Hypoglycin- from ackee: a review.

Fletcher, K.
30.0069   **JM**   1966   Observations on the origin of liver fat in infantile malnutrition. *Am J Clin Nutr* 19(3), Sept.: 170-173.   **[28]**   [*PS*]

Floch, Hervé Alexandre
30.0070   **FG**   1953   Etude du problème de l'alimentation en Guyane Francaise [Study of the nutritional problem in French Guiana]. *Archs Inst Past Guy* 298, Oct. 10: 1-7.   **[28]**
30.0071   **FG**   1955   Aspects nutritionnels de problèmes de pathologie guyanaise [Nutri-tional factors in the problems of Guianese pathology]. *Archs Inst Past Guy* 379, Oct. (5p.)   **[28]**
62.0042   **FG**   1955   A propos d'alimentation en Guyane Francaise. Elevage de porcs et arbre à pain [On nutrition in French Guiana. Pig-raising and the breadfruit tree].
30.0072   **FG**   1956   Dosage des carotenes (Provitamines A) dans les fruits guyanais. Intérêt du fruit de l'"aouara" *astrocaryum vulgare* [Amount of carotenes (Provitamins A) in Guianese fruit. Relevance of the fruit "aouara" *astrocaryum vulgare*]. *Archs Inst Past Guy* 413, Nov. (8p.)   **[60]**
30.0073   **FG**   1956   Dosage des carotenes (Provitamines A) dans les legumes guyanais, Intérêt de l'"épinard de Cayenne" *basella cordifolia* [Proportion of carotene (Provitamins A) in the Guianese vegetables. Relevance of "Cayenne spinach" *basella cordifolia*]. *Archs Inst Past Guy* 414, Nov. (5p.)   **[60]**

30.0074   **FG**   1956   Sur l'avitaminose PP en Guyane Francaise [On avitaminosis PP in French Guiana]. *Archs Inst Past Guy* 411, Oct.: (6p.)   **[28]**

Floch, Hervé Alexandre & Gelard, A.
30.0075   **FG**   1954   Dosage de l'acide ascorbique dans des fruits guyanais [Amount of ascorbic acid in Guianese fruits]. *Archs Inst Past Guy* 337, Aug. (6p.)   **[60]**
30.0076   **FG**   1954   Establissement des standards alimentaires adaptés aux conditions spéciales de notre Département guyanais [The setting of nutritional standards adapted to the specific conditions of our Guianese *Département*]. *Archs Inst Past Guy* 347, Dec. 5: (16p.)
30.0077   **FG**   1954   Valeur alimentaire de produits guyanais [Nutritional value of Guianese produce]. *Archs Inst Past Guy* 335, Aug.(7p.)   **[60]**
30.0078   **FG**   1955   "La cerise ronde de Cayenne", *malpighia punicifolia L.* Sa richesse exceptionnelle en vitamine C [The "round cherry of Cayenne," *malpighia punicifolia L.* Its exceptional richness in vitamin C]. *Archs Inst Past Guy* 368, July (6p.)   **[60]**
30.0079   **FG**   1955   Sur quelques points touchant l'alimentation-nutrition en Guyane Francaise ayant des possibilités d'amélioration rapide [Regarding some aspects of diet and nutrition in French Guiana which are amenable to quick improvement]. *Archs Inst Past Guy* 16(358), Apr.: (6p.)   [*RIS*]

Floch, Hervé Alexandre & Lecuiller, A.
30.0080   **FG**   1951   Sur l'alimentation en Guyane [On nutrition in Guiana]. *Archs Inst Past Guy* 242, Sept. (7p.)
30.0081   **FG**   1951   Sur les levures alimentaires et leur utilisation éventuelle en Guyane Francaise [On food yeasts and their possible utilization in French Guiana]. *Archs Inst Past Guy* 239, Sept. (6p.)
30.0082   **FG**   1953   Enquête sur la consommation alimentaire réelle et la valeur âlimentaire de la ration guyanaise [Survey of the actual food intake and the food value of the Guianese diet]. I. [Enquête]. *Archs Inst Past Guy* 277, Jan. (10p.)
30.0083   **FG**   1953   Enquête sur la consommation alimentaire réelle et la valeur âlimentaire de la ration guyanaise [Survey of the actual food intake and the food value of the Guianese diet]. II. Discussion. *Archs Inst Past Guy* 285, June (8p.)
30.0084   **FG**   1953   Enquête sur la consommation alimentaire réelle et la valeur âlimentaire de la ration guyanaise [Survey of the actual food intake and the food value of the Guianese diet]. III. Analyses de produits alimentaires guyanais [Analyses of Guianese food products]. *Archs Inst Past Guy* 286, June (6p.)

Floch, Hervé Alexandre; Riviérez, E. & Sureau, P.
30.0085   **FG**   1952   Pellagre et vitamine PP en Guyane Francaise [Pellagra and vitamin PP in French Guiana]. *Archs Inst Past Guy* 267, July (8p.)   **[28]**

Floch, Hervé Alexandre; Riviérez, Maurice & Sureau, Pierre
30.0086   **FG**   1953   Sur la pellagre en Guyane Francaise [Concerning pellagra in French Guiana]. *B Soc Path Exot* 46(2): 245-252.   **[28]**   [*ACM*]

Fonaroff, Arlene

30.0087   JM   1968   Differential concepts of protein-calorie malnutrition in Jamaica: an exploratory study of information and beliefs. *J Trop Pediat* 14(2), June: 81-105. (Monograph No. 4.)   [*PS*]

30.0088   JM   1975   Cultural perceptions and nutritional disorders: a Jamaican case study. *B Pan Am Heal Org* 9(2): 112-123. **[20,28,29]**   [*ACM*]

Fonaroff, L. Schuyler

28.0443   JM   1968   ECOLOGICAL PARAMETERS OF THE KWASHIORKOR—MARASMUS SYNDROME IN JAMAICA.

30.0089   JM   1969   Settlement typology and infant malnutrition in Jamaica. *Trop Geogr Med* 21(2), June: 177-185. **[9,17]**   [*PS*]

Fortuné, Roger

30.0090   GC   1961   Les bons plats de chez nous [Our tasty dishes]. *Rev Guad* 3-4 trimesters (45): 27-29. **[19]**   [*RIS*]

Foster, Isabel

30.0091   BC   1973   Comparative prices of foods in four Caribbean countries. *Cajanus* 6(1), Jan.-March: 37-44.   [*RIS*]

Fox, H. C.; Campbell, V. S. & Elliot, J. A.

30.0092   JM   1968   A mixed vegetable protein food for child feedings in Jamaica. *Inf B Scient Res Coun* 8(2-4), March: 52-68.   [*RIS*]

Fox, H. C.; Campbell, V. S. & Morris, J. C.

30.0093   JM   1968   The dietary and nutritional status of Jamaican infants and toddlers. *Inf B Scient Res Coun* 8(2-4), March: 33-51.   [*RIS*]

Fox, H. C.; Maynard, A. I. P. & James, Philip

30.0094   JM   1967   High protein supplementary feeding of five pre-school children. *Inf B Scient Res Coun* 7(4), March: 100-105.   [*RIS*]

Francis, Oliver M.

28.0451   GU   1943   Social, economic and dietetic features of tuberculosis in British Guiana.

30.0095   GU   1947   Nutritional aspects of cost of living survey, 1942. *Bri Gui Med Annual* 207-217. **[41]**   [*RIS*]

Gans, Bruno

18.0111   GC   1967   The nutritional status of West Indian immigrants.

Garrow, J. S.

30.0096   JM   1965   Total body-postassium in kwashiorkor and marasmus. *Lancet,* II for 1965 (7410), Sept. 4: 455-458. **[28]**   [*PS*]

28.0482   JM   1966   "Kwashiorkor" and "marasmus" in Jamaican infants.

30.0097   JM   1967   Loss of brain potassium in Kwashiorkor. *Lancet,* II for 1967 (7517), Sept. 23: 643-645. **[28]**   [*PS*]

Garrow, J. S.; Fletcher, K. & Halliday, D.

30.0098   JM   1965   Body composition in severe infantile malnutrition. *J Clin Invest* 44(3), Jan.: 417-425. **[28]**   [*PS*]

Garrow, J. S.; Picou, D. & Waterlow, J. C.

30.0099   JM   1962   The treatment and prognosis of infantile malnutrition in Jamaican children. *W I Med J* 11(4), Dec.: 217-227.   **[28]**   [*COL*]

Garrow, J. S. & Pike, M. C.

30.0100   JM   1967   The long-term prognosis of severe infantile malnutrition. *Lancet*, I for 1967 (7480), Jan. 7: 1-4.   **[28]**   [*PS*]

30.0101   JM   1967   The short-term prognosis of severe primary infantile malnutrition. *Br J Nutr* 21: 155-165.   **[28]**   [*PS*]

Giglioli, George

30.0102   GU   1958   An outline of the nutritional situation on the sugar estates of British Guiana in respect to the eradication of malaria: recent developments in the production of green vegetables and fruit by individual units. *W I Med J* 7(4), Dec.: 251-256.   **[12,28,42,61]**
                                                                                                              [*COL*]

Gooding, H. J.

30.0103   BC   1958   Some problems of food crop improvement in Caribbean, with special reference to starchy tubers. *W I Med J* 7(4), Dec.: 257-266.   **[60]**   [*COL*]

Goodwin, Peter

43.0173   JM   1975   Jamaica's crop of good ideas.

Gourlay, R. John

30.0104   JM   1963   Haemoglobin levels in relation to dietary iron and protein in a semiurban community in Jamaica. *W I Med J* 12(1), Mar.: 28-33.   **[28]**   [*COL*]

Grantham-McGregor, Sally M. & Back, E. H.

30.0105   JM   1970   Breast-feeding in Kingston, Jamaica. *Archs Dis Childh* 45(241), June: 404-409.   **[28]**   [*PS*]

30.0106   JM   1970   A note on infant feeding in Kingston. *W I Med J* 19(2), June: 111-115.   **[28]**   [*PS*]

Green, Lena

54.0418   JM   1962   Some seaweeds of economic importance growing in Jamaican waters.

Greenwood-Barton, L. H.

30.0107   JM   1957   The establishment and administration of food standards in Jamaica. *Chem Indus* 2, Jan. 12: 34-40.   **[33,45]**   [*COL*]

Grey, Winifred

30.0108   GC   1965   CARIBBEAN COOKERY. London, Collins: 256p.   [*RIS*]

Gupta, P. N. Sen

30.0109   BC   1971   Meeting protein and amino acid needs of infants and children. *W I Med J* 20(3), Sept.: 150-154.   [*PS*]

Gurney, J. M.; Fox, Helen & Neill, J.

30.0110   JM   1972   A rapid survey to assess the nutrition of Jamaican infants and young children in 1970. *Trans Roy Soc Trop Med Hyg* 66(4): 653-662.   **[27]**   [*PS*]

Gurney, Michael & Cook, Robert
30.0111   BC   1973   The price of groceries in the Caribbean, 1972-1973. *Cajanus* 6(1), Jan.-Mar.: 40-44.   [*RIS*]

Habib, George G.
28.0586   TR   1964   Nutritional vitamin B12 deficiency among Hindus.

Halliday, D.
30.0112   JM   1967   Chemical composition of the whole body and individual tissues of two Jamaican children whose death resulted primarily from malnutrition. *Clin Sci* 33(2): 365-370.   **[28]**   [*PS*]

Harney, Lenore
30.0113   KNA   1958   The effect of additional dietary skimmed milk on the nutrition of children of the colony of St. Kitts Nevis Anguilla using deaths from malnutrition in the age-group 1-4 years as indicator. *W I Med J* 7(3), Sept.: 211-214.   **[28]**   [*COL*]

Harris, Donald J.
41.0224   JM   1964   Econometric analysis of household consumption in Jamaica.

Harrison, John B. & Bancroft, C. K.
60.0105   GU   1917   Food plants of British Guiana.
43.0188   GU   1926   Food plants of British Guiana.

Hawkes, Alex D.
30.0114   JM   1972   THE RUM COOKBOOK. Kingston, William Collins and Sangster Ltd.: 64p.   [*NYP*]

Heesterman, J. E.
30.0115   GC   1953   Standardising milk fat content. *Car Commn Mon Inf B* 6(12), July: 273-274.   [*AGS*]

Henry, M. U.
30.0116   GC   1973   The role of nutritionists and dietitians in Caribbean health services. *Cajanus* 6(4), Oct.-Dec.: 234-245.   **[28]**   [*RIS*]

Hertzig, M. E.; Birch, H. G.; Richardson, S. A. & Tizard, J.
30.0117   JM   1972   Intellectual levels of school children severely malnourished during the first two years of life. *Pediatrics* 49(6), June: 814-824.   **[32]**
                                    [*PS*]

Heywood, Peter
30.0118   JM   1973   Malnutrition lowers cane cutters' productivity. *Cajanus* 7(3), July-Sept.: 181-184.   **[42]**   [*RIS*]

Holder, Geoffrey
30.0119   GC   1973   CARIBBEAN COOKBOOK. New York, The Viking Press: 95p.   [*RIS*]

Hooft, C. F. S. van der
30.0120   SR   1968   Een onderzoek naar het visgebruik van een deel van de bevolking van Paramaribo [Research on fish consumption of part of the population of Paramaribo]. *Voeding* 29(12), Dec. 15: 553-558.
                                    [*NYP*]

Ho Ping Kong, H. & Alleyne, G. A. O.

30.0121   JM   1971   Studies on acid excretion in adults with sickle-cell anaemia. *Clin Sci* 41(6), Dec.: 505-518.   **[27]**   *[PS]*

Horne, Louise

30.0122   TR   1972   School feeding in Trinidad and Tobago. *Cajanus* 5(3), July-Sept.: 228-231.   **[32]**   *[RIS]*

Husbands, Madre

30.0123   BB   1972   Organization of the Barbados school lunch programme. *Cajanus* 5(3), July-Sept.: 222-227.   **[32]**   *[RIS]*

Jadan, Doris & Jadan, Ivan

30.0124   VI   1968   A VIRGIN ISLAND COOKPOT CALYPSO: FIFTY RECIPES. St. Thomas, V.I.: 48p.   *[RIS]*

James, W. P. T.

30.0125   JM   1968   Intestinal absorption in protein-calorie malnutrition. *Lancet*, I for 1968 (7538), Feb. 17: 333-335.   **[28]**   *[PS]*

28.0678   JM   1968   Patterns of infant feeding in Jamaica.

30.0126   JM   1970   Sugar absorption and intestinal motility in children when mal-nourished and after treatment. *Clin Sci* 39(2), Aug.: 305-318.   *[PS]*

James, W. P. T. & Coore, H. G.

30.0127   JM   1970   Persistent impairment of insulin secretion and glucose tolerance after malnutrition. *Am J Clin Nutr* 23(4), April: 386-389.   **[28]** *[PS]*

James, W. P. T.; Drasar, B. S. & Miller, C.

28.0679   JM   1972   Physiological mechanism and pathogenesis of weanling diarrhea.

Jean, Sally Lucas

28.0681   UV   1933   Virgin Islands: school health program—utilization of existing facilities.

Jelliffe, D. B.

30.0128   GC   1970   The Caribbean Food and Nutrition Institute. *Am J Clin Nutr* 23(11), Nov.: 1409-1411.   *[PS]*

28.0682   BC   1971   The biological basis and public health aims of young child feeding.

30.0129   BC   1971   The Caribbean Food and Nutrition Institute. *W I Med J* 20(1), March: 51-59.   *[PS]*

30.0130   BC   1971   Guidelines to young child feeding in the contemporary Caribbean. *W I Med J* 20(3), Sept.: 243-251.   **[28]**   *[PS]*

Jelliffe, D. B. & McKigney, J.

30.0131   GC   1969   The Caribbean Food and Nutrition Institute. An interdisciplinary approach to child nutrition. *Clin Pediat* 8(2), Feb.: 98-105.   *[PS]*

Jelliffe, E. F. Patrice

30.0132   GC   1971   A new look at weaning multimixes for the Caribbean—a means of improving child nutrition. *Cajanus* 4(3): 185-228.   **[28]**   *[RIS]*

28.0685   JM   1971   Nutrition education on the maternity ward (or what mothers believe they have learnt on the maternity ward).

30.0133   BC   1971   Nutritional status of infants and pre-school children: a review of surveys since 1960. *W I Med J* 20(3), Sept.: 145-149.   **[28]**   *[PS]*

Jelliffe, E. F. Patrice & Jelliffe, D. B.

27.0084   **SV**   1968   Anthropometry in action. (I) Dental second year malnutrition (practical age-grouping in young children in areas without birth verification).

27.0085   **GC**   1969   The arm circumference as a public health index of protein-calorie malnutrition of early childhood. (IX) Experience in the Caribbean.

Johnson, I. E.

43.0217   **GC**   1972   Agricultural development policy in relation to human nutrition.

Jones, Catherine Joy

18.0156   **BC,UK**   1971   IMMIGRATION AND SOCIAL ADJUSTMENT: A CASE STUDY OF WEST INDIAN FOOD HABITS IN LONDON.

Kentch, Sally & Beverly, Heather

30.0134   **BA**   1973   Agricultural methods and food preparation on San Salvador. *In* Thomas, Garry L., ed. ANTHROPOLOGICAL FIELD REPORTS FROM SAN SALVADOR ISLAND. San Salvador, Bahamas, Island Environment Studies, Reports 1973: 9-24.   [*RIS*]

Krochmal, Connie & Krochmal, Arnold

30.0135   **GC**   1974   CARIBBEAN COOKING. New York, Quadrangle/The New York Times Book Co.: 261p.   [*SCH*]

Kruijer, G. J.

8.0121   **JM**   1957   The impact of poverty and undernourishment on man and society in rural Jamaica.

Kuyp, Edwin van der

1.0167   **SR**   1962   Literatuuroverzicht betreffende de voeding en de voedingsgewoonten van de Boslandcreool in Suriname [Bibliography about nutrition and food habits of the Bush Negroes in Surinam].

Lambert de Ortiz, Elisabeth

30.0136   **GC**   1967   Caribbean cook book. *House Garden* 131(1), Jan.: 139-144.   [*COL*]

Landman, Jacqueline P. & Shaw-Lyon, Violet

30.0137   **JM**   1976   Breast feeding in decline in Kingston, Jamaica, 1973. *W I Med J* 25(1), March: 43-57. **[28,34]**   [*PS*]

Larkin, Frances A.

28.0767   **DM**   1971   Pattern of weaning in Dominica.

Lees, Ronald E. M.

30.0138   **SL**   1964   Malnutrition: the pattern and prevention in St. Lucia. *W I Med J* 13(2), June: 97-102. **[28]**   [*COL*]

30.0139   **SL**   1966   Malnutrition: the infant at risk. *W I Med J* 15(4), Dec.: 211-216. **[28]**   [*PS*]

Lewis, Marva

30.0140   **BZ**   1975   Carib recipes. *National Stud* 3(6), November: 26-38. **[13]**   [*RIS*]

Lherisson, Fritz

30.0141   GC   1972   Child nutrition in the Caribbean: a résumé of the present situation and UNICEF'S current role. *Cajanus* 5(1), Jan.-Mar.: 7-18.   **[28]**
                                                                                                                          [RIS]

Lodeon, Jeanue

30.0142   MT   1971   Cuisine créole: recettes martiniquaises [Creole cuisine: recipes from Martinique]. *Parallèles* 38, 1st trimester: 36-50.   *[RIS]*

Losonczi, E.

30.0143   BZ   1958   Social anthropology in health education with particular reference to nutrition. *W I Med J* 7(3), Sept.: 206-210.   **[8,32]**   *[COL]*

Low, Deen

30.0144   DM   1969   Daily food for Dominican families. *Cajanus* 8, April: 135-145.   **[28]**
                                                                                                                          [RIS]

Low, Doreen Iris Deen

30.0145   SL,SK   1970   EVALUATING NUTRITION EDUCATION PROGRAMS ON TWO CARIBBEAN ISLANDS. Ph.D. dissertation, University of California (Berkeley).   **[28,32]**   *[PhD]*

Lunn, John A.; Miridjanian, Anoush; Fontares, Presentación; Jacobs, Elliot; Rosen, Samuel & Christakis, George

28.0812   BA   1974   Epidemiologic reconnaissance of hypertension in the Bahamas: with special reference to depot fat composition and its implications in relation to cardiovascular disease prevalence.

Luyken, R.

30.0146   NW   1958   Over voedingsproblemen in de tropen in verband met het voedingsonderzoek op de Bovenwindse Eilanden [On problems of nutrition in the tropics in relationship to the nutritional research on the Windward Islands]. *W I G* 38: 86-96.   **[28]**   *[COL]*

30.0147   SR   1962-63   Voedingsfysiologisch onderzoek in Suriname [Research in nutritional physiology in Suriname]. *N W I G* 42: 190-200.   **[28]**   *[RIS]*

30.0148   SR   1969   Nutrition research in Surinam. *Neth Found Adv Trop Res* (WOTRO), Report for the Year 1968: 34-37.   *[RIS]*

Luyken, R. & Luyken-Koning, F. W. M.

30.0149   NW   1959   Nutrition research on the Windward Islands (Netherlands Antilles). *Trop Geogr Med* 11(2), June: 103-114.   *[COL]*

30.0150   SR   1960   Studies on the physiology of nutrition in Surinam. I. General remarks. *Trop Geogr Med* 12(3): 229-232.   **[28]**   *[COL]*

30.0151   SR   1960   Studies on the physiology of nutrition in Surinam. II. Serum protein levels. *Trop Geogr Med* 12(3): 233-236.   **[28]**   *[COL]*

30.0152   SR   1960   Studies on the physiology of nutrition in Surinam. III. Urea excretions. *Trop Geogr Med* 12(3): 237-242.   **[28]**   *[COL]*

30.0153   SR   1960   Studies on the physiology of nutrition in Surinam. IV. Nitrogen balance studies. *Trop Geogr Med* 12(4): 303-307.   **[28]**   *[COL]*

30.0154   SR   1960   Studies on the physiology of nutrition in Surinam. V. Amylase, lipase and cholinesterase activity of the serum of diverse population growth. *Trop Geogr Med* 12(4): 308-312.   **[28]**   *[COL]*

30.0155	SR	1960	Studies on the physiology of nutrition in Surinam. VI. Cholestrol content of the blood serum. *Trop Geogr Med* 12(4): 313-314. **[28]** *[COL]*
30.0156	SR	1961	Studies on the physiology of nutrition in Surinam. VII. Serum iron. *Trop Geogr Med* 13(1): 42-45. **[28]** *[COL]*
30.0157	SR	1961	Studies on the physiology of nutrition in Surinam. VIII. Metabolism of calcium. *Trop Geogr Med* 13(1): 46-54. **[28]** *[COL]*
30.0158	SR	1961	Studies on the physiology of nutrition in Surinam. IX. Somato-metrical data. *Trop Geogr Med* 13(2): 123-130. **[28]** *[COL]*
30.0159	SR	1969	Studies on physiology of nutrition in Surinam. XII. Nutrition and development of muscular, skeletal, and adipose tissues in Surinam children. *Am J Clin Nutr* 22(4), April: 519-526. *[PS]*

Luyken, R.; Luyken-Koning, F. W. M.; Cambridge, T. H.; Dohle, T. & Bosch, R.

30.0160	SR	1967	Studies on physiology of nutrition in Surinam. X. Protein metabolism and influence of extra calcium on the growth and calcium metabolism in boarding school children. *Am J Clin Nutr* 20(1), Jan.: 34-42. *[PS]*

Luyken, R.; Luyken-Koning, F. W. M. & Dam-Bakker, A. W. I. van

30.0161	NW	1959	Nutrition survey on the Windward Islands (Netherlands Antilles). *Trop Geogr Med* 11(1), Mar.: 49-56. **[28]** *[COL]*

Luyken, R.; Luyken-Koning, F. W. M. & Immikhuizen, M. J. T.

30.0162	SR	1971	Goedkope eiwitrijke kindervoeding voor Suriname [Cheap protein-rich baby food for Surinam]. *Sur Landb* 19(1): 55-62. *[RILA]*
28.0814	SR	1971	Lactose intolerance in Surinam.

McCarthy, M. C.

30.0163	TR	1966	Dietary and activity patterns of obese women in Trinidad. *J Am Diet Assoc* 48(1), Jan.: 33-37. **[28]** *[PS]*

McCulloch, W. E.

28.0817	GC	1955	YOUR HEALTH IN THE CARIBBEAN.
30.0164	BC	1958	Thirty-five years' experience of colonial nutrition. *W I Med J* 7(3), Sept.: 200-205. **[28]** *[COL]*

McDowall, M. F.

28.0820	TR	1971	Feeding of the newborn in hospital—paediatrician's view.

McKay, David A.; Warren, Kenneth S.; Cook, Joseph A. & Jordan, Peter

28.0824	SL	1973	Immunologic diagnosis of schistosomiasis. III. The effects of nutritional status and infection intensity on intradermal test results in St. Lucian children.

McKenzie, Keith

28.0830	JM	1974	Priorities for child care.

McKigney, John I.

30.0165	GC	1968	Economic aspects of infant feeding practices in the West Indies. *J Trop Pediat* 14(2), June: 55-59. **[28,41]** *[PS]*

30.0166	BC	1969	Food imports: milk. *Cajanus* 2(4), No. 10, Aug.: 257-265. **[47]**

[RIS]

30.0167	BC	1971	Cost/value and selection of milks for use in artificial feeding. *W I Med J* 20(3), Sept.: 213-217. **[41]** [*PS*]
41.0321	BC	1971	Family incomes and nutrient cost of foods in the Caribbean area.
30.0168	JM	1971	The uniqueness of human milk. Economic aspects. *Am J Clin Nutr* 24(8), Aug.: 1005-1012. **[28,41]** [*PS*]

McLean, A. E. M.

30.0169	JM	1966	Enzyme activity in the liver and serum of malnourished children in Jamaica. *Clin Sci* 30(1), Feb.: 129-138. [*PS*]

Mahadevan, P.

30.0170	GC	1968	Animal protein supplies for the Caribbean. *Cajanus* 6, Dec.: 2-12. **[28]** [*RIS*]
30.0171	GC	1968	The role of the UWI Faculty of Agriculture in relation to the food needs of the Caribbean. *Cajanus* 1, Feb.: 27-30. **[32]** [*RIS*]

May, Jacques M. & McLellan, Donna L.

30.0172	BZ	1972	THE ECOLOGY OF MALNUTRITION IN MEXICO AND CENTRAL AMERICA: MEXICO, GUATEMALA, BRITISH HONDURAS, HONDURAS, EL SALVADOR, NICARAGUA, COSTA RICA AND PANAMA. New York, Hafner Publishing Company: 395p. [*NYP*]
30.0173	GC	1973	THE ECOLOGY OF MALNUTRITION IN THE CARIBBEAN: THE BAHAMAS, CUBA, JAMAICA, HISPANIOLA (HAITI AND THE DOMINICAN REPUBLIC), PUERTO RICO, THE LESSER ANTILLES, AND TRINIDAD AND TOBAGO. New York, Hafner Press: 490p. (Studies in Medical Geography, 12) **[43]** [*RIS*]
30.0174	GG	1974	THE ECOLOGY OF MALNUTRITION IN EASTERN SOUTH AMERICA: VENEZUELA, GUYANA, SURINAM (AND THE NETHERLANDS ANTILLES), FRENCH GUIANA, BRAZIL, URUGUAY, PARAGUAY, AND ARGENTINA. New York, Hafner Press: 558p. (Studies in Medical Geography, 13) [*AGS*]

Mentus, Ric

30.0175	BC	1975	Which comes first—beef or milk? *Cajanus* 8(6): 340-342. [*RIS*]

Meredith, Howard V.

27.0095	GC	1968	Body size of contemporary groups of pre-school children studied in different parts of the world.
27.0096	GC	1969	Body size of contemporary youth in different parts of the world.
27.0097	GC	1970	Body size of contemporary groups of one-year-old infants studied in different parts of the world.

Miall, W. E.; Desai, Patricia & Standard, K. L.

30.0176	JM	1970	Malnutrition, infection and child growth in Jamaica. *J Biosoc Sci* 2(1), Jan.: 31-44. **[28]** [*COL*]

Mills, Don

43.0303	JM	1968	Nutrition and economic growth.

Mitrasing, F. E. M.

30.0177   SR,GU   1969   HET SURINAAMS-GUIANEES GRENSGESCHIL: EEN RECHTSKUNDIG RE-SEARCH [THE BORDER CONFLICT SURINAM-GUYANA: LEGAL RE-SEARCH]. Paramaribo, Suriname Druk D.A.G.: 39p. **[5,37]** [*RILA*]

Mohammed, I.

30.0178   TR   1972   Protein-calorie malnutrition in South Trinidad. *Cajanus* 5(3), July-Sept.: 244-249.   [*RIS*]

Morris, Miriam

30.0179   BC   1971   Cultural differences and the feeding of young children in the Caribbean. *W I Med J* 20(3), Sept.: 135-138. **[20]**   [*PS*]

Morrison, C. J.

30.0180   JM   1970   Improving nutrition in Jamaica—suggestions towards a strategy of action. *Cajanus* 3(3), June: 178-183. **[28]**   [*RIS*]

Moser, C. A.

41.0356   JM   1957   THE MEASUREMENT OF LEVELS OF LIVING WITH SPECIAL REFERENCE TO JAMAICA.

Murray, Wm. C. G.

30.0181   SV   1942   Infant feeding and nutrition in St. Vincent. *Car Med J* 4(3): 92-96. **[28]**   [*COL*]

Nehaul, B. B. G.

28.0921   GU   1943   Report on the physical development and health of a sample of school children in the Island of Leguan, British Guiana, 1941.

Neilson, Helen R.

30.0182   GC   1972   Candi's role and contribution to improved nutrition and dietary services. *Cajanus* 5(3), July-Sept.: 167-171. **[28]**   [*RIS*]

Neumark, S. Daniel

43.0318   GC   1951   The importance of agriculture in Caribbean economy.

Nichols, B. L.; Alleyne, G. A. O.; Barnes, D. J. & Hazlewood, C. F.

30.0183   JM   1969   Relation between muscle potassium and total body potassium in infants with malnutrition. *J Pediat* 74(1), Jan.: 49-57.   [*PS*]

Nicholson, C. C.

30.0184   GU   1947   Nutritional survey of pupils of elementary schools, Mahaicony District, February-March, 1947. *Bri Gui Med Annual* 141-151. **[28,32]**   [*RIS*]

30.0185   GU   1956   Assessment of the nutritional status of elementary school children of British Guiana by periodic sampling surveys, and evaluation of the beneficial effects of supplementary feeding. *W I Med J* 5(4), Dec.: 240-246. **[28,32]**   [*COL*]

Nocks, Barry N.

30.0186   BZ   1967   Nutrition study in British Honduras. *Am J Clin Nutr* 20(7), July: 661-671.   [*PS*]

Omawale

30.0187   GU   1976   The future of textured vegetable protein (T.V.P.) production in Guyana: agricultural and nutritional considerations. *Cajanus* 9(2): 98-112.   **[43]**   [*RIS*]

Ortiz, Elisabeth Lambert

30.0188   GC   1973   THE COMPLETE BOOK OF CARIBBEAN COOKING. New York, M. Evans and Company: 450p.   [*NYP*]

Ostovar, Kurosh

59.0059   TR   1973   ISOLATION AND CHARACTERIZATION OF MICROORGANISMS INVOLVED IN THE FERMENTATION OF TRINIDAD'S CACAO BEANS.

Parize, Méréa

30.0189   GD   1971   Cuisine créole: recettes guadeloupéennes [Creole cuisine: recipes from Guadeloupe]. *Parallèles* 38, 1st trimester: 15-29.   [*RIS*]

Parry, John Horace

43.0342   JM   1962   Salt fish and ackee: an historical sketch of the introduction of food crops into Jamaica.

Pawar, M. S.

61.0117   GU   1968   Rice.

Pena, Patricia

30.0190   GC   1972   Teaching the diabetic diet in the Caribbean. *Cajanus* 5(3), July-Sept.: 172-178.   **[28,32]**   [*RIS*]

Picou, D.; Alleyne, G. A. O. & Seakins, Anne

30.0191   JM   1965   Hydroxyproline and creatinine excretion in infantile protein malnutrition. *Clin Sci* 29(3): 517-523.   [*PS*]

Picou, D.; Halliday, D. & Garrow, J. S.

30.0192   JM   1966   Total body protein, collagen and non-collagen protein in infantile malnutrition. *Clin Sci* 30(2), April: 345-351.   [*PS*]

Picou, D. & Taylor-Roberts, T.

30.0193   JM   1969   The measurement of total protein synthesis and catabolism and nitrogen turnover in infants in different nutritional states and receiving different amounts of dietary protein. *Clin Sci* 36(2), April: 283-296.   [*PS*]

Pike, Lennox A.

28.1017   BZ   1967   Observations on the feeding of babies with gastroenteritis on an acidified milk formula.

Pineau, A.

28.1018   GD   1960   Médecine et psychiatrie rurale en Guadeloupe [Rural medicine and psychiatry in Guadeloupe]. *Concours Méd* 82(4).

28.1019   GD   1960   Médecine et psychiatrie rurale en Guadeloupe [Rural medicine and psychiatry in Guadeloupe]. *Concours Méd* 82(5).

Platt, B. S.

30.0194   BC   1946   NUTRITION IN THE BRITISH WEST INDIES. London, H.M.S.O., 38p. (Colonial no. 195.)   [COL]

Ramsey, F. C.

30.0195   BC   1974   The place of nutrition in the priorities of maternal and child health. *In* International Confederation of Midwives. REPORT OF THE CARIBBEAN WORKING PARTY, BRIDGETOWN, BARBADOS, 16-24 MAY, 1974. [Bridgetown, Barbados]: 65-70. **[28]**   [RIS]

Reddy, S. K.

30.0196   SV   1968   Practical problems with obtaining valid and reliable information on household food utilisation. *J Trop Pediat* 14(2), June: 66-70.   [PS]

30.0197   GC   1970   Some misconceptions about nutrition which are common in the West Indies. *Cajanus* 4(2): 94-103.   [RIS]

30.0198   JM,BB   1971   Artificial feeding in Jamaica and Barbados. *W I Med J* 20(3), Sept.: 198-207. **[28]**   [PS]

30.0199   JM,BB   1971   Transition to family diet in Jamaica and Barbados. *W I Med J* 20(3), Sept.: 218-226.   [PS]

Reynal, Louise de

30.0200   FC   1971   Recettes créoles [Creole recipes]. *Paralleles* 38, 1st trimester: 51-54.   [RIS]

Reynolds, C. Roy

30.0201   JM   1972   Inter-disciplinary attention focuses on nutrition problems. *Jam J* 6(4), Dec.: 12-14.   [RIS]

Rhodes, Katerina

30.0202   JM   1957   Two types of liver disease in Jamaican children. *W I Med J* 6(1), Mar.: 1-29; 6(2), June: 73-93; 6(3), Sept.: 145-178. **[28]**   [COL]

Richardson, Stephen A.

30.0203   JM   1975   Physical growth of Jamaican school children who were severely malnourished before 2 years of age. *J Biosoc Sci* 7(4), Oct.: 445-462. **[28]**   [COL]

Richardson, Stephen A.; Birch, H. G. & Hertzig, Margaret E.

28.1074   JM   1973   School performance of children who were severely malnourished in infancy.

Richardson, Stephen A.; Birch, H. G. & Ragbeer, C.

30.0204   JM   1975   The behaviour of children at home who were severely malnourished in the first 2 years of life. *J Biosoc Sci* 7(3), July: 255-267. **[9,31]**   [COL]

Roberts, D. F.; Triger, D. R. & Morgan, R. J.

28.1076   JM   1970   Glucose-6-phosphate dehydrogenase deficiency and haemoglobin level in Jamaican children.

Roberts, Lydia J.

33.0161   GC   1952   First Caribbean Conference on Home Economics and Education in Nutrition.

Robinson, C. K.

43.0381	GC	1952	Food crops for local consumption.
43.0382	TR	1953	The food production programme of Trinidad and Tobago.

Robinson, J. B. D. & Parry, Joan M.

30.0205   BB   1949   Ascorbic acid content of some local Barbados foods. *Nature* 164 (4169), Sept. 24: 531-532.

Rodway, James & Aiken, James

54.0857   GU   1913   Some of our food fishes.

Roopnarinesingh, S. S.; Morris, D. & Chang, E.

28.1096   JM   1971   The underweight Jamaican parturient.

Roopnarinesingh, S. S. & Pathak, U. N.

28.1097   JM   1970   Obesity in the Jamaican parturient.

Roth, Walter Edmund

30.0206   GU   1912   On the native drinks of the Guianese Indian. *Timehri* 3d ser., 2(19A), July: 128-134. **[13]**   [*AMN*]

Sar, A. van der

28.1122   CU   1951   Incidence and treatment of kwashiorkor in Curacao.

Sar, A. van der & Kroon, T. A. J.

30.0207   CU   1956   Avitaminosis A and subclinical vitamin C deficiency in Curacao. *Docum Med Geogr Trop* 8(2), June: 144-150. **[28]**   [*COL*]

Seaforth, Compton E.

60.0199   JM   1962   The ackee—Jamaica's national fruit.

Sessler, Wa. M. & Spoon, W.

54.0911   NL   1952   Over het gebruik van wilde salie op de Benedenwindse Eilanden [On the use of wild sage in the Leeward Islands].

Shaw, Earl Bennett

43.0403   JM   1943   The food front in the Greater Antilles.

Slater, Mary

30.0208	GC	1965	Cooking the Caribbean way. London, Spring Books: 256p. [*RIS*]
30.0209	GC	1970	Caribbean cooking for pleasure. London, The Hamlyn Publishing Group Ltd.: 164p. [*SCH*]

Sprauve, M. E. & Dodds, M. L.

30.0210   VI   1965   Dietary survey of adolescents in the Virgin Islands. *J Am Diet Assoc* 47(4), Oct.: 287-291. **[27]**   [*PS*]

Springer, Rita G.

30.0211   GC   1968   Caribbean cookbook. London, Evans Bros. Ltd.: 288p.   [*NYP*]

Standard, K. L.

30.0212	JM	1958	A pilot nutrition survey in five low-income areas in Jamaica. *W I Med J* 7(3), Sept.: 215-221. [*COL*]
27.0133	BB	1964	Weights and heights of children in Barbados, West Indies, 1961.

Standard, K. L.; Desai, Patricia & Miall, W. E.

27.0134   JM   1969   A longitudinal study of child growth in a rural community in Jamaica.

Standard, K. L.; Lovell, H. G. & Garrow, J. S.

27.0135   BB,JM   1966   The validity of certain physical signs as indices of generalised malnutrition in young children.

Staveren, W. A. van; Tiggelman-Krugten, V. A. H.; Ferrier, B.; Maggillavry, Ch. J. & Dubois, G.

30.0213   SR   1971   Food habits of infants and preschool children in Surinam. *J Am Diet Assoc* 58(2), February: 127-132.   [*PS*]

Stehlé, Henri & Stehlé, Marie E.

54.0969   GD   1963   Les ravets de la Guadeloupe: ces commensaux indésirables [The turnips of Guadeloupe, those undesirable table companions].

Stephenson, Derick

28.1220   JM   1969   Dental caries, environment and diet in Jamaica.

St. George, John

30.0214   TR   1971   Dietary deficiency and pre-eclamptic toxaemia—a preliminary communication. *W I Med J* 20(3), Sept.: 166-169.   **[28]**   [*PS*]

Stoopler, Mark; Frayer, William & Alderman, Michael H.

30.0215   JM   1974   Prevalence and persistence of lactose malabsorption among young Jamaican children. *Am J Clin Nutr* 27(7), July: 728-732.   **[28]** [*PS*]

Straw, K. H.

30.0216   BB   1954   Household budgets and nutritional analysis of food consumption in Barbados. *Social Econ Stud* 3(1), June: 5-38.   **[9,41]**   [*RIS*]

Strong, M. S.

30.0217   JM   1959   Jamaicans change their eating habits. *Caribbean* 13(12), Dec.: 234-235.   [*COL*]

Symonds, Bruce

28.1258   TR   1956   Fatty liver disease in South Trinidad.

Symonds, Bruce & Mohammed, I.

30.0218   TR   1956   "Sugar babies" in South Trinidad. *W I Med J* 5(3), Sept.: 159-166.   **[28]**   [*COL*]

Taitt, D. J.

30.0219   GU   1943   Malnutrition at No. 1 Government Dispensary, Georgetown, B.G., 1943. *Br Gui Med Annual* 26: 114-124.   [*ACM*]

Thorburn, Marigold J.; Hutchinson, S. & Alleyne, G. A. O.

30.0220   JM   1972   Chromosome abnormalities in malnourished children. *Lancet* 1(7750), Marchill: 591p.   **[28]**   [*PS*]

Tulloch, J. A.

30.0221   JM   1958   Some aspects of myocardial infarction in Jamaica. *W I Med J* 7(4), Dec.: 235-243.   **[28]**   [*COL*]

Twyford, I. T.

30.0222   GC   1967   Banana nutrition: a review of principles and practice. *J Sci Food Agric* 18, May: 177-183.   [*PS*]

Usborne, Vivian

30.0223   SV   1963   The home treatment of infant malnutrition in a rural district of St. Vincent. *W I Med J* 12(4), Dec.: 253-255.   **[28]**   [*COL*]

Vernon, Cynthia

28.1343   JM   1971   Special needs of the young child in Jamaica.

Verteuil, Eric de

30.0224   TR   1943   Radio talk on "Food problems during war time." *Car Med J* 5(2): 82-86.   [*COL*]

Verwey-Burke, Norma Grace

30.0225   SR,NE   1971   VERANDERINGEN IN VOEDINGSGEWOONTEN VAN SURINAAMSE HUIS-HOUDENS IN AMSTRDAM [CHANGES IN THE FOOD HABITS OF SURINAME HOUSEHOLDS IN AMSTERDAM]. Amsterdam, The Netherlands, Joko: 118p. (Dissertation, Universiteit van Amsterdam)   **[18]**   [*RILA*]

Vinke, B.; Piers, A. & Irausquin-Cath, H.

28.1349   CU   1969   Folic acid and Vitamin B_{12} deficiencies in negroid hospital patients on Curaçao.

Vinke, B. & Sar, A. van der

30.0226   CU   1956   Megaloblastic nutritional anaemia in Curacao. *Docum Med Geogr Trop* 8(2), June: 151-163.   [*COL*]

Vinke, B.; Sar, A. van der; Faber, J. G. & Vries, J. A. de

30.0227   CU   1960   Penicillin in nutritional megaloblastic anaemia in Curacao. *Trop Geogr Med* 12(1), Mar.: 26-30.   **[28]**   [*COL*]

30.0228   CU   1960   Serum vitamin B_{12} levels and response to the treatment of megaloblastic anaemia in Curacao. *Trop Geogr Med* 12(1), Mar.: 31-37.   **[28]**   [*COL*]

Visser, W. J.; Bellot, S. M.; Duursma, S. A. & Luyken, R.

30.0229   SR   1974   Osteoporosis in Surinam. *Nutr Metab* 16(4): 208-214.   **[28]**   [*ACM*]

Waby, Mrs. J. F.

30.0230   GU   1917   War cookery: the preparation and cooking of locally grown vegetable foodstuffs. *J Bd Agric Br Gui* 10(3-4), Apr.-July: 178-197.   **[60]**   [*AMN*]

30.0231   GU   1925   The preparation and cooking of locally grown vegetable foodstuffs. *J Bd Agric Br Gui* 18(4), Oct.: 52-70.   **[60]**   [*AMN*]

Warner, Joyce; Brooks S. E. H.; James, W. P. T. & Louisy, Sheila

28.1375   JM   1972   Juvenile dermatitis herpetiformis in Jamaica: clinical and gastro-intestinal features.

Waterlow, J. C.

30.0232   JM   1974   The history of the Tropical Metabolism Research Unit—U.W.I. *W I Med J* 23(3), Sept.: 151-159.   [*PS*]

28.1383   JM   1974   Some aspects of childhood malnutrition as a public health problem.

30.0233   JM   1975   Amount and rate of disappearance of liver fat in malnourished infants in Jamaica. *Am J Clin Nutr* 28(11), Nov.: 1330-1336. **[28]**
  [PS]

Waterlow, J. C.; Garrow, J. S. & Millward, D. J.
30.0234   JM   1969   The turnover of [⁷⁵Se] Selenomethionine in infants and rats measured in a whole body counter. *Clin Sci* 36(3), June: 489-504.   *[PS]*

Waterman, James A.
30.0235   TR   1945   Nutrition in Trinidad, with special reference to milk during pregnancy and infancy. *Car Med J* 7(2-3): 95-112. **[28,34]** *[COL]*
28.1393   TR   1948   Peroneal palsy complicating labour and the puerperium.

Went, L. N.; Channer, D. M.; Harding, R. Y. & Clunes, B. E.
30.0236   JM   1960   The effect of iron and protein supplementations on the haemoglobin level of healthy female students. *W I Med J* 9(3), Sept.: 209-213. **[28]**   *[COL]*

Wertheimer, F. W.; Brewster, R. H. & White, C. L.
30.0237   TR   1967   Periodontal disease and nutrition in Trinidad. *J Periodontol* 38(2), March-April: 100-104. **[28]**   *[PS]*

Wheeler, Erica F.
30.0238   JM   1974   "Cornmeal and condensed milk": assessment of a Jamaican supplementary food mixture. *W I Med J* 23(2), June: 69-74.   *[PS]*

White, Alison
30.0239   TR   1974   The breast-feeding campaign in Trinidad and Tobago. *Cajanus* 7(5), Oct.: 205-213.   *[RIS]*

Wilson, Dorothy
30.0240   BC   1971   Nutritional requirements in pregnancy and lactation. *W I Med J* 20(3), Sept.: 155-158.   *[PS]*

Wolfe, Linda
30.0241   GC   1970   THE COOKING OF THE CARIBBEAN ISLANDS. New York, Time-Life Books: 208p.   *[RIS]*

Wood, J. K.; Milner, P. F. & Pathak, U. N.
30.0242   JM   1968   The metabolism of iron-dextran given as a total-dose infusion to iron deficient Jamaican subjects. *Br J Haematol* 14(2), Feb.: 119-129. **[28]**   *[PS]*

Yang, Y. H.
30.0243   GC   1973   Soybean foods for the Caribbean. *Cajanus* 6(1), Jan.-March: 6-21.
   [RIS]

Yde, Jens
43.0475   GU   1960   Agriculture and division of work among the Waiwai.

Zeegelaar, F. J.; Sanchez, H.; Luyken, R.; Luyken-Koning, F. W. M. &
Staveren, W. A. van
30.0244   SR   1967   Studies on physiology of nutrition in Surinam. XI. The skeleton of
aged people in Surinam. *Am J Clin Nutr* 20(1), Jan.: 43-45.   **[27]**
                                                                                           [PS]

Zephirin, M.
28.1485   GC   1969   Hospital food service in the Caribbean.
28.1486   GC   1972   The food service supervisor.

Chapter 31

PSYCHIATRY AND MENTAL HEALTH

Mental illness; mental retardation; psychology.
See also: **[9]** Socialization, family and kinship; **[20]** Values and norms; **[33]** Social and legal issues.

Abel, Theodora M.

31.0001	MS	1960	Differential responses to projective testing in a Negro peasant community: Montserrat, B.W.I. *Int J Social Psych* 6(3-4), Autumn: 218-224. **[10,11]** [*RIS*]
31.0002	MS	1962	Mental health and cross-cultural evaluations. *Int Ment Heal Res Newsl* 4(3-4), Fall-Winter: 1, 4-5. [*RIS*]

Abel, Theodora M. & Metraux, Rhoda

31.0003	MS	1959	Sex differences in a Negro peasant community; Montserrat, B.W.I. *J Proj Tech* 23(2): 127-133. **[10,11]** [*RIS*]

Abraham-van der Mark, Eva E.

9.0002	CU	1970	Differences in the upbringing of boys and girls in Curaçao, correlated with differences in the degree of neurotic instability.

Adams, Paul L.

31.0004	GC	1970	The social psychiatry of Frantz Fanon. *Am J Psych* 127(6), Dec.: 809-814. **[5]** [*PS*]

Alvarez, G. A.

31.0005	GU	1966	Some historico-psychiatric events and aspects of a recent psychiatric experience in British Guiana. *Psych Q Suppl* 40(1): 100-111. [*COL*]

Aronoff, Joel

31.0006	SK	1965	THE INTER-RELATIONSHIP OF PSYCHOLOGICAL AND CULTURAL SYSTEMS: A CASE STUDY OF A RURAL WEST INDIAN VILLAGE. Ph.D. dissertation, Brandeis University, 370p. **[8,42,52]** [*RIS*]
31.0007	BC	1967	PSYCHOLOGICAL NEEDS AND CULTURAL SYSTEMS: A CASE STUDY. Princeton, New Jersey, Van Nostrand: 241p. **[9,42,52]** [*RIS*]
31.0008	SK	1970	Psychological needs as a determinant in the formation of economic structures: a confirmation. *Hum Rel* 23(2), April: 128-138. **[8,42]** [*COL*]

Bagley, Christopher

31.0009	GC	1968	Migration, race and mental health: a review of some recent research. *Race* 9(3), Jan: 343-356. **[16,17]** [*COL*]
31.0010	BC,UK	1969	The social aetiology of schizophrenia in immigrant groups. *Race Today* 1(6), Oct.: 170-174. **[18]** [*RIS*]
31.0011	BC,UK	1971	Mental illness in immigrant minorities in London. *J Biosoc Sci* 3(4), Oct.: 449-459. **[18]** [*COL*]
31.0012	BC,UK	1975	The background of deviance in black children in London. *In* Verma, Gajendra K. & Bagley, Christopher, eds. RACE AND EDUCATION ACROSS CULTURES. London, Heinemann Educational Books Ltd.: 283-293. **[11,18,33]** [*RIS*]
18.0012	BC,UK	1975	Sequels of alienation: a social psychological view of the adaptation of West Indian migrants in Britain.

Beaubrun, Michael H.

28.0105	TR	1962	Huntington's chorea in Trinidad.
31.0013	TR	1963	The role of father in Trinidad adolescence. *In* Carter, Samuel E., ed. THE ADOLESCENT IN THE CHANGING CARIBBEAN: PROCEEDINGS OF THE THIRD CARIBBEAN CONFERENCE FOR MENTAL HEALTH, APRIL 4-11, 1961, UCWI, JAMAICA. Kingston, The Herald, p.75-77. **[9]** [*RIS*]
31.0014	TR	1964	Care of the mentally retarded in Trinidad and Tobago: review of ten years progress, and plans for the future. *In* REPORT OF CONFERENCE ON CHILD CARE IN TRINIDAD AND TOBAGO [HELD BY] TRINIDAD AND TOBAGO ASSOCIATION FOR MENTAL HEALTH, SUB-COMMITTEE ON CHILDREN AND YOUTH, APR. 18, 1964. Port of Spain, Government Printer, p.16-18. **[33]** [*RIS*]
31.0015	GC	1965	The Caribbean. *In* A MENTAL HEALTH ASSOCIATION: ITS STRUCTURE AND ROLE. Proceedings of the Special Meeting of Member Associations of the World Federation for Mental Health held in Berne, August 1964. Genève, Suisse, World Federation for Mental Health: 44-51. [*RIS*]
31.0016	GC	1965[?]	Keynote address. *In* FAMILY RELATIONSHIPS: [PROCEEDINGS OF THE] FOURTH CARIBBEAN CONFERENCE FOR MENTAL HEALTH, CURACAO, APRIL 16-23, 1963, NETHERLANDS ANTILLES. [Willemstad? Boek -en Offset Drukkerij "De Curacaosche Courant"], p.27-35. **[9]** [*RIS*]
31.0017	GC	1966	Psychiatric education for the Caribbean. *W I Med J* 15(1), March: 52-62. [*PS*]
31.0018	TR	1966	Socioeconomic change, population explosion and the changing phases of mental health programs in developing countries. *Am J Orth-psych* 36, Jan.: 84-89. **[7]** [*PS*]
31.0019	GC	1969	Planning and utilization of mental health resources within the Caribbean. In PAPERS OF THE FIRST CARIBBEAN PSYCHIATRIC ASSOCIATION MEETING, OCHO RIOS, JAMAICA: 10P. [*RIS*]
8.0009	JM	1975	Cannabis or alcohol: the Jamaican experience.
31.0020	GC	1975	The view from Monkey Mountain. *J Am Acad Psychoan* 3(3): 257-266. **[29]** [*RIS*]

Beaubrun, Michael H.; Bannister, P.; Lewis, L. F. E.; Mahy, G.; Royes, K. C.; Smith, P. & Wisinger, Z.

31.0021	BC	1975	The West Indies. *In* Howells, John G., ed. WORLD HISTORY OF PSYCHIATRY. New York, Brunner/Mazel: 507-527. **[5]**

Beaubrun, Michael H. & Firth, Hedy

33.0033   TR   1969   A transcultural analysis of Alcoholics Anonymous Trinidad/London.

Beaubrun, Michael H. & Knight, Frank

33.0034   JM   1973   Psychiatric assessment of 30 chronic users of cannabis and 30 matched controls.

Beaubrun, Michael H. & Voorhoeve, A. C.

31.0022   JM,TR   1970   A survey of nurses' attitudes to psychiatric patients in two general hospitals in Jamaica and Trinidad. *W I Med J* 19(3), Sept.: 184-187.
[PS]

Bennett, C. V.

31.0023   BB   1965[?]   Nursing and mental health in the family. *In* FAMILY RELATIONSHIPS: [PROCEEDINGS OF THE] FOURTH CARIBBEAN CONFERENCE FOR MENTAL HEALTH, CURACAO, APR. 16-23, 1963, NETHERLANDS ANTILLES. [Willemstad? Boek- en Offset Drukkerij "De Curacaosche Courant"], p. 124-128.   **[28]**   [RIS]

Benoit, Guy

31.0024   GD   1963   Attitudes and problems of adolescents in Guadeloupe. *In* Carter, Samuel E., ed. THE ADOLESCENT IN THE CHANGING CARIBBEAN: PROCEEDINGS OF THE THIRD CARIBBEAN CONFERENCE FOR MENTAL HEALTH, APRIL 4-11, 1961, UCWI, JAMAICA. Kingston, The Herald, p.35-37.   **[9,33]**   [RIS]

31.0025   GD   1965[?]   Essai sur la structure familiale vecue en Guadeloupe [Essay on family structure in Guadeloupe]. *In* FAMILY RELATIONSHIPS: [PRO-CEEDINGS OF THE] FOURTH CARIBBEAN CONFERENCE FOR MENTAL HEALTH, CURACAO, APR. 16-23, 1963, NETHERLANDS ANTILLES. [Willemstad? Boek- en Offset Drukkerij "De Curacaosche Courant"], p.142-150.   **[9]**   [RIS]

Blanchy, S. & Bourgeois, M.

31.0026   FG   1975   La psychiatrie en Guiane Française. Aspects formales, institutionnels et statistiques [Psychiatry in French Guiana. Formal, institutional and statistical aspects]. *Ann Medico-psychol* 1(1); Jan.: 51-75.   **[28]**   [PS]

Blom, F. E. A.

31.0027   GC   1963   Conflicting values and cultural identifications facing the Caribbean adolescent today. *In* Carter, Samuel E., ed. THE ADOLESCENT IN THE CHANGING CARIBBEAN: PROCEEDINGS OF THE THIRD CARIBBEAN CONFERENCE FOR MENTAL HEALTH, APRIL 4-11, 1961, UCWI, JAMAICA. Kingston, The Herald, p.33-34.   **[20]**   [RIS]

Boles, Glen

31.0028   GC   1965[?]   Children's drawings from seven Caribbean islands. *In* FAMILY RELATIONSHIPS: [PROCEEDINGS OF THE] FOURTH CARIBBEAN CONFERENCE FOR MENTAL HEALTH, CURACAO, APR. 16-23, 1963, NETHERLANDS ANTILLES. [Willemstad? Boek- en Offset Drukkerij "De Curacaosche Courant"], p.88-106.   [RIS]

Bourguignon, Erika

23.0016   **SV**   1973   An assessment of some comparisons and implications.

Bourguignon, Erika, ed.

23.0017   **SV**   1973   RELIGION, ALTERED STATES OF CONSCIOUSNESS, AND SOCIAL CHANGE.

Braithwaite, Lloyd E.

31.0029   **GC**   1961   Social and economic changes in the Caribbean. *In* CHILDREN OF THE CARIBBEAN—THEIR MENTAL HEALTH NEEDS: PROCEEDINGS OF THE SECOND CARIBBEAN CONFERENCE FOR MENTAL HEALTH, Apr. 10-16, 1959, Saint Thomas, Virgin Islands, San Juan, P.R., Dept. of the Treasury, Purchase and Supply Service—Print. Division, p.50-58. **[8]**   [*RIS*]

31.0030   **GC**   1963   The changing social scene. *In* Carter, Samuel E., ed. THE ADOLES-CENT IN THE CHANGING CARIBBEAN: PROCEEDINGS OF THE THIRD CARIBBEAN CONFERENCE FOR MENTAL HEALTH, APR. 4-11, 1961, UCWI, JAMAICA. Kingston, The Herald, p.18-24. **[16,20]**   [*RIS*]

Brodber, Erna

1.0035   **BC**   1972   SOCIAL PSYCHOLOGY IN THE CARIBBEAN: A BIBLIOGRAPHY AND SOME COMMENTS ON LAGUNAE AND AREAS OF SATURATION.

31.0031   **BC**   1974   Social psychology in the English-speaking Caribbean—a bibli-ography and some comments. *Social Econ Stud* 23(3), Sept.: 398-417. **[1,9]**   [*RIS*]

Brody, Eugene B.

34.0015   **JM**   1974   Mental health and population control.

Brown, Marvin & Amoroso, Donald M.

20.0011   **TR**   1975   Attitudes toward homosexuality among West Indian male and female college students.

Bullard, M. Kenyon

31.0032   **BZ**   1973   THE RECOGNITION OF PSYCHIATRIC DISORDER IN BRITISH HONDURAS. Ph.D. dissertation, University of Oregon: 299p.   [*PhD*]

Burke, Aggrey W.

31.0033   **JM,UK**   1973   The consequences of unplanned repatriation. *Br J Psych* 123(572), July: 109-111. **[17]**   [*COL*]

31.0034   **TR**   1974   Attempted suicide in Trinidad and Tobago. *W I Med J* 23(4), Dec.: 250-255.   [*PS*]

31.0035   **TR**   1974   Socio-cultural aspects of attempted suicide among women in Trinidad and Tobago. *Br J Psych* 125(0), Oct.: 374-377. **[10]**
                                                                               [*ACM*]

31.0036   **TR**   1974   Socio-cultural determinants of psychiatric disorder among women in Trinidad and Tobago. *W I Med J* 23(2), June: 75-79. **[10]**   [*PS*]

31.0037   **BC**   1975   Trends in Caribbean psychiatry. Part 1: the problems. *W I Med J* 24(4), Dec.: 281-222.   [*PS*]

Campbell, Albert A.

31.0038   **ST**   1943   St. Thomas Negroes—a study of personality and culture. *Psychol Monogr* 55(5): 1-90. **[11]**   [*COL*]

Campbell, Thelma P.

31.0039   **GC**   1963   The role of youth clubs in preparing for maturity. *In* Carter, Samuel E., ed. THE ADOLESCENT IN THE CHANGING CARIBBEAN: PROCEEDINGS OF THE THIRD CARIBBEAN CONFERENCE FOR MENTAL HEALTH, APR. 4-11, 1961, UCWI, JAMAICA. Kingston, The Herald, p.190-193.   **[33]**   [*RIS*]

Carstairs, G. M.

31.0040   **JM**   1973   Editorial: WFMH is alive and well and living in Jamaica. *Aus N Z J Psych* 7(4), Dec.: 223-225.   [*ACM*]

Carter, Samuel E., ed.

31.0041   **GC**   1963   THE ADOLESCENT IN THE CHANGING CARIBBEAN: PROCEEDINGS OF THE THIRD CARIBBEAN CONFERENCE FOR MENTAL HEALTH. Apr. 4-11, 1961, UCWI, Jamaica. Kingston, The Herald, 250p.   **[33]**
                                                                          [*RIS*]

Chruściel, T. L.

28.0242   **JM**   1975   Recent progress in the long-term pharmacological research on cannabis.

Clark, Isobel

32.0118   **UV**   1963   The insular training school programme for dependent, neglected and delinquent children in the Virgin Islands.

Close, Kathryn

31.0042   **GC**   1961   Youth in the Caribbean—reaching for maturity. *Children* 8(4), July-Aug.: 123-129.   **[9]**   [*RIS*]

Cohen, Yehudi A.

8.0036   **JM**   1953   A STUDY OF INTERPERSONAL RELATIONS IN A JAMAICAN COMMUNITY.

31.0043   **JM**   1955   Character formation and social structure in a Jamaican community. *Psychiatry* 18(3), Aug.: 275-296.   **[8,9]**   [*RIS*]

31.0044   **JM**   1955   A contribution to the study of adolescence: adolescent conflict in a Jamaican community. *J Indian Psychoan Inst* 9: 139-172.   **[8,9]**

31.0045   **JM**   1956   Structure and function: family organization and socialization in a Jamaican community. *Am Anthrop* 58(4), Aug.: 664-686.   **[8,9]**
                                                                          [*RIS*]

Collis, Robert & Knight, Frank

31.0046   **JM**   1970   Tropical encounter. *Jam Nurse* 12(2), Aug.: 8-10 passim.   [*AJN*]

Comitas, Lambros

33.0047   **JM**   1976   Cannabis and work in Jamaica: a refutation of the amotivational syndrome.

Cordice, Gideon

31.0047   **SV**   1965   MENTAL HEALTH IN ST. VINCENT. Paper presented at the Caribbean Seminar on Mental Health, Kingston, Jamaica, 5-11 September: 4p.
                                                                          [*RIS*]

Cromwell, Leta

32.0144   **UV**   1963   Project for discovering and assisting the mentally retarded child in the school.

Curti, Margaret Wooster

31.0048   CM   1960   Intelligence tests of white and colored school children in Grand Cayman. *J Psychol* 49(1), Jan.: 13-27.   [11,15]   [*COL*]

Dalton, Robert H.

33.0058   UV   1968   CHILDHOOD BEHAVIOR PROBLEMS IN SOCIAL FOCUS: A STUDY OF THE INSULAR TRAINING SCHOOL U.S. VIRGIN ISLANDS.

Davidson, J. R. T.

31.0049   JM   1972   Post-partum mood change in Jamaican women: a description and discussion on its significance. *B J Psych* 121(565), Dec.: 659-663.   [20,28]   [*COL*]

Davidson, Lewis

31.0050   JM   1963   The adolescent's struggle for emancipation. *In* Carter, Samuel E., ed. THE ADOLESCENT IN THE CHANGING CARIBBEAN: PROCEEDINGS OF THE THIRD CARIBBEAN CONFERENCE FOR MENTAL HEALTH, APR. 4-11, 1961, UCWI, JAMAICA. Kingston, The Herald, p.165-169.   [33]   [*RIS*]

De Freitas, Christine

31.0051   AR   1965   Mental Health in Aruba. Paper presented at the Caribbean Seminar on Mental Health, Kingston, Jamaica, 5-11 September: 13p.
                                                                              [*RIS*]

De Souza, Joan & Beaubrun, Michael H.

31.0052   BC   1967   An evaluation of the U.W.I. programme of community psychiatric care (résumé). *In* Beaubrun, Michael H., ed. RÉSUMÉ OF SIXTH CARIBBEAN CONFERENCE FOR MENTAL HEALTH HELD IN BARBADOS, 31ST JULY TO 4TH AUGUST, 1967: 6-7.   [*RIS*]

Despinoy, M. & Camelio, A.

31.0053   FA   1967   La psychopathologie aux Antilles et ses relations avec les structures sociales [Psychopathology in the Antilles and its relation to social structures]. *Bibl Psych Neurol* 132: 272-301.   [8]   [*PS*]

Deydier, Joseph

56.0089   FG   1905   La Guyane Francaise en 1904: son avenir économique [French Guiana in 1904: its economic future].

Doob, Leonard William

31.0054   JM   1958   The effect of the Jamaican patois on attitude and recall. *Am Anthrop* 60(3), June: 574-575.   [25]   [*RIS*]

Dummett, A.

31.0055   GU   1965   Mental health in British Guiana. Paper presented at the Caribbean Seminar on Mental Health, Kingston, Jamaica, 5-11 September: 6p.
                                                                              [*RIS*]

Elder, J. D.

22.0121   TR   1968   The male/female conflict in calypso.

Feldman, H. & Marriott, J. A. S.

31.0056   JM   1970-71 Diagnostic patterns and child/parent separation in children attending the Jamaican child guidance clinic. *Br J Social Psychiat* 4(4): 220-230. **[9]** [*COL*]

Feldman, H. & Morris, D.

31.0057   JM   1972   The validity of the Rutter scale for the identification of disturbed primary school children in Jamaica. *W I Med J* 21(2), June: 114-118. **[32]** [*PS*]

Fill, J. Herbert

31.0058   UV   1963   The sexual dilemma of the Caribbean adolescent. *In* Carter, Samuel E., ed. THE ADOLESCENT IN THE CHANGING CARIBBEAN: PROCEEDINGS OF THE THIRD CARIBBEAN CONFERENCE FOR MENTAL HEALTH, APR. 4-11, 1961, UCWI, JAMAICA. Kingston, The Herald, p.170-178. **[9]** [*RIS*]

31.0059   UV   1965[?] Teacher-child-parent inter-relationships in the U.S. Virgin Islands. *In* FAMILY RELATIONSHIPS: [PROCEEDINGS OF THE] FOURTH CARIBBEAN CONFERENCE FOR MENTAL HEALTH, CURACAO, APR. 16-23, 1963, NETHERLANDS ANTILLES. [Willemstad? Boek- en Offset Drukkerij "De Curacaosche Courant"], p.114-123. **[9,32]** [*RIS*]

Fisher, Lawrence E.

31.0060   BB   1971   Court remands to the Barbados Mental Hospital. *In* REPORT ON THE EIGHTH BIENNIAL CONFERENCE OF THE CARIBBEAN FEDERATION FOR MENTAL HEALTH. Paramaribo, Surinam Council on Social Welfare: 46-50. [*RIS*]

31.0061   BB   1973   THE IMAGERY OF MADNESS IN VILLAGE BARBADOS. Ph.D. dissertation, Northwestern University: 411p. **[20]** [*PhD*]

Garrett, James F.

31.0062   GC   1970   The economic benefits of programmes for the retarded. *In* Thorburn, Marigold J., ed. MENTAL RETARDATION IN THE CARIBBEAN: NEEDS, RESOURCES, APPROACHES. PROCEEDINGS OF THE FIRST CARIBBEAN MENTAL RETARDATION CONFERENCE, MONA, JAMAICA. Jamaica, The Jamaica Association for Mentally Handicapped Children: 1-4. **[41]** [*TCL*]

Giggs, John

31.0063   BC,UK   1973   High rates of schizophrenia among immigrants in Nottingham. *Nurs Times* 69(38), Sept. 20: 1210-1212. **[18]** [*ACM*]

Goodman, F. D.

23.0100   SV   1969   Glossolalia: speaking in tongues in four cultural settings.

Gordon, E. B.

18.0116   BC,UK   1965   Mentally ill West Indian immigrants.

Gourdon, J.

31.0064   GD   1965[?] Hygiène mentale et relations familiales [Mental health and family relations]. *In* FAMILY RELATIONSHIPS: [PROCEEDINGS OF THE] FOURTH CARIBBEAN CONFERENCE FOR MENTAL HEALTH, CURACAO, APR. 16-23, 1963, NETHERLANDS ANTILLES. [Willemstad? Boek- en Offset Drukkerij "De Curacaosche Courant"] p.136-141. **[9]** [*RIS*]

Gourlay, R. John

28.0536   **JM**   1961[?]   The importance of health in a developing community.

Gourlay, R. John et al.

31.0065   **JM**   1961   Aggressive behaviour in a small rural community in Jamaica: the report of a cooperative epidemiological study. *W I Med J* 10(3), Sept.: 175-183.   [*COL*]

Graham, P. J. & Meadows, C. E.

18.0117   **BC**   1967   Psychiatric disorder in the children of West Indian immigrants.

Green, Helen Bagenstose

31.0066   **JM**   1960   Comparison of nurturance and independence training in Jamaica and Puerto Rico with consideration of the resulting personality structure and transplanted social patterns. *J Social Psychol* 51(1), Feb.: 27-63.   [*COL*]

31.0067   **TR**   1964   Socialization values in the Negro and East Indian subcultures of Trinidad. *J Social Psychol* 64(1), Oct.: 1-20.   **[11,12,20]**   [*RIS*]

Grinder, Robert E.

27.0075   **JM**   1964   Negro-white differences in intellectual performance: a receding controversy.

Grinder, Robert E.; Spotts, Wendy S. & Curti, Margaret Wooster

31.0068   **JM**   1964   Relationships between Goodenough draw-a-man test performance and skin color among preadolescent Jamaican children. *J Social Psychol* 62: 181-188.   **[11]**   [*RIS*]

Hadley, C. V. D.

31.0069   **BC**   1949   Personality patterns, social class, and aggression in the British West Indies. *Hum Rel* 2(4): 349-362.   **[8]**   [*COL*]

Hagerty, T. F.

31.0070   **AR**   1963   The Junior Achievement Programme in Aruba. *In* Carter, Samuel E., ed. THE ADOLESCENT IN THE CHANGING CARIBBEAN: PROCEEDINGS OF THE THIRD CARIBBEAN CONFERENCE FOR MENTAL HEALTH, APR. 4-11, 1961, UCWI, JAMAICA. Kingston, The Herald, p.187-189.   **[33,41]**   [*RIS*]

Harding, Timothy & Knight, Frank

33.0092   **JM**   1973   Marihuana-modified mania.

Hawke, William A.

31.0071   **GC**   1970   The pre-school environment and mental retardation. *In* Thorburn, Marigold J., ed. MENTAL RETARDATION IN THE CARIBBEAN: NEEDS, RESOURCES, APPROACHES. PROCEEDINGS OF THE FIRST CARIBBEAN MENTAL RETARDATION CONFERENCE, MONA, JAMAICA. Jamaica, The Jamaica Association for Mentally Handicapped Children: 14-16.   [*TCL*]

Henney, Jeannette H.

23.0119   **SV**   1968   "MOURNING" A RELIGIOUS RITUAL AMONG THE SPIRITUAL BAPTISTS OF ST. VINCENT: AN EXPERIENCE IN SENSORY DEPRIVATION.

23.0121   **SV**   1973   The Shakers of St. Vincent: a stable religion.

Henric, S.
9.0065   **GD**   1965[?]   La famille guadeloupéenne [The Guadeloupe family].

Herskovits, Melville Jean
31.0072   **GC**   1952   Some psychological implications of Afroamerican studies. *In* Tax, Sol, ed. ACCULTURATION IN THE AMERICAS: PROCEEDINGS AND SELECTED PAPERS OF THE XXIXth INTERNATIONAL CONGRESS OF AMERICANISTS. Chicago, University of Chicago Press, p.152-160. **[11,14]**   [*AGS*]

Herzog, John D.
32.0288   **BB**   1968   HOUSEHOLD COMPOSITION AND BOY'S SCHOOL PERFORMANCE IN BARBADOS, WEST INDIES.
32.0289   **BB**   1974   Father-absence and boy's school performance in Barbados.

Hewitt, W.
31.0073   **JM**   1963   The attitudes of courts towards young offenders: the juvenile courts in Jamaica. *In* Carter, Samuel E., ed. THE ADOLESCENT IN THE CHANGING CARIBBEAN: PROCEEDINGS OF THE THIRD CARIBBEAN CONFERENCE FOR MENTAL HEALTH, APR. 4-11, 1961, UCWI, JAMAICA. Kingston, The Herald, p.147-149. **[33]**   [*RIS*]

Hickling, Frederick W.
31.0074   **JM**   1975   Psychiatric care in a general hospital unit in Jamaica. *W I Med J* 24(2), June: 67-75.   [*PS*]
31.0075   **JM**   1975   Social class and mental illness in a general hospital psychiatric unit in Jamaica. *W I Med J* 24(2), June: 76-83. **[10]**   [*PS*]
31.0076   **JM**   1976   The effects of a community psychiatric service on the mental hospital population in Jamaica. *W I Med J* 25(2), June: 101-106.
                                                                          [*RIS*]

Hoetink, Harry
9.0076   **GC**   1965   Contemporary research; the Caribbean family and its relation to the concept of mental health.

Hylson-Smith, K.
18.0150   **GC,UK** 1968   A study of immigrant group relations in North London.

Jelliffe, D. B.
31.0077   **JM**   1954   Mongolism in Jamaican children. *W I Med J* 3(3), Sept.: 164-165. **[28]**   [*COL*]

Joseph, A.
31.0078   **TR**   1963   Problems of the Trinidad adolescent. *In* Carter, Samuel E., ed. THE ADOLESCENT IN THE CHANGING CARIBBEAN: PROCEEDINGS OF THE THIRD CARIBBEAN CONFERENCE FOR MENTAL HEALTH, APR. 4-11, 1961, UCWI, JAMAICA. Kingston, The Herald, p.38-40. **[33]** [*RIS*]

Kendall, W. E., ed.
31.0079   **GC**   1957   Constructive mental hygiene in the Caribbean. PROCEEDINGS OF THE FIRST CARIBBEAN CONFERENCE ON MENTAL HEALTH. March 14-19, 1957, Aruba, Netherlands Antilles, Assen, Netherlands, Royal Van Gorcum, 176p. **[33]**   [*RIS*]

Kerr, Madeline

31.0080	JM	1953	Some areas in transition: Jamaica. *Phylon* 14(4), Dec.: 410-412. **[16]** [*COL*]
31.0081	JM	1955	The study of personality deprivation through projection tests. *Social Econ Stud* 4(1), Mar.: 83-94. [*RIS*]
31.0082	JM	1963	PERSONALITY AND CONFLICT IN JAMAICA. 2d ed. London, Collins, 221p. [*RIS*]

Kiev, Ari

31.0083	JM,UK	1963	Beliefs and delusions of West Indian immigrants to London. *Br J Psych* 109(460), May: 356-363. **[18,23]** [*RIS*]
31.0084	BC,UK	1964	Psychiatric illness among West Indians in London. *Race* 5(3), Jan.: 48-54. **[18]** [*RIS*]
18.0167	BC,UK	1964	Psychotherapeutic aspects of Pentecostal sects among West Indian immigrants to England.
18.0168	BC,UK	1965	Psychiatric morbidity of West Indian immigrants in an urban group practice.
23.0160	JM	1969	Ras Tafari.

Kruijer, G. J.

31.0085	SM,SE,ST	1953	St. Martin and St. Eustatius Negroes as compared with those of St. Thomas: a study of personality and culture. *W I G* 34(4): 225-237. **[11]** [*RIS*]
8.0121	JM	1957	The impact of poverty and undernourishment on man and society in rural Jamaica.

Lee, George W.

31.0086	GC	1970	Sheltered facilities and occupation for the mentally handicapped. *In* Thorburn, Marigold J., ed. MENTAL RETARDATION IN THE CARIBBEAN: NEEDS, RESOURCES, APPROACHES. PROCEEDINGS OF THE FIRST CARIBBEAN MENTAL RETARDATION CONFERENCE, MONA, JAMAICA. Jamaica, The Jamaica Association for Mentally Handicapped Children: 39-41. **[33]** [*TCL*]

Lefley, Harriet P.

31.0087	BA	1972	Modal personality in the Bahamas. *J Cross-Cult Psychol* 3(2), June: 135-147. **[20,26]** [*TCL*]

Levy, Roy

31.0088	GC	1963	The doctor looks at the adolescent. *In* Carter, Samuel E., ed. THE ADOLESCENT IN THE CHANGING CARIBBEAN: PROCEEDINGS OF THE THIRD CARIBBEAN CONFERENCE FOR MENTAL HEALTH, APR. 4-11, 1961, UCWI, JAMAICA. Kingston, The Herald, p.43-44. [*RIS*]

Lewis, L. F. E.

31.0089	TR	1953	Psychiatry in relation to the general practitioner. *Car Med J* 15(1-2): 40-46. **[28]** [*COL*]
31.0090	TR	1956	The use of chlorpromazine and of serpasil in the treatment of psychotic patients. *Car Med J* 18(1-2): 51-66. **[28]** [*COL*]
31.0091	GC	1957	Lecture on First Caribbean Conference on Mental Health held at Aruba on 14th-19th March, 1957. *Car Med J* 19(1-2): 53-59. [*COL*]

Lewis, Thomas H.

31.0092   SR   1975   A culturally patterned depression in a mother after loss of a child. *Psychiatry* 38(1), Feb.: 92-95. **[9,13,28,29]**   [*PS*]

Lloyd-Still, R. M.

31.0093   BB   1955   Folie à deux: report of two cases. *W I Med J* 4(2), June: 129-131.   [*COL*]

31.0094   BC   1955   The mental hospital. *Car Med J* 17(3-4): 135-138. **[5,28]**   [*COL*]

McCandless, Frederick D.

31.0095   GU   1968   Suicide and the communication of rage: a cross-cultural case study. *Am J Psych* 125(2), Aug.: 197-205. **[11,12,15]**   [*PS*]

McCartney, Timothy O.

31.0096   BA   1971   NEUROSES IN THE SUN. Nassau, Bahamas, Executive Ideas of the Bahamas, Ltd.: 166p. **[9,20]**   [*RIS*]

Mahabir, Rodney J.

31.0097   TR   1964   The care of the emotionally distrubed child—a brief survey. *In* REPORT OF THE CONFERENCE ON CHILD CARE IN TRINIDAD AND TOBAGO [HELD BY] TRINIDAD AND TOBAGO ASSOCIATION FOR MENTAL HEALTH, SUB-COMMITTEE ON CHILDREN AND YOUTH, COMMUNITY EDUCATION CENTRE, ST. ANN'S, APR. 18TH, 1964. [Port of Spain?] Government Printery, p.14-15. **[33]**   [*RIS*]

31.0098   TR   1965   MENTAL HEALTH ACTIVITIES—TRINIDAD AND TOBAGO. Paper presented at the Caribbean Seminar on Mental Health, Kingston, Jamaica, 5-11 September: 29p.   [*RIS*]

31.0099   TR   1965   Thoughts on adolescence. *Educ J Trin Tob* 1(1), Jan.: 5-11.   [*TCL*]

Marriott, J. A. S.

31.0100   JM   1968   Psychiatric symptomatology in Jamaican medical patients. *W I Med J* 17(2), June: 109-116. **[28]**   [*PS*]

31.0101   JM   1973   Family background and psychiatric disorders. Experience with admissions to the University Hospital of the West Indies. *Can Psych Assoc J* 18(3), June: 209-214. **[9]**   [*ACM*]

Menkman, W. R.

37.0569   CU   1930-31 Curacaosche toestanden [Curacao's conditions].

Metraux, Rhoda & Abel, Theodora M.

31.0102   MS   1957   Normal and deviant behavior in a peasant community: Montserrat, B.W.I. *Am J Orth-Psych* 27(1), Jan.: 167-184. **[10,20]**

Meyer, A.

31.0103   MT,CU   1968   Superstition and magic in the Caribbean—some psychiatric consequences. *Psych Neurol Neurochi* 71(5), Sept.-Oct.: 421-434. **[23]**   [*PS*]

21.0063   CU   1969   Enige socio-psychologische opmerkingen over Curaçao [Some sociopsychological remarks about Curaçao].

21.0064   NA   1973   De Antilliaanse persoonlijkheid [The Antillean personality].

Mischel, Walter

31.0104   TR   1961   Delay of gratification, need for achievement and acquiescence in another culture. *J Ab Social Psychol* 62(3), May: 543-552.   [*RIS*]

| 31.0105 | TR | 1961 | Father-absence and delay of gratification: cross-cultural comparisons. *J Ab Social Psychol* 63(1), July: 116-124. **[9]**   [*RIS*] |
| 31.0106 | TR | 1961 | Preference for delayed reinforcement and social responsibility. *J Ab Social Psychol* 62(1): 1-7.   [*RIS*] |

Mischel, Walter & Mischel, Frances
| 31.0107 | TR | 1958 | Psychological aspects of spirit possession. *Am Anthrop* 60(2, pt. 1), Apr.: 249-260. **[23]**   [*COL*] |

Moyston, B.
| 31.0108 | JM | 1963 | Problems of the Jamaican adolescent. *In* Carter, Samuel E., ed. THE ADOLESCENT IN THE CHANGING CARIBBEAN: PROCEEDINGS OF THE THIRD CARIBBEAN CONFERENCE FOR MENTAL HEALTH, APR. 4-11, 1961, UCWI, JAMAICA. Kingston, The Herald, p.41-42. **[20]** [*RIS*] |

Munroe, Robert L. & Munroe, Ruth H.
| 31.0109 | BZ | 1971 | Male pregnancy symptoms and cross-sex identity in three societies. *J Social Psychol* 84(1), June: 11-25. **[11]**   [*COL*] |

Murphy, H. B. M. & Sampath, H. M.
| 31.0110 | ST | 1967 | MENTAL ILLNESS IN A CARIBBEAN COMMUNITY: A MENTAL HEALTH SURVEY OF ST. THOMAS, V.I. Montreal, McGill University, Department of Psychiatry: 145p.   [*RIS*] |

Murray-Aynsley, J.
| 31.0111 | BB | 1965 | Mental health in Barbados. Paper presented at the Caribbean Seminar on Mental Health, Kingston, Jamaica, 5-11 September: 3p.   [*RIS*] |

Nalin, D. R.
| 31.0112 | GU | 1973 | Epidemic of suicide by malathion poisoning in Guyana. Report of 264 cases. *Trop Geogr Med* 25(1), March: 8-14. **[12,28]**   [*PS*] |

Neehall, John
| 31.0113 | TR | 1970 | The families of mentally handicapped children in Trinidad. *In* Thorburn, Marigold J., ed. MENTAL RETARDATION IN THE CARIBBEAN: NEEDS, RESOURCES, APPROACHES. PROCEEDINGS OF THE FIRST CARIBBEAN MENTAL RETARDATION CONFERENCE, MONA, JAMAICA. Jamaica, The Jamaica Association for Mentally Handicapped Children: 45-48. **[9]**   [*TCL*] |

Nicol, A. R.
| 31.0114 | GC | 1971 | Psychiatric disorder in the children of Caribbean immigrants. *J Child Psychol Psych* 12, Dec.: 273-287. **[18]**   [*PS*] |

O'Mard, C. M.
| 31.0115 | AT | 1963 | Special problems of the senior school child in Antigua. *In* Carter, Samuel E., ed. THE ADOLESCENT IN THE CHANGING CARIBBEAN: PROCEEDINGS OF THE THIRD CARIBBEAN CONFERENCE FOR MENTAL HEALTH, APR. 4-11, 1961, UCWI, JAMAICA. Kingston, The Herald, p.117-120. **[20,32]**   [*RIS*] |

Owen, G. H.

31.0116 JM 1963 Vocational guidance and education for adolescents. *In* Carter, Samuel E., ed. THE ADOLESCENT IN THE CHANGING CARIBBEAN: PROCEEDINGS OF THE THIRD CARIBBEAN CONFERENCE FOR MENTAL HEALTH, APR. 4-11, 1961, UCWI, JAMAICA. Kingston, The Herald, p.181-183. **[32,33]**   [*RIS*]

Pineau, A.

28.1018 GD 1960 Médecine et psychiatrie rurale en Guadeloupe [Rural medicine and psychiatry in Guadeloupe]. *Concours Méd* 82(4).

28.1019 GD 1960 Médecine et psychiatrie rurale en Guadeloupe [Rural medicine and psychiatry in Guadeloupe]. *Concours Méd* 82(5).

Pinto, Heather

31.0117 TR 1965[?] Group therapy among alcoholics. *In* Family relationships [proceedings of the] Fourth Caribbean Conference for Mental Health, Curacao, Apr. 16-23, 1963, Netherlands Antilles. [Willemstad? Boek- en Offset Drukkerij "De Curacaosche Courant"] p.169-176. **[33]**   [*RIS*]

Prince, Raymond

23.0238 JM 1969 The Ras Tafari of Jamaica: a study of group beliefs and social stress.

Prince, Raymond; Greenfield, Rochelle & Marriott, John

33.0154 JM 1972 Cannabis or alcohol? Observations on their use in Jamaica.

Rauch, Ralph Jerome

31.0118 SK 1968 SOME SOCIOLOGICAL DETERMINANTS OF A MENTAL HEALTH PROGRAM ON THE ISLAND OF ST. KITTS. Ph.D. dissertation, Yale University: 158p. **[8]**

Raveau, F. H. M.

18.0238 FC 1967 Caste and race in the psychodynamics of acculturation.

Reisel, J. H.

28.1057 NA 1969 Epidemiological and psychosomatic aspects in essential hypertension.

Ribstein, Michel

31.0119 MT 1963 Juvenile delinquency in Martinique. *In* Carter, Samuel E., ed. THE ADOLESCENT IN THE CHANGING CARIBBEAN: PROCEEDINGS OF THE THIRD CARIBBEAN CONFERENCE FOR MENTAL HEALTH, APR. 4-11, 1961, UCWI, JAMAICA. Kingston, The Herald, p.150-152. **[33]**
[*RIS*]

Ribstein, Michel; Certhoux, A. & Lavenaire, A.

31.0120 MT 1967 Alcoolisme au rhum: étude de la symptomologie et analyse de la personalité de l'homme martiniquais alcoolique au rhum [Alcoholism caused by rum. Study of the symptomatology and analysis of the personality of the male rum alcoholic of Martinique]. *Ann Medicopsychol* 125(4), April: 537-548. **[28]**   [*PS*]

Richardson, Stephen A.; Birch, H. G. & Ragbeer, C.

30.0204   JM   1975   The behaviour of children at home who were severely malnourished in the first 2 years of life.

Roberts, Arthur C. & Russell, Nicholas C.

31.0121   TR   1969   Social sequelae of suicide attempts: a comparative study of two ethnic groups in Trinidad. *In* PAPERS OF THE FIRST CARIBBEAN PSYCHIATRIC ASSOCIATION MEETING, OCHO RIOS, JAMAICA: 6p. **[11,12]**   [*RIS*]

Rodgers, William B. & Long, J. M.

9.0129   BA   1968   Male models and sexual identification: a case from Out Island Bahamas.

Roeher, G. Allan

31.0122   GC   1970   The adjustment of the community to the mentally retarded. *In* Thorburn, Marigold J., ed. MENTAL RETARDATION IN THE CARIBBEAN: NEEDS, RESOURCES, APPROACHES. PROCEEDINGS OF THE FIRST CARIBBEAN MENTAL RETARDATION CONFERENCE, MONA, JAMAICA. Jamaica, The Jamaica Association for Mentally Handicapped Children: 51-54. **[33]**   [*TCL*]

Rowe, Richard R. & Thorndike, Robert L.

31.0123   UV   1963   VIRGIN ISLANDS INTELLIGENCE TESTING SURVEY. New York, Institute of Psychological Research, Teachers College, Columbia University, 104p. **[32]**   [*TCL*]

Royes, K. C.

31.0124   JM   1963   Adolescents seeking psychiatric advice. *In* Carter, Samuel E., ed. THE ADOLESCENT IN THE CHANGING CARIBBEAN: PROCEEDINGS OF THE THIRD CARIBBEAN CONFERENCE FOR MENTAL HEALTH, APR. 4-11, 1961, UCWI, JAMAICA. Kingston, The Herald, p.145-146.
                                                                    [*RIS*]
31.0125   JM   1965   Mental health in Jamaica. Paper presented at the Caribbean Seminar on Mental Health, Kingston, Jamaica, 5-11 September: 11p.   [*RIS*]
31.0126   JM   1966   Bellevue Hospital, Kingston, Jamaica. *Jam Nurse* 6(3), Dec.: 19-22 passim. **[5]**   [*AJN*]

Rubin, Vera

21.0083   TR   1959   Approaches to the study of national characteristics in a multi-cultural society.
31.0127   TR   1963   The adolescent: his expectations and his society. *In* Carter, Samuel E., ed. THE ADOLESCENT IN THE CHANGING CARIBBEAN: PROCEEDINGS OF THE THIRD CARIBBEAN CONFERENCE FOR MENTAL HEALTH, APR. 4-11, 1961, UCWI, JAMAICA. Kingston, The Herald, p.56-67. **[9,20,32,33]**   [*RIS*]
31.0128   GC   1963   Report on the census of Caribbean mental hospitals. *In* Carter, Samuel E., ed. THE ADOLESCENT IN THE CHANGING CARIBBEAN: PROCEEDINGS OF THE THIRD CARIBBEAN CONFERENCE FOR MENTAL HEALTH, APR. 4-11, 1961, UCWI, JAMAICA. Kingston, The Herald, p.224-228. **[28]**   [*RIS*]
9.0134   GC   1965[?] The West Indian family retrospect and prospect.

Rubin, Vera & Comitas, Lambros
33.0170   **JM**   1976   GANJA IN JAMAICA: THE EFFECTS OF MARIJUANA USE.

Rutter, Michael; Yule, William; Berger, Michael; Yule, Bridget; Morton, Janis & Bagley, Christopher
9.0136   **BC,UK**   1974   Children of West Indian immigrants: I. Rates of behavioural deviance and of psychiatric disorder.

Sampath, H. M.
31.0129   **ST**   1969   Suicide and attempted suicide in a Caribbean resort island: a cross-cultural study of St. Thomas—U.S. Virgin Islands. Paper presented at the Joint Meeting of the American Psychiatric Association and the Caribbean Psychiatric Association, Jamaica Hilton, Ocho Rios, May 13: 37p.   [*RIS*]

Schaffner, Bertram
31.0130   **GC**   1959   Progress in mental health in the Caribbean. *Caribbean* 13(2), Feb.: 26-29, 44.   [*COL*]
31.0131   **GC**   1963   Special problems in setting up a mental health programme in an international region: the Caribbean. *Wld Ment Heal* 15(2): 80-90.   [*RIS*]

Scott, John P.
31.0132   **UV**   1963   Recreation programs for adolescents in the Virgin Islands. *In* Carter, Samuel E., ed. THE ADOLESCENT IN THE CHANGING CARIBBEAN: PROCEEDINGS OF THE THIRD CARIBBEAN CONFERENCE FOR MENTAL HEALTH, APR. 4-11, 1961, UCWI, JAMAICA. Kingston, The Herald, p.124-125.   **[33]**   [*RIS*]

Sereno, Renzo
23.0266   **GC**   1948   Obeah: magic and social structure in the Lesser Antilles.

Shillingford, Dorian
31.0133   **DM**   1965   MENTAL HEALTH IN DOMINICA. Paper presented at the Caribbean Seminar on Mental Health, Kingston, Jamaica, 5-11 September: 3p.   [*RIS*]

Singer, Philip; Aarons, Louis & Araneta, Enrique
31.0134   **GU**   1967   Integration of indigenous healing practices of the Kali cult with Western psychiatric modalities in British Guana. *Revta Interam Psicol* 1(2), June: 103-113.   **[29]**   [*RIS*]

Smith, M. G.
8.0215   **JM**   1963   Aimless, wandering adolescent groups.

Spencer, D. J.
31.0135   **BA**   1970   Cannabis induced psychoses. *W I Med J* 19(4), Dec.: 228-230.   **[29,33]**   [*PS*]
31.0136   **BA**   1972   Suicide in the Bahamas. *W I Med J* 21(2), June: 119-124.   [*PS*]

Stewart-Prince, G.
18.0266   **BC,UK**   1972   Mental health problems in pre-school West Indian children.

Stoffle, Richard William
8.0229   BB   1969   Barbadian social networks: an analysis of male clique and family participation.

St. Pierre, Maurice
46.0221   GU   1967   The sociology of work in a Guyanese mining town.

Tancock, Catherine Bridget
18.0269   BB,US   1961   A study of household structure and child training in a lower class Barbadian group.

Teresa, Joan
32.0564   TR   1966   Education of mentally deficient children.

Thorburn, Marigold J.
33.0192   JM   1972   Facilities for the mentally retarded in Jamaica: a report on the present situation.

Thorburn, Marigold J., ed.
31.0137   GC   1970   Mental retardation in the Caribbean: needs, resources, approaches. Proceedings of the First Caribbean Mental Retardation Conference, Mona, Jamaica. Jamaica, The Jamaica Association for Mentally Handicapped Children: 62p.   [33]   [TCL]

Tidrick, Kathryn
31.0138   JM   1973   Skin shade and need for achievement in a multiracial society: Jamaica, West Indies. *J Social Psychol* 89(1), Feb.: 25-33.   [20]
                                                                                                   [COL]

Triseliotis, J. P.
18.0275   BC,UK   1968   Psycho-social problems of immigrant families.

Turfboer, R.
33.0198   AR   1970   The typical Aruban alcoholic in the nineteen fifties.

Walters, Elsa H.
32.0589   GC   1963   Training the teacher to work with adolescents.

Webb, R. A. J.
31.0139   BB   1961   Characteristics of first admissions to a mental hospital: a preliminary report. *W I Med J* 10(4), Dec.: 276-279.   [COL]

Weinstein, Helen S. & Weinstein, Edwin A.
31.0140   UV   1965[?]   Gender role and family relationships. *In* Family relationships: [proceedings of the] Fourth Caribbean Conference for Mental Health, Curacao, Apr. 16-23, 1963, Netherlands Antilles. [Willemstad? Boek- en Offset Drukkerij "De Curacaosche Courant"], p.107-113.   [9]   [RIS]

Welsh, Bronte
31.0141   KNA   1965[?]   Paper on mental health and family relationship. *In* Family relationships: [proceedings of the] Fourth Caribbean Conference for Mental Health, Curacao, Apr. 16-23, 1963, Netherlands Antilles. [Willemstad? Boek- en Offset Drukkerij "De Curacaosche Courant"], p.177-180.   [9]   [RIS]

Wever, O. R.

33.0213   **AR**   1970   Some medical and sociopathological aspects of alcoholism in Aruba and its actual treatment.

Windt, H. L. de

33.0220   **NA**   1970   Neuropsychiatric aspects of alcoholism in the Netherlands Antilles, especially referring to Aruba.

Winkel, C. M.

31.0142   **CU**   1965   Mental health in Curaćao. Paper presented at the Caribbean Seminar on Mental Health, Kingston, Jamaica, 5-11 September: 5p.
                                                                                        [*RIS*]

31.0143   **NA**   1973   Geestelijke gezondheidszorg [Mental health care]. *In* Statius van Eps, L. W. & Luckman-Maduro, E., eds. VAN SCHEEPSCHIRURGIJN TOT SPECIALIST. Assen, The Netherlands, Van Gorcum & Comp. B.V.: 160-162. (Anjerpublikatie 15)   [*RILA*]

Wisinger, Zoltan

31.0144   **GC**   1967   Tourism and psychiatric emergencies. *W I Med J* 16(3), Sept.: 166-170.   **[51]**   [*PS*]

Wittkower, Eric D.

31.0145   **GC**   1970   Transcultural psychiatry in the Caribbean: past, present, and future. *Am J Psych* 127(1), July: 162-166.   **[28]**   [*PS*]

Woo-Ming, Geoffrey

31.0146   **GC**   1970   The identification and assessment of mentally retarded in the Caribbean. *In* Thorburn, Marigold J., ed. MENTAL RETARDATION IN THE CARIBBEAN: NEEDS, RESOURCES, APPROACHES. PROCEEDINGS OF THE FIRST CARIBBEAN MENTAL RETARDATION CONFERENCE, MONA, JAMAICA. Jamaica, The Jamaica Association for Mentally Handicapped Children: 6-8.   [*TCL*]

Wray, Samuel R.

9.0189   **JM**   1975   Psychologically disturbed children: a comparative analysis of three clinic populations.

Yawney, Carole D.

33.0228   **TR**   1969   Drinking patterns and alcoholism in Trinidad. I. Patterns of alcohol use. II. Pathological drinkers.

Chapter 32

EDUCATION

Works that deal with various facets of formal education; cross-listed abbreviated references include children's textbooks on all subject matter.

See also: [9] Socialization, family and kinship.

Abell, Helen C.
32.0001   BC   1956   Home economics—report on a course. *Caribbean* 9(10), May: 220, 229. **[33]**   [*COL*]

Abraham-van der Mark, Eva E.
9.0002   CU   1970   Differences in the upbringing of boys and girls in Curaçao, correlated with differences in the degree of neurotic instability.

Adams, Anthony C. I.
28.0006   JM   1965   Teaching international community medicine.

Adhin, J. H.; Tuinman, J. & Witte, C. J. de
25.0003   SR   1972   NEDERLANDS VOOR DE KLEUTER IN SURINAME [DUTCH FOR THE TODDLER IN SURINAM].

Aeth, H. R. X. d'
32.0002   BC   1956   SECONDARY SCHOOLS IN THE BRITISH CARIBBEAN: AIMS AND METHODS. London, Longmans Green, 119p.   [*UNL*]

Aeth, Richard d'
32.0003   BC   1961   The growth of the University College of the West Indies. *Br J Educ Stud* 9(2), May: 99-116.   [*TCL*]

Agostini, Malcolm Allister
32.0004   GU   1972   A STUDY OF THE DIPLOMA OF EDUCATION CURRICULUM, UNIVERSITY OF GUYANA, IN RELATION TO THE PROFESSIONAL CONCERNS OF THE 1969-1971 GRADUATES. Ed.D. dissertation, State University of New York (Buffalo): 146p.   [*PhD*]

Aiken, James
32.0005   GU   1913   Some axioms of corporate education. *Timehri* 3d ser., 3(20A), Sept.: 51-62.   [*AMN*]

Alcala, V. O.

32.0006	GC	1952	Trade and industrial education. *Car Commn Mon Inf B* 6(4), Nov.: 81-83. **[45]** *[AGS]*
32.0007	GC	1953	Agricultural training. *Car Commn Mon Inf B* 6(8), Mar.: 176-178. **[43]** *[AGS]*
46.0005	GC	1953	Apprenticeship and on-the-job training.
32.0008	GC	1953	Business education. *Car Commn Mon Inf B* 6(10), May: 223-224, 230. **[41]** *[COL]*
32.0009	GC	1953	Home economics education in the Caribbean. *Car Commn Mon Inf B* 6(9), Apr.: 199-201. **[33]** *[AGS]*
32.0010	GC	1953	Services and benefits of guidance. *Car Commn Mon Inf B* 7(5), Dec.: 103-104. **[41]** *[COL]*
32.0011	GC	1953	Survey of existing facilities for vocational training in the Caribbean. *In* DEVELOPMENT OF VOCATIONAL EDUCATION IN THE CARIBBEAN. Port of Spain, Caribbean Commission, p.5-24. **[43]** *[RIS]*
32.0012	GC	1954	Caribbean education. *Car Commn Mon Inf B* 8(3), Oct.: 54-55, 58-60. *[COL]*
32.0013	FA	1954	French Caribbean education. *Car Commn Mon Inf B* 7(10), May: 217-218, 235. *[COL]*

Alers, M. H.

25.0004	SR,NE	1974	TAALPROBLEMEN VAN SURINAAMSE KINDEREN IN NEDERLAND [LANGUAGE PROBLEMS OF SURINAMESE CHILDREN IN THE NETHERLANDS].

Alexander, George

50.0005	JM	1974	CECE approaches to pupil assessment in early childhood education.

Alexis, Bertille

7.0006	BC	1970	THE RELATIONSHIP BETWEEN THE EXISTING HUMAN RESOURCES PROBLEMS AND EDUCATION, TRAINING AND EMPLOYMENT OPPORTUNITY.

Alfrey, Phyllis Shand

33.0006	BC	1963	Social education in the West Indies.

Alladin, M. P.

32.0014	GC	1968	Research in arts and crafts. *In* PAPERS PRESENTED AT THE PRIORITIES IN EDUCATIONAL RESEARCH SEMINAR, 2-3 MAY, 1968. Trinidad, University of the West Indies: 7p. **[22]** *[RIS]*

Alleyne, Albert

32.0015	TR	1965	Problems of pre-vocational courses in Trinidad and Tobago. *Educ J Trin Tob* 1(5), Nov.: 12-16. *[TCL]*

Alleyne, Garth O'Garvin

32.0016	TR	1973	A LINEAR PROGRAMMING MODEL OF EDUCATIONAL PLANNING FOR TRINIDAD AND TOBAGO, 1968-1975. Ph.D. dissertation, University of California (Los Angeles): 286p. *[PhD]*

Alleyne, Michael

32.0017	TR	1969	A STUDY OF SECONDARY EDUCATION IN THE DEVELOPMENT OF TRINIDAD AND TOBAGO. Ph.D. dissertation, Claremont Graduate School: 227p. *[PhD]*
32.0018	TR	1972	Educational planning in Trinidad and Tobago. *Car Stud* 11(4), Jan.: 73-81. *[RIS]*

Anderson, Betty

32.0019   SL   1962   Literacy teaching. *In* Brown, John, ed. AN APPROACH TO ADULT
                      EDUCATION. Castries, St. Lucia, Govt. Print. Off., p.20-23.   **[25]**
                                                                              [RIS]

Anderson, Kenneth Vivian McLean

32.0020   JM   1972   AN ANALYSIS OF CERTAIN FACTORS AFFECTING THE SCHOLASTIC
                      ACHIEVEMENT OF LOWER SOCIO-ECONOMIC AS COMPARED WITH MID-
                      DLE SOCIO-ECONOMIC CHILDREN IN JAMAICA. Ann Arbor, Michigan,
                      University Microfilms: 159p. (Ed.D. dissertation, Cornell Univer-
                      sity, 1966)   **[8]**   *[RIS]*

Anderson, L. E.

32.0021   JM   1972   Philosophy of education in a Jamaican teachers' college. *Torch*
                      21(3), Christmas, 19-29.   *[RIS]*

32.0022   JM   1973   AUTHORITARIANISM AND ACHIEVEMENT IN A JAMAICA TEACHERS'
                      COLLEGE. Ph.D. dissertation, University of the West Indies.   **[20]**

Anderson, Wolseley Wellington

32.0023   GU   1971   FACTORS INFLUENCING PUBLIC EXPENDITURE ON EDUCATION IN
                      GUYANA (1953-1967). Ph.D. dissertation, University of Toron-
                      to.   **[33]**   *[PhD]*

Andic, Fuat M.

32.0024   GC   1968   THE EFFORTS OF THE INSTITUTE OF CARIBBEAN STUDIES FOR COOP-
                      ERATION AMONG THE UNIVERSITIES OF THE REGION: COMMUNIQUE AT
                      THE CONFERENCE OF THE INSTITUTE VIZIOZ. LES EFFORTS DE
                      L'INSTITUT D'ETUDES DES CARAÏBES POUR LA COOPERATION ENTRE
                      LES UNIVERSITÉS DE LA RÉGION: COMMUNIQUÉ POUR LA CONFERENCE
                      DE L'INSTITUT VIZIOZ. University of Puerto Rico, Institute of
                      Caribbean Studies: 13p.   **[38]**   *[RIS]*

Archer, Douglas Kentish

32.0025   JM   1973   THE EDUCATIONAL SYSTEM AND NATION BUILDING IN JAMAICA
                      (1944-70). Ph.D. dissertation, Northwestern University: 159p.   **[2]**
                                                                              [PhD]

Archimède

28.0042   GD   1965   L'hygiène scolaire dans le département de la Guadeloupe. Bilan
                      général de l'année scolaire 1962-1963 [School hygiene in the
                      department of Guadeloupe. General review of the 1962-1963 school
                      year].

Asbeck, W. D. H. van

23.0005   SR   1919   De Evangelische of Moravische Broeder-Gemeente in Suriname
                      [The Evangelical or Moravian Brethern in Surinam].

32.0026   US,SR   1921-22   Negers en onderwijs in de Vereenigde Staten van America [Negroes
                      and education in the U.S.A.]. *W I G* 3: 650-664.   **[11,18]**   *[COL]*

Ashcraft, Norman

32.0027   BZ   1970   Educación y desarrollo económico en Honduras Británica [Edu-
                      cation and economic development in British Honduras]. *América
                      Indígena* 30(2), April: 395-408.   **[41]**   *[NYP]*

32.0028   BZ   1972   Educational planning in a developing society—the case of British
                         Honduras. *Car Q* 18(3), Sept.: 23-33.   [*RIS*]

Ashcraft, Norman & Grant, Cedric
32.0029   BZ   1968   The development and organization of education in British Hon-
                         duras. *Comp Educ Rev* 12(2), June: 171-179.   [*COL*]

Ashcroft, M. T. & Antrobus, A. C. K.
27.0007   SV,GC   1970   Heights and weights of schoolchildren in St. Vincent.

Ashcroft, M. T.; Buchanan, I. C. & Lovell, H. G.
27.0011   KNA   1965   Heights and weights of primary schoolchildren in St. Christopher-
                         Nevis-Anguilla, West Indies.

Ashcroft, M. T. & Lovell, H. G.
27.0015   JM   1965   Changes in mean size of children in some Jamaican schools
                         between 1951 and 1964.
27.0016   JM   1966   Heights and weights of Jamaican primary schoolchildren.
27.0017   JM   1966   The validity of surveys of heights and weights of Jamaican
                         schoolchildren.

Ashcroft, M. T.; Lovell, H. G.; George, M. & Williams, A.
27.0018   JM   1965   Heights and weights of infants and children in a rural community of
                         Jamaica.

Ashcroft, M. T.; Urquhart, A. E. & Gentle, G. H. K.
28.0060   JM   1965   Treponemal serological tests in Jamaican school children.

Ashruf, G. J.; Dors, H. G.; Eersel, Chr. H.; Sietaram, K.; Muntslag, F. G. &
Chin A Foeng, J. A.
25.0020   SR   1972   PRATEN EN SCHRIJVEN: KLAS 2, DEEL A. [TALKING AND WRITING:
                         CLASS 2, VOLUME A].

Asquith, Justice et al.
32.0030   BC   1945   REPORT OF THE COMMISSION ON HIGHER EDUCATION IN THE
                         COLONIES. London, H.M.S.O. 119p. (Cmd. 6647.)   [*COL*]

Augustus, Earl
46.0013   TR   1967[?]   CIPRIANI LABOUR COLLEGE: RELATED DOCUMENTS.

Bacchus, Kassim
32.0031   BC   1969   Education and decolonization. *New Wld Q* 5(1-2), Dead Season-
                         Croptime: 63-73.   **[37]**   [*RIS*]

Bacchus, M. K.
32.0032   GU   1966   Social factors in secondary school selection in British Guiana.
                         Social Econ Stud 15(1), March: 40-52.   [*RIS*]
32.0033   BC   1967   The development of educational planning with special reference to
                         the West Indies—I. *Tchr Educ* 7(3), Feb.: 221-231.   [*TCL*]
32.0034   GU   1968   A quantitative assessment of the levels of education required in
                         Guyana by 1975. *Social Econ Stud* 17(2), June: 178-196. **[46]**
                                                                                  [*RIS*]
32.0035   GU   1969   Patterns of educational expenditure in an emergent nation: a study
                         of Guyana 1945-65. *Social Econ Stud* 18(3), Sept.: 282-301. **[41]**
                                                                                  [*RIS*]

| 32.0036 | GU | 1970 | EDUCATION AND SOCIO-CULTURAL INTEGRATION IN A "PLURAL" SOCIETY. Montreal, McGill University, Centre for Developing-Area Studies: 42p. (Occasional Paper Series No. 6) **[8]**   [*COL*] |

| 32.0037 | GU | 1971 | Changing attitudes to educational expenditure in a developing nation. *Social Econ Stud* 20(2), June: 164-175.   [*RIS*] |

Bacus, M. Kazim

| 32.0038 | GU | 1974 | The primary school curriculum in a colonial society. *J Curric Stud* 6(1), May: 15-29. **[20]**   [*TCL*] |

Bagley, Christopher

| 18.0009 | BC,UK | 1968 | The educational performance of immigrant children. |
| 18.0010 | BC,UK | 1971 | A comparative study of social environment and intelligence in West Indian and English children in London. |

Bagley, Christopher & Verma, Gajendra K.

| 16.0002 | BC,UK | 1975 | Inter-ethnic attitudes and behaviour in British multi-racial schools. |

Baier, Erich G.

| 32.0039 | NA | 1974 | A new conception of workers' education for the Netherlands Antilles. *Kristòf* 1(6), Dec.: 272-279. **[46]**   [*RIS*] |

Bailey, Beryl Loftman

25.0023	JM	1962	A LANGUAGE GUIDE TO JAMAICA.
25.0024	GC	1962	Language studies in the independent university.
32.0040	JM	1963	Teaching of English noun-verb concord in primary schools in Jamaica. *Car Q* 9(4), Dec.: 10-14. **[25]** [*RIS*]
25.0026	JM	1966[?]	Some problems involved in the language teaching situation in Jamaica.

Bain, Rodney

| 23.0007 | BA | 1967 | Missionary activity in the Bahamas, 1700-1830. |

Baksh, Ahamad

| 8.0008 | GU | 1974 | The mobility of degree level graduates of the University of Guyana. |

Baksh, Ishmael

32.0041	TR	1974	SOME FACTORS RELATED TO EDUCATIONAL EXPECTATION AMONG EAST INDIAN AND NEGRO STUDENTS ATTENDING PUBLIC SECONDARY SCHOOL IN TRINIDAD. Ph.D. dissertation, University of Alberta (Canada): 251p. **[8,11,12,20]**
32.0042	TR	1975	The development of public secondary education in Trinidad and Tobago. *Int Educ* 4(1): 10-19. [*TCL*]
32.0043	TR	1975	Selected variables and educational expectation among high school students in Trinidad. *Car J Educ* 2(2), Dec.: 87-100. **[20]** [*RIS*]

Bancroft, C. K.

| 45.0007 | GU,SR | 1917 | The making of panama hats: a suitable industry for British Guiana. |

Bannister, A. A.

| 32.0044 | GU | 1951 | Amerindian education in British Guiana. *Timehri* 4th ser., 1(30), Nov.: 57-59. **[13]** |

Barnes, S.

28.0079   SR   1968   Malaria eradication in Surinam; prospects of success after five years of health education.

Baron van Lynden, W. E. K.

43.0016   SR   1932-33 Landbouwvoorlichting en landbouwonderwijs in Suriname [Agricultural guidance and agricultural education in Surinam].

Barteau, Harry Carman

32.0045   GC   1973   LATIN AMERICAN STUDIES PROGRAMS IN AMERICAN-SPONSORED INDEPENDENT SCHOOLS IN THE CARIBBEAN REGION. Ph.D. dissertation, Miami University: 149p.   [*PhD*]

Bastien, J. V.

32.0046   TR   1965   Social studies. *Educ J Trin Tob* 1(2), March: 11-14.   [*TCL*]

Baugh, Edward

32.0047   BC   1970   English studies in the University of the West Indies: retrospect and prospect. *Car Q* 16(4), Dec.: 48-60.   [*RIS*]

Beals, Paul Wiley

32.0048   BZ   1973   A STUDY OF EDUCATIONAL AND OCCUPATIONAL PERCEPTIONS IN BELIZE (BRITISH HONDURAS), CENTRAL AMERICA. Ph.D. dissertation, George Peabody College for Teachers: 226p.   [*PhD*]

Beetham, David

18.0023   BC,UK 1967   IMMIGRANT SCHOOL LEAVERS AND THE YOUTH EMPLOYMENT SERVICE IN BIRMINGHAM.

Bell, Wendell

8.0011   JM   1965   Social change and elites in an emergent nation.

Benítez, Jaime

32.0049   GC   1968   CRISIS EN EL MUNDO Y EN LA EDUCACIÓN [THE WORLD AND THE EDUCATIONAL CRISIS]. Puerto Rico, Conference of the Caribbean Universities, Nov. 21-23: 7-17.   [*RIS*]

Benn, Bernard W.

32.0050   TR   1967   THE INFLUENCE OF THE CAMBRIDGE EXAMINATIONS ON THE TEACHING OF ENGLISH LANGUAGE IN THE APPROVED SECONDARY SCHOOLS OF TRINIDAD. Ed.D. dissertation, Teachers College, Columbia University, New York: 137p.   [*TCL*]

32.0051   BC   1971   Metropolitan standards and their effects on Caribbean teaching. *Car Stud* 11(2), July: 85-89.   **[25]**   [*RIS*]

Bennett, B. A.

18.0025   BC   1966   Journey to the West Indies.

Bennett, J. Harry, Jr.

32.0052   BB   1950   Sir John Gay Alleyne and the Mansion School, Codrington College, 1775-1797. *J Barb Mus Hist Soc* 17(2-3), Feb.-May: 63-78.   **[5]**

[*AMN*]

Bennett, Joseph

32.0053   BZ   1973   Aspects of educational development in Belize, 1935-1965. *J Beliz Aff* 2, Dec.: 66-88. **[5]**   *[RIS]*

32.0054   BZ   1973   Some aspects of educational development in Belize, 1915-1935. *J Beliz Aff* 1, June: 14-30. **[5]**   *[RIS]*

Bennett, P. S.

32.0055   JM   1973   Farming. *Torch* 22(1), Easter: 11-15. **[43]**   *[RIS]*

Bent, R. A.; Clough, G. H. & Jordan, R. S.

32.0056   LW,WW   1966   ECONOMIC DEVELOPMENT IN THE EASTERN CARIBBEAN ISLANDS. (SERIES 3: EDUCATION.) University of the West Indies, Institute of Social and Economic Research (Eastern Caribbean). **[41]**   *[RIS]*

Bent, Rupert

32.0057   JM   1963   Provision for the education of the adolescent in Jamaica. *In* Carter, Samuel E., ed. THE ADOLESCENT IN THE CHANGING CARIBBEAN: PROCEEDINGS OF THE THIRD CARIBBEAN CONFERENCE FOR MENTAL HEALTH, APR. 4-11, 1961; UCWI, JAMAICA. Kingston, The Herald, p.113-116.   *[RIS]*

Bergman, Jim & Coard, Bernard

18.0026   BC,UK   1972   Trials and tribulations of a self-help group.

Best, Lloyd

32.0058   GC   1965   Working notes toward a system of higher education in the W.I. —Part 1. *New Wld F* 1(10), March 19: 13-22.   *[RIS]*

32.0059   GC   1965   Working notes toward a system of higher education in the W.I. —Part 2. *New Wld F* 1(11), April 2: 15-25.   *[RIS]*

Bhatnagar, Joti

18.0027   BC,UK   1970   IMMIGRANTS AT SCHOOL.

Bickel, Wanda Lea

32.0060   JM   1972   AN ANALYTICAL AND DEVELOPMENTAL STUDY OF THE EDUCATIONAL PROGRAMS AND PLANS FOR JAMAICA. Ph.D. dissertation, St. Louis University: 284p.   *[PhD]*

Bindley, T. Herbert

32.0061   BB   1910   The evolution of a colonial college. *Natn Rev* 55(329), July: 847-857. **[5]**   *[NYP]*

Binney, E. M.

32.0062   GC   1966   CARIBBEAN THINKING EXERCISES. London, University of London Press Ltd.: 159p.   *[RIS]*

Bird, Edris

32.0063   BC   1975   Adult education and the advancement of women in the West Indies. *Convergence* 8(1): 57-67. **[10]**   *[TCL]*

Bishop, G. D.

32.0064   JM   1962   The shortage of science teachers in underdeveloped territories. *Car Q 8(4), Dec.: 42-44.*   *[RIS]*

32.0065 BC 1964 The practice of education. *Car Q* 10(1). Mar.: 31-37. [*RIS*]

Black, Clinton V.
5.0070 JM 1973 A NEW HISTORY OF JAMAICA.

Blackman, J. E.
56.0026 GC 1919 AN OUTLINE OF THE GEOGRAPHY OF THE WEST INDIES.

Blair
32.0066 GU 1901 The system of education in British Guiana. *In* EDUCATIONAL
SYSTEMS OF THE CHIEF COLONIES OF THE BRITISH EMPIRE. London,
H.M.S.O., p.751-795. (Dominion of Canada, Newfoundland, West
Indies. Board of Education. Special reports on educational subjects,
v.4.) **[5]**   [*NYP*]

Blauch, Lloyd E. & Reid, Charles F.
32.0067 UV 1939 Education in the Virgin Islands. *In* PUBLIC EDUCATION IN THE
TERRITORIES AND OUTLYING POSSESSIONS. Washington, U.S. Govt.
Print. Off., p.133-163. (Advisory Committee on Education, Staff
study no. 16.)   [*NYP*]

Bobb, Geraldine Eudora
32.0068 TR 1975 PROFESSIONAL PREPARATION OF SECONDARY SCHOOL TEACHERS IN
TRINIDAD AND TOBAGO: IMPLICATIONS FOR CURRICULUM DESIGN
AND INSTRUCTION. Ph.D., Teachers College, Columbia University:
225p.   [*RIS*]

Boheemen, H. van
32.0069 SR 1947 Onderwijshervorming in Suriname [School reform in Surinam].
W I G 28: 353-367.   [*COL*]
32.0070 SR 1951 Surinaamse onderwijszorgen [Education Problems in Surinam].
W I G 32: 65-91. **[25]**   [*COL*]

Bolland, O. Nigel
32.0071 JM 1971 Literacy in a rural area of Jamaica. *Social Econ Stud* 20(1), March:
28-51. **[8]**   [*RIS*]

Bone, Louis W.
32.0072 GG 1962 SECONDARY EDUCATION IN THE GUIANAS. Chicago, University of
Chicago, 70p. (Comparative Education Center, Comparative education monographs, no. 2.) **[8,41]**   [*TCL*]

Boodhoo, Isaiah James
32.0073 TR 1974 A CURRICULUM MODEL IN ART EDUCATION FOR THE PRIMARY
SCHOOLS OF TRINIDAD AND TOBAGO. Ed.D. dissertation, Indiana
University: 203p. **[21,22]**   [*PhD*]

Booth, Norman H.
32.0074 TR 1958 West Indian Island. *Adult Educ* 30(4), Spring: 263-270. [*NYP*]

Borely, Clive
32.0075 TR 1966 Teaching Trinidadian(s) English. *Educ J Trin Tob* 2(2): 1-6. **[25]**
                                                                   [*TCL*]

Bowker, Gordon
18.0035   BC   1968   THE EDUCATION OF COLOURED IMMIGRANTS.

Box, Gloria & Cady, Dorothy
32.0076   JM   1969   HELPING DISABLED READERS IN THE JUNIOR SECONDARY SCHOOL: A PROGRESS REPORT ON THE WORK DONE IN JAMAICA IN 1967-68. Kingston, Jamaica, University of the West Indies, Institute of Education: 24p.   [*RIS*]

Bracken, Michael B.
28.0152   GC   1970   Health education—old wine in new medicine bottles?

Braithwaite, Lloyd E.
38.0033   BC   1957   'Federal' associations and institutions in the West Indies.
32.0077   BC   1958   The development of higher education in the British West Indies. *Social Econ Stud* 7(1), Mar.: 1-64.   **[8,20,43]**   [*RIS*]
8.0019   BC   1960   The present status of the social sciences in the British Caribbean.
32.0078   BC   1965   The role of the university in the developing society of the West Indies. *Social Econ Stud* 14(1), Mar.: 76-87.   [*RIS*]

Braithwaite, R. H.
32.0079   TR   1965   The changing face of education. *Educ J Trin Tob* 1(4), July: 28-32.
                                                                    [*TCL*]

Braun, Charles A.
32.0080   BZ   1970   AN HISTORICAL STUDY OF THE DEVELOPMENT OF TECHNICAL EDUCATION IN BRITISH HONDURAS (BELIZE). Ph.D. dissertation, Wayne State University: 162p.   [*PhD*]

Breet, Ralph R. van
32.0081   AR   1975   Doorstromingsproblematiek en demokratisering in het Arubaanse onderwijs [The problem of student flow and democratization in the Aruban educational system]. *Kristòf* 2(6), Dec.: 292-303.   [*RIS*]

Bremmer, Theodore A.
32.0082   BC   1975   Science education in the Caribbean: curricular and other concerns. *In* Singham, A. W., ed. THE COMMONWEALTH CARIBBEAN INTO THE SEVENTIES. Montreal, McGill University, Centre for Developing Area Studies: 170-178.   **[20]**   [*RIS*]

Broadway, W. E.
32.0083   TR   1934   School gardens in Trinidad and Tobago. *Proc Agric Soc Trin Tob* 34(6), June: 217-220.   **[43]**   [*AMN*]

Broomes, Desmond
32.0084   BB   1966   SENSE AND SHAPE OF EDUCATIONAL STATISTICS. Barbados, University of the West Indies, Institute of Education: 32p.   [*RIS*]
32.0085   BC   1967   A STUDY OF THE MATHEMATICS PERFORMANCES OF STUDENTS AT TEACHERS' COLLEGES IN ANTIGUA, BARBADOS, GRENADA, ST. LUCIA AND ST. VINCENT DURING 1966. Cave Hill, Barbados University of the West Indies, Institute of Education: 31p.   [*RIS*]
32.0086   SL   1974   Teacher training with special reference to teaching primary school mathematics in developing countries. *Car J Educ* 1, June: 42-51.
                                                                    [*RIS*]

32.0087   **BC,SL**   1976   Structure, form and organisation for the evaluation of curriculum. *Car J Educ* 3(1), Jan.: 22-50.   [*RIS*]

Brown, Harold W.

28.0187   **GC**   1965   Government and medicine in the Caribbean.

Brown, John

32.0088   **LW**   1961   THE MEANING OF 'EXTRA-MURAL' IN THE LEEWARD ISLANDS. *In* Brown, John, ed. LEEWARDS: WRITINGS, PAST AND PRESENT, ABOUT THE LEEWARD ISLANDS. [Bridgetown?] Barbados, Dept. of Extra-Mural Studies, Leeward Islands, University College of the West Indies, p.5-11. **[21]**   [*RIS*]

32.0089   **SL**   1962   Education and development of St. Lucia. *In* Brown, John, ed. AN APPROACH TO ADULT EDUCATION. Castries, St. Lucia, Govt. Print. Off., p.44-59. **[28,43]**   [*RIS*]

32.0090   **SL**   1962   Lines of approach to adult education. *In* Brown, John, ed. AN APPROACH TO ADULT EDUCATION. Castries, St. Lucia, Govt. Print. Off., p.1-14.   [*RIS*]

Brown, John, ed.

32.0091   **SL**   1962   AN APPROACH TO ADULT EDUCATION. Castries, St. Lucia, Govt. Print Off., 59p.   [*RIS*]

Bruinsma, John H.

28.0195   **GC**   1970   A study of the movement and location of U.W.I. medical graduates, classes 1954-1965.

Brunn, Stanley D.

32.0092   **BC**   1968   The High School Geography Project of the Association of American Geographers (Part II). *In* Floyd, Barry, ed. NEW VIEWPOINTS IN GEOGRAPHY: PROCEEDINGS OF A CONFERENCE FOR TEACHERS OF GEOGRAPHY IN THE CARIBBEAN, AUGUST 27-SEPTEMBER 1, 1967. Kingston, Jamaica, University of the West Indies, Geography Department: 36-49. **[56]**   [*AGS*]

Bullen, Jean & Livingstone, Helen F.

32.0093   **BB**   1949   Of the state and advancement of the College. *In* Klingberg, Frank J., ed. CODRINGTON CHRONICLE: AN EXPERIMENT IN ANGLICAN ALTRUISM ON A BARBADOS PLANTATION, 1710-1834. Berkeley and Los Angeles, University of California Press, p.107-122. (Publications in history no. 37.) **[42]**   [*COL*]

Buma, S.

28.0198   **NA**   1975   Het schaal-probleem in de organisatie van de volksgezondheid II [The problem of scale in the organization of public health II].

Burgin, Trevor & Edson, Patricia

18.0045   **BC,UK**   1967   SPRING GROVE: THE EDUCATION OF IMMIGRANT CHILDREN.

Burnett, Muriel M.

32.0094   **JM**   1973   Study-visit by English educators to Jamaica, October, 1972. *Torch* 22,(1), Easter: 16-20.   [*RIS*]

Butcher, LeRoi
18.0047   BC,CA   1971   The Anderson affair.

Butterworth, Eric
18.0048   BC,UK   1967   A hardening colour Bar? 3.—the school
18.0050   BC,UK   1967   The presence of immigrant schoolchildren: a study of Leeds.

Bynoe, Jacob Galton
32.0095   JM,GU   1972   SOCIAL CHANGE AND HIGH SCHOOL OPPORTUNITY IN GUYANA AND JAMAICA: 1957-1967. Ph.D. dissertation, University of British Columbia: 333p. **[8,41]**   [*NYP*]

Cadbury, George
32.0096   JM   1960   Planned education in Jamaica. *Venture* 12(4), Apr.: 4-5.   [*COL*]

Camacho, Andrew
32.0097   BC   1970   Education and educational opportunity. *In* Cross, Malcolm, ed. WEST INDIAN SOCIAL PROBLEMS: A SOCIOLOGICAL PERSPECTIVE. Port-of-Spain, Trinidad, Columbus Publishers Ltd.: 99-117.   [*RIS*]

Cameron, Norman E.
32.0098   GU   1955   Thoughts on agricultural education in British Guiana. *Timehri* 4th ser., 1(34), Sept.: 55-61. **[43]**
32.0099   GU   1961   Chronology of educational development in British Guiana from 1808 to 1957. *Timehri* 4th ser., no. 40, Oct.: 57-60. **[5]**   [*AMN*]
32.0100   GU   1968   150 YEARS OF EDUCATION IN GUYANA (1808-1957): WITH SPECIAL REFERENCE TO POST-PRIMARY EDUCATION. Georgetown, Guyana, Labour Advocate Job Printing Dept.: 90p. **[5]**   [*RIS*]

Campbell, Carl
32.0101   JM   1965   The development of vocational training in Jamaica: first steps. *Car Q* 11(1-2), March & June: 13-35. **[5]**   [*RIS*]
32.0102   BC   1967   Towards an imperial policy for the education of Negroes in the West Indies after emancipation. *Jam Hist Rev* 7(1-2): 68-102. **[5,11]**   [*RIS*]
6.0025   JM   1970   Social and economic obstacles to the development of popular education in post-emancipation Jamaica, 1834-1865.
23.0042   JM   1971   Denominationalism and the Mico Charity schools in Jamaica, 1835-1842.
32.0103   TR   1975   The establishment of Queen's Collegiate School in Trinidad 1857-1867. *Car J Educ* 2(2), Dec.: 71-86. **[5]**   [*RIS*]

Campbell, Ella
45.0027   JM   1953   Industrial training methods and techniques.

Campbell, J. S.
32.0104   TR   1962   School gardening: an integral part of primary school education in Trinidad and Tobago. *J Agric Soc Trin Tob* 62(2), June: 169-176. **[43]**   [*AMN*]

Capper, T.
32.0105   JM   1901   The system of education in Jamaica. *In* EDUCATIONAL SYSTEMS OF THE CHIEF COLONIES OF THE BRITISH EMPIRE. London, H.M.S.O., p.575-749. (Dominion of Canada, Newfoundland, West Indies. Board of Education. Special reports on educational subjects, v.4.) **[5]**   [*NYP*]

| 32.0106 | JM | 1901 | Teaching the principles of agriculture in elementary schools. *W I B* 2(1): 61-72. **[43]** [*AMN*] |
| 32.0107 | JM | 1907 | Agriculture in elementary schools of Jamaica. *W I B* 8(3): 297-301. **[43]** [*AMN*] |

Carew, Jan

32.0108   BC   1976   Identity, cultural alienation and education in the Caribbean. *Social Stud Educ* 7, June: 33-37. (Special issue: Commonwealth Caribbean Social Studies Conference Proceedings. Vol. I.) **[21,25,26]**

Carley, Mary Manning

32.0109   JM   1942   EDUCATION IN JAMAICA. Kingston, Institute of Jamaica with the assistance of Jamaica Welfare, Ltd., 30p. (Social survey series, no. 1.) [*COL*]

Carmen, Mrs.

28.0220   JM   1974   Family life education—its relevance for health workers.

Carrington, Lawrence D.

32.0110   TR   1968   Language research in Trinidad and Tobago. *In* PAPERS PRESENTED AT THE PRIORITIES IN EDUCATIONAL RESEARCH SEMINAR, 2-3 MAY, 1968. Trinidad, University of the West Indies: 5p. [*RIS*]

25.0048   SL,DM   1969   Deviations from standard English in the speech of primary school children in St. Lucia and Dominica: a preliminary survey. Part I.

Carrington, Lawrence D. & Borely, C. B.

32.0111   TR   1969   AN INVESTIGATION INTO ENGLISH LANGUAGE LEARNING AND TEACHING PROBLEMS IN TRINIDAD AND TOBAGO. St. Augustine, Trinidad, University of the West Indies, Institute of Education, Project 15 Progress Report: 82p. **[25]** [*RIS*]

Carrington, Lawrence D.; Borely, C. B. & Knight, H. E.

32.0112   TR   1972   AWAY ROBIN RUN! A CRITICAL DESCRIPTION OF THE TEACHING OF THE LANGUAGE ARTS IN THE PRIMARY SCHOOLS OF TRINIDAD AND TOBAGO. St. Augustine, Trinidad, University of the West Indies, Institute of Education, Project 15: 60p. **[25]** [*RIS*]

25.0049   TR   1972   LINGUISTIC EXPOSURE OF TRINIDADIAN CHILDREN.

25.0050   TR   1974   Linguistic exposure of Trinidadian children.

Carrington, Vivien

37.0125   JM   1971   INTRODUCTION TO CIVICS FOR JAMAICAN SCHOOLS.

Carrington, Vivien & Frater, Eric

32.0113   JM   1965   The University and our schools. *Torch* 15(3), Sept.: 7-12. [*RIS*]

Carter, E. H.; Digby, G. W. & Murray, R. N.

5.0155   GC   1959   HISTORY OF THE WEST INDIAN PEOPLES. BOOK III: FROM EARLIEST TIMES TO THE 17TH CENTURY.

Casseres, R.

25.0052   NA   1974   De moedertaal: een pedagogisch uitgangspunt [The mother tongue: from an educational point of view].

Cassidy, Frederic G.
25.0055 GC 1959 English language studies in the Caribbean.

Cave, George N.
25.0065 GU 1970 Some sociolinguistic factors in the production of standard language in Guyana and implications for the language teacher.
32.0114 GU 1971 PRIMARY SCHOOL LANGUAGE IN GUYANA: AN INVESTIGATION OF ORAL LANGUAGE AT THE STANDARD ONE LEVEL. Georgetown, Guyana Teachers' Association: 67p. **[25]** [*RIS*]

Cespedes, Francisco S.
32.0115 GC 1960 Public elementary education in the Caribbean. *In* Wilgus, A. Curtis, ed. THE CARIBBEAN: CONTEMPORARY EDUCATION. Gainesville, University of Florida Press, p.51-64. [*RIS*]

Chai, Hon-Chan
32.0116 GU 1968 EDUCATION AND NATIONAL DEVELOPMENT IN PLURAL SOCIETIES: A CASE STUDY OF GUYANA. Ph.D. dissertation, Harvard University: 87p. **[8]**

Chambers, George
37.0134 TR 1972 What a government expects from training.

Chamoiseau, Miguel
32.0117 MT 1969 Les élèves des classes terminales de lycée (une approche socio-démographique des lycéennes de Fort de France) ["Senior class" lycée students (a socio-demographic approach to the high school girls of Fort de France)]. *Cah Cent Etud Reg Ant-Guy* 18: 97-112.
  [*RIS*]

Chapman, G. P.
43.0078 JM 1965 First steps in the development of a university research programme.

Chen, Gerald
28.0238 TR 1967 Organization for health planning in Trinidad and Tobago: working document.

Clark, Isobel
32.0118 UV 1963 The insular training school programme for dependent, neglected and delinquent children in the Virgin Islands. *In* Carter, Samuel E., ed. THE ADOLESCENT IN THE CHANGING CARIBBEAN: PROCEEDINGS OF THE THIRD CARIBBEAN CONFERENCE FOR MENTAL HEALTH, APR. 4-11, 1961, UCWI, JAMAICA. Kingston, The Herald, p.153-157. **[31,33]** [*RIS*]

Clarke, Anthony Stephen
32.0119 TR 1973 AN ANALYSIS OF STUDENTS' SELF-ESTEEM AND STUDENTS' ATTITUDES TOWARD CULTURE IN SECONDARY SCHOOLS IN TRINIDAD. Ph.D. dissertation, University of Nebraska (Lincoln): 151p. **[20]** [*PhD*]

Clarke, Austin
32.0120 BB 1966-67 Harrison College and me. *New Wld Q* 3(1-2), Dead Season and Croptime, Barbados Independence Issue: 31-34. [*RIS*]

Clarke, F. J.

28.0248   **SL**   1962   Adult education and the health of the community.

Clayson, David

32.0121   **JM**   1973   Public health training among the rural poor in Jamaica: some effects on medical students' concept modification and self-evaluation. *Psych Q* 47(1): 124-131.   **[28]**   [*ACM*]

32.0122   **JM**   1973   Public health training in the urban ghetto and among the rural poor: comparative effects on medical students' concept modification and self-evaluation. *Int J Social Psych* 19(1-2), Spring-Summer: 82-87.   **[28]**   [*ACM*]

Coard, Bernard

18.0059   **BC,UK**   1971   HOW THE WEST INDIAN CHILD IS MADE EDUCATIONALLY SUBNORMAL IN THE BRITISH SCHOOL SYSTEM: THE SCANDAL OF THE BLACK CHILD IN SCHOOLS IN BRITAIN.

Coates, A. G.

56.0063   **JM**   1965   Geography in Jamaica.

Coleridge, K. R. S.

32.0123   **SR**   1966   PROBLEMEN IN VERBAND MET HET ALGEMEEN LEERPLAN VOOR DE SURINAAMSE BASISSCHOLEN [PROBLEMS CONNECTED WITH THE GENERAL EDUCATIONAL PLAN FOR SURINAMESE ELEMENTARY SCHOOLS]. Paramaribo, Suriname, Gouvernements-Avondopleiding voor de Onderwijzers- en Hoofdakte: 42p.   [*RILA*]

Collings, Dorothy

32.0124   **BC**   1973   Library education in the English-speaking Caribbean. *Unesco B Libr* 27(1), Jan.-Feb.: 12-17.   **[1]**   [*TCL*]

1.0060   **BC**   1975   Library education in the English-speaking Caribbean.

Collins, Rev.

32.0125   **JM**   1907   The agricultural and industrial experiment. *W I B* 8(3): 305-307.   **[23,43]**   [*AMN*]

Collins, Sydney

8.0040   **JM**   1956   Social mobility in Jamaica, with reference to rural communities and the teaching profession.

8.0041   **JM**   1960   The school teacher in his role as leader in West Indian and African societies.

Comvalius, Th. A. C.

22.0079   **SR**   1946   Oud-Surinaamsche rhythmische dansen in dienst van de lichamelikje opvoeding [Old Surinamese rhythmic dances in the service of physical education].

Cook, Katherine M.

32.0126   **UV**   1934   PUBLIC EDUCATION IN THE VIRGIN ISLANDS. Washington, U.S. Govt. Print. Off., 31p. (U.S. Dept. of the Interior, Office of Education, Pamphlet no. 50.)   [*COL*]

Cooke, Dennis
32.0127 BC 1967 The study of children's play: the exercise. *Torch* 17(2), Sept.: 8-16.
[*RIS*]

Coombs, Godfrey
32.0128 JM 1967 Compulsory education. *Torch* 17(3), Dec.: 13-16. [*RIS*]

Cooper, John Irwin
32.0129 BC 1949 The West Indies, Bermuda, and the American mainland colleges. *Jam Hist Rev* 2(1), Dec.: 1-6. **[5]** [*COL*]

Corbin, Carlyle G., Jr.
32.0130 UV 1975 INSTITUTIONAL CONSEQUENCES OF IMPORTED EDUCATION TO THE U.S. VIRGIN ISLANDS. Kingshill, St. Croix, International Institute, Caribbean Regional Office: 53p. **[20,21]** [*RIS*]

Cororan, T. C.
32.0131 TR 1966 Our school choirs and the Music Festival. *Educ J Trin Tob* 2(2): 16-20. **[22]** [*TCL*]

Cousins, Herbert H.
32.0132 JM 1907 Some problems of agricultural education at Jamaica. *W I B* 8(3): 288-292. **[43]** [*AMN*]

Craig, Dennis R.
32.0133 JM 1965 The written English of some 14-year-old Jamaican and English children. *In* Jones, J. Allen, ed. LANGUAGE TEACHING, LINGUISTICS AND THE TEACHING OF ENGLISH IN A MULTILINGUAL SOCIETY: REPORT OF THE CONFERENCE, APRIL 6-9, 1964. Kingston, Jamaica, University of the West Indies, Faculty of Education: 52-59. [*RIS*]
[25]
32.0134 BC 1966 Some developments in language teaching in the West Indies. *Car Q* 12(1), March: 25-34. **[25]** [*RIS*]
32.0135 JM 1966 Teaching English to Jamaican Creole speakers: a model of a multi-dialect situation. *Language Learning* 16(1-2): 49-61. **[25]**
[*COL*]
32.0136 JM 1967 Some early indications of learning a second dialect. *Language Learning* 17(3-4): 133-140. **[25]** [*COL*]
32.0137 BC 1969 AN EXPERIMENT IN TEACHING ENGLISH: A DEVELOPMENT OF TEACHING METHODS AMONG PRIMARY SCHOOL CHILDREN IN THE WEST INDIES. Caribbean Universities Press: 72p. [*RIS*]
32.0138 BC 1971 Education and Creole English in the West Indies: some sociolinguistic factors. *In* Hymes, Dell, ed. PIDGINIZATION AND CREOLIZATION OF LANGUAGES: PROCEEDINGS OF A CONFERENCE HELD AT THE UNIVERSITY OF THE WEST INDIES, MONA, JAMAICA, APRIL 1968. London, Cambridge University Press: 371-391. **[25]** [*RIS*]
32.0139 GU 1971 English in secondary education in a former British colony: a case study of Guyana. *Car Stud* 19(4), Jan.: 113-151. **[25]** [*RIS*]
32.0140 JM 1973 Reading and the creole speaker. *Torch* 22(2), Summer: 10-16. **[25]**
[*RIS*]
32.0141 BC 1974 Language education research in the Commonwealth Caribbean. *Car J Educ* 1, June: 23-36. **[25]** [*RIS*]

Craig, Dennis R. & Carter, Sheila

32.0142   JM   1976   The language learning aptitudes of Jamaican children at the beginning of secondary school. *Car J Educ* 3(1), Jan.: 1-21. **[25]**
                 [*RIS*]

Creary, Jean

32.0143   JM   1965   Mathematics for children speaking Jamaican creole. *Car Q* 11(1-2), March & June: 85-94. **[25]**   [*RIS*]

Cromwell, Leta

32.0144   UV   1963   Project for discovering and assisting the mentally retarded child in the school. *In* Carter, Samuel E., ed. THE ADOLESCENT IN THE CHANGING CARIBBEAN: PROCEEDINGS OF THE THIRD CARIBBEAN CONFERENCE FOR MENTAL HEALTH, APR. 4-11, 1961, UCWI, JAMAICA. Kingston, The Herald, p.121-123. **[31,33]**   [*RIS*]

Cross, Malcolm

32.0145   GC   1973   Education and job opportunities. *In* Moss, Robert, ed. THE STABILITY OF THE CARIBBEAN: REPORT OF A SEMINAR HELD AT DITCHLEY PARK, OXFORDSHIRE, U.K. MAY 18-20, 1973. Washington, D.C., Georgetown University, Center for Strategic and International Studies: 51-76. **[40,46]**   [*RIS*]

Cross, Malcolm & Schwartzbaum, Allan M.

32.0146   TR   1969   Social mobility and secondary school selection in Trinidad and Tobago. *Social Econ Stud* 18(2), June: 189-207. **[8]**   [*RIS*]

Cruickshank, E. K.

28.0287   JM   1952   The University College Hospital of the West Indies.

Cummings, Leslie P.

56.0075   GU   1965   GEOGRAPHY OF GUYANA.

32.0147   BC   1968   Directions in geographic education. *In* Floyd, Barry, ed. NEW VIEWPOINTS IN GEOGRAPHY: PROCEEDINGS OF A CONFERENCE FOR TEACHERS OF GEOGRAPHY IN THE CARIBBEAN, AUGUST 27-SEPTEMBER 1, 1967. Kingston, Jamaica, University of the West Indies, Geography Department: 13-24. **[56]**   [*AGS*]

32.0148   BC   1968   Introduction to the use of computers in geographical analysis. *In* Floyd, Barry, ed. NEW VIEWPOINTS IN GEOGRAPHY: PROCEEDINGS OF A CONFERENCE FOR TEACHERS OF GEOGRAPHY IN THE CARIBBEAN, AUGUST 27-SEPTEMBER 1, 1967. Kingston, Jamaica, University of the West Indies, Geography Department: 49-60. **[56]**   [*AGS*]

Cummins, G. T. M. & Vaillant, Henry W.

34.0021   BB   1966   The training of the nurse-midwife for a national program in Barbados combining the IUD and cervical cytology.

Cundall, Frank

32.0149   JM   1914   THE MICO COLLEGE JAMAICA. Kingston, Gleaner Co., 98p. **[5]**
                 [*NYP*]

Cutteridge, J. O.

56.0076   GC   1951   GEOGRAPHY OF THE WEST INDIES AND ADJACENT LANDS.

Daley, Rene
32.0150 JM 1972 History, aims and functioning of the National Curriculum Development Council. *Torch* 21(3), Christmas: 1-5. [*RIS*]

Dalton, H. A.
32.0151 BB 1907 Agricultural education in secondary schools at Barbados. *W I B* 8(3): 286-288. [43] [*AMN*]

Dalton, Robert H.
32.0152 ST 1968 EDUCATION AND THE SOCIAL CLIMATE: A FOLLOW-UP STUDY OF CHILDREN FIVE YEARS LATER. St. Thomas, Virgin Islands, Department of Health: 10p. [9,20] [*RIS*]

Daly, Vere T.
32.0153 GU 1967 THE MAKING OF GUYANA—BOOK 1. Georgetown, Guyana, The Daily Chronicle Ltd.: 158p. (Independence Histories) [5] [*RIS*]

Daniskas, J.
32.0154 NC 1970 Muziekonderwijs in Suriname en de Nederlandse Antillen [Music education in Surinam and the Netherlands Antilles]. *In* STICUSA JAARVERSLAG 1970. Amsterdam, The Netherlands, Nederlandse Stichting voor Culturele Samenwerking met Suriname en de Nederlandse Antillen: 64-68. [22] [*NYP*]

Davis, Harold B.
32.0155 BC 1972 Co-ordination of personnel management training in public and private sectors. *In* TRAINING OF PUBLIC SERVICE TRAINERS: REPORT ON A PILOT COURSE, ST. AUGUSTINE, TRINIDAD, AUG. 10-SEPT. 18, 1970. New York, United Nations: 73-77. [37,45] [*UNL*]

Davis, J. Clark
32.0156 UV 1973 DEVELOPMENT OF A PLANNING AND EVALUATION DIVISION WITHIN THE DEPARTMENT OF EDUCATION, VIRGIN ISLANDS: FINAL REPORT. Washington, U.S. DHEW, National Institute of Education: 50p. [*TCL*]

Davis, Tula Joy
32.0157 JM 1973 THE SOCIAL STUDIES IN THE SECONDARY SCHOOLS OF JAMAICA. Ann Arbor, Michigan, University Microfilms: 229p. (Ph.D. dissertation, George Peabody College for Teachers, 1971) [*RIS*]

Dawson, Mary
32.0158 JM 1974 Suggestion for study of plants and animals of the local community. *Torch* 23(1), Easter: 7-14. [54] [*RIS*]

Day, Glen A.
32.0159 JM 1964 Reflections on our local examinations. *Torch* 14(2), June: 8-14. [*TCL*]

Debysingh, R.
32.0160 GC 1968 Secondary school organization. *In* PAPERS PRESENTED AT THE PRIORITIES IN EDUCATIONAL RESEARCH SEMINAR, 2-3 MAY, 1968. Trinidad, University of the West Indies: 3p. [*RIS*]

Deighton, Horace et al.

32.0161   BC   1905   Teaching the principles of agriculture in colleges and schools in the
West Indies. *W I B* 6(2): 197-216.   **[43]**   [*AMN*]

Dejnozka, E. L.

32.0162   UV   1972   America educational achievement in the Virgin Islands, 1917-1963.
J Negro Hist 57(4), Oct.: 385-394.   [*COL*]

Dejnozka, Edward J.

32.0163   UV   1973   Navajos and Virgin Islanders: educational parallels. *Integ Educ*
11(6), Nov.-Dec.: 17-19.   [*TCL*]

Deonanan, Carlton R.

32.0164   TR   1973   IMPLICATIONS FOR TEACHING HIGH SCHOOL ENGLISH COMPOSITION IN
TRINIDAD AND TOBAGO, WEST INDIES, FROM DEVELOPING TRENDS IN
THE UNITED STATES OF AMERICA. Ann Arbor, Michigan, University
Microfilms: 209p. (Ed.D. dissertation, Utah State University 1971.)
[*RIS*]

Derrick, June

18.0076   BC,UK   1966   TEACHING ENGLISH TO IMMIGRANTS.
18.0077   BC,UK   1968   School—the meeting point.

Desai, Patricia; Standard, K. L. & Miall, W. E.

28.0314   JM   1970   Socio-economic and cultural influences on child growth in rural
Jamaica.

Desantis, Lydia

32.0165   JM   1973   Teaching others to teach. *Nurs Outlook* 21(10), Oct.: 658-664.
[*ACM*]

De Suze, Jos. B.

56.0087   TR   1965   THE NEW TRINIDAD AND TOBAGO.

Deutch, Rachel F.

32.0166   FC   1969   Suggestions for the teaching of Negro literature of French expression. *Fr Rev* 42(5), April: 706-717.   **[25]**   [*COL*]

Dickinson, Thomas H. et al.

32.0167   UV   1929   REPORT OF THE EDUCATIONAL SURVEY OF THE VIRGIN ISLANDS.
Hampton, Va., The Press of the Hampton Normal and Agricultural
Institute, 69p.   [*COL*]

Dillon, A. Barrow

56.0090   BZ   1923   GEOGRAPHY OF BRITISH HONDURAS.

Dilworth, W. W.

32.0168   JM   1965   Teaching language arts on the basis of pupils' needs, errors and
background experiences. *Torch* 15(3), Sept.: 26-30.   **[25]**   [*RIS*]

Dip, C. E.

32.0169   NA   1972   Rede gehouden ter gelegenheid van de opening van het college-jaar
1972-1973 op 11 september 1972 van de Rechtshogeschool van de
Nederlandse Antillen [Speech at the opening of the academic year
1972-1973 of the Law School of the Netherlands Antilles, September 11, 1972. *Justicia* 8(2): 33-42.   **[33]**   [*COL*]

Dip, Carlos

32.0170 NA 1976 Tirso Sprockel and higher education in the Netherlands Antilles. *Car Ed B* 3(3), Sept.: 41-45. [*RIS*]

Dolly, Reynold Cartwright

45.0045 TR 1963 The adolescent in industry.

Dolphin, Celeste

48.0048 GU 1959 Good afternoon, schools.

Dottin, Ambrose Cornelius

32.0171 TR 1973 SECONDARY EDUCATION AND EMPLOYMENT IN TRINIDAD AND TOBAGO: IMPLICATIONS FOR EDUCATIONAL PLANNING. Ed.D. dissertation, Columbia University: 265p. [46] [*PhD*]

Dowdeswell, W. H.

32.0172 BZ 1970 Field studies in British Honduras. *J Biol Educ* 4(3), Sept.: 177-181. [54] [*TCL*]

D'Oyley, Vincent

18.0083 BC,CA 1976 A critique of ideas and insights from one black locating in the diaspora.

Droogleever Fortuyn, A. B.

32.0173 SR 1947 Middelbaar onderwijs in Suriname [Middle education in Surinam]. *W I G* 28: 97-106. [*COL*]

Duinman, J. C. J.

32.0174 SR 1967 Suriname op school [Surinam in schools]. *Geogr Tijdschr* Nieuwe Reeks, 1(4), Oct.: 315-319. [56] [*AGS*]

Duke, James T.

20.0020 JM 1963 EQUALITARIANISM AMONG EMERGENT ELITES IN A NEW NATION.

Duperly, Doris

32.0175 JM 1973 An account of the Secondary Schools' Drama Festival committee. *Torch* 22(3), Christmas: 35-38. [22] [*RIS*]

Durstine, Richard M. & Hudson, Barclay M.

32.0176 BB 1972 Barbados: marginal costs for marginal decisions—the case of team teaching. *In* Coombs, Philip H. & Hallak, Jacques, eds. EDUCATIONAL COST ANALYSIS IN ACTION: CASE STUDIES FOR PLANNERS—II. Paris, UNESCO, International Institute for Educational Planning: 131-168. [*TCL*]

Dwyer, Audley Lloyd

32.0177 JM 1973 A PROPOSAL FOR IMPROVING THE TEACHING OF ENGLISH IN THE LOWER PRIMARY GRADES IN JAMAICAN SCHOOLS Ann Arbor, Michigan, University Microfilms: 196p. (Ed.D. dissertation, Columbia University, 1971) [25] [*RIS*]

Dyer, Clifford Victor

32.0178 TR 1974 A STUDY TO DETERMINE CURRICULUM FOR INDUSTRIAL ARTS IN THE JUNIOR SECONDARY SCHOOLS OF TRINIDAD AND TOBAGO. Ed.D. dissertation, Arizona State University: 322p. [*PhD*]

Dyer, P. B.

32.0179   TR   1965   Interview with Dr. Jean Piaget. *Educ J Trin Tob* 1(3), May: 16-21.
                                                                                    [*TCL*]

32.0180   TR   1967   THE EFFECTS OF ENVIRONMENTAL VARIABLES ON THE ACHIEVEMENT OF ELEMENTARY SCHOOL CHILDREN IN TRINIDAD, WEST INDIES. Ph.D. dissertation, University of Alberta: 111p. **[9]**

32.0181   TR   1968   The effect of the home on the school in Trinidad. *Social Econ Stud* 17(4), Dec.: 435-441. **[9]**   [*RIS*]

32.0182   GC   1968   Towards increased educability. *In* PAPERS PRESENTED AT THE PRIORITIES IN EDUCATIONAL RESEARCH SEMINAR, 2-3 MAY, 1968. Trinidad, University of the West Indies: 6p.   [*RIS*]

Dyson, Alice

7.0042   GC   1967   Population trends in the eastern Caribbean.

Eadie, Hazel Ballance

32.0183   TT   1930   A school in Treasure Island. *Hibbert J* 28(4), July: 684-698.   [*COL*]

Ebanks, G. Edward

17.0030   JM   1968   Differential internal migration in Jamaica, 1943-1960.

Eber, Dorothy Harley

18.0085   BC,CA   1969   CANADA MEETS BLACK POWER: THE COMPUTER CENTRE PARTY, PART ONE.

Edmondson, Locksley

32.0184   GC   1976   Educational challenges of the Caribbean connection with Africa. *Car Ed B* 3(3), Sept.: 17-40. **[21]**   [*RIS*]

Edson, P.

18.0086   BC,UK   [n.d.]   Background information: West Indians.
18.0087   BC,UK   [n.d.]   Teaching techniques: West Indians.

Edwards, P. A.

32.0185   BC   1971   EDUCATION FOR DEVELOPMENT IN THE CARIBBEAN. Bridgetown, Barbados, CADEC (Caribbean Ecumenical Consultation for Development): 15p. (Study Paper No. 3) **[23]**   [*RIS*]

Edwards, V. R.

32.0186   JM   1966   The Secondary School within the Jamaican society. *Torch* 17(1), March: 5-8.   [*RIS*]

Edwards, W. J.

32.0187   GU   1975   A guided composition programme for Form I children in Guyana. *Engl Lang Tch* 29(3), April: 197-206. **[25]**   [*TCL*]

Egerton, John

32.0188   UV   1967   Education in the Virgin Islands. *South Educ Rpt* 3(4), Nov.: 18-22.
                                                                                    [*COL*]

Einaar, J. F. E.

32.0189   FA,NC   1946   Education in the Netherlands and French West Indies. *J Negro Educ* 15(3), Summer: 444-461.   [*COL*]

Embra, Shirley
18.0090   **BC,CA**   1959   Caribbean students club.

Ennever, Olive N.
32.0190   **JM**   1968   Training of the assistant nurse—developments in Jamaica. *Jam Nurse* 8(1), April-May: 24-25.   **[28]**   [*AJN*]

Ennever, Olive; Marsh, M. & Standard, K. L.
28.0362   **JM**   1969   Programa de adiestramiento de asistentes en salud de la comunidad [Training program for assistants in community health].

Escoffery, Gloria
22.0126   **BC**   1968   The bicycle lamp: an artist's reflections on art teaching.

Evans, F. C.
56.0102   **JM**   1968   A FIRST GEOGRAPHY OF JAMAICA.
56.0103   **TR**   1968   A FIRST GEOGRAPHY OF TRINIDAD AND TOBAGO.

Evans, P. C. C.
18.0092   **BC,UK**   [n.d.]   Some education problems in English schools.
32.0191   **JM**   1965   SCHOOL AND SOCIETY IN RURAL JAMAICA: A SURVEY OF RURAL ELEMENTARY SCHOOLS IN JAMAICA, WITH PARTICULAR REFERENCE TO THE LIVES CHILDREN LEAD IN THEIR COMMUNITIES AND THE OCCUPATIONS THEY FOLLOW WHEN THEY LEAVE SCHOOL. Ph.D. dissertation, University of London (Institute of Education): 624p. **[8,9]**

Evans, Vernon
22.0130   **TR**   1963[?]   The future of music in the West Indies. (ii) Art music.

Eyre, L. Alan
32.0192   **BC**   1966   The teaching of geography in the Caribbean. *Car Q* 12(2), June: 36-48.   **[56]**   [*RIS*]
56.0107   **GC**   1968   A NEW GEOGRAPHY OF THE CARIBBEAN.

Fagan, S. W.
32.0193   **JM**   1959   The experiment in secondary education in the Kingston Senior School. *Torch* 10(1), May: 26-29.   [*TCL*]
32.0194   **JM**   1972   Implementing the language arts syllabus—some consideration. *Torch* 21(1-2), Easter/Summer: 12-15.   [*RIS*]

Farley, Rawle
32.0195   **BC**   1957   The role of the university in industrial relations. *Caribbean* 10(11), June: 264-265, 268.   **[46]**   [*COL*]
46.0074   **BC**   1958   TRADE UNION DEVELOPMENT AND TRADE UNION EDUCATION IN THE BRITISH CARIBBEAN.
32.0196   **BC**   1958   UNIVERSITIES AND THE EDUCATION OF WORKING PEOPLE. Georgetown, Daily Chronicle, 39p. **[5,8,46]**   [*RIS*]

Farley, Rawle, ed.
32.0197   **BC**   [n.d.]   LABOUR EDUCATION IN THE BRITISH CARIBBEAN: REPORT OF A LABOUR EDUCATION SURVEY CONDUCTED JUNE-JULY, 1959, AND OF THE CONFERENCE HELD AT THE UNIVERSITY OF THE WEST INDIES, MONA, JAMAICA, AUG. 4th-9th, 1959. Georgetown: "Daily Chronicle", 119p. (Department of Extra-mural Studies, University of the West Indies.) **[46]**   [*RIS*]

Farrell, Joseph P.

32.0198   GC   1967   Education and pluralism in selected Caribbean societies. *Comp Educ Rev* 11(2), June: 160-181.   **[8]**   [*RIS*]

Feldman, H. & Morris, D.

31.0057   JM   1972   The validity of the Rutter scale for the identification of disturbed primary school children in Jamaica.

Ferguson, Stephen

32.0199   BC,UK   1974   West Indian medical graduates of Edinburgh to 1800. *J Hist Med All Sci* 29(1), Jan.: 111-114.   **[18,28]**   [*PS*]

Ferrier, J. H. E.

32.0200   SR   1954   The organisation of education in Surinam. *Car Commn Mon Inf B* 7(6), Jan.: 125-127.   [*COL*]

Field, C. D.

32.0201   JM   1967   Biophysical science in the University of the West Indies. *Inf B Scient Res Coun* 8(1), June: 13-18.   **[28]**   [*RIS*]

Figueroa, John Joseph

32.0202   BC   1964   Staffing and examinations in British Caribbean secondary schools. London, Evans, 21p.   [*RIS*]

32.0203   BC   1965   Needs and problems. *In* Jones, J. Allen, ed. Language teaching, linguistics and the teaching of English in a multilingual society: report of the Conference, April 6-9, 1964. Kingston, Jamaica, University of the West Indies, Faculty of Education: 10-17.   [*RIS*]

32.0204   BC   1966   Notes on the teaching of English in the West Indies. *New Wld Q* 2(4), Cropover: 17-27.   **[25]**   [*RIS*]

32.0205   JM   1969   Education for Jamaica's needs. *Car Q* 15(1), March: 5-33.   [*RIS*]

32.0206   BC   1971   Society, schools and progress in the West Indies. Oxford, Pergamon Press: 208p.   [*RIS*]

Figueroa, Peter M. E.

18.0098   BC,UK   1976   The employment prospects of West Indian school-leavers in London, England.

Fill, J. Herbert

31.0059   UV   1965[?]   Teacher-child-parent inter-relationships in the U.S. Virgin Islands.

Fish, Cynthia, ed.

32.0207   GC   1973[?]   The admission and academic placement of students from the Caribbean: a workshop report. San Juan, Puerto Rico, The North-South Center: 198p.   [*TCL*]

Fitzherbert, Katrin

18.0100   BC,UK   1968   The West Indian background.

Floyd, Barry

32.0208   BC   1967   "New viewpoints in geography": a teachers' conference. *Car Q* 13(3), Sept.: 30-37.   **[56]**   [*RIS*]

Floyd, Barry, ed.

32.0209   BC   1968   NEW VIEWPOINTS IN GEOGRAPHY: PROCEEDINGS OF A CONFERENCE FOR TEACHERS OF GEOGRAPHY IN THE CARIBBEAN, AUGUST 27-SEPTEMBER 1, 1967. Kingston, Jamaica, University of the West Indies, Geography Department: 136p. **[56]**   [AGS]

Foner, Nancy

8.0074   JM   1971   SOCIAL CHANGE AND SOCIAL MOBILITY IN A JAMAICAN RURAL COMMUNITY.

32.0210   JM   1972   Competition, conflict, and education in rural Jamaica. *Hum Org* 31(4), Winter: 395-402. **[20]**   [COL]

32.0211   JM   1973   STATUS AND POWER IN RURAL JAMAICA: A STUDY OF EDUCATIONAL AND POLITICAL CHANGE. New York: Teachers College Press: 172p. **[8,20,37]**   [RIS]

32.0212   JM,UK   1975   The meaning of education to Jamaicans at home and in London. *New Community* 4(2), Summer: 195-202. **[18,20]**   [NYP]

Forsythe, Dennis

16.0030   BC,CA   1971   By way of introduction: the Sir George Williams affair.

Forsythe, Dennis, ed.

16.0031   BC,CA   1971   LET THE NIGGERS BURN! THE SIR GEORGE WILLIAMS UNIVERSITY AFFAIR AND ITS CARIBBEAN AFTERMATH.

Fox, Robert

32.0213   JM   1963   New courses: business studies at the College of Arts, Science and Technology. *Torch* 13(3), Sept.: 12-15. **[45]**   [TCL]

45.0051   JM   1967   Education and training of management in Jamaica.

Francis, Ettle

32.0214   JM   1970   Baccalaureate degree for West Indian nurses. *Jam Nurse* 10(3), Dec.: 18-19. **[28]**   [AJN]

Frank, Francine Wattman

25.0114   NL   1974   Language and education in the Leeward Netherlands Antilles.

Fredericks, Marcel A. & Mundy, Paul

28.0457   GU   1967   Social backgrounds and some selected attitudes of physicians in a developing nation, their bearing on medical education for the Caribbean.

Fredholm, A.

32.0215   TR   1912   Agricultural education in Trinidad—past, present and future. *Proc Agric Soc Trin Tob* 12(4), Apr.: 96-103. **[43]**   [AMN]

Friday, Wellington R. L.

32.0216   BC   1975   RESTRUCTURING HIGHER EDUCATION IN THE NON-CAMPUS TERRITORIES OF THE BRITISH CARIBBEAN AS A STRATEGY FOR DEVELOPMENT—PROBLEMS AND PROSPECTS. Ph.D. dissertation, University of Southern California: 450p. **[18]**   [PhD]

Froidevaux, Henri

32.0217   FC   1900   L'OEUVRE SCOLAIRE DE LA FRANCE DANS NOS COLONIES [THE FRENCH EDUCATIONAL TASK IN THE COLONIES]. Paris, Librairie maritime et coloniale, 365p. **[5]**   [COL]

Furlonge, Errol A.

32.0218   TR   1969   THE DEVELOPMENT OF SECONDARY EDUCATION IN TRINIDAD AND TOBAGO. Ph.D. dissertation, University of Sheffield: 421p.

Gabriel, Rehenia A.

32.0219   UV   1968   AN OPERATIONS AND PROCEDURES MANUAL FOR ELEMENTARY SCHOOL GUIDANCE PROGRAMS IN THE UNITED STATES VIRGIN ISLANDS. PART I: BASIC RESEARCH, PART II: THE MANUAL. Ed.D dissertation, New York University: 290p.   [*PhD*]

Gale, Laurence

32.0220   GU   1969   EDUCATION AND DEVELOPMENT IN LATIN AMERICA: WITH SPECIAL REFERENCE TO COLOMBIA AND SOME COMPARISON WITH GUYANA, SOUTH AMERICA. New York, Frederick A. Praeger: 178p.   [*COL*]

Galton, C. T., Bp.

32.0221   GU   1912   Elementary education in British Guiana. *Timehri* 3d ser., 2(19A), July: 106-112.   **[23]**   [*AMN*]

Gatcliffe, T. A.

32.0222   TR   1965   Do we educate for life? *Educ J Trin Tob* 1(5), Nov.: 3-7.   [*TCL*]

Gayle, H. Haughton

32.0223   JM   1967   Some legal aspects of corporal punishment and supervision in schools. *Torch* 17(1), March: 1-3.   **[33]**   [*RIS*]

George, Walter F.

28.0490   JM   1974   An approach to VD control based on a study in Kingston, Jamaica.

Gerig, Zenas E.

32.0224   JM   1967   AN ANALYSIS OF SELECTED ASPECTS OF JAMAICAN CULTURE WITH IMPLICATIONS FOR ADULT EDUCATIONAL PROGRAMS IN THE CHURCH. Ph.D. dissertation, Indiana University: 157p.   **[21]**   [*PhD*]

Germanacos, C. L.

32.0225   JM   1965   The advisory or supervisory services of a Ministry of Education. *Torch* 15(3), Sept.: 1-5.   [*RIS*]

Gianetti, G. G.

32.0226   TR   1974   Growth and development of I.C.T.A. *Trop Agric* 51(4), Oct.: 462-467.   [*AGS*]

Gill, C. H. S.

45.0057   JM   1968   Setting up training schemes in a Jamaican mining company.

Girling, R. K.

32.0227   JM   1972   A cost-effectiveness evaluation of alternative technologies for teaching mathematics in Jamaica. *Social Econ Stud* 21(1), March: 72-89.   **[41]**   [*RIS*]

45.0058   JM   1974   EDUCATION, TECHNOLOGY AND DEVELOPMENT/UNDER-DEVELOPMENT: A CASE STUDY OF AGRO-INDUSTRY IN JAMAICA.

Girvan, Norman

37.0288   **JM**   1968   After Rodney—the politics of student protest in Jamaica [October counter-revolution in Jamaica].

Goddard, Dennis E.

56.0129   **BB**   1966   A JUNIOR HISTORY OF BARBADOS.

Goilo, E. R.

25.0136   **NL**   1974   HABLEMOS PAPIAMENTO [LETS SPEAK PAPIAMENTO].

Goldman, R. J. & Taylor, Francine M.

18.0113   **GC,UK**   1966   Coloured immigrant children: a survey of research, studies and literature on their educational problems and potential—in Britain.

Gomes, Carlton

32.0228   **TR**   1972   Education. *In* Boyke, Roy, ed. PATTERNS OF PROGRESS. Port-of-Spain, Trinidad, Key Caribbean Publications: 69-71.   [*RIS*]

Gomes Casseres, B.

32.0229   **CU**   1974   Onderwijs en economie op Curaçao, 1900-1940 [Education and economy on Curaçao, 1900-1940]. *Kristòf* 1(2), April: 63-71.   **[41]**   [*RIS*]

Goodridge, Rudolph

32.0230   **GC**   1974   The professional preparation of graduate teachers—a perspective for the Caribbean. *Car J Educ* 1(2), Dec.: 48-57.   [*RIS*]

Goodridge, Vincent

32.0231   **BC**   1976   The development of social studies programmes for Caribbean secondary schools; considerations and perspectives. *Social Stud Educ* 7, June: 46-50. (Special issue: Commonwealth Caribbean Social Studies Conference Proceedings. Vol. I.)

Gordon, Shirley C.

32.0232   **TR**   1962   The Keenan report, 1869. Part I: The elementary school system in Trinidad. *Car Q* 8(4), Dec.: 3-16.   **[5]**   [*RIS*]

32.0233   **BC**   1963   A CENTURY OF WEST INDIAN EDUCATION. London, Longmans, 312p. **[5]**   [*RIS*]

32.0234   **TR**   1963[?]   Documents which have guided educational policy in the West Indies—3: Patrick Joseph Keenan's report 1869—Pt. II: Secondary and higher education. *Car Q* 9(1-2): 11-25.   **[5]**   [*RIS*]

32.0235   **BB**   1963   Documents which have guided educational policy in the West Indies: the Mitchinson report, Barbados 1875. *Car Q* 9(3), Sept.: 33-43. **[5]**   [*RIS*]

32.0236   **JM**   1963   Documents which have guided educational policy in the West Indies—no. 5. Report upon the condition of the juvenile population of Jamaica, 1879. *Car Q* 9(4), Dec.: 15-24.   [*RIS*]

32.0237   **JM**   1964   Documents which have guided educational policy in the West Indies: the Lumb report, Jamaica, 1898. *Car Q* 10(1), Mar.: 12-24. **[5]**   [*RIS*]

32.0238   **TR**   1964   Documents which have guided educational policy in the West Indies: Education Commission report, Trinidad, 1916. *Car Q* 10(2), June: 19-39.   **[5]**   [*RIS*]

32.0239	GU	1964	Documents which have guided educational policy in the West Indies: report of the Commissioner of Education, British Guiana, 1925. *Car Q* 10(3), Sept.: 34-40. **[5]** [*RIS*]
32.0240	BC	1964	Documents which have guided educational policy in the West Indies, No. 8: report of the Commissioners Mayhew and Marriott on secondary and primary education in Trinidad, Barbados, Leeward Islands and Windward Islands, 1931-1932. *Car Q* 10(4), Dec.: 3-32. **[5]** [*RIS*]
32.0241	BC	1966	The Caribbean textbook project, UWI. *Torch* 16(1), March: 18-21. [*RIS*]
32.0242	BC	1968	REPORTS AND REPERCUSSIONS IN WEST INDIAN EDUCATION, 1835-1933. London, Ginn and Co. Ltd.: 190p. **[5]** [*RIS*]

Goslinga, W. J.

| 32.0243 | NA | 1948 | Netherlands educational system used in Caribbean. *Car Commn Mon Inf B* 2(3), Oct.: 67-68.   [*COL*] |
| 37.0301 | CU | 1948 | Overheidszorg voor onderwijs en volksontwikkeling [Governmental involvement in the educational system and mass education]. |

Goulbourne, De Costa Harold

| 46.0085 | JM | 1975 | TEACHERS AND PRESSURE GROUP ACTIVITIES IN JAMAICA, 1894-1967: A STUDY OF THE JAMAICA UNION OF TEACHERS AND THE JAMAICA TEACHERS' ASSOCIATION IN THE COLONIAL AND INDEPENDENT POLITICAL SYSTEMS. |

Goveia, Elsa V.

| 32.0244 | BC | 1969 | The U.W.I. and the teaching of West Indian history. *Car Q* 15(2-3), June-Sept.: 60-63. **[5]**   [*RIS*] |

Gradussov, Alex

| 32.0245 | JM | 1966 | Aims of education in Jamaica. *New Wld Q* 2(4), Cropover: 33-38.   [*RIS*] |

Graham, Daisy Agatha

| 32.0246 | JM | 1975 | A CRITICAL ANALYSIS OF TRENDS AND PATTERNS OF SECONDARY EDUCATION IN JAMAICA. Ed.D. dissertation, Columbia University: 261p.   [*PhD*] |

Graham, J. W.

| 32.0247 | JM | 1938 | A century of education in Jamaica. *Can-W I Mag* 27(7), July: 7-9. **[5]**   [*NYP*] |

Grant, D. R. B.

32.0248	JM	1964	Some problems in the teaching of English. *Torch* 14(2), June: 1-7. **[25]** [*TCL*]
32.0249	JM	1965	A study of some common language and spelling errors of elementary school children in Jamaica. *In* Jones, J. Allen, ed. LANGUAGE TEACHING, LINGUISTICS AND THE TEACHING OF ENGLISH IN A MULTILINGUAL SOCIETY: REPORT OF THE CONFERENCE, APRIL 6-9, 1964. Kingston, Jamaica, University of the West Indies, Faculty of Education: 71-77. [*RIS*]
32.0250	GC	1974	Early childhood education in the Caribbean. *Car J Educ* 1, June: 7-11. [*RIS*]

Grant, Louis Strathmore

32.0251   BC   1966   Training for medicine in the West Indies. *Car Q* 12(1), March: 11-24.   **[28]**   [*RIS*]

Grant, Trixie

32.0252   JM   1972   Research in testing: mental ability and reading achievement. *Torch* 21(1-2), Easter/Summer: 23-28.   [*RIS*]

Gray, Cecil

32.0253   BC   1963   Teaching English in the West Indies. *Car Q* 9(1-2): 67-77.   **[25]**   [*RIS*]

32.0254   BC   1965   Higgledy, piggledy, my black hen: poetry in secondary education. *Car Q* 11(3-4), Sept.-Dec.: 36-53.   [*RIS*]

32.0255   BC   1969   New training for secondary teaching. *Car Q* 15(1), March: 34-44.   [*RIS*]

32.0256   JM   1971   Jamaican English—a report of a pilot experiment in remedial English teaching through role-playing and dialogues. *Car Q* 17(2), June: 25-35.   **[25]**   [*RIS*]

32.0257   BC   1975   Curricula, syllabuses and examinations in English. *Car Q* 21(3), Sept.: 41-57.   **[25]**   [*RIS*]

Gray, Cecil, comp.

32.0258   BC   1969   RESPONSE: A COURSE IN NARRATIVE COMPREHENSION AND COMPOSITION FOR CARIBBEAN SECONDARY SCHOOLS. London, Thomas Nelson and Sons Ltd.: 180p.   [*RIS*]

Green, Helen Bagenstose

20.0031   TR   1965   Values of Negro and East Indian school children in Trinidad.

Green, John

32.0259   BC   1973   The language situation in English-speaking Caribbean. *Torch* 22(2), Summer: 2-9.   **[25]**   [*RIS*]

Grenz, Wolfgang

1.0126   GC   1966   DAS BILDUNGSWESEN IN DER GESAMTENTWICKLUNG LATEINAMERIKAS [EDUCATION AND DEVELOPMENT IN LATIN AMERICA].

Gresle, François

32.0260   MT   1969   Les enseignants et l'école: une analyse socio-démographique des instituteurs et des professeurs de la Martinique [The teachers and the school: a socio-demographic analysis of teachers and professors in Martinique]. *Cah Cent Etud Reg Ant-Guy* 19: 156p.   [*RIS*]

Griffiths, V. L.

32.0261   BC   1955   EXTERNAL TEACHER TRAINING: A STUDY OF THE PROBLEM OF THE PUPIL-TEACHER AND PROBATIONARY TEACHER SYSTEMS IN THE BRITISH CARIBBEAN. [Mona?] Centre for the Study of Education, University College of the West Indies, 33p.   [*RIS*]

Gunness, Robert N.

32.0262   TR   1966   "There is no place like home" for the handicapped child. *Educ J Trin Tob* 2(1): 1-7.   **[33]**   [*TCL*]

Haglund, Elsa

32.0263   GC   1953   Home economics in the Caribbean. *Car Commn Mon Inf B* 6(12),
                          July: 275, 280.   **[33]**   [*AGS*]

32.0264   GC   1954   Caribbean training course in home economics. *Car Commn Mon Inf
                          B* 7(6), Jan.: 128-130.   **[33]**   [*COL*]

Hall, Kenneth

32.0265   JM   1975   African studies in the Jamaican curriculum. *Torch* 23(2-3), June:
                          46-52.   **[21]**   [*RIS*]

Hall, Marshall

32.0266   BC   1974   Thoughts on the need for cooperation among the countries of the
                          Caribbean in management training. *In* MANAGEMENT STUDIES IN
                          THE COMMONWEALTH CARIBBEAN. Association of Caribbean Uni-
                          versities and Research Institutes: 3-7. (UNICA Survey Series, No.
                          1)   **[38,45]**   [*RIS*]

Hamilton, Marlene

32.0267   JM   1975   The relationship of Cambridge GCE results with the Jamaican
                          graduate output from U.W.I. *Car J Educ* 2(2), Dec.: 101-118.   [*RIS*]

Hammond, S. A.

32.0268   BC   1945   COST OF EDUCATION. [Bridgetown?] Barbados, Advocate Co., 32p.
                          (Development and welfare bulletin, no. 15.)   [*RIS*]

32.0269   BC   1946   Education in the British West Indies. *J Negro Educ* 15(3), Summer:
                          427-449.   [*COL*]

Harbin, John

32.0270   GR,SV   1905   Agriculture in the elementary schools of Grenada and St. Vincent,
                            1902-4. *W I B* 6(2): 223-227.   **[43]**   [*AMN*]

Harley, Milton; Hyde, Eugene & Segree, Norma

32.0271   JM   1968   The Jamaica School of Arts and Crafts (a discussion). *Car Q*
                          14(1-2), March-June: 83-90.   **[22]**   [*RIS*]

Harrigan, Norwell

32.0272   BV   1961   Education in the British Virgin Islands. *In* Brown, John, ed.
                          LEEWARDS: WRITINGS, PAST AND PRESENT ABOUT THE LEEWARD
                          ISLANDS. [Bridgetown?] Barbados, Dept. of Extra-Mural Studies,
                          Leeward Islands, University College of the West Indies, p.18-23.
                                                                                          [*RIS*]

32.0273   UV   1972   HIGHER EDUCATION IN THE MICRO-STATE: A THEORY OF RARAN
                          SOCIETY. Ph.D. dissertation, University of Pittsburgh: 196p.   **[40]**
                                                                                          [*PhD*]

Harris, John

32.0274   BC   1936   The vicissitudes of a legacy. *Spectator* 157(5642), Aug. 14: 265-
                          266.   **[5]**   [*NYP*]

Harrison, John

22.0167   BC   1950[?]   Art for West Indian children.

Haskell, H. N.

32.0275   **BB**   1941   Some notes on the foundation and history of Harrison College. *J Barb Mus Hist Soc* 8(4), Aug.: 187-193; 9(1), Nov.: 3-16. **[5]**
                            [*AMN*]

32.0276   **BB**   1942   Some notes on the foundation and history of Harrison College. *J Barb Mus Hist Soc* 9(2), Feb.: 59-81. **[5]**   [*AMN*]

32.0277   **BB**   1952   Some notes on the foundation and history of Harrison College. *J Barb Mus Hist Soc* 19(2), Feb.: 74-80; 19(3), May: 112-120; 19(4), Aug.: 153-163. **[5]**   [*AMN*]

Hauch, Charles C.

32.0278   **GC**   1960   College and university public education in the Caribbean. *In* Wilgus, A. Curtis, ed. THE CARIBBEAN: CONTEMPORARY EDUCATION [PAPERS DELIVERED AT THE TENTH CONFERENCE ON THE CARIBBEAN HELD AT THE UNIVERSITY OF FLORIDA, DEC. 3-5, 1959]. Gainesville, University of Florida Press, p.65-88. (Publications of the School of Inter-American Studies, ser. 1, v. 10.)   [*RIS*]

32.0279   **GC**   1960   EDUCATIONAL TRENDS IN THE CARIBBEAN: EUROPEAN AFFILIATED AREAS. Washington, U.S. Govt. Print. Off., 153p. (Bulletin no. 26.)

Haveman, H. A.

32.0280   **NA**   1971   Het m.a.v.o. in de Nederlandse Antillen [The "m.a.v.o." in the Netherlands Antilles]. *Pedag Forum* 5(9), Nov.: 342-345.   [*RILA*]

Hawkes, Nicolas

13.0080   **BC,UK**   1966   IMMIGRANT CHILDREN IN BRITISH SCHOOLS.

Hayden, Howard

32.0281   **BB**   1945[?]   A POLICY FOR EDUCATION. [Bridgetown?] Barbados: Advocate Co., 49p.   [*RIS*]

Hellinga, W. Gs.

32.0282   **SR**   1955   LANGUAGE PROBLEMS IN SURINAM: DUTCH AS THE LANGUAGE OF THE SCHOOLS. Amsterdam, North-Holland Pub. Co., 123p. **[25]**

Henderson, Alexander

32.0283   **UV**   1969   Virgin Islands. *In* Pearson, Jim B. & Fuller, Edger, eds. EDUCATION IN THE STATES: HISTORICAL DEVELOPMENT AND OUTLOOK. Washington, D.C., National Education Association of the United States: 1463-1475.   [*TCL*]

Hendricksen, H. E.

32.0284   **TR**   1912   Agricultural education. *Proc Agric Soc Trin Tob* 12(5), May: 131-135. **[43]**   [*AMN*]

Hendry, J. A.

32.0285   **BC**   1974   UNESCO/UWI/UNICEF/Project/RLA/142 and the new technologists in education. *Car J Educ* 1, June: 52-57.   [*RIS*]

Henry, Ralph

32.0286   **TR**   1968   Some problems in the economics of education in Trinidad and Tobago. *In* PAPERS PRESENTED AT THE PRIORITIES IN EDUCATIONAL RESEARCH SEMINAR, 2-3 MAY, 1968. Trinidad, University of the West Indies: 7p.   [*RIS*]

41.0232   TR   1974   Earnings and education in Trinidad and Tobago: some evidence for 1970.

Herklots, G. A. C.
32.0287   BC   1955   The Imperial College of Tropical Agriculture. *New Commonw,* Br Car Suppl 30(11), Nov. 28: xv-xvii. **[43]**   [*AGS*]

Herskovits, Melville Jean & Herskovits, Frances S.
24.0089   SR   1936   SURINAME FOLK-LORE (with transcriptions and Suriname songs and musicological analysis by Dr. M. Kolinski).

Hertzig, M. E.; Birch, H. G.; Richardson, S. A. & Tizard, J.
30.0117   JM   1972   Intellectual levels of school children severely malnourished during the first two years of life.

Hery, Pierre
51.0050   MT   1966   La Martinique à son Ecole Hôtelière [The Hotel School of Martinique].

Herzog, John D.
32.0288   BB   1968   HOUSEHOLD COMPOSITION AND BOY'S SCHOOL PERFORMANCE IN BARBADOS, WEST INDIES. Ph.D. thesis, Harvard University: 308p. **[9,31]**   [*RIS*]
32.0289   BB   1974   Father-absence and boy's school performance in Barbados. *Hum Org* 33(1), Spring: 71-83. **[9,31]**   [*COL*]

Heusden, Edgard van
32.0290   SR   1970   De Stichting voor Buitengewoon Onderwijs [The Foundation for Extraordinary Education]. *In* Janssen, Cornelius, ed. SURINAME: HET WERK VAN DE FRATERS VAN TILBURG ONDER DE VIJFSTER-RENVLAG. Tilburg, The Netherlands, Fraters van O. L. Vrouw, Moeder van Barmhartigheid: 61-65. **[23]**   [*RILA*]

Hiller, Herbert L.
51.0051   GC   1974   Caribbean tourism and the university.

Hilton, Jennifer
20.0036   BC,UK   1972   The ambitions of school children.

Holbrook, Sabra
2.0209   UV   1974   AMERICAN VIRGIN ISLANDERS ON ST. CROIX, ST. JOHN, AND ST. THOMAS.

Holdsworth, H.
1.0143   JM   1953   The Library of the University College.

Honoré, Serge
32.0291   FC   1976   Actions éducative et culturelle aux Antilles et en Guyane [Educational and cultural activities in the Antilles and [French] Guiana]. *B Inf Cenaddom* No. 29, Jan.-Feb.: 20-24.   [*RIS*]

Horne, Louise
30.0122   TR   1972   School feeding in Trinidad and Tobago.

Horst, Raoul van der

32.0292   SR   1970   Het studieconvict Boniface te Paramaribo [The Boniface religious boarding school in Paramaribo]. *In* Janssen, Cornelius, ed. SURI-NAME: HET WERK VAN DE FRATERS VAN TILBURG ONDER DE VIJFSTERRENVLAG. Tilburg, The Netherlands, Fraters van O. L. Vrouw, Moeder van Barmhartigheid: 32-41 (Intercom-Fraters No. 7). **[23]**   [*RILA*]

Hotchkiss, J. C.

32.0293   BC   1952   Eastern Caribbean Farm Institute. *Car Commn Mon Inf B* 5(8), Mar.: 233-234. **[43]**   [*AGS*]

32.0294   GC   1953   Progress of the Eastern Caribbean Farm Institute. *Car Commn Mon Inf B* 7(1), Aug.: 13-14, 24. **[43]**   [*AGS*]

Hotchkiss, J. C. & Hotchkiss, Mrs. J. C.

43.0205   BC   1954   The education of the small scale farmer and his family for better farm and home living in the British Caribbean.

Houghton, V. P.

32.0295   BC,UK   1966   Intelligence testing of West Indian and English children. *Race* 8(2), Oct.: 147-156. **[18]**   [*COL*]

Houte, I. C. van

25.0175   SR   1963   Het bilinguisme van de Hindostaanse kinderen in Suriname [Bilingualism of Hindustani children in Surinam].

Howes, H. W.

32.0296   GC   1955   FUNDAMENTAL, ADULT, LITERACY AND COMMUNITY EDUCATION IN THE WEST INDIES. [Paris?] UNESCO Education Clearing House, 79p. (Educational studies and documents no. 15.) **[33]**   [*NYP*]

Hoyos, F. A.

32.0297   BB   1945   TWO HUNDRED YEARS: A HISTORY OF THE LODGE SCHOOL. [Bridgetown?] Advocate Co., 111p. **[5]**

32.0298   BB   1948   Barbados aims at high level education. *Car Commn Mon Inf B* 2(5), Dec.: 115-116.   [*COL*]

5.0433   BB   1953   OUR COMMON HERITAGE.

Hoyte, D. A. N. & Persaud, T. V. N.

32.0299   BC   1972   A survey of teaching in human anatomy at University of the West Indies. *W I Med J* 21(3), Sept.: 183-185. **[28]**   [*PS*]

Huggins, H. D.

32.0300   BC   1949   Institute of Social and Economic Research at U.C.W.I. *Car Commn Mon Inf B* 3(4), Nov.: 129-130.   [*COL*]

8.0113   BC   1949   Special science research.

Hugill, J. A. C.

46.0121   JM   1957   Jamaica's shortage of mechanics and artisans.

Hummelen, J. A.

32.0301   SR   1965   Vakonderwijs in Suriname [Vocational education in Surinam]. *Schakels* S59: 23-28.   [*NYP*]

25.0181   NA   1967   Veeltaligheid en taalproblemen [Polyglottism and language problems].

Husbands, Madre
30.0123   **BB**   1972   Organization of the Barbados school lunch programme.

Hutchinson, Edward
32.0302   **JM**   1974   The national literacy programme in Jamaica. *Convergence* 7(1): 79-81.   [*TCL*]

Hutchinson, Joseph
32.0303   **TR**   1974   The role of I.C.T.A. in tropical agriculture. *Trop Agric* 51(4), Oct.: 459-461.   [*AGS*]

Hutchinson, Lynette C. & Ottley, Daphne M.
32.0304   **GC**   1968   Priorities in educational research: centres of the learning process —libraries. *In* PAPERS PRESENTED AT THE PRIORITIES IN EDUCATIONAL RESEARCH SEMINAR, 2-3 MAY, 1968. Trinidad, University of the West Indies: 3p. **[1]**   [*RIS*]

Hutton, A. B.
32.0305   **AT**   1929   A good report. *Morav Miss* 27(5), May: 36-37.   [*NYP*]

Irvine, James et al.
32.0306   **BC**   1945[?] REPORT OF THE WEST INDIES COMMITTEE OF THE COMMISSION ON HIGHER EDUCATION IN THE COLONIES. London, H.M.S.O., 81p.
                                                                         [*COL*]

Isaacs, Ian
32.0307   **BC**   1966   The "new" mathematics in West Indian schools. *New Wld Q* 2(4), Cropover: 29-31.   [*RIS*]
32.0308   **JM**   1975   The mathematical performances of a selected sample of third year students in Jamaican post-primary schools. *Car J Educ* 2(1), June: 15-23   [*RIS*]
32.0309   **JM**   1976   Environmental and other factors affecting the performance in mathematics of third-year students in Jamaican post-primary schools. *Car J Educ* 3(1), Jan.: 51-65. **[20]**   [*RIS*]

James, S. A.
32.0310   **SL**   1962   Adult education and community development. *In* Brown, John, ed. AN APPROACH TO ADULT EDUCATION. Castries, St. Lucia, Govt. Print. Off., p.33-38. **[8,33]**   [*RIS*]

James, Sybil
32.0311   **JM**   1972   Teaching literature in a dialect/standard situation. *Car Q* 18(3), Sept: 73-76.   [*RIS*]
32.0312 **GU,JM**   1976   A SURVEY OF SELECTED CLASSROOM SPACES USING AN OBSERVATION INVENTORY DESIGNED FOR THE PURPOSE. Ed.D. dissertation, Teachers College, Columbia University: 202p.   [*RIS*]

Jarvis, José Antonio
32.0313   **UV**   1929   A brief survey of education in the Virgin Islands. *Opportunity* 7(1), Jan.: 16-18.   [*COL*]

Jean, Sally Lucas
28.0681   **UV**   1933   Virgin Islands: school health program—utilization of existing facilities.

Johanson, Richard Keith

32.0314   JM   1969   THE DEVELOPMENT OF AN INFORMATION SYSTEM FOR THE MINISTRY OF EDUCATION IN JAMAICA. Ph.D. dissertation, Harvard University: 90p.

Johnson, Doris Louise Sands

32.0315   BA   1962   A GUIDE FOR THE ESTABLISHMENT OF AN ADVISORY COUNCIL TO THE BAHAMAS BOARD OF EDUCATION (BASED UPON A STUDY OF ADVISORY SERVICES TO THE CENTRAL BRITISH EDUCATIONAL AUTHORITY FROM 1899 TO 1959). Ed.D. dissertation, New York University: 289p.
   [*PhD*]

Johnston, Franklin A. J.

32.0316   JM,TR   1971   EDUCATION IN JAMAICA AND TRINIDAD IN THE GENERATION AFTER EMANCIPATION. D.Phil. dissertation, University of Oxford: 500p. **[5]**

Jones, J. Allen

32.0317   BC   1965   The need for a Standard. *In* Jones, J. Allen, ed. LANGUAGE TEACHING, LINGUISTICS AND THE TEACHING OF ENGLISH IN A MULTILINGUAL SOCIETY: REPORT OF THE CONFERENCE, APRIL 6-9, 1964. Kingston, Jamaica, University of the West Indies, Faculty of Education: 18-22. **[25]**   [*RIS*]

32.0318   JM   1966   English in the Commonwealth: 9. The West Indies. *Engl Lang Tch* 20(2), Jan.: 145-152. **[25]**   [*TCL*]

Jones, J. Allen, ed.

32.0319   BC   1965   LANGUAGE TEACHING, LINGUISTICS AND THE TEACHING OF ENGLISH IN A MULTILINGUAL SOCIETY: REPORT OF THE CONFERENCE, APRIL 6-9, 1964. Kingston, Jamaica, University of the West Indies, Faculty of Education: 90p. **[25]**   [*RIS*]

Jordan, Alma

1.0158   BC   1966   THE DEVELOPMENT OF LIBRARY SERVICE IN THE WEST INDIES THROUGH INTER-LIBRARY CO-OPERATION.

Joseph, H.

32.0320   TR   1965   Teacher training. *Educ J Trin Tob* 1(2), March: 36-39.   [*TCL*]

Jourdain, Elodie

25.0196   FA   1954   Is Creole a key to education?

Juglall, W. E.

32.0321   SR   1963   Het onderwijs aan nakomelingen van Brits-Indische immigranten in Suriname [The education of descendants of British Indian immigrants in Surinam]. *In* Lutchman, W. I., ed. VAN BRITS-INDISCH MIGRANT TOT BURGER VAN SURINAME. The Hague, Drukkerij Wieringa, p.83-89. **[12]**

Julien, K. S.

32.0322   BC   1966   The education of the engineer in the West Indies. *Car Q* 12(2), June: 3-7.   [*RIS*]

Justus, Joyce Bennett

20.0040 **DM** 1973 THE UTMOST FOR THE HIGHEST: A STUDY OF ADOLESCENT ASPIRATIONS IN DOMINICA, WEST INDIES.

Kandel, I. L. et al.

32.0323 **JM** 1943[?] REPORT OF THE COMMITTEE APPOINTED TO ENQUIRE INTO THE SYSTEM OF SECONDARY EDUCATION IN JAMAICA. Kingston [Govt. Printer?], 26p.   *[TCL]*

Kaude, Jüri V. & Johnson, Clive

32.0324 **JM** 1973 The launching of a postgraduate training program in diagnostic radiology in the West Indies. *J Med Educ* 48(10), Oct.: 955-957. **[28]**   *[PS]*

Kawwa, Taysir

18.0166 **UK,BC** 1965 A STUDY OF THE INTERACTION BETWEEN NATIVE AND IMMIGRANT CHILDREN IN AN ENGLISH SCHOOL, WITH SPECIAL REFERENCE TO ETHNIC PREJUDICE.

Kelly, Pamela

32.0325 **JM** 1974 Thoughts on the teaching of West Indian literature. *Torch* 23(1), Easter: 29-35.   *[RIS]*

Kendall, M. N.

32.0326 **BC** 1972 Overseas nursing students in Britain. *Int Nurs Rev* 19(3): 246-260. **[18,28]**   *[PS]*

Kerr, John F.

32.0327 **BC** 1969 CURRICULUM CHANGE IN EMERGENT COUNTRIES: AN INDIVIDUAL STUDY OF THE CONTRIBUTION BY BRITISH AGENCIES TOWARDS CURRICULUM DEVELOPMENT IN EMERGENT COUNTRIES. University of Leicester, School of Education: 38p.   *[RIS]*

Kidd, J. Roby

32.0328 **BC** 1958 ADULT EDUCATION IN THE CARIBBEAN. [Kingston?] Jamaica, Extra-Mural Dept. of the University College of the West Indies, 293p.   *[RIS]*

Kidd, J. Roby & Nettleford, R. M.

32.0329 **BC** 1969 The role of the Extra-Mural Department. *Car Q* 15(2-3), June-Sept: 21-38.   *[RIS]*

Kiemen, Mathias C.

32.0330 **GC** 1960 Catholic schools in the Caribbean. *In* Wilgus, A. Curtis, ed. THE CARIBBEAN: CONTEMPORARY EDUCATION [PAPERS DELIVERED AT THE TENTH CONFERENCE ON THE CARIBBEAN HELD AT THE UNIVERSITY OF FLORIDA, DEC. 3-5, 1959]. Gainesville, University of Florida Press, p.51-64. (Publications of the School of Inter-American Studies, ser. 1, v. 10.) **[23]**   *[RIS]*

King, Ruby

32.0331 **BC** 1976 Approaches to teaching/learning situations in social studies. *Social Stud Educ* 7, June: 59-64. (Special issue: Commonwealth Caribbean Social Studies Conference Proceedings. Vol. I.)

King, St. Clair et al.
32.0332 TR 1976 REPORT OF WORKING PARTY ON EDUCATION. Port-of-Spain, Government of Trinidad and Tobago: 154p.

Kiven Tunteng, P.
18.0169 BC,CA 1973 Racism and the Montreal computer incident of 1969.

Klingberg, Frank J.
6.0165 BB 1938 British humanitarianism at Codrington.
32.0333 BC 1939 The Lady Mico Charity Schools in the British West Indies, 1835-1842. *J Negro Hist* 24(3), July: 291-344. **[5,11,23]** [*COL*]

Knight, H. E.; Carrington, L. D. & Borely, C. B.
32.0334 TR 1972 PRELIMINARY COMMENTS ON LANGUAGE ARTS TEXTBOOKS IN USE IN THE PRIMARY SCHOOLS OF TRINIDAD AND TOBAGO. St. Augustine, Trinidad, University of the West Indies, Institute of Education, Project 15: 37p. **[25]** [*TCL*]
32.0335 TR 1974 Preliminary comments on Language Arts textbooks in use in the primary schools of Trinidad and Tobago. *Car J Educ* 1(2), Dec.: 24-47. **[25]** [*RIS*]

Knox, John
32.0336 TR 1966 Educating the blind in today's changing world. *Educ J Trin Tob* 2(1): 14-17. **[33]** [*TCL*]

Krimpen, A. van
20.0041 SR 1974 VERSLAG VAN EEN ENQUÊTE ONDER LEERLINGEN VAN SURINAAMSE SCHOLEN [ACCOUNT OF A QUESTIONNAIRE AMONG STUDENTS OF SURINAMESE SCHOOLS].

Kroon, E. W.
25.0205 NA 1972 PAPYAMENTU VOOR BEGINNERS [PAPIAMENTO FOR BEGINNERS].

Kruijer, G. J.
32.0337 JM 1952 De 4-H Clubs van Jamaica. *W I G* 33(3-4): 213-221. **[8,22,43]** [*COL*]
32.0338 NA 1953 Sociologische fundamentenen van het onderwijs [Sociological basis of education]. *In* Kruijer, G. J.; Veenenbos, J. S. & Westermann, J. H., comps. BOVENWINDENRAPPORT. Amsterdam, Voorlichtingsinstituut voor het Welvaartsplan Nederlandse Antillen, 18p.

Kuyp, Edwin van der
28.0752 SR 1969 FUTUROLOGIE VAN DE GEZONDHEID IN SURINAME DEEL I: REDE UITGESPROKEN TER GELEGENHEID VAN DE PROKLAMATIE VAN DE FAKULTEIT DER MEDISCHE WETENSCHAPPEN VAN DE UNIVERSITEIT VAN SURINAME OP VRIJDAG 26 SEPTEMBER 1969 [THE FUTURE OF HEALTH IN SURINAM PART I: SPEECH AT THE OPENING OF THE MEDICAL FACULTY OF THE UNIVERSITY OF SURINAM ON FRIDAY, SEPTEMBER 26, 1969].

Landsheere, Gilbert L. de

32.0339   JM   1962   L'éducation et la formation du personnel enseignant dans un pays en plein développement: la Jamaïque [Education and teacher training in a fast-developing country: Jamaica]. *Int Rev Educ* 8(1): 41-60.   [*COL*]

Lane, Bess B.

32.0340   UV   1934   Education in the Virgin Islands. *J Negro Educ* 3(1), Jan.: 42-49.   [*COL*]

Langton, Kenneth P.

9.0090   JM   1965   THE POLITICAL SOCIALIZATION PROCESS—THE CASE OF SECONDARY SCHOOL STUDENTS IN JAMAICA.

Lassale, Jean-Pierre

32.0341   FC   1975   Problèmes de coopération culturelle [Problems of cultural cooperation]. *B Inf Cenaddom* 28: 16-19.   **[21,26]**   [*RIS*]

Lastra, Yolanda

32.0342   GC   1968   Literacy. *In* Sebeok, Thomas A., ed. CURRENT TRENDS IN LINGUISTICS, IV: IBERO-AMERICAN AND CARIBBEAN LINGUISTICS. The Hague, Mouton: 415-463.   **[25,33]**   [*RIS*]

Latimer, J.

6.0173   BC   1965   The foundation of religious education in the British West Indies.

Latour, M. D.

32.0343   CU   1948   Het R. K. bijzonder onderwijs [Roman Catholic private schools]. *In* ORANJE EN DE ZES CARAÏBISCHE PARELEN. Amsterdam, J. H. de Bussy: 143-150.   **[23]**   [*UCLA*]

Lauriers, L. A.

32.0344   SR   1958   Geen ontwikkeling zonder onderwijs [No development without education]. *In* Walle, J. van de & Wit, H. de, eds. SURINAME IN STROOMLIJNEN. Amsterdam, Wereld Bibliotheek, p.94-103.

Lauwerys, Joseph A. & Scanlon, David G., eds.

45.0090   JM,GU   1968   EDUCATION WITHIN INDUSTRY.

Lawley, David Baxter

32.0345   TR   1952   Trinidad's new school for the blind. *Car Commn Mon Inf B* 5(11), June: 301-302.   **[33]**   [*AGS*]

Lawton, David

25.0218   JM   1964   Some problems of teaching a creolized language to Peace Corps members.

Leacock, Courtenay

32.0346   TR   1968   Modern language teaching. *Tchr J* March: 23-26.   [*RIS*]

Lee, Frank F.

18.0178   BC,UK   1960   A comparative analysis of coloured grade school children: Negroes in the U.S. and West Indians in Britain.

Lee, Rosemary
18.0181 BC,UK 1965 The education of immigrant children in England.

Leechman, Alleyne
32.0347 GU 1912 Science as a school subject in British Guiana. *J Bd Agric Br Gui* 6(2), Oct.: 62-70. [AMN]
32.0348 GU 1913 Science as a school subject in British Guiana. *J Bd Agric Br Gui* 6(3), Jan.: 117-122. [AMN]

Leeuwen, H. D. van
32.0349 SR 1966 Continued elementary education, a sociological study of the functions of the ULO in Surinam society. *Neth Found Adv Trop Res* (WOTRO), Report for the Years 1964 and 1965: 31-36. [RIS]
32.0350 SR 1968 Verandering en onderwijs in Suriname [Change and education in Surinam]. *Sociol Gids* 15(6), Nov.-Dec.: 379-392. **[7]** [NYP]

Leeuwen, J. P. H. van; Rademakers, Th. H. J. & Zwart, J. J. van der
56.0208 NC 1971 WERELDKENNIS, AARDRIJKSKUNDE—METHODE VOOR M.A.V.O.: DE OVERZEESE RIJKSDELEN SURINAME EN DE NEDERLANDSE ANTILLEN [KNOWLEDGE OF THE WORLD, GEOGRAPHY METHOD FOR "M.A.V.O.": THE OVERSEAS PARTS OF THE KINGDOM, SURINAM AND THE NETHERLANDS ANTILLES].

Le Page, R. B.
32.0351 BC 1968 Problems to be faced in the use of English as the medium of education in four West Indian territories. *In* Fishman, Joshua A.; Ferguson, Charles A. & Das Gupta, Jyotirindra, eds. LANGUAGE PROBLEMS OF DEVELOPING NATIONS. New York, John Wiley and Sons, Inc.: 431-442. **[25]** [TCL]

Lewis, Gordon K.
32.0352 BC 1959 Technical and human resources in the Caribbean. *In* Wilgus, A. Curtis, ed. THE CARIBBEAN: NATURAL RESOURCES [PAPERS DELIVERED AT THE NINTH CONFERENCE ON THE CARIBBEAN HELD AT THE UNIVERSITY OF FLORIDA, DEC. 4-6, 1958]. Gainesville, University of Florida Press, p.219-238. (Publications of the School of Inter-American Studies, ser. 1, v. 9.) [RIS]

Lewis, W. Arthur
32.0353 JM 1961 Education and economic development. *Social Econ Stud* 10(2), June: 113-127. **[41]** [RIS]
32.0354 JM 1964 Secondary education and economic structure. *Social Econ Stud* 13(2), June: 219-232. **[41]** [RIS]

Leys, J. J.
32.0355 SR 1915 Agricultural instruction in Surinam. *J Bd Agric Br Gui* 9(1), Nov.: 11-14. **[43]** [AMN]

Lichtveld, Lou
32.0356 SR 1950 Educational problems in bilingual countries in the Caribbean. *Car Hist Rev* 1, Dec.: 125-132. **[25]** [COL]
32.0357 NA 1954-55 The social and economic background of education in Surinam and the Netherlands Antilles. *Vox Guy* 1(4-5), Nov.-Jan.: 35-48. **[8]**

Lier, Rudolf A. J. van

32.0358   SR   1968   Universiteit en maatschappij in het perspectief der ontwikkeling: rede uitgesproken ter gelegenheid van de
opening van de Universiteit van Suriname op 1 November 1968
[University and society from the perspective of development:
speech at the opening of the University of Surinam, November 1, 1968]. Deventer, The Netherlands, Van Loghum Slaterus:
23p. **[8]**   [*RILA*]

Limburg Stirum, O. E. G. Graaf van

37.0494   SR   1926-27 Voorwaardelijke veroordeeling [The probation system].

Lindo, Locksley

11.0059   JM   1970   Francis Williams—a "free" Negro in a slave world.

Little, Alan

32.0359   BC,UK   1975   The educational achievement of ethnic minority children in London
schools. *In* Verma, Gajendra, K. & Bagley, Christopher, eds. Race
and education across cultures. London, Heinemann Educa-
tional Books Ltd.: 48-69. **[8,11,18]**   [*RIS*]

18.0191   BC,UK   1975   Performance of children from ethnic minority backgrounds in
primary schools.

Little, Alan; Mabey, Christine & Whitaker, Graham

18.0192   BC,UK   1968   The education of immigrant pupils in inner London primary
schools.

London, Clement B. G.

32.0360   TR   1974   A strategy for the organization of social studies in the
junior secondary schools of Trinidad-Tobago: implications
for curriculum design. Ed.D. dissertation, Teachers College,
Columbia University: 430p.   [*RIS*]

Lormeau, C. J.

32.0361   MT   1968   L'Ecole de Vente de la Martinique [The Sales School in Mar-
tinique]. *B Cham Com Indus Mart* 1-6, 1st semester: 15-18.   [*RIS*]

Losonczi, E.

30.0143   BZ   1958   Social anthropology in health education with particular reference to
nutrition.

Low, Doreen Iris Deen

30.0145   SL,SK   1970   Evaluating nutrition education programs on two Caribbean
islands.

Lowe, Gilbert Antonio

20.0047   JM   1966   Education, occupation of fathers and parental contributions to
educational expenses as factors in career aspiration among male
Jamaican students.

Lowenthal, David & Comitas, Lambros, eds.

2.0295   GC   1973   Consequences of class and color: West Indian perspectives.

Lub, G. K.

32.0362 SR 1965 Onderwijzersopleiding en hoger onderwijs [Teacher education and higher education]. *Schakels* S59: 13-17. [*NYP*]

32.0363 SR 1965 Reorganisatie bij het onderwijs [Reorganization of education]. *Schakels* S59: 6-9. [*NYP*]

32.0364 SR 1965 Schooltypen en het lager onderwijs [Types of schools and elementary education]. *Schakels* S59: 1-5. [*NYP*]

32.0365 SR 1965 Voortgezet onderwijs [Secondary education]. *Schakels* S59: 10-12. [*NYP*]

Lutchman, Harold A.

32.0366 GU 1970 Administrative change in an ex-colonial setting: a study of education administration in Guyana, 1961-64. *Social Econ Stud* 19(1), March: 26-56. **[37]** [*RIS*]

37.0508 BC 1972 Some limitations in dealing with the problems of public administration in the Commonwealth Caribbean.

Lute, Edward

32.0367 TR [n.d.] Naparima in the fifties. *In* NAPARIMA COLLEGE; DIAMOND JUBILEE, 1900-1960. San Fernando, Trinidad, Rahaman's Printery: 9-22.

Lynch, Louis

32.0368 BB 1963 Parent-pupil-teacher relationships. *In* Carter, Samuel E., ed. THE ADOLESCENT IN THE CHANGING CARIBBEAN: PROCEEDINGS OF THE THIRD CARIBBEAN CONFERENCE FOR MENTAL HEALTH, APR. 4-11, 1961, UCWI, JAMAICA. Kingston, The Herald, p.111-112. **[20]** [*RIS*]

MacFayden, Eric

32.0369 TR 1949 I.C.T.A. fills key position in British Empire. *Car Commn Mon Inf B* 2(7), Feb.: 177-178. **[43]** [*COL*]

McFie, J. & Thompson, J. A.

18.0198 GC,UK 1970 Intellectual abilities of immigrant children.

McKenzie, Earl

32.0370 JM 1973 Art education and the teaching of history. *Torch* 22(3), Christmas: 11-15. [*RIS*]

32.0371 JM 1974 Art and the teaching of history: some lesson ideas. *Torch* 23(1), Easter: 15-17. [*RIS*]

McNeal, Julia

18.0200 BC,UK 1971 Education.

MacPherson, Phyllis Claire

32.0372 JM 1961 DEVELOPING A CURRICULUM FOR CHILDREN AND YOUTH IN JAMAICA, THE WEST INDIES. Ed.D. project, Teachers College, Columbia University, 411p. [*TCL*]

McWhinnie, Harold J.

32.0373 GR 1962 Teaching art in Grenada. *Oversea Educ* 34(3), Oct.: 128-131. **[22]** [*COL*]

Madosingh, A. E.

32.0374   TR   1965   Agricultural science. *Educ J Trin Tob* 1(2), March: 22-24.   [*TCL*]

Mahabir, Harold Gilks

32.0375   TR   1973   A STUDY OF ELEMENTARY STUDENTS COMING FROM VARYING SOCIO-ECONOMIC BACKGROUNDS IN TRINIDAD-TOBAGO AND THE EFFECT THESE BACKGROUNDS HAVE ON NATIONAL EXAMINATIONS. Ed.D. dissertation, Boston University School of Education.   [8]

Mahadevan, P.

32.0376   BC   1965   The University's Faculty of Agriculture. *Car Q* 11(1-2), March-June: 36-49.   [43]   [*RIS*]

30.0171   GC   1968   The role of the UWI Faculty of Agriculture in relation to the food needs of the Caribbean.

32.0377   BC   1972   A rationale for collaborative working arrangements in agriculture between universities in North America and the University of the West Indies. *In* RESOURCE DEVELOPMENT IN THE CARIBBEAN. Montreal, McGill University, Centre for Developing-Area Studies: 3-11.   [43]   [*RIS*]

Manley, Douglas R.

32.0378   JM   1963   Mental ability in Jamaica (an examination of the performance of children in the Jamaican common entrance examination, 1959). *Social Econ Stud* 12(1), Mar.: 51-71.   [8]   [*RIS*]

32.0379   JM   1969   The School Certificate Examination, Jamaica, 1962. *Social Econ Stud* 18(1), March: 54-71.   [*RIS*]

Manswell, Claris

32.0380   TR   1966   The Princess Elizabeth Home for physically handicapped children. *Educ J Trin Tob* 2(1): 18-21.   [33]   [*TCL*]

Maraj, J. A.

32.0381   BC   1967   A Caribbean plan for primary education. *Car Q* 13(2), June: 27-32.   [*RIS*]

32.0382   GC   1968   Some pre-conditions or "prior to priorities". *In* PAPERS PRESENTED AT THE PRIORITIES IN EDUCATIONAL RESEARCH SEMINAR, 2-3 MAY, 1968. Trinidad, University of the West Indies: 7p.   [*RIS*]

Marckwardt, Albert H.

25.0244   JM   1962   Applied linguistics.

Markle, Gower

32.0383   BC   [n.d.]   Report of Labour Education Survey. *In* Farley, Rawle, ed. LABOUR EDUCATION IN THE BRITISH CARIBBEAN: REPORT OF A LABOUR EDUCATION SURVEY CONDUCTED JUNE-JULY, 1959, AND OF THE CONFERENCE HELD AT THE UNIVERSITY OF THE WEST INDIES, MONA, JAMAICA, AUG. 4th-9th, 1959. Georgetown, "Daily Chronicle", p.56-101. (Department of Extra-Mural Studies, University of the West Indies.)   [46]   [*RIS*]

Marriott, F. C. & Mayhew, Arthur

32.0384   BC   1933   REPORT OF A COMMISSION TO CONSIDER PROBLEMS OF SECONDARY AND PRIMARY EDUCATION IN TRINIDAD, BARBADOS, LEEWARD IS-LANDS AND THE WINDWARD ISLANDS, 1931-32. London, H.M.S.O., 127p. (Colonial no. 79.)   [*NYP*]

Martin, C. M.
32.0385   LW   1901   Results of ten years' experience with compulsory enactments in the Leeward Islands. *W-I B* 2(1): 72-78.   [*AMN*]

Mason, Joyce
32.0386   SL   1962   Adult education and family life. *In* Brown, John, ed. AN APPROACH TO ADULT EDUCATION. Castries, St. Lucia, Govt. Print. Off., p.30-33. **[9,33]**   [*RIS*]

Masson, J. N.
32.0387   TR   1965   Courses in technical institutes and vocational schools in Trinidad and Tobago. *Educ J Trin Tob* 1(5), Nov.: 17-22.   [*TCL*]

Mathews, Thomas G.
32.0388   BC   1969   Caribbean cooperation in the field of higher education. *In* Preiswerk, Roy, ed. REGIONALISM AND THE COMMONWEALTH CARIBBEAN: PAPERS PRESENTED AT THE "SEMINAR ON THE FOREIGN POLICIES OF CARIBBEAN STATES," APRIL-JUNE, 1968. Trinidad, University of the West Indies, Institute of International Relations: 151-156. **[38]**   [*RIS*]

Mathurin-Mair, Lucille
32.0389   BC   1969   The student and the university's civilising role. *Car Q* 15(2-3), June-Sept.: 8-19.   [*RIS*]

Maxwell, Marina
18.0208   BC,UK   1969   Violence in the toilets: the experiences of a black teacher in Brent Schools.

Mayers, Harold
32.0390   TR   1965   The Common Entrance Class. *Educ J Trin Tob* 1(4), July: 13-15.   [*TCL*]

Mayhew, Arthur
32.0391   BC   1938   EDUCATION IN THE COLONIAL EMPIRE. London, Longmans, Green, 290p.   [*NYP*]

Maynard, Fitz G. & Maynard, Olga Comma
37.0564   TR   [n.d.]   THE NEW ROAD: A SHORT STUDY IN CITIZENSHIP.

Meek, George
32.0392   JM   1963   Jamaica's Youth Corps. *Américas* 15(4), Apr.: 13-15.   [*AGS*]

Melville, Edwina
2.0309   GU   1956   THIS IS THE RUPUNUNI.

Menkman, W. R.
32.0393   SR   1939   Landbouwopvoeding der Surinaamsche jeugd [Agricultural education of the Surinam youth]. *W I G* 21: 14-19. **[43]**   [*COL*]

Mercurius, Cecil K. S.
32.0394   BC   1963-64   The role of education in developing countries. Pt. II. *Social Scient* 2: 14-16.   [*RIS*]

Mierlo, C. G. M. van

32.0395   NA   1972   Plannen voor onderwijsvernieuwing [Plans for education renewal]. *In* HET ONDERWIJS IN DE NEDERLANDSE ANTILLEN. The Hague, The Netherlands, Kabinet voor Surinaamse en Nederlands-Antilliaanse Zaken: 26-29.   [*RILA*]

Mijs, A. A.

32.0396   SR   1974   ONDERWIJS EN ONTWIKKELING VAN SURINAME [EDUCATION AND DEVELOPMENT OF SURINAM]. Amsterdam, Universiteit van Amsterdam, Sociografisch Instituut FSW: 359p. (Onderzoekprojekt Sociale Ontwikkelingsstrategie Suriname 1969, Deelrapport nr. 7)   **[8]**
                                                                           [*RIS*]

Millard, I. S.

36.0059   JM   1950   The village schoolmaster as community development leader.

Miller, Colin G.

28.0872   JM   1974   University of the West Indies, Department of Paediatrics: past —present—and future.

Miller, Errol L.

32.0397   JM   1967   Ambitions of Jamaican adolescents and the school system. *Car Q* 13(1), March: 29-33.   **[20]**   [*RIS*]

20.0054   JM   1970   A STUDY OF SELF CONCEPT AND ITS RELATIONSHIP TO CERTAIN PHYSICAL, SOCIAL, COGNITIVE AND ADJUSTMENT VARIABLES IN A SELECTED GROUP OF JAMAICAN SCHOOLGIRLS.

32.0398   JM   1971   Education and society in Jamaica. *Savacou* 5, June: 51-70.   **[8,10]**
                                                                           [*RIS*]

32.0399   JM   1972   Reappraising the sixth form idea. *Car Q* 18(3), Sept.: 7-22.   [*RIS*]

32.0400   JM   1974   Government's expenditure on education: are the priorities right? *Jam J* 8(1), March: 23-25.   [*RIS*]

Miller, H. C., ed.

43.0302   GC   1966   REPORT ON THE CARIBBEAN CONFERENCE ON AGRICULTURAL EXTENSION.

Mills, G. E.

32.0401   BC   1966   Education and training for the Public Service in the West Indies. *In* Mills, G. E., ed. REPORT OF A CONFERENCE ON TRAINING OF PUBLIC OFFICERS HELD IN BARBADOS, FEB. 12-13, 1965. Mona, Jamaica, University of the West Indies, Department of Government: 8-21.   **[37]**   [*RIS*]

Mills, G. E., ed.

32.0402   BC   1966   REPORT OF A CONFERENCE ON TRAINING OF PUBLIC OFFICERS HELD IN BARBADOS, FEB. 12-13, 1965. Mona, Jamaica, University of the West Indies, Department of Government: 44p.   **[37]**   [*RIS*]

Mills, G. E. & Williams, R. L.

32.0403   BC   1974   Reflections on management education in the Commonwealth Caribbean. *In* MANAGEMENT STUDIES IN THE COMMONWEALTH CARIBBEAN. Association of Caribbean Universities and Research Institutes: 8-28. (UNICA Survey Series, No. 1)   **[45]**   [*RIS*]

Mitchell, David I.

23.0200 BC 1964 Principles and policies for a program of leadership education for the Sunday church schools of the Methodist
Church in the English-speaking Caribbean.

Molen, G. van der

45.0107 SR 1976 Economic impacts of education and personnel management.

Molen, W. van der

32.0404 SR 1965 De ontwikkeling van het kleuteronderwijs [The development of
nursery schools]. *Schakels* S59: 18-22. [*NYP*]

Moore, Edw. Fitz.

56.0237 GU 1943 A modern geography of British Guiana.

Morais, Allan I.

32.0405 GC 1952 Statistical organisation in the Caribbean. *Car Commn Mon Inf B*
6(4), Nov.: 84-86. [*AGS*]

32.0406 GC 1953 Practical training for the Caribbean. *Car Commn Mon Inf B* 6(11),
June: 244-246. [*AGS*]

32.0407 GC 1953 Rudimentary practices in statistical presentation. *W I B* 7(2), Sept.:
25-28. [*AMN*]

32.0408 GC 1953 Statistical education in the Caribbean. *Car Commn Mon Inf B* 6(9),
Apr.: 193-194, 196. [*AGS*]

Mordecai, Pamela

32.0409 JM 1975 The use of electronic media; T.V., radio and films in the teaching of
English—an overview. *Jam J* 9(2-3): 78-83. **[25]** [*RIS*]

Morris, Mervyn

18.0213 BC,UK 1965 Feeling, affection, respect.

Morse, Richard M.

32.0410 GC 1960 Technical and industrial education in the Caribbean. *In* Wilgus, A.
Curtis, ed. The Caribbean: contemporary education [papers
delivered at the Tenth Conference on the Caribbean held at
the University of Florida, Dec. 3-5, 1959]. Gainesville, University of Florida Press, p.162-175. (Publications of the School of
Inter-American Studies, ser.1, v. 10.) **[43,46]** [*RIS*]

Morton, Allen Glenn

18.0215 BC,PA 1972 The private schools of the British West Indians in Panama.

Mose, George Elliot

33.0141 TR 1964 A paper prepared for the Conference on Child Care in Trinidad and
Tobago.

32.0411 TR 1966 Training the socially handicapped child. *Educ J Trin Tob* 2(1):
22-28. **[33]** [*TCL*]

Moser, C. A.

41.0356 JM 1957 The measurement of levels of living with special reference
to Jamaica.

Moses, Yolanda T.

10.0037   **MS**   1975   What price education: the working women of Montserrat.

Mulford, H. P.

32.0412   **SC**   1910   Our work in St. Croix: laying of the corner stone at our school at Friedensthal. *Morav Miss* 8(8), Aug.: 159-160.   [*NYP*]

Murray, R. N.

32.0413   **BC**   1967   The Institute of Education of the University of the West Indies. *Car Q* 13(4), Dec.: 15-22.   [*RIS*]

32.0414   **JM**   1968   A Jamaican perspective of educational evaluation and planning. *Torch* 18(1), Easter: 1-5.   [*RIS*]

32.0415   **BC**   1976   Social studies in the Commonwealth Caribbean. *Social Stud Educ* 7, June: 7-11. (Special issue: Commonwealth Caribbean Social Studies Conference Proceedings. Vol. I.)

Myers, Marjorie

32.0416   **JM**   1965   English research at Moneague Training College 1960-62. *In* Jones, J. Allen, ed. LANGUAGE TEACHING, LINGUISTICS AND THE TEACHING OF ENGLISH IN A MULTILINGUAL SOCIETY: REPORT OF THE CONFERENCE, APRIL 6-9, 1964. Kingston, Jamaica, University of the West Indies, Faculty of Education: 63-70.   [*RIS*]

Narayan, Ongkar

32.0417   **GU**   1972   ENGLISH IN GUYANA'S SECONDARY SCHOOLS: A CASE STUDY IN EDUCATIONAL DEVELOPMENT. Ed.D dissertation, Pennsylvania State University: 118p.   [*PhD*]

Naughton, Ezra A.

32.0418   **VI**   1973   THE ORIGIN AND DEVELOPMENT OF HIGHER EDUCATION IN THE VIRGIN ISLANDS. Ph.D. dissertation, Catholic University of America: 347p.   [*PhD*]

Nawijn, Tj.

32.0419   **SR**   1913   Elementary education in Surinam. *J Bd Agric Br Gui* 6(3), Jan.: 107-112.   [*AMN*]

Nehaul, B. B. G.

28.0921   **GU**   1943   Report on the physical development and health of a sample of school children in the Island of Leguan, British Guiana, 1941.

Nettleford, Rex

32.0420   **TR**   1957   Extra-mural work in Trinidad. *Extra-Mural Reptr* 4(1), Jan.-Mar.: 1-3.   [*RIS*]

32.0421   **JM**   1961[?]   New goals in education. *In* Cumper, George, ed. REPORT OF THE CONFERENCE ON SOCIAL DEVELOPMENT IN JAMAICA. Kingston, Standing Committee on Social Services, p.94-97.   [*RIS*]

37.0615   **JM,GU,BZ**   1962   Political education in the developing Caribbean.

32.0422   **BC**   1970   UNIVERSITY ADULT EDUCATION IN THE WEST INDIES—A PROGRAMME IN TRANSITION. Mona, Jamaica, University of the West Indies: 33p.

                                                                                                        [*RIS*]

Newman, A. J.
2.0333   JM   1946[?]   JAMAICA: THE ISLAND AND ITS PEOPLE.
32.0423   JM   1968   The story of Mico College. *Jam J* 2(2), June: 7-11.   [*RIS*]

Newton, E. & Braithwaite, R. H.
32.0424   TR   1975   New directions in education in Trinidad and Tobago—challenge and response. *Comp Educ* 11(3), Oct.: 237-246.   [*TCL*]

Nichols, Donald Arthur
25.0258   SC   1974   AUDITORY DISCRIMINATION BY VIRGIN ISLANDS CHILDREN OF DIFFERENT DIALECTS OF ENGLISH.

Nicholson, C. C.
30.0184   GU   1947   Nutritional survey of pupils of elementary schools, Mahaicony District, February-March, 1947.
30.0185   GU   1956   Assessment of the nutritional status of elementary school children of British Guiana by periodic sampling surveys, and evaluation of the beneficial effects of supplementary feeding.

Nicholson, R. M.
32.0425   BB   1967   SECONDARY COMPREHENSIVE SCHOOLS IN BARBADOS: A REVIEW. Barbados, University of the West Indies, Institute of Education: 24p.   [*RIS*]

Nicholson, R. M., ed.
32.0426   BC   1971   REPORT OF CONFERENCE ON TEACHER EDUCATION IN THE EASTERN CARIBBEAN, ST. KITTS, APRIL 19-23, 1971. University of the West Indies, Institute of Education: 217p.   [*RIS*]
32.0427   BC   1972   REPORT OF CONFERENCE ON TEACHER EDUCATION IN THE EASTERN CARIBBEAN, DOMINICA, APRIL 10-14, 1972. University of the West Indies, Institute of Education: 252p.   [*RIS*]

Nicol, J. L.
32.0428   BC   1956   Education. *Statist* Sept.: 62-64.

Norman, Alma
32.0429   JM   1965   History can be fun. *Torch* 15(2), June: 17-24. **[22]**   [*RIS*]

Norris, R. A.
32.0430   BC,UK   1971   Developing a curriculum in English for West Indian children. *Urban Educ* 6(2-3), July-Oct.: 243-259. **[18,25]**   [*NYP*]

Nosel, José
32.0431   MT   1969   Les étudiants à la Martinique [Students in Martinique]. *Cah Cent Etud Reg Ant-Guy* 18: 32-96.   [*RIS*]

Oakley, Robin, ed.
18.0218   BC,UK   1968   NEW BACKGROUNDS: THE IMMIGRANT CHILD AT HOME AND AT SCHOOL.

Ocampo-Londono, Alfonso
32.0432   GC   1967   Education—a look ahead in the Caribbean. *In* Wilgus, A. Curtis, ed. THE CARIBBEAN: ITS HEMISPHERIC ROLE. Gainesville, University of Florida Press: 127-137. (Caribbean Conference Series 1, vol. 17)   [*RIS*]

Oedayrajsingh Varma, C. C. S.

16.0075   **SR**   1968   Een sociometrisch onderzoek naar de etnische factor bij de keuze van klasgenoten op enkele scholen in Suriname [Sociometric research on the ethnic factor in choosing classmates in some schools in Surinam].

Oers, J. F. van

32.0433   **NA**   1971   Education in the Netherlands Antilles in the period 1816-1874. *Neth Found Adv Trop Res* (WOTRO), Report for the year 1970: 25-28.
         [*RIS*]

Ogilvie, Bruce

32.0434   **BC**   1968   Teaching aids and equipment for the geography room. *In* Floyd, Barry, ed. NEW VIEWPOINTS IN GEOGRAPHY: PROCEEDINGS OF A CONFERENCE FOR TEACHERS OF GEOGRAPHY IN THE CARIBBEAN, AUGUST 27-SEPTEMBER 1, 1967. Kingston, Jamaica, University of the West Indies, Geography Department: 78-91. **[56]**   [*AGS*]

O'Mard, C. M.

31.0115   **AT**   1963   Special problems of the senior school child in Antigua.

Omoruyi, Omo

9.0104   **GU**   1975   A common experiential setting as a source of discontinuity in the socialization process in a plural society: Guyana as a case study.

O'Neil, Maud E.

35.0056   **BB**   1949   Of the buildings in progress with which to house the College.

Onneweer, M. C.

32.0435   **NA**   1972[?]   V.W.O. en H.A.V.O. ["V.W.O." and "H.A.V.O." (secondary schools)]. *In* HET ONDERWIJS IN DE NEDERLANDSE ANTILLEN. The Hague, The Netherlands, Kabinet voor Surinaamse en Neder-lands-Antilliaanse Zaken: 19-21.   [*RILA*]

Osborne, Christopher

45.0114   **TR**   1956   Handicraft in Trinidad.

Oudschans Dentz, Fred

32.0436   **CU,SR,GU**   1933-34   Stichtingen en fondsen in de West [Institutions and foundations in the West.] *W I G* 15: 390-406.   [*COL*]

32.0437   **CU,SR,GU**   1934-35   Stichtingen en fondsen in de West [Institutions and foundations in the West]. *W I G* 16: 1-6.   [*COL*]

32.0438   **CU**   1942   De geschiedenis van het Collegium Neerlandicum, de eerste en eenige middelbare onderwijsinrichting op Curacao, 1866-1871 [The history of the Collegium Neerlandicum, the first and only advanced education institute on Curacao, 1866-1871]. *W I G* 24: 269-277. **[5]**
         [*COL*]

22.0280   **SR**   1949   Geschiedkundige aantekeningen over het cultureele leven in Suri-name [Historical annotation about the cultural life in Surinam].

32.0439   **SR**   1955-56   Grepen uit de geschiedenis van het onderwijs in Suriname in de 17e en 18e eeuw [Aspects of the history of school education in Surinam in the 17th and 18th centuries]. *W I G* 36: 174-182. **[5]**
         [*COL*]

Ovens, Gerald H. C.
32.0440   JM   1955   A colonial medical school. *W I Med J* 4(4), Dec.: 260-263.   **[28]**
[*COL*]

Owen, G. H.
31.0116   JM   1963   Vocational guidance and education for adolescents.

Oxaal, Ivar
37.0651   TR   1967   The intellectual background to the democratic revolution in Trinidad.

Padmore, H. J.
32.0441   GR   1946   Adult education in Grenada. *Oversea Educ* 18(1), Oct.: 401-403.

Páez, Joaquín
32.0442   GC   1974   Educational Technology Project progress report. *Car Ed B* 1(3), Sept.: 17-21.   **[38]**   [*RIS*]
32.0443   GC   1975   Proyecto de Tecnología Educativa [Educational Technology project]. *Car Ed B* 2(2), May: 33-43.   **[38]**   [*RIS*]

Page, H. J.
43.0334   TR   1949   Agricultural research at the Imperial College of Tropical Agriculture, Trinidad, B.W.I.

Palache, J. Thomas
32.0444   JM   1907   Agricultural instructors and their work. *W I B* 8(3): 310-312.   **[43]**
[*AMN*]

Palacio, Joseph
32.0445   BZ   1976   Anthropology in Belize. *Curr Anthrop* 17(3), Sept.: 485-490.   **[8,40]**
[*COL*]

Palm, J. Ph. de
25.0265   CU   1969   HET NEDERLANDS OP DE CURAÇAOSE SCHOOL [THE DUTCH LANGUAGE IN THE CURAÇAO SCHOOL].

Palmer, Donavan
32.0446   TR   1968   Local surveys. *Tchr J* March: 12-15.   [*RIS*]
32.0447   BC   1976   The strategies behind the development of a social studies curriculum. *Social Stud Educ* 7, June: 51-54. (Special issue: Commonwealth Caribbean Social Studies Conference Proceedings. Vol. I.)

Parker, Paul C.
32.0448   GC   1972   CHANGE AND CHALLENGE IN CARIBBEAN HIGHER EDUCATION: THE DEVELOPMENT OF THE UNIVERSITY OF THE WEST INDIES AND THE UNIVERSITY OF PUERTO RICO. Ann Arbor, Michigan, University Microfilms: 536p. (Ph.D., The Florida State University, 1971)
[*RIS*]

Parkin, Bingham Lloyd
32.0449   JM   1969   A STUDY OF CONTROL FOR JAMAICA'S SYSTEM OF TEACHER PREPARATION IN RELATION TO SOCIAL PROGRESS: 1944-1966. Ed.d. dissertation, State University of New York (Albany): 379p.   **[40]**   [*PhD*]

Pass, Mrs. E. A. de
8.0178   **TR**   1929   The West Indies Boy Scouts.

Patterson, H. Orlando
32.0450   **JM**   1962   The social structure of a university hall of residence. *Pelican* 9(3), Mar.: 22-39.   **[8]**

Patterson, Sheila
18.0225   **BC,UK**   1969   IMMIGRATION AND RACE RELATIONS IN BRITAIN, 1960-1967.

Patterson, V. I.
35.0059   **JM**   1963   New schools for a new nation.

Pearse, Andrew C.
32.0451   **TR**   1952[?]   Outside the walls. *Car Q* 2(4): 36-49.   [*RIS*]
32.0452   **GC**   1955   Vocational and community education in the Caribbean. *In* Wilgus, A. Curtis, ed. THE CARIBBEAN: ITS CULTURE [PAPERS DELIVERED AT THE FIFTH CONFERENCE ON THE CARIBBEAN HELD AT THE UNIVERSITY OF FLORIDA, DEC. 2-4, 1954]. Gainesville, University of Florida Press, p.118-135. (Publications of the School of Inter-American Studies, ser. 1, v. 5.)   [*RIS*]
32.0453   **BC**   1956   Ethnography and the lay scholar in the Caribbean. *W I G* 36(2-4), May: 133-146.   **[8,19,22,24]**   [*RIS*]

Pena, Patricia
30.0190   **GC**   1972   Teaching the diabetic diet in the Caribbean.

Perkins, Bryce
32.0454   **BB**   1967   TEAM TEACHING IN BARBADOS: A HANDBOOK FOR TEACHERS. Barbados, Ministry of Education: 43p.   [*RIS*]

Persaud, Ganga
32.0455   **JM**   1975   The socializing functions of teacher-education: system maintenance or change? *Car J Educ* 2(1), June: 37-58.

Persaud, Trivedi V. N.
32.0456   **BC**   1970   Medical education in the English-speaking Caribbean. *Br J Med Educ* 4(1), March: 76-81.   **[28]**   [*PS*]

Perusse, Roland I., comp.
32.0457   **GC**   1975   WORLD-WIDE DIRECTORY OF CARIBBEANISTS. Hato Rey, Puerto Rico, Caribbean Studies Associations: 135p.   [*RIS*]

Petter, G. S. V.; Harlow, F. J. & Matheson, J. A. L.
32.0458   **BC**   1957   REPORT OF THE MISSION OF HIGHER TECHNICAL EDUCATION IN THE BRITISH CARIBBEAN. London, H.M.S.O., 30p. (Colonial report no. 336.)   [*RIS*]

Phillips, A. S.
32.0459   **BC**   1966   Teacher education in the British Caribbean. *Car Q* 12(1), March: 3-10.   [*RIS*]

Phillips, H. Hudson
32.0460 BC 1931 The West Indian and higher education. *W I Comm Circ* 46(843), Jan. 22: 27-28. [*NYP*]

Ponge, Robert
25.0280 GC 1975 Foreign language teaching and the two cultures.

Powell, Dorian L.
20.0066 JM 1972 Occupational choice and role conceptions of nursing students.

Preiswerk, Roy
32.0461 GC 1971 The teaching of International Relations in the Caribbean. *Car Q* 17(1), March: 16-22. **[39]** [*RIS*]

Prescod, Sybil
32.0462 JM 1963 Reading retardation: a problem in some of Jamaica's senior schools. *Torch* 13(4), Dec. 22-27. [*TCL*]
32.0463 JM 1965 The remedial reading experiment. *Torch* 15(2), June: 11-15. [*RIS*]

Preston, Andrew C.
32.0464 GC 1960 Teacher training in the Caribbean. *In* Wilgus, A. Curtis, ed. THE CARIBBEAN: CONTEMPORARY EDUCATION [PAPERS DELIVERED AT THE TENTH CONFERENCE ON THE CARIBBEAN HELD AT THE UNIVERSITY OF FLORIDA, DEC. 3-5, 1959]. Gainesville, University of Florida Press, p.155-161. (Publications of the School of Inter-American Studies, ser. 1, v. 10.) [*RIS*]

Prins, F. W.
32.0465 NA 1967 Waarom een nieuw schoolplan? [Why a new school plan]? *Schakels* NA47: 27-32. [*NYP*]
32.0466 NA 1971 Het Antilliaanse onderwijs: een toekomstvisie [The Antillean educational system: a look in the future]. *Pedag Forum* 5(9), Nov.: 347-353. [*RILA*]

Prins-Winkel, A. C.
25.0284 NL 1973 KABES DURU? VERSLAG VAN EEN ONDERZOEK NAAR DE ONDERWIJSSITUATIE OP DE BENEDENWINDSE EILANDEN VAN DE NEDERLANDSE ANTILLEN, IN VERBAND MET HET PROBLEEM VAN DE VREEMDE VOERTAAL BIJ HET ONDERWIJS [KABES DURU? REPORT OF AN INVESTIGATION OF THE EDUCATIONAL SITUATION IN THE LEEWARD ISLANDS OF THE NETHERLANDS ANTILLES, IN CONNECTION WITH THE FOREIGN LANGUAGE USED IN EDUCATION.

Pujadas, Leo
32.0467 TR 1969 A note on educational development in Trinidad and Tobago, 1956-1966. *Trin Res Papers* 6, June: 1-46. [*RIS*]

Punch, L. D. "Lully"
32.0468 TR [n.d.] SCOUTING MEMORIES. [Port of Spain?] Ideal Printery, 123p. **[22]** [*RIS*]

Ragbeer, M. M. S.
32.0469 BC 1972 Post-graduate medical education in the Commonwealth Caribbean. *W I Med J* 21(3), Sept.: 147-154. **[28]** [*PS*]

32.0470   BC   1974   The medical faculty U.W.I.—a brief review of twenty-five years of
                           activity—1949-1974. *W I Med J* 23(3), Sept.: 113-128. **[28]**   *[PS]*

Ramchand, Kenneth
18.0236   BC,UK   1965   The colour problem at the university: a West Indian's changing
                           attitudes.

Ramcharan-Crowley, Pearl
32.0471   SL,DM   1973   Creole culture: outcast in West Indian schools. *In* Ianni, Francis A.
                           J. & Storey, Edward, eds. CULTURAL RELEVANCE AND EDUCATIONAL
                           ISSUES: READINGS IN ANTHROPOLOGY AND EDUCATION. Boston,
                           Little, Brown and Co., Inc.: 438-443. **[20]**   *[TCL]*

Read, Margaret
32.0472   BC   1955   EDUCATION AND SOCIAL CHANGE IN TROPICAL AREAS. London,
                           Thomas Nelson, 130p. **[26]**

Reece, J. E.
32.0473   BB   1907   Agricultural teaching in elementary schools of Barbados. *W I B*
                           8(3): 302-304. **[43]**   *[AMN]*

Reid, Charles Frederick
32.0474   UV   1938   Federal support and control of education in the territories and
                           outlying possessions. *J Negro Educ* 7(3), July: 400-412.   *[COL]*
32.0475   UV   1941   EDUCATION IN THE TERRITORIES AND OUTLYING POSSESSIONS OF THE
                           UNITED STATES. New York, Teachers College, Columbia University,
                           p.443-495.   *[TCL]*

Reid, L. H. E.
32.0476   JM   1963   The common entrance examination. *Torch* 13(3), Sept.: 1-6.   *[TCL]*
32.0477   JM   1972   Selection for teacher education in Jamaica. *Torch* 21(3), Christmas:
                           9-15.   *[RIS]*
32.0478   JM   1974   Educational research and the new societies. *Car J Educ* 1, June:
                           37-41.   *[RIS]*

Renes, P. B.
32.0479   SR   1971   DE PERSONEELSVOORZIENING VAN HET LAGER ONDERWIJS IN SURI-
                           NAME [THE STAFFING OF PRIMARY SCHOOLS IN SURINAM]. The
                           Hague, The Netherlands, Centrum voor de Studie van het Onder-
                           wijs in Veranderende Maatschappijen (CESO): 221p. **[7]**   *[RILA]*

Rens, J. van
32.0480   NA   1971   Het Economisch Toeristisch Administratief Onderwijs [Economic
                           Touristic Administrative Education]. *Pedag Forum* 5(9), Nov.:
                           339-342.   *[RILA]*
32.0481   NA   1972[?]   Economisch, toeristisch en administratief onderwijs [Economic,
                           tourist and administrative education]. *In* HET ONDERWIJS IN DE
                           NEDERLANDSE ANTILLEN. The Hague, The Netherlands, Kabinet
                           voor Surinaamse en Nederlands-Antilliaanse Zaken: 14-16. *[RILA]*

Richard, Gustave
32.0482   GD   1962   Propos sur la Quinzaine de l'école publique [Remarks on Public
                           Education Fortnight]. *Rev Guad* 13(47), 2d trimester: 31-32.   *[RIS]*

Richards, Leopold A.

32.0483   JM   1974   THE CAREER ASPIRATIONS OF SECONDARY SCHOOL STUDENTS IN JAMAICA IN RELATION TO EDUCATIONAL PROGRAMMES AND MANPOWER NEEDS. Ed.D. dissertation, Rutgers University: 215p. **[20,46]**   *[PhD]*

Richardson, Beryl

61.0125   GU   1969   SUGAR IN GUYANA.

Richardson, Stephen A.; Birch, H. G. & Hertzig, Margaret E.

28.1074   JM   1973   School performance of children who were severely malnourished in infancy.

Richardson, V. A.

32.0484   TR   1965   Some problems of policy in technical education. *Educ J Trin Tob* 1(5), Nov.: 8-11.   *[TCL]*

Riske, Roger & Rust, Val D.

32.0485   TR   1975   Nonformal education and the labor force in Port of Spain, Trinidad. *In* La Belle, Thomas J., ed. EDUCATIONAL ALTERNATIVES IN LATIN AMERICA: SOCIAL CHANGE AND SOCIAL STRATIFICATION. Los Angeles, U.C.L.A. Latin American Center Publications: 293-333. (Volume 30, U.C.L.A. Latin American Studies Series) **[20,46]**   *[TCL]*

Roberts, George W.

32.0486   TR   1967   A note on school enrollment in Trinidad and Tobago, 1960. *Social Econ Stud* 16(2), June: 113-126.   *[RIS]*

7.0167   JM   1968   Demographic aspects of rural development: the Jamaican experience.

Roberts, George W. & Abdulah, N.

32.0487   BC   1965   Some observations on the educational position of the British Caribbean. *Social Econ Stud* 14(1), Mar.: 144-153.   *[RIS]*

Roberts, J. R.

18.0245   JM,UK   1967   The Jamaican child at school in Britain.

Roberts, Lydia J.

33.0161   GC   1952   First Caribbean Conference on Home Economics and Education in Nutrition.

Roberts-Holmes, Joy

18.0246   JM,UK   1973   Culture shock: remedial teaching and the immigrant child.

Robinson, Arthur N. R.

32.0488   TR   1967   THE ROLE OF THE TEACHER IN THE DEVELOPMENT OF A NATIONALIST SPIRIT: LECTURE DELIVERED TO THE TEACHERS AT THE TEACHERS' TRAINING COLLEGE, WRIGHTSON ROAD, ON THURSDAY, 22ND JUNE, 1967. Port-of-Spain, Trinidad, PNM Publishing Co., Ltd.: 15p. **[21]**   *[RIS]*

Robinson, Joyce L.
1.0244   **JM**   1967   Schools Library Service in Jamaica.

Robinson, Kenneth E.
32.0489   **BE**   1952   EDUCATION IN BERMUDA. Ph.D. dissertation, Harvard University.
                                                                           [*PhD*]

Romain, Ralph
5.0789   **TR**   1966   HISTORY READER FOR THE CHILDREN OF TRINIDAD AND TOBAGO.
32.0490   **GC**   1968   A planner's view of priorities. *In* PAPERS PRESENTED AT THE
                                    PRIORITIES IN EDUCATIONAL RESEARCH SEMINAR, 2-3 MAY, 1968.
                                    Trinidad, University of the West Indies: 6p.   [*RIS*]

Romanette, Irmine
32.0491   **MT**   1925   L'enseignement secondaire des jeunes filles à la Martinique [Sec-
                                    ondary education for girls in Martinique]. *Rev Univ* 34(3), Mar.:
                                    202-215.   **[5,10]**   [*COL*]

Römer, R. A.
32.0492   **NA**   1971   Over de toekomst van ons onderwijs [About the future of our
                                    educational system]. *Pedag Forum* 5(9), Nov.: 345-347.   [*RILA*]
32.0493   **NA**   1975   Hoger onderwijs in de Nederlandse Antillen [Higher education in
                                    the Netherlands Antilles]. *Kristòf* 2(3), June: 125-131.   [*RIS*]
32.0494   **NA**   1976   Education in Caribbean perspective—the Sprockel period. *Car Ed
                                    B* 3(3), Sept.: 47-51.   [*RIS*]

Rosaz, Jean
32.0495   **GC**   1969   L'université des Antilles: pour quoi faire? [A university of the
                                    Antilles: why?] *Cah Cent Etud Reg Ant-Guy* 18: 1-20.   [*RIS*]

Roussier, Paul
32.0496   **MT**   1930   Une maison d'éducation pour les jeunes personnes à la Martinique
                                    au temps où l'impératrice Joséphine était enfant [An educational
                                    institution for young ladies in Martinique at the time when Empress
                                    Josephine was a child]. *Rev Hist Colon Fr* 23(2), Mar.-Apr.:
                                    137-182.   **[5,10]**   [*NYP*]

Rowe, Richard R. & Thorndike, Robert L.
31.0123   **UV**   1963   VIRGIN ISLANDS INTELLIGENCE TESTING SURVEY.

Rubin, Vera
20.0074   **TR**   1961   Family aspirations and attitudes of Trinidad youth.
31.0127   **TR**   1963   The adolescent: his expectations and his society.
32.0497   **GC**   1967   Deprivation and disadvantage: nature and manifestation. Paper
                                    presented at UNESCO Conference on Deprivation and Disad-
                                    vantage, Hamburg: 62p.   **[8]**   [*RIS*]

Rubin, Vera & Zavalloni, Marisa
20.0077   **TR**   1969   WE WISH TO BE LOOKED UPON: A STUDY OF THE ASPIRATIONS OF
                                    YOUTH IN A DEVELOPING SOCIETY.

Ruddock, L. C.
32.0498   **JM**   1966   Why do we study civics. *Torch* 16(1), March: 12-15.   [*RIS*]
37.0743   **JM**   1967   CIVICS FOR YOUNG JAMAICANS.

Ruinard, J.

43.0388   SR   1967   Het Centrum voor Landbouwkundig Onderzoek in Suriname [The Centre for Agricultural Research in Surinam].

Ruscoe, Gordon C.

32.0499   JM   1963   DYSFUNCTIONALITY IN JAMAICAN EDUCATION. Ann Arbor, University of Michigan, 144p. (School of Education, Comparative education dissertation series no. 1.) **[41]**

Russell, Phyllis Macpherson

32.0500   JM   1974   Determining qualitative change in education. *Jam J* 8(2-3), Summer: 76-79.   [*RIS*]

Rutter, Michael; Yule, William & Berger, Michael

18.0252   BC,UK   1974   The children of West Indian migrants.

Ryan, T. E.

32.0501   MS   1962   Education in Montserrat. *Corona* 14(1), Jan.: 15-18.

Sammy, George M.

32.0502   BC   1969   The role of the modern university. *Car Q* 15(4), Dec.: 47-51.   **[33]**   [*RIS*]

Sammy, James S.

32.0503   TR   [n.d.]   A tribute to Rev. Dr. Walls. *In* NAPARIMA COLLEGE; DIAMOND JUBILEE, 1900-1960. San Fernando, Trinidad, Rahaman's Printery: 27-30.

Samson, Ph. A.

32.0504   SR   1948   Een middelbare school in Suriname [A high school in Surinam]. *W I G* 29: 289-295.   [*COL*]

Sánchez, I. E.

32.0505   BZ   1974   Education and manpower needs in Belize. *National Stud* 2(6), November: 31-36.   [*RIS*]

32.0506   BZ   1976   Opinion: the high cost of graduating. *Belizean Stud* 4(4), July: 33-35.   [*RIS*]

Sanders-Karel, Th. J.

32.0507   NA   1972[?]   Het kleuteronderwijs [Nursery schools]. *In* HET ONDERWIJS IN DE NEDERLANDSE ANTILLEN. The Hague, The Netherlands, Kabinet voor Surinaamse en Nederlands-Antilliaanse Zaken: 4-6.   [*RILA*]

Schalkwijk, F. G.

32.0508   NC   1926-27   Keuze en opleiding van naar West-Indie uit te zenden rechterlijke en bestuursambtenarem [Selection and training of judicial and government officials for the West Indies]. *W I G* 8: 557-566.   **[37]**   [*COL*]

32.0509   NC   1928-29   Een Westindische leergang [A West Indian course]. *W I G* 10: 320-322.   [*COL*]

Schoch, C. F.

32.0510   SR   1924-25   Het Van Eeden Fonds [The Van Eeden Foundation]. *W I G* 6: 27-29.   [*COL*]

Schreiber, Jan

18.0253   **BC,CA**   1970   In the course of discovery: West Indian immigrants in Toronto schools.

Schwartzbaum, Alan M. & Cross, Malcolm

32.0511   **TR**   1970   Secondary school environment and development; the case of Trinidad and Tobago. *Social Econ Stud* 19(3), Sept.: 368-388.   **[20]**
[*RIS*]

Seaga, Edward

32.0512   **JM**   1955   Parent-teacher relationships in a Jamaican village. *Social Econ Stud* 4(3), Sept.: 289-302.   **[9]**
[*RIS*]

Searle, Chris

21.0085   **TB**   1972   The Forsaken lover: white words and black people.

Sedoc-Dahlberg, Betty

18.0256   **SR,NE**   1971   Surinaamse studenten in Nederland: een onderzoek rond de problematiek van de toekomstige intellektuele kader-vorming in Suriname [Surinamese students in the Nether-lands: research on the problems of the shaping of the intellectual framework of Surinam in the future].

Setchell, Anne

32.0513   **BC**   1970   Report of the Caribbean conference for adult education: April 5-11, 1970, Georgetown, Guyana. *Continuous Learning* 9(3), May-June: 107-110.   [*COL*]

Shah, Sair Ali

32.0514   **GC**   1968   Research in certain aspects of curriculum development with par-ticular reference to mathematics and science for primary schools. *In* Papers at the Priorities in Educational Research Seminar, 2-3 May, 1968. Trinidad, University of the West Indies: 3p.   [*RIS*]

Shaw, Frederick

32.0515   **JM**   1958   School and society in Jamaica: the Titchfield School. *J Educ Sociol* 32(3), Nov.: 107-117.   [*RIS*]

Sherlock, Philip M.

32.0516   **GC**   1950[?]   Education in the Caribbean area. *Car Q* 1(3): 9-18.
32.0517   **BC**   1952[?]   The extra-mural programme. *Car Q* 2(3): 4-13.   [*RIS*]
32.0518   **BC**   1955   The dynamic of nationalism in adult education. *Extra-Mural Reptr* 2(4-5), Oct.-Dec.   **[21]**   [*RIS*]
32.0519   **BC**   1957   Aims and priorities in education. *In* Report and proceedings [of] His Royal Highness the Duke of Edinburgh's Study Con-ference on the Human Problems of Industrial Communities within the Commonwealth and Empire, 9-27 July 1956 [Oxford University] vol. 2: Background papers. London, Oxford Uni-versity Press, p.185-190.   [*RIS*]
32.0520   **BC**   1957   Education in the Federation of the West Indies. *Sch Soc* 85(2120), Nov. 23: 356-358.   [*COL*]
32.0521   **BC**   1957   Outside the walls. *Caribbean* 10(6-7), Jan.-Feb.: 168-170, 186.
[*COL*]

| 5.0837 | JM | 1966 | JAMAICA, A JUNIOR HISTORY. |

32.0522 BC 1967 "Into the limitless morning before us." *Torch* 17(3), Dec.: 5-11. [*RIS*]

32.0523 GC 1968 ASSOCIATION OF CARIBBEAN UNIVERSITIES. LA ASOCIACIÓN DE UNIVERSIDADES DEL CARIBE. Puerto Rico, Conference of the Caribbean Universities; Nov. 21-23: 19-31. **[38]** [*RIS*]

5.0838 BZ 1969 BELIZE; A JUNIOR HISTORY.

Shorey, Leonard
32.0524 BB 1972 A functional role for teachers' organizations in Barbados. *Car Q* 18(3), Sept: 34-42. [*RIS*]

32.0525 GC 1972 Towards professionalism in teaching in the West Indies. *Torch* 21(1-2), Easter/Summer: 29-32. [*RIS*]

Sieuchand, A. C.
56.0286 TR 1967 TRINIDAD AND TOBAGO: A JUNIOR GEOGRAPHY.

Simmons, George
32.0526 BB 1963 THE HISTORY OF CODRINGTON COLLEGE, BARBADOS, 1710-1875. Ph.D. dissertation, Harvard University. **[5]** [*PhD*]

32.0527 BB 1966-67 The legitimacy of Codrington College. *New Wld Q* 3(1-2), Dead Season and Croptime, Barbados Independence Issue: 39-49. [*RIS*]

32.0528 BB 1972 West Indian higher education—the story of Codrington College. *Car Q* 18(3), Sept.: 51-72. [*RIS*]

Simms, William
32.0529 JM 1900 Agricultural education. *W I B* 1: 77-94. **[46]** [*AMN*]

32.0530 JM 1900 The proposed agricultural department and agricultural teaching in Jamaica. *W I B* 1: 260-266. **[43]** [*AMN*]

32.0531 JM 1901 Agricultural education and its place in general education. *W I B* 2(1): 56-61. **[43]** [*AMN*]

32.0532 JM 1907 Agricultural and scientific teaching in the secondary schools of Jamaica. *W I B* 8(3): 280-281. **[43]** [*AMN*]

Singh, Paul G.
32.0533 GU 1972 In defence of academic freedom. *Thunder* 4(1), Jan.-March: 1-14. [*RIS*]

Singh, Ramlaykha
32.0534 GU 1973 AN ANALYSIS OF STUDENT-TEACHING PROGRAMS IN THE UNITED STATES WITH IMPLICATIONS FOR THE GOVERNMENT TRAINING COLLEGE IN GUYANA. Ed.D. dissertation, University of Northern Colorado: 148p. [*PhD*]

Singham, A. W.
32.0535 BC 1966 Some underlying theoretical issues in Public Administration training. *In* Mills, G. E., ed. REPORT OF A CONFERENCE ON TRAINING OF PUBLIC OFFICERS HELD IN BARBADOS, FEB. 12-13, 1965. Mona, Jamaica, University of the West Indies, Department of Government: 22-27. **[37]** [*RIS*]

Smith, Colin Henderson

32.0536   JM   1973   THE EXCELSIOR SIXTH FORM TEACHER TRAINING PILOT PROJECT
                         1970-1972 JAMAICA—A STUDY IN CHANGE. Ph.D. dissertation, Mich-
                         igan State University: 230p.   [*PhD*]

Smith, Gloria Mary

32.0537   JM   1973   THE NEW JUNIOR SECONDARY SCHOOLS OF JAMAICA. Ph.D. disser-
                         tation, Michigan State University: 279p.   [*PhD*]

Smith, Karl A.

34.0104   BC   1969   The role of the University of the West Indies in family planning.

Smith, M. G.

20.0080   JM   1960   Education and occupational choice in rural Jamaica.

Smith, M. G. & Kruijer, G. J.

8.0220   JM   1957   A SOCIOLOGICAL MANUAL FOR EXTENSION WORKERS IN THE CAR-
                         IBBEAN.

Solomon, Denis

32.0538   BC   1975   Foreign language teaching: a plea for new objectives. *Car J Educ*
                         2(2), Dec.: 119-128.   **[25]**   [*RIS*]

Solomon, Patrick

1.0264   TR   1965   The role of libraries in our changing community.

Speckmann, Johan Dirk

32.0539   SR   1962-63 Enkele uitkomsten van een sociologisch onderzoek onder de
                         Hindostaanse leerlingen van de mulo-school in Nieuw Nickerie
                         [Results of a sociological investigation among the Hindustani pupils
                         of a high school in New Nickerie]. *N W I G* 42: 208-211.   **[12]**
                                                                                   [*COL*]

Spitz, Georges

37.0822   MT   1955   La Martinique et ses institutions depuis 1948 [Martinique and its
                         administration since 1948].

Springer, Hugh W.

32.0540   BC   1960   Oriens ex occidente lux. *Car Q* 6(4): 246-257.   [*RIS*]
32.0541   BC   1962   The historical development, hopes and aims of the University
                         College of the West Indies. *J Negro Educ* 31(1), Winter: 8-15.
                                                                                   [*COL*]
32.0542   BC   1963   New ventures: the Institute of Education of the University of the
                         West Indies. *Torch* 13(2), June: 1-5.   [*TCL*]

Sprockel, P. T. M.

32.0543   NA   1967   Onderwijs [Education]. *Schakels* NA47: 8-13.   [*NYP*]
32.0544   NA   1967   Onderwijsvoorzieningen [Educational institutions]. *Schakels* NA47:
                         1-7.   [*NYP*]
32.0545   NA   1971   De Antillen en hun onderwijs [The Antilles and their educational
                         system]. *Pedag Forum* 5(9), Nov.: 322-329.   [*RILA*]
32.0546   NA   1972[?] De Nederlandse Antillen en het onderwijs [The Netherlands
                         Antilles and the educational system]. *In* HET ONDERWIJS IN DE
                         NEDERLANDSE ANTILLEN. The Hague, The Netherlands, Kabinet
                         voor Surinaamse en Nederlands-Antilliaanse Zaken: 1-3. [*RILA*]

Standard, K. L.; Cruickshank, R. & Ennever, O.

28.1209   **JM**   1969   Evaluación por los alumnos de una pasantía de medicina de la comunidad en Jamaica [Evaluation by the students of a community medicine clerkship in Jamaica].

28.1210   **JM**   1970   Analysis of students' evaluation of a five-week clerkship in community medicine in Jamaica, West Indies.

Standard, K. L. & Ennever, O.

32.0547   **JM**   1974   Training health auxiliaries. *W I Med J* 23(4), Dec.: 217-225. **[28]**
                                [PS]

28.1212   **JM**   1975   Training of health auxiliaries in the West Indies.

Standard, K. L.; Lovell, H. G. & Harney, L.

27.0136   **BB**   1966   Heights and weights of Barbadian schoolchildren.

Standish, P.

25.0315   **BC**   1973   Foreign language acquisition and some sociolinguistic factors affecting the case of the English speaking Caribbean.

Stanford, Olly N.

32.0548   **TR**   1945   The 4-H clubs movement. *Proc Agric Soc Trin Tob* 45(3), Sept.: 211-221. **[22,43]**   *[AMN]*

Stark, J.; Lajoie, P. & Green, A. J.

57.0133   **SL**   1966   Soil and land use surveys No. 20, St. Lucia.

Stembridge, E. C.

32.0549   **JM**   1939   Romance of a charity-intended marriage "dot" that benefited thousands. *W I Comm Circ* 54(1057), Apr. 6: 133-134, 141. **[5]**
                                [NYP]

32.0550   **BB**   1939   Soldier-poet who founded a college. *W I Comm Circ* 54(1064), July 13: 301-302; 54(1065), July 27: 328. **[5]**   *[NYP]*

Stewart, D. B.

32.0551   **JM**   1962   A developing medical school in the tropics. *J Med Educ* 37(9), Sept.: 1000-1011. **[28]**   *[COL]*

Stewart, V. S.

32.0552   **TR**   1965   Bridging the gap between Primary and Secondary Schools. *Educ J Trin Tob* 1(4), July: 16-20.   *[TCL]*

Stimpson, Alison

32.0553   **JM**   1974   Making the scene in art education. *Torch* 23(1), Easter: 18-28. **[22]**
                                [RIS]

St. Pierre, Maurice

46.0223   **JM**   1972   Strike or struggle? Unrest on the Mona campus of the University of the West Indies.

Stuart, G. Moody

32.0554   **TR**   1919   Agricultural college and re-organization of the Imperial Department of Agriculture. *Proc Agric Soc Trin Tob* 19(2-3), Feb.-Mar.: 36-42. **[43]**   *[AMN]*

32.0555   BC   1920   Agricultural college for the West Indies. *Proc Agric Soc Trin Tob*
                         20(3), Mar.: 94-97.   **[43]**   [*AMN*]

Stuart, K. L.
32.0556   JM   1974   The Department of Medicine—the University of the West Indies
                         1948-1973. *W I Med J* 23(3), Sept.: 129-136.   **[28]**   [*PS*]

Sukdeo, Iris D.
32.0557   GU   1975   Relevance of democratic centralism in education in the Soviet
                         Union to development in Guyana. *Guy J Sociol* 1(1), Oct.:
                         70-91.   **[37]**   [*RIS*]

Tajfel, Henri & Dawson, John, eds.
18.0268 BC,UK 1965   DISAPPOINTED GUESTS: ESSAYS BY AFRICAN, ASIAN, AND WEST
                         INDIAN STUDENTS.

Tancoo, Solomon M.
32.0558   TR   1965   The Common Entrance Examination. *Educ J Trin Tob* 1(4), July:
                         1-4.   [*TCL*]
32.0559   TR   1966   THE DIFFERENTIATION OF MENTAL ABILITIES BETWEEN THE AGES OF 13
                         AND 15 AMONG SECONDARY SCHOOL PUPILS IN TRINIDAD. Ph.D.
                         dissertation, University of London: 431p.
32.0560   GC   1968   Educational research and testing. *In* PAPERS PRESENTED AT THE
                         PRIORITIES IN EDUCATIONAL RESEARCH SEMINAR, 2-3 MAY, 1968.
                         Trinidad, University of the West Indies: 8p.   [*RIS*]

Taylor, G. T.
52.0111 SL   1960   Fisheries training school in St. Lucia.

Taylor, Margaret & Gordon, Hopeton
32.0561   JM   1971   A SURVEY OF ADULT EDUCATION IN JAMAICA. Jamaica, Ministry of
                         Youth and Community Development, National Council of Jamai-
                         can Organisations and Department of Extra-Mural Studies, U.W.I.:
                         29p.

Taylor, T. W. J.
32.0562   BC   1952   The University College of the West Indies. *Car Commn Mon Inf B*
                         5(8), Mar.: 235-238.   [*AGS*]

Telemaque, H. M.
32.0563   TR   1965   The English syllabus. *Educ J Trin Tob* 1(2), March: 3-6.   [*TCL*]

Teresa, Joan
32.0564   TR   1966   Education of mentally deficient children. *Educ J Trin Tob* 2(1):
                         8-13.   **[31]**   [*TCL*]

Thakur, Parsram Sri
32.0565   US,BC 1975   A COMPARISON OF WEST INDIAN AND AMERICAN UNDERGRADUATES
                         ON SELECTED COGNITIVE FACTORS. Ph.D. dissertation, New York
                         University: 151p.   **[20]**   [*RIS*]

Thom, James Theophilus
32.0566   GU   1969   THE PARENTAL, SOCIO-ECONOMIC, ENVIRONMENTAL AND OTHER FAC-
                         TORS DETERMINING THE NATURE AND EXTENT OF THE DISPARITY IN
                         THE PERFORMANCE OF PRIMARY SCHOOL CHILDREN IN SELECTION
                         TESTS FOR SECONDARY SCHOOL ENTRANCE IN GUYANA. Ph.D. dis-
                         sertation, University of London: 454p.   **[8,20]**

Thomas, Clive Y.

32.0567   GU   1974   Management education in Guyana: a brief description. *In* MANAGEMENT STUDIES IN THE COMMONWEALTH CARIBBEAN. Association of Caribbean Universities and Research Institutes: 35-56. (UNICA Survey Series, No. 1)   **[45]**   [*RIS*]

Thomas-Hope, Elizabeth

7.0205   JM   1975   An approach to the delimitation of school districts: the example of primary schools in the parish of St. Ann, Jamaica.

Thomasson, F. H.

42.0163   GU   1968   Training in the sugar industry in Guyana.

Thompson, Adolph A.

46.0229   BC   1952   University education in labour-management relations in British Guiana, the British West Indies and Puerto Rico in 1951-1952.

46.0230   BC   1953[?]   University education in labour-management relations.

Thompson, John Timothy

46.0231   BZ   1973   SECONDARY EDUCATION AND EMPLOYMENT IN BELIZE: A TRACER STUDY OF RECENT GRADUATES.

Thorne, A. A.

32.0568   GU   1911   Education in British Guiana. *Timehri* 3d ser., 1(18B), July: 113-119. **[5]**   [*AMN*]

32.0569   GU   1912   Education in British Guiana. *Timehri* 3d ser., 2(19A), July: 113-116. **[5]**   [*AMN*]

Tidrick, Kathryn

17.0107   JM   1971   Need for achievement, social class, and intention to emigrate in Jamaican students.

Tikasingh, Ancel Jagjit

32.0570   TR   1972   TEACHER EDUCATION IN TRINIDAD: A HISTORY. Ann Arbor, Michigan, University Microfilms: 226p. (Ph.D. dissertation, University of California, Berkeley, 1969.)   **[5]**   [*RIS*]

Toby, D.; Hosien, E. & Foster, K.

32.0571   GC   1974   The student in the Medical Faculty of the University of the West Indies—after 25 years. *W I Med J* 23(4), Dec.: 192-195. **[28]**   [*PS*]

Toran, Carey D.

32.0572   SV   1973   Education in St. Vincent: Biabou. *In* Fraser, Thomas M., ed. WINDWARD ROAD: CONTRIBUTIONS TO THE ANTHROPOLOGY OF SAINT VINCENT. Amherst, University of Massachusetts, Department of Anthropology: 58-72. (Research Reports No. 12)   [*RIS*]

Townsend, H. E. R. & Brittan, E.

18.0274   BC,UK   1972   ORGANIZATION IN MULTIRACIAL SCHOOLS.

Townsend, J. W.

32.0573   TR   1965   Physical education. *Educ J Trin Tob* 1(2), March: 30-32.   [*TCL*]

Turner, D. A.

32.0574   JM   1974   Science in the 70's: Observations on science education in Jamaica. *Car Q* 20(2), June: 15-22.   [*RIS*]

Tuyl, Ethelbert van

32.0575   SR   1970   Taman Putro: hoe ons Javaans Internaat onstond en tot bloei kwam [Taman Putro: how our Javanese Boarding school came into existence and prospered]. *In* Janssen, Cornelius, ed. SURINAME: HET WERK VAN DE FRATERS VAN TILBURG ONDER DE VIJFSTERRENVLAG. Tilburg, The Netherlands, Fraters van O. L. Vrouw, Moeder van Barmhartigheid: 42-47. (Intercom-Fraters No. 7) **[15,23]**   [*RILA*]

Valdez, Pedro

32.0576   TR   1965   Our secondary schools in relation to the needs of our times. *Educ J Trin Tob* 1(4), July: 21-24.   [*TCL*]

Vallejo, Nilo

28.1335   GC   1965   Health education in the Caribbean.

Varlack, Pearl

32.0577   VI   1974   TEACHER EDUCATION IN THE VIRGIN ISLANDS: A STRATEGY FOR CURRICULUM DESIGN. Ph.D. dissertation, University of Pittsburgh: 170p.   [*PhD*]

Vaughan, B. N. Y.

32.0578   JM   1966   Ecumenical conference on education. *Torch* 16(1), March: 8-10. **[23]**   [*RIS*]

Vérin, Pierre

25.0380   BC,MT   1958   The rivalry of Creole and English in the West Indies.

Verma, Gajendra

16.0095   BC,UK   1975   Inter-group prejudice and race relations.

Verma, Gajendra & Bagley, Christopher, eds.

16.0096   BC,UK   1975   RACE AND EDUCATION ACROSS CULTURES.

Vernon, Frances

18.0278   GU,US   1972   Guyana at Tuskegee.

Vernon, Philip E.

32.0579   JM   1964   Psychology and learning in the primary school. *Torch* 14(1), Mar.: 1-12.   [*TCL*]
27.0146   BC   1965   Environmental handicaps and intellectual development: part I.
27.0147   BC   1965   Environmental handicaps and intellectual development: part II.
9.0183   JM   1969   Jamaica; Main investigation in Jamaica.

Vernon, R.

57.0148   TR   1966   A PRELIMINARY INVESTIGATION INTO TRINIDAD SOIL NUTRIENT STATUS USING MAIZE AS A TEST PLANT.

Vincent-Brown, Wayne

32.0580   BC   1967   Introducing young West Indian poets. *Torch* 17(1), March: 32-36.
                                    [*RIS*]

Volwerk, J. H.

32.0581 NA 1971 Technisch onderwijs in de Nederlandse Antillen: problemen en perspectieven [Vocational education in the Netherlands Antilles: problems and perspectives]. *Pedag Forum* 5(9), Nov.: 329-339.
[*RILA*]

32.0582 NA 1972[?] Beroepsonderwijs [Professional education]. *In* HET ONDERWIJS IN DE NEDERLANDSE ANTILLEN. The Hague, The Netherlands, Kabinet voor Surinaamse en Nederlands-Antilliaanse Zaken: 10-13. [*RILA*]

Voorhoeve, Jan

25.0390 SR 1961 A project for the study of Creole language history in Surinam.

Voskuil, J. J.

25.0400 SR 1956 HET NEDERLANDS VAN HINDOESTAANSE KINDEREN IN SURINAME: ONDERZOEK NAAR DE INVLOED VAN DE MOEDERTAAL BIJ HET AANLEREN VAN EEN VREEMDE CULTUURTAAL [THE DUTCH OF THE HINDUSTANI CHILDREN IN SURINAM: STUDY OF THE INFLUENCE OF THE MOTHER LANGUAGE ON THE LEARNING OF A FOREIGN LANGUAGE].

Wagar, Constance Edwarda

32.0583 TR 1970 A HISTORY OF ART EDUCATION IN TRINIDAD, 1851-1968. Ph.D. dissertation, University of Toronto: 118p. **[5,22]**

Wagenaar Hummelinck, P.

32.0584 SR 1948 Enkele nadere gegevens betreffende den "Cursus HBS B" te Paramaribo over de periode van zijn bestaan [Some further data about the "High School Course B" in Paramaribo during the period of its existence]. *W I G* 29: 7-12. [*COL*]

Walker, Joyce

32.0585 BC 1968 English literature for non-specialists. *Car Q* 14(4), Dec.: 25-36.
[*RIS*]

Walmsley, D.; Cornforth, I. S. & Ahmad, N.

57.0152 TR 1969 METHODS OF ESTIMATING AVAILABLE NUTRIENTS IN TRINIDAD AND TOBAGO SOILS.

Walters, Cynthia R.

32.0586 JM 1967 The role of physical education in our developing country. *Torch* 17(2), Sept.: 22-25. [*RIS*]

Walters, Elsa H.

32.0587 JM 1958 LEARNING TO READ IN JAMAICA: A STUDY OF BACKGROUND CONDITIONS. Mona, Jamaica, Centre for the Study of Education, University College of the West Indies, 51p. [*TCL*]

32.0588 BC 1960 TEACHER TRAINING COLLEGES IN THE WEST INDIES. London, Oxford University Press, 149p.

32.0589 GC 1963 Training the teacher to work with adolescents. *In* Carter, Samuel E., THE ADOLESCENT IN THE CHANGING CARIBBEAN: PROCEEDINGS OF THE THIRD CARIBBEAN CONFERENCE FOR MENTAL HEALTH, APR. 4-11, 1961, UCWI, JAMAICA. Kingston, The Herald, p.106-110. **[31]** [*RIS*]

32.0590	JM	1967	Education in Jamaica. *In* COMMONWEALTH CHILDREN IN BRITAIN. London, National Council of Social Service: 69-78. [*RIS*]
32.0591	BC	1970	Some experiments in training personnel for the education of young children in the British Caribbean. *Int Rev Educ* 16(1): 110-119. [*COL*]

Walters, Elsa H. & Castle, E. B.
32.0592   BC   1967   PRINCIPLES OF EDUCATION: WITH SPECIAL REFERENCE TO TEACHING IN THE CARIBBEAN. London, George Allen & Unwin Ltd.: 211p.
          [*RIS*]

Walters, Elsa H. & Grant, Margaret
32.0593   BC   1963   SCHOOL METHODS WITH YOUNGER CHILDREN: A HANDBOOK FOR TEACHERS IN THE CARIBBEAN. London, Evans Brothers.

Wardlaw, C. W.
32.0594   GC   1941   Foundations of tropical agriculture. *Nature* 147(3723), Mar. 8: 282-286.   **[43]**   [*AGS*]

Warmington, Cynthia M.; Robinson, Joyce L. & McLaughlin, Rosalind
1.0296   JM   1972   JAMAICA LIBRARY SERVICE: 21 YEARS OF PROGRESS IN PICTURES, 1948-1969.

Warner, Keith Q.
11.0084   FC   1974   Négritude: a new dimension in the French classroom.

Washburn, B. E.
32.0595   JM   1929   JAMAICA HEALTH STORIES AND PLAYS. Kingston, Govt. Print Off., 110p.   **[28]**   [*COL*]

Watts, Francis
32.0596   BC   1910   Systems of agricultural education. *W I B* 10(4): 331-337.   **[43]**
          [*AMN*]
32.0597   BC   1914   On agricultural education and its adjustment to the needs of the students. *W I B* 14(3): 171-180.   **[43]**   [*AMN*]

Weatherly, U. G.
8.0244   GC   1923   The West Indies as a sociological laboratory.

Weever, P. M. de
43.0455   GU   1921   Our future peasantry.

Weijtingh, C. R.
32.0598   SR   1942   Eenige aanvullingen op de Encyclopaedie van West-Indië: Het onderwijs in Suriname [Some additions to the Encyclopedia of the West Indies: Education in Suriname]. *W I G* 24: 227-245.   [*COL*]
32.0599   CU   1942   Eenige aanvullingen op de Encyclopaedie van West-Indië: Het onderwijs op Curacao [Some additions to the Encyclopedia of the West Indies: Education on Curacao]. *W I G* 24: 289-308.   [*COL*]

Wel, F. J. van
25.0402   SR   [n.d.]   Het Nederlands in Suriname [The Dutch language in Surinam].

Wel, Freek van

25.0403 SR 1974 De toekomst van het Nederlands in Suriname [The future of the Dutch language in Surinam].

Wesley, Charles H.

32.0600 BC 1932 Rise of Negro education in the British Empire. *J Negro Educ* 1(3-4), Oct.: 354-366. **[5,11,23]** [*COL*]

32.0601 BC 1933 Rise of Negro education in the British Empire. *J Negro Educ* 2(1), Jan.: 68-82. **[5,11,23]** [*COL*]

Whitbourne, Dahlia

28.1430 JM 1965 History of the school medical services, Kingston, Jamaica (1934-1959).

Wight, J.

25.0408 JM 1971 Dialect in school.

Wiles, Silvaine

18.0285 BC,UK 1968 Children from overseas (1).
18.0286 BC,UK 1968 Children from overseas (2).

Wilgus, A. Curtis, ed.

32.0602 GC 1960 THE CARIBBEAN: CONTEMPORARY EDUCATION [papers delivered at the Tenth Conference on the Caribbean held at the University of Florida, Dec. 3-5, 1959]. Gainesville, University of Florida, 290p. (Publications of the School of Inter-American Studies, ser. 1, v. 10.) [*RIS*]

Wilkinson, Henry C.

32.0603 BE 1963 Dowding's College. *Bermuda Hist Q* 20(2), Summer: 44-51. [*COL*]

Williams, C. Holman B.

32.0604 BC 1960 Faculty of Agriculture—University College of the West Indies. *Car Q* 6(4): 243-245. **[43]** [*RIS*]

Williams, Eric Eustace

32.0605 BC 1944 Establishment of a University of the West Indies. *J Negro Educ* 13(4), Fall: 565-568. [*COL*]

32.0606 BC 1945 The idea of a British West Indian University. *Harv Educ Rev* 15(3), May: 182-191. [*TCL*]

32.0607 GC 1946 Education in dependent territories in America. *J Negro Educ* 15(3), Summer: 543-551. [*COL*]

32.0608 BC 1950 EDUCATION IN THE BRITISH WEST INDIES. [Port of Spain?] Trinidad, Teachers' Economic and Cultural Association, 167p. [*RIS*]

32.0609 GC 1954 In support of text books with a Caribbean flavour. *Car Commn Mon Inf B* 8(4-5), Nov.-Dec.: 69-71, 104. [*COL*]

32.0610 GC 1955 In support of text books with a Caribbean flavour. *Car Commn Mon Inf B* 8(6), Jan.: 114-115, 119. [*COL*]

38.0236 BC 1956 FEDERATION: TWO PUBLIC LECTURES.

32.0611 GC 1975 The University in the Caribbean in the late XXth century (1980-1999). *Car Ed B* 2(1), Jan.: 3-31. [*RIS*]

Williams, Eric Eustace, ed.

32.0612   GC   1953   Evaluation of existing facilities for vocational training in the Caribbean and proposals for their improvement. Prepared jointly by Lucien Dulau [et al.] and coordinated by Eric Williams. *In* DEVELOPMENT OF VOCATIONAL EDUCATION IN THE CARIBBEAN. Port of Spain, Caribbean Commission, p.25-44.   **[43]**   [*RIS*]

Williams, J. R.

32.0613   JM   1905   Popular agricultural education in Jamaica. *W I B* 6(2): 227-237.   **[43]**   [*AMN*]

Williams, R. L.

32.0614   BC   1965   THE SUPPLY OF ESSENTIAL SKILLS IN LESS DEVELOPED COUNTRIES. Mona, Jamaica, University of the West Indies, Institute of Social and Economic Research: 84p.   [*RIS*]

Wilson, Alan L.

5.0991   BE   1969   Richard Norwood and Berkhamsted School.

Wilson, D. G.

25.0414   JM   1969   Bi-lingualism.

Wilson, Donald

32.0615   JM   1972   Curriculum development thrust. *Torch* 22(1), Easter: 6-10.   [*RIS*]
32.0616   BC   1975   Role playing and second dialect teaching in the West Indies. *Car J Educ* 2(2), Dec.: 129-137.   **[25]**   [*RIS*]

Wilson, P. N.

32.0617   BC   1961   Agricultural education in the West Indies. *J Agric Soc Trin Tob* 61(4), Dec.: 461-488.   **[43]**   [*AMN*]
32.0618   TR   1963   The teaching and research programme of the Department of Agriculture (I.C.T.A.), University of the West Indies. *J Agric Soc Trin Tob* 63(3), Sept.: 285-302.   **[43]**   [*AMN*]

Wilson, Sybil Everesta

32.0619   JM   1972   INSTRUCTIONAL NEEDS OF BEGINNING PRIMARY SCHOOL TEACHERS IN JAMAICA AND EXPRESSED SATISFACTION WITH IN-COLLEGE TRAINING. Ph.D. dissertation, University of Toronto.   [*PhD*]

Windt, S. E. de

33.0221   NA   1972[?]   Rechtspositie onderwijzend personeel [Legal position of teachers].

Wolferen, M. D. van

32.0620   NA   1972[?]   Het lager onderwijs [Elementary education]. *In* HET ONDERWIJS IN DE NEDERLANDSE ANTILLEN. The Hague, The Netherlands, Kabinet voor Surinaamse en Nederlands-Antilliaanse Zaken: 7-9.   [*RILA*]

Worrell, Keith

32.0621   BC,UK   1972   All-black schools. . .an answer to underperformance? *Race Today* 4(1), Jan.: 7-10.   **[18]**   [*RIS*]

Worthington, E. B.

56.0339   JM   1971   Ecology and conservation: Jamaica.

Wortley, E. J.
32.0622 JM 1907 General science in elementary schools of Jamaica. *W I B* 8(3): 292-296. **[43]** [*AMN*]

Wortman, Judith
34.0126 TR,JM 1975 Training nonphysicians in family planning services and a directory of training programs.

Wunderink, R.
18.0291 SR,NE 1972 Suralco bursalen in Nederland [Suralco grant-holders in the Netherlands].

Wynter, H. L.
32.0623 BC 1964 Some thoughts on adult education. *Car Q* 10(1), Mar.: 62-63. [*RIS*]

Ying, Neville
32.0624 JM 1972 The mathematics project. *Torch* 21(1-2), Easter-Summer: 1-11.
[*RIS*]

York, Edward
32.0625 BE 1963 Schooling in Bermuda. *Bermuda Hist Q* 20(1), Spring: 17-29. [*COL*]

Yule, William; Berger, Michael; Rutter, Michael & Yule, Bridget
32.0626 BC,UK 1975 Children of West Indian immigrants: II. Intellectual performance and reading attainment. *J Child Psychol Psych* 16(1), Jan.: 1-17. **[9,18]** [*COL*]

Yustos, A. Lopez
1.0311 GC 1972 Education in the West Indies: a bibliography.

Zavalloni, Marisa
20.0092 TR 1960 Youth and the future: values and aspirations of high school students in a multicultural society in transition—Trinidad, W.I.

Zinn, Lorraine M.
32.0627 UV 1975 ADULT BASIC EDUCATION TEACHER COMPETENCY INVENTORY: VIRGIN ISLANDS. Kansas City, University of Missouri, Center for Resource Development in Adult Education: 118p. [*TCL*]

Chapter 33

SOCIAL AND LEGAL ISSUES

Social services; social welfare; social problems; family and other social legislation; drug use; police; penal institutions.

See also: **[28]** Health and public health; **[30]** Food and nutrition; **[31]** Psychiatry and mental health; **[32]** Education; **[25]** Housing and architecture; **[36]** Rural and urban development; **[41]** General economics; **[46]** Employment and labor issues.

			Abbott, Simon
18.0001	**BC,UK**	1971	Introduction.
18.0002	**BC,UK**	1971	Conclusions.
			Abbott, Simon, ed.
18.0004	**BC,UK**	1971	THE PREVENTION OF RACIAL DISCRIMINATION IN BRITAIN.
			Abdul, E. R. & Timmerman, H.
33.0001	**NA**	1974	Een vergelijking tussen het druggebruik van middelbare scholieren in Nederland en de NederLandse Antillen. [A comparison between the drug use of high school students in the Netherlands and the Netherlands Antilles]. *Ned Tijdschr Crim* 16, Sept.: 184-189. [*NYP*]
			Abell, Helen C.
32.0001	**BC**	1956	Home economics—report on a course.
			Abraham, Julian A.
33.0002	**CU**	[n.d.]	THE FEMALE IN THE POLICE FORCE: A CONSULTATION DONE IN CURAÇAO. [Curaçao]: 51p. **[10]** [*RIS*]
			Adhin, J. H.
9.0006	**SR**	1969	De figuur van de "Huwelijksbeambte" in het Surinaamse huwelijksrecht. I [The figure of the "Special Marriage Functionary" in Surinamese marriage law. I].
9.0007	**SR**	1969	De figuur van de "Huwelijksbeambte" in het Surinaamse huwelijksrecht. II [The figure of the "Special Marriage Functionary" in Surinamese marriage law. II].
9.0008	**SR**	1969	Dispensatie van vereiste toestemming bij huwelijk van meerderjarige kinderen beneden dertig jaar (artikel 101 Surinaams B. W.) [Dispensation of the required permission for marriage of people of age under 30 years old (Article 101 Surinam Civil Code)].
9.0009	**SR**	1969	Huwelijksontbinding door verstoting [Dissolution of marriage by repudiation].

33.0003	SR	1969	Juridische organisatie-vormen van godsdienstige groeperingen in Surineme [Legal organizational forms of religious groups in Surinam]. *In* Carpentier Alting, Z. H., et al., eds. EEN EEUW SURINAAMSE CODIFICATIE: GEDENKBOEK (1869-1 MEI 1969). Paramaribo, Surinaamse Juristen-Vereniging: 152-160. **[23]** [*RILA*]
33.0004	SR	1969	Ontstaan en ontwikkeling van de z.g. Aziatische huwelijkswetgeving [Origin and development of Asian marriage law]. *In* Carpentier Alting, Z. H., et al., eds. EEN EEUW SURINAAMSE CODIFICATIE: GEDENKBOEK (1869-1 MEI–1969). Paramaribo, Surinaamse Juristen-Vereniging: 93-142. **[9,12]** [*RILA*]
9.0010	SR	1969	Toepassing van Rooms-Hollands recht in Suriname [Application of Roman-Dutch law in Surinam].
9.0011	SR	1969	Worden godsdienstige huwelijken door het Surinaamse recht erkend [Are religious marriages recognized by Surinam law]
9.0012	SR	1970	De formule "Opgaan in de groep" in het Surinaamse huwelijksrecht. I [The formula "Merging into the group" in Surinamese marriage law. I].
9.0013	SR	1970	De formule "Opgaan in de groep" in het Surinaamse huwelijksrecht. II [The formula "Merging into the group" in Surinamese marriage law. II].
9.0014	SR	1971	STUITING IN HET SURINAAMSE HUWELIJKSRECHT [OPPOSITION TO MARRIAGE IN SURINAMESE MARRIAGE LAW].
9.0015	SR	1975	Surinamisering van het huwelijksrecht [Surinamization of marriage laws].

Ahamad, B.

33.0005	TR	1967	The state of crime in Trinidad and Tobago. *Trin Res Papers* 3, June: 1-25. [*RIS*]

Alcala, V. O.

32.0009	GC	1953	Home economics education in the Caribbean.
36.0002	GC	1959	Highlights of the conference on social development in the West Indies.

Alexis, Francis

56.0001	BC	1976	Law and natural resources.

Alfrey, Phyllis Shand

33.0006	BC	1963	Social education in the West Indies. *Chron W I Comm* 78(1380), Jan.: 20-23. **[32]** [*NYP*]

Alleyne, Keith Hennessey Conrad

33.0007	SV	1970	THE LAWS OF ST. VINCENT IN FORCE ON THE 31ST DAY OF DECEMBER 1966. Kingstown, St. Vincent, Government Printer, 9 vols. [*COL*]

Anderson, Wolseley Wellington

32.0023	GU	1971	FACTORS INFLUENCING PUBLIC EXPENDITURE ON EDUCATION IN GUYANA (1953-1967).

Angrosino, Michael V.

12.0005	TR	1972	OUTSIDE IS DEATH: ALCOHOLISM, IDEOLOGY AND COMMUNITY ORGANIZATION AMONG THE EAST INDIANS OF TRINIDAD.
12.0006	TR	1974	OUTSIDE IS DEATH: COMMUNITY ORGANIZATION, IDEOLOGY AND ALCOHOLISM AMONG THE EAST INDIANS OF TRINIDAD.

Ashworth, Ann & Waterlow, J. C.
30.0027   **JM**   1974[?] NUTRITION IN JAMAICA, 1969-70.

Awad, Mohamed
33.0008   **BC,SR**   1966   REPORT ON SLAVERY. New York, United Nations: 314p. (United Nations Publication No. 67. XIV. 2.) **[6,39]**   [*COL*]

Bagley, Christopher
31.0012   **BC,UK**   1975   The background of deviance in black children in London.

Ballentine, Frank Schell
39.0013   **BE**   1901   A visit to the Boers in Bermuda.

Ballysingh, Marion C.
33.0009   **JM**   1961[?] Social services in Jamaica. a) Inter-relationship of Government and voluntary agencies and services. b) The voluntary social services of Jamaica. *In* Cumper, George, ed. REPORT OF THE CONFERENCE ON SOCIAL DEVELOPMENT IN JAMAICA. Kingston, Standing Committee on Social Services, p.27-29, 30,37. **[37]**   [*RIS*]

Bannister, P.
33.0010   **BB**   1974   The problem of drug abuse in Barbados. *In* Tongue, Eva & Blair, Brenda, eds. PROCEEDINGS OF THE INTERNATIONAL CONFERENCE ON THE PREVENTION OF ADDICTIONS IN DEVELOPING COUNTRIES. Nassau, Bahamas: 49-59.   [*RIS*]

Barker, Aubrey
36.0005   **GC**   1958   Progress, planning and people.

Basdeo, Sahadeo
12.0010   **TR**   1975   The 1934 Indian labour disturbances in Trinidad: a case study in colonial labour relation.

Bates, R. K.
56.0014   **TR**   1967   Legal aspects of the disposal of trade effluents.

Bayitch, S. A.
33.0011   **GC**   1969   Inter-American legal developments. *Law Am* 1(1), Feb.: 50-67.
    [*COL*]
33.0012   **GC**   1969   Inter-American legal developments. *Law Am* 1(2), June: 42-64.
    [*COL*]
33.0013   **GC**   1969   Inter-American legal developments. *Law Am* 1(3), Oct.: 61-89.
    [*COL*]
48.0011   **GC**   1970   Aircraft mortgage in the western hemisphere: recent developments.
33.0014   **GC**   1970   Inter-American legal developments. *Law Am* 2(1), Feb.: 39-66.
    [*COL*]
33.0015   **GC**   1970   Inter-American legal developments. *Law Am* 2(2), June: 200-228.
    [*COL*]
33.0016   **GC**   1970   Inter-American legal developments. *Law Am* 2(3), Oct.: 400-430.
    [*COL*]
33.0017   **GC**   1971   Inter-American legal developments. *Law Am* 3(1), Feb.: 41-77.
    [*COL*]
33.0018   **GC**   1971   Inter-American legal developments. *Law Am* 3(2), June: 274-316.
    [*COL*]

| 33.0019 | GC | 1971 | Inter-American legal developments. *Law Am* 3(3), Oct.: 507-562. [COL] |

33.0019   GC   1971   Inter-American legal developments. *Law Am* 3(3), Oct.: 507-562.
                                                                                    [COL]
33.0020   GC   1972   Inter-American legal developments. *Law Am* 4(1), Feb.: 57-99.
                                                                                    [COL]
33.0021   GC   1972   Inter-American legal developments. *Law Am* 4(2), June: 250-290.
                                                                                    [COL]
33.0022   GC   1972   Inter-American legal developments. *Law Am* 4(3), Oct.: 474-513.
                                                                                    [COL]
33.0023   GC   1973   Inter-American legal developments. *Law Am* 5(1): 42-97.   [COL]
33.0024   GC   1973   Inter-American legal developments. *Law Am* 5(2): 307-343.   [COL]
33.0025   GC   1973   Inter-American legal developments. *Law Am* 5(3): 518-558.   [COL]

Beaubrun, Michael H.

31.0014   TR   1964   Care of the mentally retarded in Trinidad and Tobago: review of ten years progress, and plans for the future.
33.0026   TR   1967   Alcohol treatment in Trinidad and Tobago. *Transcult Psych Res* 4, April: 58-60.   **[28]**   [RIS]
33.0027   TR   1967   Treatment of alcoholism in Trinidad and Tobago, 1956-65. *Br J Psych* 113(499), June: 643-658.   **[28]**   [COL]
33.0028   JM   1968   Alcoholism and drinking practices in a Jamaican suburb. *Transcult Psych Res* 5, April: 77-79.   **[28]**   [RIS]
33.0029   JM   1968   Alcoholism and drinking practices in a Jamaican suburb. *Alcoholism* 4(1): 21-37.   **[28]**   [RIS]
33.0030   TR,JM   1970   Socio-cultural factors affecting the incidence and treatment of alcoholism in the Caribbean. *In* Proceedings of the First Aruban and Antillean Congress on Alcoholism, Aruba, Netherlands Antilles, September 11-12-13, 1970. Aruba, De Wit Stores Inc.: 122-134.   **[10,11,12]**   [RILA]
33.0031   GC   1971   Problems of drug use and abuse. *Jam Nurse* 11(3), Dec.: 8-10 passim.   **[28]**   [AJN]
33.0032   JM   1973[?]   The pros and cons of cannabis use in Jamaica. *Medi-News Car* 1(2): 27-29.   [RIS]

Beaubrun, Michael H. & Firth, Hedy

33.0033   TR   1969   A transcultural analysis of Alcoholics Anonymous Trinidad/ London. Paper presented at Joint Meeting of the Caribbean Psychiatric Association and the American Psychiatric Association, Ocho Rios, Jamaica, May 10-14: 27p.   **[7,28,31]**   [RIS]

Beaubrun, Michael H. & Knight, Frank

33.0034   JM   1973   Psychiatric assessment of 30 chronic users of cannabis and 30 matched controls. *Am J Psych* 130(3), March: 309-311.   **[31]**   [PS]

Beckles, W. A., comp.

37.0041   BB   1937   The Barbados disturbances (1937); review—reproduction of the evidence and report of the Commission.

Bell, Wendell & Oxaal, Ivar

37.0047   BC   1964   Decisions of Nationhood: Political and Social Development in the British Caribbean.

Benbow, Colin
39.0016   **BE**   1962   Boer prisoners of war in Bermuda.

Benoit, Guy
31.0024   **GD**   1963   Attitudes and problems of adolescents in Guadeloupe.

Bergh, E. van den & Rondeel, A. J.
33.0035   **SR**   1969   Overzicht van de in het Surinaams Burgerlijk Wetboek aange-
brachte veranderingen gedurende de periode van 1869 tot heden,
benevens van enkele belangrijke verschillen met het Nederlands
Burgerlijk Wetboek [Survey of the changes made in the Surinamese
Civil Code since 1869 to present, as well as some important
differences from the Dutch Civil Code]. *In* Carpentier Alting, Z. H.,
et al., eds. Een eeuw Surinaamse codificatie: gedenkboek
(1869-1 mei-1969). Paramaribo, Surinaamse Juristen-Vereniging:
29-38.   **[5]**   [*RILA*]

Berleant-Schiller, Riva
9.0024   **GC**   1972   Mating is marriage in the Caribbean.

Bigelow, Poultney
3.0045   **BE**   1902   Bermuda and the Boers; also, Its importance on the new highway of
commerce.

Bissett-Johnson, A.
33.0036   **TR**   1965   West Indian views of palm tree justice and section 17 of the
Married Women's Property Act. *Int Com Law Q* 14(1), Jan.:
308-312.   **[10]**   [*COL*]

Bolt, Christine
6.0020   **UK,BC**   1969   The anti-slavery movement and reconstruction: a study in
Anglo-American cooperation, 1833-77.

Bolten, D. G. J.
28.0135   **SR**   1925-26   Muggenbestrijding [The fight against gnats].

Bonne, C.
28.0140   **SR**   1923-24   Organizatie van den geneeskundigen dienst in Suriname [Organi-
zation of the medical services in Surinam].
28.0141   **SR**   1925-26   De opleiding en de positie van den districtsgeneesheer in Suriname
[The training and the position of the district medical officer in
Surinam].

Boom, W. R.
33.0037   **NA**   1972   Reclassering in de Nederlandse Antillen [Rehabilitation in the
Netherlands Antilles]. *Ant Jurbl* 22(3-4): 777-785.   [*COL*]

Bornn, Roy W.
33.0038   **UV**   1949   Further extension of social security to Virgin Islands. *Car Commn
Mon Inf B* 2(10), May: 289-291.   **[37]**   [*COL*]

Bottoms, A. E.
18.0031   **BC,UK**   1967   Delinquency amongst immigrants.

Boucly, Felix

33.0039   FG   1932   DE LA TRANSPORTATION DES CONDAMNÉS AUX TRAVAUX FORCÉS [ON THE TRANSPORT OF SENTENCED CONVICTS]. Paris, Librairie Arthur Rousseau, 132p.   [37]   [COL]

Boyd, P. I.

28.0150   BC   1975   The health programme of the Caricom Secretariat.

Brana-Shute, Gary

33.0040   GC   1976   CRIME AND VIOLENCE IN THE CARIBBEAN. COMMITTEE REPORT OF WORKSHOP PROCEEDINGS HELD JANUARY 31-FEBRUARY 2, 1976- SANTO DOMINGO, DOMINICAN REPUBLIC. San Juan, Puerto Rico, Association of Caribbean Universities and Research Institutes: 25p.
                                                                                                            [RIS]

Brodber, Erna

1.0035   BC   1972   SOCIAL PSYCHOLOGY IN THE CARIBBEAN: A BIBLIOGRAPHY AND SOME COMMENTS ON LAGUNAE AND AREAS OF SATURATION.

33.0041   JM   1974   ABANDONMENT OF CHILDREN IN JAMAICA. Jamaica, University of the West Indies, Institute of Social and Economic Research: 104p. (Law and Society in the Caribbean No. 3)   [9]   [RIS]

8.0026   JM   1975   A STUDY OF YARDS IN THE CITY OF KINGSTON.

Bullamore, Henry W.

28.0197   JM   1973   The inequality of access to public services: the case of Port Antonio, Jamaica.

Bunge, William

56.0049   DS,GD,MG   1973   Exploration in Guadeloupe: region of the future.

Burke, E. N.

33.0042   JM   1952   Jamaica welfare. *Car Commn Mon Inf B* 6(2), Sept.: 25-28.   [AGS]

Burton, E. A.

33.0043   BE   1955   The policing of Bermuda from the earliest times. *Bermuda Hist Q* 12(3), Autumn: 87-107.   [5]   [COL]

Calver, W. A.

33.0044   BB   1945[?]   REPORTS ON THE BARBADOS POLICE FORCE AND THE BARBADOS (BRIDGETOWN) FIRE BRIGADE. [Bridgetown?] Barbados, Advocate Co., 62p.   [RIS]

Camp, George

37.0116   GU   1963   The "Georgetown strike"—a lie of the Western press.

Campbell, Thelma P.

31.0039   GC   1963   The role of youth clubs in preparing for maturity.

Carter, Samuel E., ed.

31.0041   GC   1963   THE ADOLESCENT IN THE CHANGING CARIBBEAN: PROCEEDINGS OF THE THIRD CARIBBEAN CONFERENCE FOR MENTAL HEALTH.

Catterall, Helen Tunnicliff

6.0032   **JM**   1968   Jamaica.

Champagnie, L. E.

28.0233   **JM**   1967   Area study of Montego Bay in the parish of St. James.

Chapman, John L.

35.0011   **SV**   1951   Aided self-help housing in St. Vincent.

Charpentier, S. & Charpentier, G.

33.0045   **FG**   1954   An Indianist experiment in French Guiana. *Boln Indig* 14(2), June: 133-141. **[13,14]**   *[COL]*

Cheetham, Juliet

18.0057   **BC,UK**   1972   Immigrants, social work, and the community.

Clark, Isobel

32.0118   **UV**   1963   The insular training school programme for dependent, neglected and delinquent children in the Virgin Islands.

Clyne, Monica

33.0046   **GR**   1970   Day care in Grenada. *Cajanus* 3(6), Dec.: 323-329.   *[RIS]*

Comitas, Lambros

33.0047   **JM**   1976   Cannabis and work in Jamaica: a refutation of the amotivational syndrome. *In* Dornbush, Rhea L.; Fink, Max & Freedman, Alfred M., eds. CHRONIC CANNABIS USE. *Ann N Y Acad Sci* 282: 24-32. **[28,31]**   *[RIS]*

Cook, A. P.

33.0048   **BC**   1975   Some influences on the behaviour of the West Indian adolescent —and some problems. *Guy J Sociol* 1(1), Oct.: 100-114. **[20]** *[RIS]*

Costello, M.

35.0019   **GU**   1952   Rural housing problems: with notes on self-help housing and the possibilities of prefabrication.

Cox, R. G.

33.0049   **BB**   1948   SCHEME FOR FIRE PREVENTION AND PROTECTION, BARBADOS, B.W.I. Port of Spain, Fire Brigade Headquarters, 40p.   *[RIS]*

Craig, Susan E.

36.0030   **TR**   1974   COMMUNITY DEVELOPMENT IN TRINIDAD AND TOBAGO: 1943-1973: FROM WELFARE TO PATRONAGE.

Croes, H. S.

33.0050   **AR**   1970   Some juridical aspects of alcoholism in Aruba. *In* PROCEEDINGS OF THE FIRST ARUBAN AND ANTILLEAN CONGRESS ON ALCOHOLISM, ARUBA, NETHERLANDS ANTILLES, SEPTEMBER 11-12-13, 1970. Aruba, De Wit Stores Inc.: 118-121.   *[RILA]*

Cromwell, Leta

32.0144   **UV**   1963   Project for discovering and assisting the mentally retarded child in the school.

33.0051   UV   1970   Some facts about alcoholism in the U.S. Virgin Islands. *In* PROCEEDINGS OF THE FIRST ARUBAN AND ANTILLEAN CONGRESS ON ALCOHOLISM, ARUBA, NETHERLANDS ANTILLES, SEPTEMBER 11-12-13, 1970. Aruba, De Wit Stores Inc.: 192-195.   [*RILA*]

Cross, A. R. N.; Buxton, R. J. & Tapper, C.
33.0052   BC   1967   Criminal law, evidence and procedure. *In* Wade, H. W. R., ed. ANNUAL SURVEY OF COMMONWEALTH LAW: 1966. London, Butterworth and Co. (Publishers) Ltd.: 180-230. (Chapter 4)   [*COL*]
33.0053   BC   1968   Criminal law, evidence and procedure. *In* Wade, H. W. R., ed. ANNUAL SURVEY OF COMMONWEALTH LAW: 1967. London, Butterworth and Co. (Publishers) Ltd.: 220-279. (Chapter 5)   [*COL*]

Cross, Malcolm, ed.
2.0088   BC   1970   WEST INDIAN SOCIAL PROBLEMS; A SOCIOLOGICAL PERSPECTIVE.

Crowley, Daniel J.
49.0022   JM,TR   1953   American credit institutions of Yoruba type.

Cumper, George E.
33.0054   JM   1961[?]   The success of the Conference: a personal evaluation. *In* Cumper, George, ed. REPORT OF THE CONFERENCE ON SOCIAL DEVELOPMENT IN JAMAICA. Kingston, Standing Committee on Social Services, p.114-121.   **[8]**   [*RIS*]

Cumper, George E., ed.
33.0055   JM   1961[?]   REPORT OF THE CONFERENCE ON SOCIAL DEVELOPMENT IN JAMAICA. Kingston, Standing Committee on Social Services, 181p.   **[8]**   [*RIS*]

Cumper, Gloria
33.0056   JM   1972   SURVEY OF SOCIAL LEGISLATION IN JAMAICA. Jamaica, University of the West Indies, Institute of Social and Economic Research: 122p. (Law and Society in the Caribbean No. 1)   **[37]**   [*RIS*]

Cundall, Frank
37.0167   BC   1906   POLITICAL AND SOCIAL DISTURBANCES IN THE WEST INDIES: A BRIEF ACCOUNT AND BIBLIOGRAPHY.

Dalhuysen, B.
33.0057   AR   1970   Internal medical aspects of alcoholism and experiences with it in Aruba. *In* PROCEEDINGS OF THE FIRST ARUBAN AND ANTILLEAN CONGRESS ON ALCOHOLISM, ARUBA, NETHERLANDS ANTILLES, SEPTEMBER 11-12-13, 1970. Aruba, De Wit Stores Inc.: 100-105.   **[28]**   [*RILA*]

Dalton, Robert H.
33.0058   UV   1968   CHILDHOOD BEHAVIOR PROBLEMS IN SOCIAL FOCUS: A STUDY OF THE INSULAR TRAINING SCHOOL U.S. VIRGIN ISLANDS. St. Thomas, Virgin Islands, Department of Health: 42p.   **[9,31]**   [*RIS*]

Daly, Stephanie
10.0011   TR   1975   THE LEGAL STATUS OF WOMEN IN TRINIDAD AND TOBAGO.

Davidson, Lewis
33.0059 JM 1961[?] Acceptance of social change. *In* Cumper, George, ed. REPORT OF THE CONFERENCE ON SOCIAL DEVELOPMENT IN JAMAICA. Kingston, Standing Committee on Social Services, p.111-113. **[8,20]** *[RIS]*
31.0050 JM 1963 The adolescent's struggle for emancipation.

Davis, Kortright, ed.
33.0060 GC,LW 1973 VOICES FOR CHANGE FROM CADEC (CHRISTIAN ACTION FOR DEVELOPMENT IN THE CARIBBEAN). Antigua, Benjies: 62p. **[37]** *[RIS]*

Deakin, Nicholas & Cohen, Brian
16.0021 BC,UK 1971 Other measures against racial discrimination.

Declareuil, Jean
37.0193 FG 1927 LES SYSTÈMES DE TRANSPORTATION ET DE MAIN-D'OEUVRE PÉNALE AUX COLONIES DAN LE DROIT FRANCAIS [THE COLONIAL PENAL TRANSPORTATION AND FORCED LABOR SYSTEMS IN FRENCH LAW].

De Piro, M. Stilon
34.0023 GC 1973 Social security and family planning.

Desai, Patricia; Clarke, L. M. & Heron, C. E.
28.0313 JM 1970 Do child welfare clinics influence growth?

Devèze, Michel
5.0247 FG 1965 CAYENNE: DÉPORTÉS ET BAGNARDS [CAYENNE: EXILES AND PRISONERS].

Dip, C. E.
32.0169 NA 1972 Rede gehouden ter gelegenheid van de opening van het college-jaar 1972-1973 op 11 september 1972 van de Rechtshogeschool van de Nederlandse Antillen [Speech at the opening of the academic year 1972-1973 of the Law School of the Netherlands Antilles, September 11, 1972.

Dodd, David J.
33.0061 GU 1975 Some reflections on the evolution of delinquent careers in greater Georgetown. *Guy J Sociol* 1(1), Oct.: 28-41. **[20]** *[RIS]*

Dolly, Reynold Cartwright
45.0045 TR 1963 The adolescent in industry.

Dolly-Besson, June
33.0062 JM 1969 SELECTED CASES IN JAMAICA SOCIAL WELFARE. Mona, Jamaica, University of the West Indies: 136p. **[36]** *[RIS]*

Dresden, D. & Goudriaan, J.
33.0063 CU 1947 RAPPORT WELVAARTSPLAN NEDERLANDSE ANTILLEN 1946 [REPORT ABOUT THE WELFARE PLAN, NETHERLANDS ANTILLES 1946]. Willemstad, 67p. **[43]** *[NYP]*

Driessen, W. C. H.
33.0064 AR 1970 Alcoholism, guilt and disease. *In* PROCEEDINGS OF THE FIRST ARUBAN AND ANTILLEAN CONGRESS ON ALCOHOLISM, ARUBA, NETHERLANDS ANTILLES, SEPTEMBER 11-12-13, 1970. Aruba, De Wit Stores Inc.: 196-200. **[23]** *[RILA]*

Eckstein, Michael Eusey

33.0065   SC   1967   VIOLATIONS OF VALUES: A STUDY OF THE DIVERSE SOCIAL CONSE-
                         QUENCES OF CRIME IN ST. CROIX. Ph.D. dissertation, Columbia
                         University: 260p.   [20]   [PhD]

Edmonds, Juliet

33.0066   BB   1973   Child care and family services in Barbados. *Social Econ Stud* 22(2),
                         June: 229-248.   [9,34]   [RIS]

Edwards, Adolph

37.0214   JM   1968   THE DEVELOPMENT OF CRIMINAL LAW IN JAMAICA UP TO 1900.

Eekelaar, J. M.

9.0044   BC   1968   Family law.
9.0045   BB,JM,TR 1971   Family law.

Elder, J. D.

33.0067   TR   1970   Drug addiction and society. *In* Cross, Malcolm, ed. WEST INDIAN
                         SOCIAL PROBLEMS; A SOCIOLOGICAL PERSPECTIVE. Port-of-Spain,
                         Trinidad, Columbus Publishers Ltd.: 63-81.   [28]   [RIS]

Elsenhout, R.

23.0081   SR   1970   Een visie op het werk van de fraters in Suriname [An opinion on the
                         work of the fathers in Surinam].

Emanuels, D. H.

33.0068   SR   1969   Afwijkend recht voor afzonderlijke bevolkingsgroepen in de ges-
                         chiedenis van Suriname [Special laws for different population
                         groups in the history of Surinam]. *In* Carpentier Alting, Z. H. et al.,
                         eds. EEN EEUW SURINAAMSE CODIFICATIE: GEDENKBOEK (1869-1
                         MEI-1969. Paramaribo, Surinaamse Juristen-Vereniging: 161-
                         168.   [5,15,23]   [RILA]

Ensing, D.

33.0069   CU   1956-57 Over jeugdzorg op Curacao [About care for the youth on Curacao].
                         W I G 37: 212-218.   [COL]

Erpecum, K. J. van

33.0070   SR   1969   Vijf en zeventig jaren burgerlijk recht [Seventy five years of civil
                         law]. *In* Carpentier Alting, Z. H., et al., eds. EEN EEUW SURINAAMSE
                         CODIFICATIE: GEDENKBOEK (1869-1 MEI-1969). Paramaribo, Suri-
                         naamse Juristen-Vereniging: 175-178.   [5,37]   [RILA]

Fauvel, Luc

37.0232   FA   1955   Les conséquences économiques et sociales de l'assimilation admin-
                         istrative des Antilles Francaises [The economic and social con-
                         sequences of the political assimilation of the French Antilles].

Floch, Hervé Alexandre

28.0407   FG   1951   L'assistance sociale aux lépreux et à leurs familles [Social welfare
                         for the lepers and their families].

Forbes, Urias

37.0245 **AT,DM,KNA** 1969   Subsidiary law-making process: Antigua, Dominica and St. Kitts, 1960-1968 (a critique).

37.0248 **AT,DM,KNA** 1972   Aspects of administrative law in the West Indies: a study of recent developments in Antigua, Dominica and St. Kitts.

Forde, Norma

33.0071   **BB**   1975   The evolution of marriage law in Barbados. *J Barb Mus Hist Soc* 35(1), March: 33-46. **[9]**   [*AMN*]

Fox, Annette Baker

33.0072   **GC**   1949   FREEDOM AND WELFARE IN THE CARIBBEAN: A COLONIAL DILEMMA. New York, Harcourt, Brace, 272p. **[37]**   [*RIS*]

Francis, Sybil E.

36.0038   **JM**   1969   The evolution of community development in Jamaica.

Fraser, H. Aubrey

33.0073   **BC**   1972[?]   The law and the illegitimate child. *In* Haynes, Lilith M., ed. FAMBLI: THE CHURCH'S RESPONSIBILITY TO THE FAMILY IN THE CARIBBEAN. Trinidad, CARIPLAN: 124-143. **[9]**   [*RIS*]

33.0074   **BC**   1974   The law and cannabis in the West Indies. *Social Econ Stud* 23(3), Sept.: 361-385. **[5,28]**   [*RIS*]

33.0075   **BC**   1974   The law and cannabis use in the West Indies. *In* Tongue, Eva & Blair, Brenda, eds. PROCEEDINGS OF THE INTERNATIONAL CONFERENCE ON THE PREVENTION OF ADDICTIONS IN DEVELOPING COUNTRIES. Nassau, Bahamas: 97-128.   [*RIS*]

Fraser, Thomas M.

33.0076   **SV**   1972[?]   Conclusion: the volcano takes its toll. *In* Fraser, Thomas M.; Ciski, Robert; Hourihan, John J.; Morth, Grace E. & Mulcahy, F. David. LA SOUFRIERE: CULTURAL REACTIONS TO THE THREAT OF VOLCANIC ERUPTION ON THE ISLAND OF SAINT VINCENT, 1971-1972. Amherst, University of Massachusetts: 101-113. **[20,53]**   [*RIS*]

33.0077   **SV**   1972[?]   A plan for evacuation. *In* Fraser, Thomas M.; Ciski, Robert; Hourihan, John J.; Morth, Grace E. & Mulcahy, F. David. LA SOUFRIERE: CULTURAL REACTIONS TO THE THREAT OF VOLCANIC ERUPTION ON THE ISLAND OF SAINT VINCENT, 1971-1972. Amherst, University of Massachusetts: 63-77. **[53]**   [*RIS*]

Frean, D. E.

33.0078   **GU**   1953   The British Council in British Guiana. *Timehri* 4th ser., 1(32), Nov.: 12-16.

Freitas, Q. B. de

28.0466   **GU**   1942   Some observations on the proposed scheme for British Guiana for the improvement of public health and sanitary measures.

Gaay Fortman, B. de

41.0189   **CU**   1938   Economische en sociale vraagstukken in Curacao [Economic and social problems in Curacao].

Gates, Ralph Charles

43.0167   **GC**   1961   A MONOGRAPH ON COOPERATIVE DEVELOPMENT IN THE CARIBBEAN.

Gayle, H. Haughton

32.0223   **JM**   1967   Some legal aspects of corporal punishment and supervision in schools.

George, Walter F.

28.0490   **JM**   1974   An approach to VD control based on a study in Kingston, Jamaica.

Gerber, William

46.0083   **GC**   1968   Supplementary benefits in Latin America and the Caribbean.

Gershenfeld, Walter J.

46.0084   **JM**   1974   COMPULSORY ARBITRATION IN JAMAICA 1952-1969.

Ginsbergen, G. van

9.0054   **NA**   1968   De uitsluiting van adoptie van afstammelingen van een der adoptanten [The exclusion of adoption of descendants of one of the adopting parents].

Glover, J. N.

33.0079   **TC**   1970   THE LAWS OF THE TURKS AND CAICOS ISLANDS: VOL. I. Turks and Caicos Islands, The Government of the Turks and Caicos Islands: 706p.   [*COL*]

33.0080   **TC**   1970   THE LAWS OF THE TURKS AND CAICOS ISLANDS: VOL. II. Turks and Caicos Islands, The Government of the Turks and Caicos Islands: 707-1506.   [*COL*]

33.0081   **TC**   1972   THE LAWS OF THE TURKS AND CAICOS ISLANDS: VOL. III. Turks and Caicos Islands, The Government of the Turks and Caicos Islands: 1511-2198.   [*COL*]

33.0082   **TC**   1974   THE LAWS OF THE TURKS AND CAICOS ISLANDS: CONTINUATION VOLUME 1971-1973. Turks and Caicos Islands, The Government of the Turks and Caicos Islands: 401p.   [*COL*]

Gobin, Maurice

33.0083   **TR**   1969   Social security for Trinidad and Tobago. *Int Social Sec Rev* 22(2): 227-250.   [*COL*]

Govaerts, C. H.

33.0084   **NA**   1969   Beschouwing over het domiciliebeginsel in het Antilliaans internationaal privaatrecht enin het interregionaal pr vaatrecht van het Koninkrijk [Comment on the domicile principle in Antillean international private law and in the intra-regional private law of the Kingdom]. *In* HONDERD JAAR CODIFICATIE IN DE NEDERLANDSE ANTILLEN. Arnhem, The Netherlands, S. Gouda Quint/D. Brouwer en Zoon: 63-80.   **[39]**   [*RILA*]

Graham-Perkins, Justice; Fraser, Justice; Persaud, Justice; Lewis, Justice & Williams, Justice

33.0085   **BC**   1974   THE WEST INDIAN REPORTS: VOLUME 17: 1971. London, Butterworth and Co. (Publishers) Ltd.: 544p.   [*COL*]

Grant, Louis Strathmore & Anderson, S. E.
28.0545   **BC**   1955   The problem of medical care in the Caribbean.

Green, Monica
33.0086   **BC**   1966   The Save the Children Fund in the West Indies. *Int Social Work* 9(2), April: 38-43.   [*NYP*]

Greenwood-Barton, L. H.
30.0107   **JM**   1957   The establishment and administration of food standards in Jamaica.

Grunert, Richard E., ed.
33.0087   **UV**   1967   Third circuit decision of interest. *V I Bar J* 1(1), Jan.: 63-68.   [*COL*]

Grunert, Richard E. & Spencer, J. Michael, eds.
33.0088   **UV**   1969   Third circuit cases of interest. *V I Bar J* 3(1), May: 50-55.   [*COL*]

Gunness, Robert N.
32.0262   **TR**   1966   "There is no place like home" for the handicapped child.

Hadel, Richard E.
33.0089   **BZ**   1975   Fires of Belize. *National Stud* 3(5), September: 1-10.   **[5]**   [*RIS*]

Hagerty, T. F.
31.0070   **AR**   1963   The Junior Achievement Programme in Aruba.

Haglund, Elsa
32.0263   **GC**   1953   Home economics in the Caribbean.
32.0264   **GC**   1954   Caribbean training course in home economics.
33.0090   **GC**   1955   Towards better living. *Caribbean* 9(4), Nov.: 78-81.   [*COL*]
33.0091   **GC**   1956   Better home and family living in the Caribbean. *Afr Women* 2(1), Dec.: 1-4.   [*NYP*]
35.0036   **GC**   1958   HOUSING AND HOME IMPROVEMENT IN THE CARIBBEAN.

Hale, Edward Everett
39.0075   **BE**   1901   The Boer prisoners in Bermuda (a letter).

Hallema, A.
37.0325   **SR,CU**   1934-35 Het jaar 1872 in de geschiedenis van het gevangeniswezen in de West [The year 1872 in the history of the prison system in the West].

Harding, Timothy & Knight, Frank
33.0092   **JM**   1973   Marihuana-modified mania. *Archs Gen Psych* 29(5), Nov.: 635-637.   **[31]**   [*ACM*]

Harricharan, Wilfred Rupert
46.0105   **TR**   1968   THE EMPLOYMENT PROBLEM IN AN EMERGING SOCIETY—THE CASE OF TRINIDAD AND TOBAGO.

Hausman, Robert M.
48.0073   **UV**   1969   Economic regulation of Virgin Islands air transportation.

Heasman, Kathleen
33.0093   **BB,JM,SL**   1968   Some impressions of community development in the Caribbean. *Community Dev J* 3(4), Oct.: 195-200.   **[8]**   [*TCL*]

Henriques, Fernando

33.0094   GC   1965   PROSTITUTION IN EUROPE AND THE AMERICAS. New York, The
                         Citadel Press: 378p. **[6,9]**   [*COL*]

Henriquez, E. C.

33.0095   CU   1969   Familiegronden (Tera di Famia) en oude fideicommissen (filo-
                         commis) op het eiland Curaçao [Family lands and old fidei-
                         commissum properties on the island of Curaçao]. *In* HONDERD JAAR
                         CODIFICATIE IN DE NEDERLANDSE ANTILLEN. Arnhem, The Nether-
                         lands, S. Gouda Quint/D. Brouwer en Zoon: 81-103. **[44]**   [*RILA*]

Hewitt, W.

31.0073   JM   1963   The attitudes of courts towards young offenders: the juvenile courts
                         in Jamaica.

Hiro, Dilip

18.0141   BC,UK   1973   BLACK BRITISH, WHITE BRITISH.

Hockin, Margaret L.

33.0096   GC   1950   More bread for the Caribbean. *Car Commn Mon Inf B* 4(3), Oct.:
                         531-534.   [*COL*]

Hoffman, Louis

33.0097   UV   1967   Report of the president: Virgin Islands Bar Association. *V I Bar J*
                         1(1), Jan.: 34-41.   [*COL*]

Hope, Kempe R.

37.0370   GU   1976   Guyana's National Service Programme.

Horn, Edwin

35.0042   BC   [n.d.]   THE WEST INDIES: REPORT OF A SURVEY ON HOUSING, NOVEMBER
                          1956-MAY 1957.

Hourihan, John J.

37.0372   SV   1972[?]   Evacuation as a political resource.
33.0098   SV   1972   Evacuation camps. *In* Fraser, Thomas M., Ciski, Robert; Hourihan,
                         John J.; Morth, Grace E. & Mulcahy, F. David. LA SOUFRIERE:
                         CULTURAL REACTIONS TO THE THREAT OF VOLCANIC ERUPTION ON
                         THE ISLAND OF SAINT VINCENT, 1971-1972. Amherst, University of
                         Massachusetts: 78-82. **[53]**   [*RIS*]
46.0117   SV   1973   Youth employment: Stubbs.

Howes, H. W.

32.0296   GC   1955   FUNDAMENTAL, ADULT, LITERACY AND COMMUNITY EDUCATION IN
                         THE WEST INDIES.

Hoyt, Elizabeth E.

46.0118   JM   1960   Voluntary unemployment and unemployability in Jamaica with
                         special reference to the standard of living.

Huber, H. C. U. J.

9.0079   SR   1969   Enkele opmerkingen over de specifieke regeling betreffende de
                         toestemming tot erkenning in het Surinaams Burgerlijk Wetboek
                         [Some remarks on the specific regulation of consent to legitimize in
                         the Surinam Civil Code].

Huggins, John
33.0099 BC 1944 West Indies development and welfare organization. *In* Frazier, E. F. & Williams, E., eds. THE ECONOMIC FUTURE OF THE CARIBBEAN. Washington, D.C., Howard University Press, p.69-72.

Hutchinson, Frank L.
33.0100 JM 1956 Hunger and help in the Caribbean: Jamaica, Puerto Rico, Haiti. *Natn Coun Outlook* 6(10), Dec.: 10-12. **[23]** [*NYP*]

Ibberson, Dora
33.0101 JM 1953 The training of welfare officers. *Community Dev B* 5(1), Dec.: 10-13. [*NYP*]
33.0102 BC 1956 Social welfare in the West Indies. *Statist* Sept.: 58-60.

Jagan, Cheddi
41.0262 GU 1964 THE ANATOMY OF POVERTY IN BRITISH GUIANA.

James, Charles
33.0103 BC 1972 The Queensbury rules of self-defence. *Int Comp Law Q* 21(2), April: 357-361. [*COL*]

James, S. A.
32.0310 SL 1962 Adult education and community development.

Janssen, J. H. G.
33.0104 AR 1970 Some general aspects of alcoholism in Aruba. *In* PROCEEDINGS OF THE FIRST ARUBAN AND ANTILLEAN CONGRESS ON ALCOHOLISM, ARUBA, NETHERLANDS ANTILLES, SEPTEMBER 11-12-13, 1970. Aruba, De Wit Stores Inc.: 18-28. [*RILA*]

Jenkins, R. W. & Patterson, D. A.
54.0548 JM 1973 The relationship between chemical composition and geographical origin of cannabis.

Jephcott, Pearl
33.0105 GU 1956 REPORT ON THE NEEDS OF THE YOUTH OF THE MORE POPULATED COASTAL AREAS OF BRITISH GUIANA: WITH PARTICULAR REFERENCE TO THE RECREATION AND INFORMAL EDUCATION OF THOSE AGED 13-19. [Georgetown, B.G.], Social Welfare Division, Local Government Dept., 27p. **[8,22]** [*RIS*]

Jha, J. C.
33.0106 TR 1975 The background of the legalisation of non-Christian marriages in Trinidad and Tobago. *In* EAST INDIANS IN THE CARIBBEAN: A SYMPOSIUM ON CONTEMPORARY ECONOMIC AND POLITICAL ISSUES. JUNE 25-28, 1975. St. Augustine, Trinidad, University of the West Indies, Faculty of Social Sciences and Institute of African and Asian Studies: 41p. **[9,12]** [*RIS*]

John, Augustine
18.0154 BC,UK 1970 RACE IN THE INNER CITY: A REPORT ON HANDSWORTH, BIRMINGHAM.

John, Gus
18.0155   **BC,UK**   1972   The social worker and the young blacks.

Johnson, Russell B. & Ekern, George P.
33.0107   **SC**   1969   The Public Surveyor's Protocols of St. Croix. *V I Bar J* 3(1), May:
20-34.   **[5,44]**   [*COL*]

Jones, K.
18.0159   **BC,UK**   1967   Immigrants and the social services.

Joseph, A.
31.0078   **TR**   1963   Problems of the Trinidad adolescent.

Kadleigh, Sergei
35.0045   **JM**   1961[?]   Our housing needs.

Kane, Arthur
23.0154   **JM**   1969   Social action and the church in Jamaica.

Kendall, W. E., ed.
31.0079   **GC**   1957   Constructive mental hygiene in the Caribbean.

Key, W. S.
39.0095   **BE**   1902   The Boer prisoners in Bermuda.

Kielstra, J. C.
41.0278   **SR**   1925   WIRTSCHAFTLICHE UND SOZIALE IN NIEDERLÄNDISCH-WESTINDIEN
[ECONOMIC AND SOCIAL PROBLEMS IN THE DUTCH WEST INDIES].

Kloos, Peter
13.0116   **SR**   1969   Tribale samenleving en nationale staat: over rechtspleging bij
hedendaagse Caraiben in Suriname [Tribal society and national
state: on the administration of justice among present-day Caribs in
Surinam].

Knox, John
32.0336   **TR**   1966   Educating the blind in today's changing world.

Köbben, A. J. F.
14.0039   **SR**   1969   Law at the village level: the Cottica Djuka of Surinam.

Krausz, Ernest
18.0171   **BC,UK**   1971   ETHNIC MINORITIES IN BRITAIN.

Kruijer, G. J.
33.0108   **SR**   1952   "Social welfare work" in Brits West-Indie en het maatschappelijk
werk in Suriname's Tienjarenplan [Social welfare work in the British
West Indies and social work in Surinam's Ten Year Plan]. *W I G*
33: 199-212.   [*COL*]
9.0088   **JM**   1968   JAMAICA'S SOCIAL PROBLEMS: A REPORT INDICATING A WAY OUT;
PART I [PART II: CLARIFICATIONS AND ADDITIONAL DETAILS; PART
III: SCIENTIFIC EVIDENCE].

Kruijer, G. J.; Veenenbos, J. S. & Westermann, J. H.
41.0294   **NW**   1953   Richtlijnen voor de economische en sociale ontwikkeling der Bovenwindse Eilanden [Directives for the economic and social development of the Windward Islands].

Kushnick, Louis
16.0054   **BC,UK**   1971   British anti-discrimination legislation.

Laan, R.
33.0109   **NA**   1968   Landsverordening tot regeling van het verlenen van rechtsbijstand aan onvermogenden [Land regulation for legal aid to indigents]. *Justicia* 4(2): 31-33.   [*COL*]

Laclé, Clyve
33.0110   **AR**   1970   The task of the social worker in the treatment of alcoholism. *In* PROCEEDINGS OF THE FIRST ARUBAN AND ANTILLEAN CONGRESS ON ALCOHOLISM, ARUBA, NETHERLANDS ANTILLES, SEPTEMBER 11-12-13, 1970. Aruba, De Wit Stores, Inc.: 76-79.   [*RILA*]

Lambert, B.
33.0111   **NA**   1952   Situation sociale et médicale aux Antilles Néerlandaises [The social and medical situtation in the Dutch West Indies]. *Civilizations* 2(3), Sept.: 407-411. **[28]**   [*COL*]

Lambert, J. R.
18.0173   **BC,UK**   1970   CRIME, POLICE AND RACE RELATIONS.

Lampe, P. H. J.
28.0760   **SR**   1926-27 Enkele opmerkingen over den sociaal-hygienischen toestanden en dé geneeskundige verzorging van Suriname [Some remarks about the social-hygienic conditions and medical care in Surinam].
28.0761   **SR**   1927   SURINAME, SOCIAAL-HYGIENISCHE BESCHOUWINGEN [SURINAM, SOCIAL-HYGIENIC OBSERVATIONS].
28.0762   **SR**   1927-28 Suriname, sociaal-hygienische beschouwingen [Surinam, social-hygienic observations].

Lashley, T. O.
35.0048   **BB**   1945[?] REPORT ON A HOUSING SURVEY OF EIGHT SLUM TENANTRIES IN BRIDGETOWN, JUNE 1944-APR. 1945.
35.0049   **BB**   1953   Barbados attacks the housing problem.

Lastra, Yolanda
32.0342   **GC**   1968   Literacy.

Lawley, David Baxter
32.0345   **TR**   1952   Trinidad's new school for the blind.

Layne, Frederick et al.
33.0112   **BB**   1964   A PLAN FOR THE IMPLEMENTATION AND ADMINISTRATION OF THE PROPOSED SOCIAL SECURITY SCHEME FOR BARBADOS. [Bridgetown?] Barbados, Govt. Print. Off., 77p. **[37,49]**

Lazar, Leonard
49.0066   BC   1967   Taxation.

Le Clère, Marcel
33.0113   FG   1973   LA VIE QUOTIDIENNE DANS LES BAGNES [DAILY LIFE IN THE PENAL COLONIES]. Paris, Hachette Littérature: 309p.   **[5]**

Lee, George W.
31.0086   GC   1970   Sheltered facilities and occupation for the mentally handicapped.

Lee, Ulric
33.0114   TR   1959   REPORT TO THE HONOURABLE THE PREMIER BY THE HONOURABLE ULRIC LEE ON THE REORGANISATION OF THE PUBLIC SERVICE. [Port of Spain?] Trinidad, Govt. Print. Off., 334p.   **[37,41]**   [*RIS*]

Leflore, James Edward
36.0054   TR   1973   AN ANALYSIS OF A THIRD-WORLD SLUM SETTLEMENT: A CASE STUDY OF URBANISM IN TRINIDAD.

Leger, Marcel
28.0789   FG   1917   Parasitisme intestinal à la Guyane Francaise dans la population locale et dans l'élément pénal [Intestinal parasitism in French Guiana, among the local population and among the penal element].
28.0790   FG   1918   La lèpre à la Guyane Francaise dans l'élément penal: documents statistiques [Leprosy in French Guiana among the penal element: statistical documentation].
28.0791   FG   1920   La Guyane Francaise: questions de salubrité et de réglementations sanitaires [French Guiana: matters of sanitation and public health regulations].

Lewis, Cecil P.
33.0115   MS   1965   THE REVISED LAWS OF MONTSERRAT. London, Waterlow and Sons Ltd., 9 vols.: 5254p.   [*NYP*]
33.0116   BV   1965   THE REVISED LAWS OF THE VIRGIN ISLANDS. London, Waterlow and Sons Ltd., 8 vols.: 4689p.   [*NYP*]

Lewis, E. P.
9.0091   TR   1964   ADOPTION AND FOSTER HOMES.

Lewis, L. F. E. & Moses, E. A.
33.0117   TR   1974   Policies and programmes for the prevention of drug abuse in Trinidad and Tobago. *In* Tongue, Eva & Blair, Brenda, eds. PROCEEDINGS OF THE INTERNATIONAL CONFERENCE ON THE PREVENTION OF ADDICTIONS IN DEVELOPING COUNTRIES. Nassau, Bahamas: 129-135.   [*RIS*]

Lieber, Michael
33.0118   TR   1975   The economics and distribution of *Cannabis sativa* in urban Trinidad. *Econ Botany* 29(2), April-June: 164-170.   [*COL*]

Limburg Stirum, O. E. G. Graaf van
37.0490   SR,FG   1923-24 Suriname en de Fransche strafkolonies [Surinam and the French penal colonies].
37.0491   SR,FG   1924-25 De opheffing der strafkolonie: Fransch Guyana en haar mogelijke gevolgen voor Suriname [The abolition of the penal colony in French Guiana and its possible results for Surinam].

37.0492	**SR,FG**	1925-26 De strafkolonies in Fransch Guyana [The penal colonies of French Guiana].
37.0494	**SR**	1926-27 Voorwaardelijke veroordeeling [The probation system].

Liverpool, N. J. O.

37.0497	**BC**	1965 THE DEVELOPMENT OF THE LAW OF SUCCESSION IN THE WEST INDIES.

Lloyd, Antony J. & Robertson, Elaine E.

33.0119	**TR**	1971 SOCIAL WELFARE IN TRINIDAD AND TOBAGO. Trinidad, Antilles Research Associates: 95p. [*COL*]

Lochhead, A. V. S.

33.0120	**TR**	1956[?] REPORT ON ADMINISTRATION OF THE SOCIAL SERVICES IN TRINIDAD AND TOBAGO: WITH PARTICULAR REFERENCE TO CO-ORDINATION. [Port of Spain, Govt. Print. Off.?] **[37]**

Lopez, H. Th.

9.0093	**NA**	1968 Ontwerp tot regeling der adoptie [Draft for the regulation of adoption].

Luckhoo, Joseph; Fraser, Justice; Persaud, Justice; Lewis, Justice P. C. & Williams, Justice

33.0121	**BC**	1970 THE WEST INDIAN REPORTS: VOLUME 12: 1968. London, Butterworth & Co. (Publishers) Ltd.: 529p. [*COL*]
33.0122	**BC**	1971 THE WEST INDIAN REPORTS: VOLUME 13: 1968-1969. London, Butterworth & Co. (Publishers) Ltd.: 528p. [*COL*]
33.0123	**BC**	1971 THE WEST INDIAN REPORTS: VOLUME 14: 1969-1970. London, Butterworth & Co. (Publishers) Ltd.: 532p. [*COL*]
33.0124	**BC**	1972 THE WEST INDIAN REPORTS: VOLUME 16. London, Butterworth & Co. (Publishers) Ltd.: 549p. [*COL*]

Luke, Stephen

33.0125	**BC**	1954[?] DEVELOPMENT AND WELFARE IN THE WEST INDIES 1953. London, Colonial Office, 129p. ([Gt. Brit. Colonial Office], Development and welfare in the West Indies.) [*RIS*]
33.0126	**BC**	1955[?] DEVELOPMENT AND WELFARE IN THE WEST INDIES 1954. [Bridgetown?] Barbados, Advocate Co., 129p. ([Gt. Brit. Colonial Office], Development and welfare in the West Indies.) [*RIS*]
33.0127	**BC**	1955 Organising development and welfare on the spot. *New Commonw, Br Car Suppl* 10(10), Nov. 14: ii-iv. [*AGS*]
33.0128	**BC**	1956 The work of the Development and Welfare Organisation. *Statist* Sept.: 11.
33.0129	**BC**	1957 DEVELOPMENT AND WELFARE IN THE WEST INDIES, 1955-1956. London, H.M.S.O. 140p. (Colonial no. 335.)
33.0130	**BC**	1958 DEVELOPMENT AND WELFARE IN THE WEST INDIES, 1957. London, H.M.S.O., 144p. (Colonial no. 337.)

Lutchman, Harold A.

37.0509	**GU**	1973 The office of Ombudsman in Guyana.

McCarthy, M.

33.0131	**UV**	1974 Problems of addiction and coping strategies in the U.S. Virgin Islands. *In* Tongue, Eva & Blair, Brenda, eds. PROCEEDINGS OF THE INTERNATIONAL CONFERENCE ON THE PREVENTION OF ADDICTIONS IN DEVELOPING COUNTRIES. Nassau, Bahamas: 61-78. [*RIS*]

MacCormick, Neil

33.0132   BC   1971   Social services and controls. *In* Wade, H. W. R., ed. ANNUAL SURVEY OF COMMONWEALTH LAW: 1970. London, Butterworth and Co. (Publishers) Ltd.: 666-685. (Chapter 21)   **[41]**   [*COL*]

MacDonald, Judy Smith

25.0242   GR   1973   Cursing and context in a Grenadian fishing community.

MacInnes, C. M.

33.0133   BC   1955   Development and welfare in the British West Indies. *In* DEVELOPMENT TOWARDS SELF-GOVERNMENT IN THE CARIBBEAN: A SYMPOSIUM HELD UNDER THE AUSPICES OF THE NETHERLANDS UNIVERSITIES FOUNDATION FOR INTERNATIONAL CO-OPERATION AT THE HAGUE, Sept. 1954. The Hague, W. van Hoeve, p.224-236.   [*RIS*]

McNamara, Rosalind

33.0134   GC   1960   Family improvement in the Caribbean. *Caribbean* 14(2), Feb.: 28-29.   [*COL*]

MacPherson, John

33.0135   BC   1947   DEVELOPMENT AND WELFARE IN THE WEST INDIES, 1945-46. London, H.M.S.O., 162p. ([Gt. Brit. Colonial Office], Development and welfare in the West Indies; Colonial no. 212.)

Madden, F.

41.0325   BC   1954   Social and economic conditions of the British West Indies.

Mahabir, Rodney J.

31.0097   TR   1964   The care of the emotionally distrubed child—a brief survey.

Mahy, G. E.

33.0136   GR,WW   1974   Strategies for the prevention of drug abuse in Grenada and the other Windward Islands. *In* Tongue, Eva & Blair, Brenda, eds. PROCEEDINGS ON THE INTERNATIONAL CONFERENCE ON THE PREVENTION OF ADDICTIONS IN DEVELOPING COUNTRIES. Nassau, Bahamas: 41-47.   [*RIS*]

Manswell, Claris

32.0380   TR   1966   The Princess Elizabeth Home for physically handicapped children.

Marier, Roger

33.0137   JM   1953   SOCIAL WELFARE WORK IN JAMAICA. Paris, UNESCO, 166p. (Monographs on fundamental education, 7.)   [*RIS*]

Marsh, J. D.

33.0138   UV   1974   Court modernization in the Virgin Islands. *Judicature* 58(2), Aug.-Sept.: 86-91.   [*COL*]

Marshall, Gloria Albertha

49.0077   BC   1959   BENEFIT SOCIETIES IN THE BRITISH WEST INDIES: THE FORMATIVE YEARS.

Mason, G. B.

28.0844   **BC**   1922   The British West Indies medical services.

Mason, Joyce

32.0386   **SL**   1962   Adult education and family life.

Mathews, Thomas G.

8.0154   **UV**   1970   Social configuration and its implications.

Merwin, John D.

33.0139   **UV**   1969   The U.S. Virgins come of age. *V I Bar J* 3(1), May: 35-43. **[1]**
    [COL]

Metry, F.

33.0140   **NA**   1972   Fiscale aftrek voor onderhoud van natuurlijke kinderen [Fiscal deduction for support of natural children]. *Ant Jurbl* 22(3-4): 791-796.   *[COL]*

Moorehead, George A.

28.0905   **SC,ST**   1973   Utilization of Methadone Hydrochloride for opiate addiction.

Morpurgo, A. J.

9.0102   **SR**   1966   Enige aantekeningen over de Aziatische Huwelijksbesluiten [Some notes on the Asian marriage legislation].

Mose, George Elliot

33.0141   **TR**   1964   A paper prepared for the Conference on Child Care in Trinidad and Tobago. *In* REPORT OF CONFERENCE ON CHILD CARE IN TRINIDAD AND TOBAGO [held by] Trinidad and Tobago Association for Mental Health, Sub-Committee on Children and Youth, Community Education Centre, St. Ann's, Apr. 18th 1964. [Port of Spain?] Govt. Printer, p.26-29. **[32]**

32.0411   **TR**   1966   Training the socially handicapped child.

Moser, C. A.

41.0356   **JM**   1957   THE MEASUREMENT OF LEVELS OF LIVING WITH SPECIAL REFERENCE TO JAMAICA.

Murray, Winston Churchill

5.0641   **BC**   1970   LABOR, POLITICS AND SOCIAL LEGISLATION IN THE BRITISH WEST INDIES 1834-1970.

Nahas, Gabriel G. & Greenwood, Albert

33.0142   **JM**   1974   The first report of the National Commission on marihuana (1972): signal of misunderstanding or exercise in ambiguity. *B NY Acad Med* 50(1), Jan.: 55-75. **[28]**   *[ACM]*

Nicolas, François

33.0143   **FC**   1975   Les récents avantages sociaux accordés aux habitants des Départements d'Outre-Mer [Recent social advantages accorded to inhabitants of the French Overseas departments]. *B Inf Cenaddom* 28: 23-25.   *[RIS]*

Niet, M. de

33.0144   SR   1935-36 Overheidszorg voor de rijpere jeugd in Suriname [Government care for young adults in Surinam]. *W I G* 17: 33-48.   [*COL*]

Niles, Blair

37.0622   FG   1927   Devil's Island.

37.0623   FG   1928   CONDEMNED TO DEVIL'S ISLAND: THE BIOGRAPHY OF AN UNKNOWN CONVICT.

Odle, Maurice A.

46.0166   BC   1974   PENSION FUNDS IN LABOUR SURPLUS ECONOMIES: AN ANALYSIS OF THE DEVELOPMENTAL ROLE OF PENSION PLANS IN THE CARIBBEAN.

O'Higgins, Paul & Hepple, B. A.

46.0168   BC   1969   Labour law.

46.0169   BC   1970   Labour law.

46.0170   BC   1971   Labour law.

Okpaluba, Chuks

37.0632   GC   1974   Fundamental human rights, the courts and the independent West Indian constitutions.

Oldenboom, J. F.

33.0145   AR   1970   Criminological and police aspects of alcoholism in Aruba. *In* PROCEEDINGS OF THE FIRST ARUBAN AND ANTILLEAN CONGRESS ON ALCOHOLISM, ARUBA, NETHERLANDS ANTILLES, SEPTEMBER 11-12-13, 1970. Aruba, De Wit Stores Inc.: 96-99.   [*RILA*]

Olivier, Sydney, 1st Baron Ramsden

46.0175   BC   1938   The scandal of West Indian labour conditions, by Lord Olivier.

Orde-Browne, G.

46.0176   BC   1939   LABOUR CONDITIONS IN THE WEST INDIES.

Oudschans Dentz, Fred

33.0146   SR   1954   Een welvaartsplan voor Suriname in 1770 voorgesteld door Gouverneur Jan Nepveu [A welfare plan for Surinam proposed by Governor Jan Nepveu in 1770]. *W I G* 35(1-2), Apr.: 91-94.   **[5]**   [*RIS*]

Ouensanga, Louis

33.0147   FA,FR   1970   Les prestations familiales aux Antilles [Family insurance benefits in the Antilles]. *Droit Social* 33(5), May: 247-254.   **[9,49]**   [*COL*]

Owen, G. H.

31.0116   JM   1963   Vocational guidance and education for adolescents.

Parris, Michael

33.0148   GU   1975   Delinquency in the Linden area. *Guy J Sociol* 1(1), Oct.: 1-18.   **[36]**   [*RIS*]

Patchett, Keith

9.0112   BC   1959   Some aspects of marriage and divorce in the West Indies.

Patchett, Keith & Jenkins, Valerie

1.0220   **BC**   1973   A BIBLIOGRAPHICAL GUIDE TO LAW IN THE COMMONWEALTH CARIBBEAN.

Paterson, Alexander

37.0662   **BC**   1943   REPORT OF MR. ALEXANDER PATERSON ON HIS VISITS TO THE REFORMATORY AND PENAL ESTABLISHMENTS. . .OF JAMAICA, BRITISH HONDURAS, THE BAHAMAS, THE LEEWARD AND WINDWARD ISLANDS, BARBADOS, TRINIDAD AND TOBAGO, BRITISH GUIANA. . .20TH DECEMBER, 1936-10TH MAY, 1937.

Patterson, Sybil

33.0149   **GU**   1968   Self-help projects—philosophy and achievements. *Cajanus* 4, August: 59-65.   [*RIS*]

Péan, Charles

37.0666   **FG**   1953   THE CONQUEST OF DEVIL'S ISLAND.
5.0714   **FG**   1969   LE CHRIST EN TERRE DE BAGNE [CHRIST IN THE LAND OF THE PENAL COLONY].

Pennink, B. J.

33.0150   **NA**   1969   Opmerkingen over zetelverplaatsing [Remarks on relocation]. *In* HONDERD JAAR CODIFICATIE IN DE NEDERLANDSE ANTILLEN. Arnhem, The Netherlands, S. Gouda Quint/D. Brouwer en Zoon: 105-116.   [*RILA*]

Penrose, Clement A.

28.0984   **BA**   1905   Sanitary conditions in the Bahama Islands.

Peterson, E.

28.1014   **ST,SJ**   1919   Infectious and contagious diseases on the islands of St. Thomas and St. John, Virgin Islands of the United States, March-September 1918.

Pinto, Heather

31.0117   **TR**   1965[?]   Group therapy among alcoholics.

Plantz, C. Irving

33.0151   **NA**   1971   TOEKOMSTVERZORGING [FUTURE CARE]. Curaçao, Boekhandel Salas: 24p. **[46]**   [*RILA*]

Podlewski, H.

33.0152   **BA**   1974   Drug abuse in the Bahamas. *In* Tongue, Eva & Blair, Brenda, eds. PROCEEDINGS OF THE INTERNATIONAL CONFERENCE ON THE PREVENTION OF ADDICTIONS IN DEVELOPING COUNTRIES. Nassau, Bahamas: 33-39.   [*RIS*]

Pollard, Francis C. R.

9.0115   **GU**   1975   Urban poverty and the family in Guyana.

Polman, J.

33.0153   **CU**   1948   Het Kadaster [The Land Register]. *In* ORANJE EN DE VES CARAÏBISCHE PARELEN. Amsterdam, J. H. de Bussy: 167-169. **[44]**
     [*UCLA*]

Prince, Raymond; Greenfield, Rochelle & Marriott, John

33.0154   JM   1972   Cannabis or alcohol? Observations on their use in Jamaica. *B Narc*
24(1), Jan.-March: 1-9.   **[31]**   [*RIS*]

Prins, J.

9.0118   SR   1963   Een Surinaams rechtsgeding over een Moslimse verstoting [A
Surinam lawsuit about a Moslem divorce].

Quintus Bosz, A. J. A.

33.0155   SR   1969   De weg tot de invoering van de nieuwe wetgeving in 1869 en de
overgang van het oude naar het nieuwe burgerlijk recht [The road to
the introduction of the new legislation in 1869 and the transition
from the old to the new Civil Code]. *In* Carpentier Alting, Z. H., et
al., eds. EEN EEUW SURINAAMSE CODIFICATIE: GEDENKBOEK (1869-1
MEI-1969). Paramaribo, Surinaamse Juristen-Vereniging: 7-
25.   **[5,37]**   [*RILA*]

Ramdat Misier, L. F.

37.0698   SR   1969   Een eeuw Surinaamse rechterlijke organisatie en burgerlijke rechtsvordering [A century of Surinamese judicial organization and civil
procedure].

Ramkeesoon, Gemma

33.0156   TR   1964   Voluntary welfare services for the child. *In* REPORT OF CONFERENCE
ON CHILD CARE IN TRINIDAD AND TOBAGO [held by] Trinidad and
Tobago Association for Mental Health, Sub-Committee on Children and Youth, Community Education Centre, St. Ann's, Apr.
18th 1964. [Port of Spain?] Govt. Printery, p.23-25.   **[28]**   [*RIS*]

Rance, Hubert Elvin

35.0063   TR   . 1951   Government expenditures in Trinidad and Tobago.

Rankine, J. D.

41.0422   BB   [n.d.]   A TEN YEAR DEVELOPMENT PLAN FOR BARBADOS: SKETCH PLAN OF
DEVELOPMENT, 1946-56.

Rattray, K. O.

45.0125   JM   1966   THE PROTECTION IN INTERESTS IN JAMAICAN COMPANY LAW: A STUDY
IN THE FORMATION, FLOTATION AND MANAGEMENT OF COMPANIES IN
DEVELOPING ECONOMY.

Ray, Michael

9.0121   GU   1935   Bamboo marriage.

Raynor, Lois

33.0157   BC,UK   1968   Agency adoptions of non-white children in the United Kingdom: a
quantitative study. *Race* 10(2), Oct.: 153-162.   **[9,18]**   [*COL*]

Reid, G. B.

23.0244   TR   1969   Social action and the church in Trinidad and Tobago.

Reid, Molly A.

44.0054   BB   1973   The growth of a twentieth century fiction: the foreclosure suit in
Barbados.

Ribstein, Michel
31.0119   MT   1963   Juvenile delinquency in Martinique.

Richardson, J. Henry
33.0158   GU   1955   REPORT ON SOCIAL SECURITY IN BRITISH GUIANA, APRIL, 1954. Georgetown, Reprinted for the Government of British Guiana by "The Argosy" Co., 17p.   **[37,41]**   [*RIS*]
33.0159   BC   1956   Social security problems with special reference to the British West Indies. *Social Econ Stud* 5(2), June: 139-169.   **[37]**   [*RIS*]

Richardson, John Henry
41.0427   BE   1943   REVIEW OF ECONOMIC CONDITIONS, POLICY AND ORGANISATION IN BERMUDA.
41.0428   BA   1944   REVIEW OF BAHAMIAN ECONOMIC CONDITIONS AND POST-WAR PROBLEMS.

Robert, Gerard
33.0160   GD   1935   LES TRAVAUX PUBLICS DE LA GUADELOUPE [PUBLIC WORKS IN GUADELOUPE]. Paris, Librairie militarie L. Fournier, 294p.   **[2]**
[*AGS*]

Roberts, Lydia J.
33.0161   GC   1952   First Caribbean Conference on Home Economics and Education in Nutrition. *Dep St B* 27(694), Oct. 13: 576-579.   **[30,32]**   [*COL*]

Roberts, Walter Adolphe et al.
33.0162   JM   1937   ONWARD JAMAICA. New York, Jamaica Progressive League of New York, 8p.   [*NYP*]
33.0163   JM   1938   WE ADVOCATE A SOCIAL AND ECONOMIC PROGRAM FOR JAMAICA. New York, Jamaica Progressive League of New York, 7p.   [*NYP*]

Roberts-Wray, Kenneth
33.0164   BC,UK   1966   COMMONWEALTH AND COLONIAL LAW. London, Stevens and Sons: 1008p.   **[37,40]**   [*COL*]

Roeher, G. Allan
31.0122   GC   1970   The adjustment of the community to the mentally retarded.

Rogers, Claudia
8.0189   JM   1976   ILLEGAL ENTREPRENEURSHIP AND SOCIAL NETWORKS IN RURAL JAMAICA.

Rondeel, A. J.
33.0165   SR   1965   Het rechtsbegrip "legaat" in het Surinaams B.W. en in het ontwerp nieuw Nederlands B.W. [The legal term "legacy" in the Surinamese Civil Code and in the proposed new Dutch Civil Code]. *Sur Jurbl* 6, Dec.: 29-32.   [*RILA*]

Rose, F. G.
28.1100   GU   1926   Leprosy statistics and legislation in British Guiana.

Roseman, Curtis C.; Bullamore, Henry W.; Price, Jill M.; Snow, Ronald W. & Bower, Gordon L.

33.0166   JM   1973   SOCIAL PROBLEMS IN A SMALL JAMAICAN TOWN. Urbana-Champaign, University of Illinois: 82p. (Department of Geography Paper No. 6) **[8]**   [*AGS*]

Rosen, Robert C.

34.0092   JM   1973   LAW AND POPULATION GROWTH IN JAMAICA.

Royes, W. C.

33.0167   JM   1961[?]   Government and statutory social services in Jamaica. *In* Cumper, George, ed. REPORT OF THE CONFERENCE ON SOCIAL DEVELOPMENT IN JAMAICA. Kingston, Standing Committee on Social Services, p.38-44. **[37]**   [*RIS*]

Rubin, Vera

31.0127   TR   1963   The adolescent: his expectations and his society.

33.0168   JM   1971   Variations and patterns in the cultural response to cannabis use. *Int Ment Heal Res Newsl* 13(1), Spring: 5-10.   [*RIS*]

33.0169   JM   1974   Cultural aspects of cannabis use in Jamaica. *In* Tongue, Eva & Blair, Brenda, eds. PROCEEDINGS OF THE INTERNATIONAL CONFERENCE ON THE PREVENTION OF ADDICTIONS IN DEVELOPING COUNTRIES. Nassau, Bahamas: 81-96.   [*RIS*]

Rubin, Vera & Comitas, Lambros

33.0170   JM   1976   GANJA IN JAMAICA: THE EFFECTS OF MARIJUANA USE. Garden City, New York, Anchor Press/Doubleday: 217p. **[28,31]**   [*RIS*]

Samlalsingh, Ruby S.

33.0171   GU   1959   Application of social welfare principles to the rural development programme on sugar estates in British Guiana. *In* CONFERENCE ON SOCIAL DEVELOPMENT IN THE WEST INDIES, MAR. 16-20, 1959, TRINIDAD. Port of Spain, Ministry of Labour and Social Affairs, The West Indies, p.44-51. **[36,42]**   [*RIS*]

Sammy, George M.

32.0502   BC   1969   The role of the modern university.

Samson, D.

37.0751   SR   1969   Onze honderdjarige wetgeving en het notariaat [Our hundred year old legislation and the office of notary public].

37.0752   SR   1969   Onze vijf en zeventig-jarige wetgeving en het notariaat [Our seventy five year old legislation and the office of notary public].

Samson, Ph. A.

33.0172   SR   1966   Oud-Hollands recht in Suriname [Old-Dutch law in Surinam]. *Justicia* 2(2): 37-41. **[5]**   [*COL*]

Saunier, Gabriel

5.0809   FG   1971   LA RÉALITÉ SUR LE BAGNE EN NOUVELLE-CALÉDONIE ET EN GUYANE FRANÇAISE [THE REALITY OF THE PENAL COLONY IN NEW CALEDONIA AND IN FRENCH GUIANA].

Schiltkamp, J. A. & Smidt, J. Th. de, eds.

5.0815   SR   1973   WEST INDISCHE PLAKAATBOEK: PLAKATEN, ORDONNANTIËN EN ANDERE WETTEN, UITGEVAARDIGD IN SURINAME 1667-1816 [WEST INDIAN BOOK OF EDICTS: EDICTS, ORDINANACES AND OTHER LAWS ISSUED IN SURINAM 1667-1816].

Schlesinger, Benjamin
9.0141   **JM**   1968   Divorce in Jamaica: a new phenomenon.

Schlesinger, Benjamin & Sio, Arnold A.
33.0173   **JM**   1968   The Canadian volunteer program in Jamaica. *Adult Leadership* Oct:
173-174, 195-204.   [*COL*]

Scott, John P.
31.0132   **UV**   1963   Recreation programs for adolescents in the Vrigin Islands.

Seel, George
33.0174   **BC**   1952[?] DEVELOPMENT AND WELFARE IN THE WEST INDIES, 1951. [Bridge-
town, Barbados? Printed by] Advocate Co. [for Comptroller for
Development and Welfare in the West Indies], 113p. ([Gt. Brit.
Colonial Office], Development and welfare in the West Indies.)
[*RIS*]
33.0175   **BC**   1953[?] DEVELOPMENT AND WELFARE IN THE WEST INDIES, 1952. [Bridge-
town, Barbados? Printed by] Advocate Co. [for Comptroller for
Development and Welfare in the West Indies], 104p. ([Gt. Brit.
Colonial Office], Development and Welfare in the West Indies.)
[*RIS*]

Senior, Olive
37.0770   **JM**   1972   THE MESSAGE IS CHANGE: A PERSPECTIVE ON THE 1972 GENERAL
ELECTIONS.

Sherlock, Philip M.
33.0176   **JM**   1950[?] Experiment in self-help. *Car Q* 1(4): 31-34.

Simey, Thomas S.
37.0782   **BC**   1944[?] PRINCIPLES OF PRISON REFORM.
33.0177   **BC**   1945   The welfare of the West Indies. *Geogr Mag* 18(7), Nov.: 293-301.
[*AGS*]
33.0178   **BC**   1946   WELFARE AND PLANNING IN THE WEST INDIES. Oxford, Clarendon
Press, 267p.   **[2,9]**   [*RIS*]
33.0179   **JM**   1962   Sociology, social administration, and social work. *Car Q* 8(4), Dec.:
37-41.   [*RIS*]

Simpson, George Eaton
36.0080   **JM**   1954   Begging in Kingston and Montego Bay.

Sivanandan, A.
18.0261   **BC,UK** 1976   Race, class and the state: the black experience in Britain.

Sjiem Fat, P. V.
33.0180   **NA**   1972   De Landsverordening Hazardspelen 1948, P. B. 1948 no. 138 [The
land regulation games of chance 1948, P. B. 1948 no. 138]. *Justicia*
8(4): 97-117.   **[22]**   [*COL*]

Smith, Allan C.
33.0181   **BE**   1960   An outline of the history of the courts in Bermuda. *Bermuda Hist Q*
17(3), Autumn: 96-106.   [*COL*]

Smith, M. G.

8.0215   JM   1963   Aimless, wandering adolescent groups.

Smith, M. G.; Augier, F. R. & Nettleford, Rex

23.0286   JM   1960   THE RAS TAFARI MOVEMENT IN KINGSTON, JAMAICA.

Spencer, D. J.

31.0135   BA   1970   Cannabis induced psychoses.

Sprockel, J. H. & Debrot, I. C.

33.0182   CU   1948   Sociale verordeningen [Social ordinances]. *In* ORANJE EN DE ZES CARAÏBISCHE PARELEN. Amsterdam, J. H. de Bussy: 151-154.
[*UCLA*]

Stewart-Prince, G.

18.0266   BC,UK   1972   Mental health problems in pre-school West Indian children.

Stockdale, Frank A.

33.0183   BC   1943[?]   DEVELOPMENT AND WELFARE IN THE WEST INDIES: PROGRESS REPORT FOR 1942-1943. [Bridgetown?] Barbados, Advocate Co., 14p. (Development and welfare bulletin no. 4.)   [*COL*]

28.1231   BC   1943   Development and welfare in the West Indies 1940-1942.

33.0184   BC   1943   DEVELOPMENT AND WELFARE IN THE WEST INDIES 1940-42. London, H.M.S.O., 93p. ([Gr. Brit. Colonial Office] Development and welfare in the West Indies; Colonial no. 184.)   [*COL*]

33.0185   BC   1945   The British West Indies. *United Emp* 36(4), July-Aug.: 135-140.
[*AGS*]

33.0186   BC   1945   DEVELOPMENT AND WELFARE IN THE WEST INDIES 1943-1944. London, H.M.S.O., 115p. ([Gt. Brit. Colonial Office] Development and welfare in the West Indies; Colonial no. 189.)   [*AGS*]

Stone, Carl

33.0187   JM   1975   Urban social movements in post-War Jamaica. *In* Singham, A. W., ed. THE COMMONWEALTH CARIBBEAN INTO THE SEVENTIES. Montreal, McGill University, Centre for Developing Area Studies: 71-93. **[8,21,37,40]**   [*RIS*]

36.0085   JM   1975   Urbanization as a source of political disaffection—the Jamaican experience.

Stone, O. M.

9.0175   BC   1967   Family law.

Surrency, E. C.

33.0188   BB   1965   Report on court procedures in the colonies: 1700. *Am J Legal Hist* 9: 69-83. **[5]**   [*COL*]

33.0189   BB   1966   Complaints concerning the administration of justice in the Barbados Islands. *Am J Legal Hist* 10: 237-244. **[5]**   [*COL*]

Suthoff, C. & Gorsira, M. P.

33.0190   CU   1948   De politie en haar ontwikkeling [The police and its development]. *In* ORANJE EN DE ZES CARAÏBISCHE PARELEN. Amsterdam, J. H. de Bussy: 233-238.   [*UCLA*]

Swaby, Raphael A.
48.0162   JM   1974   Some problems of public utility regulation by a statutory board in Jamaica: the Jamaica omnibus services case.

Sydes, William
33.0191   BE   1951   Account of life in the Convict Hulks. *Bermuda Hist Q* 8(1), Jan.-March: 29-39.   **[5]**   [*COL*]

Thomas, Richard & Chesher, Gregory
28.1275   JM   1973   The pharmacology of marihuana.

Thompson, E. W.
23.0302   BC   1940   The return of the West Indies.
23.0303   GC   1943   Eyes on the West Indies.

Thorburn, Marigold J.
33.0192   JM   1972   Facilities for the mentally retarded in Jamaica: a report on the present situation. *W I Med J* 21(1), March: 25-35.   **[31]**   [*PS*]

Thorburn, Marigold J., ed.
31.0137   GC   1970   MENTAL RETARDATION IN THE CARIBBEAN: NEEDS, RESOURCES, APPROACHES.

Tietze, Christopher
34.0119   BB   1957   THE FAMILY PLANNING SERVICE IN BARBADOS.
34.0120   BB   1958   THE EFFECTIVENESS OF THE FAMILY PLANNING SERVICE IN BARBADOS.

Tietze, Christopher & Alleyne, Charles
34.0121   BB   1959   A family planning service in the West Indies.

Tjon Sie Fat, Howard Cyril
28.1301   NW   1954   ONDERZOEK NAAR DE SOCIAAL-HYGIENISCHE TOESTAND OP DE BOVENWINDSE EILANDEN DER NEDERLANSE ANTILLEN [INVESTIGATION OF SOCIAL-HYGIENIC CONDITIONS ON THE WINDWARD ISLANDS OF THE NETHERLANDS ANTILLES].

Tongue, Eva & Blair, Brenda, eds.
33.0193   GC   1974   PROCEEDINGS OF THE INTERNATIONAL CONFERENCE ON THE PREVENTION OF ADDICTIONS IN DEVELOPING COUNTRIES. Nassau, Bahamas: 198p.   [*RIS*]

Towers, K. E.
33.0194   GU   1952   Social welfare projects in British Guiana. *Int Rev Missions* 41(164), Oct.: 471-477.

Triseliotis, J. P.
18.0276   BC,UK   1972   The implications of cultural factors in social work with immigrants.

Triseliotis, J. P., ed.
18.0277   BC,UK   1972   SOCIAL WORK WITH COLOURED IMMIGRANTS AND THEIR FAMILIES.

Trotman, Donald A. B.
33.0195   BC   1972[?]   Reactions [to H. A. Fraser: The Law and the illegitimate child]. *In* Haynes, Lilith M., ed. FAMBLI: THE CHURCH'S RESPONSIBILITY TO THE FAMILY IN THE CARIBBEAN. TRINIDAD, CARIPLAN: 146-151.   **[9]**   [*RIS*]

Try Ellis, W.Ch de la

33.0196   CU   1948   Civielrechtelijke beschouwingen [Remarks about Civil Law]. *In* ORANJE EN DE ZES CARAÏBISCHE PARELEN. Amsterdam, J. H. de Bussy: 217-232.   [*UCLA*]

Tucker, Terry

33.0197   BE   1973   BERMUDA'S CRIME AND PUNISHMENT, 17TH CENTURY STYLE. Hamilton, Bermuda, Island Press: 36p.   [5]   [*RIS*]

Turfboer, R.

33.0198   AR   1970   The typical Aruban alcoholic in the nineteen fifties. *In* PROCEEDINGS OF THE FIRST ARUBAN AND ANTILLEAN CONGRESS ON ALCOHOLISM, ARUBA, NETHERLANDS ANTILLES, SEPTEMBER 11-12-13, 1970. Aruba, De Wit Stores Inc.: 70-75.   [31]   [*RILA*]

Veer, Johan J. van der

23.0310   SR   1968   DE DAAD BIJ HET WOORD: ZENDINGSWERK IN SURINAME [SUITING THE ACT TO THE WORD: MISSIONARY WORK IN SURINAM].

Verteuil, Eric de

28.1346   TR   1943   The urgent need for a medical health policy for Trinidad.

Verwey, R. A.

33.0199   CU   1938   De sociale ontwikkelingsgang van Curacao [The tempo of social development of Curacao]. *W I G* 20: 161-174.   [*COL*]

Victor, Clivin

33.0200   BC   1970   Juvenile delinquency. *In* Cross, Malcolm, ed. WEST INDIAN SOCIAL PROBLEMS; A SOCIOLOGICAL PERSPECTIVE. Port-of-Spain, Trinidad, Columbus Publishers Ltd.: 45-62.   [36]   [*RIS*]

Villiers, Gerard de

5.0933   FG   1970   PAPILLON ÉPINGLÉ [PAPILLON PINNED DOWN].

Vismans, R.

33.0201   AR   1970   Pastoral care and alcoholism in Aruba. *In* PROCEEDINGS OF THE FIRST ARUBAN AND ANTILLEAN CONGRESS ON ALCOHOLISM, ARUBA, NETHERLANDS ANTILLES, SEPTEMBER 11-12-13, 1970. Aruba, De Wit Stores Inc.: 80-87.   [23]   [*RILA*]

Vizetelly, Frank H.

39.0171   BE   1901   The Boers in Bermuda.

Vollers, J. L.

37.0865   SR   1974   DE BESTUURLIJKE STRUCTUUR VAN SURINAME [THE ADMINISTRATIVE STRUCTURE OF SURINAM].

Voogt, W. J.

41.0511   NA   1968   De werkgelegenheidssituatie in de Nederlandse Antillen in verband met de ontwikkelingshulp [The employment situation in the Netherlands Antilles in connection with development aid].

Voort, P. P. C. H. van de

33.0202   AR   1970   Some juridicial considerations in defence of the Aruban alcoholic. *In* PROCEEDINGS OF THE FIRST ARUBAN AND ANTILLEAN CONGRESS ON ALCOHOLISM, ARUBA, NETHERLANDS ANTILLES, SEPTEMBER 11-12-13, 1970. Aruba, De Wit Stores Inc.: 188-191.   [*RILA*]

Vroon, L. J.

33.0203   SR   1963-64 Voorgeschiedenis, opzet en resultaten van het Surinaamse Tien-jarenplan [History, aim and results of the Surinam Ten-Year Welfare Plan]. *N W I G* 43: 25-74.   [*RIS*]

41.0514   SR   1965   Vraagstukken rond de maatschappelijke ontwikkeling van Suriname I [Problems connected with the social development of Surinam I].

41.0515   SR   1965   Vraagstukken rond de maatschappelijke ontwikkeling van Suriname II [Problems connected with the social development of Surinam II].

Waddington, Justice; Fraser, Justice Aubrey; Persaud, Justice & Lewis, Justice P. C.

33.0204   BC   1967   THE WEST INDIAN REPORTS: VOLUME 9: 1965-1966. London, Butterworth and Co. (Publishers) Ltd.: 537p.   [*COL*]

Waddington, Justice; Fraser, Justice; Persaud, Justice; Lewis, Justice P. C. & Williams, Justice

33.0205   BC   1968   THE WEST INDIAN REPORTS: VOLUME 10: 1966-1967. London, Butterworth and Co. (Publishers) Ltd.: 562p.   [*COL*]

33.0206   BC   1969   THE WEST INDIAN REPORTS: VOLUME 11: 1967-1968. London, Butterworth and Co. (Publishers) Ltd.: 538p.   [*COL*]

Waddington, Justice; Hyatali, Justice; Stoby, Kenneth; Persaud, Justice & Lewis, Justice

33.0207   BC   1966   THE WEST INDIAN REPORTS: VOLUME 8: 1965. London, Butterworth and Co. (Publishers) Ltd.: 571p.   [*COL*]

Wade, H. W. R., ed.

33.0208   BC   1967   ANNUAL SURVEY OF COMMONWEALTH LAW: 1966. London, Butterworth and Co. (Publishers) Ltd.: 873p.   [37]   [*COL*]

33.0209   BC   1968   ANNUAL SURVEY OF COMMONWEALTH LAW: 1967. London, Butterworth and Co. (Publishers) Ltd.: 816p.   [37]   [*COL*]

33.0210   BC   1969   ANNUAL SURVEY OF COMMONWEALTH LAW: 1968. London, Butterworth and Co. (Publishers) Ltd.: 857p.   [37]   [*COL*]

33.0211   BC   1970   ANNUAL SURVEY OF COMMONWEALTH LAW: 1969. London, Butterworth and Co. (Publishers) Ltd.: 792p.   [37]   [*COL*]

33.0212   BC   1971   ANNUAL SURVEY OF COMMONWEALTH LAW: 1970. London, Butterworth and Co. (Publishers) Ltd.: 712p.   [37]   [*COL*]

Washbrook, R. A.

18.0283   JM,UK   1970   The homeless offender: an English study of 200 cases.

Waterman, James A.

28.1391   TR   1944   A national health service with special reference to Trinidad.

Waterman, James A. et al.
28.1399   TR   1963   Voluntary pre-payment health insurance scheme.

Watkins, Edwin Horatio
5.0947   JM   1968   THE HISTORY OF THE LEGAL SYSTEM OF JAMAICA FROM 1661 TO 1900.

Wells, A. F. & Wells, D.
49.0108   BC   1953   FRIENDLY SOCIETIES IN THE WEST INDIES.

Wever, O. R.
33.0213   AR   1970   Some medical and sociopathological aspects of alcoholism in Aruba and its actual treatment. *In* PROCEEDINGS OF THE FIRST ARUBAN AND ANTILLEAN CONGRESS ON ALCOHOLISM, ARUBA, NETHERLANDS ANTILLES, SEPTEMBER 11-12-13, 1970. Aruba, De Wit Stores Inc.: 135-187. **[28,31]**   [*RILA*]
33.0214   AR   1975   Over het alcoholisme op Aruba [Concerning alcoholism in Aruba]. *N W I G* 50(2-3), Sept.: 89-106.   [*RIS*]

Whetton, Jim
33.0215   JM   1965   Approach to control of juvenile delinquency in Jamaica. *Torch* 15(2), June: 5-10.   [*RIS*]

White, G.
10.0055   BC   1967   Rudie, oh Rudie.

Wight, Gerald
35.0093   TR   1951   A proposal for the future financing of public housing in Trinidad and Tobago.

Wijnholt, M. R.
33.0216   SR   1965   STRAFRECHT IN SURINAME [CRIMINAL LAW IN SURINAM]. Deventer, The Netherlands, N. V. Uitgeversmaatschappij Æ. E. Kluwer: 221p. **[5,14]**   [*COL*]
5.0974   SR   1969   De betekenis van de lste mei 1869 voor het huidlige strafrecht [The significance of May 1, 1869 for present criminal law].
33.0217   NA,NE   1969   Iets over inter-regionaal strafrecht en de "uitwijzing" van Surinaamse en Antilliaanse delinquenten uit Nederland [Some remarks on intra-regional criminal law and "deportation" of Surinamese and Antillean criminals from the Netherlands]. *In* HONDERD JAAR CODIFICATIE IN DE NEDERLANDSE ANTILLEN. Arnhem, The Netherlands, S. Gouda Quint/D. Brouwer en Zoon: 315-343. **[18]**
                                                                                  [*RILA*]

Williams, Eric Eustace
33.0218   BC   1947   The new British Colonial policy of development and welfare. *Am Perspec* 1(7), Dec.: 437-451.   [*COL*]

Williams, L. R.
33.0219   TR   1973[?]   Social work and social ills in Trinidad and Tobago. *Medi-News Car* 1(2): 17-19.   [*RIS*]

Williamson, C.
37.0915   BC   1952   Britain's new colonial policy: 1940-1951.

Wills, Aeneas Ebenezer
46.0241   **BC**   1967   STATUTORY PROTECTION OF THE WORKER IN THE WEST INDIES.

Windt, H. L. de
33.0220   **NA**   1970   Neuropsychiatric aspects of alcoholism in the Netherlands Antilles, especially referring to Aruba. *In* PROCEEDINGS OF THE FIRST ARUBAN AND ANTILLEAN CONGRESS ON ALCOHOLISM, ARUBA, NETHERLANDS ANTILLES, SEPTEMBER 11-12-13, 1970. Aruba, De Wit Stores Inc.: 91-95. **[31]**   [*RILA*]

Windt, S. E. de
33.0221   **NA**   1972[?]   Rechtspositie onderwijzend personeel [Legal position of teachers]. *In* HET ONDERWIJS IN DE NEDERLANDSE ANTILLEN. The Hague, The Netherlands, Kabinet voor Surinaamse en Nederlands Antiliaanse Zaken: 22-25. **[32]**   [*RILA*]

Wiseman, H. V.
38.0244   **BC**   1948   THE WEST INDIES, TOWARDS A NEW DOMINION?

Wong, Paul G.
35.0096   **SR**   1953   The aided self-help housing programme in Surinam.

Wooding, Hugh
33.0222   **TR**   1966   Law reform necessary in Trinidad and Tobago. *Can Bar J* 9(4), Aug.: 292-298.   [*COL*]

Wright, James
33.0223   **JM**   1947   Lucky Hill Community Project. *Trop Agric* 24(10-12), Oct.-Dec.: 137-144. **[36,43]**   [*AGS*]

Wright, Jerome Wendell
8.0247   **BA**   1973   LEGAL CHOICE IN DISPUTE SETTLEMENT ON THE ISLAND OF MAYAGUANA, BAHAMAS.

Yardley, D. C. M.
33.0224   **BC**   1967   Fundamental rights and civil liberties. *In* Wade, H. W. R., ed. ANNUAL SURVEY OF COMMONWEALTH LAW: 1966. London, Butterworth and Co. (Publishers) Ltd.: 105-141 (Chapter 2).   [*COL*]
33.0225   **BC**   1968   Fundamental rights and civil liberties. *In* Wade, H. W. R., ed. ANNUAL SURVEY OF COMMONWEALTH LAW: 1967. London, Butterworth and Co. (Publishers) Ltd.: 111-140 (Chapter 2).   [*COL*]
33.0226   **BC**   1969   Fundamental rights and civil liberties. *In* Wade, H. W. R., ed. ANNUAL SURVEY OF COMMONWEALTH LAW: 1968. London, Butterworth and Co. (Publishers) Ltd.: 123-157 (Chapter 2).   [*COL*]

Yawney, Carole D.
33.0227   **TR**   1968   DRINKING PATTERNS AND ALCOHOLISM AMONG EAST INDIANS AND NEGROES IN TRINIDAD. M.A. thesis, McGill University, Department of Anthropology: 120p. **[11,12]**   [*RIS*]
33.0228   **TR**   1969   Drinking patterns and alcoholism in Trinidad. I. Patterns of alcohol use. II. Pathological drinkers. *Transcult Psych Res* 6, Oct.: 176-178. **[31]**   [*RIS*]

Young, Allan

37.0924   **GU**   1958   THE APPROACHES TO LOCAL SELF-GOVERNMENT IN BRITISH GUIANA.

Zaal, G. Ph.

28.1484   **SR**   1937   Het drinkwatervraagstuk in Suriname en het stadium zijner oplossing [The problem of drinking water in Surinam and the stage of its solution].

Zielhuis, L.

8.0249   **SR**   1974   Community development in Surinam.

Zoutendijk, Henk

33.0229   **SR**   1972   Vormingswerk in Suriname [Social work in Surinam]. *In* STICUSA JAARVERSLAG 1972. Amsterdam, the Netherlands, Nederlandse Stichting voor Culturele Samenwerking met Suriname en de Nederlandse Antillen: 41-45.   [*NYP*]

Chapter 34

FERTILITY AND FAMILY PLANNING

Including works on: contraception; birthrates; maternal care.
See also: [7] Demography and human resources; [9] Socialization, family and kinship.

Alderman, Michael H. & Ferguson, Robert
34.0001   JM   1976   The impact of a family planning clinic in rural Jamaica. *W I Med J* 25(1), March: 11-16.   **[20]**   [*PS*]

Andrews, Norma
7.0007   TR   1975   Trinidad and Tobago.

Andrews, Norma & Alleyne, Michael
34.0002   TR   1972   HANDBOOK ON FAMILY LIFE EDUCATION. Trinidad and Tobago, Ministry of Health: 27p.   **[9]**   [*IPPF*]

Awon, M. P.
34.0003   TR   1973   Family planning programmes in Trinidad and Tobago. *In* CARIBBEAN REGIONAL EMPLOYERS' SEMINAR ON POPULATION AND FAMILY WELFARE PLANNING, PORT-OF-SPAIN, 10-14 APRIL, 1973. Geneva, International Labour Office: 154-160.   [*IPPF*]

Back, Kurt W.
34.0004   JM   1963   A model of family planning experiments: the lessons of the Puerto Rican and Jamaican studies. *Marr Fam Liv* 25(1), Feb.: 14-19.
                                                                          [*TCL*]

Back, Kurt W. & Stycos, J. Mayone
34.0005   JM   1959   THE SURVEY UNDER UNUSUAL CONDITIONS: THE JAMAICA HUMAN FERTILITY INVESTIGATION. Ithaca, N.Y., Society for Applied Anthropology, Cornell University, 52p. (Monograph no. 1.)   **[20]**
                                                                          [*RIS*]

Balakrishnan, T. R.
34.0006   BB   1973   A cost benefit analysis of the Barbados family planning programme. *Popl Stud* 27(2), July: 353-364.   [*COL*]

Benoist, Jean
7.0014   GC   1971   Population structure in the Caribbean area.

Bertram, G. C. L.
34.0007   GU   1962   The Indians of British Guiana. *Popul Rev* 6(2), July: 114-117.   **[12]**

Bhagwansingh, Andrew
28.0122   TR   1974   Maternal and child health and family planning programme —Trinidad and Tobago.

Blake, Judith
34.0008   JM   1955   FAMILY INSTABILITY AND REPRODUCTIVE BEHAVIOUR IN JAMAICA: CURRENT RESEARCH IN HUMAN FERTILITY. New York, Milbank Memorial Fund, p.24-41.   **[9]**   [*RIS*]
34.0009   JM   1958   A reply to Mr. [Lloyd E.] Braithwaite. *Social Econ Stud* 7(4), Dec.: 234-237.   **[9]**   [*RIS*]

Blake, Judith; Stycos, J. Mayone & Davis, Kingsley
34.0010   JM   1961   FAMILY STRUCTURE IN JAMAICA: THE SOCIAL CONTEXT OF REPRODUCTION. Glencoe, Ill., Free Press, 262p.   **[8,9,20]**   [*RIS*]

Bracken, Michael B. & Kasl, Stanislav V.
34.0011   JM   1973   Factors associated with dropping out of family planning clinics in Jamaica. *Am J Publ Heal* 63(3), March: 262-271.   [*PS*]

Braithwaite, Lloyd E.
34.0012   BC   1957   Sociology and demographic research in the British Caribbean. *Social Econ Stud* 6(4), Dec.: 523-571.   **[7,8,9]**   [*RIS*]
17.0016   JM   1961[?]   Population, migration and urbanization.

Braithwaite, Lloyd E. & Roberts, George W.
34.0013   TR   1967   Mating patterns and prospects in Trinidad. *Trin Res Papers* 4, Dec.: 120-127.   **[7,9]**   [*IPPF*]

Brawer, Milton Jacob
34.0014   TR   1965   FERTILITY DIFFERENCES, FAMILY STRUCTURE AND MODERNIZATION IN TWO POPULATIONS IN TRINIDAD. Ann Arbor, Michigan, University Microfilms, Inc.: 245p. (Ph.D. dissertation, Columbia University)   **[9,11,12]**   [*RIS*]

Brody, Eugene B.
34.0015   JM   1974   Mental health and population control. *MH* 58(1), Winter: 12-14.   **[20,31]**   [*ACM*]
34.0016   JM   1974   Psychocultural aspects of contraceptive behavior in Jamaica. *J Nerv Ment Dis* 159(2), Aug.: 108-119.   **[20]**   [*ACM*]

Brody, Eugene B.; Ottey, Frank & Lagranade, Janet
34.0017   JM   1974   Couple communication in the contraceptive decision making of Jamaican women. *J Nerv Ment Dis* 159(6), Dec.: 407-412.   **[20]**
                                                                                           [*ACM*]

Burrowes, J. T.
28.0202   JM   1966   The intra-uterine contraceptive device in Jamaica (a preliminary review).

Byrne, Joycelin

34.0018   BB   1966   A fertility survey in Barbados. *Social Econ Stud* 15(4), Dec.: 368-378. **[7]**   [*RIS*]

7.0019   BC   1973   LEVELS OF FERTILITY IN THE COMMONWEALTH CARIBBEAN 1921-1965.

Cannon, Jo Ann

9.0032   DM   1970   MATING PATTERNS AS ENVIRONMENTAL ADAPTATIONS IN DOMINICA, BRITISH WEST INDIES.

Clare, Lionel A.

28.0246   BZ   1974   Maternal and child health—family planning programme in Belize.

Craigen, A. J.

28.0284   GU   1912   Practice of midwifery at the Public Hospital, Georgetown.

Cummins, G. T. M.

34.0019   GC   1974   What constitutes maternal and child care in the Caribbean. *In* INTERNATIONAL CONFEDERATION OF MIDWIVES. REPORT OF THE CARIBBEAN WORKING PARTY, BRIDGETOWN, BARBADOS, 16-24 MAY, 1974. (Bridgetown, Barbados): 47-50. **[28]**   [*RIS*]

Cummins, G. T. M.; Lovell, H. G. & Standard, K. L.

34.0020   BB   1965   Population control in Barbados. *Am J Publ Heal* 55(10), Oct.: 1600-1608. **[7]**   [*PS*]

Cummins, G. T. M. & Vaillant, Henry W.

34.0021   BB   1966   The training of the nurse-midwife for a national program in Barbados combining the IUD and cervical cytology. *In* FAMILY PLANNING AND POPULATION PROGRAMS: A REVIEW OF WORLD DEVELOPMENTS. Chicago, University of Chicago Press: 451-454. **[28,32]**   [*COL*]

Cumper, George E.

34.0022   JM   1966   The fertility of common law unions in Jamaica. *Social Econ Stud* 15(3), Sept.: 189-202.   [*RIS*]

De Piro, M. Stilon

34.0023   GC   1973   Social security and family planning. *In* CARIBBEAN REGIONAL EMPLOYERS' SEMINAR ON POPULATION AND FAMILY WELFARE PLANNING, PORT-OF-SPAIN, 10-14 APRIL, 1973. Geneva, International Labour Office: 103-118. **[33]**   [*IPPF*]

D'Onofrio, Carol N.; Minkler, Donald H. & Pulley, Hamlet C.

34.0024   JM   1974   EVALUATION OF THE JAMAICAN FAMILY PLANNING PROGRAM 1974. Washington, D.C., American Public Health Association: 241p.
                                                    [*RIS*]

Ebanks, G. Edward

34.0025   BB   1969   Social and demographic characteristics of family planning clients in Barbados. *Social Econ Stud* 18(4), Dec.: 391-401. **[7]**   [*RIS*]

34.0026   BB   1970   Users and non-users of contraception: tests of stationarity applied to members of a family planning programme. *Popul Stud* 24(1), March: 85-91.   [*COL*]

34.0027	BB	1971	Family planning among health clinic patients in Barbados. *Social Biology* 18(2), June: 137-147. [*COL*]
34.0028	BB	1974	PATTERNS OF CONTRACEPTIVE USE AMONG CLIENTS OF THE BARBADOS FAMILY PLANNING ASSOCIATION. Ann Arbor, Michigan, University Microfilms: 253p. (Ph.D. dissertation, Cornell University, 1968.) [*RIS*]
7.0043	BB	1975	Barbados.
7.0044	JM	1975	Jamaica.

Ebanks, G. Edward; George, P. M. & Nobbe, Charles E.

| 34.0029 | BB | 1974 | Fertility and number of partnerships in Barbados. *Popul Stud* 28(3), Nov.: 449-461.   **[9]**   [*COL*] |
| *7.0045* | BB | 1975 | Emigration and fertility decline: the case of Barbados. |

Edmonds, Juliet

| *33.0066* | BB | 1973 | Child care and family services in Barbados. |

Ewan, H. M. Gordon

| *28.0373* | JM | 1967 | Methods of contraception: an assessment of their usefulness in Jamaica. |

Farley, John U. & Leavitt, Harold J.

| 34.0030 | JM | 1968 | Private sector logistics in population control: a case in Jamaica. *Demography* 5(1),: 449-459.   [*COL*] |

Ferguson, Joyce D.

| 34.0031 | JM | 1968 | The family planning programme at Operation Friendship. *Jam Nurse* 8(3), Dec.: 24-25.   [*AJN*] |

Floch, Hervé Alexandre

28.0416	FG	1956	Influence de la lutte antipaludique sur la natalité, la mortinatalité et la mortalité infantile en Guyane Francaise [Influence of the fight against malaria on birthrate, stillbirth rate, and infantile mortality in French Guiana].
28.0417	FG	1956	Influence du paludisme sur la natalité, mortinatalité et mortalité infantile [The influence of malaria on the birthrate, stillbirth rate, and infantile mortality].
28.0419	FG	1956	Natalité, mortinatalité, mortalité infantile et paludisme [Birthrate, stillbirth rate, infantile mortality, and malaria].

Fock, Niels

| *9.0047* | GG | 1960 | South American birth customs in theory and practice. |

Francis, Sybil E.

| 34.0032 | JM | 1971 | The role of social work in family planning in Jamaica. *Jam Nurse* 11(1), April: 13, passim.   [*AJN*] |

Frejka, Tomas

| *7.0052* | TR | 1974 | Alternative projections to a stationary population: Trinidad and Tobago. |

Gardiner, J.

| *28.0479* | JM | 1966 | Induction of labour up to thirty-six weeks. |

Gardner, Richard Eugene

9.0050 **DM** 1974 THE ALLOCATION OF SCARCE GOODS AND VALUES: A COMPARATIVE ANALYSIS OF MATING PATTERNS IN DOMINICA, WEST INDIES.

Gemmink, Joh.

7.0055 **SR** 1966 REPRODUCTIE-PATRONEN BINNEN EEN RACIAAL EN CULTUREEL HETEROGENE BEVOLKING [REPRODUCTION PATTERNS IN A RACIALLY AND CULTURALLY HETEROGENEOUS POPULATION].

7.0057 **SR** 1971 EEN NEDERLANDSCH KOLONISTEN-GESLACHT IN SURINAME 1805-1950 [A DUTCH COLONIST-LINEAGE IN SURINAM 1805-1950].

Grantham-McGregor, Sally M. & Back, E. H.

34.0033 **JM** 1972 Family planning during the first year after delivery by women in Kingston, Jamaica. *W I Med J* 21(4), Dec.: 249-252. [*PS*]

Greenfield, Sidney M.

34.0034 **BB** 1966 ENGLISH RUSTICS IN BLACK SKIN: A STUDY OF MODERN FAMILY FORMS IN A PRE-INDUSTRIALIZED SOCIETY. New Haven, Conn., College and University Press: 208p. **[11]** [*COL*]

Harewood, Jack

7.0070 **TR** 1967 Population growth of Trinidad and Tobago in the twentieth century.

34.0035 **GC** 1968 Recent population trends and family planning activity in the Caribbean area. *Demography* 5(2): 874-893. **[7]** [*COL*]

7.0072 **BC** 1972 Algunos pensamientos acerca de los probables efectos de las disminuciones recientes de la fecundidad y el crecimiento de la población en el Caribe Británico [Some thoughts on the probable effects of the recent drop in fertility and population growth in the British Caribbean].

34.0036 **TR** 1973 Changes in the use of birth control methods. *Popul Stud* 27(1), March: 33-57. [*COL*]

7.0074 **TR** 1975 THE POPULATION OF TRINIDAD AND TOBAGO.

Harewood, Jack & Abdulah, Norma

34.0037 **TR** 1971 FAMILY PLANNING IN TRINIDAD AND TOBAGO IN 1970 (PRELIMINARY REPORT ON THE FAMILY PLANNING SURVEY—FEMALES). Trinidad, University of the West Indies, Institute of Social and Economic Research: 63p. [*RIS*]

34.0038 **TR** 1972 WHAT OUR WOMEN KNOW THINK AND DO ABOUT BIRTH CONTROL. St. Augustine, Trinidad, University of the West Indies, Institute of Social and Economic Research: 42p. [*RIS*]

Higman, B. W.

6.0143 **JM** 1973 Household structure and fertility on Jamaican slave plantations: a nineteenth-century example.

Hinds, P.

34.0039 **BB** 1974 The role of the hospital midwife in family planning programmes. *In* International Confederation of Midwives. REPORT OF THE CARIBBEAN WORKING PARTY, BRIDGETOWN, BARBADOS, 16-24 MAY, 1974. [Bridgetown, Barbados]: 104-109. **[28]** [*RIS*]

Hoyos, M. D. & Armstrong, G. A.

34.0040   BB   1975   The profile of family planning defaulters in a Barbadian general practice. *W I Med J* 24(3), Sept.: 122-128.   [28]   [*PS*]

Ibberson, Dora

34.0041   JM   1956   A note on the relationship between illegitimacy and the birthrate. *Social Econ Stud* 5(1), Mar.: 93-99.   [9]   [*RIS*]

Isaacs, Stephen L.

34.0042   AT,BB   1975   Nonphysician distribution of contraception in Latin American and the Caribbean. *Fam Plan Persp* 7(4); July-Aug.: 158-164.   [*RIS*]

Jacobs, Len & Jacobs, Beth

34.0043   GC   1967   THE FAMILY AND FAMILY PLANNING IN THE WEST INDIES. London, George Allen and Unwin, Ltd.: 86p.   [*RIS*]

Jenkins, Veronica

34.0044   BA   1973   Fertility and birth control on San Salvador. *In* Thomas, Garry L., ed. ANTHROPOLOGICAL FIELD REPORTS FROM SAN SALVADOR ISLAND. San Salvador, Bahamas, Island Environment Studies, Reports 1973: 77-81.   [*RIS*]

Kanagaratnam, Kandiah

34.0045   JM,TR   1973   The concern and contribution of the World Bank in population planning. *Int J Heal Serv* 3(4), Fall: 709-718.   [39]   [*PS*]

Kildare-Donaldson, Evan; Daley, Errol A. & Sorhaindo, B. A.

28.0727   DM   1972   Tubal ligations in Dominica.

Kruijer, G. J.

34.0046   JM   1958   Family size and family planning: a pilot survey among Jamaican mothers. *W I G* 38(3-4), Dec.: 144-150.   [9,20]   [*RIS*]

Kumar, Sushil

34.0047   AT   1973   A SURVEY OF USERS AND NONUSERS OF CONTRACEPTIVES IN ANTIGUA. Columbia, Maryland, Westinghouse Population Center, Health Systems Division: 217p.   [20]   [*IPPF*]

34.0048   AT   1975   AN ASSESSMENT OF COMMUNITY-BASED CONTRACEPTIVE DISTRIBUTION IN ANTIGUA, WEST INDIES. Columbia, Maryland, Westinghouse Population Center: 60p.   [*RIS*]

34.0049   GC   1975   OVERVIEW 1973-1974: CONTRACEPTIVE SERVICES, FAMILY PLANNING PROGRAMS, WESTERN HEMISPHERE REGION. New York, International Planned Parenthood Federation, Medical Division: 16p.   [*IPPF*]

Kunike, Hugo

19.0038   GG   1912   Der Fisch als Fruchtbarkeitssymbol bei den Waldindianern Sudamerikas [The fish as a fertility symbol among the South American forest Indians].

Lampe, P. H. J.

34.0050   BC   1951   A study on human fertility in the British Caribbean territories. *Car Econ Rev* 3(1-2), Oct.: 93-178.   [*RIS*]

34.0051   BC   1952   Human fertility in the British West Indies. *Car Commn Mon Inf B* 5(8), Mar.: 231-232, 243.   [*COL*]

Lamur, H. E.
34.0052 SR 1974 Fertility decline in Surinam. *Boln Estud Latam Car* 16, June: 28-49. **[7]** [*RIS*]

Landman, Jacqueline P. & Shaw-Lyon, Violet
30.0137 JM 1976 Breast feeding in decline in Kingston, Jamaica, 1973.

Leon, S.
34.0053 GU 1973 Geboortenregeling [Birth control]. *In* Statius van Eps, L. W. & Luckman-Maduro, E., eds. VAN SCHEEPSCHIRURGIJN TOT SPECIALIST. Assen, The Netherlands, Van Gorcum & Comp. B.V.: 67-70. (Anjerpublikatie 15). [*RILA*]

Léridon, Henri
34.0054 MT 1970 Fertility in Martinique. *Nat Hist* 79(1), Jan.: 57-59. **[9]** [*COL*]
34.0055 MT 1971 Les facteurs de la fécondité en Martinique [Fertility factors in Martinique]. *Population* 26(2), March-April: 277-300. [*COL*]
34.0056 MT 1972 Le fecundidad según el tipo de unión en Martinica [Fertility according to the type of union in Martinique]. *In* CONFERENCIA REGIONAL LATINOAMERICANA DE POBLACIÓN, MEXICO 1970: ACTAS 1. Guanajuato, Mexico, El Colegio de México: 373-378. **[9]** [*COL*]

Léridon, Henri; Zucker, Elisabeth & Cazenave, Maïté
34.0057 MT 1970 FÉCONDITÉ ET FAMILLE EN MARTINIQUE: FAITS, ATTITUDES, ET OPINIONS [FERTILITY AND FAMILY IN MARTINIQUE: FACTS, ATTITUDES, AND OPINIONS]. Institute National d'Etudes Démographiques, Travaux et Documents, Cahier 56. Paris, Presses Universitaires de France: 186p. **[9]** [*COL*]

Lovell, Belle
34.0058 BZ 1974 The traditional birth attendant—Belize. *In* International Confederation of Midwives. REPORT OF THE CARIBBEAN WORKING PARTY, BRIDGETOWN, BARBADOS, 16-24 MAY, 1974. [Bridgetown, Barbados]: 119-122. **[28,29]** [*RIS*]

McMillan, Robert T.
34.0059 TR 1967 Demographic and socio-economic correlatives of fertility in Trinidad and Tobago. *Trin Res Papers* 4, Dec.: 196-213. **[7]** [*RIS*]

Mandle, Jay R.
34.0060 TR 1973 THE RECENT DECLINE IN FERTILITY IN TRINIDAD AND TOBAGO. Berkeley, University of California, International Population and Urban Research: 23p. (Preliminary Paper No. 5) **[7]** [*RIS*]
34.0061 GU 1975 Guyana: pro-natalist policies. *In* Segal, Aaron, ed. POPULATION POLICIES IN THE CARIBBEAN. Lexington, Massachusetts, D. C. Heath & Company: 89-102. **[7,17]** [*RIS*]

Manicom, Jacqueline
34.0062 GD 1962 A propos de la limitation des naissances en Guadeloupe [Regarding birth control in Guadeloupe]. *Rev Guad* 13(48), 3d trimester: 8-10.
[*RIS*]

Mapp, Lionel McHenry
28.0837   **TR**   1952   Midwives versus middies in a rural community.

Marino, Anthony
9.0098   **BC**   1970   Family, fertility and sex ratios in the British Caribbean.

Meyer, H.
7.0124   **SR**   1961-62   Suriname en het Wereldbevolkingsvraagstuk [Surinam and the problem of world population].

Morgan, B. I. & Stratmann, C. J.
34.0063   **JM**   1971   The Jamaican male and family planning. *W I Med J* 20(1), March: 5-11.   [*PS*]

Nag, Moni
7.0130   **BB**   1971   The influence of conjugal behavior, migration and contraception on natality in Barbados.
34.0064   **BB**   1971   Pattern of mating behaviour, emigration and contraceptives as factors affecting human fertility in Barbados. *Social Econ Stud* 20(2), June: 110-133.   **[9,17]**   [*RIS*]
34.0065   **BB**   1972   Comportamiento conyugal, migración y anticoncepción que afectan a la fecundidad humana en Barbados [Patterns of mating behavior, migration and contraceptives as factors affecting human fertility in Barbados]. *In* Conferencia regional latinoamericana de población, Mexico 1970: actas 1. Guanajuato, Mexico, El Colegio de México: 379-386.   **[9,17]**   [*COL*]

Noel, Desmond
28.0937   **GR,GN**   1974   Maternal and child health/family planning programme in Grenada, Carriacou and Petit Martinique.

Nortman, Dorothy & Hofstatter, Ellen
7.0133   **BB,JM,TR**   1974   Population and family planning programs: a factbook.

Omphroy-Spencer, G.
28.0945   **JM,BC**   1974   What are the priorities for maternal care?

Otterbein, Keith F.
34.0066   **BA**   1966   The Andros Islanders: a study of family organization in the Bahamas. Lawrence, University of Kansas Press, Social Science Studies, 14: 152p.   **[9,11]**   [*COL*]

Pailler, G.
7.0141   **MT**   1965   La vitalité démographique du département de la Martinique [Vital demographic statistics of the department of Martinique].

Pathak, U. N.
28.0969   **JM**   1966   Intra-amniotic saline induction for termination of early pregnancy.
34.0067   **JM**   1971   Post-partum sterilization. *W I Med J* 20(1), March: 17-24.   [*PS*]

Patterson, A. W.
34.0068   **JM**   1973   Family planning programs in Jamaica. *In* Caribbean Regional Employers' Seminar on Population and Family Welfare Planning, Port-of-Spain, 10-14 April, 1973. Geneva, International Labour Office: 149-153.   [*IPPF*]

28.0973	**JM**	1974	Maternal and child health and family planning.

Piotrow, P. T. & Lee, Calvin M.

34.0069	**GC**	1974	Oral contraceptives—50 million users. *Popul Rpts* [A] series A(1), April: A1-28. [*ACM*]

Potts, Malcolm

34.0070	**AT**	1973	CONTRACEPTIVE DISTRIBUTION IN COLOMBIA AND ANTIGUA. London, International Planned Parenthood Federation: 19p. [*RIS*]

Powell, Dorian L.

1.0228	**JM**	1974	A select bibliography.
10.0045	**JM**	1976	Female labour force participation and fertility: an exploratory study of Jamaican women.

Price, Jill M.

34.0071	**JM**	1973	Familial and locational factors associated with aspects of teenage sexual behavior in Portland Parish, Jamaica. *In* Roseman, Curtis C., et al. SOCIAL PROBLEMS IN A SMALL JAMAICAN TOWN. Urbana-Champaign, University of Illinois: 41-55. (Department of Geography Paper No. 6) **[9]** [*AGS*]

Ram, Bali & Ebanks, G. Edward

34.0072	**BB**	1973	Stability of unions and fertility in Barbados. *Social Biol* 20(2), June: 143-250. **[7]** [*PS*]

Ramos, Carlos G.

34.0073	**CU**	1975	The Catholic church and birth control: Curaçao and Puerto Rico. *In* Segal, Aaron, ed. POPULATION POLICIES IN THE CARIBBEAN. Lexington, Massachusetts, D.C. Heath and Company: 159-175. **[23]** [*RIS*]

Ramzy, Nadia

34.0074	**JM**	1968	Family planning on the north coast of Jamaica. *Trans Kansas Acad Sci* 71(1), Spring: 1-6. [*COL*]

Reynolds, Jack

34.0075	**TR**	1971	Family planning dropouts in Trinidad: report of a small study. *Social Econ Stud* 20(2), June: 176-187. [*RIS*]

Roberts, George W.

34.0076	**BC**	1953	Motherhood tables of the 1946 census. *Social Econ Stud* 2(2-3), Oct.: 175-186. **[7,9]** [*RIS*]
34.0077	**BC**	1955	Cultural factors in fertility in the British Caribbean. *In* PROCEEDINGS OF THE WORLD POPULATION CONFERENCE IN ROME, 1954. New York, United Nations, p.977-988. **[9,20]** [*RIS*]
34.0078	**GC**	1955	Some aspects of mating and fertility in the West Indies. *Popul Stud* 8(3), Mar.: 199-227. **[9]** [*NYP*]
7.0165	**GC**	1966	Populations of the non-Spanish-speaking Caribbean.
7.0166	**GC**	1967	Reproductive performance and reproductive capacity in less industrialized societies.
34.0079	**JM**	1968	The present fertility position in Jamaica. *In* Szabady, Egon, ed. WORLD VIEWS OF POPULATION PROBLEMS. Budapest, Akadémiai Kiadó: 259-275. **[7]** [*COL*]

34.0080	GC	1968	Some problems of fertility control in developing societies. *In* ADVANCES IN FERTILITY CONTROL. Amsterdam, Excerpta Medica Foundation: 33-37. **[7]** [*RIS*]
34.0081	BC	1971	SOME ISSUES IN THE MEASUREMENT OF FERTILITY. Mona, Jamaica, University of the West Indies: 31p. **[7]** [*RIS*]
34.0082	BC	1972	Fecundidad diferencial por tipo de unión y algunas de sus implicaciones en las Islas occidentales [Differences in fertility by type of union and some of its implications in the West Indies]. *In* CONFERENCIA REGIONAL LATINOAMERICANA DE POBLACIÓN, MEXICO 1970: ACTAS 1. Guanajuato, Mexico, El Colegio de México: 364-372. **[9]** [*COL*]
34.0083	BC	1975	FERTILITY AND MATING IN FOUR WEST INDIAN POPULATIONS. Mona, Jamaica, University of the West Indies, Institute of Social and Economic Research: 341p. **[7,9,10]** [*RIS*]

Roberts, George W., ed.

7.0174	JM	1974	RECENT POPULATION MOVEMENTS IN JAMAICA.

Roberts, George W. & Braithwaite, Lloyd E.

34.0084	TR	1960	Fertility differentials by family type in Trinidad. *In* Rubin, Vera, ed. CULTURE, SOCIETY, AND HEALTH. New York, New York Academy of Sciences, p.963-980. (*Annals of the New York Academy of Sciences*, v. 84, art. 17.) **[9,11,12]** [*RIS*]
34.0085	TR	1961	A gross mating table for a West Indian population. *Popul Stud* 14(3), Jan.: 198-217. **[9,11]** [*RIS*]
9.0126	TR	1962	Mating among East Indian and non-Indian women in Trinidad.
34.0086	TR	1967	Fertility differentials by family type in Trinidad. *Trin Res Papers* 4, Dec.: 102-119. **[9]** [*IPPF*]
34.0087	TR	1967	Fertility differentials in Trinidad. *Trin Res Papers* 4, Dec.: 95-101. **[7,9,10]** [*IPPF*]
34.0088	TR	1967	A gross mating table for a West Indian population. *Trin Res Papers* 4, Dec.: 128-147. **[7,9]** [*IPPF*]
34.0089	TR	1967	Mating among East Indian and non-Indian women in Trinidad. *Trin Res Papers* 4, Dec.: 148-185. **[7,9,13]** [*IPPF*]

Roberts, George W.; Cummins, G. T.; Byrne, Joycelin & Alleyne, C.

34.0090	BB	1967	Knowledge and use of birth control in Barbados. *Demography* 4(2): 576-600. [*COL*]

Roopnarinesingh, S. S.

34.0091	TR	1975	Teenage pregnancy in Trinidad. *W I Med J* 24(3), Sept.: 129-132. **[28]** [*PS*]

Rosen, Robert C.

34.0092	JM	1973	LAW AND POPULATION GROWTH IN JAMAICA. Medford, Massachusetts, Fletcher School of Law and Diplomacy: 44p. (Law and Population Monograph Series Number 10) **[7,33]** [*IPPF*]

Rotchell, Yvonne E.

28.1105	BB	1976	An evaluation of paracervical block anaesthesia for use in minor gynaecological surgery.

Russell, Aubrey

34.0093   JM   1963   Field test of simple, foam-producing chemical contraceptive. *W I Med J* 12(1), Mar.: 23-27.   [*COL*]

Salas, Rafael M.

34.0094   GC   1973   The United Nations fund for population activities. *Int J Heal Serv* 3(4), Fall: 679-687. **[7,39]**   [*PS*]

Salzano, Francisco M., ed.

7.0182   GC   1971   THE ONGOING EVOLUTION OF LATIN AMERICAN POPULATIONS.

Scantlebury, Elayne

28.1135   BB   1974   Maternal child health/family planning in Barbados.

Schlesinger, Benjamin

9.0142   JM   1968   Family patterns in Jamaica: review and commentary.

Segal, Aaron

34.0095   GC   1969   Le planning familial dans la Caraïbe [Family planning in the Caribbean]. *Cah Cent Etud Reg Ant-Guy* (15): 14p.   [*RIS*]

7.0185   BA   1975   Bahamas.

Segal, Aaron, ed.

7.0187   GC   1975   POPULATION POLICIES IN THE CARIBBEAN.

Simpson, R. E. D.

34.0096   BC,UK   1970   Birthrates: a five year comparative study. *Race Today* 2(8), Aug.: 256-265. **[18]**   [*RIS*]

Sinclair, Hazel

34.0097   JM   1974   The role of the district midwife in family planning. *In* INTERNATIONAL CONFEDERATION OF MIDWIVES. Report of the Caribbean Working Party, Bridgetown, Barbados, 16-24 May, 1974. [Bridgetown, Barbados]: 101-103. **[28]**   [*RIS*]

Sinclair, Sonja A.

34.0098   JM   1974   Fertility. *In* Roberts, G. W., ed. RECENT POPULATION MOVEMENTS IN JAMAICA. Kingston, Jamaica, C.I.C.R.E.D. Series (Committee for International Coordination of National Research in Demography, Paris, France): 124-168. **[7]**   [*RIS*]

34.0099   JM   1974   A fertility analysis of Jamaica: recent trends with reference to the parish of St. Ann. *Social Econ Stud* 23(4), Dec.: 588-636. **[5,7]**

    [*RIS*]

Slavin, Stephen

34.0100   BB   1973   AN EVALUATION OF THE ECONOMIC COST AND EFFECTIVENESS OF THE BARBADOS FAMILY PLANNING ASSOCIATION. Ph.D. dissertation, New York University: 364p. **[7,41]**   [*PhD*]

Slavin, Stephen & Bilsborrow, Richard E.

34.0101   BB   1974   The Barbados Family Planning Association and fertility decline in Barbados. *Stud Fam Plan* 5(10), Oct.: 325-332.   [*PS*]

Smith, Karl A.

34.0102   JM   1968   Current research on family planning in Jamaica. *In* Kiser, E. V., ed. CURRENT RESEARCH ON FERTILITY AND FAMILY PLANNING IN LATIN AMERICA. *Millbank Mem Fund Q* 46(3, Part 2), July: 257-268.

[*ACM*]

34.0103   JM   1969   Problems, attitudes and programmes of family planning in Jamaica. *J Med Educ* 44(11, part 2), Nov.: 165-166.   [*PS*]

34.0104   BC   1969   The role of the University of the West Indies in family planning. *Car Q* 15(2-3), June-Sept.: 100-103.   **[32]**   [*RIS*]

34.0105   JM   1971   SOME SOCIO-CULTURAL AND MEDICAL PROBLEMS RELATED TO FAMILY PLANNING IN JAMAICA, WEST INDIES. D.P.H. Essay, Yale University, Department of Epidemiology and Public Health: 376p.   [*RIS*]

34.0106   DM   1972   The need for a family planning programme in Dominica, West Indies. *W I Med J* 21(2), June: 125-134.   [*PS*]

Smith, Karl A. & Johnson, Raymond L.

34.0107   JM   [n.d.]   MEDICAL OPINION ON ABORTION IN JAMAICA: A NATIONAL DELPHI SURVEY OF PHYSICIANS, NURSES, AND MIDWIVES. Kingston, Jamaica, University of the West Indies, Department of Social and Preventive Medicine: 29p.   **[20,28]**   [*IPPF*]

Smith, Robert H.

34.0108   JM   1973   CONTRACEPTIVE DISTRIBUTION IN THE COMMERCIAL SECTOR OF JAMAICA. Columbia, Maryland, Westinghouse Population Center, Health Systems Division: 222p.   [*IPPF*]

Smith, Theodore Frederick

34.0109   JM   1971   THE DIFFUSION OF CONTRACEPTIVE INNOVATION AMONG THE URBAN POOR IN JAMAICA. Ph.D. dissertation, Indian University, Graduate School of Business. 365p.   **[10]**   [*PhD*]

Steele, Wesley

16.0090   JM   1954   ENGULFED BY THE COLOR TIDE; STUDIES FROM JAMAICA: CONSEQUENCES OF THE SLAVE TRADE AND BRITISH COLONIALISM.

St. George, John

34.0110   TR   1969   Factors influencing the high incidence of grand multiparity in Trinidad and Tobago. *Obstet Gynec* 34(5), Nov.: 685-689.   **[20]**

[*PS*]

Stycos, J. Mayone

34.0111   JM   1954   Unusual applications of research: studies of fertility in underdeveloped areas. *Hum Org* 13(1), Spring: 9-12.   **[7]**   [*COL*]

34.0112   JM   1965   Experimentos sobre cambios sociales: los estudios de fecundidad en el Caribe [Experiments on social changes: fecundity studies in the Caribbean]. *In* Kahl, Joseph A., ed. LA INDUSTRIALIZACIÓN EN AMÉRICA LATINA. México, Fondo de Cultura Económica: 54-66.   **[7]**   [*NYP*]

34.0113   JM   1968   HUMAN FERTILITY IN LATIN AMERICA: SOCIOLOGICAL PERSPECTIVES. Ithaca, New York, Cornell University Press: 318p.   **[9,20]**   [*RIS*]

Stycos, J. Mayone & Arias, Jorge, eds.
7.0200   **GC**   1966   POPULATION DILEMMA IN LATIN AMERICA.

Stycos, J. Mayone & Back, Kurt
34.0114   **JM**   1958   Contraception and Catholicism in Jamaica. *Eng Q* 5(4), Dec.: 216-220. **[9,20,23]**   [*RIS*]

Stycos, J. Mayone & Blake, Judith
9.0176   **JM**   1954   The Jamaican Family Life Project: some objectives and methods.

Sukdeo, Fred
7.0201   **GU**   1970   DYNAMICS OF POPULATION GROWTH, WITH REFERENCE TO GUYANA.

Talbot, Frederick
34.0115   **BC**   1968   Family life and family planning programmes in the Caribbean. *In* REPORT OF CONSULTATION ON SOCIAL AND ECONOMIC DEVELOPMENT IN THE EASTERN CARIBBEAN HELD IN ST. VINCENT NOV. 26-30, 1968. Port-of-Spain, Trinidad, Superservice Printing Co.: 33-36.   [*RIS*]

Talbot, Frederick; Mc Neil, Jesse Jai & Talbot, Sylvia
34.0116   **BC**   1967   THE WANTED CHILD. REPORT OF 1967 FAMILY PLANNING SURVEY OF FIVE ISLANDS IN THE CARIBBEAN. New York, National Council of Churches of Christ in the U.S.A.: 58p. **[23]**   [*RIS*]

Tekse, Kalman
34.0117   **JM**   1968   A STUDY OF FERTILITY IN JAMAICA. Jamaica, Department of Statistics: 27p. **[7]**   [*RIS*]

Thomas, Thelma
34.0118   **JM**   1967   The nurses' contribution to the Jamaica Ministry of Health's family planning programme. *Jam Nurse* 7(1), April-May: 12 passim.   [*AJN*]

Tietze, Christopher
34.0119   **BB**   1957   THE FAMILY PLANNING SERVICE IN BARBADOS. New York, 14p. (United Nations Technical Assistance Programme, Report TAA/BAR/1.) **[9,33]**   [*RIS*]
34.0120   **BB**   1958   THE EFFECTIVENESS OF THE FAMILY PLANNING SERVICE IN BARBADOS. New York, 17p. (United Nations Technical Assistance Programme, Report TAA/BAR/4.) **[9,33]**   [*RIS*]

Tietze, Christopher & Alleyne, Charles
34.0121   **BB**   1959   A family planning service in the West Indies. *Fert Ster* 10(3), May-June: 259-271. **[9,33]**   [*RIS*]

Vaillant, Henry W.; Cummins, G. T.; Richart, R. M. & Barron, B. A.
34.0122   **BB**   1968   Insertion of Lippes loop by nurse-midwives and doctors. *Br Med J* 3(5619), Sept. 14: 671-673.   [*PS*]

Veeder, Nancy Walker
34.0123   **JM**   1974   PRENATAL CARE UTILIZATION AND PERSISTENCE PATTERNS IN A DEVELOPING NATION: A STUDY OF ONE HUNDRED AND EIGHTY-FIVE PREGNANT WOMEN ATTENDING TWO PRENATAL CLINICS IN KINGSTON, JAMAICA, WEST INDIES. Ph.D. dissertation, Brandeis University: 262p. **[28]**   [*PhD*]

Waterman, James A.

| 28.1388 | BC | 1942 | A suggested maternity scheme for the West Indies. |

30.0235   TR   1945   Nutrition in Trinidad, with special reference to milk during pregnancy and infancy.

Williams, L. L.

34.0124   JM   1966   Post-partum insertion of a standard Lippes loop. *In* FAMILY PLANNING AND POPULATION PROGRAMS: A REVIEW OF WORLD DEVELOPMENTS. Chicago, University of Chicago Press: 443-449. **[28]**   [*COL*]

Williams, L. L. & Patterson, A. W.

34.0125   JM   1971   Four years' experience with the Lippes Loop as a method of family planning. *W I Med J* 20(1), March: 12-16.   [*PS*]

Wortman, Judith

34.0126   TR,JM   1975   Training nonphysicians in family planning services and a directory of training programs. *Popul Rpts* Series J(6), Sept.: 89-108. **[28,32]**
                                                                                                                  [*ACM*]

Wynter, Hugh H.

34.0127   JM   1973   An experience of 200 cases of "culdoscopic" sterilization—an out-patient procedure. *W I Med J* 22(2), June: 107-111.   [*PS*]

Wynter, Hugh H.; Morris, David & Stockhausen, B. Yvonne

34.0128   JM   1973   Use of age/parity analysis in the assessment of primary IUCD acceptors (U.H.W.I.—October, 1964-February, 1966). *W I Med J* 22(2), June: 73-76.   [*PS*]

Wythenshawe, Lord Simon of

7.0223   BB   1954   POPULATION AND RESOURCES OF BARBADOS.

Yoyo, Michel

34.0129   MT   1969   Le planning familial à la Martinique [Family planning in Martinique]. *Cah Cent Etud Reg Ant-Guy* 15: 3p.   [*RIS*]

Chapter 35

HOUSING AND ARCHITECTURE

Public and private housing developments; construction industry; housing conditions; architectural studies; furniture.
See also: **[36]** Rural and urban development.

Acworth, A. W.
35.0001   BC   1949   TREASURE IN THE CARIBBEAN: A FIRST STUDY OF GEORGIAN BUILDINGS IN THE BRITISH WEST INDIES. London, Pleiades Books, 36p. **[5]**   [*COL*]

Ashurst, P. R. & Firth, A. R.
45.0005   JM   1971   Pilot plant operations in a developing country—considerations of design and construction.

Atkinson, G. Anthony
35.0002   BC   1953   Architecture in the trade winds. *Weather* 8(10), Oct.: 313-315.   [*RIS*]

Barker, Aubrey
36.0005   GC   1958   Progress, planning and people.

Barnett, A. S.; Pickvance, C. G. & Ward, R. H.
18.0019   BC,UK   1970   Some factors underlying racial discrimination in housing: a preliminary report on Manchester.

Benoist, Jean
42.0022   GD,MT   1968   Types de plantations en Guadeloupe et Martinique [Plantation types in Guadeloupe and Martinique].

Bertrand, Anca
35.0003   GC   1968   La maison antillaise [Houses in the Antilles]. *Parallèles* 29, 4th trimester: 14-25.   [*RIS*]
35.0004   FA   1968   Meubles anciens des Antilles françaises: queslques éléments d'histoire [Antique furniture of the French Antilles: some historical elements]. *Parallèles* 27, June-July-Aug: 4-13. **[5]**   [*RIS*]

Brandon, David
18.0039   BC,UK   1973   NOT PROVEN.

Brandt, Donald P.
35.0005   BZ   1975   Birth pains of Belmopan. *Places* 2(1), March: 14-20.   [*AGS*]

Brown, Audrey
5.0101   SK   1962   La Chateau de la Montagne, Saint Christopher.

Bueneman, E. R.
35.0006   TB   1958   The Tobago story—example of cooperation at all levels. *Caribbean* 12(1), Aug.: 6-10.   [*COL*]

Buisseret, David
35.0007   JM   1973   The Stony Hill barracks. *Jam J* 7(1-2), March-June: 22-24.   **[5]**
                                                                         [*RIS*]

Burgess, Charles J.
35.0008   GC   1951   Issues in Caribbean housing improvement. *In* ASPECTS OF HOUSING IN THE CARIBBEAN. Port of Spain, Caribbean Commission, p.203-212.   [*RIS*]

Burney, Elizabeth
35.0009   BC,UK   1967   HOUSING ON TRIAL: A STUDY OF IMMIGRANTS AND LOCAL GOVERN-MENT. London, Oxford University Press: 267p.   **[18,36]**   [*COL*]
18.0046   BC,UK   1971   Housing.

Burns, L. V.
63.0033   JM   1942   Roofing shingles in Jamaica.

Bynoe, Peter
35.0010   TR   1962   THE ARCHITECTURE OF TRINIDAD AND TOBAGO, 1562-1962. Port of Spain, Guardian Commercial Printery, 15p.   [*RIS*]

Chapman, John L.
35.0011   SV   1951   Aided self-help housing in St. Vincent. *In* ASPECTS OF HOUSING IN THE CARIBBEAN. Port of Spain, Caribbean Commission, p.98-102.   **[33]**   [*RIS*]

Chatillon, Marcel
35.0012   GD   1967   Meubles anciens de la Guadeloupe [Antique furniture in Guade-loupe]. *Parallèles* 27, June-July-Aug.: 24-31.   **[5]**   [*RIS*]

Clarke, Colin G.
7.0021   JM   1970   An overcrowded metropolis: Kingston, Jamaica.
36.0025   GC   1974-75   Problems of employment and housing in West Indian towns.

Concannon, T. A. L.
35.0013   JM   1963   Preservation of national monuments in Jamaica. *Car Q* 9(3), Sept.: 3-9.   **[5]**   [*RIS*]
35.0014   JM   1965   The great houses of Jamaica. *In* Cargill, Morris, ed. IAN FLEMING INTRODUCES JAMAICA. New York, Hawthorn Books, Inc.: 117-126.   **[3]**   [*RIS*]
35.0015   JM   1967   Houses of Jamaica. *Jam J* 1(1), Dec.: 35-39.   [*RIS*]
35.0016   JM   1970   Our architectural heritage: houses of the 18th and 19th century with special reference to Spanish Town. *Jam J* 4(2), June: 23-28.   **[5]**
                                                                         [*RIS*]

5.0181	JM	1972	Restoration of Rose Hall Great House.

Connell, Neville

23.0054	BB	1953	St. George's Parish Church, Barbados.
35.0017	BB	1959	18th century furniture and its background in Barbados. *J Barb Mus Hist Soc 26(4), Aug.: 162-190.* **[5]** [*AMN*]

Conway, Dennis

7.0027	TR	1975	The residential mosaic of Port of Spain, 1960.

Costello, M.

35.0018	GU	1951	The possibilities of prefabrication. *In* ASPECTS OF HOUSING IN THE CARIBBEAN. Port of Spain, Caribbean Commission, p.63-66. [*RIS*]
35.0019	GU	1952	Rural housing problems: with notes on self-help housing and the possibilities of prefabrication. *Timehri* 4th ser., 1(31), Nov.: 16-20. **[33,36]**

Cox, John

5.0189	BE	1970	Governor Nathaniel Butler and the State House, St. George's, Bermuda.

Cox, William M.

5.0190	BE	1963	Mount Wyndham: an historic Bermuda home.

Cross, Beryl

35.0020	BC	1954	From shack to self-help in the West Indies. *Venture* 6(5), Sept.: 8-9. [*COL*]

Currie, Leonard J.

35.0021	GC	1965	Housing and health in the Caribbean. *In* Wilgus, A. Curtis, ed. THE CARIBBEAN: ITS HEALTH PROBLEMS. Gainesville, University of Florida Press: 18-32. (Caribbean Conference Series 1, Vol. 15.) **[28]** [*RIS*]

DeForest, Jeanne

35.0022	BC	1968	A home in the Caribbean. *Car Beachcomb* 4(5), Sept.-Oct.: 15-16. [*NYP*]

Delawarde, Jean-Baptiste

56.0083	MT	1935	ESSAI SUR L'INSTALLATION HUMAINE DANS LES MORNES DE LA MARTINIQUE [ESSAY ON THE HUMAN SETTLEMENT ON THE BLUFFS OF MARTINIQUE].

Dennert, H.

35.0023	BN	1968	Oude woningen op Bonaire [Old houses on Bonaire]. *Schakels* NA54: 34-39. [*NYP*]
35.0024	NW	1968	Oude woningen op de Bovenwindse eilanden [Old houses on the Windward Islands]. *Schakels* NA54: 40-47. [*NYP*]
35.0025	AR	1968	Het oude woonhuis op Aruba [The old houses on Aruba]. *Schakels* NA54: 28-33. [*NYP*]

Desai, Patricia; Standard, K. L. & Miall, W. E.

28.0314	JM	1970	Socio-economic and cultural influences on child growth in rural Jamaica.

De Syllas, L. M.

35.0026   BB   1944[?]   REPORT ON PRELIMINARY HOUSING SURVEY OF TWO BLOCKS OF CHAPMAN'S LANE TENANTRY, BRIDGETOWN (JUNE-JULY, 1944); AND COMMENTS ON THE REPORT BY THE TOWN PLANNING ADVISOR AND THE HOUSING BOARD. [Bridgetown?] Barbados, Advocate Co., 8p.

[*RIS*]

Doran, Edwin Beal, Jr.

35.0027   GC   1962   The West Indian hip-roofed cottage. *Calif Geogr* 3: 97-104.   **[19]**

[*RIS*]

Drayton, Evan

35.0028   GU   1955   More houses for British Guiana. *Caribbean* 8(10), May: 221-223, 236.   [*COL*]

Dybbroe, Ole

35.0029   JM   1967   Design for comfort in tropical environment. *In* Floyd, Barry, ed. PROCEEDINGS OF A CONFERENCE ON CLIMATOLOGY AND RELATED FIELDS IN THE CARIBBEAN, MONA, JAMAICA, UNIVERSITY OF THE WEST INDIES, SEPT. 20-22, 1966. Scientific Research Council, Technical Information Service: 81-90.   **[55]**   [*RIS*]

Eberlein, Harold Donaldson

35.0030   UV   1935   Housing in the Virgin Islands. *Architecture* 71(1), Jan.: 1-4.   **[36]**

[*COL*]

Eyre, L. Alan

36.0036   JM   [n.d.]   THE SHANTY TOWN—A REAPPRAISAL.

Farrar, P. A.

23.0085   BB   1935   Christ church.

Floch, Hervé Alexandre & Cornu, G.

35.0031   FG   1956   Problèmes de l'habitat à Cayenne. Le Casier sanitaire des immeubles [Housing problems in Cayenne. A sanitation register of the property]. *Archs Inst Past Guy* 415, Dec. (32p.).   **[28]**

Francis, Sybil E.

35.0032   JM   1953   A land settlement project in Jamaica. *Car Commn Mon Inf B* 7(4), Nov.: 83, 86.   **[36]**   [*COL*]

Franklin, George H.

51.0041   BC   1968   Tourism and the preservation of amenities: the problem of reconciliation: II-the West Indies.

Goyeneche, Eugene

5.0339   MT   1956   Historical monuments of Martinique.

Gradussov, Alex

5.0341   JM   1971   The deceit of motive: looking back on the Georgian age in Jamaica.

Groome, J. R.

35.0033   GR   1964   Sedan-chair porches: a detail of Georgian architecture in St. George's. *Car Q* 10(3), Sept.: 31-33.   [*RIS*]

Groote, J. F.

35.0034   CU   1948   Woningbouw en stadsuitbreiding [Housing and urban development]. *In* ORANJE EN DE ZES CARAÏBISCHE PARELEN. Amsterdam, J. H. de Bussy: 161-166.   [*UCLA*]

Haddon, Roy F.

35.0035   BC,UK   1970   A minority in a Welfare State: the location of West Indians in the London housing market. *New Atlan* 2(1): 80-133.   **[18,36]**   [*COL*]

Haglund, Elsa

35.0036   GC   1958   HOUSING AND HOME IMPROVEMENT IN THE CARIBBEAN. [Port of Spain?] Trinidad, Food and Agriculture Organization and Caribbean Commission, 216p.   **[9,33]**   [*RIS*]

Hanson, Donald R.

35.0037   GC   1955   Caribbean housing. *Caribbean* 8(6), Jan.: 116-119.   [*COL*]
35.0038   GC   1965   Some housing problems in the Caribbean. *In* Wilgus, A. Curtis, ed. THE CARIBBEAN: ITS HEALTH PROBLEMS. Gainesville, University of Florida Press: 9-17. (Caribbean Conference Series 1, Vol. 15)   [*RIS*]

Hartog, J.

36.0045   CU,AR   1947   De voorgenomen uitbreiding van Willemstad op Curacao, Oranjestad en St. Nicolaas op Aruba [The contemplated expansion of Willemstad in Curacao, of Oranjestad and St. Nicolaas in Aruba].

5.0388   SM   1974   THE COURTHOUSE OF ST. MAARTEN: LIFE AND WORK OF DR. WILLEM HENDRIK RINK, COMMANDER AND GOVERNOR OF THE ISLAND 1790-1806.

Heaton, John Langdon

35.0039   BE   1902   Coral-stone and palm. The homes of Bermuda. *House Garden* 2(4), April: 164-174.   **[3]**   [*COL*]

Heesterman, J. E.

35.0040   GC   1951   New materials and methods of construction. *In* ASPECTS OF HOUSING IN THE CARIBBEAN. Port of Spain. Caribbean Commission, p.213-217.   [*RIS*]
35.0041   GC   1955   Information on standardisation of milling sizes of sawn timber and of prefabricated wooden parts of housing in the Caribbean area. *In* CARIBBEAN TIMBERS, THEIR UTILISATION AND TRADE WITHIN THE AREA: REPORT OF THE TIMBER CONFERENCE HELD AT KENT HOUSE, TRINIDAD, APR. 15-22, 1953. Port of Spain, Caribbean Commission, p.59-66.   [*RIS*]

Hendrick, S. Purcell

23.0118   JM   1911   A SKETCH OF THE HISTORY OF THE CATHEDRAL CHURCH OF ST. JAGO DE LA VEGA, SPANISH TOWN IN THE PARISH OF ST. CATHERINE, JAMAICA.

Horn, Edwin

35.0042   BC   [n.d.]   THE WEST INDIES: REPORT OF A SURVEY ON HOUSING, NOVEMBER 1956-MAY 1957. [Bridgetown?] Barbados, Development and Welfare Organization, 16p.   **[33,44]**

Howells, D. A.

35.0043   JM   1966   Note on the design of structures to resist earthquakes. *Inf B Scient Res Coun* 7(2), Sept.: 42-44.   **[53]**   [*RIS*]

Howes, J. R.

62.0063   TR   1956   Livestock buildings at the college New Farm.

Johnstone, H. M.

35.0044   TR   1959   Queens Hall, Trinidad—the beginning of a new era of cultural development. *Can-W I Mag* 49(10), Oct.: 19-20, 22.   **[26]**   [*NYP*]

Kadleigh, Sergei

35.0045   JM   1961[?]   Our housing needs. *In* Cumper, George, ed. REPORT OF THE CONFERENCE ON SOCIAL DEVELOPMENT IN JAMAICA. Kingston, Standing Committee on Social Services, p.105-107.   **[33]**   [*RIS*]

King, Robert L.

28.0728   GC   1965   Health facilities construction in the Caribbean.

Kloos, Peter

13.0121   SR   1972   Huizen en dorpen van de Caraiben van de Marowijne, Suriname [House form and settlement pattern of the Maroni River Caribs of Surinam].

Kuip, E. van der

28.0744   AR,CU   1969   *Trypanosomiasis cruzi* in Aruba and Curacao.

Laird, Colin

35.0046   TR   1954   Trinidad town house. *Car Q 3(4), Aug.: 188-198.*   [*RIS*]

Lampe, P. H. J.

35.0047   GC   1951   Housing and health in the Caribbean. *In* ASPECTS OF HOUSING IN THE CARIBBEAN. Port of Spain, Caribbean Commission, p.15-22.   **[28]**   [*RIS*]

Lashley, T. O.

35.0048   BB   1945[?]   REPORT ON A HOUSING SURVEY OF EIGHT SLUM TENANTRIES IN BRIDGETOWN, JUNE 1944-APR. 1945. Bridgetown, Housing Board Office, 47p.   **[33,36]**   [*RIS*]

35.0049   BB   1953   Barbados attacks the housing problem. *Car Commn Mon Inf B* 7(5), Dec.: 110-112.   **[33,36]**   [*COL*]

Lefroy, John Henry, ed.

35.0050   BE   1970   A full account of the first Assembly, August 1, 1620. *Bermuda Hist Q* 27(2), Summer: 42-48.   **[5]**   [*COL*]

Le Pasteur

35.0051   MT   1966   Qu'est-ce que l'épargne-logement? [What is cheap lodging?] *B Cham Com Indus Mart* 2-3, Feb.-March: 91-93.   [*RIS*]

Lichtveld, Lou

35.0052   SR   1960   Native arts in modern architecture. *Caribbean* 14(4), Apr.: 87-89.   **[19,22]**   [*COL*]

McIntyre, Raymond
35.0053   JM   1967   The relevance of climate to Jamaican architecture. *Inf B Scient Res Coun* 7(4), March: 113-116.   [*RIS*]

May, Arthur J.
35.0054   BC   1933   The architecture of the West Indies. *W I Comm Circ* 48(899), Mar. 16: 105-107; 48(900), Mar. 30: 125-126; 48(901), Apr. 13: 147-148; 48(902), Apr. 27: 167-168; 48(904), May 25: 207-208; 48(905), June 8: 227-229.   **[5,19]**   [*NYP*]

Norton, A. V.
35.0055   JM   1970   The Kingston metropolitan area: a description of its land use patterns. *In* ESSAYS ON JAMAICA. Kingston, Jamaican Geographical Society and University of the West Indies, Geology & Geography Department: 34-44.   **[36]**   [*AGS*]

O'Neil, Maud E.
35.0056   BB   1949   Of the buildings in progress with which to house the College. *In* Klingberg, Frank. J., ed. CODRINGTON CHRONICLE: AN EXPERIMENT IN ANGLICAN ALTRUISM ON A BARBADOS PLANTATION, 1710-1834. Berkeley and Los Angeles, University of California Press, p.27-39. (Publications in history no. 37.)   **[5,32,42]**   [*COL*]

Otterbein, Keith F.
35.0057   BA   1975   CHANGING HOUSE TYPES IN LONG BAY CAYS: THE EVOLUTION OF FOLK HOUSING IN AN OUT ISLAND BAHAMIAN COMMUNITY. New Haven, Connecticut, Human Relations Area Files Press: 123p.   **[26]**   [*RIS*]

Oudschans Dentz, Fred
50.0119   SR   1920-21   De bauxietnijverheid en de stichting van een nieuwe stad in Suriname [The bauxite industry and the founding of a new city in Surinam].

Paquette, Romain
35.0058   GD,MT   1969   Divergences de politique en matière d'habitation populaire dans les villes antillaises: une ville française et une ville anglaise [Differences in popular lodging policies in West Indies: a French town and a English town]. *Rev Geogr Montr* 23(2): 123-136.   [*NYP*]

Patterson, V. I.
35.0059   JM   1963   New schools for a new nation. *Torch* 13(4), Dec.: 12-20.   **[32]**
    [*TCL*]

Pawson, M.
5.0712   JM   1971   A seventeenth century plantation house.

Peacocke, Nora E.
35.0060   GC   1953   Building research in the Caribbean. *Car Commn Mon Inf B* 6(9), Apr.: 197-198.   [*AGS*]

Peters, Fred E.
35.0061   MS   1931   SAINT ANTHONY'S CHURCH, MONTSERRAT, WEST INDIES. Bridgetown, Advocate Co., 11p.   **[5,23]**

Pinto, Geoffrey de Sola
35.0062   JM   1972   "Georgian": a part of our architectural environment. *Jam Archi* 9:
                         44-48.   [*NYP*]

Rance, Hubert Elvin
35.0063   TR   1951   Government expenditures in Trinidad and Tobago. *In* ASPECTS OF
                         HOUSING IN THE CARIBBEAN. Port of Spain, Caribbean Commission,
                         p.111-112. **[33,37]**   [*RIS*]

Reijenga, T. W. & Asselt, W. P. van
28.1055 SR   1968   *Schistosomiasis mansoni* in a Surinam polder.

Reynal, Adeline de
35.0064   MT   1968   Meubles anciens de la Martinique: notes sur le mobilier antillais
                         [Antique furniture of Martinique: notes on West Indian furniture].
                         Parallèles 27, June-July-Aug.: 14-23. **[5]**   [*RIS*]

Richards, Judith E.
35.0065   JM   1967   The chandeliers from Old King's House, Spanish Town. *Jam J* 1(1),
                         Dec.: 13-15. **[5]**   [*RIS*]

Richards, Neil O.
35.0066   JM   1971   Vernacular housing: a stylistic base? *Jam Archi* 8: 30-37.   [*NYP*]
36.0065 JM   1972   Land development patterns in Jamaica.

Roberts, Walter Adolphe
35.0067   JM   1962   Old King's House, Spanish Town. *Chron W I Comm* 77(1372), May:
                         230-233. **[5]**   [*NYP*]

Rose, Dexter L.
35.0068   JM   1968   A SURVEY OF HOUSING CONDITIONS IN TRENCH TOWN, SEPTEMBER,
                         1967. Kingston, Jamaica, Department of Statistics: 61p. **[8,9]**
                                                                                   [*NYP*]
35.0069   JM   1970   A SURVEY OF HOUSING CONDITIONS IN DELACREE PEN, JANUARY,
                         1969. Kingston, Jamaica, Department of Statistics: 66p. **[8,9]**
                                                                                   [*NYP*]

Roux, G.
35.0070   FC   1957   Housing in the French Caribbean Departments. *Caribbean* 10(6-7),
                         Jan.-Feb.: 154-155.   [*COL*]

Savarey, Eunice
35.0071   SK   1954   St. Kitts housing project. *Can-W I Mag* 44(12), Dec.: 2-3.   [*NYP*]

Senior, Clarence
35.0072   GC   1954   Housing and sanitation in the Caribbean. *In* Wilgus, A. Curtis, ed.
                         THE CARIBBEAN: ITS ECONOMY [PAPERS DELIVERED AT THE FOURTH
                         ANNUAL CONFERENCE ON THE CARIBBEAN HELD AT THE UNIVERSITY
                         OF FLORIDA, DEC. 3-5, 1953]. Gainesville, University of Florida
                         Press, p.177-190. (Publications of the School of Inter-American
                         Studies, ser. 1, v.4.) **[28]**   [*RIS*]

Shaw, Earl Bennett
8.0198   SC   1934   The villages of St. Croix.

Slater, Mary
35.0073   BC   1971   A place in the sun. *W I Chron* 86(1480), May: 187-189.   [*NYP*]

Sloman, E.
35.0074   GU   1912   St. George's Cathedral. *Timehri* 3d ser., 2(19), Dec.: 373-376. **[5,23]**   [*AMN*]

Smart, Lawrence H.
35.0075   BE   1954   Structural problems. *Bermuda Hist Q* 11(1), Spring: 16-18. **[23]**   [*COL*]

Smeathers, R.
63.0109   TR   1943   The manufacture of shingles from local woods in Trinidad and Tobago.

Smit, B.
35.0076   CU   1968   Oude bouwwerken op Curaçao [Old buildings on Curaçao]. *Schakels* NA54: 20-27.   [*NYP*]

Stevens, Peter
35.0077   BB   1959   Planning and preservation. *J Barb Mus Hist Soc* 26(3), May: 111-119. **[5]**   [*AMN*]

Stevens, Peter H. M.
36.0084   BC   1957   Planning in the West Indies.

Stockdale, Frank A.; Gardner-Medwin, R. & Syllas, S. M. de
35.0078   BC   1948   Recent planning developments in the colonies. *J Roy Inst Br Archit* 55(4), Feb.: 140-148. **[36]**   [*NYP*]

Stow, John
35.0079   BE   1953   The house itself. *Bermuda Hist Q* 10(2), Summer: 50-53. **[5]**   [*COL*]
23.0296   BE   1954   The spirit of the founders; the first few years; the growth of the building.

Temminck Groll, C. L.
35.0080   SR   1970   An inventory of the historical monuments of Surinam. *Neth Found Adv Trop Res* (WOTRO),Report for the Year 1969: 25-29. **[5]**   [*RIS*]
5.0885   SR   1973   Het Hoekhuis en de Dixie Bar [The House on the Corner and the Dixie Bar].

Temminck Groll, C. L., comp.
35.0081   SR   1973   DE ARCHITEKTUUR VAN SURINAME 1667-1930 [THE ARCHITECTURE OF SURINAM 1667-1930]. Zutphen, The Netherlands, De Walburg Pers: 363p. (Suriname en zijn historie II) **[5]**   [*NYP*]

Trowbridge, James W.
36.0087   JM   1973[?] URBANIZATION IN JAMAICA.

Tucker, Ethel
35.0082   BE   1955   The Bridge House, Somerset. *Bermuda Hist Q* 12(4), Winter: 118-123. **[5]** [*COL*]

Tucker, Terry
23.0307   BE   1974   St. Anne's Church.

Volders, J. L.
35.0083   SR   1966   BOUWKUNST IN SURINAME: DRIEHONDERD JAREN NATIONALE ARCHITECTUUR [ARCHITECTURE IN SURINAM: 300 YEARS OF NATIONAL ARCHITECTURE]. Hilversum, G. van Saane, Lectura Architectonica: 152p. **[5]** [*NYP*]
35.0084   SR   1975   Houten huizen, een eigen Surinaamse bouwkunst [Wooden houses, a unique Surinamese architecture]. *Suralco Mag* June: 1-7. [*UCLA*]

Voort, P. P. C. H. van de
35.0085   NA   1973   De behoefte aan woningen in de Nederlandse Antillen [The need for houses in the Netherlands Antilles]. *Econ Stat Ber* 58(2914), August 22: 751-754. [*COL*]

Waterman, Thomas T.
35.0086   BB   1946   Some early buildings of Barbados. *J Barb Mus Hist Soc* 13(3-4), May-Nov.: 140-148. **[5]** [*AMN*]

Watlington, Hereward T.
23.0316   BE   1956   Old Devonshire Church.
35.0087   BE   1959   Bermuda architecture and anecdote. *Bermuda Hist Q* 16(1), Spring: 9-27. **[5]** [*COL*]
5.0953   BE   1967   Verdmont: a history of the property.
35.0088   BE   1971   The Bridge House, St. George's Bermuda. *Bermuda Hist Q* 28(1), Spring: 9-18. **[5]** [*COL*]

Wel, F. J. van
35.0089   CU   1968   De architectuur van Willemstad [The architecture of Willemstad]. *Schakels* NA54: 1-4. [*NYP*]
35.0090   CU   1968   Oude landhuizen op Curaçao [Old country houses on Curaçao]. *Schakels* NA54: 12-19. [*NYP*]
35.0091   CU   1968   Stadsaanleg en woningbouw van Willemstad [The city planning and housing construction of Willemstad]. *Schakels* NA54: 5-11. [*NYP*]
35.0092   SR   1970   Plantagehuizen [Plantation houses]. *Schakels* S74: 19-23. [*NYP*]

Wight, Gerald
35.0093   TR   1951   A proposal for the future financing of public housing in Trinidad and Tobago. *In* ASPECTS OF HOUSING IN THE CARIBBEAN. Port of Spain, Caribbean Commission, p.113-119. **[33,37]** [*RIS*]

Wilkinson, Henry
35.0094   BE   1953   Furniture of the (Tucker) House. *Bermuda Hist Q* 10(2), Summer: 63-66. **[5]** [*COL*]

Willis, Margaret
20.0087   JM   1971   Housing aspirations and changing life-styles in Jamaica.

Wint, J. McL.

35.0095   GC   1967   Hurricane precautions for tropical buildings. *In* Floyd, Barry, ed. Proceedings of a Conference on Climatology and Related Fields in the Caribbean, Mona, Jamaica, University of the West Indies, Sept. 20-22, 1966. Scientific Research Council, Technical Information Service: 91-101. **[55]**   [*RIS*]

Wong, Paul G.

35.0096   SR   1953   The aided self-help housing programme in Surinam. *Car Commn Mon Inf B* 6(7), Feb.: 155-156. **[33]**   [*AGS*]

Woodhouse, W. M.

35.0097   BC   1954   Building and housing in the West Indies. *Prefabrication* 1(10), Aug.: 13-18.   [*RIS*]

35.0098   BC   1955   Housing in the West Indies. *Corona* 7(6), June: 227-231.   [*RIS*]

35.0099   BC   1956   Housing in the West Indies. *Statist* Sept.: 66, 68.

35.0100   BC   1962   Developments in the local building industries of the Commonwealth. *J Roy Soc Arts* 110(5073), Aug.: 639-704. **[45]**   [*RIS*]

Chapter 36

RURAL AND URBAN DEVELOPMENT

Cooperatives; community development; town planning; urbanization; urban problems; urban research.
See also: [7] Demography and human resources; [35] Housing and architecture.

Ahrens, H.

46.0003   **SR**   1922-23 Kolonisatie op particulier land in Suriname met Javanen onder contract onder de thans geldende immigratie wetten [Colonization with Javanese contract laborers on privately owned land in Surinam under the current immigration laws].

Alcala, V. O.

36.0001   **GC**   1957   About community development ... a review. *Caribbean* 10(8), Mar.: 192-195.   [*COL*]

36.0002   **GC**   1959   Highlights of the conference on social development in the West Indies. *Caribbean* 13(6), June: 114-116. **[33]**   [*COL*]

Alexander, John J. G.

36.0003   **JM**   1946   Growing pains in Jamaica. *America* 75(21), Aug. 24: 494-495.

    [*COL*]

Auchinleck, Gilbert; Smith, G. Whitfield & Bertrand, Walter

44.0001   **GN,GR**   1914   Government schemes of land settlement in Grenada and the Grenadines.

Bailey, Wilma

8.0006   **JM**   1976   What the yard is said to be.

Bangou, Henri

36.0004   **GD**   1968   Pointe-à-Pitre 1968. *Perspectives d'Outre Mer* 72, April (1st Trimester): 5-10.   [*RIS*]

Barker, Aubrey

36.0005   **GC**   1958   Progress, planning and people. *Caribbean* 11(11), June: 251-254. **[33,35]**   [*COL*]

Beckett, J. Edgar

36.0006   **GU**   1918   Some stray thoughts on our people. *Timehri* 3d ser., 5(22), Aug.: 91-97.   [*AMN*]

36.0007   GU   1919   Some home truths. *Timehri* 3d ser., 6(23), Sept.: 186-195.   [*AMN*]
36.0008   GU   1921   Progress? *Timehri* 3d ser., 7(24), Aug.: 131-147.   [*AMN*]

Beringuier, Christian
36.0009   MT   1967   L'espace régional martiniquais [Regional planning in Martinique]. *Cah O-M* 20(78), April-June: 150-184.   **[7]**   [*AGS*]

Bernard, Hector
52.0018   FC   1949   Jamaica peasant farmers set example in cooperation.

Bertrand, Anca
36.0010   FA   1968   Répercussions sociologiques de l'urbanisation [Sociological repercussions of urbanization]. *Parallèles* 29, 4th trimester: 59-66.   [*RIS*]

Binnendijk, A. L. & Hunter, L. J.
7.0016   JM   1974   Implications for rural development from a long-range planning model: an illustration for Jamaica.

Bluck, Laura A.
36.0011   BE   1956   The evolution of the town of Hamilton, 1747-1857. *Bermuda Hist Q* 13(3), Autumn: 111-135.   **[5]**   [*COL*]

Bonner, A.
36.0012   BC   1956   Cooperation in the British West Indies. *Venture* 8(6), Nov.: 4-5.   [*COL*]

Bowen, Noel P.
36.0013   GC   1954   Cooperatives in the Caribbean. *Car Commn Mon Inf B* 7(9), Apr.: 191-193, 208, 216.   [*COL*]

Braithwaite, E. A.
36.0014   GC   1954   Cooperatives in the Caribbean. *Car Commn Mon Inf B* 7(10), May: 219-220, 232; 77(11), June: 241-242, 260; 8(1), Aug.: 20-22; 8(4-5), Nov.-Dec.: 80-81.   [*COL*]

Braithwaite, Lloyd E.
17.0016   JM   1961[?]   Population, migration and urbanization.

Briggs, Ronald & Conway, Dennis
36.0015   TR   1975   The evolution of urban ecological structure: theory and a case study, Port of Spain, Trinidad. *Social Sci Q* 55(4), March: 871-888.   **[7,8]**   [*COL*]

Brodber, Erna
8.0026   JM   1975   A STUDY OF YARDS IN THE CITY OF KINGSTON.

Broom, Leonard
36.0016   BC   1953   Urban research in the British Caribbean: a prospectus. *Social Econ Stud* 1(1), Feb.: 113-119.   [*COL*]
36.0017   JM   1960   Urbanization and the plural society. *In* Rubin, Vera, ed. SOCIAL AND CULTURAL PLURALISM IN THE CARIBBEAN. New York, New York Academy of Sciences, p.880-891. (*Annals of the New York Academy of Sciences*, v. 83, art. 5.)   **[8]**   [*RIS*]

Bruijne, G. A. de

17.0017 **SR,NE** 1969 Surinamers naar Nederland: een nieuwe vorm van urbanisatie [Surinamese to the Netherlands: a new form of urbanization].

Bryce, Wyatt E. et al.

36.0018 **JM** 1962 Historic Port Royal. Kingston, Tourist Trade Development Board, 80p. **[5]** *[SCH]*

Burney, Elizabeth

35.0009 **BC,UK** 1967 Housing on trial: a study of immigrants and local government.

Carley, Verna A. & Starch, Elmer A.

36.0019 **JM** 1955 Report on community development programs in Jamaica, Puerto Rico, Bolivia, and Peru, by Team Number II. Washington, D.C., International Cooperation Administration, 76p.
[UNL]

Case, Gerald O.

45.0029 **GU** 1946 Problems affecting industrialisation of the interior of British Guiana.

Chambolle, Thierry

36.0020 **MT** 1967 Le port de Fort-de-France [The port of Fort-de-France]. *B Cham Com Indus Mart* 1-6, 1st semester: 40-49. *[RIS]*

Cheesman, W. J. W.

36.0021 **GC** 1956 Handbook for cooperative personnel in the Caribbean. [Port of Spain?] Trinidad, Food and Agriculture Organization of the United Nations and the Caribbean Commission, 252p.

Clarke, Colin G.

46.0038 **JM** 1966 Population pressure in Kingston, Jamaica: a study of unemployment and overcrowding.

36.0022 **JM** 1966 Problemas de planeación urbana en Kingston, Jamaica [Problems of urban planning in Kingston, Jamaica]. *In* Conferencia Regional Latinoamericana: tomo I. Mexico, Sociedad Mexicana de Geografía y Estadística: 411-431. **[7]** *[COL]*

36.0023 **JM** 1967 Aspects of the urban geography of Kingston, Jamaica. D.Phil. dissertation, University of Oxford: 491p. **[56]**

7.0021 **JM** 1970 An overcrowded metropolis: Kingston, Jamaica.

36.0024 **JM** 1973 The slums of Kingston. *In* Comitas, Lambros & Lowenthal, David, eds. Work and family life: West Indian perspectives. Garden City, N.Y., Anchor Press/Doubleday: 175-187. **[8]** *[RIS]*

7.0023 **JM** 1974 Jamaica overflows.

36.0025 **GC** 1974-75 Problems of employment and housing in West Indian towns. *J Geogr Assoc Trin Tob* 4: 5-15. **[35,46]** *[RIS]*

36.0026 **GC** 1974 Urbanization in the Caribbean. *Geography* 59(3), July: 223-232.
[NYP]

36.0027 **BC** 1975 The Commonwealth Caribbean. *In* Jones, Ronald, ed. Essays on world urbanization. London, George Philip and Sons Ltd.: 341-350. **[7]** *[RIS]*

7.0024 **JM** 1975 Ecological aspects of population growth in Kingston, Jamaica.

36.0028   **JM**   1975   KINGSTON, JAMAICA: URBAN DEVELOPMENT AND SOCIAL CHANGE, 1692-1962. Berkeley, University of California Press: 270p.   **[5,7,56]**
                                                                                                      [*RIS*]

Clarke, F. J.
36.0029   **BB**   1908   Origin and establishment of the Barbados co-operative cotton factory. *W I B* 9(3): 243-246.   **[61]**   [*AMN*]

Coleridge, P. E.
8.0039   **SR**   1958   Vrouwenleven in Paramaribo [Women's life in Paramaribo].

Collins, Sydney
8.0040   **JM**   1956   Social mobility in Jamaica, with reference to rural communities and the teaching profession.

Costello, M.
35.0019   **GU**   1952   Rural housing problems: with notes on self-help housing and the possibilities of prefabrication.

Craig, Susan E.
36.0030   **TR**   1974   COMMUNITY DEVELOPMENT IN TRINIDAD AND TOBAGO: 1943-1973: FROM WELFARE TO PATRONAGE. Mona, Jamaica, University of the West Indies, Institute of Social and Economic Research: 138p. (Working Paper No. 4)   **[33,37]**   [*RIS*]

Crane, Alfred V.
28.0285   **GU**   1924   The Georgetown sewerage scheme.

Cruickshank, J. Graham
36.0031   **GU**   1918   "King William's people." *Timehri* 3d ser., 5(22), Aug.: 104-119.   **[5]**
                                                                                                      [*AMN*]

Cumper, George E.
36.0032   **GU,BZ**   1950[?]   This is the Evans Report. *Car Q* 1(3): 39-44.   **[17]**
41.0115   **JM**   1958   Expenditure patterns, Kingston, Jamaica, 1954.

Cumper, Gloria
3.0134   **JM**   1967   New pattern for Kingston.

David, Wilfred L.
36.0033   **GU**   1976   PLANNING FOR NATIONAL DEVELOPMENT. Mona, Jamaica, University of the West Indies, Institute of Social and Economic Research: 68p. (Working Paper No. 10)   **[41]**   [*RIS*]

Davies, E. D.
36.0034   **TB**   1957   Cocoa co-ops. *Caribbean* 11(3), Oct.: 60-62, 72.   **[47,59]**   [*COL*]

Dolly-Besson, June
33.0062   **JM**   1969   SELECTED CASES IN JAMAICA SOCIAL WELFARE.

Dyer, H. Thornley
36.0035   **BC**   1970   Foreshore reclamation schemes for urban expansion in the Caribbean. *Car Cons Assoc Environ Newsl* 1(2), Oct.: 29-30.   [*RIS*]

Eberlein, Harold Donaldson
35.0030   **UV**   1935   Housing in the Virgin Islands.

Egerton, Walter
48.0051   **GU**   1915   A railway and hinterland development.

Ericksen, E. Gordon
7.0048   **BC**   1962   THE WEST INDIES POPULATION PROBLEM: DIMENSIONS FOR ACTION.

Eyre, L. Alan
36.0036   **JM**   [n.d.]   THE SHANTY TOWN—A REAPPRAISAL. Kingston, Jamaica, University
                                   of the West Indies, Geography Department: 17p. (Research Notes
                                   3) **[35]**   *[AGS]*
36.0037   **JM**   1972   The shantytowns of Montego Bay, Jamaica. *Geogr Rev* 62(3), July:
                                   394-413. **[17]**   *[AGS]*

Field, Arthur J., ed.
46.0078   **GC**   1967   URBANIZATION AND WORK IN MODERNIZING SOCIETIES.

Foreman, R. A.
44.0020   **SL**   1958   LAND SETTLEMENT SCHEME FOR SAINT LUCIA: BASED ON A SURVEY OF
                                   THE AGRICULTURAL AND SOCIAL CONDITIONS OF THE ISLAND ON A
                                   VISIT FROM 24.3.58-25.4.58.

Frampton, A. de K. et al.
2.0147   **TB**   1957   DEVELOPMENT PLAN FOR TOBAGO: REPORT OF THE TEAM WHICH
                                   VISITED TOBAGO IN MARCH/APRIL, 1957.
2.0148   **SV**   1959   REPORT AND RECOMMENDATIONS FOR THE DEVELOPMENT OF SAINT
                                   VINCENT BY TEAM OF EXPERTS FOLLOWING ITS VISIT IN NOVEMBER,
                                   1957.

Francis, Sybil E.
35.0032   **JM**   1953   A land settlement project in Jamaica.
36.0038   **JM**   1969   The evolution of community development in Jamaica. *Car Q*
                                   15(2-3), June-Sept.: 40-58. **[33,37]**   *[RIS]*

Furley, Peter
21.0030   **BZ**   1971   A capital waits for its country.

Gardner-Medwin, R. J.
36.0039   **BC**   1948   Major problems of town planning in the West Indies. *Car Commn
                                   Mon Inf B* 2(1), Aug.: 15-16, 18.   *[COL]*

Gates, Ralph Charles
47.0110   **BC**   1959   Marketing of fresh vegetables in the Caribbean islands.

Giglioli, George
28.0503   **GU**   1958   The mosquito and sand-fly nuisance in Georgetown and its
                                   suburbs.

Gilbert, S. M.
36.0040   **TR**   1931   Co-operation. *Proc Agric Soc Trin Tob* 31(5), May: 185-193. *[AMN]*

Gonggrijp, J. W.

36.0041   SR   1955   Some remarks on the Brokopondo Project. *Vox Guy* 1(6): 145-148.
                                                                                [*RIS*]

Gordon, G. C. L.

36.0042   GU   1957   The development of co-operation in British Guiana. *Timehri* 4th
                         ser., 1(36), Oct.: 55-60.

Goudet, Françoise

36.0043   GD   1973   LE QUARTIER DE L'ASSAINISSEMENT À POINT-À-PITRE (GUADELOUPE):
                         CONTRIBUTION Á L'ÉTUDE DES PHÉNOMÈNES DE CROISSANCE ET DE
                         RÉNOVATION URBAINES EN MILIEU TROPICAL [A SQUATTER SETTLE-
                         MENT IN POINT-À-PITRE (GUADELOUPE): CONTRIBUTION TO THE
                         STUDY OF THE PHENOMENA OF URBAN GROWTH AND RENEWAL IN A
                         TROPICAL ENVIRONMENT]. Talence, France, Centres d'Etudes de
                         Géographie Tropicale: 144p. (Travaux et Documents de Gé-
                         ographie Tropicale, no. 10)   **[7]**   [*AGS*]

Grant, Andrew

48.0062   GU   1930   Railways necessary to progress.
48.0063   GU   1931   Railroad construction advocated.

Grant, C. H.

37.0304   GU   1965   The politics of community development in British Guiana 1954-57.

Greer, Scott; McElrath, Dennis L.; Minar, David W. & Orleans, Peter, eds.

8.0089   BC   1968   THE NEW URBANIZATION.

Gretton, R. H.

36.0044   GC   1957   THE ROLE OF THE COOPERATIVE MOVEMENT IN ECONOMIC DEVEL-
                         OPMENT, WITH SPECIAL REFERENCE TO THE AREA SERVED BY THE
                         CARIBBEAN COMMISSION. [Port of Spain?] Caribbean Commission,
                         18p.

Haan, J. H. de

43.0177   SR   1953   The Lelydorp project.
43.0178   SR   1955   De landstreekontwikkeling in Suriname [Development of rural
                         regions in Surinam].

Haan, J. H. de & Hendriks, J. A. H.

43.0179   SR   1954   Lelydorp project—a pilotscheme for land-development in Surinam.

Haddon, Roy F.

35.0035   BC,UK 1970   A minority in a Welfare State: the location of West Indians in the
                         London housing market.

Hartog, J.

36.0045   CU,AR 1947   De voorgenomen uitbreiding van Willemstad op Curacao, Oran-
                         jestad en St. Nicolaas op Aruba [The contemplated expansion of
                         Willemstad in Curacao, of Oranjestad and St. Nicolaas in Aruba].
                         W I G 28: 42-46.   **[35]**   [*COL*]

Heesterman, J. E.
51.0049   **BN**   1957   A development plan for Bonaire.

Hendriks, J. A. H.
43.0195   **SR**   1956   HET LELYDORPPLAN IN SURINAME: INLEIDING TOT HET VRAAGSTUK
VAN DE LANDONTWIKKELING OP ARME GRONDEN IN EEN TROPISCH
GEBIED [THE LELYDORP PLAN IN SURINAM: INTRODUCTION TO THE
PROBLEM OF LAND DEVELOPMENT OF INFERIOR SOILS IN A TROPICAL
AREA].

Hervé, P.
43.0200   **FG**   1964   Le polder de Marie-Anne: l'aménagement des terres basses de la
Guyane par la S.A.T.E.C. [The Marie-Anne polder: the utilization
of the Guiana lowlands by the S.A.T.E.C.].

Hill, Luke M.
36.0046   **GU**   1911   Nomenclature of Georgetown: its streets and districts. *Timehri* 3d
ser., 1(18A), Jan.: 42-52. **[5,19]**   [*AMN*]
36.0047   **GU**   1915   The municipality of Georgetown. *Timehri* 3d ser., 3(20B), May:
227-235. **[5]**   [*AMN*]

Hubbard, Raymond
36.0048   **JM**   1970   THE SPATIAL PATTERN AND MARKET AREAS OF URBAN SETTLEMENT IN
JAMAICA. Kingston, Jamaica, University of the West Indies, De-
partment of Geography: 15p. (Research Notes 1)   [*RIS*]

Hussein, Ahmed & Taylor, Carl C.
36.0049   **JM,TR**   1953   REPORT OF THE MISSION ON RURAL COMMUNITY ORGANIZATION
AND DEVELOPMENT IN THE CARIBBEAN AREA AND MEXICO. [New
York?] United Nations, March, 45p. **[8]**

Imrie, John
41.0257   **TR**   1958   REPORT ON THE FINANCE OF THE THREE MUNICIPALITIES AND THE
WORKING OF THE COUNTY COUNCILS IN TRINIDAD AND TOBAGO.

Issa, Abe
51.0056   **BC**   1959[?]   A SURVEY OF THE TOURIST POTENTIAL OF THE EASTERN CARIBBEAN:
WITH PARTICULAR REFERENCE TO THE DEVELOPMENT OF BEACHES,
THE BUILDING OF HOTELS, AND THE PROVISION OF ANCILLARY
FACILITIES AND AMENITIES FOR THE TOURIST INDUSTRY.

Jones, G. A.
43.0238   **LW,WW**   1933   Recent agricultural developments in some of the Leeward and
Windward Islands.

Kane, Arthur
36.0050   **JM**   1973   The church and urbanization in the Caribbean. *Jam J* 7(4), Dec.:
32-37. **[23]**   [*RIS*]

Kearns, Kevin C.
36.0051   **BZ**   1973   Belmopan: perspective on a new capital. *Geogr Rev* 63(2), April:
147-169.   [*AGS*]

Klein, W. C.

41.0282   **GG**   1940   Economische binnenland-penitratie in de vier Guyana's [Penetration into the interior regions of the four Guianas for economic reasons].

Kluvers, B. J.

48.0094   **SR**   1921-22 Een wegtracé door het moeras naar Coronie [A road plan for traversing the swamps to Coronie].

Kool, R.

41.0290   **SR**   1956   Paramaribo; het economische leven van een stad in een tropisch land [Paramaribo; economic life of a town in a tropical land].

Kruijer, G. J.

36.0052   **SR**   1951   Urbanisme in Suriname [Urbanism in Surinam]. *Tijdschr Ned Aar Genoot* 68(1), Jan.: 31-63.   **[7]**   [*RIS*]

43.0259   **JM**   1958   Het Christianagebied; een landhervormings project in Jamaica [The Christiana Area—a land reform project in Jamaica].

Kruijer, G. J. & Nuis, A.

43.0260   **JM**   1960   REPORT ON AN EVALUATION OF THE FARM DEVELOPMENT SCHEME: FIRST PLAN: 1955-1960.

Lamont, Norman et al.

36.0053   **TR**   1918   Report of the Co-operative Sugar Factories Committee. *Proc Agric Soc Trin Tob* 18(10), Oct.: 894-902.   **[42,61]**   [*AMN*]

Lashley, T. O.

35.0048   **BB**   1945[?] REPORT ON A HOUSING SURVEY OF EIGHT SLUM TENANTRIES IN BRIDGETOWN, JUNE 1944-APR. 1945.

35.0049   **BB**   1953   Barbados attacks the housing problem.

Leflore, James Edward

36.0054   **TR**   1973   AN ANALYSIS OF A THIRD-WORLD SLUM SETTLEMENT: A CASE STUDY OF URBANISM IN TRINIDAD. Ph.D. dissertation, Syracuse University: 290p.   **[33]**   [*PhD*]

Leighton, Fred

45.0091   **BC**   1951   REPORT ON HANDICRAFTS AND COTTAGE INDUSTRIES IN THE BRITISH WEST INDIES.

45.0092   **BC**   1952   Handicrafts and cottage industries in the British West Indies.

Lewis, A. B.

43.0271   **GC**   1951   A land improvement programme for the Caribbean.

Lighton, G.

36.0055   **GU**   1950   British Guiana. II: Georgetown and its trade. *Geography* 35: 228-239.   [*AGS*]

McDonald, Frank

36.0056   **BV**   1969   THE BRITISH VIRGIN ISLANDS: PROBLEMS OF RAPID DEVELOPMENT. New York, Institute of Current World Affairs: 4p.   [*RIS*]

Marie-Saint-Germain, M. G.
36.0057   **GD**   1968   La construction en Guadeloupe (Building in Guadeloupe). *Perspectives d'Outre Mer* 72, April (1st Trimester): 11-12.   [*RIS*]

Maunder, W. F.
48.0111   **JM**   1954   Development of internal transport in Jamaica.
48.0112   **JM**   1954   Expenditure on internal transport in Jamaica.
48.0113   **JM**   1954   Kingston public passenger transport.

Mensah, Phyllis Joyce
36.0058   **JM**   1974   DECISION MAKING AND URBANISATION: KINGSTON, JAMAICA. Ph.D. dissertation, University of Liverpool: 573p.

Millard, I. S.
36.0059   **JM**   1950   The village schoolmaster as community development leader. *Mass Educ B* 1(3), June: 42-45. **[32]**   [*NYP*]

Miller, H.
43.0300   **JM**   1958   The role of surveys in planning agricultural development in Jamaica.

Mintz, Sidney W.
8.0157   **JM**   1958   Historical sociology of the Jamaican church-founded free village system.

Miscall, Leonard
48.0117   **TR**   1944   Jungle roadbuilding.

Moss, Guido
48.0121   **TR**   1961   BUS TRANSPORTATION IN TRINIDAD AND TOBAGO [BY THE] NATIONAL CITY MANAGEMENT CO., CHICAGO, ILL. [GUIDO MOSS, ENGINEER].

Newling, Bruce E.
36.0060   **JM**   1962   THE GROWTH AND SPATIAL STRUCTURE OF KINGSTON, JAMAICA. Ph.D. dissertation, Northwestern University, 195p. **[7,56]**

Norton, A. V.
35.0055   **JM**   1970   The Kingston metropolitan area: a description of its land use patterns.

Oberg, Kalervo
43.0325   **SR**   1964   A STUDY OF FARM PRODUCTIVITY IN THE SANTO BOMA SETTLEMENT PROJECT SURINAM.

Oberg, Kalervo & Hindori, George
43.0326   **SR**   1963   GROOT HENAR POLDER: POLDER SETTLEMENT STUDY NO. II.

Oberg, Kalervo & May, Edward
43.0327   **SR**   1961   POLDER SETTLEMENT STUDY NO. I: LA POULE.

Olivier, Sydney, 1st Baron Ramsden
43.0329   **JM**   1915   Recent development in Jamaica: internal and external, by Sir Sydney Olivier.

Ottley, C. R.

5.0679   **TR**   1962   THE STORY OF PORT OF SPAIN, CAPITAL OF TRINIDAD, WEST INDIES, FROM THE EARLIEST TIMES TO THE PRESENT DAY.

Oudschans Dentz, Fred

50.0119   **SR**   1920-21 De bauxietnijverheid en de stichting van een nieuwe stad in Suriname [The bauxite industry and the founding of a new city in Surinam].

Paget, Hugh

36.0061   **JM**   1946   The founding of Mandeville. *Jam Hist Rev* 1(2), Dec.: 172-180.   **[5]**
                                                                                                 [*COL*]

Panhuys, L. C. van

48.0130   **SR**   1922-23 Denkbeelden en plannen nopens een kustspoorweg in Suriname [Plans and ideas about a coastal railroad in Surinam].
36.0062   **SR**   1933-34 Ir. A. A. Meyers over het kolonisatievraagstuk [Ir. A. A. Meyers about the problem of colonization]. *W I G* 15: 102-104.   [*COL*]

Paquette, Romain

36.0063   **MT**   1965   AN ANALYSIS OF THE CONCENTRATION AND DISPERSAL OF SETTLEMENT IN MARTINIQUE. M.A. thesis, McGill University, 181p.   **[56]**
43.0339   **GU**   1968   LOT CULTIVATION—ITS ROLE IN ADJUSTMENT TO TROPICAL URBAN LIFE. A CASE STUDY: MACKENZIE, GUYANA.
36.0064   **MT**   1969   Une cité planifiée et une cité spontanée (Fort-de-France, Martinique) [A planned city and a "spontaneous" city (Fort-de-France, Martinique)]. *Cah Geogr Québec* 29, Sept.: 169-186.   [*COL*]

Parris, Michael

33.0148   **GU**   1975   Delinquency in the Linden area.

Pascoe S., J.

41.0401   **GC**   1966   Community development trends in the region.

Peacocke, Nora E.

43.0344   **GC**   1953   Research in relation to extension services in the Caribbean.

Philibert, Jean-Marc

17.0076   **GD**   1969   UN CAS DE MIGRATION URBAINE EN GUADELOUPE [A CASE OF URBAN MIGRATION IN GUADELOUPE].
17.0077   **MG,GD** 1972   Les Marie-Galantais à Pointe-à-Pitre. Quelques problèmes posés par l'étude de le migration urbaine [Marie-Galanteans in Pointe-à-Pitre. Some problems presented by the study of urban migration].

Pound, F. J.

43.0359   **TR**   1946   The extension services of the Department of Agriculture.

Pyttersen, Tj.

48.0136   **GU,SR** 1923-24 Waarom landwegen in Demarary wél en in Suriname niet noodzakelijk waren [Why country roads were necessary in Demerara and unnecessary in Surinam].

Richards, Neil O.

36.0065   JM   1972   Land development patterns in Jamaica. *Jam J* 6(4), Dec.: 4-11. **[35]**   [*RIS*]

Roberts, George W.

7.0167   JM   1968   Demographic aspects of rural development: the Jamaican experience.

Roberts, Walter Adolphe, ed.

36.0066   JM   1955   THE CAPITALS OF JAMAICA. Kingston, Pioneer Press, 112p. **[5]**

Robinson, H. E.

36.0067   TR   1954   The Cooperative Citrus Growers Association: a record of cooperation and progress. *J Agric Soc Trin Tob* 54(2), June: 153-159. **[60]**   [*AMN*]

Robinson, Joyce L.

1.0245   JM   1973   Rural library development in Jamaica.

Rodgers, William B.

8.0187   BA   1965   THE WAGES OF CHANGE: AN ANTHROPOLOGICAL STUDY OF THE EFFECTS OF ECONOMIC DEVELOPMENT ON SOME NEGRO COMMUNITIES IN THE OUT ISLAND BAHAMAS.

Romalis, Rochelle S.

43.0385   SL   1969   The rural entrepreneur and economic development: the case of St. Lucia.

Rose, John C. & Lewis, Anthony C.

36.0068   SL   1949   REPORT ON THE NEW TOWN PLANNING PROPOSALS; REDEVELOPMENT OF CENTRAL AREA, CASTRIES, ST. LUCIA 1948. Castries, St. Lucia Govt., 31p.   [*RIS*]

Rosen, Joseph A.

17.0089   GU   1939   Problem of large scale settlement of refugees from middle European countries in British Guiana.

Roth, Vincent

36.0069   GU   1919   Some lesser known potentialities of the northwestern district. *Timehri* 3d ser., 6(23), Sept.: 133-135.   [*AMN*]

Roux, Antoine de

7.0181   MT   1966   La population de Fort-de-France en 1985 et les perspectives de concentration urbaine en Martinique [The population of Fort-de-France in 1985 and the perspectives of urban density in Martinique].

36.0070   MT   1967   Le centre de Fort-de-France: ses possibilités d'adaptation à la vie moderne [Downtown Fort-de-France: its possibilities for adapting to modern life]. *Cah Cent Etud Reg Ant-Guy* 12: 5-86.   [*RIS*]

36.0071   MT   1968   Le futur Fort-de-France [The future Fort-de-France]. *Perspectives d'Outre Mer* 72, April (1st Trimester): 43-47. **[41]**   [*RIS*]

Sable, Martin H.

1.0253   GC   1971   LATIN AMERICAN URBANIZATION: A GUIDE TO THE LITERATURE, ORGANIZATIONS AND PERSONNEL.

Samlalsingh, Ruby S.

33.0171   GU   1959   Application of social welfare principles to the rural development programme on sugar estates in British Guiana.

Saxe, Allen

36.0072   TR   1968   URBAN SQUATTERS IN TRINIDAD: THE POOR IN A MASS SOCIETY. M.A. thesis, Brandeis University: 47p.   **[8]**   [*RIS*]

Sebastian, S. & Buchanan, I. C.

28.1150   AG   1965   Feasibility of concrete septic privies for sewage disposal in Anguilla, B.W.I.

Seggar, W. H.

13.0194   GU   1952   The Mazaruni Amerindian district.
36.0073   GU   1954   Some aspects of development of a remote interior district. *Timehri* 4th ser., 1(33), Oct.: 30-40.   **[13]**
36.0074   GU   1959   Community development amongst Amerindians. *Timehri* 4th ser., 38, Sept.: 21-24.   **[8,13]**   [*AMN*]

Sertima, J. van

36.0075   GU   1915   The municipality of New Amsterdam. *Timehri* 3d ser., 3(20B), May: 237-252.   **[5]**   [*AMN*]
36.0076   GU   1921   Progress in New Amsterdam. *Timehri* 3d ser., 7(24), Aug.: 24-28.
                                                                              [*AMN*]

Shaw, Earl Bennett

7.0191   VI   1935   Population adjustments in our Virgin Islands.

Shephard, C. Y.

43.0409   GC   1954   Background to agricultural extension in the Caribbean.
47.0250   GC   1954   Marketing and processing problems.
47.0251   BC   1954   Organisation for the processing and marketing of the products of small scale farming.
43.0411   JM   1955   Agricultural extension.
59.0081   TB   1957   Cooperative cocoa fermentaries in Tobago.
36.0077   TR   1957   Postscript. *Caribbean* 11(3), Oct.: 63-64.   **[59]**   [*COL*]

Sherlock, Philip M.

36.0078   BC   1958   The co-operative movement in the British Caribbean. *Int Lab Rev* 77(4), Apr.: 325-341.   [*COL*]

Simons, R. D.

36.0079   SR   1958   Stad en platteland [The city and the rural areas]. *In* Walle, J. van de & Wit, H. de, eds. SURINAM IN STROOMLIJNEN. Amsterdam, Wereld Bibliotheek, p.44-58.   **[8]**

Simpson, George Eaton

36.0080   JM   1954   Begging in Kingston and Montego Bay. *Social Econ Stud* 3(2), Sept.: 197-211.   **[8,20,33]**   [*RIS*]

Sinclair, Dennis William

36.0081   JM   1975   JAMAICA WICKER WORKS: A CASE STUDY OF A SMALL INDUSTRY IN THE DEVELOPMENT OF RURAL JAMAICA. Ph.D. dissertation, University of Michigan: 275p.   **[45]**   [*PhD*]

Smith, M. G.

9.0153   CR   1962   WEST INDIAN FAMILY STRUCTURE.

Staniforth, A. R.

36.0082   GU,SV,TR   1944   Co-operative credit societies in the South Caribbean area. *Trop Agric* 21(12), Dec.: 219-227.   [*AGS*]

36.0083   GU,SV,TR   1945   Co-operative credit societies in the South Caribbean area. *Trop Agric* 22(1), Jan.: 3-8.   [*AGS*]

Stehlé, Henri

43.0422   FC   1950   New agricultural research centre set up for French Caribbean Departments.

Stevens, Peter H. M.

36.0084   BC   1957   Planning in the West Indies. *Town Ctry Plann* 25(12), Dec.: 503-508.   **[35]**   [*COL*]

Stevenson, N. S.

63.0114   BZ   1938   The evolution of vegetation survey and rural planning in British Honduras.

Stockdale, Frank A., ed.

43.0425   BB   1941   AGRICULTURAL DEVELOPMENT IN BARBADOS: DESPATCHES FROM THE COMPTROLLER FOR DEVELOPMENT AND WELFARE IN THE WEST INDIES TO HIS EXCELLENCY THE GOVERNOR OF BARBADOS.

Stockdale, Frank A.; Gardner-Medwin, R. & Syllas, S. M. de

35.0078   BC   1948   Recent planning developments in the colonies.

Stone, Carl

36.0085   JM   1975   Urbanization as a source of political disaffection—the Jamaican experience. *Br J Sociol* 26(4), Dec.: 448-464.   **[8,20,33]**   [*COL*]

Sylvestre, Henri

36.0086   MT   1967   Les zones industrielles [The industrial zones]. *B Cham Com Indus Mart* 1-6, 1st semester: 58-65.   [*RIS*]

Tegani, Ulderico

3.0589   CU   1929   Willemstad di Curacao [Willemstad of Curacao].

Thomas, Robert N.

17.0105   GC   1971   Internal migration in Latin America: an analysis of recent literature.

Trowbridge, James W.

36.0087   JM   1973[?]   URBANIZATION IN JAMAICA. New York, The Ford Foundation: 30p. (International Urbanization Survey)   **[35]**   [*RIS*]

Turner, Wm. T.

49.0103   JM   1907   The Christiana People's Co-operative Bank Limited.

Victor, Clivin

33.0200   BC   1970   Juvenile delinquency.

Villaronga, Mariano

36.0088   GC   1962   El cooperativismo en el Caribe [Cooperative ventures in the Caribbean]. *Boricua* 1(4), Mar.: 32-33, 95.   **[49]**   [*NYP*]

Wakefield, A. J. et al.

43.0445   TR   1943   REPORT OF THE AGRICULTURAL POLICY COMMITTEE OF TRINIDAD AND TOBAGO.

Watts, Francis

44.0063   GR,CR,SV   1914   Efforts in aid of peasant agriculture in the West Indies.
43.0448   MS   1915   Agricultural industries of Montserrat.
43.0449   DM   1915   The development of Dominica.

Webster, Aimée

36.0089   JM   1961   Small farmers' role in Jamaica's economy. *New Commonw* 39(1), Jan: 65-66.   **[10]**   [*AGS*]

Wel, F. J. van

36.0090   SR   1970   De groei van Paramaribo [The growth of Paramaribo]. *Schakels* S75: 28-34.   [*NYP*]

Wells, A. F. & Wells, D.

49.0108   BC   1953   FRIENDLY SOCIETIES IN THE WEST INDIES.

Wengen, G. D. van

15.0092   SR   [n.d.]   DE JAVANEN IN DE SURINAAMSE SAMENLEVING [THE JAVANESE IN THE SURINAMESE SOCIETY].

Wit, Y. B. de

7.0221   SR   1966   Is Paramaribo te groot [Is Paramaribo too large]?

Wooding, Hugh

36.0091   JM,TR   1947   Co-operation and agriculture. *Proc Agric Soc Trin Tob* 47(4), Dec.: 311-317.   [*AMN*]

Wright, James

33.0223   JM   1947   Lucky Hill Community Project.

Young, Allan

36.0092   GU   1957   SOME MILESTONES IN VILLAGE HISTORY. [Georgetown?] British Guiana, British Guiana Village Chairmen's Conference, 22p. (A series of six radio talks.)   **[5,37]**

Young, J. G.

36.0093 **JM** 1946 Who planned Kingston? *Jam Hist Rev* 1(2), Dec.: 144-153. **[5]**
[COL]

Zielhuis, L.

8.0249 **SR** 1974 Community development in Surinam.

POLITICAL
ISSUES

Chapter 37

POLITICS AND GOVERNMENT

Political events; electoral politics; political unrest; political development; constitutional law.

See also: [8] The nature of society; [33] Social and legal issues; [38] Intraregional issues; [39] International issues; [40] Post-colonial issues.

Abarbanel, Albert

37.0001   JM   1951   Bustamente of Jamaica—promises and pistols. *Reporter* 4(12), June 12: 24-26.   [*COL*]

Abbott, George C.

41.0001   BC   1963   The future of economic co-operation in the West Indies in the light of the break-up of the Federation.

37.0002   KNA   1971   Political disintegration: the lessons of Anguilla. *Gov Opp* 6(1), Winter: 58-74.   **[40]**   [*COL*]

Abénon, Lucien

37.0003   GD   1965   Les luttes électorales et la vie politique à la Guadeloupe de 1870 à 1885 [Electoral struggles and political life in Guadeloupe from 1870 to 1885]. *B Soc Hist Guad* 3-4: 29-32.   **[5]**   [*RIS*]

Adam, B. H.

37.0004   NC   1965   Tien jaar Statuut 1954-1964. De wetgeving [Ten years of the Statute, 1954-1964. The legislation]. *N W I G* 44(1-2), April: 3-15.   [*RIS*]

Adhin, J. H.

37.0005   NC   1972   Landsbesluiten: alleen uitvoeringsbesluiten of ook autonome besluiten? [Land decisions: only executive or also autonomous decisions?] *Ant Jurbl* 22(3-4): 785-791.   [*COL*]

Alexander, Robert J.

37.0006   GU   1955   Communist power cracks in British Guiana. *Int Free Trade Un* 11(10), Oct.: 1p.   [*RIS*]

Alleyne, Mervin C.

37.0007   JM   1963   Communication and politics in Jamaica. *Car Stud* 3(2), July: 22-61.   **[25,48]**   [*RIS*]

Allum, Desmond

37.0008   TR   1973   Legality vs. Morality: a plea for Lt. Raffique Shah. *In* Lowenthal, David & Comitas, Lambros, eds. THE AFTERMATH OF SOVEREIGNTY: WEST INDIAN PERSPECTIVES. Garden City, N.Y., Anchor Press/ Doubleday: 331-348.   **[8]**   [*RIS*]

Ameyde, M. F. van
37.0009   SR   1967   De niet-militaire activiteiten van de Troepenmacht in Suriname [The non-military activities of the military forces in Surinam]. *Schakels* S65/NA49: 32-34.   [*NYP*]

Anderson, Robert W.
38.0002   GC   1967   Social science ideology and the politics of national integration.

Anderson, William A. & Dynes, Russell R.
46.0006   CU   1973   Organizational and political transformation of a social movement: a study of the 30th of May Movement in Curaçao.
37.0010   CU   1975   SOCIAL MOVEMENTS, VIOLENCE, AND CHANGE: THE MAY MOVEMENT IN CURAÇAO. Columbus, Ohio State University Press: 175p. **[16,40,46]**   [*RIS*]

Andic, Fuat M. & Mathews, Thomas G., eds.
2.0008   GC   1965   THE CARIBBEAN IN TRANSITION: PAPERS ON SOCIAL, POLITICAL AND ECONOMIC DEVELOPMENT. SECOND CARIBBEAN SCHOLARS' CONFERENCE, MONA, JAMAICA, APRIL 14-19, 1964.

Anglin, Douglas G.
37.0011   BC   1961   The political development of the West Indies. *In* Lowenthal, David, ed. THE WEST INDIES FEDERATION. New York, Columbia University Press, p.35-62. **[38]**   [*RIS*]

Archibald, Charles H.
37.0012   GC   1962   Cold war in the Caribbean. *Venture* 14(10), Nov.: 7-8.   [*COL*]
37.0013   TR   1962   Trinidad: crossroads of the Caribbean. *New Commonw* 40(11), Nov.: 689-691.   [*AGS*]

Arden-Clarke, Charles
37.0014   TR   1958   REPORT OF THE CHAGUARAMAS JOINT COMMISSION. London, H.M.S.O., 61p. (Colonial no. 338.)

Argueta Ruiz, José Dolores
39.0004   BZ   1966   ESTADOS UNIDOS FIEL DE LA BALANZA EN EL CASO DE BELICE [THE UNITED STATES, BALANCE OF LOYALTY IN THE CASE OF BELIZE].

Armet, Auguste
37.0015   MT   1974   A propos des élections législatives 1973 à la Martinique: Césaire, le Parti Progressiste Martiniquais et les électeurs du Centre [A propos the 1973 legislative elections in Martinique: Césaire, the PPM, and the voters of the central region]. *Cah Césairiens* 1, Printemps: 26-31.   [*RIS*]

Armstrong, W. H. R.
37.0016   GC   1960   The Sea Devils of the Caribbean; an account of German U-boat activity in the West Indies during World War II. *J Barb Mus Hist Soc* 28(1), Nov.: 29-48.   [*AMN*]

Arntz, W.
37.0017   SR   1925-26 Het Suriname vraagstuk [The Surinam problem]. *W I G* 7: 252-264.   [*COL*]

Aruoture, Felix Robinson Okeroto
37.0018   JM   1970   AN EVOLUTIONARY AND COMPARATIVE STUDY OF JAMAICAN CONSTITUTIONAL LAW. Ph.D. dissertation, University of London: 433p.

Aspinall, Algernon E.
37.0019   BC   1940   British West Indian bases for the U.S.A. *Crown Colonist* 10(108), Nov.: 491-493. **[39]**   [NYP]
37.0020   BC   1940   Constitutional changes in the British West Indies. *J Comp Leg Int Law* 3d ser., 22(4), Nov.: 129-135.   [COL]
37.0021   JM   1941   New chapter in Jamaica's history. *Crown Colonist* 11(114), May: 207-209.

Assenderp, Andre L. van
37.0022   NC   1957   The Netherlands Caribbean: a study in regional autonomy. *In* Wilgus, A. Curtis, ed. THE CARIBBEAN: CONTEMPORARY INTERNATIONAL RELATIONS [PAPERS DELIVERED AT THE SEVENTH CONFERENCE ON THE CARIBBEAN HELD AT THE UNIVERSITY OF FLORIDA, DEC. 6-8, 1956]. Gainesville, University of Florida Press, p.69-88. (Publications of the School of Inter-American Studies, ser. 1, v. 7.)   [RIS]

Astwood, J. C.
37.0023   BE   1970   The Parliamentary system and the role of "Speaker". *Bermuda Hist Q* 27(2), Summer: 33-41.   [COL]

Augelli, John P.
56.0004   VI   1955   The British Virgin Islands: a West Indian anomaly.

Augier, F. R.
37.0024   BC   1965   F. G. Spurdle, early West Indian government. *Jam Hist Rev* 5(1), May: 71-75. **[5]**   [RIS]
5.0027   JM   1966   The consequences of Morant Bay: before and after 1865.

Auguste, Armet
37.0025   MT   1971   Césaire et le Parti Progressiste Martiniquais: le nationalisme progressiste [Cesaire and the PPM: the progressive nationalism]. *Nou Opt* 1(2), May: 57-84. **[11,21]**   [RIS]

Ayearst, Morley
37.0026   BC   1954   A note on some characteristics of West Indian political parties. *Social Econ Stud* 3(2), Sept.: 186-196.   [RIS]
37.0027   BC   1960   THE BRITISH WEST INDIES: THE SEARCH FOR SELF-GOVERNMENT. New York, New York University Press, 258p.   [RIS]

Bacchus, Kassim
32.0031   BC   1969   Education and decolonization.

Bacchus, M. K.
37.0028   GU   1967   The ministerial system at work: a case study of Guyana. *Social Econ Stud* 16(1), March: 34-56.   [RIS]
37.0029   GU   1967   Relationship between professional and administrative officers in a government department during a period of administrative change. *Sociol Rev* 15(2), July: 155-178.   [COL]

Bahadoorsingh, Krishna

37.0030   TR   1966   TRINIDAD ELECTORAL POLITICS: THE PERSISTENCE OF THE RACE FACTOR. Ph.D. dissertation, Indiana University: 186p. **[16]** *[PhD]*

37.0031   TR   1968   TRINIDAD ELECTORAL POLITICS: THE PERSISTENCE OF THE RACE FACTOR. London, Institute of Race Relations, Special Series: 98p. **[16,11,12]**   *[RIS]*

Bailey, Sydney D.

37.0032   BC   1949   Constitutions of the British Colonies. I: Colonies in the western hemisphere. *Parl Aff* 2(2), Spring: 156-174. **[38]**   *[COL]*

37.0033   BC   1950   CONSTITUTIONS OF THE BRITISH COLONIES. London, Hansard Society, 52p. (Hansard Society pamphlet no. 9.)   *[COL]*

Baker, Cecil Sherman

37.0034   UV   1935   Looking back at the turbulent Virgins: a Navy retrospect. *U S Navl Inst Proc* 61(9), Sept.: 1260-1276.   *[NYP]*

Bakker, J.

37.0035   SR   1928-29 De betuursregeling van Suriname [The governmental arrangement of Surinam]. *W I G* 11: 313-319. **[41]**   *[COL]*

Ballysingh, Marion C.

33.0009   JM   1961[?] Social services in Jamaica. a) Inter-relationship of Government and voluntary agencies and services. b) The voluntary social services of Jamaica.

Baptiste, F. A.

39.0014   AR,CU 1973   The seizure of the Dutch authorities in Willemstad, Curaçao, by Venezuelan political exiles in June 1929, viewed in relation to the Anglo-French landings in Aruba and Curaçao in May 1940.

Baptiste, Owen

37.0036   TR   1976   The PNM: 20 years later. *People Mag Car* 2(13), Aug.: 17-22.   *[RIS]*

Bara, Judith Linda Lorimer

37.0037   BC   1975   AN AGGREGATE ECOLOGICAL ANALYSIS OF VOTING BEHAVIOUR IN FOUR COMMONWEALTH STATES. Ph.D. dissertation, University of London: 334p.

Bari, Valeska

37.0038   UV   1925-26 What to do with the Virgin Islands? *Nth Am Rev* 222, Dec., Jan., Feb.: 266-273.   *[COL]*

Barnett, Lloyd G.

37.0039   JM   1966   CONSTITUTIONAL LAW OF JAMAICA: A STUDY IN THE EVOLUTION AND ADAPTATION OF RESPONSIBLE CABINET GOVERNMENT AND CONSTITUTIONALISM IN AN EMERGENT NATION. Ph.D. dissertation, University of London: 899p.

Barnett, W. L.

54.0065   JM   1951   GANJA.

61.0005   JM   1951   NOTES ON JAMAICA RUM.

Barratt, P. J. H.
5.0039   BA   1972   GRAND BAHAMA.

Barrett, Leonard
23.0008   JM   1968   THE RASTAFARIANS: A STUDY IN MESSIANIC CULTISM IN JAMAICA.

Bartels, Dennis
20.0005   GU   1974   The influence of folk models upon historical analysis: a case study
                        from Guyana.

Bartels, E.
51.0003   GC   1956   Government can help.

Bartlett, C. J.
5.0043   GC   1970   A new balance of power: the 19th century.

Bartlett, Kenneth A.
37.0040   UV   1957   The U.S. Virgin Islands Corporation. *Caribbean* 10(6-7), Jan.-Feb.:
                        165-167.   [*COL*]

Beasley, Cyril George
41.0029   BB   1952   A FISCAL SURVEY OF BARBADOS.

Beckford, George L.
60.0013   JM,WW 1965   Issues in the Windward-Jamaica banana war.
43.0024   JM   1967   Possible effects on Jamaican agriculture of Britain's entry into the
                        E.E.C.

Beckles, W. A., comp.
37.0041   BB   1937   THE BARBADOS DISTURBANCES (1937); REVIEW—REPRODUCTION OF
                        THE EVIDENCE AND REPORT OF THE COMMISSION. [Bridgetown?]
                        Barbados, Advocate Co. **[33]**

Bell, Henry Hesketh
3.0035   DM   1946[?] GLIMPSES OF A GOVERNOR'S LIFE.

Bell, Wendell
37.0042   JM   1960   Images of the United States and the Soviet Union held by Jamaican
                        elite groups. *Wld Polit* 12(2), Jan.: 225-248. **[8,20]**   [*COL*]
37.0043   JM   1962   Equality and attitudes of elites in Jamaica. *In* Singham, A. &
                        Braithwaite, L. E., eds. SPECIAL NUMBER [OF *Social Econ Stud*] ON
                        THE CONFERENCE ON POLITICAL SOCIOLOGY IN THE BRITISH CAR-
                        IBBEAN, DEC. 1961. *Social Econ Stud* 11(4), Dec.: 409-
                        432. **[8,20,41]**   [*RIS*]
37.0044   JM   1964   JAMAICAN LEADERS: POLITICAL ATTITUDES IN A NEW NATION.
                        Berkeley and Los Angeles: University of California Press,
                        229p. **[8,20,21]**   [*RIS*]
8.0011   JM   1965   Social change and elites in an emergent nation.
37.0045   GC   1967   Ethnicity, decisions of nationhood, and images of the future. *In*
                        Bell, Wendell & Freeman, Walter E., eds. ETHNICITY AND NATION-
                        BUILDING: COMPARATIVE, INTERNATIONAL AND HISTORICAL PER-
                        SPECTIVES. Beverly Hills, California, Sage Publications: 283-
                        300. **[20,21]**   [*COL*]
40.0004   BC   1973   New states in the Caribbean: a grounded theoretical account.

Bell, Wendell, ed.

37.0046   BC   1967   THE DEMOCRATIC REVOLUTION IN THE WEST INDIES: STUDIES IN
                         NATIONALISM, LEADERSHIP, AND THE BELIEF IN PROGRESS. Cam-
                         bridge, Mass., Schenkman Pub. Co., Inc.: 232p.   **[20,21]**   *[RIS]*

Bell, Wendell & Freeman, Walter E., eds.

21.0003   GC   1974   ETHNICITY AND NATION-BUILDING: COMPARATIVE, INTERNATIONAL,
                         AND HISTORICAL PERSPECTIVES.

Bell, Wendell & Oxaal, Ivar

37.0047   BC   1964   DECISIONS OF NATIONHOOD: POLITICAL AND SOCIAL DEVELOPMENT
                         IN THE BRITISH CARIBBEAN. Denver, University of Denver, 99p.
                         (Monograph Series in World Affairs.)   **[20,33]**

37.0048   BC   1967   The nation-state as a unit in the comparative study of social change.
                         In Moore, Wilbert E. & Cook, Robert M., eds. READINGS ON SOCIAL
                         CHANGE. Englewood Cliffs, New Jersey, Prentice-Hall: 169-
                         181.   **[38,40]**   *[RIS]*

Beloux, François

37.0049   MT   1969   Un poète politique: Aimé Césaire [Political poet: Aimé Césaire].
                         Mag Lit 34, Nov.: 27-32.   **[21]**   *[NYP]*

Benjamins, H. D.

37.0050   SR   1920-21 De grenzen van Surinam [The borders of Surinam]. *W I G* 2:
                         333-350.   *[COL]*

Benn, Denis M.

37.0051   GC   1973   THE GROWTH AND DEVELOPMENT OF POLITICAL IDEAS IN THE
                         CARIBBEAN. Ph.D. dissertation, University of Manchester.

Bennett, J. Harry, Jr.

23.0013   BB   1951   The S.P.G. and Barbadian politics, 1710-1720.

Berger, W. Y. Z.

37.0052   TR   1942   "Joe" in Trinidad. *Car-W I Mag* 31(9), Sept.: 19-22   *[NYP]*

Best, Lloyd

37.0053   GC   1967   Independent thought and Caribbean freedom. *New Wld Q* 3(4),
                         Cropover: 13-34.   **[40]**   *[RIS]*

11.0009   BC   1970   Black power and doctor politics.

11.0010   TR   1970   BLACK POWER AND NATIONAL RECONSTRUCTION; PROPOSALS FOL-
                         LOWING THE FEBRUARY REVOLUTION.

37.0054   BC,TR 1971   GOVERNMENT AND POLITICS IN THE WEST INDIES. San Fernando,
                         Trinidad, Tapia House: 8p. & 4p. (Tapia Pamphlets 4-5, June 13.)
                                                                                        [RIS]

37.0055   TR   1973   The February Revolution. *In* Lowenthal, David & Comitas, Lam-
                         bros, eds. THE AFTERMATH OF SOVEREIGNTY: WEST INDIAN PER-
                         SPECTIVES. Garden City, N. Y., Anchor Press/Doubleday: 306-329.
                                                                                        [RIS]

Bhagwandin, Khemraj

39.0029   GU   1971   Transactions of the XVI Congress of the People's Progressive Party:
                         address.

Biervliet, Harold

37.0056   SR   1974   Jaggernath Lachmon en de Vooruitstrevende Hervormings-Partij [Jaggernath Lachmon and the Progressive Reform-Party]. *Haagse Post* 61(43), Oct. 26: 22-25.   [*UCLA*]

Bijlsma, R.

5.0062   SR   1923-24 De brieven van Gouverneur van Aerssen van Sommelsdijck aan de Directeuren der Societeit van Suriname uit het jaar 1648 [The letters written by Governor van Aerssen van Sommelsdijck to the Director of the Society of Surinam in the year 1648].

5.0063   SR   1924-25 De brieven van Gouverneur van Aerssen van Sommelsdijck aan de Directeuren der Societeit van Suriname uit het jaar 1648 [The letters written by Governor van Aerssen van Sommelsdijck to the Director of the Society of Surinam in the year 1648].

5.0064   SR   1925-26 De brieven van Gouverneur van Aerssen van Sommelsdijck aan de Directeuren der Societeit van Suriname uit het jaar 1648 [The letters written by Governor van Aerssen van Sommelsdijck to the Director of the Society of Surinam in the year 1648].

Birac, Anthony

37.0057   JM   1942   Jamaica. *New Stsm Natn* 24(605), Sept. 26: 203.

Bird, V. C.

46.0021   AT   1950   Labour in the Leewards.

Biswamitre, C. R.

37.0058   SR   1947   Suriname en Linggadjati [Surinam and Linggadjati]. *W I G* 28: 321-328.   [*COL*]

Black, Clinton V.

1.0023   GU   1955   REPORT ON THE ARCHIVES OF BRITISH GUIANA.

Blair, Patricia Wohlgemuth

37.0059   GC   1967   THE MINISTATE DILEMMA. Carnegie Endowment for International Peace: 98p. (Occasional Paper No. 6)   **[38]**   [*RIS*]

Blancan, André

37.0060   GD   1904   LA CRISE DE LA GUADELOUPE: SES CAUSES, SES REMÈDES [THE CRISIS IN GUADELOUPE: ITS CAUSES AND REMEDIES]. Paris, Librairie nouvelle de droit et de jurisprudence, 206p. (Ph.D. dissertation.)   [*COL*]

Blanshard, Paul

37.0061   GC   1947   DEMOCRACY AND EMPIRE IN THE CARIBBEAN: A CONTEMPORARY REVIEW. New York, Macmillan, 379p.   **[41]**   [*NYP*]

Blant, Robert le

37.0062   DS   1947   Les mauvais sujets à la Désirade, 1763-1767 [Undesirable individuals in Desirade, 1763-1767]. *Rev Hist Colon* 33: 84-95.   **[5]**
                                                          [*NYP*]

Blij, Harm J. de

37.0063   SR   1970   Cultural pluralism and the political geography of decolonization: the case of Surinam. *Penn Geogr* 8(2), July: 1-11.   **[8]**   [*AGS*]

Blin, G.

28.0129 FG 1914 L'uncinariose chez les chercheurs d'or et les forcats du Maroni [Uncinariasis among the gold prospectors and convicts of Maroni].

Blood, Hilary

37.0064 BZ 1960 British Honduras: land of opportunity. *J Roy Commonw Soc* new ser., 3, May-June: 83-86. [*AGS*]

37.0065 JM 1962 And now—Jamaica. *New Commonw* 40(8), Aug.: 501-504. [*AGS*]

37.0066 BC 1966 Parliament in small territories. *In* Burns, Alan, ed. PARLIAMENT AS AN EXPORT. London, George Allen and Unwin Ltd.: 246-263.

[*COL*]

Bogoslovsky, V. A.

37.0067 GU 1969 Narodnaya progressivnaya partiya Gaiani v borbe za podlinnyv nezabisimoct, democratiyv u cotzialii progrecc strani [The new progressive Guyanese parties in the struggle for true independence, democracy and socialist progress for their countries]. *In* Grigulevich, I. R., ed. GVIANA: GAIANA, FRANTZUZKAYA-GAIANA, SURINAM. Moskva, Izdatelstvo "Natchka": 56-75. **[40]** [*UNL*]

Bohtlingk, F. R.

37.0068 NC 1954 Les nouveaux rapports politiques entre les Pays-Bas, le Surinam et les Antilles Néerlandaises [The new political relations between the Netherlands, Surinam, and the Netherlands Antilles]. *Civilisations* 4(3): 419-422. [*COL*]

37.0069 NC 1956 Wat moet bij rijkswet worden geregeld? [What should be regulated by federal law?]. *Ned Jurbl* May 12: 411-415.

Bone, Louis U.

5.0080 GU 1965 Atkinson deal.

Boodhoo, Ken

37.0070 GU,TR 1974 The case of the missing majority. *Car R* 6(2), April-May-June: 3-7. **[11,12]** [*RIS*]

Boom, W. R.

37.0071 NA 1965 De Cassatieregeling voor de Nederlandse Antillen [The Appeal regulation of the Netherlands Antilles]. *Justicia* 1, April: 29-38.

[*COL*]

Boos, W. J. & Harris, H. A.

46.0023 TR 1959 REPORT OF THE COLONY WHITLEY COUNCIL ON THE KING COMMISSION. REPORT WITH COMMENTS OF THE CIVIL SERVICE ASSOCIATION ON THE LEE REPORT. STRUCTURE AND ORGANIZATION OF THE PUBLIC SERVICE.

Bordewijk, H. W. C.

37.0072 CU,SR 1914 HANDELINGEN OVER DE REGLEMENTEN OP HET BELEID DER REGERING IN DE KOLONIËN SURINAME EN CURACAO [PROCEEDINGS ON THE REGULATIONS GOVERNING THE POLICY OF THE GOVERNMENT IN THE COLONIES OF SURINAM AND CARACAO]. The Hague, Nijhoff, 876p.

[*NYP*]

Bornn, Roy W.
33.0038   **UV**   1949   Further extension of social security to Virgin Islands.

Boromé, Joseph A.
37.0073   **DM**   1969   How Crown Colony government came to Dominica by 1898. *Car Stud* 9(3), Oct.: 26-67. **[5]**   *[RIS]*

Boucly, Felix
33.0039   **FG**   1932   DE LA TRANSPORTATION DES CONDAMNÉS AUX TRAVAUX FORCÉS [ON THE TRANSPORT OF SENTENCED CONVICTS].

Bough, James A.
37.0074   **GC**   1947   The United Nations and the Caribbean territories. *Car Commn Mon Inf B* 1(5), Dec.: 18-21.   *[COL]*
37.0075   **UV**   1970   General introduction to the constitutional evolution of the Virgin Islands. *In* Bough, James A. & Macridis, Roy C., eds. VIRGIN ISLANDS, AMERICA'S CARIBBEAN OUTPOST: THE EVOLUTION OF SELF-GOVERNMENT. Wakefield, Massachusetts, The Walter F. Williams Publishing Company: 119-127.   *[UNL]*

Bough, James A. & Macridis, Roy C., eds.
37.0076   **UV**   1970   VIRGIN ISLANDS, AMERICA'S CARIBBEAN OUTPOST: THE EVOLUTION OF SELF-GOVERNMENT. Wakefield, Massachusetts, The Walter F. Williams Publishing Company: 232p. **[4]**   *[UNL]*

Bowden, Alan & Carto, W. L.
37.0077   **GU**   1965   British Guiana. *New Commonw* 43(9), Sept.: 459-466. **[41]** *[NYP]*

Bowden, Alan; Smith, E. P. & Pierce, John F.
41.0060   **TR**   1965   Focus: Trinidad and Tobago.

Bowstead, William, ed.
41.0062   **BC**   [n.d.]   THE COMMERCIAL LAWS OF THE WORLD. VOL. 17: BRITISH DOMINIONS AND PROTECTORATES IN AMERICA.

Boyea, Samuel
37.0078   **GU**   1953   Dent in the crown: leftists win in Guiana. *Nation* 177(10), Sept. 5: 193-194.   *[COL]*

Boyke, Roy, ed.
37.0079   **TR**   1972   PATTERNS OF PROGRESS: TRINIDAD AND TOBAGO, 10 YEARS OF INDEPENDENCE. Port-of-Spain, Trinidad, Key Caribean Publications: 128p.   *[RIS]*

Boyle, Andrew
37.0080   **GU**   1953   Red threat in British Guiana. *America* 90(10), Dec. 5: 261-263.

Braam, H. L.
37.0081   **NA**   1970   HOE ONS LAND GEREGEERD WORDT [HOW OUR COUNTRY IS GOVERNED]. Oranjestad, Aruba, De Wit N.V.: 117p.   *[RILA]*

Bradley, C. Paul
37.0082   **JM**   1960   Mass parties in Jamaica: structure and organization. *Social Econ Stud* 9(4), Dec.: 375-416.   *[RIS]*

| 37.0083 | GU | 1961 | The party system in British Guiana and the general election of 1961. *Car Stud* 1(3), Oct.: 1-26. [*RIS*] |

37.0083 GU 1961 The party system in British Guiana and the general election of 1961. *Car Stud* 1(3), Oct.: 1-26. [*RIS*]

37.0084 GU 1963 Party politics in British Guiana. *West Polit Q* 16(2), June: 353-370. [*COL*]

Brakel, C. J.

37.0085 NA 1967 Over de toestand op de Nederlanse Antillen (1) [About the situation in the Netherlands Antilles (1)]. *Social Democ* 24(6), June: 396-408. [*COL*]

Brana-Shute, Rosemary

10.0007 SR 1976 Women, clubs, and politics: the case of a lower-class neighborhood in Parimaribo, Suriname.

Brathwaite, Shirley

37.0086 BC 1976 The question of political repression. *B E Car Aff* 2(9), Nov.: 12-14. [*RIS*]

37.0087 GR 1976 Reflections on the pending elections in Grenada. *B E Car Aff* 2(8), Oct.: 15-17. [*RIS*]

Brereton, Ashton S.

37.0088 BC 1963-64 West Indian perspective. *Social Scient* 2: 16-18. **[21]** [*RIS*]

Brisk, William J.

37.0089 AG 1968 ANGUILLA AND THE MINI-STATE DILEMMA. New York University. Center for International Studies, Policy Paper 5: 40p. **[39]** [*COL*]

37.0090 AG 1969 THE DILEMMA OF A MINI STATE: ANGUILLA. Columbia, S. C., University of South Carolina, Institute of International Studies: 93p. (Studies in International Affairs, 7.) **[41,46,51]** [*COL*]

Broderick, Margaret

37.0091 BC 1968 Associated Statehood—a new form of decolonisation. *Int Comp Law Q* (4th series) 17(2), April: 368-403. **[38,40]** [*COL*]

Brown, Adlith

41.0079 JM 1975 Planning as a political activity: some aspects of the Jamaican experience.

Brown, E. Ethelred

37.0092 JM 1937 INJUSTICES IN THE CIVIL SERVICE OF JAMAICA. New York, Jamaica Progressive League of New York, 8p. **[46]** [*NYP*]

Brown, G. Arthur

41.0081 JM 1958 Economic development and the private sector.

Brown, Noel

37.0093 JM 1963 JAMAICA AND THE WEST INDIES FEDERATION: A CASE STUDY ON THE PROBLEMS OF POLITICAL INTEGRATION. Ph.D. dissertation, Yale University, 472p. **[38]** [*COL*]

Brown, Richard H.

37.0094 GU 1966 Decolonisation. *New Wld F* 1(35), March 4: 10-21. **[40]** [*RIS*]

Brown, W. Aggrey
8.0028   JM   1974   NEW PERSPECTIVES ON COLOR, CLASS AND POLITICS IN JAMAICA.

Brown, W. J.
37.0095   JM   1948   Jamaica boss. *Spectator* 180(6240), Jan. 30: 127-128.   **[41]**   [*NYP*]

Brown, Wayne
5.0110   JM   1975   EDNA MANLEY. THE PRIVATE YEARS: 1900-1938.

Bruce, V. E.
37.0096   TR   1965   The new civil service. *BLATT* 2(4), special issue: 34-41.   [*RIS*]

Brummer, A. F. J.
37.0097   NC   1932-33 De titel Excellentie [The title "Excellency"]. *W I G* 14: 285-286.
                                                                                    [*COL*]

Brunn, Stanley D.; Ford, John J. & McIntosh, Terry
37.0098   GC   1971   The state of political geography research in Latin America *In*
                            Lentnek, Barry; Carmin, Robert L. & Martinson, Tom L., eds.
                            GEOGRAPHIC RESEARCH ON LATIN AMERICA: BENCHMARK 1970:
                            PROCEEDINGS OF THE CONFERENCE OF LATIN AMERICANIST
                            GEOGRAPHERS, VOLUME ONE. Muncie, Indiana, Ball State Univer-
                            sity: 265-287.   **[38,39,40]**   [*COL*]

Bryan, C. S.
37.0099   GC   1941   Geography and the defense of the Caribbean and the Panama
                            Canal. *Ann Assoc Am Geogr* 31(2), June: 83-94.   [*AGS*]

Buiskool, J. A. E.
37.0100   SR   1954   DE STAATSINSTELLINGEN VAN SURINAME, IN DE HOOFDZAKEN MEDE
                            VERGELEKEN MET DIE VAN NEDERLAND EN DE NEDERLANDSE AN-
                            TILLEN [THE POLITICAL INSTITUTIONS OF SURINAM, ALSO AS COM-
                            PARED WITH THOSE OF THE NETHERLANDS AND THE NETHERLANDS
                            ANTILLES]. The Hague, Nijhoff, 659p.   [*NYP*]

Burgess, G. & Hunn, J. K.
37.0101   GU   1966   REPORT ON PUBLIC ADMINISTRATION IN GUYANA. Georgetown,
                            Guyana, The Government Printery: 115p.   **[46]**   [*RIS*]

Burnham, L. F. S.
37.0102   GU   1968   THE CASE OF PEDRO BERIA; SPECIAL BROADCAST PRESS CONFERENCE,
                            NOVEMBER 30, 1968. Georgetown, Guyana, The Government
                            Printery: 19p.   [*RIS*]
37.0103   GU   1968   'A GREAT FUTURE TOGETHER' (THE PRIME MINISTER'S REPORT TO THE
                            NATION ON GUYANA'S 2ND ANNIVERSARY OF INDEPENDENCE, 25 MAY,
                            1968. Georgetown, Guyana, Lithographic Co. Ltd. (for the Guyana
                            Information Service): 24p.   [*RIS*]
37.0104   GU   1969   THE SMALL MAN, A REAL MAN IN THE COOPERATIVE REPUBLIC,
                            GUYANA. SPEECHES BY THE PRIME MINISTER IN THE NATIONAL
                            ASSEMBLY ON THE REPUBLIC MOTION. Georgetown, Guyana Litho-
                            graphic Co., Ltd. (for the Ministry of Information): 12p.   [*RIS*]
37.0105   GU   1970   A DESTINY TO MOULD: SELECTED DISCOURSE BY THE PRIME MINISTER
                            OF GUYANA. Trinidad and Jamaica, Longman Caribbean Ltd.,
                            (compiled by C. A. Nascimento and R. A. Burrowes): 275p.   **[41]**
                                                                                    [*RIS*]

37.0106   GU   1973   FOUR TALKS TO THE NATION: 1973 ELECTION RADIO ADDRESSES TO
THE NATION. Guyana, Ministry of Information and Culture: 31p.
[*RIS*]

37.0107   GU   1973   THE YEAR OF THE BREAKTHROUGH: ADDRESS TO THE NATION ON THE
THIRD ANNIVERSARY OF THE CO-OPERATIVE REPUBLIC OF GUYANA,
FEB. 23, 1973. Guyana, Ministry of Information, Culture and
Youth: 16p.   [*RIS*]

37.0108   GU   1974   THE SURVIVAL OF OUR NATION: ADDRESS TO THE NATION. Georgetown, Guyana Lithographic Co. Ltd. (for the Ministry of Information and Culture): 8p.   [*RIS*]

Burns, Alan
37.0109   BC   1949   Weaknesses of British West Indian administration. *Crown Colonist*
19(208), Mar.: 147-149.   [*NYP*]

Burt, Arthur E.
37.0110   JM   1962   The first instalment of representative government in Jamaica, 1884.
Social Econ Stud 11(3), Sept.: 241-259.   **[5]**   [*RIS*]

Byles, G. Louis
37.0111   JM   1948   The Jamaican experiment. *Parl Aff* 1(2), Spring: 56-69.   [*COL*]

Cabot, John M.
37.0112   GC   1953   Forces for change in the Caribbean. *Dep St B* 29(756), Dec. 21:
855-859.   [*COL*]

Cacho, C. P.
37.0113   BZ   1967   British Honduras: a case of deviation in Commonwealth Caribbean
decolonization. *New Wld Q* 3(3), High Season: 33-44.   **[40]**   [*RIS*]

Caires, David de
41.0089   GU   1963   Regional integration.
37.0114   GU   1966   Socialism and the Guyanese situation. *New Wld F* 1(43), July 11:
13-21.   [*RIS*]

Caires, David de & Fitzpatrick, Miles
37.0115   GU   1966   Twenty years of politics in our land. *New Wld Q* 2(3), May, Guyana
Independence Issue: 39-45.   **[5]**   [*RIS*]

Camp, George
37.0116   GU   1963   The "Georgetown strike"—a lie of the Western press. *Wld Trade Un
Mov* 10, Oct.: 10-15.   **[33,46]**   [*COL*]

Campbell, Carl
37.0117   TR   1975   The death of the Cabildo of Port of Spain, Trinidad, 1832-1840. *In*
SOCIAL GROUPS AND INSTITUTIONS IN THE HISTORY OF THE CARIB-
BEAN: PAPERS PRESENTED...AT THE VI ANNUAL CONFERENCE OF
CARIBBEAN HISTORIANS. PUERTO RICO, APRIL 4-9, 1974. [Rio
Piedras, Puerto Rico], Association of Caribbean Historians: 26-
49.   **[5]**   [*RIS*]

Campbell, Jock
37.0118   BC   1962   Facing up to facts in the Caribbean. *Chron W I Comm* 77(1373),
June: 279-280.   **[38]**   [*NYP*]

37.0119   BC   1963   The West Indies: can they stand alone? *Int Aff* 39(3), July:
                         335-344. **[38]**   *[AGS]*

Campbell, Roy B.
37.0120   JM   1948   West Indian crisis. *America* 78(24), Mar. 13: 659-660.   *[COL]*

Caraib, Frair
40.0009   GD   1967   La Guadeloupe opprimée [Guadeloupe oppressed].

Cariss, Andrew Calvert
37.0121   JM   1973   The official attitude towards the elected members in the Jamaica
                         Legislative Council 1918-1938. *Jam J* 7(3), Sept.: 6-10. **[5]**   *[RIS]*

Carnegie, A. R.
37.0122   BC   1971   Judicial review of legislation in the West Indian constitutions. *Publ
                         Law* Winter: 276-287.   *[COL]*
37.0123   JM   1972   JAMAICA. Dobbs Ferry, New York, Oceana Publications: 90p.
                         (Constitutions of the Countries of the World Series)   *[RIS]*

Carnegie, James
37.0124   JM   1973   SOME ASPECTS OF JAMAICA'S POLITICS: 1918-1938. Kingston, Insti-
                         tute of Jamaica: 194p. (Cultural Heritage Series, Volume 4)   **[5]**
                                                                                        [RIS]

Carpentier Alting, Z. H.
5.0151   SR   1969   Schetsmatig overzicht van de wijzigingen in het Surinaams Wetboek
                         van Koophandel sinds 1 mei 1869 [Survey of the changes in the
                         Surinamese Maritime Law since May 1, 1869].

**Carpentier Alting, Z. H.; Adrin, J. H.; Koole, W. J. J.; Quintus Bosz, A. J. A.;
Rondeel, A. J. & Schroeff, G. J. C. van der, eds.**
5.0152   SR   1969   EEN EEUW SURINAAMSE CODIFICATIE: GEDENKBOEK (1869-1 MEI-
                         1969) [ONE CENTURY OF SURINAM CODIFICATION: COMMEMORATIVE
                         VOLUME(1869-MAY 1-1969)].

Carrington, Vivien
37.0125   JM   1971   INTRODUCTION TO CIVICS FOR JAMAICAN SCHOOLS. Trinidad and
                         Jamaica, Longman Caribbean: 138p. **[32]**   *[RIS]*

Carroll, John Joseph
37.0126   JM,UK 1973   THE GOVERNMENT OF JAMAICA, 1900-1913, WITH SPECIAL REFERENCE
                         TO THE ROLE OF SIR SYDNEY OLIVIER. Ph.D. dissertation, University
                         of London: 326p. **[5]**

Carter, Martin
37.0127   GU   [n.d.] The race crisis—British Guiana. *In* CARIBBEAN INSTITUTE AND
                         STUDY CENTER FOR LATIN AMERICA (CISCLA). REPORT: FIRST
                         INSTITUTE ON BRITISH GUIANA. San German, P.R., Inter American
                         University: 6-14. **[16]**   *[RIS]*
37.0128   GU   1966   A question of self-contempt. *New Wld Q* 2(3), May, Guyana
                         Independence Issue: 10-12. **[5]**   *[RIS]*

Caute, David
5.0156   **FA**   1970   FRANTZ FANON.

Cavassori, Ermes
37.0129   **BZ**   1958   L'Honduras Britannico fra Inghilterra, Guatemala e Messico [British Honduras between England, Guatemala and Mexico]. *Universo* 38(6), Nov.-Dec.: 991-1000.   [*AGS*]

Cazalet
37.0130   **FG**   1909   La Guyane et ses bagnes [Guiana and its penal colonies]. *B Soc Geogr Toul* 28: 36-42.   [*NYP*]

Cell, John W.
37.0131   **BC**   1970   BRITISH COLONIAL ADMINISTRATION IN THE MID-NINETEENTH CENTURY: THE POLICY MAKING PROCESS. New Haven, Yale University Press: 344p.   **[5]**   [*COL*]

Césaire, Aimé
37.0132   **NA**   1961   Crise dans les Départements d'Outre-Mer ou crise de la départementalisation? [Crisis in the Overseas *Départements*, or crisis of departmentalization?] *Rev Guad* 43, Jan.-Mar.: 52-54.   [*RIS*]

Chamberland, Greg
37.0133   **TR**   1973   Patterns of crisis. *In* Harding, Colin & Roper, Christopher, eds. LATIN AMERICAN REVIEW 1 OF BOOKS. Palo Alto, California, Ramparts Press: 159-168.   [*RIS*]

Chambers, George
37.0134   **TR**   1972   What a government expects from training. *In* TRAINING OF PUBLIC SERVICE TRAINERS: REPORT ON A PILOT COURSE, ST. AUGUSTINE, TRINIDAD, AUG. 10-SEPT. 18, 1970. New York, United Nations: 36-39.   **[32]**   [*UNL*]

Chandisingh, Ranji
37.0135   **GU**   1971   The XXI anniversary of the PPP. *Thunder* 2(2), April-June: 43-52
                                                                                                [*RIS*]

Chapman, Esther
37.0136   **JM**   1945   Political experiment in Jamaica: a promising start. *Crown Colonist* 15(166), Sept.: 599-600.   [*AGS*]
37.0137   **JM**   1946   Jamaican political experiment: machinery at work. *Crown Colonist* 16(170), Jan.: 15-16.   [*AGS*]
2.0064   **JM**   1954   DEVELOPMENT IN JAMAICA: YEAR OF PROGRESS, 1954.

Charles, Henri
41.0100   **GD**   1947   La Guadeloupe: un cas d'émancipation coloniale et de rétablissement économique après la guerre [Guadeloupe: a case history of political emancipation and economic revival after the war].

Chatelain, Jean
37.0138   **FC**   1948   Le statut des nouveaux Départements d'Outre-Mer [The status of the new overseas territories]. *Rev Jur Polit Un Fr* 2(3), July-Sept.: 285-316.   [*COL*]

Cheltenham, Richard Lionel

37.0139   BB   1970   CONSTITUTIONAL AND POLITICAL DEVELOPMENT IN BARBADOS, 1946-1966. Ph.D dissertation, University of Manchester: 287p.

Chilstone, E. M.

37.0140   BB   1939   Tercentenary of the Barbados House of Assembly—growth of representative government. *W I Comm Circ* 54(1062), June 15: 251-252; 54(1063), June 29: 275-277. **[5]**   [*NYP*]

Chisholm, Hester Dorothy

37.0141   LW,UV   1938   A COLONIAL EVALUATION OF THE BRITISH LEEWARD ISLANDS AND THE VIRGIN ISLANDS OF THE UNITED STATES. M.A. thesis, Clark University, 73p. **[2]**

Christian, Sydney T.

37.0142   LW   1955   Constitutional changes in the Leeward Islands. *New Commonw British Caribbean Supplement* 30(10), Nov. 14: xiv-xv.   [*AGS*]

Chutkan, Noelle

37.0143   JM   1975   The administration of justice in Jamaica as a contributing factor in the Morant Bay Rebellion of 1865. *Savacou* 11-12, Sept.: 78-85. **[5]**   [*RIS*]

Clarke, C. P.

5.0167   BB   1968   Imperial forces in Barbados.

Clarke, Colin G.

37.0144   AG   1971   Political fragmentation in the Caribbean: the case of Anguilla. *Can Geogr* 15(1): 13-29. **[38,40]**   [*AGS*]

8.0034   TR   1972   The political ecology of a town in Trinidad.

Clementi, Cecil

37.0145   GU   1937   A CONSTITUTIONAL HISTORY OF BRITISH GUIANA. London, Macmillan, 546p. **[5]**   [*NYP*]

Coggins, J. C.

37.0146   TR   1971   Race, economics and politics in Trinidad: the search for indigenous values. *Round Table* 61(241), Jan.: 153-159. **[16]**   [*COL*]

Collins, B. A. N.

37.0147   GU   1963   La structure constitutionnelle et administrative de la Guyane Britannique [The constitutional and administrative structure of British Guiana]. *Civilisations* 13(3): 294-307.   [*RIS*]

46.0040   GU   1964   The civil service of British Guiana in the general strike of 1963.

37.0148   GU   1965   Acceeding to independence: some constitutional problems of a polyethnic society (British Guiana). *Civilizations* 15(3): 376-403. **[40]**   [*COL*]

37.0149   GU   1965-66   "Consultative democracy" in British Guiana. *Parl Aff J Hans Soc* 19(1), Winter: 103-112. **[40]**   [*COL*]

37.0150   GU   1965   The end of a colony. II: British Guiana 1965. *Polit Q* 36(4), Oct.-Dec.: 406-416. **[40]**   [*COL*]

37.0151   GU   1966   Independence for Guyana. *Wld Today* 22(6), June: 260-268. **[40,46]**   [*COL*]

1.0061   BC   1967   A select bibliography on public administration in the British Caribbean.

37.0152 BC 1967 Some notes on Public Service Commissions in the Commonwealth Caribbean. *Social Econ Stud* 16(1), March: 1-16. **[39]** [*RIS*]

Cook, Mercer
37.0153 FA 1940 The literary contribution of the French West Indian. *J Negro Hist* 25(4), Oct.: 520-530. **[22]** [*AMN*]

Coore, David
37.0154 JM 1961[?] Government and the community. *In* Cumper, George, ed. REPORT OF THE CONFERENCE ON SOCIAL DEVELOPMENT IN JAMAICA. Kingston, Standing Committee on Social Services, p.108-110. [*RIS*]

Corneiro, Francisco
37.0155 UV 1970 Notes on the office of the governor of the Virgin Islands. *In* Bough, James A. & Macridis, Roy C., eds. VIRGIN ISLANDS, AMERICA'S CARIBBEAN OUTPOST: THE EVOLUTION OF SELF-GOVERNMENT. Wakefield, Massachusetts, The Walter F. Williams Publishing Company: 139-144. [*UNL*]

Cornu, Henri
37.0156 FA 1935 UNE EXPÉRIENCE LÉGISLATIVE À LA RÉUNION, À LA MARTINIQUE ET À LA GUADELOUPE [A LEGISLATIVE EXPERIMENT IN REUNION, MARTINIQUE, AND GUADELOUPE]. Paris, Editions Domat-Montchrestien, 155p. **[41]** [*NYP*]

Costa Gomez, F. M. da
37.0157 NC 1935-36 Het amendement-Marchant of art. 94 van de Grondwet van 1917 en de West-Indische staatsdelen [The Marchant amendment of article 94 of the Constitution of 1917 and the West Indian possessions]. *W I G* 17: 374-386. [*COL*]

Cotter, C. S.
37.0158 JM 1959 Ocho Rios in Jamaican history. *Jam Hist Rev* 3(2), Mar.: 34-38. **[5]** [*COL*]

Cotter, Graham
37.0159 JM 1948 Toward responsible government in Jamaica. *Can Forum* 28(334), Nov.: 177-178; 28(335), Dec.: 202-203. [*COL*]

Coutinho, D.
37.0160 SR 1924-25 Schorsing van koloniale verordeningen [Suspension of colonial regulations]. *W I G* 6: 561-574. [*COL*]

Cox, Idris
37.0161 GU 1963 Freedom struggle in British Guiana. *Int Aff* 9(10), Oct.: 67-70. [*COL*]

Craig, Hewan
37.0162 TR 1952 THE LEGISLATIVE COUNCIL OF TRINIDAD AND TOBAGO. London, Faber & Faber, 195p. [*RIS*]

Craig, Susan E.
36.0030 TR 1974 COMMUNITY DEVELOPMENT IN TRINIDAD AND TOBAGO: 1943-1973: FROM WELFARE TO PATRONAGE.

Craton, Michael

5.0195 BC 1971 The role of the Caribbean Vice Admiralty Courts in British imperialism.

Crile, George

37.0163 JM 1974 Our man in Jamaica. *Harper's Mag* 249(1493), Oct.: 87-96.   [*TCL*]

Croft, W. D.; Springer, H. W. & Christopherson, H. S.

47.0075 BC 1958 REPORT OF THE TRADE AND TARIFFS COMMISSION.

Crowe, Harry J.

47.0076 BC 1920 Canadian-West Indian union.

37.0164 BC 1920 Separate West Indian Dominion, or confederation with Canada. *Can-W I Mag* 8(5), Mar.: 460-461. **[39,47]**   [*NYP*]

41.0114 BC 1923 Mr. Harry J. Crowe on confederation with the West Indies.

47.0077 JM 1925 How Canada-West Indies federation might be achieved.

37.0165 JM 1925 The political side of the question. *Can-W I Mag* 13(6), Apr.: 155-157. **[41,47]**   [*NYP*]

Cummings, Felix

37.0166 GU 1964 British Guiana in transition. *Freedomways* 4(3), Summer: 392-404.
                          [*RIS*]

Cumper, George E.

41.0121 BB 1962 The differentiation of economic groups in the West Indies.

Cumper, Gloria

33.0056 JM 1972 SURVEY OF SOCIAL LEGISLATION IN JAMAICA.

Cumpston, I. M., ed.

5.0202 BC 1967 The West Indies: economic difficulties and political problems.

Cundall, Frank

37.0167 BC 1906 POLITICAL AND SOCIAL DISTURBANCES IN THE WEST INDIES: A BRIEF ACCOUNT AND BIBLIOGRAPHY. Published for Institute of Jamaica by the Educational Supply Co., 35p. **[1,5,8,16,33,41]**   [*NYP*]

37.0168 JM 1919 Jamaica governors [some items have title: Governors of Jamaica]. *W I Comm Circ*: (1) Edward Doyley. 34(529), Jan. 9: 8; 34(530), Jan. 23: 19-20; (2) Thomas, Seventh Baron Windsor. 34(544), Aug. 7: 208-210; (3) Sir Charles Lyttelton. 34(546), Sept. 4: 245-246; (4) Sir Thomas Modyford. 34(553), Dec. 11: 333-334; 34(554), Dec. 25: 351-352. **[5]**   [*NYP*]

37.0169 JM 1920 Jamaica governors [some items have title: Governors of Jamaica]. *W I Comm Circ*: 35(555), Jan. 8: 6; 35(556), Jan. 22: 23; (5) Sir Thomas Lynch. 35(560), Mar. 18: 79-80; 35(561), Apr. 1: 24; 35(563), Apr. 29: 124-125; 35(564), May 13: 139-140; 35(566), June 10: 171-172; (6) Sir Henry Morgan. 35(579), Dec. 9: 378-379; 35(580), Dec. 23: 398-399. **[5]**   [*NYP*]

37.0170 BC 1920 Royal visits to the West Indies. *W I Comm Circ* 35(571), Aug. 19: 241; 35(572), Sept. 2: 260-261; 35(573), Sept. 16: 276-277; 35(574), Sept. 30: 290; 35(575), Oct. 14: 307. **[5]**   [*NYP*]

37.0171   JM   1921   Jamaica governors [some items have title: Governors of Jamaica].
                          W I Comm Circ: 36(581), Jan. 6: 13-14; 36(582), Jan. 20: 31-32;
                          36(583), Feb. 3: 53-54; 36(584), Feb. 17: 68-69; (7) John, Lord
                          Vaughan. 36(597), Aug. 18: 349-350; 36(598), Sept. 1: 368-369;
                          36(599), Sept. 15: 396; (8) Charles, Earl of Carlisle. 36(601), Oct. 13:
                          436-437; 36(602), Oct. 27: 458-459; 36(603), Nov. 10: 480-481.   **[5]**
                                                                                    [NYP]

37.0172   JM   1922   Jamaica governors [some items have title: Governors of Jamaica].
                          W I Comm Circ: (9) Sir Hender Molesworth. 37(607), Jan. 5: 14-15;
                          37(608), Jan. 19: 39-40; 37(609), Feb. 2: 58-59; 37(610), Feb. 16: 81;
                          37(611), Mar. 2: 104; (10) Christopher, Duke of Albemarle. 37(617),
                          May 25: 250-251; 37(618), June 8: 271-273; (11) Sir Francis
                          Watson, President. 371(624), Aug. 31: 404-405; 37(625), Sept. 14:
                          427-428; (12) William, 2nd Earl of Inchiquin. 37(626), Sept. 28:
                          455-456; 37(627), Oct. 12: 478-479; (13) John White, President.
                          37(630), Nov. 23: 542-543; 37(631), Dec. 7: 570-571; 37(632), Dec.
                          21: 593-594.   **[5]**   *[NYP]*

37.0173   JM   1923   Jamaica governors [some items have title: Governors of Jamaica].
                          W I Comm Circ: (14) John Bourden, President. 38(650), Aug. 30:
                          384-385.   **[5]**   *[NYP]*

37.0174   JM   1936   THE GOVERNORS OF JAMAICA IN THE SEVENTEENTH CENTURY. Lon-
                          don, West India Committee, 177p.   **[5]**   *[COL]*

37.0175   JM   1937   THE GOVERNORS OF JAMAICA IN THE FIRST HALF OF THE EIGHTEENTH
                          CENTURY. London, West India Committee, 229p.   **[5]**   *[COL]*

Curry, Herbert Franklin, Jr.

37.0176   BZ   1956   British Honduras: from public meeting to crown colony. *The
                          Americas* 13(1), July: 31-42.   **[5]**   *[COL]*

Curtin, Philip D.

37.0177   GC   1955   The United States in the Caribbean. *Curr Hist* 29(172), Dec.:
                          364-370.   **[39]**   *[COL]*

Dabreo, Sinclair

40.0017   BC   1974[?]   LESSONS FROM THE CARIBBEAN REVOLUTION.

Da Costa, H. L.

5.0223   JM   1966   The constitutional experiment in the twelve years before the Morant
                          Bay rebellion.

Da Costa, Harvey & Phillips, Fred A.

37.0178   BC   1960   A summary of constitutional advances. *Car Q* 6(2-3), May: 230-235.
                                                                                    [RIS]

Daley, Wesley Walton

37.0179   JM   1973   POLITICAL GROWTH IN JAMAICA: 1938-1969, FROM COLONY TO
                          NATIONHOOD. Ann Arbor, Michigan, University Microfilms: 276p.
                          (Ph.D. dissertation, Howard University, 1971)   *[RIS]*

Dalley, F. W.

46.0051   BC   1956   The labour position: the trade unions and the political parties.

Dalton, L. C.

37.0180 GU 1912 Abolition of Roman-Dutch law in British Guiana. *Timehri* 3d ser., 2(19A), July: 94-100.   [*AMN*]

37.0181 GU 1915 Some controverted points of local law with respect to leases. *Timehri* 3d ser., 3(20B), May: 215-221. **[44]**   [*AMN*]

37.0182 GU 1917 The civil law of British Guiana, with notes and comments. *Timehri* 3d ser., 4(21), June: 160-243.   [*AMN*]

Daniel, George T.

46.0052 BC 1957 Labor and Nationalism in the British Caribbean.

Darbyshire, Taylor

37.0183 BC 1937 The King in the West Indies. *W I Comm Circ* 52(1008), May 20: 185-186.   [*NYP*]

Darlington, Charleen Arnett

20.0018 BA 1973 A brief examination of political attitudes on San Salvador on the eve of political independence.

Darrell, Owen H.

37.0184 BE 1957 The British Garrison and the imperial connection. *Bermuda Hist Q* 14(3), Autumn: 94-98. **[5]**   [*COL*]

David, Wilfred L.

37.0185 GC 1968 Democracy, stability and economic development. *Car Q* 14(4), Dec.: 7-24. **[41]**   [*RIS*]

Davis, Harold B.

32.0155 BC 1972 Co-ordination of personnel management training in public and private sectors.

Davis, Hassoldt

3.0139 FG 1952 THE JUNGLE AND THE DAMNED.

Davis, Kortright, ed.

33.0060 GC,LW 1973 VOICES FOR CHANGE FROM CADEC (CHRISTIAN ACTION FOR DEVELOPMENT IN THE CARIBBEAN).

Davis, Stephen

37.0186 JM 1976 Roots of reggae: the extraordinary Rastafarians. *New Age* 2(6), Nov.: 18-27. **[8,11,23]**   [*RIS*]

Davson, Edward R.

37.0187 BC 1919 Problems of the West Indies. *W I Comm Circ* 34(554), Dec. 25: suppl. (7p.) **[38]**   [*NYP*]

Dawson, Eric E.

37.0188 UV 1970 The legislature: its structure and power. *In* Bough, James A. & Macridis, Roy C., eds. VIRGIN ISLANDS, AMERICA'S CARIBBEAN OUTPOST: THE EVOLUTION OF SELF-GOVERNMENT. Wakefield, Massachusetts, The Walter F. Williams Publishing Company: 128-138.   [*UNL*]

Deakin, Nicholas, ed.
37.0189   BC,UK   1965   COLOUR AND THE BRITISH ELECTORATE, 1964: SIX CASE STUDIES. New York, Frederick A. Praeger: 172p.   **[16,18]**   [COL]

Debrot, I. C.
37.0190   NC   1960-61 Een coördinerende en stimulerende cultuurpolitiek [A coordinating and stimulating cultural policy]. N W I G 40: 185-189.   [COL]

Debrot, N.
37.0191   GC   1953   Politieke aspecten in het Caraibische gebied [Political aspects in the Caribbean]. W I G 34: 160-172.   [COL]

DeCaires, David & Fitzpatrick, Miles
37.0192   GU   1969   TWENTY YEARS OF POLITICS IN OUR LAND. In CARIBBEAN DEVELOPMENT AND THE FUTURE OF THE CHURCH: PROCEEDINGS OF A CONFERENCE HELD AT GEORGETOWN, JAN. 6-8. Georgetown, Guyana, Guyana Institute for Social Research and Action.   [SCH]

Declareuil, Jean
37.0193   FG   1927   LES SYSTÈMES DE TRANSPORTATION ET DE MAIN-D'OEUVRE PÉNALE AUX COLONIES DAN LE DROIT FRANCAIS [THE COLONIAL PENAL TRANSPORTATION AND FORCED LABOR SYSTEMS IN FRENCH LAW]. Toulouse, Impr. J. Fournier, 189p. (Ph.D. dissertation, University of Toulouse.)   **[5,33,46]**   [COL]

Demas, William G.
41.0136   BC   1972   The economic environment of the 1970's.

Dench, Morgan
37.0194   FG   1947   The Devil's island. Contemp Rev 172, Oct.: 237-239.   [COL]

Dennert, H.
5.0245   NA   1967   Antillianen in de Tweede Wereldoorlog [Antilleans in the Second World War].

Des Forges, Charles & Imrie, J. D.
37.0195   TR   1950   REPORT ON LOCAL GOVERNMENT (FINANCIAL RELATIONSHIPS). [Port of Spain?] Trinidad, Govt. Print. Off., 109p.   **[41]**   [RIS]

Despres, Leo A.
37.0196   GU   1964   The implications of nationalist politics in British Guiana for the development of cultural theory. Am Anthrop 66(5), Oct.: 1051-1075.   **[8,19,21]**   [RIS]
8.0059   GU   1967   CULTURAL PLURALISM AND NATIONALIST POLITICS IN BRITISH GUIANA.

Dessarre, Eve
2.0107   JM,TR,FA   1965   CAUCHEMAR ANTILLAIS [ANTILLES NIGHTMARE].

Deure, A. van der
37.0197   SR   1919-20 Rechtszekerheid van de grondeigendommen in Surinam [Legal security of the landed properties in Surinam]. W I G 1(2): 193-213.   **[44]**   [COL]

Dew, Edward

37.0198   SR   1974   Elections: Surinam style. *Car R* 6(2), April-May-June: 20-25.   [*RIS*]

Dijkstra, Jan

37.0199   SR   1973   SURINAME-GEGEVENS: INFORMATIE OVER SURINAME VOOR EEN BETER
                         BEGRIP OMTRENT DE GEBEURTENISSEN VAN FEBRUARI 1973 [SURINAM
                         DATA: INFORMATION ABOUT SURINAM NECESSARY FOR A BETTER
                         UNDERSTANDING OF THE INCIDENTS OF FEBRUARY 1973]. Voorburg,
                         The Netherlands, Protestantse Stichting tot Bevordering van het
                         Bibliotheekwezen en de Lectuur-voorlichting in Nederland: 40p.
                         (Act-If 16)   **[40]**   [*RILA*]

Dip, C. E.

37.0200   NA   1969   Kent de Staatsregeling het codificatie-beginsel [Does the Consti-
                         tution incorporate the codification principle]? *In* HONDERD JAAR
                         CODIFICATIE IN DE NEDERLANDSE ANTILLEN. Arnhem, The Nether-
                         lands, S. Gouda Quint/D. Brouwer en Zoon: 1-6.   [*RILA*]

37.0201   NA   1971   Is het Landsbesluit van de 2de augustus 1971 no. 6 (P.B. 1971, no.
                         116) inderdaad onbevoegd genomen [Has the Land decision of
                         August 2, 1971 no. 6 (P.B. 1971, no. 116) really been made
                         incompetently]? *Justicia* 7(3): 65-72.   [*COL*]

37.0202   NA   1973   Enige beschouwingen rond artikel 2 van de Antilliaanse Staats-
                         regeling [Some remarks on Article 2 of the Antillean Constitution].
                         Ant Jurbl 23(3): 927-945.   [*COL*]

Dirks, Robert

8.0062   TT   1971   NETWORKS, GROUPS, AND LOCAL-LEVEL POLITICS IN AN AFRO-
                         CARIBBEAN COMMUNITY.

Diufeal, F.

37.0203   MT   1960   Kommunisty Martiniki. *Problemy Mira Sots* 2: 69.   [*COL*]

Dodge, Peter

8.0065   SR   1966   Ethnic fragmentation and politics: the case of Surinam.
8.0066   SR   1966   Fragmentación étnica y estructura política: el caso de Surinam
                         [Ethnic fragmentation and political structure: the case of Surinam].

Domingo, W. A.

37.0204   JM   1938   Jamaica seeks its freedom. *Opportunity* 16(12), Dec.: 370-372.
                                                                                       [*COL*]

Duffus, J. A. H.

37.0205   JM   1963   Conduct of arbitration II—rules of procedure, of evidence, etc., in
                         voluntary and legal arbitrations. *In* Eaton, G. E., ed. PROCEEDINGS
                         OF INDUSTRIAL RELATIONS CONFERENCE ON THE THEORY AND
                         PRACTICE OF ARBITRATION, Nov. 1962. Mona, Institute of Social
                         and Economic Research, University of the West Indies, p.67-
                         81.   **[46]**   [*RIS*]

Dufougeré, W.

37.0206   FG   1921   De l'utilisation rationnelle de la main-d'oeuvre pénale en Guyane
                         [On the rational use of forced labor in Guiana]. *B Soc Path Exot*
                         14(5), May: 258-265.   **[28,30,46]**   [*ACM*]

Duke, James T.

37.0207   **JM**   1967   Egalitarianism and future leaders in Jamaica. *In* Bell, Wendell, ed. THE DEMOCRATIC REVOLUTION IN THE WEST INDIES. Cambridge, Mass., Schenkman Pub. Co., Inc.: 115-139. **[8,20]**   *[RIS]*

Duncan, Ebenezer

37.0208   **BC**   1947   THE POLITICAL CONSTITUTION OF THE WESTINDIAN COMMONWEALTH. Kingstown, St. Vincent, Govt. Print. Off., 23p. **[38]**   *[RIS]*

5.0263   **SV**   1963   A BRIEF HISTORY OF ST. VINCENT WITH STUDIES IN CITIZENSHIP.

Duncan, Neville C.

37.0209   **JM**   1970   The political process, and attitudes and opinions in a Jamaican Parish Council. *Social Econ Stud* 19(1), March: 89-113. **[20]** *[RIS]*

37.0210   **SV**   1975   THE VINCENTIAN ELECTIONS. Cave Hill, Barbados, University of the West Indies, Institute of Social and Economic Research (Eastern Caribbean): 43p. (Occasional paper No. 3)   *[RIS]*

Dunn, W. N.

37.0211   **GC**   1971   Law and the political development of new states: review and commentary. *Social Econ Stud* 20(1), March: 15-27.   *[RIS]*

Durrant, Fay

1.0097   **GC**   1971   A bibliographical aid to the study of government and politics in the West Indies.

Dusseldorp, D. B. W. M. van

37.0212   **SR**   1967   MEERDIMENSIONALE OVERHEIDSPLANNING: DE OVERHEIDSPLANNING VAN SURINAME IN DE PERIODE 1952-1964 GETOETST AAN EEN RELATIOMODEL [MULTI-DIMENSIONAL GOVERNMENTAL PLANNING: THE GOVERNMENTAL PLANNING OF SURINAM IN THE PERIOD 1952-1964 TESTED AGAINST A RELATION MODEL]. Wageningen, The Netherlands, H. Veenman en Zonen N.V.: 215p. (Dissertation, Landbouwhogeschool Wageningen) **[41]**   *[RILA]*

Eaton, George E.

46.0065   **JM**   1974   Osmond Dyce—labour leader: a life and its times, 1918-1970.

37.0213   **JM**   1975   ALEXANDER BUSTAMENTE AND MODERN JAMAICA. Kingston, Jamaica, Kingston Publishers Ltd.: 276p. **[5]**   *[RIS]*

Edwards, Adolph

37.0214   **JM**   1968   THE DEVELOPMENT OF CRIMINAL LAW IN JAMAICA UP TO 1900. Ph.D. dissertation, University of London (LSE): 640p. **[33]**

Ehrensaft, Philip

41.0154   **TR**   1968   Authentic planning or Afro-Asian Appalachia?

Einaar, J. F. E.

37.0215   **SR**   1934   BIJDRAGE TOT DE KENNIS VAN HET ENGELSCH TUSSCHENBESTUUR VAN SURINAME 1804-1816 [CONTRIBUTION TO KNOWLEDGE ABOUT THE ENGLISH INTERREGNUM IN SURINAM, 1804-1816]. Leiden, Dubbeldeman, 227p. (Ph.D. dissertation, Leiden, 1934.) **[5]**   *[NYP]*

Ellis, J. J. A.

37.0216   CU   1948   Bestuursindeling [The administration]. *In* ORANJE EN DE ZES CARAÏBISCHE PARELEN. Amsterdam, J. H. de Bussy: 198-201.

[*UCLA*]

37.0217   CU   1948   De Rechtsbedeling [The judicial process]. *In* ORANJE EN DE ZES CARAÏBISCHE PARELEN. Amsterdam, J. H. de Bussy: 208-216.

[*UCLA*]

Ellis, J. W.; Gorsira, M. P. & Nuyten, F. C. J.

37.0218   NA   1954   DE ZELFSTANDIGHEID DER EILANDGEBIEDEN [THE INDEPENDENCE OF THE ISLAND TERRITORIES]. Willemstad, Curacao.

Ellis, Walter Glenn

37.0219   JM   1973   THE JAMAICAN CIVIL SERVICE: AN EXPLORATORY ANALYSIS OF HIGHER CIVIL SERVANTS IN FOUR MINISTRIES. Ann Arbor, Michigan, University Microfilms: 192p. (Ph.D. dissertation, University of Washington, 1971) **[46]** [*RIS*]

Emmanuel, Patrick

37.0220   LW,WW   1976   Independence and viability: elements of analysis. *In* Lewis, Vaughan A., ed. SIZE, SELF-DETERMINATION AND INTERNATIONAL RELATIONS: THE CARIBBEAN. Mona, Jamaica, University of the West Indies, Institute of Social and Economic Research: 1-15. **[39]**

[*RIS*]

Ernste, Th.

41.0156   SR   1966   De politieke, economische en strategische positie van Suriname [The political, economic and strategic position of Surinam].

41.0157   NA   1967   De politiek-economische en strategische betekenis van de Nederlandse Antillen [The political, economic and strategic significance of the Netherlands Antilles].

Erp, Th. E. J. van

37.0221   AR   1948   De politie [The police]. *In* ORANJE EN DE ZES CARAÏBISCHE PARELEN. Amsterdam, J. H. de Bussy: 430-432. [*UCLA*]

Erpecum, K. J. van

33.0070   SR   1969   Vijf en zeventig jaren burgerlijk recht [Seventy five years of civil law].

Evans, E. W.

37.0222   BC   1954   Constitutional development in the British West Indies. *In* PROCEEDINGS OF THE SYMPOSIUM INTERCOLONIAL, JUNE 27-JULY 3, 1952. Bordeaux, Delmas, p.136-143. [*RIS*]

37.0223   BC   1955   A survey of the present constitutional situation in the British West Indies. *In* DEVELOPMENTS TOWARDS SELF-GOVERNMENT IN THE CARIBBEAN. A symposium held under the auspices of the Netherlands Universities Foundation for International Co-operation at The Hague, Sept. 1954. The Hague, W. van Hoeve: 23-33. [*RIS*]

Evans, Geoffrey et al.

17.0034   GU,BZ   1948   REPORT OF THE BRITISH GUIANA AND BRITISH HONDURAS SETTLEMENT COMMISSION.

Evans, Harry

46.0070   GU   1962   Profsoiuzy Britanskoi Gviany na raspute [The trade unions of British Guiana in disarray] [by] Garri Evans.

Evans, Luther Harris

37.0224   UV   1935   Unrest in the Virgin Islands. *For Policy Rep* 11(2), Mar. 27: 14-24.
                                                                                                      [NYP]

5.0285   UV   1945   THE VIRGIN ISLANDS: FROM NAVAL BASE TO NEW DEAL.

Evers, M. A.

37.0225   CU   1923-24 Een bezoek van den Gouverneur van Curacao aan Venezuela in 1921 [A visit of the Governor of Curacao to Venezuela in 1921]. *W I G* 5: 318-331.   [COL]

Faber, Michael

37.0226   JM   1964   A "swing" analysis of the Jamaican election of 1962: a note. *Social Econ Stud* 13(2), June: 302-310.   [RIS]

Falls, Cyril

37.0227   JM   1962   A window on the world: Jamaica moves to independence. *Illus London News* 24(6420), Aug. 18: 240.   **[41]**   [RIS]

Farley, Rawle

41.0159   GU   1955   The economic circumstances of the British annexation of British Guiana (1795-1815).

37.0228   GU   1955   The unification of British Guiana. *Social Econ Stud* 4(2), June: 168-183.   **[5]**   [RIS]

45.0048   BC   1958   NATIONALISM AND INDUSTRIAL DEVELOPMENT IN THE BRITISH CARIBBEAN.

46.0075   BC   1958   TRADE UNIONS AND POLITICS IN THE BRITISH CARIBBEAN.

41.0160   GU   1962   Kaldor's budget in retrospect: reason and unreason in a developing area: reflections on the 1962 budget in British Guiana.

Farley, Rawle & Hughes, Colin

37.0229   GU   1952   El Dorado's new constitution. *Venture* 3(12), Jan.: 9.   [COL]

Farrelly, Alexander

37.0230   US,UV   1967   The doctrine of incorporation and federal labor policy in the Virgin Islands. *V I Bar J* 1(1), Jan.: 11-32.   **[40,46]**   [COL]

Farrugia, Laurent

37.0231   GD   1968   LE FAIT NATIONAL GUADELOUPÉEN [GUADELOUPE BECOMES A NATION]. Ivry-sur-Seine, Laurent Farrugia: 201p.   [COL]

Fauvel, Luc

37.0232   FA   1955   Les conséquences économiques et sociales de l'assimilation administrative des Antilles Francaises [The economic and social consequences of the political assimilation of the French Antilles]. *In* DEVELOPMENTS TOWARDS SELF-GOVERNMENT IN THE CARIBBEAN. A symposium held under the auspices of the Netherlands Universities Foundation for International Co-operation at The Hague, Sept. 1954. The Hague, W. van Hoeve: 176-200.   **[33,41,43]**   [RIS]

Felhoen Kraal, Johanna L. G.

37.0233   NA   1954   Notices sur les principes d'administration des Antilles Néerlandaises et leur relation avec la situation économique et sociale
[Notes on the administrative regulations of the Dutch Antilles and
their relationship to the socio-economic situation]. *In* PROCEEDINGS
OF THE SYMPOSIUM INTERCOLONIAL, JUNE 27-JULY 3, 1952. Bordeaux, Impr. Delmas, p.159-166.   [*RIS*]

Ferdinand, Prince Edgar

37.0234   TR   1964   CITIZENSHIP FOR TRINIDAD AND TOBAGO. Port of Spain, PNM Pub.
Co., 182p.

Ferkiss, Barbara & Ferkiss, Victor C.

16.0029   GU,TR   1971   Race and politics in Trinidad and Guyana.

Fernandes, A. S. J.

41.0162   SR   1925-26   De Surinaamsche begrooting voor 1925 in de Staten-Generaal [The
budget of Surinam for 1925 before the States-General].

37.0235   SR   1925-26   Ministerieele bedreiging van de onafhankelijkheid van het opperste
gerechtshof van Suriname [Ministerial threat to the independence of
the highest court of justice of Surinam]. *W I G 7: 207-288.*   [*COL*]

Field-Ridley, Shirley

37.0236   GU   1969[?]   The concept of the co-operative republic. Debate in the Guyana
National Assembly on Friday, August 29: 12p.   [*RIS*]

Findlay, D. G. A.

5.0295   SR   [n.d.]   HET POLITIEK COMPLOT VAN KILLINGER C. S. IN SURINAME [THE
POLITICAL CONSPIRACY OF KILLINGER AND HIS ASSOCIATES IN
SURINAME].

Findling, John E.

37.0237   BB   1973   The Lowther-Gordon controversy: church and state in Barbados,
1711-1720. *J Barb Mus Hist Soc* 34(3), March: 131-144.   **[5,23]**
                                                            [*NYP*]

Finnis, J. M. & Carnegie, A. R.

37.0238   BC   1969   Constitutional law. *In* Wade, H. W. R., ed. ANNUAL SURVEY OF
COMMONWEALTH LAW: 1968. London, Butterworth and Co. (Pub-
lishers) Ltd.: 1-122. (Chapter 1)   **[38]**   [*COL*]

37.0239   BC   1970   Constitutional law. *In* Wade, H. W. R., ed. ANNUAL SURVEY OF
COMMONWEALTH LAW: 1969. London, Butterworth and Co. (Pub-
lishers) Ltd.: 1-88. (Chaper 1)   **[38]**   [*COL*]

Finnis, J. M. & Gould, B. C.

37.0240   BC   1971   Constitutional law. *In* Wade, H. W. R., ed. ANNUAL SURVEY OF
COMMONWEALTH LAW: 1970. London, Butterworth and Co. (Pub-
lishers) Ltd.: 1-65. (Chapter 1)   [*COL*]

Fisher, Ruth Anna

15.0033   JM   1943   Note on Jamaica.

Fitzpatrick, Miles

37.0241   GU   1965   Portrait of Moses Bhagwan. *New Wld F* 1(18), July 9: 9-20.   [*RIS*]

37.0242   GU   1969   Political problems of Guyana today. *In* CARIBBEAN DEVELOPMENT AND THE FUTURE OF THE CHURCH: PROCEEDINGS OF A CONFERENCE HELD IN GEORGETOWN, JAN. 6-8. Georgetown, Guyana, Guyana Institute for Social Research and Action.   [*SCH*]

Fliek, F. C.

5.0296   NA   1969   Het reglement op de inrichting en de samenstelling van de rechterlijke macht: de geboorte in het bewogen leven van een honderdjarige [The regulation on the jurisdictions and the composition of the judicial power: the birth and full life of a centenary].

Foner, Nancy

8.0074   JM   1971   SOCIAL CHANGE AND SOCIAL MOBILITY IN A JAMAICAN RURAL COMMUNITY.

37.0243   JM   1973   Party politics in a Jamaican community. *Car Stud* 13(2), July: 51-64. **[10]**   [*RIS*]

32.0211   JM   1973   STATUS AND POWER IN RURAL JAMAICA: A STUDY OF EDUCATIONAL AND POLITICAL CHANGE.

Foot, Hugh

37.0244   JM   1964   A START IN FREEDOM. London, Hodder and Stoughton, p.113-142.

Forbes, Urias

37.0245   AT,DM,KNA   1969   Subsidiary law-making process: Antigua, Dominica and St. Kitts, 1960-1968 (a critique). *Int Comp Law Q* 18(3), July: 533-557.   **[33]**   [*COL*]

37.0246   NV   1971   The Nevis local council: a case of formalism in structural change. *Car Stud* 11(2), July: 21-32.   [*RIS*]

37.0247   BC   1972   Administrative environment of the 1970's. *In* TRAINING OF PUBLIC SERVICE TRAINERS: REPORT ON A PILOT COURSE, ST. AUGUSTINE, TRINIDAD, AUG. 10-SEPT. 18, 1970. New York, United Nations: 57-62.   [*UNL*]

37.0248   AT,DM,KNA   1972   Aspects of administrative law in the West Indies: a study of recent developments in Antigua, Dominica and St. Kitts. *Int Comp Law Q* 21(1), Jan.: 95-118.   **[33]**   [*COL*]

Forsythe, Dennis

17.0036   BC   1972   Migration and radical politics.

18.0106   GC,US   1976   West Indian radicalism in America: an assessment of ideologies.

Fox, Annette Baker

33.0072   GC   1949   FREEDOM AND WELFARE IN THE CARIBBEAN: A COLONIAL DILEMMA.

Francis, L. B.

39.0064   JM   1965   Jamaica assumes treaty rights and obligations: some aspects of foreign policy.

Francis, Sybil E.

36.0038   JM   1969   The evolution of community development in Jamaica.

Franck, Thomas M.

38.0074   **BC**   1968   Why federations fail.

Franck, Thomas M., ed.

38.0075   **BC**   1968   WHY FEDERATIONS FAIL: AN INQUIRY INTO THE REQUISITES FOR SUCCESSFUL FEDERALISM.

Freitas, G. V. de

37.0249   **GU**   1961   British Guiana clears the decks. *New Commonw* 39(1), Jan.: 15-16.

                                                  [*AGS*]

Freitas, Q. B. de

37.0250   **GU**   1941   Notes on the trial of a nurse-midwife on the charge of murder held in the Criminal Court of Georgetown, Demarara, from 22nd April to 5th May, 1941. *Car Med J* 3(2): 120-126. **[28]**   [*COL*]

Gaay Fortman, B. de

37.0251   **CU**   1919   De rechtsbedeling op onze Bovenwindse Eilanden en de herziening van de rechterlijke macht en van de rechtspleging in de kolonie Curacao [The administration of justice in our Windward Islands and the revision of judiciary powers and of the judicature in the colony of Curacao]. *W I G* 1(1): 85-101.   [*COL*]

37.0252   **NA**   1920-21 Vreendelingen [Foreigners]. *W I G* 2: 315-321.   [*COL*]

2.0152   **NA**   1921-22 De vooruitgang der Nederlandsche West-Indische eilanden [The progress of the Dutch West Indian islands].

37.0253   **CU**   1921-22 Nog een staatsrechterlijke kwestie [Another constitutional-legal problem]. *W I G* 3: 637-640.   [*COL*]

37.0254   **NA**   1921-22 Een staatsrechterlijk vraagstuk [A constitutional problem]. *W I G* 3: 337-341.   [*COL*]

37.0255   **CU**   1922-25 Over de bestuursinrichting van Curacao [On the organization of the government of Curacao]. *W I G* 4: 289-304, 533-551 (1922/23); 5: 535-560 (1923/24); 6: 385-404 (1924/25).   [*COL*]

5.0310   **CU**   1924-25 Een bladzijde uit de geschiedenis van Curacao [A page from the history of Curacao].

37.0256   **CU**   1925-26 Een aanvulling van Bordewijks ontstaan en ontwikkeling van het staatsrecht van Curacao [An addition to Bordewijk's origin and development of the constitutional law of Curacao]. *W I G* 7: 505-506.   [*COL*]

37.0257   **CU**   1926-27 De oprichting der Curacaosche shutterij [The establishment of the citizen-soldiery in Curacao]. *W I G* 8: 97-118.   [*COL*]

41.0178   **CU**   1928-29 De Curacaosche begrooting voor 1929: over den politieken toestand van Curacao [The budget of Curacao for the year 1929: about the political situation in Curacao].

5.0312   **SR**   1928-29 In Suriname vóór honderd jaar [In Surinam a hundred years ago].

6.0088   **SR**   1930-31 Suriname op den drempel van de afschaffing der slavernij [Surinam on the threshold of the abolition of slavery].

37.0258   **CU**   1933-34 Vrijheid van drukpers en recht van vergadering [Freedom of the press and the right of assembly]. *W I G* 15: 241-251. **[48]**   [*COL*]

37.0259   **CU**   1934-35 Staatkundige geschiedenis van Curacao [Political history of Curacao]. *W I G* 16:209-221. **[5]**   [*COL*]

41.0186   **CU**   1935-36 Staatkundige geschiedenis van Curacao: de Curacaosche begrooting voor 1935 [Political history of Curacao: the budget of Curacao for the year 1935].

41.0187　**CU**　1936-37　Staatkundige geschiedenis van Curacao: de Curacaosche begrooting voor 1936 [Political history of Curacao: the budget of Curacao for the year 1936].

41.0188　**CU**　1937　Staatkundige geschiedenis van Curacao: de Curacaosche begrooting voor 1937 [Political history of Curacao: the budget of Curacao for the year 1937].

41.0189　**CU**　1938　Economische en sociale vraagstukken in Curacao [Economic and social problems in Curacao].

41.0190　**CU**　1938　Staatkundige geschiedenis van Curacao: de Curacaosche begrooting voor 1938 [Political history of Curacao: the budget of Curacao for the year 1938].

37.0260　**CU**　1939　Het Plan-Jas [The proposed plan of Jas]. *W I G* 21: 173-178.　[*COL*]

41.0191　**CU**　1939　Staatkundige geschiedenis van Curacao: de Curacaosche begrooting van 1939 [Political history of Curacao: the budget of Curacao for the year 1939].

41.0192　**CU**　1940　Staatkundige geschiedenis van Curacao: de Curacaosche begrooting voor 1940 [Political history of Curacao: the budget of Curacao for the year 1940].

37.0261　**CU**　1942　Aanvulling van de Encyclopaedie van Nederlandsch West-Indië: Bestuursregeling van Curacao [Addition to the Encyclopedia of the Netherlands West Indies: Government rule of Curacao]. *W I G* 24: 214-226.　[*COL*]

37.0262　**CU**　1943　Aanvulling van de Encyclopaedie van Nederlandsch West-Indië: De gouverneurs van Curacao [Addition to the Encyclopedia of the Netherlands West Indies: The governors of Curacao]. *W I G* 25: 380-382.　**[5]**　[*COL*]

37.0263　**CU**　1946　Politieke beschouwingen over Curacao [Political observations about Curacao]. *W I G* 27: 257-279.　[*COL*]

37.0264　**CU**　1947　Schets van de politieke geschiedenis der Nederlandsche Antillen in de Twintigste eeuw (Curacao) [Sketch of the political history of the Netherlands Antilles in the twentieth century (Curacao)]. The Hague, W. van Hoeve, 71p.　**[5]**　[*RIS*]

37.0265　**CU**　1948　Een half jaar politiek [Half a year of politics]. *W I G* 29: 257-272.　[*COL*]

37.0266　**NA**　1948　Het Staatsdeel in de Staten-Generaal [The overseas Kingdom in the States General]. *In* Oranje en de zes Caraïbische parelen. Amsterdam, J. H. de Bussy: 51-60.　[*UCLA*]

37.0267　**NA**　1949　De ontwikkeling van den politieken toestand op de Nederlandse Antillen [The development of the political situation of the Netherlands Antilles]. *W I G* 30: 237-243.　[*COL*]

37.0268　**NA**　1949　De verkiezingen in de Nederlandse Antillen [The elections in the Netherlands Antilles]. *W I G* 30: 129-135.　[*COL*]

7.0054　**NA**　1959　Toelating, verblijf, vestiging, en uitzetting in de Nederlandse Antillen [Admission, residence, settlement and expulsion in the Netherlands Antilles].

Gaay Fortman, W. F. de

37.0269　**NA**　1969　Maatschappelijke verhoudingen en codificatie [Social circumstances and codification]. *In* Honderd jaar codificatie in de Nederlandse Antillen. Arnhem, The Netherlands, S. Gouda Quint/D. Brouwer en Zoon: 53-62.　[*RILA*]

Gammans, L. D.

37.0270 JM 1947 Self-governing Jamaica. *Spectator* 178(6189), Feb. 7: 169-170.
 [NYP]

Gant, Liz

37.0271 TR 1974 New directions? Trinidad and the Caribbean. *Black Wld* May: 61-77. *[NYP]*

Garcia-Zamor, Jean-Claude

37.0272 BC 1970 Development administration in the Commonwealth Caribbean. *Int Rev Adm Sci* 36(3): 1-14. *[COL]*

37.0273 GC 1971 Micro-bureaucracies and development administration. Paper prepared for the National Conference on Comparative Administration, Syracuse, New York, April 1-4: 21p. *[RIS]*

37.0274 BC 1972 A typology of Creole bureaucracies. *Int Rev Adm Sci* 38(1): 49-60.
 [COL]

Garcon, Maurice

37.0275 FG 1933 Apropos de la Guyane [Concerning Guiana]. *Edn Hebd J Deb* 40(2067), Oct. 6: 539-541. *[COL]*

Gaskin, Winifred

37.0276 GU [n.d.] The People's National Congress. *In* CARIBBEAN INSTITUTE AND STUDY CENTER FOR LATIN AMERICA (CISCLA). REPORT: FIRST INSTITUTE ON BRITISH GUIANA. San German, P.R., Inter American University: 27-33. *[RIS]*

Gastmann, Albert

37.0277 NC 1964 THE PLACE OF SURINAM AND THE NETHERLAND ANTILLES IN THE POLITICAL AND CONSTITUTIONAL STRUCTURE OF THE KINGDOM OF THE NETHERLANDS. Ph.D. dissertation, Columbia University: 341p. **[2]** *[PhD]*

37.0278 NC 1968 THE POLITICS OF SURINAM AND THE NETHERLANDS ANTILLES. Rio Piedras, University of Puerto Rico, Institute of Caribbean Studies: 185p. (Caribbean Monograph Series, No. 3). *[RIS]*

37.0279 NC 1971 The Charter of the Kingdom. *In* Mathews, T. G. & Andic, F. M., eds. POLITICS AND ECONOMICS IN THE CARIBBEAN. Rio Piedras, University of Puerto Rico, Institute of Caribbean Studies: 103-120. (Special Study No. 8) *[RIS]*

37.0280 SR 1971 The politics of Surinam. *In* Mathews, T. G. & Andic, F. M., eds. POLITICS AND ECONOMICS IN THE CARIBBEAN. Rio Piedras, University of Puerto Rico, Institute of Caribbean Studies: 141-148. (Special Study No. 8) *[RIS]*

37.0281 NA 1971 The politics of the Netherlands Antilles. *In* Mathews, T. G. & Andic, F. M., eds. POLITICS AND ECONOMICS IN THE CARIBBEAN. Rio Piedras, University of Puerto Rico, Institute of Caribbean Studies: 121-127. (Special Study No. 8) *[RIS]*

Gautam, Brijendra Pratap

37.0282 GU 1966 Guyana: attainment of independence. *United Asia* 18(3), May-June: 152-156. *[COL]*

Gelder, J. van

37.0283   SR   1967   Troepenmacht in Suriname gedurende deze eeuw [Military forces in Surinam during this century]. *Schakels* S65/NA49: 16-20.   [*NYP*]

Gerlings, H. J. Marius

37.0284   NC   1971   Het Koninkrijksstatuut [The Statute of the Kingdom]. *N W I G* 48(2-3), Dec.: 135-157.   [*RIS*]

37.0285   NC   1975   Nederland, Suriname en de Nederlandse Antillen: souvereine staten [The Netherlands, Surinam and the Netherlands Antilles: sovereign states]. *N W I G* 50(1), Jan.: 3-6.   [*RIS*]

Getrouw, C. F. G.

37.0286   SR   1946   Suriname en de oorlog [Surinam and the War]. *W I G* 27: 129-136.   **[41]**   [*COL*]

Gibbs, Bernard, ed.

2.0159   SV   1947[?]   A PLAN OF DEVELOPMENT FOR THE COLONY OF ST. VINCENT, WINDWARD ISLANDS, BRITISH WEST INDIES.

Giles, Bryant Whitmore

39.0068   BZ   1956   THE "BELIZE" QUESTION: A PROBLEM OF ANTI-COLONIALISM IN THE NEW WORLD.

Giles, Walter I.

37.0287   JM   1956   JAMAICA: A STUDY OF BRITISH COLONIAL POLICY AND THE DEVELOPMENT OF SELF-GOVERNMENT. Ph.D. dissertation, Georgetown University, 2v. (703p.)   **[38]**

Girvan, Norman

37.0288   JM   1968   After Rodney—the politics of student protest in Jamaica [October counter-revolution in Jamaica]. *New Wld Q* 4(3), High Season: 59-68.   **[32]**   [*RIS*]

Glantz, Oscar

20.0027   GC,US   1976   Personal efficacy, system-blame, and violence orientation: a test of the blocked-opportunity theory.

Glass, Ruth

21.0032   JM   1962   Ashes of discontent.

Glusa, Rudolf

37.0289   GC   1962   ZUR POLITISCHEN GEOGRAPHIE WESTINDIENS [ON THE POLITICAL GEOGRAPHY OF THE WEST INDIES]. Münster, Max Kramer, 134p. (Ph.D. dissertation, Westfälischen Wilhelms-Universität zu Münster, 1962)   **[56]**   [*AGS*]

Gocking, C. V.

37.0290   JM   1960   Early constitutional history of Jamaica (with special reference to the period 1838-1866). *Car Q* 6(2-3), May: 114-133.   **[5]**   [*RIS*]

Godfrey, J. E.

28.0521   GU   1904   A few introductory remarks on the regulations passed by the recent Quarantine Conference.

37.0291 GU 1912 Village administration and local government in British Guiana. *Timehri* 3d ser., 2(19B), Dec.: 337-356. **[5,8]** [*AMN*]

Goldberg, J. & Sutherland, E. S.
28.0525 JM 1963 Studies on Gonorrhoea. I: Some social and sexual parameters of male patients in Kingston, Jamaica.

Golding, Will
37.0292 BE 1952 Servants on horse-back. *Bermuda Hist Q* 9(1), Jan.-March: 183-213. (Originally published in 1648) **[5]** [*COL*]

Gomes, Albert
5.0331 TR 1974 THROUGH A MAZE OF COLOUR.

Gomes, Ralph C.
21.0034 GU 1972 Colonialism, nationalism, fractionalism, and self-identity among Guyanese leaders.
20.0029 GU 1975 A social psychology of leadership: elite attitudes in Guyana.

Gomes Casseres, Charles
37.0293 NA 1975 Our future. . .di nos e ta? [Our future. . .it is ours?] *Kristòf* 2(1), Feb.:
— 1-27. **[40]** [*RIS*]

Goode, Richard
41.0201 JM 1956 Taxation and economic development in Jamaica.

Gordijn, W.
22.0148 NC 1965 Tien jaar Statuut 1954-1964. Culturele ontwikkelingen in Rijks-verband [Ten years of Statute 1954-1964. Cultural developments in context of the Kingdom].

Gordon, William E.
37.0294 JM 1939 Jamaicans strive for dominion status. *Crown Colonist* 9(91), June: 361. **[38]** [*NYP*]
37.0295 JM 1939 A new constitution for Jamaica. *United Emp* new ser., 30(9), Sept.: 1007-1010.
37.0296 JM 1942 Jamaica rejects a constitution. *Contemp Rev* 161(913), Jan.: 51-54. [*NYP*]
37.0297 JM 1955 Socialist planning for Jamaica. *Contemp Rev* 188(1079), Nov.: 326-329. [*COL*]
41.0207 JM 1957 Imperial policy decisions in the economic history of Jamaica, 1664-1934.
37.0298 JM 1963 Jamaica: from colony to state. *Contemp Rev* 203, Apr.: 187-191. [*COL*]

Gorkom, J. A. J. van
37.0299 NC 1955 Partnership in a kingdom. *Caribbean* 8(7), Feb.: 130-133, 151-152. [*COL*]

Goslinga, Cornelius Ch.
23.0102 GC 1956 Kerk, Kroon en Cariben [Church, crown and Caribs].
5.0336 CU 1968 Papachi Sassen: Drie onrustige jaren op Curaçao: 1870-1873 [Papachi Sassen: Three turbulent years in Curacao: 1870-1873].

37.0300   CU   1975   CURAÇAO AND GUZMAN BLANCO: A CASE STUDY OF SMALL POWER
                         POLITICS IN THE CARIBBEAN. The Hague, Martinus Nijhoff: 140p.
                         (Verhandelingen van het Koninklijk Instituut voor Taal-, Land en
                         Volkenkunde No. 76)   **[5]**   [*UCLA*]

Goslinga, W. J.
37.0301   CU   1948   Overheidszorg voor onderwijs en volksontwikkeling [Governmental
                         involvement in the educational system and mass education]. *In*
                         ORANJE EN DE ZES CARAÏBISCHE PARELEN. Amsterdam, J. H. de
                         Bussy: 126-142.   **[32]**   [*UCLA*]

Goulbourne, De Costa Harold
46.0085 JM   1975   TEACHERS AND PRESSURE GROUP ACTIVITIES IN JAMAICA, 1894-1967:
                         A STUDY OF THE JAMAICA UNION OF TEACHERS AND THE JAMAICA
                         TEACHERS' ASSOCIATION IN THE COLONIAL AND INDEPENDENT POLIT-
                         ICAL SYSTEMS.

Graff, Edward de
37.0302   GU   1962   Cheddi Jagan y el futuro de la Guayana Británica [Cheddi Jagan
                         and the future of British Guiana]. *Cuadernos* 57, Feb.: 83-86.
                                                                             [*COL*]

Grant, C. H.
37.0303   GU   1965   The District Commissioner system in British Guiana. *J Local Adm
                         Overseas* 4(4), Oct.: 244-259.   [*COL*]
37.0304   GU   1965   The politics of community development in British Guiana 1954-57.
                         Social Econ Stud 14(2), June: 170-182.   **[36]**   [*RIS*]
46.0087 BZ   1966   The civil service strike in British Honduras: a case study of politics
                         and the civil service.
37.0305   GU,BZ 1967   Rural local government in Guyana and British Honduras. *Social
                         Econ Stud* 16(1), March: 57-76.   **[8]**   [*RIS*]
40.0027 BZ   1969   POLITICAL CHANGE IN BRITISH HONDURAS: A STUDY OF DECOLONI-
                         SATION AND NATIONAL INTEGRATION.
37.0306   GU   1973   Political sequel to Alcan nationalization in Guyana: the inter-
                         national aspects. *Social Econ Stud* 22(2), June: 249-271.   **[39,50]**
                                                                             [*RIS*]
37.0307   BZ   1976   THE MAKING OF MODERN BELIZE: POLITICS, SOCIETY AND BRITISH
                         COLONIALISM IN CENTRAL AMERICA. Cambridge, Cambridge Uni-
                         versity Press: 400p.   **[5,8,40]**   [*RIS*]

Grant, R. W.
37.0308   GU   1970   THE EMERGENCE OF PARTY POLITICS IN GUYANA, 1945-1957. Ph.D.
                         dissertation, University of Toronto.   [*PhD*]
37.0309   BC   1972   Party politics and contemporary socio-political movements in the
                         Commonwealth Caribbean. *In* RESOURCE DEVELOPMENT IN THE
                         CARIBBEAN. Montreal, McGill University, Centre for Developing-
                         Area Studies: 157-163.   **[40]**   [*RIS*]

Gratiant, Gilbert
37.0310   MT   1961   ILE FÉDÉRÉE FRANCAISE DE LA MARTINIQUE [THE FEDERATED
                         FRENCH ISLAND OF MARTINIQUE]. Paris, Louis Soulanges, 110p.
                                                                             [*NYP*]

Green, James W.
8.0086   **GC**   1972   Review essay: culture and colonialism in the West Indies.

Greene, Edward
37.0311   **TR**   1971   An analysis of the general elections in Trinidad and Tobago 1971. *In* Munroe, Trevor & Lewis, Rupert, eds. READINGS IN GOVERNMENT AND POLITICS OF THE WEST INDIES. Mona, Jamaica, University of the West Indies: 136-145.   [*RIS*]

Greene, J. E.
37.0312   **GU**   1972   Participation, integration and legitimacy as indicators of developmental change in the politics of Guyana. *Social Econ Stud* 21(3), Sept.: 243-283. **[8]**   [*RIS*]
37.0313   **GU**   1972   POLITICAL CLEAVAGES AND POLITICAL MOBILISATION IN GUYANA: THE 1968 GENERAL ELECTION. Ph.D. dissertation, University of British Columbia.   [*PhD*]
37.0314   **GU**   1974   The politics of economic planning in Guyana. *Social Econ Stud* 23(2), June: 186-203. **[41]**   [*RIS*]
37.0315   **GU**   1974   RACE VS. POLITICS IN GUYANA: POLITICAL CLEAVAGES AND POLITICAL MOBILISATION IN THE 1968 GENERAL ELECTION. Jamaica, University of the West Indies, Institute of Social and Economic Research: 198p. **[8]**   [*RIS*]
2.0168   **GC**   1974   A review of political science research in the English-speaking Caribbean: toward a methodology.
37.0316   **BC**   1976   Institutionalization of party systems. *In* Lewis, Vaughan A., ed. SIZE, SELF-DETERMINATION AND INTERNATIONAL RELATIONS: THE CARIBBEAN. Mona, Jamaica, University of the West Indies, Institute of Social and Economic Research: 203-226. **[40]**   [*RIS*]

Greenwood, Thomas
46.0089   **BC**   1921   East Indian emigration: the Indian government's policy.

Greer, Scott; McElrath, Dennis L.; Minar, David W. & Orleans, Peter, eds.
8.0089   **BC**   1968   THE NEW URBANIZATION.

Greiner, F.
37.0317   **SR**   1920-21   Suriname en de oorzaken van de achterlijkheid dezer Nederlandsche kolonie [Surinam and the causes for the backwardness of this Dutch colony]. *W I G* 2: 285-310.   [*COL*]

Griffith, J. A. G.
18.0120   **BC,UK**   1960   Legal aspects of immigration.

Grimble, June A.
46.0090   **JM**   1951   The Jamaica story.

Groot, Silvia W. de
14.0011   **SR**   1963   VAN ISOLATIE NAAR INTEGRATIE: DE SURINAAMSE MARRONS EN HUN AFSTAMMELINGEN, OFFICIELE DOCUMENTEN BETREFFENDE DE DJOEKA'S (1845-1863) [FROM ISOLATION TO INTEGRATION: THE SURINAM MAROONS AND THEIR DESCENDANTS, OFFICAL DOCUMENTS CONCERNING THE DJUKA TRIBE (1845-1863)].

37.0318	**SR**	1970	Bosnegers en politiek: gesprek met E. Josephzoon [Bush Negroes and politics: a conversation with E. Josephzoon]. *Gids* 133(9): 305-308. **[14]** [*COL*]
37.0319	**SR**	1970	De Surinaamse Socialistische Unie: gesprek met het presidium (H. F. Herrenberg, voorzitter) [The Surinam Socialist Union: a conversation with its president, H. F. Herrenberg]. *Gids* 133(9): 322-324. [*COL*]
37.0320	**SR**	1970	Zelfstandigheid en West-Suriname: gesprek met minister F. E. Essed [Independence and Western Surinam: a conversation with F. E. Essed]. *Gids* 133(9): 269-274. [*COL*]
16.0037	**SR**	1972	Zelfstandigheid nu, integratie later: twee Surinamers geven hun opinie [Independence now, integration later: two Surinamese give their opinion].

Grunewald, Donald

5.0346	**BZ**	1965	The Anglo-Guatemalan dispute over British Honduras.

Guggenheim, Hans

22.0158	**TR**	1968	SOCIAL AND POLITICAL CHANGE IN THE ART WORLD OF TRINIDAD DURING THE PERIOD OF TRANSITION FROM COLONY TO NEW NATION.

Gutierrez Castro, Edgar A.

37.0321	**GC**	1974	Notas finales sobre Colabor 1 [Final notes on Colabor 1]. *Car Ed B* 1(2), New Series, May: 31-39. **[47]** [*RIS*]

Haack, Olaf

37.0322	**UV**	1916	Dansk-vestindisk straffelovgivning [Danish-West Indian penal law]. *Nord Tidsskr Straf* 4, Jan.: 19-26.

Habron, John D.

38.0087	**JM**	1970	ISLANDS IN TRANSITION: THE DOMINICAN REPUBLIC, PUERTO RICO, JAMAICA.

Haliar, André

5.0348	**FC**	1965	DANS LES DÉPARTEMENTS D'OUTRE-MER: DU COLBERTISME AU GAULLISME [OVERSEAS TERRITORIES: FROM COLBERTISM TO GAULLISM].

Hall, Douglas

5.0349	**JM**	1968	The colonial legacy in Jamaica.

Hall, Neville A. T.

37.0323	**BB,JM**	1965	CONSTITUTIONAL AND POLITICAL DEVELOPMENTS IN BARBADOS AND JAMAICA, 1783-1815. Ph.D. dissertation, University of London: 457p. **[5]**
5.0352	**BB**	1971	Governors and generals: the relationship of civil and military commands in Barbados, 1783-1815.
5.0353	**BB**	1972	Law and society in Barbados at the turn of the 19th century.
5.0354	**JM**	1972	Public office and private gain: a note on administration in Jamaica in the later eighteenth century.

Hallema, A.

37.0324	**CU**	1934-35	Eenige gegevens over oude gevangenissen, aard der gevangenisstraf, etc. op Curacao gedurende de 17de en 18de eeuw [Some data about old prisons, nature of imprisonment, etc. on Curacao during the 17th and 18th centuries]. *W I G* 16: 192-204. **[5]** [*COL*]

37.0325   **SR,CU**   1934-35 Het jaar 1872 in de geschiedenis van het gevangeniswezen in de West [The year 1872 in the history of the prison system in the West]. *W I G* 16: 33-47, 49-64. **[5,33]** *[COL]*

Hallett, Hugh et al.
37.0326   **GU**   1960   REPORT OF THE BRITISH GUIANA ELECTORAL BOUNDARIES COMMISSION, 1960. Georgetown, Lithographic Co., printers to the Govt. of British Guiana, 63p.   *[RIS]*

Halperin, Ernst
37.0327   **GU**   1965   Racism and Communism in British Guiana. *J Inter-Amer Stud* 7(1), Jan.: 95-134. **[16]**

Hamilton, Bruce
37.0328   **BB**   1944   The Barbados Executive Committee: an experiment in government. *J Barb Mus Hist Soc* 11(3), May: 115-131. **[5]**   *[AMN]*

Hamilton, W. B.; Robinson, Kenneth & Goodwin, C. D. W., eds.
37.0329   **BC**   1966   A DECADE OF THE COMMONWEALTH, 1955-1964. Durham, North Carolina, Duke University Press: 567p. **[39]**   *[COL]*

Hammond, S. A.
46.0093   **BB,LW,BV**   1952   REPORT ON AN ENQUIRY INTO THE ORGANIZATION AND SALARIES OF THE CIVIL SERVICE.

Handler, Jerome S. & Shelby, Lon, eds.
5.0361   **BB**   1973   A seventeenth century commentary on labor and military problems in Barbados.

Hannerz, Ulf
37.0330   **CM**   1974   CAYMANIAN POLITICS: STRUCTURE AND STYLE IN A CHANGING ISLAND SOCIETY. Stockholm, Department of Social Anthropology, University of Stockholm: 198p. (Stockholm Studies in Social Anthropology, 1.)   *[RIS]*

Hanson, David
20.0033   **BZ**   1974   Politics, partisanship, and social position in Belize.

Harlow, Vincent Todd
37.0331   **GU**   1951   British Guiana and British colonial policy. *United Emp* 42(6), Nov.-Dec.: 305-309.   *[RIS]*

Harper-Smith, James W.
37.0332   **GU**   1965   The Colonial Stock Acts and the British Guiana Constitution of 1891. *Social Econ Stud* 14(3), Sept.: 252-263. **[5,41]**   *[RIS]*

Harris, Britton
45.0068   **GC**   1953   The role of government in industrial development in the Caribbean.

Harris, Coleridge
37.0333   **WW**   1960   The constitutional history of the Windwards. *Car Q* 6(2-3), May: 160-176. **[5]**   *[RIS]*

Hart, Richard

37.0334   GU   1966   Approach to the problems of socialism. *New Wld F* 1(31), Jan. 7:
15-19.   [*RIS*]

37.0335   GU   1966   Approach to the problems of socialism. *New Wld F* 1(32), Jan. 21:
8-14.   [*RIS*]

5.0375   JM   1972   Jamaica and self-determination, 1660-1970.

Hartley-Brewer, Michael

37.0336   BC,UK   1965   Smethwick. *In* Deakin, Nicholas, ed. COLOUR AND THE BRITISH
ELECTORATE, 1964: SIX CASE STUDIES. New York, Frederick A.
Praeger: 77-105.   **[16,18]**   [*COL*]

Hartog, J.

37.0337   CU   1946   Oud rechtsgebruik op Curacao herleefd: een voortvluchtige militair
ingedaagd [Old legal custom on Curacao revived: a runaway soldier
summoned]. *W I G* 27: 137-138.   [*COL*]

Hatch, John

37.0338   GU   1958   Delicate balance in British Guiana. *New Stsm* 55(1407), Mar. 1:
258-260.   [*COL*]

Hauofa, Epeli

37.0339   TR   1968   VILLAGE-GOVERNMENT COMMUNICATION: A CASE STUDY IN TRINI-
DAD. M.A. thesis, McGill University, Department of Anthropology:
110p.   **[8]**   [*RIS*]

Haywood, E. J.

37.0340   GU   1945   The British Guiana Regiment. *Emp Dig* 2(5), Feb.: 29-32.   [*NYP*]

Hazard, John N.

41.0230   GU   1968   Guyana's alternative to socialist and capitalist legal models.

Heemstra, J.

15.0039   SR   1952-53   De Indonesiërs in Suriname [The Indonesians in Surinam].

Heidler, J. B.

5.0400   JM   1929   The Jamaica insurrection and English men of letters.

Helsdingen, W. H. van

37.0341   NA   1951   De zelstandigheid der eilandgebieden in de Nederlandse Antillen
[The independence of the islands of the Netherlands Antilles].
W I G 32: 193-205.   [*RIS*]

37.0342   AR   1954   Aruba en de separacion [Aruba's wish to secede]. *W I G* 35(3), Oct.:
113-133.   [*RIS*]

37.0343   NA   1954   Voorlopige balans over de uitvoering van de Eilandenregeling
Nederlandse Antillen [Preliminary assessment of the application of
the Netherlands Antilles Islands regulation]. *W I G* 35(1-2), Oct.:
72-90.   **[41]**   [*RIS*]

37.0344   NC   1955   Het Statuut voor het Koninkrijk der Nederlanden [The Statute for
the Kingdom of the Netherlands]. *W I G* 35: 182-191.   [*COL*]

37.0345   NA   1955   Voorlopige balans over de uitvoering van de Eilandenregeling
Nederlandse Antillen [Preliminary assessment of the application of
the Netherlands Antilles Islands regulation]. *W I G* 35:72-89.
[*COL*]

37.0346   NC   1956   De wetgeving betreffende Koninkrijksaangelegenheden in 1955 [The legislation regarding the affairs of the Kingdom in 1955]. *Ned Jurbl* Apr. 21: 334-342.   [*RIS*]

Hendrickson, Embert
37.0347   GU   1971   New directions for Republican Guyana. *Wld Today* 27(1), Jan.: 33-39.   [*COL*]

Henfrey, Colin
37.0348   GU   1961   The Amerindians of British Guiana. *Venture* 13(9), Oct.: 8-9. **[13]**   [*COL*]
13.0081   GU   1961   S.O.S. from Guiana.
37.0349   GU   1972   Foreign influence in Guyana: the struggle for independence. *In* Kadt, Emanuel de, ed. PATTERNS OF FOREIGN INFLUENCE IN THE CARIBBEAN. LONDON, OXFORD UNIVERSITY PRESS: 49-81. **[39]**   [*RIS*]

Henri, Edmond
37.0350   FG   1912   ETUDE CRITIQUE DE LA TRANSPORTATION EN GUYANE FRANCAISE. RÉFORMES REALISABLES [CRITICAL STUDY OF TRANSPORTATION IN FRENCH GUIANA. WORKABLE IMPROVEMENTS]. Paris, Librairie de la Société du recueil Sirey, 220p. (Ph.D. dissertation, University of Paris, 1912.)   [*COL*]

Henry, Frances
2.0198   TR   1966   The role of the fieldworker in an explosive political situation.

Henry, Frances, ed.
21.0041   GC   1976   ETHNICITY IN THE AMERICAS.

Hermans, Hans G.
37.0351   NC   1955   A queen calls. *Caribbean* 9(3), Oct.: 59-61.   [*COL*]
37.0352   NC   1958   Constitutional development of the Netherlands Antilles and Surinam. *In* Wilgus, A Curtis, ed. THE CARIBBEAN: BRITISH, DUTCH, FRENCH, UNITED STATES [PAPERS DELIVERED AT THE EIGHTH CONFERENCE ON THE CARIBBEAN HELD AT THE UNIVERSITY OF FLORIDA, DEC. 5-7, 1957]. Gainesville, University of Florida Press, p.53-72. (Publications of the School of Inter-American Studies, ser. 1, v. 8.) **[5]**   [*RIS*]

Hewitt, J. M.
37.0353   BB   1954[?]   TEN YEARS OF CONSTITUTIONAL DEVELOPMENT IN BARBADOS. Bridgetown, Barbados, Cole's Printery, 41p.

Higdon, E. K.
37.0354   JM   1943   Democracy gains in the Caribbean. *Chr Cent* 60(43), Oct. 27: 1237, 1240.   [*COL*]

Higham, C. S. S.
37.0355   LW,GR   1926   The General Assembly of the Leeward Islands. *Engl Hist Rev* 41(162), Apr.: 190-209; 41(163), July: 366-388. **[5]**   [*COL*]
37.0356   BC   1926   Sir Henry Taylor and the establishment of crown colony government in the West Indies. *Scott Hist Rev* 23(90), Jan.: 92-96. **[5]**   [*COL*]

Hill, Frank

5.0414   JM   1976   Bustamante and his letters.

Hill, L. C.

37.0357   JM   1943   Report on the reform of local government in Jamaica. Kingston, Govt. Printer, 49p.   [*NYP*]

37.0358   JM   1945   Jamaica gets reform program. *Natn Munic Rev* 34(3), Mar.: 116-121.   [*NYP*]

Hinden, Rita

41.0236   JM   1941   Jamaican paradox.

37.0359   GU   1954   The case of British Guiana. *Encounter* 2, Jan.: 18-22.   [*COL*]

Hoare, Samuel

37.0360   BZ   1921   The problem of crown colony government in the Caribbean. *Nineteenth Cent After* 89(530), Apr.: 606-616.   [*TCL*]

Hoetink, Harry

37.0361   NA   1972   The Dutch Caribbean and its Metropolis. *In* Kadt, Emanuel de, ed. Patterns of foreign influence in the Caribbean. London, Oxford University Press: 103-120.   **[5,39]**   [*RIS*]

37.0362   NA   1974   De Antillen en de toekomst: een science-fiction [The Antilles and the future: a science-fiction]. *Kristòf* 1(1), Feb.: 26-31.   [*RIS*]

Holmes, Maurice et al.

37.0363   BC   1949   Report of the Commission on the Unification of the Public Services in the British Caribbean area 1948-49. London, H.M.S.O., 75p. (Colonial no. 254.)   [*COL*]

Holstein, Casper

37.0364   UV   1925   The Virgin Islands. *Opportunity* 3(34), Oct.: 304-306.   [*COL*]

37.0365   UV   1926   The Virgin Islands: past and present. *Opportunity* 4(47), Nov.: 344-345.   [*COL*]

Honoré, A. M.; Finnis, J. M. & Irani, P. K.

37.0366   BC   1968   Constitutional law. *In* Wade, H. W. R., ed. Annual survey of Commonwealth law: 1967. London, Butterworth and Co. (Publishers) Ltd.: 1-110. (Chapter 1)   [*COL*]

Hope, F. E.

41.0242   BC   1967   Estimating capital formation in the area including the problem of government capital formation.

Hope, Kempe R.

37.0367   GU   1973   Anmerkungen zum genossenschaftlichen Sozialismus in Guayana [Notes on cooperative socialism in Guyana]. *Ann Gemeinwirtschaft* 42(4), Oct.-Dec.: 417-426.   **[40]**   [*COL*]

37.0368   GU   1973   A note on co-operative socialism in Guyana. *Ann Pub Co-op Econ,* Sept.: 1-8.   [*NYP*]

37.0369   GU   1975   Co-operative socialism and the Co-operative movement in Guyana. *Rev Int Co-op* 68(2): 3-12.   **[41]**   [*COL*]

37.0370   GU   1976   Guyana's National Service Programme. *J Adm Overseas* 15, Jan.: 34-38.   **[33,40]**   [*COL*]

Hope, Kempe R. & David, Wilfred L.

41.0244   **GU**   1974   Planning for development in Guyana: the experience from 1945 to 1973.

Horowitz, David L.

37.0371   **GU**   1966   Pigment problems in Guyana. *New Leader* 49(14), July 4: 16-18. **[16]**   [*COL*]

Hourihan, John J.

37.0372   **SV**   1972[?]   Evacuation as a political resource. *In* Fraser, Thomas M.; Ciski, Robert; Hourihan, John J.; Morth, Grace E. & Mulcahy, F. David. LA SOUFRIERE: CULTURAL REACTIONS TO THE THREAT OF VOLCANIC ERUPTION ON THE ISLAND OF SAINT VINCENT, 1971-1972. Amherst, University of Massachusetts: 83-100. **[33]**   [*RIS*]

37.0373   **SV,GR**   1975   RULE IN HAIROUN: A STUDY OF THE POLITICS OF POWER. Ph.D. dissertation, University of Massachusetts: 283p. **[8]**   [*RIS*]

Hoyos, F. A.

37.0374   **BB**   1947[?]   THE STORY OF THE PROGRESSIVE MOVEMENT: ACHIEVEMENTS OF A DECADE. [Bridgetown?] Barbados, Beacon Printery.

37.0375   **BB**   196-[?]   THE ROAD TO RESPONSIBLE GOVERNMENT. [Bridgetown?] Barbados, Letchworth Press, 104p.

37.0376   **BC**   1963   THE RISE OF WEST INDIAN DEMOCRACY: THE LIFE AND TIMES OF SIR GRANTLEY ADAMS. [Bridgetown?] Barbados, Advocate Press, 228p. **[38,46]**   [*RIS*]

Hoyte, Desmond

37.0377   **GU**   1973   THE GREAT ADVANCE IN INFRASTRUCTURE DEVELOPMENT UNDER THE P.N.C. GOVERNMENT. ADDRESS AT THE 16TH ANNUAL DELEGATES' CONGRESS OF THE PEOPLE'S NATIONAL CONGRESS, MAY 2-10. Lacytown, Guyana, Design and Graphics: 20p.   [*RIS*]

Hubbard, H. J. M.

37.0378   **GU**   1966   Guyana: another U.S. satellite? *New Wld Rev* 34(8), Aug.-Sept.: 35-40. **[40]**   [*COL*]

8.0112   **GU**   1969   RACE AND GUYANA: THE ANATOMY OF A COLONIAL ENTERPRISE.

Huck, Susan L. M.

2.0221   **BZ**   1962   BRITISH HONDURAS: AN EVALUATION.

Huggins, H. D., ed.

41.0250   **BC**   1958   [Proceedings of the] Study Conference on Economic Development in Underdeveloped Countries [held at the University College of the West Indies, Aug. 5-15, 1957].

Hughes, Colin A.

37.0379   **BC**   1953   Semi-responsible government in the British West Indies. *Polit Sci Q* 68(3), Sept.: 338-353.   [*COL*]

37.0380   **JM**   1955   Adult suffrage in Jamaica, 1944-1955. *Parl Aff* 8(3), Summer: 344-352.   [*COL*]

37.0381   **BC**   1955   Power and responsibility: a sociological analysis of the political situation in the British West Indies. *In* DEVELOPMENTS TOWARDS SELF-GOVERNMENT IN THE CARIBBEAN. A symposium held under the auspices of the Netherlands Universities Foundation for International Co-operation at The Hague, Sept. 1954. The Hague, W. van Hoeve: 95-111.   [*RIS*]

Hullu, J. de

37.0382   NC   1922-23 Memorie van den Amerikaanschen Raad over de Hollandsche
bezittingen in West-Indie in Juli 1806 [Memorandum of the
American Council about the Dutch possessions in the West Indies
in July 1806]. *W I G* 4: 387-400.   **[5]**   [*COL*]

Humphreys, Robert Arthur

37.0383   BZ   1948   The Anglo-Guatemalan dispute. *Int Aff* 24(3), July: 387-404.   **[5]**
                                                                                        [*AGS*]

37.0384   BZ   1961   THE DIPLOMATIC HISTORY OF BRITISH HONDURAS, 1638-1901. London, Oxford University Press, 196p.   **[5]**   [*RIS*]

Hunte, Keith

5.0446   BB   1966-67 Duncan O'Neale: apostle of freedom.

Huntley, Eric

37.0385   GU   1966   Socialism and the Guyanese situation. *New Wld F* 1(39), April 29:
8-15.   [*RIS*]

Hurwitz, Samuel J. & Hurwitz, Edith

15.0043   JM   1965   The New World sets an example for the Old: the Jews of Jamaica
and political rights 1661-1831.

Hutchinson, Lionel

37.0386   BB   1951   BEHIND THE MACE: AN INTRODUCTION TO THE BARBADOS HOUSE OF
ASSEMBLY. Bridgetown, Advocate Co., 47p.

Huurman, D.

37.0387   GC   1947   Nederland tezamen met Groot-Brittannie, de Vereenigde Staten
van Noord Amerika en Frankrijk in West-Indie [The Netherlands
together with Great Britain, the USA and France in the West
Indies]. *W I G* 28: 47-57.   [*COL*]

37.0388   NC   1948   Britse federatieve voorstellen en Nederlandse federatiemogelijkheden in West Indië [British federation proposals and Dutch
federation possibilities in the West Indies]. *W I G* 29: 33-
47.   **[38,39]**   [*COL*]

Huying, A. F. H.

37.0389   SR   1967   De Surinaamse vrijwilligers [The Surinamese volunteers]. *Schakels*
S65/NA49: 21-23.   [*NYP*]

Hyde, Douglas

37.0390   GU   1962   Communism in Guiana. *Commonweal* 75(19), Feb. 2: 487-489.
                                                                                        [*COL*]

Hylton, Patrick

22.0191   BC   1975   The politics of Caribbean music.

Ibene, Hegesippe

37.0391   GD   1962   Svoboda i nezavisimost-nasha zavetnaia tsel [Freedom and independence—our sworn goal]. [By] Ezhezipp Ibene. *Part Zhizn* 12:
65-68.   [*COL*]

Ifill, Max B.

37.0392   TR   1964   THE SOLOMON AFFAIR: A TALE OF IMMORALITY IN TRINIDAD. [Port of Spain?] People's Democratic Society, 20p. (Citizens' series no. 1.)
           [*RIS*]

Ince, Basil A.

37.0393   AG   [n.d.]   The limits of Caribbean diplomacy: the invasion of Anguilla. *New Wld Q* 5(3): 48-57. **[39,40]**   [*RIS*]

37.0394   AG   1970   The diplomacy of new states: the Commonwealth Caribbean and the case of Anguilla. *S Atlan Q* 69(3), Summer: 382-396. **[39,40]**
           [*COL*]

37.0395   TR   1970   POLITICS BEFORE THE PEOPLE'S NATIONAL MOVEMENT: A STUDY OF PARTIES AND ELECTIONS IN BRITISH TRINIDAD. Ann Arbor, Michigan, University Microfilms, Inc.: 260p. (Ph.D. dissertation, New York University, Department of Government and International Relations) **[5]**   [*RIS*]

37.0396   GU   1974   DECOLONIZATION AND CONFLICT IN THE UNITED NATIONS: GUYANA'S STRUGGLE FOR INDEPENDENCE. Cambridge, Massachusetts, Schenkman Publishing Co.: 202p. **[39,40]**   [*RIS*]

40.0032   GR   1974   The decolonization of Grenada in the U.N.

12.0035   GU   1975   Race and ideology in the foreign relations of independent Guyana: the case of the East Indians.

Ingrams, Harold

37.0397   GU,BZ   1954   Our American colonies—what next? *New Commonw* 27(13), June 24: 645-647.   [*AGS*]

Irish, J. A. George

37.0398   MS   1974   ALLIOUAGANA IN AGONY: NOTES ON MONTSERRAT POLITICS. Plymouth, Montserrat: 27p.   [*RIS*]

Jacob, Charles

37.0399   GU   1969   Guyana: victim of electoral fraud. *Polit Aff* 48(5), May: 23-28.
           [*COL*]

Jacobs, H. P.

37.0400   BC   1957   Centralisation and separatism in the Antilles. *W I Rev* new ser., 2(10), Oct.: 33-38.   [*NYP*]

37.0401   JM   1965   Jamaica: the new phase. *Chron W I Comm* 80(1408), May: 244-246.
           [*NYP*]

37.0402   JM   1966   The Morant Bay Revolt. *Chron W I Comm* 81(1416), Jan: 13-15. **[5]**   [*NYP*]

37.0403   JM   1966   The parish of St. Thomas on the eve of the Morant Bay rebellion. *B Jam Hist Soc* 4(77), Sept.: 136-143. **[5]**   [*NYP*]

5.0466   JM   1973   SIXTY YEARS OF CHANGE, 1806-1866 [PROGRESS AND REACTION IN KINGSTON AND THE COUNTRYSIDE].

Jacobs, Richard

37.0404   GR   1974   The movement towards Grenadian independence. *In* INDEPENDENCE FOR GRENADA—MYTH OR REALITY? Proceedings of a Conference on the Implications of Independence for Grenada sponsored by the Institute of International Relations and the Dept. of Govt., U.W.I., St. Augustine, Trinidad, Jan. 11-13, 1974: 21-33. **[40]**
           [*RIS*]

Jacobs, W. Richard

37.0405   JM   1973   Appeals by Jamaican political parties: a study of newspaper advertisements in the 1972 Jamaican general election campaign. *Car Stud* 13(2), July: 19-50.   [*RIS*]

Jagan, Cheddi

37.0406   GU   1954   FORBIDDEN FREEDOM. New York, International Publishers, 96p.
                                                                                  [*RIS*]

37.0407   GU   1961   TOWARDS UNDERSTANDING. Washington, D.C., National Press Club, 7p.   [*RIS*]

37.0408   GU   1962   Socialism and democracy. *Mon Rev* 13(10), Feb.: 461-466.   [*NYP*]

41.0262   GU   1964   THE ANATOMY OF POVERTY IN BRITISH GUIANA.

37.0409   GU   1964   Let it not be said that we have failed. *Mon Rev* 15(11), Mar.: 612-615. **[41]**   [*NYP*]

37.0410   GU   1965   Guiana's struggle against reaction and racism for democracy and independence. *New Wld F* 1(29), Dec. 10: 16-20.   [*RIS*]

37.0411   GU   1965   Guiana's struggle against reaction and racism for democracy and independence. *New Wld F* 1(30), Dec. 24: 13-19.   [*RIS*]

37.0412   GU   1965   Western democracy on trial in British Guiana. *Labour Monthly* 47(11), Nov.: 494-501.   [*COL*]

37.0413   GU   1966   Cheddi Jagan on the situation in British Guiana. *New Times* 11, March: 18-20.   [*COL*]

37.0414   GU   1966   THE WEST ON TRIAL: MY FIGHT FOR GUYANA'S FREEDOM. London, Michael Joseph Ltd.: 471p. **[5]**   [*RIS*]

37.0415   GU   1968   Guyana: drift toward dictatorship. *New Wld Rev* 36(4), Fall-Winter: 35-39.   [*COL*]

37.0416   GU   1968   SOCIALISM FOR GUYANA. Georgetown, Guyana, People's Progressive Party Education Committee: 19p.   [*RIS*]

39.0090   GU,US   1968   Toward dictatorship in Guyana.

37.0417   GU   1969   Guyana's fraudulent election. *New Wld Rev* 37(1): 62-68.   [*COL*]

37.0418   TR   1971   The February revolt. *Thunder* 2(1), Jan.-March: 11-24. **[40]** [*RIS*]

37.0419   GU   1971   Transactions of the XVI Congress of the People's Progressive Party: address and resolution. *Thunder* 2(1), Jan.-March: 38-44. **[40]**
                                                                                  [*RIS*]

37.0420   GU   1972   Address. (Delivered at the XVII Congress of the PPP, September 2-3.) *Thunder* 4(3), July-Sept.: 2-23.   [*RIS*]

37.0421   GU   1972   The three kinds of nationalisations: capitalist, reformist and socialist. *New Wld Q* 5(4), Cropover: 64-68.   [*RIS*]

37.0422   BC   1972   A WEST INDIAN STATE: PRO-IMPERIALIST OR ANTI-IMPERIALIST. New Guyana Co., Ltd.: 72p. **[38]**   [*RIS*]

Jagan, Derek

37.0423   GU   1971   Transactions of the XVI Congress of the People's Progressive Party: address. *Thunder* 2(1), Jan.-March: 49-52.   [*RIS*]

Jagan, Janet

37.0424   GU   1962   What happened in British Guiana? *Mon Rev* 13(12), Aug.: 559-567.
                                                                                  [*COL*]

37.0425   GU   1973   ARMY INTERVENTION IN THE 1973 ELECTIONS IN GUYANA. Georgetown, P.P.P.: 93p.   [*SCH*]

James, C. L. R.

37.0426	BC	1933	THE CASE FOR WEST INDIAN SELF-GOVERNMENT. London, Leonard & Virginia Woolf at the Hogarth Press, 32p. [*NYP*]
37.0427	TR	1962	PARTY POLITICS IN THE WEST INDIES. San Juan, Trinidad, Vedic Enterprises, 175p. [*RIS*]
37.0428	GC	1964	Parties, politics and economics in the Caribbean. *Freedomways* 4(3), Summer: 312-318. [*RIS*]
46.0124	TR	1970	The Caribbean confrontation begins.
37.0429	GC	1970	Excerpt from: *Party politics in the West Indies* (1962). *Radical America* 4(4), May: 50-60. **[8]** [*RIS*]
37.0430	GC	1972	Parties, politics and economics in the Caribbean. *In* McDonald, Vincent R., ed. THE CARIBBEAN ECONOMIES: PERSPECTIVES ON SOCIAL, POLITICAL AND ECONOMIC CONDITIONS. New York, MSS Information Corporation: 28-34. [*COL*]
37.0431	BC	1975	The revolutionary. *In* Singham, A. W., ed. THE COMMONWEALTH CARIBBEAN INTO THE SEVENTIES. Montreal, McGill University, Centre for Developing Area Studies: 179-187. **[21,40]** [*RIS*]

James, Eric George

37.0432	JM	1956	ADMINISTRATIVE INSTITUTIONS AND SOCIAL CHANGE IN JAMAICA, BRITISH WEST INDIES—A STUDY IN CULTURAL ADAPTATION. Ph.D. dissertation, New York University, 638p. **[8,19]** [*COL*]

Jean, Clinton

41.0265	TR	1970	ECONOMY AND SOCIAL TRANSFORMATION IN TRINIDAD AND TOBAGO.

John, George

37.0433	TR	1972	Trinidad, Tobago and the Caribbean. *In* Boyke, Roy, ed. PATTERNS OF PROGRESS. Port-of-Spain, Trinidad, Key Caribbean Publications: 93-95. [*RIS*]

John, Kenneth

37.0434	SV	1967	Political crisis in St. Vincent. *New Wld Q* 3(3), High Season: 51-56. [*RIS*]
37.0435	SV	1973	St. Vincent: a political kaleidoscope. *In* Lowenthal, David & Comitas, Lambros, eds. THE AFTERMATH OF SOVEREIGNTY: WEST INDIAN PERSPECTIVES. Garden City, N.Y., Anchor Press/ Doubleday: 81-91. [*RIS*]

Johnson, Caswell L.

37.0436	JM,TR	1975	Political unionism and the collective objective in economies of British colonial origin: the cases of Jamaica and Trinidad. *Am J Econ Sociol* 34(4), Oct.: 365-379. **[40,46]** [*COL*]

Johnson, H. B. D.

5.0485	TR	1970	CROWN COLONY GOVERNMENT IN TRINIDAD, 1870-1897.

Johnson, Harry G.; Demas, William G.; Meier, Gerald M. & Balogh, T.

47.0145	BC	1960	Symposium on the Report of the Trade and Tariffs Commission.

Jones, Chester Lloyd

2.0242	GC	1931	CARIBBEAN BACKGROUNDS AND PROSPECTS.
5.0488	GC	1970	THE CARIBBEAN SINCE 1900.

Jones, Edwin

37.0437 JM,TR,GU 1970 PRESSURE GROUP POLITICS IN THE WEST INDIES—A CASE STUDY OF COLONIAL SYSTEMS: JAMAICA, TRINIDAD AND BRITISH GUIANA. Ph.D. dissertation, University of Manchester: 267p. **[40]**

37.0438 JM 1970 The role of statutory boards in the political process in Jamaica. *Social Econ Stud* 19(1), March: 114-134. [*RIS*]

37.0439 JM 1974 Administrative institution-building in Jamaica—an interpretation. *Social Econ Stud* 23(2), June: 264-291. [*RIS*]

37.0440 BC 1974 Some notes on decision-making and change in Caribbean administrative systems. *Social Econ Stud* 23(2), June: 292-310. [*RIS*]

37.0441 BC 1975 Tendencies and change in Caribbean administrative systems. *Social Econ Stud* 24(2), June: 239-256. **[40]** [*RIS*]

37.0442 BC 1976 Bureaucracy as a problem-solving mechanism in small states: a review in terms of the current literature. *In* Lewis, Vaughan A., ed. SIZE, SELF-DETERMINATION AND INTERNATIONAL RELATIONS: THE CARIBBEAN. Mona, Jamaica, University of the West Indies, Institute of Social and Economic Research: 73-97. [*RIS*]

Jones, Edwin & Mills, G. E.

40.0036 BC 1975 Cambio e inovación institucional en los paises de habla inglesa del Caribe [Institutional innovation and change in the English-speaking Caribbean].

Jones, Grant D.

13.0104 BZ 1971 La estructura política de los Mayas de Chan Santa Cruz: el papel del respaldo inglés [Political structure of the Mayas of Chan Santa Cruz: the role of British support].

Jonkers, E. H.

37.0443 SR 1965 Tien jaar Statuut 1954-1964. Enkele facetten van de economische ontwikkeling van Suriname [Ten years of Statute 1954-1964. Some aspects of the economic development of Surinam]. *N W I G* 44(1-2), April: 16-49. **[41]** [*RIS*]

Joseph, Cedric L.

5.0495 BC 1973 The strategic importance of the British West Indies, 1882-1932.

Joseph, Franz M. & Koppel, Richard U.

41.0272 CU 1961 Curacao organizations.

Joshua, M. S.

37.0444 WW 1966 Government and politics of the Windward Islands. *In* Mathews, T. G.; Latortue, G.; Joshua, M. S.; Andic, F. M.; Andic, S. & Thorne, A. P., eds. POLITICS AND ECONOMICS IN THE CARIBBEAN: A CONTEMPORARY ANALYSIS OF DUTCH, FRENCH AND BRITISH CARIBBEAN. Rio Piedras, University of Puerto Rico, Institute of Caribbean Studies: 196-258. (Special Study No. 3) [*RIS*]

Josse, Victor C.

37.0445 KNA 1967 THE ANATOMY OF THE CONSTITUTION: EIGHT BROADCAST TALKS ON THE MAIN FEATURES OF THE ST. KITTS-NEVIS-ANGUILLA CONSTITUTION. St. Kitts, University of the West Indies, Department of Extra-Mural Studies: 59p. [*RIS*]

Judah, George Fortunatus

15.0046　JM　1909　The Jews' tribute in Jamaica.

Junker, L.

14.0028　SR　1932-33 Het einde van een dynastie—de dood van Jankosoe [The end of a dynasty—the death of Jankosoe].

14.0029　SR　1932-33 Een Staat in den Staat [A State within the State].

37.0446　SR　1947　De benoeming van een grootopperhoofd der Boschnegers [The appointment of a headman of the Bush Negroes]. *W I G* 28: 107-118. **[14]**　　　　　　　　　　　　　　　　　　　[*COL*]

Kalff, S.

37.0447　NC　1927-28 Vreemdelingen in het Westindische leger [Foreigners in the West Indian army]. *W I G* 9: 161-179. **[5,16]**　　　　[*COL*]

37.0448　CU　1931-32 Curacaosche troebelen [Troubles of Curacao]. *W I G* 13: 80-94. **[5]**　　　　　　　　　　　　　　　　　　　　[*COL*]

Kasteel, Annemarie C. T.

37.0449　NA　1956　DE STAATKUNDIGE ONTWIKKELING DER NEDERLANDSE ANTILLEN [THE POLITICAL EVOLUTION OF THE NETHERLANDS ANTILLES]. The Hague, W. van Hoeve, 351p. (Ph.D. dissertation, Rijksuniversiteit te Leiden.) **[5]**　　　　　　　　　　　　　　　　[*COL*]

Kasteleyn, J. S. C. & Kluvers, B. J.

41.0275　SR　1919-20 Resumé van het rapport (1919) der studie-commissie van het Surinaamse studie-syndicaat [Résumé of the report (1919) of the study committee of the Surinam study syndicate].

Katznelson, Ira

18.0164　JM,UK　1970　The politics of racial buffering in Nottingham, 1954-1968.

18.0165　BC,UK　1973　BLACK MEN, WHITE CITIES: RACE, POLITICS, AND MIGRATION IN THE UNITED STATES, 1900-30, AND BRITAIN, 1948-68.

Kaufmann, William W.

5.0501　GC　1967　BRITISH POLICY AND THE INDEPENDENCE OF LATIN AMERICA, 1804-1828.

Kelly, James B.

37.0450　JM　1963　The Jamaican independence constitution of 1962. *Car Stud* 3(1), Apr.: 18-83.　　　　　　　　　　　　　　　　　　[*RIS*]

Kelsick, Cecil A.

37.0451　LW　1960　Constitutional history of the Leewards. *Car Q* 6(2-3), May: 177-209. **[5]**　　　　　　　　　　　　　　　　　　[*RIS*]

Kensmil, Harry

37.0452　SR　1970　Hoe de Surinamer politiek bewust werd [How the Surinamese developed political consciousness]. *Gids* 133(9): 328-332.　　[*COL*]

Kesler, C. K.

37.0453　SR　1930-31 Déporté's in Suriname tijdens het bewind van den Gouverneur Friderici [Deportees in Surinam during the rule of Governor Friderici]. *W I G* 12: 558-572.　　　　　　　　　　　　[*COL*]

King, Winston M.
41.0279   **GU**   1967   GUYANA'S CABINET SUB-COMMITTEE ON ECONOMIC MATTERS.

Kitzinger, Sheila
23.0162   **JM**   1969   Protest and mysticism: the Rastafari cult of Jamaica.

Klerk, Cornelis Johannes Maria de
46.0133   **SR**   1953   DE IMMIGRATIE DER HINDOESTANEN IN SURINAME [THE IMMIGRATION OF HINDUS TO SURINAM].

Knappert, L.
23.0169   **SM**   1928-29 Een heksenproces op Sint Maarten [A witch trial on St. Maarten].

Knight, Rudolph H.
37.0454   **BC**   1960   La planificación y la política en el Caribe Británico [Economic planning and politics in the British West Indies]. *Revta Cienc Social* 4(1), Mar.: 193-213. **[41]**

Knowles, Yereth
11.0054   **GU**   1972   Guyana: Black power?

Knox, A. D.
45.0086   **JM**   1956   Note on pioneer industry legislation.

Knox, Graham
37.0455   **JM**   1963   British colonial policy and the problems of establishing a free society in Jamaica, 1838-1865. *Car Stud* 2(4), Jan.: 3-13. **[5,8,16]**
                                                                                                                          [*RIS*]
37.0456   **JM**   1965   Political change in Jamaica (1866-1906) and the local reaction to the policies of the Crown Colony Government. *In* Andic, F. M. & Mathews, T. G., eds. THE CARIBBEAN IN TRANSITION: PAPERS ON SOCIAL, POLITICAL AND ECONOMIC DEVELOPMENT. Second Caribbean Scholars' Conference, Mona, Jamaica, April 14-19, 1964. Rio Piedras, University of Puerto Rico, Institute of Caribbean Studies: 141-162. **[5]**   [*RIS*]

Kol, H. van
37.0457   **SR**   1919   De Koloniale Staten [The Colonial Council]. *W I G* 1(1): 5-23.
                                                                                                                          [*COL*]

Koopmans, K.
5.0532   **SR**   1967   Historische ontwikkeling van de krijgsmacht in Suriname [Historical development of the military force in Surinam].

Kopytoff, Barbara Klamon
37.0458   **JM**   1976   Jamaican maroon political organization: the effects of the treaties. *Social Econ Stud* 25(2), June: 87-105. **[6,14]**   [*RIS*]

Kovrov, Iu.
41.0291   **GU**   1954   Proizvol angliiskikh kolonizatorov v Britanskoi Gviane [The tyranny of English colonialists in British Guiana].

Krarup-Nielson, A.

37.0459   FG   1935   HELL BEYOND THE SEAS. London, John Lane, 259p.   [*NYP*]

Kroll, Morton

37.0460   TR   1967   Political leadership and administrative communications in new nation states: the case study of Trinidad and Tobago. *Social Econ Stud* 16(1), March: 17-33. **[21]**   [*RIS*]

Kross, R. F.

37.0461   SR   1972   REBEL OP DE VALREEP: EEN ANALYSE NA DE PERSCONFERENTIE VAN DE HEER J. LACHMON [LAST MOMENT REBEL: AN ANALYSIS AFTER THE PRESS CONFERENCE OF MR. J. LACHMON]. Paramaribo, Suriname, Biswakon & Biswakon: 35p.   [*RILA*]

Kruijer, G. J.

40.0041   SR   1974   Neokolonie in rijksverband 2: twee ontwikkelingsstrategieën voor Suriname [Neo-colony in context of the Kingdom 2: Two development strategies for Surinam].

Kuper, Adam

2.0257   JM   1976   CHANGING JAMAICA.

Kwayana, Eusi

37.0462   GU   1974   Burnhamism and Jaganism: the politics of the old order. *Race Today* 6(3), March: 86-88. **[16]**   [*RIS*]

Lacey, Terence John

37.0463   JM   1975   THE MAINTENANCE OF INTERNAL SECURITY IN A DEVELOPING COUNTRY. A CASE STUDY OF JAMAICA, 1960-1970, IN THE CONTEXT OF THE REGIONAL SECURITY ARRANGEMENTS. Ph.D. dissertation, University of Manchester: 655p.

Lafond, Georges

37.0464   GU   1954   La Guyane et Monroe [(French) Guiana and Monroe]. *Hommes Mondes* 9, Feb.: 377-388.   [*COL*]

LaGrosillière, J.

37.0465   MT   1903   LA QUESTION DE LA MARTINIQUE [THE QUESTION OF MARTINIQUE]. Paris, Editions du Mouvement socialiste.

La Guerre, John Gaffar

37.0466   TR   1972   The general elections of 1946 in Trinidad and Tobago. *Social Econ Stud* 21(2), June: 184-204.   [*RIS*]

12.0050   TR   1974   The East Indian middle class today.

16.0057   TR   1976   Afro-Indian relations in Trinidad and Tobago: an assessment.

Laing, Malcolm B.

37.0467   GU   1950[?]   Local government in British Guiana. *Car Q* 1(4): 35-37.

Lampe, W. F. M.

5.0534   NA   1968   IN DE SCHADUW VAN DE GOUVERNEURS: MÉMOIRES [IN THE SHADOW OF THE GOVERNORS: MEMOIRS].

Landis, Joseph B.

16.0058	GU	1973	RACE RELATIONS AND POLITICS IN GUYANA.
37.0468	GU	1974	Racial polarization and political conflict in Guyana. *In* Bell, Wendell & Freeman, Walter E., eds. ETHNICITY AND NATION-BUILDING: COMPARATIVE, INTERNATIONAL AND HISTORICAL PERSPECTIVES. Beverly Hills, California, Sage Publications: 255-267. [8,16] [COL]

Lange, H. M. de

37.0469   CU   1969   Curaçao (al weer) vergeten [Curaçao (already) forgotten]. *Wending* 24(5-6), July-Aug.: 316-320.   [COL]

Langton, Kenneth P.

9.0090   JM   1965   THE POLITICAL SOCIALIZATION PROCESS—THE CASE OF SECONDARY SCHOOL STUDENTS IN JAMAICA.

37.0470   JM   1966   Political partisanship and political socialization in Jamaica. *Br J Sociol* 17(4), Dec.: 419-429. [20]   [COL]

Langton, Kenneth P. & Karns, David

8.0126   JM   1969   The relative influence of the family, peer group, and school in the development of political efficacy.

Lashley, L. A. G. O.

37.0471   SR   1954-55   Het Koninkrijk is dood, leve het Koninkrijk [The Kingdom is dead, long live the Kingdom]. *Vox Guy* 1(4-5), Nov.-Jan.: 12-16. [5]

Lasserre, Guy & Mabileau, Albert

37.0472   FA   1972   The French Antilles and their status as Overseas Departments. *In* Kadt, Emanuel de, ed. PATTERNS OF FOREIGN INFLUENCE IN THE CARIBBEAN. London, Oxford University Press: 82-102. [2,39]
                                                                          [RIS]

Latortue, Gérard

37.0473   FC   1966   Political status of the French Caribbean. *In* Mathews, T. G.; Latortue, G.; Joshua, M. S.; Andic, F. M.; Andic, S. & Thorne, A. P. POLITICS AND ECONOMICS OF THE CARIBBEAN: A CONTEMPORARY ANALYSIS OF THE DUTCH, FRENCH AND BRITISH CARIBBEAN. Rio Piedras, University of Puerto Rico, Institute of Caribbean Studies: 148-183. (Special Study No. 3)   [RIS]

40.0046   FC,NA   1971   The European lands.

37.0474   FC   1971   Political status of the French Caribbean. *In* Mathews, T. G. & Andic, F. M., eds. POLITICS AND ECONOMICS IN THE CARIBBEAN. Rio Piedras, University of Puerto Rico, Institute of Caribbean Studies: 169-189. (Special Study No. 8)   [RIS]

Laurence, K. O., ed.

37.0475   TR   1969   "The Trinidad Water Riot of 1903: reflections of an eyewitness" (based principally on the Report of the Commission of Enquiry which followed the riot). *Car Q* 15(4), Dec.: 5-22. [5]   [RIS]

Lavigne, Pierre

46.0142   FC   1953   La législation industrielle dans les départements francais de la Caraïbe [Industrial legislation in the French territories of the Caribbean].

Lawrence, B. C.

37.0476   JM   1968   Prolegomena to reform of Jamaican local government. *Car Q* 14(4), Dec.: 37-47.   [*RIS*]

Layne, Frederick et al.

33.0112   BB   1964   A PLAN FOR THE IMPLEMENTATION AND ADMINISTRATION OF THE PROPOSED SOCIAL SECURITY SCHEME FOR BARBADOS.

Leborgne, Yvon

21.0049   FA   1962   Le climat social [The social environment].

Ledlie, J. C.

37.0477   GU   1917   Roman-Dutch law in British Guiana and a West Indian court of appeal. *J Soc Comp Leg* 17, Nov.: 210-222.

Lee, J. M.

37.0478   BC   1967   COLONIAL DEVELOPMENT AND GOOD GOVERNMENT: A STUDY OF IDEAS EXPRESSED BY THE BRITISH OFFICIAL CLASSES IN PLANNING DECOLONIZATION, 1939-1964. Oxford, Clarendon Press: 311p.   **[5]**
                                                                                    [*RIS*]

Lee, Ulric

33.0114   TR   1959   REPORT TO THE HONOURABLE THE PREMIER BY THE HONOURABLE ULRIC LEE ON THE REORGANISATION OF THE PUBLIC SERVICE.

Leeuwen, W. C. J. van

37.0479   NA   1972   DE NEDERLANDSE ANTILLEN TUSSEN NEDERLAND EN VENEZUELA: POSITION-PAPER [THE NETHERLANDS ANTILLES BETWEEN THE NETHERLANDS AND VENEZUELA: POSITION-PAPER]. Willemstad, Staten van de Nederlandse Antillen, Parlementaire Staatkundige Commissie: 58p.   **[39]**   [*RILA*]

Lemaire, W. C.

5.0542   NA   1967   De Koninklijke Marine in de Nederlandse Antillen [The Royal Navy in the Netherlands Antilles].

37.0480   NA   1967   De marine man in de Nederlandse Antillen [The sailor in the Netherlands Antilles]. *Schakels* S65/NA49: 43-49.   [*NYP*]

Lestrade, Swinburne & Gonsalves, Ralph

38.0121   LW,WW   1972   Political aspects of integration of the Windward and Leeward Islands.

Le Veness, Frank Paul

37.0481   BC   1973   Development politics in the Commonwealth Caribbean. Paper prepared for the 1973 Annual Meeting of the American Political Science Association, New Orleans, Sept. 4-8: 35p.   [*RIS*]

37.0482   BA   1974   Development politics in the Commonwealth Caribbean: a case study of the Commonwealth of the Bahamas. Prepared for the Southwestern Political Science Association, Dallas, Texas: 28p.
                                                                                    [*RIS*]

Lewis, A. M.

37.0483   KNA   1967   CRITICISMS OF THE ADMINISTRATION OF JUSTICE IN ST. CHRISTOPHER-NEVIS-ANGUILLA. Farquharson Institute of Public Affairs: 5p.
                                                                                    [*RIS*]

Lewis, Gordon K.

37.0484	GC	1961	The Caribbean: colonization and culture. *Stud Left* 1(4): 26-42. **[5,6,16,19]** [*RIS*]
37.0485	TR	1962	The Trinidad and Tobago general election of 1961. *Car Stud* 2(2), July: 2-30. [*RIS*]
2.0282	BC	1967	The social legacy of British colonialism in the Caribbean.
37.0486	BC	1968	THE GROWTH OF THE MODERN WEST INDIES. New York, Monthly Review Press: 506p. **[5,41]** [*RIS*]
37.0487	GC	1971	The politics of the Caribbean. *In* Szulc, Tad, ed. THE UNITED STATES AND THE CARIBBEAN. Englewood Cliffs, N.J., Prentice-Hall, Inc.: 5-35. [*RIS*]

Lewis, Patrick Albert

37.0488	BC	1974	A HISTORICAL ANALYSIS OF THE DEVELOPMENT OF THE UNION-PARTY SYSTEM IN THE COMMONWEALTH CARIBBEAN, 1935-1968. Ph.D. dissertation, University of Cincinnati: 319p. [*PhD*]

Lewis, Sybil & Mathews, Thomas G., eds.

2.0285	GC	1967	CARIBBEAN INTEGRATION: PAPERS ON SOCIAL, POLITICAL, AND ECONOMIC INTEGRATION. THIRD CARIBBEAN SCHOLARS' CONFERENCE, GEORGETOWN, GUYANA, APRIL 4-9, 1966.

Lewis, Vaughan A.

39.0101	BC	1976	The Commonwealth Caribbean and self-determination in the international system.
37.0489	JM	1976	Review article: electoral behaviour in Jamaica. *Social Econ Stud* 25(2), June: 176-181. **[40]** [*RIS*]

Lewis, Vaughan A., ed.

40.0050	BC	1976	SIZE, SELF-DETERMINATION AND INTERNATIONAL RELATIONS: THE CARIBBEAN.

Lewis, W. Arthur

38.0133	BC	1965	THE AGONY OF THE EIGHT.

Lichtveld, Lou

2.0286	SR	1953	SURINAME'S NATIONALE ASPIRATIES (EEN AANLEIDING TOT DISCUSSIES OVER DE GRONDSLAGEN VAN EEN AL-OMVATTEND ONTWIKKELINGSPLAN) [SURINAM'S NATIONAL ASPIRATIONS (LEADING TO DISCUSSION OF THE PRINCIPLES OF A GENERAL PLAN OF DEVELOPMENT)].

Lier, Rudolf A. J. van

8.0135	GC	1951	The problem of the political and social elite in the West Indies and the Guyanas.
8.0136	NC	1955	Social and political conditions in Suriname and the Netherlands Antilles: Introduction.

Limburg Stirum, O. E. G. Graaf van

50.0095	SR	1923-24	De Surinamsche mijnwetgeving [The mining laws of Surinam].
37.0490	SR,FG	1923-24	Suriname en de Fransche strafkolonies [Surinam and the French penal colonies]. *W I G* 5: 95-109. **[33]** [*COL*]
37.0491	SR,FG	1924-25	De opheffing der strafkolonie: Fransch Guyana en haar mogelijke gevolgen voor Suriname [The abolition of the penal colony in French Guiana and its possible results for Surinam]. *W I G* 6: 371-376. **[33]** [*COL*]

37.0492	SR,FG	1925-26	De strafkolonies in Fransch Guyana [The penal colonies of French Guiana]. *W I G* 7: 49-80, 97-120. **[33]** [COL]
37.0493	SR	1925-26	De wet op de staatsinrichting van Suriname [The law about the form of government of Surinam]. *W I G* 7: 449-480. [COL]
37.0494	SR	1926-27	Voorwaardelijke veroordeeling [The probation system]. *W I G* 8: 370-374. **[32,33]** [COL]

Lindsay, Louis

| 37.0495 | JM | 1976 | Colonialism and the myth of resource insufficiency in Jamaica. *In* Lewis, Vaughan A., ed. SIZE, SELF-DETERMINATION AND INTERNATIONAL RELATIONS: THE CARIBBEAN. Mona, Jamaica, University of the West Indies, Institute of Social and Economic Research: 45-72. **[41,42]** [RIS] |

Linton, Neville

| *38.0134* | BC | 1971 | Regional diplomacy of the Commonwealth Caribbean. |

Listowel, William Francis Hare, 5th Earl of; Farley, Rawle; Hinden, Rita & Hughes, Colin

| 37.0496 | BC | 1952 | CHALLENGE TO THE BRITISH CARIBBEAN. London, Fabian Publications, 37p. (Research series no. 150.) **[38]** |

Liverpool, N. J. O.

| 37.0497 | BC | 1965 | THE DEVELOPMENT OF THE LAW OF SUCCESSION IN THE WEST INDIES. Ph.D. dissertation, University of Sheffield: 224p. **[33]** |

Lochhead, A. V. S.

| *33.0120* | TR | 1956[?] | REPORT ON ADMINISTRATION OF THE SOCIAL SERVICES IN TRINIDAD AND TOBAGO: WITH PARTICULAR REFERENCE TO CO-ORDINATION. |

Logemann, J. H. A.

| 37.0498 | NC | 1955 | The constitutional status of the Netherlands Caribbean territories. *In* DEVELOPMENTS TOWARDS SELF-GOVERNMENT IN THE CARIBBEAN. A symposium held under the auspices of the Netherlands Universities Foundation for International Co-operation at The Hague, Sept., 1954. The Hague, W. van Hoeve, p.46-72. [RIS] |

Lohier, Michel

| *5.0561* | FG | 1969 | LES GRANDES ÉTAPES DE L'HISTOIRE DE LA GUYANE FRANÇAISE (1498-1968) [GREAT STEPS IN THE HISTORY OF FRENCH GUIANA (1498-1968)]. |

Lopez, H. Th.

| 37.0499 | NA | 1967 | Is de eilandsontvanger bevoegd zelfstandig in rechten op te treden? [Does the island receiver have the authority to act on his own?] *Justicia* 3(3): 69-73. [COL] |

Lotan, Yael

| *21.0053* | JM | 1964 | Jamaica today. |

Lowenthal, David

| *2.0293* | FG | 1960 | French Guiana: myths and realities. |
| 37.0500 | BC | 1962 | Levels of West Indian Government. *In* Singham, A. & Braithwaite, L. E., eds. SPECIAL NUMBER [of *Social Econ Stud*] ON THE CONFERENCE ON POLITICAL SOCIOLOGY IN THE BRITISH CARIBBEAN, DEC. 1961. *Social Econ Stud* 1(4), Dec.: 363-391. **[20,21]** [RIS] |

Lowenthal, David & Comitas, Lambros, eds.

2.0294   GC   1973   THE AFTERMATH OF SOVEREIGNTY: WEST INDIAN PERSPECTIVES.

Lutchman, Harold A.

37.0501   GU   [n.d.]   THE 1891 CONSTITUTIONAL CHANGE AND REPRESENTATION IN THE FORMER BRITISH GUIANA. Guyana, Critchlow Labour College Political Science Series: 29p. **[5]**   [*RIS*]

37.0502   GU   1967   MIDDLE CLASS COLONIAL POLITICS: A STUDY OF GUYANA, WITH SPECIAL REFERENCE TO THE PERIOD 1920-1931. Ph.D. dissertation, University of Manchester: 474p. **[5,10]**

32.0366   GU   1970   Administrative change in an ex-colonial setting: a study of education administration in Guyana, 1961-64.

37.0503   GU   1970   The Co-Operative Republic of Guyana. *Car Stud* 10(3), Oct.: 97-115.   [*RIS*]

5.0571   GU   1970   Patronage in colonial society: a study of the former British Guiana.

37.0504   GU   1970   SOME ASPECTS OF: THE CROWN COLONY SYSTEM OF GOVERNMENT WITH SPECIAL REFERENCE TO GUYANA. Georgetown, Guyana, C.L.C. Political Science Series: 57p.   [*RIS*]

37.0505   GU   1972   CONSTITUTIONAL DEVELOPMENTS IN GUYANA DURING THE SECOND WORLD WAR. Georgetown, University of Guyana, Department of Political Science: 30p. (Occasional Papers No. 1)   [*RIS*]

37.0506   GU   1972   Guyana: a review of recent political developments. *In* Irving, Brian, ed. GUYANA: A COMPOSITE MONOGRAPH. Hato Rey, Puerto Rico, Inter American University Press: 13-31. **[16,38]**   [*RIS*]

37.0507   GU   1972   Race and bureaucracy in Guyana. *J Comp Adm* 4(2), August: 225-252. **[16]**   [*COL*]

37.0508   BC   1972   Some limitations in dealing with the problems of public administration in the Commonwealth Caribbean. *In* TRAINING OF PUBLIC SERVICE TRAINERS: REPORT ON A PILOT COURSE, ST. AUGUSTINE, TRINIDAD, AUG. 10-SEPT. 18, 1970. New York, United Nations: 68-72. **[32]**   [*UNL*]

37.0509   GU   1973   The office of Ombudsman in Guyana. *Car Stud* 13(1), April: 62-77. **[33]**   [*RIS*]

Macaulay, Thomas B.

47.0172   BC   1919   Canada and the West Indies—the case of commercial union.

McColgan, Kathleen

37.0510   JM   1955   Jamaica survey. *New Commonw*, British Caribbean Supplement, 30(9), Oct. 31: vii-ix.   [*AGS*]

McConney, E. J., comp.

17.0062   BB   1963   Prisoners of the '45 rising.

McCormack, Ed

37.0511   JM   1976   Bob Marley with a bullet. *Rolling Stone* Aug. 12: 37-41. **[8,11,22,23]**   [*RIS*]

McCowan, Anthony

37.0512   GU   1956   British Guiana. *In* RACE AND POWER: STUDIES OF LEADERSHIP IN FIVE BRITISH DEPENDENCIES. London, The Bow Group, p.17-36.   [*RIS*]

McCoy, H. M.

37.0513   CM   1963-64 The civil servant in the Cayman Islands. *Social Scient* 1: 6, 12.
                                                                                                      [*RIS*]

MacDermot, T. H.

37.0514   JM   1922   Jamaica, past and present. *Dalh Rev* 2(3), Oct.: 271-284.   **[5]**
                                                                                                      [*COL*]

37.0515   JM   1922   The political constitution of Jamaica. *United Emp* new ser., 13(10),
                         Oct.: 642-650.   **[5]**

McDonald, Frank

37.0516   TR   1969   DOCTOR POLITICS: ERIC WILLIAMS AND THE P.N.M. New York,
                         Institute of Current World Affairs: 23p.   [*RIS*]

37.0517   GU   1969   GUYANA; JAGAN ON THE LEFT, BURNHAM ON THE RIGHT. New York,
                         Institute of Current World Affairs: 27p.   **[16]**   [*RIS*]

37.0518   TR   1969   THE RACE FACTOR IN TRINIDAD POLITICS. New York, Institute of
                         Current World Affairs: 7p.   **[16]**   [*RIS*]

37.0519   TR   1969   THE RADICAL ALTERNATIVES. New York, Institute of Current World
                         Affairs: 20p.   **[47]**   [*RIS*]

41.0313   JM   1970   JAMAICA. PT. I: AN ECONOMIC OVERVIEW; PT. II: A POLITICAL
                         OVERVIEW; PT. III: THE CONFRONTATION TO COME.

37.0520   TR   1970   TRINIDAD: BLACK POWER AND NATIONAL RECONSTRUCTION. New
                         York, Institute of Current World Affairs: 26p.   **[11,16,21]**   [*RIS*]

37.0521   TR   1970   TRINIDAD: THE FEBRUARY REVOLUTION. New York, Institute of
                         Current World Affairs: 31p.   [*RIS*]

McDonald, Ian

37.0522   GU   1966   Some thoughts on socialism. *New Wld F* 1(34), Feb. 18: 12-20.
                                                                                                      [*RIS*]

McDonald, Vincent R., ed.

41.0315   GC   1972   THE CARIBBEAN ECONOMIES: PERSPECTIVES ON SOCIAL, POLITICAL
                         AND ECONOMIC CONDITIONS.

McFarlane, Dennis

37.0523   BC   1964   A comparative study of incentive legislation in the Leeward Islands,
                         Windward Islands, Barbados and Jamaica. *Social Econ Stud* 13(3),
                         Sept., suppl.: 63p.   **[45]**   [*RIS*]

MacInnes, C. M.

37.0524   BC   1955   Constitutional development of the British West Indies. *In* DEVEL-
                         OPMENTS TOWARD SELF-GOVERNMENT IN THE CARIBBEAN. A sym-
                         posium held under the auspices of the Netherlands Universities
                         Foundation for International Co-operation at The Hague, Sept.
                         1954. The Hague, W. van Hoeve, p.3-22.   **[5]** ·   [*RIS*]

McIntyre, W. D.

37.0525   BC   1967   COLONIES INTO COMMONWEALTH. New York, Walker and Com-
                         pany: 391p.   **[5,40]**   [*COL*]

Mack, Raymond W.

16.0063   BB   1967   Race, class, and power in Barbados.

Mackenzie, V. St. Clair, ed.

37.0526   GU   1923   LAWS OF BRITISH GUIANA (1803-1921) Rev. ed. London, Waterlow, 6v. **[5]**   [*NYP*]

McKitterick, T. E. M.

37.0527   GU   1962   The end of a colony. *Polit Q* 33(1), Jan.-Mar.: 30-40.   [*COL*]

McKitterick, Tom

37.0528   GU   1957   Common sense in British Guiana. *Venture* 9(7), Dec.: 8-9.   [*COL*]

37.0529   GU   1957   The political scene in British Guiana. *Venture* 8(11), Apr.: 6-7.
                                                                                          [*COL*]

37.0530   GU   1962   What next for British Guiana? *Venture* 14(4), Apr.: 7-8.   [*COL*]

Macmillan, W. M.

37.0531   BC   1960   THE ROAD TO SELF RULE: A STUDY IN COLONIAL EVOLUTION. New York, Frederick A. Praeger, 296p. **[5]**   [*COL*]

Macridis, Roy C.

40.0055   UV   1970   The evolution of the islands—some concluding remarks.

37.0532   UV   1970   Political attitudes in the Virgin Islands. *In* Bough, James A. & Macridis, Roy C., eds. VIRGIN ISLANDS, AMERICA'S CARIBBEAN OUTPOST: THE EVOLUTION OF SELF-GOVERNMENT. Wakefield, Massachusetts, The Walter F. Williams Publishing Company: 193-207. **[20]**   [*UNL*]

Makiesky, Susan R.

46.0151   AT   1969   POLITICS AND TRADE UNIONS: AN ANTIGUAN CASE-STUDY.

Malcolm, Harcourt

37.0533   BA   1921   A HISTORY OF THE BAHAMAS HOUSE OF ASSEMBLY. Nassau, Nassau Guardian: 83p. **[5]**   [*NYP*]

Malik, Yogendra K.

37.0534   TR   1970   THE DEMOCRATIC LABOUR PARTY OF TRINIDAD: AN ATTEMPT AT THE FORMATION OF A MASS PARTY IN A MULTI-ETHNIC SOCIETY. Ann Arbor, Michigan, University Microfilms: 431p. (Ph.D. dissertation, University of Florida, 1966) **[12]**   [*RIS*]

12.0059   TR   1971   EAST INDIANS IN TRINIDAD: A STUDY IN MINORITY POLITICS.

Manley, Michael

37.0535   JM   1970   Overcoming insularity in Jamaica. *For Aff* 49(1), Oct.: 100-110. **[39]**   [*COL*]

37.0536   JM   1974   THE POLITICS OF CHANGE: A JAMAICAN TESTAMENT. London, André Deutsch Ltd.: 223p.   [*RIS*]

46.0153   JM   1975   A VOICE AT THE WORKPLACE: REFLECTIONS ON COLONIALISM AND THE JAMAICAN WORKER.

Manley, Robert Henry

40.0056   GU   1975   DECOLONIZATION AND NATIONAL DEVELOPMENT IN GUYANA, 1966-1974: THE ROLE OF EXTERNAL ENVIRONMENTS.

Manville, Marcel

37.0537   FC   1962   Chronique de la répression [Chronicle of repression]. *Esprit* 30(305), Apr.: 551-555.   [*NYP*]

Marden, Luis

37.0538   BC   1942   Americans in the Caribbean. *Natn Geogr Mag* 81(6), June: 723-
                                758.   [3]   [*AGS*]

Mark, Francis X.

46.0155   GU   1965   Organized labour in British Guiana.

Marquand, Hilary

37.0539   GU   1956   A new step in British Guiana. *Venture* 8(2), June: 3.   [*COL*]

Mars, Perry

37.0540   GU   1975   The nature of political violence. *Social Econ Stud* 24(2), June:
                                221-238.   [*RIS*]

Marsden, E. J.

37.0541   TR   1945   Trinidad's war effort. *Can-W I Mag* 35(5), June: 29, 31, 33.   [*NYP*]

Marshall, A. H.

37.0542   GU   1955   REPORT ON LOCAL GOVERNMENT IN BRITISH GUIANA. Georgetown,
                                Argosy Co., 109p.

Marshall, Arthur Calder

37.0543   TR   1938   Trinidad wants to be American. *Liv Age* 355(4467), Dec.: 322-324.
                                                                                [*COL*]

Marshall, Woodville K.

5.0590   BB,WW   1971   The termination of the apprenticeship in Barbados and the Wind-
                                ward Islands: an essay in colonial administration and politics.

Marten, Neil

37.0544   AG   1969   THEIR'S NOT TO REASON WHY: A STUDY OF THE ANGUILLAN
                                OPERATION AS PRESENTED TO PARLIAMENT. Crawley, England, Con-
                                servative Political Centre, 22p.   [5]   [*RIS*]

Martin, Kingsley

23.0193   JM   1961   The Jamaican volcano.

Martin, Lawrence & Martin, Sylvia

37.0545   GC   1941   Outpost no. 2: the West Indies. *Harper's Mag* 182, Mar.: 359-368.
                                                                                [*COL*]

Martin, Tony

37.0546   TR   1973   Revolutionary upheaval in Trinidad, 1919: views from British and
                                American sources. *J Negro Hist* 58(3), July: 313-326.   [5,11]   [*COL*]
37.0547   BC   1975   Repression and resistance in West Indian history. *Pan-Afr J* 8(2),
                                Summer: 125-138.   [5]   [*RIS*]

Martineau, Alfred

37.0548   FA   1935   Il y à cent ans: les droits civils et politiques, le Conseil colonial [One
                                hundred years ago: civil and political rights, the colonial Council].
                                In Denis, Serge, ed. NOS ANTILLES. Orléans, Luzeray, 163-175.   [5]
                                                                                [*AGS*]

Mason, Philip

8.0152   GC   1970   The Caribbean.

Mathews, Thomas G.

37.0549   GC   1965   The Caribbean kaleidoscope. *Curr Hist* 48(281), Jan.: 32-39.   **[41]**
                                                                                                            [*COL*]

37.0550   NA   1966   Charter of the Kingdom of The Netherlands. *In* Mathews, T. G.;
                              Latortue, G.; Joshua, M. S.; Andic, F. M.; Andic, S. & Thorne,
                              A. P., eds. POLITICS AND ECONOMICS IN THE CARIBBEAN: A CON-
                              TEMPORARY ANALYSIS OF THE DUTCH, FRENCH AND BRITISH CAR-
                              IBBEAN. Rio Piedras, University of Puerto Rico, Institute of
                              Caribbean Studies: 70-82. (Special Study No. 3)   [*RIS*]

37.0551   BC   1966   Jamaica, Trinidad and the British West Indies. *In* Mathews, T. G.;
                              Latortue, G.; Joshua, M. S.: Andic, F. M.; Andic, S. & Thorne,
                              A. P., eds. POLITICS AND ECONOMICS IN THE CARIBBEAN: A CON-
                              TEMPORARY ANALYSIS OF THE DUTCH, FRENCH AND BRITISH CAR-
                              IBBEAN. Rio Piedras, University of Puerto Rico, Institute of
                              Caribbean Studies: 184-195. (Special Study No. 3)   [*RIS*]

37.0552   GC   1966   Overview: introductory summary. *In* Mathews, T. G.; Latortue, G.;
                              Joshua, M. S.; Andic, F. M.; Andic, S. & Thorne, A. P., eds.
                              POLITICS AND ECONOMICS IN THE CARIBBEAN: A CONTEMPORARY
                              ANALYSIS OF THE DUTCH, FRENCH AND BRITISH CARIBBEAN. Rio
                              Piedras, University of Puerto Rico, Institute of Caribbean Studies:
                              1-33. (Special Study No. 3)   **[41]**   [*RIS*]

37.0553   SR   1966   Political picture in Surinam. *In* Mathews, T. G.; Latortue, G.;
                              Joshua, M. S.; Andic, F. M.; Andic, S. & Thorne, A. P. POLITICS
                              AND ECONOMICS IN THE CARIBBEAN: A CONTEMPORARY ANALYSIS OF
                              THE DUTCH, FRENCH AND BRITISH CARIBBEAN. Rio Piedras, Uni-
                              versity of Puerto Rico, Institute of Caribbean Studies: 92-103.
                              (Special Study No. 3)   [*RIS*]

37.0554   NA   1966   Politics and government of the Netherlands Antilles. *In* Mathews,
                              T. G.; LaTortue, G.; Joshua, M. S.; Andic, F. M.; Andic, S. &
                              Thorne, A. P., eds. POLITICS AND ECONOMICS IN THE CARIBBEAN: A
                              CONTEMPORARY ANALYSIS OF THE DUTCH, FRENCH AND BRITISH
                              CARIBBEAN. Rio Piedras, University of Puerto Rico, Institute of
                              Caribbean Studies: 83-91. (Special Study No. 3)   [*RIS*]

37.0555   BC   1971   The Commonwealth countries of the Caribbean. *In* Mathews, T. G.
                              & Andic, F. M., eds. POLITICS AND ECONOMICS IN THE CARIBBEAN.
                              Rio Piedras, University of Puerto Rico, Institute of Caribbean
                              Studies: 245-251. (Special Study No. 8)   [*RIS*]

37.0556   GC   1971   Political overview. *In* Mathews, T. G. & Andic, F. M. POLITICS AND
                              ECONOMICS IN THE CARIBBEAN. Rio Piedras, University of Puerto
                              Rico, Institute of Caribbean Studies: 1-9. (Special Study No. 8)
                                                                                        [*RIS*]

37.0557   GC   1973   Whatever happened to polarization in the Caribbean. *Car R* 5(1),
                              Jan.-Feb.-March: 26-30.   [*RIS*]

Mathews, Thomas G. & Andic, Fuat M., eds.

37.0558   GC   1971   POLITICS AND ECONOMICS IN THE CARIBBEAN. Rio Piedras, Univer-
                              sity of Puerto Rico, Institute of Caribbean Studies: 284p. (Special
                              Study No. 8)   **[41]**   [*RIS*]

Mathews, Thomas G.; Latortue, Gérard; Joshua, M. S.; Andic, Fuat M.;
Andic, Suphan & Thorne, Alfred P.

37.0559   GC   1966   POLITICS AND ECONOMICS IN THE CARIBBEAN: A CONTEMPORARY
ANALYSIS OF THE DUTCH, FRENCH AND BRITISH CARIBBEAN. Rio
Piedras, University of Puerto Rico, Institute of Caribbean Studies:
301p. (Special Study No. 3) **[41]**   [*RIS*]

Matthews, Basil

37.0560   GC   1943   The West Indies: bridge and laboratory of inter-Americanism.
Commonweal 37(19), Feb. 26: 464-467.   [*COL*]

Matthews, Harry G.

39.0108   JM   1969   JAMAICA IN THE UNITED NATIONS, 1962-1966.

16.0069   BC   1971   RACIAL DIMENSIONS OF THE UNITED NATIONS BEHAVIOR: THE
COMMONWEALTH CARIBBEAN.

Mau, James A.

20.0051   JM   1965   The threatening masses: myth or reality?

37.0561   JM   1967   Images of Jamaica's future. *In* Bell, Wendell, ed. THE DEMOCRATIC
REVOLUTION IN THE WEST INDIES. Cambridge, Mass., Schenkman
Pub. Co., Inc.: 197-223. **[20,41]**   [*RIS*]

37.0562   JM   1968   SOCIAL CHANGE AND IMAGES OF THE FUTURE: A STUDY OF THE
PURSUIT OF PROGRESS IN JAMAICA. Cambridge, Mass., Schenkman
Publishing Co., Inc.: 145p. **[20]**   [*RIS*]

Maude, John

37.0563   BB   1949   REPORT ON LOCAL GOVERNMENT IN BARBADOS. [Bridgetown? Barbados, Govt. Printer] 52p. (Supplement to Official Gazette, Nov. 28,
1949.)   [*UNL*]

May, R. J.

38.0154   BC   1969   FEDERALISM AND FISCAL ADJUSTMENT.

Maynard, Fitz G. & Maynard, Olga Comma

37.0564   TR   [n.d.]   THE NEW ROAD: A SHORT STUDY IN CITIZENSHIP. [Port of Spain?]
Granderson Bros. Printer, 68p. **[32]**   [*RIS*]

Mazin, E.

37.0565   FA   1921   LES ANTILLES FRANCAISES: ÉTUDE JURIDIQUE ET ÉCONOMIQUE [THE
FRENCH ANTILLES: A JUDICIAL AND ECONOMIC STUDY]. Toulouse,
Impr. Languedocienne, 157p. (Ph.D. dissertation.) **[41]**   [*COL*]

Mbanefo, Louis; Moses, Macdonald & Marshall, Osley Roy

37.0566   TR   1965   REPORT OF THE COMMISSION OF ENQUIRY INTO SUBVERSIVE ACTIV-
ITIES IN TRINIDAD AND TOBAGO. [Port of Spain?] Govt. Printery,
70p. (Trinidad and Tobago, House paper no. 2 of 1965.) [*RIS*]

Meisler, Stanley

46.0159   GU,BZ   1964   Meddling in Latin America: dubious role of AFL-CIO.

Menéndez Valdés, Manuel

37.0567   FG   1930   FRENCH JUSTICE: SEVEN MONTHS UNDER SENTENCE OF DEATH.
London, Faber and Faber, 256p.   [*NYP*]

Menkman, W. R.

37.0568	NC	1929-30 Moederlandsche verantwoordelijkheid en Westindische autonomie [The responsibility of the mother country and West Indian autonomy]. *W I G* 11: 403-411. **[41]** [*COL*]
37.0569	CU	1930-31 Curacaosche toestanden [Curacao's conditions]. *W I G* 12: 53-72. **[31,41]** [*COL*]
37.0570	SR	1931-32 Nederland en Suriname, een nabertrachting [The Netherlands and Surinam, in retrospect]. *W I G* 13:569-575. **[41]** [*COL*]
37.0571	SR	1931-32 Nederland en Suriname [The Netherlands and Surinam]. *W I G* 13: 365-377. **[41]** [*COL*]
6.0198	CU	1935-36 Slavenhandel en rechtsbedeeling op Curacao op het einde der 17ᵉ eeuw [Slave trade and administration of justice on Curacao at the end of the 17th century].
5.0611	SR	1935-36 Suriname onder Engelsch bewind [Surinam under English rule].
5.0612	NA	1936-37 De Nederlanders in de Caraïbische wateren: een nabetrachting [The Dutch in the Caribbean seas: in retrospect].
43.0298	SR	1940 Landbouw-economische politiek in Suriname [Agricultural-economic policy in Surinam].
37.0572	SR,CU	1947 Federalisme en seperatisme in Westindië [Federalism and separatism in the West Indies]. *W I G* 28: 368-371. [*COL*]
37.0573	CU	1949 Curacao gedurende de oorlogsjaren [Curacao during the war years]. *W I G* 30: 105-115. [*COL*]

Metcalf, George

5.0622	JM	1965 Royal government and political conflict in Jamaica 1729-1783.

Michels, J.

37.0574	SR	1954-55 Suriname's binnenlands bestuur [Surinam's internal government]. *Vox Guy* 1(4-5), Nov.-Jan.: 73-78.

Midas, André

37.0575	BC	1957 Constitutional evolution. *Caribbean* 10(10), May: 236-240. **[38]** [*COL*]

Miles, G. E.

37.0576	BC,UK	1966 Education and training for the public service in the West Indies. *J Adm Overseas* 5(3), July: 155-166. [*COL*]

Miller, Jake C.

40.0058	UV,US	1974 The Virgin Islands and the United States: definition of a relationship.

Millette, James

5.0627	TR	1964 Constitutional development in Trinidad: 1783-1810.
5.0628	TR	1966 The Civil Commission of 1802: an account and an explanation of an issue in the early constitutional and political history of Trinidad.
37.0577	TR	1970 The genesis of Crown Colony government: Trinidad, 1783-1810. Trinidad, Moko Enterprises Ltd.: 295p. **[5]** [*RIS*]
16.0070	GC	1974 Race and class: factors in the history of protest movements since 1789.

Mills, G. E.

32.0401	BC	1966	Education and training for the Public Service in the West Indies.
37.0578	BC	1970	Public administration in the Commonwealth Caribbean: evolution, conflicts and challenges. *Social Econ Stud* 19(1), March: 5-25. [*RIS*]
37.0579	BC	1973	The environment of Commonwealth Caribbean bureaucracies. *Int Rev Adm Sci* 39(1): 14-24. [*COL*]
45.0106	BC	1974	Public policy and private enterprise in the Commonwealth Caribbean.

Mills, G. E., ed.

32.0402	BC	1966	REPORT OF A CONFERENCE ON TRAINING OF PUBLIC OFFICERS HELD IN BARBADOS, FEB. 12-13, 1965.
37.0580	BC	1970	Problems of administrative change in the Commonwealth Caribbean. *Social Econ Stud* 19(1), March (Special Number): 146p. **[38,40]** [*RIS*]
37.0581	BC	1974	Issues of public policy and public administration in the Commonwealth Caribbean. *Social Econ Stud* 23(2), June (Special Number): 145-360. **[41,45,48]** [*RIS*]

Mills, G. E. & Robertson, Paul D.

37.0582	JM	1974	The attitudes and behaviour of the senior civil service in Jamaica. *Social Econ Stud* 23(2), June: 311-343. **[20]** [*RIS*]

Mintz, Sidney W.

37.0583	GC	1967	Caribbean nationhood in anthropological perspective. *In* Lewis, Sybil & Mathews, Thomas G., eds. CARIBBEAN INTEGRATION: PAPERS ON SOCIAL, POLITICAL, AND ECONOMIC INTEGRATION. Third Caribbean Scholars' Conference, Georgetown, Guyana, April 4-9, 1966. Rio Piedras, University of Puerto Rico, Institute of Caribbean Studies: 141-154. **[21]** [*RIS*]

Miranda, J. C. de, Jr.

37.0584	SR	1969	Het handelsrecht [Maritime law]. *In* Carpentier Alting, Z. H., et al., eds. EEN EEUW SURINAAMSE CODIFICATIE: GEDENKBOEK (1869-1 MEI-1969). Paramaribo, Surinaamse Juristen-Vereniging: 179-183. **[5,47]** [*RILA*]

Mitchell, Harold

37.0585	GC	1963	EUROPE IN THE CARIBBEAN: THE POLITICS OF GREAT BRITAIN, FRANCE AND THE NETHERLANDS TOWARDS THEIR WEST INDIAN TERRITORIES IN THE TWENTIETH CENTURY. Edinburgh, W. & R. Chambers, 211p. **[41]** [*RIS*]
37.0586	GC	1967	CARIBBEAN PATTERNS: A POLITICAL AND ECONOMIC STUDY OF THE CONTEMPORARY CARIBBEAN. London, W. and R. Chambers Ltd.: 520p. (Also published in Athens, Ohio, Ohio University Press, under the title: *Contemporary Politics and Economics in the Caribbean.* **[41]** [*RIS*]
37.0587	GC	1969	Conflict and cooperation in tomorrow's Caribbean. *Int J* 24(3), Summer: 559-570. **[47]** [*COL*]
38.0161	GC	1970	Islands of the Caribbean.

Mitrasing, F. E. M.

37.0588   SR   1959   TIEN JAAR SURINAME: VAN AFHANKELIJKHEID TOT GELIJK-
GERECHTIGDHEID [TEN YEARS SURINAM: FROM DEPENDENCY TO
EQUALITY]. Leiden, Drukkerij "Luctor et Emergo," 348p.   [*NYP*]

5.0629   SR   1965   Een blik terug: de prae-parlementaire vertegenwoordigingen bezien
in (staatsrechts-) historisch perspectief [Looking back: the pre-
parliament representatives through public law and historical per-
spectives].

37.0589   SR   1966   CONSTITUTIONELE REGELINGEN VAN SURINAME: VERZAMELING VAN
RECHTSREGELINGEN BETREFFENDE DE SURINAAMSE STAAT [CONSTI-
TUTIONAL REGULATIONS OF SURINAM: A COLLECTION OF STATUTES
CONCERNING THE SURINAMESE STATE]. The Hague, Staatsdrukkerij:
296p.   [*COL*]

5.0630   SR   1966   De geboorte van het Surinaams parlement [The birth of the
Surinamese parliament].

30.0177   SR,GU   1969   HET SURINAAMS-GUIANEES GRENSGESCHIL: EEN RECHTSKUNDIG RE-
SEARCH [THE BORDER CONFLICT SURINAM-GUYANA: LEGAL RE-
SEARCH].

Monte, E.

37.0590   NL   1955   ANTILLIAANS PROCESRECHT [LEGAL PROCEEDINGS IN THE ANTILLES].
Schiedam, Roelants, 196p.

Moore, Richard B.

37.0591   GC   1964   Caribbean unity and freedom. *Freedomways* 4(3), Summer: 295-
311. **[5]**   [*RIS*]

Mordecai, John

37.0592   BC   1966-67   Federation and after. *New Wld Q* 3(1-2), Dead Season and
Croptime, Barbados Independence Issue: 87-96. **[38]**   [*RIS*]

37.0593   BC   1968   THE WEST INDIES: THE FEDERAL NEGOTIATIONS. London, George
Allen and Unwin Ltd.: 484p. **[5]**   [*RIS*]

Morère, Pierre

5.0636   BC   1970   ASPECTS DE LA POLITIQUE COLONIALE ANGLAISE AUX ANTILLES
[ASPECTS OF ENGLISH COLONIAL POLITICS IN THE ANTILLES].

Morgan, D. J.

47.0201   BC   1962   Imperial preference in the West Indies and in the British Caribbean,
1929-55: a quantitative analysis.

Morrel, W. P.

5.0639   BC   1969   BRITISH COLONIAL POLICY IN THE MID-VICTORIAN AGE: SOUTH
AFRICA, NEW ZEALAND, THE WEST INDIES.

Morrell, Gladys C. de C.

37.0594   BE   1957   History of the I.O.D.E. in Bermuda. *Bermuda Hist Q* 14(2),
Summer: 64-70.   [*COL*]

Moskos, Charles C., Jr.

37.0595   BC   1963   THE SOCIOLOGY OF POLITICAL INDEPENDENCE: A STUDY OF INFLU-
ENCE, SOCIAL STRUCTURE AND IDEOLOGY IN THE BRITISH WEST
INDIES. Ph.D. dissertation, University of California, Los Angeles,
244p. **[9,20,21,40]**

| 37.0596 | BC | 1967 | Attitudes toward political independence. *In* Bell, Wendell, ed. THE DEMOCRATIC REVOLUTION IN THE WEST INDIES. Cambridge, Mass., Schenkman Pub. Co., Inc.: 49-67. **[20,21]** [*RIS*] |
| *21.0067* | JM | 1967 | THE SOCIOLOGY OF POLITICAL INDEPENDENCE: A STUDY OF NATIONALIST ATTITUDES AMONG WEST INDIAN LEADERS. |

Moskos, Charles C., Jr. & Bell, Wendell

37.0597	BC	1964	Attitudes towards democracy among leaders in four emergent nations. *Br J Sociol* 15(4), Dec.: 317-337. **[8,20]** [*RIS*]
21.0068	BC	1964	West Indian nationalism.
37.0598	BC	1965	Attitudes toward democracy among leaders in four emergent nations. *Stud Comp Int Dev* 1(14): 217-228. **[20]** [*COL*]
8.0166	GU,TR	1965	Cultural unity and diversity in new states.
8.0167	BC	1965	Some implications of equality for political, economic, and social development.
37.0599	BC	1967	Attitudes toward democracy. *In* Bell, Wendell, ed. THE DEMOCRATIC REVOLUTION IN THE WEST INDIES. Cambridge, Mass., Schenkman Pub. Co., Inc.: 68-85. **[20]** [*RIS*]
37.0600	BC	1967	Attitudes toward equality. *In* Bell, Wendell, ed. THE DEMOCRATIC REVOLUTION IN THE WEST INDIES. Cambridge, Mass., Schenkman Pub. Co., Inc.: 100-114. **[8,20]** [*RIS*]
37.0601	BC	1967	Attitudes toward global alignments. *In* Bell, Wendell, ed. THE DEMOCRATIC REVOLUTION IN THE WEST INDIES. Cambridge, Mass., Schenkman Pub. Co., Inc.: 86-99. **[20]** [*RIS*]
20.0060	BC	1967	Political attitudes in new nations: examples from the British Caribbean.
20.0061	BC	1968	Ideological foundations of development in the West Indies.

Moss, Robert

| 37.0602 | GC | 1973 | The stability of the Caribbean: report of the proceedings of the conference. *In* Moss, Robert, ed. THE STABILITY OF THE CARIBBEAN: REPORT OF A SEMINAR HELD AT DITCHLEY PARK, OXFORDSHIRE, U.K., MAY 18-20, 1973. Washington, D.C., Georgetown University, Center for Strategic and International Studies: 9-27. **[39,40]** [*RIS*] |

Moss, Robert, ed.

| 37.0603 | GC | 1973 | THE STABILITY OF THE CARIBBEAN: REPORT OF A SEMINAR HELD AT DITCHLEY PARK, OXFORDSHIRE, U.K., MAY 18-20, 1973. Washington, D.C., Georgetown University, Center for Strategic and International Studies: 137p. **[39,40]** [*RIS*] |

Mullings, F. A. R.

| 37.0604 | JM | 1969 | Adminstrative aspects of planning in Jamaica. *In* ADMINISTRATIVE ASPECTS OF PLANNING: PAPERS OF A SEMINAR. New York, United Nations: 274-283. **[41]** [*UNL*] |

Mullings, Llewellyn Maximillian

| *41.0358* | JM | 1964 | AN ANALYSIS OF THE ECONOMIC IMPLICATIONS OF POLITICAL INDEPENDENCE FOR JAMAICA. |

Mulzac, Una G.

| 37.0605 | GU | 1963 | The general strike in British Guiana. *New Wld Rev* 31(11), Dec.: 32-36. [*COL*] |

Munroe, Trevor

37.0606	JM	[n.d.]	The PNP 1938-1944: a view of the early nationalists movement in Jamaica. *In* Singham, A. W. et al., comps. READINGS IN GOVERNMENT AND POLITICS OF THE WEST INDIES. Kingston, Jamaica, Instant Letter Service Co., Ltd.: 221-227. [*RIS*]
37.0607	JM	1969	POLITICAL CHANGE AND CONSTITUTIONAL DEVELOPMENT IN JAMAICA, 1944-62. D.Phil. dissertation, University of Oxford: 337p.
40.0059	BC	1971	DEVELOPED IDEALISM AND EARLY MATERIALISM: 'LEFT' CARIBBEAN THOUGHT IN TRANSITION.
41.0359	JM	1971	JAMAICAN POLITICAL ECONOMY 1962-1970: SURVEY AND PROSPECTS.
37.0608	JM	1972	THE POLITICS OF CONSTITUTIONAL DECOLONIZATION: JAMAICA, 1944-1962. Jamaica, University of the West Indies, Institute of Social and Economic Research: 239p. **[40]** [*RIS*]
37.0609	JM	1974	The Bustamante letters 1935. *Jam J* 8(1), March: 3-15. **[5]** [*RIS*]

Munroe, Trevor & Lewis, Rupert, eds.

37.0610	GC	1971	READINGS IN GOVERNMENT AND POLITICS OF THE WEST INDIES. Mona, Jamaica, University of the West Indies: 270p. [*RIS*]

Murch, Arvin

37.0611	FA	1968	Political integration as an alternative to independence in the French Antilles. *Am Sociol Rev* 33(4), Aug.: 544-562. **[40]** [*COL*]
37.0612	FC	1971	BLACK FRENCHMEN: THE POLITICAL INTEGRATION OF THE FRENCH ANTILLES. Cambridge, Massachusetts, Schenkman Publishing Co., Inc.: 156p. **[40]** [*RIS*]
40.0060	FA	1972	POLITICAL INTEGRATION AS AN ALTERNATIVE TO INDEPENDENCE IN THE FRENCH ANTILLES.

Murray, D. J.

37.0613	BC	1965	THE WEST INDIES AND THE DEVELOPMENT OF COLONIAL GOVERNMENT. Oxford, Clarendon Press, 264p. **[5]**

Murray, Gideon

37.0614	BC	1919	Canada and the British West Indies. *United Emp* 10(2), Feb.: 54-58. **[38,39]** [*AGS*]

Murray, R. N.

5.0640	JM	1960	The road back—Jamaica after 1866.

Murray, Winston Churchill

5.0641	BC	1970	LABOR, POLITICS AND SOCIAL LEGISLATION IN THE BRITISH WEST INDIES 1834-1970.

Nadir, Henri Rousseau

41.0362	FA	1956	Les Antilles existent [The Antilles do exist].

Naipaul, V. S.

3.0434	AG,SK	1969	Anguilla: the shipwrecked 6000.
3.0435	AG,SK	1969	St. Kitts: Papa and the power set.
3.0436	BC	1970	Power to the Caribbean people.

Nardin, J.-C.

5.0645	TB	1969	LA MISE EN VALEUR DE L'ÎLE DE TABAGO (1763-1783) [THE DEVELOPMENT OF THE ISLAND OF TOBAGO (1763-1783)].

Nettleford, Rex

37.0615 JM,GU,BZ 1962 Political education in the developing Caribbean. *Car Q* 7(4), Apr.: 203-212. **[32]** *[RIS]*

37.0616 JM 1971 Manley and the politics of Jamaica—towards an analysis of political change in Jamaica 1938-1968. *Social Econ Stud* 20(3), Sept.: suppl.: 1-72. **[5]** *[RIS]*

Nettleford, Rex, ed.

37.0617 JM 1971 NORMAN WASHINGTON MANLEY AND THE NEW JAMAICA: SELECTED SPEECHES AND WRITINGS, 1938-1968. London, Trinidad and Jamaica, Longman Caribbean: 393p. **[5]** *[RIS]*

Newman, Peter Kenneth

16.0074 GU 1962 Racial tension in British Guiana.

Ney, Robert Morse

37.0618 BZ,GU,JM 1938 THE COLONIAL VALUE OF BRITISH HONDURAS, BRITISH GUIANA AND JAMAICA. M.A. thesis, Clark University, 128p. **[2]**

Niet, M. de

37.0619 SR 1969 Vijf en zeventig jaren strafrecht [Seventy-five years of criminal law]. *In* Carpentier Alting, Z. H., et al., eds. EEN EEUW SURINAAMSE CODIFICATIE: GEDENKBOEK (1869-1 MEI-1969). Paramaribo, Surinaamse Juristen-Vereniging: 184-187. **[5]** *[RILA]*

Niger, Paul

37.0620 FA 1962 L'assimilation, forme suprême du colonialisme [(Political) assimilation, the supreme goal of colonialism]. *Esprit* 30(305), Apr.: 518-532.

Nikolia, A.

37.0621 MT 1961 Sbrosim tsepi kolonializma! [Let us smash the chains of colonialism!] *Part Zhizn* 24: 60-63. *[COL]*

Niles, Blair

37.0622 FG 1927 Devil's Island. *Forum N Y* 78(6), Dec.: 836-847. **[33]** *[COL]*

37.0623 FG 1928 CONDEMNED TO DEVIL'S ISLAND: THE BIOGRAPHY OF AN UNKNOWN CONVICT. New York, Harcourt, Brace, 376p. **[33]** *[NYP]*

Nita, A. P.

37.0624 CU 1969 CAMBIONAN SOCIAL CU UN YIU DI TERA TA SONJA CUNE DEN E PARTINAN IGUAL DI E REINADO NOBO [SOCIAL CHANGES THE NATIVE IS DREAMING OF IN THE EQUAL PARTS OF THE NEW KINGDOM]. Willemsted, Curaçao: 16p. (Originally published in 1952) **[8]** *[SCH]*

Norman, Frank A.

46.0164 BC 1952 WHITEHALL TO WEST INDIES.

Norris, Katrin

21.0072 JM 1962 JAMAICA: THE SEARCH FOR AN IDENTITY.

Nowicka, Ewa

23.0212 JM 1974 The Ras Tafari movement—its genesis and functions.

Nunan, Joseph J.

37.0625   GU   1912   Roman-Dutch law and the West Indian Appeal Court: a reply. *Timehri* 3d ser., 2(19A), July: 101-105.   [*AMN*]

37.0626   GU   1915   West Indian law and appeals. *Timehri* 3d ser., 3(20B), May: 253-256.   [*AMN*]

37.0627   BC   1917   West Indian Appeal Court. *Timehri* 3d ser., 4(21), June: 306-315.

Nunes, F. E.

37.0628   JM   1974   The declining status of the Jamaican Civil Service. *Social Econ Stud* 23(2), June: 344-357.   [20]   [*RIS*]

37.0629   TB   1974   A ministry and its community: Tobago—a case study in participation. *Social Econ Stud* 23(2), June: 176-185.   [*RIS*]

Nunes, F. E. & Draper, Gordon

45.0112   BC   1974   NOTES ON ORGANIZATION AND CHANGE IN THE CARIBBEAN: INTRODUCTORY READINGS IN ORGANIZATIONAL THEORY AND BEHAVIOUR.

O'Connor, Harvey

37.0630   JM   1952   Jamaica: the colonial dilemma. *Mon Rev* 3(9), Jan.: 268-277; 3(10), Feb.: 307-314.   [*COL*]

Odlum, George

37.0631   SL   1962   The structure of local and island government. *In* Brown, John, ed. AN APPROACH TO ADULT EDUCATION. Castries, St. Lucia, Govt. Print. Off., p.24-29.   [*RIS*]

Okpaluba, Chuks

37.0632   GC   1974   Fundamental human rights, the courts and the independent West Indian constitutions. *In* INDEPENDENCE FOR GRENADA—MYTH OR REALITY? Proceedings of a Conference on the Implications of Independence for Grenada sponsored by the Institute of International Relations and the Dept. of Govt., U.W.I., St. Augustine, Trinidad, Jan. 11-13, 1974: 79-90.   [33]   [*RIS*]

Olch, Isaiah

37.0633   GC   1940   A résumé of national interests in the Caribbean area. *U S Nvl Inst Proc* 66(2), Feb.: 165-176.   [5]   [*AGS*]

Olivier, Sydney, 1st Baron Ramsden

37.0634   BC   1938   Freedom Day, by Lord Olivier. *Contemp Rev* 872, Aug.: 154-162.   [*AGS*]

O'Loughlin, Carleen

41.0382   LW,WW   1963-64 Economic problems of the Leeward and Windward Islands.

2.0338   LW,WW   1968   ECONOMIC AND POLITICAL CHANGE IN THE LEEWARD AND WINDWARD ISLANDS.

O'Meally, Jaime

37.0635   JM   1938   WHY WE DEMAND SELF-GOVERNMENT. New York, Jamaica Progressive League of New York, 16p.   [*NYP*]

Omoruyi, Omo

20.0063   GU   1975   Use of multiple symbols of association as a measure of cohesion in a plural society.

Ooft, C. D.

37.0636   SR   1965   "Aanloop" tot een rechtsvergelijkende studie van het Nederlandse en het Surinaamse staatrecht. I. ["Running start" for a comparative legal study of Dutch and Surinamese public law. I]. *Justicia* 1, April: 44-51.   [*COL*]

37.0637   SR   1965   "Aanloop" tot een rechtsvergelijkende studie van het Nederlandse en het Surinaamse staatsrecht. II. ["Running start" for a comparative legal study of Dutch and Surinamese public law. II]. *Justicia* 1, July: 76-87.   [*COL*]

37.0638   SR   1966   Aanloop tot een rechtsvergelijkende studie van het Nederlandse en het Surinaamse Staatsrecht [Running start for a comparative legal study of Dutch and Surinamese Public Law]. Alphen aan de Rijn, The Netherlands, N. Samson N.V.: 46p.   [*RILA*]

37.0639   SR   1972   Ontwikkeling van het constitutionele recht van Suriname [Development of the constitutional law of Surinam]. Assen, The Netherlands, Van Gorcum & Comp. N.V./Dr. H. J. Prakke & H. M. G. Prakke: 316p. [5]   [*NYP*]

Ooft, C. D., ed.

37.0640   SR   1970   Naar een onafhankelijk Suriname [To an independent Surinam]. Progressieve Surinaamse Volkspartij: 44p.   [*RILA*]

Oorschot, J. W. van

37.0641   SR   1919   Eene militaire beschouwing omtrent de kolonie Suriname [A military viewpoint of the colony of Surinam]. *W I G* 1(1): 178-185.   [*COL*]

Ottley, C. R.

37.0642   TR   1964   A historical account of the Trinidad and Tobago police force from the earliest times. [Port of Spain?] Trinidad, Published by the author [printed by Robert MacLehose, University Press], 152p. [5]   [*RIS*]

Oudschans Dentz, Fred

37.0643   SR,CU   1927-28   Het Nederlanderschap in Suriname en Curacao [Dutch citizenship in Surinam and Curacao]. *W I G* 9: 131-136.   [*COL*]

37.0644   SR   1928-29   Nogmaals het wapen van Suriname [Surinam's coat of arms once again]. *W I G* 10: 35-43. [5]   [*COL*]

37.0645   NC   1932-33   De titel Excellentie [The title "Excellency"]. *W I G* 14: 179-181.   [*COL*]

37.0646   SR,CU   1934-35   Het Nederlanderschap in Suriname en Curacao [Dutch citizenship in Surinam and Curacao]. *W I G* 16: 205.   [*COL*]

41.0393   SR   1941   Een blik op den toestand van Suriname bij den overgang van het Engelsche bestuur op dat der Bataafsche Republiek in 1802 [The conditions in Surinam at the time of the change from English rule to that of the Batavian Republic].

37.0647   SR   1943   Aanvulling van de Encyclopaedie van Nederlandsch West-Indië: De Gouverneurs van Suriname [Addition to the Encyclopedia of the Dutch West Indies: The Governors of Surinam]. *W I G* 25: 345-348. [5]   [*COL*]

37.0648   SR   1948   De afzetting van het Groot-Opperhoofd der Saramaccaners Koffy in 1835 en de politieke contracten met de Boschnegers in Suriname [The dismissal of Koffy, the headman of the Saramaccans, in 1835, and the political contracts with the Bush Negroes in Surinam]. *Bijd Volk* 104: 33-43. [5,14]

Overbeek, H. E.

37.0649   NA   1966   Korps Politie Nederlandse Antillen [Police Corps Netherlands Antilles]. *Schakels* S63/NA46: 43-52.   [*NYP*]

Oxaal, Ivar

37.0650   TR   1965   WEST INDIAN INTELLECTUALS IN POWER. Ph.D. dissertation, U.C.L.A.: 370p.   [*PhD*]

37.0651   TR   1967   The intellectual background to the democratic revolution in Trinidad. *In* Bell, Wendell, ed. THE DEMOCRATIC REVOLUTION IN THE WEST INDIES. Cambridge, Mass., Schenkman Pub. Co., Inc.: 20-48. **[5,32]**   [*RIS*]

5.0693   TR   1968   BLACK INTELLECTUALS COME TO POWER: THE RISE OF CREOLE NATIONALISM IN TRINIDAD AND TOBAGO.

16.0078   TR   1971   RACE AND REVOLUTIONARY CONSCIOUSNESS: A DOCUMENTARY INTERPRETATION OF THE 1970 BLACK POWER REVOLT IN TRINIDAD.

37.0652   TR   1975   The dependency economist as grassroots politician in the Caribbean. *In* Oxaal, Ivar; Barnett, Tony & Booth, David, eds. BEYOND THE SOCIOLOGY OF DEVELOPMENT: ECONOMY AND SOCIETY IN LATIN AMERICA AND AFRICA. London, Routledge and Kegan Paul Ltd.: 28-49. **[40]**   [*RIS*]

Paiewonsky, Ralph M.

37.0653   UV   1967   MESSAGES OF THE GOVERNOR OF THE VIRGIN ISLANDS: FROM NOV. 28, 1965 - APRIL 2, 1967. Orford, New Hampshire, Equity Publishing Corp: 198p.   [*RIS*]

37.0654   UV   1969   MESSAGES OF THE GOVERNOR OF THE VIRGIN ISLANDS: FROM FEB. 2, 1967 - DEC. 24, 1968. Orford, New Hampshire, Equity Publishing Corp: 257p.   [*RIS*]

Panhuys, L. C. van

37.0655   SR   1924-25 De Gouverneur-Generaal Willem Benjamin van Panhuys [Governor-General Willem Benjamin van Panhuys]. *W I G* 6: 289-320. **[5]**   [*COL*]

37.0656   SR   1926-27 De Nederlandsche Regeering tegenover de kolonie Suriname in 1816 [The Dutch Government versus the colony of Surinam in 1816]. *W I G* 8: 463-472. **[5]**   [*COL*]

37.0657   SR   1934-35 Mr. Lammers over het bestuur van Suriname in 1816 [Mr. Lammers on the government of Surinam in 1816]. *W I G* 16: 151-162. **[5]**   [*COL*]

Pares, Richard

5.0698   GC   1936   WAR AND TRADE IN THE WEST INDIES 1739-1763.

37.0658   GC   1937   Prisoners of war in the West-Indies in the eighteenth century. *J Barb Mus Hist Soc* 5(1), Nov.: 12-17. **[5]**   [*AMN*]

Parker, Franklin D.

37.0659   FC   1958   Political development in the French Caribbean. *In* Wilgus, A. Curtis, ed. THE CARIBBEAN: BRITISH, DUTCH, FRENCH, UNITED STATES [PAPERS DELIVERED AT THE EIGHTH CONFERENCE ON THE CARIBBEAN HELD AT THE UNIVERSITY OF FLORIDA, DEC. 5-7, 1957]. Gainesville, University of Florida Press, p.97-104. (Publications of the School of Inter-American Studies, ser. 1, v.8.) **[5]**   [*RIS*]

Parkinson, E. C. L.

37.0660   JM   1971   The evolution of Jamaican law. *Jam J* 5(2-3), June-Sept.: 24-27.

[*RIS*]

Parris, Carl D.

41.0399   TR   1976   Size or class: factors affecting Trinidad and Tobago's foreign economic policy.

Parry, John Horace

37.0661   BC   1954   The Patent Offices in the British West Indies. *Engl Hist Rev* 69(271), Apr.: 200-225.   **[5]**   [*COL*]

Patchett, Keith & Jenkins, Valerie

1.0220   BC   1973   A BIBLIOGRAPHICAL GUIDE TO LAW IN THE COMMONWEALTH CARIBBEAN.

Paterson, Alexander

37.0662   BC   1943   REPORT OF MR. ALEXANDER PATERSON ON HIS VISITS TO THE REFORMATORY AND PENAL ESTABLISHMENTS...OF JAMAICA, BRITISH HONDURAS, THE BAHAMAS, THE LEEWARD AND WINDWARD ISLANDS, BARBADOS, TRINIDAD AND TOBAGO, BRITISH GUIANA...20TH DECEMBER, 1936-10TH MAY, 1937. [Port of Spain?] Printed by A. L. Rhodes, Govt. Printer, 25p. (West Indian no. 234.)   **[33]**   [*RIS*]

Paton, Walker

37.0663   BB   1944   Barbados and the war. *Can-W I Mag* 33-34(11), Nov.: 65-67.

[*NYP*]

Pattee, Richard

37.0664   JM   1946   Tumult in the Antilles: Jamaica. *America* 74(26), Mar. 30: 648-650.   **[46]**   [*COL*]

Patterson, H. Orlando

37.0665   GC   1966   Franz Fanon: my hope and hero. *New Wld Q* 2(3), May, Guyana Independence Issue: 93-95.   **[5]**   [*RIS*]

Péan, Charles

37.0666   FG   1953   THE CONQUEST OF DEVIL'S ISLAND. London, Max Parrish, 187p.   **[33]**   [*SCH*]

Penson, Lillian M.

37.0667   GU   1926   The making of a crown colony: British Guiana, 1803-33. *Trans Roy Hist Soc* 4th ser., 9: 107-134.   **[5]**   [*COL*]

5.0720   BC   1971   THE COLONIAL AGENTS OF THE BRITISH WEST INDIES: A STUDY IN COLONIAL ADMINISTRATION, MAINLY IN THE EIGHTEENTH CENTURY.

Perkins, Whitney T.

37.0668   UV   1962   DENIAL OF EMPIRE. Leyden, A. W. Sythoff, 381p.   [*COL*]

Phelps, O. W.

46.0179   JM   1960   Rise of the labour movement in Jamaica.

Phillips, Andrew P.

21.0076   **AT**   1967   Management and workers face an independent Antigua.

Phillips, Fred A.

37.0669   **BC**   1966   Politics and the administration of justice in newly independent countries. *Univ Toronto Law J* 16(2): 395-404.   [*COL*]

37.0670   **BC**   1968   Service commissions and constitutional change in the Caribbean. *J Adm Overseas* 7(2), April: 358-366.   [*COL*]

Pierre, Lennox & La Rose, John

37.0671   **TR**   1955   FOR MORE AND BETTER DEMOCRACY FOR A DEMOCRATIC CONSTI-TUTION FOR TRINIDAD AND TOBAGO. Port of Spain, West Indian Independence Party of Trinidad and Tobago, 38p.

Pitt, David

37.0672   **TR**   1949   Trinidad's new Constitution. *Venture* 1(2), Mar.: 5, 8-9.   [*COL*]

Platt, Raye R.

37.0673   **GC**   1926   A note on political sovereignty and administration in the Carib-bean. *Geogr Rev* 16(4), Oct.: 623-637.   **[5]**   [*AGS*]

Plénel, Alain

37.0674   **FA**   1963   Libération nationale et assimilation à la Martinique et à la Guadeloupe [National liberation and (political) assimilation in Martinique and Guadeloupe]. *Temps Mod* 18(205), June: 2197-2234.   **[5,41]**   [*COL*]

Pollak, Harry H.

37.0675   **GU**   1957   What about British Guiana? *Am Fed* 64(7), July: 28-29.   **[46]**
                                                                                                                    [*COL*]

Pope-Hennessy, James

37.0676   **BC**   1964   The Federation Riots, Barbados 1875-1876. *In his* VERANDAH: SOME EPISODES IN THE CROWN COLONIES 1867-1889. London, George Allen and Unwin, p.157-182.   **[5]**   [*COL*]

Pos, H.

37.0677   **NA**   1955   Mijmeringen naar aanleiding van het proefschrift "Antilliaans procesrecht" [Contemplations on the dissertation "Legal procedures in the Antilles"]. *Vox Guy* 1(6): 185-192.

Pos, R. H.

37.0678   **NC**   1954-55 De ontwikkeling der Westinidsche rijksdelen onder het Statuut voor het Koninkrijk der Nederlanden [The development of the West Indian Provinces under the Constitution of the Kingdom of The Netherlands]. *Vox Guy* 1(4-5), Nov.-Jan.: 3-5.

Post, K. W. J.

37.0679   **JM**   1969   The politics of protest in Jamaica, 1938: some problems of analysis and conceptualization. *Social Econ Stud* 18(4), Dec.: 374-390.   **[5]**
                                                                                                                    [*RIS*]

Poyer, John

37.0680   BB   1954   History of the administration of the Rt. Hon. Lord Seaforth, etc., etc., etc. *J Barb Mus Hist Soc* 21(4), Aug.: 160-174. **[5]**   [*AMN*]

Praag, C. S. van

18.0235   **NC,NE**   1971   Het Overheidsbeleid inzake allochtone groepen [The government policy concerning groups of aliens].

Premdas, Ralph R.

37.0681   GU   1970   POLITICAL PARTIES IN A BIFURCATED STATE: THE CASE OF GUYANA. Ph.D. dissertation, University of Illinois (Urbana-Champaign): 272p.   [*PhD*]

37.0682   GU   1972   Elections and political campaigns in a racially bifurcated state: the case of Guyana. *J Inter-Amer Stud* 14(3), Aug.: 271-296. **[8,16]**   [*COL*]

37.0683   GU   1972   VOLUNTARY ASSOCIATIONS AND POLITICAL PARTIES IN A RACIALLY FRAGMENTED STATE: THE CASE OF GUYANA. Georgetown, University of Guyana, Department of Political Science: 42p. (Occasional papers, 2) **[8]**   [*RIS*]

37.0684   GU   1973   Competitive party organizations and political integration in a racially fragmented state: the case of Guyana. *Car Stud* 12(4), Jan.: 5-35. **[8]**   [*RIS*]

37.0685   GU   1973   PARTY POLITICS AND RACIAL DIVISION IN GUYANA. Denver, Colorado, University of Denver, Center on International Race Relations: 36p. **[8,16]**   [*COL*]

37.0686   GU   1974   The rise of the first mass-based multi-racial party in Guyana. *Car Q* 20(3-4), Sept.-Dec.: 5-20.   [*RIS*]

Prescod, Colin

37.0687   BC   1975   The 'people's cause' in the Caribbean. *Race and Class* 17(1), Summer: 71-75. **[40]**   [*COL*]

37.0688   GU   1976   Guyana's socialism: an interview with Walter Rodney. *Race and Class* 18(2), Autumn: 109-128. **[40]**   [*RIS*]

Prest, A. R.

41.0412   BC   1957   A FISCAL SURVEY OF THE BRITISH CARIBBEAN.

41.0413   BC   1960   Public finance.

Prins, J.

37.0689   SR   1952   Vragen inzake Bosneger-volksrecht [Questions concerning public rights of the Bush Negroes]. *W I G* 33: 53-76. **[14]**   [*COL*]

37.0690   SR   1961   De Surinaamse bevolking en haar Districtscommissarissen [The Surinam population and its District Commissioners]. *Mens Mij* 36(5), Sept.-Oct.: 375-385.   [*RIS*]

Proctor, Jesse Harris, Jr.

37.0691   BC   1962   British West Indian society and government in transition 1920-1960. *In* Singham, A. & Braithwaite, L. E., eds. SPECIAL NUMBER [of *Social Econ Stud*] ON THE CONFERENCE ON POLITICAL SOCIOLOGY IN THE BRITISH CARIBBEAN, DEC. 1961. *Social Econ Stud* 11(4), Dec.: 273-304.   [*RIS*]

Punch, L. D. "Lully"

37.0692 TR 1967 A JOURNEY TO REMEMBER (39 YEARS IN THE CIVIL SERVICE). Trinidad and Tobago, Ideal Printery: 176p. **[2]** [*RIS*]

Quintus Bosz, A. J. A.

37.0693 SR 1960-61 Misvattingen omtrent de staatkundige ontwikkeling van Suriname [Misunderstandings about the political development of Surinam]. *N W I G* 40: 3-16. **[5]** [*COL*]

33.0155 SR 1969 De weg tot de invoering van de nieuwe wetgeving in 1869 en de overgang van het oude naar het nieuwe burgerlijk recht [The road to the introduction of the new legislation in 1869 and the transition from the old to the new Civil Code].

Rabinowitz, Victor

37.0694 GU 1962 Guiana rightist riots no surprise to Jagan. *Natn Guardian* 14(20), Feb. 26: 3. [*NYP*]

Ragatz, Lowell Joseph

42.0123 BC 1928[?] ABSENTEE LANDLORDISM IN THE BRITISH CARIBBEAN 1750-1833.

1.0231 BC 1931 A CHECKLIST OF HOUSE OF LORDS SESSIONAL PAPERS RELATING TO THE BRITISH WEST INDIES AND TO THE WEST INDIAN SLAVE TRADE AND SLAVERY, 1763-1834.

Rajbansee, Joseph

46.0182 BC [n.d.] CIVIL SERVICE ASSOCIATIONS & UNIONS IN THE COMMONWEALTH CARIBBEAN.

37.0695 TR 1967 THE TRANSFER OF AN ADMINISTRATIVE PRACTICE: THE APPLICABILITY OF THE UNITED STATES INCENTIVE AWARD PROGRAM TO THE IMPROVEMENT OF PUBLIC ADMINISTRATION IN TRINIDAD AND TOBAGO. Ph.D. dissertation, American University: 265p. [*PhD*]

43.0367 BC 1972 Politico-administrative aspects of agricultural development: a Caribbean perspective.

37.0696 BC 1972 Public personnel systems in the Commonwealth Caribbean. *In* TRAINING OF PUBLIC SERVICE TRAINERS: REPORT ON A PILOT COURSE, ST. AUGUSTINE, TRINIDAD, AUG. 10-SEPT. 18, 1970. New York, United Nations: 63-67. [*UNL*]

37.0697 GC 1972 Size and bureaucracy in the Caribbean. *J Comp Adm* 4(2), August: 205-224. **[41]** [*COL*]

Ramdat Misier, L. F.

37.0698 SR 1969 Een eeuw Surinaamse rechterlijke organisatie en burgerlijke rechtsvordering [A century of Surinamese judicial organization and civil procedure]. *In* Carpentier Alting, Z. H., et al., eds. EEN EEUW SURINAAMSE CODIFICATIE: GEDENKBOEK (1869-1 MEI-1969). Paramaribo, Surinaamse Juristen-Vereniging: 44-52. **[5,33]** [*RILA*]

37.0699 SR 1971 De rechter in ambtenarenzaken in Suriname [The judge in civil servant cases in Surinam]. *In* UIT HET RECHT: RECHTSGELEERDE OPSTELLEN AANGEBODEN AAN MR. P. J. VERDAM [OUT OF THE LAW: LEGAL PAPERS PRESENTED TO P. J. VERDAM LLM]. Deventer, The Netherlands, Kluwer: 261-273. [*COL*]

Ramsahoye, Fenton

37.0700   GU   [n.d.]   The People's Progressive Party. *In* Caribbean Institute and Study Center for Latin America (CISCLA). Report: First Institute on British Guiana. San German, P.R., Inter American University: 15-26. [*RIS*]

Rance, Hubert Elvin

35.0063   TR   1951   Government expenditures in Trinidad and Tobago.
41.0421   TR   1953   Trinidad report.

Ras Dizzy

11.0076   JM   1967   Notes and commentary. II. The Rastas Speak.

Rawlins, Randolph

37.0701   GU   1963   What really happened in British Guiana. *J Inter-Amer Stud* 5(1), Jan.: 140-147. [*COL*]

Ray, Ellen

37.0702   JM   1976   CIA and local gunmen plan Jamaican coup. *CounterSpy* 3(2): 36-41, 63. **[39]** [*RIS*]

Rayner, Thomas Crossley, ed.

37.0703   GU   1905   Laws of British Guiana. New and rev. ed. London, Waterlow, 5v. **[5]** [*NYP*]

Regnier, Françoise

40.0065   GD,MT   1967   Les Antilles françaises ne sont pas décolonisées [The French Antilles are not decolonized].

Reid, Carmen Shirley

5.0756   GU   1968   The constitutional development of Guyana.

Reid, Vic

37.0704   JM   1969   Norman Washington Manley: a profile written for the Jamaican Information Service. Kingston, The Jamaican Information Service: 20p. [*RIS*]

Reidy, Joseph W.

37.0705   GC   1967   Growth and possible change in Caribbean America's political capacity. *In* Wilgus, A. Curtis, ed. The Caribbean: its hemispheric role. Gainesville, University of Florida Press: 13-27. (Caribbean Conference Series 1, vol. 17) **[38]** [*RIS*]

Reis, Charles

37.0706   TR   1929[?]   A history of the Constitution or government of Trinidad from the earliest times to the present day, vol. 1. Port of Spain, Author's Press, 291p. [*COL*]
37.0707   TR   1947   The government of Trinidad and Tobago: law of the Constitution. Port of Spain, Trinidad, Yuille's Printerie, 336p.

Renkema, W. E.

5.0758   CU   1976   Anno 1869: Curaçao los van Nederland? Dat nooit!!! [Anno 1869: Curaçao independent of the Netherlands? Never!!!]

Rennie, Bukka

10.0046   **TR**   1973   HISTORY OF THE WORKING-CLASS IN THE 20TH CENTURY—(1919-1956)—THE TRINIDAD AND TOBAGO EXPERIENCE.

37.0708   **GC**   1975   "The conflicting tendencies in the Caribbean revolution." *Pan-Afr J* 8(2), Summer: 153-176.   **[39]**   [*RIS*]

37.0709   **TR**   1975   REVOLUTION AND SOCIAL DEVELOPMENT—A DIRECT ADDRESS TO THE UNEMPLOYEDS OF TRINIDAD AND TOBAGO. Trinidad and Tobago, New Beginning Movement: 44p.   **[46]**   [*RIS*]

Rennie, Bukkha

37.0710   **BC**   1974   The Caribbean revolution de-mystified. *Race Today* 6(5), May: 142-146.   **[46]**   [*RIS*]

Reno, Philip

37.0711   **GU**   1964   THE ORDEAL OF BRITISH GUIANA. N.Y., Monthly Review Press: 132p.   [*RIS*]

Rest, C. P. M. van

43.0374   **SR**   1974   HET DEPARTEMENT VAN LANDBOUW, VEETEELT EN VISSERIJ [THE DEPARTMENT OF AGRICULTURE, CATTLE-BREEDING AND FISHING].

Reuters, H. M. J.

22.0307   **SR**   1967   Welzijnszorg bij de Troepenmacht in Suriname [Welfare of the military forces in Surinam].

Revert, Eugene

56.0266   **GC**   1951   Géographie politique du monde caraïbe [Political geography of the Caribbean].

37.0712   **MT**   1955   Les institutions de la Martinique jusqu'à l'assimilation [The administration of Martinique up to the Assimilation Act of 1946]. *In* DEVELOPMENTS TOWARDS SELF-GOVERNMENT IN THE CARIBBEAN. A symposium held under the auspices of the Netherlands Universities Foundation for International Co-operation at The Hague, Sept. 1954. The Hague, W. van Hoeve, p.34-45.   [*RIS*]

Richardson, C. Howard

37.0713   **GC**   1971   American research on the political geography of Latin America. *In* Lentnek, Barry; Carmin, Robert L. & Martinson, Tom L., eds. GEOGRAPHIC RESEARCH ON LATIN AMERICA: BENCHMARK 1970: PROCEEDINGS OF THE CONFERENCE OF LATIN AMERICANIST GEOGRAPHERS, VOLUME ONE. Muncie, Indiana, Ball State University: 288-298.   **[38,39,40]**   [*COL*]

Richardson, E. C.

37.0714   **TR**   [n.d.]   TRINIDAD: REVOLUTION OR EVOLUTION; A CRITICAL ANALYSIS. Port of Spain, Vedic Enterprises, 19p.   [*RIS*]

43.0379   **TR**   196-[?]   P.N.M. AND ITS AGRICULTURAL POLICY.

Richardson, J. Henry

33.0158   **GU**   1955   REPORT ON SOCIAL SECURITY IN BRITISH GUIANA, APRIL, 1954.

33.0159   **BC**   1956   Social security problems with special reference to the British West Indies.

Richardson, Leigh

37.0715   BZ   1955   P.U.P. plan for British Honduras. *New Commonw* 29(1), Jan. 10: 12-13.   [*AGS*]

Rickards, Colin

37.0716   GC   1963   Caribbean power. London, Dennis Dobson, 247p.   [*RIS*]

Riemens, H.

37.0717   NA   1960   De internationale positie van de Nederlandse Antillen [The international position of the Netherlands Antilles]. *Int Spectator* 14(17), Oct. 8: 407-427.

37.0718   NC   1969   Suriname, de Nederlandse Antillen en Latijns Amerika [Surinam, the Netherlands Antilles and Latin America]. *Int Spectator* 23(6), March 22: 469-476.   [*COL*]

Roberts, Walter Adolphe

37.0719   BC   1934   British West Indian aspirations. *Curr Hist* 40(5), Aug.: 552-556.
                                                                        [*COL*]

37.0720   JM   1936   Self-government for Jamaica. New York, Jamaica Progressive League of New York, 16p.   [*NYP*]

37.0721   BC   1941   Caribbean headaches. *Nation* 153(12), Sept. 20: 251-253. **[16,50]**
                                                                        [*COL*]

37.0722   BC   1941   Future of the British Caribbean. *Surv Graphic* 30(4), Apr.: 229-234.
                                                                        [*COL*]

37.0723   GC   1941   Strategy in the Caribbean. *Nation* 152(15), Apr. 12: 428-431.   [*COL*]

37.0724   BC   1944   The future of colonialism in the Caribbean: the British West Indies. *In* Frazier, E. F. & Williams, E., eds. The economic future of the Caribbean. Washington, Howard University Press, p.37-39.   [*COL*]

5.0773   JM   1952   Sir Henry Morgan, buccaneer and Governor.

37.0725   JM   1959   The Act of Havana. *Jam Hist Rev* 3(2), Mar.: 66-69.   [*COL*]

Robertson, Glory

5.0782   JM   1972   Death of a constitution.

Robertson, James

37.0726   GU   1954   Report of the British Guiana Constitutional Commission 1954. London, H.M.S.O., 91p. (Cmd. 9274.)

Robertson, Keith J.

37.0727   GU   1972   Strategies applied to the process of administration reform. *In* Training of public service trainers: report on a pilot course, St. Augustine, Trinidad, Aug. 10-Sept. 18, 1970. New York, United Nations: 91-96.   **[7]**   [*UNL*]

Robertson, Paul D.

37.0728   JM   1972   Party "organization" in Jamaica. *Social Econ Stud* 21(1), March: 30-43.   [*RIS*]

20.0068   JM   1975   Ruling class attitudes in Jamaica: the bureaucratic component.

Roberts-Wray, Kenneth

33.0164   BC,UK   1966   Commonwealth and colonial law.

Robinson, Arthur N. R.

37.0729   TR   1967   THE PRESERVATION OF OUR DEMOCRACY: AN ADDRESS DELIVERED TO
                         THE FEDERATION OF WOMEN'S INSTITUTE AT QUEEN'S HALL ON
                         APRIL 22, 1967. PNM Publishing Company, Ltd.: 8p.   [RIS]

41.0435   TR   1971   THE MECHANICS OF INDEPENDENCE: PATTERNS OF POLITICAL AND
                         ECONOMIC TRANSFORMATION IN TRINIDAD AND TOBAGO.

Robinson, Kenneth

37.0730   FA   1954   The end of empire: another view. *Int Aff* 30(2), Apr.: 186-195.
                                                                                   [AGS]

37.0731   NC,FC   1956   Alternatives to independence. *Polit Stud* 4(3), Oct.: 225-249.

Roche, Jean Cazenave de la

37.0732   FA   1943   Tension in the French West Indies. *For Aff* 21(3), Apr.: 560-565.
                                                                                   [AGS]

Rodes, Félix

37.0733   GD   1972   LIBERTÉ POUR LA GUADELOUPE; 169 JOURS DE PRISON [FREEDOM
                         FOR GUADELOUPE; 169 DAYS IN PRISON]. Paris, Editions du
                         Témoignage Chrétien: 361p.   [40]   [NYP]

Rodney, Walter

40.0066   BC   1975   Contemporary political trends in the English-speaking Caribbean.

Rodríguez Beteta, Virgilio

39.0143   BZ   1965   SOLIDARITY AND RESPONSIBILITIES OF THE UNITED STATES IN THE
                         BELIZE CASE.

Rogers, Howard Aston

37.0734   LW,WW   1970   THE FALL OF THE OLD REPRESENTATIVE SYSTEM IN THE LEEWARD AND
                         WINDWARD ISLANDS, 1854-1877. Ph.D. dissertation, University of
                         Southern California: 377p.   [5]   [PhD]

Rolison, William Edward

40.0067   GU   1974   BRITISH COLONIAL POLICY AND THE INDEPENDENCE OF GUYANA.

Romalis, Coleman

37.0735   BB,SL   1969   BARBADOS AND ST. LUCIA: A COMPARATIVE ANALYSIS OF SOCIAL AND
                         ECONOMIC DEVELOPMENT IN TWO BRITISH WEST INDIAN ISLANDS.
                         Ph.D. dissertation, Washington University, Department of Soci-
                         ology: 243p.   [5,41]   [RIS]

Römer, Hans

37.0736   UV   1936   Die Virgin-Islands: ein unerfreuliches Kapitel der amerikanischen
                         Kolonialpolitik [The Virgin Islands; a displeasing chapter of
                         American colonial policy]. *Z Polit* 26(10), Oct.: 578-586.   [COL]

Römer, R. A.

37.0737   CU   1975   Race and class in political perspective: the case of Frente Obrero.
                         Kristòf 2(6), Dec.: 253-263.   [10]   [RIS]

Romondt, Ph. F. W.

6.0250   NW   1941   Pieter Hassell.

Romondt, W. H. A.
37.0738   SR   1922-23 De ontwikkeling van het kiersrecht in Suriname [The development of suffrage in Surinam]. *W I G* 4: 99-114.   [*COL*]

Rorty, James
37.0739   NV   1961 Independence, like it or not. *Commonweal* 74(20), Sept. 8: 491-493. **[38,51]**   [*RIS*]

Rosario, Elco
37.0740   NA   1974 Desentralisashon i sentralisashon den Estado Antiyano Ulandes II [Decentralization and centralization of the Netherlands Antilles]. *Kristòf* 1(4), Aug.: 185-194.   [*RIS*]

Rose, Dexter L.
41.0439   BC   1967 Notes on a possible set of accounts for the public sector.

Rose, F. G.
28.1100   GU   1926 Leprosy statistics and legislation in British Guiana.

Roth, Vincent
37.0741   GU   1952 Amerindians and the state: a brief history of the Guiana Amerindians vis-a-vis the government. *Timehri* 4th ser., 1(31), Nov.: 8-15. **[13]**

Rousseau, Louis
37.0742   FG   1925 Faillite morale et utilitaire de la transportation en Guyane: état sanitaire général de la colonie pénitentiaire [The moral and practical failure of the (penal) traffic to (French) Guiana: general sanitary conditions in the penal colony]. *Acad Sci Colon Cr Séanc* 2: 225-243.   [*NYP*]

Royes, W. C.
33.0167   JM   1961[?] Government and statutory social services in Jamaica.

Rubin, Vera
20.0075   BC   1962 Culture, politics and race relations.

Ruddock, L. C.
37.0743   JM   1967 CIVICS FOR YOUNG JAMAICANS. London, Collins: 191p. **[32]** [*RIS*]

Russell, Patricia
37.0744   BE   1945 Origin of Court of Vice-Admiralty. *Bermuda Hist Q* 2(1), Jan.-March: 36-39. **[5]**   [*NYP*]

Rutter, Owen
37.0745   TR   1941 Trinidad's contribution to the empire war effort. *Crown Colonist* 11(118), Sept.: 399-400.   [*AGS*]

Ryan, Selwyn
5.0799   TR   1966 THE TRANSITION TO NATIONHOOD IN TRINIDAD AND TOBAGO, 1797-1962.
37.0746   TR   1972 RACE AND NATIONALISM IN TRINIDAD AND TOBAGO: A STUDY OF DECOLONIZATION IN A MULTIRACIAL SOCIETY. Toronto, University of Toronto Press: 509p. **[16,2,5]**   [*RIS*]

37.0747   BE   1976   Politics in an artificial society: the case of Bermuda. *In* Henry,
                         Frances, ed. ETHNICITY IN THE AMERICAS. The Hague, Mouton:
                         159-192. **[8,21]**   [*RIS*]

Sablé, Victor
37.0748   FC   1955   LA TRANSFORMATION DES ISLES D'AMÉRIQUE EN DÉPARTEMENTS
                         FRANCAIS [THE CONVERSION OF THE AMERICAN ISLANDS INTO
                         FRENCH *Départements*]. Paris, Editions Larose, 200p. **[5]**   [*AGS*]
37.0749   FA   1972   LES ANTILLES SANS COMPLEXES: UNE EXPÉRIENCE DE DÉCOLONI-
                         SATION [THE UNCOMPLICATED ANTILLES? AN EXPERIENCE IN DE-
                         COLONIZATION.] Paris, Éditions G.-P. Maisonneuve & Larose:
                         309p. **[40]**   [*RIS*]

Saint-Ruf, Germain
5.0801   GD   1965   L'ÉPOPÉE DELGRÈS: LA GUADELOUPE SOUS LA RÉVOLUTION FRAN-
                         ÇAISE: 1789-1802 [THE DELGRÈS EPOCH: GUADELOUPE UNDER THE
                         FRENCH REVOLUTION].

Samaroo, Brinsley
37.0750   TR   1969   CONSTITUTIONAL AND POLITICAL DEVELOPMENT OF TRINIDAD, 1898-
                         1925. Ph.D. dissertation, University of London: 275p. **[5]**
5.0803   TR   1971   Cyrus Prudhomme David—a case study in the emergence of the
                         black man in Trinidad politics.
5.0804   TR   1972   The Trinidad Workingmen's Association and the origins of popular
                         protest in a crown colony.

Samson, D.
37.0751   SR   1969   Onze honderdjarige wetgeving en het notariaat [Our hundred year
                         old legislation and the office of notary public]. *In* Carpentier Alting,
                         Z. H., et al., eds. EEN EEUW SURINAAMSE CODIFICATIE: GEDENKBOEK
                         (1869-1 MEI-1969). Paramaribo, Surinaamse Juristen-Vereniging:
                         71-83. **[5,33]**   [*RILA*]
37.0752   SR   1969   Onze vijf en zeventig-jarige wetgeving en het notariaat [Our seventy
                         five year old legislation and the office of notary public]. *In*
                         Carpentier Alting, Z. H., et al., eds. EEN EEUW SURINAAMSE
                         CODIFICATIE: GEDENKBOEK (1869-1 MEI-1969). Paramaribo, Suri-
                         naamse Juristen-Vereniging: 188-192. **[5,33]**   [*RILA*]

Samson, Ph. A.
23.0256   SR   1940   De oplossing van het eedsvraagstuk in Suriname [The solution of
                         the problem of oath-taking in Surinam].
23.0257   SR   1946   Afgoderij als strafbaar feit [Idolatry as a penal offense].
37.0753   SR   1947   Kiesverenigingen in Suriname [Political parties in Surinam]. *W I G*
                         28: 161-174.   [*COL*]
37.0754   SR   1949   Uit de geschiedenis van de Surinaamse balie [From the history of
                         Surinam (judicial) bar]. *W I G* 30: 172-181.   [*COL*]
48.0143   SR   1950   De Surinaamse pers gedurende het Engelse tussenbestuur [The
                         Surinam press during the English interregnum].
37.0755   SR   1951   Koninklijke besluiten in Surinam [Royal Government decisions in
                         Surinam]. *W I G* 32: 129-142.   [*COL*]
48.0144   SR   1951   Persdelicten in Suriname [Legal actions against the press in
                         Surinam].

37.0756   **SR**   1956-57 Iets over de Surinaamsche Scherpschuttersvereeniging [About the Rifle-Club in Surinam]. *W I G* 37: 219-222. **[22]**   [COL]

37.0757   **SR**   1969 Onze wetgeving drie-kwart eeuw oud [Our legislation is three quarters of a century old]. *In* Carpentier Alting, Z. H., et al., eds. EEN EEUV SURINAAMSE CODIFICATIE: GEDENKBOEK (1869-1 MEI-1969]. Paramaribo, Surinaamse Juristen-Vereniging: 172-174. **[5]**
                                                          [RILA]

Sanders, Andrew

13.0187   **GU**   1972 Amerindians in Guyana: a minority group in a multiethnic society.

Sanjurjo, Maria Antonina

37.0758   **FC**   1938 AN APPROACH TO THE COLONIAL EVALUATION OF THE FRENCH WEST INDIES AND FRENCH GUIANA. M.A. thesis, Clark University, 137p. **[2]**

Saul, Samuel Berrick

41.0445   **BC**   1957 The economic significance of "constructive imperialism."

41.0446   **BC**   1958 The British West Indies in depression.

Schalkwijk, F. G.

37.0759   **CU**   1924-25 De reorganisatie van de rechterlijke macht en van de rechtspleging der kolonie Curacao in de praktijk [The reorganization of the judiciary power and the administration of justice in the colony of Curacao in practice]. *W I G* 6: 609-624.   [COL]

32.0508   **NC**   1926-27 Keuze en opleiding van naar West-Indie uit te zenden rechterlijke en bestuursambtenarem [Selection and training of judicial and government officials for the West Indies].

Schiltkamp, J. A.

5.0814   **NA**   1969 Bestuur en rechtspraak in de Nederlandse Antillen ten tijde van de West-Indische Compagnie [Administration and judicial decisions in the Netherlands Antilles at the time of the West India Company].

Schiltkamp, J. A. & Smidt, J. Th. de, eds.

5.0815   **SR**   1973 WEST INDISCHE PLAKAATBOEK: PLAKATEN, ORDONNANTIËN EN ANDERE WETTEN, UITGEVAARDIGD IN SURINAME 1667-1816 [WEST INDIAN BOOK OF EDICTS: EDICTS, ORDINANACES AND OTHER LAWS ISSUED IN SURINAM 1667-1816].

Schroeder, Herbert

37.0760   **LW**   1949 Sturm um die Inseln Unterm Wind [Storm over the Leeward Islands]. *Dt Rdsch* 75(6), June: 504-509.   [COL]

Schroeff, G. J. C. van der

37.0761   **SR**   1969 Honderd jaar advocatuur in Suriname [Hundred years of legal practice in Surinam]. *In* Carpentier Alting, Z. H., et al., eds. EEN EEUW SURINAAMSE CODIFICATIE: GEDENKBOEK (1869-1 MEI-1969). Paramaribo, Surinaamse Juristen-Vereniging: 84-89. **[5]** [RILA]

Schroeff, G. J. C. van der & Adhin, J. H.

37.0762   **SR**   1969 Eenhondered jaar Wetboek van Strafvordering [One hundred years of Criminal Procedure]. *In* Carpentier Alting, Z. H., et al., eds. EEN EEUW SURINAAMSE CODIFICATIE: GEDENKBOEK (1869-1 MEI-1969). Paramaribo, Surinaamse Juristen-Vereniging: 64-67. **[5]** [RILA]

Schuyler, Robert Livingston

37.0763   BC   1925   The constitutional claims of the British West Indies; the controversy over the slave registry bill of 1815. *Polit Sci Q* 40(1), Mar.:
1-36. **[6]**   [*COL*]

Schwartz, Barton M.

37.0764   TR   1965   Extra-legal activities of the village pandit in Trinidad. *Anthrop Q*
38(2), Apr.: 62-71. **[12,19]**   [*RIS*]

Schwarz, Ernst

37.0765   JM   1955   Progressive government in Jamaica: the Manley Plan. *Facts Fig*
4(3-4), Mar.-Apr.: 1-4.   [*NYP*]

Scott, Winthrop R.

41.0448   GG   1943   War economy of the Guianas.

Scroggs, William

37.0766   JM   1962   Jamaicans are English. *W I Econ* 4(7), Jan.: 11-12. **[5,21]**   [*RIS*]
37.0767   JM   1962   Political pluralism. *W I Econ* 4(12), June: 2.   [*RIS*]

Segal, Aaron

37.0768   BA   1974   Bahama watching. *Car R* 6(3), July-Aug.-Sept.: 40-43. **[40]** [*RIS*]

Segal, Aaron & Earnhardt, Kent C.

7.0188   GC   1969   Politics and population in the Caribbean.

Seggar, W. H.

37.0769   GU   1959   Amerindian local authority elections: upper Mazaruni Amerindian
district. *Timehri* 4th ser., 38, Sept.: 86-88. **[13]**   [*AMN*]

Semmel, Bernard

16.0087   JM   1962   The issue of "race" in the British reaction to the Morant Bay
Uprising of 1865.

Senior, Olive

37.0770   JM   1972   The message is change: a perspective on the 1972 General
Elections. Kingston, Jamaica, Kingston Publishers Ltd.:
98p. **[33]**   [*RIS*]

Seppen, G.

37.0771   CU   1947   Enkele maritieme gedachten over de defensie van Curacao [Some
maritime thoughts about the defense of Curacao]. *W I G* 28: 65-73.
[*COL*]

Shahabuddeen, Mohamed

37.0772   GU   1970   Constitutional development in Guyana. Ph.D. dissertation,
University of London: 883p. **[40]**

Shaw, Earl Bennett

37.0773   BC   1941   Our new Atlantic defenses. *J Geogr* 40(2), Feb.: 41-56.   [*AGS*]

Shenfield, A. A.

41.0458   BC   1958   Economic advance in the West Indies.

Sherlock, Philip M.

37.0774   JM,TR   1962   Nouvelles nations dans les Antilles [New nations in the Caribbean]. *Civilisations* 12(3): 404-406. **[5,38]** [RIS]

37.0775   JM,TR   1963   Prospects in the Caribbean. *For Aff* 41(4), July: 744-756. **[16,20,21]** [RIS]

20.0079   BC   1972   The socio-cultural environment of the 1970's.

Sherman, Alfred

37.0776   BC,UK   1965   Deptford. *In* Deakin, Nicholas, ed. COLOUR AND THE BRITISH ELECTORATE, 1964: SIX CASE STUDIES. New York, Frederick A. Praeger: 106-119. **[16,18]** [COL]

Shilstone, E. M.

37.0777   BB   1934   The evolution of the general assembly of Barbados. *J Barb Mus Hist Soc* 1(4), Aug.: 187-191. **[5]** [AMN]

37.0778   BB   1935   The thirteen Baronets. *J Barb Mus Hist Soc* 2(2), Feb.: 89-92. **[5]** [AMN]

Shoman, A.

37.0779   BZ   1973   The birth of the nationalistic movement in Belize, 1950-1954. *J Beliz Aff* 2, Dec.: 3-40. **[21]** [RIS]

Shuttleworth, Alan

37.0780   BC,UK   1965   Sparkbrook. *In* Deakin, Nicolas, ed. COLOUR AND THE BRITISH ELECTORATE, 1964: SIX CASE STUDIES. New York, Frederick A. Praeger: 54-76. **[16,18]** [COL]

Silberman, Leo

37.0781   BZ   1954   Trouble in British Honduras. *Contemp Rev* 186, July: 21-25. [COL]

Silverman, Marilyn

12.0085   GU   1976   The role of factionalism in political encapsulation: East Indian villagers in Guyana.

Simey, Thomas S.

37.0782   BC   1944[?]   PRINCIPLES OF PRISON REFORM. Bridgetown, Advocate Co., 26p. (Development and welfare bulletin no. 10.) **[33]** [COL]

Simms, Peter

37.0783   GU   1966   TROUBLE IN GUYANA: AN ACCOUNT OF PEOPLE, PERSONALITIES AND POLITICS AS THEY WERE IN BRITISH GUYANA. London, George Allen and Unwin Ltd.: 198p. **[5]** [RIS]

Simons, R. D.

37.0784   SR   1947   Suriname's ontvoogding en het welvaartsplan [Surinam's emancipation and the welfare plan]. *W I G* 28: 222-235. [COL]

Simpson, George Eaton

23.0272   JM   1955   Culture change and reintegration found in the cults of West Kingston, Jamaica.

23.0273   JM   1955   Political cultism in West Kingston, Jamaica.

23.0274   JM   1955   The Ras Tafari movement in Jamaica: a study of race and class conflict.

23.0277   JM   1962   The Ras Tafari movement in Jamaica in its millennial aspect.

Simpson-Holley, Barry

5.0845   TR   1973   Members for Trinidad.

Singh, Fieldin

37.0785   GU   [n.d.]   The United Force. *In* Caribbean Institute and Study Center for Latin America (CISCLA). REPORT: FIRST INSTITUTE ON BRITISH GUIANA. San German, P.R., Inter American University: 34-39.
[*RIS*]

Singh, Jai Narine

37.0786   GU   1954   GUAYANA: HACIA LA LIBERTAD [GUIANA: TOWARD FREEDOM]. Caracas, Tip. Vargas, 63p.   [*COL*]

Singh, Paul G.

37.0787   BC   [n.d.]   The development of local government in the Commonwealth Caribbean. *Stud Comp Loc Gov* 3(1), Summer: 28-40.   [*COL*]

37.0788   BC   1970   Problems of institutional transplantation: the case of the Commonwealth Caribbean local government system. *Car Stud* 10(1), April: 22-33.   **[19]**   [*RIS*]

8.0204   GU   1972   GUYANA: SOCIALISM IN A PLURAL SOCIETY.

37.0789   BC   1972   LOCAL DEMOCRACY IN THE COMMONWEALTH CARIBBEAN: A STUDY OF ADAPTATION AND GROWTH. Trinidad and Jamaica, Longman Caribbean: 146p.   [*RIS*]

Singham, A. W.

37.0790   GU,GR   1965   Three cases of constitutionalism and cuckoo politics: Ceylon, British Guiana and Grenada. *New Wld Q* 2(1), Dead Season: 23-33.   **[24]**   [*RIS*]

32.0535   BC   1966   Some underlying theoretical issues in Public Administration training.

37.0791   BC   1967   Legislative-executive relations in smaller territories. *In* Benedict, Burton, ed. PROBLEMS OF SMALLER TERRITORIES. London, The Athlone Press: 134-148.   [*RIS*]

11.0082   BC   1967   The political socialization of marginal groups.

37.0792   GR   1968   THE HERO AND THE CROWD IN A COLONIAL POLITY. New Haven, Yale University Press: 389p. (Caribbean Series no. 12)   **[8]**   [*RIS*]

Singham, A. W., ed.

2.0432   BC   1975   THE COMMONWEALTH CARIBBEAN INTO THE SEVENTIES: PROCEEDINGS OF A CONFERENCE HELD ON 28-30 SEPTEMBER, 1973, AT HOWARD UNIVERSITY, WASHINGTON, D. C.

Singham, A. W. & Braithwaite, Lloyd E., eds.

37.0793   BC   1962   Special number on the Conference on Political Sociology in the British Caribbean, Dec. 1961. *Social Econ Stud* 11(4), Dec.: 456p.
[*RIS*]

Singham, A. W.; Jones, E. S.; Gordon, D.; Levy, Catherine & Munroe, T. G., comps.

37.0794   GC   [n.d.]   READINGS IN GOVERNMENT AND POLITICS OF THE WEST INDIES. Kingston, Instant Letter Service Co. Ltd: 518p.   [*RIS*]

Singham, A. W. & Singham, N. L.
37.0795   GC   1973   Cultural domination and political subordination: notes toward a theory of the Caribbean political system. *Comp Stud Soc Hist* 15(3), June: 258-288.   [*COL*]

Sires, Ronald Vernon
5.0848   JM   1936   JAMAICA IN DECLINE, 1834-1856.
37.0796   JM   1940   Constitutional change in Jamaica, 1834-60. *J Comp Leg Int Law* 3d ser., 22(4): 178-190.   **[5]**
37.0797   JM   1953   Governmental crisis in Jamaica, 1860-1866. *Jam Hist Rev* 2(3), Dec.: 1-26.   **[5]**   [*RIS*]
37.0798   GU   1954   British Guiana: the suspension of the constitution. *Polit Q* 7(4), Dec.: 554-569.   [*RIS*]
37.0799   JM   1954   The Jamaica Constitution of 1884. *Social Econ Stud* 3(1), June: 64-81.   **[5]**   [*RIS*]
37.0800   JM   1955   The experience of Jamaica with a modified crown colony government. *Social Econ Stud* 4(2), June: 150-167.   **[5]**   [*RIS*]
37.0801   BC   1957   Government in the British West Indies: an historical outline. *Social Econ Stud* 6(2), June: 108-132.   **[5]**   [*RIS*]

Sjiem Fat, P. V.
37.0802   NA   1965   De Algemene Maatregel van Rijksbestuur ter uitvoering van de Cassatieregeling voor de Nederlandse Antillen [The State Order in Council for the execution of the Appeal regulation of the Netherlands Antilles]. *Justicia* 1, April: 38-44.   [*COL*]
37.0803   NA   1965   Vonnis, eindvonnis en beslissing [Judgement, verdict and decision]. *Justicia* 1, Jan.: 3-16.   [*COL*]
37.0804   NA   1967   Twee jaar Cassatie regeling [Two years of the Appeal regulation]. *Justicia* 3(1): 3-6.   [*COL*]
37.0805   NA   1968   Aanpassing Antilliaanse wetgeving aan cassatie regeling gewenst [Adaptation of the Antillean legislation to the appeal regulation is required]. *Justicia* 4(1): 1-5.   [*COL*]
37.0806   NA   1969   HONDERD JAAR ADVOCATUUR IN DE NEDERLANDSE ANTILLEN [HUNDRED YEARS OF LEGAL PRACTICE IN THE NETHERLANDS ANTILLES]. *In* HONDERD JAAR CODIFICATIE IN DE NEDERLANDSE ANTILLEN. Arnhem, The Netherlands, S. Gouda Guint/D. Brouwer en Zoon: 185-291.   **[5]**   [*RILA*]
37.0807   NA   1971   Rechterskeuze [Selection of judges]. *Justicia* 7(3): 77-83.   [*COL*]

Skinnard, Frederick W.
37.0808   JM   1946   Evolving Jamaica. *Spectator* 177(6175), Nov. 1: 443-444.   **[50]**
[*NYP*]

Slepneva, G.
37.0809   GU   1959   Britanskaia Gviana [British Guiana]. *Mezhdunarodnaia Zhizn* 7: 139-141.   [*COL*]

Sloan, Jennie A.
37.0810   GU   1938   Anglo-American relations and the Venezuelan boundary dispute. *Hisp Am Hist Rev* 18(4), Nov.: 486-506.   **[5]**   [*COL*]

Smith, Cuthbert Brooke

37.0811   **BE**   1957   Some military records of Bermuda, and, Infantry units stationed in Bermuda. *Bermuda Hist Q* 14(3), Autumn: 80-93. **[5]**   *[COL]*

Smith, M. G.

37.0812   **BC**   1962   Short-range prospects in the British Caribbean. *In* Singham, A. & Braithwaite, L. E., eds. SPECIAL NUMBER [of *Social Econ Stud*] ON THE CONFERENCE ON POLITICAL SOCIOLOGY IN THE BRITISH CARIBBEAN, DEC. 1961. *Social Econ Stud* 11(4), Dec.: 392-408. **[8,38]** *[RIS]*

8.0218   **GR**   1965   Structure and crisis in Grenada, 1950-1954.

Smith, M. G.; Augier, F. R. & Nettleford, Rex

23.0286   **JM**   1960   THE RAS TAFARI MOVEMENT IN KINGSTON, JAMAICA.

Smith, Raymond Thomas

37.0813   **GU**   1963   British Guiana's prospects. *New Soc* 44, Aug. 1: 6-8. **[8]**   *[RIS]*

37.0814   **GU**   1971   Race and political conflict in Guyana. *Race* 12(4), April: 415-427. **[16]**   *[RIS]*

Smith, Robert Worthington

6.0273   **JM**   1945   The legal status of Jamaican slaves before the anti-slavery movement.

Smith, S. A. de; Leigh, L. H. & Hasson, R. A.

37.0815   **BC**   1967   Constitutional law. *In* Wade, H. W. R., ed. ANNUAL SURVEY OF COMMONWEALTH LAW: 1966. London, Butterworth and Co. (Publishers) Ltd.: 1-104. (Chapter 1)   *[COL]*

Smith, T. E.

37.0816   **JM,TR,GU**   1960   ELECTIONS IN DEVELOPING COUNTRIES: A STUDY OF ELECTORAL PROCEDURES USED IN TROPICAL AFRICA, SOUTH-EAST ASIA AND THE BRITISH CARIBBEAN. London, Macmillan, 278p.   *[RIS]*

Smithers, David

37.0817   **KNA**   1967   Anguilla's UDI. *Venture* 19(9), Oct.: 15-18.   *[COL]*

Solnick, Bruce B.

5.0857   **GC**   1970   THE WEST INDIES AND CENTRAL AMERICA TO 1898.

Spackman, Ann

37.0818   **TR**   1965   Constitutional development in Trinidad and Tobago. *Social Econ Stud* 14(4), Dec.: 283-320.   *[RIS]*

37.0819   **TR**   1967   The Senate of Trinidad and Tobago. *Social Econ Stud* 16(1), March: 77-100. **[20]**   *[RIS]*

37.0820   **JM**   1969   Electoral law and administration in Jamaica. *Social Econ Studies* 18(1), March: 1-53.   *[RIS]*

5.0860   **GU**   1973   Official attitudes and official violence: the Ruimveldt massacre, Guyana, 1924.

45.0140   **GU**   1975   The role of private companies in the politics of empire: a case study of bauxite and diamond companies in Guyana in the early 1920s.

Spiers, Maurice
37.0821   BC,UK   1965   Bradford. *In* Deakin, Nicholas, ed. COLOUR AND THE BRITISH ELECTORATE, 1964: SIX CASE STUDIES. New York, Frederick A. Praeger: 120-156. **[16,18]**   [*COL*]

Spitz, Georges
37.0822   MT   1955   La Martinique et ses institutions depuis 1948 [Martinique and its administration since 1948]. *In* DEVELOPMENTS TOWARDS SELF-GOVERNMENT IN THE CARIBBEAN. A symposium held under the auspices of the Netherlands Universities Foundation for International Co-operation at The Hague, Sept. 1954. The Hague, W. van Hoeve, p.112-124. **[32,41]**   [*RIS*]

Springer, Hugh W.
37.0823   BB   1967   Barbados as a sovereign state. *J Roy Soc Arts* 115(5131), June: 627-641. **[40]**   [*COL*]

Sprock, René
41.0467   NA   1975   De overheidsfinanciën van de Nederlandse Antillen naar doel en economische categorie in 1972 [The finances of the government of the Netherlands Antilles by purpose and economic category in 1972].

Spurdle, Frederick G.
5.0862   BB,JM,LW   [n.d.]   EARLY WEST INDIAN GOVERNMENT: SHOWING THE PROGRESS OF GOVERNMENT IN BARBADOS, JAMAICA AND THE LEEWARD ISLANDS, 1660-1783.

Staal, G. J.
37.0824   SR   1921-22 De grondwetsherziening en Suriname [The revision of the Constitution in Surinam]. *W I G* 3: 545-564.   [*COL*]
37.0825   SR   1921-22 Het voorspel der installatie van den posthouder bij de Aucaners [The prelude to the installation of the representative among the Aucaner]. *W I G* 3: 630-636. **[14,16]**   [*COL*]
37.0826   SR   1926-27 De wet op de staatsinrichting van Suriname [The law about the form of government of Surinam]. *W I G* 8: 85-91.   [*COL*]

Stewart, Walter Elmore
37.0827   GU   1967   THE DEVELOPMENT OF THE GUYANA CONSTITUTION, 1891-1953. Ph.D. dissertation, Columbia University: 480p. **[5]**   [*PhD*]

St. Hill, C. A. P.
41.0473   BC   1970   Towards the reform of the public services: some problems of transitional bureaucracies in Commonwealth Caribbean states.

Stokes, Anthony
37.0828   BC   1969   A VIEW OF THE CONSTITUTION OF THE BRITISH COLONIES IN NORTH AMERICA AND THE WEST INDIES. London, Dawsons of Pall Mall: 561p. (Originally published in 1783.) **[5]**   [*RIS*]

Stone, Carl
8.0230   JM   1972   Social class and partisan attitudes in urban Jamaica.
8.0231   TR,JM   1972   STRATIFICATION AND POLITICAL CHANGE IN TRINIDAD AND JAMAICA.
8.0232   JM   1973   CLASS, RACE AND POLITICAL BEHAVIOUR IN URBAN JAMAICA.

37.0829	JM	1974	ELECTORAL BEHAVIOUR AND PUBLIC OPINION IN JAMAICA. Jamaica, University of the West Indies, Institute of Social and Economic Research: 107p. **[8,20]** [*RIS*]
37.0830	JM	1974	Political aspects of postwar agricultural policies in Jamaica (1945-1970). *Social Econ Stud* 23(2), June: 145-175. **[43]** [*RIS*]
33.0187	JM	1975	Urban social movements in post-War Jamaica.
8.0233	JM	1976	Class, community, and leadership on a Jamaican sugar plantation.

Story, Christopher

| 37.0831 | GU | 1963 | Political development in British Guiana. *Q Rev* 301(635), Jan.: 77-88. [*COL*] |

St. Pierre, Maurice

37.0832	GU	1972	The Co-operative Republic—idea or ideology? *In* ESSAYS ON THE CO-OPERATIVE REPUBLIC OF GUYANA. Georgetown, Guyana, Critchlow Labour College Series No. 2: 15p. **[40]** [*RIS*]
37.0833	GU	1972	The sociology of decolonization: the case of Guyana bauxite. *New Wld Q* 5(4), Cropover: 50-62. **[40,50]** [*RIS*]
46.0223	JM	1972	Strike or struggle? Unrest on the Mona campus of the University of the West Indies.

Suárez, Andrés

| *1.0272* | GC | 1973 | Mexico, Central America, the Caribbean and the Guianas. |

Sukdeo, Iris D.

| *32.0557* | GU | 1975 | Relevance of democratic centralism in education in the Soviet Union to development in Guyana. |

Swinfen, D. B.

| 37.0834 | BC | 1970 | IMPERIAL CONTROL OF COLONIAL LEGISLATION, 1813-1865: A STUDY OF BRITISH POLICY TOWARDS COLONIAL LEGISLATIVE POWERS. London, Clarendon Press/Oxford: 202p. **[5]** [*COL*] |

Swing, Raymond Gram

| 37.0835 | UV | 1935 | Justice in the Virgin Islands. *Nation* 40(3629), Jan. 23: 95-96. [*COL*] |
| 37.0836 | UV | 1935 | Storm over the Virgin Islands. *Nation* 141(3655), July 24: 95-96. [*COL*] |

Sykes, J. W.

| 37.0837 | BC | 1966 | Development and decline of Crown Colony government. *Bermuda Hist Q* 23(1), Spring: 9-16. **[5]** [*COL*] |

Taylor, S. A. G.

| 37.0838 | JM | 1949 | Military operations in Jamaica 1655-1660: an appreciation. *Jam Hist Rev* 1(2), Dec.: 7-25. **[5]** [*COL*] |

Teulières, André

| 37.0839 | FC | 1970 | L'OUTRE-MER FRANÇAIS: HIER. . .AUJORD'HUI. . .DEMAIN [FRENCH OVERSEAS DEPARTMENTS: YESTERDAY. . .TODAY. . .TOMORROW]. Paris, Editions Berger-Levrault: 483p. **[5,40]** [*COL*] |

Thakur, Andra P.
8.0237 **GU** 1973 GUYANA: THE POLITICS OF RACE AND CLASS 1953-64.

Thamar, Maurice
37.0840 **FG** 1935 LES PEINES COLONIALES ET L'EXPÉRIENCE GUYANAISE [COLONIAL PENAL SENTENCES AND THE GUIANA EXPERIMENT]. Paris, Impr. Georges Subervie, 202p. (Ph.D. dissertation, University of Paris.) **[5]**

Theuns, H. L.
16.0092 **SR** 1975 Ras, politiek en ideologie in Suriname [Race, politics and ideology in Surinam].
40.0073 **SR** 1975 Suriname als Nederlands probleem [Surinam as a Dutch problem].

Thomas, Bert J.
37.0841 **DM** 1976 Revolutionary activity in the Caribbean: some notes on the Dreads of Dominica. *Guy J Sociol* 1(2), April: 75-92. **[8]**   *[RIS]*

Thomas, C. C.
37.0842 **BC** 1966 Constitutional theory and practice in the West Indies. *Jb Öff Rechts Geg* 15: 683-762. **[38]**   *[COL]*

Thomas, Clive Y.
37.0843 **GU** 1973 Meaningful participation: the fraud of it. *In* Lowenthal, David & Comitas, Lambros, eds. THE AFTERMATH OF SOVEREIGNTY: WEST INDIAN PERSPECTIVES. Garden City, N.Y., Anchor Press/ Doubleday: 351-366. **[20,50]**   *[RIS]*
37.0844 **GU** 1976 Bread and justice: the struggle for socialism in Guyana. *Mon Rev* 28(4), Sept.: 23-35. **[40]**   *[COL]*

Thomas, Cuthbert J.
37.0845 **DM** 1973 FROM CROWN COLONY TO ASSOCIATE STATEHOOD: POLITICAL CHANGE IN DOMINICA, THE COMMONWEALTH WEST INDIES. Ph.D. dissertation, University of Massachusetts: 378p. **[5,40]**   *[PhD]*

Thomas, Michael
37.0846 **JM** 1976 Jamaica at war: the Rastas are coming! *Rolling Stone* Aug. 12: 32-36. **[8,11,23]**   *[RIS]*

Thomas, Tony & Riddell, John
37.0847 **TR** 1971 BLACK POWER IN THE CARIBBEAN: THE 1970 UPSURGE IN TRINIDAD. New York, Pathfinder Press: 15p. **[11]**   *[RIS]*

Thompson, Era Bell
37.0848 **GC** 1967 Black leaders of the West Indies. *Ebony* 22(12), Oct.: 76-89. **[11]**   *[NYP]*

Thorndike, Tony
40.0075 **GR** 1974 Grenada: maxi-crisis for a mini-state.

Thorne, Alfred P.
41.0494 **JM** 1956 Some general comments on the Hicks Report.

Tinker, Hugh

12.0107   **BC**   1975   British policy towards a separate Indian identity in the Caribbean, 1920-1950.

Toledano, Luis

37.0849   **JM**   1947   Tropical Gilbert and Sullivan. *New Stsm Natn* 33(831), Jan. 25: 68.

Tomasek, Robert D.

37.0850   **GU**   1959   British Guiana: a case study of British colonial policy. *Polit Sci Q* 74(3), Sept.: 393-411.   [*AGS*]

Tooke, Charles W.

41.0501   **UV**   1900   The Danish colonial fiscal system in the West Indies.

Trigt, Ivo van

40.0076   **NA**   1969   Rondom een gouverneursbenoeming [Concerning a governor's appointment].

37.0851   **SR**   1969   Suriname en Nederland [Surinam and the Netherlands]. *Streven* 7, April: 672-678.   [*NYP*]

40.0077   **NA**   1970   Tweespalt in de Antillen [Discord in the Antilles].

Trotman, Donald A. B.

37.0852   **GU**   1973[?]   GUYANA AND THE WORLD: COMMENTARIES ON NATIONAL AND INTERNATIONAL AFFAIRS (1968-1973). United Nations Association of Guyana: 100p.   **[39]**   [*RIS*]

Tucker, Gerald Etienne

20.0082   **JM**   1973   AFRO-EUROPEAN POLITICAL CULTURE AND DEVELOPMENT IN JAMAICA.

Tucker, Henry

37.0853   **BE**   1970   The new Constitution. *Bermuda Hist Q* 27(4), Winter: 94-98.   [*COL*]

Turgeon, Maurice

37.0854   **MT**   1943   "Vichy" in Martinique. *Can-W I Mag* 32(4), Apr.: 9-10.   [*NYP*]

Tuttle, Andrew C.

38.0225   **GC**   1967   THE WEST INDIES FEDERATION: POLITICS AND PROSPECTS.

Tuyl Schuitemaker-van Steenbergen, E.

37.0855   **SR**   1951   Politieke ontwikkeling in Suriname na de inwerkingtreding der Interim-Regeling [Political development in Surinam after the introduction of the Interim-Rule]. *W I G* 32: 154-167.   [*COL*]

Updike, John

3.0617   **AG**   1968   Letter from Anguilla.

Vandenbosch, Amry

37.0856   **AR,CU**   1931   Dutch problems in the West Indies. *For Aff* 9(2), Jan.: 350-352.   **[41]**   [*AGS*]

Varsier, Orphélia

37.0857   **MT**   1966   De la profession d'Expert-Compatable [The profession of Chartered Accountant]. *B Cham Com Indus Mart* 1, Jan.: 35-37.   [*RIS*]

37.0858   MT   1966   De la profession d'Expert Compatable (suite) [The profession of Chartered Accountant (continued)]. *B Cham Com Indus Mart* 2-3, Feb.-March: 102-103.   [*RIS*]

Vaughan, H. A.
5.0926   BB   1966-67 Samuel Prescod: the birth of a hero.

Veerasawmy, J. A.
37.0859   GU   1919   The Noitgedacht murder. *Timehri* 3d ser., 6(23), Sept.: 116-132. **[23]**   [*AMN*]

Venables, Robert
37.0860   GC,JM   1965   THE NARRATIVE OF GENERAL VENABLES; WITH AN APPENDIX OF PAPERS RELATING TO THE EXPEDITION TO THE WEST INDIES AND THE CONQUEST OF JAMAICA, 1654-1655. New York, Johnson Reprint Corp.: 180p. (Originally published in 1900; Royal Historical Society Publications No. 60) **[5]**   [*COL*]

Verner, Joel Gordon
37.0861   BC   1973   The recruitment of cabinet ministers in the former British Caribbean: a five-county study. *J Dev Areas* 7(4), July: 635-652.   [*COL*]

Verrier, Anthony
37.0862   GU   1966   Guyana and Cyprus: techniques of peace-keeping. *J Roy United Serv Inst* 111(644), Nov.: 298-306. **[39]**   [*COL*]

Verton, Peter
37.0863   NA   1973   KIEZERS EN POLITIEKE PARTIJEN IN DE NEDERLANDSE ANTILLEN [VOTERS AND POLITICAL PARTIES IN THE NETHERLANDS ANTILLES]. Aruba, De Wit Stores N. V.: 66p.   [*RIS*]

Vignon, Robert
2.0476   FG   1954   La Guyane Francaise au sein de la Communauté Francaise (situation politique, juridique et économique) [French Guiana at the heart of the French community].

Villaronga, Mariano
37.0864   GU   1962   Quién es Cheddi Jagan: patriota, demagogo, communista?. . . [Who is Cheddi Jagan: patriot, demagogue, Communist?] *Boricua* 1(6), May: 50-51, 90.   [*NYP*]

Vollenhoven, C. van
5.0936   SR   1916   Politieke contracten met de Boschnegers in Suriname [Political contracts with the Bush Negroes of Surinam].

Vollers, J. L.
37.0865   SR   1974   DE BESTUURLIJKE STRUCTUUR VAN SURINAME [THE ADMINISTRATIVE STRUCTUUR OF SURINAM]. Amsterdam, Universiteit van Amsterdam, Sociografisch Instituut FSW: 194p. (Onderzoekprojekt Sociale Ontwikkelingsstrategie Suriname 1969, Deelrapport nr. 12) **[33,46]**   [*RIS*]

Voort, P. P. C. H. van de

37.0866   NA   1971   Reorganisatie van de rechterlijke macht [Reorganization of the judicial power]. *Justicia* 7(3): 73-76.   [*COL*]

Vries, F. P. de

37.0867   NA   1955-56 Enige aspecten der ontwikkeling van de Nederlands-Antilliaanse vertegenwoordiging in Nederland [Some aspects of the development of the Dutch-Antillean representation in the Netherlands]. *W I G* 36: 165-173.   [*COL*]

41.0513   NA   1965   Tien jaar Statuut 1954-1964. Motieven en perspectieven van de Nederlands-Antilliaanse economie [Ten years of Statute 1954-1964. Motives and perspectives of the economy of the Netherlands Antilles).

Waard, J. de

41.0516   SR   1954-55 De economische bepalingen van het Statuut [The economic provisions of the Constitution].

Waddell, David A. G.

37.0868   BZ   1957   British Honduras and Anglo-American relations. *Car Q* 5(1), June: 50-59.   **[5]**   [*RIS*]

37.0869   BZ   1959   British Honduras and Anglo-American relations: a correction. *Car Q* 5(4), June: 292.   **[5]**   [*RIS*]

37.0870   BZ   1959   Great Britain and the Bay Islands 1821-61. *Hist J* 2(1): 59-77.   **[5]**   [*RIS*]

37.0871   BZ   1961   Developments in the Belize question 1946-1960. *Am J Int Law* 55(2), Apr.: 459-469.   **[39]**   [*RIS*]

5.0941   BC   1965   Las Antillas británicas y la independencia hispano-americana: informe preliminar sobre investigaciones [The British Antilles and Spanish-American independence: preliminary report on investigations].

37.0872   BZ   1967   Case study: British Honduras. *In* Benedict, Burton, ed. PROBLEMS OF SMALLER TERRITORIES. London, The Athlone Press: 56-67.   **[7]**   [*RIS*]

Wade, H. W. R., ed.

33.0208   BC   1967   ANNUAL SURVEY OF COMMONWEALTH LAW: 1966.
33.0209   BC   1968   ANNUAL SURVEY OF COMMONWEALTH LAW: 1967.
33.0210   BC   1969   ANNUAL SURVEY OF COMMONWEALTH LAW: 1968.
33.0211   BC   1970   ANNUAL SURVEY OF COMMONWEALTH LAW: 1969.
33.0212   BC   1971   ANNUAL SURVEY OF COMMONWEALTH LAW: 1970.

Wageningen, G. J. van

37.0873   NA   1971   Is het Landsbesluit van de 2de augustus 1971 no. 6 (P.B. 1971, 116) onbevoegd genomen en dus van rechtswege nietig [Has the Land decision of August 2, 1971 no. 6 (P.B. 1971, 116) been made without authority and is it therefore void]? *Justicia* 7(2): 33-35.   [*COL*]

Walker, Dorsey

46.0237   JM   1948   THE ROLES OF JAMAICAN MIGRANT LABOR AND THOSE INDUSTRIES OF THE CARIBBEAN AREA THAT REQUIRE HEAVY LABOR IN CONSIDERATION OF THE POLITICAL ADAPTATION OF MODERN JAMAICA, 1895-1946.

Walker, H. De R.

3.0629   **BC**   1902   THE WEST INDIES AND THE EMPIRE: STUDY AND TRAVEL IN THE WINTER OF 1900-1901.

Walle, J. van de

37.0874   **CU**   1946   De internationale ontwikkeling in West Indië gedurende den oorlog [The international development in West India during the war]. *W I G* 27: 1-17.   [*COL*]

37.0875   **JM**   1947   Rondom de nieuwe Constitutie van Jamaica [About the new Constitution of Jamaica]. *W I G* 28: 129-144.   [*COL*]

Walters, Enid

20.0084   **JM**   1971   The political attitudes of Jamaican sixth formers.

Watkins, Edwin Horatio

5.0947   **JM**   1968   THE HISTORY OF THE LEGAL SYSTEM OF JAMAICA FROM 1661 TO 1900.

Watson, Hilbourne A.

40.0083   **BC**   1975   Leadership and imperialism in the Commonwealth Caribbean.

Watts, R. L.

38.0233   **BC**   1970   MULTICULTURAL SOCIETIES AND FEDERALISM.

Wearing, Brian

37.0876   **GU**   1972   Guyana. *Rev Interam Rev* 1(2), Winter: 142-148.   [*RIS*]
37.0877   **GU**   1972   Guyana: present political situation. *In* Irving, Brian, ed. GUYANA, A COMPOSITE MONOGRAPH. Hato Rey, Puerto Rico, Inter American University Press: 32-39.   [*RIS*]

Weatherhead, Basil

37.0878   **BB**   1956   The Barbados police force: the Barbados regiment. *Can-W I Mag* 46(1), Jan.: 11, 13, 15, 17.   [*NYP*]

Weel, A. H. W. van

37.0879   **CU**   1948   Het Wetgevend lichaam [The legislature]. *In* ORANJE EN DE ZES CARAÏBISCHE PARELEN. Amsterdam, J. H. de Bussy: 202-207.
                                                                      [*UCLA*]

Weever, Guy E. L. de

37.0880   **GU**   1933   The British Guiana Constitution. *Natn Rev* 101[606], Aug.: 209-214.
                                                                      [*NYP*]

Weijtingh, C. R.

37.0881   **SR**   1938   Eenige aanvullingen op de Encyclopaedie van West-Indië: De krijgsmacht in Suriname [Some additions to the Encyclopedia of the West Indies: The power of the Army in Surinam]. *W I G* 20: 276-281, 372-374.   [*COL*]

Weitjens, W. M. A.

37.0882   **NW,CU**   1931-32   Het bestuur van de Bovenwindsche Eilanden [The government of the Windward Islands]. *W I G* 13: 231-239.   [*COL*]

Wells, Henry

37.0883   UV   1955   Outline of the constitutional development of the United States Virgin Islands. *In* Developments towards self-government in the Caribbean. A symposium held under the auspices of the Netherlands Universities Foundation for International Co-operation at The Hague, Sept. 1954. The Hague, W. van Hoeve, p.86-92. **[5]**   *[RIS]*

37.0884   UV   1955   Outline of the nature of United States Virgin Islands politics. *In* Developments towards self-government in the Caribbean. A symposium held under the auspices of the Netherlands Universities Foundation for International Co-operation at The Hague, Sept. 1954. The Hague, W. van Hoeve, p.145-147. **[16,20]**   *[RIS]*

37.0885   UV   1955   Outline of the possibilities for future constitutional development in the United States Virgin Islands. *In* Developments towards self-government in the Caribbean. A symposium held under the auspices of the Netherlands Universities Foundation for International Co-operation at The Hague, Sept. 1954. The Hague, W. van Hoeve, p.222-223.   *[RIS]*

37.0886   UV   1970   Puerto Rico's commonwealth status and its relevance to the U.S. Virgin Islands: an outline. *In* Bough, James A. & Macridis, Roy C., eds. Virgin Islands, America's Caribbean outpost: the evolution of self-government. Wakefield, Massachusetts, The Walter F. Williams Publishing Company: 174-183.   *[UNL]*

Wendt, Herbert

37.0887   GC   1966   Hurricane over the Caribbean. *In* Wendt, Herbert, ed. The red, white, and black continent: Latin America—land of reformers and rebels. Garden City, New York, Doubleday and Company, Inc.: 48-100. (Chapter 2). **[40]**   *[COL]*

Westlake, Donald E.

40.0085   AG   1972   Under an English heaven.

Westmaas, David

37.0888   GU   1971   The local government elections—a national scandal. *Thunder* 2(1), Jan.-March: 53-64.   *[RIS]*

Weston, S. Burns

37.0889   GC   1944   The Caribbean: laboratory for colonial policy. *Antioch Rev* 4(3), Fall: 370-382.   *[COL]*

Westra, P.

37.0890   SR   1919   De Koloniale Staten van Suriname [The Colonial Council of Surinam]. *W I G* 1(1): 208-215. **[5]**   *[COL]*

White, A. D. M.

37.0891   GU   1929   Bush rum in British Guiana. *Pol J* 2: 211-217.   *[COL]*

Whitehead, Henry S.

37.0892   UV   1926   The grievance of the Virgin Islands. *Independent* 117(3979), Sept. 4: 271-273, 280. **[41]**

Whitson, Agnes M.

37.0893   JM   1929   THE CONSTITUTIONAL DEVELOPMENT OF JAMAICA, 1660 TO 1729. Manchester, Manchester University Press, 182p. (Publications of the University of Manchester [no. 190] Historical series, no. 52.) **[5]**   [*RIS*]

Wight, Gerald

35.0093   TR   1951   A proposal for the future financing of public housing in Trinidad and Tobago.

Wight, Martin

37.0894   BC   1946   THE DEVELOPMENT OF THE LEGISLATIVE COUNCIL, 1606-1945. London, Faber and Faber, 187p.   [*COL*]

Wilkin, H. C.

37.0895   TR   1945   Military activities in Trinidad. *Can-W I Mag* 35(5), June: 60-65.   [*NYP*]

Wilkinson, Henry

37.0896   BE   1945   The Governor, the Council & Assembly in Bermuda during the first half of the eighteenth century. *Bermuda Hist Q* 2(2), April-June: 69-84. **[5]**   [*NYP*]

Will, H. A.

5.0980   JM,TR   1966   Problems of constitutional reform in Jamaica, Mauritius and Trinidad, 1880-95.

37.0897   JM,TR,GU   1968   THE COLONIAL OFFICE AND PROBLEMS OF CONSTITUTIONAL REFORM IN JAMAICA, TRINIDAD AND BRITISH GUIANA, 1880-1903. Ph.D. dissertation, University of London: 422p. **[5]**

5.0982   BC   1970   CONSTITUTIONAL CHANGE IN THE BRITISH WEST INDIES, 1880-1903: WITH SPECIAL REFERENCE TO JAMAICA, BRITISH GUIANA AND TRINIDAD.

Will, Wilbur Marvin

37.0898   BB   1972   POLITICAL DEVELOPMENT IN THE MINI-STATE CARIBBEAN: A FOCUS ON BARBADOS. Ph.D. dissertation, University of Missouri (Columbia): 373p. **[5,40]**   [*PhD*]

Willemse, Age

41.0527   NA   1975   Het begrotingsbeleid in de Antillen [The budget policy in the Antilles].

Williams, Dalbert Adolphus

37.0899   JM   1968   CROWN COLONY GOVERNMENT IN JAMAICA 1866-1914. Ph.D. dissertation, Catholic University of America: 149p. **[5]**   [*PhD*]

Williams, Douglas

37.0900   BC   1958   Constitutional developments in the British West Indies. *In* Wilgus, A. Curtis, ed. THE CARIBBEAN: BRITISH, DUTCH, FRENCH, UNITED STATES [PAPERS DELIVERED AT THE EIGHTH CONFERENCE ON THE CARIBBEAN HELD AT THE UNIVERSITY OF FLORIDA, DEC. 5-7, 1957]. Gainesville, University of Florida Press, p.3-10. (Publications of the School of Inter-American Studies, ser. 1, v. 8.) **[38]**   [*RIS*]

Williams, Eric Eustace

| 37.0901 | GC | 1942 | Crossways of the Caribbean. *Surv Graphic* 31(11), Nov.: 510-514, 564. **[16]** [*COL*] |

42.0178 BC 1943 Laissez faire, sugar and slavery.

6.0302 BC 1954 THE BRITISH WEST INDIES AT WESTMINSTER. PART I: 1789-1823.

37.0902 TR 1955 THE CASE FOR PARTY POLITICS IN TRINIDAD AND TOBAGO. Port of Spain, Teachers Economic and Cultural Association, 24p. (Public Affairs pamphlet no. 4.) [*RIS*]

37.0903 TR 1955 CONSTITUTION REFORM IN TRINIDAD AND TOBAGO. Port of Spain, Teachers Economic and Cultural Association. (Public affairs pamphlets no. 2.)

38.0236 BC 1956 FEDERATION: TWO PUBLIC LECTURES.

2.0514 TR 1960 PERSPECTIVES FOR THE WEST INDIES.

16.0102 GC 1960 Race relations in Caribbean society.

2.0516 TR 1964 Trinidad and Tobago: international perspectives.

37.0904 TR 1965 AN ADDRESS (DELIVERED AT THE NINTH ANNUAL CONVENTION OF THE PNM ON SEPTEMBER 24). Port-of-Spain, Trinidad, PNM Publishing Co., Ltd.: 24p. [*RIS*]

37.0905 TR 1965 THE DEVELOPING NATION IN THE MODERN WORLD (ENCAENIA ADDRESS, THURSDAY, MAY 20, 1965). Fredericton, N. B., Univ. of New Brunswick: 9p. [*RIS*]

46.0240 TR 1965 REFLECTIONS ON THE INDUSTRIAL STABILISATION BILL.

37.0906 TR 1965 REORGANISATION OF THE PUBLIC SERVICE: THREE SPEECHES. Port-of-Spain, Trinidad, P.N.M. Publishing Co. Ltd.: 131p. **[41]** [*RIS*]

37.0907 TR 1966 A REVIEW OF THE POLITICAL SCENE. ADDRESS TO THE SPECIAL P.N.M. CONVENTION, SEPT. 11. Port-of-Spain, Trinidad, P.N.M. Publishing Co. Ltd.: 19p. [*RIS*]

37.0908 BC 1969 BRITAIN AND THE WEST INDIES (NOEL BUXTON LECTURE, THE UNIVERSITY OF ESSEX). London, and Harlow, England, Longmans, Green and Co., Ltd.: 23p. **[39]** [*RIS*]

37.0909 TR 1970 NATIONWIDE BROADCAST, 10TH MAY, 1970. Trinidad, Government Printery: 4p. [*RIS*]

37.0910 TR 1972 Patterns of progress. *In* Boyke, Roy, ed. PATTERNS OF PROGRESS: TRINIDAD AND TOBAGO, 10 YEARS OF INDEPENDENCE. Port-of-Spain, Trinidad, Key Caribbean Publications: 13-23. [*RIS*]

37.0911 TR 1973 ADDRESS BY THE POLITICAL LEADER (DELIVERED ON FRIDAY 28TH SEPTEMBER, 1973, AT THE CHAGUARAMAS CONVENTION CENTER). Trinidad, PNM: 36p. [*RIS*]

37.0912 TR 1973 Proportional representation in Trinidad and Tobago: the case against. *Round Table* 63(250), April: 233-245. [*COL*]

37.0913 TR 1974 THE ENERGY CRISIS 1973-1974: THREE ADDRESSES. Arima, Trinidad, Trinidad and Tobago Printing and Packaging Ltd.: 14p. [*RIS*]

Williams, George

37.0914 BC 1968 Government programmes: a brief résumé. *In* REPORT OF CONSULTATION ON SOCIAL AND ECONOMIC DEVELOPMENT IN THE EASTERN CARIBBEAN HELD IN ST. VINCENT NOV. 26-30, 1968. Port-of-Spain, Trinidad, Superservice Printing Co.: 30-32. [*RIS*]

Williams, Victor

41.0537 TR 1969 Planning techniques and organization in Trinidad and Tobago.

Williamson, C.

37.0915 BC 1952 Britain's new colonial policy: 1940-1951. *S Atlan Q* 51, July: 366-373. **[33]** *[COL]*

Wiseman, H. V.

38.0244 BC 1948 THE WEST INDIES, TOWARDS A NEW DOMINION?

Wit, H. de

37.0916 SR 1958 Baas in eigen huis [Master in one's own house]. *In* Walle, J. van de & Wit, H. de, eds. SURINAME IN STROOMLIJNEN. Amsterdam, Wereld Bibliotheek, p.117-133.

Wolf, Sig. W.

37.0917 SR 1971 SURINAME ZOEKEND NAAR EIGEN IDENTITEIT [SURINAM LOOKING FOR ITS OWN IDENTITY]. Roermond, The Netherlands, Centrum Oriëntatie Latijns-Amerika (COLAM): 18p. **[40]** *[RILA]*

Wooding, Hugh

37.0918 TR 1960 The constitutional history of Trinidad and Tobago. *Car Q* 6(2-3), May: 143-159. **[5]** *[RIS]*

37.0919 BC 1968 A COLLECTION OF ADDRESSES. Trinidad and Tobago, Government Printing Office: 182p. *[RIS]*

Wooding, Hugh, ed.

38.0247 AG,UK 1970 REPORT OF THE COMMISSION OF INQUIRY APPOINTED BY THE GOVERNMENTS OF THE UNITED KINGDOM AND ST. CHRISTOPHER-NEVIS-ANGUILLA TO EXAMINE THE ANGUILLA PROBLEM.

37.0920 TR 1972 THINKING THINGS THROUGH. Trinidad, Government Printery: 112p. *[CEIP]*

Woolcott, David

37.0921 BC,UK 1965 Southall. *In* Deakin, Nicholas, ed. COLOUR AND THE BRITISH ELECTORATE, 1964: SIX CASE STUDIES. New York, Frederick A. Praeger: 31-53. **[16,18]** *[COL]*

Worswick, G. D. N.

41.0540 JM 1956 Financing development.

Wouk, Jonathan

37.0922 GU 1967 British Guiana: a case study in British colonial and foreign policy. *Polit Scient* 3(2), Jan.-June: 41-59. **[39]** *[COL]*

Wouw, J. J. van

43.0468 SR 1949 Het departement van landbouw-economische zaken in Suriname in 1945 [The department of agricultural-economic affairs in Surinam in 1945].

Wrong, Hume

5.1004 BC 1969 GOVERNMENT OF THE WEST INDIES.

Wytema, H. J.

37.0923 CU,SR 1931 OPPERBESTUUR EN ALGEMEEN BESTUUR OVER NEDERLANDSCH INDIE, SURINAME EN CURACAO [SOVEREIGN RULE AND GENERAL RULE OVER THE DUTCH EAST INDIES, SURINAM, AND CURACAO]. Groningen, Wolters, 92p.

Young, Allan

36.0092	GU	1957	SOME MILESTONES IN VILLAGE HISTORY.
37.0924	GU	1958	THE APPROACHES TO LOCAL SELF-GOVERNMENT IN BRITISH GUIANA. London, Longmans, Green, 246p. **[5,8,33]** [*RIS*]

Young, J. G.

37.0925	JM	1945	The beginnings of civil government in Jamaica. *Jam Hist Rev* 1(1), June: 49-65. [*NYP*]
48.0174	JM	1959	Old road laws of Jamaica.

Zaal, G. Ph.

49.0111	SR	1938	Loterijen in Suriname [Lotteries in Surinam].

Zaheeruddeen, Mohamed

37.0926	GU	1973	FROM SELF-DESTRUCTION TO SELF-RELIANCE. Address presented at the 16th Annual Delegates' Congress of the P.N.C., 2nd May: 12p. [*RIS*]

Zeidenfelt, Alex

48.0175	GC	1950	Transportation in the Caribbean during World War II.
37.0927	JM	1952	Political and constitutional developments in Jamaica. *J Polit* 14(3), Aug.: 512-540.

Zeidler, Gerhard

37.0928	FG	1940	CAYENNE—HELL LET LOOSE! Berlin, German Information Service, 81p. [*COL*]

Chapter 38

INTRAREGIONAL ISSUES

The British West Indies Federation; political, economic, social integration; inter-territorial cooperation; cooperative regional projects.

See also: **[37]** Politics and government; **[39]** International issues; **[40]** Post-colonial issues.

Abbott, George C.

41.0001 **BC** 1963 The future of economic co-operation in the West Indies in the light of the break-up of the Federation.

Abbott, Richard L.

47.0001 **BC** 1969 The Caribbean Free Trade Association. *Law Am* (2).

47.0002 **BC** 1969 The Caribbean Free Trade Association. *Law Am* (3).

Adams, F. Cunningham

38.0001 **BC** 1961 Nations, like men, have their infancy. *In* Brown, John, ed. LEEWARDS: WRITINGS, PAST AND PRESENT, ABOUT THE LEEWARD ISLANDS. [Bridgetown?] Barbados, Dept. of Extra-Mural Studies, Leeward Islands, University College of the West Indies, p.71-73.

[*RIS*]

Anderson, Robert W.

38.0002 **GC** 1967 Social science ideology and the politics of national integration. *In* Lewis, Sybil & Mathews, Thomas G., eds. CARIBBEAN INTEGRATION: PAPERS ON SOCIAL, POLITICAL, AND ECONOMIC INTEGRATION. THIRD CARIBBEAN SCHOLARS' CONFERENCE, GEORGETOWN, GUYANA, APRIL 4-9, 1966. Rio Piedras, University of Puerto Rico, Institute of Caribbean Studies: 21-37. **[37]** [*RIS*]

Andic, Fuat M.

41.0009 **GC** 1967 Fiscal aspects of economic integration with special reference to selected Caribbean countries.

32.0024 **GC** 1968 THE EFFORTS OF THE INSTITUTE OF CARIBBEAN STUDIES FOR COOPERATION AMONG THE UNIVERSITIES OF THE REGION: COMMUNIQUE AT THE CONFERENCE OF THE INSTITUTE VIZIOZ. LES EFFORTS DE L'INSTITUT D'ETUDES DES CARAÏBES POUR LA COOPERATION ENTRE LES UNIVERSITÉS DE LA RÉGION: COMMUNIQUÉ POUR LA CONFERENCE DE L'INSTITUT VIZIOZ.

38.0003   GC   1974   CARIFTA, CARIBANK and CARICOM: a brief survey. *In* Studies on the economic integration of the Caribbean and Latin America. Association of Caribbean Universities and Research Institutes (UNICA): 37-51.   **[47,49]**   [*RIS*]

Andic, Fuat M. & Gutiérrez, Elías
47.0010   GC   1966   Caribbean trade patterns.

Anglin, Douglas G.
37.0011   BC   1961   The political development of the West Indies.

Archibald, Charles H.
38.0004   BC   1956   British Caribbean Federation. *Venture* 7(11), Apr.: 6-7.   [*COL*]
38.0005   BC   1958   First steps in West Indies Federation. *New Commonw* 35(11), May 26: 509-510.   [*AGS*]
38.0006   BC   1959   West Indian Federation: federal and territorial conflict. *Venture* 10(8), Jan.: 6-7.   [*COL*]
38.0007   BC   1961   Adrift in the Caribbean. *Venture* 13(10), Nov.: 5.   [*COL*]
38.0008   BC   1961   Question-mark over the Caribbean. *New Commonw* 39(7), Aug.: 505-508.   [*AGS*]
38.0009   BC   1962   The failure of the West Indies Federation. *Wld Today* 18(6), June: 233-242.   [*COL*]

Armstrong, Eric
38.0010   JM,TR   1967   Import substitution in Jamaica and Trinidad and Tobago: incentive legislation in Trinidad and Tobago. Jamaica, University of the West Indies, Institute of Social and Economic Research: 32p. (Studies in Regional Economic Integration, 2(5), Part A) **[47]**   [*RIS*]

Armstrong, Percy E.
38.0011   BC   1945   British West Indies' approach to federation. *Crown Colonist* 15(167), Oct.: 677-678.   [*AGS*]

Aspinall, Algernon E.
38.0012   BC   1919   West Indian Federation: its historical aspect. *United Emp* new ser., 10(2), Feb.: 58-63. **[5]**   [*AGS*]

Auguiac, Max
38.0013   FC   1968-69 La réforme régionale [Regional reform]. *B Cham Com Indus Mart,* 4th trimester/1st trimester: 49-55.   [*RIS*]

Ayearst, Morley
38.0014   BC   1957   Political aspects of Federation. *Social Econ Stud* 6(2), June: 247-261.   [*RIS*]

Baa, Enid M., ed.
1.0013   GC   1970   Conference on sharing Caribbean resources for instruction and research, May 17-19, 1969.

Bahadoorsingh, Krishna
38.0015   BC   1969   The East Caribbean Federation attempts. *In* Preiswerk, Roy, ed. Regionalism and the Commonwealth Caribbean: papers presented at the "Seminar on the Foreign Policies of Caribbean States", April-June, 1968. Trinidad, University of the West Indies, Institute of International Relations: 157-169.   [*RIS*]

Bailey, Sydney D.

37.0032   **BC**   1949   Constitutions of the British Colonies. I: Colonies in the western hemisphere.

38.0016   **BC**   1952   A British Caribbean Federation. *Fortnightly* new ser., 1028, Aug.: 84-89.   [*NYP*]

Ballah, Lennox F.

38.0017   **GC**   1974   Applicability of the archipelago and mare clausum to the Caribbean Sea. *In* PACEM IN MARIBUS: CARIBBEAN STUDY PROJECT WORKING PAPERS AND SELECTION FROM DIALOGUE AT PREPARATORY CONFERENCE, JAMAICA, OCTOBER, 1972. Malta, Malta University Press: 276-304. (Chapter 13)   **[39,56]**   [*RIS*]

Balogh, Thomas

47.0013   **BC**   1960   Making of a customs union.

Beauregard, C. F.

38.0018   **GC**   1963   The Caribbean organization and development in the Caribbean. *Chron W I Comm* 78(1391), Dec.: 644-646.   [*NYP*]

Beckford, George L. & Grant, Cedric

38.0019   **BZ**   1967   British Honduras: two views. *New Wld Q* 3(4), Cropover: 51-55.
                                                                            [*RIS*]

Bell, Wendell

38.0020   **JM**   1960   Attitudes of Jamaican elites toward the West Indies Federation. *In* Rubin, Vera, ed. SOCIAL AND CULTURAL PLURALISM IN THE CARIBBEAN. New York, New York Academy of Sciences, p.862-879. (*Annals of the New York Academy of Sciences*, v. 83, art. 5.)   **[8,20]**
                                                                            [*RIS*]

Bell, Wendell & Oxaal, Ivar

37.0048   **BC**   1967   The nation-state as a unit in the comparative study of social change.

Benham, Frederic C.

47.0020   **BC**   1945   BRITISH WEST INDIAN INTER-COLONIAL TRADE IN THE WEST INDIES.

Best, Lloyd

38.0021   **TR**   1965   Chaguaramas to slavery? *New Wld Q* 2(1), Dead Season: 43-70.
                                                                            [*RIS*]

41.0042   **GC**   1967   Current development strategy and economic integration in the Caribbean.

Birch, A. H.

38.0022   **BC**   1950   A British Caribbean Federation: the next dominion? *Parl Aff* 14(1), Winter: 152-162.   [*COL*]

Blair, Patricia Wohlgemuth

37.0059   **GC**   1967   THE MINISTATE DILEMMA.

Blanc, O.

21.0006   **GD,MT**   1965   La France des Antilles [The France of the Antilles].

Blanshard, Paul
38.0023   BC   1949   Twilight of Caribbean imperialism. *Nation* 168(4), Jan. 22: 92-94.
                                                                                                                 [*COL*]

Blood, Hilary
38.0024   BC   1955   The birth of a new nation. *Listener* 54(1400), Dec. 29: 1109-1110.
                                                                                                                 [*COL*]
38.0025   BC   1956   Federation in the Caribbean. *Corona* 8(5), May: 166-169.   [*AGS*]
38.0026   BC   1957   The West Indian Federation. *J Roy Soc Arts* 105(5009), Aug. 2:
                                          746-757.   [*AGS*]
38.0027   BC   1958   British Caribbean Federation. *J Roy Commonw Soc* 1(2), July-Aug.:
                                          158-162.   [*AGS*]
38.0028   BC   1958   Final stages in the West Indies. *Corona* 10(5), May: 166-168.   [*AGS*]

Bloomfield, Arthur
49.0010   BC   [n.d.]   Central banking arrangements for the West Indian Feder-
                                          ation.

Bobb, Lewis E.
38.0029   BC   1966   The federal principle in the British West Indies: an appraisal of its
                                          use. *Social Econ Stud* 15(3), Sept.: 239-265.   [*RIS*]

Bolt, Anne
2.0036   BC   1961   A diversity of islands: The West Indian Federation.

Bough, James A.
38.0030   GC   1949   The Caribbean Commission. *Int Org* 3(4), Nov.: 643-655.

Boyd, P. I.
28.0150   BC   1975   The health programme of the Caricom Secretariat.

Bradshaw
41.0064   BC   1958   Financial problems of the federation.

Brady, Alexander
38.0031   BC   1958   The West Indies: a new Federation. Toronto, Canadian Institute
                                          of International Affairs, 16p. (Behind the headlines, v. 17, no. 5.)
                                                                                                                 [*RIS*]

Braine, Bernard
38.0032   BC   1953   To be or not to be. . .? in the West Indies. *New Commonw* 25(7),
                                          Mar. 30: 324-325.   [*AGS*]

Braithwaite, Lloyd E.
38.0033   BC   1957   'Federal' associations and institutions in the West Indies. *Social
                                          Econ Stud* 6(2), June: 286-328.   **[8,23,32,41]**   [*RIS*]
38.0034   BC   1957   Progress toward Federation, 1938-1956. *Social Econ Stud* 6(2), June:
                                          133-184.   **[5,41]**   [*RIS*]

Brent-Harris, K. B.
47.0036   BC   1970   The compatibility of the CARIFTA agreement and the General
                                          Agreement of Tariffs and Trade with particular reference to Article
                                          XXIV of the GATT.

Brewster, Havelock & Thomas, Clive Y.
41.0077   GC   1967   THE DYNAMICS OF WEST INDIAN ECONOMIC INTEGRATION.

Broderick, Margaret
37.0091   BC   1968   Associated Statehood—a new form of decolonisation.

Brown, Adlith
38.0035   AT   1976   Caribbean mini-states and the Caribbean Common Market: the case of Antigua. *In* Lewis, Vaughan A., ed. SIZE, SELF-DETERMINATION AND INTERNATIONAL RELATIONS: THE CARIBBEAN. Mona, Jamaica, University of the West Indies, Institute of Social and Economic Research: 122-157.   **[41,42,45]**   [*RIS*]

Brown, Noel
37.0093   JM   1963   JAMAICA AND THE WEST INDIES FEDERATION: A CASE STUDY ON THE PROBLEMS OF POLITICAL INTEGRATION.

Brunn, Stanley D.; Ford, John J. & McIntosh, Terry
37.0098   GC   1971   The state of political geography research in Latin America

Bryden, John M.
43.0057   BC   1968   THE CONTRIBUTION OF AGRICULTURE TO ECONOMIC GROWTH IN THE FORMER FEDERATION OF WEST INDIES, 1955-66: A STATISTICAL ANALYSIS.

Buckmaster, Michael H.
38.0036   BC   1962   What prospect for the Windwards? *New Commonw* 40(2), Feb.: 89-92.

Burgess, Charles J.
48.0031   GC   1954   Problems of intra-Caribbean transportation.

Burns, Alan
38.0037   BC   1955   Towards a Caribbean Federation. *For Aff* 34(1), Oct.: 128-140.
                                                                        [*AGS*]

Cahnman, Werner J.
38.0038   BC   1948   The West-Indian Federation. *Jew Fron* 15(1), Jan.: 16-18.   [*COL*]

Caires, David de
41.0089   GU   1963   Regional integration.

Campbell, Jock
37.0118   BC   1962   Facing up to facts in the Caribbean.
37.0119   BC   1963   The West Indies: can they stand alone?

Carstairs, C. Y.
38.0039   BC   1950   Federation. *J Barb Mus Hist Soc* 17(2-3), Feb.-May: 84-92.   [*AMN*]

Castañeda, Jorge
38.0040   GC   1974   The patrimonial sea as a regional concept. *In* PACEM IN MARIBUS: CARIBBEAN STUDY PROJECT WORKING PAPERS AND SELECTION FROM DIALOGUE AT PREPARATORY CONFERENCE, JAMAICA, OCTOBER, 1972. Malta, Malta University Press: 341-365. (Chapter 16)   **[39]**   [*RIS*]

Clarke, Colin G.

37.0144   **AG**   1971   Political fragmentation in the Caribbean: the case of Anguilla.

Clingan, Thomas A., Jr.

39.0041   **GC**   1972   The oceans.

38.0041   **GC**   1973   The oceans. *Law Am* 5(1): 181-197.   [*COL*]

Coard, Bernard

40.0012   **BC**   1974   The meaning of political independence in the Commonwealth Caribbean.

Collart, Yves

38.0042   **BC**   1969   Regional conflict resolution and the integration process in the Commonwealth Caribbean. *In* Preiswerk, Roy, ed. REGIONALISM AND THE COMMONWEALTH CARIBBEAN: PAPERS PRESENTED AT THE "SEMINAR ON THE FOREIGN POLICIES OF CARIBBEAN STATES", APRIL-JUNE, 1968. Trinidad, University of the West Indies, Institute of International Relations: 170-188.   [*RIS*]

Collins, B. A. N.

38.0043   **BC**   1969   The Caribbean Regional Secretariat. *In* Preiswerk, Roy, ed. REGIONALISM AND THE COMMONWEALTH CARIBBEAN: PAPERS PRESENTED AT THE "SEMINAR ON THE FOREIGN POLICIES OF CARIBBEAN STATES", APRIL-JUNE, 1968. Trinidad, University of the West Indies, Institute of International Relations: 108-115.   [*RIS*]

Collins, Charles O.

40.0013   **BZ**   1973   THE POLITICAL GEOGRAPHY OF NATION-BUILDING: THE CASE OF BELIZE.

Collymore, Clinton

38.0044   **BC**   1972   Caribbean integration. *Thunder* 4(1), Jan.-March: 15-23.   [*RIS*]

Coon, F. Seal

38.0045   **GU**   1951   British Guiana's attitude towards Federation. *New Commonw* 22(6), Dec.: 474.

Corkran, Herbert

38.0046   **GC**   1961   CHANGING PATTERNS OF INTERNATIONAL ORGANIZATION IN THE CARIBBEAN. Ph.D. dissertation, Indiana University: 406p.   **[40]**
                                                                            [*PhD*]

38.0047   **GC**   1966   FROM FORMAL TO INFORMAL INTERNATIONAL COOPERATION IN THE CARIBBEAN. Dallas, Texas, Southern Methodist University: 34p. (Arnold Foundation Monograph 17)   [*RIS*]

39.0044   **GC**   1970   PATTERNS OF INTERNATIONAL COOPERATION IN THE CARIBBEAN, 1942-1969.

Cozier, Edward L.

38.0048   **BC**   1957   Foreshadows of Federation. *Caribbean* 10(10), May: 241-244.   **[5]**
                                                                            [*COL*]

Crabot

56.0070   **BC**   1959   Naissance d'une nation: la Féderation des Antilles Britanniques [Birth of a nation: the British West Indies Federation].

Crassweller, Robert D.

39.0046   **GC**   1972   THE CARIBBEAN COMMUNITY: CHANGING SOCIETIES AND U.S. POLICY.

Crocker, John

38.0049   **BC**   1973   A new era in Caribbean thinking. *W I Chron* 88(1507), Aug.: 319-322. **[47]**   [*NYP*]

Croft, W. D.; Springer, H. W. & Christopherson, H. S.

47.0075   **BC**   1958   REPORT OF THE TRADE AND TARIFFS COMMISSION.

Crowe, Harry J.

38.0050   **BC**   1920   Political union between Canada and the West Indies. *Can-W I Mag* 8(9), July: 576-577. **[47]**   [*NYP*]

38.0051   **BC**   1921   The future relations of Canada and Jamaica. *Can-W I Mag* 9(4), Feb.: 96-97. **[47]**   [*NYP*]

Cumper, George E., ed.

41.0126   **BC**   1960   ECONOMY OF THE WEST INDIES.

Curry, Herbert Franklin, Jr.

38.0052   **BC**   1958   THE MOVEMENT TOWARDS FEDERATION OF THE BRITISH WEST INDIAN COLONIES, 1634-1945. Ph.D. dissertation, University of Wisconsin, 306p. **[5]**   [*NYP*]

Dale, Edmund H.

38.0053   **BC**   1961   The West Indies: a Federation in search of a capital. *Can Geogr* 5(2), Summer: 44-52.

38.0054   **BC**   1962   The state-idea: missing prop of the West Indies Federation. *Scott Geogr Mag* 78(3), Dec.: 166-176.   [*COL*]

David, Wilfred L.

47.0081   **GU**   1969   A large country in CARIFTA: the case of Guyana.

Davson, Edward R.

37.0187   **BC**   1919   Problems of the West Indies.

DeCastro, Steve

38.0055   **BC**   [n.d.]   Caribbean economic integration and the West Indians. *New Wld Q* 5(3): 27-35. **[41]**   [*RIS*]

Demas, William G.

47.0085   **BC**   1960   The economics of West Indies customs union.

38.0056   **BC**   1967   Planning and the price-mechanism in the context of Caribbean economic integration. *In* Lewis, Sybil & Mathews, Thomas G., eds. CARIBBEAN INTEGRATION: PAPERS ON SOCIAL, POLITICAL, AND ECONOMIC INTEGRATION. THIRD CARIBBEAN SCHOLARS' CONFERENCE, GEORGETOWN, GUYANA, APRIL 4-9, 1966. Rio Piedras, University of Puerto Rico, Institute of Caribbean Studies: 77-100. **[47]**   [*RIS*]

38.0057   **BC**   1974   WEST INDIAN NATIONHOOD AND CARIBBEAN INTEGRATION. Barbados, CCC Publishing House: 74p. (Challenges in the New Caribbean series, No. 1) **[21,40]**   [*RIS*]

40.0020   **BC**   1975   CHANGE AND RENEWAL IN THE CARIBBEAN.

38.0058   **BC**   1976   Some thoughts on the Caribbean community. *B E Car Aff* 2(8), Oct.: 1-3. **[47]**   [*RIS*]

Denny, P.

47.0087 BC 1970 A consideration of Article 36 of CARIFTA in the context of conflict resolution in the Caribbean.

Domingo, W. A.

38.0059 BC 1956 BRITISH WEST INDIAN FEDERATION: A CRITIQUE. Kingston, Gleaner Co., 19p.

Dominice, Christian

39.0050 BC 1969 The denuclearization of Latin America.

Drummond, Andrew T.

38.0060 BC 1917 The future of the West Indies. *W I Comm Circ* 32(448), June 14: 224-228. **[41]**   [*NYP*]

Duncan, Ebenezer

37.0208 BC 1947 THE POLITICAL CONSTITUTION OF THE WESTINDIAN COMMONWEALTH.

Dupuy, René-Jean

38.0061 FC 1974 The legal position of Guadeloupe and Martinique in the framework of a Caribbean regional regime. *In* PACEM IN MARIBUS: CARIBBEAN STUDY PROJECT WORKING PAPERS AND SELECTION FROM DIALOGUE AT PREPARATORY CONFERENCE, JAMAICA, OCTOBER, 1972. Malta, Malta University Press: 325-340. (Chapter 15)   [*RIS*]

Eckenstein, Christopher

38.0062 BC 1969 The rationale and obstacles of regional integration among developing countries. *In* Preiswerk, Roy, ed. REGIONALISM AND THE COMMONWEALTH CARIBBEAN: PAPERS PRESENTED AT THE "SEMINAR ON THE FOREIGN POLICIES OF CARIBBEAN STATES", APRIL-JUNE, 1968. Trinidad, University of the West Indies, Institute of International Relations: 25-32.   [*RIS*]

38.0063 BC 1969 Regional integration among unequally developed countries. *In* Preiswerk, Roy, ed. REGIONALISM AND THE COMMONWEALTH CARIBBEAN: PAPERS PRESENTED AT THE "SEMINAR ON THE FOREIGN POLICIES OF CARIBBEAN STATES", APRIL-JUNE: 1968. Trinidad, University of the West Indies, Institute of International Relations: 41-55.   [*RIS*]

Elias, Taslim Olawale

38.0064 BC 1960 FEDERATION VS. CONFEDERATION AND THE NIGERIAN FEDERATION. Port of Spain, Office of the Premier of Trinidad and Tobago, 50p.   [*RIS*]

Emery, Byron Elwyn

38.0065 BC 1963 REGIONAL INTEGRATION AND DISINTEGRATION IN THE BRITISH CARIBBEAN AREA. Ph.D. dissertation, University of Michigan: 322p.   [*PhD*]

Emmart, A. D.

38.0066 GC [n.d.] CARIBBEAN COOPERATION. Washington, D.C., Anglo-American Caribbean Commission.   [*AGS*]

Etienne, Flory
38.0067 GC 1952 LA COMMISSION DES CARAÏBES [THE CARIBBEAN COMMISSION]. Paris, Maurice Lavergne, 192p. (Ph.D. dissertation, University of Paris.)
[*COL*]

Etzioni, Amitai
38.0068 BC 1965 A union that failed: the Federation of the West Indies (1958-1962). *In his* POLITICAL UNIFICATION: A COMPARATIVE STUDY OF LEADERS AND FORCES. New York, Holt, Rinehart and Winston, p.138-183.
[*RIS*]

Fawcett, J. E. S.
39.0059 GU,UK 1967 International law.
39.0060 BC 1968 International law.
39.0061 KNA 1969 International law.

Ferraté F., Luis A.
38.0069 GC 1974 A model for environmental design. *In* PACEM IN MARIBUS: CARIBBEAN STUDY PROJECT WORKING PAPERS AND SELECTION FROM DIALOGUE AT PREPARATORY CONFERENCE, JAMAICA, OCTOBER, 1972. Malta, Malta University Press: 170-193. **[41,56]**   [*RIS*]

Fertig, Norman Ross
38.0070 BC 1958 THE CLOSER UNION MOVEMENT IN THE BRITISH WEST INDIES. Ph.D. dissertation, University of Southern California, 316p. **[5]**   [*NYP*]

Finnis, J. M. & Carnegie, A. R.
37.0238 BC 1969 Constitutional law.
37.0239 BC 1970 Constitutional law.

Flanz, Gisbert H.
38.0071 BC 1968 West Indian Federation. *In* Franck, Thomas M., ed. WHY FEDERATIONS FAIL: AN INQUIRY INTO THE REQUISITES FOR SUCCESSFUL FEDERALISM. New York, New York University Press: 91-123. [*RIS*]

Foot, Hugh
38.0072 BC 1957 Great Britain and the building of a new self-governing nation in the Caribbean. *In* Wilgus, A. Curtis, ed. THE CARIBBEAN: CONTEMPORARY, INTERNATIONAL RELATIONS [PAPERS DELIVERED AT THE SEVENTH CONFERENCE ON THE CARIBBEAN HELD AT THE UNIVERSITY OF FLORIDA, DEC. 6-8, 1965]. Gainesville, University of Florida Press, p.53-58. (Publications of the School of Inter-American Studies, ser. 1, v. 7.)   [*RIS*]

Forbes, Urias
38.0073 BC 1970 The West Indies Associated States: some aspects of the constitutional arrangements. *Social Econ Stud* 19(1), March: 57-88. [*RIS*]

Forsythe, Dennis
20.0024 GC 1974 Repression, radicalism and change in the West Indies.

Francis, Fitzgerald
49.0043 BC 1969 The Caribbean Development Bank.

Franck, Thomas M.

38.0074   **BC**   1968   Why federations fail. *In* Franck, Thomas M., ed. WHY FEDERATIONS FAIL: AN INQUIRY INTO THE REQUISITES FOR SUCCESSFUL FEDERALISM. New York, New York University Press: 167-199. (Chapter 5)   **[37]**
                                                                                                          [*COL*]

Franck, Thomas M., ed.

38.0075   **BC**   1968   WHY FEDERATIONS FAIL: AN INQUIRY INTO THE REQUISITES FOR SUCCESSFUL FEDERALISM. New York, New York University Press: 213p.   **[37]**   [*COL*]

Franco Holguín, Jorge

47.0101   **GC**   1969   Problems of developing inter-regional trade and production in the Caribbean/Latin American area.

Freitas, G. V. de

38.0076   **BC**   1956   Wanted—a federal capital. *New Commonw* 32(3), Aug.: 118-119.
                                                                                                          [*AGS*]

Galindo Pohl, Reynaldo

38.0077   **GC**   1974   Pacem in maribus in the Caribbean region. *In* PACEM IN MARIBUS: CARIBBEAN STUDY PROJECT WORKING PAPERS AND SELECTION FROM DIALOGUE AT PREPARATORY CONFERENCE, JAMAICA, OCTOBER, 1972. Malta, Malta University Press: 414-440. (Chapter 18)   **[39]**   [*RIS*]

Garcia-Amador, F. V.

47.0107   **BC**   1972   Latin American economic integration.

Giles, Walter I.

37.0287   **JM**   1956   JAMAICA: A STUDY OF BRITISH COLONIAL POLICY AND THE DEVELOPMENT OF SELF-GOVERNMENT.

Gillette, H. P. S.

28.0514   **BC**   1960   Comments of Dr. Thomas's report of the chest service for the Federation of the West Indies.

Girvan, Norman

38.0078   **BC**   1966   West Indian unity. *New Wld F* 1(45), Aug. 8: 10-23.   [*RIS*]
38.0079   **TR**   1967   Prospects for a Caribbean economic community. *Enterprise* May: 15-29.   **[47]**   [*RIS*]
50.0057   **GC**   1967   Regional integration vs. company integration in the utilization of Caribbean bauxite.
39.0069   **BC**   1969   Integration from the viewpoint of the Caribbean: system of resource allocation in the private sector.

Glassner, Martin Ira

39.0070   **JM,TR**   1970   The foreign relations of Jamaica and Trinidad and Tobago, 1960-1965.

Goban, M. O.

38.0080   **BC**   1951   Federation in the West Indies? *Contemp Rev* 180, Sept.: 145-148.
                                                                                                          [*COL*]

Gomes, Albert

38.0081   BC   1959   The ides of September—for the W. I. Federation. *Can-W I Mag* 49(9), Sept.: 1-2.   [*NYP*]

Gordon, Garnet H.

38.0082   BC   1961   The West Indies before and after Jamaica's quitvote. *Commonw J* 4(6), Nov.-Dec.: 274-279.   [*COL*]

Gordon, William E.

37.0294   JM   1939   Jamaicans strive for dominion status.

Gottschalk, Kurt P.

38.0083   BZ   1969   BRITISH HONDURAS (BELIZE) AND REGIONAL ECONOMIC INTEGRATION: AN ANALYSIS OF ALTERNATIVE CHOICES. Winston-Salem, Wake Forest University, Overseas Research Center: 55p. (Developing Nations Monograph Series 1) **[41]**   [*RIS*]

Greenidge, C. W. W.

38.0084   BC   1950   The British Caribbean Federation. *Wld Aff* 4(3), July: 321-334.   [*AGS*]

38.0085   BC   1952   West Indian Federation. *W I Comm Circ* 68(1266), June: 145-146.   [*NYP*]

38.0086   BB   1956   Barbados and the Pope Hennessy riots. *W I Comm Circ* 71(1303), July: 183-184. **[5]**   [*NYP*]

Habron, John D.

38.0087   JM   1970   ISLANDS IN TRANSITION: THE DOMINICAN REPUBLIC, PUERTO RICO, JAMAICA. Toronto, Canadian Institute of International Affairs: 18p. **[37]**   [*CEIP*]

Hall, Marshall

32.0266   BC   1974   Thoughts on the need for cooperation among the countries of the Caribbean in management training.

Hamilton, Bruce

38.0088   BB   1950   Barbados and British West Indian Confederation, 1871-1885. *Car His Rev* 1, Dec.: 80-109. **[5]**   [*RIS*]

38.0089   BB   1951   Barbados and British West Indian Confederation, 1871-1885. *Car His Rev* 2, Dec.: 47-78. **[5]**   [*RIS*]

38.0090   BB   1956   BARBADOS AND THE CONFEDERATION QUESTION, 1871-1885. London, Crown Agents for Overseas Governments & Administrations, 149p. **[5]**

Harewood, Jack

46.0098   JM,TR   1960   Overpopulation and underemployment in the West Indies.

Harrigan, Norwell & Varlack, Pearl

38.0091   VI   1973   Inter-relationships of the Virgin Islands. *VI Forum* 1(4): 24-31.   [*RIS*]

Hatch, John

38.0092   BC   1958   Birth of a nation. *Venture* 9(10), Mar.: 4.   [*COL*]

38.0093   BC   1958   DWELL TOGETHER IN UNITY. London, Fabian Society, 40p. (Fabian tract 313.)   [*COL*]

Hawkins, Irene
47.0124   **GC**   1975   The club of 46.

Heimsath, Surjit Mansingh
38.0094   **BC**   1972   BACKGROUND TO FAILURE OF THE WEST INDIES FEDERATION: AN
INQUITY INTO BRITISH RULE IN THE CARIBBEAN, 1920-1947. Ph.D.
dissertation, American University: 528p.   **[40]**   [*PhD*]

Helminiak, Thomas Walter
28.0629   **SL**   1972   THE SUGAR-BANANAS SHIFT OF ST. LUCIA, WEST INDIES: BILHARZIA
AND MALARIA DISEASE CAUSAL LINKAGES.

Hewitt-Myring, Philip
38.0095   **BC**   1949   West Indian future. *Spectator* 182(6298), Mar. 11: 317-318.   [*NYP*]
38.0096   **BC**   1955   British Caribbean Federation. *Parl Aff* 8(4), Autumn: 436-444.
[*COL*]

Hill, Anthony
40.0030   **BC**   1973   Economic stability in the mini-states.

Hinden, Rita
38.0097   **BC**   1953   Federating the West Indies. *Corona* 5(3), Mar.: 97-100.   [*AGS*]

Hinkson, Victor & Taylor, Don
47.0129   **BC**   1970   Carifta two years later.

Holmes, Olive
38.0098   **BC,VI**   1944   Anglo-American Caribbean Commission—pattern for colonial co-
operation. *For Policy Rep* 20(19), Dec. 15: 238-247.   [*AGS*]

Hooker, James R.
38.0099   **TR**   1972   Anatomy of a meeting: Trinidad in a non-carnival mood. *Am Univ
Field Staff* 7(1): 1-7. (Mexico and Caribbean Area Series)   **[16]**
[*CEIP*]

Hope, Kempe R.
47.0130   **BC**   1974   CARIFTA and Caribbean trade: an overview.

Hoyos, F. A.
37.0376   **BC**   1963   THE RISE OF WEST INDIAN DEMOCRACY: THE LIFE AND TIMES OF SIR
GRANTLEY ADAMS.

Hughes, Colin A.
38.0100   **BC**   1958   Experiments towards closer union in the British West Indies. *J
Negro Hist* 43(2), Apr.: 85-104.   **[5]**   [*COL*]

Hunte, George Hutchinson
16.0050   **BC**   1946   West Indian unity: measures and machinery.
51.0054   **BC**   1957   Tourism: a federal approach.
51.0055   **BB**   1959   Barbados in the federal tourist picture.

Hunte, K. R.
41.0254   **BB**   1961   TO WORK TOGETHER IN UNITY: FOR THE ECONOMIC BETTERMENT OF
THE WEST INDIES FEDERATION.

Hunte, Keith

40.0031   BC   1970   The last days of empire in the Caribbean: the tribulations of regionalism.

Huurman, D.

37.0388   NC   1948   Britse federatieve voorstellen en Nederlandse federatiemogelijkheden in West Indië [British federation proposals and Dutch federation possibilities in the West Indies].

Jacobs, H. P.

38.0101   BC   1956   This Federation. *Pepperpot* [6]: 21-23.

38.0102   BC   1957   The Federal constitution: its mechanism and meaning. *W I Rev* new ser., 2(10), Oct.: 19, 21, 111.   [*NYP*]

Jagan, Cheddi

47.0137   BC   1968   CARIBBEAN UNITY AND CARIFTA.

37.0422   BC   1972   A WEST INDIAN STATE: PRO-IMPERIALIST OR ANTI-IMPERIALIST.

James, C. L. R.

38.0103   BC   1962   FEDERATION: "WE FAILED MISERABLY"; HOW AND WHY. San Juan, Trinidad, Vedic Enterprises, 32p.   [*RIS*]

Jandray, Frederick

38.0104   BC   1958   The new Federation of the West Indies. *Dep St B* 38(985), May 12: 768-769.   [*COL*]

Jeannet, Gilles

47.0140   BC   1974   CARIFTA: intégration économique dans la Caraïbe [CARIFTA: economic integration in the Caribbean].

Jefferson, Owen

47.0142   JM   1967   The case for regional economic collaboration in the West Indies.

38.0105   BC   1969   Integration from the viewpoint of the Caribbean: institutional arrangements and the economic integration of the Caribbean and Latin America. *In* Waters, Maurice, ed. THE CARIBBEAN AND LATIN AMERICA: POLITICAL AND ECONOMIC RELATIONS. VOLUME I. Jamaica, University of the West Indies: 53-57.   [*RIS*]

Jones, A. Creech

38.0106   BC   1958   Salute to Federation. *W I Comm Circ* 73(1324), Apr.: 99-100.
                                                                                 [*NYP*]

38.0107   BC   1958   A visit to the West Indies. *Venture* 10(2), June: 4.   [*COL*]

Jordan, Henry P.

38.0108   GC   1944   Regional experiment in the Caribbean. *Curr Hist* 6(33), May: 398-404.   [*COL*]

Keirstead, B. S. & Levitt, Kari

48.0089   BC   [n.d.]   INTER-TERRITORIAL FREIGHT RATES AND THE FEDERAL SHIPPING SERVICE.

Kelly, James B.

38.0109   BC   1962   The end of Federation: some constitutional implications. *W I Econ* 4(9), Mar.: 11-26.

Kim, Jung-Gun
38.0110   GC   1967   Non-member participation in the South Pacific Commission and the Caribbean Organisation. *Car Q* 13(4), Dec.: 24-30.   **[39]**   [*RIS*]

King, K. F. S.
38.0111   GU   1973   A GREAT FUTURE TOGETHER: THE DEVELOPMENT AND EMPLOYMENT PLAN [ADDRESS BY THE MINISTER OF ECONOMIC DEVELOPMENT]. La Penitence, Guyana, Design and Graphics: 28p.   **[46]**   [*UNL*]

Kissler, Betty Jane
38.0112   GU   1971   VENEZUELA-GUYANA BOUNDARY DISPUTE: 1899-1966. Ph.D. dissertation, University of Texas (Austin): 249p.   [*PhD*]

Knaplund, Paul
38.0113   BC   1962   Introduction to Federation of the West Indies. *Social Econ Stud* 6(2), June: 99-108.   **[5]**   [*RIS*]

Knight, H. Gary
38.0114   GC   1974   Impacts of some law of the sea proposals on Gulf and Caribbean resource development. *In* PACEM IN MARIBUS: CARIBBEAN STUDY PROJECT WORKING PAPERS AND SELECTION FROM DIALOGUE AT PREPARATORY CONFERENCE, JAMAICA, OCTOBER, 1972. Malta, Malta University Press: 366-413 [Chapter 17].   **[39,52]**   [*RIS*]

Knox, A. D.
47.0157   BC   1960   Trade and customs union in the West Indies.

Kok, Michiel
38.0115   GC   1973   Pogingen tot economische integratie in het Caribisch gebied vanaf het begin der tweede wereldoorlog tot heden en de rol die de Nederlandse Antillen daarbij gespeeld hebben [Attempts at economic integration in the Caribbean from the beginning of World War II until now and the role of the Netherlands Antilles here-in]. *Econ Not* 1, Jan.: 2-8.   **[47]**   [*RILA*]

Kontak, W. J. F.
38.0116   GC   1963   SOME IMPORTANT CARIBBEAN QUESTIONS. Antigonish, N. S., St. Francis Xavier University, 65p.   [*RIS*]

Krieger, David
38.0117   GC   1974   A Caribbean community for ocean development. *Int Stud Q* 18(1), March: 75-103.   **[41]**   [*COL*]
38.0118   GC   1974   A Caribbean community for ocean development. *In* PACEM IN MARIBUS: CARIBBEAN STUDY PROJECT WORKING PAPERS AND SELECTIONS FROM DIALOGUE AT PREPARATORY CONFERENCE, JAMAICA, OCTOBER, 1972. Malta, Malta University Press: 441-481 (Chapter 19).   **[39]**   [*RIS*]

Kruijer, G. J.
38.0119   NC   1956   Samenwerking Suriname en Nederlandse Antillen [Cooperation between Surinam and the Netherlands Antilles]. *Oost West* 49(2): 3-5.

Laing, Edward A.
40.0044 **WW,UK** 1974 Crown indivisibility, governmental liability and other problems in West Indies Associated States.

Leprette, Jacques
38.0120 **GC** 1960 De la Commission des Caraïbes à l'Organisation des Caraïbes [From the Caribbean Commission to the Caribbean Organization]. *Annuar Fr Dr Int* 6: 685-706. [*COL*]

Lestrade, Swinburne & Gonsalves, Ralph
38.0121 **LW,WW** 1972 Political aspects of integration of the Windward and Leeward Islands. *Car Q* 18(2), June: 28-35. **[37]** [*RIS*]

Le Veness, Frank Paul
38.0122 **BC** 1974 REGIONAL INTEGRATION: THE CASE OF THE COMMONWEALTH CARIBBEAN. Prepared for International Studies Association, St. Louis, Missouri: 37p. **[47]** [*RIS*]

Levo, Edith Miriam
38.0123 **BC** 1957 THE FEDERATION OF THE BRITISH WEST INDIES: DEVELOPMENT AND PROSPECTS. M. A. thesis, Clark University, 108p.

Levy, Claude
38.0124 **BC** 1950 PROBLEMS IN BRITISH WEST INDIAN FEDERATION. Ph.D. dissertation, University of Colorado, 266p. **[5]**

Lewinski, Wilhelm
38.0125 **BC** 1970 Die West-Indische Föderation [The West Indies Federation]. *Z Polit* 17(4), Nov.: 472-483. [*COL*]

Lewis, Gordon K.
38.0126 **BC** 1957 The British Caribbean Federation: the West Indian background. *Polit Q* 28(1), Jan.-Mar.: 49-65. [*COL*]
38.0127 **BC** 1957 La Federación Británica del Caribe; el trasfondo de las Indias Occidentales [The British Caribbean Federation: the West Indian background]. *Revta Cienc Social* 1(1), Mar.: 139-171. [*AGS*]
38.0128 **BC** 1957 West Indian Federation: the constitutional aspects. *Social Econ Stud* 6(2), June: 215-246. [*RIS*]

Lewis, Vaughan A.
38.0129 **BC** 1972 Small states in the international society: with special reference to the Associated States. *Car Q* 18(2), June: 36-47. **[39]** [*RIS*]
38.0130 **GC** 1976 Problems and possibilities of Caribbean Community. *Social Stud Educ* 7, June: 26-33. (Special issue: Commonwealth Caribbean Social Studies Conference Proceedings. Vol. I.) **[47]**

Lewis, Vaughan A. & Singham, A. W.
38.0131 **GC** 1967 Integration, domination and the small-state system: the Caribbean. *In* Lewis, Sybil & Mathews, Thomas G., eds. CARIBBEAN INTEGRATION: PAPERS ON SOCIAL, POLITICAL, AND ECONOMIC INTEGRATION. Third Caribbean Scholars' Conference, Georgetown, Guyana, April 4-9, 1966. Rio Piedras, University of Puerto Rico, Institute of Caribbean Studies: 119-140. **[39]** [*RIS*]

Lewis, W. Arthur

38.0132   BC   1962   PROPOSALS FOR AN EASTERN CARIBBEAN FEDERATION, COMPRISING THE TERRITORIES OF ANTIGUA, BARBADOS, DOMINICA, GRENADA, MONTSERRAT, ST. KITTS-NEVIS-ANGUILLA, ST. LUCIA AND ST. VINCENT. Port of Spain, Government of the West Indies, 8p.   [RIS]

38.0133   BC   1965   THE AGONY OF THE EIGHT. [Bridgetown?] Barbados, Advocate Commercial Printery.   [37]   [RIS]

Linton, Neville

38.0134   BC   1971   Regional diplomacy of the Commonwealth Caribbean. *Int J* 26(2), Spring: 401-417.   [37]   [COL]

Listowel, William Francis Hare, 5th Earl of; Farley, Rawle; Hinden, Rita & Hughes, Colin

37.0496   BC   1952   CHALLENGE TO THE BRITISH CARIBBEAN.

Logan, Rayford W.

38.0135   BC   1944   The possibilities of a Caribbean Federation. *In* Frazier, E. F. & Williams E., eds. THE ECONOMIC FUTURE OF THE WEST INDIES. Washington, D.C., Howard University Press, p.55-58.

Lowenthal, David

38.0136   BC   1957   Two federations. *Social Econ Stud* 6(2), June: 185-196.   [5]   [RIS]

38.0137   BC   1958   The West Indies chooses a capital. *Geogr Rev* 48(3): 336-364.   [RIS]

38.0138   BC   1961   The social background of West Indian Federation. *In* Lowenthal, David, ed. THE WEST INDIES FEDERATION. New York, Columbia University Press, p.63-96.   [21]   [RIS]

38.0139   BC   1961   THE WEST INDIES FEDERATION. New York, Columbia University Press, 142p.   [RIS]

Lusaka, Paul John Firmino

38.0140   BC   1964   THE DISSOLUTION OF THE WEST INDIES FEDERATION. M.A. thesis, McGill University, 215p.

Lutchman, Harold A.

37.0506   GU   1972   Guyana: a review of recent political developments.

McColl, E. Kimbark

38.0141   BC   1951-52 Poverty and politics in the Caribbean. *Int J* 7(1), Winter: 12-22.   [AGS]

McCowan, Anthony

38.0142   GU   1957   British Guiana and Federation. *Corona* 9(3), Mar.: 85-88.   [AGS]

McDermott, T. W. L.

38.0143   BC   1933   Federation of the West Indies: Is it desirable? *Can-W I Mag* 22(8), July: 239-240.   [5]   [NYP]

McDonald, Vincent R.

38.0144   BC   1971   The Caribbean Free Trade Association: provisions and implications. *Rev Black Polit Econ* 1(3), Winter-Spring: 65-77.   [47]   [RIS]

McDonald, Vincent R., ed.
41.0315   **GC**   1972   THE CARIBBEAN ECONOMIES: PERSPECTIVES ON SOCIAL, POLITICAL AND ECONOMIC CONDITIONS.

McFarlane, Malcolm Randolph Murchison
38.0145   **GU,JM,TR**   1974   THE MILITARY IN THE COMMONWEALTH CARIBBEAN: A STUDY IN COMPARATIVE INSTITUTIONALIZATION. Ph.D. dissertation, University of Western Ontario (Canada). **[40]**   *[PhD]*

MacInnes, C. M.
38.0146   **BC**   1955   British Caribbean Federation. *In* DEVELOPMENTS TOWARDS SELF-GOVERNMENT IN THE CARIBBEAN. A symposium held under the auspices of the Netherlands Universities Foundation for International Co-operation at the Hague, Sept. 1954. The Hague, W. van Hoeve, p.151-175.   *[RIS]*

McIntosh, C. E., ed.
43.0276   **BC**   1973   PROCEEDINGS OF THE EIGHTH WEST INDIAN AGRICULTURAL ECONOMICS CONFERENCE, HELD AT HILTON HOTEL, TRINIDAD, APRIL 1-7, 1973.

McIntyre, Alistair
38.0147   **BC**   1968   Caribbean: free ports among the islands. *CERES* 1(6), Nov.-Dec.: 38-41. **[47]**   *[COL]*

McIntyre, Alister
47.0177   **BC**   1966   Caribbean Economic Community: some issues of trade policy in the West Indies.
47.0178   **JM**   1967   External economic relations for an integrated Commonwealth Caribbean.

Mahabir, Dennis J.
38.0148   **BC**   1957   The Caribbean Federation. *India Q* 13(1), Jan.-Mar.: 32-40.   *[AGS]*

Maingot, Anthony P.
38.0149   **BC**   1969   National sovereignty, collective security and the realities of power in the Caribbean area. *In* Preiswerk, Roy, ed. REGIONALISM AND THE COMMONWEALTH CARIBBEAN: PAPERS PRESENTED AT THE "SEMINAR ON THE FOREIGN POLICIES OF CARIBBEAN STATES", APRIL-JUNE, 1968. Trinidad, University of the West Indies, Institute of International Relations: 220-245. **[39]**   *[RIS]*

Manigat, Leslie F.
39.0104   **GC**   1969   Les Etats-Unis et le secteur caraïbe de l'Amérique Latine [The United States and the Caribbean region of Latin America].

Manley, Norman Washington
38.0150   **BC**   1951   Political future of British West Indies. *Venture* 3(2), Mar.: 4-5.   *[COL]*

Marasciulo, Edward
38.0151   **GC**   1971   Quasi-economic political units in Latin America. *In* Lentnek, Barry; Carmin, Robert L. & Martinson, Tom L., eds. GEOGRAPHIC RESEARCH ON LATIN AMERICA: BENCHMARK 1970: PROCEEDINGS OF THE CONFERENCE OF LATIN AMERICANIST GEOGRAPHERS, VOLUME ONE. Muncie, Indiana, Ball State University: 412-414.   *[COL]*

Marryshow, Julian A.

41.0335   BC   1954   The Regional Economic Committee of the British West Indies, British Guiana and British Honduras.

Marshall, Bernard

38.0152   LW,WW   1972   Attempts at Windward/Leeward federation. *Car Q* 18(2), June: 9-15. **[5]**   [*RIS*]

Martin, C. I.

47.0181   SV,BC   1971   The functioning of the agricultural marketing protocol of the CARIFTA agreement with particular reference to exports from St. Vincent.

Mathews, Thomas G.

38.0153   GC   1966   The West Indies after the Federation. *Current History* 50(293), Jan.: 27-31, 52-53. **[41]**   [*COL*]

32.0388   BC   1969   Caribbean cooperation in the field of higher education.

May, R. J.

38.0154   BC   1969   FEDERALISM AND FISCAL ADJUSTMENT. Oxford, Clarendon Press: 192p. **[37,49]**   [*COL*]

Meier, Gerald M.

47.0184   BC   1960   Effects of a customs union on economic development.

Meikle, Louis S.

38.0155   BC   1969   CONFEDERATION OF THE BRITISH WEST INDIES VERSUS ANNEXATION TO THE UNITED STATES OF AMERICA: A POLITICAL DISCOURSE ON THE WEST INDIES. New York, Negro Universities Press: 279p. (Originally published in 1912) **[5,39]**   [*RIS*]

Mendez, Jorge

38.0156   BC   1969   Multi-national coordination of plans and policies in the process of integration. *In* Preiswerk, Roy, ed. REGIONALISM AND THE COMMONWEALTH CARIBBEAN: PAPERS PRESENTED AT THE "SEMINAR ON THE FOREIGN POLICIES OF CARIBBEAN STATES", APRIL-JUNE, 1968. Trinidad, University of the West Indies, Institute of International Relations: 56-67.   [*RIS*]

Menkman, W. R.

38.0157   NC   1948   Westindische samenwerking [West Indian cooperation]. *W I G* 29: 368-372.   [*COL*]

Merrill, Gordon Clark

2.0313   GC   1958   The British West Indies—the newest Federation of the Commonwealth.

19.0045   BC   1961   The survival of the past in the West Indies.

Messina, Milton

47.0189   GC   1971   LA INTEGRACIÓN ECONÓMICA DEL CARIBE [ECONOMIC INTEGRATION OF THE CARIBBEAN].

Midas, André

38.0158   GC   1957   A brief historical sketch of the West Indian Conference. *Caribbean*
11(4), Nov.: 74-77.   [*COL*]

37.0575   BC   1957   Constitutional evolution.

Millette, James

38.0159   BC   1969   The West Indies: the federal negotiations (review article). *Social
Econ Stud* 18(4): 408-420.   [*RIS*]

Mills, G. E., ed.

37.0580   BC   1970   Problems of administrative change in the Commonwealth Caribbean.

Milne, R. Stephen

38.0160   BC   1974   Impulses and obstacles to Caribbean political integration. *Int Stud
Q* 18(3), Sept.: 291-316.   [*COL*]

Mitchell, Harold

41.0350   BC   1957   Finance and Federation.

38.0161   GC   1970   Islands of the Caribbean. *Curr Hist* 58(342), Feb.: 107-110.   **[37]**
[*COL*]

Mitchell, J. F.

47.0197   BC   1972   The Carifta marketing protocol, its creation and maintenance.

Mitchell, Philip

38.0162   BC   1950   A federal plan for the British Caribbean. *Corona* 2(5), May:
175-178.

Mohammed, Kamaluddin

47.0198   BC   1969   CARIBBEAN INTEGRATION; A REVIEW.

38.0163   BC   1969   Common services in the Caribbean. *In* Preiswerk, Roy, ed.
REGIONALISM AND THE COMMONWEALTH CARIBBEAN: PAPERS PRE-
SENTED AT THE "SEMINAR ON THE FOREIGN POLICIES OF CARIBBEAN
STATES", APRIL-JUNE, 1968. Trinidad, University of the West Indies,
Institute of International Relations: 116-129.   [*RIS*]

Mordecai, John

37.0592   BC   1966-67 Federation and after.

Morgan, D. J.

47.0201   BC   1962   Imperial preference in the West Indies and in the British Caribbean,
1929-55: a quantitative analysis.

Mudie, Francis et al.

38.0164   BC   1956   REPORT OF THE BRITISH CARIBBEAN FEDERAL CAPITAL COMMISSION.
London, H.M.S.O., 44p. (Colonial no. 328.)   [*AGS*]

Mulchansingh, Vernon C.

47.0203   BC   1968   CARIFTA: NEW HORIZONS IN THE WEST INDIES.

Mullings, Llewellyn Maximillian

41.0358   JM   1964   AN ANALYSIS OF THE ECONOMIC IMPLICATIONS OF POLITICAL INDE-
PENDENCE FOR JAMAICA.

Murkland, Harry B.
38.0165   BC   1958   The West Indies unite: British colonies take first step toward independence. *The Americas* July: 3-9.   [*AGS*]

Murray, C. Gideon
38.0166   BC   1912   A UNITED WEST INDIES. London, West Strand Pub. Co., 127p.   **[5]**
                                                                                                  [*NYP*]

Murray, Gideon
37.0614   BC   1919   Canada and the British West Indies.

Neally, Willis
38.0167   BC   1948   THE CARIBBEAN COMMISSION AS AN INTERNATIONAL INSTRUMENT FOR REGIONAL COLLABORATION. Ph.D. dissertation, Stanford University.
                                                                                                  [*PhD*]

Olivier, Sydney, 1st Baron Ramsden
38.0168   BC   1937   The future in the West Indies, by Lord Olivier. *Crown Colonist* 7(66), May: 196.   [*NYP*]

O'Loughlin, Carleen
41.0382   LW,WW   1963-64 Economic problems of the Leeward and Windward Islands.

Orrego-Vicuña, Francisco & Tolosa, Alberto O. C.
47.0216   BC   1973   Latin American economic integration.
47.0217   BC   1973   Latin American economic integration.

Osborne, William Adolphus
38.0169   BC   1956   SOME PROBLEMS OF FEDERATION IN THE BRITISH CARIBBEAN. Ph.D. dissertation, Clark University, 291p.

Páez, Joaquín
32.0442   GC   1974   Educational Technology Project progress report.
32.0443   GC   1975   Proyecto de Tecnología Educativa [Educational Technology project].

Paget, Hugh
38.0170   BC   1950   The West Indies. *United Emp* 41(3), May-June: 164-167.

Passalacqua-Christian, Luis A.
38.0171   BC   1969   The role of the Caribbean Economic Development Corporation (CODECA) in Caribbean cooperation. *In* Preiswerk, Roy, ed. REGIONALISM AND THE COMMONWEALTH CARIBBEAN: PAPERS PRESENTED AT THE "SEMINAR ON THE FOREIGN POLICIES OF CARIBBEAN STATES", APRIL-JUNE, 1968. Trinidad, University of the West Indies, Institute of International Relations: 141-150.   [*RIS*]

Persaud, Bishnodat
47.0227   BC   1969   The Agricultural Marketing Protocol of CARIFTA and the economic integration of agriculture.

Perusse, Roland I.
38.0172   GC   1971   A STRATEGY FOR CARIBBEAN ECONOMIC INTEGRATION. San Juan, Puerto Rico, North-South Press: 212p.   **[40,41]**   [*RIS*]

Pollard, Duke E.

38.0173 BC 1974 Institutional and legal aspects of the Caribbean community. *Car Stud* 14(1), April: 39-74. **[47]** [*RIS*]

Poole, Bernard L.

38.0174 GC 1951 THE CARIBBEAN COMMISSION: BACKGROUND OF COOPERATION IN THE WEST INDIES. Columbia, S.C., University of South Carolina Press, 303p. [*COL*]

Preiswerk, Roy

39.0126 BC 1969 The new regional dimensions of the foreign policies of Commonwealth Caribbean States.

Preiswerk, Roy, ed.

38.0175 BC 1969 REGIONALISM AND THE COMMONWEALTH CARIBBEAN: PAPERS PRESENTED AT THE "SEMINAR ON THE FOREIGN POLICIES OF CARIBBEAN STATES", APRIL-JUNE, 1968. Trinidad, University of the West Indies, Institute of International Relations: 273p. **[39]** [*RIS*]

Procope, Bruce

38.0176 BC 1960 The temporary federal mace. *Car Q* 6(2-3), May: 142. **[22]** [*RIS*]

Proctor, Jesse Harris, Jr.

38.0177 BC 1955 The development of the idea of Federation of the British Caribbean territories. *Revta Hist Am* 39, June: 61-105. [*RIS*]

38.0178 BC 1955 THE EFFORT TO FEDERATE THE BRITISH CARIBBEAN TERRITORIES, 1945-1953. Ph.D. dissertation, Harvard University, 618p. [*RIS*]

38.0179 BC 1956 Britain's pro-Federation policy in the Caribbean: an inquiry into motivation. *Can J Econ Polit Sci* 22(3), Aug.: 319-331. [*RIS*]

38.0180 BC 1956 The functional approach to political union: lessons from the effort to federate the British Caribbean territories. *Int Org* 10(1): 35-48. [*RIS*]

38.0181 BC 1957 The international significance of the Federation of British Caribbean territories. *In* Wilgus, A. Curtis, ed. THE CARIBBEAN: CONTEMPORARY INTERNATIONAL RELATIONS [PAPERS DELIVERED AT THE SEVENTH CONFERENCE ON THE CARIBBEAN HELD AT THE UNIVERSITY OF FLORIDA, DEC. 6-8, 1956]. Gainesville, University of Florida Press, p. 59-68. (Publications of the School of Inter-American Studies, ser. 1, v. 7.) **[39]** [*RIS*]

38.0182 TR 1961 East Indians and the Federation of the British West Indies. *India Q* 17(4), Oct.-Dec.: 370-395. **[12]** [*RIS*]

Pye, Norman

38.0183 BC 1935 The geographical factors involved in the problem of British West Indian federation. *Globe* 15, May: 6-11. **[56]** [*AGS*]

Rampersad, Frank B.

47.0234 BC 1969 The Caribbean Free Trade Association.

Ramphal, S. S.

38.0184 BC 1959 The West Indies—constitutional background to Federation. *Publ Law* Summer: 128-151. **[5]** [*COL*]

38.0185	BC	1960	Federalism in the West Indies. *Car Q* 6(2-3), May: 210-229. **[5]**
			[*RIS*]
38.0186	GU	1968	DEVELOPMENT OR DEFENCE: THE SMALL STATE THREATENED WITH AGGRESSION (PART OF AN ADDRESS DELIVERED IN THE GENERAL DEBATE OF THE 23RD SESSION OF THE U.N. GENERAL ASSEMBLY, 3 OCTOBER 1968). Georgetown, Guyana, Ministry of External Affairs: 14p. [*CEIP*]
38.0187	BC	1973	West Indian nationhood—myth, mirage or mandate? *In* Lowenthal, David & Comitas, Lambros, eds. THE AFTERMATH OF SOVEREIGNTY: WEST INDIAN PERSPECTIVES. Garden City, N. Y., Anchor Press/ Doubleday: 237-262. **[40]** [*RIS*]

Ramsaran, Ramesh

38.0188	BC	1974	Commonwealth Caribbean integration: progress, problems and prospects. *Inter-Am Econ Aff* 28(2), Autumn: 39-50. [*COL*]
47.0235	TR	1975	Trinidad and Tobago's trade performance in the Caribbean Free Trade area (Carifta).

Rance, Hubert Elvin

38.0189	BC	1953	Towards a Federation of the British West Indies. *In* Wilgus, A. Curtis, ed. THE CARIBBEAN: CONTEMPORARY TRENDS [PAPERS DELIVERED AT THE THIRD ANNUAL CONFERENCE ON THE CARIBBEAN HELD AT THE UNIVERSITY OF FLORIDA, DEC. 18-20, 1952]. Gainesville, University of Florida Press, p.241-256. (Publications of the School of Inter-American Studies, ser. 1, v. 3.) [*RIS*]
38.0190	BC	1954	Towards a Federation of the British West Indies. *Car Hist Rev* 3-4, Dec.: 1-12. [*RIS*]

Rattray, K. O.; Kirton, Allan & Robinson, Patrick

39.0132	GC	1974	The effect of the existing law of the sea on the development of the Caribbean region and the Gulf of Mexico.

Rawlins, Randolph

38.0191	GC	1958	Federation and confederation. *Corona* 10(3), Mar.: 98-100. [*AGS*]

Reid, George Lincoln

38.0192	BC	1972	A COMPARATIVE STUDY OF THE FOREIGN POLICIES OF VERY SMALL STATES, WITH SPECIAL REFERENCE TO THE COMMONWEALTH CARIBBEAN. Ph.D. dissertation, University of Southampton: 499p. **[39]**

Reidy, Joseph W.

37.0705	GC	1967	Growth and possible change in Caribbean America's political capacity.

Reive, R. v. H.

39.0133	BC	1970	The international competence of the associated states in the CARIFTA treaty.

Renwick, David

47.0238	BC	1975	In deep water.

Revert, Eugene

38.0193	GC	1954	La Commission Caraïbe [The Caribbean Commission]. *In* PROCEEDINGS OF THE SYMPOSIUM INTERCOLONIAL, JUNE 27-JULY 3, 1952. Bordeaux, Impr. Delmas, p.144-146. [*RIS*]

Richards, Vincent Arnold
38.0194   BC   1975   AN APPROACH TO MULTI-COUNTRY DEVELOPMENT PLANNING AND INDUSTRIAL PROGRAMMING FOR THE EAST CARIBBEAN COMMON MARKET. Ph.D. dissertation, Cornell University: 428p. **[41,47]**
[*PhD*]

Richardson, C. Howard
37.0713   GC   1971   American research on the political geography of Latin America.

Richardson, W. A.
38.0195   TR   1959   Trinidad—the Federal Capital. *Can-W I Mag* 49(10), Oct.: 13-16.
[*NYP*]

Riemens, H.
39.0136   GC   1967   Latijns Amerika en de Caribische emancipatie [Latin America and the Caribbean emancipation].

Riesgo, Raymond R.
47.0240   BC   1961   The federation of the West Indies. 1) A bright opportunity for trade. 2) Jamaica and Trinidad, thriving markets.

Roberts, E. J. Ph.
38.0196   GC   1969   De overeenkomst tot oprichting van een Caribische vrijhandelsassociatie [Caribbean Free Trade Association Agreement]. *Justicia* 5(1): 5-29. **[47]**
[*COL*]

Roberts, George W.
38.0197   BC   1957   Some demographic considerations of West Indian federation. *Social Econ Stud* 6(2), June: 262-285. **[5,7]**
[*RIS*]

Robinson, C. L.
48.0141   BC   1970   The allocation of the Federal Palm and the Federal Maple according to international law.

Rodríguez, Raul Sosa
38.0198   BC   1969   Economic cooperation and integration between Latin American and Caribbean Countries. *In* Preiswerk, Roy, ed. REGIONALISM AND THE COMMONWEALTH CARIBBEAN: PAPERS PRESENTED AT THE "SEMINAR ON THE FOREIGN POLICIES OF CARIBBEAN STATES", APRIL-JUNE, 1968. Trinidad, University of the West Indies, Institute of International Relations: 214-219. **[39,47]**
[*RIS*]

Rorty, James
37.0739   NV   1961   Independence, like it or not.

Salmon, C. S.
5.0802   BC   1971   THE CARIBBEAN CONFEDERATION: A PLAN FOR THE UNION OF THE FIFTEEN BRITISH WEST INDIAN COLONIES.

Sanders, William
38.0199   GC   1966   The Conference System in the Caribbean. *In* Wilgus, A. Curtis, ed. THE CARIBBEAN: CURRENT UNITED STATES RELATIONS. Gainesville, University of Florida Press: 193-207. (Caribbean Conference Series 1, Vol. 16) **[39]**
[*RIS*]

Sanz de Santamaría, Carlos
38.0200   BC   1969   Integration from the viewpoint of Latin America. *In* Waters, Maurice, ed. THE CARIBBEAN AND LATIN AMERICA: POLITICAL AND ECONOMIC RELATIONS. Volume I. Jamaica, University of the West Indies: 63-67. **[39]**   [*RIS*]

Schneider, Fred D.
38.0201   BC   1959   British policy in West Indian Federation. *Wld Aff Q* 30(3), Oct.: 241-265.

Seel, G. F.
41.0449   BC   1953[?]   FINANCIAL ASPECTS OF FEDERATION OF THE BRITISH WEST INDIAN TERRITORIES.

Seel, George
38.0202   BC   1956   Federation. *Statist* Sept.: 7-9.
38.0203   BC   1957   Some Federation memories. *W I Rev* new ser., 2(10), Oct.: 23-25.
  [*NYP*]

Seers, Dudley
38.0204   BC   1957   Federation of the British West Indies: the economic and financial aspects. *Social Econ Stud* 6(2), June: 197-214. **[41]**   [*RIS*]

Segal, Aaron
38.0205   GC   1968   THE POLITICS OF CARIBBEAN ECONOMIC INTEGRATION. Rio Piedras, University of Puerto Rico, Insitute of Caribbean Studies: 156p. (Special Study, 6.) **[47]**   [*RIS*]

Shenfield, A. A.
41.0458   BC   1958   Economic advance in the West Indies.

Shepheard, Walwyn P. B.
38.0206   BC   1900   The West Indies and confederation. *J Soc Comp Leg* new ser., 2(2): 224-232. **[5]**   [*NYP*]

Sherlock, Philip M.
21.0086   BC   1956[?]   Federation: let's meet the family.
37.0774   JM,TR   1962   Nouvelles nations dans les Antilles [New nations in the Caribbean].
38.0207   BC   1963   Une fédération restreinte? [A limited federation?] *Civilisations* 13(1-2): 212-213.   [*RIS*]
32.0523   GC   1968   ASSOCIATION OF CARIBBEAN UNIVERSITIES. LA ASOCIACIÓN DE UNIVERSIDADES DEL CARIBE.
38.0208   GC   1974   Reflections on the Caribbean community and Caribbean integration. *In* STUDIES ON THE ECONOMIC INTEGRATION OF THE CARIBBEAN AND LATIN AMERICA. Association of Caribbean Universities and Research Institutes (UNICA): 10-15.   [*RIS*]

Simey, Thomas S.
38.0209   BC   1957   A new capital for the British West Indies. *Town Plann Rev* 28(1), Apr.: 63-70.   [*AGS*]

Simmonds, K. R.
38.0210   TR   1967   The Central American Common Market. *Int Comp Law Q* 16(4), Oct.: 911-945. **[41]**   [*COL*]

39.0152	**BZ**	1968	The Belize mediation.
38.0211	**BC**	1970	International economics organisations in Central and Latin America and the Caribbean: regionalism and sub-regionalism in the integration process. *Int Comp Law Q* 19(3), July: 376-397. **[39,47]** [*COL*]
38.0212	**KNA,UK**	1972	Anguilla: an interim settlement. *Int Comp Law Q* 21(1), Jan.: 151-157. **[40]** [*COL*]

Sklar, Barry & Hagen, Virginia, eds.

39.0154	**GC**	1973	INTER-AMERICAN RELATIONS: A COLLECTION OF DOCUMENTS, LEGISLATION, DESCRIPTIONS OF INTER-AMERICAN ORGANIZATIONS, AND OTHER MATERIAL PERTAINING TO INTER-AMERICAN AFFAIRS.

Smith, David August

48.0155	**GC**	1959	A GEOGRAPHIC ANALYSIS OF INTER-ISLAND TRANSPORTATION IN THE LESSER ANTILLES AND HAWAIIAN ISLANDS.

Smith, Frances McReynolds

38.0213	**GC**	1958	The Caribbean Commission: prototype of regional cooperation. *In* Wilgus, A. Curtis, ed. THE CARIBBEAN: BRITISH, DUTCH, FRENCH, UNITED STATES [PAPERS DELIVERED AT THE EIGHTH CONFERENCE ON THE CARIBBEAN HELD AT THE UNIVERSITY OF FLORIDA, DEC. 5-7, 1957]. Gainesville, University of Florida Press, p.276-299. (Publications of the School of Inter-American Studies, ser. 1, v. 8.) [*RIS*]

Smith, Gerald Grogan

38.0214	**BC**	1955	THE PROPOSED BRITISH CARIBBEAN FEDERATION. Ph.D. dissertation, Syracuse University, 250p. [*NYP*]

Smith, M. G.

37.0812	**BC**	1962	Short-range prospects in the British Caribbean.

Smith, R. G. C.

47.0258	**BC**	1959	The West Indies.

Smith, Raymond Thomas

21.0087	**GU**	1958	British Guiana.
19.0058	**BC**	1967	Social stratification, cultural pluralism, and integration in West Indian societies.

Somersall, T.

39.0157	**BC**	1968	Monetary cooperation and economic integration in the Commonwealth Caribbean.

Springer, Hugh W.

38.0215	**BC**	1961	The West Indies emergent: problems and prospects. *In* Lowenthal, David, ed. THE WEST INDIES FEDERATION. New York, Columbia University Press, p.1-16. **[40,41,43]** [*RIS*]
38.0216	**BC**	1962	Federation in the Caribbean: an attempt that failed. *Int Org* 16(4), Autumn: 758-775.
38.0217	**BC**	1962	REFLECTIONS ON THE FAILURE OF THE FIRST WEST INDIAN FEDERATION. Cambridge, Center for International Affairs, Harvard University, 66p. (Occasional papers in international affairs, no. 4.)

St. Cyr, E. B. A.
39.0158   BC   1969   Foreign aid to the Caribbean from the angle of integrative efforts.

Stephenson, Yvonne, comp.
1.0269   BC   1972   A BIBLIOGRAPHY ON THE WEST INDIAN FEDERATION.

Stern, Peter M.; Augelli, John P.; Lowenthal, David & Alexander, Lewis M.
38.0218   BC   1956   British Caribbean Federation. *Focus* 7(1), Sept. (6p.)   [*AGS*]

Stewart, Alice R.
38.0219   BC   1950   Canadian-West Indian union, 1884-1885. *Can Hist Rev* 31(4), Dec.:
                         369-389.   **[5]**   [*COL*]
38.0220   BC   1951   Documents on Canadian-West Indian relations, 1883-1885. *Car
                         Hist Rev* 2, Dec.: 100-133.   **[5]**

Stockdale, Frank A.
38.0221   GC   1947   The work of the Caribbean Commission. *Int Aff* 23(2), Apr.:
                         213-220.   [*AGS*]

Taussig, Charles W.
38.0222   GC   1946   A four-power program in the Caribbean. *For Aff* 84(4), July:
                         699-710.   [*AGS*]

Thomas, C. C.
37.0842   BC   1966   Constitutional theory and practice in the West Indies.

Thompson, George
38.0223   BC   1960   The West Indies Federation. *Venture* 12(8), Sept.: 5-6.   [*COL*]

Tucker, Terry
38.0224   BE,TC   1974   The Turks and Caicos Islands group in its relationship to Bermuda.
                           Bermuda Hist Q 31(4), Winter: 78-89.   **[5]**   [*COL*]

Tuttle, Andrew C.
38.0225   GC   1967   THE WEST INDIES FEDERATION: POLITICS AND PROSPECTS. Ph.D.
                         dissertation, Claremont Graduate School and University Center:
                         181p.   **[37]**   [*PhD*]

Uchegbu, P. E. A.
38.0226   BC,UK   1973   The Caribbean Development Bank: implications for integration. *J
                           Wld Trade Law* 7(5), Sept.-Oct.: 568-586.   **[41,49]**   [*COL*]

Venner, Dwight
38.0227   LW,WW   1972   The advantages of economic integration in the Windward and
                           Leeward Islands. *Car Q* 18(2), June: 16-27.   **[41]**   [*RIS*]

Walker, P. C. Gordan
38.0228   BC   1955   No easy path for Caribbean federation. *New Commonw* 30(8), Oct.
                         17: 364-365.   [*AGS*]

Wallace, Elisabeth
38.0229   BC   1961   The West Indies: improbable Federation? *Can J Econ Polit Sci*
                         27(4), Nov.: 444-459.

38.0230   BC   1962   The West Indies Federation: decline and fall. *Int J* 17(3), Summer: 269-288.

Washington, S. Walter
38.0231   BC   1960   Crisis in the British West Indies. *For Aff* 38(4), July: 646-655.   [*RIS*]

Waterman, James A.
28.1395   BC   1958   The impact of federation on medicine in the West Indies.

Watts, R. L.
38.0232   BC   1966   NEW FEDERATIONS: EXPERIMENT IN THE COMMONWEALTH. Oxford, Clarendon Press: 417p.   [*RIS*]
38.0233   BC   1970   MULTICULTURAL SOCIETIES AND FEDERALISM. Ottawa, Information Canada: 187p. (Studies of the Royal Commission on Bilingualism and Biculturalism, 8)   **[8,37]**   [*COL*]

Weston, S. Burns
38.0234   GC   1944   The Anglo-American Caribbean Commission. *In* Frazier, E. F. & Williams, E., eds. THE ECONOMIC FUTURE OF THE CARIBBEAN. Washington, D.C., Howard University Press, p.73-74.

Wilgus, A. Curtis, ed.
2.0507   GC   1957   THE CARIBBEAN: CONTEMPORARY INTERNATIONAL RELATIONS [PAPERS DELIVERED AT THE SEVENTH CONFERENCE ON THE CARIBBEAN HELD AT THE UNIVERSITY OF FLORIDA, DEC. 6-8, 1956].

Williams, Douglas
37.0900   BC   1958   Constitutional developments in the British West Indies.

Williams, Eric Eustace
38.0235   GC   1955   MY RELATIONS WITH THE CARIBBEAN COMMISSION, 1953-1955. Port of Spain, Ben Durham Print. Works, 51p.
38.0236   BC   1956   FEDERATION: TWO PUBLIC LECTURES. [Port of Spain?] Trinidad, People's National Movement, 60p.   **[32,37]**   [*RIS*]
2.0514   TR   1960   PERSPECTIVES FOR THE WEST INDIES.
38.0237   BC   1963   THE FUTURE OF THE WEST INDIES AND GUYANA. Address delivered at Queens College, Georgetown, Guyana, under the auspices of the Extra-mural Department, University of the West Indies, 13th March 1963. Port of Spain, Govt. Print. Off., 39p.   **[5]**   [*RIS*]
38.0238   GC   1965   REFLECTIONS ON THE CARIBBEAN ECONOMIC COMMUNITY: A SERIES OF SEVEN ARTICLES. Port-of-Spain, Trinidad, P.N.M. Publishing Co., Ltd.: 39p. (reprinted from *The Nation,* Sept. 14-Dec. 11)   [*RIS*]
39.0180   GC   1973   The foreign policy of the Caribbean states.
38.0239   BC   1973   A new federation for the Commonwealth Caribbean? *Polit Q* 44(3), July-Sept.: 242-256.   [*COL*]

Williams, Eric Eustace, ed.
38.0240   BC   1954   The historical background of the British West Indian Federation: select documents. *Car Hist Rev* 3-4, Dec.: 13-69.   **[5]**   [*RIS*]

Wiltshire, Rosina
38.0241   BC   1974   REGIONAL INTEGRATION AND CONFLICT IN THE COMMONWEALTH CARIBBEAN. Ph.D. dissertation, The University of Michigan: 202p.   **[40]**   [*PhD*]

38.0242   BC   1976   Mini-states, dependency and regional integration in the Caribbean.
                        In Lewis, Vaughan A., ed. SIZE, SELF-DETERMINATION AND INTER-
                        NATIONAL RELATIONS: THE CARIBBEAN. Mona, Jamaica, University
                        of the West Indies, Institute of Social and Economic Research:
                        98-121. **[40]**   [*RIS*]

         Wionczek, Miguel S., ed.
38.0243   GC   1969   CARIFTA. *In* Wionczek, Miguel S., ed. ECONOMIC COOPERATION IN
                        LATIN AMERICA, AFRICA, AND ASIA: A HANDBOOK OF DOCUMENTS.
                        Cambridge, Massachusetts, The MIT Press: 126-158. (Chapter
                        3) **[41,47]**   [*UNL*]

         Wiseman, H. V.
38.0244   BC   1948   THE WEST INDIES, TOWARDS A NEW DOMINION? London, Fabian
                        Publications, 45p. (Research series no. 130.) **[33,37,41,43]**   [*RIS*]

         Woetzel, Robert
39.0182 BC   1969   The Organization of American States and Caribbean security.

         Wolf, Donna Marie
40.0088 JM   1973   THE CARIBBEAN PEOPLE OF COLOR AND THE CUBAN INDEPENDENCE
                        MOVEMENT.

         Wolf, Sig. W.
38.0245   GC   1967   Politieke en economische integratie in het Caribische gebied [Po-
                        litical and economic integration in the Caribbean area]. *Int Spec-
                        tator* 21(6), March 22: 490-498.   [*COL*]

         Wooding, Hugh
38.0246   BC   1967   LEGAL PROBLEMS OF POLITICAL INTEGRATION IN THE CARIBBEAN. St.
                        Augustine, Trinidad, University of the West Indies: 11p. (Lecture
                        delivered on June 28, 1967 at the Institute of International
                        Relations)   [*RIS*]

         Wooding, Hugh, ed.
38.0247   AG,UK   1970   REPORT OF THE COMMISSION OF INQUIRY APPOINTED BY THE
                        GOVERNMENTS OF THE UNITED KINGDOM AND ST. CHRISTOPHER-
                        NEVIS-ANGUILLA TO EXAMINE THE ANGUILLA PROBLEM. London,
                        Her Majesty's Stationary Office: 131p. (Miscellaneous No.
                        23) **[37]**   [*CEIP*]

         Yaukey, Raymond S.
47.0285 BC   1972   The Caribbean Free Trade Association.

Chapter 39

INTERNATIONAL ISSUES

External boundary issues; political issues between Caribbean and non-Caribbean societies; the Caribbean in the international political arena; foreign political influence or intervention; international law.

Alexander, Lewis M., ed.

39.0001   GC   1973   GULF AND CARIBBEAN MARITIME PROBLEMS. Kingston, Rhode Island, University of Rhode Island: 107p. (Law of the Sea Institute Workshop No. 2)   [*COL*]

Allen, Devere

39.0002   GC   1943   THE CARIBBEAN: LABORATORY OF WORLD COOPERATION. New York, League for Industrial Democracy, 40p. (Pamphlet series.)   [*COL*]

Alvarado, Rafael

39.0003   BZ   1958   LA CUESTIÓN DE BELICE [THE BELIZE QUESTION]. [Guatemala City?] Guatemala, Secretaría de Información de la Presidencia de la República, 60p.   **[5]**   [*AGS*]

Alvarez Uriarte, Miguel

47.0008   BC   1969   World and hemisphere trade policies affecting the Caribbean area.

Andic, Fuat M.

41.0010   FC,NC   1969   La Caraïbe face à la Communauté Economique Européene: le cas des Antilles néerlandaises, de Surinam, des Antilles françaises et de la Guyane Française [The Caribbean facing the European Economic Community: the case of the Netherlands Antilles, Surinam, the French Antilles and French Guiana].

41.0011   FC,NC   1969   The development impact of the EEC on the French and Dutch Caribbean.

Argueta Ruiz, José Dolores

39.0004   BZ   1966   ESTADOS UNIDOS FIEL DE LA BALANZA EN EL CASO DE BELICE [THE UNITED STATES, BALANCE OF LOYALTY IN THE CASE OF BELIZE]. Guatemala, Editorial del Ejército: 75p.   **[37]**   [*COL*]

Armstrong, Elizabeth H.

39.0005   GC   1946   Report on the West Indian Conference. *Dep St B* 14(359), May 19: 840-845.   [*AGS*]

39.0006   GC   1949   West Indian Conference: third session. *Dep St B* 20(503), Feb. 20: 221-226.   [*AGS*]

1309

Arroyo, Manuel
39.0007   BZ   1947-48 A questão de Belice, Honduras Britânicas [The question of Belize,
British Honduras]. *Revta Soc Brasil Geogr* 54: 23-41. **[5]**   [*AGS*]

Aspinall, Algernon E.
37.0019   BC   1940 British West Indian bases for the U.S.A.

Asturias, Francisco
39.0008   BZ   1941 BELICE. 2ND ED. ENL. [Guatemala City?] Guatemala: Tipografía
Nacional de Guatemala, Publicaciones de La Revista de la Facul-
tad de Ciencias Jurídicas y Sociales, 177p. **[5]**   [*AGS*]

Augelli, John P.
39.0009   GC   1975 Geographic concepts and the Caribbean crisis area. *J Geogr* 74(7),
Oct.: 393-402. **[56]**   [*AGS*]

Awad, Mohamed
33.0008   BC,SR 1966 REPORT ON SLAVERY.

Azevedo Costa, J. A. de
39.0010   FG   1945 Litígio entre o Brasil e a Franca—a questão do Território de Amapá
[Litigation between Brazil and France—the question of the Ter-
ritory of Amapá]. *Revta Soc Geogr Rio Jan* 52: 92-100. **[5]**   [*AGS*]

Baker, Marcus
39.0011   GU   1900 Anglo-Venezuelan boundary dispute. *Natn Geogr Mag* 11(4), Apr.:
129-144. **[5]**   [*AGS*]

Baldwin, Richard
39.0012   GU   1948 Rupununi and its neighbor—Rio Branco. *Timehri* 4th ser., 1(28),
Dec.: 47-53.

Ballah, Lennox F.
38.0017   GC   1974 Applicability of the archipelago and mare clausum to the Caribbean
Sea.

Ballentine, Frank Schell
39.0013   BE   1901 A visit to the Boers in Bermuda. *Outlook* 69(10), Nov. 9: 633-
637. **[33]**   [*COL*]

Baptiste, F. A.
39.0014   AR,CU 1973 The seizure of the Dutch authorities in Willemstad, Curaçao, by
Venezuelan political exiles in June 1929, viewed in relation to the
Anglo-French landings in Aruba and Curaçao in May 1940. *Car
Stud* 13(1), April: 36-61. **[5,37]**   [*RIS*]

Baptiste, Owen
39.0015   BZ   1976 The Belize question: can Cuba refuse to help if there's trouble from
Guatemala. *People Mag Car* 2(13), Aug.: 41-46.   [*RIS*]

Barrett, Raymond J.
5.0041   GC   1971 The United States and the Caribbean.

Benbow, Colin

39.0016   BE   1962   BOER PRISONERS OF WAR IN BERMUDA. Hamilton, Bermuda His-
                           torical Society. (Occasional Publication No. 3)   **[5,33]**   [*NYP*]

Benjamins, H. D.

39.0017   SR   1921-22 Suriname's westgrens und kein Ende [Surinam's western borderline
                           ad infinitum]. *W I G* 3: 393-401.   [*COL*]

39.0018   SR   1922-23 Nogmaals Suriname's westgrens [Surinam's westerly border once
                           again]. *W I G* 4: 401-420.   [*COL*]

39.0019   SR   1923   Minister de Graaff en de Corantijn kwestie [Minister de Graaff and
                           the Courantyne problem]. *W I G* 6: 259-276.   [*COL*]

39.0020   SR   1924-25 De Corantijnkwestie twee stappen vooruit [The Courantyne prob-
                           lem: two steps in the right direction]. *W I G* 6: 338-365.   [*COL*]

39.0021   SR   1925-26 Een nieuw geluid in de Corantijn kwestie [A new possibility in the
                           Courantyne problem]. *W I G* 7: 311-345.   [*COL*]

39.0022   SR   1926-27 De Corantijnsche kwestie op den goeden weg? [Is the Courantyne
                           problem going in the right direction?] *W I G* 8: 293-314.   [*COL*]

39.0023   SR   1927-28 Hoe staat het thans met de Corantijn kwestie? [What is the present
                           situation of the Courantyne problem?] *W I G* 9: 389-416.   [*COL*]

39.0024   SR   1928-29 De Courantijnkwestie bij Buitenlandsche Zaken [The Courantyne
                           problem before the Ministry of Foreign Affairs]. *W I G* 10: 571-584.
                                                                                          [*COL*]

39.0025   SR   1930-31 Surinaamsche grenskwesties, het einde in zicht [Surinam's border
                           problems; the end is in sight]. *W I G* 11: 367-388.   [*COL*]

39.0026   SR   1931-32 De Corantijnkwestie: nieuw licht op oude bescheiden [The Couran-
                           tyne problem: new light upon old documents]. *W I G* 13: 49-62.
                                                                                          [*COL*]

Berle, Adolf A.

39.0027   GC   1966   The Cold War in the Caribbean. *In* Wilgus, A. Curtis, ed. THE
                           CARIBBEAN: CURRENT UNITED STATES RELATIONS. Gainesville, Uni-
                           versity of Florida Press: 208-215. (Caribbean Conference Series 1,
                           Vol. 16)   [*RIS*]

Bernard, Augustin

39.0028   FG   1901   Le contesté franco-brésilien [The Franco-Brazilian [boundary] dis-
                           pute]. *Quest Diplom Colon* 11, Jan.: 31-37.   [*COL*]

Bhagwandin, Khemraj

39.0029   GU   1971   Transactions of the XVI Congress of the People's Progressive Party:
                           address. *Thunder* 2(1), Jan.-March: 45-49.   **[37]**   [*RIS*]

Bianchi, William J.

39.0030   BZ   1959   BELIZE: THE CONTROVERSY BETWEEN GUATEMALA AND GREAT BRIT-
                           AIN OVER THE TERRITORY OF BRITISH HONDURAS IN CENTRAL
                           AMERICA. New York, Las Américas Pub. Co., 142p.   **[5]**   [*AGS*]

Blaine, J. C. D.

47.0026   JM,TR   1957   Trade relations of the United Kingdom and the United States in the
                           Caribbean.

Bland, C. L.
47.0027   **BC**   1966   Canada and the Commonwealth Caribbean.

Bloomfield, L. M.
39.0031   **BZ**   1953   THE BRITISH HONDURAS-GUATEMALA DISPUTE. Toronto, Carswell
                              Co., 231p.   **[5]**   [*COL*]

Boersner, Demetrio
39.0032   **BC**   1969   Latin American attitudes towards the Caribbean. *In* Preiswerk,
                              Roy, ed. REGIONALISM AND THE COMMONWEALTH CARIBBEAN:
                              PAPERS PRESENTED AT THE "SEMINAR ON THE FOREIGN POLICIES OF
                              CARIBBEAN STATES", APRIL-JUNE, 1968. Trinidad, University of the
                              West Indies, Institute of International Relations: 189-197.   [*RIS*]

Boodhoo, Ken
40.0007   **TR**   1974   EXTERNAL INFLUENCES ON THE BEHAVIOUR OF A SMALL STATE:
                              PENETRATION OF THE TRINIDAD POLITICAL SYSTEMS.

Boulle, Pierre
5.0088   **BC**   1975-76 The West Indies in French policy on the eve of the American
                              Revolution.

Brent-Harris, K. B.
47.0036   **BC**   1970   The compatibility of the CARIFTA agreement and the General
                              Agreement of Tariffs and Trade with particular reference to Article
                              XXIV of the GATT.

Briceño-Picón, Mario
39.0033   **GU**   1966   CARTILLA PATRIÓTICA: LA INFAMÍA DE ESEQUIBO [PATRIOTIC NOTE:
                              THE INFAMY OF ESEQUIBO]. Caracas, Ediciones Independencia: 78p.
                                                                                                [*COL*]

Brisk, William J.
37.0089   **AG**   1968   ANGUILLA AND THE MINI-STATE DILEMMA.

Brousseau, Georges
56.0042   **FG**   1901   LES RICHESSES DE LA GUYANE FRANCAISE ET DE L'ANCIEN CONTESTÉ
                              FRANCO-BRÉSILIEN [THE NATURAL RESOURCES OF FRENCH GUIANA
                              AND THE BOUNDARY DISPUTE BETWEEN FRANCE AND BRAZIL].

Brown, Noel
39.0034   **BC**   1969   The OAS and regional non-members. *In* Waters, Maurice, ed. THE
                              CARIBBEAN AND LATIN AMERICA: POLITICAL AND ECONOMIC RELA-
                              TIONS. Jamaica, University of the West Indies: 31-40.   [*RIS*]

Brunn, Stanley D.; Ford, John J. & McIntosh, Terry
37.0098   **GC**   1971   The state of political geography research in Latin America

Buck, Wilbur F.
47.0043   **GC**   1971   AGRICULTURE AND TRADE OF THE CARIBBEAN REGION: BERMUDA,
                              THE BAHAMAS, THE GUIANAS, AND BRITISH HONDURAS.

Buckmire, George E.
47.0044   **BC**   1971   The future possibilities of Caribbean export crops in the metropolitan markets.

Burgess, Charles J.
47.0045   **BC**   1956   Trade relations between the British West Indies and Canada.

Burr, George Lincoln
39.0035   **GU**   1900   The Guiana boundary: a postscript to the work of the American
Commission. *Am Hist Rev* 6(1), Oct.: 49-64.   **[5]**   [*COL*]

Cabrera Sifontes, Horacio
2.0055   **GU**   1970   GUAYANA ESEQUIBO.

Calderón Quijano, José Antonio
39.0036   **BZ**   1944   BELICE 1663(?)-1821: HISTORIA DE LOS ESTABLECIMIENTOS BRI-
TÁNICOS DEL RÍO VALIS HASTA LA INDEPENDENCIA DE HISPANO-
AMÉRICA [BELIZE 1663(?)-1821: HISTORY OF THE BRITISH SETTLE-
MENTS OF THE VALIS RIVER UNTIL THE INDEPENDENCE OF SPANISH
AMERICA]. Seville, Victoria-Artes Gráficas, 503p. (Publicaciones de
la Escuela de Estudios Hispanoamericanos de la Universidad de
Sevilla, general no. 5, 2nd ser., no. 1.)   **[5]**   [*AGS*]

Canaday, Ward M.
39.0037   **GC**   1949   U.S. economic policy in the Caribbean. *Dep St B* 20(521), June 26:
813-819.   **[41]**   [*COL*]

Canales Salazar, Felix
39.0038   **BZ**   1946   DERECHOS TERRITORIALES DE LA REPÚBLICA DE HONDURAS SOBRE
HONDURAS BRITÁNICA O BELICE, ISLAS DEL CISNE Y COSTAS DE LOS
INDIOS MOSQUITOS [TERRITORIAL RIGHTS OF THE REPUBLIC OF
HONDURAS OVER BRITISH HONDURAS OR BELIZE, SWAN ISLANDS,
AND THE MOSQUITO INDIAN COAST]. Mexico, 91p.   **[5]**   [*AGS*]

Casserly, F. L.
47.0054   **JM**   1947   Retrospect of Canada—Jamaica trade.

Castañeda, Jorge
38.0040   **GC**   1974   The patrimonial sea as a regional concept.

Charpentier, Geneviève
47.0057   **FA**   1937   LES RELATIONS ÉCONOMIQUES ENTRE BORDEAUX ET LES ANTILLES AU
XVIIIᵉ SIÈCLE. [ECONOMIC RELATIONS BETWEEN BORDEAUX AND THE
ANTILLES IN THE 18TH CENTURY].

Clegern, Wayne M.
39.0039   **BZ**   1958   New light on the Belize dispute. *Am J Int Law* 52(2), Apr.: 280-297.
[*AGS*]
39.0040   **BZ**   1962   British Honduras and the pacification of Yucatán. *The Americas*
18(3), Jan.: 243-254.   [*COL*]

Clingan, Thomas A., Jr.
39.0041   **GC**   1972   The oceans. *Law Am* 4(3), Oct.: 576-584.   **[38]**   [*COL*]

Collier, H. C.
39.0042   BZ   1947   Selling British Honduras short. *Can-W I Mag* 36(11), Jan.: 11-12.
                                                                                    [*NYP*]

Collins, B. A. N.
37.0152   BC   1967   Some notes on Public Service Commissions in the Commonwealth
                         Caribbean.

Comitas, Lambros
39.0043   JM   1965   Lessons from Jamaica. *In* Textor, Robert B., ed. CULTURAL
                         FRONTIERS OF THE PEACE CORPS. Cambridge, Massachusetts, The
                         M.I.T. Press: 201-219.   [*COL*]

Corkran, Herbert
39.0044   GC   1970   PATTERNS OF INTERNATIONAL COOPERATION IN THE CARIBBEAN,
                         1942-1969. Dallas, Southern Methodist University Press:
                         285p. **[5,38]**   [*RIS*]

Corrêa, P. H. da Rocha
39.0045   GG   1965   O BRASIL E AS GUIANAS [BRAZIL AND THE GUIANAS]. Catanduva,
                         Irmãos Boso Editôres e Livreiros: 112p.   [*NYP*]

Crassweller, Robert D.
39.0046   GC   1972   THE CARIBBEAN COMMUNITY: CHANGING SOCIETIES AND U.S. POLICY.
                         New York, Praeger Publishers: 470p. **[38]**   [*RIS*]

Crowe, Harry J.
47.0076   BC   1920   Canadian-West Indian union.
37.0164   BC   1920   Separate West Indian Dominion, or confederation with Canada.
47.0077   JM   1925   How Canada-West Indies federation might be achieved.

Cummings, Felix
39.0047   GU   [n.d.]   GUYANA BEFORE THE UNITED NATIONS. Georgetown, New Guiana
                         Co., Ltd. (for the People's Progressive Party): 16p.   [*RIS*]

Cundall, Frank
39.0048   JM   1925   JAMAICA'S PART IN THE GREAT WAR, 1914-1918. London, West India
                         Committee for the Institute of Jamaica: 155p.   [*NYP*]

Curtin, Philip D.
37.0177   GC   1955   The United States in the Caribbean.

Dell, Sidney
47.0083   GC   1969   Strategies for economic development open to the public.

Devine, Fred W.
28.0316   GC   1965   CARE in the Caribbean.

Dill, Thomas Melville
39.0049   BE   1944   Bermuda and the War of 1812. *Bermuda Hist Q* 1(3), July-Sept.:
                         137-148. **[5]**   [*NYP*]

Dominice, Christian

39.0050   **BC**   1969   The denuclearization of Latin America. *In* Preiswerk, Roy, ed. REGIONALISM AND THE COMMONWEALTH CARIBBEAN: PAPERS PRESENTED AT THE "SEMINAR ON THE FOREIGN POLICIES OF CARIBBEAN STATES", APRIL-JUNE, 1968. Trinidad, University of the West Indies, Institute of International Relations: 257-283. **[38]**   [*RIS*]

Donner, Walther R. W.

47.0090   **SR**   1966   El efecto económico de la asociación de Surinam con el Mercado Común Europeo [The economic effect of the relationship of Surinam with the European Common Market].

41.0142   **SR**   1967   The impact of the agriculture policy of the European Economic Community on the economies of the associated countries.

Dookhan, Isaac

5.0254   **VI**   1973   Vieques or Crab Island: source of Anglo-Spanish colonial conflict.

5.0258   **GC**   1975   War and trade in the West Indies 1783-1815: a preliminary survey.

Doxey, G. V.

39.0051   **BC**   1966   The Commonwealth in the Americas: Canada takes the initiative. *Round Table* 56(224), Oct.: 387-393. **[41]**   [*COL*]

39.0052   **BC**   1969   The OAS and regional non-members—the Canadian picutre. *In* Waters, Maurice, ed. THE CARIBBEAN AND LATIN AMERICA: POLITICAL AND ECONOMIC RELATIONS. Jamaica, University of the West Indies: 17-23.   [*RIS*]

Echavarría Olózaga, Hernán

39.0053   **GC**   1974   Regional collaboration in the Caribbean. *In* STUDIES ON THE ECONOMIC INTEGRATION OF THE CARIBBEAN AND LATIN AMERICA. Association of Caribbean Universities and Research Institutes (UNICA): 1-9. **[41]**   [*RIS*]

Edmondson, Locksley

21.0023   **GC**   1974   Caribbean nation-building and the internationalization of race: issues and perspectives.

21.0024   **GC**   1974   The internationalization of black power: historical and contemporary perspectives.

Edmundson, George

39.0054   **GU**   1923   The relations of Great Britain with Guiana. *Trans Roy Hist Soc* 4th ser., 6: 1-21. **[5]**   [*COL*]

Emmanuel, Patrick

37.0220   **LW,WW**   1976   Independence and viability: elements of analysis.

Escalona Ramos, Alberto

39.0055   **BZ**   1940   Belice pertenece a México o a Guatemala? [Does Belize belong to Mexico or to Guatemala?]. *Revta Mex Geogr* 1(1), July-Sept.: 33-60. **[5]**   [*AGS*]

Essed, F. E.

39.0056   **SR,FG**   1965   De bepaling van de grenslijn tussen twee grondgebieden in grensriveiren: de evenregigheidalijn ("Proportional line") [The proportional line as the boundary line between two countries, separated by a river]. *Tijdschr Ned Aar Genoot* Tweede Reeks, 82(4), Oct.: 348-358.   [*AGS*]

Fagon, Donald O'Connor

39.0057   GC   1973   THE GEOPOLITICS OF THE CARIBBEAN SEA AND ITS ADJACENT LANDS. Ph.D. dissertation, The Catholic University of America: 387p. **[5,40]**   *[PhD]*

Fauchille, Paul

39.0058   GU   1905   LE CONFLIT DE LIMITES ENTRE LE BRÉSIL ET LA GRANDE-BRETAGNE ET LA SENTENCE ARBITRALE DU ROI D'ITALIE [THE BOUNDARY DISPUTE BETWEEN BRAZIL AND GREAT BRITAIN AND THE ARBITRATION RULING OF THE KING OF ITALY]. Paris, A. Pedone, 131p. **[5]**   *[NYP]*

Fawcett, J. E. S.

39.0059   GU,UK   1967   International law. *In* Wade, H. W. R., ed. ANNUAL SURVEY OF COMMONWEALTH LAW: 1966. London, Butterworth and Co. (Publishers) Ltd.: 699-716. (Chapter 18)   **[38]**   *[COL]*

39.0060   BC   1968   International law. *In* Wade, H. W. R., ed. ANNUAL SURVEY OF COMMONWEALTH LAW: 1967. London, Butterworth and Co. (Publishers) Ltd.: 709-724. (Chapter 19)   **[38]**   *[COL]*

39.0061   KNA   1969   International law. *In* Wade, H. W. R., ed. ANNUAL SURVEY OF COMMONWEALTH LAW: 1968. London, Butterworth and Co. (Publishers) Ltd.: 785-801. (Chapter 19)   **[38]**   *[COL]*

Fergusson, C. Bruce

47.0097   BC   1966   The West Indies and the Atlantic Provinces: background of the present relationship.

Fonteyne, Jean-Pierre L.

39.0062   GC   1976   The Caribbean Sea: values and options in the light of changing international law. *In* Lewis, Vaughan A., ed. SIZE, SELF-DETERMINATION AND INTERNATIONAL RELATIONS: THE CARIBBEAN. Mona, Jamaica, University of the West Indies, Institute of Social and Economic Research: 264-284.   **[50,52,56]**   *[RIS]*

Fossum, Paul R.

39.0063   GU   1928   The Anglo-Venezuelan boundary controversy. *Hispan Am Hist Rev* 8(3), Aug.: 299-329.   **[5]**   *[COL]*

Francis, L. B.

39.0064   JM   1965   Jamaica assumes treaty rights and obligations: some aspects of foreign policy. *Int Comp Law Q* 14(2), April: 612-627.   **[37]**   *[COL]*

Franco Holguín, Jorge

47.0101   GC   1969   Problems of developing inter-regional trade and production in the Caribbean/Latin American area.

Fraser, Duncan

47.0102   BC   1966   The West Indies and Canada: the present relationship.

Friede, Juan

39.0065   GU   1969   España y la independencia (Guayana y los Llanos) [Spain and independence (Guyana and the Llanos)]. *Boln Cult Bibli* 12(4): 21-28.   **[5]**   *[COL]*

Gafar, John
47.0105 BC 1974 The terms of trade experience of the Caribbean Common Market countries.

Galavis Seidel, José Antonio
39.0066 GC 1973 Coastal states' perceptions of mineral regimes in the Gulf and Caribbean areas. *In* Alexander, Lewis M., ed. GULF AND CARIBBEAN MARITIME PROBLEMS. Kingston, Rhode Island, University of Rhode Island: 25-29. (Law of the Sea Institute Workshop No. 2) **[50,53]**
[COL]

Galindo Pohl, Reynaldo
39.0067 GC 1973 Eventual consequences of the new law of the sea in the Caribbean zone. *In* Alexander, Lewis M., ed. GULF AND CARIBBEAN MARITIME PROBLEMS. Kingston, Rhode Island, University of Rhode Island: 36-39. (Law of the Sea Institute Workshop No. 2) [COL]
38.0077 GC 1974 Pacem in maribus in the Caribbean region.

Garcin, William
47.0108 MT 1966 L'avenir de la Martinique dans le Marché Commun [The future of Martinique in the Common Market].

Giles, Bryant Whitmore
39.0068 BZ 1956 THE "BELIZE" QUESTION: A PROBLEM OF ANTI-COLONIALISM IN THE NEW WORLD. Ph.D. dissertation, Yale University: 301p. **[37]**
[PhD]

Girvan, Norman
39.0069 BC 1969 Integration from the viewpoint of the Caribbean: system of resource allocation in the private sector. *In* Waters, Maurice, ed. THE CARIBBEAN AND LATIN AMERICA: POLITICAL AND ECONOMIC RELATIONS. VOLUMES I. Jamaica, University of the West Indies: 57-60. **[38,45]** [RIS]

Girvan, Norman, ed.
41.0197 GC 1973 Dependence and underdevelopment in the New World and the Old.

Girwar, S. Norman
61.0062 BC 1973 The role and future of sugar in the Commonwealth Caribbean in the light of Britain's entry into the E.E.C.

Glassner, Martin Ira
39.0070 JM,TR 1970 The foreign relations of Jamaica and Trinidad and Tobago, 1960-1965. *Car Stud* 10(3), Oct.: 116-153. **[38,41]** [RIS]

Gonsalves, Ralph E.
39.0071 BB 1976 Barbados' foreign policy: Adams at the United Nations—a review. *B E Car Aff* 2(8), Oct.: 3-6. [RIS]

Goodman, Eileen
41.0202 JM 1962 Canada in Jamaica.

Gordon, Lincoln

39.0072   GC   1972   The United States and the Caribbean. *In* Kadt, Emanuel de, ed. PATTERNS OF FOREIGN INFLUENCE IN THE CARIBBEAN. London, Oxford University Press: 170-180.   [*RIS*]

Govaerts, C. H.

33.0084   NA   1969   Beschouwing over het domiciliebeginsel in het Antilliaans internationaal privaatrecht enin het interregionaal pr vaatrecht van het Koninkrijk [Comment on the domicile principle in Antillean international private law and in the intra-regional private law of the Kingdom].

Grant, C. H.

39.0073   BZ   1970   British Honduras and Guatemala. *Venture* 22(6), June: 22-26.
     [*COL*]

37.0306   GU   1973   Political sequel to Alcan nationalization in Guyana: the international aspects.

Green, Irene

7.0064   JM   1966   THE EFFECTS OF THE POPULATION EXPLOSION ON JAMAICA'S INTERNATIONAL RELATIONS.

Groot, Silvia W. de

39.0074   SR,GU   1970   Kroniek van een grensconflict [Chronicle of a border conflict]. *Gids* 133(9): 325-328.   [*COL*]

Hale, Edward Everett

39.0075   BE   1901   The Boer prisoners in Bermuda (a letter). *Outlook* 69(2), Sept.: 141. **[33]**   [*COL*]

39.0076   BE   1902   The Boer prisoners (a letter). *Outlook* 70(17), April 26: 1029.   [*COL*]

Hale, Edward Everett & Whitman, Mrs. Bernard

39.0077   BE   1901   The Boer prisoners at Bermuda. *Outlook* 69(13), Nov. 30: 849.
     [*COL*]

Hamilton, W. B.; Robinson, Kenneth & Goodwin, C. D. W., eds.

37.0329   BC   1966   A DECADE OF THE COMMONWEALTH, 1955-1964.

Hargreaves, Reginald

5.0364   GC,UK   1968   THE BLOODYBACKS: THE BRITISH SERVICEMAN IN NORTH AMERICA AND THE CARIBBEAN, 1655-1783.

Harrod, Jeffrey

46.0106   JM   1972   TRADE UNION FOREIGN POLICY: A STUDY OF BRITISH AND AMERICAN TRADE UNION ACTIVITIES IN JAMAICA.

Hawkins, Irene

47.0123   BC   1972   The choice of agreement.
47.0124   GC   1975   The club of 46.

Henfrey, Colin

37.0349   GU   1972   Foreign influence in Guyana: the struggle for independence.

Hermes, João Severiano da Fonseca

39.0078   **BZ**   1939   Questão de limites entre Guatemala e Honduras Ingleza [Boundary controversy between Guatemala and British Honduras]. *Revta Soc Geogr Rio* Jan 46: 13-30. **[5]**   [*AGS*]

Hines, Calvin Warner

5.0418   **GC**   1968   UNITED STATES DIPLOMACY IN THE CARIBBEAN DURING WORLD WAR II.

Hodgson, Robert D.

2.0205   **GC**   1973   The American Mediterannean: one sea, one region?

Hoetink, Harry

37.0361   **NA**   1972   The Dutch Caribbean and its Metropolis.

Houben, P.-H. J. M.

39.0079   **NC**   1965   DE ASSOCIATIE VAN SURINAME EN DE NEDERLANDSE ANTILLEN MET DE EUROPESE ECONOMISCHE GEMEEENSCHAP [THE ASSOCIATION OF SURINAM AND THE NETHERLANDS ANTILLES WITH THE EUROPEAN ECONOMIC COMMUNITY]. Leiden, A. W. Sijthoff: 124p. (Europese Integratie No. 5) **[41]**   [*COL*]

Hubbard, H. J. M.

39.0080   **GU**   1966   THE VENEZUELAN BORDER ISSUE: A SELL-OUT BY THE COALITION GOVERNMENT IN GUYANA. Georgetown, People's Progressive Party: 40p.   [*RIS*]

39.0081   **GU**   1967   VENEZUELAN BORDER ISSUE AND OCCUPATION OF ANKOKO: A SELL-OUT BY THE COALITION GOVERNMENT. Georgetown, Guyana, People's Progressive Party: 64p.   [*RIS*]

Hurtado, Héctor

47.0134   **GC**   1974   Venezuela and the Caribbean: integration of integration.

Hurtado Aguilar, Luis A.

39.0082   **BZ**   1958[?]   BELICE ES DE GUATEMALA: TRATADOS, SITUACIÓN JURÍDICA, ACTUACIONES, OPINIONES [BELIZE BELONGS TO GUATEMALA: TREATIES, JURIDICAL SITUATION, PROCEEDINGS, RULINGS]. [Guatemala City?] Guatemala, Secretaría de Información de la Presidencia de la República, 128p. **[5]**   [*AGS*]

Huurman, D.

37.0388   **NC**   1948   Britse federatieve voorstellen en Nederlandse federatiemogelijkheden in West Indië [British federation proposals and Dutch federation possibilities in the West Indies].

Ince, Basil A.

37.0393   **AG**   [n.d.]   The limits of Caribbean diplomacy: the invasion of Anguilla.

37.0394   **AG**   1970   The diplomacy of new states: the Commonwealth Caribbean and the case of Anguilla.

39.0083   **GU**   1970   The Venezuela-Guyana boundary dispute in the United Nations. *Car Stud* 9(4), Jan.: 5-26. **[5]**   [*RIS*]

37.0396   **GU**   1974   DECOLONIZATION AND CONFLICT IN THE UNITED NATIONS: GUYANA'S STRUGGLE FOR INDEPENDENCE.

40.0032   **GR**   1974   The decolonization of Grenada in the U.N.

12.0035	**GU**	1975	Race and ideology in the foreign relations of independent Guyana: the case of the East Indians.
39.0084	**TR**	1976	The administration of foreign affairs in a very small developing country: the case of Trinidad and Tobago. *In* Lewis, Vaughan A., ed. SIZE, SELF-DETERMINATION AND INTERNATIONAL RELATIONS: THE CARIBBEAN. Mona, Jamaica, University of the West Indies, Institute of Social and Economic Research: 307-339. [*RIS*]

Ireland, Gordon

39.0085	**GG**	1938	BOUNDARIES, POSSESSIONS, AND CONFLICTS IN SOUTH AMERICA. Cambridge, Harvard University Press, 345p. [*COL*]

Iribarren Borges, Ignacio

39.0086	**GU**	1965	Alocución pronunciada por el Doctor Iribarren Borges respecto al problema de la Guayana Esequiba [Address made by Doctor Iribarren Borges with respect to the problem of Guyana Esequibo]. *Documentos* 22, July-Sept.: 436-444. [*COL*]

Jagan, Cheddi

39.0087	**GU**	1966	U.S. INTERVENTION IN GUYANA. Georgetown, New Guiana Co. Ltd.: 31p. **[40]** [*RIS*]
39.0088	**GU**	1967	THE ROLE OF THE C.I.A. IN GUYANA AND ITS ACTIVITIES THROUGH-OUT THE WORLD. Georgetown, Guyana, People's Progressive Party: 15p. **[40]** [*RIS*]
39.0089	**GU**	1968	BORDER CONSPIRACY EXPOSED (TEXT OF LEGISLATIVE SPEECH ON VENEZUELAN DECREE). Georgetown, Guyana, People's Progressive Party: 32p. [*RIS*]
39.0090	**GU,US**	1968	Toward dictatorship in Guyana. *Minor One* 10(6), June: 13-15. **[37]** [*COL*]
40.0033	**GU**	1969	Intrigues of U.S. imperialism in Guyana.

Jainarain, Iserdeo

41.0263	**BC**	1976	TRADE AND UNDERDEVELOPMENT: A STUDY OF THE SMALL CARIBBEAN COUNTRIES AND LARGE MULTINATIONAL CORPORATIONS.

Jefferson, Owen

47.0141	**JM**	1967	Agricultural and commercial policies of the E.E.C.
47.0143	**BC**	1967	The comparative merits of West Indian association with Canada, the European Economic Community, the Latin American Free Trade Association and the Central American Common Market.
47.0144	**BC**	1967	The terms of association between countries at different stages of development as reflected in some recent trade agreements.

Jenney, E. Ross

28.0686	**GC**	1965	The Pan American Health Organization in WHO and the Caribbean.

Jones, Chester Lloyd

39.0091	**GC**	1970	CARIBBEAN INTERESTS OF THE UNITED STATES. New York, Arno Press and the New York Times: 379p. (Originally published in 1916) **[5]** [*RIS*]

Jones, R. A.

49.0055   **BC**   1968   The arguments for and against remaining on a foreign exchange standard.

Joseph, Cedric L.

39.0092   **GU**   1970   The Venezuela-Guyana boundary arbitration of 1889: an appraisal. Part I. *Car Stud* 10(2), July: 56-89.   **[5]**   [*RIS*]

39.0093   **GU**   1971   The Venezuela-Guyana boundary arbitration of 1889: an appraisal. Part II. *Car Stud* 10(4), Jan: 35-74.   **[5]**   [*RIS*]

5.0495   **BC**   1973   The strategic importance of the British West Indies, 1882-1932.

Kadt, Emanuel de, ed.

39.0094   **GC**   1972   PATTERNS OF FOREIGN INFLUENCE IN THE CARIBBEAN. London, Oxford University Press: 188p.   [*RIS*]

Kanagaratnam, Kandiah

34.0045   **JM,TR**   1973   The concern and contribution of the World Bank in population planning.

Kerr, Wilfred Brenton

5.0508   **BE**   1936   BERMUDA AND THE AMERICAN REVOLUTION: 1760-1783.

Kesteven, Geoffrey L.

56.0179   **GC**   1973   A sketch for a survey of Gulf and Caribbean fisheries.

Key, W. S.

39.0095   **BE**   1902   The Boer prisoners in Bermuda. *Outlook* 70(7), Feb. 15: 424-427.   **[33]**   [*COL*]

Kim, Jung-Gun

38.0110   **GC**   1967   Non-member participation in the South Pacific Commission and the Caribbean Organisation.

Kitzinger, Uwe

39.0096   **JM**   1965   THE BACKGROUND TO JAMAICA'S FOREIGN POLICY. Kingston, Jamaica, Farquharson Institutue of Public Affairs: 20p.   [*RIS*]

Knaplund, Paul

39.0097   **BC**   1953   JAMES STEPHEN AND THE BRITISH COLONIAL SYSTEM, 1813-1847. Madison, University of Wisconsin Press: 315p.   **[6]**   [*COL*]

Knight, H. Gary

38.0114   **GC**   1974   Impacts of some law of the sea proposals on Gulf and Caribbean resource development.

Krieger, David

38.0117   **GC**   1974   A Caribbean community for ocean development.

Kruijer, G. J.

40.0040   **SR**   1974   Neokolonie in rijksverband 1: Suriname's positie in het internationale machtssysteem [Neo-colony in the context of the Kingdom 1: Surinam's position in the international system of powers].

Kunz, Josef L.

39.0098   BZ   1946   Guatemala vs. Great Britain: in re Belice. *Am J Int Law* 40(2), Apr.:
383-390.   [5]   [*AGS*]

Lall, Sanjoya

45.0088   JM   1972   BALANCE OF PAYMENT EFFECTS OF PRIVATE FOREIGN INVESTMENT IN
DEVELOPING COUNTRIES: SUMMARY OF CASE STUDIES OF INDIA, IRAN,
JAMAICA AND KENYA.

Lasserre, Guy & Mabileau, Albert

37.0472   FA   1972   The French Antilles and their status as Overseas Departments.

Leach, Richard H.

39.0099   BC   1973   The changing Caribbean Commonwealth. *Wld Today*, May: 216-
226.   [16,41]   [*COL*]

Leeuwen, W. C. J. van

37.0479   NA   1972   DE NEDERLANDSE ANTILLEN TUSSEN NEDERLAND EN VENEZUELA:
POSITION-PAPER [THE NETHERLANDS ANTILLES BETWEEN THE NETH-
ERLANDS AND VENEZUELA: POSITION-PAPER].

Levitt, Kari & McIntyre, Alister

39.0100   BC   1967   CANADA—WEST INDIES ECONOMIC RELATIONS. Montreal, McGill
University: 181p.   [41,47]   [*UNL*]

Lewis, Vaughan A.

38.0129   BC   1972   Small states in the international society: with special reference to
the Associated States.

40.0048   BA   1974   The Bahamas in international politics: issues arising for an archipelago state.

39.0101   BC   1976   The Commonwealth Caribbean and self-determination in the
international system. *In* Lewis, Vaughan A., ed. SIZE, SELF-DETER-
MINATION AND INTERNATIONAL RELATIONS: THE CARIBBEAN. Mona,
Jamaica, University of the West Indies, Institute of Social and
Economic Research: 227-247.   [37,40]   [*RIS*]

Lewis, Vaughan A., ed.

40.0050   BC   1976   SIZE, SELF-DETERMINATION AND INTERNATIONAL RELATIONS: THE
CARIBBEAN.

Lewis, Vaughan A. & Singham, A. W.

38.0131   GC   1967   Integration, domination and the small-state system: the Caribbean.

Lewisohn, Florence

5.0553   SE   1975-76   St. Eustatius: depot for revolution.

Leyton Rodríguez, Ruben

39.0102   BZ   1971   LA PUERTA DE GUATEMALA EN EL CARIBE Y, LA INSEGURIDAD DE
AMÉRICA [GUATEMALA'S DOOR TO THE CARIBBEAN AND, THE INSE-
CURITY OF AMERICA]. Guatemala, Impresora Kelly: 212p.   [*NYP*]

Lord, W. T.

39.0103   GU   1961   Experiences of a government surveyor. *Timehri* 4th ser., no. 40,
Oct.: 61-75.   [*AMN*]

McCracken, John
56.0223   **GC**   1973   Comments re shipping and marine pollution.

McDonald, Frank
40.0054   **BC**   1971   THE COMMONWEALTH CARIBBEAN. III. THE POLITICS OF POWER.

McIntyre, Alister
47.0175   **BC**   1965   Aspects of development and trade in the Commonwealth Caribbean (preliminary draft).
49.0073   **BC**   1968   West Indian membership of the Sterling Area: a regional view.

McIntyre, Alister & Watson, Beverly
45.0100   **BC**   1970   STUDIES IN FOREIGN INVESTMENT IN THE COMMONWEALTH CARIBBEAN: NO. 1 TRINIDAD AND TOBAGO.

Maingot, Anthony P.
38.0149   **BC**   1969   National sovereignty, collective security and the realities of power in the Caribbean area.

Makinson, David Harold
5.0580   **BB**   1962   BARBADOS; A STUDY OF NORTH AMERICAN-WEST INDIAN RELATIONS, 1739-1789.

Manigat, Leslie F.
39.0104   **GC**   1969   Les Etats-Unis et le secteur caraïbe de l'Amérique Latine [The United States and the Caribbean region of Latin America]. *Rev Fr Sci Polit* 19(3), June: 645-683.   **[38,40]**   [*COL*]

Manley, Michael
37.0535   **JM**   1970   Overcoming insularity in Jamaica.

Mann, O. Nelson
39.0105   **GC**   1966   A program for maintaining relations between the Atlantic Provinces and the West Indies: is it feasible? *In* THE WEST INDIES AND THE ATLANTIC PROVINCES OF CANADA. CONFERENCE ORGANIZED BY CANADIAN NATIONAL COMMISSION FOR UNESCO, MAY 18-20, 1966. Halifax, Canada, Dalhousie University, Institute of Public Affairs: 63-65.   [*RIS*]

Marcos López, Francisco
39.0106   **BZ**   [n.d.]   QUIEBRA Y REINTEGRACIÓN DEL DERECHO DE GENTES: GIBRALTAR, BELICE, LAS MALVINAS [THE BREAKING AND RESTORATION OF HUMAN RIGHTS: GIBRALTAR, BELIZE, LAS MALVINAS]. [Guatemala City?] Guatemala, Talleres de Impr. Hispania, 78p.   **[5]**
[*AGS*]

Mathews, Thomas G.
39.0107   **GC**   1967   Problems and leaders in the Caribbean. *In* Wilgus, A. Curtis, ed. THE CARIBBEAN: ITS HEMISPHERIC ROLE. Gainesville, University of Florida Press: 28-40. (Caribbean Conference Series 1, vol. 17)
[*RIS*]

Matthews, Harry G.

39.0108   **JM**   1969   JAMAICA IN THE UNITED NATIONS, 1962-1966. Ann Arbor, Michigan, University Microfilms, Inc.: 164p. [Ph.D. dissertation, Claremont Graduate School and University Center]   **[20,37]**   [*UNL*]

Mecham, John Lloyd

39.0109   **GC,US**   1965   The general Caribbean policies of the United States. *In* Mecham, John Lloyd, ed. A SURVEY OF UNITED STATES-LATIN AMERICAN RELATIONS. Boston, Houghton Mifflin Company: 239-275.   **[5]**
                                                                       [*COL*]

Meikle, Louis S.

38.0155   **BC**   1969   CONFEDERATION OF THE BRITISH WEST INDIES VERSUS ANNEXATION TO THE UNITED STATES OF AMERICA: A POLITICAL DISCOURSE ON THE WEST INDIES.

Mendoza, José Luis

39.0110   **BZ**   1942   INGLATERRA Y SUS PACTOS SOBRE BELICE [GREAT BRITAIN AND ITS TREATIES ON BELIZE]. [Guatemala City?] Guatemala, Secretaría de Relaciones Exteriores, 287p.   **[5]**   [*AGS*]

Mestre, José A.

45.0105   **GC**   1966   Investments.

Meyers, H., ed.

39.0111   **BC**   1970   SOME PROBLEMS OF INTERNATIONAL LAW IN THE COMMONWEALTH CARIBBEAN. Mona, Jamaica, University of the West Indies: 144p.
                                                                       [*RIS*]

Mintz, Sidney W., ed.

6.0208   **GC**   1974   SLAVERY, COLONIALISM AND RACISM.

Monteforte Toledo, Mario

39.0112   **BC**   1969   Political cooperation in the light of cultural and historical factors. *In* Waters, Maurice, ed. THE CARIBBEAN AND LATIN AMERICA: POLITICAL AND ECONOMIC RELATIONS. VOL. I. Jamaica, University of the West Indies: 8-13.   [*RIS*]

Monzón, T. M.

39.0113   **NA**   1974   Naar een nieuwe juridische orde voor de exploitatie van de rijkdommen der zee en de implicaties hiervan voor de Antillen [Toward a new legal order for the exploitation of the ocean's resources and the implications thereof for the Antilles]. *Kristòf* 1(5), Oct.: 224-230.   **[55]**   [*RIS*]

39.0114   **NA**   1974   Naar een nieuwe juridische orde voor de exploitatie van de rijkdommen der zee en de implicaties hiervan voor de Antillen (Deel II) [Toward a new legal order for the exploitation of the ocean's resources and the implications thereof for the Antilles (Part II)]. *Kristòf* 1(6), Dec.: 257-260.   **[55]**   [*RIS*]

39.0115   **NA**   1975   Naar een nieuwe juridische orde voor de exploitatie van de rijkdommen der zee en de implicaties hiervan voor de Antillen (Deel III) [Toward a new legal order for the exploitation of the ocean's resources and the implications thereof for the Antilles (Part III)]. *Kristòf* 2(2), April: 73-84.   **[55]**   [*RIS*]

Morison, Samuel Eliot
5.0638   **GC**   1974   THE EUROPEAN DISCOVERY OF AMERICA: THE SOUTHERN VOYAGES.

Moss, Robert
37.0602   **GC**   1973   The stability of the Caribbean: report of the proceedings of the conference.

Moss, Robert, ed.
37.0603   **GC**   1973   THE STABILITY OF THE CARIBBEAN: REPORT OF A SEMINAR HELD AT DITCHLEY PARK, OXFORDSHIRE, U.K. MAY 18-20, 1973.

Murray, Gideon
37.0614   **BC**   1919   Canada and the British West Indies.

Nitoburg, E. L.
39.0116   **SR**   1969   Konflicti po nasledctbv. (k istori Gaiano-Venesvelskovo i Gaiano-surinamskovo pogranichnix sporov) [Conflicts of "inheritance": in the history of Venezuelan Guiana and Dutch-Guiana boundary disputes]. *In* Grigulevich, I. R., ed. GVIANA: GAIANA, FRANT-ZUZKAYA-GAIANA, SURINAM. Moscow, Izdatelstvo "Natchka": 229-246. **[5]**   [*UNL*]

Noel, Jesse A.
5.0659   **TR**   1966   Síntesis de la evolucíon histórica de la Isla de Trinidad (1498-1776) [Synthesis of the historical evolution of the island of Trinidad].

Noorden, D. van
39.0117   **NC**   1966   Enige gedachten omtrent het optreden der Lands-regeringen bij het tot stand brengen van internationale overeenkomsten [Some thoughts on the role that the Land governments play in the negotiation of international agreements]. *Justicia* 2(4): 113-118.
                                                                  [*COL*]
39.0118   **NC**   1969   Enige opmerkingen omtrent de associatieband van de Nederlandse Antillen en Suriname met de Europese Economische Gemeenschap [Some remarks on the association of the Netherlands Antilles and Surinam with the European Economic Community]. *Justicia* 3(2): 37-42. **[41]**   [*COL*]

O'Dell, D. J.
47.0212   **BC**   1970   On interpreting Article 16 (security exceptions) of the "Agreement Establishing the Caribbean Free Trade Area."

Odell, Peter R.
39.0119   **GC**   1972   The Caribbean and the outside world: geopolitical considerations. *In* Kadt, Emanuel de, ed. PATTERNS OF FOREIGN INFLUENCE IN THE CARIBBEAN. London, Oxford University Press: 18-31. **[5]**   [*RIS*]

Oduber Quiros, Daniel
39.0120   **BC**   1969   The OAS and regional members. *In* Waters, Maurice, ed. THE CARIBBEAN AND LATIN AMERICA: POLITICAL AND ECONOMIC RELA-TIONS. VOLUME I. Jamaica, University of the West Indies: 42-47.
                                                                  [*RIS*]

Ojer, Pablo
5.0664   GU   1969   ROBERT H. SCHOMBURGK: EXPLORADOR DE GUAYANA Y SUS LINEAS
DE FRONTERA [ROBERT H. SCHOMBURGK: EXPLORER OF GUYANA
AND ITS BOUNDARIES].

Paërl, Eric
45.0116   NC   1971   NEDERLANDSE MACHT IN DE DERDE WERELD: EEN INVENTARISATIE
VAN ECONOMISCHE BELANGEN [DUTCH POWER IN THE THIRD WORLD:
TAKING AN INVENTORY OF ECONOMIC INTERESTS].

Parris, Carl D.
41.0399   TR   1976   Size or class: factors affecting Trinidad and Tobago's foreign
economic policy.

Parris, Ronald Glenfield
40.0063   BB   1972   Inequality and control in a colonial bureaucracy: Barbados,
1955-1962.
16.0079   BB   1974   RACE, INEQUALITY AND UNDERDEVELOPMENT IN BARBADOS, 1627-
1973.

Perazzo, Nicolás
39.0121   GU   1965   FRONTERAS DE VENEZUELA [VENEZUELAN BORDERS]. Caracas,
Vargas: 107p.   [COL]

Pérez Aparicio, Josefina
5.0721   TR   1966   PÉRDIDA DE LA ISLA DE TRINIDAD [THE LOSS OF THE ISLAND OF
TRINIDAD].

Perkins, Dexter
39.0122   GC   1966   THE UNITED STATES AND THE CARIBBEAN. Cambridge, Mass.,
Harvard University Press: 197p.   [RIS]

Persaud, Bishnodat
47.0228   BC   1971   An enlarged EEC and the Commonwealth Caribbean.

Pindling, Lynden O.
39.0123   BA   1974   Hydrospace and the law of the sea. *Car R* 6(3), July-Aug.-Sept.: 6-9.
[RIS]

Plank, John N.
39.0124   BC   1967   Neighborly relations in the Caribbean. *In* Wilgus, A. Curtis, ed. THE
CARIBBEAN: ITS HEMISPHERIC ROLE. Gainesville, University of
Florida Press: 161-170. (Caribbean Conference Series 1, vol. 17)
[RIS]

Pollard, H. J.
51.0089   AT   1974   INTERNATIONAL TOURISM AND THE ECONOMIC DEVELOPMENT OF
SMALL TERRITORIES: THE CASE OF ANTIGUA, WEST INDIES.

Poveda Ramos, Gabriel
39.0125   GC   1974   The Andean Group and the integration of the Caribbean. *In*
STUDIES ON THE ECONOMIC INTEGRATION OF THE CARIBBEAN AND
LATIN AMERICA. Association of Caribbean Universities and Research Institutes (UNICA): 52-63.   **[41]**   [RIS]

Preiswerk, Roy

39.0126   BC   1969   The new regional dimensions of the foreign policies of Commonwealth Caribbean States. *In* Preiswerk, Roy, ed. REGIONALISM AND THE COMMONWEALTH CARIBBEAN: PAPERS PRESENTED AT THE "SEMINAR ON THE FOREIGN POLICIES OF CARIBBEAN STATES", APRIL-JUNE, 1968. Trinidad, University of the West Indies, Institute of International Relations: 1-24. **[38]**   [*RIS*]

39.0127   BC   1969   The relevance of Latin America to the foreign policy of Commonwealth Caribbean states. *J Inter-Amer Stud* 11(2), April: 245-271. **[47]**   [*COL*]

32.0461   GC   1971   The teaching of International Relations in the Caribbean.

Preiswerk, Roy, ed.

38.0175   BC   1969   REGIONALISM AND THE COMMONWEALTH CARIBBEAN: PAPERS PRESENTED AT THE "SEMINAR ON THE FOREIGN POLICIES OF CARIBBEAN STATES", APRIL-JUNE, 1968.

39.0128   GC   1970   DOCUMENTS ON INTERNATIONAL RELATIONS IN THE CARIBBEAN. Rio Piedras, University of Puerto Rico, Institute of Caribbean Studies: 853p. [also published by the University of West Indies, Trinidad, Document and Monograph Series of the Institute of International Relations, 1]   [*RIS*]

Preston, Richard A.

39.0129   BC   1971   Caribbean defense and security: a study of the implications of Canada's "special relationship" with the Commonwealth West Indies. *S Atlan Q* 70(3), Summer: 317-331.   [*COL*]

Proctor, Jesse Harris, Jr.

38.0181   BC   1957   The international significance of the Federation of British Caribbean territories.

Ramphal, S. S.

39.0130   GU   1967   BUILDING THE FOUNDATIONS: THE TEXT OF A LECTURE ENTITLED "FOREIGN AFFAIRS AND THE NEW STATE: THE GUYANA EXPERIENCE." Georgetown, Guyana Government Printery: 28p.   [*RIS*]

39.0131   GU   1973   STATEMENT AT THE MEETING OF THE SECURITY COUNCIL AT PANAMA CITY, PANAMA ON TUESDAY, MARCH 15, 1973. New York, Permanent Mission of Guyana to the United Nations: 31p.   [*CEIP*]

Rattray, K. O.; Kirton, Allan & Robinson, Patrick

39.0132   GC   1974   The effect of the existing law of the sea on the development of the Caribbean region and the Gulf of Mexico. *In* PACEM IN MARIBUS: CARIBBEAN STUDY PROJECT WORKING PAPERS AND SELECTION FROM DIALOGUE AT PREPARATORY CONFERENCE, JAMAICA, OCTOBER, 1972. Malta, Malta University Press: 251-275. (Chapter 12) **[38,56]**
       [*RIS*]

Ray, Ellen

37.0702   JM   1976   CIA and local gunmen plan Jamaican coup.

Reid, George Lincoln

38.0192   BC   1972   A COMPARATIVE STUDY OF THE FOREIGN POLICIES OF VERY SMALL STATES, WITH SPECIAL REFERENCE TO THE COMMONWEALTH CARIBBEAN.

Reive, R. v. H.

39.0133   BC   1970   The international competence of the associated states in the CARIFTA treaty. *In* Meyers, H., ed. SOME PROBLEMS OF INTERNATIONAL LAW IN THE COMMONWEALTH CARIBBEAN. Mona, Jamaica, University of the West Indies: 1-16. **[38,47]**   [*RIS*]

Renforth, William Eldon

45.0126   GC   1974   A COMPARATIVE STUDY OF JOINT INTERNATIONAL BUSINESS VENTURES WITH FAMILY FIRM OR NON-FAMILY FIRM PARTNERS: THE CARIBBEAN COMMUNITY EXPERIENCE.

Rennie, Bukka

37.0708   GC   1975   "The conflicting tendencies in the Caribbean revolution."

Reyner, Anthony S. & Hope, Walter B.

39.0134   GU   1967   Guyana's disputed borders: a factual background. *Wld Aff* 130(2), July-August-Sept.: 107-113.   [*COL*]

Ribeiro, Darcy

5.0762   GC   1971   THE AMERICAS AND CIVILIZATION.

Richardson, C. Howard

37.0713   GC   1971   American research on the political geography of Latin America.

Richardson, Q. B.

56.0270   NA   1975   Aandacht voor de bestrijding van de zeevervuiling op de Derde VN Zeerechtconferentie [Attention to the control of sea pollution at the Third UN Conference on the Law of the Sea].

Richardson, Q. B. & Monzón, T. M.

39.0135   NA   1975   Overdracht van technologie [Export of technology]. *Kristòf* 2(4), August: 157-161.   [*RIS*]

Riemens, H.

39.0136   GC   1967   Latijns Amerika en de Caribische emancipatie [Latin America and the Caribbean emancipation]. *Int Spectator* 21(6), March 22: 477-489. **[38]**   [*COL*]

Roberts, E. J. Ph.

39.0137   NC   1967   De verdragsrelaties tussen het Koninkrijk en Latijns-Amerika op het gebied van de handel [The treaty relations between the Kingdom and Latin America concerning trade]. *Ant Jurbl* 17(1): 4-13. **[47]**   [*COL*]

39.0138   NA   1968   De associatie van de Nederlandse Antillen met de Europese Economische Gemeenschap in zijn uitvoering: relevante teksten, II [The association of the Netherlands Antilles with the European Economic Community: relevant texts, II]. *Justicia* 4(2): 34-46.

        [*COL*]

39.0139   NA   1968   De associatie van de Nederlandse Antillen met de Europese Economische Gemeenschap in zijn uitvoering: relevante teksten, III [The association of the Netherlands Antilles with the European Economic Community: relevant texts, III]. *Justicia* 4(4): 113-119.

        [*COL*]

39.0140	NA	1968	De Verdragsbetrekkingen met Venezuela [The Treaty relations with Venezuela]. *Justicia* 4(3): 79-93. [*COL*]
39.0141	NA	1969	De verdragsrelaties van het Koninkrijk der Nederlanden betreffende de burgerluchtvaart [The treaty relations of the kingdom of The Netherlands regarding passenger aviation]. *Justicia* 5(3): 73-79. **[48]** [*COL*]
39.0142	GC	1972	Het toetredingsverdrag inzake de uitbreiding van de E.E.G. en het Koninkrijk der Nederlanden [The entrance treaty regarding the extension of the E.E.C. and the kingdom of The Netherlands]. *Justicia* 8(1): 1-3. [*COL*]

Robinson, C. L.

48.0141	BC	1970	The allocation of the Federal Palm and the Federal Maple according to international law.

Rodríguez, Raul Sosa

38.0198	BC	1969	Economic cooperation and integration between Latin American and Caribbean Countries.

Rodríguez Beteta, Virgilio

39.0143	BZ	1965	SOLIDARITY AND RESPONSIBILITIES OF THE UNITED STATES IN THE BELIZE CASE. Guatemala, Tipografía Nacional: 137p. **[5,37]** [*NYP*]

Rodway, James

39.0144	GU	1911	Our boundary war scare. *Timehri* 3d ser., 1(18C), Dec.: 239-247. **[5]** [*AMN*]

Rondón Lovera, César

5.0790	GU	1966	DESDE EL ORINOCO HASTA EL ESEQUIBO: CRÓNICA EN GRADO ELEMENTAL [FROM THE ORINOCO TO THE ESEQUIBO: A SIMPLE CHRONICLE].

Ross, Rodney Anson

39.0145	UV	1975	BLACK AMERICANS AND HAITI, LIBERIA, THE VIRGIN ISLANDS, AND ETHIOPIA, 1929-1936. Ph.D. dissertation, University of Chicago. **[16]** [*PhD*]

Rout, Leslie B., Jr.

39.0146	GU	1971	WHICH WAY OUT? A STUDY OF THE GUYANA-VENEZUELA BOUNDARY DISPUTE. East Lansing, Michigan State University, Latin American Studies Center: 130p. [*TCL*]

Ryan, Selwyn

39.0147	TR	1972	Third World unit? *In* Boyke, Roy, ed. PATTERNS OF PROGRESS. Port-of-Spain, Trinidad, Key Caribbean Publications: 104-111. [*RIS*]

Salas, Rafael M.

34.0094	GC	1973	The United Nations fund for population activities.

Sanders, William

38.0199	GC	1966	The Conference System in the Caribbean.

Santiso Galvez, Gustavo

39.0148   BZ   1941   EL CASO DE BELICE A LA LUZ DE LA HISTORIA Y EL DERECHO INTERNACIONAL [THE BELIZE QUESTION IN THE LIGHT OF HISTORY AND INTERNATIONAL LAW]. [Guatemala City?] Guatemala, Tip. Nacional, 346p. (Thesis, University of Mexico.) **[5]**   [*AGS*]

Sanz de Santamaría, Carlos

38.0200   BC   1969   Integration from the viewpoint of Latin America.

Schoenrich, Otto

39.0149   GU   1949   The Venezuela-British Guiana boundary dispute. *Am J Int Law* 43(3), July: 523-530. **[5]**   [*AGS*]

Siebert, Wilbur H.

39.0150   BA,BC   1913   THE LEGACY OF THE AMERICAN REVOLUTION TO THE BRITISH WEST INDIES AND BAHAMAS; A CHAPTER OUT OF THE HISTORY OF THE AMERICAN LOYALISTS. Columbus, Ohio State University Contributions in History and Political Science No. 1: 50p. **[5]**   [*NYP*]

Silvert, Kalman H.

39.0151   GC   1971   The Caribbean and North America. *In* Szulc, Tad, ed. THE UNITED STATES AND THE CARIBBEAN. Englewood Cliffs, N.J., Prentice-Hall, Inc.: 193-210.   [*RIS*]

Simmonds, K. R.

39.0152   BZ   1968   The Belize mediation. *Int Comp Law Q* 17(4), Oct.: 996-1009. **[38]**
                                                                               [*COL*]

38.0211   BC   1970   International economics organisations in Central and Latin America and the Caribbean: regionalism and sub-regionalism in the integration process.

Skeete, Charles A.

39.0153   BC   1973   Association and the agricultural policies of the E.E.C. *In* PROCEEDINGS OF THE EIGHTH WEST INDIAN AGRICULTURAL ECONOMICS CONFERENCE, HELD AT THE HILTON HOTEL, TRINIDAD, APRIL 1-7, 1973. St. Augustine, Trinidad, University of the West Indies, Department of Agricultural Economics and Farm Management: 56-60. **[47]**   [*RIS*]

Sklar, Barry & Hagen, Virginia, eds.

39.0154   GC   1973   INTER-AMERICAN RELATIONS: A COLLECTION OF DOCUMENTS, LEGISLATION, DESCRIPTIONS OF INTER-AMERICAN ORGANIZATIONS, AND OTHER MATERIAL PERTAINING TO INTER-AMERICAN AFFAIRS. Washinton, DC, U.S. Government Printing Office: 780p. **[38]**
                                                                               [*CEIP*]

Sluisdom, E. E.

39.0155   SR,GU   1969   Rondom de grensgeschillen in de Guyana's [On the border conflicts in the Guyanas]. *In* ENIG ZICHT OP SURINAME. Amsterdam, The Netherlands, Vrije Universiteit, Geografisch Instituut: V1-V5.
                                                                               [*AGS*]

Sluiter, Engel

39.0156   SR   1933   Dutch Guiana: a problem in boundaries. *Hisp Am Hist Rev* 13(1), Feb.: 2-22. **[5]**   *[AGS]*

Smith, H. Carington

3.0550   GU   1938   On the frontier of British Guiana and Brazil.

Somersall, T.

39.0157   BC   1968   Monetary cooperation and economic integration in the Commonwealth Caribbean. *In* PAPERS PRESENTED AT THE REGIONAL CONFERENCE ON DEVALUATION, FEBRUARY 2-4, 1968. [Mona, Jamaica], University of the West Indies, Institute of Social and Economic Research: 231-239. **[38,41]**   *[RIS]*

St. Cyr, E. B. A.

39.0158   BC   1969   Foreign aid to the Caribbean from the angle of integrative efforts. *In* Preiswerk Roy, ed. REGIONALISM AND THE COMMONWEALTH CARIBBEAN: PAPERS PRESENTED AT THE "SEMINAR ON THE FOREIGN POLICIES OF CARIBBEAN STATES", APRIL-JUNE, 1968. TRINIDAD, UNIVERSITY OF THE WEST INDIES, INSTITUTE OF INTERNATIONAL RELATIONS: 130-140. **[38]**   *[RIS]*

Stewart, G. P.

39.0159   BA   1970   Straight baselines for the Bahamas. *In* Meyers, H., ed. SOME PROBLEMS OF INTERNATIONAL LAW IN THE COMMONWEALTH CARIBBEAN. Mona, Jamaica, University of the West Indies: 109-144.   *[RIS]*

Szulc, Tad, ed.

39.0160   GC   1971   THE UNITED STATES AND THE CARIBBEAN. Englewood Cliffs, N.J., Prentice-Hall, Inc: 1212p.   *[RIS]*

Theberge, James D., ed.

39.0161   GC   1972   SOVIET SEAPOWER IN THE CARIBBEAN: POLITICAL AND STRATEGIC IMPLICATIONS. New York, Praeger Publications: 175p. (Praeger Special Studies in International Politics and Public Affairs)   *[RIS]*

39.0162   GC   1973   RUSSIA IN THE CARIBBEAN. PART ONE: PANELISTS' FINDINGS, RECOMMENDATIONS AND COMMENTS. Washington, D.C., Georgetown University, Center for Strategic and International Studies: 36p. **[40]**   *[RIS]*

39.0163   GC   1973   RUSSIA IN THE CARIBBEAN. PART TWO: A SPECIAL REPORT. Washington, D.C., Georgetown University, Center for Strategic and International Studies: 166p. **[40]**   *[RIS]*

Thomas, Clive Y.

47.0269   BC   1966   The West Indies Canada Conference.

Toro, Elías

39.0164   GU   1905   POR LAS SELVAS DE GUAYANA: DELIMITACIÓN DE VENEZUELA CON GUAYANA BRITÁNICA [THROUGH THE FORESTS OF GUIANA: THE BOUNDARY BETWEEN VENEZUELA AND BRITISH GUIANA]. Caracas, Tip. Herrera Irigoyen, 289p. **[5]**   *[COL]*

Toth, Charles W.
5.0899   **GC**   1975-76 Introduction: the American Revolution and the Caribbean.

Trotman, Donald A. B.
37.0852   **GU**   1973[?] GUYANA AND THE WORLD: COMMENTARIES ON NATIONAL AND INTERNATIONAL AFFAIRS (1968-1973).

Tudor, J. Cameron
39.0165   **BC**   1966   A program for maintaining relations between the Atlantic Provinces and the West Indies: it is feasible? *In* THE WEST INDIES AND THE ATLANTIC PROVINCES OF CANADA. CONFERENCE ORGANIZED BY CANADIAN NATIONAL COMMISSION FOR UNESCO, MAY 18-20, 1966. Halifax, Canada, Dalhousie University, Institute of Public Affairs: 66-68.   [*RIS*]

Turk, Richard Wellington
5.0919   **GC,ST** 1968   STRATEGY AND FOREIGN POLICY: THE UNITED STATES NAVY IN THE CARIBBEAN, 1865-1913.

Tyson, George F., Jr.
5.0920   **BC**   1975-76 The Carolina Black Corps: legacy of revolution (1782-1798).

Uchegbu, Amechi
39.0166   **GC**   1976   The law of the sea and small states in the Caribbean. *In* Lewis, Vaughan A., ed. SIZE, SELF-DETERMINATION AND INTERNATIONAL RELATIONS: THE CARIBBEAN. Mona, Jamaica, University of the West Indies, Institute of Social and Economic Research: 285-306. **[50,52,56]**   [*RIS*]

Ugarte, Manuel
39.0167   **BZ**   1940   Guatemala's claims in British Honduras. *Liv Age* 357(4480), Jan.: 438-439. **[5]**

Vasco, G.
39.0168   **FG**   1901   L'arbitrage du contesté franco-brésilien [The arbitration of the Franco-Brazilian [boundary] dispute]. *Rev Fr Etr Colon* 26(266), Feb.: 70-76.   [*NYP*]

Verrier, Anthony
37.0862   **GU**   1966   Guyana and Cyprus: techniques of peace-keeping.

Verrill, Addison E.
39.0169   **BE**   1908   Relations between Bermuda and the American colonies during the Revolutionary War. *CAAST* 13: 47-64. **[5]**   [*COL*]

Villiers, J. A. J. de
39.0170   **GU**   1912   The boundaries of British Guiana. *United Emp* new ser., 3(6), June: 505-513. **[5]**   [*AGS*]

Vivó Escoto, Jorge A.
2.0478   **BC**   1967   Belice: país y pueblo; evolución económica y política [Belize: country and town; economic and political evolution].

Vizetelly, Frank H.
39.0171   BE   1901   The Boers in Bermuda. *Outlook* 69(13), Nov.: 849-851. **[33]**
                                                                                     [*COL*]

Waddell, David A. G.
39.0172   BZ   1961   As Honduras Británicas e a reivindicacão guatemalteca [British Honduras and the Guatemalan claim]. *Revta Brasil Polit Int* 4(15), Sept.: 55-71.   [*NYP*]
37.0871   BZ   1961   Developments in the Belize question 1946-1960.

Waters, Maurice, ed.
39.0173   GC   1969   THE CARIBBEAN AND LATIN AMERICA: POLITICAL AND ECONOMIC RELATIONS. VOLUME I. (SYMPOSIUM HELD AT THE UNIVERSITY OF THE WEST INDIES, MONA, JAMAICA). Jamaica, University of the West Indies: 112p. **[41,47]**   [*RIS*]
39.0174   GC   1969   WESTERN HEMISPHERE INTERNATIONAL RELATIONS AND THE CARIBBEAN AREA. VOLUME II. (SYMPOSIUM HELD AT THE UNIVERSITY OF THE WEST INDIES, MONA, JAMAICA). Jamaica, University of the West Indies: 111p. **[41,47]**   [*RIS*]

Weinstein, Brian
5.0961   FG,FC   1972   EBOUÉ.

White, John W.
39.0175   BC,SR   1957   United States technical assistance in the Caribbean. *In* Wilgus, A. Curtis, ed. THE CARIBBEAN: CONTEMPORARY INTERNATIONAL RELATIONS [PAPERS DELIVERED AT THE SEVENTH CONFERENCE ON THE CARIBBEAN HELD AT THE UNIVERSITY OF FLORIDA, DEC. 6-8, 1956]. Gainesville, University of Florida Press, p.129-134. (Publications of the School of Inter-American Studies, ser. 1, v. 7.)   [*RIS*]

Wilgus, A. Curtis, ed.
2.0507   GC   1957   THE CARIBBEAN: CONTEMPORARY INTERNATIONAL RELATIONS [PAPERS DELIVERED AT THE SEVENTH CONFERENCE ON THE CARIBBEAN HELD AT THE UNIVERSITY OF FLORIDA, DEC. 6-8, 1956].
39.0176   GC   1966   THE CARIBBEAN: CURRENT UNITED STATES RELATIONS. Gainesville, University of Florida Press: 243p. (Caribbean Conference Series 1, Vol. 16)   [*RIS*]
39.0177   GC   1967   THE CARIBBEAN: ITS HEMISPHERIC ROLE. Gainesville, University of Florida Press: 202p. (Caribbean Conference Series 1, vol. 17) [*RIS*]

Willcock, Roger
39.0178   BE   1973   The Bermuda-Colombian 'war' of 1936. *Bermuda Hist Q* 30(2), Summer: 37-52.   [*COL*]

Williams, Donn Alan
39.0179   FG   1975   BRAZIL AND FRENCH GUIANA: THE FOUR-HUNDRED YEAR STRUGGLE FOR AMAPA. Ph.D. dissertation, Texas Christian University: 235p. **[5]**   [*PhD*]

Williams, Eric Eustace
2.0516   TR   1964   Trinidad and Tobago: international perspectives.
37.0908   BC   1969   BRITAIN AND THE WEST INDIES (NOEL BUXTON LECTURE, THE UNIVERSITY OF ESSEX).

39.0180   **GC**   1973   The foreign policy of the Caribbean states. *Round Table* 63(249), Jan.: 77-88.   **[38]**   [*COL*]

Winks, Robin W.
39.0181   **BC**   1968   Canadian-West Indian union: a forty-year minuet. London, University of London, Athlone Press: 54p. (Published for the Institute of Commonwealth Studies, Commonwealth Paper No. 11)
                                                                                                          [*RIS*]

Winters, Robert H.
47.0283   **BC**   1966   Interest of Canada in the West Indies.

Wionczek, Miguel S.
45.0156   **GC**   1969   The roles [of] foreign investment in the development of the Caribbean/Latin American area: South American view.
40.0087   **GC,US**   1969-70   United States investment and the development of Middle America.

Woetzel, Robert
39.0182   **BC**   1969   The Organization of American States and Caribbean security. *In* Preiswerk, Roy, ed. Regionalism and the Commonwealth Caribbean: papers presented at the "Seminar on the Foreign Policies of Caribbean States", April-June, 1968. Trinidad, University of the West Indies, Institute of International Relations: 246-256.   **[38]**   [*RIS*]

Wouk, Jonathan
37.0922   **GU**   1967   British Guiana: a case study in British colonial and foreign policy.

Zuill, William Sears
44.0067   **BE**   1953   The Gibraltar of the West: a history of Admiralty and War Department lands.

Chapter 40

POST-COLONIAL ISSUES

Socio-political concerns; problems engendered by dependent economies; political problems of newly independent ex-colonies and territories approaching independence.

See also: **[8]** The nature of society; **[37]** Politics and government; **[38]** Intraregional issues; **[41]** General economics.

Abbott, George C.
37.0002   **KNA**   1971   Political disintegration: the lessons of Anguilla.

Anderson, William A. & Dynes, Russell R.
37.0010   **CU**   1975   SOCIAL MOVEMENTS, VIOLENCE, AND CHANGE: THE MAY MOVEMENT IN CURAÇAO.

Andic, Fuat M. & Gutiérrez, Elías
47.0010   **GC**   1966   Caribbean trade patterns.

Andrews, Valerie; Brodie, Ben & Forde, Kenneth
40.0001   **BC**   1975   On the tasks facing Caribbean students and intellectuals. *In* Singham, A. W., ed. THE COMMONWEALTH CARIBBEAN INTO THE SEVENTIES. Montreal, McGill University, Centre for Developing Area Studies: 188-191. **[21]**   [*RIS*]

Ashcraft, Norman
40.0002   **BZ**   1973   COLONIALISM AND UNDERDEVELOPMENT: PROCESSES OF POLITICAL ECONOMIC CHANGE IN BRITISH HONDURAS. New York, Teacher's College Press: 180p.   **[10,41]**   [*TCL*]

Aubinière, Général
40.0003   **FG**   1966   Le centre spatial guyanais [The Guianese space center]. *Rev Defense Natn* 22, April: 634-641.   [*COL*]

Baum, Daniel Jay
49.0007   **BC**   1974   THE BANKS OF CANADA IN THE COMMONWEALTH CARIBBEAN: ECONOMIC NATIONALISM AND MULTINATIONAL ENTERPRISES OF A MEDIUM POWER.

Beckford, George L.
42.0019   **GC**   1972   PERSISTENT POVERTY: UNDERDEVELOPMENT IN PLANTATION ECONOMIES OF THE THIRD WORLD.

Beckford, George L., ed.

41.0032   BC   1975   CARIBBEAN ECONOMY: DEPENDENCE AND BACKWARDNESS.

Bell, Wendell

40.0004   BC   1973   New states in the Caribbean: a grounded theoretical account. *In* Eisenstadt, S. N. & Rokkan, Stein, eds. BUILDING STATES AND NATIONS: ANALYSES BY REGION. VOLUME II. Beverly Hills, California, Sage Publications: 177-208.   **[20,37]**   [*NYP*]

Bell, Wendell & Moskos, C. C., Jr.

40.0005   BC   1965   Some implications of equality for political, economic and social development. *Int Rev Community Dev* 13-14: 219-246.   **[20]**   [*COL*]

Bell, Wendell & Oxaal, Ivar

37.0048   BC   1967   The nation-state as a unit in the comparative study of social change.

Benedict, Burton, ed.

2.0024   BC   1967   PROBLEMS OF SMALLER TERRITORIES.

Best, Lloyd

37.0053   GC   1967   Independent thought and Caribbean freedom.

Bhagwandin, Khemraj

40.0006   BC   1972   Erosion of human rights and fundamental freedom in the Commonwealth Caribbean and Guyana. *Thunder* 4(2), April-June: 5-10.   [*RIS*]

Blackman, Courtney N.

49.0009   JM   1968   CENTRAL BANKING IN A DEPENDENT ECONOMY: THE JAMAICAN EXPERIENCE, 1961-1967.

Bogoslovsky, V. A.

37.0067   GU   1969   Narodnaya progressivnaya partiya Gaiani v borbe za podlinnyv nezabisimoct, democratiyv u cotzialii progrecc strani [The new progressive Guyanese parties in the struggle for true independence, democracy and socialist progress for their countries].

Bolland, O. Nigel

5.0079   BZ   1975   THE FORMATION OF A COLONIAL SOCIETY: BELIZE, FROM CONQUEST TO CROWN COLONY.

Boodhoo, Ken

40.0007   TR   1974   EXTERNAL INFLUENCES ON THE BEHAVIOUR OF A SMALL STATE: PENETRATION OF THE TRINIDAD POLITICAL SYSTEMS. Ph.D. dissertation, University of the West Indies.   **[39,45]**

Bosch, Juan

5.0086   GC   1970   DE CRISTÓBAL COLÓN A FIDEL CASTRO: EL CARIBE FRONTERA IMPERIAL [FROM CHRISTOPHER COLUMBUS TO FIDEL CASTRO: THE IMPERIAL CARIBBEAN FRONTIER].

Brand, W.

40.0008   NC   1973   Hulp aan Suriname en de Nederlandse Antillen [Aid to Surinam and the Netherlands Antilles]. *Int Spectator* 27(4), Feb. 22: 139-144.   **[41]**   [*NYP*]

Brewster, Havelock
41.0076   **GC**   1973   Economic dependence: a quantitative interpretation.

Broderick, Margaret
37.0091   **BC**   1968   Associated Statehood—a new form of decolonisation.

Brown, Richard H.
37.0094   **GU**   1966   Decolonisation.

Bruijne, G. A. de
41.0087   **SR**   1969   Het isolement van Suriname [The isolation of Surinam].

Brunn, Stanley D.; Ford, John J. & McIntosh, Terry
37.0098   **GC**   1971   The state of political geography research in Latin America

Cacho, C. P.
37.0113   **BZ**   1967   British Honduras: a case of deviation in Commonwealth Caribbean decolonization.

Caraib, Frair
40.0009   **GD**   1967   La Guadeloupe opprimée [Guadeloupe oppressed]. *Temps Mod* 23(256), Sept.: 442-494.   **[37]**   [*COL*]

Carlozzi, Carl A.
56.0058   **GC**   1972   An ecological overview of Caribbean development programs.

Carmichael, Trevor Austin
40.0010   **BC**   1973   INTEGRATION AND DEPENDENCY IN THE COMMONWEALTH CARIB-BEAN: A STUDY IN POLITICAL ECONOMY. Ph.D. dissertation, Wayne State University: 176p.   [*PhD*]

Chapman, Donald
40.0011   **JM**   1962   Jamaica cuts loose. *Venture* 14(1), Jan.: 4, 8.   [*COL*]

Chin, H. E.
41.0103   **SR**   1971   Suriname: ontwikkelingshulp en economische ontwikkeling [Surinam: economic aid and economic development].

Clarke, Colin G.
37.0144   **AG**   1971   Political fragmentation in the Caribbean: the case of Anguilla.
21.0013   **GC**   1976   Insularity and identity in the Caribbean.

Coard, Bernard
40.0012   **BC**   1974   The meaning of political independence in the Commonwealth Caribbean. *In* INDEPENDENCE FOR GRENADA—MYTH OR REALITY? Proceedings of a Conference on the Implications of Independence for Grenada sponsored by the Institute of International Relations and the Dept. of Govt., U.W.I., St. Augustine, Trinidad, Jan. 11-13, 1974: 69-75.   **[38]**   [*RIS*]

Collins, B. A. N.
37.0148   **GU**   1965   Acceeding to independence: some constitutional problems of a polyethnic society (British Guiana).
37.0149   **GU**   1965-66   "Consultative democracy" in British Guiana.

37.0150	GU	1965	The end of a colony. II: British Guiana 1965.
37.0151	GU	1966	Independence for Guyana.

Collins, Charles O.
40.0013   BZ   1973   THE POLITICAL GEOGRAPHY OF NATION-BUILDING: THE CASE OF BELIZE. Ph.D. dissertation, University of Kansas: 211p.   **[7,38]**
                                                                                   [PhD]

Constandse, A. L.
40.0014   SR   1973   Suriname, eenzaam in de frontlinie [Surinam, alone at the front]. *Gids* 136(2): 128-132.   *[COL]*

Coombs, Orde, ed.
21.0014   GC   1974   IS MASSA DAY DEAD? BLACK MOODS IN THE CARIBBEAN.

Corkran, Herbert
38.0046   GC   1961   CHANGING PATTERNS OF INTERNATIONAL ORGANIZATION IN THE CARIBBEAN.

Craton, Michael
5.0192   BA   1968   A HISTORY OF THE BAHAMAS.

Cross, Malcolm
32.0145   GC   1973   Education and job opportunities.

Cumper, George E.
40.0015   GC   1974   Dependence, development, and the sociology of economic thought. *Social Econ Stud* 23(3), Sept.: 465-482.   **[41]**   *[RIS]*

Dabreo, Sinclair
40.0016   BC   1971   THE WEST INDIES TODAY: A THESIS ON THE FORCES, STRUGGLES, FRUSTRATIONS, AND PEOPLES OF THE WEST INDIES. Barbados, Letchworth Press: 117p.   *[IPPF]*
40.0017   BC   1974[?]   LESSONS FROM THE CARIBBEAN REVOLUTION. Castries, St. Lucia, Sinclair Dabreo: 120p.   **[21,37]**

Darbeau, D.
40.0018   BC   1968   Neo-colonialism in the...Commonwealth Caribbean. *Pelican:* 22-24.   *[RIS]*

Davis, Horace B.
42.0044   GU   1967   The decolonization of sugar in Guyana.

Demas, William G.
40.0019   BC   1974   How to be independent. *Car R* 6(4), Oct.-Nov.-Dec.: 9-16.   **[41]**
                                                                                   [RIS]
38.0057   BC   1974   WEST INDIAN NATIONHOOD AND CARIBBEAN INTEGRATION.
40.0020   BC   1975   CHANGE AND RENEWAL IN THE CARIBBEAN. Barbados, CCC Publishing House: 60p. (Challenges in the New Caribbean series, No. 2)   **[21,38,46]**   *[RIS]*
41.0137   BC   1975   Situation and change.

Dijkstra, Jan

37.0199 **SR** 1973 SURINAME-GEGEVENS: INFORMATIE OVER SURINAME VOOR EEN BETER BEGRIP OMTRENT DE GEBEURTENISSEN VAN FEBRUARI 1973 [SURINAM DATA: INFORMATION ABOUT SURINAM NECESSARY FOR A BETTER UNDERSTANDING OF THE INCIDENTS OF FEBRUARY 1973].

Dupuis, Jacques

40.0021 **CU** 1969 Les paradoxes de Curaçao: A travers les provinces de l'Empire Shell [The paradoxes of Curaçao: through the provinces of the Shell Empire]. *Cah O-M* 22(85), Jan.-March: 63-74. **[41,45]** [*COL*]

Fagon, Donald O'Connor

39.0057 **GC** 1973 THE GEOPOLITICS OF THE CARIBBEAN SEA AND ITS ADJACENT LANDS.

Farrell, T. M. A.

45.0049 **TR** 1974 THE MULTINATIONAL CORPORATIONS, THE PETROLEUM INDUSTRY AND ECONOMIC UNDERDEVELOPMENT IN TRINIDAD AND TOBAGO.

Farrelly, Alexander

37.0230 **US,UV** 1967 The doctrine of incorporation and federal labor policy in the Virgin Islands.

Forsythe, Dennis

18.0105 **BC** 1973 WEST INDIAN RADICALISM ABROAD.
20.0024 **GC** 1974 Repression, radicalism and change in the West Indies.

Frucht, Richard

2.0151 **NV** 1966 COMMUNITY AND CONTEXT IN A COLONIAL SOCIETY: SOCIAL AND ECONOMIC CHANGE IN NEVIS, BRITISH WEST INDIES.

Giacottino, Jean-Claude

40.0022 **BB** 1967 La Barbade indépendante [Independent Barbados]. *Cah O-M* 20(79), July-Sept.: 209-227. [*AGS*]

Girvan, Norman

50.0054 **GU** [n.d.] The denationalization of Caribbean bauxite: Alcoa in Guyana.
45.0059 **GC** 1970 Multinational corporations and dependent underdevelopment in mineral-export economies.
50.0058 **JM,GU,SR** 1971 Bauxite: the need to nationalize, part 1.
50.0059 **GU** 1971 The Guyana-Alcan conflict and the nationalization of Demba.
50.0060 **GC** 1971 Making the rules of the game: company-country agreements in the bauxite industry.
50.0061 **GU** 1972 Bauxite: the need to nationalize, part II.
45.0060 **JM** 1972 FOREIGN CAPITAL AND ECONOMIC UNDERDEVELOPMENT IN JAMAICA.
40.0023 **BC** 1973 The development of dependency economics in the Caribbean and Latin America: review and comparison. *Social Econ Stud* 22(1), March: 1-33. **[41]** [*RIS*]
40.0024 **BC** 1973 Teorías de dependencia económica en el Caribe y la América Latina: un estudio comparativo [Theories of economic dependency in the Caribbean and Latin America: a comparative study]. *Tri Econ* 40(160), Oct.-Dec.: 855-891. **[41]** [*COL*]
20.0026 **GC** 1975 ASPECTS OF THE POLITICAL ECONOMY OF RACE IN THE CARIBBEAN AND IN THE AMERICAS.

Girvan, Norman, ed.
41.0197   **GC**   1973   Dependence and underdevelopment in the New World and the Old.

Girvan, Norman & Jefferson, Owen, eds.
40.0025   **GC**   1971   READINGS IN THE POLITICAL ECONOMY OF THE CARIBBEAN. Kingston, New World Group Ltd.: 287p.   **[41]**   [*RIS*]

Gomes, Ralph C.
20.0029   **GU**   1975   A social psychology of leadership: elite attitudes in Guyana.

Gomes Casseres, Charles
37.0293   **NA**   1975   Our future. . .di nos e ta? [Our future. . .it is ours?]
40.0026   **CU**   1976   Dilemmas of development planning. *Kristòf* 3(3), Sept.: 97-113.
                                                                            [*RIS*]

Grant, C. H.
40.0027   **BZ**   1969   POLITICAL CHANGE IN BRITISH HONDURAS: A STUDY OF DECOLONI-
                                 SATION AND NATIONAL INTEGRATION. Ph.D. dissertation, University
                                 of Edinburgh: 410p.   **[37]**
37.0307   **BZ**   1976   THE MAKING OF MODERN BELIZE: POLITICS, SOCIETY AND BRITISH
                                 COLONIALISM IN CENTRAL AMERICA.

Grant, R. W.
37.0309   **BC**   1972   Party politics and contemporary socio-political movements in the
                                 Commonwealth Caribbean.

Greene, J. E.
37.0316   **BC**   1976   Institutionalization of party systems.

Guérin, Daniel
2.0179   **GC**   1956   LES ANTILLES DÉCOLONISÉES [THE INDEPENDENT ANTILLES].

Hall, Douglas
8.0092   **JM**   1972   The ex-colonial society in Jamaica.

Hanley, Eric R.
61.0067   **GU**   1975   Rice, politics and development in Guyana.

Harrigan, Norwell
32.0273   **UV**   1972   HIGHER EDUCATION IN THE MICRO-STATE: A THEORY OF RARAN
                                 SOCIETY.

Harris, David
2.0187   **AG**   1969   Anguilla's tradition of independence.

Hartog, J.
5.0381   **CU**   1968   CURAÇAO: FROM COLONIAL DEPENDENCE TO AUTONOMY.

Hawkins, Irene
40.0028   **BC**   1973   Aid and the European Community. *W I Chron* 88(1500), Jan.:
                                 7-10.   **[41]**   [*NYP*]
40.0029   **BC**   1973   Anxiety over economic survival. *W I Chron* 88(1511), Dec.:
                                 481-483.   **[41]**   [*NYP*]
45.0069   **BC**   1974   Paying for the privilege.

Heimsath, Surjit Mansingh

38.0094   **BC**   1972   BACKGROUND TO FAILURE OF THE WEST INDIES FEDERATION: AN INQUITY INTO BRITISH RULE IN THE CARIBBEAN, 1920-1947.

Hélène, Appolon

21.0040   **GC**   1970   "L'ANTILLAITISME": PRÉFIGURATION DU MONDE DE DEMAIN ["L'ANTILLAITISME": VISION OF TOMORROW'S WORLD].

Herman, Paula

2.0200   **BZ**   1975   British Honduras: a question of viability.

Hill, Anthony

40.0030   **BC**   1973   Economic stability in the mini-states. *In* Moss, Robert, ed. THE STABILITY OF THE CARIBBEAN: REPORT OF A SEMINAR HELD AT DITCHLEY PARK, OXFORDSHIRE, U.K. MAY 18-20, 1973. Washington D. C., Georgetown University, Center for Strategic and International Studies: 38-50. **[38]**   [*RIS*]

Hoetink, Harry

21.0043   **GC**   1972   National identity, culture, and race in the Caribbean.

Hoeven, P. van der

41.0239   **NC**   1973   Commentaar: hulp aan Suriname en de Nederlandse Antillen [Commentary: aid to Surinam and the Netherlands Antilles].

Hope, Kempe R.

37.0367   **GU**   1973   Anmerkungen zum genossenschaftlichen Sozialismus in Guayana [Notes on cooperative socialism in Guyana].

37.0370   **GU**   1976   Guyana's National Service Programme.

Hubbard, H. J. M.

37.0378   **GU**   1966   Guyana: another U.S. satellite?

Hunte, Keith

40.0031   **BC**   1970   The last days of empire in the Caribbean: the tribulations of regionalism. *Round Table* 60(240), Nov.: 387-594. **[38]**   [*COL*]

Ince, Basil A.

37.0393   **AG**   [n.d.]   The limits of Caribbean diplomacy: the invasion of Anguilla.

37.0394   **AG**   1970   The diplomacy of new states: the Commonwealth Caribbean and the case of Anguilla.

37.0396   **GU**   1974   DECOLONIZATION AND CONFLICT IN THE UNITED NATIONS: GUYANA'S STRUGGLE FOR INDEPENDENCE.

40.0032   **GR**   1974   The decolonization of Grenada in the U.N. *In* INDEPENDENCE FOR GRENADA—MYTH OR REALITY? Proceedings of a Conference on the Implications of Independence for Grenada sponsored by the Institute of International Relations and the Dept. of Govt., U.W.I., St. Augustine, Trinidad, Jan. 11-13, 1974: 43-51. **[37,39]**   [*RIS*]

Jacobs, Richard

37.0404   **GR**   1974   The movement towards Grenadian independence.

Jagan, Cheddi
39.0087   GU   1966   U.S. INTERVENTION IN GUYANA.
39.0088   GU   1967   THE ROLE OF THE C.I.A. IN GUYANA AND ITS ACTIVITIES THROUGH-
                          OUT THE WORLD.
40.0033 GU   1969   Intrigues of U.S. imperialism in Guyana. *Polit Aff* 48(12), Decem-
                          ber: 17-25. **[39]**   [*COL*]
40.0034 GU   1969   Ten scha nad Gaianoi [The shadow of the U.S.A. over Guyana]. *In*
                          Grigulevich, I. R., ed. GVIANA: GAIANA, FRANTZUZKAYA-GAIANA,
                          SURINAM. Moscow, Izdatelstvo "Natcha": 43-55.   [*UNL*]
37.0418   TR   1971   The February revolt.
37.0419   GU   1971   Transactions of the XVI Congress of the People's Progressive Party:
                          address and resolution.
50.0078   GU   1972   THE TRUTH ABOUT BAUXITE: NATIONALISATION.

Jainarain, Iserdeo
41.0263   BC   1976   TRADE AND UNDERDEVELOPMENT: A STUDY OF THE SMALL CARIBBEAN
                          COUNTRIES AND LARGE MULTINATIONAL CORPORATIONS.

James, C. L. R.
37.0431   BC   1975   The revolutionary.

Jefferson, Owen
41.0269   BC   1972   External dependence and economic development: a Common-
                          wealth Caribbean perspective.

Jeffrey, H. B.
40.0035 GU   1975   Capitalist discipline and socialist construction. *Guy J Sociol* 1(1),
                          Oct.: 92-99.   [*RIS*]

Johnson, Caswell L.
37.0436   JM,TR   1975   Political unionism and the collective objective in economies of
                            British colonial origin: the cases of Jamaica and Trinidad.

Jones, Edwin
37.0437   JM,TR,GU   1970   PRESSURE GROUP POLITICS IN THE WEST INDIES—A CASE STUDY OF
                                COLONIAL SYSTEMS: JAMAICA, TRINIDAD AND BRITISH GUIANA.
37.0441   BC   1975   Tendencies and change in Caribbean administrative systems.

Jones, Edwin & Mills, G. E.
40.0036 BC   1975   Cambio e inovación institucional en los paises de habla inglesa del
                          Caribe [Institutional innovation and change in the English-speaking
                          Caribbean]. *Revta LatinoAmer Admin Pub* 4, Aug.: 17-40. **[37]**
                                                                                  [*RIS*]

Kearns, Kevin C.
40.0037 BZ   1968   Prospects of sovereignty and economic viability for British Hon-
                          duras. *Prof Geogr* 21(2), March: 97-103.   [*AGS*]

Kross, R.
40.0038 SR   1969   Suriname en Nederland [Surinam and The Netherlands]. *In* ENIG
                          ZICHT OP SURINAME. Amsterdam, The Netherlands, Vrije Uni-
                          versiteit, Geografisch Instituut: 128-132. **[5]**   [*AGS*]

Kruijer, G. J.

40.0039   SR   1973   SURINAME, NEOKOLONIE IN RIJKSVERBAND [SURINAM, NEOCOLONY IN
THE CONTEXT OF THE KINGDOM]. Meppel, The Netherlands, Boom:
309p. **[8,41]**   [*RILA*]

40.0040   SR   1974   Neokolonie in rijksverband 1: Suriname's positie in het internationale machtssysteem [Neo-colony in the context of the King-
dom 1: Surinam's position in the international system of powers].
Intermediair 10(13), March 29: 1-11. **[39]**   [*RILA*]

40.0041   SR   1974   Neokolonie in rijksverband 2: twee ontwikkelingsstrategieën voor
Suriname [Neo-colony in context of the Kingdom 2: Two devel-
opment strategies for Surinam]. *Intermediair* 10(25), June 21:
13-23. **[37]**   [*RILA*]

Labeur, Cees

40.0042   SR   1975   Gesprek met Premier Henck Arron van Suriname: "Nederland
heeft gewoon te geven wat wij nodig hebben" [Conversation with
Prime-Minister Henck Arron of Surinam: "The Netherlands simply
have to give us what we need"]. *Elseviers Mag* 31(15), April 12:
16-19.   [*NYP*]

40.0043   SR   1975   Gouden handdruk voor Suriname: rumoerig einde van een koloniaal tijdperk [A golden handshake for Surinam: tumultuous end to a
colonial era]. *Elseviers Mag* 31(13), March 29: 14-18.   [*NYP*]

Lagerberg, C. & Vingerhoets, J.

41.0297   SR   1974   Ontwikkelingssamenwerking met onafhankelijk Suriname [Devel-
opment co-operation with an independent Surinam].

Laing, Edward A.

40.0044   WW,UK   1974   Crown indivisibility, governmental liability and other problems in
West Indies Associated States. *Int Comp Law Q* 23(1), Jan.:
127-142. **[38]**   [*COL*]

Lasserre, Guy

40.0045   FC   1970   Problèmes économiques et sociaux des Antilles Françaises [Eco-
nomic and social problems of the French Antilles]. *Geographica* 22,
April: 19-43. **[46]**   [*AGS*]

Latortue, Gérard

40.0046   FC,NA   1971   The European lands. *In* Szulc, Tad, ed. THE UNITED STATES AND
THE CARIBBEAN. Englewood Cliffs, N.J., Prentice-Hall, Inc.: 173-
190. **[37]**   [*RIS*]

Levitt, Kari & Best, Lloyd

41.0305   GC   1975   CHARACTER OF CARIBBEAN ECONOMY.

Lewis, Gordon K.

8.0131   GC   1974   On the dangers of composing a West Indian anthology.

Lewis, Vaughan A.

40.0047   GC   1970   Comment on multinational corporations and dependent underdevelopment in mineral export economies. *Social Econ Stud* 19(4),
Dec.: 527-533. **[45]**   [*RIS*]

40.0048 **BA** 1974 The Bahamas in international politics: issues arising for an archipelago state. *J Inter-Amer Stud* 16(2), May: 131-152. **[39]** *[COL]*

39.0101 **BC** 1976 The Commonwealth Caribbean and self-determination in the international system.

37.0489 **JM** 1976 Review article: electoral behaviour in Jamaica.

40.0049 **BC** 1976 Some questions and conclusions. *In* Lewis, Vaughan A., ed. SIZE, SELF-DETERMINATION AND INTERNATIONAL RELATIONS: THE CARIBBEAN. Mona, Jamaica, University of the West Indies, Institute of Social and Economic Research: 340-345. *[RIS]*

Lewis, Vaughan A., ed.
40.0050 **BC** 1976 SIZE, SELF-DETERMINATION AND INTERNATIONAL RELATIONS: THE CARIBBEAN. Mona, Jamaica, University of the West Indies, Institute of Social and Economic Research: 358p. **[37,39]** *[RIS]*

Lindsay, Louis
40.0051 **JM** 1975 THE MYTH OF INDEPENDENCE: MIDDLE CLASS POLITICS AND NON-MOBILIZATION IN JAMAICA. Mona, Jamaica, University of the West Indies, Institute of Social and Economic Research: 71p. *[RIS]*

Litvak, Isaiah & Maule, Christopher
50.0099 **GU** 1975 Nationalisation in the Caribbean bauxite industry.

Lotan, Yael
40.0052 **JM** 1972 Jamaica today. *In* McDonald, Vincent R., ed. THE CARIBBEAN ECONOMIES: PERSPECTIVES ON SOCIAL, POLITICAL, AND ECONOMIC CONDITIONS. New York, MSS Information Corporation: 192-196. **[21]** *[COL]*

Lutchman, Harold A.
40.0053 **GU** 1971 Some administrative problems of the co-operative republic in Guyana. *J Adm Overseas* 10(2), April: 87-99. **[41]** *[AMN]*

McDonald, Frank
40.0054 **BC** 1971 THE COMMONWEALTH CARIBBEAN. III. THE POLITICS OF POWER. New York, Institute of Current World Affairs: [8p.] **[39]** *[RIS]*

McFarlane, Malcolm Randolph Murchison
38.0145 **GU,JM,TR** 1974 THE MILITARY IN THE COMMONWEALTH CARIBBEAN: A STUDY IN COMPARATIVE INSTITUTIONALIZATION.

McIntyre, Alister
47.0175 **BC** 1965 Aspects of development and trade in the Commonwealth Caribbean (preliminary draft).

47.0176 **BC** 1965 Decolonization and trade policy in the West Indies.

McIntyre, W. D.
37.0525 **BC** 1967 COLONIES INTO COMMONWEALTH.

Macridis, Roy C.
40.0055 **UV** 1970 The evolution of the islands—some concluding remarks. *In* Bough, James A. & Macridis, Roy C., eds. VIRGIN ISLANDS, AMERICA'S CARIBBEAN OUTPOST: THE EVOLUTION OF SELF-GOVERNMENT. Wakefield, Massachusetts, The Walter F. Williams Publishing Company: 184-189. **[37]** *[UNL]*

Mandle, Jay R.
41.0329   GU   1976   Continuity and change in Guyanese underdevelopment.

Manigat, Leslie F.
39.0104   GC   1969   Les Etats-Unis et le secteur caraïbe de l'Amérique Latine [The United States and the Caribbean region of Latin America].

Manley, Robert Henry
40.0056   GU   1975   DECOLONIZATION AND NATIONAL DEVELOPMENT IN GUYANA, 1966-1974: THE ROLE OF EXTERNAL ENVIRONMENTS. Ph.D. dissertation, State University of New York (Albany): 350p. [37]   [PhD]

Manyoni, Joseph R.
21.0059   GC   1973   Emergence of Black Power.

Maxwell, Ken
40.0057   JM   1971   Greater local control of Jamaican wealth. W I Chron 86(1477), Feb.: 55-57. [45]   [NYP]

Miller, Jake C.
40.0058   UV,US   1974   The Virgin Islands and the United States: definition of a relationship. Wld Aff 136(4), Spring: 297-305. [37]   [COL]

Miller, Nugent
41.0349   GR   1974   The scope to monetary and financial independence.

Millette, James
16.0070   GC   1974   Race and class: factors in the history of protest movements since 1789.

Mills, G. E., ed.
37.0580   BC   1970   Problems of administrative change in the Commonwealth Caribbean.

Moskos, Charles C., Jr.
37.0595   BC   1963   THE SOCIOLOGY OF POLITICAL INDEPENDENCE: A STUDY OF INFLUENCE, SOCIAL STRUCTURE AND IDEOLOGY IN THE BRITISH WEST INDIES.

Moskos, Charles C., Jr. & Bell, Wendell
8.0166   GU,TR   1965   Cultural unity and diversity in new states.
20.0060   BC   1967   Political attitudes in new nations: examples from the British Caribbean.

Moss, Robert
37.0602   GC   1973   The stability of the Caribbean: report of the proceedings of the conference.

Moss, Robert, ed.
37.0603   GC   1973   THE STABILITY OF THE CARIBBEAN: REPORT OF A SEMINAR HELD AT DITCHLEY PARK, OXFORDSHIRE, U.K. MAY 18-20, 1973.

Mullings, Llewellyn Maximillian

41.0358   **JM**   1964   AN ANALYSIS OF THE ECONOMIC IMPLICATIONS OF POLITICAL INDE-
PENDENCE FOR JAMAICA.

Munroe, Trevor

40.0059   **BC**   1971   DEVELOPED IDEALISM AND EARLY MATERIALISM: 'LEFT' CARIBBEAN
THOUGHT IN TRANSITION. Mona, Jamaica, University of the West
Indies: 52p. **[21,37]**   [*RIS*]

41.0359   **JM**   1971   JAMAICAN POLITICAL ECONOMY 1962-1970: SURVEY AND PROSPECTS.

37.0608   **JM**   1972   THE POLITICS OF CONSTITUTIONAL DECOLONIZATION: JAMAICA,
1944-1962.

Murch, Arvin

37.0611   **FA**   1968   Political integration as an alternative to independence in the French
Antilles.

37.0612   **FC**   1971   BLACK FRENCHMEN: THE POLITICAL INTEGRATION OF THE FRENCH
ANTILLES.

40.0060   **FA**   1972   POLITICAL INTEGRATION AS AN ALTERNATIVE TO INDEPENDENCE IN
THE FRENCH ANTILLES. Ann Arbor, Michigan, University Micro-
films: 262p. (Ph.D. dissertation, Yale University, 1968.) **[2,21,37]**
                                                          [*RIS*]

Nemo, Général

40.0061   **FC**   1966   Terres françaises d'Amérique: à propos du Cinquiéme Plan [French
territories in America: the Fifth Plan]. *Rev Defense Natn* 22, Feb.:
224-233. **[41]**   [*COL*]

Oxaal, Ivar

37.0652   **TR**   1975   The dependency economist as grassroots politician in the Caribbean.

Oxaal, Ivar; Barnett, Tony & Booth, David, eds.

41.0394   **GU,TR**   1975   BEYOND THE SOCIOLOGY OF DEVELOPMENT: ECONOMY AND SOCIETY
IN LATIN AMERICA AND AFRICA.

Oxtoby, F. E.

45.0115   **US,UV**   1970   The role of political factors in the Virgin Islands watch industry.

Paërl, Eric

45.0116   **NC**   1971   NEDERLANDSE MACHT IN DE DERDE WERELD: EEN INVENTARISATIE
VAN ECONOMISCHE BELANGEN [DUTCH POWER IN THE THIRD WORLD:
TAKING AN INVENTORY OF ECONOMIC INTERESTS].

40.0062   **SR**   1972   KLASSENSTRIJD IN SURINAME [CLASS STRUGGLE IN SURINAM]. Nijmegen, The Netherlands, Socialistische Uitgeverij: 63p. (sunschrift
59) **[45,46]**   [*RILA*]

Palacio, Joseph

32.0445   **BZ**   1976   Anthropology in Belize.

Parkin, Bingham Lloyd

32.0449   **JM**   1969   A STUDY OF CONTROL FOR JAMAICA'S SYSTEM OF TEACHER PREPA-
RATION IN RELATION TO SOCIAL PROGRESS: 1944-1966.

Parris, Ronald Glenfield
40.0063 **BB** 1972 Inequality and control in a colonial bureaucracy: Barbados, 1955-1962. *J Black Stud* 3(1), Sept.: 57-74. **[39,41,45]** [*COL*]

Payne, Thomas
42.0110 **GU** 1976 Sugar and the Guyanese society.

Pérez, Louis A.
51.0087 **GC** 1973-74 Aspects of underdevelopment: tourism in the West Indies.

Perusse, Roland I.
38.0172 **GC** 1971 A STRATEGY FOR CARIBBEAN ECONOMIC INTEGRATION.

Phillips, Andrew P.
21.0076 **AT** 1967 Management and workers face an independent Antigua.

Prescod, Colin
37.0687 **BC** 1975 The 'people's cause' in the Caribbean.
37.0688 **GU** 1976 Guyana's socialism: an interview with Walter Rodney.

Ramphal, S. S.
38.0187 **BC** 1973 West Indian nationhood—myth, mirage or mandate?

Rattray, K. O.
45.0125 **JM** 1966 THE PROTECTION IN INTERESTS IN JAMAICAN COMPANY LAW: A STUDY IN THE FORMATION, FLOTATION AND MANAGEMENT OF COMPANIES IN DEVELOPING ECONOMY.

Reckord, Barry
40.0064 **GC** 1967 The racial double-standard. *New Wld Q* 3(3), High Season: 65-68.
[*RIS*]

Regnier, Françoise
40.0065 **GD,MT** 1967 Les Antilles françaises ne sont pas décolonisées [The French Antilles are not decolonized]. *Croiss Jeunes Natn* 69, Sept.: 13-15. **[37]** [*COL*]

Reno, Philip
50.0136 **GU,JM,SR** 1970 Aluminum profits and Caribbean people.

Richardson, C. Howard
37.0713 **GC** 1971 American research on the political geography of Latin America.

Roberts-Wray, Kenneth
33.0164 **BC,UK** 1966 COMMONWEALTH AND COLONIAL LAW.

Rodes, Félix
37.0733 **GD** 1972 LIBERTÉ POUR LA GUADELOUPE; 169 JOURS DE PRISON [FREEDOM FOR GUADELOUPE; 169 DAYS IN PRISON].

Rodney, Walter
40.0066 **BC** 1975 Contemporary political trends in the English-speaking Caribbean. *Black Scholar* 7(1), Sept.: 15-21. **[8,37]** [*NYP*]

Rolison, William Edward
40.0067   **GU**   1974   BRITISH COLONIAL POLICY AND THE INDEPENDENCE OF GUYANA. Ph.D. dissertation, University of Missouri (Columbia): 426p. **[5,37]**   [*PhD*]

Römer, R. A.
40.0068   **NA**   1974   Dimensies van onafhankelijkheid [Dimensions of independence]. *Kristòf* 1(6), Dec.: 247-254.   [*RIS*]

Ryan, Selwyn
21.0084   **GC**   1971   Politics in the Caribbean: black power or black powerlessness.

Sablé, Victor
37.0749   **FA**   1972   LES ANTILLES SANS COMPLEXES: UNE EXPÉRIENCE DE DÉCOLONISATION [THE UNCOMPLICATED ANTILLES? AN EXPERIENCE IN DECOLONIZATION.]

Sanderson, Agnes G.
43.0394   **GC**   1965   NOTES ON THE AGRICULTURAL ECONOMIES OF DEPENDENT TERRITORIES IN THE WESTERN HEMISPHERE AND PUERTO RICO.

Segal, Aaron
37.0768   **BA**   1974   Bahama watching.

Shahabuddéen, Mohamed
37.0772   **GU**   1970   CONSTITUTIONAL DEVELOPMENT IN GUYANA.

Sherlock, Philip M.
5.0839   **GC**   1973   WEST INDIAN NATIONS: A NEW HISTORY.

Simmonds, K. R.
38.0212   **KNA,UK**   1972   Anguilla: an interim settlement.

Singham, A. W., ed.
2.0432   **BC**   1975   THE COMMONWEALTH CARIBBEAN INTO THE SEVENTIES: PROCEEDINGS OF A CONFERENCE HELD ON 28-30 SEPTEMBER, 1973, AT HOWARD UNIVERSITY, WASHINGTON, D. C.

Soest, Jaap van
40.0069   **NA**   1976   The Dutch in the Netherlands Antilles, 1900-1950: political retreat and economic expansion. *Kristòf* 3(2), April: 49-65. **[5]**   [*RIS*]

Somer, Herman
41.0464   **SR**   1973   SURINAME.

Springer, Hugh W.
38.0215   **BC**   1961   The West Indies emergent: problems and prospects.
37.0823   **BB**   1967   Barbados as a sovereign state.

St. Hill, C. A. P.
41.0473   **BC**   1970   Towards the reform of the public services: some problems of transitional bureaucracies in Commonwealth Caribbean states.

Stone, Carl

33.0187   **JM**   1975   Urban social movements in post-War Jamaica.

Stone, Montgomery

41.0477   **GC**   1975   Misrepresentation of self-management in the Caribbean.

St. Pierre, Maurice

37.0832   **GU**   1972   The Co-operative Republic—idea or ideology?

37.0833   **GU**   1972   The sociology of decolonization: the case of Guyana bauxite.

40.0070   **GU**   1975   Race, the political factor and the nationalization of the Demerara Bauxite Company, Guyana. *Social Econ Stud* 24(4), Dec.: 481-503. **[8,16,45,50]**   [*RIS*]

Sykes, Lynn R. & Ewing, Maurice

40.0071   **GC**   1965   The seismicity of the Caribbean region. *J Geophys Res* 70(20), Oct. 15: 5065-5074.   [*COL*]

Taylor, Frank

8.0236   **JM**   1975   JAMAICA—THE WELCOMING SOCIETY: MYTHS AND REALITY.

Terpstra, G. H.

41.0484   **SR**   1973   De sociaal-economische problemen van Suriname [The socio-economic problems of Surinam].

Teulières, André

37.0839   **FC**   1970   L'OUTRE-MER FRANÇAIS: HIER. . .AUJORD'HUI. . .DEMAIN [FRENCH OVERSEAS DEPARTMENTS: YESTERDAY. . .TODAY. . .TOMORROW].

Theberge, James D., ed.

39.0162   **GC**   1973   RUSSIA IN THE CARIBBEAN. PART ONE: PANELISTS' FINDINGS, RECOMMENDATIONS AND COMMENTS.

39.0163   **GC**   1973   RUSSIA IN THE CARIBBEAN. PART TWO: A SPECIAL REPORT.

Theuns, H. L.

40.0072   **NA**   1971   Hulpverlening aan de Nederlandse Antillen [Aid to the Netherlands Antilles]. *Int Spectator* 25(5), March 8: 499-521. **[41]**   [*COL*]

40.0073   **SR**   1975   Suriname als Nederlands probleem [Surinam as a Dutch problem]. *Civis Mundi* 11(4), Jan.: 10-15. **[37]**   [*RIS*]

Thomas, Clive Y.

42.0160   **GU**   [n.d.]   SUGAR ECONOMICS IN A COLONIAL SITUATION: A STUDY OF THE GUYANA SUGAR INDUSTRY.

41.0487   **GU**   1965   MONETARY AND FINANCIAL ARRANGEMENTS IN A DEPENDENT MONETARY ECONOMY: A STUDY OF BRITISH GUIANA, 1945-1962.

49.0101   **BC**   1966   The end of empire?

40.0074   **GC**   1972   The political economy of exploitation in the Caribbean. *Black Lines* 2(2-3), Winter-Spring: 39-49.   [*RIS*]

41.0489   **GC**   1974   Black exploitation in the Caribbean: is there a Caribbean economic system?

37.0844   **GU**   1976   Bread and justice: the struggle for socialism in Guyana.

Thomas, Cuthbert J.

37.0845   **DM**   1973   FROM CROWN COLONY TO ASSOCIATE STATEHOOD: POLITICAL CHANGE IN DOMINICA, THE COMMONWEALTH WEST INDIES.

Thorndike, Tony
40.0075   GR   1974   Grenada: maxi-crisis for a mini-state. *Wld Today*30(10), October: 436-444. **[37]**   [*COL*]

Thorne, Alfred P.
42.0164   GU   1971   Comments on a monograph on exploitation and some relevant reminiscences.

Trigt, Ivo van
40.0076   NA   1969   Rondom een gouverneursbenoeming [Concerning a governor's appointment]. *Streven* 11-12, Aug.-Sept.: 1171-1178. **[37]**   [*NYP*]
46.0234   CU   1969   Waaraan ging Willemstad ten onder [What caused Willemstad to go under?]
40.0077   NA   1970   Tweespalt in de Antillen [Discord in the Antilles]. *Streven* 6, March: 556-563. **[37]**   [*NYP*]

Varlack, Pearl & Harrigan, Norwell
40.0078   BV   1971   Anegada—feudal development in the twentieth century. *Car Q* 17(1), March: 5-15.   [*RIS*]

Veen, L. B. van der
40.0079   CU   1976   Reflections on local aspects of behavior change. *Kristòf* 3(3), Sept.: 116-122.   [*RIS*]

Vogt, Robert C.
40.0080   TR   1975   THE DEVELOPMENT OF A SENSE OF POLITICAL COMMUNITY IN A PLURAL SOCIETY: NATION-BUILDING IN TRINIDAD. Ph.D. dissertation, State University of New York (Buffalo): 215p. **[8]**   [*PhD*]

Von der Ohe, Werner
40.0081   GC   1975   THE EUROPEAN COMMUNITIES AND ITS FORMER COLONIES IN AFRICA, THE CARIBBEAN, AND THE PACIFIC—AN EMPIRICAL TEST OF CERTAIN EMERSONIAN EXCHANGE-THEORETICAL PROPOSITIONS. Ph.D. dissertation, Michigan State University: 248p.   [*PhD*]

Watson, Beverly
40.0082 BB,DM,GU 1974   SUPPLEMENTARY NOTES ON FOREIGN INVESTMENT IN THE COMMONWEALTH CARIBBEAN. University of the West Indies, Institute of Social and Economic Research: 92p. (Working Paper No. 1) **[41,45]**   [*RIS*]

Watson, Hilbourne A.
40.0083   BC   1975   Leadership and imperialism in the Commonwealth Caribbean. *In* Singham, A. W., ed. THE COMMONWEALTH CARIBBEAN INTO THE SEVENTIES. . . Montreal, McGill University, Centre for Developing Area Studies: 43-67. **[37,45]**   [*RIS*]

Watty, Frank
44.0064   DM   1970   Alien land ownership and agricultural development issues, problems and the policy framework.

Wel, F. J. van
40.0084   GU   1971   Zoeklicht op Guyana (II) [Spot-light on Guyana (II)]. *Oost West* 64, Nov.: 12-15.   [*NYP*]

Wendt, Herbert
37.0887 GC   1966   Hurricane over the Caribbean.

Westlake, Donald E.
40.0085 AG   1972   UNDER AN ENGLISH HEAVEN. New York, Simon and Schuster: 278p. **[37]**   [*RIS*]

Will, Wilbur Marvin
37.0898 BB   1972   POLITICAL DEVELOPMENT IN THE MINI-STATE CARIBBEAN: A FOCUS ON BARBADOS.

Williams, Eric Eustace
40.0086 GC   1961   MASSA DAY DONE. Port of Spain, PNM Pub. Co., 19p. **[20]**   [*RIS*]

Wiltshire, Rosina
38.0241 BC   1974   REGIONAL INTEGRATION AND CONFLICT IN THE COMMONWEALTH CARIBBEAN.
38.0242 BC   1976   Mini-states, dependency and regional integration in the Caribbean.

Wionczek, Miguel S.
40.0087 GC,US   1969-70 United States investment and the development of Middle America. *Stud Comp Int Dev* 5(1): 1-17. **[39,45]**   [*COL*]

Wolf, Donna Marie
40.0088 JM   1973   THE CARIBBEAN PEOPLE OF COLOR AND THE CUBAN INDEPENDENCE MOVEMENT. Ph.D. dissertation, University of Pittsburgh: 474p. **[11,16,38]**   [*PhD*]

Wolf, Sig. W.
37.0917 SR   1971   SURINAME ZOEKEND NAAR EIGEN IDENTITEIT [SURINAM LOOKING FOR ITS OWN IDENTITY].

Worrell, DeLisle
40.0089 BC,CA   1971   Canadian economic involvement in the West Indies. *In* Forsythe, Dennis, ed. LET THE NIGGERS BURN! THE SIR GEORGE WILLIAMS UNIVERSITY AFFAIR AND ITS CARIBBEAN AFTERMATH. Montreal, Black Rose Books: 41-55.   [*NYP*]